SOCIETY, CULTURE, AND PERSONALITY

SOCIETY, CULTURE, AND PERSONALITY:

Their Structure and Dynamics

A SYSTEM OF GENERAL SOCIOLOGY

By PITIRIM A. SOROKIN

COOPER SQUARE PUBLISHERS, INC.

New York   1962

Contents

v

Part Four—Social Differentiation and Stratification

equality)—Multibonded Stratification—Additional Sub-Forms of the Unibonded and Multibonded Strata—Conclusions

Population (Society) as an Agglomeration of Unibonded and Multibonded Groups—How to Analyze the Group Structure of a Population—
The Problem of Classification of the Types of Population Agglomerations
("Societies")—Main Types—Criticism of the Traditional Theory of Society
and Individual—Criticism of the Unilinear Theories of Social Differentiation and Stratification, of Solidarity and Antagonism—General Conclusion to the Structural Analysis of Social Phenomena

Part Five—Structures of the Cultural and Personality Aspects of the Superorganic Universe

Ideological, Behavioral, and Material Cultures of Individuals and Groups
—Integrated, Unintegrated, and Contradictory Relationships of Cultural
Phenomena—Integration, Unintegration, and Contradiction of Ideological
Culture—Main Vast Ideological Systems, Combined Systems, and Supersystems—Integration of Ideological, Behavioral, and Material Cultures
of an Individual—Integration, Unintegration, and Contradiction of
the Culture of a Whole Interaction Group—Integration, Unintegration,
and Contradiction of the Cultures of a Conglomeration of Interacting
Groups

Extent of Integration of the Total Ideological, Behavioral, and Material
Culture of an Individual—The Structure of the Total Ideological, Be-
havioral, and Material Culture of an Organized Group, and of an Area
as an Agglomeration of Groups—Relationship Between Organized Social
Groups and Integrated Cultural Systems—Critical Remarks on Prevalent
Theories of Cultural Integration

Relationship Between the Social and Cultural Structures and the Individual's Self, Mind, and Conduct—The Mental Development of an Individual
and the Development of Sociocultural Structure—Pluralism of "Selves" in
the Individual as a Reflection of the Pluralism of Groups—The Cultural
Content of the Souls of the Individual as a Reflection of the Cultures of
His Groups and of Additional Factors—Social and Cultural Position of
an Individual in the Sociocultural World

Impossibility of Locating Sociocultural Phenomena in Geometric Space—
Location of Sociocultural Phenomena in Sociocultural Space—Structure of
Sociocultural Space and Distance—Concluding Remarks on Structure of
Sociocultural Universe

Part Six—Dynamics of the Recurrent Social Processes

Foreword

Since its original edition this volume has been published in Spanish, Portuguese and Hindi translations. For the last few years its American edition has been out of print. Now, like my *Social and Cultural Dynamics,* and *Social Mobility,* it is re-issued by the Cooper Square Publishers, Inc., to whom I bring my thanks for this service.

The new edition is a reprint of the original edition of this work. Of course, if I were younger and were not interested more in writing new works than in revising the old ones, I could have "freshened" it by adding bibliography of the works that appeared after its publication and, perhaps, by changing here and there informational material of this or that chapter. However, these superficial alterations would not have changed anything important in the system of general sociology with its main propositions and generalizations developed and—logically and empirically—corroborated in the book.

The system, propositions and generalizations have seemingly stood well the acid test of time—what among other things is witnessed by some forty-two translations of my volumes into all main languages of humanity and by an already large and rapidly growing literature—books about my books, Ph.D. theses, and multitude of articles—devoted to an analysis, evaluation, and criticism of my theories. As the central cognitive value of any science, and especially of the generalizing sciences, like sociology, consists exactly in the validity of their conceptual system and its propositions and generalizations, these symphomatic facts are a sufficient justification for reprint of this volume.

PITIRIM A. SOROKIN

Winchester, Mass.
July, 1962

Preface

So much fact-finding sociological work has been done during the past few decades that the greatest need of contemporary sociology is not so much a further collection of facts as assimilating the existing data, presenting them in a sound, logical order, and rebuilding the framework of sociology as a systematic science. Otherwise we are in danger of being lost in a maze of intractable facts.

In a modest and imperfect way this work endeavors to meet this need. It attempts to present a system of sociology as a generalizing science of sociocultural phenomena possessing its own set of referential principles, its own meaningful-causal method, and its own special task among the other social and humanistic disciplines. The work unfolds a systematic theory of the structure and dynamics of social, cultural, and personality systems. It is little concerned with physical, biological, and other "presociological" problems; instead it confines itself to a study of sociocultural phenomena in their structural and dynamic aspects.

It remains faithful to the general principles of science, but it modifies these principles to fit the peculiar nature of sociocultural phenomena. Its meaningful-causal method, and the logic of sociocultural systems as contrasted with that of congeries, are examples of such a modification.

In harmony with the generalizing nature of sociology, the bulk of the empirical propositions consists of more or less generalized formulae of meaningful-causal uniformities (structural and dynamic), of the main types of sociocultural systems, or of the typical ways in which social, cultural, and personality systems emerge, function, change, and decline. A

description of specific, nontypical cases is omitted. The concrete corroboration and illustration of the general formulae can be supplied by any intelligent teacher, student, or reader.

The generalizing propositions do not aim to be precise, but only to be approximately valid. At the present stage of our knowledge of the complex constellations of sociocultural systems and congeries absolute exactness is hardly attainable. When it is attempted, the result is ordinarily a misleading preciseness acquired at the expense of approximate validity.

The tentative generalizations are based upon the existing body of empirical evidence: experimental, semi-experimental, statistical, historical, and clinical, and on other observational data. For the sake of economy the work does not reproduce the concrete data and procedures of the enormous body of empirical studies utilized. Instead, it simply takes their results, critically analyzes and compares them, and derives from their totality what seems to be the soundest conclusion. A minimum of empirical evidence is given in the text; the bulk of it may be found in the works referred to in the footnotes. For the same reason—that of economy—the literature cited in the footnotes is intentionally reduced to a minimum.

The analysis of each basic problem includes a critical survey of the existing theories in the field, followed by a constructive solution.

I am indebted to the Harvard Committee for Research in the Social Sciences for financial assistance in the preparation of the manuscript. To the American Book Company and E. P. Dutton & Co. I am indebted for permission to use some of the text matter and diagrams in my *Social and Cultural Dynamics* and *Crisis of Our Age*. Grateful acknowledgment is due Professor F. S. Chapin for his editorial advice. From the English manuscript the work is being translated into Czech and Spanish. My sincere thanks are due all the firms who

ventured to publish it under the present difficult conditions attending the publication of large scholarly works.

PITIRIM A. SOROKIN

Harvard University

KEY TO ABBREVIATIONS

AA—*American Anthropologist*
AJS—*American Journal of Sociology*
ASR—*American Sociological Review*
JAOS—*Journal of the American Oriental Society*
LPS—*Journal of Legal and Political Sociology*
SF—*Social Forces*
SR—*Social Research*
SSR—*Sociology and Social Research*
Calamity —P. A. Sorokin, *Man and Society in Calamity* (New York, 1942)
Crisis —P. A. Sorokin, *Crisis of Our Age* (New York, 1941)
Dynamics—P. A. Sorokin, *Social and Cultural Dynamics* (4 vols., New York, 1937-41)
Theories —P. A. Sorokin, *Contemporary Sociological Theories* (New York, 1928)
Mobility —P. A. Sorokin, *Social Mobility* (New York, 1927)

PART ONE

---

*Sociology: Its Object,
Method and Development*

Chapter 1. Sociology as a Science

I. Sociology and Other Sciences

1. The Superorganic World

The physical sciences study inorganic phenomena; biology investigates the *organic* world; the social sciences are concerned with *superorganic* phenomena. As the presence of life distinguishes living structures and processes, so the presence of mind or thought in its developed form, differentiates the superorganic phenomena from the organic. Just as the vital phenomena are superimposed upon the inorganic, so the superorganic world is superimposed upon the organic. Just as only a small fraction of physical phenomena (plants and animals) display the phenomena of life, so only a small fraction of vital phenomena manifest mind in the developed form of science and philosophy, religion and ethics, the fine arts, technological inventions, and social institutions. Superorganic phenomena so developed are found only in man and the man-made world. Other species exhibit only rudimentary forms of the superorganic. Sociology and the other social sciences consider man and the man-made world only with reference to superorganic mind or thought.

The social and humanistic sciences do not analyze the chemical composition of human bodies, or of church buildings, airplanes, or any other part of the man-made world; this is the task of organic and inorganic chemistry. Likewise they do not study the physical prop-

erties of the human world; this is the concern of physics. Human anatomy and physiology belong to the realm of biology. Social scientists, to be sure, must know the conclusions of the physical and biological sciences concerning man; but these conclusions do not form an integral part of sociology or the social sciences. They are "presociology" or "presocial science." The task of sociology and social science begins where the physical and biological study of man and his world ends.[1]

Later on we shall see that the physicochemical and biological properties of man do indeed enter the field of social science, but only so far as they are inextricably connected with the superorganic, either as its instruments and vehicles or as factors that condition or are conditioned by the superorganic.

2. Delineation of the Superorganic

The superorganic is equivalent to mind in all its clearly developed manifestations. Superorganic phenomena embrace language; science and philosophy; religion; the fine arts (painting, sculpture, architecture, music, literature, and drama); law and ethics; mores and manners; technological inventions and processes from the simplest tools up to the most intricate machinery; road-making; building construction; the cultivation of fields and gardens; the domestication and training of animals, etc.; and

---

[1] Most of the introductory texts in sociology are largely filled with such "presociological" information taken from mechanics, physics, chemistry, and especially biology. If for pedagogical purposes an insertion of "presociological" information is advisable, its enormous inflation at the cost of a strictly sociological study of man and the human world is hardly justifiable. In this work most of the "presociological" knowledge of man is assumed to be known; therefore, its insertion is reduced to the minimum.

social organizations. These are all superorganic phenomena because they are the articulations of mind in various forms; none of them arise mainly in response to blind reflexes or instincts.[2]

3. Where the Superorganic Is Found

In other words, in its developed forms the superorganic is found exclusively in the realm of interacting human beings and the products of their interaction.

Outside the human species only the rudiments of superorganic behavior can be observed, such as reflexes and instincts; sensations, feelings, and emotions; traces of reproductive imagination; elementary association of images; and rudimentary ability to learn by experience. Several animal species, such as ants and bees, have complex societies; but these societies result from inherited reflexes and instincts. To the latter are due also such marvelous activities as the construction of webs by spiders, nests by birds, and lodges by beavers. Without a highly developed nervous system and brain an animal can learn little by personal experience, no matter how much it is taught. When the Kelloggs tried to educate a seven-month-old chimpanzee under conditions identical with those surrounding their son who was of about the same age, the chimpanzee at first excelled the boy in various activities determined by its anatomy, inherited instincts, and reflexes. It learned to perform such acts as eating with a spoon, drinking from a glass, and opening doors. But it could not understand human speech, except for a few simple words and phrases; nor could it learn to speak, or to solve arithmetical and other problems of a moderate degree of difficulty.[3] Not being endowed with higher mental powers, animals do not develop linguistic, scientific, philosophical, or other superorganic systems. The little they learn is achieved principally through the mechanism of conditioned reflexes.[4]

As already indicated, the superorganic is observed mainly in the realm of interacting human beings and in the products of such interaction. No one isolated from birth from other human beings can develop his mind to any considerable degree. Kaspar Hauser, Anna, the Hessian boy, the girl of Songi, the girl found in a forest near Châlons in 1731, Amala and Kamala the "wolf children," and others similarly isolated from other human beings were found to be unable to speak, to recall past experience, or to solve simple mental problems. They resembled, in fact, animals

[2] The best definition of the superorganic is given by E. De Roberty. He rightly indicates that the transition from the inorganic to the organic and then to the superorganic is gradual. Vital phenomena have rudimentary mental processes like irritability, sensation, feeling, emotion, and association of images. But no species except man has the highest forms of mind represented by four main classes of social thought: (a) abstract concepts and laws of scientific thought; (b) generalizations of philosophy and religion; (c) symbolic thought of the fine arts; and (d) rational applied thought, in all disciplines from technology, agronomy, and medicine, up to ethics, social planning, and engineering. This superorganic thought is the "stuff" of sociocultural phenomena. Concrete historical events and sociocultural phenomena always represent a mixture of physical, biological, and superorganic phenomena. See E. De Roberty, Nouveau Programme de sociologie (Paris, 1904). Social scientists who state that social phenomena are in their nature psychological or mental say, in a less distinct form, the same thing. This means that practically all representatives of the psychological and sociologistic schools in sociology (and they make up the main streams of social thought) are in implicit or explicit agreement with the thesis of this work. See P. A. Sorokin, Contemporary Sociological Theories (New York, 1928), Chps. 8-13. See also A. L. Kroeber, "The Superorganic," AA (April-June, 1917).

[3] See W. N. and L. A. Kellogg, The Ape and the Child (New York, 1933); also J. Wolff, "Effectiveness of Token-Reward for Chimpanzees," Comparative Psychology Monograph, Vol. XII (No. 5, 1936); W. Köhler, The Mentality of Apes (New York, 1925); R. M. Yerkes, Almost Human (New York, 1925); H. Hart and A. Pantzer, "Have Sub-Human Animals a Culture?" AJS, Vol. XXX (May 1925); N. D. M. Hirsch, Genius and Creative Intelligence (Cambridge, 1931).

On the mechanism of building complex social organizations by bees, ants, and other animals, see W. M. Wheeler, Ants, Their Structure, Development, and Behavior (New York, 1916) and Social Life Among the Insects (New York, 1923); W. Wagner, Biological Foundations of Comparative Psychology, 2 Vols. in Russian (St. Petersburg, 1916); A. D. Imms, Social Behavior in Insects (New York, 1931); W. B. Allee, The Social Life of Animals (New York, 1938).

[4] See I. Pavlov, Lectures on Conditioned Reflexes (New York, 1928).

rather than intelligent persons.[5] Scientific knowledge, philosophical thought, aesthetic tastes, and other superorganic traits are not inherited biologically but are learned from other human beings through incessant interaction with the man-made world as the repository of superorganic values. If any one of us were isolated at birth from the human world, how much of our culture could he discover by himself? The most elementary language, the simplest rules of addition and subtraction, the elementary notions of physics and biology, the use of simple tools like the lever, the wheel, and the bow and arrow, or the production and use of fire, easily learned by a boy of seven, would exceed the ability of 99 per cent of us, even if we lived a hundred years and had the brain of a Sir Isaac Newton. It required many generations of interacting human beings to make such discoveries and inventions. Under conditions of complete isolation from the sociocultural world it would take centuries and millennia before isolated individuals could do this, if they ever could. Individual experience is very limited. Isolated from others, one would be deprived of the infinitely rich accumulated experiences of millions of generations. Therefore his mind would be doomed to remain at the most rudimentary level. Even the developed mind of an intelligent person begins to deteriorate if he is cut off for a long time from interaction with the human and man-made world.

Science, philosophy, religion, ethics, technology, the fine arts, and social structures have been created and enriched by the interacting activities of countless human generations. Any specific increment of the superorganic may arise from the interaction of the innovator and the preexisting culture; but this prior accumulation is itself the product of interaction among human beings. In this sense superorganic culture may be regarded as the direct or indirect product of human interaction.

[5] See M. Halbwachs, *Les cadres sociaux de la mémoire* (Paris, 1925), pp. viii-ix, 49 ff.; K. Davis, "A Case of Extreme Social Isolation of a Child," *AJS*, Vol. XLV (January, 1940); M. H. Small, "On Some Psychic Relations of Society and Solitude," *Pedagogical Seminary* (April, 1900); A. Gesell, *Wolf Child and Human Child* (New York, 1941).

4. Human Personality as a Product of Sociocultural Forces

At birth one is not yet a human personality or an agent of the superorganic life. His personality and name; his scientific ideas, religious beliefs, aesthetic tastes, moral convictions, and manners and mores; his occupation, economic position, and social status; his destiny and life career—none of these are yet determined. He is like a phonograph, capable of playing any record. A well-constructed phonograph, to be sure, plays any record better than a poorly constructed phonograph. But what records it will play—whether a Beethoven symphony or jazz—does not depend upon the phonograph. Similarly, a person born with a superior constitution may develop a better mind and play his "sociocultural records" better than one born with inferior hereditary endowments; but what "sociocultural records" he will play depends relatively little upon the organic or biological factors. Whether one's name is Smith or Jones; whether he is a Protestant or a Buddhist; whether he speaks the English or the Turkish language; whether he is a Republican or a Democrat, a janitor or a king, a citizen of Russia or of Siam, a monogamist or a polygamist; or whether he wears Oriental or American clothing—these and other sociocultural characteristics are not inherited biologically but are acquired in the process of interaction with the human beings among whom one is born, reared, and educated.

Joseph Rinehart, born of American parents in the United States, was at the age of three deserted by his parents, adopted by a Chinese family, taken to China, and reared there for nineteen years, becoming Fung Kwok Keung, typically Chinese in language, ideas and beliefs, manners and way of life.[6] Identical twins, born with identical organisms, develop their minds to a different degree and have different sociocultural characteristics, if they are placed in different sociocultural environments. Mabel and Mary, identical twins, one reared on an American farm, the other in an American city, showed 17.7 points of variation in the Stanford-Binet mental test, as well as marked differences in manners and mores, in spite of

[6] See A. Scheinfeld, *You and Heredity* (New York, 1939), pp. 354 ff.

the fact that the sociocultural discrepancy between rural and urban American environments is not pronounced.[7] In another case of twins, Johnny, who was born lighter and weaker than Jimmy but was especially encouraged in his motor activities, was taller and heavier at the age of seven months than Jimmy.[8] Other identical twins, reared in slightly different environments, varied in I.Q. 7.7 points more than twins reared in the same environment.[9] Two organisms may differ from each other slightly, if at all; but one may become a king or dictator, the other a slave or serf. Two organisms may be very different biologically—for instance, respectively weak and strong in physique and respectively feeble and brilliant in mentality; yet both of them may become kings or multimillionaires[10] by the fiat of sociocultural conditions. In spite of wide variations in biological heredity, children born and reared in an English-speaking society acquire English as their native language; in a Roman Catholic environment from 80 to 100 per cent of the children become Roman Catholics, and so on.

This means that in respect to his sociocultural traits and life career everyone is conditioned by the superorganic environment in which he is born and reared. Even certain biological characteristics are indirectly deter-

mined by sociocultural influences. In many societies the members are commanded to kill babies born with certain tabooed traits. Other societies prohibit intermarriage between the upper and the lower castes, between slaves and masters, or between certain ethnic, racial, and religious groups. In this way sociocultural factors condition and control, to a considerable extent, the kind of biological organisms that are begotten or exterminated.

The role of the biological forces in all these respects is limited to two functions. First, an organism endowed with a superior heredity will perform better the sociocultural functions assigned it by the superorganic milieu. Second, biological organisms born with certain characteristics are necessarily restricted by them; for instance, a congenital idiot will be unable to become a professor, nor can a constitutionally weak person become a heavyweight champion. Otherwise, as sociocultural personalities we are what we are by reason of sociocultural forces, and we behave in the way in which these forces impel us to behave. The cardinal importance of the superorganic world in determining human personality will be treated more fully in later chapters.

The subject matter of sociology and the social sciences is generally distinguished in the ways noted above from that of the physical and biological sciences.

II. Sociology Among the Social Sciences

1. Generalizing and Individualizing Sciences

The superorganic or sociocultural universe is studied by all the social and humanistic disciplines. The question arises, therefore, how sociology differs from economics, politics, history, psychology, and other social sciences. Though in a deeper sense all scientific disciplines make one indivisible science, for practical purposes a division of labor requires

specialization in each discipline. Physics differs from chemistry and both from biology, though the boundary lines between them are relative and overlapping. Physical mechanics overlaps with geometry and mathematics; both overlap with chemistry, and all three with biology, giving us organic chemistry and mathematical physics. The difference between sociology and the other social disciplines is also relative;

---

[7] See H. H. Newman, "Mental and Physical Traits of Identical Twins Reared Apart," *Journal of Heredity*, Vol. xxiii (1932), pp. 2-18.

[8] M. McGraw, *Growth; A Study of Johnny and Jimmy* (New York, 1935).

[9] See H. H. Newman, F. N. Freeman, and K. J. Holzinger, *Twins; A Study of Heredity and Environment* (Chicago, 1937).

[10] Among monarchs and multimillionaires there have been both strong and weak constitutions, and feeble as well as brilliant mentalities. Consult P. A. Sorokin, "Monarchs and Rulers," *SF*, Vol. IV (September, 1925; March, 1926) and "American Millionaires and Multimillionaires," *SF*, Vol. III (May, 1925). See there other literature on these problems.

nevertheless, they are as distinct as physics, chemistry, and biology.

Within the great team of social and humanistic disciplines that deal with the superorganic world, sociology has its own distinctive task and performs its functions in a manner tangibly different from that of other members of the team. First, in contradistinction to history and other *individualizing* sciences, sociology is a *generalizing* science. Whereas history concentrates its attention upon the study of the sociocultural phenomena that are unique and unrepeated in time and space (the United States as a distinctive nation; Christianity as a unique religion; Abraham Lincoln as a particular man; the Thirty Years' War as dissimilar from all other wars), sociology studies the properties of the superorganic that are repeated in time and space, that is to say, those common to all sociocultural phenomena (general sociology) or else to all varieties of a given class of sociocultural phenomena—to all wars, all nations, all revolutions, all religions, etc. (special sociologies). By virtue of this generalizing quality sociology differs profoundly from history and other individualizing humanistic disciplines.[11]

2. Contrast with Other Social Sciences

In no less degree does the task of sociology differ from that of such generalizing social sciences as economics, political science, and the science of law. Economics too is a generalizing science, in that it seeks to discover and formulate the properties, relationships, and uniformities that are repeated in time and space and are common either to all economic phenomena (such as the laws of demand and supply or of marginal utility, in general economics), or to all economic phenomena of a certain class (like Gresham's law in the special economics of money, the law of diminishing returns in the special economics of agriculture, and so on). The same can be said, with proper modifications, of any other generalizing social science.

Sociology differs from such disciplines in several ways. In the first place, each of these sciences deals with only one compartment of the sociocultural universe, economics with the economic compartment, politics with the political compartment. Sociology deals, along its special lines, with all compartments of that universe. For instance, economics studies business organizations as a variety of society; political science analyzes the state as a specific kind of society; the science of religion investigates the church as a special form of society. General sociology, on the other hand, is concerned with society as a genus, with the properties and relationships that are found in any society, be it a business firm, a church, a state, a club, the family, or anything else. To take another example: Economics deals with business cycles and fluctuations; political science studies cycles and fluctuations in political life. Sociology sees cycles and fluctuations as generic social phenomena appearing in practically all social processes: economic, political, artistic, religious, philosophical, and their interconnections with one another. The same is true of such social processes as competition and exploitation, domination and subordination, stratification and differentiation, solidarity and antagonism, and so forth. Each of these processes appears not only in single compartments of the superorganic but in practically all compartments of sociocultural life, and as such requires a study of its generic form and of the connections which each special form bears to the other special forms of the same process. Such a study transcends the boundary lines of any compartmentalized discipline. It demands a special science that deals with the generic form of all these phenomena and with the interrelations of all the main varieties with one another. This task has been performed by sociology. Schematically this may be expressed as follows. Let the designated classes of social phenomena consist of the following elements and relationships:

economic: a, b, c, n, m, f
political: a, b, c, h, d, j
religious: a, b, c, g, i, q
and so on.

Granting that all the other varieties of sociocultural phenomena have the same common

---

[11] On the profound difference between the generalizing and the individualizing sciences see H. Rickert, *Die Grenzen der Naturwissenschaftlichen Begriffsbildung* (Tübingen, 1902); A. Xénopol, *La théorie de l'histoire* (Paris, 1908); A. Tschuproff, *Essays in the Theory of Statistics* (St. Petersburg, 1909).

elements and relationships, *a, b, c*—and since they all belong to the same genus of sociocultural phenomena they cannot help having them—a study of these common elements *a, b, c,* would comprise the first task of sociology. On the the other hand, an investigation of how the noncommon elements, for instance, *n, h, g,* are connected with one another—how, for instance, business cycles are related to cycles in the movement of criminality, scientific theories, suicide, artistic tastes, revolutions, etc.—this constitutes its second main task. Neither of these tasks is discharged by any of the compartmentalized social sciences, nor do either of them logically belong to such a science. They comprise the specific domain of sociology.

Along with this deep difference between the tasks of sociology and those of the other generalizing social sciences stands the important difference in their fundamental presuppositions concerning the *nature of man and the interrelations of social phenomena*. The compartmentalized character of economics forces it to postulate *homo economicus*—the purely economic creature controlled by economic self-interest and utilitarian rationality, to the utter exclusion of noneconomic religious beliefs and nonutilitarian moral convictions, of antiegotistic altruism and profitless artistic values, of nonrational mores and irrational passions. In conformity with this, economic phenomena are assumed to be entirely isolated from other sociocultural phenomena and undisturbed by religious, legal, political, artistic, or moral forces. In a similar one-sided manner have been conceived *homo politicus* in the political realm, *homo religiosus* in the religious sphere, and so on.

In contradistinction to these presuppositions, *homo socius* of sociology is viewed as a generic and manifold *homo*, simultaneously and inseparably economic, political, religious, ethical, and artistic, partly rational and utilitarian, partly nonrational and even irrational, with all these aspects incessantly influencing one another. Consequently each class of sociocultural phenomena is viewed by sociology as connected with all the other classes (with varying degrees of interdependence), as influenced by and affecting the rest of the sociocultural universe. In this sense sociology studies man and the sociocultural universe as they really are, in all their manifoldness—as genuine wholes, in distinct contrast to the other sciences, which, for analytical purposes, view them artificially in merely one aspect, entirely isolated from the whole.

From these two fundamental differences follow several others that distinguish the essential principles and methods of sociology from those of other social sciences.

a. *Theories on Cause of Suicide.* The preceding discussion indicates clearly the specific functions of sociology among the various social and humanistic disciplines, as well as the cognitive importance of these functions. Without a discipline performing these functions— whether it is called sociology or abracadabra— no adequate knowledge of important sociocultural phenomena is possible. Even such a minor phenomenon as suicide cannot be adequately understood, especially in its causes, without a study of its occurrence in man's sociocultural universe as a whole. In order to demonstrate this, as well as the functions of sociology, in concrete form, let us pause for a concise analysis of suicide and its causes. The phenomenon is dealt with by biology and medicine, psychiatry, psychology, history, economics, political science, law, ethics, and other biological, social, and humanistic disciplines. Each of these seeks the causes in its own particular field. Biologists and physicians look for them in poor health and similar biological conditions; psychiatrists, in the field of mental disease and derangement; psychologists, in this or that painful experience, such as unrequited love, disillusionment, and fear of scandal or punishment. Geographers seek the causes in climatic and other geographic conditions; economists, in economic factors, such as poverty, depression, and bankruptcy. To a certain extent each of such theories is true. But none is adequate, because none can account for the whole series of fundamental properties of suicide, such as the kind of persons involved, the frequency of its distribution among various societies; periods of increase and decrease; and so on.

History cannot answer these questions at all; it merely describes unique or dissimilar occurrences of suicide among various historical persons. A description of the conditions under which Seneca opened his veins is not a causal analysis and does not even attempt to be one. The recording of an unhappy love affair or of a mental disease does not give the cause, for millions of persons under similar conditions have not committed suicide. The same is true of any special case of suicide studied in accordance with one of these disciplines. A merely atomistic or singularistic study of this or that case does not unravel its cause, for we lack the inductive conditions needed to put our finger on the real cause among hundreds of variables. Suicide has to be investigated as a phenomenon recurrent in various societies and periods. As such it becomes not a special case but a general process or typical phenomenon exhibited by many societies at different times. When it is treated thus, we obtain the data of its frequency in various groups and periods. Possessing these data, we are in a position to test the special theories of the physicians, biologists, psychologists, psychiatrists, economists, and geographers. The test proves that their theories contain at best only a small part of the truth, not the whole truth.

Let us take, for example, an economic interpretation of suicide causation. Hurlburt's[12] study of suicide in the United States for the years 1902-1925 appears to support the economic causes of suicide. The curve of business fluctuations and the curve of suicide in the United States for these years seem to synchronize fairly well, the periods of depression being marked by an increase in suicide and the periods of prosperity by its decrease.

Similar results are obtained by L. I. Dublin and B. Bunzel from data of the Metropolitan Life Insurance Company for the years 1910-1931. The coefficient of correlation between the monthly business index and the monthly suicide index during the period 1910-1931 is relatively high, namely, $-.47 \pm .05$. Kröse, Morselli, Durkheim, and Halbwachs have noted a similar increase in suicide during periods of depression; Halbwachs summarizes

a considerable set of data showing a similar relationship between periods of depression and suicide in Prussia, Germany, Austria, and France. In Austria the crash of 1872 was attended by an increase of about 50 per cent in the suicide rate. In Prussia and Germany the curve of suicide from 1881 to 1913 moved inversely to that of prices and parallel with the number of bankruptcies and financial failures.[13]

Though it may appear that suicide cycles are conditioned and sufficiently explained by economic causes, somewhat more rigorous analysis shows that such an explanation is only a partial truth. First, even in these data the association of suicide and poverty or financial stress is far from convincing. None of these studies yields a high coefficient of correlation between the two phenomena. Thus other factors and conditions are needed to account for the fluctuations of the suicide curve. Second, if economic causes were indeed the main factor of suicide, we should expect that suicide would tend to decrease in a given country, with an increase of economic well-being. The actual situation is quite otherwise. In almost all European countries real wages and the standard of living rose 200 to 300 per cent or more during the nineteenth century, especially during the second half. Yet the suicide curve in almost all these countries failed to decrease; indeed, it actually increased during that period. During the last sixty or seventy years the rate of suicide per 10,000 population has risen in Italy from 2.8 to 8.3; in France from 7.1 to 23; in England from 7.3 to 11; in Prussia from 10.6 to 20.5; in the United States from 3.18 (in 1860) to 11.9 (in 1922). In Denmark, Norway, Switzerland, and Germany alone it either failed to increase or else moved erratically.[14] In all these countries the standard of living improved notably from around 1840 to 1914.

Such a relationship shows at once that the

---

[12] W. C. Hurlburt, "Prosperity, Depression, and the Suicide Rate," *AJS*, Vol. XXXVII (1932), p. 715; L. I. Dublin and B. Bunzel, *To Be or Not To Be* (New York, 1933), p. 102.

[13] See M. Halbwachs, *Les Causes du suicide* (Paris, 1930), pp. 355-374, and other data there.

[14] See the data: E. Ferri, "A Century of Homicides and Suicides in Europe," *Bulletin de l'Institut International de statistique*, Vol. XXII, 3-a

Livraison, 433 ff.; W. A. Bunger, "Le suicide comme phenomène social," *Revue de l'Institut de Sociologie*, XVI (1936), pp. 332-333. P. A. Sorokin and C. Zimmerman, *Principles of Rural-Urban Sociology* (New York, 1929), p. 179. For other data see the quoted works of Halbwachs, Dublin and Bunzel, and the literature given in these works. These rates may be uncorrected, but the correction does not change the result.

long-time trend of suicide is not accounted for by the economic factors of poverty and prosperity. The same conclusion appears when we examine the distribution and frequency of suicide by countries and regions. Many agricultural countries, such as the Balkan States or Russia in the nineteenth century, have been poorer than many western industrial nations. And yet the suicide rate in these poorer countries has been lower than in the more prosperous ones. In the Middle Ages, Europe was poorer economically than in the nineteenth or twentieth century; yet the suicide rate of medieval Europe seems to have been very low. Furthermore, if economic prosperity were the main inhibiting factor and poverty the main cause, we should expect that poor people would regularly show a higher rate of suicide than rich people. Yet the data present a very different picture. If anything, the well-to-do, especially the very rich, tend to exhibit a higher rate than the poor.[15]

These observations are sufficient to show that economic factors alone cannot explain either the distribution of suicide or its main trends and fluctuations. They explain some of its minor fluctuations, in certain periods and in certain countries (mainly industrialized and economically minded), but that is all.[16]

Any theory that tries to account for the phenomenon with reference to one special factor, without due regard to the given society and culture as a whole, is equally fallacious. However convincing at first glance may be an attempted explanation of suicide in terms of physiographical factors such as the climate and the seasons, a more thorough analysis of the phenomena shows that neither the climate nor the change of season nor longitude and latitude are the real causes of social phenomena. Suicide has a fairly uniform seasonal fluctuation that reaches its maximum in May or June in the European countries; but the reason for the increase during these months is not their weather or temperature but the intensity of social life and social conflicts. If the suicide curve falls to its minimum during July, August, and September, the reason again is not the climate or other physiographical factors but the relaxation of social life (vacations, etc.) and a decrease in the social factors in suicide.[17] Although the climate and other geographic factors may be contributing agencies, they are not the basic factors, and in no way do they explain the distribution of suicide in space or its fluctuation in time.

The theories of physicians, psychiatrists, and psychologists contain the same fault. For a long time these men have tried to explain suicide as illness, attributing it to mental disease, disorder, or abnormality. "Suicide is always a malady and an act of mental alienation." So runs the formula.[18] The principal arguments in favor of such theories are the supposedly high percentage of the mentally abnormal among the persons who commit suicide (in some cases alleged to reach almost 100 per cent), the parallel movement of suicide and mental disease, and the like. Although it is true that some of the data cited are unquestionable, the interpretation of these facts by the theory is doubtful, its claims are enor-

[15] See the data by occupational economic classes in Sorokin and Zimmerman, *Principles*, Ch. 7; Sorokin, Zimmerman, and Galpin, *A Systematic Source Book in Rural Sociology*, Ch. 3, pp. 116-121, 178-179 (Minneapolis, 1932). See other data in the quoted works of Halbwachs, Bunger, Dublin and Bunzel, Durkheim, Kröse, and others.

[16] Though even in these minor fluctuations the causative role is due not exactly to the economic factors as such but to the social disorganization in which the depressions, bankruptcies, and sharp economic changes are one of the manifestations, and to the subsequent psychosocial isolation that follows such a disorganization. This is supported by the fact that not only a sharp depression but a sudden economic prosperity is often followed by an increase of suicide. On the other hand, when a sharp economic change (in either direction) does not mean social disorganization and does not lead to psychosocial isolation of individuals it does not produce an increase of suicide.

[17] About the cosmic theories of suicide see H. Morselli, *Suicide* (English tr. New York, 1882); Dublin and Bunzel, *op. cit.*, Ch. 7; J. R. Miner, "Suicide and Its Relation to Climatic and Other Factors," *American Journal of Hygiene*, Monographic Series No. 2 (July, 1922). For an excellent criticism of this interpretation see E. Durkheim, *Le Suicide*, Ch. 3 (Paris, 1912), M. Halbwachs, *op. cit.*, Ch. 4-6.

[18] Bourdin, *Du suicide considéré comme maladie* (Paris, 1845), p. 9. For theories of the prevalent attitude of society toward suicide see A. Bayet, *Le Suicide et la morale* (Paris, 1922). Contemporary psychiatric theories are summarized in Dublin and Bunzel, Ch. 22, and in Halbwachs, pp. 375 ff.

mously exaggerated, and the greater part of the evidence is fallacious.

(1) The percentage of the mentally abnormal among the victims of suicide has in most cases been enormously exaggerated. As the respective studies have been made more accurate, the earlier figures on the mentally abnormal have tended to decrease to as low a proportion as 10 per cent or even less.[19] (2) The nature of many a mental disease is still vague and does not lend itself to definite diagnosis. Hence a wide margin of uncertainty exists even in cases which are supposedly diagnosed as mental abnormality. Not infrequently the very fact that a person has committed suicide induces an automatic diagnosis of abnormality. (3) What mental state is or is not abnormal depends, with a few exceptions (such as idiocy), upon sociocultural conditions. In this sense it is conditional and cannot be diagnosed in a psychiatrist's laboratory; rather it depends upon the prevalent social norms. Mental processes regarded by psychiatrists as abnormal, may by various societies be considered normal —even brilliant, virtuous, saintly, inspired, or heroic. In the opinion of many psychiatrists, most of the saints and mystics of the Middle Ages were abnormal or diseased, whereas in the Middle Ages they were regarded as saintly or gifted, and as such were highly esteemed.[20] In view of this relativity there is reason to question the claims that such phenomena as melancholic depression, suicidal obsession, hysteria, chronic delirium, superexcitability, or even so-called insanity are necessarily forms of mental disease, for the proper standard of reference cannot be a norm per se but must be the norm of a particular culture. If a certain percentage of those who commit suicide display these traits, this does not necessarily mean that they are mentally deranged.[21] This

also explains the supposedly high percentage of the mentally abnormal in those who commit suicide. (4) It does not follow from the possession of certain mental abnormalities that they are the cause of suicide. Mental diseases are often acquired rather than inherited; they result from the particular social conditions in which the victim happens to be placed. In many cases social conditions (A) generate simultaneously an increase of mental abnormality, such as melancholic depression (B), and the suicidal tendency (C). In such cases B is not the cause of C, but both B and C are effects of the common cause A (the given social conditions). Careful study reveals in many cases a relationship of this kind, but does not support the oversimplified interpretation characteristic of the psychiatrist's theory. (5) Decisive evidence derived from actual observation clearly contradicts the psychiatrist's theory in its exaggerated forms. The studies of Durkheim, Halbwachs, Kröse, and others indicate that the countries, regions, or classes which show a higher rate of mental disease do not exhibit a higher rate of suicide, and vice versa. The relationship between these two phenomena displays no positive correlation or association. Likewise, the dynamic movement of the two curves through a period of time does not yield a concomitant variation. In most European countries both suicide and mental disease have tended to increase during the last eighty or ninety years, but their growth has been neither parallel nor mutually consistent. Furthermore, judged by the norms of psychiatry, the population of the Middle Ages was mentally more abnormal (as suggested by the waves of mental "epidemics," flagellation, mysticism, ecstasy, mass hysteria, etc.) than today's population. Yet there is no reason to believe that suicide in the Middle Ages was more frequent than now; indeed, it is reasonably certain that its

[19] See the data in M. Halbwach's work, quoted, Ch. 13; S. J. Kröse, *Die Ursachen of Selbstmordhäufigkeit* (Freiburg, 1906); also his "Die Selbstmörde, 1893-1908" in *Vierteljahrhefte zur Statistik des deutschen Reichs*, Vol. I (1910), p. 108. Dublin and Benzel, *op. cit.*, Ch. 22.

[20] For what is and what is not mental disease, and the dependence of diagnosis upon social conditions, see the studies of A. L. Kroeber and the Shermans in A. Benthley, *Mental Disease* (New York, 1934); R. Benedict, *The Patterns of Culture* (Boston, 1934), Chps. 1-2.

[21] According to the prevalent norms of contemporary psychiatry, ideal mental health seems to be complete mental mediocrity: intellectually neither too bright nor too dull; fairly emotional, but not too emotional, etc. Most men of genius—great poets (with their Bohemian habits of intemperance), artists, mystics, founders of religions, and the like—would appear to be insane, mentally unbalanced, or abnormal. This shows the relativity of the psychiatric norms of mental health and abnormality.

rate was lower than in the nineteenth or twentieth century. Such facts disprove the exaggerated claims of psychiatric theories and show their inability to account for the essential traits of suicide, its distribution in society, or its fluctuation in time.[22]

The foregoing criticism of the psychiatric theory is applicable also, with slight changes, to the medical theories of suicide (bad health, poor sanitary conditions, and the like). We have no reason to suppose that the health of the contemporary population of the West is poorer than was that of the population of the Middle Ages. Yet the suicide rate has been higher in the nineteenth and twentieth centuries than in the Middle Ages. Again, we are not justified in assuming that the health of Europeans or Americans at the end of the nineteenth century and during the prewar years of the twentieth century was poorer than in the years 1700-1850. At least, medical science enthusiastically asserts the progressive improvement of health, the decrease of mortality and morbidity, and the increasing duration of life in the course of the last hundred years. If this is so, then an increase in the rate of suicide among this population clearly contradicts the theory of poor health as the cause of suicide. Furthermore, there is little warrant for believing that the health of the English or Germans is poorer than that of the Spanish or Italians. Yet since the close of the nineteenth century the first two nations have shown a notably higher rate of suicide than the second two.[23]

b. *Durkheim's Explanation of Suicide.* These considerations indicate that no causal theories of suicide which ignore social organization and cultural patterns can account for its essential factors. What, then, does account for its distribution in space and fluctuations in time? Durkheim seems to have answered the problem satisfactorily, at least approximately so. The essence of his theory consists in regarding the total character of the respective society and culture as the cause of suicide. When the entire network of social relationships

is well integrated, when there is a high degree of social cohesion, people feel themselves to be vital parts of the society to which they belong and are free from a sense of psychosocial isolation or loneliness or of being "forgotten persons." Such a type of organization exerts a powerful inhibiting effect upon the tendency to commit suicide. The culture of such a society operates in the same direction. Since the society is integrated, and since its unity is felt by its members, its culture is also unified. Its values are accepted and cherished by all its members, being regarded as superindividual, universal, unchallengeable, and sacrosanct. Such a culture discourages suicide and becomes a potent antisuicidal factor. Conversely, a society with a low degree of cohesiveness, its members being loosely attached to one another and to the group, with a confused network of social norms, with its cultural values "atomized," "relativized," devoid of universal acceptance, and a matter of mere personal preference—such a society is a potent generator of suicide, regardless of climatic conditions or the economic, psychiatric, and health conditions of its members. Such is the essence of the hypothesis. It views a given society and culture as a whole and endeavors thus to account for the distribution of suicide in space and time.

What are the facts that corroborate the theory? They are so numerous and so relevant that they render it more adequate and valid than any other theory of suicide. (1) The factors of sociocultural cohesion and psychosocial isolation explain why, in a given society, the divorced exhibit a higher rate of suicide than the single, and the single than the married; why childless families show a higher rate than families with children; and why the greater the number of children the lower the rate of suicide. Divorced persons have been the most highly isolated psychosocially (especially in the past, when divorce was a scandal entailing social ostracism). The least isolated are families with many children, whose members are bound together by the closest of ties. (2) In the light of this theory it is easily comprehensible why the rural classes show a lower rate of suicide than the urban classes; (3) why among various occupations those which are better integrated show a lower rate than the less integrated and more individualistic occu-

---

[22] See data and criticism of the theory in Durkheim, *op. cit.*, Ch. 1; Halbwachs, *op. cit.*, Ch. 13.

[23] See the comparative rates in the quoted works of Bunger, Ferri, Halbwachs, Sorokin and Zimmerman.

pational groups; (4) why the well-to-do reveal a higher rate than the poorer people, and why an especially high rate is typical of vagabonds and other persons without any occupation or permanent ties. (5) It explains why in countries where a communal and "familistic" type of organization is preserved (as in many predominantly agricultural, only slightly industrialized or urbanized countries) the suicide rate tends to be lower than in highly urbanized, industrialized, and "individualized" countries, even though the latter may be economically better off than the former.

(6) The factors of sociocultural cohesion and psychosocial isolation demonstrate why atheists and free-thinkers (that is, persons not bound by religious ties) show a higher rate of suicide than persons affiliated with the leading religious organizations; and why among the latter the Catholics, the Eastern Orthodox Christians, and the Orthodox Jews reflect a lower rate than the more free-thinking and less dogmatic Protestants. (7) It explains why throughout the nineteenth and twentieth centuries the suicide trend has increased in most European countries. (8) It shows why with the onset of major social movements (whether a popular war, revolution, or reform) the curve of suicide suddenly drops as the sense of individuality gives place to that of joint membership in a common cause, and why it rises again at the close of the movement, when the sense of social oneness fades and psychosocial isolation reappears. (9) It shows why periods of sudden shattering of the network of social relationship, as during economic crises, are followed by an increase of suicide. (10) It shows why there is a higher rate of suicide among men than among women. (11) It explains the annual or daily curve of suicide. (12) It explains why, even in contemporary society, the sick and the mentally diseased exhibit a somewhat higher percentage of suicide than normal persons; sickness and abnormality often accentuate the psychosocial isolation of such persons.[24]

These and many other traits of suicide—its distribution among various groups of the population and its fluctuation in time—are all com-

[24] See the data and analysis of this theory in the quoted works of Durkheim, Halbwachs, Sorokin and Zimmerman, Kröse, and others.

prehensible in the light of this theory. To repeat: without considering the whole character of a given social organization and culture we cannot understand its frequency distribution and its dynamic aspects. A specialized, or "atomistic," approach permits, at best, an understanding of fragmentary parts—never of the entire causation. Hence the cognitive necessity of viewing society as a whole, which is the standpoint of sociology.

3. Limitations of the Compartmentalized Disciplines

What has been said of the causation of suicide applies still more pertinently to the causation of crime, revolution, war, and practically all other sociocultural phenomena. Unless they are studied as *repeated* phenomena, viewed at the same time in the matrix of the *whole* of the respective society and culture, none of them can be adequately understood or their real causes discovered. For instance, if one asks why criminality in the United States shows a higher rate than in certain other nations, what are the causes of the fluctuations of a specific crime or of all crimes, or why the severity of punishment for various crimes now increases and now decreases, none of these questions can be properly answered without a study of crime as a recurrent factor in the general structure of the society and culture in question. It can be confidently asserted that no specialized causal theory of crime—biological, psychiatric, economic, geographic, ecological, educational—can adequately account for its frequency in various societies and groups, for its fluctuation in the course of time, for its prevalent types, or even explain why certain actions are regarded as criminal while others are not. The inadequacy of such one-sided theories is due precisely to their "atomistic," singularistic, and compartmentalized approach, their neglect of the generalizing approach that views society and culture as a whole. This is even more true of large-scale sociocultural phenomena, such as wars and revolutions. Even compartmentalized phenomena, as studied from the standpoint of economics or political science, law or ethics, the fine arts, or history, cannot be fully understood without a consideration of the sociocultural constellation in which they recur. K.

Mannheim correctly observes that—for instance, in political science—"sooner or later one is confronted with the question *why* do the countries at the same period and on the same plane of development have wholly different types of constitutions and forms of government, and *why* when the technique and constitution belonging to one country are taken over by another do they change their form in the adopting country? . . . Thus the political scientist is thrown back on certain unknown entities which he labels 'the national spirit' or 'the cultural heritage of a people.' " This means that it is necessary to consider society and culture as a whole. The same is true when he considers the problem of power and domination or many economic problems. ". . . It is for instance becoming increasingly evident that the choices made by individuals in their capacity as consumers are not fortuitous, but conform to certain collective standards which . . . are determined by non-economic 'social' factors. *What* social factors? To be able to answer this and similar questions, the economist, like the political scientist, seeks as it were a theory of the constants and variables in the formation of human wants."[25] Again it is necessary to go beyond the confines of a special field.

In medicine it is routine procedure for every competent physician, before diagnosing the disease of the patient, to investigate his whole organism and its life history. In the social sciences this routine unfortunately is neither established nor its necessity well understood. As in medicine the specialized approach here is fruitful and reasonable only when the whole of the sociocultural universe is recognized by this or that science. Otherwise it is bound to be inadequate and often misleading. In the great team of the social sciences sociology has been performing exactly this role.[26]

The above gives a sufficient idea of the specific functions of sociology in the team of the social and humanistic sciences; what these functions are in concrete forms; and why such a science is necessary whether it is called sociology or abracadabra.

4. Sociology as a Special Science

Though sociology is a generalizing science dealing with the sociocultural universe as a whole, this does not mean that it is an encyclopedic survey of all the social sciences or that it is a vague philosophical synthesis. The study of the common and current properties, relationships, and uniformities of sociocultural phenomena involves as much specialization as does a study of the unique or segmentary traits and relationships. *In spite of its generalizing nature sociology remains a strictly special science*. Though the president or treasurer of a firm deals with the company as a whole it does not follow that his work is not specialized or that he does the work of all the firm's employees; for the same reason sociology, studying the sociocultural universe as a whole, does not attempt to do the work of the other social sciences. Just as the task of a treasurer or president is not impossible, so the tasks of generalizing sciences—like physics and chemistry, which deal with the repeated properties and relationships of the whole material universe; or general biology, which studies the properties and repeated relationships of the living world, and sociology, which does the same in regard to the superorganic world—these tasks do not necessarily surpass the capacity of a single science. Perhaps they are more difficult than the tasks of a very narrow specialty, but that they are in no way impossible is evidenced by the very existence of such disciplines.

5. Interdependence Between Sociology and Other Sciences

In its generalizing functions sociology depends upon the findings of other special sciences; but every science depends upon several others and the special sciences depend upon the generalizing sciences no less, rather more in fact. Physics uses mathematics, mechanics, geometry, and chemistry; and each

[25] K. Mannheim, "The Place of Sociology," *Conference on the Social Sciences: Their Relations in Theory and in Teaching* (London, 1935), pp. 3 ff. See also M. Weber, "Wirtschaftssoziologie," in *Wirtschaft und Gesellschaft* (Tübingen, 1922); A. Löwe, *Economics and Sociology* (London, 1935).

[26] The urgency of the standpoint of the whole is increasingly recognized by biology, psychology, and other disciplines. See, for instance, W. Köhler, *Gestalt Psychology* (New York, 1929); R. H. Wheeler, "Organismic Vs. Mechanistic Logic," *Psychological Review* (July, 1935).

of these disciplines employs the others. It is impossible for a scholar to work upon any important problem without making use of the findings of other disciplines and scholars. No special problem in physics or chemistry can be solved without a knowledge of the body of these generalizing disciplines. The same is true of special problems in biology and of the main principles of general biology. The specialized science of geology depends much more upon general physics, chemistry, and biology than these depend upon geology.

Similarly, if sociology depends upon history, economics, political science and other compartmentalized social disciplines, these depend no less upon the generalizing science of sociology. Generalizing sociological theories of Plato and Aristotle have exerted a great influence upon the political, economic, legal, historical and other special sciences right up to the present moment. The same is true, in various degrees, of the generalizing conclusions of the works of Augustine and Thomas Aquinas, Hobbes and Machiavelli, Ibn Khaldun and Vico, Montesquieu and Locke, Rousseau and Bossuet, Auguste Comte and Herbert Spencer, Hegel and Marx, Spengler, Durkheim, Tarde, Max Weber, and Pareto. One can cite hundreds of historical, economic, political, anthropological, psychological . . . linguistic and even synological works written along the lines of either Augustinian (Orosius's *History*), or Thomistic, Machiavellian, Hobbesian, Hegelian, Spencerian, Comtean, or Marxian sociological principles.

Emergence of any important sociological system has invariably influenced a series of compartmentalized disciplines, in their leading principles, interpretations, problems studied, methods and techniques of investigation. Almost all the special social and humanistic disciplines in the second half of the nineteenth century were built up along either Hegelian or Comtian-Spencerian principles. Those of more recent times have been enormously affected by Marxian sociology in economic interpretations of data; by Tardian-Durkheimian, Weberian, Paretian and Spenglerian sociological principles and methods.

Even more, the emergence of sociology as a systematic science has been followed by "sociologization" of all the special disciplines in the last few decades. Their content, methods, interpretations, including even those whose authors have been inimical to sociology, have become increasingly sociological and have led to the appearance in all these disciplines of the sociological or institutional schools in jurisprudence and history (so called social histories), in economics and political science, in anthropology and psychology (social psychology), in sciences that examine fine arts and ethics, religion and even logic. Such a "sociologization" of these disciplines is eloquent evidence of the influence of sociology upon them. The dependence between sociology and the other social sciences is mutual; it is interdependence, not a one-sided dependence of sociology upon the other sciences.[27]

As a generalizing discipline general sociology

[27] If sociology has been enormously influenced by biology, then biology has also been affected by sociology in many ways. Darwin's theory of evolution and of the struggle for existence was suggested by Malthus' work; Spencer's formula of evolution or progress is still the most generally used formula of biological evolution, while several biological concepts like the division of labor and differentiation were taken from sociology. See G. Tarde, "La théorie organique des sociétés" in *Annales de l'Institut International de sociologie*, Vol. IV. In the last few decades biology has increasingly emphasized the social factors in causation of many biological phenomena, especially in the aetiology of various diseases and of transformation and modification of organisms, not to mention the emergence of various offshoots of biology—"ecology," "animal sociology," "plant sociology," and the like. In all these respects the impact of sociology has been so considerable that several prominent biologists entitle their studies "Soziologie innerer Krankheiten," "Soziologie Geschlechtskrankheiten," "Ueber den Einfluss der Berufe auf das Herz," "Krankheit und soziale Lage," and the like. Several corresponding studies with sociological titles are to be found in the *Handbuch der soziale Hygiene* (Berlin, 1926-29), all volumes; or M. Mosse and G. Tugendreich (ed.), *Krankheit und soziale Lage* (Munich, 1913). Some branches of medical science, psychiatry, for example, are becoming increasingly sociological. These and many other facts unmistakably show that biology and sociology influence one another. Later on in this work it will be shown that even mathematics, physics, and chemistry are socially conditioned in their nature and development. The sociology of knowledge has contributed to the demonstration of this condition, making these sciences aware of the psychosocial implications of many of their propositions.

has to be somewhat abstract and theoretical, and for this reason may appear to many a "practical man" as an impractical academic preoccupation, divorced from concrete actuality and devoid of practical utilitarian value. Here as well as in all such reasonings of too practical men (who, according to Lao-tzu are the most impractical), the fallacy of their conclusion is evident. Mathematics is possibly the most abstract and theoretical of all the sciences. And yet its practical importance is unquestionable. Algebra and calculus are more abstract than arithmetic. And yet who would conclude they are less important practically than arithmetic? General theoretical physics, chemistry, and biology are much more abstract and "impractical" than a cookbook or instruction book for a Chevrolet or other automobile. And yet without theoretical physics, chemistry, and biology neither an automobile nor a good cookbook could be produced. The same is true of sociology as a generalizing, theoretical, and somewhat abstract discipline. Its practical influence—whether good or bad does not concern us here—has been rather startling. In most of the great social revolutions, reforms, and reconstructions it is sociology of this or that kind which has been the leading ideology and guide. Thus Lockean sociology played this part in the Revolution of 1688 and the establishment of the liberal democratic regime in England; the thinking of Voltaire, Rousseau, and other Encyclopedists had a similar role in the French Revolution of 1789 and subsequent years. In our own time Marxian sociology has been the driving intellectual scheme and "the gospel" of the Communist revolution in Russia; the racial sociologies of A. Gobineau, H. S. Chamberlain, and others became the credo of the Nazi revolution and the Third Reich. From the sociology of Confucius to that of the present the practical effects of this study have been influential (although often fallacious sociologies, unhappily, instead of the valid ones). This fact is sufficient to dispel the illusions of the too practical men in this field.

To summarize: sociology is a generalizing science of sociocultural phenomena viewed in their generic forms, types, and manifold interconnections.

6. General and Special Sociologies

Like biology, which is divided into general and special biologies (botany, zoology, and their further subdivisions), and like economics, which is divided into general and special economics (banking and money, transportation and agriculture), sociology can also be divided into general and special sociologies. *General sociology* studies (a) the properties and uniformities common to all sociocultural phenomena in their structural and dynamic aspects as well as (b) the recurring interrelationships between the sociocultural and the cosmic phenomena; the sociocultural and the biological phenomena; the various classes of sociocultural phenomena.

Structural general sociology studies (a) the structure and composition of the generic sociocultural phenomenon (corresponding to the study of the structure of a cell as a phenomenon of life or that of an atom in physics); (b) the main structural types of the groups or institutions into which human population is differentiated and stratified and their relationship to one another; (c) the main structural types of the cultural systems and their relationships with one another; (d) the structure and types of personality embedded in social groups and cultural systems.

Dynamic general sociology investigates (a) recurring social processes, such as social contact, interaction, socialization, conflict, domination, subordination, adaptation, amalgamation, migration, mobility; how social systems are born, how they acquire and lose members; how they distribute these within the system, how they become organized and disorganized, and how all these processes affect the personality of the individuals involved; (b) recurring cultural processes—invention, diffusion, integration and disintegration, conversion and the accumulation of cultural traits and systems—and how they affect the personality of the individuals involved; (c) rhythms, tempos, periodicities, trends and fluctuations in social and cultural processes, together with the general problem of sociocultural change and evolution; (d) recurring sociocultural processes in persons, and how and why persons change.

Special sociologies each do the same in regard to a special class of sociocultural phenomena chosen for intensive study. The most de-

General		Special
Structural[28]	Dynamic	
Theory of:	Theory of the recurring:	Theory of structure and dynamics of the respective class of sociocultural phenomena studied in their generic and repeated aspects and relationship.
a. social systems and congeries;	a. social processes and change;	
b. cultural systems and congeies;	b. cultural processes and change;	
c. personalities in their structural aspect, main types, and interrelations.	c. personality processes and change in their types, interrelationships, rhythms, trends, and causal factors.	

veloped special sociologies are at present: sociology of population, rural sociology, urban sociology; sociology of the family, of law, of religion, of knowledge; sociology of war, of revolution, of social disorganization; sociology of crime and punishment (criminology); sociology of the fine arts; sociology of economic phenomena; and several others.

In a schematic form the main divisions of sociology can be represented as above.

This delineation of sociology is logically more adequate[29] and better corresponds to what sociology has actually been than other definitions, such as the science "of culture," "of society," "of human relations," "of social interaction," "of forms of social relationships," and the like. These definitions are far too loose. They do not point out the specific characteristics of sociology or differentiate it from other social sciences. On the other hand, the sound part of these definitions is well incorporated into the above delineation.

This tabular definition presents the logical structure of sociology as a scientific discipline

regardless of who carries on the studies; whether a sociologist ex-officio or historian, economist, or engineer. From the fact that Sir Isaac Newton wrote his *Principia* and his *Observations upon the Prophecies of Daniel* it does not follow that both works belong to the same science; one is a great treatise in mechanics, the other in theology, though both were written by the same man. Likewise, many important sociological works were written by historians like F. de Coulanges, by engineers like Le Play and Herbert Spencer, or mathematicians like August Comte. Many sociological generalizations are found in treatises on history, philosophy, economics, and other sciences. And conversely, some ex-officio sociologists have written books that do not belong to sociology but fall into the domain of some other science. Even in textbooks of sociology one can find large portions that belong to pre-sociology or other disciplines. This difference between the logical nature of sociology and the ex-officio authorship of a sociological study must be kept clearly in mind.[30]

[28] One can easily see that in this division of sociology into structural and dynamic I follow Comte's division of sociology into social statics and dynamics. So far it has been the most fruitful of all the divisions.

[29] Theoretical sociology studies the sociocultural universe as it is, in contradistinction from *normative* sociology, that sets forth the ideal sociocultural world as it ought to be; and from *practical or applied* sociology which, like medicine or agronomy, consists in a scientific arrangement of the most efficient ways and means for a realization of a certain objective—elimination of poverty, war, etc. Like many applied disciplines, applied sociology, or the art of social engineering, must use not only the data of sociology but of several other sciences. And as with any applied discipline its validity depends upon the level of knowledge attained by theoretical sociology; as long as this is low, no successful and efficient applied social engineering is possible. In this work we are concerned only with theoretical sociology. On the difference between the theoretical, normative, and applied disciplines see my "Sociology and Ethics" in W. F. Ogburn and A. Goldenweiser, *The Social Sciences and Their Interpretations* (Boston, 1927) and H. Poincaré, *Dernières pensées*, Ch. on "Science and Ethics" (Paris, 1913).

[30] On sociology as a science see P. A. Sorokin, "Sociology as a Science," and S. Rice, "What is Sociology," both in *SF*, Vol. X (1931); see there other articles on this topic in subsequent numbers. K. Mannheim, "The Place of Sociology," in *Conference on the Social Sciences: Their Relations in Theory and Teaching* (London, 1935); R. Thurnwald (ed.), *Soziologie von Heute*, (Leipzig, 1932); articles by A. Walther, H. Freyer, F. Plenge, P. A. Sorokin, M. Ginsberg, W. Ogburn, R. MacIver, S. R. Steinmetz, F. Tönnies, R. Thurnwald; in W. Ogburn and A. Goldenweiser (ed.), *The Social Sciences and Their Interrelations* (Boston, 1927); L. von Weise, *Sociology* (New York, 1941).

III. Methods and Referential Principles

In essence the methods and referential principles of sociology are the same as those of science generally. But every basic science modifies these principles, methods, and technical procedures in conformity with the nature of the phenomena. For instance, chemistry's principles and techniques are different from those of physics and biology. Similarly, sociology has its own modifications of the principles and procedures demanded by the peculiar nature of sociocultural phenomena, especially by their components of meaning-value-norm. (See further Chapters 3, 4, et passim.) It

operates with such categories as causality, time, space, and others (as we shall see further), but in a manner notably different from that of the natural sciences. In its study it uses logical-mathematical and syllogistic deductive methods, moderately exploits intuitive insight (always checked by other methods), widely applies empirical observation in all its forms: induction, statistical analysis, case or clinical observation, even experiment; but again with considerable modification of each of these methods and techniques, so as to adjust to the specific character of superorganic phenomena.[31]

---

[31] On method see E. Durkheim, *The Rules of Sociological Method* (Chicago, 1938); C. Ellwood, *Methods in Sociology* (Durham, 1933); F. Znaniecki, *The Method of Sociology* (New York, 1934); S. Rice (ed.), *Methods in Social Sciences* (New York, 1931); P. A. Sorokin, *Sociocultural Causality, Space, Time* (Durham, 1943); R. M. MacIver, *Social Causation* (Boston, 1942); L. Bernard (ed.), *Fields and Methods of Sociology* (New York, 1933); V. Pareto, *Mind and Society* (New York, 1935), Vol. I, Ch. 1; W. Dilthey, *Einleitung in die Geisteswissenschaften* (Leipzig, 1883); M. Weber, *Gesammelte Aufsätze zur Wissenschaftslehre* (Tübingen, 1922); H. Rickert, *op. cit.*; P. A. Sorokin, *Social and Cultural Dynamics* (New York, 1937-41), Vols. I, IV; W. Thomas and F. Znaniecki, *The Polish Peasant* (New York, 1927), Vol. I, "Methodological Note"; A. Toynbee, *A Study of History* (Oxford, 1936), Vol. I; E. Greenwood, *Experimental Sociology* (New York, 1945).

Chapter 2. Development of Sociology

I. In the Orient, Greece, Rome, Medieval Europe, and Arabia

Though the word "sociology" as coined by August Comte is of relatively recent origin, yet unsystematized observations and generalizations of a sociological character are as old as those of any social science. They have been represented in a great number of ancient works. Human knowledge in the remote past was as yet undifferentiated into the diverse separate scientific disciplines now prevailing. As a result most of the works of the past have contained in undifferentiated form the elements of what was later called religion, poetry, philosophy, natural science, and the social sciences. Parts of these works are often clearly sociological in character. Many portions of the *Texts of Confucianism*—the Confucian theories of the five fundamental social relationships, filial piety, benevolence and reciprocity as the essence of sociality, ritual, ceremony, poetry, and music as the means of social control—are neither political nor philosophical in character, but distinctly sociological. The same is true of portions of the *Texts of Taoism*, of the works of Mencius, Motze, and other Chinese social thinkers. Similarly, many parts of the works of ancient Hindu thinkers, in particular *The Laws of Manu, Brihaspati, Narada*, and the *Institutes of Vishnu* are largely sociological studies outlining the repeated characteristics and relationships common to all or to a special class of sociocultural phenomena.[1]

Still more true is this of the Greek, Roman, and medieval scholars. Even the pre-Socratic thinkers in Greece, such as Solon, Parmenides, Heraclitus, Pindar, and Protagoras, offered many sociological generalizations. Thucydides' *History of the Peloponnesian War* contains sections constituting a special sociology of revolution, war, and political regimes, not to mention generalizations on the relationship between various classes of sociocultural phenomena. Plato's *Republic*, his *Laws*, and some of the *Dialogues*, for instance like the *Statesman*, as well as Aristotle's *Politics*, and to a lesser degree, *Nichomachean Ethics*, are largely treatises in general and special sociologies, as is evidenced in their analyses of society (*koinon*), of the forms of friendship as the types of sociality, of social differentiation and stratification. Further proof of their sociological content is to be found in their generalized theories of revolution, of the cycles of sociopolitical regimes, of the correlations between types of personality, culture, and sociopolitical regimes, and so on. Polybius' *Histories* abound with sociological analyses. The works of Strabo, Varro, Cicero, Lucretius, Columella, C. Ptolemy (his *Tetrabyblos*); those of many lesser known authors like the historians Dicaearchus, Florus and Diodorus Siculus; the rhetoricians Censorinus (his *De Die Natali*), Celsus, Sextus Empiricus; the scientific poet Marcus Mani-

[1] See B. Sarkar. *The Positive Background of Hindu Sociology* (Allahabad, 1937); K. Motvani, *Manu* (Madras, 1934); M. Granet, *La pensée chinoise* (Paris, 1934); J. Hertzler, *The Social Thought of the Ancient Civilizations* (New York, 1929).

19

lius, and others, are similarly fruitful. Especially great was the contribution of the great Roman jurists to structural sociology and to what is now called "institutional" and "formal" sociology. In their works, later incorporated into the *Corpus Juris Civilis* of Justinian, they gave an unexcelled analysis and definition of all the basic social institutions and the main forms of social relationships: marriage, the family, the state, property, and possessions; *potestas, imperium, dominium, manus, status, contractus,* and so on.[2]

Sociological studies were continued by Augustine, Irenaeus, and other Church Fathers whose works contain a number of sociological observations and generalizations in various fields of sociology, as well as by several medieval thinkers—Erigena, John of Salisbury, Joachim de Flore; and by a number of medieval jurists and scholastics such as Dante, Pierre du Bois, Marsilio of Padua, Albertus Magnus, Thomas Aquinas, Roger Bacon, Nicolas of Cusa, and others. Most textbooks ignore the medieval period as though it were empty of

either political or economic, sociological or philosophical theories. In fact it is much richer in works of all these fields than is usually thought and needs more study than has hitherto been given.[3]

Before the fourteenth century, however, sociology hardly constituted a systematic discipline. In the fourteenth century it made such an appearance with the publication of the *Historical Prolegomena* (1377) by a great Arabian thinker and statesman, Ibn Khaldun (1332-1406). In this extensive work, under the name of a "New History," Ibn Khaldun systematically discussed almost all the main problems of contemporary general and special sociology in terms of the nomadic and civilized societies. Large portions of this work appear quite modern even at the present time. Side by side with Plato, Aristotle, G. Vico, and August Comte, Ibn Khaldun is certainly one of the founders of sociology (as well as of a scientific history). Unfortunately the work of Ibn Khaldun remained unknown to western thinkers almost up to the nineteenth century.[4]

II. From the Renaissance to Modern Times

With the Renaissance and the Reformation interest in sociological problems notably increased and led to numerous inquiries during the sixteenth and seventeenth centuries. A large part of the works of Erasmus, Machiavelli, G. Botero, François Holtman, Francis Bacon, J. Bodin, J. Harrington, Montaigne, and Pascal were sociological. The same is true of the utopians Thomas More, Campanella, and others; of the social contractualists Althusius, R.

Hooker, Suarez, Marianna, Pufendorf, Grotius, Hobbes, Spinoza, Locke, and others; of the political arithmeticians and cameralists J. Graunt, W. Petty, G. King, Deparcieux, J. Süssmilch, and others.

Two developments in the seventeenth and in part the eighteenth centuries deserve special mention.

First, there was the emergence of the so-called "social physics" during these centuries,

[2] On early Greek sociology, see W. Jaeger, *Paideia,* 3 Vols. (Oxford, 1939-44); A. Menzel, *Griechische Soziologie* (Wien, 1936). R. Ihering, *Geist des römischen Rechts,* 3 Vols. (Berlin, 1894-1907); R. Sohm, *Institutionen* (Berlin, 1911). P. Willems, *Le droit public romain* (Paris, 1910). E. F. Kitzer, "Early Western Social Thought," *American Catholic Social Review,* VI, pp. 201-212.

[3] For medieval political and sociological theories see O. Gierke, *Das deutsche Genossenschaftsrecht,* 4 Vols. (Berlin, 1868-1913); *Political Theories of the Middle Age,* tr. by F. Maitland (Cambridge, 1900); P. Janet, *Histoire de science politique* (Paris, 1887); C. H. McIlwain, *The Growth of Political Thought in the West* (New York, 1932); R. W. and A. Carlyle, *A History of Medieval*

Political Theory in the West, 5 Vols. (Edinburgh, 1903-28); F. J. C. Hearnshaw (ed.), *Social and Political Ideas of Some Great Mediaeval and Later Thinkers,* 8 Vols. (London, 1923-33); H. E. Barnes and H. Becker, *Social Thought from Lore to Science* (Boston, 1938), Vol. I; E. Troeltsch, *Die Soziallehren der Christlichen Kirchen und Gruppen* (Tübingen, 1923); English translation (London, 1931).

[4] See French translation of his work under the title *Prolégoménes Historiques,* tr. by M. G. de Slane in the *Notices et extraits des manuscripts de la Bibliothéque Impérial publiés par l'Institut Impérial de France* (Paris, 1862-68), Tomes XIX, XX, XXI.

in which Descartes, Cumberland, Spinoza, Hobbes, Leibniz, Malebranche, Berkeley, and especially E. Weigel tried to build social science along the mechanistic and quantitative lines of Newtonian mechanics. With their social physics, and "sociometrika" they were unexcelled pioneers of all the subsequent mechanistic, physical, mathematical, statistical, behavioristic, and sociometric interpretations of sociocultural phenomena.[5]

The second important event was the publication of two versions of the *New Science* by Giambattista Vico (1668-1744). Hardly noticed and very little appreciated during the life of Vico, this work came into its own in the nineteenth century as one of the most important in the history of sociology and social science. It is the first systematic treatise in social and cultural dynamics and deservedly puts its author among the true founders of sociology.

During the eighteenth and the first third of the nineteenth centuries the sociological work of the preceding centuries continued on an ever expanding and differentiated scale. Political arithmeticians and cameralists of this period contributed greatly to the study of population. Malthus' famous work was a culmination of this sociology of population. Physiocrats such as F. Quesnay, Mercier de la Rivière, Mirabeau the Elder, and others, were busy not only with purely economic or political questions but to an even greater extent with the basic problems of society, culture, the laws that govern sociocultural phenomena, and the problems of rural and urban sociology.

Among the larger number of social thinkers during this period who made important contributions to sociology were Montesquieu, who wrote the first systematic sociology of law and mores (his *Spirit of Law*); Adam Ferguson, who gave a system of general sociology in his main works; J. de Maistre and E. Burke, who wrote important sociologies of revolution; Adam Smith, whose work on moral sentiments and on the social aspects of the wealth of nations were important contributions to the sociology of ethical and economic phenomena; Voltaire, and especially, Turgot, Condorcet, Saint Simon, Herder, and Hegel, who laid down the theory of sociocultural evolution and progress; Savigny and Puchta, who through their studies of the origin and crystallization of social institutions and law said most of what one finds in the contemporary sociology of folkways and mores as developed by Herbert Spencer, W. Sumner, and others; Jeremy Bentham and other utilitarians, who demonstrated the role of utilitarian factors in sociocultural phenomena generally and in ethical and jural phenomena particularly and who, in the form of "the moral arithmetics," tried to analyze these phenomena quantitatively and to measure them sociometrically. Important contributions in various fields of sociology were made also by Beccaria, Bossuet, Rousseau, Grimm, Brisot, Condillac, Mably, La Mettrie, Morelli, Hume, Kant, Fichte, Blackstone, Godwin, and many others in the period.[6]

With the publication of the *Cours de philosophie positive* (six volumes, 1830-1842) by August Comte (1798-1857), sociology acquired its own name and a definite system. Comte defined it as a generalizing science of social order (or structure) and social progress (or dynamics). He divided it respectively into social statics and dynamics. Because of his great contribution to sociology Comte became one of its founders. Somewhat later, in England, an exceptionally important role in the development of sociology was played by Herbert Spencer (1820-1903). Comte's and Spencer's works, in addition to those of Hegel (1770-1831), have truly become the cornerstones of subsequent sociology.

[5] For social physics of that century and subsequent imitations of it see E. Spektorsky, *The Problems of Social Physics of the Seventeenth Century*, 2 Vols. in Russian (Warsaw and Kiev, 1910-17); P. A. Sorokin, *Contemporary Sociological Theories* (New York, 1928) Ch. 1.

[6] For the German sociology of these centuries see H. Stoltenberg, *Geschichte der deutschen Gruppwissenschaft* (Leipzig, 1937); for other countries see J. P. Lichtenberger, *Development of Social Theory* (New York, 1923); Barnes and Becker, *op. cit.*, Vol. I; C. A. Ellwood, *A History of Social Philosophy* (New York, 1938); F. House, *Development of Sociology* (New York, 1936). For history of rural sociology see P. A. Sorokin, C. Zimmerman and C. Galpin, *A Systematic Source Book in Rural Sociology* (Minneapolis, 1930), Vol. I. For a history of the theories of social rhythms, cycles, and periodicities see P. A. Sorokin, *Social and Cultural Dynamics* (New York, 1941), Vol. IV; W. C. Lehmann, *Adam Ferguson and the Beginning of Modern Sociology* (New York, 1930).

III. Recent and Contemporary Sociology

The post-Comtean phase of the development of sociology, right up to the present time, has been so prolific and fruitful and so diversified and differentiated that only its most outstanding characteristics can be mentioned here.

(1) The number of general and special works in sociology has enormously increased in all the civilized countries of the world.

(2) A considerable number of special sociological journals and periodicals have made their appearance, not only in European and American countries but also in China, Japan, and India.

(3) Sociology courses and departments in colleges and universities have been increasingly introduced, and sociology has become a full-fledged discipline in the university curriculum. In the United States this penetration of sociology into the academic world has been particularly great, so that nowadays sociology departments and courses rank near the top in the number of enrolled students.

(4) The "academization" of sociology has created a need for books on this subject and has resulted in the production of more and more sociological texts, particularly in the United States.

(5) Sociologists have been increasingly called as experts into governmental, public, and private service; and especially into what is called social work or social service.

(6) While sociology has been affected by other sciences—social, biological, and physical —it has since Comte influenced the other social, humanistic, philosophical, and even biological sciences to a greater and greater degree. This or that "sociological viewpoint" has increasingly penetrated all these disciplines: history, economics, the science of government, psychology, anthropology, the sciences of religion, fine arts, linguistics, philosophy, ethics, and law. In the decades of domination by the Comtean, Spencerian, and Darwinian sociologies, most historical, political, economic, and other works had been written along the lines of the Comte-Spencer theories of positivism and of progressive evolution. During the vogue of Marxian sociology

a large portion of the works in the above disciplines showed the stamp of the "economic interpretation" of historical, psychological, economic, religious, and philosophical data studied by these disciplines. Biology has borrowed several sociological concepts—the division of labor, differentiation, integration; furthermore, biologists are examining general and special sociocultural factors in the study and interpretation of many of their own problems, especially the study and treatment of many diseases. In psychiatry this dependence upon sociology has become habitual; in other medical fields, the very terms "sociology of venereal disease," "sociology of epidemics," "sociology of heart-disease" and so on, show clearly the extent of this influence. In dozens of other ways sociology has been modifying other disciplines, even those whose scholars either attempt to deny this modification or assume a negative attitude.

(7) Sociology is constantly growing more factual, less speculative; its research methods have become increasingly inductive, precise, and objective. Side by side with improved qualitative analysis, there has been a great development in quantitative analysis and techniques, in observational and experimental methods of study of social and cultural phenomena. As a result contemporary sociology is much nearer to the natural sciences in objectivity, preciseness, and inductiveness of method than are most of the other social and humanistic disciplines.

(8) While recent sociology has inclined toward synthesis, it has in the same period become progressively more specialized and differentiated. Particular sociologies appear and, in their turn, are split into still narrower problems and subproblems. Specialization has gone so far that, in order to achieve a genuine comprehension of the whole sociocultural universe, it is now imperative that a fruitful and valid synthesis be prepared, before the study becomes hopelessly enmeshed in fragmentary, disconnected, and irrelevant facts and problems. Attempts to meet this need have been made in a number of synthesizing works. Such

attempts are likely to increase in the future.

The preoccupations and character of contemporary sociology can be seen from a concise enumeration of the main currents of recent sociological thought and research.

1. Cosmosociology

Continuing the works of Strabo, Ptolemy, Ibn Khaldun, and Montesquieu, to mention but a few predecessors, a large number of studies have been devoted to an investigation of uniformities in the relationship between geographic conditions (climate, sun-spots, flora, fauna, configuration of the locality, etc.), and sociocultural phenomena (the distribution of population on the earth, its density and size; its racial and ethnic characteristics, its vital processes, health, energy, and mental efficiency; its morbidity and suicide; criminality and insanity; economic phenomena such as kinds of clothing, food, buildings, character and distribution of industries, fluctuation of business conditions; religion, philosophy, science, fine arts, law and ethics; forms of political organization, war and peace; and finally, the emergence, evolution, and decline of civilizations). In spite of the exaggerated influence generally attributed to geographic factors in their relation to sociocultural life, and in spite of several mistakes committed in these studies, they have given us a more solid and precise picture of uniformities in the interrelationship between the geographic and sociocultural realms. They have improved geographical sociology and have created social geography as an important branch of general geography. F. Ratzel, F. Le Play, H. de Tourville, E. Demolins, L. Metchnikoff, E. Reclus, P. Mougeolle, Vidal de la Blache, J. Bruhnes, E. Huntington, E. Dexter, E. Semple, Morselli, H. Moore, R. de Ward, W. Jevons, and many others have distinguished themselves in this field.[7]

2. Biosociology

In a similar manner the earlier investigations of the relationship between biological and sociocultural phenomena have been ener-

getically pursued during recent times. (a) Many a sociologist has attempted to analyze human society in terms of a biological organism, to note in what respects the social organism in its structure and processes is similar to, and in what respects it is dissimilar from, the biological organism. Some insight and knowledge has been gained through this *bio-organismic* interpretation of sociocultural phenomena, though the results have been rather modest. The works of P. Lilienfeld, J. Bluntschli, Herbert Spencer, A. Schäffle, R. Worms, J. Novikov, and still more recently, of C. Gini, La Ferriére, and Kjellen, have been the most important contributions in this field. (b) A large number of scholars have been busy elucidating the role of such biological factors as biological constitution, race, and heredity upon human affairs and sociocultural life. Arthur de Gobineau, H. S. Chamberlain, and a legion of such popularizers as M. Grant, and more recently the crowd of Nazi ideologists have given a whole philosophy of history interpreted through these factors. From the behavior of an individual on up to the rise and decline of civilizations, almost every sociocultural phenomenon has been viewed as controlled by these factors of race and heredity. (c) V. de Lapouge, O. Ammon, and other *anthropometrists*, on the basis of a study of the anthropometric traits of races and of a large number of measurements, gave support to the preceding theories, extolling the superiority of the Nordic race, and asserting its leading role in human history. They went on to formulate several laws of social stratification, social selection, urbanization, and the rise and decline of nations and social classes, all interpreted through the racial and hereditary biological factors. In a special detail of this current of sociological thought, C. Lombroso and quite recently E. Hooton have attempted to prove that criminality and its forms are caused by the biological constitutions of individuals. Others have advanced the same theory in regard to genius, mental ability, and the creative achievements of human beings.

(d) Still another variety of this biological interpretation of social phenomena has been carried on by many a *geneticist, eugenist, biometrician,* and *biologist* who ascribed paramount importance to the factors of heredity,

---

[7] See the theories, facts, literature, and criticism in P. A. Sorokin, *Contemporary Sociological Theories,* Chs. 2, 3. G. Dykmans, *Introduction critique à la science économique,* Vol. II (Bruxelles, 1945).

selection, and other biological conditions. F. Galton, K. Pearson, and an enormous number of other scholars have been promoting this kind of study. (e) Another subcurrent of this biological interpretation has been supplied by the Darwinian school, which uses concepts such as the struggle for existence, survival of the fittest, biological selection, and heredity, in an attempt to explain a large set of sociocultural phenomena—war, social antagonism, revolution, the rise and decline of nations, norms of ethics and law, and so on. The works of Gumplowitz, Ratzenhofer, Woltmann, Vaccaro, and Nasmith are samples of this stream of biosociological thought. (f) Another branch of biosociology is represented by the *demographic school*, which makes numerous and often painstaking studies of the influence of population density and size in conditioning various sociocultural phenomena. These statistical studies of vital processes (births, deaths, marriages, divorces, morbidity, etc.) give us a *special sociology of the population*, so far as they emphasize the purely biological factors of population density and size as instrumental in determining forms of social organization, political regimes, the success or failure of ideologies of equality, various religious beliefs, law norms, and so on. The works of A. Coste, M. Kovalevsky, C. Bouglé, C. Gini, R. Pearl, J. Brownlee, G. Yule, Stevenson, F. Carli, E. and A. Kulishers, A. Carr-Saunders are typical for this school of sociology. (g) Finally, all the theories that particularly stress the important role of instincts, reflexes, biological drives, and the unconscious biological forces in human behavior, mentality, and sociocultural life, belong to the biosocial branch of sociology. The works of Freud, Jung, and other psychoanalysts; of H. Blüher, W. McDougall, H. Ellis, W. Trotter, J. Watson, and other behaviorists represent this branch of biosociology.

Taken as a whole all these varieties of investigation into the relationship of biological and sociocultural phenomena have amassed a prodigious amount of impressive facts in this field and have disclosed a series of important uniformities and correlations between these classes of phenomena. They have thrown light upon many problems, both general and special, as to the extent to which biological factors condition sociocultural phenomena, and vice versa. On the other hand, most of these investigations have exaggerated the influence of biological factors; some of their findings have proved fallacious. Generally these mistakes have been discovered and corrected by the criticism of other sociologists and biosociologists.[8]

When we turn from a study of the cosmic (or geographic) and biological phenomena to the sociocultural universe in its structural and dynamic aspects, its classes and types, we find a variety of approaches, methods, and conceptual schemes used by different scholars. This variety can easily be reduced to three main schools of sociology: (1) mechanistic; (2) psychological; (3) sociologistic or sociocultural; with each school differentiated into several branches. While in theory these schools and their branches partially contradict one another, they can be legitimately differentiated in terms of the specific set of phenomena upon which each concentrates its attention, as well as the specific methodological and conceptual scheme it uses. The fact that the "psychological school" studies primarily the psychological aspects of the sociocultural universe while the "sociologistic school" stresses the sociocultural aspects per se does not necessarily mean that their theories are contradictory. Rather it signifies a specific standpoint from which the manifold sociocultural universe is studied. The results obtained from each angle supplement in most of the cases, rather than contradict, the results obtained from other standpoints. The net outcome of such divergence is a more adequate and many-sided knowledge of the manifold sociocultural universe. This needs to be emphasized in order to avoid the frequent mistake of interpreting this diversity as a sign of the immaturity of sociology. Since the universe itself is many-sided there must logically be several standpoints, each of which specializes in the study of one of the main aspects. Such a specialization is found, as a matter of fact, in any basic science, from physics and chemistry to biology. Let us now briefly survey the three main schools just mentioned.

---

[8] See the detailed analysis, criticism, and literature of the biosocial school in P. A. Sorokin, *Contemporary Sociological Theories*, Chs. 4-7, 11.

3. Mechanistic School

Following the social physics of the seventeenth century and enchanted by the progress of the physicochemical sciences, many a sociologist has recently tried to develop sociology as a branch of these sciences by imitating their terminology, referential principles, and laws. In most cases the mechanistic school merely transported these principles into the sociocultural field and applied them uncritically. H. C. Carey and other scholars attempted to create a *social physics* and tried to interpret economic and other social phenomena in terms of physical mechanics and physics. Others, like Voronoff, Haret, Portuondo y Barcelo, M. Lins, and Ferreira, tried to create *social mechanics* in the same imitative way. Still others, like E. Solvay, W. Ostwald, Bekhtereff, Winiarsky, and Carver, endeavored to interpret sociocultural phenomena in terms of *energetics and mechanics*. A few—K. Lewin, J. Brown, and others—mainly imitated geometry in their efforts to create "topological" sociology and psychology. Finally, a number of very recent works have ventured to describe and analyze social facts in a general imitation of natural scientific methods, without forcing their principles too far or limiting their imitative efforts strictly to mechanics, physics, or geometry. They have taken anything in the physicochemical and geometrical sciences that appealed to their fancy as suitable for imitation. Most of these attempts, as those of Lundberg, Dodd, Chapple, Coon, and others, have been eclectic, deficient in a knowledge of the principles and theories of mathematical and physicochemical sciences, and therefore immature and fruitless. Others, mainly following the methods of the natural sciences in a broad sense and properly modifying whatever principles they borrowed from these sciences (equilibrium, causation, and so on), have succeeded somewhat better in their task and have contributed to our understanding of the sociocultural universe. V. Pareto's *Mind and Society* is an example of one of those more fruitful works. However, even Pareto and a few others have made their contribution not so much through an imitation of the concepts and methods of the natural sciences as through incessant violation of their own proclaimed methods and principles and through an actual study of sociocultural phenomena by methods and techniques adapted to the true nature of these phenomena. Otherwise, the efforts of the strict partisans of social geometry or topology, social physics, social mechanics, social energetics, and so on, have remained largely sterile.[9]

4. Psychological School

Since by definition the sociocultural or superorganic phenomena are mental in their nature, the difference between psychological and sociologistic studies is relative. When an investigator takes a psychological factor, for example instincts, wishes, ideas, emotions, or residues, and uses it as a variable for an interpretation of social facts and processes, his study falls within the realm of psychology. When he takes social factors, say the structure of a society or culture, and through these tries to explain certain mental traits and phenomena, his study falls within the realm of sociology. The boundary line, however, is very indefinite, as witnessed by social psychology, which is as much psychology as sociology.

In the sociology of the recent period a large number of studies have been published taking this or that psychological element of man as an independent variable and endeavoring to trace its effects in sociocultural life; in other words, attempting to establish causal connections between the psychological and social aspects of the sociocultural universe. These studies can be divided into several parts, depending upon the nature of the psychological factor taken as an explanatory principle. (a) First we have the *instinctivist* and *reflexological* psychosociologies that take instincts or a special instinct, like the "parental instinct" or the "instinct of sex," "gregariousness," "herd," "self-preservation," as the important factor, and through it try to account for a number of constant and varying social phenomena. For instance, the phenomena of war is explained as the "fighting" or "herd instinct"; the institutions of marriage and the family, as the sex and parental instincts, and so forth. The *Social Psychology* of W. McDougall, the *Instinct of*

[9] For a detailed survey, criticism, and literature of this school see P. A. Sorokin, *Contemporary Sociological Theories*, Ch. 1, and *Sociocultural Causality, Space, Time.*

the Herd by W. Trotter, *Sex and Society* by W.
I. Thomas, and *The Instinct of Workmanship*
by Veblen serve as examples of such interpretation of social phenomena. (b) Very near to
the instinctivist theories are the psychoanalytical sociologies of Freud, Jung, and others in
their sociological theorizing. Instead of speaking in terms of instincts they refer to subconscious complexes and drives, particularly the
libido or sex complex, and by this key attempt
to explain almost every sociocultural phenomenon, from religion to the existence of society
itself. (c) Not very different from these two
branches is *behavioristic* psychosociology,
which also takes as explanatory variables certain biological drives, reflexes, and instincts,
but differs from the above two subcurrents in
its insistence upon a purely objective, external
observation of overt actions without any use of
various subjective or introspective notions. For
a while fashionable, strict behaviorism is now
largely out of date even in the field of psychology. Strictly behavioristic studies have hardly
been realized in sociology. Misusing the discoveries of I. Pavlov and of others, particularly in the field of the conditioned reflexes
(which Pavlov called a "physiology of the
nervous system," but not psychology or sociology), the extreme behaviorists mistook the
study of the physiology of the nervous system
for psychology and sociology and met insur-
mountable obstacles to an understanding and
interpretation of social phenomena in terms of
this biological discipline. The works of A.
Benthley and G. Seliony, and the more immature attempts of some others (Lundberg,
Coon, etc.) can serve as examples of these
behavioristic endeavors. Although in the field
of physiology the works of Pavlov, Lashley,
and others have been fruitful, in the field of
sociology they have remained for the most
part sterile and have thrown no light upon any
important class of sociocultural phenomena. (d)
Finally, a large number of introspective studies
have given analysis and interpretation of sociocultural realities in terms of emotions, sentiments, affections, feelings, wishes, ideas, interests, attitudes, and other inner psychological
experiences. By studying the social manifestations of these psychological variables and
connecting them with certain social conditions,
the introspective branch has produced many

books that have enriched our knowledge of
various aspects of the sociocultural world. The
works of G. Tarde, of V. Pareto (whose sociology after all is mainly a study of the role of
sentiments in social affairs), of G. Lebon, L.
Ward, G. Ratzenhofer, C. Ellwood, W. Sumner
and A. Keller, W. I. Thomas, F. Znaniecki,
and Leo Petrajitsky (in his remarkable psychological theory of law and ethics) are samples of
the best works in this field. Of all the branches
of the psychological school this one has been
most fruitful, so far as sociology is concerned.[10]

5. Sociologistic or Sociocultural School

All the above schools are not so much interested in the sociocultural universe as such as
in its geographical and biological patterns, or
in the socially contingent mental processes of
man. They are busy mainly with an investigation of the effects of these cosmic, biological,
and psychological factors upon sociocultural
phenomena; but the nature of these phenomena, their structural and dynamic properties,
relationships, and uniformities, are touched
upon only indirectly and incidentally, only
so far as is necessary to elucidate the main
considerations. A study of the sociocultural
universe as such, in all its essential aspects, is
precisely the main task of the sociologistic or
sociocultural school.

Consequently, only this school gives us real
sociology in the strict sense of the term. The
other schools surveyed—namely cosmosociol-
ogy, biosociology, and psychosociology,—are
but peripheral and derivative disciplines.

Much of the work done by the sociologistic
school has centered around three main problems: first, an analysis of the essential characteristics of the sociocultural phenomena in their
structural aspects; second, a study of the main
and recurring forms of social processes in their
dynamic aspects; third, an elucidation of the
uniform relationships and interdependence between various classes of sociocultural phenomena. In accordance with these tasks we can
classify the main subcurrents of this school.

a. *Studies of the General Structural Properties of Sociocultural Phenomena.* The works
of E. De Roberty, E. Durkheim, M. Halb-

---

[10] See the analysis, criticism, and literature of
that school in P. A. Sorokin, *Contemporary
Sociological Theories,* Ch. 11.

wachs, Fauconnet, Mauss, A. Espinas, J. Izoulet, Levy-Brühl, C. Cooley, and others showed
that superorganic or sociocultural phenomena
arise from the "intercerebral interaction" of
human beings. Just as the interaction of chemical elements, for instance H_2 and O, give a
resultant—water—quite different from hydrogen and oxygen taken in isolation; just as the
interaction of cells results in a multicellular
organism different from its component cells
taken separately; so the interaction of human
beings produces a sociocultural phenomenon, a
real society or sociocultural system, quite unlike the totality of its individual members taken
in the state of isolation. The structural and
dynamic properties of any continuous system
of interpersonal or intergroup action differ
radically from those of a mere arithmetical
sum of these individuals. Interaction changes
their biological and psychological characteristics and gives a sociocultural reality different
from either biological or psychological realities.
Consequently, sociocultural phenomena do not
require explanation from the standpoint of the
psychological properties of their members,
quite the reverse; psychological characteristics
need to be elucidated from the standpoint of
the properties of the sociocultural interaction
into whose matrix they are embedded. Without
a knowledge of the society and culture into
which a given individual was born and reared
none of his personality traits—beliefs, ideas,
convictions, tastes, likes, and dislikes—can be
understood; his whole mentality, his manners
and mores, his ways of conduct and life, are
entirely incomprehensible. Not only his whole
psychosocial personality but many of his biological properties are molded and conditioned
by the sociocultural universe in which he
is reared.

Having demonstrated the uniqueness of
sociocultural phenomena these scholars have
then proceeded to study their general structural
and dynamic properties. From the structural
standpoint they have analyzed the main forms
of interaction and the appropriate types of
sociocultural structures: antagonistic and
solidary; organized and unorganized; familistic,
contractual, and compulsory; *Gemeinschaft*
and *Gesellschaft*, mechanical and organic
types; centralized and decentralized groupings,
and so on.

These investigators have subjected every
organized and durable system of interaction
(society) to a detailed analysis of its generic
characteristics: the values and norms (legal
and otherwise) that regulate the conduct of
its members; the institutions that arise from
interpersonal relationships; the differentiation
of the functions or roles of members; the
stratification of these into hierarchical ranks,
together with the status that defines the position of every member in the system (intergroup differentiation and stratification). From
such a social cytology they have passed to a
study of the structural morphology, anatomy,
and taxonomy of sociocultural systems; the
age-sex-racial groups; the family; the state;
the territorial, occupational, national, religious,
and other groups into which mankind is differentiated; and then to a study of the castes,
orders, social classes, and other hierarchies
into which mankind is stratified (intergroup
differentiation and stratification). In addition,
the typical functional configurations of these
groups and institutions with their *raisons
d'etre* have been carefully investigated.

Concomitantly with such a cytology, anatomy, and taxonomy of social structures these
scholars have subjected the cultural aspects
of the superorganic world to a similar structural analysis; they have singled out for study
the universal components of culture; integrated
cultural systems and unintegrated or disintegrated cultural congeries; the main cultural
systems of language, science, philosophy, religion, fine arts, law, and ethics, their interrelationships with one another and their constellations in cultural "supersystems."

In this way the sociologistic school has given
us a real cytology, histology, morphology,
anatomy, and taxonomy of sociocultural structures. It has convincingly demonstrated the
peculiar reality and individuality of sociocultural systems, their self-regulation, and the
logic of their functioning and dynamics—all
of which are incomprehensible from a purely
biological or psychological standpoint.

b. *Studies of Recurring Processes; Dynamics
of Sociocultural Phenomena.* No less attention has been given by the sociologistic school
to a study of the dynamic properties and uniformities of sociocultural phenomena, which
discipline has given us both analysis and

systematics of the main recurrent sociocultural processes ("sociocultural physiology") and a generalized theory of the change and evolution of sociocultural systems. G. Tarde, F. Tönnies, G. Simmel, L. von Wiese; G. Richard, and others; and in the United States, E. Ross, C. Cooley, R. Park, E. Burgess, E. Bogardus, C. Case, and other scholars have analyzed and systematized a great number of such recurring processes as sociocultural isolation, contact, conflict, competition, war, adaptation, amalgamation, co-operation, domination-subordination, imitation, acculturation, social control, and many others. A number of other sociologists like C. Gini, C. Cooley, W. Sumner, and A. Keller have investigated such recurring processes to learn how sociocultural systems are generated and how they become organized; how they recruit and lose their members, distribute them within the society, move them around (phenomena of migration and social mobility), effect changes in their organization, norms, mores, and so on.

Still others like Tarde, Lowie, Goldenweiser, Gilfillan, F. S. Chapin, W. Ogburn, C. Wissler, and others have investigated the how and why of such ever repeated cultural processes as invention, diffusion, conversion, symbiosis, borrowing, and transformation of cultural phenomena. A good many sociologists have also thrown light upon such recurring uniformities in sociocultural dynamics as rhythms, periodicities, tempo, and the temporal orders of their change. Finally, a series of scholars— A. Toynbee, O. Spengler, A. Kroeber, P. Ligeti, F. Chambers, P. A. Sorokin, and others —have attempted to give a systematic integrated theory of the life cycles or recurring phases in the life history of the most inclusive cultural supersystems. As a result of this extensive study of the dynamic aspects of the sociocultural universe we now know a great deal more about their physiology and evolution.

c. *Studies of the Interrelationships of Various Classes of Sociocultural Phenomena.* A large portion of the efforts of the sociologistic school has been devoted to an analysis of the interrelationships of various classes of sociocultural phenomena in their static and dynamic aspects: economic, technological, political, religious, scientific, legal, ethical, artistic, and others.

Some scholars have tried to demonstrate a one-sided dependence of sociocultural phenomena upon one or another sociocultural variable selected. Marxians and many other partisans of the economic and technological interpretation of history have taken the economic or technological factor as the primary one and have tried to prove the dependence of scientific, political, philosophic, religious, ethical, legal, artistic, and other phenomena upon their selected factor. (In the United States, Veblen, Ogburn, Chapin, and many others represent this position. In modified form, A. Weber, L. Weber, and others represent it in Europe, and MacIver and some others in this country.)

At the present time, regardless of whether or not the economic or technological factor is the primary one we have, on the one hand, a series of rather detailed studies of the interrelationship between economic phenomena, and on the other hand, the bodily and mental characteristics of the population, the movement of vital processes; suicide, crime, migration, mobility; forms of social and political institutions, strikes, internal disturbances, revolutions, war; the character of law, ethics and religion, forms of fine arts, and so on. These factual and detailed studies of the interrelationships between economic and other classes of sociocultural phenomena have clarified, to a considerable degree, their interdependence.

Other scholars have taken, instead of the economic category, some other class of sociocultural phenomena as the principal factor, and have traced its influence upon the superorganic processes. Thus, F. de Coulanges, Max Weber, C. Ellwood, E. Durkheim, C. Bouglé, J. Frazer, B. Kidd, J. Wach, and many others chose religion and magical beliefs as the independent variables, showing their influence upon, and relationship with, economic, political, legal, artistic, and other classes of social phenomena.

Still others like Herbert Spencer, Savigny, Puchta, Westermarck, W. G. Sumner, A. Keller, and in regard to law, Leo Petrajitsky, R. Stammler, R. Ihering, R. Pound, P. Vinogradoff, N. Timasheff, G. Gurvitch, and others have considered folkways and mores, customs and laws as independent variables and have studied their interrelationships with other classes of the sociocultural universe. Still others have taken as their independent variable the family (Le Play, Demolins, and others); science (De Roberty and others); philosophy, fine arts, political ideologies, and so on. In spite of many mistakes and their inflation of the role of whatever factor they happened to select as the primary one, these studies have disclosed many significant social and cultural uniformities.

Other sociologists working in this field began their studies, not with the assumption of a one-sided dependence of sociocultural phenomena upon some single factor taken as primary, but with the unbiased objective of studying the relationship between various elements of the superorganic as they are really given in the sociocultural universe: between classes of phenomena whose causal relationships are close and between classes in which they are loose and remote; where and when they exhibit one-sided dependence or two-sided interdependence; what functions each class of phenomenon performs in the sociocultural whole and how these functions are related to other classes of our universe. This setting of the problem moved the study to a different and more scientific plane, yielding results more adequate and valid than one-sided studies. From this setting some sociologists, such as Max Weber, intentionally took their variable as a conditional one, rather than as a primary factor. Thus Weber, in terms of his variable, religion and the *Wirtschaftsethik*, studied the interdependence between forms of religion and forms of economy, especially between Protestantism and capitalism. Many other investigators have made similar studies of the interdependence of various sociocultural factors. Others have gone even further in this analysis, perceiving that the interrelations between sociocultural phenomena may vary all the way from integrated systems to unintegrated congeries. It is increasingly recognized that any study which fails to appreciate this distinction cannot arrive at definitely valid conclusions.

Investigation of any integrated system of sociocultural phenomena shows that all the main elements are interdependent, in varying degrees of intensity. When, therefore, we notice that a change in one of the classes (say the economic), within an integrated culture, is accompanied by a simultaneous or delayed change in another of the classes (say the religious), we do not assign to one of these classes preponderant influence but rather view all these changes as a manifestation of alteration within the sociocultural systems as a whole. When an organism passes from childhood to puberty its anatomic, physiological, and psychological properties undergo many changes: stature and weight increase, glandular activities are transformed, mustache and beard appear in males, intelligence and experience grow. All these changes are due not to the increase of stature or to the growth of the mustache, but are all the many-sided manifestations of a change experienced by the organism as a whole. Similar are the interrelations, both static and dynamic, among the component classes within a sociocultural system. For instance, when we study western society and culture at the end of the Middle Ages and during subsequent centuries we notice that scientific discoveries and inventions appear at an increasing rate, a capitalistic economy emerges and grows, the fine arts undergo a fundamental shift from predominantly religious to predominantly secular and sensate forms; absolutistic ethics and mores give way to relative utilitarian ethics; idealism decreases, materialism increases; Protestantism appears and grows, and hundreds of other changes occur. According to Karl Marx these phenomena are due to the shifting of economic-technological conditions; according to Max Weber, they are due to the change in religion, more specifically, to Protestantism. As a matter of fact throughout this transmutation of western society and culture neither one of these "primary" factors was responsible for the change of the others but rather the change experienced by *the whole dominant sociocultural system* of the West was responsible for all the manifold developments in its economic, religious, political, and other subsystems; just as the change in stature, weight, glands, and mentality in an organism passing from childhood to puberty is caused by the whole process of growth. In unintegrated and disintegrated sociocultural congeries no such interdependence is found. This relatively new setting of the problem as to the relationship between various classes of sociocultural phenomena antiquates to a degree the older and traditional approaches to sociocultural causality and promises much more fruitful results than those hitherto achieved.

Such are the main currents of the sociologistic school.[11] The foregoing survey has given some idea of general sociology, its main problems, and its principal schools and methods of study.

6. Special Sociologies

Side by side with the development of general sociology there has been marked progress in the special sociologies, particularly in the more recent period. A large number of these, all rather well developed, have now appeared. Some of the most important of these are the sociology of population, the family, the territorial community; the state, religion, law; social classes, castes, racial and ethnic groups; occupations and professions, fine arts, knowledge; criminology, rural and urban sociology; the sociology of war and revolution; social mobility, experimental sociology, the sociology of calamities and catastrophes, and several others. In all these fields vast factual material has been collected, qualitatively and quantitatively analyzed, correlated with other socio-

---

[11] For further details see P. A. Sorokin, *Contemporary Sociological Theories*, Chps. 8-19, 12-13; regarding the last point, see P. A. Sorokin, *Social and Cultural Dynamics*, Vol. IV, and *Sociocultural Causality, Space, Time*.

cultural variables, and traced to several valid uniformities.

To summarize: The recent period of sociology has been marked by a quantitative and qualitative growth. The logical structure of sociology as a science has been progressively clarified; a large number of generalizations made by previous social thinkers have been rigorously tested and, as a result, some of them have been rejected as invalid; others have been corrected, and new valid uniformities discovered. Sociology itself has tended to become more and more factual and inductive, its methods more scientific, its techniques better adapted to the nature of the phenomena studied. Though in the last two decades mere factfinding studies have gone too far at the cost of conceptual systematization, resulting in a collection of many irrelevant facts; though in the quest for precise methods and techniques many spurious and pseudo-precise procedures have been used and a series of fruitless imitations of natural science have been practiced; nevertheless these mistakes are being progressively corrected and the false attempts have proved to be shortlived, however fashionable for the moment they may have been. At present, when sociology has at its disposal a vast universe of factual material, it is entering the stage of a new synthesis and a further clarification of its logical structure. There is hardly any doubt that it will eventually succeed in these tasks.

BIBLIOGRAPHY

INTRODUCTORY TEXTS

The following are representative of a large number of introductory texts

Ellwood, C. A., *Sociology, Principles and Problems* (New York, 1943).

Freyre, G., *Sociologia* (Rio de Janeiro, 1945).

Haesaert, J., *Essai de Sociologie* (Bruxelles, 1946).

MacIver, R. M., *Society: a Textbook of Sociology* (New York, 1937).

Ogburn, W., and Nimkoff, M., *Sociology* (Boston, 1940).

Panunzio, C., *Major Social Institutions* (New York, 1939).

Park, R., and Burgess, E., *Introduction to the Science of Sociology* (Chicago, 1924).

Poviña, A., *Cursos de Sociologia* (Cordoba, 1945).

Ross, E. A., *Principles of Sociology* (New York, 1938).

Sutherland, R., and Woodward, J., *Introductory Sociology* (Philadelphia, 1939).

Todorov, C., *Obtcha Sociologia* (Sophia, 1946).

Young, K., *Sociology* (New York, 1942).

HISTORY AND SURVEY OF CONTEMPORARY SOCIOLOGICAL THEORIES

Abel, T., *Systematic Sociology in Germany* (New York, 1929).

Barnes, H., and Becker, H., *Social Thought from Lore to Science*, 2 Vols. (Boston, 1938).

Barth, P., *Die Philosophie der Geschichte als Soziologie* (Leipzig, 1921).

Bernard, L. and J., *Origins of American Sociology* (New York, 1943).

Bogardus, E., *The Development of Social Thought* (New York, 1940).

Ellwood, C. A., *A History of Social Philosophy* (New York, 1938).

Hecker, J., *Russian Sociology* (London, 1926).

House, F., *Development of Sociology* (New York, 1936).

Lichtenberger, J., *Development of Social Theory* (New York, 1923).

Parsons, T., *The Structure of Social Action* (New York, 1937).

Sorokin, P. A., *Contemporary Sociological Theories* (New York, 1928).

Stoltenberg, H., *Geschichte der deutschen Gruppwissenschaft* (Leipzig, 1937).

Troeltsch, E., *Die soziallehren der Christlichen Kirchen und Gruppen* (Tübingen, 1923).

IMPORTANT MONOGRAPHIC WORKS IN GENERAL SOCIOLOGY

Comte, A., *Positive Philosophy*, tr. by Martineau, 2 Vols. (New York, 1855).

Comte, A., *System of Positive Polity*, 2 Vols. (London, 1875).

Hegel, G. W. F., *Philosophy of History* (New York, 1900).

Ibn Khaldun, *Prolégomènes historiques*, 3 Vols. (Paris, 1862-68).

Spencer, Herbert, *Principles of Sociology*, 3 Vols. (London, 1896).

Vico, G., *Principi di una scienza nuova* (Milano, 1854).

For Geographic Schools

Dechesne, L., *La localisation des diverses productions* (Bruxelles, 1945).

Demolins, E., *Anglo-Saxon Superiority* (London, 1898).

Dykmans, G., *Introduction critique à la science économique*, Vol. II (Bruxelles, 1945).

Huntington, E., *Mainsprings of Civilization* (New York, 1945).

Le Play, F., *Les ouvriers europeens*, 3 Vols. (Paris, 1879).

Ratzel, F., *Anthropogeographie*, 2 Vols. (Leipzig, 1891).

For Organismic Theories

Kistiakowski, B., *Gesellschaft und Enzelwesen* (Berlin, 1899).

Mikhailovsky, N., *What Is Progress?*

Mikhailovsky, N., *Struggle for Individuality*.

Mikhailovsky, N., *Darwinism and the Social Sciences* (all in Russian, St. Petersburg, 1884).

Novicov, J., *Conscience et volonté sociale* (Paris, 1897).

Schäffle, A., *Bau und Leben des socialen Körpers*, 2 Vols. (Leipzig, 1896).

Worms, R., *Philosophie des sciences sociales*, 3 Vols. (Paris, 1913).

On the Anthroporacial and Demographic Schools

Ammon, O., *Die Natürliche Auslese beim Menschen* (Jena, 1893).

Bouglé, C., *Les Idées égalitaires* (Paris, 1908).

Carli, F., *L'equilibrio delle nazioni secondo la demografia applicata* (Bologna, 1919).

Carr-Saunders, A. M., *The Population Problem* (Oxford, 1912).

Chamberlain, H. S., *The Foundations of the Nineteenth Century* (London, 1911).

Coste, A., *Les principes d'une sociologie objective* (Paris, 1899).

Dahlberg, G., *Race-Reason and Rubbish* (New York, 1942).

Dixon, R. B., *The Racial History of Man* (New York, 1923).

Galton, F., *Hereditary Genius* (London, 1892).

Gini, C., *I fattori demografici dell'evoluzione delle nazioni* (Torino, 1912).

Gobineau, A. De, *Essai sur l'inégalité des races humaines*, 4 Vols. (Paris, 1853-55).

Lapouge, V. de, *Les selections sociales* (Paris, 1896).

Montagu, M. F. A., *Man's Most Dangerous Myth: the Fallacy of Race* (New York, 1942).

Pearson, K., *The Scope and Importance to the State of the Science of National Eugenics* (London, 1909).

Terman, L., *Genetic Study of Genius* (New York, 1925).

Woods, F., *Mental and Moral Heredity in Royalty* (New York, 1906).

See also the bibliography for the special sociology of population.

On the Psychological School

Baldwin, M., *The Individual and Society* (Boston, 1911).

Bekhtereff, W., *General Foundations of Reflexology* (Russia, 1922).

Benthley, A., *Process of Government* (New York, 1908).

Benthley, A., *Relativity in Man and Society* (1926).

Bergson, H., *Les deux sources de la morale et de la religion* (Paris, 1932).

Bernard, L., *Instinct* (New York, 1924).

Ellwood, C. A., *Psychology of Human Society* (New York, 1925).

Freud, S., *Group Psychology and Analysis of Ego*, tr. by J. Strachey.

Freud, S., *Totem and Taboo* (New York, 1918).

Graham, W., *Human Nature in Politics* (London, 1919).

McDougall, W., *An Introduction to Social Psychology* (Boston, 1923).

Pareto, V., *Mind and Society*, 4 Vols. (New York, 1935).

Patten, S., *The Theory of Social Forces* (Philadelphia, 1896).

Pavlov, I., *Conditioned Reflexes* (London, 1930).

Petrajitsky, Leo, *Introduction to the Theory of Law and Ethics* (Russian, St. Petersburg, 1907).

Petrajitsky, Leo, *Theory of Law and Ethics*, 2 Vols. (Russian, St. Petersburg, 1911).

Ratzenhofer, G., *Die soziologische Erkenntnis* (Leipzig, 1898).

Small, A., *General Sociology* (Chicago, 1905).

Sorokin, P. A., *Man and Society in Calamity* (New York, 1942).

Tarde, G., *The Laws of Imitation* (New York, 1903).

Tarde, G., *Social Laws* (New York, 1899).

Tarde, G., *La logique sociale* (Paris, 1895).

Tarde, G., *L'opposition universelle* (Paris, 1897).

Tarde, G., *La philosophie pénale* (Paris, 1890).

Tarde, G., *Etudes de psychologie sociale* (Paris, 1898).

Thomas, W. I., *Sex and Society* (7th ed.) (New York, 1920).

Thomas, W. I., and Znaniecki, F., *The Polish Peasant*, 2 Vols. (New York, 1927).

Thorndike, E., *Human Nature and Social Order* (New York, 1940).

Trotter, W., *Instincts of Herd in Peace and War* (London, 1916).

Veblen, T., *The Instinct of Workmanship* (New York, 1914).

Ward, L., *Dynamic Sociology*, 2 Vols. (New York, 1883).

Ward, L., *Psychic Factors of Civilization* (New York, 1893).

Ward, L., *Pure Sociology* (New York, 1903).

Ward, L., *Applied Sociology* (New York, 1906).

There is also a large literature in social psychology. See Social Psychology.

On the Mechanistic and Geometric School

Bagehot, W., *Physics and Politics* (New York, 1884).

Barcelo, A. P., *Essais de mecanique sociale* (Paris, 1925).

Brown, J., *Psychology and Social Order* (New York, 1936).

Carey, H. C., *Principles of Social Science* (Philadelphia, 1858).

Chapple, E., and Coon, C., *Principles of Anthropology* (New York, 1942).

Dodd, S., *Dimensions of Society* (New York, 1942).

Ferreira, P., *Teoria do espaco social* (Rio de Janeiro, 1939).

Haret, S., *Mechanique sociale* (Paris, 1910).

Lewin, K., *Principles of Topological Psychology* (New York, 1936).

Lins, M., *Espaco-Tempo e Relacoes Sociaes* (Rio de Janeiro, 1940).

Lundberg, G., *Foundations of Sociology* (New York, 1939).

MacIver, R. M., *Social Causation* (Boston, 1942).

Ostwald, W., *Energetische Grundlagen der Kulturwissenschaften* (Leipzig, 1909).

Pintschovius, K., *Das Problem des socialen raumes* (Berlin, 1934).

Sorokin, P. A., *Sociocultural Causality, Space, Time* (Durham, 1943).

Spektorsky, E., *The Problems of Social Physics in the 17th Century*, 2 Vols. (Russian, Kiev, Warsaw, 1910; 1917).

On the Sociologistic School

Adams, B., *The Law of Civilization and Decay* (New York, 1897).

Bauer, A., *Les classes sociales* (Paris, 1902).

Bernard, L., *Social Control* (New York, 1940).

Berr, H., *La synthèse en histoire* (Paris, 1911).

Bouglé, C., *Leçons de sociologie sur l'évolution des valeurs* (Paris, 1922).

Bouglé, C., *Essais sur le régime des castes* (Paris, 1908).

Briefs, G., *The Proletariat* (New York, 1938).

Carr-Saunders, A., and Wilson, P., *The Professions* (Oxford, 1933).

Case, C., *Social Process and Human Progress* (New York, 1931).

Chapin, F. S., *Contemporary American Institutions* (New York, 1935).

Chapin, F. S., *Cultural Change* (New York, 1928).

Cooley, C., *Social Organization* (New York, 1924).

Cooley, C., *Social Process* (New York, 1906).

De Roberty, E., *Nouveau programme de sociology* (Paris, 1904).

De Roberty, E., *Sociologie de l'action* (Paris, 1908).

Dowd, J., *Control in Human Societies* (New York, 1936).

Draghicesco, D., *Du role de l'individu dans le déterminisme social* (Paris, 1906).

Draghicesco, D., *Vérité et revelation*, 2 Vols. (Paris, 1939).

Dupréel, E., *La rapport sociale* (Paris, 1912).

Durkheim, E., *The Rules of Sociological Method* (Chicago, 1938).

Durkheim, E., *Elementary Forms of Religious Life* (London, 1915).

Durkheim, E., *Le suicide* (Paris, 1911).

Durkheim, E., *On the Division of Labor* (New York, 1933).

Durkheim, E., *L'éducation morale* (Paris, 1925). All volumes of *L'Année sociologique* edited by Durkheim.

Fahlbeck, P., *Die Classen und Gesellschaft* (Jena, 1923).

Gurvitch, G., *Essais de sociologie* (Paris, n.d.).

Halbwachs, M., *Les cadres sociaux de la mémoire* (Paris, 1925).

Halbwachs, M., *Les causes du suicide* (Paris, 1930).

Hertzler, J. O., *Social Institutions* (New York, 1930).

Hobhouse, L., *Social Development* (London, 1924).

Izoulet, J., *La cité moderne* (Paris, 1908).

Kovalevsky, M., *Coutume contemporaine et loi ancienne* (Paris, 1888).

Kroeber, A., *Configurations of Culture Growth* (Berkeley, 1944).

Landtman, G., *Origin of the Inequality of Social Classes* (Chicago, 1938).

Levy-Brühl, L., *La moral et la science des mœurs* (Paris, 1903).

Levy-Brühl, L., *La mentalité primitive* (Paris, 1922).

Ligeti, P., *Der Weg aus dem Chaos* (München, 1931).

Marx, K., *A Contribution to the Critique of Political Economy* (New York, 1904).

Mazzarella, J., *Les types sociaux et le droit* (Paris, 1900).

Moreno, L. J., *Who Shall Survive?* (Washington, 1934).

Mosca, G., *The Ruling Class* (New York, 1938).

Niceforo, A., *Les classes pauvres* (Paris, 1905).

Northrop, F., *The Meeting of East and West* (New York, 1946).

Ogburn, W., *Social Change* (New York, 1922).

Ogburn, W. (ed.)., *Recent Social Trends*, 2 Vols. (New York, 1933).

Richard, G., *La sociologie générale* (Paris, 1912).

Ross, E., *Social Control* (New York, 1902).

Simmel, G., *Soziologie* (Berlin, 1908).

Sorokin, P. A., *Social Mobility* (New York, 1927).

Sorokin, P. A., *Social and Cultural Dynamics*, 4 Vols. (New York, 1937-41).

Spengler, O., *The Decline of the West*, 2 Vols. (New York, 1929).

Spengler, O., *Der Mensch und der Technik* (Münich, 1933).

Stammler, R., *Wirtschaft und Recht* (Leipzig, 1896).

Sumner, W. G., *Folkways* (Boston, 1907).

Sumner, W., and Keller, A., *The Science of Society*, 4 Vols. (New Haven, 1927).

Tönnies, F., *Fundamental Concepts of Sociology* (New York, 1940).

Toynbee, A., *A Study of History*, 6 Vols. (Oxford, 1936-39).

Veblen, T., *The Theory of the Leisure Class* (New York, 1899).

Vierkandt, A., *Die Stetigkeit in Kulturwandel* (Leipzig, 1908).

Warner, L., and Lunt, P., *The Status System of a Modern Community* (New Haven, 1942).

Weber, A., *Ideen zur Staats- und Kultursoziologie* (Karlsruhe, 1927).

Weber, L., *Le rhythme du progrés* (Paris, 1913).

Weber, M., *Gesammelte Aufsätze zur Religionssoziologie*, 3 Vols. (Tübingen, 1922).

Weber, M., *Gesammelte Aufsätze zur Wissenschaftslehre* (1922).

Weber, M., *Wirtschaft und Gesellschaft* (Tübingen, 1921-22).

Wiese, L. von, *System der allgemeinen Soziologie* (München, 1933).

Wood, M., *The Stranger* (New York, 1934).

Ziegenfuss, W., *Versuch über das Wesen der Gesellschaft* (Leipzig, 1935).

SPECIAL SOCIOLOGIES. REPRESENTATIVE WORKS

Sociology of Population

Gini, C., and others, *Population* (Chicago, 1930).

Glass, D. V., *The Struggle for Population* (Oxford, 1936).

Landis, P., *Population Problems* (New York, 1943).

Lorimer, F., and Osborn, F., *Dynamics of Population* (New York, 1934).

Pearl, R., *Natural History of Population* (New York, 1939).

Thompson, W., *Population Problems* (New York, 1938).

See also the works quoted in Demographic School.

Rural Sociology

Sanderson, D., *Rural Sociology and Rural Social Organization* (New York, 1942).

Smith, T., *Sociology of Rural Life* (New York, 1940).

Sorokin, P. A., Zimmerman, C., and Galpin, C. S., *Systematic Source Book in Rural Sociology*, 3 Vols. (Minneapolis, 1930-32).

Urban Sociology

Carpenter, N., *The Sociology of City Life* (New York, 1931).

Gist, N., and Halbert, L., *Urban Sociology* (New York, 1939).

Mumford, L., *The Culture of Cities* (New York, 1938).

Woolston, H., *Metropolis* (New York, 1938).

Sociology of the Family

Becker, H., and Hill, R. (eds.). *Marriage and the Family* (Boston, 1942).

Burgess, E., and Locke, M., *The Family* (New York, 1946).

Groves, E., *The Family and Its Functions* (New York, 1940).

Ogburn, W., and Groves, E., *American Marriage and Family* (New York, 1928).

Westermark, E., *History of Human Marriage*, 2 Vols. (London, 1921).

Zimmerman, C., and Frampton, M., *Family and Society* (New York, 1935).

Sociology of Law

Commons, J., *Legal Foundations of Capitalism* (New York, 1924).

Cruet, J., *La vie du droit et l'impuissance des lois* (Paris, 1908).

Ehrlich, E., *Grundlagen der Soziologie des Rechts* (München, 1913).

Gurvitch, G., *Sociology of Law* (New York, 1942).

Kelsen, H., *Society and Nature* (Chicago, 1943).

Petrajitsky, Leo., *Introduction to the Theory of Law and Ethics* (Russian, St. Petersburg, 1907).

Petrajitsky, Leo., *Theory of Law and Ethics*, 2 Vols. (St. Petersburg, 1911).

Pound, R., *Contemporary Juristic Law* (New York, 1940).

Stammler, R., *Wirtschaft und Recht* (Leipzig, 1896).

Timasheff, N., *An Introduction to the Sociology of Law* (Cambridge, 1939).

Sociology of War, Revolution, and Disorganization

Bauer, A., *Essai sur les révolutions* (Paris, 1908).

Elliott, M., and Merrill, F., *Social Disorganization* (New York, 1939).

Ford, J., *Social Deviation* (New York, 1939).

Gasset, J. O., *The Revolt of the Masses* (New York, 1937).

Kropotkin, P., *Mutual Aid* (London, 1902).

Lebon, G., *The Psychology of Revolution* (New York, 1913).

Novicov, J., *Les luttes entre sociétés humaines* (Paris, 1897).

Pettee, G., *The Process of Revolution* (New York, 1938).

Sorokin, P. A., *Social and Cultural Dynamics*, Vol. III (New York, 1937).

Sorokin, P. A., *Man and Society in Calamity* (New York, 1942).

Sorokin, P. A., *Sociology of Revolution* (Philadelphia, 1925).

Steinmetz, R., *Soziologie des Krieges* (Leipzig, 1929).

Wright, Q., *A Study of War*, 2 Vols. (Chicago, 1942).

Sociology of Fine Arts

Boas, F., *Primitive Art* (Oslo, 1927).

Chambers, F., *Cycles of Taste* (Cambridge, 1928).

Deonna, W., *L'archéologie*, 3 Vols. (Paris, 1912).

Efimoff, N., *Sociology of Literature* (Russian-Leningrad, 1927).

Hausenstein, W., *Die Kunst und die Gesellschaft* (Leipzig, 1926).

Lalo, C., *Esquisse d'une esthetique musicale scientifique* (Paris, 1908).

Ligeti, P., *Der Weg aus dem Chaos* (München, 1931).

Lowes, J., *Convention and Revolt in Literature* (Boston, 1926).

Petrie, W., *Revolutions of Civilization* (London, 1912).

Schücking, L., *Die Soziologie der literarischen Geschmacksbieldung* (München, 1923).

Sorokin, P. A., *Social and Cultural Dynamics*, Vol. I (New York, 1937).

Wölfflin, H., *Principles of Art History* (New York, 1932).

Sociology of Knowledge

Mannheim, K., *Ideology and Utopia* (New York, 1936).

Merton, R. K., "The Sociology of Knowledge," in *Twentieth Century Sociology*, ed. by G. Gurvitch (New York, 1945).

Pareto, V., *The Mind and Society*, 4 Vols. (New York, 1935).

Scheler, M., *Schriften zur Soziologie der Weltanschauungslehre*, 3 Vols. (Leipzig, 1923-24).

Scheler, M., *Die Wissenformen und die Gesellschaft* (Leipzig, 1926).

Sorokin, P. A., *Social and Cultural Dynamics*, 4 Vols. (New York, 1937).

Sorokin, P. A., *Sociocultural Causality, Space, Time* (Durham, 1943).

Sociology of Religion

Bouglé, C., *Les idées egalitaires* (Paris, 1908).

Bouglé, C., *Leçons de sociologie sur l'evolution des valeurs* (Paris, 1922).

Bouglé, C., *Essais sur le régime des castes* (Paris, 1908).

Coulanges, F. de, *The Ancient City* (Boston, 1900).

Durkheim, E., *Elementary Forms of Religious Life* (London, 1915).

Durkheim, E., *L'education morale* (Paris, 1925).

Ellwood, C. A., *The Reconstruction of Religion* (New York, 1922).

Frazer, J., *Psyche's Task* (London, 1913).

Guignebert, C., *L'evolution des dogmes* (Paris, 1910).

James, W., *The Varieties of Religious Experience* (New York, 1928).

Johnson, P. E., *Psychology of Religion* (New York, 1945).

Kidd, B., *Social Evolution* (New York, 1894).

Lebon, G., *Psychology of Socialism* (New York, 1909).

Leuba, J., *The Belief in God and Immortality* (Boston, 1916).

Wach, J., *Sociology of Religion* (Chicago, 1943).

Weber, M., *Gesammelte Aufsatze zur Religions soziologie*, 3 Vols. (Tübingen, 1922).

Criminology

Bonger, W. A., *An Introduction to Criminology* (London, 1936).

Hooton, E., *Crime and the Man* (Cambridge, 1939).

Reckless, W., *Criminal Behavior* (New York, 1940).

Sutherland, E., *Criminology* (Philadelphia, 1939).

Tarde, G., *La philosophie pénale* (Paris, 1890).

Wood, A., and Waite, J., *Crime and Its Treatment* (New York, 1943).

Sociological Periodicals

In many countries the sociological journals that existed before the war have been discontinued, either because of the war or because of various dictatorial regimes (in Germany, Russia, France, Belgium, and many other countries). The following journals still exist or have been resumed.

In Czechoslovakia: *Sociologická Revue.*

In England: *The Sociological Review.*

In France: *Cahiers Internationaux de Sociologie.*

In the United States: *American Journal of Sociology.*
American Sociological Review.
Social Forces.
Social Research.
Sociology and Social Research.
Journal of Legal and Political Sociology.
Rural Sociology.
Social Science.

In Mexico: *Revista Mexicana de sociologia.*

In Brazil: *Sociologia.*

In Argentina: *Boletin del Instituto de Sociologia.*

In Bolivia: *Revista de Sociologia Boliviana.*

In Venezuela: *Revista Interamericana de Sociologia.*

Sociological Encyclopedias

Handwörterbuch der Soziologie, 4 Vols. (Stuttgart, 1931).

Fairchild, H. P., *Dictionary of Sociology* (New York, 1943).

Baldus, H., and Willems, E., *Dicionario de Etnologia e Sociologia* (Sao Paulo, 1939).

Trujilo, C. A. E., *Diccionario abreviado de Sociologia* (La Habana, 1944).

Squillace, F., *Diccionario de Sociologia* (Barcelona, n.d.).

PART TWO

Structural Sociology

Chapter 3. Generic Structure of Sociocultural Phenomena

I. Meaningful Human Interaction as the Generic Social Phenomenon

A study of the structural aspect of sociocultural phenomena begins with an analysis of the generic properties common to all sociocultural phenomena—past, present, and future.

By "generic sociocultural phenomenon" is not meant the "simplest unit." Imitating the poorly understood natural sciences, sociologists are still looking for the "simplest unit" of social phenomena, analogous to the atom in physics or the cell in biology. Some, like the partisans of the organismic, mechanistic, and psychological schools in sociology, find this "unit" in the individual. Others, like Giddings, define it as a "socius" or "fellowship." Still others, such as Moreno and Znaniecki, conceive it as the "role" which the individual performs. Many identify it with "social relationship." A large group of sociologists, realizing that an isolated individual cannot constitute a social phenomenon, look for the simplest unit in "the most elementary society," meaning thereby the family, as in the case of Le Play and his school, or "the most primitive society," undifferentiated and poorly integrated, as in the case of Spencer and Durkheim.[1]

This quest for the simplest social unit is based largely upon a misconception. (1) Physics and general biology begin their study of structural properties with the atom and the cell, respectively, as the generic elements of physical and biological structures—not because they are the simplest units. Every physicist and biologist is fully aware of the extremely complex structures of atoms and cells. Again, these disciplines begin their study of the structural properties of their respective fields not with this or that specific atom and cell but with the atom and cell in the generic form common to all atoms and cells. (2) An individual or even a million isolated individuals do not constitute a social phenomenon, to say nothing of its simplest unit. An individual represents merely a physical, biological, or psychological phenomenon; therefore he can become the object of study of a physicist, biologist, or psychologist, but not of a sociologist. Nor can such a unit perform the "role" of an individual. Without an entire drama there can be no role; for a role is possible only in the context of all

---

[1] On the unit of the organismic, mechanistic, psychological, and Le Play schools see my *Theories* (New York, 1928), Chps. 1-2 and 4. On other units see F. Giddings, *Inductive Sociology* (New York, 1901), pp. 10 ff.; L. J. Moreno, "Sociometry and Cultural Order," *Sociometry*, Vol. VI (1943), pp. 304 ff.; F. Znaniecki, *The Social Rôle of the*

Man of Knowledge (New York, 1940), pp. 13 ff.; Herbert Spencer, *Principles of Sociology* (London, 1885), Vol. I, Ch. 10 (classifications of societies into the "simple," "compound," "doubly compound," and so on); E. Durkheim, *The Rules of Sociological Method* (Chicago, 1938), Ch. 4; B. Malinowski, *A Scientific Theory of Culture* (Chapel Hill, 1944), pp. 39 ff.

the roles of the drama. Whatever an isolated individual may do, none of his actions constitutes a social phenomenon or its simplest unit. A role can become a social role only in the presence of the social matrix. Only in such a setting can the role become an element of a social phenomenon, just as a chromosome is a constituent of a cell or an electron a constituent of an atom; but neither the role, nor the chromosome, nor the electron forms the simplest unit of the social, biological, or physical structure. On the other hand, an individual taken as a *socius*, or personality, is one of the most complex of social phenomena. To say that a *socius* is an ultimate, irreducible unit is equivalent (as E. C. Hayes rightly observes) to calling a bouquet of flowers the simplest and ultimate unit of plant structures.[2]

Likewise the family is not the simplest or a generic social phenomenon: quantitatively the family is not the smallest social unit; qualitatively the structure of the family is highly complex. In addition, the family has many differential characteristics not found in other social groups. For this reason the family cannot serve as the simplest form or the generic model of social structures. The same is true of primitive societies—the postulated "simple societies" of Spencer and Durkheim,—and of Malinowski's "institution" as a unit. These are neither the smallest nor the simplest units of social structures. The internal organization of a primitive clan or tribe is highly complex— much more intricate than, for instance, the structure of most of the modern "associational" organizations, such as literary, scientific, and other specialized groups. Likewise, primitive beliefs, mythology, literature, music, and so on are often much more complex than those of nonprimitive peoples. In brief, the so-called primitive societies and cultures cannot be regarded as the simplest units, as social atoms or cells, or as generic social phenomena. Still less can Malinowski's "institution" be taken for such a unit. As we shall see in Chapter 4, an institution as an organized group is neither generic nor the simplest social unit but a

special form of the generic social phenomenon, often very complex in structure. Finally, general sociology is not a theory of the simplest social phenomenon but of the generic properties, relationships, and uniformities of sociocultural phenomena.[3]

The most generic model of any sociocultural phenomenon is the meaningful interaction of two or more human individuals. By "interaction" is meant any event by which one partly tangibly influences the overt actions or the state of mind of the other. In the absence of such an influence (unilateral or mutual) no sociocultural phenomenon is possible. A million completely isolated human beings do not represent a social phenomenon or a society, since they do not influence one another. By "meaning" is to be understood "anything which, for some mind, stands as a sign of something else. The generic significance of meaning is that in which A means B if A operates as representing B, if it stands for B, or calls it to mind."[4] A meaningful interaction is any interaction where the influence exerted by one party over another has a meaning or value superimposed upon the purely physical and biological properties of the respective actions. If the interaction is not meaningful in this sense, it is not a sociocultural phenomenon but a purely physical or biological phenomenon —a proper object of study for physics and biology, but not for sociology or the social sciences. If a person shoots another person, the physicochemical properties of the gun, the trajectory of the bullet, the force with which it struck the victim, the biological aspects of the wound or of the organs penetrated by the bullet, the cause of death, and the like, are proper subjects of investigation by specialists in the fields of physics, chemistry, and biology. Only when such an interaction acquires the meaning or value of "murder" or "manslaughter," of "heroic action" in exterminating the enemy in war, or of "action in self-defense," does it become a sociocultural or superorganic phenomenon and fall within the field of the criminologist, sociologist, or social scientist.

---

[2] See E. C. Hayes, "Classification of Social Phenomena," *AJS*, Vol. XVII, pp. 109-10.

[3] See P. A. Sorokin, "Remarques," *Revue international de sociologie* (March, 1935). See further the criticism of Spencer's and Durkheim's con-

ception of the simple society and their morphological classifications of social structures (Ch. 9).

[4] C. I. Lewis, "The Modes of Meaning," *Philosophy and Phenomenological Research*, Vol. IV (1943), p. 236.

Similarly, if an interaction consists in sexual intercourse, in its purely physical and biological properties it does not constitute a sociocultural phenomenon. When, however, it is a case of prostitution or rape, or is incident to marital relations—even though biologically it may be identical in all these cases—it acquires a value or meaning superimposed upon the biophysical factors and becomes a meaningful interaction. The act of plunging a knife into a person's body, taken without any superimposed value or meaning, is not a sociocultural phenomenon. Its biophysical properties are studied not by the social but by the biophysical sciences. Only when it is viewed as an act of "murder," as a "surgical operation," as an "act of war," or as a "religious sacrifice to the gods" does it become a sociocultural phenomenon, even though in all these radically different sociocultural meanings the biophysical aspect may remain essentially identical.

The term "tangible" is incorporated in the definition to denote that only a tangible, or observable, interaction can be a genuine social phenomenon. Though, theoretically, perhaps everything may be connected with everything else in this world, and every individual influences infinitesimally the rest of mankind, actually there are tangible and intangible influences, in spite of the possibility that "tout se lie, tout s'enchaîne dans ce monde." As Cournot brilliantly remarked,

Nobody would seriously contend that by stamping on the ground with one's foot one could deflect the navigators of the other hemisphere from their course or shake the system of Jupiter's satellites; at any rate the disturbance would be so infini-tesimal that it could not be manifest through any effect noticeable by us, and therefore we should be fully justified in disregarding it. It is not impossible that an insignificant event occurring in China or Japan has some influence upon what happens in Paris or London. But generally it is quite certain that the manner in which a Parisian bourgeois plans his day is not influenced by what is happening in an isolated Chinese city which has never been entered by a European. These are like two little worlds in each of which one can observe the chain of cause and effects which develop simultaneously but without a mutual connection and without exerting any influence one upon another.[5]

Hence a tangible, observable, or noticeable degree of influencing and conditioning is a necessary characteristic of sociocultural phenomena. Thus no nominal or purely statistical group constitutes a phenomenon of interaction as a real social group, a social system, or society. One might, for instance, divide all males in the United States into two classes: those wearing brown shoes and those wearing black shoes, and then, computing the total number of such males, reduce the figures to percentages. These classes would be purely nominal or statistical; for there would be scarcely any evidence of a more tangible or intensive interaction between the males with black shoes or between those with brown shoes than between members belonging to opposite groups. A similar generalization applies to all other nominal groups and classes.

After this preliminary definition of the generic sociocultural phenomenon we can turn to a more detailed analysis of its structure.

II. Components of the Generic Sociocultural Phenomenon

Every process of meaningful human interaction consists of three components, each component, in turn, being made up of many elements that determine its concrete forms. These components are (1) thinking, acting, and reacting human beings as subjects of interaction; (2) meanings, values and norms for the sake of which the individuals interact, realizing and exchanging them in the course of the interaction; (3) overt actions and material phenom-

---

[5] A. Cournot, Essai sur les fondements de nos connaissances et sur les caractères de la critique philosophique, Vol. I (Paris, 1851). Compare A. A. Thchuproff, Studies in Theory of Statistics (St. Petersburg, 1909), pp. 99 ff. (in Russian).

ena as vehicles or conductors through which immaterial meanings, values, and norms are objectified and socialized.[6]

THE SUBJECTS OF INTERACTION; THEIR PROPERTIES

In homosociology[7] the subjects of interaction are either human individuals (in interpersonal interaction) or organized groups of human beings (in inter-group interaction).

The biological and psychological properties of human beings are investigated by biology and psychology. A sociologist must know these properties, but their study does not belong to the domain of sociology. For our purposes it is sufficient to remember the following biopsychological properties of *homo sapiens*: (1) Possession of a well-developed nervous system, with its receptors, conductors, and effectors, which enables man to react to the stimuli exerted by other human beings. (2) Ability to perform a wide variety of overt actions. (3) Possession of mind, with its elements of sensations, perceptions, ideas, imagination, memory, emotions, feelings, and volitions. Man is a thinking, emotional, affective, volitional organism, able to act and react in the superorganic world of meanings, values, and norms. (Why and how he has become such a creature does not concern us at this point.) (4) Biological and psychological heterogeneity in respect to race, sex, age, and other physical characteristics, as well as mental make-up—intelligence, emotionality, will power, and so on.

1. Number of Interacting Individuals

As to the number of interacting individuals we can distinguish the following interpersonal types: (a) Between two individuals (a pair, or dyad), as, for instance, between husband and wife, parent and child, two friends, teacher and pupil, master and slave, buyer and seller, physician and patient. The intimate forms of dyads exhibit a number of characteristics peculiar to them and distinguishing them from the nonintimate varieties. (b) Between three individuals (a triad), as, for instance, between the accuser, the accused, and the judge; a maiden and two competitors for her hand; husband, wife, and paramour; or father, mother, and child. (c) Between four, five, or more individuals. (d) Between one and many, illustrated by a radio speaker and his listeners or by an artist and his audience. (e) Between many and many, as between the members of an unorganized crowd, or between buyers and sellers of a certain commodity who are unorganized and scattered, acting without any special co-ordination. However, this last type assumes, as a rule, the form of interaction between organized groups, in the sense presently to be defined (see Chapter 4).

Similarly, intergroup interaction may occur between two groups, between three, four, or more, between one and many, or between collectivities of many groups. The number of the subjects of interaction is important because it accounts for many special characteristics of the process of interaction.[8]

---

[6] The three-componential structure of sociocultural phenomena, systematically developed in my *Dynamics*, has been noted before and after publication in a somewhat vaguer form by an ever-increasing number of social scientists. Unfortunately many of these have failed to clarify and systematically unfold their conceptions. See, for instance, W. I. Thomas, *Primitive Behavior* (New York, 1937), pp. 8 ff.; B. Malinowski, *A Scientific Theory of Culture*, p. 36; R. Linton and C. Kluckhohn in *AA*, 45 (1943), pp. 216 ff.; M. Mead, *Competition and Cooperation Among Primitive Peoples* (New York, 1937), pp. 458 ff.; Linton's material, kinesthetik, and psychological orders of culture; Malinowski's material, human, and spiritual orders of it; Kluckhohn's "overt and covert" cultures; Thomas's human agents, points of view (meanings, values), and patterns as their expression; M. Mead and A. Radcliff-Brown's individuals,

their interrelations, nonhuman material involved in interaction. All these are a somewhat more indefinite and undeveloped variation of the theory given in the *Dynamics*.

[7] In biosociology, which studies the biological interactions of plant and animal organisms, the subjects of interaction are plants and animals.

[8] See L. von Wiese, *System der allgemeinen Soziologie* (München, 1933), pp. 447-507; G. Simmel, "The Number of Members as Determining the Sociological Form of the Group," *AJS*, Vol. VIII (1902), pp. 1-46, 158-196; L. J. Moreno, "Interpersonal Therapy," *Sociometry*, Vol. I (1937), pp. 9-76; H. Becker and R. Useem, "Sociological Analysis of the Dyads," *ASR*, Vol. VII (1942), pp. 13-26; T. Geiger, *Die Gestalten der Gesellung* (Karlsruhe, 1920), Ch. 3. The role of the number of subjects of interaction is discussed more fully in subsequent chapters.

2. Qualities of Interacting Individuals

From the standpoint of the qualities of the subjects of interaction, we find an enormous number of varieties (to be discussed at a later stage). Here we need consider only one characteristic, namely, the biopsychological and sociocultural *homogeneity or heterogeneity* (similarity or dissimilarity) of the interacting individuals or groups. Interaction between individuals of the same race, nationality, tribe, territorial group, family, sex, age, religion, political party, occupation, economic status, and so on, and especially between those who possess similar sociocultural values, always differs in many ways from that of individuals who differ in these respects.

3. Character of Actions

Actions and reactions may be catalytic, active, passive, or tolerant. Overt actions and reactions are a part of the component of vehicles; yet certain aspects of these may conveniently be studied here as properties of the subjects of interaction. The extremely diverse relations through which the interacting parties influence one another may be reduced to four main forms: those that exert an influence merely through the *known existence* of the party or parties (the *catalytic* form); through performing *overt actions*; through *abstention from overt action*; through active *toleration*.

a. *Catalytic Actions.* A catalytic agent in chemistry is a substance (such as platinum black or aluminum chloride) which, though it does not participate in a chemical reaction and does not change its character, notably intensifies and accelerates the reaction. An analogous phenomenon is found in social interaction. The mere thought of an enemy, a loved one, or a hero with whom a person is not and perhaps never has been in contact may notably influence his mind, mood, or overt behavior. Such influences, exerted through the mere existence of the other party, without any actual contact,

may be designated as *catalytic*. Sociology and the social sciences hardly ever mention this factor and are hardly aware of it. Nevertheless it functions daily and is as important as the other three factors enumerated. The mere existence of the Soviet regime or of the Fascist form of government has exerted, during the last two decades, an enormous influence on the Communist and Fascist movements throughout the world, on the forms of government and of economic organization. This influence has been far greater than that exerted by all the paid agents and propagandists taken together.

b. *Overt Actions; Toleration.* Influences exerted through *overt acts* (striking a blow, shooting, giving money, kissing, etc.) and through *abstention* from overt action, or passivity, are too familiar to require further comment. A few remarks are in order concerning the factor of *toleration*. This is regularly confused with the passive mode of abstention from action. Nevertheless, as Leo Petrajitsky has pointed out,[9] it is fundamentally different. In contradistinction to the passive mode of nonaction, toleration may demand the most strenuous inner effort, frequently much more strenuous than that required for overt action. The conduct of one of the Christian martyrs, who, while being roasted on an iron grill, calmly said to his executioners, "This side is already done; it is time to turn me over," affords a striking example of this factor of toleration and of the intense effort of will which it requires. The norms of the Sermon on the Mount, usually interpreted as prescribing inactivity and passivity, prescribe, in fact, the method of active toleration—of loving one's enemies, offering the other cheek, and not responding to hatred and animosity in kind. The ethics of Christianity are not the ethics of passive nonaction but of sublime toleration.[10]

c. *Effective and Ineffective Actions.* Overt action, abstention from action, and toleration are infinitely diverse in their concrete

---

[9] See Leo Petrajitsky, *Teoria prava i morali* (St. Petersburg, 1910), Vol. II, pp. 430 ff.

[10] F. Dostoievski rightly interpreted it as such. Zosima, in his *Brothers Karamazoff*, says: "Seeing the sins of men, one sometimes wonders whether one should react to them by force or by humble love. Always decide to fight them by humble love. If it is carried through, the whole world can be conquered. Loving humbleness is the most effective force, the most terrific, the most powerful, unequaled by any other force in the world." By "humble love" is meant precisely the way of toleration. Rightly understood, the tolerance shown by a truly democratic regime toward dissenting opinions, beliefs, and tastes is not passive indifference, precluding the fullest appreciation of one's own values and a sense of loyalty to them.

forms. From the standpoint of *causal effectiveness* there are actions producing an intense
effect and actions exerting only an insignificant
influence. If a visitor passes his hand over his
beard, his action does not appreciably affect
me. If he shoots me, this may influence my
physical and mental states very decisively.
Sometimes a fiery outburst of words elicits no
appreciable reaction on the part of the hearer.
Conversely, a single word, quietly spoken, may
produce a devastating effect upon the person
to whom it is addressed. What kind of actions
are effective and what are not depends upon
many conditions.

d. *Durable and Shortlived Actions.* Overt
action, abstention from action, and toleration
vary also in the *duration of their effectiveness.*
There are actions whose effect evaporates
almost instantly, such as the greetings of
friends, paying for a package of cigarettes at
a store, and hundreds of other petty actions
performed daily. Other actions exert an influence for a long time, sometimes until the
death of the parties or even longer. Thus, the
first kiss and the first declaration "I love you"
may be remembered long after their performance. The sex act may be followed by the conception and birth of a child—consequences
that may affect the career of the mother permanently. Other examples are afforded by the
marriage ceremony, baptism, the buying of
property, graduation from college, and the
adoption of a certain occupation. Which
actions are lasting in their effects and which
are shortlived depends upon many conditions,
such as time, place, persons, the kind of society
and culture, the biological and psychological
nature of the actions.[11]

The durability of actions is important; for if
their effects were too ephemeral, no society
with continuous interactions would be possible. On the other hand, actions with only
transitory effects alleviate the business of
living; for if every interaction produced lasting
effects, no one could preserve the integrity of

his personality, and no one's nervous system
would be able to stand the strain.

e. *Conscious and Nonconscious Actions.*
Some interactions are performed consciously,
others unconsciously. If they are unconscious
(that is, unconditioned or conditioned reflexes), they are not superorganic and hence
do not belong to the field of sociology. If,
however, certain actions of one party are unconscious and the other subjects of the interaction respond to them with conscious actions,
the interaction is sociocultural and falls within
the domain of sociological study. Unconscious
actions of one party responded to consciously
by others are fairly numerous; for instance, the
interaction of a sleeping baby and its mother;
that of a feverish or unconscious patient and
his physician; or that of a felled boxer and his
victorious opponent. The habitual actions of a
party automatically performed without intention either to offend or cheer the other party,
often are taken by the other party(ies) as intentional and reacted to in a conscious way.
An inadvertent word or phrase, or a gesture or
motion automatically performed, is not infrequently misinterpreted as a deliberate offense,
challenge, or the like. In their totality such
interactions occupy a large place in the total
constellation of sociocultural interactions.

f. *Purposive and Nonpurposive Actions.*
The conscious processes of action, abstinence
from action, and toleration fall into two main
classes: *purposive*, motivated by a conscious
goal, and performed for the sake of its attainment; and *nonpurposive*, motivated solely by
past and present experience, including inculcated norms, and performed without any conscious idea of the future. In purposive actions,
although they too are generated by past and
present experience, there is always an idea of
the future goal, or end, and of the means of its
attainment.[12]

Many thinkers, including utilitarians, hedon-
ists, and rationalists, have held that all conscious actions are purposive, or means to an
end.[13] Others go still further and regard all
social actions as means for the attainment of

---

[11] Most of the theories of utilitarian moralists
(such as Jeremy Bentham), economists, and psychologists as to which actions are lasting and which
are shortlived in their influence are faulty, enunciating the principles of what *ought* to be rather than
of what actually *is*, in this respect.

[12] See a good analysis of purposeful actions in
D. Draghicesco, *L'Ideal Createur* (Paris, 1914).
[13] See, for instance, R. Ihering, *Der Zweck im
Recht*, 2 Vols. (Leipzig, 1877-1883); *The Struggle for Law* (Chicago, 1897).

certain ends.[14] There are even scholars who view as conscious and purposive practically every action of the amoeba and similar organisms, and all the changes of inorganic matter (such as oxidation) as learning by experience or as a manifestation of memory.[15] This is the crudest form of anthropomorphism. If we were to accept this viewpoint, the terms "learning," "remembering," "conscious," and "purposeful" would lose all meaning; the distinction between learning and the combustion of coal, remembering and the oxidation of oil, the formation of purposes and the rotting of leaves, or consciousness and any inorganic process, would disappear. No less fallacious are the theories that regard all human actions as conscious and purposive. The existence of unconditioned and partly conditioned reflexes, of instinctive, unconscious, and subconscious actions, with their mechanisms of "drives" and stimulation, suffices to refute all such theories.[16]

Fallacious also are the theories identifying conscious and purposeful action and viewing all social actions as purposeful means to ends. (1) Interactions of the unconscious-conscious type are clearly not purposeful on the part of the unconscious party. (2) The writers in question misuse the teleological terms "means" and "end," confusing them with the quite different categories of cause and effect, anterior and posterior. Pareto, in his division of human actions into logical and nonlogical, speaks of "subjective and objective ends," meaning by "subjective end" a conscious purpose and by "objective end" any consequence of an action. According to him, the objective end is found even where there is no subjective purpose; for instance, in the reflexes of men and animals. One may properly speak of the objective consequence or effect of a reflex action or of anterior and posterior actions in a chronological sequence; but how can one correctly speak of an "objective end or purpose" in connection with actions devoid of any conscious purpose or end? The term "objective end" is as para-

doxical as "armless arm" or "purposeless purpose." It requires one to view as teleological and anthropomorphic every nonteleological physical and biological phenomenon, strips teleological phenomena of their purposive character, identifies profoundly different phenomena, differentiates identical phenomena, and leads to a vague pseudo-conception of universal means and ends devoid of any precise meaning. As a result, when this "purposeless purpose" is used as a fundamental category in any analysis, a host of other errors follow, as in the case of Pareto and other theorists.

(3) A large proportion of even conscious actions are not purposive in motivation or character, as demonstrated by Leo Petrajitsky and others. Most human and animal actions are performed not for the sake of achieving some purpose but in response to very different motivations. Actions directed toward a certain *purpose*, or *for the sake of* something, must be distinguished from actions *because of*. The point is that the ability to arouse the emotions and through these to induce action belongs not only to ideas concerning the *future* but in no less degree to those concerning the past, as, for instance, the memory of an insult suffered. If a given action elicits in another person a sense of hatred, indignation, contempt, admiration, or love, the emotion is discharged in the form of indignant, contemptuous, or eulogistic words, or in the act of striking, applauding, kissing, or embracing, without any thought of the achievement of any purpose. In fact, if one were to express contempt, righteous indignation, or admiration for the sake of this or that purpose, it would be a sure sign that his demonstration was not sincere but a mere pose or burlesque. Many forms of human behavior by their very nature preclude a purposive motivation envisaging the future and presuppose a motivation derived from past experience. All such motivations and actions, where stimulating ideas, images, and emotions are grounded in past experience and events rather

---

[14] V. Pareto, *Trattato di sociologia generale* (Torino, 1916), Vol. I, pp. 65 ff.; B. Malinowski, *op. cit.*, pp. 40, 43, 52 ff., so far as he defines all institutions "as organized systems of purposeful activities." Also T. Parsons, *The Structure of Social Action* (New York, 1937).

[15] See W. I. Thomas, *Primitive Behavior*, Chps. 3 and 4; also C. L. Hull, "Goal Attraction," *Psy-*

chological Review, Vol. XXXVIII, p. 505; A. P. Mathews, *Physiological Chemistry* (New York, 1935), p. 76.

[16] Concerning these actions and the mechanism of their stimulation (instead of misapplied term "motivation") see G. Murphy and T. Newsholme, *Experimental Social Psychology* (New York, 1936), Ch. 2; see literature there.

than in future purposes, are called by Petrajit-sky "fundamental motivation and actions," in contradistinction to the purposive ones, where the ideas and representations always relate to the future.[17]

Conscious but nonpurposive actions are illustrated also by acts performed contrary to one's purpose. A habitual alcoholic, seeing a bottle of liquor, cannot resist the temptation, and drinks contrary to his avowed purpose to refrain from the use of alcohol. A fat person or a glutton eats tempting food in spite of his decision to go on a reducing diet or to practice abstinence. A sexual profligate sins in spite of his determination to reform. A combatant flees from an enemy contrary to his resolve to fight courageously. In all such cases the conscious purpose is thwarted by overt conduct equally conscious but nonpurposive. The real motivating force is not a purpose but a biological drive, a conditioned reflex (or habit), or a certain objective stimulus, such as alcohol, a nude body, tempting food, or a terrifying animal or foe.

There is a common belief that to do something without any purpose is nonsense. But nature would have acted very stupidly, from the standpoint of the preservation and development of life, if organisms were so constituted that without purposeful calculation no action would be possible. Such a situation would have entailed a gigantic waste of vital energy and time, especially detrimental when safety or the successful performance of biological functions demands an instantaneous adjustment to conditions. The complex mental process of purposeful motivation requires a comparatively long time. What would happen to a person if he were obliged to incur such delay before jumping aside when an automobile horn is sounded or dodging when threatened with a sudden blow is self-evident.[18]

Another variety of conscious but nonpurposeful motivation is the "actional," "self-suffi-cient," or "normative" motivation, to use Petra-jitsky's terminology. Here the role of the ideas and images that stimulate emotion processes and through these elicit actions is played by the images of *action patterns themselves*. If an honest man is bribed to perform an act of calumny, forgery, or poisoning, the very imagining, or mental representation, of such an evil action calls forth repulsive inhibiting emotions. These emotions are often strong enough to nullify the attraction of the bribe or of other rewards offered by way of purposeful utilitarian motivation. Other "actional" ideas—for instance, those relating to good, noble, or heroic actions—call forth congenial emotions and lead to the performance of the respective actions. Ideas of this kind are manifested often in the form of judgments approving or rejecting the respective act not as a means to a given end but for its own sake; for instance, "A lie is shameful," Thou shalt not lie," or "Always speak the truth." Such a self-sufficient normative motivation with norms consisting of a simple "Thou shalt" or "Thou shalt not," applies to the conduct of children as well as of grown-up persons. The studies of Piaget show that the first stage in the moral development of children—the stage of their "heteronomous morality"—consists precisely in such normative judgments and motivations, where the rules (imposed by grown-ups) are regarded as sacrosanct. Some 67 per cent of all their norms are of this type.[19] A large proportion of the norms of conduct of grown-ups are also of this character, the rest being made up of self-sufficient norms reenforced by utilitarian and other considerations. The judgments based upon such "actional" ideas and emotional attractions or repulsions may be called "normative judgments." As Petrajitsky has pointed out, these "normative" motivations, judgments, and convictions constitute the reactions, relationships,

---

[17] Leo Petrajitsky, *Theory of Law and Ethics* (Russian, St. Petersburg, 1910), Vol. I, pp. 15 ff.

[18] Petrajitsky, *op. cit.*, pp. 17 ff. The same conclusion is reached from the standpoint of I. Pavlov's theory of conditioned responses. Not only all the unconditioned but most of the conditioned responses are nonpurposeful in their origin and functions. E. Durkheim's and W. G. Summer's theories of the origin and development of social norms, institutions, folkways, and mores and G. Tarde's theory of imitative acts are a further corroboration of the existence of nonpurposive conscious actions and of their predominance in human conduct.

[19] J. Piaget, *The Moral Judgment of the Child* (London, 1932), pp. 312, *passim*.

and convictions of *law and ethics*.[20] (See Chapter 4.)

The above is sufficient to show the fallacy of the opinion that all conscious actions are purposeful. If we assign the proper meaning to the terms "purposeful" and "teleological" and to the correlated terms "means" and "end," it is clear that conscious actions are not always purposeful and that the conscious motivations called by Petrajitsky "fundamental," "actional," and "normative" are nonpurposeful. The same conclusion is reached if one approaches the problem from the standpoint of Pavlov's theory of conditioned and unconditioned responses.

In the light of this conclusion the inadequacy of the schema "means and end," even in application to conscious actions and social relationships, is evident. Since the basic assumption is false, the results of this pseudo-teleological analysis of social phenomena have been either negligible or (more often) misleading. Only with reference to purposeful phenomena is the schema applicable and helpful, and they constitute merely a small fraction of sociocultural phenomena.

MEANINGS, VALUES, AND NORMS IN GENERIC SOCIOCULTURAL PHENOMENON

Meanings and values superimposed upon the biophysical properties of interacting persons form the second component of sociocultural phenomena. Meanings may be classified as follows: (1) cognitive *meanings,* in the narrow sense of the term, such as the meaning of Plato's philosophy, the Christian *Credo,* a mathematical formula, or the Marxian theory of surplus value; (2) meaningful *values,* such as the economic value of land or other property, the value of religion, science, education, or music, of democracy or monarchy, of life or health; (3) *norms* referred to as a standard, like the norms of law and ethics, norms of etiquette, technical norms, or prescriptions for constructing machinery, writing a poem, cooking meat, or growing vegetables. These three classes of meanings are inherent aspects of meaningful phenomena. Any meaning in a narrow sense is a value (cognitive or other). Any value presupposes a norm of conduct with reference to its realization or rejection—for instance, the value of wealth, of the Kingdom of God, of virtue, of health, and the corresponding means of attaining or avoiding such an end. On the other hand, any norm—juridical, ethical, technical, or otherwise—is necessarily a meaning and a positive or negative value. Hence the terms "meaning," "value," and "norm" will be used interchangeably to denote a general class of meaningful phenomena[21] superimposed upon the biophysical properties of persons and objects, actions and events.

Stripped of their meaningful aspects, all the phenomena of human interaction become merely biophysical phenomena and, as such, properly form the subject matter of the biophysical sciences. The purposeful or nonpurposeful, solidary or antagonistic, cooperative or noncooperative, harmonious or discordant, loving or hating, contractual or familistic, religious or irreligious, moral or immoral, scientific or artistic—such sociocultural characteristics are inherent not in the biophysical properties of interaction but in the meaningful component superimposed upon these. The same is true of all the social systems of interaction, such as the state, the family, the Church, universities, academies of science, political parties, labor unions, or armies and navies. In the chemical universe there is no science or philosophy element, no trade-union molecule, no educational or religious reaction. In the physical universe there are no phenom-

---

[20] Leo Petrajitsky, *op. cit.,* Vol. I, pp. 15-21. Both volumes give a brilliant analysis of motivation and actions, and an unsurpassed analysis of the phenomena of law and ethics. E. Husserl's and my analysis of so-called *normative judgments* further corroborates Petrajitsky's conclusions. See E. Husserl, *Logische Untersuchungen* (Halle, 1922), Vol. I, Ch. 1.

[21] Tönnies' division of social phenomena into five classes—social entities (*Wesenheiten*) of the *Gemeinschaft* and *Gesellschaft,* social relationships, social norms, social values and social endeavors (*Bezugsgebilden*)—is defective. Better is his division of what I call "meaning component" into norms, values, and endeavors. However, his "endeavors" are very vague. The classification of meanings (in the generic sense) into norms, meanings, and values appears to be sounder, both logically and causally. See F. Tönnies, *Einführung in die Soziologie* (Stuttgart, 1931); cf. C. Loomis, Introduction to *Tönnies' Fundamental Concepts of Sociology* (New York, 1940).

ena such as the state or the Church, no purposeful, ethical, antagonistic or solidary, contractual, or artistic relationships. In the biological world one does not find a religious cell, a juridical chromosome, a moral tissue, a political organ, a biological species of trade union or university, or—if biology is divested of its anthropomorphic elements—any solidary or antagonistic, contractual or familistic, relationships.[22]

Stripped of its meaningful component, Plato's *Republic* becomes a material object (a book) with certain physical and chemical properties. The *Victory of Samothrace* proves to be nothing but a piece of marble, with a certain geometric form and a certain physicochemical composition. Beethoven's *Ninth Symphony* resolves itself into a complex of sounds; that is, into air waves of varying lengths and amplitudes. The national flag becomes merely a piece of cloth attached to a stick. Cooperation becomes an "addition or multiplication of forces"; war, a "subtraction of forces"; social organization, an "equilibrium of forces"; law, a "correlation of forces";[23] consciousness, an "electron-proton aggregation" (A. P. Weiss); emotion, a particular "stimulus-response relationship" (W. S. Hunter); fear, "the behavior of a subject of specified characteristics reacting to a stimulus of specified characteristics

within the specified field of forces" (G. Lundberg); and so on.[24] In brief, without the component of meaning all sociocultural phenomena become purely physical or biological. As such they are legitimately studied by only the biophysical sciences, whose categories and laws are applicable to human beings considered as merely organisms or aggregations of matter.[25]

The component of meanings, values, and norms is quite different from the third component of sociocultural phenomena—that of material vehicles—and can in no wise be identified with the physical or biological properties either of the latter or of the subjects of interaction. This is unquestionably shown by the fact that *one and the same meaning* (for instance, that of the Christian *Credo*) can be materialized or objectified in a variety of material vehicles: saying it aloud (sounds, or air waves, serve as the vehicle); writing or printing it on paper, stone, or a steel plate; recording it on a phonograph record; broadcasting it over the radio. The meaning of the *Credo*, however, remains the same in spite of the wide variety of the vehicles and of their physical and chemical properties.

The meaning of enmity may be manifested in a variety of overt actions, such as shooting, poisoning, drowning, hanging, burning, or

---

[22] As we shall see, what relationships are solidary and what are antagonistic is determined not so much by the nature of overt actions and reactions as by their inner meaning. Overtly we can distinguish actions and reactions only in terms of spatial approach and withdrawal of the interacting parties. If, however, we call all interactions in which the parties approach one another solidary, then two armies closing in a mortal combat in the closest spatial proximity represent the most solidary interaction, while armies withdrawing from one another after the armistice represent antagonistic interaction. Without the meaning component we cannot tell which reactions are solidary and which are antagonistic and if we try to do so, the result will be absurd, as the above case shows. For this reason the characterization of associative processes as those where parties approach one another, and dissociative processes as those where they withdraw from one another, has proved extremely unsatisfactory. This is aptly illustrated by L. von Wiese and H. Becker. Cf. Wiese and Becker, *Systematic Sociology* (New York, 1932), pp. 5 and 37 ff.

[23] B. Voronov, *Osnovania soziologii* (St. Petersburg, 1909).

[24] For a survey and criticism of such theories of "social physics," "social mechanics," and "behavioristic sociology," cf. my *Theories* (New York, 1928), Ch. 1 and pp. 617 ff.

[25] In that case no amateur "social physics," "social mechanics," or "behavioristic sociobiology" is necessary. At best, such amateur disciplines only duplicate authentic physics, chemistry, and biology; more often this homemade "social biophysics" distorts the natural as well as the social sciences, adding nothing to our knowledge. For a criticism of these theories, cf. my *Theories*, Ch. 1 and my *Sociocultural Causality, Space, Time* (Duke University Press, 1943), Ch. 1 *passim*. See also C. A. Ellwood, *Methods in Sociology* (Duke University Press, 1933), Ch. 1 *passim*. "The social value is opposed to the natural thing, which has a content but, as a part of nature, has no meaning for human activity, and is treated as valueless; when the natural thing assumes a meaning, it becomes thereby a social value," declare W. I. Thomas and F. Znaniecki. It is to be regretted they did not draw all the appropriate conclusions from this sound principle. Cf. Thomas and Znaniecki, *The Polish Peasant* (New York, 1927), Vol. I, p. 21.

knifing the hated party; torturing his loved ones; ruining him economically; or denouncing him to the authorities. The overt actions all manifest the meaning of enmity, in distinction from that of love, sympathy, charity, solidarity, and the like. The same may be said of any sociocultural phenomenon: the meaning may be externalized through the most diverse biophysical vehicles. Conversely the same material phenomenon may serve as a vehicle for externalizing the widest range of meanings, values, and norms. The identical sum of money (in identical material and denominations) may serve now as a means of assisting the needy, now for paying a debt, now as a bribe, now for seducing a girl, now for the purchase of a material commodity, and so forth. The money as a vehicle has not changed; the meanings it manifests are radically different.[26] Likewise, an overt action may remain externally the same in all its essentials, but its meanings may be widely dissimilar. The sex act means now prostitution, now seduction, now adultery, now rape, now the legitimate intercourse of a married couple. The external acts of shaking one's fist, spanking, or firing a gun may vary in intent from play to dead-seriousness. A kiss may be the caress of Judas or that of profound love; verbal expressions may range from a meaningless "How do you do?" or a hypocritical "I admire you" to sincere manifestations of the respective meanings. Otherwise there could be no lying, hypocrisy, or insincerity.

The human organism may remain biologically unchanged, but the meanings superimposed upon it may vary widely and radically. Czar Nicholas II did not alter biologically when he was deposed from his exalted position and relegated to the status of a prisoner. Similarly, without any biological change the political criminal Lenin suddenly became a dictator, and the obscure Robespierre was elevated overnight to the headship of the powerful Jacobin group. This shift of values is exemplified even in the case of the dead. No physical, chemical, or biological change took place in the dust of the French kings who had passed away long before the French Revolution. Yet during the revolution their meaning as revered or respected sovereigns was transformed into that of hateful tyrants and oppressors. In our personal relations such shifts of meaning are daily occurrences: a person who yesterday was our enemy today becomes a friend, though nothing has meanwhile changed in his physical or biological organism. Today's lovers are tomorrow's enemies; revered persons become despised; the famous become infamous.[27]

The identity of meanings, values, and norms manifested in the most diverse material vehicles, and the identity of vehicles incarnating widely different meanings, reveal (1) the presence of the component of meanings, values, and norms in all sociocultural phenomena; (2) its profound difference from the other two components (human beings and material vehicles); and (3) the relatively loose relationship between the component of meanings and those of vehicles and human agents. Since any meaning may manifest itself through different vehicles and human agents, and since any vehicle or human agent may incorporate different meanings, their relationship is "polygamous" rather than "monogamous," loose rather than close. (For a further discussion of this principle, compare the section on vehicles and conductors of interaction.)

The component of meaning may affect the conduct of human beings and the nature of vehicles so much that their biophysical properties become comparatively irrelevant. A stick may become the highly sacred *churinga* of the Australian; a piece of wood supposed to have belonged to the cross of Jesus is transformed into a precious miracle-working relic; a piece of cheap cloth on a stick may become the national flag of a country, for which lives are gladly sacrificed. An ordinary human organism—perhaps even sick and infirm—may become a saint or prophet, or a deified monarch or glorified revolutionary

---

[26] For the diverse character of money as a vehicle, cf. especially G. Simmel, *Philosophie des Geldes* (Leipzig, 1900), and P. Rykatchev, *Vlast deneg (The Power of Money,* Moscow, 1911).

[27] Cf. M. Sherif, *The Psychology of Social Norms* (New York, 1936), pp. 28 ff. A series of experimental studies shows that no values, even the affective values of pleasantness and unpleasantness, are necessarily inherent in the respective objects, but may be attached to almost any object. Cf. J. Beebe-Center, *Pleasantness and Unpleasantness* (New York, 1934); E. F. Wells, "The Effect of Attitude upon Feeling," *AJS,* Vol. XLII (1930), pp. 573-580.

leader. Conversely, a strong and excellently endowed physical organism may become a prostitute or even a criminal. The properties designated as "sacred," "saintly," "heroic," "virtuous," "beloved," etc. and their opposites inhere not in the biophysical traits of the respective objects or persons but in the meanings that are superimposed upon them.

Thus what is materially identical is often fundamentally different socioculturally, by virtue of the difference of meanings or values imputed to it; vice versa, what is different biophysically is often identical socioculturally. Identical actions (for instance, carrying a gun) performed by the same person in the same location may be now criminal, now lawful. On the other hand, highly diverse material objects, persons, and overt actions may be identical socioculturally. *Hence the application of the principles of identity and difference on the basis of the meanings manifested by material objects, overt actions, and persons often leads to results radically different from those arrived at on the basis of their biophysical properties.*

The preceding analysis clearly shows the absurdity of the so-called naturalistic and behavioristic study of sociocultural phenomena. If it were consistently carried out, it would be necessary to classify all sociocultural phenomena as identical or different solely on the basis of their biophysical properties, in which case there would be no political, economic, religious, scientific, aesthetic, or juridical classes of phenomena, since each of these classes is composed of the most heterogeneous objects, persons, actions, events, and processes. For the same reason one could not properly speak of solidary or antagonistic, militant or peaceful, cooperative or conflicting, purposeful or nonpurposeful, relationships and actions; nor could one speak of the family, the state, the Church, political parties, trade unions, scientific societies, classes or castes, or any other form of organized groups. Moreover,

classifying phenomena on the basis of their biophysical nature, such investigators would have to treat as identical what socioculturally is absolutely different. All cases of shooting would become identical (for instance, there would be no difference between shooting as murder, shooting in war, and shooting for practice), and all sex acts would be identical, whether associated with prostitution, rape, or the marital relation. All objects made of the same material (such as wood) would have to be put in the same class, whether a wooden cross, a wooden swastika, wooden toys, or wooden furniture. Buildings of the same materials and form would necessarily be regarded as identical, whether a church, a Communist club, a warehouse, a concert hall, or an armory. All persons with the same physical traits would likewise have to be classed as identical, though they might be members of different nations, religions, classes, occupations, economic strata, and so on.

If a genuine naturalistic and behavioristic social science is actually attempted, the result is a series of the grossest absurdities. No wonder that, in spite of vociferous manifestoes, none of them has ever carried its program even through its first stages. In their factual analysis the investigators invariably forget their declarations and proceed to classify and analyze sociocultural phenomena on the basis of their meaning component rather than on the basis of the biophysical properties of the vehicles or human agents. Thus all of them speak of economic, religious, scientific, or political variables and factors; of the Church, the state, the family, and other social systems whose identity is based on their meaning-component; of solidary and antagonistic, legal and criminal, and other meaningful relations and actions. But, starting with a wrong assumption and not realizing clearly the structural composition of sociocultural phenomena, they classify and analyze them erroneously.[28]

---

[28] Glaring examples of the contradictions of these pseudo-naturalists and pseudo-behaviorists are found in the introductory chapter of Pareto's *Mind and Society*, which treats sociology as the strictly "logico-experimental" natural science. In all his subsequent chapters, operating with sentiments, residues, derivation, derivatives, ideologies, religions, and economic and other phenomena, he incessantly transgresses his methodological principles, fortunately contributing something valuable precisely because of this radical departure from his own avowed principles. Still more naive examples of such a contradiction are given by S. Dodd in his *Dimensions of Society* (New York, 1942), by G. Lundberg in his *Foundations of Sociology* (New York, 1939), and by E. D. Chapple and C. S. Coon in their *Principles of Anthropology* (New York, 1942).

Finally, *the component of meanings transforms not only the sociocultural nature of its vehicles and human agents but also the causal relationships between them: it creates tangible causal interdependence between the vehicles and human beings where, on the basis of their biophysical properties, such interdependence does not exist; conversely, it precludes causal dependence where otherwise it would exist.*[29] The human members and vehicles that compose Harvard University or the Roman Catholic Church or the United States of America are highly heterogeneous in their biophysical properties. Take the case of Harvard University, with its various buildings, the corpses in its medical school, the fantastic array of objects in its museums, the books in its libraries, and the different organisms that constitute its human members. On the basis of their biophysical properties this heterogeneous collection of objects and persons cannot have any tangible causal interdependence. Nevertheless, if any important change occurs in any important part of these vehicles and human agents (say, the Widener Library is burned, or the president and members of the corporation are changed), this may at once affect virtually all the rest of the university. For instance, an extraordinary expenditure for rebuilding the library may lead to cuts in the budgets of all the departments, thus influencing even the number of corpses in the medical school, not to mention the tangible changes in many of the vehicles and human members of the university. Likewise, a new president and a new corporation may introduce a new policy affecting in many ways the vehicles and human members of the institution. This causal interdependence between sociocultural phenomena where on the basis of purely biophysical properties such a dependence does not exist represents a general law.

Conversely, the component of meanings frequently precludes a causal tie which would otherwise exist. If there were no sociocultural norms of religion, law, or ethics prohibiting,

for instance, unlawful sexual relations, and theft, or admonishing one to sacrifice his property and even his life in the interest of an ideal, the interrelationships or interactions of human beings would have been very different from what they are. If there were no values and norms guaranteeing civil and political rights, freedom and independence would be nonexistent in thousands of human relationships; the biophysically stronger would dominate the weaker; and the weaker would be causally dependent upon the stronger. If, for a moment, we imagine the human universe as being ruled and controlled only by its biophysical properties, without any religious, legal, ethical, scientific, or aesthetic meanings, we can readily perceive that the causal relationships in that universe, in the actions and reactions of its members, would be fundamentally different from what they actually are. An enormous proportion of the causal relationships that now exist would be absent, and vice versa.[30]

The foregoing discussion makes it abundantly clear that meanings, values, and norms are a universal component of sociocultural phenomena and are of paramount importance for an understanding of the structural and dynamic properties as well as causal relationships of these phenomena.

MATERIAL VEHICLES AS A UNIVERSAL COMPONENT OF SOCIOCULTURAL PHENOMENA

1. Definition of Vehicles

Since pure meanings, values, and norms are immaterial, spaceless, and timeless, they cannot be transmitted directly from mind to mind, unless possibly by telepathy or extrasensory transmission.[31] If such a direct transmission of ideas or meanings exists, it is exceedingly rare, accessible to a very limited number of people and under highly exceptional conditions.[32] The

---

[29] This is a further reason for the futility of the strictly naturalistic study of causal relationships in the sociocultural universe. Such a study would overlook almost all the causal relationships in this universe and would predicate many where they really do not exist.

[30] For a development of this point, cf. my *Sociocultural Causality, Space, Time,* Chps. 1, 2, *passim.*

[31] Cf. J. B. Rhine, *Extra-sensory Perception* (Boston, 1935) and *New Frontiers of Mind* (New York, 1937).

[32] For this reason G. Gurvitch is wrong in opposing "sociability by interpenetration," as a direct inner liaison between minds based on actual collective intuitions, where the symbols (vehicles)

overwhelming majority of meaningful interactions between human beings occur not through extrasensory perception but through the instrumentality of the sensory vehicles— overt actions and material objects—that externalize, materialize, objectify, and socialize the immaterial meanings. In order to transmit to another person the meaning "2 plus 2 is 4," we may tell him this, that is, through the actions of our vocal apparatus, objectify the meaning in certain sounds which, impinging upon his ears, are retransformed in his mind (through his nervous system) into the meaning. Or we may write it on paper, the figures becoming the material vehicle through which the idea is transmitted. Or we may use certain gestures, as in the case of deaf-mutes. The same is true of any other meaning and its transmission to others. If any meaning or system of meanings stays in the mind of the person who conceives it, and does not become objectified in any vehicle, it obviously remains inaccessible to other persons and perishes with the death of its author, if not sooner.

All sensory overt actions, material objects, and physical, chemical, and biological processes and forces used for the externalizing, objectifying and socializing of meanings are vehicles of meaningful interaction. As such they compose the third universal component of sociocultural phenomena. The schema of meaningful interaction is as follows: Subject A objectifies his meaning N in a vehicle X, in oral or written form; the vehicle X comes into contact with the appropriate sense organ of B and is perceived; and in the mind of B it is retransformed into the meaning N. Languages, both oral and written; gestures and pantomime; music and other meaningful sounds; paintings and sculpture; and such material objects as tools, implements, machines, weapons, clothing, buildings, monuments, cultivated fields, paved roads, and artificial dams—in brief, all material phenomena essential to the meaningful interaction of human beings—are vehicles of sociocultural phenomena. They all objectify various meanings, socialize them and render them accessible to others.

Hence it is inaccurate to speak of sociocultural phenomena as though they consisted exclusively of human beings; besides human beings they admit immaterial meanings and their material vehicles as equally essential and universal components. The structure of empirical sociocultural phenomena is thus not single but three-componential. This principle is often overlooked, with the result that a series of theoretical and practical blunders are incessantly committed by those who perceive merely a single component—only human beings *or* meanings *or* vehicles.

2. Vehicles as Conductors of Interaction

As already indicated, without vehicles as conductors meaningful interaction is impossible. Even the purely physical interaction of human beings would be reduced in that case to a meager minimum. Even if the so-called distance receptors—organs capable of receiving stimuli from a distance—are taken into account, the range of physical interaction would not be substantially widened. A few miles would constitute the limit beyond which no physical interaction would be possible. This is also true with regard to time, for without the aid of conductors any physical interaction between two or more people not in proximity at a given moment—especially between the dead and the living, or between past, present, and future generations—would be precluded.

However, we know that interaction goes on between persons separated by thousands of miles (through letters, telegrams, the radio, etc.) and even between the dead and the living. Plato, Shakespeare, Beethoven, and Raphael still influence our state of mind and our actions when we read, listen to, or look at their works. Such an interaction is obviously possible only through the media of vehicles as conductors.

3. Principal Types of Vehicles

In their concrete forms the conductors of interaction are numerous and diverse. We must distinguish, first, *physical and symbolic conductors. Physical* conductors are those in

---

play either no part or a secondary role, to "sociability by convergence," where the individual minds communicate exclusively through symbolic vehicles.

He does not demonstrate how, in the absence of vehicles, collective intuitions can be formed and meaningful communication carried on. Cf. his *Essai de sociologie* (Paris, 1938), pp. 1-112.

which the physical qualities of the vehicle are used to modify the state of mind and the overt actions of another. Thus a stone, bullet, or atomic bomb directed at an enemy affects him through its physical properties, including the force of the impact. *Symbolic* conductors exert an influence not so much by virtue of their physical properties as by virtue of the symbolic meaning attached to them. A spoken word exerts an influence not so much through the physical qualities of sound as through the meaning it conveys. A single word, quietly uttered, frequently proves more effective than the loudest and most deafening noise. Symbolic conductors require that one understand the language spoken or written in order to translate the sounds or signs into their proper meaning. Otherwise they remain mere gibberish. It goes without saying that symbolic conductors play a paramount role in the world of meaningful interactions.

According to the *physical* form of energy or matter used, the principal conductors of interaction are the following: (a) *Sound conductors*, where air waves convey the message. Speech, music, and various noises are examples of this type of conductors. (b) *Light and color conductors*, where radiant energy is employed. Street lights and pictures furnish examples. (c) *Pantomimic conductors* consisting of gestures and expressive movements. (d) *Thermal conductors*, where the energy of heat is used to influence the conduct or mind of others. (e) *Mechanical conductors*, where mechanical energy is used for this purpose. Striking, stroking, and stinging are illustrations of this type. (f) *Chemical conductors*, where chemical properties are used for interaction. (g) *Electrical and radio conductors*. (h) *Material-object conductors*, where a complex of physicochemical and biological properties is used in the form of a given object for the purpose of interaction. In object conductors not this or that specific property is important but the specific complex of qualities, as in the case of an engagement ring, a family heirloom, the national flag, or a dollar bill.

This enumeration of the basic types of conductors shows that almost all physicochemical energies are used as the vehicles of interaction. It indicates also the fallacy of regarding language (oral or written) as the only instrument of meaningful interaction.

Let us undertake a detailed examination of each of these forms.

a. *Sound conductors.* Sounds as such, functioning both as physical and as symbolic conductors, quite apart from their symbolic qualities, may affect our mind and behavior. The following case of the influence of sounds independently of their symbolic significance affords a pertinent example. The subject was required to raise repeatedly, with the middle finger of his right hand, a weight of three kilograms until the finger was completely exhausted. It was found that certain sound stimuli enabled him to lift the weight more times in immediate succession. Thus in sixteen experiments he raised it 850 times when a certain quint was sounded, but when this tone combination was lowered in pitch by half a tone he could lift it only 50 times in succession.[33] In this case the sound acted solely as a physical agent.

From our own experience we know that certain loud noises, without any meaning attached to them, affect our mind and conduct. The question of noise in our big cities has become a serious problem.

The primary role of sound conductors, however, is that of symbolic vehicles. Among symbolic sound conductors the most important are *speech* and *music*. Owing to their flexibility, accessibility, and ease of transmission these symbolic conductors constitute the most important agents of meaningful interaction.

Speech is the basic medium for the objectification and transmission of meanings, even those of the most complex and subtle character. There is no exaggeration in the statement that superorganic sociocultural life is made possible solely through the existence of language. Not only meaningful interaction but even thought itself (especially abstract thought) is hardly possible without the use of words.

It is by means of speech that human beings for the most part regulate their mutual behavior. When we want to stimulate others to a specific act or to restrain them, we nearly always employ oral symbols, as in the injunc-

---

[33] G. Bohn, *La Nouvelle Psychologie animale* (Paris, 1911), pp. 166-168.

tions: "Hands up!" "Do that," or "Don't do this!" Wherever people meet—in Congress or the market place, at church or at home, in a classroom or a court—oral conductors play a significant social role.[34]

Words are like electric currents which pass between human beings. Their effects are at times amazing: a word may kill a man! It is no mere coincidence that in many religions, as in Brahmanism, words are conceived of as magic forces ruling the world, and even the will of the gods. The Scriptures declare, "In the beginning was the Word, and the Word was with God, and the Word was God."[35]

Music is the second basic form of symbolic sound conductors. By its nature it is suited more for the objectification and transmission of feelings, emotions, moods, or elusive mental states that defy verbal expression than of ideas or acts, and is therefore more often used for emotional than intellectual communication. A talented musician at the piano binds his hearers to himself by invisible ties; the sound waves resulting from the movements of his fingers on the keys transmit his emotions to his listeners, creating in them waves of psychic experience. Some of these waves induce a depressed state—sadness, despondency, or grief, with their corresponding overt reactions— while others elicit a sense of mirth, happiness, or joy, accompanied by the appropriate movements. An emotional and often ideological whole is thus created of the individuals composing a concert audience. The exciting or de-

pressing influence of music, says Bohn, has been known since ancient days. "Besides funeral marches, accompanied by depressing moods and slow movements, there is also exciting music compelling people to move their bodies vigorously in marching or dancing, a thing which could not be even imagined without the music."[36]

Men have often ascribed to sacred forms of music magical and mystic influences which rule the universe, gods, and men. In several forms music has exerted a striking effect upon the listeners (as well as the performers), both good and bad. Its sociocultural role has been always highly significant.[37]

Besides speech and music, sound conductors function in a number of other ways. The firing of a cannon at Petrograd once meant that it was noon; the whistle of a locomotive signifies the departure of the train; factory whistles are blown to indicate a new shift; the ringing of a bell in a classroom marks the beginning of the hour; church bells announce a religious service; a telephone bell apprizes us that someone wishes to speak to us.

b. *Light and Color Conductors.* In social life these agents function chiefly in symbolic form. Together with sound conductors, the color and light conductors form the commonest and most important method for objectifying and transmitting meanings or values.

The most significant of these is *written* language. In the broadest sense, written language includes all that has been marked by man on

---

[34] In addition to the actual meaning of words, the voice itself, through its pitch and timbre, acts as an additional stimulus. Cf. C. Darwin, *The Expression of the Emotions* (New York, 1873), pp. 83-95.

[35] It is interesting to note that among preliterate peoples speech reactions seem to have been an inseparable part of man's organism, the whole organism, so to speak, participating in their performance. As with animals which use the entire body for elementary forms of communication (see R. Yerkes and A. Yerkes, "Social Behavior of Infrahuman Primates," in C. Murchison, *Handbook of Social Psychology* Clark University Press, 1935), "speech involved for primitive man much more extensive patterns of physiological action than is the case with civilized man today." Speech was then not so easily manipulated nor so sharply separated from other vital functions of the organism as today. Hence it was not used to say what one did not mean, as is frequently the case

with us. Words were employed for real thinking and communication, and so were often considered sacred. In "civilized" man the excessive use of words and the corresponding mental calisthenics have cheapened language and led to its misuse, which, as in schizophrenics, may finally react disruptively upon one's mental integrity. Herein lies one of the chief sources of many mental and social troubles of our times. For an interesting analysis along this line, cf. Trigant Burrow, "Fallacies of the Senses," *Scientia*, 1935; "Neurosis and War," *The Journal of Psychology*, 1941; and W. Galt, "Our Mother Tongue," *Psychoanalytic Review*, 1943. Though the "bioorganismic" interpretation of the authors is questionable, the facts they cite are accurate and well stated.

[36] G. Bohn, *La Nouvelle Psychologie animale*, pp. 166-168.

[37] On the types of music, their dynamics, and their social role, cf. my *Dynamics*, Vol. I, Ch. 12, for the theories and literature.

various objects (paper, stone, walls, the human body, etc.) by means of signs or figures for the purpose of expressing various meanings, values, and norms. Written language in this sense covers not only alphabetic writing but also hieroglyphics, the cuneiform of the ancient Assyrians, and the symbolic signs of primitive man, as well as the conventional signs and symbols used in mathematics.

In the civilized world, books are the most widely used form of light conductors, each book representing a complex transmitting the thoughts and feelings of its author to the reader. A library may be regarded as a large telephone exchange where hundreds of people are connected daily with scores of authors, both living and dead, in order to converse with them inaudibly. It may be stated without exaggeration that the person who first employed such conductors for communication with others made the most revolutionary invention of all times. Printing and all technical progress in this field have played an extremely significant part in the growth of human culture. According to J. W. Danzel,

The higher human culture rises, the greater is its dependence upon the results of the work of previous generations, and the greater is the necessity for a medium to record the experience of the past. This medium is written language. Here thought is tied to permanent symbols and is thereby liberated from the instantaneousness of its existence. Moreover, serving as a means of preservation of the spiritual wealth of the ages, the social role of written language is of especial importance, for it guarantees the continuity of social life far beyond the limits of that of the individual. It is the medium of communication between those separated in space, and it is the tie between past, contemporary, and future generations. Mauthner very clearly defines this function: "Let us imagine for a moment," he says, "that in all civilized countries all graphic signs—books, etc.—were suddenly destroyed, and their use forgotten forever. Such destruction would make a ruin out of our civilization, converting it into a relic similar to the clocks of the old cathedrals which no one can wind because the keys have been lost."[38]

The second fundamental type of color and light conductors is represented by *pictures and paintings*, consisting physically of a mass of colored spots arranged in a definite order and form. They convey to us the artists' thoughts, ideas, and emotions, even if they are no longer living. In addition to permitting this interaction between the artist and ourselves, pictures serve to unite us with one another by creating common psychic experiences and moods. From the naive scrawling of a child to the ingenious creations of the great masters they serve the need of communication between human minds.

There are many other forms of light and color conductors in everyday life: lamps on the mast of a boat indicate the presence of a ship; light effects in a play are used to evoke a gay or other mood in the audience. Color conductors are, indeed, all around us: red and green traffic lights symbolize, respectively, "Stop!" and "Go!" Black often signifies mourning; a crimson rose, ardent love; red banners, revolutionary ideas and hopes; colored state flags, their respective nations; colored chevrons or gold braid, military ranks. The color of clothing may likewise symbolize various meanings: the whiteness of the wedding dress means purity; the black habit worn by monks is a sign of their renunciation of the world, and so on.

c. *Pantomimic Conductors.* The third class of conductors, *pantomimic or motor*, are again either physical or symbolic. Mere physical actions are sufficient in themselves to alter the state of mind or the overt conduct of others; if in addition a meaning is attached to them, their influence becomes all the more effective. In our daily life constant use is made of symbolic pantomimic conductors: the meaning "Get out of here!" may be expressed by a gesture indicating the door; a nod of the head indicates assent; while negation may be expressed by merely shaking the head, indifference by a shrug of the shoulders, love by caresses, rage by clenching the fists, satisfaction and joy by smiling, greeting by raising the hat.

Pantomimic conductors of vehicles combined in vast systems are capable of transmitting very complex meanings. Among such systems are the ceremonials of primitive peoples,

[38] J. W. Danzel, *Die Anfänge der Schrift* (Leipzig, 1912), pp. 1-2. See also A. C. Woolner, *Languages in History and Politics* (Oxford University Press, 1938); J. Vendryes, *Le Langage* (Paris, 1921); and C. Serrus, *La Langue, les Sens et la Pensée* (Paris, 1941).

church rituals, state ceremonies, processions, parades, and the like.[39] Silent motion pictures, which are a combination of pantomimic and light conductors, transmit complex dramas, comedies, and tragedies without the medium of spoken words. Pantomimic vehicles in the form of gestures make up the language of deaf-mutes, of members of certain primitive societies, and, in part, of children.[40]

d. *Thermal, Mechanical, Chemical and Electrical Conductors.* These groups of conductors influence behavior largely through their direct physical effects on the human organism, but they function also as symbolic conductors. *Thermal* conductors function in a host of ways. A person who sets fire to a house or a forest, or an airman who drops incendiary bombs upon a city, markedly conditions the state of mind and the behavior of others; for fear, panic, injury, illness, and even death, as well as poverty, may ensue. A central heating system provides another type of thermal conductor, since through altering the temperature the janitor or the owner of the house may indirectly influence the behavior of the tenants. Other instances are afforded by hot water bottles, refrigerators, and ice packs. The heat generated by firemen or stokers on locomotives or boats is a conductor of this type; for through it the convenience and even the fate of the passengers may be definitely determined. *Mechanical* conductors are exemplified by blows, shots, etc. which inflict bodily injury; surgical operations; caresses and embraces; and other acts distinguished from pure pantomime. *Chemical* conductors are employed incessantly in thousands of forms to influence the conduct or mentality of others. A cook or housewife, through the chemical properties of food, affects the behavior of the consumers and their state of mind. So does a grocer through selling contaminated food to his cus-

tomers; a doctor or nurse through the administration of medicine to patients; a murderer through poisoning his victim; or a hospitable friend through offering whisky to his guest.

Electric and radio conductors function in a variety of ways, but mainly as physical conductors transmitting through a distance or broadcasting over vast areas the sound, color and light, pantomimic, mechanical, and other conductors used to objectify and convey meanings to others. The telephone, telegraph, and radio serve as conductors of conductors but not directly of meanings. In other cases, as in radiotherapy, electricity and radio waves serve as direct conductors of meanings. Transformed into other forms of energy they function as thermal, mechanical, and other types of conductors. In all these and many other ways their role in human interaction is enormous.

e. *Object Conductors.* Material objects—a dollar bill, a lock of hair, a wedding ring, a family heirloom, a scepter, a cross, a national flag, a trophy cup, the "keys of the city" presented to a distinguished visitor, Notre Dame Cathedral, the White House, the Lincoln Memorial—exemplify object conductors. In thousands of forms object conductors function in social interaction as physical and especially as symbolic conductors.[41] As such they objectify a wide range of meanings and convey them to others, influencing their state of mind and their overt actions. In a sense the whole of material culture—tools, utensils, machinery, weapons, cultivated fields and gardens, roads, buildings, and entire cities—represents object conductors. Those who created such objects—often past generations—influence our state of mind and overt actions through the physical and especially the symbolic properties of these conductors. We have to follow the course of streets and roads as they were laid out even

[39] Legal interaction abounds in pantomimic symbolic conductors used for objectification and transmission of such meanings as respective rights and duties, contracts, or the acquisition of property. Contemporary court procedure consists also in part of a use of these conductors. For symbolic conductors in legal relationships, cf. Leo Petrajitsky, *A Theory of Law,* Vol. I, pp. 54-57, and J. Chassan, *Essai sur la symbolique du droit* (Paris, 1842), pp. 54-56, 123-25. For political symbolism, cf. T. Arnold, *Symbols of Government* (New Haven,

1935), and J. Marshall, *Swords and Symbols* (New York, 1939); for military symbolism, C. Jaray, *Du formalisme au "Débrouillez-vous"* (Paris, 1910); for religious symbolism, Durkheim, *The Elementary Forms of Religious Life* (London, 1915).

[40] See L. Levy-Brühl, *How Natives Think,* (tr. by L. A. Clare, New York, 1925), pp. 158-167.

[41] Especially interesting is the role of *money* as an object conductor objectifying and transmitting a wide variety of meanings from the sublimest to the most despicable. See G. Simmel, *Philosophie des Geldes* (Leipzig, 1900).

though it may be crooked or round-about. The Bunker Hill Monument, the Lincoln Memorial, a historic castle, palace, cathedral, or house, evoke in us a series of images, ideas, and emotions, and induce such overt actions as buying postcards depicting these objects, giving tips to the guides, or even consecrating our lives to the realization of the values represented by these monuments and the historic persons associated with them.

Human beings may be compared to polyps; as the activities of the latter lead progressively to the formation of coral reefs,[42] so the processes of human interaction continuously produce new layers of material culture and new sets of conductors. Their gradual accumulation, layer by layer, results in the formation of a new environment around the interacting individuals, an environment entirely distinct from the physical, a sociotechnical milieu. All of us live in such an environment. It surrounds us at every step. It constantly transmits to us stimuli initiated by former generations and thus definitely conditions our experiences and conduct. Durkheim is right in asserting that "society consists not only of individuals but also of material objects which play an essential role in social life" and that "social facts are often objectified to such a degree that they become parts of the material world."[43]

This is important to bear in mind in order to avoid the common mistake of considering components of interaction as consisting only of individuals, meanings, or material vehicles (conductors). All three components, as has been said, are indispensable for any social phenomenon. In the absence of the meaning component there are only physical or biological phenomena. If the human agent component is lacking, despite the vehicle component (as in the case of the excavated cities and monuments of Egypt, Babylonia, and Summeria), we have only a dead shell.[44] If the vehicles are absent, the meaningful interaction process is equally impossible. A correct understanding of the three-componential structure is very important for an adequate grasp of the reality or nominality of social groups, of the logic of change of sociocultural phenomena, of their causal connections, and so on.

4. The Chain of Conductors

In a large proportion of meaningful interactions the parties use a chain of different conductors joined to one another with human beings as the linking agents. The whole mechanism of transmission may be compared to a complex system of cogwheels, one of which sets in motion the next, and so on, until the whole system is completed. Let us consider a typical case.

A dictates to his secretary a telegram (sound conductor) addressed to B. She writes it out (light conductor) and then telephones it to the telegraph office (sound and electric conductors). The telegraph operator sends a radiogram (radio conductor), and at the receiving station it is again written down (light conductor) and thus presented to B. This process may be represented as follows: A (1) sound (2) light (3) sound and electricity (4) radio (5) light B.

In this chain human beings (the secretary, telegraph and radio operator, and messenger boy) serve as necessary intermediate links; they establish the contact between various inanimate conductors. Usually it is only by virtue of this "contact role" of human conductors that the combination of various conductors into one continuous chain becomes possible.

This contact role is of special importance in the interaction between individuals separated in space and time. The stimulus which one person sends from America to Europe must pass through a long series of conductors, and human beings inevitably act as the contacts. Similarly, a stimulus derived from some one

---

[42] "The human polyp is perpetually building a coral reef, on the upper surface of which the last generation lives and builds." (Lester F. Ward, *Pure Sociology* [New York, 1911], p. 16.)

[43] E. Durkheim, *Le Suicide*. The concept of the presence of material conductors in social phenomena and their immanent development through the processes of human interaction is expressed by Simmel: "Culture begins—and this is the most critical moment for its understanding—with the fusion of two elements neither of which is of greater significance than the other: the subjective soul and the objective product of the soul." (G. Simmel, "The Concept and the Tragedy of Culture," *Logos* [St. Petersburg, 1911], pp. 4-5.)

[44] See, for instance, P. Carleton, *Buried Civilizations* (New York, 1939), and A. Toynbee, *A Study of History*, 6 Vols. (Oxford University Press, 1934-1939), *passim*.

who is dead is transmitted to us through a chain of conductors, and men are indispensable links in the process.

To resort to analogy, the "connective tissue" of society sought for by the organicists can now be easily located. It consists of the totality of the vehicles and conductor chains, with their total interaction.[45]

5. Retroactive Influence of Vehicles

A large part of human behavior and of the phenomena of human interaction cannot be fully understood unless light is thrown on one additional phase of the role of vehicles as conductors. Can the conductors influence behavior and mental states by themselves—in their own right, so to speak—and, if so, how?

The answer to this question is in the affirmative. Although depending upon man for their very existence, conductors, once created, exert a powerful retroactive influence upon his behavior and psychic states.

a. *General Retroactive Influence.* Vehicles condition behavior and states of mind, first of all, in a purely *mechanical* way. This is especially true of object conductors. As we have already seen, in the process of interaction human meanings, values, and norms, as well as actions, lead to the formation of a great number of object vehicles which, accumulating from generation to generation, constitute what is called "material culture." This material culture, representing the sum total of the vehicles, mechanically conditions the behavior and mental states of men.

Social life (the phenomena of interaction), by crystallizing itself in material objects, helps us to take root in the surrounding world, and at the same time influences us through the media of these material objects.

Roads, constructed before our time, direct the course of our affairs. A child's taste is formed through contact with the monuments of national taste and with the traditions of former generations. Sometimes these monuments (vehicles) are forgotten for a time. . . . only to reappear and start a new life in a new society. This is the characteristic trait of the Renaissance: social life, after being stowed away for a long time, reappears, changing the intellectual and moral views of persons who did not create it. In the absence of such a reawakening these persons would have felt and thought quite differently.

Legal relations under written law differ from those where the law is not codified (in written form). Though jurisprudence is better regulated under a code, it is less supple; though more systematized, it is less mobile. The material forms into which laws are put cannot be thought of, therefore, as mere combinations of words, without significance; on the contrary, they are active realities, as is proved by the difference in legal relations in the absence of these realities.[46]

This quotation makes clear the retroactive influence of the conductors, or vehicles. Once created, they live an independent life, acquiring a logic of functioning, rhythm, and tempo of their own. To cite Simmel's somewhat nebulous terminology:

Things are not under the absolute control of our purposes. Each objective spirit (conductor) possesses its own logic. At the very moment that the first principles of law, art, and mores are created, we let go the thread of their development into separate objective formations. Thus technique, in obedience to its own logic, develops one subtlety after another. The excess of specialization, increasing continuously under the demoniacal pressure of the laws inherent in labor, represents a specific case of the usual fate of all cultural elements; objects (vehicles) possess a logic of development of their own which prevents them from

---

[45] Since meanings must pass through a chain of conductors, any incorrect linking of the conductors leads to a change of meaning, which may reach the other party in a distorted form. This is especially true of sound conductors. They are particularly liable to distortion when the message is passed through two or more human beings. I have performed the following classroom experiment. Asking three of the students to leave the room, I have read to the class twenty to thirty lines of a newspaper report of some crime or other event. I have then asked one of the students to relate the story as accurately as possible to one of the

absentees, who repeated it to the second, who, in turn, passed it on to the third. When the last-named returned to the classroom and related his version of the story, it was always grossly distorted. If the transmission involved a larger number of persons and a longer time interval, and if the factor of mental bias entered into the experiment, the resulting distortion was almost unbelievable. This explains the distortion of facts typical of the testimony of even honest witnesses in court, of news reporting, of gossip, and of the development of myths, legends, and the like.

[46] E. Durkheim, *Le Suicide*, pp. 426-427.

keeping in line with the development of the human soul.[47]

As has already been said, the mere existence of the vehicles conditions our behavior and mental states. We are compelled to live in cities or villages not built by us; we use roads laid out by former generations; we pray in churches erected before we were born. Surrounded on all sides by innumerable vehicles, we constantly absorb—often unconsciously and against our will—the stimuli and meanings which these conductors emit. Sometimes (as in the case of roads) they dictate to us the direction of our movements; again, they predetermine the character of the dwelling in which we are to live; often their mere appearance (such as that of an old tower or a medieval church) terminates some of our experiences and induces others.

The problem of the retroactive influence of vehicles upon the meanings and subjects of interaction thus possesses great significance in social life and warrants more detailed treatment. Let us consider the retroactive effects of pantomimic conductors upon our mind and actions.[48] *The mechanical reproduction of a gesture frequently has a retroactive influence on the mind of the performer.* It is possible to laugh oneself into a gay mood; a dejected attitude deliberately assumed may evoke a sad mood; the mere use of the gestures and overt expressions of rage is often sufficient to produce this emotion. According to Fastrez,[49] "posture and actions have a real and profound, if indirect, influence on our manner of thinking, feeling, and willing"; and Pareto declares:[50] "The actions through which sentiments are objectified reenforce the sentiments and may even evoke them in their absence. It is a well-known psychological fact that if a person subjects himself to a physiological state which normally accompanies a definite emotion, he may through this fact alone arouse in himself the corresponding emotion."

According to Payot,[51]

The most profound practical psychologists, such as Loyola and Pascal, who dealt with the development of feelings, recommended overt religious acts as the best means for creating a religious mood. It is a known fact that the position taken by a subject in a hypnotic sleep acts as a powerful factor in bringing about the desired emotion. In fact, any emotion suggested to the subject will be aroused when corresponding muscles are brought into action. . . . Dogs who fight playfully with one another often end in a serious fight. . . . The elaborate Chinese ceremonial which was designed to strengthen the idea of authority was deliberately invented by Confucius, who, like Loyola, was convinced that gestures reenforce feelings. . . . The solemn ritual of the Catholic Church exerts a powerful influence upon the souls of people—even of those having little faith. . . . Edmund Burke is said to have asserted that he often actually experienced the emotion of rage in the course of a speech in which he had to use the gestures and facial expressions appropriate to this emotion.

Waynbaum argues, similarly, that the physiological act of laughing is apt to increase our subjective gaiety.[52] And, according to Paul Levy,

---

[47] G. Simmel, "The Concept and the Tragedy of Culture," in *Logos* (1911), pp. 15-21. Cf. H. Freyer, *Theorie des objectiven Geistes* (Berlin, 1928).

[48] The James-Lange theory of the influence of overt actions and physiological processes upon our emotions glimpses this retroactive influence, though it describes it incorrectly. As Morgan rightly indicates, the theory overemphasizes the disturbances of the vasomotor system and ties them too exclusively to the states of mind. It assumes that every change in the vasomotor system produces only one kind of emotion, and, conversely, that each emotion manifests itself in only one kind of action. The theory claims, so to speak, that the marriage of the specific meanings (emotions) and vehicles (actions or physiological changes) is monogamous. We have seen that the same meaning or emotion can be objectified by many diverse vehicles and that the same vehicle may manifest many diverse meanings. Morgan correctly states this, saying that the same emotion—for instance, fear—is expressed overtly through flight, simulation of death, attack, and other overt means. Conversely, the same vehicle or overt act may be an expression of different mental states. Cf. C. G. Lange, *The Emotions* (Baltimore, 1922); W. James, "What Is an Emotion?" in *Mind*, Vol. IX, (1884); and C. Morgan, *Habit and Instinct* (London, 1896), pp. 186-209.

[49] Cf. G. Fastrez, "Les Rites militaires," *Bulletin mensuel*, No. 11 (1911), p. 167.

[50] V. Pareto, *op. cit.*, Vol. I, p. 556.

[51] Cf. J. Payot, *Education de la volonté* (Paris, 1907).

[52] J. Waynbaum, *La Physiognomie humaine*, (Paris, 1907) p. 62.

A merry song hummed in spite of one's depressed state will eventually—quite imperceptibly—arouse a cheerful mood in the singer. . . . The connection between an idea and its overt expression is so close that one cannot be influenced without at the same time influencing the other. An act during its performance strengthens the idea that produced it. Let an overt expression of a mental state be simulated, and the idea, regardless of how weak it was, will acquire strength and assume definite shape.[53]

Such instances are innumerable. To mention only one more, many actors, repeatedly going through the gestures of the characters they portray, often actually experience in their playing the corresponding states of mind. It is obvious that gestures have a very pronounced retroactive influence on our mental life. The mechanical repetition of the same gesture or of a certain posture will arouse and strengthen a corresponding mental state. Similarly, a mental state can be inhibited by making the gestures or assuming the posture usually associated with another mental state.

This retroactive influence is true in the case of any vehicle—sound, light, or concrete object. An individual acting in a definite social capacity (as judge, priest, or tribal chief), clad in the robes appropriate to his office, in the presence of objective vehicles of a definite nature—the setting of the courtroom, the church, or the like—is often completely transformed, losing all resemblance to himself as he is in private life. Judges, after inflicting the severest penalties upon the accused, have been known, when freed from the influence of the symbolic conductors (the courtroom and their robes of office), bitterly to regret their heartlessness. As individuals they were merciful; but under the influence of these symbolic surroundings their humane characteristics were stifled. *Fiat justitia et pereat mundus* was their motto in such surroundings.

History provides us with many such cases. Robespierre, the chief instigator of the French Terror, merciless in the performance of his official duties, was in private life a highly sentimental and sensitive being who wept over the novels of Saint-Pierre. It is evident that the adoption of customs, rites, or even forms of dress in various fields of social life is not accidental. "The uniform possesses a power of its own; not without reason did law-givers attribute an enormous significance to it and to formal dress in general. The robe does not make the monk, but the respect shown to it means much to its wearer and affects his mind and conduct."[54]

A uniform imposes a certain definite manner of conduct on its wearer. . . . While the respect which must be shown to a ranking military official usually expresses itself in specified actions, as salutes, the latter, by virtue of their retroactive action, reaffirm the respect. The careless execution of these acts (a slovenly salute) has exactly the opposite effect, weakening the basic idea of respect and honor. As Simon says, the external signs of respect are without doubt powerful means of suggestion, through which respect is imprinted upon our mind. There is no better way for high officials to strengthen their position than to demand that they be shown all the marks of respect due them. Carelessness in this respect begets familiarity, gradually putting an end to the respect and honor which they should receive from their subordinates.[55]

Political prisoners experience a decisive change in mentality upon donning prisoners' garb. Officers stripped of the symbols of their rank—a sword, stars, or other insignia—and donning civilian clothing, undergo a mental change which is sometimes permanent. On the other hand, if an ordinary citizen is invested with the insignia of pomp and power, he may be transformed into a self-confident, proud, and arrogant personality.

The same is true with relation to *sound symbols*. The grant of a title of nobility transforms one mentally.[56] To be addressed as "Doctor," "Judge," or "Captain" is pleasant to the ear and exerts a similar effect.

In view of the facts cited, it is impossible to deny the retroactive influence of symbolic conductors upon our mental states. This influence is even more significant in connection with the fetishization of vehicles.

b. *The Fetishization of Vehicles, and Its Retroactive Influence.* A given biophysical

[53] Paul Levy, *L'Education de la volonté* (Paris, 1920), pp. 83, 95-96.

[54] P. Guyot, *Education et Hérédité* (Paris, 1910), p. 28.

[55] Fastrez, *op. cit.*, pp. 11, 12, 167.

[56] Cf. Herbert Spencer, *Principles of Sociology*, Vol. II, Part IV, Ch. 1.

object, functioning for a considerable length of time as the vehicle of a certain meaning, norm, or value, identifies itself with it to such an extent in the minds of the subjects of inter-action that it tends to become a self-sufficient value in its own right. It is often transformed into a fetish loved or respected, feared or hated, for its own sake. A nation's flag, which physically is but a stick with a piece of cloth attached, becomes, through constant use, an emblem of the independence, power, dignity, honor, or glory of the nation. It ceases to be regarded solely as a piece of cloth attached to a stick and becomes an idol. The sentiments and attitudes evoked by the meanings and values which it objectifies and conveys become permanently attached to it; the admiration, respect, or hatred inspired by the values which it represents are finally redirected to the banner itself. People lose sight of its actual role as a lifeless medium for the transmission of living meanings; they come to regard it as animate, imbued with a vitality and a uniqueness of its own. In short, the flag becomes a fetish, and as such deeply affects their behavior and mentality. Men willingly die as well as slay for it.[57]

Instances of the fetishization of symbolic conductors may be observed among savages as well as among civilized peoples, in all spheres of social life, at every stage, the only differences being the objects fetishized. An Australian fetishizes a piece of wood; a devout believer, an ikon or the name of a saint; a monarchist, his ruler's portrait; a Communist, the portrait of Lenin or Stalin.

A magic influence is frequently attributed to words and to sound conductors in general. In many religions a particular word is regarded as a power which rules over natural events and even directs the will of the gods; and the word as such is therefore revered. This fetishization of words is most common in primitive groups, a "mystical importance being attached to every such expression." Primitive people firmly believe that the mere act of uttering a certain word is sufficient in itself to determine formidable events.[58] This belief accounts for the existence of "secret language" and of the taboos against the use of certain words by women and children. The rules governing the use of various words are many and rigid; for example, while hunting or fishing the game is not to be referred to by name. "The inhabitants of some Malay islands are forbidden the use of many words when referring to their ruler; it cannot be said of him that he eats, sleeps, sits, or exists. . . . At his death his name is not to be uttered."

"The value and mystical power attributed to words as such are proved by the widespread use, in religious and magical ceremonies, of songs and ritual formulas whose meaning was lost long ago and which are therefore unintelligible to the hearers and even to those repeating them."[59]

Since words become identified with the meanings and values for which they stand, an argument respecting the spelling or pronunciation of a word may assume tremendous significance. For instance, in the history of the Russian Church the controversy which arose over the question of the spelling of the word "Jesus" led to a serious schism into "Niconians" and "Old Believers." Laughter occasioned by an odd name is often considered as directed at its owner. Usage has placed a taboo upon certain words as indecent, and their use in polite society is sufficient to arouse an intense and indignant reaction. To utter such words audibly in public may be deemed a crime and land the perpetrator in jail.

The mere naming of an abstraction is often sufficient to transform it into an objective reality with a value far above its own intrinsic importance. "A high degree of personification exists when an abstraction is transformed into an objective entity through a name. This personification may be made even stronger by adding to the name a definite indication of gender."[60] From such personifications anthro-

---

[57] According to Fastrez, a French soldier, when asked what the flag actually is, answered, "That for which heads are broken." (*Les Rites militaires*, p. 167.)

[58] Cf. Levy-Brühl, *Les Fonctions mentales*, pp. 174-181. Cf. also the works of Trigant Burrow and W. Galt already cited.

[59] Levy-Brühl, p. 179. Cf. also B. Spencer and F. Gillen, *The Northern Tribes of Central Australia* (London, 1904), pp. 286, 460, 462, 606, and W. I. Thomas, *Primitive Behavior* (New York, 1937), pp. 89-97.

[60] V. Pareto, *op. cit.*, Vol. I, pp. 545-546.

pomorphisms arose. The fetishization of words explains the origin of such Roman deities as Fortuna, Victoria, Juventus, Providentia, and Virtus.[61] As Pareto indicates, this deification has continued through the ages up to our own time, as is well attested by the existence of such modern deities (personified abstractions) as Progress, Democracy, Pacifism, and Socialism.[62]

This fetishization of sound conductors occurs daily in hundreds of forms, in spite of the detachment of words from the rest of our activities and the general depreciation of words caused by their excessive use and misuse. They are still endowed with magical power in oaths, in official rituals and ceremonies with rigidly prescribed formulas, and so on.[63]

Light and color conductors are similarly fetishized. The picture of a saint or of a national hero becomes in time endowed with the virtues of the subject and is capable of arousing strong emotions per se. The defense of an ikon has often led to acts of heroism and self-sacrifice. Even atheistic communists are not free from such fetishization; for the desecration of the portrait of Lenin or Stalin is to them sacrilege.[64] The same is true of heraldic emblems.

Pantomimic conductors also become fetishized—the acts of crossing oneself, kneeling, saluting a flag,[65] taking an oath, and many other rites and ceremonies. Although the fetishization of ceremonial acts is more frequent among primitive peoples,[66] many instances may be found also among civilized peoples. During the Middle Ages the refusal to perform a required act in a ceremony was sometimes regarded as open rebellion. The rules of the

Order of St. Columban prescribed that one who forgot to make the sign of the Cross at table should suffer six to twelve lashes.[67] The devout Catholic believes that by making the sign of the Cross he protects himself from evil. In many religious, military, political, and civic rituals and ceremonies today a deviation from the prescribed forms is prohibited and often punished. Sometimes even the mere violation of etiquette rule is penalized.

The fetishization of object conductors is seen in the deification of pieces of wood (Australian *churingas*), stones, plants, and animals (totems); in the reverence for flags, uniforms, medals, and amulets; and in the worship of crosses, holy statues, and relics. The fetishization of goods and money, which Marx refers to, is only a specific case of the general fetishization of object conductors.[68]

Nor is man himself excluded from the general fetishization of conductors; he is one of the most important conductors. Continually functioning as a representative of certain meanings and values, a person becomes identified with them and may gradually assume a significance far greater than what naturally belongs and is originally attributed to him. In short, he is fetishized—adored as a living god, a powerful lord, or an incarnation of all virtues. Such cases are common in primitive societies. The Zulus address their king with the following hymn:

Hail, the King of Kings, the King of Heavens! What do the mightiest of the earth avail in the presence of our great King! What avails the power of the forests against the Great Elephant! With

---

[61] Cf. J. F. Toutain, *Les Cultes païens dans l'empire romain* (Paris, 1907), Vol. I, pp. 415-416.

[62] Cf. Pareto, *op. cit.*, Vol. I, pp. 540 ff.

[63] Cf. J. W. Woodard, *Deification and Supernaturalism as Factors in Social Rigidity and Change* (Philadelphia, 1935).

[64] Pareto's statement, that these phenomena are identical in nature, is correct. "The cult of the Christian religion is passing; but in its place there has arisen the worship of socialistic and humanitarian saints, and especially of God the State, and God the Nation. There is no difference between the holy day of a Catholic saint and that of Rousseau, for which the French government appropriated thirty thousand francs. Of course, to the humanitarian a Catholic saint is a scoundrel, whereas Rousseau is a highly exemplary man; and for a Catholic the reverse holds true. But this opposition

in evaluation proves the identity of the psychology in the two cases. Church processions are dying out, but their place is being taken by demonstrations and manifestations of a political character. Enthusiasm for the Christian religion has been replaced by enthusiasm for socialism, patriotism, nationalism etc." (Pareto, *Trattato di sociologia generale*, Vol. II, p. 247).

[65] Fastrez, *op. cit.*, p. 167.

[66] In Uganda "an officer observed to salute informally is ordered for execution. . . . Another who perhaps exposes an inch of naked leg whilst squatting or has his imbugu tied contrary to regulations" is condemned to the same fate. (Herbert Spencer, *Principles of Sociology*, Vol. III, p. 220.)

[67] *Ibid.*, Vol. II.

[68] Cf. G. Simmel, *The Concept and Tragedy of Culture*, p. 20.

his trunk he crushes the branches of the trees. Thy breath on the face of thine enemies is like fire which falls on the dry ground, consuming it. Thou art the Father of Fire, who sends lightning into the clouds and compels the rain to fall. Mountains, woods, and you, green fields, hear the voice of the son of Maggoban, the King of the Heavens![69]

The aborigines of New Zealand address their chief with the following words: "Come to us, God!"

Such phenomena are prevalent also among civilized peoples: the worship of the Roman emperors and of the Pope, the quasi-deification of monarchs who can do no wrong, of dictators and other rulers, is identical with primitive fetishization. Moreover, these phenomena are observable not only among obscurantist reactionaries but also among seemingly enlightened revolutionaries.[70]

The fetishization of symbolic conductors exerts a strong retroactive influence upon man's behavior and mind. Vehicles crystallize and standardize, clarify and formalize, or distort and disfigure the meanings, values, and norms which they objectify and convey. After their emergence as conductors through the activities of human beings they powerfully affect human actions and states of mind, especially when they become self-values, or idols.

The foregoing discussion indicates how inextricably and organically all three components (meanings, human subjects, and vehicles) are linked together in one inseparable unity in the process of meaningful interaction. Hence every theory of the "sociocultural unit, atom, or cell" that attempts to reduce its components to any one or any two of these three components is untenable.

III. Personality, Society, and Culture as an Inseparable Trinity

Viewed from a slightly modified standpoint, the componential structure of sociocultural interaction presents three aspects inseparable from one another, namely: (1) *personality* as the subject of interaction; (2) *society* as the totality of interacting personalities, with their sociocultural relationships and processes; and (3) *culture* as the totality of the meanings, values, and norms possessed by the interacting persons and the totality of the vehicles which

objectify, socialize, and convey these meanings. In the classroom the instructor and the students are the *personalities*; the totality of these personalities, with the norms of their relationships, constitutes *the society of the classroom*; the scientific and other ideas which they possess and exchange, as well as the books, the blackboard, the furniture, the lamps, and the room itself, represent *the culture of this society*. None of the members of this indivisible trinity

---

[69] M. Kovalevsky, *Sociology*, in *Russian* (St. Petersburg, 1911), Vol. II, pp. 194, 195.

[70] In connection with Lenin's arrival in Petrograd the *Red Gazette* (1919), No. 57, published the following editorial: "The leader of leaders, the spiritual father and the guiding spirit and founder of the Third International, is among us. . . . Comrade Lenin! Who can pronounce his name unmoved! Some tremble in impotent hatred and rage; others, in unbounded love and loyalty!" Hundreds of articles in the Communist papers (*Izvestia, Pravda,* etc.) for the years 1918-1947 characterized Lenin and Stalin in practically the same terms as the Zulus or the native New Zealanders characterize their chiefs.

In this respect the communists are no exception. R. Michels writes in his well-known book on political parties: "In 1864 the inhabitants of the

provinces along the Rhine greeted Lassalle as a god. When the Fascisti, the first organizations of agricultural workers, were formed in Italy, both men and women placed almost supernatural trust in the leaders of the movement. Confusing, in their naïveté, the social problem with religious rites, in their parades they often carried the Cross beside the red flag. In Holland, upon being released from prison, Domela Nieuwenhuis received honors exceeding those accorded to the sovereign. The Marxian prophet Jules Guedes was idolized in northern France. The same phenomenon has been known in England and America. Nor is such worship terminated by their death. The greatest of them are canonized; even Karl Marx has not escaped this, judging by the zeal with which his followers defend him in our times—a zeal which comes close to being idolatry." (R. Michels, *Les Partis politiques* [Paris, 1920], pp. 43-46.)

(personality, society, and culture) can exist without the other two. There is no personality as a *socius*, bearer, creator, and user of meanings, values, and norms without a corresponding culture and society; only an isolated biological organism can exist in their absence. Similarly, there is no superorganic society without interacting personalities and a culture; and there is no living culture without interacting personalities and a society. Hence none of these phenomena can be properly investigated without considering the other members of the trinity. Any theory that stresses only one of these in a study of the sociocultural world, or that seeks to keep the three aspects separate, is inadequate. For pedagogical purposes they may be studied separately; but when the analysis of each member of the trinity is concluded, this element must be referred to the triadic manifold, or matrix, in which it exists.

IV. Critical Remarks

Attempts to limit the subject matter of sociology to the social aspect of superorganic phenomena and to exclude the factors of culture or personality are, as has been said, erroneous. We read, for instance, that "sociology is primarily concerned with . . . the social"—that systems of knowledge, religion, linguistics, technology, and the like do not concern it.[71] Such a theory is utterly untenable. (1) Without cultural or superorganic values human interactions would be purely biophysical rather than social phenomena. If the contention were carried to its logical conclusion, the category of the social would merge with the biophysical phenomena, and sociology would lose the basis of its very existence.

(2) If in our consideration of social interactions we excluded all cultural values, there would remain very little to be studied, nothing but various physical structures and motions, which are the proper subject matter of biology or physics. We could not properly speak of such characteristics of the interaction process as are suggested by the terms "antagonistic" and "solidary," "revolutionary," "religious," "ethical," or "scientific." Such a study certainly could not yield any knowledge of the real nature, relationships, or infinitely varied characteristics of meaningful human interactions.

(3) Without an inclusion of the cultural element—meanings, values, and norms—we could not study even the norms regulating the interaction of individuals and constituting, according to these theorists themselves, the essence of any social institution or organization. "The rules of behavior constitute . . . a certain number of more or less connected and harmonious systems which can be generally called social *institutions*, and the totality of institutions found in a concrete social group constitutes the social *organization* of this group," which is the center of sociological study (Thomas and Znaniecki, *op. cit.*, p. 33). These norms are either legal or moral standards, as embraced in official law codes or in religious, moral, and other systems. Law and ethics are as much a part of culture as are religion, the fine arts, economics and science. Their norms are closely, often inseparably, connected with all the basic values of a given group—religious, scientific, philosophical, aesthetic, economic, political, and so on. Hence, without a study of legal and moral norms, institutions and organizations could not be investigated. In that case there would be no place for a special sociology of religion, economics, or the fine arts, or for any other special sociology. In brief, the proposition flagrantly contradicts the definition of sociology and its subject matter given by the theorists themselves, and it deprives sociology of any appropriate subject matter.

(4) The consequences of the erroneous contention of such theorists are so disastrous that, fortunately, none of them has attempted to carry it to its logical conclusion. After stating the proposition they presently violate it, reintroducing by the back door, as it were, the cultural systems denied at the outset. L. von

---

[71] F. Znaniecki, *The Social Role of the Man of Science* (New York, 1940), p. 3. Cf. also L. von Wiese, *Sociology* (New York, 1941), pp. 25 ff, and W. I. Thomas and F. Znaniecki, *The Polish Peasant* (New York, 1927), Vol. I, p. 35.

Wiese does this in his classification of the primary social processes, such as estrangement, competition, adjustment, acceptance, acknowledgment, amusement, comforting, and dedicating—all of which are cultural meanings, values, or norms—as well as in his explicit study of religion, science, ethics and law, economics, and politics.[72] W. I. Thomas and F. Znaniecki do the same thing by introducing into their sociology the "set of values" (religious, moral, artistic, economic, and so on) as the fundamental category and principle of reference, and by explicitly dealing with science, knowledge, magic, medicine, religion, economics, technology, and other cultural values. The sociocultural order is indivisible, and no one can make a special science of one aspect of it, say, the social aspect, ignoring the cultural and personal aspects. Such a system of sociology would be as absurd as a scheme of botany that studied only the right side of a plant, disregarding the left side, or a zoology that concerned itself only with the skin of organisms, leaving all the internal organs and tissues to another field of science. Sociology is concerned equally with all three aspects of sociocultural phenomena, but from its specific standpoint as a generalizing science, viewing the sociocultural system as a whole.[73]

[72] Cf. his *System der Allgemeinen Soziologie* (München, 1933).
[73] Cf. R. Linton, "Culture, Society, and the Individual," *Journal of Abnormal and Social Psychology*, Vol. XXXIII, pp. 425-436.

Unsatisfactory likewise are those theories that endeavor to separate the cultural and social aspects of sociocultural phenomena on the ground that "culture is the name given to the abstracted intercorrelated customs of a social group. . . . Society seems to be the broader term, since it includes the manifestation of culture and impulse."[74] Every organized group necessarily possesses norms of law and morality. Legal and moral values are an essential part of cultural values. Therefore any organized group inevitably possesses a culture. Furthermore, neither a social group nor a person (save as a mere biological organism) can exist without the components of meanings and vehicles; that is, without a culture. For these reasons "society" cannot be a broader term than "culture," nor can they be sharply separated from one another. The only possible differentiation is that the term "social" denotes concentration on the totality of interacting human beings and their relationships, whereas "cultural" signifies concentration on meanings, values, and norms and their material vehicles (or material culture).[75]

[74] J. Dollard, "Culture, Society, Impulse and Socialization," *AJS*, Vol. XLV, pp. 50-63.
[75] For further examples of the fallacies in question, see Chapters 17 and 18. Cf. also Kluckhohn and O. Mowrer, "Culture and Personality," *AA*, Vol. XLVI (1944), pp. 1-29, and D. Bidney, "On the Concept of Culture," *AA*, Vol. XLVI (1944), pp. 30-44.

V. SUMMARY

STRUCTURE OF SOCIOCULTURAL INTERACTION

I. Subjects of Interaction and Their Properties
A. Number of interacting individuals: two, three, or more; one and many; many and many
B. Qualities of interacting individuals: homogeneous, heterogeneous
C. Character of action
1. Catalytic
2. Overt; tolerant
3. Effective; ineffective
4. Durable; shortlived
5. Conscious; unconscious
6. Purposive; nonpurposive: fundamental, habitual, normative

II. Meanings, Values, and Norms
Scientific, philosophical, religious, moral, ethical, legal, aesthetic, etc.

IV. Personality, Society and Culture as the Indivisible aspects of the Sociocultural Manifold

III. Vehicles, or Conductors
A. Definition
B. Vehicles as conductors of interaction
C. Principal types of vehicles
1. Sound conductors
2. Light and color
3. Pantomimic
4. Thermal
5. Mechanical
6. Chemical
7. Electrical and radio
8. Object conductors
D. The chain of conductors (human beings as links)
E. Retroactive influence of vehicles
1. General retroactive influence
2. Fetishization of vehicles

PART THREE

Structure of the Social Universe

Chapter 4. Organized Systems of Interaction: Groups or Institutions

I. The Main Forms of Sociocultural Interaction

For purposes of study the interaction processes and social relationships can be classified in many different ways. From the standpoint of *the component of subjects of interaction* they may be classified according to the number of the interacting subjects: two, three, many, one and many, many and many; from the standpoint of *the meaning-component* as the reason for the interaction processes, they can be divided into religious, scientific, legal, ethical, political, and many other classes; from the point of view of *the vehicle-component* interactions may be distinguished as carried on through various sound, light, color, pantomimic, thermal, mechanical, chemical, electrical and object conductors. Then, taking into consideration several combined characteristics, we can see interactions as *face to face or indirect, durable or shortlived, intensive or nonintensive, extensive* (as to the range of values and actions involved) *or narrow.* They may be *one-sided,* where a first party influences greatly the overt actions and state of mind of a second, while the second affects the first only slightly, or not at all, or *two-sided,* where the influence is mutual; *partly conscious* or *wholly conscious,* with the conscious interactions subdivided into purposeful and nonpurposeful actions, and so on.[1]

For the purposes of general sociology, however, these and similar break-downs have a subordinate value. More important are those classifications which combine several simpler forms to give the types of interaction and sociocultural systems that are ever present and play a significant role. The sociocultural universe is like an ocean in which millions of interaction processes incessantly arise. Some of these, like superficial ripplings, appear and disappear without any durable existence or result. Others, like the perennial deep tides, persist as important features of the sociocultural ocean. Every one of us enters daily into numerous superficial and shortlived interactions with many persons: in the street, a drug store, in public places. Thousands of interactions, like that between the druggist and the tourist who steps into his drug store for a package of cigarettes, arise daily and in a few minutes cease to exist, leaving no serious effect upon the mind, body, or conduct of the interacting parties. Neither do these brief interactions result in any permanent structure like an organized group or institution. Other interactions may prove durable, exerting a tangible influence upon the mind, body, and conduct, and resulting in permanent sociocultural structures. The superficial and shortlived interactions may be

[1] For an analysis of these forms see my *Dynamics,* Vol. III, Ch. 1. Such classifications cut across all "compartments" of the sociocultural world; they are equally given in economic, religious, legal, aesthetic, scientific, political, and other interaction processes. This shows again that classifications of sociology are generic and different from those of the compartmentalized social sciences.

compared with the conceived organism that dies in its pre-natal phase, while durable interactions are similar to fully grown organisms that live, function, and carry on the stream of life in the biological universe.

Our attention is naturally concentrated upon the durable, the recurring, effective, and "full grown" interaction processes that generate important sociocultural structures (social groups, cultural systems) and sociocultural persons, in contradistinction from purely biological organisms. For the totality of these interactions and persons provides the general structure of the sociocultural universe; their activi-

ties and functions create its essential dynamic processes. For this reason in our analysis of the social aspect of the superorganic we shall direct our attention to those full-grown interaction processes that are: (1) *organized*, in contrast to the *unorganized* and *disorganized*; (2) *solidary*, in distinction from *antagonistic* and *neutral*; and (3) *integrated*, in contrast to the *unintegrated*. When each of these truly basic forms of interaction is analyzed, we shall find out to what extent they are interrelated. Turn now to the organized form of interaction and its consequence, the organized group or institution.

II. *Unorganized, Organized, and Disorganized Interaction*

Interaction processes between parties may be either *unorganized, organized, or disorganized*. One hundred musicians in a hall, each playing his own instrument and his own piece of music, interact with one another but produce a phenomenon fundamentally different from the same hundred musicians in the same hall, united into one orchestra, with one conductor, with the clearly outlined rights and duties, functions and roles of each member, playing together the same musical composition, according to the composer's score and conductor's guidance. The difference between these systems of interaction is enormous. In the first place we have an unorganized interaction; in the second, organized. The total result of the activities is, in the first case, a cacophony; in the second, a symphony. If the organized orchestra falls again into the uncoordinated "noise-making" by each musician of his own piece of music, the orchestra becomes disorganized. This illustrates first, the profound difference between "interaction" and "organization," so often forgotten. The existence of interaction does not mean, as yet, that the interacting persons constitute an organized system of interaction or group. Interaction may remain on an unorganized level, as it often does. The problem thus arises: what are the characteristics of the organized interaction (group) and through what traits does it differ

from an unorganized or disorganized interaction? Let us analyze this basic problem.

CHARACTERISTICS OF THE ORGANIZED GROUP (INSTITUTION, SOCIAL SYSTEM)

A *social group, as a totality of interacting individuals, is organized when its central set of meanings and values, as the reason for their interaction, is somewhat consistent within itself and assumes the form of the law-norms precisely defining all the relevant actions-reactions of the interacting individuals in their relationship toward one another, the outsiders, and the world at large; and when these norms are effective, obligatory, and, if need be, enforced, in the conduct of the interacting persons.* The central trait of an organized interaction (group, institution, or social system) is thus the presence in it of law-norms as the conduct-regulating and behavior-controlling aspect of the component of meanings-values.[2]

In an unfolded form the definition means (1) that these norms determine in detail (a) what the *rights and duties* of each member are; (b) what, in regard to whom, when, how

[2] Practically any value-meaning contains implicitly a norm of conduct beginning with a norm of what and how to think about it and ending with how to act about it.

much, and under what conditions each member is entitled and obliged *to do or not to do, to tolerate or not to tolerate;* (c) what are the exact *functions or roles* which a member has to play; (d) what his *status* is in the system of interaction as determined by the totality of his rights-duties, functions, and roles. (2) The law norms generate the official law and government of the group with its legislative, executive, and judicial functions. (3) By defining rights and duties, the law-norms clearly indicate what relationships or forms of interaction to expect between the parties; (a) as *obligatory,* (b) as *prohibited,* and (c) as *recommended,* though not required, and under what conditions, when, and in regard to whom. (4) Through their definition of the rights-duties, functions, and status of every member and through that of the obligatory, prohibited, and recommended relationships the law-norms make a group of interacting individuals into a clearly *differentiated and stratified* body in which each member performs a specific task in the total functions of the group and in which each occupies a certain rank in its hierarchy of authorities. (5) The group usually has an economic complex of vehicles possessed, used, and operated to carry on the functions of the group and, often, to give to it its means of subsistence. (6) The group ordinarily gets a name, sign, or symbol of its identity.

These are the exact characteristics of organized interaction in contradistinction from unorganized interaction. All the traits of this organization follow from the existence in the group of definite law-norms inseparably connected with them. As soon as the law-norms emerge, the definition of the rights-duties, functions, and statuses; the establishment of the official law and government; the differentiation of relationships into obligatory, prohibited, and recommended; the group's differentiation and stratification; its vehicles (property), and name appear. For the sake of clarity and in order to avoid the prevalent vagueness of sociological definitions of organized groups—definitions which rarely distinguish law-norms from other kinds of norms—it is advisable to delineate the precise nature of law-norms and their difference from various other norms.

CHARACTERISTICS OF LAW-NORMS[3]

1. Inadequate Definitions of Law-Norms

The law-norm is a rule of conduct in a social relationship, but not every rule of conduct is a law-norm. What then are the specific traits of law-norms that distinguish them from the multitude of other norms? The most common definitions of law-norms try to characterize them in terms of (a) their obligatory character as norms enacted by the state and backed by its force; or (b) their being the expression of the common will of the people; or (c) their function in protecting and distributing the freedom and interests of the members of the group; or (d) in a combination of these characteristics with an addition of reason as a factor in their development. None of these definitions is quite satisfactory. The definition of law-norms as obligatory rules enacted (or recognized) by the state and backed by its force assumes that without the state there is no law and that only the norms enacted by the state are law-norms. This theory contains a part of the truth but not the whole truth.

First, the state as a certain form of organized group emerged fairly late in the history of mankind. Before it there were and still are clans, tribes, totemic and other groups which have lived and functioned for centuries and even thousands of years. To assume that they lived and functioned "lawlessly," without any norms of law, would be a fantastic assumption. Second, in many societies and periods, as in the Middle Ages in Europe, there were such norms as canon law, the special law of the burghers, those of guilds and of peasants, which were neither enacted by, nor needed specific recognition by the state for their vigorous functioning. Even at the present time many organized groups, different from the state, have law-norms never enacted by the state. Similarly, what is termed customary, international, canon, and even common law, was not enacted by the state, and emerged either without such an enactment or, sometimes, even contrary to the state authority, thus vitiating the claim that without the state there is no law.

[3] The subsequent analysis of law-norms follows the brilliant analysis of law by Leo Petrajitsky. See the details in his *Theory of Law and Ethics* (in Russian, St. Petersburg, 1909), Vol. I, Ch. 3 *passim.*

Third, the very existence of the state already presupposes law. So far as the state is an *organized* nation, its existence already presupposes the existence of law-norms that define its territory, its government, and its constitution, in brief, its structure and functions. Otherwise neither the boundaries of the state, nor its government, nor the actions of its government and its subjects would be lawful; there would be no way of determining what norms enacted by this or that group within the state were legal. In fact, without law-norms no state would be possible. Neither is it true that the law as the official code of the state was enacted by its supreme authority (monarch, parliament, Congress). In Rome, in Anglo-Saxon countries, and among the Mohammedans a large part of the law-norms have been enacted by judges or courts. Likewise a norm becomes a law-norm not because it is included in the law-code or the statutes of the state. Most of the people hardly know these codes and statutes at all, have hardly ever opened and read them; therefore, if such a claim were valid we should conclude that people lived and acted without any law. Such a supposition would mean further that these codes and statutes themselves are merely "dead laws"—an implication which annuls the claim itself. For these and many other reasons the criticized theory of law is inadequate.

No less fallacious is the definition of law-norms as an obligatory rule of conduct backed by force. If such a definition were true the rudest force would be a supreme law; "might makes right." A command of a gangster to the man he is "taking for a ride," of a willful ravisher to the ravished, of the murderer to his helpless victim, would be the law. Any difference between law and lawlessness, between lawful and unlawful compulsion would have disappeared. These considerations are sufficient cause to scrap the definition.

Equally inadequate is the definition of law-norms as an expression of the common will or of the will of the people. If law were such a will for the enactment of any statute everyone would have to be consulted. Factually, most of the law-norms are enacted without any consultation with most of the people of a given state or group. In autocracies and absolute monarchies no consultation of the subjects takes place in the enactment of law-norms. If the theory were true we would be forced to think that slaves who, in the past, composed a majority of the population, freely imposed upon themselves the chains of slavery by enacting the laws which sanctioned slavery; that the serfs did the same; that the laws imposed by the conqueror on the conquered were a manifestation of the common will of the conquered, and so on.

For similar reasons we cannot accept definitions of law as the protection of the freedom of group members or as the distribution and protection of their vital interests. The law-norm that gives an unlimited power to a despot over his people or to a master over his slaves and serfs certainly protects the freedom and interests of the despot and of the master; but it hardly protects those of the subjects, slaves, and serfs. On the contrary it deprives them of freedom as well as of their vital interests.

Finally, we cannot accept a definition of law-norms as norms developed by reason and representing its incarnation. Many a law-norm emerged in the way of trial and error without any systematic reasoning, conscious plan, or rational purpose. A multitude of law-norms have been based upon superstitious beliefs opposed to reason, upon errors opposite to knowledge, and upon ignorance contrary to real experience. If a law-code protecting the interests of the slave-owners was, perhaps, developed by the reason of the slave masters it certainly was not generated by the reason of the slaves, nor would it appear to them as "reasonable," "rational," or "sensible." However appealing these high-flown definitions may sound they are obviously fallacious.[4]

2. Formal Characteristics of Law-Norms

The specific formal characteristics of law-norms as distinct from other norms are as follows: *Irrespective of their content, any norms of conduct (of doing, nondoing, toleration) that attribute a certain right (the object of right) to one party (the subject of right) and a certain duty (the object of duty) to another party (the subject of duty) are law-norms.* The law-norm establishes a definite two-sided, imperative-

[4] See the details and literature in the quoted work of Petrajitsky; also my *General Theory of Law* (in Russian, Jaroslavle, 1919), Ch. 1.

attributive relationship between two parties through an indication of what one party is entitled to demand from the other and what the other party is obliged to do to meet this demand. The norms: "the creditor (the subject of right) is entitled to demand the payment of the debt as agreed per contract and the debtor is obliged to pay it"; "the general is entitled to issue the commands and the soldiers are obliged to obey them"; "the landlord is entitled to the stipulated rent from the tenant and the tenant is obliged to pay it"; these and billions of norms that have the two-sided distribution of rights and duties between the two or more parties are all law-norms, no matter what their content. All other norms that do not have these characteristics are, as we shall see, not law-norms.

In a fully formulated law-norm there are, first, *its defining part*, which indicates a definite obligatory form of conduct; second, the *sanctioning* part, which formulates the consequences of the violation of this form of conduct. For example: "the persons guilty in theft are punished by imprisonment for from one to six months." The first, or defining part, concisely prohibits the specific form of conduct (theft) which other law-norms define exactly; the second part indicates the consequences of the violation of such a norm. Here the sanction is *punishment*; in other law-norms the sanction is *compulsory realization* of the demand of the defining part, for instance, the foreclosure of a forfeited mortgaged property; in others, a *restitution* of loss incurred through the violation of a norm, for instance, of financial or moral loss. In still other norms the sanction is a *voiding* or *nullification*, for instance, voiding of the legality of a contract or will if it was made under conditions contradictory to, or devoid of, those which are prescribed by the law-norm. Side by side with sanctioned law-norms there are law-norms having no sanctions (*leges imperfectae*). These, however, are few and concern actions and relationships of little importance.

In any fully formulated law-norm there is a clear indication of: (a) *the subject of the right*, (b) *the subject of the duty*, (c) *the object of the right*, (d) *the object of the duty*, (e) *reference to the source of the law*, (f) *additional specifications of time, place, conditions, way of acting, etc.*, and (g) *the addressees of the law-activities*.

By the *subject of right* is meant the person or group entitled to that which is indicated in the law-norm. In the norm: "a creditor is entitled to demand the payment of a debt," the subject of right is entitled to demand the payment of a debt; the subject of right is "the creditor." The subjects of right have been individuals (J. Smith, buyer, seller, creditor, etc.), and *collective groups* (the state, the church, the municipality, the corporation, etc.). In the law-norms of many past peoples the individual subjects of right were not only the real physical persons as now but also nonphysical, imaginary creatures (gods, angels, devils, etc.), to whom certain rights were ascribed and with whom certain law deals were concluded. Examples of this kind of law-norm are to be found in the theme of selling a soul to a devil whereby he was entitled, after the death of the seller, to claim the soul; in the covenant between Jehovah and the Jewish people in the Bible; as well as in animals, plants, and inorganic objects (flags, religious articles, totemic animals, plants and objects, like *churinga*) to whom (in totemistic, fetishistic and other societies) many a right was ascribed and with whom many a legal deal was thought to be concluded. At the present time in so-called complex societies physical persons and groups function as the main subjects of right. Each clearly formulated law-norm indicates who (or what) is its subject of right.

By the *subject of duty* is meant that individual or collective person who is obliged to perform the duty indicated in the law-norm. In the norm "the creditor is entitled to demand the payment of a debt and the debtor is obliged to pay it," the debtor is the subject of the duty. Again the subjects of duty are individual and collective persons. In the past imaginary creatures (devils, angels, souls, deities, various spirits, etc.), as well as animals, plants, and inorganic objects were ascribed various duties and therefore functioned as the subjects of duty.

By the *object of right* in a law-norm is meant the totality of activities (doing, nondoing, nontolerating) of the subject of right to which he is entitled by the law-norm.

By the *object of duty* is meant the totality

of the actions of the subject of duty required from him by the law-norm. In a law-norm regulating the relationship of buying and selling, the object of right of the seller is the payment to him by the buyer of the price agreed (or prescribed by the norm); his object of duty is to deliver the sold object to the buyer. The object of right of the buyer, on the other hand, is to have the thing bought, while his object of duty is to pay to the buyer the price agreed upon or prescribed.

All the objects of right as concrete actions fall into three classes of activities: the right to an *acceptance of something* (e.g., money as salary), of *doing something* (issuing a command or giving an owned thing as a gift), and of *nontolerating something* (the right not to tolerate pillaging of one's property or the blows of an attacker). Similarly all the objects of duty fall, as concrete actions, into three related classes: the duty of *doing something* (delivering the object bought to the buyer, the performance of eight hours of work by a hired employee), of *tolerating something* (blows of the master by a slave, disciplinary censure from the superior to the inferior officer, arrest and imprisonment by the guilty criminal, etc.), and of *nondoing something* ("Don't kill," "Don't steal," "Don't lie," etc.).

The following is a schematic outline of the objects of rights and of duties:

Subject of Right Is Entitled to:
  Accept (objects or services)
  Do (issue a command, give his property, marry)
  Not tolerate (violence, attack, insults, nuisances, any violation of his rights)
Subject of Duty Is Obliged to:
  Do (work, deliver goods)
  Tolerate (reprimand, imprisonment, taking of his property from him)
  Not do (not to kill, not to steal, not to violate law-norms)

This threefold classification exhausts the main forms of the objects of right and of duty so far as they are expressed in activities; it shows also the relationship between each form of the objects of right and of duty.

The fully unfolded law-norm thus describes in detailed and exact form all the specific forms of the actions-reactions of the subjects of right and of duty in each case. In this sense it gives a clear-cut map of conduct to the parties.

In many, though not all law-norms, there is an additional element—*reference to the source* on which the legality and obligation of the given norm is based. For instance, "On the basis of Art. 1521, Vol. X, of the Russian Laws, a buyer is obliged to pay to the seller the price of the sold merchandise." The source of legality of this norm is the Code of the Russian Law. In Anglo-Saxon countries a reference to a certain statute, or to the Constitution of the United States, or to a decision of the Supreme Court is often given in a newly enacted law-norm. The sources of the legality of the given norm have been and are very different; now the "official law of the state"; now (for many) the commandments of God; now "the Declaration of the Rights of Man"; now a reference to this or that decision of a judge or court; now the opinion of this or that eminent jurist; now the prevailing custom, and so on. In the history of "official law" of many states such religious works as the Bible, the Koran, the Laws of Manu, the Rig-Veda, Homer's and Hesiod's works, and so on have played an exceptionally important role as sources of their legality.

Law-norms, being exact rules of conduct, often exhibit *additional specifications of time, space, and many other conditions*; they tend to be as specific as possible in their description of the relationship of the parties involved. Therefore they often contain many additional conditions, e.g.: "The tax should be paid on or before March 15, at the office of the Collector of Internal Revenue," followed by a number of specifications, sometimes with many a "whereas, if, and when" in detail indicating the specific circumstances under which the prescribed relationship is lawful or unlawful. Finally, many law-norms indicate the *addressee* of the legal actions of the norm, by which is meant neither the subject of right nor that of duty but the person (individual or collective or imaginary) in favor of whom or against whom the subjects of right and duty discharge their rights and duties. X and Y (for instance an insurance company and its client) have a contract in which Y is entitled to demand from X, and X is obliged to pay a sum of $5000 in favor of Z (a beneficiary). Z here is neither the subject of right nor that of duty but a third party, the addressee.

Often instead of the fully formulated law-norm discussed above, we find many law-norms that give an abbreviated formula, omitting this or that element (except the subjects of rights and duties and the objects of rights and duties, always present explicitly or implicitly). All norms having these formal characteristics, distinguishing them from all other rules of conduct and social relationships, are law-norms.

3. Psychological Characteristics of Law-Norms

The formal characteristics of law-norms are paralleled by their specific psychological traits. Schematically these specific traits can be described as follows: (a) an idea of the pattern of action demanded by the law norm; plus (b) a normative motivation of the respective actions; plus, (c) powerful emotional (affective and volitional) backing of the actions propelling us simultaneously to realize unhesitatingly our right and to fulfill unflinchingly our duty. In its totality the inner experience we undergo when we act according to our law-convictions is unique, not present in any other actions. If our law-convictions ascribe to us the right to ownership of a certain object, say, a watch, and to everyone the duty to abstain from the violation of our property-rights, without any hesitation we possess, use, and dispose of our watch as we please and are ready to defend our right by all lawful means from a violation by anybody. Quite different is our conduct in regard to the watch that does not belong to us. If we inadvertently put it into our own pocket, we feel guilty and spontaneously tend to make some restitution, from a sincere apology on up to a payment of the damages.

Millions of persons in normal times have the law-conviction which prohibits the killing of other human beings. The very idea of performing an act of murder immediately arouses in us a negative normative motivation followed by a powerful emotional and volitional drive inhibiting such an action as "horrible," "awful," "repellent." This emotional repulsion is similar to that aroused by the idea of eating a meal made up of rotten earthworms, rats, and vermin. This inner motivation, and not an apprehension of punishment, is the reason why these millions of people do not murder and

kill. When, however, the same persons have a law-conviction that it is their duty to fight and to kill the enemy in war, they fight and kill, without any hesitation, abhorrence, or disgust. Without such a law-conviction most of them, like the conscientious objector, would hardly be able to kill the enemy and still less would they regard such action as praiseworthy and heroic.

Thus the law-norms of all of us (no matter what may be their content) are not merely mental patterns of a certain form of conduct but *living convictions charged with all the emotional, affective, and volitional force that one possesses*. With all the power of these forces the norm urges us to realize our rights and to perform our duties. If somebody or something opposes the realization of our rights, all the energy of these emotional, affective, and volitional forces becomes at once mobilized to eliminate the opposition, to restore the violated rights, and to insist upon their realization. Often for the sake of this restoration we are ready to suffer more hardships, or to go to much greater financial expense than the violation of the right originally cost us.[5] On the other hand, the same law-convictions powerfully propel us to discharge our duty, no matter how unpleasant or disadvantageous it may be from a utilitarian standpoint. When deeply ingrafted, law-norms represent one of the most powerful forces that control our conduct; they not only indicate in the minutest detail the course of action we must follow in millions of different interactions with thousands of different persons under the most varied conditions, but they effectively drive us to such a course through the emotional, affective, and volitional forces behind them.

Our law-actions, then, are motivated by a *normative* motivation different from the purposive and other motivations of human behavior. (See above, Chapter 3.) It is a *self-sufficient* motivation in the sense that the deeply ingrafted law-conviction (norm) is a perfectly sufficient motive for a person's compliance with the norm in the realization of his right and in the discharge of his duty. No other motive is necessary in such normative

---

[5] See on this especially R. Ihering, *The Struggle for Law*, tr. by J. Lalor (Chicago, 1879).

actions. The appropriate law-conduct is performed purely out of the motive of our law-convictions with their stipulation: "the subject of right is entitled, and the subject of duty is obliged," regardless of any other motivation. The normative motivation differs from *purposive* motivation because many law-actions take place without any idea of a future purpose or end, without any future hedonistic, utilitarian, or other considerations. Now and then a utilitarian or purposive motivation may follow the normative motivation in law-conduct in the form of a purpose of avoiding punishment for the violation of a law, or for receiving some profit for a lawful action. But these purposive motivations are mere by-products, fellow-travellers neither necessary nor always present in our law-conduct motivated by normative motivation. The fear of punishment and the utilitarian advantages in law-conduct are necessary only for those who do not have strong law-convictions—persons such as the cynics, the demoralized, the criminals, the dishonest. For persons with strong law-convictions the very idea that they do not murder, do not steal, and do not take bribes, just because they are afraid of punishment or of losing some utilitarian advantage would appear insulting, and rightly so. The foregoing illustrates the utter inadequacy of all those theories which identify normative and purposive motivations with the schema of means and ends, of those which regard all human conduct as *purposive*, and of those which interpret the origin and development of law-norms and law-conduct in terms of utilitarian considerations.[6]

Normative motivation differs also from "the because of" type of motivation: blushing and mumbling because of embarrassment, reacting by insult because of preceding insult, becoming angry and shouting because of preceding irritation, and so on. This "because of" motivation is different from purposive as well as from normative motivation. In the actions motivated by the "because of" motive there is ordinarily no idea of a future purpose or end. Here man often acts even contrary to purposive motivation; for instance, irritated by the boss's im-

pudence, an employee explodes and gives him a real piece of his mind instead of carrying out the previously planned purposive action to obtain the boss's benevolence by flattery. Normative motivation differs from "because of" motivation by its self-sufficiency and by its definite pattern of compliance with some norm. In contrast to it, "because of actions" do not have any definite norm or pattern; they may assume any form, depending upon the nature of the preceding stimuli. They are devoid of the specific experience of normativeness (imperative-attributive experience) and of the ascription of duty and right which is typical of normative actions. By virtue of the above characteristics, law-norms, their motivation and their actions differ psychologically a great deal from all other norms, motivations, and actions.

4. Law-Norms as a Guide of Human Conduct

Because of their precise and detailed definition of the actions of the subjects of right and of duty in each specific case and of the enormous emotional and volitional power with which a law-conviction is charged, the law-norms of every one of us constitute the main guide and power of our conduct. Every day we have to perform thousands of actions in interaction with hundreds of different persons, under the most diverse constellations of conditions. If for a moment we imagine that none of us had any law-norm which would clearly indicate what should be our actions when we enter a store to get something, when we converse with the members of our family, when we go into the office or place of our work, meet our neighbors, call a doctor or plumber, address a policeman, interact with our superiors and inferiors, attend a public meeting, enter a church or theater, and so on; if indeed we had had no law-norms pointing out how to act in each of these and thousands of other situations, we should meet each moment of our lives with the greatest difficulty, never knowing what to do in each case. We should be lost in a jungle without map or orientation. That we do not incessantly experience

---

[6] See a brilliant analysis of human motivation in Leo Petrajitsky's *Theory of Law and Ethics*, quoted, Vol. I, Ch. 1. The utter fallacy of the utilitarian theories of ethical and law-norms and

actions has also been well demonstrated by E. Durkheim in his *De la division du travail social* (Paris, 1893; there is an English translation) and in his *Elementary Forms of Religious Life* (London, 1915).

this difficulty is due to the law-norms inculcated into every one of us. Guided by these we unhesitatingly perform each day hundreds of deeds in interaction with thousands of different persons: members of our family, our superiors and subordinates, neighbors and even strangers, the doctor, grocery man, policeman, tax collector, plumber and milkman, fellow-colleagues, friends, enemies, on up to practically everyone and everything in the world. With the exception of the few perfectly new cases for which law-norms have not been made as yet, our law-convictions solve the difficulty for everyone and everything; they point out what must be our conduct in each case. In this sense they constitute our main guide and our chief motivating force.

In the minds of all of us are thousands of law-norms or convictions, incessantly objectified and manifested in our speech-reactions ("I have the right to do this," "it is my duty to do that," "this is lawful," "this is lawless, outrageous," "this is just," "this is unjust," and so on), and in the vast majority of our actions, which follow precisely the clear indications of law-convictions. All the actions (of doing or nondoing, tolerating or nontolerating) that are performed as a realization of our rights or duties are realizations of our law-norms. In the totality of actions performed by us they occupy a larger place than any other kind of actions (those motivated by other than law-norms, those that are normless or unlawful, those due to neutral utilitarian and other reasons). We live and act, are born and die, enjoy and suffer in "the climate of law-norms" (or law-meanings and values); in this sense they penetrate all spheres of our conduct and all fields of social life. They make us indignant at the "injustice and utter depravity" of this or that action; they call forth our admiration at the discharge of a duty or the sacrifice of life by this or that party; they propel us to fight "injustice" and to protect "righteousness"; they give us the sense of certainty as to the propriety and fairness and justice of our actions in millions of daily encounters. In this sense the bulk of our conduct is but a manifestation of the law-norms we possess.

More than that, *law-norms are the essence—the skeleton, the heart, and the soul—of any organized group or institution*. The family,

the state, the church, the political party, the business firm, the occupational union, the school and college, the scientific, artistic, philanthropic, or other society, the army and the navy, even an organized criminal gang are but the objectification and materialization of the respective law-norms and law-convictions of their members. Without such norms none of these organized groups would be possible. Their written or unwritten constitutions—laws and by-laws—are the law-convictions of their members or of the largest part of them. Without law-norms no order, no stable structure, no smooth functioning of these groups, indeed no continuity of their existence would be possible.

A law-norm is neither the mere formula of this or that statute of "official law" nor "the futile and lifeless figment of the imagination of jurists," but a powerful living force in constant operation, defining, guiding, "fuelling" human conduct until it is finally socialized and congealed into organized groups or institutions. (The terms "organized group" and "institution" as used here are identical.) In this sense law is a real power that establishes, crystallizes, and overthrows all social institutions, from the family up to the State-Leviathan and even superstate organizations.

5. Distributive Functions of Law-Norms in Official Law

The preceding analysis shows that by their very nature law-norms perform two great social functions, the distributive and the organizational. In distributing rights and duties among interacting individuals, law-norms assign not only the specific functions and roles among them but also social values and burdens, material or non-material. To be entitled to some "right" means, as a rule, to be entitled to some desirable social value: property or goods; the services of the subjects of duty, their obedience and subordination, and so on. To be obliged to perform a duty means, as a rule, to carry on or to discharge some social burden: to pay taxes, to obey, to render a service, to part with wealth or even life. Without the distributive function of law-norms no boundary line between "mine" and "thine," no distinction between what each member is entitled or obliged to do; no obedience of the

subordinate to the superior; no orderly discharge of duties would be possible. Social interaction of the participants would be characterized by unceasing struggle, a real *bellum
omnium contra omnes*. Through their distributive function (*suum cuique tribuere*) law-norms
eliminate this anarchy and make an orderly
and stable social life possible.

This aspect of law-norms explains (a) why
as a rule they are clear in the assignment of
rights and duties and free from the possibility
of different interpretation; (b) why the rights
and duties they distribute are rarely if ever
indefinite or unlimited but always limited and
precise, showing where the rights of an individual end and his duties begin; (c) why
they tend to be "objectively verifiable and
provable," attaching the rights and duties to
some external, definite, easily verifiable characteristics of persons or objects such as a legal
document (proving the ownership of a person); a certain age, for instance 10 years old
instead of the indefinite term "juvenile"; a
definite sex, a specified public ceremony, and
so on.

The same distributive function of law-norms
generates *official law* with its characteristics
and the official court with its machinery of
justice and system of judicial evidence. If the
law-norm happens to be vague and liable to
different interpretations by the parties involved
there is need for an authoritative agency which
can give an interpretation obligatory upon all
parties and thereby prevent their incessant
conflict. Hence the judge and the court are
the agencies which perform this function;
they are a by-product of the law-norms implicitly given in their distributive function.
Likewise, as we shall see a little further (section 7 of this chapter), the law-convictions of
different members of an interacting group may
be and often are different, even contradictory.
Each party following its own law-norms would
chronically clash with other parties whose
law-norms were contradictory. No stable or
definite distribution of the rights and duties
in such a group would be possible. To prevent
or to remove such a situation in the group the
distributive function of law-norms generates
(in ways not discussed here) *a set of law-
norms that becomes obligatory* and enforceable for all the members of the group, irrespec-

tive of whether the law-norms of certain members coincide with or contradict this "official
law." The necessity for such an official law
is implicitly contained in the distributive function of the law-norm and becomes explicit in
any durable group of interacting individuals
(or groups).

6. Organizational Functions of Law-Norms

A second basic function of law-norms, inseparably connected with their distributive
role, is their *organizational* function, for, if the
most careful distribution of the rights and
duties of the norms were not enforced or
obediently followed by the members of the
group, their work would be unfulfilled and
therefore useless. If human beings were angels
or if their law-convictions were identical, no
compulsory enforcement would be necessary
and no sanctions would be needed. The real
situation being different, compulsory enforcement and the sanctions of official law-norms
become inevitable. This can be accomplished
only by an authoritative power-agency capable of enforcing laws and applying sanctions.

In creating such an enforcing power, the
government of the group manifests the organizational function of law-norms, thereby supplementing the distributive function. Any
authoritative power of government is thus a
direct product or manifestation of law-norms.
This authority consists not in the physical
force of the members of the government (sometimes they are very feeble persons physically),
nor in the power of various gadgets which
they have (these are operated by many human
agents subordinated to them), but in the law-
convictions of the members of the group (or
of their majority) which attribute to the government the right to govern, to legislate, to
judge (always under specified conditions),
ascribing at the same time to the members of
the group the duty to obey its orders. The
specified power of a state government over its
citizens; of the president of a university over
its members; of the Pope over the members
of the Roman Catholic Church; of a teacher
over the pupils; of a general over the army;
of a father over his children, and so on,
consists exactly in this "self-imposed obedience" of the members of the group that ascribes
to the general or the father the respective

rights of governing and commanding (legislative, judicial, executive) and to those below him the duty of obeying his "lawful orders." The law-norms determine who is the government, what are its rights, who among the governing agents are the superior and the inferior, entitled to command and obliged to obey, what orders are obligatory and which are not, under what conditions the legislative, the judicial and executive orders are binding and under which they are not, and so on, with all the meticulousness and external objectivity inherent in law-norms generally.

By performing this function the law-norms call forth the existence in any organized group of a government-power capable of enforcing their distributive function and through that of maintaining an order in the group with a minimum of conflicts among its members. Through these distributive and organizational functions the law-norms mold an interactive group of individuals into an organized group, stamped with all the other traits of organization mentioned above.

7. Official and Unofficial Law-Norms of a Group

Naturally, law-norms may vary in their content from person to person and from group to group. The law-convictions of the poor often differ from those of the rich, those of employees from those of employers, those of Communists and revolutionaries from those of anti-Communists and conservative persons. If in a group of interacting individuals such a diversity and oppositeness of law-norms prevails, no order, no peaceful social life is possible; though each member acts according to his own law-norms, perennial disputes will be unavoidable, since the law-norms conflict. Hence in any durable interacting group it is necessary to have a set of law-norms obligatory for all, backed by power and enforced, no matter whether they coincide with or contradict the law-norms of some members of the group. *The totality of the law-norms which are obligatory for all members of the group, protected and enforced by all the authoritative power of the government of the group or by the group itself, makes its official law.*

The *official* law of the state, incorporated in all its statutes and codes, regulates the most important relationships of its members and groups: its constitution, the organization of its power—legislative, executive, and judicial; the hierarchy of governmental ranks and authorities; the economic and property relationship of its members; the forms of the family, marriage, and of inheritance; the rights and duties of the government and of the citizens; the relationships and activities that are permitted and prohibited, and so on (constitutional, administrative, civil, criminal, and commercial laws of the state). The official law of the family (nowadays usually incorporated into the official law of the state) defines its nature as the union of husband(s) and wife (wives), of parents and children, establishes the conditions of marriage, separation, and divorce, and of the personal and property relationships of the members. The official law of a business organization (again nowadays incorporated into the official law of the state) determines all the essentials of its structure and functions. A religious group has its canon law, and so on.

In all groups the official law ordinarily regulates (distributes the rights and duties, and organizes the group's power or government) the most important relationships of the members within the group as well as those between the group and the outside world.

However, neither in the state nor in any large group does such an official law exhaust all the law-norms (and law-convictions) possessed by the members, which function and regulate their relationships. Side by side with official law (and respective organization) there always exist many norms of *unofficial law supplementing, correcting, or even contradicting the norms of the official law of the group,* and manifested in those law-norms (or attributive-imperative law convictions) of members, not incorporated into the official law. Nevertheless these unofficial norms perform vigorously their distributive and organizational functions, either supplementing or contradicting the norms of official law.[7]

The first reason for the existence of norms of unofficial law is that in particularly large

---

[7] The existence of such an unofficial law was known long ago. Under the names of "rules of propriety" (Confucius, Mencius), "Tao" (Lao-Tzu), "natural law," *aequitas, jus honorarium,*

social groups, with billions of varied interactions between members, the official law
cannot in advance foresee and define all
these relationships in all their individual and
peculiar circumstances. Had official law attempted to do so it would have expanded and
grown almost to infinity. For this reason official
law limits its regulation to the most important
of these relationships. Thousands of minor
situations as well as those which deviate from
the standardized relationships of official law
are ordinarily governed by the norms of unofficial law of the members of the group. A
second main reason for the existence of unofficial law is the excessive rigidity and partial
obsolescence of official law—a point to be
discussed further.[8] This factor often makes
official law unfit for the regulation of the ever-
changing and ever peculiar conditions in the
social life of interacting individuals.

Thus in the state all the relationships of its
members are regulated not only by the state's
official law but by the unofficial (for the state)
law-norms of various occupational, professional,
and religious groups; by codes of decency and
professional ethics; by the unofficial law-convictions of many of its subgroups and persons. These unofficial law-norms are unin-
corporated in the official law of the state and
sometimes even contradictory to it. A good
example is the case of the unpopular prohibition law in the United States which did not
coincide with, and even contradicted, the unofficial law-norms of a large part of the population.

In the family, side by side with official law
(at present incorporated into the official law
of the state) thousands of member relationships are regulated by their unofficial law-
convictions: the exact relationships between
husband and wife in regard to their daily
activities, their cooperation and subordination,
even the details of their sexual life, their
actual economic and other relationships, their
associations with other persons, and so on.
Similarly, only a small fraction of the relationships between parents and children are
defined by official law; the majority are left
unregulated, but unofficial law takes care of
them. This is shown by the fact that sometimes the norms of unofficial law take the
upper hand over those of official law. For instance, in many societies, like that of pre-
Nazi Germany, according to official law the
husband gave orders and the wife followed
them, economically and in many other ways.
Yet in a great many German families the
status of husband and wife was either equal
or reversed, so that sometimes the wife was
the real boss in the family. Furthermore, the
official law of the family in nations composed
of different ethnic and other groups is the
same for all the groups. Actually, the family
structure of upper and lower classes, of various
ethnic groups—whether in Russia or in the
United States, for instance—differs widely.
Most such relationships, except those regulated by official law, are controlled by the
norms of unofficial law of these families and
groups.

and others (Roman law) it has been analyzed by
many, and especially by the great Roman jurists.
Tacitus' *Quid leges sine moribus* well sums up the
conflict between official and unofficial laws and the
inefficacy of the former when contradicted by the
latter. Since ancient times the nature and the
relationship of these laws has been analyzed by
many thinkers. Recently Leo Petrajitsky has greatly
advanced our knowledge of both types of law and
their formal and causal relationship. (See his
Theory of Law and Ethics, Vol. II, Ch. 5, *passim*.)
The existence of unofficial law in any group leads
to that of an unofficial or informal organization in
the group side by side with its official or formal
organization. When the official and unofficial laws
of the group greatly differ or when they mutually
conflict, the informal organization of the group
then runs along different lines and even contradicts
its formal or official organization. This means, as
we shall see further, that the pretentious claims
of some recent theorizers to being the discoverers
of "informal organization" in groups is a rediscovery of America many centuries after it was discovered by preceding generations.

[8] W. I. Thomas and F. Znaniecki understood
this. "Group-organization embodied in socially
systematized schemes of behavior imposed as rules
[more exactly as official law-norms] upon individuals never exactly coincides with individual life-
organization consisting in personally systematized
schemes of behavior [with unofficial law-norms of
the individual]. Even in the least differentiated
groups we find socially sanctioned rules of behavior which explicitly apply only to certain classes
of individuals and we find individuals who in
organizing their conduct use some personal schemes
of their own invention besides the traditionally
sanctioned rules." (W. I. Thomas and F. Znaniecki, *The Polish Peasant in Europe and America*
[New York, 1927], p. 1127.)

With religious groups, too, their main relationships are defined by the official canon law of the church. But thousands of other relationships of their members are regulated by the unofficial law-norms of these members. This explains why in such great religious organizations as the Roman Catholic Church, in spite of the consistency of its official canon law, an enormous number of relationships of Catholics in Italy and France, in China and Australia differ greatly and are diversely regulated; the reason is the difference in the unofficial law of these groups and persons.

The existence of an informal organization side by side with the formal one in business firms has been indicated by Chester I. Barnard, F. J. Roethlisberger, W. J. Dickson, E. Mayo and others.[9] Their studies show also that the informal organization is different from the formal one. The distribution of rights and duties, of the hierarchies of domination and subordination, of authority and prestige in the informal organization does not coincide with that of the formal one. The relationships in this informal organization are regulated not by the official law of the firm but by the unofficial law-convictions of the persons involved.

Studies of J. L. Moreno, H. H. Jennings, and of other "sociometricians" have discovered in practically all social groups a deviation of the wishful "informal relationship" from the factual and formal association of the members. If and when they can choose the persons with whom each of the members would like to work, to live in the same room or building, to play together or to associate, the persons chosen deviate greatly from those with whom a member is factually working, playing, living, or associating. Accordingly their informal law-convictions ascribe prestige, rights, and duties to various members of the group along essentially different lines from those stipulated by the official distribution of prestige, rights, and duties in the group. All this means again the existence of an unofficial law in groups side by side with the official one.[10]

Likewise, what some anthropologists and social scientists call (sometimes in a very inadequate way) the discrepancy between the ideal or theoretical norm and the practice of society, between the "ideal" and "behavioral" patterns of conduct or between "covert" and "overt" culture points also to the existence of a discrepancy between official and unofficial law of groups, or to a deviation of actual conduct from the norms of official and unofficial law.[11]

Not only does every organized group have its official and unofficial law-norms, now essentially supplementing one another, now mutually contradicting, but every one of us, in the totality of our law-norms has, side by side with the law-convictions identical with the norms of the official law of the state, many law-convictions partly supplementing the official law, partly contradicting it. Some of the official law-norms appear to us obsolescent, others "unjust" and in need of elimination from the official law-norms. In such cases *summa jus* (official law) appears to us as a *summa injuria*.

Hence in their content *the norms of unofficial law may or may not coincide with the content*

---

[9] See the facts and analysis in Chester I. Barnard, *The Functions of the Executive* (Harvard University Press, 1938); F. J. Roethlisberger and W. J. Dickson, *Management and the Worker*, Ch. 9 (Harvard University Press, 1942); F. J. Roethlisberger, *Management and Morale* (Harvard University Press, 1941).

[10] See J. L. Moreno, *Who Shall Survive* (Washington, 1934); "Sociometry and the Cultural Order," *Sociometry*, Vol. VI (1943), pp. 299-344; H. H. Jennings, *Leadership and Isolation* (New York, 1943); and other copies of the *Sociometry*.

[11] See, for instance, D. Bidney, "On the Concept of Culture," *AA*, Vol. XLVI (1944), pp. 37 ff; C. Kluckhohn, "Covert Culture," *Ibid*, Vol. XLV (1943), pp. 214 ff. Unfortunately these classifications are very inexact. A discrepancy between "theory" and "practice," "ideal and behavioral" norms may mean several kinds of discrepancies: either between the ethical and law-norms (see further), or between the ethical, the official, and the unofficial law-norms, or between these and purely technical norms (see further on this) or between the lawful and unlawful conduct due to the poor inculcation of law-norms into the respective persons or groups. All these discrepancies are evidently of a very different nature. Not possessing any clear definition of law-norms these authors dump together into their respective classes very different phenomena and through that make their classifications unsatisfactory from a logical as well as from a factual standpoint. Such classifications and pseudo-concepts get us nowhere.

of official law. When they do coincide, unofficial law supplements the regulations of official law. When they do not coincide, such as in the existence of republican law-convictions within a monarchical regime, or of communistic law-norms within a Capitalistic society, or of anti-Hitlerite law-convictions within Hitler's Third Reich, then the unofficial law conflicts with the official law of the group. In such cases a struggle between official and unofficial law becomes inevitable. It may be solved by an orderly or bloody suppression of the unofficial law on the part of official law; again, by peaceful or by revolutionary replacement of the official law by the unofficial one (in which case the latter becomes the official law); or by a mutual adjustment of both laws.

Generally, *in any group there is some discrepancy between its official law and the unofficial norms, of some of its members, though normally this discrepancy is not too great.* The point is that official law, especially in vast groups like the state, cannot be incessantly changed; the change of any official law-norm involves a huge legislative machinery, working slowly and expensively, and requiring time for the enactment of even a comparatively unimportant new statute. For the change of a constitutional norm or of any important law the expense, time, energy, and machinery needed are enormous. Furthermore, the fundamental social relationships regulated by official law change but slowly, providing the society with a necessary stability and order. An incessant change of such fundamental social relationships as property, the family, and forms of government would mean a continuous revolution—economic, social, and political—which would make stable order in the society impossible. These facts explain why the norms of official law tend to "harden" and in this "hardened" form tend to stay unchanged for decades, even centuries, until a profound change in the law-convictions of the members occurs. Meanwhile sociocultural conditions change endlessly and call forth the modification of many law-norms to make them fit the new conditions. In conformity with this our unofficial law-norms can change incessantly hand in hand with the change of sociocultural conditions. Being unencumbered with formal

machinery, they can develop as fast as the circumstances demand.

It follows that unofficial law is more elastic, more changeable, and more easily meets individual conditions and intimate relationships than official law. While the latter cannot help lagging to some extent behind the changed conditions, the unofficial law is able to follow these changes promptly. *Official law, then, always lags somewhat behind unofficial law.* When the discrepancy between the two becomes considerable and when official law-norms become notably antiquated by new conditions, the official law—at least in wise groups—is changed in an orderly way by due process as provided in the official law itself; the new official law is made similar to the existing unofficial law. If and when, for some reason, such an orderly change of official law is not made in time, and the gap between official and unofficial law becomes wide, either a violent overthrow of the official law and of its government and partisans occurs in the form of a revolution, or a bloody suppression of the unofficial law and of its partisans takes place by the iron hand of the official government. In this way an incessant mutual influence of the two laws goes on; official law affects the unofficial law and the latter incessantly presses upon official law. One is the factor of societal stability par excellence; the other is the factor of social change demanded by an incessant shifting of sociocultural conditions. One is hard, fixed, inelastic, unadaptable to many peculiar and intimate situations; the other is elastic, progressive, adjustable to the most singular conditions. When their mutual discrepancy is moderate and concerns only a fraction of human relationships, they may coexist side by side, cooperating with one another and mutually stimulating one another. When the discrepancy becomes enormous and concerns important values, they clash and either are reconciled, in an orderly way, mainly through a replacement of the antiquated official law by the unofficial law, or in a disorderly way through violence and internal disturbances.[12]

---

[12] See a detailed development of many of the above points in Leo Petrajitsky's *Theory of Law and Ethics,* quoted, 2 Vols., *passim;* R. Stammler, *Wirtschaft und Recht nach der materialistische*

8. Difference Between Law-Norms and Other Norms

All the norms of conduct that do not have the above characteristics of law-norms (their two-sidedness, their attributive-imperative character, their logical elements in the form of subjects of right and duty, objects of right and duty, etc.) are not law-norms.

a. *Moral Norms.* Such are, first, the purely *moral* norms, which recommend but do not require a certain form of conduct, which are only imperative—urging or recommending a given form of conduct—but not at all attributive, i. e., not entitling anyone to demand the recommended conduct, and having only a subject and object of recommended conduct (duty) but not any subject and object of right entitled to demand it. By this one-sidedness the purely moral norms differ fundamentally from the two-sided law-norms. The following norms of the Sermon on the Mount are concrete examples: "Whosoever shall smite thee on thy right cheek, turn to him the other also," "if any man will sue thee at the law, and take away thy coat, let him have thy cloak also," and "whosoever shall compel thee to go a mile, go with him twain" (Matthew 5:39-41). These norms only urge and recommend this conduct; they do not entitle anyone to demand the right of slapping the other cheek or taking away the cloak or forcing one to go the twain. Regardless of content, any norm that is only imperative and not attributive, that only recommends a certain conduct but does not ascribe a right to demand it to any subject of right is a *moral norm*, and is a very different thing from law-norms.

From this fundamental difference between law-norms and moral norms there follow several other differences. (1) Since a law-norm is an obligatory norm, a compulsory realization of its demand is possible; a subject of duty who failed to discharge that duty can be forced to discharge it by the sanction of punishment, retribution, restitution, and so on.

For this reason law has behind it a compulsory apparatus of enforcement if the party fails in his duty. Since a moral norm is only a recommended norm, a party is free to fulfill or not to fulfill it. Therefore a coercive enforcement is perfectly alien to and incompatible with a moral norm. (2) Since a law-norm attributes a right to one party and a duty to another, in many cases for the subject of right it is unimportant by whom the duty is discharged: by the subject of duty or by some other agent who, for instance, pays a debt to a creditor. For the subject of the right is important only in that the right is realized, the debt is paid, the contracted work is done, the services rendered. Whether this is done by the subject of the duty or by some other person is a quite secondary thing in most law-relationships (though not in all). For this reason, a law-norm permits the performance of the duty not only by the subject of the duty but also by a third party. Such a substitution is impossible in a moral norm. The value of the moral act consists exactly in that it is done freely. Here it is impossible to be heroic or moral at the cost of somebody else's action. The heroism of a free sacrifice of life for the well-being of a fellow man belongs only to the one who did it; it cannot be credited to someone else. One cannot be heroic and saintly by the saintliness of someone else.

(3) For a law-norm it is of secondary importance by what motives the subject of duty is moved in the fulfillment of his duty: by the duty itself, or by the fear of punishment, or by some profit. Whatever the motive, the important thing is that the duty is discharged. Different is the situation with a moral norm; here the purity of the motive in the discharge of the recommended norm is paramount; if a person gives a dollar to a needy person expecting a ten-dollar profit from his action such an action is a commercial transaction on the part

---

Geschichtsauffassung (Leipzig, 1924); also his *Theorie der Rechtswissenschaft* (Halle, 1911); R. Ihering, *The Struggle for Law* (Chicago, 1879); K. Binding, *Die Normen und ihre Übertrebungen* (Leipzig, 1890); J. Commons, *Legal Foundations of Capitalism* (New York, 1924); N. Timasheff, *An Introduction to the Sociology of Law* (Cambridge, 1939); R. Pound, *Contemporary Juristic Law* (New York, 1940), also his *The Task of Law* (Lancaster, 1944); G. Gurvitch, *Sociology of Law* (New York, 1942); P. A. Sorokin, *General Theory of Law* (in Russian, Jaroslavl, 1919). See also the articles of LeFur, Darmstädter, Perticone, and Gurvitch in the *Archives de Philosophie du droit et de sociologie juridique*, Nos. 3-4 (1935).

of a profiteer and it is not a truly moral action. (4) The discharge of the obligatory duty of a law-norm is regarded as a normal discharge of what is expected. It does not appear as something heroic which we should admire and be grateful for. In a moral norm there is no obligation. Therefore its discharge calls forth emotions of thankfulness, admiration, and respect on the part of those in favor of whom it is done. (5) A law-norm as a two-sided obligatory norm is always *limited* in the extent and the kind of the right and duty; and being obligatory, neither of these can be infinite and unlimited. Otherwise the fulfillment of the law-norm would have been impossible and would generate endless conflict between the parties. Quite different is the situation with a moral norm; since there is no subject of right who is entitled to demand its fulfillment, and since it is free, the moral norm can be potentially infinite and unlimited. There is no limit to ethical perfection, and the further a person advances along the line of goodness the better. Therefore the indication of a limit to the goodness recommended by a moral norm is unnecessary, irrelevant, and superfluous. For this reason moral norms do not specify the limits of moral duty as do law-norms in regard to the law-duty and the law-right. These are some of the derivative differences between law-norms and moral norms.

Thus, in their logical structure as well as in their urging power, the two types of norms are distinctly different. For this reason they should not be mixed with each other. In the same person or group the main connection between their law-norms and their moral norms is that as a rule (having, however, many exceptions) the *law-norms require "a minimum" of ethical conduct while the moral norms recommend conduct that is above this minimum*—heroic or saintly actions accessible only to a few and in no way to all. As such they are only recommended for those who can reach this high level of heroism but are not required from everybody.[13] For instance, according to St. Paul, to remain virgin and chaste

is the conduct recommended to all Christians *who can reach this heroic level, but it is not* required of them. Those who cannot reach this level are entitled to satisfy their sexual urge in the form of marriage, as a lawful action embodying a minimum of ethical conduct in this field; "if they cannot contain, let them marry for it is better to marry than to burn." Finally, all Christians are prohibited from having sexual life outside of marriage; such actions would be sinful and unlawful (I Corinthians, 7 and 5). On these ethical levels the highest is the purely recommended moral conduct; next, as a minimum of ethical conduct, is the socially sanctioned marriage; finally, sexual life outside of marriage is the lowest, being sinful, unlawful, criminal conduct which is vetoed and punishable.

At the present time, the payment of taxes is required from all taxable persons; failure to do so becomes a punishable crime. Buying war-bonds is only recommended but not required from all of us. Studying our own norms of conduct, we can easily see that side by side with law-norms we have a large number of purely moral norms. We well know, by our own experience, the difference between them, we feel that it would be good if we followed this or that moral norm, for instance, devoting a large part of our energy and fortune to the alleviation of the misery of the poor, or the unemployed, or the sick. But on the other hand, if an unemployed person or a pauper should demand from us such services and fortune we might become indignant at him because we do not ascribe to him the right to demand it. Finally, if we violate this or that law-conviction of ours we feel that we are acting sinfully, lawlessly, and criminally.

b. *Technical Norms.* Law-norms differ further from purely *technical norms* which prescribe how to do this or that: how to write a novel, to broil a chicken, to plant vegetables, to shave, or to play the piano. Such purely utilitarian norms, devoid of the imperative-attributive urge, having neither subjects nor objects of right and of duty, nor practically any of the formal, psychological, and social traits of law and of moral norms, do not belong to these fields at all. However, if a technical norm, for instance, that which defines how to perform a surgical operation or a religious

---

[13] See a development of this in G. Jellineck, *Sozialethische Bedeutung von Recht, Unrecht und Strafe* (Wien, 1879); P. A. Sorokin, *Crime and Punishment, Heroism and Reward* (Russian, St. Petersburg, 1914).

When we consider further Sumner's reference to "the elements of truth" its irrelevancy to a definition of folkways and mores is rather obvious; monogamic or polygamic marriage mores are neither true nor false. The truth is a category hardly applicable to mores, folkways, law, and ethics.

Furthermore, if we were to believe Sumner, the mores of slavery and serfdom were, in "the judgment" of slaves and serfs, "conducive to societal—and their—welfare" and were neither imposed upon them "nor co-ordinated by any authority." We may be excused for refusing to accept such a statement. Moreover, so far as the official law of organized groups is an important part of Sumner's mores and folkways, one can hardly say that the official law-mores "were not co-ordinated by any authority." Beginning with the most ancient known law-codes, like the code of Hammurabi, the ancient Egyptian law and moral codes, the Ten Commandments of Moses, the Laws of Manu, Brihaspati, Gautama, Narada, the jural and moral norms of Hesiod, of Dracon, and Licurgus, and ending with the modern law-codes, most of these have certainly been codified and "co-ordinated" by the law-givers of the particular society. These and other blunders of Sumner are inevitable since his mores and folkways are a kind of grocery basket into which are dumped together official and unofficial law-norms, moral norms, "religion," "life policy," "philosophy," "truth," "societal welfare." Taking such a hodgepodge as a major premise one cannot build upon it any systematic, logically consistent, or factually adequate theory of organized groups, institutions, or society. Ballard's definition of an institution is an even worse variety of the criticized definition of law-norms, as "purposively established by the common will." So slavery was purposively established by the will of the slaves, as a part of the "common will." (See the criticism above, p. 72.)

Finally, such definitions of institutions as those of T. Parsons are about as defective as all the quoted ones. Everything in this cumbersome pile of words is unclear. (1)

Almost all law-norms, moral norms, technical norms, and rules of etiquette, are derivable from "a common value system" of the society. Does this mean that all such rules are institutions? (2) What is meant by a "common value system" is undefined by the author. Common to whom? is unspecified. What is meant by "moral authority" is undefined. What we are to understand by "immediate ends" is unclear: is it the "end" realizable in one hour? one year? ten years? twenty years? In addition the whole definition is based on a false premise (criticized above) that all human actions are purposeful and that all fall within the schema of means and end.[14]

The above is sufficient to show the gross inadequacy of prevalent definitions and conceptions dealing with the problems of organized groups, institutions, social norms, mores, folkways, customs, law and moral norms. Dealing with such a logical and factual hash nobody can arrive at any satisfactory result in these fields. Clearly a very different procedure is needed to arrive at a more adequate definition of organized groups, or institutions, as well as at a better analysis of what mores, folkways, social norms, customs, habits, and concerted behavior are. The first step in this procedure is to recognize that the heart and soul of any organized group or institution are its law-norms, as a specific form or aspect of its component of meaning-values. The second step is a clear and adequate conception of law-norms and their specific characteristics. Third, when they are adequately defined, the nature of official and unofficial law-norms, of their distributive and organizational functions, of "formal and informal organization," of moral, technical, and other norms becomes easily definable and validly differentiated from the law-norms. Fourth, having at our disposal valid definitions of each kind of norm we can easily analyze into its various components such congeries of norms as mores, folkways, concerted behavior, and other "logical grocery baskets" where side by side are squatting quite different norms and values. This has been the precise method we have followed. Finally, as we shall presently

---

[14] More adequate are the definitions of institutions given by C. Panunzio, J. O. Hertzler, and F. S. Chapin. Their main defect is that they are purely descriptive and do not stress and analyze the law-norms and their nature. See C. Panunzio, *Major Social Institutions* (New York, 1939), Ch. 1; J. O. Hertzler, *Social Institutions* (New York, 1929), Ch. 3; F. S. Chapin, *Contemporary American Institutions* (New York, 1935), Ch. 2.

observe, law-norms, in their fullest implications, contain all the other characteristics of organized groups, or institutions.

OTHER CHARACTERISTICS OF ORGANIZED GROUPS OR INSTITUTIONS

As soon as the official and unofficial law-norms of the group are given, all the other characteristics of an organized group enumerated above (see section 1) follow as their consequence and product. (1) Division of all the relationships and forms of conduct into: (a) *lawful*, (b) *moral or recommended*, (c) *prohibited or unlawful* (*tabooed, sinful*), violating the norms of law—such a division is simply a consequence of the law-norms of the group.

As indicated above, the very nature of the recommended (moral) relationships makes superfluous and unnecessary their detailed specifications and limitations once the general character of the norm, for instance "love thy neighbor," is given. Since recommended forms of conduct are free, not obligatory, the details and limits of their realization are left to the good will and wisdom of the individuals. For this reason the moral or recommended norms are rarely, if ever, greatly detailed in any organized group of interacting individuals. The very nature of the *obligatory law-relationships*, however, demands the most detailed, clear-cut, precise definition of the relationships of the parties involved, with all the specified subjects of rights and duties, objects of rights and duties, the conditions of time, space, circumstances, addressees, and so on. Hence the law-norms (official and unofficial) of a group are always formulated in great detail, and in large groups are very numerous, amounting sometimes to many thousands of norms filling lengthy codes of law, like the official laws of the state or the canon law of a vast church.

Similarly the law-norms defining *unlawful or prohibited* conduct and relationships are also detailed and numerous, not only in their enumeration and definition of what kinds of actions and relationships are prohibited but also of what sanctions follow each kind of prohibited conduct—be it murder of different degrees, theft, larceny, adultery, forgery, etc. The law grades in much detail the gravity of the prohibited actions and relations, leaving the lightest violations unsanctioned (so-called *leges imperfectae*); others sanctioned only by the *legal nullity* of the particular violation, or by a restitution of the financial harm caused to the injured party by the guilty party; finally, the gravity of prohibited conduct is expressed in a long series of sanctions of punishment beginning with fines and short detentions and ending with the most thoroughgoing forms of capital punishment or hard labor and imprisonment for life with a loss of all civil rights. For instance, most of the norms of criminal law subdivide criminal actions first into a few classes: the gravest crimes; the serious crimes; and the light violations. These groups become *the felony and misdemeanor* of Anglo-Saxon Criminal Law; *Verbrechen, Vergehen* and *Uebertrebungen* of the German criminal law; *crime, délit, contravention* of the French criminal law; *Prestuplenia, prostupki* and *pravonarushenia* of the Russian criminal law. Then within each class the unlawful actions are graded into many subgrades from the standpoint of their comparative gravity, and are punished with an appropriate severity. Though the content and the gravity of the prohibited actions and relationships fluctuate from person to person, from group to group, from period to period in the same group, nevertheless their detailed specification followed with appropriate sanctions in some form are given in any organized group.[15] The family or business firm, the religious or political group, the primitive tribe or even the criminal gang, the state or the occupational union—all of these have written or unwritten codes of actions and relationships tabooed, vetoed, prohibited, and appropriately sanctioned by fine, expulsion, suspension of membership, on up to taking a doublecrosser "for a ride," or other such grave sanctions. Nowadays, however, these grave sanctions are imposed through the agency of the state, to which the perpetrator of the grave violation is

[15] The diversity and relativity of the content and of the gravity of punishment have been, however, greatly exaggerated by the anthropologists and sociologists. The gravest kinds of unlawful actions are, after all, essentially the same in various groups and periods. See the detailed study of this in my *Dynamics*, Vol. II, Ch. 15.

transmitted and by which he is tried and condemned.

(2) Another consequence of the emergence of law-norms in an interacting group is a *detailed definition of the rights and duties, of the kind and amount of social values, of the functions or role, and of the social status of every member in regard to every other member, the group as a whole, and toward the world outside of the group.* The totality of the norms of official and unofficial law and of the moral norms of the group determines all this with the precision of a script for a play which outlines the speech and movement of an actor playing one of its parts. These norms clearly define not only what a member has to say and do in regard to any other member, but often determine as well which of several roles of the "social play" in the group a given individual has to perform: that of a slave or a master; of a ruler or a criminal; of a rich person or a pauper; of a banker or a priest; of a housewife or a spinster, and so on. If here and there, for instance in the choice of the occupation of a member, there remains a large margin left to the decision of an individual, the large margin exists only because it is left so by the law-norms; where they do not leave such a margin, for instance in a caste society, the member has to take the occupation prescribed by the law-norms. The totality of the rights and duties each individual has in a group defines also his *social status and position* in the given group, because the social status and position of an individual is nothing but the totality of his rights and duties with all the benefits and burdens, advantages and disadvantages they give. The totality of the rights and duties of a master makes his status (the *status libertatis* in the terms of Roman law) and social position different from those of a slave assigned quite different rights (if any) and duties; the same is true of the status and social position of any member of a group.

The totality of the law-norms and moral norms thus determines, from the cradle to the grave, the essential actions, reactions, functions, role, and status of each member in that segment of his life which is involved with his membership in a given group. Thus the family law and moral norms determine his conduct as a baby, son, daughter, father, mother, divorcee, or illegitimate child; the totality of the state's law and moral norms define his conduct in many important segments of his conduct and relationships; in totalitarian states almost all the segments of these are defined by the state's law and moral norms. One's religious group determines his religious conduct; the laws of his union are the script for his occupational role-playing; his political party charts, for his political behavior; his recreational or artistic or scientific societies define his sayings and doings in these fields.

When an individual belongs—voluntarily or not—to several different groups, as is the case with an overwhelming majority of individuals, he has as many different "souls," plays as many different parts, has as many different statuses as there are groups of which he is a member. In that case his *total* sociocultural functions or roles, his total status and position is the sum-total of all the rights and duties, functions and roles, statuses and positions he has in all the groups in which he participates. To summarize: the law and moral norms of a group define precisely the conduct, the relationships, the possessions, the advantages and burdens, the sayings and doings or functions and roles, social statuses and social positions of its members. All these are mere derivatives or consequences of the respective legal and moral norms of the group.[16]

(3) *Emergence of the official law and of the government of the group* has already been discussed. (4) Again as a simple consequence of the *distributive and organizational functions of law-norms there arises differentiation and stratification* of the members of the group. Since the rights and duties, the functions and the status ascribed to each member are never identical but always different, the organized

---

[16] Therefore the term: "social role" adds practically nothing to the more precisely defined term "the totality of the rights and duties" except some pedagogical value of vividness. On the other hand, when it is taken without reference to law and moral norms, it becomes vague and unsatisfactory, even when reference is made to a foggy "complex of values" as F. Znaniecki does. Still less satisfactory is the use of the "social role" as a "social unit." For examples of such a deficient use of the term "social role" see F. Znaniecki, *The Social Role of the Man of Knowledge* (New York, 1940), pp. 13 ff; T. Sarbin, "The Concept of Role-Taking," *Sociometry*, Vol. VI (1943), pp. 273-85.

group of interacting individuals becomes inescapably differentiated into parts and persons, each performing a specific role different from those of other parts and individuals. Even in such a small group as the family the functions and roles of a baby, of an adult daughter or son, of father and mother are different from one another. Likewise, the functions and roles of a small business firm's handful of workers and their foremen, of the clerks, treasurer, secretary, and president are all different. Still greater is the differentiation in large social groups like a big university, a large religious group, an occupational union, or the state. In a university we find members with the functions of janitor, stenographer, printer, trustee, president, dean, professor, and students in different departments and classes. Even in the smallest possible groups—in pairs of interacting individuals—we hardly ever find a real identity of the functions and roles of the partners, be it the pair of husband and wife, teacher and pupil, lover and beloved, father and son, leader and led.

Directly from the organizational function of the law-norms follows a stratification of any organized group into unilinear or multilinear, clear-cut or vague, long or short hierarchies of the superior and subordinated ranks and authorities, beginning with the "government" and "the governed," and with many ranks and precedences within each stratum in large social groups. In the family we have its head and the subordinated members of several ranks. In a college we find the ranks of president, trustees, deans, assistant deans, full-associate-assistant professors, instructors of various ranks, and so on down to freshmen. In the state we have a long list of superior and subordinated authorities beginning with a king or president, passing to the members of the cabinet, first, second, third assistant secretaries of the departments; the chiefs of divisions; assistant chiefs; and so on down to the lowest rank of the state officialdom and the plain citizens. In a religious group we observe likewise a gradation starting with the Pope, patriarch, chief archbishop, dalailama, or supreme priest and passing through the subordinated ranks of the metropolitans, arch-bishop, bishops, priests of various ranks, and ending with the ordinary believer. In an army there is a long ladder of ranks beginning with the Commander-in-Chief and marshals or full generals and ending with the private. In India there are some 3,000 different castes hierarchically ranked in their relative superiority and inferiority beginning with the highest Brahman caste and ending with the outcastes. Even in contemporary England there exist some seventy orders of precedence with each order, in its turn, being subdivided into several subranks. The intragroup stratification is in some form an inalienable trait of any organized group, being a mere consequence of the organizational function of its law-norms.

(5) *Definition and regulation of the possession, use and operation, management and disposal of all the vehicles of the group and of its members, specifically the economic and property vehicles, is also characteristic of the organized group.* The law-norms regulate and determine, among other things, what, when, where, and how each of the interacting members should employ all the material vehicles involved in the interaction, beginning with what words or phrases to use and ending with all the object-vehicles, property, wealth, and means of subsistence of the group and of its members. Who of the members, when, where, and which of the material vehicles shall possess, use, operate, manage, and dispose, is again determined in detail by the law-norms of the organized group. Regulating all the relevant interrelations the law-norms naturally determine also these economic, material, and property rights, and the duties of each member. Whether the group has a private property system, or communal property, or the state-property system, is determined by its law norms; which portion of the material values of the group is assigned to each member, and how, under what conditions, when, and where these portions of the vehicles are to be used is again determined by the group's law-norms. While, for instance, the ethical norms of the Christian society recommend to "go and sell that thou hast, and give to the poor" (*Matthew* 19:21), its law-norms never demanded such actions, and satisfied themselves with much less radical conduct and relationships. Law-norms regulate the conduct of the subjects of interaction, the possession, use, operation, management, and disposal of all the vehicles involved, and especially the set of

object-vehicles called economic, material, and property values. The economic or property order of an organized group is a mere consequence of its law-norms.

Summing up, we have first the law-norms (official and unofficial) regulating the conduct and relationships of the members of a group and, immediately following from these, the official laws and government; next the division of all forms of conduct and relationship into obligatory, recommended, and prohibited; the precise definition of the rights-duties, functions and role, social status and position of every member; social differentiation and stratification; last, economic order. These are the necessary, inalienable and sufficient characteristics of any organized system of interaction or organized group or social institution in contradistinction from unorganized ones.[17] If one wishes one may add to these traits *the name or the symbol of such a group* (the Lincoln family, the United States of America, the General Electric Company, the Roman Catholic Church, the American Association for the Advancement of Science, and so on, with their heraldic emblems and signs and symbols), because such organized groups ordinarily acquire some name and symbol. However, such a trait is but a mere additional derivative of the six basic characteristics above and need only be mentioned.

UNORGANIZED AND LITTLE ORGANIZED GROUPS

The unorganized or disorganized group does not have the characteristics we have just examined. It is amorphous in all these respects: the rights, duties, possessions, functions, roles, social status, and position of its members are undetermined and undefined either in broad outline or meticulous detail; so are its categories of the lawful, recommended, and prohibited forms of conduct and relationship; so are its official law and government, structure of social differentiation and stratification, economic order, and so on. Consequently all remain uncrystallized. The whole system of

social relationships and values is confused and vague. Members do not know who is ruler and who is to be ruled; what are the rights and duties of each; what is the proper form of social relationship between them; what actions and conduct are recommended, lawful, and prohibited for each party. All this remains amorphous and untidy, in an unorganized or disorganized system of interaction.

No doubt the passage from the absolutely unorganized to the perfectly organized groups or social systems of interaction is in reality gradual. We have a gradation from unorganized social groups through somewhat organized up to perfectly organized and integrated social bodies, where practically all the actions of the members and all their relationships are crystallized clearly and consistently, where each member has a definite *norm* for each of his roles in interaction for each configuration of circumstances.

1. As if Organized Groups

The main form of intermediary interacting groups is the *externally unified group* or *"as if organized groups."* By passing a law that grants important privileges to one part of the population and imposes serious disfranchisements, for instance serfdom, upon the other part, the groups of aristocracy and of serfs are created. The majority of the members of each group, especially of the serfs, may not be in any close interaction with one another, may not even know of the existence of one another, may not have any government or central committee. And yet by the objectively imposed conditions, all serfs will be forced to think and to act as serfs, each suffering from the same conditions, having the same oppressing masters, being deprived of the same values, and aspiring toward the same freedom from disfranchisements. The imposed conditions tend to make them solidary with one another and opposed to the same antagonistic group. The result is that the serfs would be behaving in a manner very similar to that when they are united through direct interaction and organization. The discriminating conditions, imposed upon the serfs as well as upon the

---

[17] This shows the extreme narrowness and vagueness of such characteristics of the social and of the organized group as Durkheim's characteristics of "exteriority and constraint" (it points out only a few secondary traits of law-norms), or as many current definitions of organized groups and institutions, criticized above.

privileged, tie the members of each class into a semblance of unity and give to each class the appearance of a real organized group, whose members, each acting individually, become spontaneously solidary and antagonistic to the same group. When a conquering group imposes serious disfranchisements upon the multitude of the conquered, it creates such a semblance of a real group. When any discriminatory measure is passed giving privileges to one part and burdens to another part of the population, it externally unites the members of each class into the quasi-real group. It is indeed something intermediary between a real organized group and a nominal *plurel* of individuals, being nearer to an organized group. The groups of that kind are numerous and play a very important part in sociocultural processes. We shall see many examples of these further on.

2. Public

Other forms of little organized groups are *Public*, for instance the listeners to a radio talk or the readers of the same newspaper, who very indirectly interact with one another. Ordinarily they are not organized and remain an amorphous body sometimes near to a mere nominal *plurel*. The size and membership of such a public is never clearly defined, and incessantly changes.

3. Crowd and Mob

When individuals interact face to face, in a spatial proximity, but have no clear characteristics of organization they constitute a mob. As a result such groups must be and are chaotic, unstable, disorderly, liable to be

swayed emotionally to many surprising actions, and so forth. As a rule they are shortlived groups, suddenly appearing and as quickly disappearing after having done something usually violent or being dispersed by an organized group. They flourish and multiply in conditions either of a lack of social organization, or in those of social disorganization when the previously existing system of law and of other meanings-values-norms disintegrate in a given group of interacting individuals. The times of revolutions, of great catastrophes and calamities, of rapid decay of the existing organized order with its system of values and meanings are those of rapid emergence and multiplication of various kinds of mobs and crowds.[18]

4. Semi-Nominal Plurels

Men of genius in various creative activities of any organized population rarely if ever make a special "union of men of genius." But the bulk of these directly and indirectly know of one another and casually interact with one another without making a real organized system of interaction. Such a group—something intermediary between a real unorganized group and a nominal plurel—may be termed a *semi-nominal plurel*. Similar is the situation with a totality of all persons of the same sex or of the same race that are somewhat interacting (mainly indirectly) with one another but remain isolated individuals having no tangible interaction. The total sex or racial group of that kind will give another example of a semi-nominal *plurel* or "as if" organized group. These four—"as if organized," public, crowd and mob, and semi-nominal plurels—are the main types of the unorganized and semi-organized groups.

---

[18] The literature on mobs, crowds, public, and similar groups is enormous. Just as at present a study of the "wishful network of social relationships" (sociometry) is in vogue (though such a network is quite superfluous in comparison with the real network of social relationship defined by the law-norms), so in the past at one time a study of these unorganized or semi-organized groups was in great vogue, so much so that a study of infinitely more important organized social groups was neglected. At the present time this one-sided fashion is about over.

On crowds, mobs, etc., see G. Tarde, *The Laws of Imitation*, (New York, 1903); *L'opinion et la foule* (Paris, 1901); *Etudes de psychologie sociale* (Paris, 1898); G. Lebon, *The Crowd* (New York, 1897), *The Psychology of Socialism* (New York, 1901); E. D. Martin, *The Behavior of Crowds* (New York, 1920). Respective chapters in the texts of social psychology like K. Young, *Social Psychology* (New York, 1930), Chps. 20, 21; R. T. LaPiere, *Collective Behavior* (New York, 1938), Chps. 17-20.

Chapter 5. Solidary, Antagonistic, and Mixed Systems of Interaction

I. Definitions

Interaction is *solidary* when the aspirations (meanings-values) and overt actions of the interacting parties concur and are mutually helpful for the realization of their objectives.

It is *antagonistic* when the desires (meanings-values) and overt actions of the parties are opposite and mutually hinder one another.

It is *mixed* when the aspirations (meanings-values) and overt behavior of the parties are partly solidary, partly antagonistic. It is mixed also when the aspirations of the parties harmoniously coincide but their objective behavior defeats the realization of the objectives, for instance, when a person desires to help his sick friend but gives him, by mistake, a poison instead of medicine. Here we have a solidarity of desires and an antagonism of overt conduct. Interaction is also mixed when the meanings, values, and purposes of the parties are conflicting but their overt actions help (inadvertently) the realization of their aspirations; for instance, when *A*, desirous of becoming rich at the cost of *B*, and *B* wishing to be rich at the cost of *A*, act in such a way that they enrich each other.

Thus only those interactions where both the inner aspirations (meanings-values) and the overt actions are solidary or antagonistic are fully one or the other. All the other interactions are mixed: solidary inwardly and antagonistic overtly, antagonistic covertly and solidary overtly; partly solidary and partly antagonistic in their inner and overt aspects.[1]

[1] This shows again that no purely behavioristic description of overt actions can give us solidary or antagonistic or mixed interactions. For this reason all the semi-behavioristic descriptions, like the above "associative" and "dissociative" definitions of L. von Wiese and H. Becker, do not and cannot define any of these forms of interaction (see footnote on p. 48). Even such overt actions as killing are not necessarily antagonistic interactions, as, for instance, actions of a surgeon resulting in the death of the patient or those of Abraham sacrificing Isaac. On the other hand, even such actions as an embrace and kiss are not necessarily solidary actions—for instance, the embraces and kisses of Judas, of the ravisher and the ravished, of the prostitute and her clients. Still less can one get these forms of interaction by defining them as "approach" and "avoidance" in the sense of physical approach and avoidance. Any strictly behavioristic attempt to define these interactions in the terms of overt actions is hopeless. On the other hand, a definition based entirely upon the meanings (aspirations, desires, wishes) of the parties is also inadequate as has been shown in the text. For an adequate definition of these interactions (as well as of any other) all the components of the interactions—its subjects, their meanings (aspirations and objectives), and the vehicles (overt actions and other forms of the objectification of the meanings) must be fully considered.

II. Difference Between Solidary-Antagonistic and Organized-Unorganized Forms of Interaction

Many social scientists identify organized interaction with solidary, and unorganized with antagonistic. It is true that the ideally organized group includes solidarity of its members as one of its characteristics. Nevertheless, the categories solidary-antagonistic and organized-unorganized are very different. An interaction system (group) may be well organized in the sense defined in the preceding chapter, and yet contain a great deal of antagonism in the interrelationships of its members. And vice versa, the interacting parties may be solidary and yet remain unorganized. A model prison as a system of interaction is a conspicuously organized group; the rights and duties of the prisoners and of the administration are well defined; their functions and roles and status are clear-cut; so are their differentiation and stratification. The prison has its government, property, name, and symbol (the Charlestown Prison, Sing Sing, etc.). In spite of that, the whole group is essentially antagonistic. The unofficial convictions of the prisoners and the official law of the prison greatly conflict; the aspirations and the actions of the prisoners and of the administration are, to a great extent, contradictory; even the relationships among the various groups of the prisoners are to some extent conflicting. This gives an example of an organized but essentially antagonistic system of interaction. The system of interaction between masters and slaves, conquerors and conquered, is ordinarily organized, but remains predominantly antagonistic.

As a matter of fact, in almost all the organized groups—the state, business firms, armies and navies, the family, schools, religious groups, political parties, occupational unions—there is usually present an element of antagonistic relationship. Membership in all these groups involves many a burdensome duty: taxes, military service, tiresome work, subordination to a disliked boss, and so on. Without some pressure on the part of the official law and authorities such duties would not be performed. Likewise, the ambitions and aspirations of the members often clash; often they profoundly dislike one another. Not infrequently they hinder a realization of the objectives of their fellows.

The purely solidary organized groups are rare, limited mainly to small groups like the "perfect family" or to the interaction of devoted friends. Otherwise, side by side with the solidary relationships, there are always to a greater or less degree antagonistic relationships in the overwhelming majority of organized groups.

The decisive evidence for this in practically all organized groups is the existence of *coercion and sanctions* in their official law. Sanctions mean a compulsory enforcement of group norms. If there were no antagonism between the aspirations of the members and the norms of the official law, or between the opinions of its various members, or between their unofficial opinions and the norms of the official law, and if the desires of all members were perfectly harmonious—under these conditions all members would do their duty freely, without coercive sanctions. Since the official law of all organized groups has some kind of sanctions, from discharge and expulsion to punishment and compulsory enforcement, this means that side by side with the solidary relationships there exists in any organized group some amount of antagonism. The same fact is disclosed by the discrepancy between the existing relationships in the groups and their "wishful" or informal relationships.[2]

Other conditions being equal, *the greater the antagonism in the interaction of the members of a group the greater the amount and severity of punishment and coercion (sanctions) used for the maintenance and enforcement of its official law.* This explains, and is corroborated by, the severity, cruelty, and abundance of sanctions in the official law imposed by a hated conqueror upon the conquered; by pitiless masters upon unmanageable slaves; by an

---

[2] See the sociometric studies of Moreno, Jennings, and those of Barnard and others quoted above.

unpopular dictatorial government upon rebellious subjects; by revolutionaries upon counterrevolutionaries, or vice versa; by the Holy Inquisition upon incorrigible heretics; by a prison guard upon rioting prisoners, and so on. The same is true of any organized group with widespread and intense antagonism among its members.[3]

On the other hand, in an organized group of perfectly solidary, harmonious, and sinless angels, no coercion, punishment, or other severe sanction would be necessary, and not even any official law. Their wishes and their legal and ethical convictions being perfectly solidary, they would all spontaneously fulfill their legal and ethical duties, and these duties would harmonize with their wishes and aspirations. From this standpoint the very existence of official law with its sanctions in any organized group is evidence of a lack of perfect solidarity among its members.[4]

Summarizing: (1) organized groups range from the free solidary type (given rarely) through the mixed type—partly solidary, partly antagonistic—to the predominantly antagonistic type, where order and official law are maintained mainly through unlimited coercion.

(2) The greater the discrepancy between (a) the official law of the group and the unofficial law of its members, (b) between the law norms of the members, and (c) between their wishes and aspirations, the more antagonistic such an organized group will be. The less these discrepancies are, the more solidary the group will be.

(3) The more antagonistic the organized group is, the greater are the amount and severity of sanctions (compulsion, punishment) used for the maintenance and enforcement of its official law and order.

The totality of these considerations is sufficient to show the essential difference between the organized and solidary and the unorganized and antagonistic forms of interaction and groups.

III. Forms of Solidarity and Antagonism

1. Direct and Indirect

Solidary and antagonistic interactions have many varieties and can be classified in many different ways.[5] They may be mutual and one-sided; short-lived and durable; direct (face-to-face) and indirect. The direct interaction is that where the parties influence one another directly, where their actions are specifically addressed to one another. When the parties interact face to face, or send a letter, a telegram, a gift, money, or poison to one another, all such interactions are direct interactions, no matter what kind of conductors are used to transmit the stimuli from one party to another. In the indirect interaction the parties influence one another without addressing their actions specifically to the other parties, often not even suspecting their existence. Interactions between a producer and a consumer, between a writer and his readers, and between a legislator and the bulk of the citizens are examples of this form of interaction. If not literally, nevertheless essentially this classification is close to C. H. Cooley's classification of the primary and secondary groups. Cooley's "primary" group is really not a merely "face-to-face interacting group" but something much more complex, and essentially similar to what

[3] See a systematic corroboration of this proposition in my *Dynamics*, Vol. II, Ch. 15.

[4] See Leo Petrajitzky, *Politika Prava* (St. Petersburg, 1907).

[5] See various classifications of solidary and antagonistic interrelationships in Max Scheler, *Das Wesen und die Formen der Sympathie* (2nd ed., 1929); *Der Formalismus in der Ethik und die materiale Wertethik* (2nd ed., 1931); F. Tönnies, *Fundamental Concepts of Sociology* (Eng. tr. of Tönnies' *Gemeinschaft und Gesellschaft* by C. Loomis, New York, (1940); J. Delevsky, *Les antagonismes sociaux* (Paris, 1924); R. Park and

E. Burgess, *Introduction to the Science of Sociology* (Chicago, 1924), Chps. 8-10; F. Savorgnan, "Les antagonisms sociaux," *Scientia* (1914); E. Ross, *Principles of Sociology* (New York, 1938), Chps. 13-27; L. von Wiese, *System der allgemeinen Soziologie*, quoted, Part III. For a survey of the main classifications of solidary interactions see G. Gurvitch, *Essais de sociologie* (Paris, 1938); G. Devereux and E. Loeb, "Antagonistic Acculturation," *ASR*, Vol. VIII (1943), 133 ff.

I call the "familistic" form of social relationship. Many sociologists that accept Cooley's primary group as just a face-to-face interacting group misinterpret Cooley's conception.[6]

2. Least to Most Intense

Antagonisms and solidarities range from the least to the most intense; from a mere coldness between parties to the most intense hatred satiated only by the extermination of the enemy and by vilification of him even after death; from mere tolerance of a person to a joyful readiness to sacrifice everything for him. In this range from the slightest to the most intense, solidarity has many shades: politeness, benevolent neutrality, kindness, sympathy, infatuation, friendliness, loyalty, compassion, admiration, devotion, adoration, respect, reverence, benevolence, up to unlimited all-bestowing and all-forgiving love. This last form of solidarity, where one is loved for his own sake, and not for various utilitarian or hedonistic reasons, where the ego of the loving person is entirely merged in that of the beloved, is the highest form of solidarity. Exactly this most intense and noblest form of love is prescribed, in regard to all human beings, by the ethical norms of the Sermon on the Mount. "Love your enemies, do good to them which hate you, bless them that curse you. . . . And as ye would that men should do to you, do ye also to them likewise" (Luke 6:27-31); "Greater love hath no man than this, that a man lay down his life for his friends" (John 15:13). Likewise antagonism has many shades and varieties, such as coldness, competition, rivalry, antipathy, dislike, repulsion, disgust, and anger, up to downright animosity and unlimited and insatiable hatred.

3. Narrow to Universal

In *extensity*, antagonism and solidarity range from the narrowest, covering only an insignificant fraction of the life and values of the parties, up to the universal, coextensive with almost all the values and the entire life of the interacting parties. The solidarity of a tourist

buying a trinket from a clerk; of a waiter in a café and his customer; of a householder and a plumber—these are examples of the narrow solidarity limited to a comparatively insignificant fragment of one's life and values. The solidarity of the members of a good family whose life is merged into a single whole, a "we" consciousness where every joy and every sorrow of one becomes the joy and sorrow of the others, where all the values—physical, material, mental, and moral—are merged together, where solidarity is coextensive with all their values and lives, is an example of the broad type of solidarity. The competition of two bidders for the same table at an auction or of two football teams for a touchdown are examples of narrow antagonism. The unquenchable hatred of two mortal enemies that hate everything the other approves and admires, all of whose values collide and conflict, is an example of the broad type of antagonism. From a theoretical as well as a practical standpoint, the narrow, casual solidarities and antagonisms are much less important than the broad and intense ones. The latter provide the most potent and intense sociocultural dramas and tragedies.

4. Interpersonal and Intergroup

From the standpoint of *the subjects of solidary and antagonistic interaction* we have (a) interpersonal and (b) intergroup solidarities and antagonisms: between states, nations, ethnic groups, races, families, castes, orders and classes, religious, economic, occupational, political, ethical, artistic, scientific, philosophical, territorial, and other groups or sociocultural systems.

5. From Standpoint of Motivation

From the point of view of motivation we have interpersonal and intergroup solidarities and antagonisms generated by "fundamental," "conditioned," "normative," and "purposeful" motivations often combined with one another (see above, Chapter 3, Section II). In the *fundamental and the conditioned motivation* the attitudes of solidarity or antagonism are neither purposively planned, nor foreseen in advance, nor do they have any preliminary motives of utility or advantage. They arise spontaneously as a result of certain character-

---

[6] See C. H. Cooley, *Social Organization* (New York, 1924), Ch. 3. E. Faris' interpretation of primary group is faithful to the real spirit of Cooley's conception. Cf. E. Faris, *The Nature of Human Nature* (New York, 1937), Ch. 4.

istics of the other party—for instance, a certain appearance, such as color or some other racial trait; or certain beliefs, such as religious convictions; or certain affiliations, such as one's nationality—or as a result of certain actions and reactions of the parties in the past or the present. The parties have no mutual sense of either solidarity or antagonism before their first meeting; but in the process of interaction, now suddenly, now gradually, such attitudes appear and finally, in a crystallized form, emerge and become solidary or antagonistic relationships. We all know of "love at first sight" or profound dislike at the first encounter. In such cases the attitudes of love or antipathy appear quite suddenly. Attitudes appear in us of their own accord, sometimes even contrary to our purposes or plans, as a result of some characteristic trait—for instance, dirty finger nails, crude table manners, an unpleasant odor, a shrill voice, the "wrong color," or a bad pronunciation. Not infrequently this trait is fairly trivial; in other cases, it is significant.

Often love and hatred do not arise at first sight, but grow gradually, accumulate, and finally crystallize into the respective attitudes of solidarity or antagonism. From that moment these attitudes become a cause of the perpetuation of the respective forms of interaction. Many persons as well as many nations and groups are in solidary or antagonistic relationship with other persons and groups largely because of past experience, with the attitude thus developed. In some cases this is the only reason for their solidarities and antagonisms, possessing the parties contrary to their purposes and their utilitarian advantages. The parties hate one another because they cannot help it. A party loves the other party even though the love may be his perdition. A nation dislikes another nation because of the animosity aroused in past experience. Not infrequently the individuals and groups who are the victims of this fundamental motivation and of conditioned motivation are well aware of the blind character of their sympathy or hatred; of its highly irrational and harmful influence; of its unworthiness and indecency. Sometimes they even try to fight it through this or that purposive or normative motivation—considerations of profit and advantage, commands of law and ethical norms, and so on. And yet they fail in that endeavor as frequently as they succeed. Such experiences show clearly the role of the fundamental and the conditioned motivation in generating solidarities and antagonisms. These occupy a very large place among the total solidarities and antagonisms of every person or group. A large part of interstate, international, interracial, interethnic, interreligious, and interpolitical group antagonisms are due to conditioned or fundamental motivation.[7] This is one of the chief reasons why it is so difficult to eradicate them; why most utilitarian, rational, "enlightened" propaganda, preaching, and teaching have been so ineffective. In spite of the teaching of Christianity or Buddhism that all men are the children of God, in spite of all the declarations of the equality of man, in spite of all the economic and other disadvantages of intergroup tensions, nevertheless interracial, interethnic, international, inter-

---

[7] What F. Tönnies calls "the immediate and instinctive sympathy and antipathy," the "natural volitions" (*Wesenwille*), "the simple, emotional (impulsive) and therefore irrational volition and action," in contrast to the "rational volition and action in which the means are arranged" in accordance with the end, is a vague description of what we call conditioned and fundamental motivations, "because of." Tönnies's description of how the *Gemeinschaft* originated through this "natural volition" or, as he sometimes says, through "instinctive" sympathy, is a somewhat unprecise description of how the solidary and antagonistic attitudes emerge through conditioned and fundamental motivation. His "rational volition" and his description of how through this volition the *Gesellschaft* emerges is close to what is called in this work the purposive motivation. See F. Tönnies, *Fundamental*

Concepts of Sociology, quoted, pp. 5, 14 ff., 37 ff. Likewise Max Scheler's "emotional contagion," "involuntary intuition," and co-living (*Miterleben*) through which, in his opinion, arise two forms of solidarity (*Masse* and *Lebensgemeinschaft*), are again motivations similar to our "conditioned and fundamental motivations" (though less precisely described); while his contractual motivation that generates his *Gesellschaft's* type of solidarity is but another term for the purposive motivation. Furthermore, C. H. Cooley's analysis of how the primary groups arise in the process of "intimate association" and spontaneous interchange of ideas, sentiments, and experiences runs along lines very similar to our fundamental and conditioned motivations. See Max Scheler, *Das Wesen und die Formen der Sympathie*, and his *Der Formalismus in der Ethik*; C. H. Cooley, *op. cit.*, Chps. 3-4.

religious, interoccupational, and other antagonisms and tensions are still as much in evidence as ever.

Other antagonisms and solidarities are generated by *purposive* considerations of utility and disutility, of advantage or disadvantage, of pleasure and pain. The variety and extent of these motivated antagonisms and solidarities are large. They are present in interpersonal and intergroup interactions. The attitudes of the interacting parties are premeditated and conform to the schema of the means and the end. Persons or groups who start a business relationship with a clear purpose to derive from it a profit; persons who meet to enjoy mutual kisses and embraces; a criminal gang murdering its victim in order to get his money; an employee flattering his boss to obtain promotion; a scholar praising another scholar in order to be praised by him—such relationships are examples of purposively motivated solidarities and antagonisms. In the final analysis they are a variety of motivation for the sake of this or that *utility or hedonistic satisfaction* expected to be derived from the interacting party. The party here is not an end in himself but merely a means of extracting (one-sidedly or mutually) some utilitarian advantage or sensory pleasure. He has value only so far as he can serve this utilitarian or hedonistic purpose.

Finally, many antagonisms and solidarities have a *self-sufficient, normative motivation, legal and ethical.* We have solidary or antagonistic relationships with those for whom the norms prescribe a solidary or antagonistic attitude. We are antagonistic toward an enemy, criminals, unbelievers, an exploiting or inferior race, a barbaric nation, and so on. But we are solidary with all democratic nations, peace-loving people, heroes, honest and decent persons, law-abiding individuals and groups—in brief, with all those to whom our law and ethical convictions dictate friendly terms. The solidarities and antagonisms motivated normatively are very numerous. They appear and develop in the conduct of a person or of a group with the inculcation of the respective ethical and legal norms. J. Piaget and others have shown that up to three or four years of

age a child is devoid of legal and ethical norms. After that, one-sidedly imposed norms are implanted in the child; eventually they become autonomous, inner legal and ethical convictions motivating his normative actions, solidarities, and antagonisms.[8] If the norms change, as they often do, the respective normative antagonisms and solidarities also change.[9]

Solidarities and antagonisms generated by *similarities and dissimilarities* of interacting parties have been classified as (a) mechanical solidarity, based on the similarities of the sentiments and beliefs of the parties (E. Durkheim and many others), and (b) organic solidarity, due to the division of labor and the dissimilarities of the parties, each party needing the supplementation and cooperation of the other parties. The first form of solidarity is supposed to be illustrated by primitive and other groups (like the army) with little division of labor and with similar mores, convictions, beliefs, and sentiments on the part of the individual members. The second form of solidarity is assumed to be illustrated by complex societies with a well-developed division of labor and with dissimilar sentiments, beliefs, convictions, and mores on the part of the members, each of whom needs the cooperation of the other members.[10] There are many variations of this theory of classification.

6. According to Meanings or Values

We can distinguish (a) total or encyclopedic antagonisms and solidarities, in which all the values of the parties clash or agree, and (b) special antagonisms and solidarities, including the biosocial (involving the values of life, health, and survival and those of sex, age, and race), economic, political, linguistic, religious, scientific, philosophical, artistic, and ethico-juridical, or such a combination of these as the values of prestige, authority, fame, and leadership. While total antagonism or solidarity is a purely theoretical case, rarely, if ever, found in actual interaction, the special forms are very numerous, more or less narrow, and often combined into clusters of antagonisms and solidarities.

---

[8] J. Piaget, *The Moral Judgment of the Child.*
[9] This shows again the inadequacy of any theory that attempts to reduce the motivation of soli-

darities and antagonisms to a purposive motivation of means and end.
[10] See E. Durkheim, *On the Division of Labor* (New York, 1933).

The above classes represent practically all the important forms of solidary and antagonistic interactions. In a work of general sociology they need no further analysis. However, there remain several important problems that require further study. (1) Can these numerous forms of antagonism and solidarity—somewhat mechanically assigned to the above classes—be reduced to a few fundamental types that are actually embodied in the empirical social world and that constitute the main forms of the combined antagonistic-solidary relationships? (2) What role do similarity and dissimilarity of the parties play in the generation of solidarity and antagonism? Are there special forms of solidarity based upon similarity and dissimilarity? (3) What are the main factors that generate solidarities and antagonisms of the interacting parties? An elucidation of these questions is highly important theoretically as well as practically. Let us pass to such an inquiry.

IV. Familistic, Mixed (Contractual), and Compulsory Types of Interaction

Chemical elements exist in the chemical universe not only in an isolated form but also in combination with other elements as molecules, or constituents of compounds. Similarly, in actual social life solidary and antagonistic relationships appear not only in pure forms but also in various combinations of these forms. As in chemistry, such combinations are numerous. Of these combined types three are particularly important. They are met in almost any human society past and present, primitive and modern, oriental and occidental. These forms are *familistic* (predominantly solidary); *mixed* (partly solidary, partly antagonistic), of which the *contractual* relationships are especially typical; *compulsory* (pre-eminently antagonistic). Let us look more closely at each of these forms.

1. Familistic Type

Let us select from the above varieties of solidary-antagonistic interaction the following: (a) predominantly solidary; (b) total or broad in extensity; (c) of high intensity; (d) durable; (e) direct; (f) mutual, or two-sided; (g) marked by the fundamental, normative, and purposive types of motivation, all working harmoniously with one another; (h) based upon a deep sense of the sociocultural oneness of the parties; (i) possessing leadership or government that is natural and spontaneous and truly paternalistic, with a leader who is merely a *primus inter pares*. A combination of these nine forms makes up the familistic system of interaction, or social relationship. Such

is its "chemical" formula. Upon this basis we can depict its living physiognomy.

Concrete examples are given by the relationships between a loving mother and her baby; between the mutually devoted members of the family; and between true friends, in the Aristotelian sense of real friendship.[11] In these systems of interaction almost the whole circle of life activities of the parties is involved in the process of interaction, and certainly all their important values. Their whole lives are intermingled and organically united into one "we." There is almost none of the "It does not concern me" or "Mind your own affairs" attitude. On the contrary, what concerns one party concerns the others—the joys and sorrows, successes and failures of one party are shared by the others and elicit their concurrence, aid, and sympathy. The solidarity of the parties is intense and as close as the interdependence of various parts of an organism. Like these parts the subjects of the familistic interaction may be very different in hundreds of overt characteristics: in age and sex, health and vigor, stature, pigmentation, intelligence, temperament, occupation, nationality, race, and so on. And yet they are all similar in their mutual attachment, in their strong sense of interdependence, and ordinarily in their main sociocultural values and main norms of conduct.

Their lives are interfused to such an extent

---

[11] See Aristotle, *The Nicomachean Ethics*, Bks. VIII and IX, in Everyman's Library edition, pp. 201-216 particularly.

that the parties seek one another, need one another, and help one another spontaneously (through the fundamental and normative motivations), regardless of any utilitarian or hedonistic considerations. A loving mother cares for her sick and feeble-minded baby even more than for a healthy baby, in spite of the fact that such care of a defective baby is not a source of pleasure or profit. Utilitarian, purposeful motivation is sometimes present in these relationships; but not infrequently it is absent, and sometimes such relationships obtain in spite of and contrary to purposive, utilitarian ends. Members of a family cherish and help their "black sheep" even though from a purely utilitarian standpoint they know they should not; a hopeless suitor loves his sweetheart even though he derives from his love not pleasure but sorrow and distress. Such an attachment is not due to any contract, covenant, or calculation of pleasure and pain, advantage and disadvantage. A devoted mother passes a sleepless night with her child not because of an implicit or explicit contract between her and the child or between herself and society. Her action is the result of a spontaneous organic impulse. Much the same is true of real friends. If one befriends another on the basis of a mere contract, or from motives of profit or pleasure, he is a pseudo-friend. A real friend, as Aristotle rightly observes, is "one who . . . does what is good (or what he believes to be good) for another for that other's sake, and one wishes his friend to . . . live for that friend's own sake,"[12] and not because the friend gives him pleasure or is useful to him. Or, as Cicero puts it, in "that genuine and perfect friendship," the friends "are so intimately one that no advantage can attend either which does not equally communicate itself to

both; they are strong in the strength, rich in the opulence, and powerful in the power of each other. They can scarcely, indeed, be considered in any respects as separate individuals, and wherever the one appears the other is virtually present."[13]

In other words, in such a relationship there is spontaneous internal unity between the individuals, a complete merging of their selves in a single "we." As already observed, such a relationship yields, as a by-product, pleasure and utility; but it entails also sorrow and sacrifice. However, the sacrifice is regarded not as a disadvantage or as the personal loss of some value, but as a privilege freely and gladly bestowed.[14]

The normative motivation, cooperating with the fundamental motivation in generating the familistic relationship, functions here not only as law-norms but especially as an unlimited ethical motivation, free from legal and contractual limits, with their "so much—no more and no less." Legal and contractual limits are as much out of place in these relationships as they would be in the interrelationships between various organs of the same body where each organ was concerned only with itself and served the others only "so much—no more and no less."

As a consequence no detailed *external* delineation of the rights and duties, of "how much" and "under which circumstances," and other specifications and limitations of the law-norms imposed upon the parties by an external authority is necessary for that kind of relationship. They become superfluous in a truly familistic interaction or group, where there is no formal *domination and subordination*, no master and servant, no arbitrary government

---

[12] Aristotle, *The Nicomachean Ethics*, Bk. IX, 1166a. See generally his analysis of the three fundamental forms of friendship: the real friendship, where the motive is the friendship itself as an absolute end; the pseudo-friendships where the motive is either pleasure or utility rendered by the partners. The real friendship is the first form only. The other two are pseudo-friendships. "They whose motive is utility have no friendship for one another really, but only in so far as some good arises to them from one another. And they whose motive is pleasure are in like case"; . . . they love the friend "not in so far as the friend beloved *is* but in so far as he is useful or pleasurable. . . .

Such friendships are of course very liable to dissolution . . . when they are no longer pleasurable. It is the nature of utility not to be permanent but constantly varying: so, of course, when the motive which made them friends is vanished, the friendship likewise dissolves: since it existed only relatively to those circumstances." The same is true of pleasure as the motive of friendship. *Ibid.*, Bk. VIII, 1156a, pp. 185-186, in the mentioned edition.

[13] Cicero "*On Friendship*," p. 179, in Everyman's Library Edition.

[14] See an enlightening analysis of sacrifice in E. Dupréel, "Le renoncement" in *Archives de la Société Belge de Philosophie*, II (1930), fascicule No. 2.

and suppressed subjects. Its place is taken either by the paternalistic leadership of a good father in relation to a child or by a brotherly or comradely fellowship,[15] with the leader as a servant of the others. This leadership government tends to approach the kind of leadership that, in contrast to the dominion and domination of princes, was preached by Jesus: "Whosoever will be great among you, let him be your servant" (Matthew 20:26-27). "If any man desire to be first, the same shall be last of all, and servant of all" (Mark 9:35). In this social service the leader is the *primus inter pares.* Such a leadership is ordinarily informal, without meticulously circumscribed rights and duties. First and foremost, it is geniuely devoted to the needs of the group or of the interacting members.

The next trait of these relationships is the coexistence of *internal freedom of the individuals with the external appearance of its limitation.* Observed outwardly, from a behavioristic standpoint, the familistic relationship may often appear as a severe limitation of the freedom of the parties. From the standpoint of a frivolous or superficial observer, the fact that a mother stays with her children instead of going out or giving parties, passes many a sleepless night instead of comfortably resting, spends her money buying necessities for her children instead of purchasing a new dress for herself; "slaves" for them and sacrifices not only pleasures but even her health instead of freely enjoying her own life—for such an observer all this is "frightful slavery," a drastic limitation of her freedom. Likewise, when a loving father inflicts some "pedagogical" punishment upon a child (spanks him, puts him to bed, etc.), prohibits him from doing various things, deprives him of this or that pleasure (for instance, eating too much candy), tries to impose upon him a certain discipline, seeks to inculcate in him various good habits, and all this for the child's own good and perhaps at the expense of pain to himself—such actions

again appear, from the standpoint of a superficial behaviorist, a limitation of the freedom of the children. And so in other familistic relationships. However, when one puts himself in the position of the mother or father, most of these "limitations of freedom" appear in a different light. The mother and father do not feel that "slaving" for their children is a limitation of their freedom; on the contrary, they are glad to do it and prefer it to the freedom of the "flapper." Even most children do not feel the punishment imposed upon them by their parents as something inimical, intended to injure or hurt them. On the contrary, they often realize that it was motivated by affection, very quickly forget it, and in no way hold a resentful attitude towards their parents because they are punished or limited in the realization of their desires. The same is to be said of the relationship of friends and other familistic cases. One may reprimand his friend most severely; and yet much a criticism is absolutely different from a reprimand by an outsider or by a "contractual" partner. In brief, the familistic relationship permits us to reconcile duty and discipline with freedom, sacrifice with liberty, and external inhibition of the actions of the members with their internal sense of freedom.[16]

In this respect again the familistic relationship differs greatly from compulsory as well as contractual bonds. In compulsory bonds there is no freedom for the subjugated party; in the mixed contractual relationship, rarely and within much more narrow limits can it be reconciled with discipline, sacrifice, order, "common interests," and the like.

The familistic relationship *eliminates or reduces to the minimum the feeling of being a stranger or outsider among its members.* It is the relationship in which the whole life of each member in all its important aspects and values tends to be merged into a warm and hearty collective "we." To use Modestine's definition of marriage, it is the *consortium omnis vitae,*

---

[15] Cf. F. Tönnies, *Fundamental Concepts of Sociology,* pp. 21-22.

[16] Here Cooley's observation is quite accurate. In the primary relationships (which, as mentioned, are somewhat similar to our familistic relationships), Cooley says, "it is not supposed that the unity of the primary group is one of mere harmony

and love." . . . It admits "self-assertion and various passions; but these passions are socialized by sympathy, and come under the discipline of a common spirit. The individual will be ambitious, but the chief object of his ambition will be some desired place in the thought of the others, and he will feel allegiance to common standards of service." C. H. Cooley, *op. cit.,* pp. 24 ff.

divini et humani juris communicatio. All aspects and spheres of life of the members are reduced to oneness, being familiar and understandable to all the members. Nothing "private" tends to exist in the extreme type of the familistic relationship. The ideal familistic relationship is the opposite pole to the stranger, the outsider, and the private as a sociological category.[17] Such is the ideal form of the familistic interaction or relationship. In actual social life it has many gradations and degrees of purity, beginning with the almost pure form (outlined here), passing through less and less pure forms—with less intensity and extensity of solidarity, with a less integrated "we," a more pronounced ego of the parties, and marked utilitarian and hedonistic motivations —until we come to such a diluted form that it imperceptibly merges with the mixed (contractual form) of interaction.

The analyzed form is styled "familistic" because most often and in the purest form it is met in the relationship between the members of a good and harmonious family.[18] In a more diluted form it exists, of course, in many non-familistic groups: between devoted friends, between the members of a religious organization, even between the members of the state, a regiment, a college, and many other groups. On the other hand, the term "familistic" must not lead to the conclusion that all or even the majority of the social relationships among members of the family are familistic, especially in application to the modern family, where, besides the familistic, the mixed contractual form constitutes a considerable part of its total system of interactions.

2. The Mixed (Contractual) Type[19]

Solidarity is limited in its *extensity*. It covers only a few, often very narrow, values in the interaction of the parties and never their whole life or even its greater part. It may concern economic, or political, or other specific values, always limited, as in the interrelations of an employer and his employees, a householder and a plumber, a landlord and a tenant. Beyond this limited sector of solidarity the other sectors of their interrelationship may be and often are antagonistic or, at best, neutral. The limited sector of their solidarity tends always to be specified and circumscribed by the parties, with the proviso "so much— no more and no less." This limitation takes place in advance in the contractual variety of relationships, at the moment of the conclusion of the contract. In other cases it may grow gradually, but it is always given implicitly or explicitly in the mixed form. *The intensity of the solidarity* in the narrow sector may be high or low, depending upon the values involved and the attitude of the parties. Even intense solidarity in this sector does not preclude antagonisms in other sectors of their

---

[17] See M. M. Wood, *The Stranger*, Chps. 1, 2, *passim.* The author sums up the literature on the stranger, grasps the essence of the problem, and gives a fairly thoughtful analysis of it. Unfortunately, it is not pushed deep and far enough by the author, or by Simmel and several others who have studied it.

[18] The familistic relationship in the above sense is similar to the general nature of the five fundamental relationships of Confucius, whose entire social and political system is built upon this principle, also to the concept of real friendship of Aristotle and Cicero. In more recent times, as will be shown further, the type of social relationship in the patriarchal family analyzed by Le Play, the type of the *Gemeinschaft* relationship of F. Tönnies, Makarewicz, B. Kistiakowsky, Max Scheler and (partly) of G. Richard, is also near to—though far from being identical with—the familistic relationship in the above sense. See besides the quoted works of Aristotle and Cicero, the *Hsiao King* and *The Li Ki*, among the texts of Confucianism, in the *Sacred Books of the East*, Vols. III, XXVII;

F. Tönnies, *Gemeinschaft und Gesellschaft* (Eng. tr. by C. P. Loomis), *Fundamental Concepts of Sociology* (New York, 1940); H. Makarewicz, *Einführung in die Philosophie des Strafrechts*, (Stuttgart, 1906), pp. 36 ff.; B. Kistiakowsky, *Gesellschaft und Einzelwesen* (Berlin, 1899); G. Richard, *La sociologie générale et les lois sociologiques* (Paris, 1912); Le Play's works; Sorokin, *Theories*, Ch. 2; C. Zimmerman and M. Frampton, *Family and Society* (New York, 1935).

[19] Hans Speier, in his discerning analysis of this type of relationship, states that "since the nature of what Professor Sorokin calls "the contractual relationship" is not "contract," it must be defined in entirely different terms, *ASR*, Vol. II (1937), p. 926. He is right in that it is a mixed intermediary form where a contract enters mainly in the way of its origin. If, however, the term is used, as a subterm, the reason is that most of the contractual relations exhibit exactly the traits of the mixed form. Hence the advisability of a subsidiary use of the term for denoting a large subclass of the mixed type.

relationships. In addition, as we shall see, even intense solidarity is, as a rule, of a strictly utilitarian or hedonistic nature, never attaining the sublime heights of the pure familistic solidarity.

The duration of the solidarity is ordinarily limited and specified, especially in the contractual variety of these relationships. *Solidarity is usually mutual,* but sometimes, as in a pseudo-contractual relationship, it is one-sided, giving an advantage to one party and entailing a disadvantage, and therefore dissatisfaction, for the other party. In almost every contractual variety of mixed relationship the main motivation of solidarity is of the *purposive, implicitly egoistic, utilitarian type, often supplemented and moderated by the legal normative motivation.* It may be *direct or indirect.* The *sense of sociocultural oneness* of the parties is usually lacking. The egos of the parties remain unmerged in any real "we," even in the solidary sector. In other sectors their egos are either "strangers" or even inimical to one another. *Leadership turns into a formal government, into a formal domination and subordination with or without genuine social service.* These elements make up the "chemical formula" of the mixed form of interaction, with its many varieties.

a. *Benevolent Neutrality.* The mildest variety of the mixed type of interaction is present where the parties hold an attitude of slightly benevolent neutrality or ungrudging tolerance with respect to some of the other party's aspirations and activities, paralleled by a slightly hostile and somewhat grudging toleration vis-à-vis its other aspirations and activities. Here both solidarity and antagonism are present in their mildest forms, barely distinguishable from mutual indifference. When *A* and *B* view a hobby of the other with a mild sense of amusement, while each regards another hobby as a nuisance, this furnishes an example of the least pronounced form of the mixed relationship. When, in World War II, some of the nations, like Turkey, exhibited benevolent neutrality now toward the Allies, now toward Germany, their relationships to the Allies, and to Germany, were of this mixed type.

b. *Passive Resistance-Reluctant Cooperation.* A somewhat more pronounced variety of the mixed relationship is furnished by inter-actions where passive resistance of one party to some of the values and activities of the other is paralleled by reluctant cooperation of an egotistic, utilitarian type in regard to its other values and activities. When American and European capitalists cooperated with the Communist Soviet government in business, both parties remained passively inimical in regard to other activities and values. When many Hindus, following Mahatma Gandhi, passively resist British rule in India, while reluctantly cooperating with the British in many other fields, we have another illustration of this variety of mixed relationships.

c. *Competitive Cooperation.* It is even more conspicuous in various interactions of competition and rivalry combined with cooperation in the sense of "fair play." An alliance of otherwise antagonistic individuals or nations against a common enemy is another species of the mixed form. So far as fighting the common enemy (in court, on a battlefield, or in political actions) is concerned, they are solidary; otherwise they are mutually distrustful, often antagonistic, and liable to double-cross one another as soon as the common enemy is defeated. The history of wars is full of such instances. Others are furnished by the everyday alliances and double-crossings of various individuals and groups. Competition and rivalry in business, love, politics, science, the fine arts, sports, or court litigation is always antagonistic in nature. In some cases it assumes the form of "cutthroat" competition. However, it is often followed by the solidarity of the parties in other fields—in obeying the rules of fair play, in being a "good sport," sometimes in actually helping the defeated party. A conspicuous variety of this type is found in the political interactions of two parties competing for the election of members, and in the "loyal opposition" of the minority party to the majority government in the British Parliament. In a different form it is common in the silent or noisy rivalry in science, the arts, and other fields where the competition is carried on under fair and just conditions and where the parties remain "good fellows" in other relationships. A scientific or literary or art critic denouncing the defects of a given work and at the same time recognizing its merits often stands in this mixed relationship with the author.

d. *Simultaneous Love and Hate.* Finally, the most conspicuous case is supplied by those relationships where the parties profoundly hate one another with reference to certain characteristics and actions, and at the same time respect and admire one another with regard to other characteristics and values. Turbulent lovers or a husband and wife, now loving and now hating each other, and the leaders of revolutionary factions (like those depicted by Victor Hugo in his *1793*) who do their best to exterminate their opponents but at the same time have profound respect for their courage and ability, are concrete cases of this variety. Even such intense group antagonisms as war are mitigated by some elements of solidarity, such as respecting the enemy for his courage and valor, helping prisoners through the Red Cross and other organizations, or showing mercy to the wounded.

We have seen the most important varieties of the mixed interaction. On the basis of its "chemical formula" and the varieties sketched we can now give a living portrait of this relationship, especially of its most common contractual variety. I call it "contractual" because it is most frequently found in various economic and political contractual interactions.

e. *Characteristics of the Contractual Group.* The solidarity of mixed interaction even within the limited narrow sector is always *egoistic,* a party entering into the contract does so for his own sake, uniting with the other party only so far as this provides him with an advantage (profit, pleasure, or service). He tends to get from the other party "as much as possible for as little as possible." In this sense a bargaining and calculated solidarity has been achieved; the other party is sought not for his own sake but mainly as an agency able to render some service, enjoyment, utility, or profit.[20] Outside of the limited sector of the contractual interaction the *parties remain either total strangers to one another in private life, or even inimical*

to one another. The contractual formula of the mixed form is well known. "I agree to do so and so for you, and you agree to do so and so for me. If you do not discharge your obligation, I am freed from mine; besides, you will have to bear the unpleasant consequences of breaking the contract." The parties may agree according to the classic Roman formula: *"Do ut des; facio ut facias; do ut facias; facio ut des"* ("I give to be given," "serve to be served," "give to be served," "serve to be given"). Here the parties do not merge into a single "we," but each feels and acts as an independent party, primarily concerned with his own interests. In the relationships of buying and selling, employing and rendering services, contractual governing and obeying, and thousands of other contractual relationships, the real motive for entering into the contract is a kind of utility or pleasure derived or expected from such an association by the contracting parties. In this sense the contractual group is more nominalistic and singularistic than the familistic group. The free sacrifice of individual interests to the other party or to the collective "we" is here replaced by the bond of mutual bargaining.

As a result of such egoism the *mixed (contractual) relationships cannot be unlimited or undefined. Therefore the solidarity of the mixed form is, as a rule, limited and tends to be coldly legalistic.* As each party is pursuing its own interests, there cannot be, as a rule, any assurance that one party will not double-cross the other if their convenant is not specific and definitely agreed upon. Hence a written contract, witnesses, and a notary to certify its authenticity are customary in such an agreement. Since definite distrust of the good faith of the other party is inherent in it, experts or experienced lawyers are hired to make the agreement clear and to leave no loophole through which the interests of a given party may be prejudiced by the other. Such a relationship is a lawyer's paradise, his "bread and butter," whereas familistic relationships do not need his services, or those of a public notary or even an official judge. All this means that by their very nature the mixed (contractual) relationships are limited and definitely measured: "so much—no more and no less." "Fifteen dollars a week for your honest work,

---

[20] It is the solidarity which Aristotle styles as not a real friendship but a pseudo-friendship, motivated by the intention of getting from the other party either pleasure or utility. See his *Nicomachean Ethics*, quoted.

eight hours a day." "Fifteen cents for a package of Lucky Strikes." This proviso, "exactly so much—no more and no less," appears in any contractual relationship, such as that of Shylock and the Merchant of Venice, state constitutions, covenants between rulers and the ruled, international treaties, or the covenant between "Jehovah and His people." The rights, duties, functions, services, remuneration, etc. of the contracting parties are ordinarily specified as fully as possible, with all the appropriate reservations, showing definitely what each party has the right to claim from the other and what are its own obligations. Nevertheless, breaches of the agreement and double-crossing of the other party are not infrequent, indeed, in contemporary international relationships they have become the rule rather than the exception.

The solidarity here is strictly formal and legalistic and does not go beyond the norms of the official law. And the parties feel quite virtuous, like the Pharisee of the Gospel, if they conform to the legal rule, no matter how unfair, from a higher standpoint, their adherence to the contract may be to the other party. The insistence of the Merchant of Venice on the stipulated "pound of flesh"—legally agreed upon—is an illustration of this "formal and legalistic solidarity." Bank foreclosures of a farm mortgage, the discharge of employees, the evicting of tenants for nonpayment of rent —all of these actions are legal. And the banks, the employers, and the landlords often have no ethical scruples in these respects; they are confident that they are acting legally and irreproachably. Yet from a higher ethical standpoint such Scrooges may sometimes be utterly unethical. Their insistence on their contractual rights may be a case of *summum jus, summa injuria.*

The members of the contractual group *always remain to a considerable degree mutual strangers and outsiders.* They are "fused" and bound together only in the specific respect which is covered by the sector of egoistic solidarity. In all other respects they do not concern one another, do not know one another, and do not want to be known. One calls in a plumber, carpenter, or painter, and agrees about the job to be done and the price to be paid for it. So far the parties cease to be complete strangers; but in relation to all other values and activities they continue to be strangers, frequently antagonists. Only a small segment of the personality of one contractual party is "fused" with that of the others. All the other aspects remain "private" for each member, and normally it is regarded in such a group as bad taste to try to violate this privacy and to ask the others to make their lives a *consortium omnis vitae.* Each member remains to other members a kind of "closed monad" (to quote Leibniz) in all respects except as regards the little "window" unshuttered by the agreement.

In accordance with the nature of the contract, the amount and the degree of mutual fusion may fluctuate. In the marital relations of a modern couple the husband and wife cannot fail to learn a great deal about one another, their separate personalities are interfused to a considerable degree, and privacy of life and the status of the stranger are greatly reduced. Conversely, in sales relations or in employer-employee contractual unions the parties interact very superficially and only in one very narrow respect. They remain strangers in virtually every aspect of their personalities. Their shortlived fusion concerns only the exchange of money, goods, and services. Pure contractualism and a certain degree of strangeness, with potential antagonism, are inseparable. If the members of the contractual association cease to be strangers, this means that the contractual relationship has been transformed into a familistic relationship.

It follows not only that, as compared with the familistic relationships, the contractual relationships bind the parties by fewer common values (namely, those which constitute the contract), but that these bonds of community of interests, as a rule, are comparatively shortlived. Most contracts have a definite time limit—for a day, a week, a month, a year, and so on. A large percentage of contracts are of short duration. Very few are for life, like the marriage contract; and such contracts are, rather, pseudo-contracts, essentially familistic in their nature. As soon as the time span of the contract elapses, or its conditions are fulfilled, the bond of solidarity between the parties ends. Their superficial and transitory "fusion" disappears, unless the contractual relationship is transformed into a familistic one during the period of the contract. They become again mutual strangers or even antagonists.

This mixed interaction is one of *formal domination and subordination,* in contradistinction to familistic leadership. So far as there is implicit or explicit pressure and coercion, so long as the rights and duties of each party are meticulously defined, and so far as the parties remain egocentric, the mixed group or system of interaction exhibits clearly a formal government which is superior to the governed, with its hierarchy of ranks, authorities, and precedences; which bases its authority not so much on social service as on legal, stipulated rights and privileges; and which suggests the words of Jesus: "The princes . . . exercise dominion over them, and they that are great exercise authority upon them" (Matthew 20:25). It may or may not render real social service, but instead of being a paternalistic servant it exercises governmental authority "by the grace of God," through a constitution, or through sheer physical force.

Finally, it follows that the *contractual relationship is inseparable from a high degree of freedom of each party from the other.* Since to enter or not to enter into the contract (in real contractual relationships, not in pseudo-contractual relationships under duress, which are but a variety of compulsory relationships) depends upon the choice of an individual, and since the conditions depend upon him also, he is largely free, at least outwardly. And since in real contracts his pre-contractual position is such that he can afford to choose, the individual in a contractual group is indeed given a large opportunity for the display of his singularistic freedom. In contrast to the freedom of the familistic type, the freedom of an individual here manifests itself clearly in the form of explicit choice: in the form of his recognized right to enter or not to enter into the contractual alliance; to adhere to it or to withdraw from it; to approve or disapprove various values and groups—in a word, to enjoy the liberties and inalienable rights of an individual. In the familistic relationship the interests of individual freedom and of the group rarely conflict; they ordinarily coincide, in response to the conviction that "what is good for the group is good for me," or that "what

makes the group free makes me free also." In contractual relationships such a coincidence is not so frequent. Here the individual or groups declares: "What is good for me must be good for the group or the other groups; if not, so much the worse for the others. At best I can sacrifice some of my inalienable rights if the others are willing to do the same, and if in that way the rest of my freedom can be secured and guaranteed. Otherwise it is my right and duty to fight any unjustifiable tyranny of society and other groups." All this is fundamentally different from the freedom of the familistic relationship.

Again, in various forms and proportions, *contractual relationships compose a considerable part of the network of social relationships of many different groups, comprising employers and employees, buyers and sellers, owners and tenants, as well as religious, political, state, educational, artistic, scientific, and even family groups and associations.* They have characterized also the relationships of nations and social classes and other intergroup relationships.

These are the essential traits of the mixed (contractual) type of social interaction.[21]

3. The Compulsory Type

The basic characteristic of the compulsory type is its overwhelmingly *antagonistic* nature. It may be very *intense,* animated by an unquenchable hatred, seeking the extermination of the enemy and intent on desecrating his memory; or it may be less intense, striving to inflict upon the opponent merely some damage, fine, discomfort, or shame. As in the case of the familistic relationship, its *extensity* may be all-embracing and total, one party trying to destroy all the values of the adversary, disapproving everything he has and does; or it may be circumscribed and limited in extensity, being confined to a sector of interacting activities, and in other sectors remaining wholly neutral. It may be *one-sided or mutual, direct or indirect, durable or temporary.* It may be rooted in the *fundamental, the normative, or the purposive type of motivation* or in a combination of all three. Ordinarily the intensive and exten-

[21] See other details in G. Davy, *La Foi jurée. Etude sociologique du problème du contrat. La Formation du lien contractual* (Paris, 1922).

sive types of compulsory relationships are jointly motivated by two or more of these factors acting in agreement with one another. A natural dislike caused by the fundamental motivation cooperates with the normative motivation, imposing the duty to hate, to coerce, to punish, or to defeat the adversary, and with the utilitarian motive of deriving profit and advantage from the ruthless compulsion of the adversary to obey the orders of the dominant party, to work for him, and so on. *The compulsory form of government is overtly despotic, based upon brute force supplemented by fraud. As a rule it serves only the interests of the dominant faction, at the expense of the oppressed.*

When one of the interacting parties imposes upon the other certain forms of conduct, certain duties and functions, contrary to the desire and inclination of that party, and not for the other party's welfare but in its own interest, and when it relies exclusively upon the application of physical and psychophysical coercion, the interrelation is compulsory in character. The bond which unites the parties and prevents a rupture is precisely this factor of coercion. It may assume various forms, from purely physical compulsion (including material penalties and even torture) to the more complex psychosocial type of coercion, such as destroying the other party's values, depriving it of necessities (like food, shelter, or freedom of movement), and threatening to inflict injury upon persons or groups dear to the party in question.

In brief, compulsion or coercion may assume many different forms, quantitatively as well as qualitatively. Wherever it occurs, and especially when it is applied merely in the interest of the stronger party, the relationship becomes in part or in whole compulsory. The relationships of a hated master and an inhumanly treated slave or serf, of an executioner and his victim, of a cruel conqueror and the conquered, of a despotic government and its subjects, of an extortionist and his victim, of a ravisher and the ravished, of a kidnaper and the kidnaped, etc., are clearly compulsory, though not always exclusively so, since the relationships of a master and slave, of the lord of a manor and the villeins, and so on have often

been partly familistic and partly even contractual.

A specific case is afforded by *the pseudo-familistic and pseudo-contractual relationships.* By "pseudo-familistic" is meant a relationship where the stronger party outwardly assumes the familistic attitude, claiming that "this is done with fatherly feelings," "for your own good," and the like, whereas actually the values and welfare of the weaker party are not considered, and the compulsion imposed fails to serve its welfare in any way. By "pseudo-contractual" is meant a relationship where the weaker party enters into the contract seemingly of his own accord, but actually under duress, having no choice, so that the "free agreement" is but a travesty on a truly free decision. A person dying of starvation and suffering from the lack of other necessities is often forced to make such a contract; he accepts a job for a grossly inadequate remuneration, performs some service which under normal conditions he or she would not have thought of rendering—for instance, becoming a mistress, a hired murderer, and the like. All such relationships assumed under duress are merely disguised forms of compulsory relationships. This is important to keep in mind, because many compulsory relationships, especially in recent times, have manifested themselves in this pseudocontractual form, just as many such relationships in medieval and other past societies tended to assume the pseudofamilistic forms.

Compulsory interaction always entails the despotic, tyrannical, dictatorial domination of the oppressed party. The dominant party serves only its own interests, at the expense of the subjugated and subordinated party. Its domination is based mainly, often exclusively, upon physical force (supplemented by fraud), now screened by some high-sounding ideology, now naked in its brutality. It may outwardly assume monarchical, republican, timocratic, aristocratic, oligarchic, or even democratic forms; but in spite of these appearances it is always essentially tyranny, dictatorship, and autocracy.

Furthermore, the compulsory relationship *does not give any freedom to the coerced party, while to the coercing party it gives the vicious freedom* of doing what it pleases.

In the pure compulsory relationship the parties remain to one another *total strangers*, even negative values. A slave to a cruel master may be a mere instrument—something even less human than his cattle—or, at best, a species of animal. Conversely, the coercing party is perceived not as a human personality, capable of understanding, but merely as an instrument of oppression, inhuman and perverse. There is no bridge of real understanding between the parties as human beings and personalities. The inner world of each is closed to the other; often there is not even a desire to enter it. This explains why in such relationships there are always certain ideologies, especially on the part of the oppressor, to the effect that the parties are fundamentally different in nature. Such ideologies embrace the notions of pure and impure races, master and slave races, chosen peoples and gentiles, bearers of culture and hopelessly backward races, caste and outcaste, bourgeois and proletarian, saintliness and sinfulness, and the like. It explains also why the masters or conquerors often display unbelievable cruelty toward the coerced, sometimes styling them "dogs"[22] and very often treating them worse than dogs; why in slave insurrections the oppressed frequently delight in killing or torturing their masters; why the other party tends always to be regarded in the worst possible light. Remaining total strangers, the parties speak different languages and can rarely understand each other's real personality.

In intergroup interactions the most sharply accentuated form of compulsory relationship is found in *international and civil wars, revolutions, riots, and revolts* aimed at the extermination of the enemy and the destruction of his values. Somewhat milder forms are represented by various types of "pressure" applied to the other group: economic blockade, deprivation of certain values (including freedom), threats of reprisal, establishment of courts and a police force for the protection of the interests of the dominant group, etc.

In interpersonal interactions the compulsory relationship manifests itself in a wide range of actions directed at ruining the adversary, such as extermination or torture, persecution, banishment, outcasting, imprisonment, slander and vilification, and economic throttling, often carried on through a misuse of legal and police measures. Most grave crimes and their punishment are manifestations of compulsory relationships between the criminal and the victim or between the criminal and society.

When, in interpersonal or intergroup interactions, the severity and the quantity of the coercive measures increase, this is generally a sure symptom of an increase of antagonistic relationships between the respective individ-

---

[22] A few examples are selected from the infinitely great number of situations where parties remain strangers.

"The feudal literature, which was addressed to the privileged classes only, gives only a caricature of the peasant. Disdain was general in regard to him; brute force was regarded the only method fit in dealing with him: 'Oignez vilain, il vous poindra; poignez vilain, il vous oindra.'" J. Calmette, *La société féodale*, pp. 166-167 (Paris, 1932). Characterizations of that kind were general throughout the whole medieval literature in regard to the unfree and semi-free classes, on the part of the privileged classes with which the former were connected by compulsory ties mainly.

"The literature of the Middle Ages is not favorable to the peasant. . . . Where we meet the peasant, he is first of all depicted as the coarse and clumsy yokel." See P. Meissner, *Der Bauer in der englischen Literatur* (Bonn, 1922), pp. 17 ff. See also G. von Below, *Probleme der Wirtschaftsgeschichte* (Tübingen, 1926), p. 94. Similar mentality is found in practically all the purely compulsory relationships on the part of masters toward slaves, serfs, victims, and so on in all periods and countries, including the United States.

On the other hand, a study of the mottoes, songs, and other "speech-reactions" of the coerced groups in the times of their revolts discloses an analogous mentality on their part toward their masters. "Kill the priests, kill these dogs, kill the wealthy, kill that wretched vampire—the Czar; kill all these scoundrels"—runs the Russian revolutionary hymn. Similar are the characteristics of the privileged classes in the *Carmagnole, Ça ira* and other revolutionary hymns of the French Revolution. There these classes are styled also as "the impure blood" which had to be shed. See many examples of that in P. Sorokin, *The Sociology of Revolution*, pp. 149 ff. Similar is the "ideology" of the Nazi "master-race" in regard to the "scum of the earth" of all the conquered groups. Nazi "factories of death" in Lublin and in other places, with their unbelievable cruelty, with their extermination of millions of innocent victims well illustrate the point.

In many variations the same phenomenon appears, always in any interaction of a purely compulsory type.

uals or groups; conversely, heightened antagonism between the parties regularly manifests itself in an increase of coercive measures. If, in a given society, there is an increase of grave and bloody crimes or in the severity of their punishment; if martial law replaces the normal law; if constitutional government gives place to unlimited dictatorship; or if the citizens apply more coercive measures to one another—such an intensification of coercion is a sure sign of a multiplication of social antagonisms. The same is true of international and other intergroup relationships.

4. Gradation and Scale of the Relationships

It is hardly necessary to point out that the transition from the solidary to the antagonistic type of interaction is not abrupt in the sense that there are no intermediate (more or less familistic, more or less contractual, more or less compulsory) grades between the main forms. Such intermediate forms exist, and it is frequently difficult to decide which of the three basic types of interaction a given form most closely resembles. As in other fields of classification, we have to select and stress a few fundamental forms as typically "pure," whereas in reality there is a series of forms merging into one another by imperceptible gradations. As a matter of fact, virtually every organized system of interactions represents a combination of these main forms —partly familistic, partly mixed contractual, and partly compulsory. But the proportion of each type in the totality of social relationships varies from group to group, and in the course of time even within the same group.

5. Groups Where Each Type Predominates

If we consider various social groups, we note that some of them represent one of these types in larger measure than the others. If we take such groups as the *family, the Church, or an association of genuine friends*, we find that they ordinarily possess an abundant share of familistic relationships. From the primitive family (no matter what its form) to the most modern, the relationships of the members in most cases have been largely familistic, either in a relatively rough or in a refined form, characterized by the sense of "we," the fusion of the members into a single team, mutual

solidarity, help, and altruism, and a sense of common values and responsibilities. The proportion of this "familism" varies, of course, from family to family; but as a rule it is very considerable, and in most cases it is the dominant form of relationship. The compulsory and the contractual relationships are present too, but with few exceptions they are subsidiary elements.

Religious groups have likewise nearly always been shaped after the pattern of familistic interactions. This is shown clearly by the terminology of such a group: "Our Father" (God), "We are the children of God," "God the Father," "God the Son," "the Mother of God," "Mother Church," "Holy Father," "Sisters in Christ," "Brethren," "the Spouse of Christ," and so on. Whether one takes the Bible, the writings of the Church Fathers, or religious services, prayers, and sermons, the terminology is replete with familistic terms. Even the church sacraments abound with them (for example, "rites of passage" from the status of a "stranger" or "gentile" to "brotherhood in God"). This may be said of virtually any true religion; it may also be said of real friends. Here again the relationship is invariably familistic.

If, now, we turn to a conscript army in time of peace[23] (as distinguished from such a group as the early medieval "companions in arms," which was modeled after the familistic pattern), we find that, side by side with familistic relationships, compulsory relationships are always present to a considerable degree, especially when the army is large and is recruited from many different sources. Likewise, in a state network of social relationships, especially in a despotic, dictatorial, or tyrannical state, many of the relations are compulsory, as suggested by the coercive mechanism of the state: its army, police, jails, courts, punishments, and the like. In a democratic state the mixed, or contractual, relationships are dominant, supplemented by compulsion.

Finally, when we turn to commercial and trade organizations, we find that they have always represented, to a considerable degree, a developed system of mixed, or contractual,

---

[23] On a battlefield members of the same detachment or regiment, fighting, living, and dying together become, as a rule, a familistic group.

relationships. Trade ordinarily consists of bargaining, a free exchange of commodities. Beginning with barter between Europeans and primitive peoples and ending with the contemporary system of purchase and sale in terms of cash or credit, trade and commerce have always consisted largely of contractual relationships. So also the employer-employee relationships of the capitalist régime; here the interactions of employers and laborers have been mainly of the mixed, or contractual, type.

The foregoing examples show that certain organized groups, by their very nature, are destined to exhibit one of the basic types of social relationships—the familistic, the mixed (contractual), or the compulsory type of interaction—more prominently than other organized groups.

6. Possibility of Confusion

There is danger of confusing the existing nature of the relationship with its mode of origin. A given form of interaction may originate in a contractual form, for instance, the relationship between married parties, or the relationship of *fidelitas* between the lord and his vassal in the Middle Ages. But in the course of time the contractual form may be superseded by either the familistic or the compulsory type of interaction. The relationship prescribed by a marriage contract may develop into a real familistic relationship between the husband and wife. A business contract and the subsequent meetings of the parties often lead to the establishment of true friendship between the contracting parties. Even many relationships compulsory in origin may become familistic (for instance, in the past, in marriages imposed upon one or both parties by others) or contractual. On the other hand, a weak familistic relationship sometimes degenerates into a contractual or even a compulsory one, or a contractual relationship may degenerate into a compulsory one. To repeat: *The way in which an interaction originated must be clearly distinguished from its present nature*—familistic, contractual, or compulsory. An established relationship does not always remain the same in the course of time but may assume a different form at a later period. (Cf. Chapter 29.) This is particularly important for a proper understanding of the nature of certain relationships, especially such medieval relationships as that of *fidelitas*.[24]

V. Survey and Criticism of Other Classifications of Solidarity and Antagonism

The problem of the principal types of antagonistic and solidary interactions has been widely discussed in recent sociological works.[25] Let us glance briefly at the various classifications and expositions of these relationships.

1. Theories of von Wiese, Park and Burgess, etc.

One group of such theories, common in texts of sociology, presents a rather artificial classification of solidary and antagonistic forms of social processes or relationships. Thus L. von Wiese mentions "advance, adjustment, accord, and amalgamation" as the main forms of "associative processes," and competition, opposition, and conflict as the main forms of "dissociative processes."[26] Unfortunately he gives hardly any analysis of the concrete social, psychological, or cultural characteristics of these processes. As a result the varieties of antago-

[24] See Sorokin, *Dynamics*, Vol. III, Chps. 1-4.

[25] I omit here the ancient classifications and delineations of these types by Confucius, Lao-Tzu, Plato, Aristotle, Augustine, Joachim de Flore, Thomas Aquinas, Nicolaus Cusanus, Ibn Khaldun, G. Vico, G. F. Hegel, A. Comte, Herbert Spencer, and many mystics. Though many of these classifications are excellent and as good as many recent ones (in several respects even better), their his-

torical survey is obviously outside of the tasks of this work. Their place is in the history of sociological thought. Unfortunately in the existing texts of such a history this focal problem is almost entirely omitted and the reader finds next to nothing about the problem.

[26] See his *Sociology* (New York, 1941), pp. 58 ff.

nistic and solidary interactions noted remain dryly formal and abstract. They do not include even the most intense forms of solidarity, such as all-bestowing and all-forgiving love. The subclasses of "advance, adjustment, accord, and amalgamation" often represent not solidary but mixed, sometimes even antagonistic, interactions. The advance of an army against the enemy, like the "adjustment" of the conquered by the conqueror, is not a solidary interaction. Amalgamation does not necessarily constitute or always lead to solidarity; sometimes, as in the case of coercive sex relations of dominant and subjugated races, it tends to accentuate existing antagonisms. Likewise, many forms of competition, as we have seen, are mixed, not antagonistic (dissociative), interactions. Even as steps in the development of contacts and association of previously isolated parties, these varieties and their sequence are in no way typical. The phase of adjustment does not always precede that of accord, or the phase of accord that of amalgamation. Amalgamation, especially in a coercive or semicoercive form between conquering and conquered racial or ethnic groups, sometimes takes place before any advance, adjustment, or accord. Hence the classification is sterile. With a slight modification the same can be said of many variations of this classification, such as that given by R. Park and E. Burgess, who single out such process as isolation, social contact, social interaction, competition, conflict, accommodation, assimilation, amalgamation, social control, and progress;[27] or that presented by E. A. Ross, who supplies us with numerous forms like preliminary socialization, association, domination, exploitation, opposition, and antagonism; competition, conflict, class struggle, and war; adaptation, cooperation, organiza-

tion of social effort, will, and thought; subordination, equalization, estrangement, and liberation.[28] Somewhat similar lines are followed by most of the classifications given in many textbooks.[29]

These classifications are utterly haphazard, possessing no logical *fundamentum divisionis*.[30] They divide the same form of social relationship into two or more different forms, and they unite into one form processes that are different. In addition, they fail to give a graphic exposition of the solidary, antagonistic, or mixed forms.[31]

2. Theories of Le Play, Lavrov, Kropotkin, and Cooley

Much more satisfactory are those classifications that attempt a concrete portrayal of the main varieties of solidary, antagonistic, and mixed interactions and that examine the place they occupy in various social groups. Among these we shall mention F. Le Play's types of the family and society. His characterization of what he calls the patriarchal family, the *famille-souche*, and the "prosperous society" gives a realistic portrait of a predominantly familistic group or system of interaction in my sense. His typology of what he styles the "unstable" family and society affords a fairly typical portrait of what I call the mixed or contractual form of interaction. Through these excellent and well-documented types of the familistic and mixed (or contractual) forms of social interaction Le Play outlined two forms which were subsequently reiterated by F. Tönnies in his *Gemeinschaft und Gesellschaft* and by others in their variations of the same types.[32] The difference between Le Play's types and the above types of the familistic, mixed, and compulsory forms consists in two

[27] R. Park and E. Burgess, *op. cit.*

[28] E. A. Ross, *Principles of Sociology* (New York, 1923).

[29] Cf., for instance, E. Bogardus, *Fundamentals of Social Psychology* (New York, 1924); E. Sutherland, "The Biological and Sociological Processes," *AJS, Proceedings*, Vol. XX, p. 62; R. L. Sutherland and J. L. Woodward, *Introductory Sociology* (Chicago-Philadelphia, 1940); E. R. Groves and H. E. Moore, *An Introduction to Sociology* (New York, 1940); and other introductory texts.

[30] Much more substantial and in many ways better is the analysis and classification of antagonisms given by J. Delevsky in his *Social Antago-*

nisms and the Class Struggle in History (in Russian, 1910). But even it is largely formal. For other classifications, cf. my *Theories*, pp. 327 ff.

[31] For a further criticism, cf. my *Theories*, pp. 507 ff.

[32] Cf. F. Le Play, *Les ouvriers européens* (2nd ed., Paris, 1877-1879), and *The Organization of Labor* (tr. by Emerson) (Philadelphia, 1872). For a characterization of the types of the family and society by Le Play, cf. my *Theories*, Ch. 2. Excerpts from Le Play's analysis of prosperous societies are given in P. Sorokin, C. Zimmerman, and C. Galpin, *A Systematic Source Book in Rural Sociology* (Minneapolis, 1931), Vol. II, pp. 76-94.

traits: first, he does not analyze the compulsory type in a systematic way; second, he does not give a systematic analysis of the general forms of the familistic and mixed relationships, but presents instead concrete cases of these general types. His work has great merit as an illustration of how each of these forms reflects itself in an organized family group.

Somewhat similar are the studies of the historical types of solidary and antagonistic groups made by various scholars. They do not undertake a generalized classification of these forms, but they supply concrete examples of each. Such, for instance, is the analysis of the historical forms of solidarity furnished by P. Lavrov and P. Kropotkin. Viewing sociology as a science concerned with the forms of solidarity exhibited by thinking human beings, and with the stages and factors of its development, P. Lavrov classifies the types of solidarity, in their historical development, as (a) *the solidarity of habit and custom*, established through trial and error, unconsciously arising in the process of long interaction and constituting the most ancient form; (b) *the affective and emotional solidarity of common interests*, still devoid of any critical or purposeful thought; and finally (c) *solidarity based upon a community of rational purposes, values, and convictions*. Each form is divided into subforms. Lavrov shows which forms and combinations of forms have dominated the social organization of primitive groups, and of the monarchies of the ancient East, of ancient Greece and Rome, of the Middle Ages, and of modern times. From this standpoint his work constitutes one of the most important studies of the historical forms of solidarity, with their transformations and fluctuations.[33]

Similarly, P. Kropotkin, in his study of the role of solidarity in human affairs and of its principal historical forms, has analyzed many specific historical types of solidarity and of the organization of social groups in which this or that form dominated, as well as the causes and methods of such domination and of the modification of these forms.[34] Others, like C. H. Cooley in his analysis of what he calls the primary group, have enriched our understanding of several aspects of solidary relationships and organization.[35]

The contributions of this sort are numerous. Their chief shortcoming is that they rarely attempt to give a generalized systematic theory of the solidary, the antagonistic, or the mixed form. They furnish, however, much concrete data for such a generalized and systematic theory.

3. Theories of Tönnies, Scheler, Durkheim

Let us next consider the works that do seek to establish such a theory. The most typical are the works of F. Tönnies and E. Durkheim, and those which present variations of their concepts. F. Tönnies's theory of the *Gemeinschaft* and the *Gesellschaft* ("community" and "society," though these terms do not properly translate the German) deals with two fundamental and general types exhibited in social relationships and interactions (*Verhältnisse*) in the collectives (*Samtschaften*) and in corporate bodies (*Körperschaften*). All in all, his *Gemeinschaft* is somewhat similar to what I call the familistic type, and his *Gesellschaft* to what I call the mixed or contractual type—corresponding to what Le Play outlines as the patriarchal family and society and the unstable family and society[36]—but with important differences.

Tönnies' conception of the *Gemeinschaft* and *Gesellschaft* underwent a certain change in

---

[33] See P. Lavrov (pseud. A. Dolenga), *The Most Important Moments in the Development of Thought* (in Russian, Moscow, 1903); *The Tasks of Historical Understanding* (in Russian, St. Petersburg, 1903); and *A Treatise on the History of Thought* (in his *Works*, St. Petersburg, 1918), Vol. II. In these treatises (published in their first editions in the nineteenth century) Lavrov has given us, in a much more substantial form, what later on was developed more sketchily by L. Hobhouse in his works on intellectual and ethical evolution and by Max Scheler and others in their studies of the forms of sympathy and ethics.

[34] Cf. P. Kropotkin, *Mutual Aid* (New York, 1902).

[35] C. H. Cooley, *op. cit.*

[36] Tönnies possibly did not know Le Play's works published some fifteen years before the first edition of Tönnies' *Gemeinschaft und Gesellschaft* (1887). However, he probably was influenced by Hegel, whose conception of the family versus civil society is fairly similar to Tönnies' types. (Cf. G. Richard's remarks in his *La sociologie générale et les lois sociologiques*, pp. 174 ff.)

his later formulation of these types. In his *Gemeinschaft und Gesellschaft* he defines the terms as follows: *Gemeinschaft* is a social relationship that is "real and organic," while *Gesellschaft* is an "imaginary and mechanical structure." The first is an "intimate, private, and exclusive community of life"; the second is "public life." In the *Gemeinschaft* one lives with one's family from birth, bound to it in weal and woe. One enters a *Gesellschaft* as one goes into a strange country. *Gemeinschaft* means a total community of life of the parties (*communio totius vitae*); *Gesellschaft*, a partial, temporary association of persons, otherwise independent of each other, for this or that utilitarian purpose. *Gemeinschaft* arises spontaneously, partly instinctively, through "natural will"; *Gesellschaft* is established contractually, through "rational (utilitarian) will," artificially, in a calculating way. "There exists a *Gemeinschaft* of language, of folkways or mores, or of beliefs; by way of contrast, *Gesellschaft* exists in the realm of business, travel, or sciences."[37]

Tönnies' earlier concepts of *Gemeinschaft* and *Gesellschaft* were a complex of several heterogeneous characteristics: (a) the mode of emergence (spontaneous, through instinctive or emotional "natural will," in *Gemeinschaft*, and through calculated, utilitarian "rational will" in *Gesellschaft*); (b) respectively "organic" and "mechanically artificial" traits; (c) extensive solidarity (community of life) in the one case and a narrow solidarity in the other; (d) life-long association in the one case and temporary association in the other; (e) the merging of individualities in one, and the preservation of their independence in the other; (f) living as the end, or value, of the *Gemeinschaft*, and the attainment of a utilitarian purpose as the objective of the *Gesellschaft*. The family, the tribe, and the medieval peasant community are seen as a *Gemeinschaft*; most modern associations, as a *Gesellschaft*.

In addition, Tönnies claimed in this work that there is a historical trend of societies in the course of time from the *Gemeinschaft* type to that of the *Gesellschaft*. His concepts, as has been said, were an agglomeration of several heterogeneous characteristics. Under the influence of the critics Tönnies seems to have recognized the weakness of such a scheme of construction. Accordingly, in his latest works he has sought to simplify his concepts and to make them more consistent and logical. Hence his later definition: "I call all kinds of association in which natural will predominates *Gemeinschaft*; all those which are formed and fundamentally conditioned by rational will, *Gesellschaft*."[38]

The *Gemeinschaft* presents relationships of the "fellowship type," in which two persons live together in a brotherly, comradely manner, or relationships of the "authoritative type," such as those obtaining between father and son. The Gesellschaft is exemplified by various contractual relationships of independent parties for utilitarian ends. These relations enter also into collective and social organizations, some of these (such as the family, the *Volk*, or the tribe) approximating the *Gemeinschaft* type, whereas the others approximate the Gesellschaft type.[39] There is no doubt that the later version of Tönnies' theory is logically sounder than the earlier, more complex version.

The foregoing discussion reveals the differences between my familistic, mixed, and compulsory forms and Tönnies' *Gemeinschaft and Gesellschaft* forms. He virtually ignores the antagonistic, or compulsory, type. Hence his classification is incomplete. The earlier version of his theory is defective because of its mechanical juxtaposition of disparate criteria and characteristics. Even the later version is marred by several logical and factual defects. First, some of the characteristics of both types are exceedingly vague—indeed, almost meaningless—such as the "real and organic" nature of the *Gemeinschaft* and the "imaginary and

---

[37] F. Tönnies, *Fundamental Concepts of Sociology*, pp. 37 ff. For an analysis of these concepts, cf. the introduction by the translator, C. Loomis.

[38] Tönnies' article, "Gemeinschaft and Gesellschaft" (1931), translated and included in his *Fundamental Concepts of Sociology*, p. 17. By "natural will" (*Wesenwille*) he means "simple emotional (impulsive) and therefore irrational voli-

tion and action," while by "rational will" (*Kürwille*) he means the form of volition "in which thinking has gained predominance and come to be the directing agent," in which "the means are (rationally) determined" with reference to the end. (*Ibid.*, pp. 15-17).

[39] *Ibid.*, pp. 18 ff.

mechanical structure" of the *Gesellschaft*. Second, both versions are fallacious, in that they mix the modes of origin of each form with its nature. The Gemeinschaft, or familistic form, may originate not only "instinctively," through "natural will," but also contractually and purposefully, through "rational will." As we have seen, it sometimes arises through the transformation of earlier compulsory or contractual relationships. Conversely, the *Gesellschaft* (or contractual) relationship originates now and then through compulsion, through normative motivation or even conditioned and fundamental motivation, or, in the terms of Tönnies, through "natural will."

Third, Tönnies' conceptions of "natural will" and "rational will," and of the "means and ends" associated with them, are exceedingly vague and psychologically primitive. He offers no satisfactory theory of motivation, volition, instincts, reflexes, emotions, feelings, or cognition. All these biopsychological elements are hopelessly intermingled in his writings: distinctly different motivations are identified, and his "natural" and "rational" volitions are nothing but a psychological hash. As a result, the whole construction of the *Gemeinschaft* and *Gesellschaft*, built upon these deficient concepts, is vague and unsatisfactory. Fourth, his concept of a historical trend from the *Gemeinschaft* to the *Gesellschaft* is untenable: the two forms coexisted in most past societies and continue to coexist at the present time; if there have been fluctuations in the domination of each type in this or that group, they have been temporary fluctuations, in no way representing a steady perennial trend.[40]

Some of the subsequent followers of the *Gemeinschaft* and *Gesellschaft* typology improved it at certain points, but not fundamentally. Hence the foregoing criticism applies to their variations as well.[41]

Max Scheler's classification of the forms of sociability may serve as a typical example of these variations on the theme of the *Gemeinschaft* and *Gesellschaft*. Instead of two main forms, Scheler offers four forms of sociability and their corresponding groups: (a) social unity based upon "contagion and involuntary intuition," as illustrated by the unity of the crowd (or *Masse*); (b) unity based upon living together and co-experiencing (or *Miterleben*), where the members are bound together by mutual comprehension, cooperation, and sympathy. Scheler calls this *Lebensgemeinschaft*. It is quite similar to Tönnies' *Gemeinschaft*. (c) The third type resembles Tönnies' *Gesellschaft*, representing a group of dissimilar individuals bound by contract for the attainment of commercial or other utilitarian ends. It is a contractual plurality of relationships between disparate individuals. (d) Finally, a complex collective personality (*Gesamtperson*) represents a synthesis of the *Lebensgemeinschaft* and *Gesellschaft* types. Its members may be dissimilar, and each enjoys individual freedom, as in a contractual *Gesellschaft*; but at the same time their solidarity approaches in intensity that of the *Gemeinschaft* type, each being responsible both for himself and for the entire group. They are united by love and by a common fund of supreme values. Such *Gesamtpersonen* are the nation, the state, and the Church. This fourth type constitutes the supreme form of social unity and solidarity.[42]

One can easily perceive that these four forms are very similar to Lavrov's classification and represent Tönnies' two forms (each subdivided into two subforms). The classification exhibits essentially the same virtues and defects as that of Tönnies. In addition, it possesses certain other weaknesses. Its first and fourth forms are outlined very vaguely. It con-

---

[40] For a systematic corroboration of this, cf. my *Dynamics*, Vol. III, Chps. 1-4. Tönnies, like Durkheim and many others, gives scarcely any remotely relevant factual corroboration of his trend.

[41] Cf. for instance, G. Richard, *op. cit.*, in spite of his excellent criticism of Tönnies' types; B. Kistiakowsky, *op. cit.*, though the book clarifies the problem of the society and individual; Makarewicz, *op. cit.*; T. Litt. *Individuum und Gemeinschaft* (Leipzig, 1924); and T. Geiger, *Die Gestalten der Gesellung* (Karlsruhe, 1928); and H.

Freyer, *Einleitung in die Soziologie* (Leipzig, 1931). For a further criticism of the Tönnies-Scheler theory, cf. G. Gurvitch, "Remarques sur la classification des formes de la sociabilité," *Archives de philosophie du droit et de sociologie juridique*, Nos. 3-4 (1935); also W. Ziegenfuss, *Versuch über des Wesen der Gesellschaft* (Leipzig, 1935).

[42] Max Scheler, *Das Wesen und die Formen der Sympathie*, and *Der Formalismus in der Ethik und die materiale Wertethik*.

fuses the origin and motivation of a form of sociability or unity with its nature. Solidarity or unity of a certain kind may arise in several different ways and in response to different motivations, and yet be identical in nature. Conversely, the same type of motivation or generation (through "contagion and involuntary intuition," or through "co-living and co-experiencing," or, in my terminology, through fundamental, normative, or purposive motivation) of social relationships may lead to such dissimilar forms as solidarity and antagonism. Still more objectionable is the fact that Scheler identifies the forms of social relationships (such as sociability or solidarity) with various social groups (like the state, the nation, and the Church). As we have seen, such identification of the forms of social relationships with concrete groups is impermissible. The same social group—for instance, the family, the state, or the Church—is characterized mainly now by familistic, now by contractual, and now by compulsory social relationships.[43] Conversely, the same social relationship—for instance, the familistic or the compulsory—may be the principal stuff of which the network of interactions is composed in the state, in labor unions, in the family, and in any other group. To declare that all the relationships in the state, for example, represent the highest forms of sociability is a gross factual error. Even the man on the street knows that the state system contains plenty of mixed and compulsory relationships; otherwise it would not need any army, police force, prisons, or other punitive agencies. Some states have been founded, maintained, and expanded chiefly through conquest, oppression, and naked force.

Somewhat similar to Tönnies' is Durkheim's classification of the forms of solidarity into *mechanical* forms, based on the similarity of the sentiments and beliefs of the members of the group, and *organic* forms, based on their dissimilarity and interdependence. The mechanical type of solidarity supposedly exists among groups with little division of labor, as in most primitive societies, in the early stages of the historical nations, or in such organizations as the army. Organic solidarity flourishes among societies which possess a well-developed division of labor and are differentiated and stratified, like most modern societies. The first form arises spontaneously; the second, purposively, mainly through contractual relations between the independent individuals. The societies with mechanical solidarity exhibit many other distinct characteristics, one of which is their repressive system of law aimed to re-enforce the common sentiments and beliefs through punishment of the violators of the society's norms. The societies with organic solidarity are marked mainly by a restitutive system of law intended only to ensure compensation for the damage caused by violations of the law. In the first type of society the members enjoy hardly any individuality or independence; they are all interfused and engulfed in the unity of the group. Societies with organic solidarity are nurseries of individuality, individualism, and independence, their members freely associating and contracting with one another. Historically the societies with mechanical solidarity tend to be replaced progressively by those with increasing division of labor and with organic solidarity.[44]

With certain qualifications most of the criticisms of the theory of Tönnies are applicable also to Durkheim's forms of solidarity. First, he analyzes little, if at all, the psychosocial nature of the forms and their varieties. Instead he offers a theory of two social conditions, respectively with and without division of labor, with and without similarity of the members, in which so-called mechanical solidarity and organic solidarity respectively arise. Second, like the Tönnies-Scheler theory, that of Durkheim confuses the forms of solidarity with the modes of their origin and with the social factors upon which they depend. As mentioned before, almost any form of solidarity or antagonism may arise in different ways; conversely, the same origin may lead to different forms of solidarity or antagonism. Third, as we shall see in the next chapter, Durkheim's factors of similarity or dissimilarity do not determine the forms of solidarity, nor

---

[43] Cf. my *Dynamics*, Vol. III, Chps. 1-4.
[44] Cf. E. Durkheim, *De la division du travail social* (Paris, 1893); Eng. tr. also. Cf. my *Contemporary Sociological Theories*, pp. 463ff. For a criticism of this theory of Durkheim's cf. C. Bouglé, "Théories sur la division du travail," *L'Année sociologique*, Vol. IV; G. Gurvitch, *op. cit.*; and M. Kovalevsky, *Sovremennyie soziologi* (St. Petersburg, 1905).

do they always produce solidarity, but sometimes engender antagonism. For this reason his theory of the existence of a causal connection between similarity and mechanical solidarity and between dissimilarity and organic solidarity is fallacious. In other words, the familistic, the mixed, and the compulsory relationships exist among societies with well-developed or poorly developed division of labor and among those with similar or dissimilar members.

Fourth, many other contentions of Durkheim are unfounded, such as the historical trend from mechanical to organic solidarity, from the repressive to the restitutive type of law, and so on. Fifth, his forms do not include the antagonistic or compulsory relationship and are therefore incomplete. Sixth, most of what he styles organic solidarity proves to be a mixed form of social relationship. Durkheim was idealizing the liberal capitalistic society at the end of the nineteenth century in the form of a society with organic solidarity, but later perceived that his idealization was in many respects unfounded and that the supposedly "organic solidarity" of this society was in reality conflict and disintegration.

The work of Durkheim has many important merits, but his typology of the forms of solidarity is defective. Nevertheless the Tönnies-Durkheim theories rank among the most fruitful in their particular field.

4. Concepts of "Community" and "Association"

Finally, we must consider the variation of the *Gemeinschaft-Gesellschaft* theory, quite common in textbooks of sociology, which deal with the concepts "*community*" and "*association*." If the textbooks meant by "community" a unibonded, localized territorial group, such as a city or village, the definition would be clear and the group would be merely a territorial association (a unibonded locality group). In that case it would not represent a general form of social relationship or interaction, nor could it be confounded with other unibonded associations. Like religious and artistic associations organized, respectively, around common religious and artistic values, the territorial group would be an association organized around the interests generated by

spatial proximity of the members. Unfortunately, the theories in question treat "community" and "association" along broader lines, similar to those of the *Gemeinschaft* and *Gesellschaft* types. Herein lies the source of gross logical and factual defects.

As one of the best examples of these fallacious theories let us take R. M. MacIver's concept of *community vs. association*. We are told that "any circle of people who live together, who belong together, so that they share, not this or that particular interest, but a whole set of interests wide enough and complete enough to include their lives, is a community. . . . The mark of community is that one's life may be lived wholly within it." "A community is always a group occupying a territorial area" and is at the same time an "area of common living" and an "area of effective communication."[45] This "community" is contrasted with, "association," which will be considered a little later. For the present let us look at this definition of "community." Its rough similarity to Tönnies' *Gemeinschaft* is evident. The community is conceived not as a mere local territorial association but as a universal form of social relationship. If Tönnies' concept suffers from a juxtaposition of different characteristics that neither logically nor causally belong together, MacIver's conception suffers from this defect still more. If the expression "living together, belonging together, sharing together" means intimate solidary relationships between the members of a community, and if a community is always a territorial group, are we to conclude that all persons who live in the same village, city, or territorial unity possess only solidary relationships and do not exhibit any mutually antagonistic or mixed relationships? By the terms of the definition we are forced to such a conclusion. But we know well that it would be both logically and actually false.

In his definition of community MacIver links two characteristics—solidarity and territorial proximity—which neither logically, causally, nor actually belong together. On the basis of the trait of solidarity we must designate as a "community" any set of people who sustain solidary relations with one another, no matter

[45] R. M. MacIver, *Society, Its Structure and Changes* (New York, 1931), pp. 9-12.

whether they all belong to a single locality or are scattered from China to Mexico, from Newfoundland to the South Pole. On the basis of territorial proximity we must regard as a community any group of interacting persons territorially adjacent, even such a combination as German and Russian military divisions fighting in the closest propinquity.

Let us assume, for a moment, that MacIver's definition of "community" means what Aristotle calls a self-sufficient[46] group ("wide enough and complete enough to include their lives," so that "one's life may be lived wholly within it"). Only vast social groups such as the state, the nation, or humanity can be regarded as self-sufficient; for villages, cities, and territorial groups all export and import goods to and from the outside world. Vast, self-sufficient groups exhibit, however, not only solidary but also antagonistic relations. Hence they are not communities. Self-sufficient groups have existed in the past, as they do at present; but they have been neither purely solidary nor territorially proximate groups. There are abundant instances of solidary groups, such as the Communist party, the Catholic Church, and the Jews; but they are not self-sufficient, nor do their members necessarily occupy the same territory. We know many groups whose members are territorially contiguous, but they are neither self-sufficient nor solidary. To these inconsistencies and contradictions should be added the identification of "territorial area" with "area of common living" and "area of effective communication." It is evident that no territorial area is one of common living: persons in New York, occupying the same big apartment house, often do not even know one another; on the other hand, an American soldier in Europe or on the Marianas shares a common life with his family, and his family with him, in spite of a wide spatial separation. Likewise, an area of effective communication is not identical with either a territorial area or with an area of common living. The world-wide radio network represents an area of effective communication, but the persons that use it do not constitute a solidary group sharing a common life nor do they form a territorially proximate community. These remarks are sufficient to show that MacIver's definition of "community" is a conceptual congeries made by assembling heterogeneous characteristics neither logically, causally, nor factually related. Therefore it is empty and meaningless. It is even more incoherent than Tönnies' *Gemeinschaft*.

The same may be said of MacIver's "association," which remotely resembles Tönnies' *Gesellschaft*. We are told that "an association is a group specifically organized for the pursuit of an interest or group of interests in common. It is not a community but an organization within a community." As it is organized for "particular purposes, we belong to it only by virtue of these purposes." The modern family, he declares, is "definitely an association," but not a community. The state is also an "association."[47]

As the definition of "community" is barren so also is this concept of "association." If there is any group whose members "belong together, live together, and share together a whole set of interests," the family is certainly the closest approximation to such a group (cf. Chapter 13). Yet MacIver declares it to be an association rather than a community. If there is any group approaching self-sufficiency, with territorial continuity and locus (as marks of a community), then the state is certainly the closest approximation to it. Yet it is pronounced to be an association but not a community. This is the more striking considering that a village or city is designated as a community. Again, if there is a group whose set of interests is broad, almost universal (the mark of a community), instead of being narrow and specific, then the family and the state are certainly the closest approximations to such a community group. Yet they are classified as associations.

This analysis demonstrates the logical, causal, and factual inadequacy of such pseudo-conceptions. They do not improve the concept of *Gemeinschaft* and *Gesellschaft* but render it even less tenable.[48] The same criticism applies to numerous other variations of this

---

[46] Such, according to Aristotle, is the specific trait of the state as distinguished from all other groups. (Cf. Aristotle, *Politics*, Bk. I, Ch. 2, or 1252b.)

[47] MacIver, *op. cit.*, pp. 12-13.

[48] The criticism is equally applicable to the more detailed analysis of the community given by MacIver in his monograph *Community* (New York,

view of community and association found in most textbooks of sociology.[49] Only if "community" is used in the sense of a mere nominal plural (a locality), of a real territorial group, or of a specified unibonded or multibonded group can it possess a definite meaning. As such it cannot be opposed to the term "association" in a general sense, nor can it be identified with a universal form of social relationships, processes, or groups.[50] (Cf. the subsequent chapters on unibonded and multibonded groups.)

5. Conclusion

The preceding critical survey should suffice to show that the classification of the solitary, antagonistic, and mixed relationships offered by this work embodies all the valid and significant traits of other classifications and at the same time is free from most of their defects. It is more complete than other classifications, which usually neglect the antagonistic relationships. It presents the primary forms of social relationships (or interactions) without confusing them with the modes of their origin or with the concrete forms of historically existing groups. The three basic forms of relationship enter, in various proportions and at various times, into the fabric of practically all groups. None of them is identical with any of the historical groups nor is it excluded from any of them. As we shall see later, the family, the village, the tribe, the caste or class, the state or nation, and the like must be classified from quite a different standpoint from that of the solitary, antagonistic, and mixed forms. In portraying each form I have tried to include only such traits as are actually inherent in it and to avoid ascribing to it characteristics that are purely incidental. Likewise, the traits of each form are such as logically and causally belong together, in contrast to heterogeneous

traits artificially dumped together and devoid of either logical or causal ties. Finally, in its psychological motivation my analysis is more adequate and precise than that of other conceptions.

The foregoing analysis suggests the present status of this problem in sociology and the social sciences. To an empirically minded person its protracted discussion may appear to be a purely academic preoccupation, devoid of any practical importance and divorced from actual social reality. However, the question is one of the basic problems of the social sciences in general and of sociology in particular. It is also one of the most acute practical problems of contemporary social life. The struggle between the totalitarians, the liberal democrats, and the partisans of capitalism, socialism, and communism is essentially a struggle for a familistic, a mixed (liberal contractual), or a compulsory type of national or international organization. Purely formal political organization—that of republic vs. monarchy, of federal vs. centralized government, and the like—plays a very minor role in this connection. Most of the strategic social and political issues of our time are inseparably connected with the forms under discussion. The question is: What type of social relationship should be dominant in the organization of a political regime, of an economic regime, of the family, of a territorial group, of an occupational organization or labor union, and so on? Shall these be organized along the lines of the familistic, the mixed (contractual), or the pseudo-familistic and pseudo-contractual (compulsory) patterns? Here, as in many other cases, the so-called "practical and concrete minds" prove to be very shortsighted and impractical, overlooking the really important issues and concentrating on the relatively unimportant and superficial.

1929). The defects of this conception are still more evident in MacIver's attempt to distinguish community, association, institution, mores, and society. Each of these is very poorly defined, and all overlap one another. The whole classification exemplifies an elaborate effort to create a multitude of superfluous pseudo-definitions.

[49] Cf., for instance R. C. Angell and L. J. Carr, *Introductory Sociology* (New York, 1933), Chps. 16, 17; E. C. Hughes, "Institutions," in R. Park (ed.), *An Outline of the Principles of Sociology*

(New York, 1939), Ch. 27; and W. L. Warner and P. S. Lunt, *op. cit.*, pp. 16-17.

[50] Therefore all statements about such a territorial group—that it is solidary, that it is one in its thinking, acting, interests, and so on—are invalid. We read, for instance, in Lynds's *Middletown* how Middletown thinks, how it feels, how it acts. But in Middletown there are Republicans, Democrats, Socialists, and Communists, who think and act in quite different, often opposite, ways. The same is true of its richer and poorer classes.

Chapter 6. Factors of Solidarity and Antagonism

I. Need for Studying Causes of Solidarity and Antagonism

The paramount theoretical and practical importance of the factors of solidarity and antagonism is obvious. Had we known what caused either solidarity or antagonism, and with such knowledge been able to increase the familistic and eliminate the antagonistic from interpersonal and intergroup relationships, had we but known this, all the main social tragedies —war, bloody revolution, crime, coercion and compulsion, misery and unhappiness, the contrasts of poverty and luxury, domination and enslavement—would have been eliminated or reduced to a minimum. In spite of the urgency of the situation, we know little about it; even more paradoxical is the fact that the problem has hardly ever been studied as intensely as hundreds of others in physics and chemistry, biology and the social sciences. Even now, when a quantitative and qualitative increase of solidarity in mankind means life or death to humanity, when without such an increase nothing can prevent future world wars with their apocalyptic destruction, we have thousands of special research institutes examining all sorts of matters, often quite unimportant, but we do not have a single research institute in the world dedicated to the problems of solidarity and antagonism.[1] On the basis of the existing experimental, observational, historical, sociological, and other studies,[2] the known

---

[1] With financial help of Mr. Eli Lilly and in cooperation with several scholars the author is engaged now in a research of several central problems of solidarity.

[2] Besides the works referred to in this chapter, among many studies the following are important: J. B. Maller, *Cooperation and Competition: An Experimental Study of Motivation* (New York, 1929); P. A. Sorokin, M. Tanquist, M. Parten and Mrs. C. C. Zimmerman, "An Experimental Study of Efficiency of Work Under Various Conditions," *AJS*, Vol. XXXV (1930); P. A. Sorokin, "Experimente zur Soziologie," *Zeitschrift für Völkerpsychologie und Soziologie* (March, 1928); E. A. Graves, "The Effect of Competition," unpublished thesis in Library, University of Minnesota (1934); P. J. Greenberg, "Competition in Children," *American Journal of Psychology*, Vol. XXXIV

(1932); F. Hoppe, "Erfolg und Misserfolg," *Psychol. Forschung*, Vol. XIV (1930); B. V. Belyaeff, "The Problem of the 'Collective' and Its Experimental-Psychological Study," *Psychologiya* (Russian, 1929, 1930, 1932); I. Evergettoff, "Observations of Manifestations of Sociality in Early Childhood," *Methody obiektivnago izucheniya rebenka* (Moscow, 1924); P. R. Farnworth and A. Behner, "A Note on the Attitude of Social Conformity," *Journal of Social Psychology* (1931); E. B. Hurlock, "The Use of Group Rivalry as an Incentive," *Journal of Abnormal Psychology* (1927); C. J. Leuba, "An Experimental Study of Rivalry in Young Children," *Journal of Comparative Psychology* (1933); J. L. Moreno, *Who Shall Survive* (Washington, 1934); R. Updegraff and E. K. Herbst, "An Experimental Study of the Social Behavior," *Journal of Genetic Psychology* (1933);

factors of solidarity and antagonism among interacting individuals and groups can be summarized in the following propositions, though

they give us only an imperfect and scanty knowledge of these factors.

II. Negative Propositions

Taken by themselves, without the configuration of other conditions in which they are given, the following characteristics of interacting parties are not important factors in the generation of either solidarity or antagonism.

(1) Sex of the party in the sense that neither of the sexes is more solidary or more antagonistic than the other.

(2) Race of the party in the sense that none of the races per se is either more antagonistic or more solidary than the others.

(3) Age of the party with the exception of the too young babies and quite senile persons whose interaction becomes mainly biological and falls out of the realm of the superorganic. For this reason the categories solidary-antagonistic become almost inapplicable to their behavior.

(4) Good or poor health of the parties with the exception of some specific forms of disease like highly contagious or venereal diseases endangering the other parties.

(5) Physical handsomeness or comeliness of the parties, with the possible exception of what other parties regard as an extreme ugliness.

(6) High or low intelligence, mental brilliance or dullness, with the possible exception of mental defects—idiocy and mental disease —lowering the intelligence of the party below the minimum of "normal mindfulness" or making the mentally diseased dangerous to other parties.

(7) Presence or absence in the parties of literacy or illiteracy; of school education in either elementary, or high school or college education, when the education consists mainly or exclusively in a cultivation of intellect, without training in either cooperative and altruistic or competitive and egotistic forms of conduct.

(8) High or low standard of living, wealth or poverty, with the exception of an extreme poverty denying satisfaction of the basic biological needs in food, shelter, etc.

(9) Ethnic or national traits of the parties in the sense that none of the ethnic or national groups per se is either universally and perennially more solidary or more antagonistic than the others.

(10) Technology of the parties, their living in an agricultural, pastoral, or industrial age.

(11) Even such characteristics of interacting parties as their being members of either monarchical or republican, autocratic or democratic states, Socialist or Communist or Capitalist parties, taken per se, are not uniformly effective factors of either solidarity or antagonism.

The existing body of the evidence supplied by the experimental, observational, historical and sociological studies shows that none of these characteristics of interacting parties, taken without the configuration of the reasons for the interaction, with whom, where, and under what circumstances, are uniform causes

M. A. May and L. W. Dobb, Competition and Cooperation (New York, 1937); see there additional literature; J. C. Hsia, A Study of Sociability of Elementary School Children (New York, 1928); M. Meade (ed.), Cooperation and Competition Among Primitive Peoples (New York, 1927); L. Murphy, Social Behavior (New York, 1937); A. T. Jersild and T. Markey, Conflicts Between Preschool Children (New York, 1935); M. May and H. Hartshorne, Studies in the Nature of Character, 3 Vols. (New York, 1928-1930); C. Chassell, The Relation Between Morality and Intellect (New York, 1935); I. D. Suttie, The Origins of Love and Hatred (London, 1935).

For systematic studies of war and revolution as the sharpest forms of social antagonisms see P. A. Sorokin, Social and Cultural Dynamics, Vol. III; "The Cause and Factors of War and Peace," Annual Report of the American Historical Association, Vol. III (1942, Washington); Man and Society in Calamity (New York, 1943); The Crisis of Our Age (New York, 1941); "The Conditions and Prospects for a World Without War," AJS (1944); "Theses on Group Tensions" in Approach to National Unity, ed. by L. Bryson, L. Finkelstein and R. M. MacIver (New York, 1945). See also Q. Wright, A Study of War, 2 Vols. (Chicago, 1942). See further bibliography in these works.

generating either solidarity or antagonism. In other words, we cannot say that persons with good health or high intelligence or a certain sex-age-race show uniformly either greater solidarity or greater antagonism than persons with poor health or moderate intelligence or a different sex-age-race. Statistical studies of the correlation between high or low intelligence and cooperativeness, or sociality, or altruism of the persons do not give consistently high coefficients of correlation. Historical and statistical induction also shows that intellectually brilliant men are hardly more altruistic or antagonistic than intellectually dull persons. Intellectually brighter pupils of the elementary school, high school, or college do not show consistently greater cooperativeness or sociality or altruism than dull pupils, nor do they show greater antagonism. The same is true of the literates and illiterates. Neither does historical

induction support the widely accepted opinion that increase of literacy, scientific discoveries, technological inventions, or democracy reduces social antagonisms. From the thirteenth to the twentieth century, schools, discoveries, inventions, literacy, and democracies have been all increasing; in the nineteenth and twentieth century they all increased enormously. And yet wars, revolutions, group conflicts, and crimes show that antagonisms have had unprecedented growth (see further Chapters 31, 32, 33). On the other hand these data do not entitle anyone to contend that these factors generate antagonisms.

On the basis of these and other studies similar conclusions follow in regard to other "ineffective" factors enumerated. The popular opinion that these factors generally facilitate either solidarity or antagonism is unsupported by the existing body of evidence.

III. Positive Propositions

1. Immediate Factors of Solidarity and Antagonism

The immediate and most decisive factors of either solidarity or antagonism of the interacting parties are (a) the character of their law and ethical convictions; (b) the concordance or discordance of the law and moral convictions of each party with those of the others; (c) the degree to which these norms are consistently and adequately practiced by the overt actions and vehicles of the parties. The importance of the proposition justifies a concise comment upon it.

a. *Character of Law and Ethical Convictions.* Suppose we have the kinds of law and moral norms shown here:

I

Moral Norms

Love all human beings, help them, cooperate with them, treat them according to the Golden Rule.

Law-Norms

Creditor is entitled to demand the payment of the debt from the debtor, as agreed per contract, and the debtor is obliged to pay his debt. If, however, the debtor becomes insolvent through

many and adverse circumstances in spite of all his efforts honestly to pay the debt, the creditor's claim becomes void until the debtor becomes solvent. The debtor is obliged to do his best to pay the debt when he becomes solvent. Employer must pay to the employee a fair price, no less than $1.00 per hour and more than that if his profit is high. The employee must render an honest service to the employer during the six-hour working day as agreed per contract. In case of sickness or misfortune of either party the other party must help as much as he can.

II

Moral Norms

Hate all human beings; do not help them; compete with them, try to defeat them and be victorious over them by all means at your disposal.

Law-Norms

Creditor is entitled to demand the payment of the debt from the debtor with as high an interest as he can get. In case of insolvency of the debtor the creditor is entitled to appropriate all the property of the debtor, make all the grown-up members of the debtor's family into serfs, or to put the debtor into prison until the debt is paid. Employer is entitled to pay to the employee as low a price as he can and to force the employee to work as many hours as he can enforce. The employee is entitled to demand as high a price as he can get by all means at his disposal and to work as few hours a day as he can get from the employer. In case of sickness or misfortune of either party the other party is entitled to take advantage of him and to impose upon him any condition he can in order to benefit himself.

If we assume that the interacting parties have in one case law and moral norms of the type I, in another case of the type II; if we assume further that these norms are consistently practiced in the overt actions and vehicles of the parties, it becomes evident that the interaction in the first case will be essentially solidary, in the other antagonistic. The very nature of their law and moral norms determines respectively their solidary or antagonistic character. In the first case the norms make the parties mutually sympathetic, cooperative, helpful, and more or less "familistic." In the second, the norms pit the parties one against another as rivals, competitors, enemies who are recommended and entitled to use and misuse the other party as a mere means for the benefit of the victorious party. As a result, other conditions being equal, the interacting parties whose law and moral norms are of a competitive, egocentric character, urging them to defeat, to conquer, to subjugate the other party in all fields of activity, from the football and business field up to the battle field, such a group would have more numerous and more important antagonisms than the interacting parties whose law and moral norms are permeated by the spirit of love, mutual aid, and cooperation. Western society of the last few decades has been permeated mainly by the law and moral norms based upon competition and rivalry. However beneficial such a "fighting spirit of competition" is in many other respects, its existence with various inequalities attendant to it has produced a multitude of antagonisms in the western world, terrible

wars, revolutions and endless conflicts between the racial, ethnic, national, occupational, economic, political, religious, territorial, and other groups and individuals. Experimental studies, like my own and a few others, show this clearly: competition stimulates a greater efficiency but it also brings about "strikes" and conflicts, even among four-year-old children.

Hence, a practical conclusion: *if one wants to make the interacting parties solidary, the first necessary condition is to make their law and moral norms conform to the principles of love, of the Golden Rule, mutual aid, mutual respect and sympathy*, rather than the principles of egocentric competition and rivalry, with their "fighting spirit," "cult of success," superiority of the victors, and inferiority of the defeated. Until this is actually done, all other measures cannot eliminate the antagonism or establish a real solidarity in the interaction of the parties.

b. *Concordance or Discordance of Law and Moral Norms.* The second condition of solidarity or antagonism is the concordance or discordance of the law and moral norms of each party with those of the others. If a master ascribes to himself the right A (for instance, the right of an unlimited domination over his slave) and ascribes to his slave the duty B (unlimited obedience), and if the slave likewise ascribes to his master the right A and to himself the duty B, their law-norms are concordant. If the law and moral convictions of the slave deny the right A to the master and the duty B to himself and ascribe to the master the duty to free all slaves and to himself the right to be free and not to obey the master, their law and moral norms are discordant. The *necessary condition of solidarity of the parties, especially when their law and moral norms are of a competitive, egocentric kind is the concordance of the norms of each party with those of the others.*[3]

We have seen in Chapter 4 that the law-

---

[3] As a qualification to this proposition it is to be added that the *contrast or inequality of privileges and disfranchisements in even concordant norms of the parties should not be too great and contrasting. When the inequality is too great it tends to undermine the concordance of their norms and to generate antagonisms.* In my experiments with children when they were paid equally for their "work" there was not a single strike. When they began to be paid according to the efficiency of their

work, the least efficient and therefore the least remunerated regarded the payment "unfair" and stopped work. The experiments and observations of J. Piaget show also that among all the acts considered by the children "unfair" or "wrong" 27 per cent of such acts were the acts of inequality (in the judgment of the children of 6-9 years old), and 75 per cent of the unfair acts were the acts of inequality in the judgment of the children 9-12 years old. Other experimental and observa-

norms of a person clearly indicate his rights and duties in regard to other persons and their rights and duties in regard to him. We have also seen that the purely imperative moral norms clearly point out the forms of the recommended, though not required, actions-reactions under the specified conditions. As a result when a party performs the overt actions and uses vehicles corresponding to the law-convictions of the other party, such conduct of the first party does not appear antagonistic to the other, does not violate his rights and duties, does not irritate him or make him angry; in brief, generates no animosity or antagonism. Such conduct of the first party does not generate in the other the feelings and emotions of gratitude, admiration, adoration, profound respect, and love. The party does what the other party expects of him, according to his law-convictions. If the actions and vehicles used by the other party correspond, likewise, to the first party's law-convictions, the first party also finds the conduct of the other party satisfactory, free from antagonism and violation of his rights and duties. As a result the interaction of the parties under such concordance of their law-norms becomes free from antagonism and assumes a slightly solidary character.

If now one of the parties not only adequately discharges the rights and duties expected of him by the law-convictions of the other party, but through overt actions and vehicles realizes the recommended moral norms in regard to the other party, goes in generosity far beyond the limits of the law, such conduct of the first party generates in the other feelings, emotions, and ideas of gratefulness, kindness, admiration, respect, sympathy, attachment, and love. If the other party acts in the same way in regard to the first party, the solidarity—in its various shades and gradations—becomes mutual. If such conduct is practiced by both parties continuously, their solidarity and love deepens, becomes stronger and durable.

To summarize, *if the law and moral norms*

of the interacting parties are concordant, and if the parties adequately practice these norms in their overt actions and vehicles in the process of interaction, the interaction becomes non-antagonistic or mixed, even slightly solidary, when the parties' conduct conforms to their concordant law-norms and it becomes solidary when the parties' conduct conforms to their concordant moral norms.

If the law and moral norms of the parties are discordant, that is partly different and partly contradictory to one another; if one party ascribes to himself a right which is denied by the law-norms of the other party; if one party ascribes to the other party a duty which the other party denies; under such discordance of norms and provided the parties carry on these convictions into their overt actions and vehicles, their interaction becomes inevitably antagonistic and the more so the greater are the values involved and the more irreconcilable is the contradiction of their legal and moral norms. Under such conditions the parties violate the rights and duties of one another, hinder realization of the objectives of one another, and become antagonistic. If A ascribes to himself the right to take the property of B, and to B the duty to tolerate his property dispossession; and if B denies such a right of A and such a duty of himself, their law-norms become irreconcilably conflicting; and if each party carries his law-norms into practice, their overt conduct becomes hopelessly antagonistic. If the values involved are unimportant, for instance A ascribes to himself the right to wear blue tie and denies such a right for B, with B denying A's right and his own duty, their antagonism is not very bitter. But if the values are very important, for instance A ascribes to himself a right to use B's wife for his sexual purposes, with B dissenting, the antagonism becomes more virulent, hateful, often mortal.

Thus the concordance or discordance of the law and ethical norms of the interacting parties

---

tional studies, plus the vast series of social antagonisms, riots, revolts, revolutions, strikes, etc., point to the same fact. Even the establishment of concordant moral and legal norms is difficult when the respective rights and duties of the parties are too unequal. Contrasting norms can be established only under coercion, and if established, the concordance of such norms is comparatively unstable

and liable to be broken more easily than the concordance of norms where the inequality of the rights and duties is more limited. However, the margin of inequality can still be fairly wide. See J. Piaget, *The Moral Judgment of the Child,* p. 312; P. A. Sorokin, "Experimental Study," quoted; J. B. Maller, *Cooperation and Competition,* quoted.

determine definitely and immediately the neutrality, solidarity, and antagonism of the interacting parties. In this sense these factors are the first immediate and decisive conditions of solidarity or antagonism.

c. *Degree of Consistency Between Convictions and Actions.* A third condition of solidarity or antagonism is the degree to which these norms are consistently and adequately practiced in the overt-actions and vehicles of the parties. In the preceding analysis we assumed that the parties consistently practice what their law-norms and moral norms preach. In actual reality, however, as we shall see further (Chapter 16), there has hardly existed, in the whole of human history, an individual who practiced in his overt actions and vehicles 100 per cent of his law and moral convictions. Moral norms of Christianity preach the duty of turning the other cheek to the offender, but very few Christians have practiced this norm. Liars, hypocrites, and the like do not practice many of their legal and moral norms, but practice actions and vehicles contradictory to the norms they profess. More or less discrepancy between the legal and moral norms of a person and his overt actions and vehicles exists in all human beings. In an experimental study all my students professed to be free from any discrimination against race, religion, etc.; in their actions all of them transgressed their declared norm. The discrepancy between law-norms and actions is due to different reasons: the norms of some persons are weak, ingrafted, or so superficially inculcated that the causal belt between norms and actions is either non-existent or exceedingly loose, hence functions faultily and ineffectively. As a result, the slightest biological or other temptation induces them to violate their norms and to act "freely" as they please. In other cases the norm, for instance "Don't kill," may be strongly inculcated, but the adverse force of an attack by a murderer or enemy breaks the controlling power of the norm and leads one to kill the murderer or enemy in self-defense, contrary to the norm. From these and other causes human beings do not consistently or adequately realize their own convictions in their actions and vehicles; indeed, they frequently betray their moral and law-norms.

2. Factors Determining the Character of Norms

Though the above formula is quite valid and precise, we cannot stop there but must take further steps in the analysis of our problem. We must now ask three questions: What conditions determine the loving or hating, cooperative or competitive character of the norms of the parties and their concordance or discordance? What conditions determine their consistent realization or violation of these principles in actions and vehicles of the interacting persons and groups? What conditions determine the quantitatively varying magnitude and the qualitatively different intensity of solidarity or antagonism?

The factors determining each of these variables are numerous and far from well known at the present time. Only tentatively can a few general factors be mentioned.

The loving or hating, cooperative or competitive character and the concordance or discordance of the law and moral norms are determined largely by the social and cultural milieu in which the parties were born, reared, live, and act. If, from the moment of birth on, all the interacting parties have been mainly exposed to loving and cooperative norms, and have received from their sociocultural milieu concordant norms, their law and moral convictions will be essentially altruistic and concordant. Otherwise, when the parties are exposed to conflicting and selfish competitive norms they too will be conflicting and selfishly competitive. Since the law and moral norms are not given in the organic world, they are not received through biological heredity, but are planted by the sociocultural milieu. Granting a margin of selection and the combination and invention of norms by an individual, nevertheless, as a general rule, the norms of persons (and groups) born, reared, living, and acting in a sociocultural milieu with altruistic or concordant norms, will be altruistic and concordant; those reared among discordant or competitive norms will be discordant and competitive people.

Therefore, if the social milieu of the interacting parties inculcates only altruistic and concordant norms and implants them deeply into each party, then their interaction will show less antagonism and more solidarity than that of parties exposed to competitive divergent and contradictory norms deeply ingrafted in each party. The sociocultural milieu of the contemporary western world is made up of numerous, predominantly competitive, diverse, and contradictory law and moral norms. There are Hitlerites and anti-Hitlerites, Communists and Capitalists, the poor and the rich, believers and atheists, "virtuous" and cynical men. Law and moral convictions concerning God, the sanctity of marriage, property, crime, or practically any value and norm—all are diverse, contradictory, and mainly competitive. What one group praises the other blames; what one group affirms the other denies. As a result all the persons born, reared, and exposed to such a diverse and contradictory universe of competitive norms cannot help having divergent, competitive, and discordant norms. Therefore, as we shall see, their interactions abound in antagonisms between person and person, group and group; antagonism that has almost reached the situation of the Hobbesian war of all against all. This will be shown further (Chapter 33). Persons born and exposed to a much more concordant universe of mainly cooperative law and moral norms in a preliterate tribe or clan, acquire more cooperative and concordant norms and therefore, within the tribe, have more solidary interactions than those exposed to different norms. For the same reason friends, members of the family, and other groups who have been exposed to an altruistic and a concordant body of ' norms, have more concordant norms; and when deeply inculcated with them, exhibit more solidarity and less antagonism than the members of groups exposed to the competitive divergent and contradictory norms.[4]

As a result, the concordant law and moral norms of parties lead to either neutral or solidary interaction only if and when these norms are adequately realized in the practice and vehicles of the parties. As to discordant and conflicting law and ethical norms, they

lead to antagonism when they are consistently realized by the actions of the parties; often they lead to antagonism even when they are not quite consistently put into practice. The reason for antagonism in the last case is that, though not quite consistently practiced, the norms nevertheless remain conflicting and lead mainly to antagonistic interactions for want of positive concordant norms. Such a lack of concordant norms makes the mutual actions-reactions of the parties haphazard, in part openly antagonistic so far as they objectify the conflicting norms; in part antagonistic because the actions-reactions do not follow any concordant norms. In this latter case the relationships of the parties become unpredictable and anarchistic.

To summarize: On this level of immediate factors the prescription for how to make the interacting parties solidary or antagonistic is very definite and simple. *To achieve a solidary group, first permeate its law-convictions and moral norms with the principles of love and mutual help, inculcate these norms so deeply in personality that the norms become second nature and are unfailingly translated into the actions and vehicles of the parties. Second, permeate their norms with the principle of hatred and rivalry, and make them discordant and conflicting; inculcate these feelings deeply into the parties, and you will invariably get antagonistic interaction.* We will get it in this case even when and where the conflicting norms are not consistently practiced by the parties.

These are the immediate factors of solidarity or antagonism in the interaction of either persons or groups.

3. Factors Determining Motivating and Controlling Force of Norms

To what extent and how consistently a person practices his law and moral norms in his actions and vehicles depends upon how deeply the norms are ingrained within the person or how great is their motivating and controlling

---

[4] This proposition makes the character and concordance or discordance of norms a result of the character of the sociocultural milieu in which the members were born and in which they live. The problem can and should be pushed further in this recessive chain of causes. For its further elucidation one can ask the question: Why do some of the sociocultural milieux have concordant and coop-

erative norms while others have discordant and competitives norms. Such a recessive deepening of the causal analysis is, however, outside of the tasks of this work; it is a task for a special monograph. The totality of the propositions of this chapter answer to some extent even this question.

power over the person's overt actions and vehicles; in other words, how strong and tight is the causal belt uniting the individual's norms with his overt actions and vehicles. Of many instrumental factors determining the causal relationship between the norms and overt actions the following can be mentioned.

(a) The nature of the norm is related to the basic biological needs of a person. Other conditions being equal, *the norms that demand conduct contrary to drives of the primary biological needs, that repress these needs and hinder their satisfaction, have less chance of becoming a powerful motivating force in overt actions than norms not opposed to the satisfaction of the basic biological needs.* In the first case the power of the norm is greatly weakened by the opposite pressure of the biological needs while in the second case the motivating force is reinforced by their power. For this reason the "contra-biological" norms are likely to be violated by the interacting parties more frequently than the "pro-biological" norms. Through this more frequent violation of contra-biological norms in the overt actions of the parties their interaction is bound to be more frequently antagonistic, even when their norms are concordant, than in the case of the concordant pro-biological norms.

(b) *Causal efficiency of a law or moral norm depends also upon its concordance or conflict with other law and moral norms of the same party.* When a given norm A contradicts the norms of B, C, D, of the same party (for instance, the norm "love your enemy" and the norm "killing an enemy is a heroic and patriotic action"), such a norm A and the other contradictory norms B, C, D, mutually weaken one another and have less causal effectiveness in their realization through actions. Yet when the norm A is concordant with others, say M, N, X, each of these norms is reinforced mutually by the others and each is more consistently practiced.

(c) *Causal efficiency (depth of inculcation) of a norm depends also upon the specific properties of the individual or group.* As individuals and groups are never identical and always differ from one another through biological, psychosocial, and cultural properties, the same norm A cannot be inculcated with equal success into their personality and conduct. The norm "don't drink alcohol" sincerely professed by a habitual alcoholic and by a temperate person will be violated by the alcoholic more frequently than by the temperate person. The norm "remain chaste and virgin" cannot be ingrafted as strongly in a person whose respective glands and biological constitution powerfully urge a satisfaction of the sex-drive as in a person with undeveloped glands and a biological constitution with weak sex impulses. The same can be said of a great many biological, psychological, and sociocultural differences of persons and groups.

(d) *The causal efficiency of the norm depends upon the consequences of its realization.* If the practice of the ingrafted norm is followed by positive (pleasant, desirable, welcome) effects for the party, the repeated positive consequences of the practiced norm progressively reinforce its motivating force and causal effectiveness. If the consequences turn out to be negative (painful, undesirable, unwelcome) it will be practiced less and less, will progressively weaken, and be more and more frequently violated.

(e) Regardless of the positive or negative consequences of the norm's realization in practice *the more frequently and unfailingly it is practiced, the stronger it becomes as a causal factor of actions and vehicles.* The less it is practiced the more impotent it becomes as a controlling force of the individual's actions and vehicles.

(f) Finally, the causal efficiency of the norms depends upon the concordance or discordance of all the law and moral norms of a given population. *The more mutually concordant are all the law and moral norms in a given population, the deeper each norm is bound to be inculcated into its members, the greater becomes its motivating power, and the more consistently is it translated into the overt actions of the members.* And vice versa, the greater the discrepancy and contradiction between the law and moral norms of a given population, the more frequently each norm is violated in the practice of its members. In a concordant legal and moral universe each norm reinforces the others and is reinforced by them. Each norm is universally recognized and backed by a unanimous public opinion and public pressure. No norm will have a challenging or competing norm. Each newly born member is exposed to this norm. It therefore has a monopoly in that society. Under these circumstances each norm is experienced as something sacred, inviolable, unconditionally binding. Norms like these in such a concordant moral and legal universe obtain a much greater causal effectiveness in governing overt conduct than norms discordant and conflicting with one another. By their mutual contradiction such norms weaken one another, become more and more relative and less and less universally binding; they are devoid of support by a unanimous public opinion and pressure. None of the norms has a monopoly to which alone individuals are exposed. Such norms do not have a halo of sacredness, universality, or inviolability, but are experienced as purely conventional rules to be broken at any convenient moment. For these reasons they cannot have great motivating power and are violated by the overt actions much more frequently than the norms of the concordant legal and moral universe. As we shall see further (Chapter 42) one of the tragedies of the contemporary western world is exactly this excessive discordance of its legal and moral norms, their excessive relativity and therefore comparatively weak motivating force in controlling the behavior of western populations. An emergence of rude force, assisted by the fraud of "might is right" in such conditions becomes inevitable; and with that, an increase of antagonisms in all their forms.

On the basis of the above factors of causal effectiveness in norms we can say that other conditions being equal: the more concordant is the sociocultural universe in its legal and moral norms to which interacting parties have been exposed, the less violently the concordant norms of the parties oppose their basic biological drives, the more consistent the norms of each party are with one another and with those of the other parties, the more positive are the consequences of their practice for the parties, the more frequently and unfailingly the concordant norms are practiced by the parties, the more they fit the biopsychosociocultural properties of the parties, *the more consistently and adequately legal and moral norms are realized in the actions and vehicles of the parties and therefore the more solidary be-*

comes their interaction. The converse is also true.

4. Factors Determining Intensity and Extensity of Solidarity and Antagonism

The most significant factor determining the intensity and extensity of antagonism or solidarity is the importance of the values involved. *The more important (qualitatively and quantitatively) are the values because of which and for the sake of which parties interact, the greater their solidarity or antagonism will be.* If the discordance of the parties concerns an insignificant value, for instance, whether they should buy Scotch or rye whisky, the ensuing antagonism will be slight in intensity and extensity. If their discordance involves values that are exceedingly important in the value-system of the parties, for instance, their life, freedom, love, property, religion, sociopolitical status, dignity, etc., ensuing antagonism will be intense and extended over a large sector of their values. Sometimes the antagonism is so intense and so extensive that it can be quenched only through an extermination of the other party and of all his values. The same is true of the solidarities of the parties.

This general proposition will become more precise through considering two different situations: one, where both or all parties regard a given value as similarly important or unimportant; the other, where one party regards it as important, while the other party considers it unimportant. In the first case, both or all parties have a *common fund of values*; all regard the values *A* as important or unimportant. In the other case, there is no common fund of values; what one party regards as important, the other estimates as of zero or insignificant value. *Intense solidarities and antagonisms are possible only when there is a common fund of important values. Where there is no such fund of values the relationship of the parties assumes a neutral, indifferent character, neither intensely solidary nor intensely antagonistic.* If *A* is a devotee of tennis and esteems its value highly, or if he is in love with a lady; and if *B* regards tennis of neither positive nor negative value nor cares in any way for the lady, provided that the interaction of *A* and *B* is limited only to the value of tennis or of the lady, they do not become either intensely solidary or antagonistic. "If he enjoys his hobby, let him enjoy it," is the attitude in such relationships.

Parties who have a common fund of important values (a) will be solidary if the values are abundant and the norms of the parties concordantly urge the greatest realization of the values by each party; (b) if the important values are scarce and cannot be had in unlimited abundance by each party, the parties will be solidary if their law and moral systems are permeated by love and the Golden Rule and if the scarce values are distributed among them according to these norms; (c) the parties will still be slightly solidary, and at least free from antagonism, when the scarce values are distributed according to their concordant law and moral norms; if the concordance demands an equal distribution, such a distribution will cause no antagonism; if it requires an unequal ("justly-proportional") distribution, then such a distribution will cause no antagonism. If an employer and employee are similarly convinced that their shares from an enterprise ought to be unequal, and the employer is entitled to have a much larger share than the employee, their relationship will remain free from antagonism. If an employer gives to the employee a bonus exceeding the legal share of the employee, their relationship becomes solidary. Under these conditions parties will be largely free from antagonism if the value (e.g., person loved by both parties) cannot be shared. The losing party may be saddened, but he will not become an enemy of the winning party.

Parties having a *common fund of important values* will be antagonistic when, despite an abundance of the values, their norms and respective conduct are permeated by the principles of hatred, egotism, unlimited rivalry and competition, and each party tries to get more of these values than the other. With a scarcity of values, they will be still more antagonistic under such a system. When their law and moral norms are discordant, even equal distribution of the scarce values will not help in their case if the norms and conduct of one party demand an unequal, while those of the other require an equal distribution.[5] Especially when their norms and respective conduct are quite contradictory, those of one party will affirm what those of the other party deny. Hitlerites and anti-Hitlerites agree that political or economic values are important, but the Hitlerite brand of these values is in essential contradiction with the anti-Hitlerite values; each party regards the values of the other party as important, but of negative importance. Two lovers both value highly the same lady with whom they are in love; but their norms are contradictory in the sense that one party affirms his right to marry the lady and denies such a right to the other party. The same is true in all cases of a struggle for power and domination, of states and nations, religious bodies, and other groups and persons put into that contradictory (discordant) position.

These are the most important factors or variables determining the fluctuation of intensity and extensity in solidarity and antagonism.

IV. Concrete Uniformities Derived from Above General Formula

This general formula of the factors of solidarity and antagonism makes comprehensible, illustrates, corroborates, and corrects several concrete uniformities in this field observed and formulated by many thinkers of the past and present. Three of such concrete uniformities can be mentioned in this chapter; a fourth

uniformity, extensively worked out by many investigators, will be discussed and corrected in the next chapter.

1. Effect of Increased Social Distance

Intensity of solidarity decreases with increase of social distance (discordance and con-

---

[5] Here Aristotle's generalization is quite pertinent. Under such conditions, "those who aim at equality will be ever ready for sedition, if they see those whom they esteem their equals possess more than they do." Likewise seditious become "those who are not content with equality and aim at superiority, if they think that while they deserve more they have only equal with or less than their inferiors." Aristotle, *Politics*, 130-32.

tradiction of the norms) of the parties. Everyone is most solidary with himself, as a party identical in all values and norms. Everyone of us ordinarily is most intensely, familistically solidary with the members of our family and with a few real friends, those with whom we have a large common fund of values, in regard to whom our norms are permeated by love and the Golden Rule; with whom our norms are most concordant; and in regard to whom our actions practice more adequately what our norms preach. Likewise the conditions favorable for an inculcation of these norms into our behavior are, within such a milieu of family or friends, more frequently met than in other and larger sociocultural milieux.

As the social distance between us and other human beings increases, the intensity of our solidarity progressively decreases. The intensity of our solidarity and love, especially in our actions, is considerably lower in regard to persons and groups even of the same town or city than in regard to our family and friends; it becomes still lower in regard to the other citizens of our state; and still less intense toward people as remote as the Chinese and Tasmanians. The same decrease of intensity uniformly occurs when we pass from our immediate group of co-religionists, say, Catholics, of the same parish, to the Catholics of other counties, states of the United States, then to the Catholics of other countries, then to other Christian denominations, then to the members of the non-Christian religions. The same is true in regard to occupational or political party members, and to members of any other group. In our speech reactions we may profess an equal solidarity with the whole of mankind, but in our actions we hardly ever practice this. Our solidarity rapidly decreases with social distance between ourselves and others. Experimental studies have shown this clearly and unanimously.[6]

The above propositions explain this decreasing intensity of solidarity with an increase of social distance. Our solidarity with the members of the family and friends is intense because (a) our interaction with them and interdependence is intense; (b) because most of us are taught from birth the values and norms of love and the Golden Rule, cooperation and help in regard to the members and friends; (c) because respective actions are implanted in us more persistently and in most favorable conditions for them to become efficient; (d) because our law and moral norms are more concordant with those of members of the family and friends than with norms of other, more remote groups; (e) because the values involved in the interaction of members of family and friends are most important, most extensive, covering almost all the main values of the parties.

If, on the other hand, we take some remote group, say, Russians, Chinese, or Trobrianders, many of us do not profess any particular solidarity with them. Others who profess it rarely show solidarity in their actions and if it is manifested, it is shortlived, narrow, and weak. The reasons are at hand. Our interaction with these distant peoples is at best only indirect and discontinuous; our interdependence is remote and often intangible. We are not taught as persistently, as early, and as deeply the norms of love for them; we are taught to be indifferent and even inimical to them. Our norms and other values are predominantly divergent, in a considerable part discordant with theirs; we rarely practice the norms of the Golden Rule in regard to them, or they in regard to us. The values involved in interaction are few, narrow in character, and in no way co-extensive with our life; for many there is hardly any real contact with them. For all these reasons, including the more detailed factors discussed above, the intensity of our solidarity with distant individuals and groups cannot help being weak, intermittent, sporadic, sometimes even totally lacking. Ranging on the one hand is the declining scale of the intensity of our sympathy, love, solidarity, cooperation with various groups; while on the other are the groups or persons who range along the scale of increasing discrepancy of their law and moral convictions with ours. We shall find that both series of groups are parallel. The more a given person or group is a "stranger" to us, the more discrepant are his norms from ours, the weaker is our sympathy to such persons and groups.

[6] See Sorokin, "An Experimental Study," quoted at the beginning of this chapter.

2. Solidary Effect of Uniting Against a Common Enemy

The easiest and quickest way to have a temporary solidarity of heterogeneous persons and groups is the creation of an enemy common to all of them and menacing the important values of each person or group. The emergence of Hitler's Reich and of Japan as common enemies of the Allies brought into solidary cooperation very divergent and even contradictory nations, groups, and persons. The common enemy menacing the most important values of each allied nation served as a unifying force binding together the heterogeneous motley of nations and groups. And the greater the danger to the paramount values the more efficacious is the solidarizing role of the common enemy either of several heterogeneous persons, or of states, religious groups, political factions, occupational unions, or of other groups. However important are their discordances, if there appears a common enemy with discordant norms and menacing more important values of each party than the values menaced mutually by one party in regard to those of the others, the common enemy unites them temporarily into a solidary group fighting the common enemy. When the common enemy is defeated and removed, the discordances among the previous allies reappear.

The reasons for this uniformity on which the policy of the *divide et impera* has always been built are given in the preceding formula. A common enemy becomes a paramount threat to the values of all the parties menaced by it. The enemy's norms and values are much more discordant and contradictory to the norms and values of all the prospective allies than are the norms and values of the allies with one another, and so on, hence the effective and quickly unifying role of a common enemy. However, this solidarity bound by the belt of a common enemy disappears as quickly as it arises; as soon as the enemy is eliminated, the solidarity evaporates also.

3. Explanation of Contemporary Antagonistic Trend

These factors of solidarity and antagonism explain also the contemporary hurricane of sharpest antagonisms raging over the whole

of humanity. Likewise they satisfactorily account, as we shall see further, in chapters dealing with war, revolutions, and group tensions, for the rise and decline of war and peace, of order and revolutions, and of group tensions in the dynamics of these phenomena in the history of the Graeco-Roman, western, and other populations. Modern culture and society for the last few decades have brought into contact the most divergent peoples and groups, possessing the most varied law and moral convictions, as well as other important values behind the law and moral norms. Thus the discrepancy of their norms has increased. Furthermore, western culture in recent centuries has been inculcating mainly selfish, competitive, and utilitarian norms vs. the unconditional moral norms of universal love of Christianity. In addition modern culture has progressively produced more and more conditional and relativistic, and therefore less and less binding legal and moral norms, which clash with, and contradict one another. It has made paramount mainly material, sensory values—wealth, pleasure, comfort, popularity, sexual love, worldly fame—which by their nature are scarce and cannot be possessed in abundance by all. As a result, the law and moral norms of various persons and groups have become more and more discrepant and mutually contradictory; even those norms that remain concordant are practiced less and violated more. The scarcity of material values has made the struggle for their possession more intense, less controlled by norms than by the rude force of "might is right." In such conditions, the sharp antagonisms among men and groups are bound to grow to an extent unprecedented in the preceding twenty-five centuries of the Graeco-Roman and western world. They have made the twentieth century the bloodiest, the most cruel, hate-loaded, destructive, turbulent, and antagonistic century of all. Humanity has approached a situation not far from the Hobbesian *bellum omnium contra omnes*. Almost every group is at war with other groups. The thunder of hatreds and the tornado of antagonisms roar over the whole planet. With the atomic bomb, invented under pressure of this gigantic explosion of hatred, the tornado of antagonisms menaces the very existence of humanity itself. We are harvesting the inevitable fruits of egotism instead of love; of widely discordant norms among various persons and groups; of failure in practicing what the concordant norms preach.

Peace and solidarity can be re-established only (a) if the values and norms of love and the Golden Rule replace competitive norms: (b) if the main norms become concordant and unconditionally binding for all groups and persons; (c) if these concordant norms are causally effective and practiced in the behavior of all. All the factors and conditions that work in this direction become the agencies of peace and solidarity. All that work against this direction are forces of strife and antagonism. Until these three main conditions are accomplished, no durable and just peace, no real solidarity of mankind can be realized. Those who offer various easy solutions fool themselves and others.

These are some of the concrete illustrations of the factors of solidarity and antagonism. Now let us turn to the role of similarity and dissimilarity in solidarity and antagonism. Its relative importance deserves a more detailed analysis, and the analysis will permit us to make much more concrete the above principles and to correct errors in the prevalent theories.

Chapter 7. The Roles of Similarity and Dissimilarity in Social Solidarity and Antagonism

I. Practical Importance of the Problem

Like many a preceding generation we are confronted once again with the problem of the role which similarity and dissimilarity play in solidary and antagonistic interrelationships; in the phenomena of social cohesion and disunity; and in creativity and sterility of persons and groups. In a dozen important social fields the problem confronts us not only in a theoretical way but in an urgent practical way. Thus, to have a "happy, strong, lasting marriage" shall one marry a party similar to oneself in race, stature, color, weight, nationality, religion, socio-economic status, and so on, or does such a marriage demand marrying a dissimilar party? If similar or dissimilar, what kind of similarities and dissimilarities are particularly important for the purpose? If there must be a combination of similarities and dissimilarities what sort of combination and what kind of similarities and dissimilarities will be best? The problem thus forcibly invades the field of the family and marriage and becomes of paramount practical importance to all persons of marriageable age.

No less urgent is it in practically all other fields of social cohesion and unity. In order to have a solidary and united social group, shall we strive to build such a group of members similar to one another in racial or sociocultural characteristics, or will the aspired unity and solidarity be better achieved through a racial and sociocultural diversity of its members? If the desired end may be better achieved through one of these ways, then what kind of similarities and dissimilarities will be particularly important for the particular social group?

At present the "problem of minorities" is one of the most urgent of our time. Any solution of it in terms of "assimilation and amalgamation" would imply a belief in that form of social unity and solidarity which is based upon similarities. On the other hand, its solution in terms of the maintenance and development of racial and sociocultural diversity presupposes a belief in solidarity and unity based upon dissimilarities. The same is true in regard to the cultural creativity of persons and social groups. Other conditions being equal, does creativity explode and blossom mainly in likeminded groups with identical "consciousness of kind," and with a uniform and standardized culture (religion, fine arts, political credo, scientific and philosophical views, etc.)? Does it flower for all its members mainly in groups with a multitude of diversified cultural cur-

132

rents, different religious sects, scientific and philosophical schools, political factions, heterogeneous artistic divisions, and so on?

These remarks should indicate the urgent theoretical and practical importance of the problem at the present time.

II. Main Theories

Let us now glance at the kinds of answers to the problems offered by those who have studied it in various fields. These solutions readily fall into the three main classes suggested by thinkers of past societies confronted with the problem, and are well summed up by Aristotle. He tells us:

There is much difference of opinion as to the nature of friendship. Some define it as a matter of similarity; they say that we love those who are like ourselves; whence the proverbs, "Like finds his like," "Birds of a feather flock together," and so on; others, on the contrary, say that with men who are alike it is always a case of "two of a trade." Some try to find a more profound and scientific explanation of the nature of affection. Euripides writes that "Earth yearneth for the rain, when dried up, and the majestic heaven when filled with rain yearneth to fall to earth." Heraclitus says, "Opposition unites" and "The fairest harmony springs from discord." Others maintain the opposite view, notably Empedocles, who declares that "like seek after like."[1]

If we add to these opposite views a third one, which claims a certain combination of similarities and dissimilarities as the most conclusive to friendship, solidarity, love, harmony and unity, we have all the three main solutions proffered at the present time. First, there is the theory which argues for similarity as the basis of solidarity in all kinds of groups beginning with marriage and ending with the state and other societies. F. Giddings' theory of "likemindedness" and "consciousness of kind"; the Nazi theory of "One blood, one race, one nation, one State"; all the theories of the inevitability of tensions and conflicts between different racial, ethnic, and sociocultural groups up to those of the partisans of

[1] Aristotle, *The Nicomachean Ethics*, tr. by Racknar (New York, 1926), Book VIII, 16, p. 454.

"homogamy in marriage" are varieties of this solution.

Second, there is the theory that a stable, durable, and fruitful solidarity exists mainly, if not exclusively, in groups made up of diverse racial, ethnic, or sociocultural (religious, scientific, artistic, occupational, economic, etc.) elements. All those theories which claim that in marriage and friendship "the opposite poles attract"; that durable and free solidarity is possible only in societies with a "social division of labor"; that a cross-fertilization of diverse cultural elements is the necessary condition for social or individual creativity; that the only rational policy in regard to minorities is a facilitation of their specific and unique traits; that the most fruitful and durable societies are those which represent "unity in diversity"—these and many other theories are but variations upon this second solution. Its samples will be discussed further.

Finally, the third solution gives us two main varieties. One contends that any real solidarity is based neither upon similarity nor dissimilarity but upon a certain combination of both. The same is held to be true of social antagonisms and tensions. From the standpoint of this theory both of the preceding theories are factually deficient, and logically fallacious. The other variation of this viewpoint is represented by all those theories which admit two different kinds of solidarity: one based upon similarity, the other upon dissimilarity. Both solidarities are real but they differ from one another in a number of characteristics. The well known "mechanical" and "organic" solidarities of E. Durkheim, the solidarities of F. Tönnies' *Gemeinschaft* and *Gesellschaft*; and the different cohesions implied in the concepts "community" and "association" of many sociologists are examples of this variation of the third solution.

III. The Role of Similarity-
Dissimilarity in Marriage Solidarity

Let us now examine critically which of these rival theories is valid. At the present time we have a considerable body of empirical data which permits us to test this validity. When properly analyzed the data also disclose the true complexity of the problem, often overlooked by many. We may begin our test in terms of data concerning choice in marriage, and its possible stability and happiness. A happy and stable marriage is one of the most general and most intense forms of interpersonal solidarity. Even a shortlived marriage union will have this intense solidarity at its initial stages. For this reason the factual evidence in this field becomes decidedly relevant to our problem. If the evidence shows that choice of the marriage partner is governed mainly by similarity and that happy and stable marriages are generally between parties similar to one another, such a uniformity would testify in favor of the theory of similarity. If the data show a different situation, they obviously would be supporting either the theory of dissimilarity or that of the combination of similarity-dissimilarity. Let us begin with choice in marriage. Does it follow the rule "like begets like" or does it follow the rule "opposite poles attract"?

The predominant answer seems to be in favor of like marrying like (homogamy or assortative mating). A considerable number of investigators have compared engaged or married couples in terms of their race, stature, weight, cephalic index, color of eyes and hair, age, health, longevity, and other physical characteristics; in their intelligence, temperament, nationality, religion, education, economic and occupational status; in their family background, tastes, manners, mores, and other psychological and sociocultural traits. The result obtained in most of the studies is that the actual ratio of similarity in the characteristics investigated is notably higher than that which would be expected if there were no special attraction of like to like.[2] Measured by the coefficient of correlation or of contingency the resemblance in physical traits of the couples is around .2, in psychological traits around .4 or .5. Measured by the coefficient of mean square contingency the similarity in various sociocultural characteristics fluctuates between .1 and .5. In only a few studies do the results fail to show either a homogamy or a heterogamy (attraction of the dissimilar).

Shall we conclude from this that there is a special attraction of similarity in engaged and married couples; that it is a universal rule, and that "we cannot doubt that like actually tend to mate with like in the case of man," as K. Pearson, one of the pioneers in the study of homogamy, puts it;[3] that the studies demonstrate the importance of similarity as a paramount condition for solidarity of any other group?

In spite of fairly uniform results such conclusions would be rather hasty. (1) Several technical considerations caution against a rash acceptance of such conclusions: (a) coefficients of correlation in most of the studies in regard to many traits are rather low and are hardly significant statistically; (b) in different studies the coefficients of resemblance in the same traits are inconsistent—now high, now low, sometimes positive, sometimes negative; (c) in several studies like Kretschmer's and a few others, the results favor heterogamy; (d) the objectivity of the coefficients and conclusions is greatly vitiated by arbitrary assumptions, arbitrary assignment of different weights to different items and other subjective judgments underlying the objective looking figures. For these technical reasons the validity of the

[2] See the summaries of such studies in E. Burgess and P. Wallin, "Homogamy in Social Characteristics," *AJS*, Vol. XLIX (1943), pp. 109-124; C. A. Anderson, "Our Present Knowledge of Assortative Mating," *Rural Sociology*, Vol. III (1938), pp. 296-302; H. E. Jones, "Homogamy in Intellectual Abilities," *AJS*. Vol. XXXV (1929), pp. 369-382;

H. M. Richardson, "Studies of Mental Resemblance Between Husbands and Wives and Between Friends," *Psychological Bulletin*, XXXVI (1939), pp. 104-120.
[3] K. Pearson, *Grammar of Science* (London, 1902), p. 431.

results obtained becomes rather questionable.

(2) Other considerations and facts make very questionable the existence of a special mysterious "attraction of like for like." Its nature has hardly been analyzed by its partisans and remains essentially unknown. More than that, even in the seemingly homogamic marriages it remains unknown as to whether the seeming homogamy is due to this mystical attraction or simply to the fact of a limited sphere of available contact and interaction for each of the parties. Two persons who do not meet and do not enter into contact evidently cannot fall in love, become engaged and be married. Accessibility of contact, and lasting interaction of the parties, are necessary conditions for a subsequent engagement and marriage of couples who marry by their own choice and consent. Persons living in widely separated places do not have the same chance to meet one another and to fall in love and marry as persons living in the same neighborhood. Such a fact does not mean that there is a special mysterious attraction of persons living in spatial proximity and a disattraction of persons living in widely separated places. It simply means that the opportunity of meetings, contacts, and interaction of parties living in the same block as contrasted with those living in widely separated places is entirely different. For this reason—and not by virtue of any mysterious attraction of like to like—an overwhelming proportion of marriages is between persons living in the same neighborhood. In Philadelphia, out of 5,000 marriages studied for the period 1885-1931, 67.3 per cent were between persons living within twenty blocks or less of each other. Of these 49.9 per cent of the marriages were between parties living within nine blocks of each other or less.[4] Similarly in New Haven 76 per cent of the marriages in 1940 were between persons living within twenty blocks of each other, and 35 per cent within five blocks.[5] Several other studies present a similar picture. That such a situation is due not to the special attraction of like to like but rather to a greater availability of contact for persons living in spatial propinquity is negatively corroborated by the fact of very infrequent marriages between persons who, though living in spatial propinquity, do not contact or interact with one another because of "social obstacles to interaction" as between the rich and the poor, high society and the underdogs, and the like. The contrasts in social status, wealth, religion, language, race, and many other sociocultural traits are as great obstacles to the meeting, mixing, and interacting of prospective bridegrooms and brides as a spatial isolation. As a rule the poor interact mainly with the poor; the rich with the rich; the Italians or Poles of the first generation immigrants mainly with other Italians or Poles, respectively. Hence, the opportunity for falling in love and marrying is immeasurably less for "socially separated" persons than for persons of the same social circle. This objective difference in the availability, frequency, and intimacy of contacts adequately accounts for the general prevalence of so-called homogamic marriages over the heterogamic ones. The hypothesis of the attraction of like for like would have been proved only when, in a universe of prospective parties with equally available contact and interaction for everyone with all others, it were found that persons marry more frequently those who are similar. So far none of the studies have given to us such a result in the specified universe.

This objective factor of unequal opportunity of contact and interaction accounts for a great part of the prevalence of marriages by Italians with Italians, Jews with Jews, Poles with Poles, rich with rich, Catholics with Catholics, and many other forms of so-called homogamy. A considerable body of the data well supports this theory and clearly contradicts the theory of a special attraction of like for like. If such a hypothesis were valid we should expect it to be universal, operating equally for various persons and groups. Meanwhile we find that in a Minnesota county, out of 1,000 matings, Italians mate with Italians in 828 to 970 cases (respectively by husbands and wives), Poles mate with Poles in 815 to 910, Hungarians with Hungarians in 856 to 849; but the British, Canadians, and Germans give only from 295 to 421 "homogamous"

---

[4] R. H. Abrams, "Residential Propinquity as a Factor in Marriage Selection," *ASR*, Vol. VIII (1943), pp. 288-294.

[5] R. Kennedy, "Premarital Residential Propinquity," *AJS*, Vol. XLVIII (1943), pp. 580-584.

marriages.[6] If there were any mysterious attraction of like for like, it seems that for some still more mysterious reason this attraction is effective for Italians and Poles but is very ineffective for the British, Canadians, and Germans, who appear to be greatly exempt from its power. The real explanation of the difference is, of course, much simpler and does not presuppose any mysterious attraction. The Italians, the Poles, and the Hungarians, being generally later immigrants with a peculiar sociocultural background, are much less "amalgamated" and assimilated and carry on their interaction much more within their own national groups than do the British or the Germans, hence the difference. This explanation is corroborated by the fact that the percentage of mixed marriages ethnically heterogamous is much higher in subsequent generations than in the first or second.[7]

The same result is given by other studies. R. Kennedy's study of international and interreligious marriages in New Haven shows, first, that the "homogamous" marriages between the same nationals declined from 91.2 per cent in 1870 to 75.9 per cent in 1900, and to 63.6 per cent in 1940. To explain this decline in homogamy by a supposed decline in the power of our mysterious attraction is evidently impossible. In that case the question "Why did the power of the attraction decline?" would present an almost insoluble problem. The same study shows further that the per cent of the religiously homogamous marriages is quite different for different groups; while Jews marry Jews in almost 100 per cent of the cases (97 and 94 per cent in 1930 and 1940), the Catholic religiously homogamous marriages show only 83 per cent and the Protestant marriages yield only 78 per cent.[8] Here again, for an unknown reason, our mysterious attraction seems to operate differently for different religious groups. These considerations and data leave hardly any doubt that even in so-called homogamous marriages the real cause of the homogamy is often not our mysterious attraction of like for like, but rests on the differences in availability of contact and interaction between the parties concerned, plus several other factors to be discussed further.

(3) The next set of evidence cautioning against similarity as the decisive factor in marriage selection or in "marital happiness" is that husband-wife similarity (or dissimilarity) in a number of traits does not show a high correlation with happiness or unhappiness in marriage. L. M. Terman and associates obtained no significant relationship between husband-wife similarity or dissimilarity and happy or unhappy marriages.[9] The same study shows also that the degree of husband-wife resemblance runs comparatively high in happy and unhappy marriages of office clerks and lawyers and very low in those of chemists and certified public accountants,[10] which difference, if typical, can hardly be reconciled with the hypothesis of a mysterious attraction or of a paramount importance of similarity for marriage happiness.

The study of E. Burgess and L. Cottrell found a somewhat significant correlation of happy marriages with agreement of husband and wife in regard to several items and of disagreement in unhappy marriages; but agreement and disagreement is something very different from similarity and dissimilarity of the parties in this or that physical or sociocultural characteristic. Furthermore, even in the agreement the coefficients of correlation were only moderately significant (from .2 to .5). As a detail, in this study they found that agreement in religious matters has a low correlation with happiness in marriage while the Burgess-Wallin study found that similarity in religion has the highest correlation with choice in marriage.[11] This discrepancy makes both conclusions somewhat questionable and again cautions against the theory of homogamy and similarity.

(4) Another set of contradictory evidence is

---

[6] L. Nelson, "Intermarriage Among Nationality Groups." *AJS*, Vol. XLVIII (1943), pp. 585-593; see also J. Kolemainen, "A Study of Marriage in a Finnish Community," *Ibid*, Vol. XLII (1936), p. 376.

[7] See the data in J. Kolemainen's study quoted.

[8] R. Kennedy, "Single or Triple Melting Pot," *AJS*, Vol. XLIX (1944), pp. 331-340.

[9] L. M. Terman, *Psychological Factors in Marital Happiness* (New York, 1938), pp. 19 ff.

[10] *Ibid.*, p. 19.

[11] E. Burgess and L. Cottrell, Jr., *Predicting Success or Failure in Marriage* (New York, 1939), pp. 50 ff. Compare with E. Burgess and P. Wallin, "Homogamy in Social Characteristics," quoted p. 124.

given by a widely spread phenomena of exogamy, accompanied by a prohibition of marriages with a close degree of consanquinity. If similarity and attraction of like for like is a decisive factor in choice at marriage and in marital cohesiveness and happiness, such mores, quite contradictory to the principle of similarity, simply could not appear or be widely practiced. Still less could they persist for centuries in a vast number of groups, since they expressly demand dissimilar parties for marriage. Their existence clearly testifies against the paramount importance of similarity and attraction of like for like.

(5) The decisive line of evidence against the theory that solidarity and love in marriage or in any other social group is based always and entirely upon similarity is the very fact of the highly intense love, solidarity, and devotion between persons of *different* sexes whether in marriage or out of marriage. Homosexual love has always represented an insignificant fraction of heterosexual love. This simple fact means that in marriage and in family groups bisexual heterogeneity of the parties is a rule, while their homogeneity is an exception.

The totality of these sets of evidence is sufficient to make the theory of similarity and of homogamy, as a specific attraction of like for like, undemonstrated and highly questionable.

To reject the theory of homogamy and of similarity as the paramount factor of either choice in marriage or of its happiness and stability does not mean an acceptance of the opposite theory of the attraction of opposite poles and of dissimilarity as the basis of durable and happy marital solidarity. The widely spread rule of marriage endogamy as well as a number of facts stressed by the partisans of homogamy in marriage contradict such a theory explicitly and make it even more unacceptable than the theory of similarity. As we have already seen, the Poles and Italians marry mainly Poles and Italians. The same is true of other national groups. Jews, Catholics, and Protestants marry mainly Jews, Catholics, and Protestants. The rich marry mainly the rich and the poor, the poor; the negroes marry mainly negroes, and so on. Thus there is little ground for any generalization of the theory of dissimilarity and heterogamy.

IV. Preliminary Analysis

If neither the theory of similarity nor of dissimilarity, neither homogamy nor heterogamy is acceptable, what then remains? Evidently there is the third theory, suggesting a certain combination of similar and dissimilar traits as the foundation of solidarity generally, of choice in marriage, and especially, of marriage happiness.

A body of evidence in favor of such a thesis has been given by a study of close friends or pairs of chums from this standpoint. A study of 300 pairs of chums disclosed that in a grand total of 2,962 of their behavior traits the chums were similar, and in 1,484 traits they were dissimilar. In 88 per cent of their

standards and ideals they were similar, similarity decreasing to 50 per cent in hobbies, reading habits, and shopping habits.[12]

The argument for a combination of similar and dissimilar traits is corroborated also by the contradictory results of other studies of friendships in relationship to similarity-dissimilarity characteristics. Challman, Flemming, Winslow, Richardson, and others have found several similarities between friends in nursery school children, school children, and adults; but in other respects their friends are dissimilar. On the other hand, Pintner, Forlano, Freedman, and others found very low correlation between friends and their similarities.[13]

---

[12] E. Bogardus and P. Otto, "Social Psychology of Chums," *SSR*, Vol. XX, pp. 260-270; E. Bogardus, "Social Distance," *Ibid*, Vol. XXII; 466-67.
[13] See R. C. Challman, "Factors Influencing Friendships Among Pre-School Children," *Child Development*, Vol. III (1932), pp. 46-158; E. G. Flemming, "Best Friends," *Journal of Social Psy-*

chology, Vol. III (1932), pp. 385-390; C. H. Winslow, "A Study of the Extent of Agreement Between Friends' Opinions and Their Ability to Estimate the Opinions of Each Other," *Journal of Social Psychology*, Vol. VII (1937), pp. 433-442; H. M. Richardson, "Community of Values as a

As to marriage solidarity, dissimilarity is always present in it, first of all in the fact of sexual difference, not to mention other dissimilar traits of the parties, deriving partly from biological sex-difference, partly from sociocultural and personality conditions. Likewise, a similarity in regard to the most important values of both parties seems to be necessary in order for the marriage solidarity to be intense, strong, and durable. If the data of the partisans of homogamy do not prove their thesis, they do show that in "happy" marriages there is given a higher degree of resemblance and agreement between the parties than in unhappy or divorced marriages.

The Burgess-Cottrell study, already mentioned, shows a correlation of agreement between the parties (in handling finances, recreation, religious matters, friends, intimate relations, philosophy of life, and so on) with happiness in marriage, the coefficients of correlation ranging from .3 to .7. Terman's study likewise shows that, of some 545 traits studied, in 130 items the happy marriage disclosed a higher agreement between the parties than did the unhappy or divorced marriage.[14] From daily observation we know that a durable and happy marriage is hardly possible between persons who are entirely dissimilar to one another in all the important traits and values. Such married couples would represent little more than two strangers cohabiting with one another. Neither deep unity, nor deep devotion and understanding, nor the fusion of personalities into one "we" is possible under such conditions. To summarize: some kind of combination of similarities and dissimilarities is present in any marriage; of these, a certain combination of similarity-dissimilarity traits is the de-

cisive factor in a happy choice for marriage and in a happy and stable marriage itself.

With this conclusion we have cleared the field of one-sided theories regarding marital solidarity and unity, but we have not solved the problem. Its solution requires an answer to the question: Exactly what kind of similarities and dissimilarities and what combination of them is conductive to a happy, solidary, and durable marriage? An adequate answer to this requires several preliminary steps. (1) We must recognize that there are thousands of similarities and dissimilarities between any two persons of different sexes. (2) *Not all similar and dissimilar traits are equally virulent in generating solidarity or antagonism between* such interacting parties. Some traits, such as a similarity in preference for brown shoes rather than black ones and a dissimilarity in preference for Chesterfield cigarettes by one party as against Camels by the other party, hardly exert tangible effect upon the solidarities and antagonisms of the majority of interacting persons. On the other hand, such a trait as dissimilarity in religion during the Middle Ages was very virulent in this respect, causing, as a rule, bitter animosity to heretics, schismatics, and pagans, and a solidarity between members of the same Christian religion. This means that before answering our question we must find out which of the similarities-dissimilarities are virulent, and which are neutral and ineffective. Only the virulent traits and their effective combinations are important for our purposes.

(3) The next step consists in a realization that *there is hardly any trait of similarity or dissimilarity which as such, through its biophysical properties, and regardless of the sociocultural universe in which it is given, uni-*

Factor in Friendships of College and Adult Women." *Journal of Social Psychology,* Vol. XI (1940), pp. 302-312; R. G. Pintner, Forlano, and H. Freedman, "Personality and Attitudinal Similarities Among Classroom Friends," *Journal of Applied Psychology,* Vol. XXXIII (1937), pp. 48-65; A. J. Pelletieri, *Friends* (Nashville, Tenn., 1935); E. D. Partridge, "A Study of Friendship Among Adolescent Boys," *Journal of Genetic Psychology,* Vol. XLIII (1933), pp. 472-477; P. E. Williams, "A Study of Adolescent Friendship," *Pedagogical Seminary,* Vol. XXX (1923), pp. 343-346; M. V. Seagoe, "Factors Influencing the Selection of Associates," *Journal of Educational Research,* Vol. XXVII (1933), pp. 32-40; R. B. Cat-

tell, "Friends and Enemies," *Character and Personality,* Vol. III (1934), pp. 55-63; P. Furfey, "Some Factors Influencing the Selection of Boys' Chums," *Journal of Applied Psychology,* Vol. XI (1929), pp. 47-51; E. P. Hagman, "The Companionship of Preschool Children," *University of Iowa Studies in Child Welfare,* Vol. VII (1933), No. 4; G. G. Jenkins, "Factors Involved in Children's Friendships," *Journal of Educational Psychology,* Vol. XXII (1931), pp. 440-48; E. V. Van Dyne, "Personality Traits and Friendship Formation Among Adolescent Girls," *Journal of Social Psychology,* Vol. XII (1940), p. 291-305.

[14] Burgess and Cottrell, *op. cit.,* pp. 48 ff. Terman, *op. cit.,* pp. 26 ff.

formly becomes virulent and generates either solidarity or antagonism. Religious similarity or dissimilarity is very virulent in a religious society like Medieval Europe. In the interaction of atheists and disbelievers or in an irreligious society it becomes neutral and ineffective in the generation of either antagonism or solidarity. Racial similarity or dissimilarity is very important in societies and persons that attach a great value to race, such as the caste society of India, early Jewish society and colonial American society. It ceases to be virulent for persons and societies attaching to it little or no value, like Russian society during a number of centuries, or the early society of Dutch settlers in Africa, or Brazil, and many others.[15] In such societies the persons of different races intermarry, and such marriages show hardly any specific solidarity or antagonism different from the marriages of persons belonging to the same race. Similarity or dissimilarity in political views is very virulent in persons and societies that attach a great value to them, as for instance our contemporary society, with its Nazi and anti-Nazi conflict. For persons and societies that give little value to political views it becomes unimportant and inffective. Even such biologically important characteristics as similarity or great discrepancy in the ages of married parties is very effective in societies that attach to it a great value and much less effective in societies where as a rule girls of 8 to 12 years are married to men of much more advanced age (as in India, and many other societies in the past). The same is true of practically any other trait of similarity or dissimilarity. This means that we cannot establish which traits of similarity or dissimilarity per se, in their biophysical characteristics, are universally virulent or neutral. Any trait of similarity or dissimilarity is virulent only in those persons, societies, and cultures that attach to it great importance, in which it represents a great value in their total system of values; otherwise it becomes neutral and ineffective. *The effectiveness or non-effectiveness of a trait of similarity or dissimilarity depends upon the system of values of the persons and groups involved.*

A trait which is virulent in the generation of solidarity or antagonism for the interacting parties C and D may become neutral for the parties M and N whose system of values is different from that of C and D. As a result *which traits are regarded as an important similarity or dissimilarity and which are not will be determined mainly by the system of values of the interacting parties, by their self-identification with those traits or values, and not by their biophysical nature.* A mother and her small son are as different anatomically, physiologically, psychologically, and socioculturally as they can be. And yet this obvious biophysical and "objective" dissimilarity does not prevent their regarding themselves as one "we," intimately similar, even identical to the utmost degree of oneness, their lives fused in the most intense solidary unity. Identical twin brothers are certainly similar in a large number of anatomical, physiological, psychological, and sociocultural characteristics. But if one becomes a Communist and the other an anti-Communist, this single difference may "cancel" all their similarities and make them bitter enemies. Facts of this kind could be multiplied ad infinitum. The traits that are regarded by the interacting parties as unimportant, as of little or no value, are neutral and ineffective, regardless of their "objective," biophysical characteristics.

From these conclusions a further inference follows, namely: *any* purely objective and mechanical collection of similar and dissimilar traits of the parties concerned, and their correlation with solidarity or antagonism, marriage selection or marriage happiness, does not and cannot yield a valid and generalized formula of their causal relationship. Without reference to the system of values of the interacting parties no objective similarity or dissimilarity can be either effective or neutral. Only when it is placed in the appropriate system of values does it become either effective

---

[15] On the dominant attitude in regard to race similarity-dissimilarity in Russian see P. A. Sorokin, *Russia and the United States* (New York, 1944), pp. 31 ff. On the early Dutch colonies in Africa see S. G. Millin, *The South African* (New York, 1927). On interracial intermarriage and the lack of a serious race discrimination in several early settlements of the Europeans see R. Park, "Race Relations and Certain Frontiers," in E. B. Reuter (ed.), *Race and Culture Contact* (New York, 1934), pp. 57-88; Julius Lips, *The Savage Hits Back* (New Haven, 1937), Ch. 1, *passim.*

or neutral. This explains why the results obtained by various investigators of marriage-homogamy and heterogamy, and of marital happiness and unhappiness have been inconclusive, discordant, and inconsistent. Most of them have taken various traits of similarity and dissimilarity "objectively" and mechanically, without any systematic investigation of the systems of values of the parties concerned. As a result in some studies the trait A is found to be very effective in the selection of a mate or in marital happiness; in others it is found to be playing very little or no role.

For instance in the Burgess-Wallin study of factors in marriage homogamy the highest correlation is shown by a similarity of religious affiliation and behavior (.54); while in their study of marital happiness, similarity in religion is found to occupy one of the most minor roles (.28). Terman's study likewise finds this factor unimportant for marital happiness, difference in religion occupying 29th place in frequency and 47th place in seriousness among grievances by the husband, and occupying 22nd and 44th places, respectively, for the wife. This result is however still further complicated by Terman's subsequent data showing that neither strict nor slight nor utter lack of training in religion is conducive to happy marriage; a moderate religious training seems to be most closely associated with happy marriages. Especially undesirable is very strict religious training for the wives, according to this study.[16] These discrepancies are increased further by the different role which religion or any other similarity and dissimilarity factor plays in various occupational groups studied by Terman. In other studies religious similarity is found to be playing an exceptionally great role in marriage choice. R. Kennedy's study quoted above shows that New Haven Jews marry other Jews in some 97-94 per cent of their marriages; for Catholics its importance is lower (83 per cent), and for Protestants it is still lower (78 to 79 per cent). Women students at the University of Wisconsin, coming from proprietary classes, place a very high

value on the religious affiliation of their prospective husbands (mean score .91), while the women students from professional and farmer classes place much lower value on this trait (mean score .64).[17]

Other studies give a still more varied picture of the role of religious similarity or dissimilarity in marriage selection and happiness. Add to this such facts as this, that in Medieval Europe, religious similarity of Christians was a necessary condition to any Christian marriage—demanded by secular and canon law, by mores, and by the personal happiness of the parties concerned. Consider further several variations of these legal and moral requirements as given in different countries. In pre-revolutionary Russia, for instance, Russian-Orthodox persons could marry any Christian (Catholic, Protestant), but could not marry a non-Christian without his or her conversion to Christianity. Other Russian citizens, such as Jews, pagans, and so on could marry any non-Christian. When all these diversities are considered the whole problem of the extent to which religious similarity is important in the selection of mates or in marital happiness becomes entirely indefinite. Different studies give, as we have seen, quite different results and coefficients. No uniformity in regard to its effectiveness is found. The reason for this is at hand; since religion is of unequal importance in the value systems of the different persons and groups studied, similarity or dissimilarity in religion necessarily has different degrees of effectiveness in the facilitation of choice in marriage and in marriage happiness, or more broadly, in the generation of solidarity and antagonism in the relationships of the parties. For those parties in whose value-system it occupies an important place its similarity or dissimilarity exerts an effective influence. For those parties in whose system of values it is unimportant, it becomes neutral and ineffective.

The same can be said of practically any trait of similarity or dissimilarity that has been studied. Taken objectively and mechanically, without reference to the systems of values of

---

[16] See Burgess and Wallin, *op. cit.*, p. 124; Burgess and Cottrell, *op. cit.*, pp. 50-51; Terman, *op. cit.*, pp. 96 ff., 230 ff.
[17] T. McCormic and B. Macrory, "Group Values in Mate Selection," *SF*, Vol. XXII (1944), pp. 315-

317. See also J. and M. Biesanz, "Mate Selection Standards," *SF*, Vol. XXII (1943), pp. 194-199; R. Baber, "Some Mate Selection Standards," *Journal of Social Hygiene*, Vol. XXII (1936), pp. 115-125.

the parties concerned, they are all found to be playing quite different roles in different studies. Even such purely physical traits of similarity-dissimilarity as a tubercular infection of married persons yielded in two different studies by Pope the coefficients .32 and .17; in Goring's studies,[18] .01, and .16; in Elderston's study, .30—a rather considerable range of coefficients. Similarity in alcoholism likewise gave coefficients ranging from .27 to .44 and .70 in the studies of Goring, Schuster, and Elderton. Similarity in insanity gave coefficients from .06 and higher (Goring); similarity in intelligence gave from .08 to .38 and higher (Woods, Elderton). The same is still more true of practically any sociocultural and psychological trait. For instance, while girl students at the University of Wisconsin highly rated "education" in their prospective husbands (third place in the rank order of various traits), the Costa Rican students rated it much lower (thirteenth place in the rank). While 20 per cent of the girl students and 29 per cent of the boy students at New York University were willing to marry a person of inferior moral standards to their own, only 5 per cent of the girls and 9 per cent of the boys among the Costa Rican students were ready to do so.[19] This shows again that the value attached to the same trait differs greatly even among students of the same university and still more so among different ethnic, racial, national, occupational, economic, educational, political, religious, scientific, artistic, and other groups and persons. It is hopeless to find an objective trait which, without reference to the value system of the persons involved, would be always either efficient or neutral, generating either solidarity or antagonism, happiness or unhappiness in marriage.

V. Generalized Hypotheses

The conclusions thus reached mean that in the final analysis the real factor in solidarity or antagonism is not just the overt, objective similarity or dissimilarity of the parties concerned but is rather the place which they occupy in the system of values of the persons and groups, and the character of these systems of values. Several inferences follow from this conclusion. They are equally applicable to marriage solidarity-antagonism as well as to other solidarities and antagonisms in their relationship to similarity-dissimilarity traits.

What traits (physical, biological, psychosocial) or persons or groups will be regarded by the interacting parties as similar or dissimilar is determined not only, and not so much, by the objective biosocial characteristics of these traits as by the nature of the sociocultural mentality of the parties, by the meanings and values they impose upon, and attach to them.[20] In the above mentioned case of the mother and her boy, their overt differences are obliterated by their sociocultural unity, similarity, even identity, by their oneness of the most intense and intimate kind. This "intangible similarity" cancels out and makes unimportant, sometimes even nonexistent for the parties concerned, their numerous overt dissimilarities. Millions of Christians are utterly dissimilar from one another in hundreds of ways. However, as long as they regard all Christians as the children of God, created in His own image, they become similar in Christ. The same may be true of millions of Communists. Competitors for the love of the same person, for the same wealth, prize, or popularity become similar to one another in spite of many overt dissimilarities, and so on.

Thus sociocultural similarity and dissimilarity as they are perceived by the parties concerned may not only be different from their overt, biophysical similarity-dissimilarity characteristics, but peculiar in their nature, being always meaningful, sometimes transcendental and mystical (like the declarations: "All men

[18] C. B. Goring, *Studies in National Deterioration*, No. 5 (London, 1909); E. G. Pope, *Studies in National Deterioration*, No. 2 (London, 1908).

[19] See the quoted works of McCormic and Macrory, Biesanz, and Baber.

[20] This is a mere case of the already studied general rule that the sociocultural nature of phenomena does not coincide with, and is determined not so much by, their biophysical characteristics as by the meaning superimposed upon them.

are equal" or "All Christians are similar in their being created in the image of God," "All heroes," "All sinners and criminals"); often intangible and irreducible to any overt similarity-dissimilarity; rarely purely external and sensory. They are generated, shaped, and determined by the system of values of the interacting parties. As such they have little to do with purely overt, biophysical similarities or dissimilarities.

For this reason all attempts to study the role of similarity or dissimilarity on the basis of the overtly similar or dissimilar traits are doomed to failure and cannot deliver any uniformity, even any valid conclusion. They are all vitiated at their starting point through a faulty assumption of the identity of overt, biophysical similarity or dissimilarity with sociocultural similarity-dissimilarity, which is actually quite different. This error is responsible for the fallacy of many theories in this field.

In conformity with the preceding point, if all the interacting parties (in marriage, in minority-majority groups, in different occupational, religious, political, economic, racial, ethnic, and other interacting groups and persons) view the given overtly similar (or dissimilar) traits: A,B,C,D,N (physical, biological, mental, sociocultural) as negligible values or as no values at all, as comprising even no similarity (or dissimilarity), such overt similarities-dissimilarities are innocuous in the generation of either solidarity or antagonism. Only those similarities-dissimilarities that are regarded by all or by some of the interacting parties as real and important values will be effective factors in either solidarity or antagonism.

An important sociocultural similarity can generate both solidarity and antagonism of the parties. It generates solidarity (a) when the values equally important for the interacting parties are abundant and sufficient for all; when each party can have its full share without decreasing that of the other parties. The grace of God for Christians, the national pride for patriots, the prestige of the family, party, or union—all these are, for their members, virtually inexhaustible and lead to the solidarity of the members. (b) Sociocultural similarity generates solidarity if and when the egos of the interacting parties are already

fused together in one "we." In this oneness the more of the value a member has the richer is the unified "we," and the greater becomes the share of every participant member. In the condition of such a "we" even a scarcity of the important value leads to a solidarity of the parties. The "we" may be a good family, a labor union, a religious body, a nation, a political party.

(c) Solidarity is generated if the norms of the parties governing their relationship in the field of the similarity are concordant.

An important sociocultural similarity generates antagonism of the parties (a) when the values regarded as important by all the parties are scarce, if their norms are permeated by egotistic competition and are discordant; (b) when their norms are discordant and the nature of the important value does not permit any sharing between the parties so that only one of them can have the value, for instance, marrying a girl or boy equally desired by all the parties.

An important sociocultural dissimilarity can generate both solidarity and antagonism between the socioculturally dissimilar parties. (a) If the values (or traits) of the parties are quite dissimilar, having no common ground and containing no value equally regarded as important by the parties, such values do not generate either solidarity or antagonism. The values of the other party are regarded as unimportant hobbies that provoke neither positive nor negative reaction. The same is true when some of the values of the parties are opposite but are considered unimportant and negligible.

(b) When each party regards its values and norms as important and when these values and norms are opposite, one party denying what the other party affirms, such a dissimilarity (mixed with similarity in that all parties regard the values as important) generates an antagonism between the parties. When an atheist and a believer, a Communist and an anti-Communist, regard their own values as important and give a negative importance to the values of the opponents, they become antagonistic.

(c) When the main values and norms of the parties are similar but their secondary values are diverse and mutually neutral, and especially when the other values are mutually supplementary, such a combination of similarity-dissimilarity facilitates the solidarity of the parties involved. Heterosexual marriage between parties having their main values common and differing only in secondary values; a society made up of different racial or ethnic groups each having its own values or traits, but at the same time all possessing a common system of values and concordant norms giving thus a multicolored united whole; a society with a well-developed social division of labor but with the main system of values common to all groups and segments; these are concrete types of such a solidarity. On the other hand, if such a group is made up of persons and subgroups with discordant values and norms, each person (in marriage) or subgroup (in society) having values and norms mutually discordant with those of others, such a society gives an antagonistic body, when the diverse values and norms clash, or at best, a neutral body, in which persons and subgroups are indifferent to one another. Such a "unity" is exceedingly loose and can fall to pieces from the smallest adversity. A society made up of a majority and a minority having no concordant system of values and norms cannot help becoming antagonistic. Even a minimum of mutual tolerance as the lowest form of solidarity is impossible in such a society.

From the above it follows that the combination of a basic similarity in the main values and of concordance in the norms of the parties concerned, with a supplementary diversity in their secondary values, is the most conducive to solidary relationships, provided the main values are abundant, or are distributed by all the parties involved according to their concordant norms.

An opposite and diverse character of the values and norms of the parties, when they are considered important (positively or negatively), and in which the parties have no common system of values and norms, is the most conducive to the generation of intense antagonisms. Just such a combination of the dissimilar with the similar (in that all the parties regard their own values as positively important and the opposite values as negatively important) has uniformly been the cause of the sharpest antagonisms—wars, revolutions, riots, and many inter-individual crimes.[21] (Cf. Chapter 33.)

These are the main uniformities in the generation of solidarity-antagonism by similarity-dissimilarity in the value systems of the interacting parties. The conclusions thus reached differ from prevalent opinions, and the inferences transfer the whole problem to a different plane. They show that solidarity and antagonism have little to do with either similarity or dissimilarity of atomistically taken and singularistically treated overt biophysical and psychological traits. The above analysis points out that the decisive factor is the system of values and norms of the parties involved. These systems determine which of the traits are important and are regarded as a real similarity, and which are not. The above shows also that sociocultural similarity and dissimilarity can generate solidarity as well as antagonism under specified conditions.

VI. Critical Remarks

In the light of the conclusions reached it is easy to see the main errors of the prevalent theories in this field, like those of E. Durkheim, F. Tönnies, and of the investigators of marriage-selection and happiness, of the partisans of assimilation and amalgamation of minorities, and so on. A terse enumeration of the mistakes of the Durkheimian theory of solidarity and antagonism may serve the purpose. With a slight modification this enumeration can be applied to the other theories.

(1) Durkheim errs in assuming that in primitive societies the solidarity is based only or mainly upon a similarity of the sentiments and beliefs of the members, while in advanced societies it is based upon the dissimilarity of these sentiments and beliefs. As a matter of fact in both types of societies the solidarity is based upon a combination of similarities and dissimilarities in terms of the formulae set forth

[21] On this see my *Russia and the United States* (New York, 1944), Chps. 10, 11.

above.[22] So far as societies with a social division of labor do not co-ordinate the dissimilarities of their members by a common fund of main values and norms, such a dissimilarity has invariably generated antagonism instead of solidarity. Durkheim himself had to acknowledge this in his later works.

(2) Durkheim arbitrarily assumes that the members of both types of society, whether mechanistically or organically solidary, regard themselves as similar and dissimilar in exactly those traits in which they appear similar and dissimilar to Durkheim. The factual situation is notably different.

(3) Durkheim's contention that the members of societies with mechanistic solidarity ascribe their solidarity to the similarity of their sentiments and beliefs, while the members of societies with organic solidarity ascribe it to the dissimilarity of their sentiments and beliefs, is again a perfectly dogmatic belief contradicted by logic and relevant facts.

(4) Durkheim is wrong in his claim that there is an historical trend from mechanistic to organic solidarity. As a matter of fact such a trend has hardly ever existed nor does it now exist.

(5) Many of the subordinate statements of Durkheim as, for instance, his assertion that mechanistic solidarity is connected with repressive law, while organic solidarity is connected with restitutive law and sanctions, are grossly fallacious.[23]

Any theory claiming that solidarity is always based only upon similarity or only upon dissimilarity, without a further specification and reservation, is void. Likewise all theories that ascribe antagonism either to similarity or dissimilarity are untenable. As a rule solidary as well as antagonistic relationships are generated by a combination of sociocultural similarities and dissimilarities along the lines specified above. This means that a solidary society can be created not only out of "one race, one nation, one government" with subsidiary differences of its subgroups, but also out of many diverse racial, ethnic, political, and religious groups when they have a common fund of main values and concordant norms side by side with their specific values and traits. Historically social "unity in diversity" has been as common as the mono-ethnic, mono-racial, mono-religious, and other "monolithic societies." This also means that the problems of various minorities can be solved not only in the way of "amalgamation and assimilation," that is through melting and elimination of their diverse traits and values into the traits and values of the majority, but also through a stimulation and development of the specific traits and values of the minorities side by side with a development of the common fund of values for the majority and minority. If they have and practice the value-norm of mutual respect of their differences such a common concordant value-norm provides the minimum of the common fund necessary for a solidary coexistence of different persons and groups.

No study of similar and dissimilar traits taken overtly, atomistically, without reference to the value systems of the interacting persons or groups, can yield valid results or real uniformities, in the relationship of these traits to the solidarity or antagonism of the parties. This equally concerns marital union as well as occupational, economic, religious, ethnic, racial, political, and other social groups. For the reasons mentioned above such a "behavioristic" study gives mainly misleading conclusions and generalizations.

---

[22] See substantiation of this and some of the critical points in G. Gurvitch, *Essais de Sociologie* (Paris, 1938), pp. 68 ff.

[23] See its factual criticism in my *Dynamics*, Vol. II, pp. 593 ff. The criticism equally concerns Durkheim's reformulation of his earlier generalization in his "Deux Lois de l'evolution pénale," *L'Année Sociologique*, Vol. IV, pp. 65 ff.

Chapter 8. The Organized Group as a Collective Unity

I. Spatial, Causal-Functional, and Meaningful Unities

We can distinguish six kinds of unities: (1) spatially contiguous and perceptionally similar; (2) spatially contiguous and mechanically cohesive; (3) indirect causal-functional; (4) direct causal-functional; (5) meaningful; (6) meaningful-causal-functional.

(1) A pile of sand or bricks is perceived as a unity, an object perceptionally separable from the universe of other objects. The basis of their unity is the *spatial contiguous adjacency* of the grains of sand or of the bricks that make them perceptionally different from other objects.[1]

(2) A piece of rock, a stick, a box containing all the unassembled parts of a car are perceived as unities, perceptionally circumscribed from the rest of the world. The basis of their unity is a *spatial contiguous adjacency* and a *mechanical cohesion* of their parts. These parts may be as different from one another as the elements of a rock or the parts in a box. Most of the separate objects perceived as unities in the physicochemical universe belong to these two types of unities.

(3) In my study I find a large variety of objects: books, manuscripts, typewriter, logs in the fire-place, fishing tools, clock, pictures, various boxes, furniture. In our pockets we often carry money, pen and watch, handkerchief, some letters, automobile license and

registration, comb, etc. These heterogeneous objects are not always together in a spatial adjacency; in jewelry stores watches exist without shirts, shoes, pens, combs, handkerchiefs, and all the other objects enumerated; fishing tools do not go always together with clocks, phonographs, typewriters, and so on. Neither do they have any direct-causal-functional relationship with one another; clocks and fishing tools do not always coexist or change together. All these objects are causal-functional strangers to one another. And yet somehow they all happen to be united through a common agent, the individual and his needs. Each of them is in causal-functional relationship with the individual and his needs and, through this common agent, they are indirectly connected by causal-functional ties, one with another. *All unities in which various objects have a causal-functional relationship to one common agency external to all of them, give a class of indirect causal-functional unities. A, B, C, D, M . . . ,* each being connected with the common agency X, are indirectly connected with one another, though they do not have direct causal relationship with one another, and sometimes are not in a spatial adjacency.

(4) An assembled automobile, a solar system, the Columbia Broadcasting System, and an organism are also unities, though some of them, like a solar system or the radio network, cannot be perceived as sensory unities; their parts are separated by distant space and

[1] Cf. Eubank's "Category" and "Aggregation," *The Concepts of Sociology* (Boston, 1932), pp. 117-119.

are not visible at one glance. The basis for their unity is a *tangible, causal dependence and functional interdependence* among their parts.[2] When the causal part of such a unity changes, then all the parts that are effects change also; while in functionally interdependent unity important parts change together. In such causal-functional unities there is mutual interdependence; each part depends upon the whole and the whole depends upon the parts. The functional dependence of the members of the solar systems is the reason why we regard it as a unity among the rest of the heavenly bodies. A still closer functional interdependence between the earth and the moon makes them a subunity in the looser and larger unity of the solar system. As noted, the causal-functional unities may be spatially adjacent and perceptionally concrete like an automobile or organism; or they may be spatially discontiguous and perceptionally discrete, like the solar system or the radio network, scattered around the whole planet.

(5) The science of mathematics, Plato's philosophical system, Bach's *Mass in B Minor*, Dante's *Divine Comedy*, a Christian Credo, the Civil Code of Napoleon are *meaningful, logico-aesthetic* unities. The basis of their unity is the logical or aesthetic consistency of their meanings-norms-values. All systems of meanings-norms-values that show such a consistency are meaningful, logico-aesthetic unities, beginning with a simple proposition: A is B, $2+2=4$, and ending with all the consistent scientific, philosophical, religious, ethical, artistic systems of meanings-norms-values. (See further, Chapters 17 and 18.) As pure meanings-norms-values they are immate-

rial and non-sensory, therefore spaceless and timeless. When they are objectified and materialized in actions and vehicles, they may be spatially concrete and sensorily perceptional like a statue, a picture, a building, or a book; they may also be spatially scattered and discrete, like a symphony or speech broadcast throughout the world.

(6) Sinking of Japanese ships and bombing of their cities, draft and military training of millions of American youth, decrease of regular students in colleges, rationing of many necessities, lend-lease to Russia and England, intensified production of ships, tanks, guns, planes, and so on; these and hundreds of other phenomena which by virtue of their purely physical and biological qualities are not connected causally with one another, are in fact causally interdependent because they all are the *meaningful-causal* manifestation of the war between the United States and Japan. The United States, Japan, and war are meaningful unities and all these phenomena are meaningfully-causally interdependent.

If we had two identical inventions, say of atomic bombs, made independently from one another, we should have only a meaningful tie between the two atomic bombs invented; both would give us a meaningful unity of the same kind. If, however, an invention of atomic bombs in the United States factually influenced their invention somewhere else, then the two atomic bombs would be connected not only meaningfully but also causally with each other. This example illustrates meaningful-causal (functional) unity.[3]

---

[2] By causal dependence is meant a one-sided dependence of the effect A upon the cause B, so that when B is given A is given, when B is changing A is changing, but the reverse may not be true. By functional dependence is meant mutual interdependence of two or more variables where A is the cause and effect of B and vice versa. Wind is the cause of the flower bending, while the flower is not the cause of the wind blowing. When two iron sticks, one hot, the other cold, touch one another the resulting process is an equalization of their temperatures. In this equalization neither of the sticks is the cause or the effect; both influence each other and are functionally interdependent.

[3] The above six types are a somewhat more complete and systematic classification of unities often discussed in a less systematic manner in the texts of logic and methodology. Compare C. Sigwart, *Logik* (Russian, St. Petersburg, 1908), Vol. II, p. 226; B. Kistiakowsky, *Gesellschaft und Einzelwesen* (Berlin, 1899), pp. 131 ff; A. A. Tschuproff, *Ocherki teorii statistiki* (Moscow, 1909), pp. 78-80; G. Simmel, *Ueber Soziale Differenzierung* (Leipzig, 1890), Ch. 1; J. Venn, *The Principles of Empirical and Inductive Logic* (London, 1907), Ch. 3; A. Findlay, *The Phase Rule and Its Application* (London, 1904), Chps. 1, 2; H. Höffding, *La relativité philosophique. Totalité et relation* (Paris, 1924), pp. 44 ff.

II. An Organized Group as a Causal and Meaningful Unity

The very definition of social interaction points out at once that any group of interacting individuals is first of all a *causal-functional unity* in which all components are mutually and tangibly interdependent. In any interaction system there is a triple interdependence of one part upon the other important parts, of the whole upon these parts, and of the parts upon the whole interaction system. The unity is not always apparent, as when in its membership and vehicles a group of interacting individuals is a *discrete* but not a *concrete unity*. One cannot see at once the whole Catholic Church or a nation like the United States of America. Only in a very relative way can one distinguish, from this viewpoint, two different ecological types of groups, one *with a locus territorially contiguous and circumscribed* and the other *non-contiguous and undefined*.

A territorial village or city group, some of the primitive tribes, and especially the state whose control is thought to be contiguous and exclusive over its circumscribed territory, on which no other state can exist, are examples of the first type. The Roman Catholic or Protestant Church, an International Association of Sociologists or of Rotarians give examples of the second type. In the first type the territory becomes an important vehicle-symbol of the group; in the second it does not play such an important role in the structure and functions of the group.[4] But even this difference between territorially defined and undefined groups is very relative; as a matter of fact within the territory of a state, for instance of the United States, there exist millions of other than the state groups; there are also citizens of other states, just as the citizens of the United States are scattered and live in the territory of the British Empire or Russia. Then, within the territory of the United States there are special "extraterritorial" areas occupied by the diplomatic corps of other states exempt from the control of the United States just as the United States has similar, extraterritorial areas in other states. The meanings and vehicles produced within the territory of the state beginning with industrial and agricultural products and ending with scientific, artistic, political, or religious ideologies, are scattered everywhere on this planet, just as within its own territory the meanings and vehicles of other nations and states circulate. For these reasons even the above difference between territorially contiguous and discontiguous groups is very relative. Anyhow, as a causal-functional unity the interacting group need not be either spatially contiguous, have a circumscribed territory, or be spatially adjacent. Such properties, in a very relative sense, belong only to some varieties of groups.

Likewise as a causal-functional unity the interacting group need not be *cohesive* in a mechanical sense. Any one of its components is not spatially "glued" to the others, can change its spatial place, and is incessantly on the move. In spite of this a tangible interdependence of its important parts remains and binds them into a causal-functional unity of an interacting group.

Furthermore, an organized interacting group is a *meaningful unity*. (1) The members interact because of or for the sake of certain meanings-norms-values. By definition only meaningful interaction makes a sociocultural group. (2) We have seen above (Chapter 3) how a group's causal-functional unity is determined, to a great extent, by its component of meanings; they create indirect or direct causal-functional dependence where otherwise, by virtue of the biophysical properties of the objects involved, there would be no causal-functional dependence; and vice versa, the component of meanings often eliminates the causal-functional ties between the phenomena. (3) Any organized group is a group integrated or logically consistent to some extent at least in its ethical and law-norms, meanings, and

[4] Cf G. Simmel, *Soziologie* (Münich, 1923), pp. 518-522; R. Maunier, "The Definition of the City," *AJS*, Vol. XVI, pp. 536-548; E. C. Hughes, "The Ecological Aspect of Institutions," *ASR*, Vol. I, pp. 180-189; W. Firey, *Land Use in Central Boston* (Harvard University Press, 1947).

values. We shall see that, in spite of the presence of contradictions in the official and unofficial law of the group, most of its norms are logically consistent; and, so far as they are enforced, the bulk of the overt actions of its members and of the vehicles used are consistent also with the norms and with one another. This logical consistency of the law-norms and law-actions of the members is never perfect, but its minimum is found in any group as long as it remains an organized group. Otherwise no organized group is possible (see Chapters 17 and 18). (4) Even outside of law-norms, the rest of the meanings-norms-values of the group, because of which or for the sake of which the individuals interact, are integrated to some extent into aesthetically or logically consistent systems. (5) Any long existing organized group has to have a minimum of solidarity among its most powerful members. Solidarity in all its ramifications is again a set of consistent meanings. So far as it is one of the ties binding the members of the group into a solidary unity, it is a meaningful tie. Causal-functional ties are "colorless"; neither antagonistic nor solidary per se; they are merely ties of dependence and interdependence.

These reasons are sufficient to show how and why any organized, and especially solidary groups are meaningful-causal unities.

Contrary to many social scientists and sociologists who see the meaningful unity only in the teleological groups with a common purpose of the members, and who often make the common purpose or end as the very characteristic of a group,[5] the above statements stress any organized group, no matter whether it has or does not have a common purpose. The teleological or purposive groups are but one of the forms of organized groups as meaningful-causal unities.

Still more fallacious is the denial of the meaningful unity of an organized group by pseudo-empiricists.[6] They are ready to recognize an interacting group as a causal-functional unity, but they deny its meaningful unity. Their mistakes are obvious; they overlook the fact that the very causal-functional relationships in the phenomena of meaningful interaction are already permeated by the meanings-norms-values that change even the purely biophysical causal-functional relationships of persons, actions, and vehicles. They do not realize that the bulk of law-norms, without which there is no organized group, is already a consistent and unified body of meanings, and not a mere physical phenomena of motions of various kinds. Finally, when they attempt to classify and describe various groups like the family, the state, the Church, the school, the political party, and the like, they seemingly do not understand that these terms as well as the sociocultural individuality of each of such groups and their difference from one another are determined most of all by their meanings-

---

[5] The examples of this are given in Chapter 4. See further examples of such teleological definitions of a group in G. Jellineck, *The Law of the Modern State* (Russian, St. Petersburg, 1903), pp. 110-112. In the preceding criticism of the theory of purposive motivation, of means and end, and of the teleological definition of an institution and law, the inadequacy of such conceptions has been shown. We can add here that a mere unity of purpose as such is insufficient to create a group; if a thousand persons have identical purpose but do not interact with one another, they remain a thousand separate individuals without making any group; no causal or other relationship exists between them. Furthermore, nobody can tell in regard to an overwhelming majority of the groups whether all the members have or have not any common aim; and if they have, what it is: for instance, the common aim of the state, of a territorial community, of a nation, of many a family, and so on. Finally, as we have seen, as soon as a meaningful interaction is given, the group becomes a causal

unity and this causal unity is already permeated with meaningful unity.

[6] See, for instance, Sims, *op. cit.*, pp. 235 ff., where he oscillates between rejection of meaningful unity and its factual acceptance; also G. Lundberg, *Foundations of Sociology* (New York, 1939), pp. 340 ff., 360 ff. Lundberg's case is humorous in its self-contradiction; on the one hand he ardently desires to describe everything in terms of a mere physicochemical science; on the other hand he incessantly breaks this desire by an uncritical use of the most "meaningful" terms—family, school, YMCA, church, arts—stressing irrelevant characteristics of a group like its geographical contiguity, etc., and omitting the true characteristics of the real groups. He and his like seem to be unaware that the family, university, business firm, church, and state are first of all and most of all meaningful unities which cannot be found among the strictly causal relationships and unities of the biophysical world.

norms-values. In terms of mere motions, intensity and extensity of interaction, primary or secondary contact and its frequency, geographical proximity, the size of the group and means of communication, it is absolutely impossible to grasp the nature of a religious group, the state, the family, or any other group with their distinctions. On the basis of their "deaf-mute criteria" one hundred individuals meeting in the same building, say, Symphony Hall, Boston, once a week for one hour, will always be the same group. Meanwhile one hundred individuals, and sometimes the same individuals meeting in the same Symphony Hall are often quite different groups; now a religious service, now a business meeting, now a political rally,

now a Rotary Club. Everything depends upon what kind of meanings-values-norms they objectify and realize at these meetings.

The nature of meanings-values-norms is the basic characteristic of the sociocultural individuality of a group. The other criteria—its size, frequency of contact, intensity of interaction, closeness of causal interdependence, and so on—can be useful as subsidiary characteristics, but they alone without the meanings-norms-values cannot give any notion of the sociocultural nature of a group. This is well corroborated by the pseudo-empiricists themselves in their uncritical but incessant use of the meaningful terms "business corporation," "religious," or "political" groups.

III. The Main Properties
of an Organized Sociocultural Group

1. Reality

If any organized group is a causal-meaningful unity, this means that it is as a group a real unity. For the causal and meaningful unities are not the external, accidental, and mechanical unities of the spatial adjacency of grains of sand or of the material contiguity of pieces of rock, but the highest forms of internal unification of the components of interaction by the most powerful causal and meaningful bonds. The external and mechanical unities can easily be broken and once broken they do not tend to restore their unity; a pile of sand dispersed remains dispersed, a rock broken to pieces stays broken. But causal-functional and meaningful unities, broken by an interference of external forces, tend to restore their unity, if and when they are not utterly demolished; the state conquered, the family dispersed, the religious or political group suppressed often tend to restore their unity. A logical or aesthetic consistency broken by a non-logical mind tends to persist. In spite of the billions of errors or violations of the multiplication table it is still valid and will remain valid as a logical-meaningful unity. Its distortion neither kills its validity nor damages its meaningful unity (consistency). The same can be said of any meaningful unity.

Representing this causal-meaningful unity

an organized group is truly real; it is real as an *ontological entity*, as a definite, even material structure, as a *causal-functional unity*, as a *meaningful system*. In all these senses it is real as a group or as a whole. Its components and elements are also real, as the subjects of interaction, their meanings and values, their overt actions and the vehicles of interaction; but all these have a *reality of parts and components*, different from that of the group as a whole. Water (H_2O) is real just as oxygen and hydrogen are also real; but the reality of water as a chemical compound of interacting oxygen and hydrogen is quite different from that of oxygen and hydrogen in separation. Each of the cells of our organism is real; no less real is our organism as a whole, made up by the interaction of the cells; but the reality of the organism as a whole is different from that of a mere sum of the same cells in a state of isolation. Likewise, in an organized group its reality is very different from that of its components and parts in a state of noninteraction. This means that the platform of sociological nominalists who see in an organized group only a reality of its members and other components and deny the reality of the group as a whole is untenable; they err when they deny the profound difference between the reality of the group as a whole and that of a mere sum of its elements in the state of their non-interaction. They are mistaken when they try to understand and interpret a group reality, its structure, its properties, its change, its uniformities, in the nominalistic terms of a mere sum of its parts.[7] With such an approach they can never adequately know and understand, interpret and predict either the group's structure or its properties, functions, and change. This affirms the position of the *sociological realists*, who insist upon the reality of the group as a whole and upon a profound difference between this reality and that of its parts taken in a state of noninteraction. An organized group is a unified structural, functional, and meaningful reality *sui generis*.

The prevalent implicit and explicit attitude of psychologists, sociologists, and other social scientists in recent decades has been predominantly nominalistic. They still do not see the forest behind the trees; the reality of the group behind that of its individual members and other components. They still try to interpret sociocultural phenomena mainly from the standpoint of largely imagined and fictitious properties of an individual. We must not be

surprised at the many mistakes and fruitlessness of such interpretations. On the other hand, the sociological realists should avoid the mistakes of "misplaced concreteness" made by the organismic realists who identify a group with an organism; or with the "mechanical realists" who identify it with a concrete material mechanism (the partisans of the mechanistic school in sociology); or with "the psychological realists" who identify a group with a so-called "group mind" understood as an enlarged replica of the mind of an individual. (See my *Theories*, Chs. 1, 4, 8, 9.)

The organized group is not the reality of a concrete organism, as the partisans of organismic theories claim,[8] nor that of a concrete mechanism, as the partisans of mechanistic theories contend,[9] nor that of an individual "mind" just enlarged and called the "group mind," as sociologists and psychologists often state.[10] Nor is it a kind of cosmic mind, as the Hegelians and Neo-Hegelians say;[11] nor is it the reality external to its individual members and existing irrespective of them and other components, as E. Durkheim in his earlier works ambiguously stated.[12] It is the reality

---

[7] See typical nominalistic statements in G. Tarde, *La Logique sociale* (Paris, 1913), p. viii; "Les deux élements de la sociologie," in Tarde's *Etudes de psychologie sociale* (Paris, 1889), pp. 69-75; G. Duprat, *Science sociale et democratie* (Paris, 1900), pp. 59-69. In America F. Allport is a typical nominalist. See his *Social Psychology* (New York, 1924); *Institutional Behavior* (Chapel Hill, 1933). See other literature in my *Theories*, Chs. 1, 4, 8, 9.

[8] See, for instance, Herbert Spencer, *Principles of Sociology*, Vol. I, Part II; later on in this work, however, he repudiated his organismic conception of a group. See Vol. I, Part I, Ch. 12, pp. 576-585 in the edition of London, 1885. See further the works of P. Lilienfeld, R. Worms, A. Schäffle, and others quoted and referred to in my *Theories*, Ch. 4.

[9] See my *Theories*, Ch. 1.

[10] For instance, "Societies are living beings. Society is a living consciousness or an organism of ideas." A. Espinas, *Des Sociétés animales* (Paris, 1878), p. 530; A. Posada, "Les Sociétés animales," in *Annales de l'Institut International de Sociologie*, Vol. III, p. 271. All who without any qualification talk of "public mind," "English or Russian soul," "the spirit of this or that nation" indulge in this fallacy.

[11] For instance A. Fouillet, talking of "the universe as an organism tending to create within itself

a consciousness and a will; a republic which tries to realize itself through its own idea." Postulating a consciousness, will, or republic diffused in the whole universe, he naturally views a human society as a specific centralization of the consciousness, will, and idea. A. Fouillet, *La science sociale contemporaine* (Paris, 1880), p. 413. In the United States J. E. Boodin occupies a somewhat similar position. See his "The Existence of Social Mind," *AJS* (July, 1913).

[12] Society "consists of ways of acting, thinking, and feeling, *external* to the individual, and endowed with a power of coercion. . . . *Their source is not in the individual*. . . . Thus the great movements of enthusiasm, indignation, and pity in a crowd *do not originate in any one of the particular individual consciousnesses. They come to each of us from without*. . . . Any form of activity is social . . . which has its own existence independent of its individual manifestations." E. Durkheim, *Les régles de la method sociologique* (Paris, 1912), pp. 19 ff. Or "above the individuals is society. The latter is not an imaginary and nominal entity but a system of actual real forces." "*En résumé; la société n'est nullement l'être illogique ou alogique, incohérent et fantastique qu'on se plait trop souvent à voir en elle. Tout au contraire, la conscience collective est la forme la plus haute de la vie psychique, puisque c'est un conscience de consciences.*" E. Durkheim, *Les formes elementaires de la vie*

of a causal-functional and meaningful unified system of the subjects of interaction with their properties and actions, of the meanings-norms-values they have and interchange, and of the material vehicles they use for objectification and socialization of the meanings-norms-values. As such this reality is fundamentally different from the total sum of these components taken in the state of mutual isolation.

2. Individuality

Having its own totality of meanings-values-norms, articulated by its members through the assortment of vehicles, every organized group has its own individuality distinguishing it from other groups in the sociocultural universe. Like the individual, it has its own sociocultural physiognomy, character, and traits, which taken with all its characteristics, make it unique in the whole world. The Roosevelt family, the Congregational Church, the United States of America, the American Federation of Labor, Harvard University, these and millions of other organized groups each possess their own individuality clearly distinguishing them from all other groups.

This individuality is due partly to the specific traits and combination of the components, among which the component of meanings-values-norms plays a particularly important role, its character decisively determining the individuality of the group. Without it, the individuality of the group would have been largely effaced, no matter what other components were present. If we take from the Congregational Church or the United States of America the totality of their meanings-values-norms, they would become quite "faceless," little distinguishable from and lost among many other groups in the superorganic universe. The paramount importance of meanings for the individuality of a group comes out clearly in groups where the members and the vehicles remain essentially the same, but the

component of meanings is different; in such cases we have no difficulty in distinguishing the respective groups as different individualities. A radio network like the Columbia Broadcasting System remains in its vehicles and personnel essentially the same during The Catholic Hour, a symphonic concert, a political speech, *The Invitation to Learning*, or *America's Town Meeting*. In spite of this we do not have the slightest difficulty in understanding that quite different groups are using the broadcasting system for an articulation of their meanings-norms-values. And observing such heterogeneous activities and vehicles as a Mass conducted in a cathedral, a Catholic Hour on the radio, missionary activities in China, the publication of *America*, and hundreds of other activities with the vehicles involved, we easily grasp that all these diverse activities and vehicles articulate the same system of meanings-norms-values and therefore are manifestations of the same group, the Catholic Church. The identity of the component of meanings defines the individuality of the group.

3. General and Differential Interdependence and Conductivity

From the definition of interaction and from the causal-functional and meaningful unity of an organized group, there follows a tangible interdependence of all its important parts upon one another, of the parts upon the whole, and of the whole upon the parts. Conductivity within the organized group exists in the sense that an important change in one of its important parts is transmitted to and spreads over other important parts, accomplished through the component of the vehicles functioning as the conductors of interaction.

This general triple interdependence and conductivity does not preclude the *differential interdependence and conductivity*, as well as a *"break" in the chain of the conductors* resulting in a break of conductivity to some of the

---

religieuse (Paris, 1912), pp. 633-635. Hence the constant use, by Durkheim and his followers, of terms like "collective consciousness," "collective representations," etc. The expressions: "external to individuals," "independent from individuals," and so on are certainly fallacious. Tarde and other critics of Durkheim were quite right in saying "what can remain of a university if its professors and students are excluded from it, except a mere

name?" In the preface to later editions of the *Régles*, Durkheim himself had to qualify these "rash" expressions, stating that individuals and even "some other integrating elements" '(our vehicles) compose society. See Durkheim, *The Rules of Sociological Method* (Chicago, 1938), pp. xli-lviii. In my conception no group can exist without its subjects of interaction and other components.

parts, isolated from the whole through this break or defectiveness.

Such differential interdependence, conductivity, and isolation of a part through a break in the chain of conductors is present in any mechanical or organic unity. A change in an unessential part of an automobile (for instance in its upholstery), or of an organism (for instance cutting its hair or nails), does not affect in any serious way the rest of the parts of a car or of a body. Nevertheless a change in an essential part, for instance in the car's engine or the heart of an organism, affects the car most decisively and the organism in all its essential parts. Similar differential interdependence is found in any organized group. A change in an unimportant part or of its ordinary members, does not tangibly affect the group as a whole. An essential change in any of its vital parts influences many or all of its important parts, as for instance a change in the group's government or in its fundamental values-meanings-norms or in its essential vehicles.

A break in the electric wiring connecting the lights of a car with the battery isolates the lights and results in their "insensitivity" to switching the lights on and off. A "break" in the effectors of the nervous system connecting a given organ with the central nervous system results in insensitivity of the organ to all the stimuli coming from the central nervous system. Similarly, the conductors of interaction or the "causal belts" between various members, meanings, and vehicles of a group may also be broken or put out of order. In such a situation the members, vehicles, and meanings, isolated from the rest of the group, cease to be affected by the changes in others of the group and do not affect the group by the changes within themselves. A person decisively isolated in a solitary dungeon with all means of communication severed, or lost in the jungles, is not influenced by many changes within the group. And conversely, he eventually ceases to influence it effectively by his isolated actions, meanings, or vehicles. During this war many American prisoners isolated in Japan or Manchuria were uninfluenced by changes in the United States until their liberation; in turn they ceased to affect the United States tangibly after their isolation.

If in the group there is a poor system of conductors and communication, if its "causal belts," especially between the meanings and overt actions, function poorly (see Chapters 17 and 22) many important changes of ideas, norms, and values within, say the government, the intelligentsia, the scientific or religious leaders, may not reach a large number of the group and may not affect their life, mentality, and conditions, and vice versa. A poor conductivity of that kind has often appeared in many organized groups of the past, with an aristocracy and intellectual elite notably isolated from the lower classes, especially the serfs and slaves. Many important changes within the upper classes passed without notably influencing the lower classes, and the other way around. A new important invention, discovery, artistic or religious idea may remain ineffective due to a lack of means of communication, advertizing, publication, broadcasting, financing its spread, etc., between the inventor and the rest of the group.

The above gives a preliminary idea of the general and differential interdependence and conductivity within an organized group and components. The problem is much more complex than as outlined here and its more detailed study will be found further on in Chapters 36-38 but for the present this outline may suffice.

4. Spatial Compatibility of Groups

In contradistinction to physical objects which are thought of as spatially incompatible in the sense that two objects cannot occupy the same space at the same time, *sociocultural groups can be spatially compatible*; two or more different groups can coexist on the same territory using the same set of vehicles and having nearly identical or identical members. The same set of vehicles, for instance the NBC radio network, is used by hundreds of different groups. The same building, for instance that of the Boston Symphony Hall, is used now by Boston Symphony Orchestra, now by the Community Church, now by a political party, now by the Massachusetts Institute of Technology. Finally, the same or nearly the same group of individuals can and do make now a business firm, now the family, now the board of trustees of a scientific foundation, now something else.

Since meanings-norms-values are immaterial and since they are the most important factor of the individuality of a group, the different sets of meanings-norms-values can create several different groups in spite of the identity of the vehicles and of members of these groups. The same is true of a territory. In any populated area where the population organizes several groups, there on the same territory coexist a number of social groups. In the limited territory of New York City there exist hundreds of thousands, even millions of different groups. Even in the small territory of one apartment house there coexist several different groups. Within the still more limited territory of a street car or subway car there are representatives of very different groups.

Such a statement is contradicted by a legalistic theory that in the territory of a given state there exists only this state and no other group, and especially no other state. The first part of the statement is obviously wrong. The second part of it, as we have seen before, is also inadequate, in view of so-called extraterritorial areas for the embassies of other states and in view of the coexistence of two or more states, for instance, the State of Massachusetts and the United States of America, in the same territory. The statement is also incorrect if it means that only with the permission of the state can other groups exist on the state territory; most of the thousands of groups that exist within the territory of any state appeared and settled there without asking any permission; sometimes they came even contrary to the permission of the state, for instance the revolutionary parties, religious groups, and so on that aim to overthrow a given state or its government.

In regard to territory there is this relative difference, that some of the groups can easily coexist on the same territory, while some other groups, especially the states, are territorially less compatible. The other side of this spatial compatibility of groups is that, as we shall see further, an *individual can belong not only to one but to several different groups*. Within the "space of an individual" can coexist several different groups of which he is a member. In the physical and even the biological world such a spatial compatibility of different unities, the simultaneous belonging of an atom or organism to several different unities is hardly possible at all. In the sociocultural universe it is a rule.

5. Continuity of the Group Individuality, Despite Change in Component Vehicles, Members

In a machine, for instance an automobile, one part can be replaced by another identical part without disruption of the continuity of the car. In an organism some cells incessantly die and some others incessantly replace them without ending the existence of the organism. In a sociocultural group, be it the state, the family, the Church or other groups, their members incessantly change, new generations succeed the old ones; its vehicles are in perennial modification and replacement; and yet, as long as the most essential system of its meanings-norms-vehicles remains identical to itself, the group continues to exist and to live. Its sameness remains. The members of the United States of America have changed many, many times through the succession of many generations, through immigration and emigration; the totality of the vehicles of the United States has changed most radically through some hundred and seventy years of its existence; and yet nobody thinks even for a moment that today's United States is not a continuation of the United States at the first year of its existence. The same is true of a family existing for several hundred years, of the Roman Catholic Church, and of other groups.

As noted above, the *most important condition of such a continuity of a group is the preservation of the sameness or identify of its central system of meanings-norms-values.* Without this condition the continuity of the group is impossible, even if its members and vehicles remain unchanged. If the set of values-meanings-norms of Harvard University is replaced by that of a Special Corps of the U.S. Army, the continuity of existence of Harvard University is brought to an end, even if all its professorial and student members (turned respectively into officers and soldiers) and all the vehicles—buildings, property, and so on—are left unchanged; instead of Harvard University we have an Army group.

The continuity of a group is broken further when it loses all its members; without any subjects there is no interaction and therefore no group. Its set of meanings and vehicles falls apart, having no living agent to keep them together; the vehicles become the dead material debris or broken pieces of a shell without any living body animating and operating them. The remnants of the buried civilizations of Troy or Babylonia excavated by archeologists are illustrative of such a debris of dead vehicles.

Finally, if we imagine a purely hypothetical case (impossible in the empirical reality), that the group loses all its vehicles, its existence and individuality end also. A compulsory conquest of a state and dispossession of all its vehicles appropriated by the conqueror for his state represents an approach to this hypothetical case. In such conditions, in spite of the set of meanings-values-norms of the conquered state imposed upon the mind of its previous citizens and in spite of the existence of these citizens as individuals, the continuity of a conquered state like Czechoslovakia or Poland after Hitler's conquest is brought to an end until the previous citizens re-acquire the vehicles for the restoration of the three-componential unity of the violently disrupted state. Factually, such complete loss of the vehicles of a group is not a very frequent phenomenon. A partial loss or change of the vehicles can weaken the group, can change many of its apparent traits, but does not necessarily lead to the cessation of its existence. Since the vehicles are only loosely married to the meanings and members, their quantitative or qualitative change is not fatal to the continuity of the group, as long as its central set of meanings-values-norms remains the same and so long as it has its members (see further, Chapter 22).

6. Change in Togetherness of an Organized Group

As much as an organized group is a causal-functional and meaningful unity, so far an essential change in one of its parts leads to a respective change in its other important parts. A change in the parts alters the whole group and the change of the group as a whole alters its important elements. This functioning and change in togetherness, due to the causal and meaningful ties between the parts of the group, does not always mean simultaneous and instantaneous change in all the parts. For a change in one part of the group to influence the other parts some time is necessary; now short, now long, depending upon the nature of the change, the conductivity of the group, and other conditions. The causal effects in physical and biological fields are rarely instantaneous, but usually take time for their realization; fire (the cause) heats water but even a gas heater takes a few minutes to heat water to the boiling point. Birth takes place only some nine months after conception. Tuberculosis of the lungs begins to affect the rest of the organism only some time after the infection of the lungs, while the effects of a serious heart-attack are almost instantaneous. The same we observe in an organized group. Small changes in an unimportant element may not tangibly affect the rest of the group. An important change of one of the essential parts may diffuse over the rest of the group very rapidly; some others take a much longer time. Later on (see Chapter 43) something more will be said of this.

On the other hand, a simultaneity of a change in two or more objects does not necessarily mean their change is related by causal-meaningful bonds; the simultaneity may be purely accidental, devoid of any causal connection between the phenomena. At any minute thousands of different changes occur, from headhunting of a tribe in the jungles, coronation of a king, a symphony concert, murder in a metropolis, to declaration of war between European countries. From the fact that they all occur on the same day it does not follow they are all causally and meaningfully connected. Most of the various events we read about in a newspaper belong to these accidental simultaneous changes of unrelated phenomena. Such accidental though simultaneous changes are not the change in togetherness we are discussing.

7. A Group's Self-Directing (Immanent) Change and Life-Career

A pile of sand, bricks, or fallen leaves is a passive conglomeration without its own (causal) force controlling its functions, change, and development. It is at the mercy of external forces. A wind can blow off a part of the leaves; dogs or children walloping in the pile rearrange it; stones put upon it will press the leaves, and so on. The same is true of any incidental conglomeration of sociocultural objects like the parts of an unassembled automobile scattered on the garage floor; bricks, cement, logs, boards piled up to build a house; diverse objects dumped together, and so forth. Having no causal ties between them, the members of such incidental congeries have no inner force controlling their functions and giving them a margin of freedom from all external forces.

Different is the situation with the causal-meaningful system. It has its own self-directing force that keeps its unified integrity in different conditions, that controls its functions, that determines (from within) the direction and the character of its change, and gives to it a margin of autonomy from all external forces that try to disrupt its unity, influence its functions, and condition its change. An assembled automobile as a causal mechanical system performs the functions determined by its own structure. It keeps its unity in the most diverse external conditions—in cold and hot climate, on most different roads, in rain and snow. Likewise it has a considerable margin of autonomy from all these external factors, and the better the car the wider is the margin. The same is true of an organism as a biological system. From the moment of its emergence it controls its own destiny in the most decisive way; from an acorn develops only an oak and nothing else; from a human baby, only a human being. During its life it is incessantly bombarded by thousands of external forces: chemical and physical factors; countless biological agencies from bacteria up to large organisms; flora and fauna. In spite of that it ordinarily keeps its identity and grows, unfolding its own potentialities. It has thus a considerable margin of autonomy from all forces external to it.

This is also true of an organized sociocultural group. From the moment of its emergence, in accordance with its sociocultural nature, the group determines its main functions, whether they be political, scientific, economic, religious, criminal. From the moment of its emergence it is largely a self-changing and self-directing unity that bears in itself the essentials of its life-career, the direction of its change, its phases, and its destination. As such

it has always a margin of autonomy from the external forces. In widely different milieu, conditions, and situations it keeps its own identity and integrity. In all these respects it is an immanent self-regulating and self-determining system. A group born as a family has different functions and phases of development from a political party; both have different functions and "evolutions" from those of the state, of a church, of a business concern, or of a scientific association. Each of these groups has different stages of development and this development consists largely in an unfolding of its own immanent potentialities. Such an inner cohesion, preservation of its integrity, self-determination of its functions and change, margin of autonomy is due to the fact that the organized group is a causal-functional and meaningful unity, in contrast to a mere spatial conglomeration of things dumped together. This causal-functional and meaningful unity furnishes to it, as to any system, its inner cohesion and its immanent self-directing and self-developing force, absent in unorganized groups and conglomerations.[13]

8. Roles of External Forces in Group Structure, Functions, and Change

The above does not mean that all the forces external to an organized group (or to any causal unity) have no role in conditioning the group's structure, functions, and life-career. They play an important, sometimes catastrophically decisive role, but these roles consist mainly in the following influences: (a) either acceleration or retardation, (b) either facilitation or inhibition of the unfolding of the structural, functional, and developmental potentialities of the group, and finally, (c) destruction of the group. Under extremely adverse external conditions an automobile can be smashed, an acorn can be broken, an organism can be killed, a social group can be annihilated (by a tornado, earthquake, or flood; by epi-

[13] Many investigators term this force equilibrium. While the term has a very definite meaning in physical mechanics and physicochemical sciences, it is devoid of meaning when applied to sociocultural phenomena. For this and other reasons its use in the sociocultural sciences is a liability rather than an asset. See a detailed analysis of this problem in my *Dynamics*, Vol. IV, pp. 677-693. Cf. K. Goldstein *The Organism* (New York, 1939).

demic or other biological elemental forces; by an invading enemy, by the pressures of other groups, and so on). Hitler's invasion temporarily crushed thousands of different groups in the invaded countries; it suppressed some of them permanently.

Unfavorable external conditions may retard the development of a powerful oak from an acorn, a normally growing personality from a new born baby, or the functioning of a new business firm, church, artistic association, state, family, and so on. Favorable external conditions can accelerate and facilitate a full unfolding of all the potentialities of a system or a group—a mighty oak from an acorn, an excellently developed organism, the fully unfolded mental and physical potentialities of a person, and finally the successful structural fullness, functional adequacy, and growth of a group.

These effects, however, limit the roles of the factors external to a group. No external factors can produce from an acorn any other organism but an oak; likewise, no external factors can transform the family into the business firm or church or state. Due to the discussed spatial compatibility of diverse social groups and to the possibility of the same individual's belonging to different social groups, the members of the family can constitute a political party, business firm, or religious sect. Yet such facts do not mean that the family becomes one of these groups by a mere cumulation or spatial compatibility of different groups within the area of the same individuals. A political party does not have such categories of meanings as "father-mother-son-daughter"; it does not perform the functions of the family and does not mean, behave, and objectify what the family means and does, and vice versa. The family as the family does not have the categories "Republican-Democrat-Communist," etc.; these are the categories of a political party. Likewise the family as a family does not have the categories "Catholic-Protestant-Buddhist-Taoist," or "pope-metropolitan-bishop-priest," or "marshal-general-colonel-private," or all the specific structural and functional categories of any but the family group. A group emerging as the family will continue to exist, unless crushed, as the family, and no external conditions can make out of it anything but the family. Ex-

ternal forces can crush it, dissolve it, and make out of the previous family members the members of some other group: business association, political party, or monastery. Such facts would however mean not a transformation of the family into something else but simply either a dissolution of the family and emergence of a new group, or a cumulation of different groups among the same individuals.

Such are the roles of external factors in molding the group's structure, functions, and life-destiny. Later on (Chapter 46) these principles will be developed.

9. Selectivity of the Group

Any organized group is selective, either quantitatively or qualitatively or both in the sense that it takes only certain elements from the outside world into its components, and rejects or leaves out of itself other elements. *Quantitatively* many groups have limits (different for different kinds of groups) either in membership, or in the meanings-norms-values, or in the vehicles. The maximum membership for such groups as the family or a sect (so long as it remains a sect) is fairly small and must remain small. For the other groups, like the state, a world religion, a political party, a labor union, and others, it is very large, potentially limited only by the whole of humanity. However, if a labor union should embrace the whole of mankind, it would cease to be the labor union, because if all employers and employees equally belong to the same union it becomes neither labor nor capitalist but a union of mankind. The same can be said of a world-state or one world-religion. Expansion of these groups to the size of mankind means a fundamental transformation of these groups into something very different from what they are with more limited membership, and with several groups (states, labor unions, religious organizations) of the same kind.

Likewise, any organized group is limited in the quantity of meanings-norms-values and of the vehicles it can have. No group can have —think over, use, operate—an unlimited quantity of these; otherwise it would be an omniscient and omnipotent God. So far as each of the numerous groups has to have its share of these, no single group can have an unlimited quantity of both components due to the existence, pressure, and competition of other groups for these values.

But the group's selectivity manifests itself mainly in a *qualitative selectivity*. As a rule an organized group can take as members only those individuals that meet its qualifications and demands. Every organized group has such qualifications. The "exclusive" groups that convey to members some advantages have very specific qualifications excluding all except a small group of the "aristocracy," the "upper class," "the intellectual elite," "the high caste," or "the royalty." Other groups have less rigid but quite definite qualifications. Not everyone can become a doctor, professor, engineer, a member of this or that family, kinship group, firm, club, association, religion, state, etc. Even the least privileged groups have their selectivity. Honest men so long as they remain honest cannot become members of a criminal gang; a Brahmin is ineligible for membership in the sudra caste (unless outcast and disqualified); not everyone can become a member of an unskilled labor union, of the society of the poor, and so on.

Likewise any organized group is selective in regard to the meanings-values-norms. An official law of the group cannot take in all the norms that are contradictory to it, otherwise it ceases to be a consistent body of norms in its bulk. Likewise, due to the presence in any organized group of a minimum of consistency in its meanings-values, the infiltration of the contradictory meanings and values also has a limit beyond which it cannot go; otherwise the group would become totally unintegrated and self-contradictory, impossible for an organized group. The same is true of its component of vehicles. Not every material agency can become a suitable vehicle for the manifestation of the menings-values-norms of the group, and not every vehicles fits the rest of the vehicles physically, biologically, and socioculturally. Later on (see Chapter 22) we shall see a substantiation of this principle.

10. Limited Variability of the Group

A mere consequence of the unity, individuality, self-direction, and selectivity of an organized group is its *limited possibility of variation*. Any organized group can change its secondary characteristics without losing its identity. It cannot, however, change radically all or most of its important traits, especially its central meanings-values-norms. In such a case it simply loses its identity, ceases to exist, and is replaced by another group. A given family incessantly changes in the secondary traits of all its components. But without losing its identity, it cannot change to such an extent as to drop its family characteristics and acquire those of a church. As a socially sanctioned union of husband(s) and wife (wives), of the parents and children, it may be monogamic, polyandric, polygamic, matrilineal and patrilineal, patriarchal, particularist and unstable, agnatic and cognatic, and so on. But all these variations leave untouched its central characteristics: the socially sanctioned union of husband(s) and wife (wives), of the parents and children, with all the functions derivative from it. The same is true of an organized group. The Catholic Church has varied many of its secondary traits: the number and character of its prayers, some of the rituals, some of the secondary dogmas, its vehicles, membership, and so on; but in all these variations it has preserved the central meanings-norms-values intact, likewise many of its vehicles, its hierarchy, and so on. When a variation within it greatly changed some of its central meanings-norms-values, the result was an emergence of new sects and of the Protestant religious groups, distinctly separate and different from the Catholic Church. With slight variation this principle is applicable to any organized group. It has, depending upon its nature, a different margin of variability, without losing its identity. But all of them have a limit in this. The limit exceeded, the group ceases to exist and gives place to another group. The important consequences of this principle will be shown later on (see Chapter 46).

11. Other Properties

To these general properties of an organized group we shall add the characteristics already discussed in the preceding chapters, namely: each organized group has a three-componential structure; it is a causal-functional and meaningful unity; it has a body of official and unofficial law-norms, and respectively formal and informal organization. Every organized group has some kind of government; it has a body of relationships, values, and phenomena specified as obligatory, recommended, and prohibited; it is a unity with a differentiation of rights-duties, functions, roles, and status of its members. The organized group is a body stratified into higher and lower hierarchies of authorities, ranks, strata; among its vehicles it has an economic complex of the vehicles enabling it to carry on its tasks and giving it the necessary means of subsistence; it has a name or a sign of its individuality.

These properties belong to all organized groups and exhaust their generic characteristics.

Chapter 9. Classification
of Organized Groups

I. A Critical Survey of Existing Classifications

Having now a fairly definite conception of an organized group at our disposal, we turn our attention to the study of the main types or classes of organized social groups. We know that within mankind there exist millions of such social systems. A study of such unities one by one would take a lifetime of many generations and would be largely a fruitless waste of time and energy. Instead, as science usually does, we must reduce this infinite variety of groups to a limited number of main types and in this way acquire the essential knowledge of the group-structure of the whole human population.

It goes without saying that one can classify organized groups in a great many different ways, depending upon the objective of the classification, and as a matter of fact they have been so classified. However, not every classification is equally adequate and fruitful. As the logic and history of classifications in the natural sciences show, any adequate classification of social groups must meet seven fundamental conditions, without which it is doomed to be logically defective and scientifically fruitless.

(1) It must be logical, with a definite and consistent *fundamentum divisionis*. One cannot classify chemical elements into hydrogen, oxygen, orange juice, and rubber. Likewise a classification of plants into *Myxophyta, Cormophyta*, vegetables, and poisonous plants is a logical hash without any consistent *fundamentum divisionis*.

(2) The *fundamentum divisionis* must be clear. A vague criterion of classification makes it fruitless. For instance, to classify books as "more or less large or small in size" is a bad classification, if the unit of size is not determined and if the size remains unspecified as to whether it means only the size of the pages without their number in the book or whether it means the thickness of the book.

(3) A third condition of an adequate and fruitful classification is that the selected bases of classification must be connected causally (and meaningfully for social groups) with all or most of the important structural and functional characteristics of each classified type. Then on the basis of the classificatory traits one acquires a knowledge of all the important characteristics of the group classified, of their main types and their mutual relationships in the complex universe of human population. Thus not all equally logical classifications are equally valid and fruitful. Many logical, "artificial" classifications are quite inadequate and fruitless.

An example of this in botany is Linnaeus' classification of plants according to the number of stamens, subdivided for each group by that of pistils. The classification is quite logical, even qualitative-quantitative, but largely artificial and fruitless. The number of stamens or pistils is not causally connected with other important properties of the plant species. In the same class are plants fundamentally different genetically and morphologically, while the plants belonging to the same family on the basis of their essential genetic-morphological similarity are placed in quite different classes. Consequently a knowledge of the number of stamens and pistils of a plant does not give even a remote idea of its important morphological and physiological properties. The trait selected by Linnaeus was unconnected causally with most of the important structural and functional properties of the plants, and hence was superseded in botany by a genetic-morphological classification founded upon more adequate bases.[1] The *fundamentum divisionis* of this more adequate plant taxonomy consists not of one but of several characteristics mutually related to many other morphological, physiological, and genetic properties of plants. Knowing to which class a plant belongs by a limited number of traits (the bases of classification), one knows many other properties also. For instance, the class of *Myxophyta*: "Unicellular or multicellular organisms; in vegetative stage of development their cells are devoid of cellwalls; no food synthesis; no sexual reproduction." Type *Cormophyta*: "multicellular organisms; cells always have cellwalls . . . food synthesis; in the assimilating cells chlorophyll. Side by side with vegetative reproduction always sexual reproduction. Adaptations for a development of sex organs outside of water. Regular differentiation into root, stem, and leaf."[2]

For these reasons such classifications of social groups as barefooted or wearing footwear; as having an automobile or being carless, though logically impeccable are quite artificial and fruitless. They do not give even a remote idea of the most important properties of the respective groups; they put into one

class groups fundamentally different from one another and separate into different classes those that are essentially similar; finally, they do not supply us with the most essential knowledge of the main types of groups existing within the total human population. We shall see that classifications of this type are rather numerous among sociological classifications.[3]

(4) A fourth requirement is that the classification must not mix real social groups (as causal-meaningful unities) with purely nominal or statistical classes (as the mere sum of individuals grouped together on the basis of this or that statistical characteristic). The age-classes of population, from 0 to one year, one year to five years, five to ten years, ten to twenty years; or the statistical nominal groups, persons wearing brown shoes and those having black shoes; these and similar groups are purely nominal plurels with no tangible interaction and having no causal-meaningful bonds of unity. The classifications that mix such nominal plurels with real social groups are defective logically as well as from the standpoint of their causal-meaningful adequacy.

(5) The classification must not mix the simple or elementary groups with complex combinations of these elementary types. A scientific classification of the chemical elements does not mix them with various molecules made up of a combination of the elements or with the complex chemical bodies made up of a variety of molecules. For the same reason the classification of social groups must not mix the types of simple or elementary social groups with their complex types made up of the combination of two or more of these simple types. We shall see again that many sociological classifications suffer from this defect.[4]

---

[1] On the three stages of botanical classification of plants (pre-Linnaean or purely descriptive; Linnaean, or artificial, and post-Linnaean or morphologico-genetic) see P. Wettstein, *A Textbook in Plant Taxonomy* (Rukovodstvo po sistematike *rasteny*, Moscow, 1903), Vol. I, pp. 1-26; N. Bush, *Taxonomy of Plants* (St. Petersburg, 1915), Vol. I, Introduction (Russian title *Sistematika rasteny*).

[2] Wettstein, *op. cit.*, pp. 48-50.

[3] The purely logical classifications and definitions are often called "analytical." Many sociologists think that as soon as they give some purely logical ("analytical") definition or classification of social phenomena their scientific task is accomplished. The above shows how greatly mistaken they are.

It explains also why most of the recent "analytical" definitions and classifications (being often clumsy logically) have remained quite fruitless. The reason is that their classifications and definitions have not met the third most important and difficult condition. A recent example of an artificial and purely mechanical classification and conception of groups is given in S. C. Dodd's *Dimensions of Society* (New York, 1942).

[4] See a discussion of adequate and inadequate classifications of social groups in R. Steinmetz, "Classification des types sociaux et catalogue des peuples," *L'Année sociologique*, Vol. III; F. Somlo *Zur Gründung einer beschreibenden Soziologie*

(6) The pluralistic bases of classification must not turn into eclectic congeries of various traits not bound together causally and meaningfully, and the classification itself must not degenerate into a mere descriptive catalogue of various traits of a group devoid of any causal or meaningful unity. Such a relapse into a mere eclectic description would mean the greatest possible regress into a pre-classificatory chaos. In such a stage was botanical taxonomy before Linnaeus. Though artificial and inadequate, Linnaeus' classification was a definite step forward in comparison with the purely descriptive botanical taxonomy before him. A mere description of a congeries of incidental traits is a defect commonly vitiating many classificatory attempts of anthropologists and sociologists. In their anthropological and sociological surveys[5] a multitude of questions little related to each other present a mass of informative material concerning the most different items of this or that "primitive and civilized" group. Such descriptive works are evidently raw material rather than a scientific theory; material for classification rather than the classification itself. As a piling up of purely descriptive data such works are all useful. But when they claim classificatory and other titles they become misleading.

(7) The classification must be more or less complete, giving all the main types of social groups, not enumerating a portion of the existing groups and passing by the others. One can classify all animal organisms as cow, mosquito, and others. One can classify all human beings as Americans, Chinese, and others. Such a classification is but a parody of real classification of all organisms or human beings.

In the light of these requirements for an adequate classification it is easy to see the defects of many existing classifications. Here are examples of each of the seven defects mentioned.

1. Lacking a Fundamentum Divisionis

Herbert Spencer classifies social institutions (groups) into domestic, ceremonial, political, ecclesiastical, professional, industrial.[6] Ceremonial institutions in this set quite evidently rest on a very different basis than the others. They do not make a special class of institutions but are part and parcel of all the other institutions. Domestic, political, religious, and other institutions have their own ceremonies, rituals, trophies, titles, badges and other varieties of rituals enumerated by Herbert Spencer in this class. The juxtaposition of "ceremonial" with other institutions is a breach of logical *fundamentum divisionis*. No less defective from this standpoint are such classifications as that of E. A. Ross: (a) fortuitous groups (crowd, public); (b) natural groups (the family, kindred, community); (c) likeness groups (castes, classes, sects, parties, professions, nations); (d) interest groups (tribes, states, guilds, etc.); (e) functional groups (purposeful associations); (f) authorities; (g) hierarchies.[7] It is perfectly evident that the classification does not have any consistent *fundamentum divisionis* and uses quite different criteria for different groups, for instance, fortuitous, functional, authorities, and so on. As a result authorities, hierarchies, and functions that are the characteristics of any organized group become special classes of groups. Likeness and purpose, again the traits of many groups (of the interest, the nature groups), are defined as special classes of groups.

Another example of the same shortcoming is given by R. Worms' classification of groups into ethnic, territorial, occupational, class, and sympathetic groups.[8] The "sympathetic group" here is an interloper whose basis is quite different from the other groups. The classification of R. Park and E. Burgess suffers from the same defect when it distinguishes: (a) the family, (b) language (racial) groups, (c)

(Berlin and Leipzig, 1909); E. E. Eubank, *The Concepts of Sociology* (Boston, 1932), Ch. 8.

[5] See for instance *Ethnographische Fragensammlung zur Erforschung der sozialen Lebens der Völker*, containing 2512 questions, edited by several anthropologists and sociologists: R. Steinmetz, R. Thurnwald, and others (Leipzig, 1906); *Questionnaire de sociologie et d'ethnographie* by the Paris Anthropological Society, and several others.

[6] Herbert Spencer, *The Principles of Sociology* (London, 1892), Vols. II and III.
[7] E. A. Ross, *Foundations of Sociology* (New York, 1905), p. 98.
[8] R. Worms, *Philosophie des sciences sociales* (Paris, 1908), Vol. III, pp. 64-65. In the current texts of sociology one can find many such defective classifications.

local and territorial groups, as neighborhoods, rural-urban communities; (d) conflict groups (nationalities, parties, sects, labor organizations, gangs); (e) accommodation groups (classes, castes, vocational and denomination groups). The authors themselves say frankly that it is "not quite adequate or wholly logical."[9]

B. Malinowski classifies institutions or organized groups on the basis of the need they serve: (a) the bond of reproduction creates the family, kinship, and clan groups; (b) the common interests of territorial propinquity give the neighborhod groups, from a household to a municipality and tribe; (c) "physiological" interests ·or needs produce the age and sex groups; (d) "voluntary associations" form secret societies, clubs, lodges, etc.; (e) occupational needs and values make occupational groups; (f) "rank and status" create estates, classes, and castes; (g) "comprehensive cultural values" unify tribes, nationalities, and political groups.[10]

The defects are first, that the classification is not complete. Such groups as the state, even racial and religious groups and several others are not included. The *fundamentum divisionis* is vague and inconsistent. ("Reproduction" is separated from the "physiological" needs to which it belongs; the "voluntary" class makes, by inference, all the other classes "involuntary," which is nonsense.) The assignment of the need-correlates is quite arbitrary. Holding that the family or kinship groups serve and are generated only by the need of reproduction is evidently a distortion. Into one class are put quite different groups (as we shall see further) like estates, castes, classes, racial and ethnic groups or tribes, nationalities and political groups, but closely related groups such as those of "clan" and "tribe" are placed into quite different classes. The classification has some sound points but they are hopelessly smothered in a hash of haphazard divisions and arbitrary connections of groups with postulated "need."

[9] R. Park and E. Burgess, *Introduction to the Science of Sociology*, p. 50. Another example is furnished by the classification of N. Anderson and E. Lindeman, *Urban Sociology* (New York, 1928), pp. 298-299.

[10] Malinowski, *A Scientific Theory of Culture* (Chapel Hill, 1944), Ch. 6.

Not quite consistent either is the classification of R. Maunier. All social groupings he puts into three main classes: biological groupings based on similarity of physical traits or complexion (as age-sex-parents groups and early social classes); geographic groupings based on community of habitation or territory (as tribe, village, city, nations); sociological groupings based upon the community of interests and action (as upper and lower strata, castes, social orders, religious, occupational, recreational, and other groups).[11] In spite of the elegancy of the classification it is unsatisfactory, for it classifies only some and not all of the social groups, and it regards the family or social class as purely or mainly biological. (We shall see that the family is one of the most complex groups in which biological traits and complexion are not the important part.) It further views a tribe or a nation as the territorial groups bound mainly by the bond of territorial adjacency. (We shall see tribe and nation represent complex multibonded groups in which the territorial bond is just one of several bonds; we shall see also that the city is not a simple territorial group but an agglomeration of a multitude of different groups.) In Maunier's purely sociological groupings the biological and territorial ties play no less a role than they play in the nation, the family, the social class, and so on; strata cannot be mixed with groups, for they are parts of all organized groups.

2. With a Vague Fundamentum Divisionis

The classification of A. Fouillée, dividing all peoples into several classes on the basis of the degree of harmony between the society and the individual, is one example of the vague *fundamentum divisionis*. What is the harmony here, and how it is to be measured or defined is quite vague. Classifications of P. Lavrov and others, dividing the groups into "historical and unhistorical"; of A. Vierkandt, dividing them into "the peoples of nature and the peoples of culture"; of A. Sutherland, classifying them into mentally developed and undeveloped, are

[11] R. Maunier, "Les trois formes du groupements social," in *Miscelanea scientifica a literaria dedicada ao Dr. J. Leite de Vasconcelos* (Coimbra, 1932).

further examples of vague classifications.[12] One cannot base classification on a purely incidental thing. A historian may devote many pages to the battle of Bunker Hill and hardly mention the whole history of ancient peoples, but that does not mean these other peoples did not exist and are "unhistorical." Many so-called "unhistorical peoples"—the Huns, Goths, Sarmatians, Scythians, Khazars, Turko-Mongols—are now mentioned in histories of the early stages of other "historical" peoples. From the fact that a chemist of the past did not know a chemical element it does not follow that this element either does not exist or should not be mentioned in a mature science of chemistry.

When Vierkandt and others base their division of peoples into the *Naturvölker and Kulturvölker* (or "civilized-uncivilized," "primitive-advanced" and so on), on their psychological character, on supposed presence of freedom of person, of thought, of criticism among the "peoples of culture," and on their absence among the "peoples of nature," one wonders to which of these groups Nazi Germany, Communist Russia, and all the totalitarian societies belong. Evidently to the *Naturvölker*, since there is no "freedom." On the other hand, Vierkandt put Germany and other European countries into the class of *Kulturvölker*. This joke of history speaks for itself. The criterion of "freedom" is very vague. Among one group a member is free to drink alcohol, to have many wives, to use contraceptives, and to criticize a foreman or an employer, but is unfree to criticize the king or the religion of that group. Among other peoples there is freedom of religion and criticism of the government, but no freedom

of bigamy-polygamy, of selling and drinking alcoholic beverages, of birth-control, of Sunday shows and recreations, or of criticism of labor leaders.[13] As we shall see (Chapter 30) there never has been a group unfree in all fields of conduct or free in all social relationships. Therefore a classification based upon such a criterion as "freedom" is doomed to be vague and fruitless. No wonder that recent history has made such classifications absurd. The same is true of such vague criteria as "general mental development," applied to groups and peoples. There are many other classifications with this kind of defect.

3. "Artificial"

Based upon one or few causally unconnected characteristics, some classifications are an aggravated variety of the Linnaean artificial classifications in botany. For example, A. Coste classifies types of societies on the basis of the density and size of their populations, particularly of the per cent of the urban to the total population. These criteria, in his belief, give the comparative index of the progressiveness and powerfulness of the respective societies. The obtained results are not surprising in their absurdity. Sweden happens to be less progressive and advanced than Turkey; the United States of America turns out to be less powerful than France, Germany, or Russia. Many densely populated regions of China become more progressive and powerful than most of the nations of the West. These results are sufficient to show the inadequacy of such classifications.[14]

A better variety of this type of classification is that of Herbert Spencer and E. Durkheim

---

[12] P. Lavrov, *Opyt istorii mysly* (An Essay in History of Thought), Vol. I, pp. 21-26 *passim*; A. Vierkandt, *Naturvölker und Kulturvölker* (Leipzig, 1896); A. Sutherland, *The Origin and Growth of the Moral Instinct* (London, 1898).

[13] On this see the pointed remarks of Pareto, *Trattato di sociologia generale* (Torino, 1916), Vol. II, pp. 256-88.

[14] See A. Coste, *Principes d'une sociologie objective* (Paris, 1899), pp. 160-175; also his *L'expérience des peuples* (Paris, 1900), pp. 591-610. Somewhat similar is the classification by A. Sutherland, who classifies groups on the basis of the size of their membership correlated with the level of mental development, as (1) lower primitive

groups with membership from 40 to 360; (2) barbarian groups (6,500 to 442,000 members); (3) civilized groups (from 4,200,000 up). If we are to believe this classification then the small groups of the Norsemen, the Koreans, the Melanesians must be quite similar in structure, functions, and culture. Small membership groups like the Academies of Sciences and Arts must be hopelessly backward and primitive in mentality. On the other hand, the large groups like the United States of America, China, India, the British Empire, Russia, the Roman Catholic Church, Buddhist Church, and so on, must all be similar because all have more than 100 million members. See A. Sutherland, *The Origin and Growth of the Moral Instinct* (London, 1898).

who in spite of his criticism of Spencerian classification gives a mere variation of it. Both are based upon the morphological characteristic of simplicity and complexity, starting with the undifferentiated "simple group" of Spencer and "the horde" of Durkheim and then passing to doubly compound, trebly compound, and so on. The results of such an artificial attempt are sterile and fallacious. First, the Spencerian "simple group" and the Durkheimian "horde" is a fiction that never existed; and second, Spencer's "doubly compound," "trebly compound" societies and Durkheim's "simple polysegmental," "complex polysegmental" become also largely fictitious, based upon a purely political trait of federations of unified societies. No wonder that in the Spencerian classification into one class of the "trebly compound" are put such groups as ancient Mexico, the Assyrian Empire, the Egyptian Empire, Great Britain, France, Germany, Italy, and Russia; no wonder also that the Tahitians, Fijians, and Javans become similar to the Athenian and Spartan societies, to the greater fiefs of France of the thirteenth century, and so on. The absurdity of these results speaks for itself.[15]

Another popular variety of this type is the classification of groups into *primary* and *secondary*. Mechanically applying C. H. Cooley's distinction between the direct "face to face" and indirect interaction (which Cooley indicated for other purposes), many American sociologists use this "face to face" and indirect characteristic as the main criterion for their classifications of groups. It must be evident that the mere fact as to whether an interaction is "face to face" or indirect is a relatively unimportant trait, much less important than the number of Linnaean stamens in

a plant. The brief face to face interaction we have every day with a multitude of individuals on the street, in street cars, in our offices, is quite unimportant in the mentality and behavior of the persons. An antagonistic face to face interaction of American and German soldiers on a battlefield is something absolutely different from a solidary face to face interaction. A face to face interaction—between the other players and the man with a "poker face" at a bridge party, between a criminal and judge, a mother and her child, or a commander and his soldiers—these again are very different phenomena; therefore any classification which takes this "face to face" trait for its foundation is bound to be a quite artificial classification with fundamentally different groups put into the same class and with quite similar groups put into different classes. In addition, such a classification cannot yield the essential characteristics of the groups classified on this basis.

One of the best of these is K. Young's classification. He also divides groups into primary and secondary. In the primary class are the family, neighborhood, village community, congeniality groups, play groups, crowds. In the secondary we find political, economic, religious, organized recreational groups, criminal gangs, publics. And then somewhere outside or in between these classes are mentioned race, society, and community.[16] At a glance we see that into one class are put such fundamentally different groups (different in structure and functions, meanings, members, and vehicles) as the family and crowd, the village community and play groups, religious groups and criminal gangs, political groups and publics.

In all their essential properties these groups

---

[15] See Herbert Spencer, *Principles of Sociology* (London, 1885), Vol. I, pp. 540 ff; E. Durkheim, *The Rules of Sociological Method* (Chicago, 1938), Ch. 4. Though Durkheim criticizes Spencer, his own classification has all its defects. In his *Le Suicide* and *L'année sociologique* Durkheim gave another classification of social groups into religious, familial, political, and occupational, adding to it in *L'année* a group called "the character of civilization." See Durkheim and Mauss, "Civilization et types of civilization," *L'année*, Vol. XII, p. 47; *Le Suicide*, p. 522. Likewise Spencer gave, besides the two criticized classifications, a third

one, militant and industrial types of society. This classification is much more productive for the purpose of distinguishing two types of political organizations. See Spencer, *The Principles of Sociology*, Vol. II, Chs. 17-18.

[16] K. Young, *An Introductory Sociology*, (New York, 1939), pp. 5-17. See also G. Lundberg, *Foundations of Sociology*, quoted Ch. 8, and most of the texts in introductory sociology. Much more adequate is the concept of primary group by E. Faris. It is near to what I call the familistic group. Cf. E. Faris, *The Nature of Human Nature* (New York, 1937), Ch. 4.

are as different as they can be, and vice versa, essentially similar groups like "play groups" and "organized recreational groups" are divorced from one another and put into different classes. The whole classification is as artificial as a classification "man has a nose and dog has a nose, therefore they belong to the same class of organisms." If the characteristics of the face to face and indirect interaction were divided into their main types and if these specified traits were taken as a sub-characteristic of a sub-sub-sub-division of a class of groups, they would be useful. But when these many varied and indefinite traits are made the main *fundamentum divisionis*, the above results and general fruitlessness of the classification become inevitable.

Still another variety of this "pathological" type of classification is given by many who take economic characteristics for their *fundamentum divisionis*. So far as these are offered to classify various types of economic groups, they are valuable, when their specific criteria are valid. When, however, these theorists contend that through their economic criteria they supply also the classification of all kinds of groups, with the economic criteria giving us the knowledge of all the important properties of the groups, the classifications with all their defects become artificial. Examples of such classifications are those of F. Liszt, B. Hildebrandt, K. Bücher, G. Schmoller, E. Grosse, and more recently of L. Hobhouse, G. Wheeler, and M. Ginsberg.[17]

Dividing societies into the classes hunters-fishermen, pastoral, agricultural, industrial (F. Liszt); or into those with *Naturalwirtschaft, Geldwirtschaft and Kreditwirtschaft* (B. Hildebrandt); or into lower hunters, higher hunters, Agricultural I, Pastoral I, Agricultural II, Pastoral II, Agricultural III (Hobhouse, Wheeler and Ginsberg);[18] these theories may be of considerable value so far as they outline the main

types of economic groups. If through this classification they claim (as some of them, especially Marxian theories, do) to be classifying all the essential types of groups and all their important characteristics (allegedly connected with the economic traits), then they become a variety of the artificial classifications, because a certain economic trait does not determine all the important social and cultural characteristics of the group. The causal and meaningful connection between the economic and other sociocultural variables of the groups is, in most cases, rather remote, in others non-tangible, in only a few more or less close. Therefore two societies with similar economic organization may have quite dissimilar characteristics in other respects, and vice versa.[19] It need not be added that these classifications are very incomplete and give little idea of the main types of social groups.

These samples show the concrete types of the "artificial" defective classification.

4. Mixing Real and Nominal Social Groups

F. Gidding's classification of groups into primary classes: vitality, personality, social; and then into the derivative or secondary classes: political, industrial, and economic, is a good sample of this kind of classification.[20] Gidding's vitality classes and personality classes are largely nominal groups. There is no special group of intensely interacting individuals who are particularly healthy, have many children, and low mortality; likewise we do not have a special interacting group of idiots and morons or a union of greatest geniuses. His group of the true elite made up of the healthiest, most moral, and greatest intellectual geniuses is likewise a purely fictitious group; as a real group it has hardly ever existed. Side by side with these fictitious groups the same classification gives several real groups like some of the industrial, occupational, and

---

[17] See F. Liszt, *Das nationale System der Politischen Oekonomie* (Leipzig, 1883); K. Bücher, *Die Entstehung der Volkswirtschahft* (ed. 1921); G. Schmoller, *Grundriss der Allgemeinen Volkswirtschaftslehre* (Leipzig, 1901); B. Hildebrandt, *Naturalwirtschaft, Geldwirtschaft und Kreditwirtschaft. Jahrbucher für Nationaloekonomie*, Vol. II (1864), pp. 1 ff; L. Hobhouse, G. Wheeler, and M. Ginsberg, *The Material Culture and Social Institutions of the Simpler Peoples* (London, 1915).

[18] Other classifications of economic type, including numerous Marxian classifications, are mere variations of these patterns.

[19] See the evidence of this in my *Theories*, Ch. 10. Hobhouse, Wheeler, and Ginsberg's work shows this also, that groups of the same economic class, say Agricultural I, have very different sociocultural traits.

[20] F. Giddings, *Elements of Sociology* (New York, 1912), pp. 103-118.

economic groups. Even more mixed are the real and the nominal groups in Gidding's other classification of organic structure, sex, age and kinship, this last subclassified as consanguinity, propinquity, nationality, potential nationality, ethnic race, glottic race, chromatic race, cephalic race, humanity.[21] The whole classification offers a conspicuous mixture of the real and nominal groups.

The classification of E. A. Ross, noted above, contains a mixture also, the nominal groups of "the authorities" being put side by side with the real groups. In Park and Burgess' classification, noted above, the "conflict" and "accommodation" categories are nominal, not real, because there are no groups entirely devoted to conflict or accommodation; on the other hand these relationships are given in all real groups to some extent. Most of the purely statistical classifications of a population by detailed age-groups, by sex-groups, by birth-mortality-marriage-morbidity rates, by literacy and illiteracy, and so on are mainly classifications of nominal groups, now and then mixed with the real groups.[22]

Many "evolutionary" or "genetic" classifications of groups, on the basis of their alleged place on the ladder of progress-evolution, are largely artificial and vague classifications but have in addition the defect of mixing real groups with nominal plurels. L. Morgan's lower-middle-upper savage groups, lower-middle-upper barbaric groups, and civilized groups is an example of such logically and factually sick classifications.[23] Some of the groups within each of these classes are real groups; most of the others, including the categories themselves, are purely nominal plurels. The whole assumption of the linear evolution of various groups is unsound; the specific traits demarcating one stage-group from another like

"fish subsistence," discovery of fire, invention of bow and arrow, the art of pottery, domestication of animals, use of bricks or of iron tools, up to the invention of phonetic alphabets, are quite arbitrary criteria whose time order of invention is arbitrarily (and mostly wrongly) fixed, and which in no way provides a similarity for the groups that have one of these characteristics in common. The groups using a phonetic alphabet are as different from one another in many of their essential traits as they can be. The same is true of the groups that know the art of pottery or the use of iron tools.

With slight modification the same can be said of many other evolutionary (genetic) classifications like that of R. Steinmetz, dividing groups into genetic classes according to the intellectual character of the group: sub-men groups (*Urmenschen*), primitive barbarians, groups with systematized and unified thought, cultural groups with science, humanitarian ethics, etc.[24]

In addition the criterion of "intellectual character" is as dark as in A. Sutherland's classification. Determination of this intellectual level by the intellectual top men of the groups is a still more risky operation; one can hardly determine the intellectual level of a group by the great intellectual comets that irregularly appear in it. It would be unscientific to measure by Homer and Plato and Aristotle the intellectuality of the Greeks; or by that of J. S. Erigena the intellectuality of the Irish in the eighth century; or by Lomonosov's mind or Sir Isaac Newton's intellectuality that of the Russian and English societies of the seventeenth and eighteenth centuries. If such an operation is even permissible the criterion itself is purely artificial and the groups united into one class

---

[21] F. Giddings, *Inductive Sociology* (New York, 1901), pp. 47-54. On pp. 249-265 he gives a still different and also mixed classification.

[22] See for example Mayo-Smith, *Statistics and Sociology* (New York, 1902), p. 6; G. von Mayr, *Statistik und Gesellschaftlehre* (Tübingen, 1917), Vol. III.

[23] L. H. Morgan, *Ancient Society* (New York, 1878), p. 12. Similar are the shortcomings of many other "evolutionary" classifications, as those of J. Bachofen, F. Engels, Sir John Lubbock, and other partisans of a linear social evolution.

[24] R. Steinmetz, "Classification des types sociaux," quoted pp. 136-147; this genetic classification he parallels by "systematic" classification dividing all groups into ten economic types: small collectors of gifts of nature, hunters, fishermen, nomadic agriculturists, lower agriculturists, higher agriculturists, nomadic pastoral groups, groups living in complex conditions, manufacturing groups, industrial groups. All that is said above of the economic classifications can be said of this. Another variety of a genetic classification is given by W. Wundt in his *Elemente der Völkerpsychologie* (Leipzig, 1912).

by such a criterion are nothing but nominal groups.

Another variety of this kind of classification is represented by all who introduce, side by side with specific groups, mankind as a group. In a large number of theories, like those of Turgot, Condorcet, Saint Simon, Herder, Fichte, Lessing, A. Comte, Kant, Hegel, mankind or "great society"[25] functions as the largest and most embracing group. It is evident that mankind is a nominalistic plurel that has never been, up to the present time, a real interacting group in any tangible degree; it has been nothing but the totality of human population differentiated into many groups, but not itself a real group. Putting it side by side with the real groups is a logical confusion mixing them with a nominal plurel. There are many other classifications that possess this defect of mixing nominal collections of individuals with real social groups.

5. Mixing Simple and Complex Groups

If a chemist puts among the chemical elements such molecules as H_2O or H_2SO_4, his classification will be ridiculed by other chemists. Such errors are however quite common in current classifications of social groups, which mix simple or unibonded with complex multibonded groups. In subsequent chapters we shall see that such groups as social caste, social class, nation, and many others are complex ("manybonded") groups made up, like chemical molecules, of a cumulation or combination of two or more simple (unibonded) groups. Evidently they cannot be put into the same class as the simple groups. Meanwhile in a great many classifications these complex groups are put side by side with the religious, occupational, language, or territorial groups of whose combinations they are made up. The respective classifications are devoid of logical coherence and causal relationship.

6. "Cataloguing"

If one wants to, one can pick up and enumerate several thousands of groups in Boston alone. There are thousands of different families,

precincts, political factions, street and apartment house groups, scientific, philosophic, religious, nationality, artistic, philanthropic, recreational, and other groups. If we are interested in the most detailed study of the group composition of Boston, all these groups can be enumerated and catalogued. Several volumes can be filled by their descriptions. A telephone directory is an example of such a catalogue. However, for a generalizing science such a cataloging is useless. If we attempt to follow such a descriptive method in regard to all the groups within the whole human population, a lifetime of many generations will be needed; and when such a "directory" is compiled, nobody can use it, for its confusion defeats understanding. In order to make up a directory of all the groups in even one city, some classification has to be present, otherwise even the modest task of making a usable directory cannot be achieved. Still less can such a cataloging supply a knowledge of all the main types of social groups. For these reasons when we are confronted with the pretentious claims of such catalogers of being very "factual" and "devoid of speculation" we can respectfully advise them to enjoy their own cooking if they can, and remind them that all descriptive factual material, or an alphabetic telephone directory, is not a science but only material for a science, in our case for a scientific classification of social groups.

Classifications of this kind are given in abundance in a large number of anthropological or descriptive sociological studies of this or that "middletown," "community," "city," "village," "street-corner," or "parish." Such surveys of various populations pile one item upon another in a purely mechanical or alphabetic order, never giving a real analysis of the causal-meaningful structure of the aggregates of the population studied. If such classifications of groups are really scientific work, then it has already been done, and the telephone directory is the best classification of that kind.

7. Fragmentary and Incomplete

An example of such classifications is given by many theories of the state that divide all social groups into the *state and society* (as another group different from the state or as a mere name covering all groups except states).

---

[25] For instance in G. Wallas, *The Great Society* (New York, 1914). See also Giddings' "humanity" above.

Hypnotized by the state, these authors solve the problem of classification by simply stating that "the concept of society in a narrow sense embraces all social groups with the exception of the state";[26] or that the state is the authoritative, administrative, political organization, while society is a system of interdependence of individuals arising from an unequal distribution of wealth (L. von Stein, Gneist, and others); or that the state is the highest organized group under whose roof all the other groups exist with the permission of the state (N. Lazarevsky and other theorizers of constitutional law). There is no need for a lengthy criticism of such classifications. They do not give any real classification of social groups but simply single out the state and leave all the other groups in an undifferentiated mass. Later on we shall see that their specific claim for a supreme and exclusive role of the states is also unwarranted.

Another example of the incomplete classification is that of Don L. Sturzo dividing all social groups (forms) into the family, the political society, the religious form or group.[27] We shall see that these groups are only a few among many. Other examples of this kind of classification are furnished by all those theories that divide mankind only or mainly into racial groups (Gobineau, Ammon, Lapouge, partly Gumplowicz, and others); into social classes (most of the Marxian classifications), or into religious groups only, leaving all the other groups unclassified. In a less conspicuous form the defect of incompleteness and fragmentariness is quite common for an overwhelming majority of existing classifications. When giving a set of groups they usually miss several important ones, not to mention further important subdivisions of each group.

This critical survey gives an idea of the contemporary situation in this field, of the main types of the existing classifications and the obvious mistakes made. Now we can attempt to give a classification of the main, real groups into which the human population is differentiated, as free as possible from the above defects.

II. The Meaning and Criteria
of the Powerful Social Group

As mentioned at the beginning of this chapter, the task of the classification of the social group consists not in an enumeration of millions of various social groups that exist in the sociocultural universe, from the "club of lovers of photography" and "association of the collectors of broken whisky bottles" to vast social groups like big empires and world religious groups. Such a cataloging is useless and gets us nowhere. Instead the task of sociology here is determined by its nature, to classify and to study the phenomena (here the groups) that recur in time and space as perennial social groups, omitting the unique groups unrepeated in time and space. Furthermore, even among the recurring groups at the present stage of our knowledge, the primary attention has to be given to the important social groups repeated in time or space or in both.

Which groups are to be considered important depends upon the criteria of importance. Since the supreme task of science generally and of sociology particularly is to find out the causal-functional and meaningful relationships among the phenomena studied, *the important groups in our case will be those that exert a powerful causal-meaningful influence upon individuals, upon other groups, and upon the course of sociocultural phenomena generally.* The groups like "a club of phlegmatics" or "an

[26] G. Jellineck, *Pravo sovremmennago gosudarstva* (St. Petersburg, 1903), pp. 58-61; B. Tchicherin, *Kurs gosudarstvennoi nauki* (Moscow, 1896), Part II, pp. 3 ff. With variations this conception is offered by L. von Stein, Gneist, and many other theorizers of constitutional law and of the state. See a survey of these theories in R. von Mohl, *Staatswissenschaften und Gesellschaftswissenschaften* (Tübingen, 1851), Vol. I; A. Small's "Sociology" in the earlier editions of the *Encyclopedia Americana* and also in his *Origins of Sociology* (Chicago, 1924).

[27] D. L. Sturzo, *Inner Laws of Society* (New York, 1944), pp. 25 ff.

association of collectors of last year's snow" come and go, leaving hardly any trace in the annals of history. They exert little, if any, influence upon the rest of human population, upon other groups, or upon the course of sociocultural life. In this sense they are powerless, uninfluential forces that neither causally nor meaningfully affect anything and anybody in the sociocultural universe except a few members of such groups in whose total life they are an incidental, unimportant fancy.

We can define precisely, with the help of definite criteria, which groups are socioculturally and historically powerful, as the *foci* of the effective causal-meaningful forces shaping and determining the life of their members, of the outside population, and of sociocultural processes. *Five criteria give a rough but fairly accurate measuring stick of the comparative powerfulness of social groups.*[28] They are (1) the size of the group membership, either of a single given group, or of a formation of many similar interacting groups; (2) the totality of the meanings-values-norms at the disposal of the group (the qualitative aspect of the members); (3) the totality of the vehicles possessed by the group for influencing the individuals, groups, and the sociocultural universe; (4) solidarity of the group; (5) the technical perfection of its structural and functional organization. A few comments are in order.

(1) Other conditions being equal, the group with a larger membership is more powerful than that with a small membership. A strike of 500,000 workers is a social event; a strike of 50 workers usually passes without being noticed by the inhabitants of the same city.

(2) Again, of two equal groups, the group that has a richer and more adequate fund of scientific knowledge, technological inventive ideas, better and more integrated systems of philosophy and religion, ethics and law, more rational systems of economic and political ideas, organization and oratorical talents, vitality and health, is more powerful than less favored groups. Whether the richer and poorer funds are due to the hereditary or environmental factors of the members of both groups just now is unimportant to us. What is important is the difference in the funds of meanings in the two cases.

(3) Other conditions being equal, the group that has at its disposal a richer and more adequate assortment of vehicles: machines, tools, weapons, press, telephone, telegraph, radio, means of communication, money, wealth, buildings, land, capital, books, libraries, orchestras, museums, etc., is more powerful than a group having a much poorer fund of vehicles.

(4) Likewise being identical in all other respects, a group that is solidary in the relationships of its members is more powerful than if it were antagonistic. In the first case the energy of the group is not wasted by internal frictions; in the second it is spent in useless conflict.

(5) Finally, as a subdivision of the second and third condition, the technical perfection of the structural and functional organization of the group should be mentioned specifically. A well-disciplined and well-organized group of police with a rational and clear-cut division of the functions of each member, with each member well trained in the performance of his activities, with rational differentiation and stratification, can disperse a much larger crowd with a poor technical organization. The same is observed in the army. A perfectly organized army often defeats a much larger army, poorly organized from a technical standpoint.[29] Of two orchestras, one with a perfect technical organization, the other with a poor one, the

---

[28] B. Russell in his book, *Power* (New York, 1938) pp. 145, 158, treats this problem but does not solve it in any adequate way. See also G. Mosca, *The Ruling Class*, Ch. 2; B. Kidd, *The Science of Power* (New York, 1918); G. Ferrero, *The Principles of Power* (New York, 1942).

[29] All these phenomena could easily be observed in the present war. At its initial stages, numerically much smaller army-groups of Nazis conquered and then kept in subjugation many times larger populations of Greece and Yugoslavia, Norway and Holland, Belgium and France, Poland and Denmark. Unpopular governments being in a small minority within their subjects keep their power because the government and their pretorian army and police are a much better organized group than the numerically superior population. See many facts of that kind in N. Lazarevsky, *Russian Constitutional Law* (St. Petersburg, 1911), p. 14; M. Ostrogorsky, *La democratie et les parties politiques* (Paris, 1912), pp. 157 ff; G. Mosca, *The Ruling Class* (New York, 1939), *passim*; A. Benthley, *The Process of Government* (Chicago, 1908), pp. 215 ff.

first performs the same composition much better and impresses the audience more powerfully than the poorly organized orchestra. Similar differences are notable in two schools or universities, churches or courts, and in practically all organized groups (unorganized ones being the least powerful, like a mob, a crowd, or an incidental assembly).

Each of these measuring sticks of power is practically self-evident. Taken together, they give a fairly accurate idea of the comparative powerfulness of groups. Inductively verified, the proposition is supported by history. The

groups that by their existence and activity made history, that tangibly conditioned the course of historical events or of sociocultural life have been exactly those having all or most of these characteristics.

Subsequently we shall classify and deal with the powerful groups. The ineffective groups will not be dealt with specifically, but they will not be passed by; they will fall, as subgroups, within one of the powerful groups studied. Scarcely any of them will be left outside of the powerful groups (unibonded and multibonded).

III. The Bases of Classification

Since an organized group is a causal-functional and meaningful unity, its very individuality and reality among other groups and individuals are due to its causal and meaningful ties. Only through the causal interdependence of its components does it stand out as a unity in the ocean of human population. The first scientific basis of the classification of the groups is therefore the *intensity or closeness of causal-functional interdependence* among its members and components. If among 1000 individuals not united by causal interdependence, 200 are united, these 200 make a real collective unity or group. If among these 200 members of the group, 50 individuals are, say, twice or thrice more closely interdependent, this difference in the degree of causal interdependence (intensity of interaction) makes of these 50 individuals a group within the group of 200. If among these 50 members, 10 are still more tangibly interdependent, they make a group in a group of 50 within a group of 200. Thus a tangible difference in closeness or intensity of causal-functional interdependence is the first objective basis for distinguishing the existence of groups and for their classification.

The closer interdependence of the members of the solar system makes it a causal-functional unity distinct from the rest of heavenly bodies. A still closer interdependence between the earth and the moon make them a group within the solar system. Most[30] of the citizens of the

United States, being causally interdependent in many ways (through taxes, laws, regulations, governmental agencies, and so on), make a real group—the United States of America. Within this group the federal government of the United States makes a group within the group, for the causal-functional interdependence among the members of the government is closer than among the general body of the citizens. Within the government group the executive, the legislative, and the judicial bodies make still closer groups for the same reason. Thus we have, on the basis of different *intensity* of causal-functional interdependence, groups within still larger but looser groups. There may be a long gradation of groups within groups on this objective basis of unity and reality.

However, the criterion of the intensity of causal-functional interdependence is not the only basis of the unity and individuality of social groups. They have not only causal-functional but also *meaningful* unity. Their individuality is determined by the meanings-values-norms in and around which, because of and for the sake of which, the individuals interact and make a causal unity. If within a given population there are 200 individuals with an equal causal interdependence, but the component of meanings of 100 consists in a "Roman-Catholic religion," while the component of meanings of the other 100 consists

---

[30] Though some of the citizens may have such feeble causal ties with the body of the citizens that

they may be nominal rather than real members of the United States.

in a "Republican Party," these 200 indviduals with equal intensity of causal interdependence make not one but two different collective unities. The difference in the component of meanings makes them two distinct unities, in spite of an equal intensity of their causal ties. Thus the second objective basis of the unity and individuality of a group is *the character of its component of meanings*. When the meanings-values-norms because of which and for the sake of which the individuals interact and establish their causal interdependence are different in two sets of interacting individuals, these individuals (with their actions and vehicles) make different groups. If they now interact around the values of Protestantism, now about the values of General Motors, now around the values of the Democratic party, they compose not one but three different groups "compounded" of the same individuals. We have seen that the component of the meanings-values-norms gives the specific individuality to a group (see above, Chapter 8). Here we only reiterate this statement.

Thus the main bases of group classification quite logically follow from the very nature of the causal-meaningful unity of the groups. They are inherent to and inseparable from it. They do not introduce anything foreign to the nature of the group's unity. They take care of the most important tasks of any scientific classification or definition, namely the *causal-functional* (for all the natural sciences), and the *meaningful* (for the sociocultural sciences) relationships of the phenomena studied.[31] As such these two bases (again mutually connected in the group) are the most adequate, the most logical, and most coherent bases of any classification. As we shall see, they put into one class the groups that are really similar in their essential properties and put into different classes those that are dissimilar. Likewise they enable us to observe and to classify all the main social groups, without missing any important one.[32] Being inherently united within the group the causal and meaningful bases are not an eclectic duality but a unified double *fundamentum divisionis* of the groups.

IV. Unibonded and Multibonded Groups

Since the component of meanings gives a group individuality (on the basis of the causal-functional unity), a group may have *one set of meanings-norms-values* (with their vehicles) as the central value. Or a group may have *not one but two or more sets of meaning coordinated with one another* (for instance, religious and political; economic and scientific; recreational, ethical, and economic, with their vehicles). In the first case the members of the group interact because of and for the sake of realization, enjoyment, increase, and utilization of this one set of meanings-norms-values. As a by-product on the fringes of such a central set there may be some other values, as secondary

and incidental "fellow travelers." They, however, do not play an important role in the existence and functioning of the group. Its *raison d'être* is in the central system of values-meanings-norms (with respective vehicles). This central set is defined in the official and unofficial law-norms of the group. In the second case the *raison d'être* of the group is not one, but two or three sets of values-meanings-norms and their vehicles. The group exists because of or for the sake of realization, utilization, enjoyment, multiplication, creation of two or a larger number of such values. In the first case the members of the group are

[31] For other purposes (for instance ethical or aesthetic) groups can be classified on ethical or aesthetic bases. But for strictly scientific purposes, the *causal-meaningful* basis is the only adequate one.

[32] If we were considering only the causal intensity of the interdependence, then we should miss a greater part of the important groups, with an equal intensity of interaction. If we had taken only the component of meanings, then we should miss all the groups with a different intensity of interaction and be likely to take as a real group many a nominal group. In that case the partisans of political democracy or of materialism in Europe and China of the seventeenth century would make one group, since their component of meanings is similar. In reality, not being in a causal interaction, they make not one but two different groups. United into one group they make a nominal plurel only.

unified into a real social system *by one tie*—
that of the central system of values-meanings-
norms; in the second, by *two or a greater number of such ties*. The first kind of group can be
called *unibonded*; the second, *multibonded*.[33]
*In the unibonded groups the members are
united by one central meaningful-causal bond;
in the multibonded, by two or more bonds.*

Unibonded groups correspond to chemical
elements, multibonded to chemical molecules.
Just as the molecules are a combination of
two or more elements, so the multibonded
groups are a combination of two or more unibonded ties. Just as analysis of the concrete
chemical substances consists ultimately in finding the molecules and elements of which they
are composed, so the analysis of group structures in human population consists in reduction of its complexity to the multibonded and
unibonded structures. In its concrete form any
human population inhabiting a certain area is
always a complex aggregate of several unibonded and multibonded groups. It is to be
noted that the concepts of the unibonded and
multibonded groups logically follow from the
componential structure of the groups and from
their causal-meaningful unity.

This leads to another question. What set of
meanings-values-norms can be taken as unibinding? A solution of this problem will also
throw light upon multibonded groups. What
meanings become unibinding values depends
upon persons and many different conditions.
They certainly fluctuate from person to person and from group to group. Almost any
meaning, however, may be such a value for at
least a few individuals, as a "club of stout
persons" or an association of "tall men." However, sociology is not concerned with such rare
oddities. They are few and unique, neither
permanent nor recurrent in time and space,
neither influential historically nor meaningfully

important. As such they can be passed by as
"hobby and recreational" groups.

If we look for the meanings that have been
a unibonded "magnet" for large, permanent,
historically effective groups, the classes of such
values are rather limited. Exactly what they
are can hardly be stated offhand, in view of our
limited knowledge of the problem, but a few
hypotheses can tentatively be advanced. For
instance one can say that such values must be
closely related to the satisfaction of basic
human needs. Since there is no agreement as
to what human needs are basic, however, such
a hypothesis leaves us exactly where we were.
One may tentatively classify values into their
logical classes: scientific, aesthetic, economic,
religious, political and moral, and make a corresponding list of unibonded groups.[34]

Such a classification has many merits. Its
weak point is that it may not correspond to the
actually existing groups and consequently may
remain a classification of meanings-values-
norms rather than of the actual social groups.
Such a danger is not imaginary. Our observation shows that the intellectual or cultural or
moral-legal values appear not in one group but
in several (scientific, philosophical, religious,
educational, professional, occupational, and the
family groups). The same is true of other
classes of meanings, and vice versa. The same
group, for instance, the family, maintains
values of several kinds. Therefore if we strictly
adhere to such a classification we should place
in one "intellectual" class several different
groups; on the other hand we should miss
groups like the family that do not fall into any
of the classes of meanings-values-norms given.

Taking this observational approach we find
that some unibonded groups are centered
around a *biological "landmark" of values*. The
others (the majority of the groups) have centered around *sociocultural indicators of values*.

[33] In my Russian *Sistema Soziologii* and other
previous works I called them respectively *elementary* and *cumulative*.

[34] Among the existing "artificial" classifications
of groups there are several based upon the basic
needs as classes of meanings-values-norms. Such,
for instance, are Blackmar and Gillin's classification
of sustaining, perpetuating, communicating, cultural, regulative, and protective systems of groups;
or A. Fairbanks' classification of economic, social,
political, aesthetic, intellectual, moral, and religious

activities. See G. Ratzenhofer's six main interests
of groups. W. McDougall's classification of groups
based on the main instincts, or B. Malinowski's
poorer version of McDougall's classification, and
many others. See F. Blackmar and J. Gillin, *Outlines of Sociology* (New York, 1915), p. 105; A.
Fairbanks, *Introduction to Sociology* (New York,
1910), Ch. 7; W. McDougall, *An Introduction to
Social Psychology* (Boston, 1923); G. Ratzenhofer, *Soziologie* (Leipzig, 1908); B. Malinowski,
The Scientific Theory of Culture, quoted.

Consequently we can single out the following unibonded and multibonded groups into which human population has been differentiated:

I. Important Unibonded Groups
(Centered Around the Main Values)

A. Biosocial Characteristics
 1. Race,
 2. Sex, and
 3. Age values.
B. Sociocultural Characteristics
 4. Kinship,
 5. Territorial proximity,
 6. Language (nationality),
 7. The state,
 8. Occupational,
 9. Economic,
 10. Religious,
 11. Political,
 12. Scientific, philosophical, aesthetic, educational, recreational, ethical, and other "ideological" values.
 13. A nominal group of the elite: leaders, men of genius, and historical persons.

II. Important Multibonded Groups

(Made by a Combination of Two or More Unibonded Values)

As we shall see, their number is enormous but among these the following deserve special attention:

 1. Family
 2. Clan
 3. Tribe
 4. Nation
 5. Caste
 6. Social Order
 7. Social Class

The point is that the logical classes of meanings and the classes of social groups are not coterminal and identical. The same class of values (say, scientific or ethical or legal) is used by a multitude of different groups: the family, the business firm, the state, the occupational, and other groups; and all the multibonded groups have not one but several sets of meanings (see further, Chapter 14). For this reason a purely logical classification of meanings-values-norms can hardly serve as a valid classification of important social groups. Therefore it is better to choose a different approach to our problem, as to what have been the unibonded values serving as the magnet attracting and creating influential social groups.

Guided by the above definition of unibinding values, we shall drop the speculative way of tentative hypothesis and take instead the way of observation. What groups in human population have actually been the powerful and permanent groups? We are in the position of a geographer trying to chart a little known region with its plains and hills, streams and lakes, woods and deserts. His first task is to map these as they are given to his observation. Only after that can he ask and answer the questions as to why these hills are there, and why the streams and lakes are situated in a given way. The actual geographic picture of the region is the prior consideration.

The above outline includes the most important unibonded and multibonded groups. In their totality these groups have been guiding the destiny of every individual and of all other groups. By their integral pressure the main course of sociocultural life and of human history has been largely shaped. They also determine the main lines of social differentiation. Speaking analogically, they are the main "organs" into which the "body" of the total human population is differentiated. Social differentiation of mankind is nothing but differentiation into these groups. The classification of groups is at the same time the map of the main "trenches" of social differentiation. It reveals the *horizontal* structure of the human population.

Following our study of these groups and of the main lines of social differentiation we shall study the *vertical* aspect of this structure, its social stratification. Then our view of the structure of the sociocultural universe will be essentially complete, embracing (a) the internal structure of the generic sociocultural phenomenon (social interaction in its components and forms; organized-unorganized; solidary-antagonistic, and others); (b) a study of the differentiation of human population into the main unibonded and multibonded groups with their typical formations; (c) a study of the intra- and intergroup social stratification of the human population. In this way we may obtain the relevant knowledge of the "histology, anatomy, morphology, and taxonomy" of the superorganic human universe.

The unibonded and multibonded classification of organized groups may be subdivided into several subclasses according to additional secondary characteristics. Thus among both classes we can distinguish the following groups.

1. Comparatively Large or Small

Even among groups of the same nature, as states, occupational unions, or language groups there are large and small states, occupational unions, and language groups.

2. Clearly Organized and Semi-Organized

As a rule the powerful social groups are well organized from a technical standpoint. However, there are also groups which are organized in only a fraction of their potential membership, the other part remaining "as if" organized or unorganized. Some of such groups have a large potential membership, as the race, sex, or language plurels. When such a multitude has a nucleus of organized leaders it often gains spontaneous support, by virtue of its situation and aspirations, from the unorganized members. Each of its members acts spontaneously, sometimes even without any knowledge of the actions of leaders and other members. On the battlefield of history the total weight of such semi-organized groups has been considerable. For this reason they are to be listed among the important groups. Sooner or later they pass from the unorganized to the organized state, and then they become powerful groups indeed, turning their potential strength (large membership, solidarity, organization, fund of meanings, and vehicles) into effective action.

3. Centralized, Decentralized, and Otherwise Distinguished in Government

Soviet Russia (of the period 1918-1932) with its entirely centralized government regulating almost all the relationships of the Soviet citizens and rigidly controlling all the governments of the "federated" and "autonomous" republics of Russia, is a conspicuous example of the centralized state government. In contrast to this the federal government of the United States in the nineteenth century regulated and controlled only a few social relationships of the citizens of the United States, other relationships being controlled by the state and municipal governments and by a multitude of private groups and individuals.

The governmental organization of the Roman Catholic Church is more centralized than that of the Evangelical Protestant churches. There are labor unions, universities, families, political parties, and other groups with more and less centralized governments. In some of the groups the decentralization is so great that it often amounts almost to a lack of real organization.

Governments in the organized groups yield several types classified differently by various social and political thinkers. Here we can mention but a few of the important classifications. Whether in the state, the Church, the political party, the family, business firms, or other groups we can distinguish (after Aristotle) the following types of government:

Government of One: monarchy (good form); tyranny (bad form)

Government of Few: aristocracy (good form); oligarchy (bad form)

Government of the Majority: democracy (good form); mob-rule (bad form).

Or according to Plato:

Aristocracy (the government of the wise)

Timocracy (the government of the proud with military glory and honor)

Oligarchy (the government of the rich)

Democracy (the government animated by unrestrained freedom)

Tyranny (the worst government of compulsion, coercion, and unwise cruelty).

Or we may distinguish monarchic, republican, and intermediary forms. One can use any of the several existing classifications of the forms of government treated by political scientists, though few if any of these are as accurate and fruitful as the Aristotelian and Platonic classifications, supplemented by those of the centralized and decentralized forms.

4. Stratified

All organized groups are stratified but have different kinds of stratification. These types will be studied further in Chapter 15, which gives the general theory of social stratification.

5. Having Short or Long Life-Span

As a rule powerful social groups are longlived groups, their longevity usually exceeding the life-span of one generation. Once in a while, however, social groups appear like a tornado; they suddenly come and as quickly pass, leav-

ing indelible traces of their short-lived existence. (See Chapter 33 for the data on the life-
span of various groups.)

6. Open, Closed, and Intermediary

Closed groups are those in which, to be a
member, one has to be born; in other words,
they are hereditary. Groups like race and sex
groups are closed on a biological basis; one
enters them only through the gate of birth and
leaves only through that of death. There is no
other way to enter or to quit their membership. Other closed groups are hereditary by
virtue of legal and social norms, like the groups
of the medieval estates, of slaves and serfs, of
royalty, and of caste. One inherits the status of
a noble, slave, or Brahmin through social
norms and not because one has distinct biological properties like those of male or female, of
this or that race. Socially closed (hereditary)
groups have a somewhat larger margin for an
infiltration of outsiders and a change of membership than purely biological groups. Besides
the gates of birth and death they usually have
other channels for the circulation of their members from group to group. These channels are
few and narrow, accessible to only a few individuals, but nevertheless they can be opened.

At the opposite pole are the open groups,
neither biologically nor socially hereditary. No
legal norms prohibit the individual from entering or leaving their membership. Many voluntary associations and societies belong to this
type, especially those which impose some kind
of burden rather than a privilege upon their
members. Likewise some of the occupational
groups, political parties, religious groups, and
others have open membership. Finally, in
between these poles there is a multitude of
intermediary groups. Their gates for entrance
and exit are fairly wide but not too wide to
squeeze through without effort. They range
from the groups almost closed to those almost
open. Most of the organized groups actually
are intermediary. This open-closed feature is
fairly important as a subsidiary trait in all social
groups.

7. Solidary, Antagonistic, and Mixed

The types of solidary, antagonistic, and
mixed groups (familistic, compulsory and contractual) have already been discussed. All

powerful groups must have a minimum of solidarity. However, as we shall see, in the many
bonded groups we sometimes find an antagonistic element that is a cumulation of mutually
contradictory bonds.

8. Those Having Integrated, Unintegrated, and Contradictory Cultures

As we shall see further (Chapters 17 and
18) all powerful groups have a minimum of
cultural integration in their central system of
meanings, values, and norms. But once in a
while there are fairly influential groups that
exhibit a rather low degree of integration,
especially in the causal-meaningful integration
of all its components.

9. According to the Various Combinations of Their Components

As these latter types are entirely neglected
in sociology and social sciences a little longer
comment is in order. Since a group is made up
of three components (persons, meanings,
vehicles) its properties evidently are determined by the quality and quantity of
each component. Assuming that the quality
of the components is constant, we can distinguish quantitative groups: (a) with *few
human subjects* but with a large amount of
values or vehicles or both at their disposal;
(b) with *scarcity of meanings-values* but with
a large membership or a large mass of the
vehicles (material culture) or both; (c) with
a *scarcity of vehicles* but with a large membership or rich fund of meanings-values or
both. Assuming the *quantity* of the components
is constant, one can distinguish qualitative systems of interaction made up of *all three components* excellent and well harmonized with
one another; *one of the components poor, the
other two good; two components poor, one
good; all three components poor* in quality.
Depending upon which of the components is
excellent or poor, and how well they are integrated with one another, each of these qualitative classes can be subdivided into several subclasses. In spite of an abstract appearance of
these subdivisions a careful analysis of the
groups along this line is important.[35]

[35] In the natural sciences this is well understood.
In a sense it is the central point in chemistry and
physics. Chemistry is a system of formulas that

Groups with *few members but with adequate meanings and vehicles at their disposal* will always have a rich, scintillating culture, exerting an influence far greater than the size of the group. By virtue of its meanings-values, such a group will always be highly stimulating whether it is religious, scientific, artistic, legal-ethical, or technological, provided that all components of such a group are harmonious. In other words in its field it will be the *leader-group*; the leading university, the leading religious group, the leading artistic group, the leading legal, economic, or political group. In the political field such a group will compose a powerful aristocracy, whether of a conquering population or of a subjugated society. In the latter case it can retain its power and control in spite of the great majority of the conquered population, if this population is poor in its meanings-values and its vehicles.

If the interacting members are *few* and have *poor* meanings-values and vehicles at their disposal, such a group is destined to pass without leaving a trace in the annals of history; never a leader and always led by other groups; never a creator but a backward receiver of the crumbs from the table of the more creative groups; never conquering but always conquered. A backward primitive tribe, a small group of "unskilled" laborers; of serfs, of slaves, generally of the lowest class of a given population, are examples of such social groups.

If a small group has rich meanings-values at its disposal but a *scarcity of vehicles*, such a system characterizes the new creators and coming leaders, as a new religious sect like the early Christians, a new scientific or philosophic group, new technological inventors, new schools in fine arts or ethics, revolutionaries in the political or economic field. None of these may as yet be recognized, nor given a vast body of vehicles for dissemination of their new values, but as a rule such leaders are destined to have recognition and eventually a larger number of followers. Tertullian's statement of the early Christian leaders: *hesterni sumus et*

vestra omnia implevimus ("We are only the men of yesterday, but we are already flooding everything of yours") is true of all such coming groups of leaders.

If a small group has a very poor fund of meanings but a *rich and vast assortment of vehicles*, such a group becomes either the primitive or "civilized" barbarians. When a primitive tribe suddenly finds itself flooded with automobiles, airplanes, telephones, telegraphs, radios, factories, and machinery, with rouge and lipsticks, cocktails and jazz-bands, it gives us one example of such a group. When a group of the *nouveau-riche* surrounds itself with all the paraphernalia of culture, with ostentatious mansions, "conspicuous consumption" (to use Veblen's expression), the best radios, clothing, and other forms of a luxurious material culture with its "rouge" and glitter, but remains a complete stranger to the meanings and values that created such a culture, we have another example. When a degenerated aristocracy holds the rich heritage of its ancestors in its external forms without the meanings and values that created and animated these forms, without the respective duties, services, and achievements, such a group is another example of "civilized barbarians."

However different the groups may be in many respects, they will all be characterized by the traits of barbarianism when placed amidst a vast universe of vehicles, having themselves a much poorer fund of the meanings-values. Such are the main systems of interaction consisting of small groups under the above four conditions.

If the *group of interacting individuals is vast* it will show the following types in accordance with the quality and quantity of the other components. (1) If it is rich in valuable meanings and vehicles well integrated with one another, it may be a leading and powerful empire, a great religious body, a dominant layer of the population; in brief, a powerful, leading, creative group. (2) If it is poor in meanings and vehicles, then it will give a vast

---

indicates of which chemical elements and in what proportion any chemical molecule is made (H_2O), and of which elements and molecules and in which proportion any material body is composed. The same is true of other natural sciences. In sociology there is scarcely any adequate and systematic

theory of the components of sociocultural phenomena and practically no theory at all as to the relative quantity and quality of each component in the sociocultural system. We have wasted an enormous amount of time and energy in studying a series of perfectly vacuous problems and overlooked many cardinal issues such as this.

body of "backward," traditional people, a low caste or class (of unskilled labor), dominated by and subordinated to other groups or classes. (3) If such a large group has a good fund of meanings but a very undeveloped system of the vehicles, then it is destined, as a rule, to acquire the vehicles, power, and prestige. Such a group is always a powerful potential leader, though it may not as yet be realized. (4) Finally, if such a vast group has a quantity of vehicles created by predecessors or other groups, but is a stranger to the values these vehicles objectify, we see again the "glittering barbarians"—primitive, sophisticated, or degenerated. Examples occur in the Greeks, Romans, Arabs, or Egyptians during periods of decay when they lived amidst the magnificent material culture of Athens, Rome, the Arabian or Egyptian empire, but were incapable of assimilating the rich universe of meanings objectified by these temples, palaces, museums, or manuscripts, and were still less capable of continuing the creative work of their predecessors. Other examples appear in the vast masses of "primitive peoples" recently invaded by the "civilization" of technological machines, factories, and business enterprises of the western nations, yet remaining strangers to the meanings and values of western culture. A vast nation with a gigantic technology, prosperous and seemingly powerful, but whose network of radio, telephone, telegraph, numerous and voluminous papers, magazines, books, movies, schools, church-pulpits, and public halls are used for exchange and dissemination of platitudes, vacuous and flat ideas of crooning and jazz of the most superfluous and superficial futilities, is another variation of this system of interaction with a fat and sumptuous mechanism of vehicles objectifying and socializing thin, poor, thoughtless meanings. If and when such a constellation appears, it presages the eventual decline of such a nation. Such are the main types of groups according to the combinations of their components.

These subclasses of unibonded and multibonded groups represent the main varieties. As we shall see they will be diagnostically useful in giving the precise formula for each of the powerful groups.

V. Interrelations of Groups

Like the members in a system of interaction the groups in their interrelationships may be either (1) solidary, or (2) antagonistic, or (3) neutral (mixed) or (4) unrelated causally and meaningfully. Two states or religious organizations may be heartily cooperating with one another; they may be in a state of war with one another; they may hold a state of mutual neutrality or a mixed combination of partly conflicting, partly solidary relationships; or they may not be connected at all.

1. The solidary groups yield two varieties of relationships: (a) *first, a subsystem within a larger system.* A precinct in a city is an administrative subgroup in the larger group of the city; the city itself is a subgroup in the larger group of the state, and the state is a subgroup in a still larger group of the United States. (b) A *second* form of solidary intergroup relationship is *co-ordination of two or more groups into a vaster federated unity.* Here none of the groups is a subsystem in the others; each is autonomous and remains so without domination or subordination. Assuming their relationship is solidary, the Federal Council of the Church is an example of this. None of the denominations of the Federal Council of the Churches of Christ is dominant or subordinated to another. Federation of states, labor unions, chambers of commerce, political parties (especially in the time of national emergency), of the church and the state, of United Nations, are further examples of the coordinated interrelationship of groups.

Likewise the antagonism may be (a) either between subsystems within a larger system or a subsystem and its system; (b) between two or more autonomous and mutually independent groups. The same applies to the neutral and mixed relationships. Finally, the noninteracting groups are merely a nominal plurel of groups making no real causal-meaningful unity.

2. Like the intragroup differentiation and stratification of their members, the interacting

groups can also be differentiated from one another and also *stratified* into the superior and inferior, upper and lower, *dominating and subordinated*. This intergroup stratification is only mentioned here. Its main forms will be considered further in Chapter 15, devoted to a study of social stratification.

The above gives a fairly complete "taxonomy" of social groups, in their main characteristics: (1) organized-unorganized; (2) solidary-antagonistic; (3) powerful-unimportant; (4) unibonded-multibonded, with a large variety of supplementary and secondary characteristics; (5) types of intergroup relationships.

With this classification in hand, we can now plunge into an analysis of the group structure of the human population. Our first task here is to show concisely[36] the actual existence and characteristics of the main unibonded groups in their mutual relationships. Our second task is to give a systematic theory of the multibonded groups in their relationships—a theory largely non-existent in contemporary sociology. Our third task is to give a structural analysis of the most typical constellations and combinations of the unibonded and multibonded groups in the total population. The accomplishment of these tasks furnishes us with an adeqate knowledge of the essentials of social differentiation of humanity into groups, as well as of the total group structure of mankind.

VI. Summary Classification of Groups

I. *Unorganized and Semi-Organized Groups*
   1. Externally united, "as if" organized
   2. Public
   3. Crowd, mob
   4. Semi-nominal plurel
   5. Purely nominal plurel

II. *Important Organized Groups*
   A. *Unibonded groups*
      1. Biosocial groupings:
         a. Race,
         b. Sex, and
         c. Age groups.
      2. Sociocultural groupings:
         a. Kinship,
         b. Territorial,
         c. Language,
         d. State,
         e. Occupational,
         f. Economic,
         g. Religious,
         h. Political,
         i. Ideological, and educational groups
         j. Nominal groups of the elite
   B. *Multibonded groups*
      1. The family
      2. Clans

   3. Tribes
   4. Nations
   5. Castes
   6. Feudal estates
   7. Classes

   C. *Structural Varieties*
      1. Large or small in size
      2. Well-organized or semi-organized
      3. Centralized or decentralized
      4. With monarchical, aristocratic, oligarchic, democratic, republican, tyrannical, and other forms of government
      5. Stratified in various ways
      6. Long and short-lived
      7. Solidary, antagonistic, mixed
      8. Integrated, unintegrated, mixed culture
      9. Rich and poor in the components of meanings and vehicles; in the quality of members
      10. With mutual intergroup relationships:
         a. Solidary (as subgroup to group, or as coordinated groups)
         b. Antagonistic
         c. Neutral
         d. Unrelated
         e. Stratified

[36] A detailed study of these is subject-matter for special sociologies and special social sciences in each of these groups. The state and political groups are the subject-matter of political science and of political sociology; the economic and occupational groups are specifically studied by economics and economic occupational sociology; religious groups are investigated in detail by the sociology of religion, and so on. General sociology touches them only so far as to give the total and general picture of the differentiation of mankind into these important groups, to note the specific role and traits of each of these groups in their mutual relationships in the sociocultural universe. All the unique characteristics of each of these groups it leaves to the respective social sciences and special sociologies.

PART FOUR

Social Differentiation and Stratification

Chapter 10. Differentiation of Human Population into Biosocial Groups

I. Preliminaries

1. Biosocial Bases of Race, Age, and Sex Groups

We begin our study of the differentiation of human population with biosocial groups. Though the values of these groups may appear as purely biological traits (race, sex, age), in real groups of this kind they are sociocultural. What traits in a given population are regarded as racial, who belongs to what race, and which race is "superior" or "inferior," these attitudes are always conditioned by the sociocultural notions of such people. The Nazi criteria of the Aryan, Nordic, or "Master Race" is a typical example. All German Nazis and their allies were regarded as Aryan Nordics, whether or not they had the exact biological traits. All anti-Nazis were regarded as non-Aryan, non-Nordic and inferior, though actually the Nordic traits were more prevalent in Norway, Denmark, Scotland, and northern Russia than among the Nazis of the German population. This clearly shows that the Nazi's "Nordic master race" as a real group was based less upon biological similarity than upon cultural characteristics. This mixture of biological and sociocultural traits is typical of real biosocial groups.

Among peoples past and present a similarity in language, religion, the state citizenship, political party, occupation, or social status has often been mistaken for racial identity, though zoologically they belonged to different types. And vice versa, persons dissimilar in one of these traits were often regarded as racially different though zoologically they belonged to the same racial type. Finally, in the populations that attached no particular value to the zoological characteristics, all persons were regarded as racially similar and equal. This means that so-called racial groups, as real social groups, have regularly been not purely zoological types, but biosocial groups, based upon sociocultural traits as much as upon purely biological characteristics.

The same can be said of age groups. The age composition of any large population is continuous from infancy to advanced senility. The purely biological ages of the persons in a given population do not leave any gaps separating one age group from the others. If therefore we find a given population divided into three or five or seven different age groups—and not nominal—with different rights and duties, status and roles, such differentiation into age groups does not directly result from biological factors. These groups are cut out by sociocultural conditions that determine the age-boundaries for each group; their status, rights, and duties; and whether the old or the young are privileged and dominant. This is supported by the fact that there is wide variation in the number, age-boundaries and sociocultural position of age groups in different populations and periods. In some populations, for instance, old age is privileged and youth is disfranchised, sometimes even to having no rights at all. In other populations the younger age groups are dominant; in still others they all have legally equal status. This means that the respective age groups as real social groups are determined not so much by the biological properties of the persons of various ages as by the sociocultural conditions.

More fixed biologically is the differentiation into the sex groups. The two sexes are so clearly separated biologically that they hardly leave any margin for variation. But the extent to which sex groups differ from one another in their status, role, rights, duties, functions, and whether one sex is placed in an inferior position—this is determined by sociocultural conditions rather than biological ones. This condition explains the variety in relations between the sexes in various populations, from that of equal status to the superiority and domination of one by the other. When we deal with races, age groups and sex groups as nominal or statistical plurels we deal with them as biological types only. When we study them as real social groups they are always biosocial unities.

2. Nominal and "As if Organized"

If individuals belonging to the same race, age, or sex do not interact with one another they remain nominal plurels and do not make real groups. A large majority of the individuals of the same race-age-sex have often been such nominal plurels. On the other hand, in many populations a portion of the persons belonging to the same race or sex or age[1] has established a real organized group. Also a large portion of persons of the same race, sex, or age has often acted "as if organized." In a given population when the privileges of one part of its population and the disfranchisements of the

other are established upon either racial or sex or age characteristics, then these classes feel and act like real organized groups, though the majority of their members may not be in direct interaction or have the agencies of organized groups. For instance the discriminatory measures introduced and maintained against the Negroes in the United States externally united them without any prior agreement into one group, to feel and act in a similar way, to realize the discrimination against them, and eventually to become "solidary" for the Negroes and antagonistic against the privileged whites, in spite of a lack of any close interaction or specific organization among the majority of the Negroes. Thus they begin to act as if they were organized.

The same is true of the sex and age groups under similar conditions. When a discriminatory status is imposed upon all women, or all the persons of a certain age, they react by similar feelings, emotions, ideas, and actions, and the total result of their activity assumes the *appearance of a concerted, pre-arranged action* of an organized group, though in fact is is neither pre-arranged nor organized in advance. Grant privileges to a part of a population and disfranchisements to another part, and these measures will create something very close to real groups of the privileged and of the disfranchised, even if their members are unaware of their unification and do not strive purposefully to organize. The members of the privileged and disfranchised groups would, in these conditions, be objectively unified in an interdependent system, forced to think and to act similarly, to be pitted against the same enemy; in brief, to act and to function *as though they were unified into a real group* by organized interaction.

This adds immensely to the power of the organized groups. As the strictly organized race-sex-age groups are ordinarily quite small, they would alone be too weak to exert much pressure on other groups and historical processes. If the racial, age, and sex groups have exerted such an influence, the secret is the addition of the potentially enormous weight of

[1] For our purposes one can take any zoological classification of race. See various classifications in R. B. Dixon, *The Racial History of Man* (New York, 1923), Ch. 1; A. L. Kroeber, *Anthropology* (New York, 1923), Ch. 3; Sorokin, *Theories*, Ch. 5; A. Haddon, *The Races of Man* (New York, 1925); A. Keith, *Man* (New York, 1913); M. F. Ashley Montagu, *Man's Most Dangerous Myth* (New York, 1942).

the "as if organized" groups. The organized and "as if organized" portions of race, sex, and age groups, acting spontaneously together, possess often a considerable power. We shall meet this again in other sociocultural groups like social class and nationality.

3. Attitudes of "For" and "Against"

As to the meanings-values that give the basis for the existence of race-age-sex groups, their main characteristic is that they tend to extol the positive value of the group. They defend either its superiority over, or its equal goodness with the other groups, and unify the members for their own and against other racial or age or sex groups that oppose either its equality or superiority. This unification against all the opponents or adverse conditions and for one's own group with its values is the main content of the norms of any such groups. Otherwise, in their concrete forms these can be very different, depending upon the sociocultural conditions.

The unifying ideology may be the Biblical theory of the "chosen people and of the bastards" (Deuteronomy, 23:2), the "twice born castes" of the *Sacred Books* of India (*Laws of Manu*, Chapters 1-4; *Gautama*, Chapter 10; *Narada*, Chapter 12); the Homeric "line of men that are the fosterlings of Zeus" quite superior to the "churl that cannot beget such sons" (*Odyssey*, IV, 60; *Iliad*, XIV, 126); the Aryan race of A. Gobineau; or the superior race of many eugenists and geneticists.[2] The content of the meanings of such groups varies in its concrete form; the perennial "for" and "against" remain, however, the constant traits of such ideologies. The same is true of similar ideologies of age and sex groups. The "ideology" of such justifies the equality or inequality, superiority or inferiority, domination-subordination of the sexes or of the age groups now on a religious basis, now on a philosophical, now on a "scientific," or again for eclectic, utilitarian, and other reasons. All the immense variety of such ideologies builds an attitude of "for" one's own group and "against" all the opposing groups.

II. Differentiation into Racial Groups and Plurels[3]

We have seen that most of the racial groups are biosocial in nature. The rank and file of the population do not consist of the professional physical anthropologists and know little of the zoological classification of the racial types, cephalic indexes, anatomical details of the structure of hair or of pigmentation or of chemical composition of various types of blood, or of other bases of biological classification of races. Only the most "visible" racial traits which force themselves spontaneously upon one's attention and establish, without anthropological instruments and research, the racial resemblance or difference between ourselves and others, only these traits have been recognized by the average man as significant. Such visible racial traits together with the sociocultural characteristics superimposed upon

them have been responsible for the prevalent groupings of persons into "races."[4]

Whether it is good or bad, there is no doubt that in any population with "racial discrimination" organized and as if organized racial groups are found with attraction and solidarity of the members; and with indifference or antagonism to the "visibly" different racial groups. Differentiation of the population into such groups manifests itself in hundreds of forms beginning with different legal status, functions, and roles of various racial groups with their respective psychology and attitudes conscious of their difference, and ending with tension and conflicts between these, with interracial domination-subordination, exploitation,

[2] For a historical and systematic survey of such ideologies of racial superiority and inferiority see my *Theories*, Ch. 5.

[3] Cf. C. C. North, *Social Differentiation* (Chapel Hill, 1926).

[4] As noted, it is outside the scope of general sociology to discuss the problem of race in its various aspects. This is the task of a special biology and sociology of races. See the main problems of such a special sociology of race, their theories, criticism, and literature in my *Theories*, Ch. 5. Here I touch race problems only in the aspect of racial groups.

discrimination, and disfranchisement, up to open race-riots and wars. These interracial tensions and struggles have in many populations continued incessantly, now in silent, now in noisy and bloody forms. And they still exist in many populations, in spite of all the preaching, teaching, and other efforts against such "race-discriminations." Here are a few concrete details of this existence of racial groups and of their tensions and conflicts.

First of all, not only in the populations with racial discrimination but even among those professing equality of races, daily observation and the records of history show that a large portion of the individuals of the same socioracial plurel are more easily attracted to each other than to the members of the visibly different racial types. In regard to them they remain either "neutral" or antagonistic. "Men of the same race, upon approaching one another, do not experience the same feeling of strangeness and opposition as the black man meeting a white, or as a hairy Ainu coming in contact with a hairless Chinese."[5] Color and color contrast are almost always a hindrance to social feeling and a bar to intermarriage. In ancient India color seems to have been one of the foundations of caste. The shock which a human being experiences on beholding a face of an unfamiliar hue is accentuated as soon as color-contrast becomes indelibly associated with mental, moral, and social differences. Each race, moreover, builds its ideal of personal beauty on the basis of its distinctive traits, and the individuals of another race are apt to strike it as ugly and repulsive.

In every race the ideal of beauty is represented by the types which exhibit more or less exactly the most recurring physical features. The artificial means employed by various peoples to enhance their beauty testify to the same: "dark races blacken their skin, flat-nosed flatten their noses, white women use face powder."[6] Among the yellow races of the Malay Archipelago yellow color is spoken of as golden.

E. A. Ross enumerates various forms of in-sulting epithets which point out the repulsion[7] aroused by strange features. Forms of abuse, as "niggers, greasers, round-heads, fuzzy-wuzzies, red-necks, red-haired devils, brown monkeys, redskins," etc., indicate features "which strike the eyes" as alien.

The surface signs of dissimilarity naturally strike the senses more forcibly, and among these the skin is perhaps the bodily characteristic which most provokes prejudice. Every race is habituated to its own skin, and a different hue excites feelings of distrust, fear, and something akin to rage.[8]

Many facts prove the existence of such disgust and antipathy. The Chinese call the white people "foreign devils." According to Livingston's testimony a white man generated a feeling of revulsion in the African aborigines. The children of the black natives at the approach of the white man of Livingston's expedition ran in horror and the women hid themselves. An Australian woman having a child from a white man, smoked and blackened it in order to give it the appearance of a native. Among some primitive peoples children of mixed parentage are looked upon as "monsters." Darwin says that the children born from the association of the first white settlers of Australia with the native women were massacred by the thoroughbred black natives. Among the Indians of California the native woman who married or committed adultery with a white man was condemned to die, and her children were killed "without remorse."[9]

The closest approach to a satisfactory classification of races as a basis of antipathy is that of grouping men according to color. The antipathies between these general groups and between their subdivision will be found to be essentially fundamental.[10]

It is no wonder that racial differences were very often picked up as the suitable bases for erecting many sociocultural privileges and disfranchisements. The role attributed to race by L. Gumplowicz was exaggerated, but racial differences were undoubtedly instrumental in

---

[5] P. Lavrov, *Essay on Philosophy of History* (Russian, Geneva, 1894), p. 601.

[6] U. G. Weatherly, "Race and Marriage," *AJS*, Vol. XV, p. 10.

[7] E. A. Rose, *Foundations*, quoted, p. 264.

[8] W. I. Thomas, "The Significance of the Orient for the Occident," *AJS*, Vol. XIII, pp. 730-731.

[9] Weatherly, *Ibid*, p. 434.

[10] A. Stone, "Race Friction Between Blacks and Whites in the U.S.," *AJS*, Vol. XIII, p. 679.

the origin of many social strata of the superior and inferior groups as in that of caste-systems. *Varna*—the Sanscrit name for caste—meant also color. The principle upon which the system of caste rests is the sense of distinction of race indicated by difference of color. "The race sentiment . . . supplied the motive principle of caste . . . and . . . tended to preserve in comparative purity the types which it favors—hence the absolute prohibition of intermarriage between the castes as the essential and most prominent characteristic of caste."[11]

When such feelings and attitudes are spread among the given population—and unfortunately they are still spread very widely—they flare up into open antagonistic interaction as soon as two or more different racial groups come in close contact with one another and have to live side by side. The antagonism manifests itself in the form of discrimination against the different race, subjugation and subordination, disfranchisement and exploitation, even extermination of the weaker racial aggregate by open fights, riots, and wars. Such antagonisms have existed not only in so-called autocratic or barbaric countries but in no lesser degree in so-called democratic countries professing the principle of equality, Christianity, and freedom, and denying racial or religious discrimination.

"When two races come together, the fate of the weaker is summed up as extermination, subordination, or amalgamation."[12] This rule has exceptions, for in many populations different racial groups live quite peacefully side by side. However the prevalent rule has been discrimination, subordination, extermination, or amalgamation of the weaker group. It is especially striking to find this rule in democratic countries such as the United States, Australia, South Africa, New Zealand, and the like. Racial prejudice, discrimination, antagonism in

organized and "as if organized" groups appear in hundreds of symptoms: formerly in the slavery of the Negroes, later in legal disfranchisements, prohibition of interracial marriages, denial of civil and political rights, segregation in restaurants, theaters, schools, churches, army, even in prison cells; and the exclusion of the Negroes from a number of social and occupational activities. These silent tensions and open race riots make the race groupings and interracial antagonism in many countries, especially in the Anglo-American ones, a serious conflict situation.[13]

The numerous attempts of the Federal Supreme Court to mitigate the antagonism have been only partially successful. *Quid leges sine moribus!* The emancipation of the Negro has weakened some of these antagonisms but has also intensified others.

Similar situations between the "red Indians" and the whites in the United States, the "yellow Orientals" and the whites, and in a smaller degree between the Jews and the Gentiles, have existed. Assimilation and amalgamation of these racial groups have not been as successful as might be expected in a country with an extraordinary assimilating and amalgamating power. Similar tensions occur between the white and the black racial groups in Australia, New Zealand, and South Africa, all very democratic countries.[14] Antagonism exists also between the white and black Christians in Africa. "There is an absolute and almost bitter refusal on the part of white Christians to mingle in any kind of fellowship with black Christians," writes Calloway.[15]

Racial prejudice and interracial antagonism exist not only in the rich or privileged classes but also in the farmer-labor and professional groups. In all these democratic countries the Negroes are excluded from white trade unions, and labor classes stimulate the exclusion of

---

[11] Cf. Sir Herbert H. Risley, *General Report on the Census of India* (1901) and the *People of India* (1915).

[12] F. A. McKenzie, "The Assimilation of the American Indian," *AJS*, Vol. XIX, p. 762.

[13] See the facts in G. T. Stephenson, *Race Distinctions in American Law* (New York, 1918), pp. 16 ff; A. Jenks, "The Legal Status of Negro-White Amalgamation in the U.S.A.," *AJS*, Vol. XXI (1916), pp. 668 ff; C. S. Johnson, *The Negro in American Civilization* (New York, 1930); R.

Park, "Racial Assimilation," *AJS*, Vol. XX, pp. 610 ff; J. Dollard, *Caste and Class in a Southern Town* (New York, 1937); P. E. Baker, *Negro-White Adjustments* (New York, 1934); G. Myrdal, *An American Dilemma* (New York, 1944).

[14] See S. G. Millin, *The South African* (New York, 1927); E. B. Reuter, *Race and Culture Contact* (New York, 1934); J. Lips, *The Savage Hits Back* (New Haven, 1937).

[15] Callaway, "Color Antipathies," *The East and the West* (1910) No. 59-61.

the Oriental and African workers as immigrants.

It may be true that the basis of this antagonism is economic. But why should the economic interests of the white American worker and those of the Chinese coolie be more antagonistic than the interests of the American and other whites? It is possible that restrictions of Negro rights might have economic causes, yet it is inconceivable that the conscious or unconscious economic policy of the American bourgeoisie as some think, is behind "orientophoby" and "mongolophoby," for what economic interests move the capitalists to discriminate between workers upon racial lines? From the economic viewpoint there is no apparent difference as to whether one exploits a black, yellow, or white worker. Why, further, do the trade unions exclude all men of black and yellow races? Whatever explanations may be advanced, the racial grouping is there and has not been eliminated.[16]

The whole history of the expansion of the white man's civilization over hundreds of primitive and cultured racial groups on all continents is a further evidence of the existence of socioracial groups and their interracial antagonisms. The history of the white man's treatment of the aborigines racially different from him has been the most pitiless conquest, cruel subjugation, exploitation, and extermination of these aboriginal socioracial groups. One of the Russian investigators of this history, A. N. Engelhardt, entitled his book *Progress as Evolution of Cruelty*. Though much cruelty has been shown also in the interrelationships of the white populations, it hardly compares with the amount displayed by the "civilizing, Christian peoples" in regard to the aboriginal races of all the continents. A large part of them has in fact been exterminated.[17]

And this antagonism has been perennial. It emerges with the beginning of human history and, varying in form, continues to exist as recent subjugation and extermination of the Indonesians and other colonial groups show. It is a common practice to build on a racial

trait a huge super-structure of privileges for one racial group and disfranchisements for another. Where races are distinguished by certain external marks these furnish a permanent physical substratum upon which and around which the irritations and animosities incidental to all human intercourse, tend to accumulate and to gain strength and volume.[18]

These antipathies and antagonisms are not instinctive, as many claim. The existence of populations with little or no interracial antagonism and discrimination; the existence of many individuals who do not have it at all; the elimination and weakening of such antagonisms through wise policies—these facts are convincing evidence against the instinctive nature of these hostilities. They are acquired from the culture and society charged with such attitudes. These attitudes are not local or isolated. They have spread widely, appeared, and reappeared in many populations, and have existed almost continuously throughout human history.

The main racial types like the Caucasian or the Mongoloid are plurels consisting of several hundred millions of individuals. Such racial plurels if they were organized would be among the most powerful social groups. The pressure of such groups would be decisive in many ways. The actual situation, however, has been quite different. *Only a small fraction of such large racial plurels has ever been organized into solidary racial groups. The larger portion has been either in the form of an "as if organized" group or in the state of a mere nominal plurel.* This explains why the huge racial plurels have exerted much more modest effects than their potential power. In spite of this, the pressure of various racial groups upon the behavior of individuals, upon other social groups and upon the course of human history has been very considerable, working incessantly and indefatigably. This pressure manifests itself in the following main ways.

So far as inherited racial characteristics are related to the behavioral and mental traits of individuals, the racial group is one of the forces that shapes the total personality of

---

[16] See several papers in a special volume of the *Annals of American Academy of Political and Social Science*, Vol. XXXIV; also C. S. Johnson, *The Negro in American Civilization*, quoted.

[17] See A. N. Engelhardt, *Progress as the Evolu-*

tion of Cruelty (Russian, St. Petersburg, 1884); Triggs, "The Decay of Aboriginal Races," *Open Court*, (1912).

[18] R. Park, *op. cit.*, p. 611.

every individual from within. Persons who are different in anatomical and physiological characteristics cannot help being also different in behavioral and mental traits. The difference should not be exaggerated as some partisans of heredity and race exaggerate it; neither does it mean a superiority or inferiority of different races.[19] Nevertheless, differences exist in racial hereditary traits which determine to a tangible degree different constitutional types of human beings with their different behavioral and mental properties.[20] When this purely biological heredity is joined by many sociocultural traits raised upon it, the individual born and reared in such a biosocial racial group is shaped by it in his anatomical, physiological, behavioral, and mental characteristics. In this sense the racial factor is one of the omnipresent and perennial molders of every individual, a constant force in sociocultural life and history.

The racial group as biosocial is also responsible for the attitudes of sympathy toward one's own kind and indifference or antagonism toward those who are different. This manifestation of its power is quite considerable and, as we have seen, perennial in the sociocultural universe.

The power of racial groups is further evident in the successful pressure upon other groups and in the modification of these groups as demanded by this or that racial group. *Its influence upon the family is shown in many ways, particularly in the prohibition of interracial marriage.* Such prohibitions are found in some of the pre-literate tribes, in the marriage laws of the caste and feudal estates, as well as in penalized restrictions of the most democratic countries of our times. In this and other ways the racial groups have influenced the family quite tangibly. Through the family and marriage the race groups have conditioned the process of social selection favoring procreation of certain racial types and disfavoring others, accentuating the racial traits in one population and effacing them in

others, facilitating the survival of one racial type and the mortality of another. The biosocial consequences of prohibition or permission of interracial marriage have been many and important.

The racial groups have effected likewise *the state groups*. (1) Racial groups with racial consciousness and discrimination tend to organize themselves into the state, and in many cases they have succeeded in controlling its policies. (2) The states created by different racial groups have often become antagonistic toward one another. Many wars and other interstate conflicts have been caused, to quite an extent, by the workings of the racial groups organized into states. (3) Within a state made up of different racial groups, the race differences have often served as the pretext for a stratification of the population into the upper or privileged classes and the enslaved or disfranchised lower classes, the stratification following the line of the so-called "superior" and "inferior" racial groups.

The *racial groups have also influenced the economic, the occupational, and other groups*. In many populations, from the caste societies of India to the modern democratic countries, the occupational and economic differentiation and stratification follow the lines of racial differences. Many privileged occupations are closed to the "inferior" races and reserved to the "superior" racial groups while the burdensome occupations are imposed upon the "lower and inferior" racial groups. Likewise the upper, wealthy classes are filled mainly or exclusively by the members of one race while the poorer classes are recruited mainly from the members of a subjugated race.[21] These tangible correlations between the racial and economic-occupational groups have existed in many countries and at all times.

There are just as significant influences of racial groups upon the *religious, political, and ideological* (scientific, philosophical, aesthetic, ethical) groups. In these and other ways the racial groups and plurels have influenced individuals and groups in the course of human

---

[19] Thus neither the alleged superior genius of the Nordic race, nor the specific mental traits ascribed to the dolichocephals, nor a host of "laws" of Ammon-Lapouge and of other geneticists and eugenists are valid. Note my *Theories*, Ch. 5. See there the data and literature.

[20] On this see my *Theories*, Ch. 5.

[21] See the facts and literature in my *Mobility*, Chps. 10-12; A. Niceforo, *Les classes pauvres* (Paris, 1905); E. B. Reuter, *Race Mixture* (New York, 1931).

history. For this reason they have to be counted among the most powerful social groups. They make, as we shall see, one of the indispensable lines in the system of sociocultural co-ordinates, determining the position of every individual and group.

Finally, the *racial group, so far as it is a biological group, is a closed system.* One enters it only through the gate of birth and leaves it only through the gate of death. There is no other avenue of escape from it and no other way to join it. Every individual has to stay in the racial group from the moment of his birth to his death. This closed character of the racial groups is one of the reasons for the slow change and limited fluctuation in the

racial composition of the human population. These changes can be effected only through (1) differential fertility of various race groups; (2) through their differential mortality, including extermination; and (3) through racial amalgamation. These processes go on incessantly changing the racial structure of a given population and of mankind. Once in a while they become extraordinary when a large portion of a racial group is exterminated or the differential fertility and mortality of various races change. Nevertheless, compared with sudden and enormous changes in the size and fluctuation of other sociocultural groups, the change in the racial composition of a population remains slow and gradual.

III. Differentiation into Sex Groups and Plurels

With little variation most of what has been said of the race groups can be said of the sex groups and plurels. Like the race groups the sex population has existed partly as nominal plurels and as if organized groups, and partly united into real biosocial groups. Like race differences the biological sex differentials[22] were seized upon as bases for notably different superstructures of rights, duties, functions, roles, and status. In this way, in most populations, real and "as if" sex groups have been established. In some populations the sex groups and plurels stand on a more or less equal basis. In others, probably in the majority of the aggregates of the population, the sexes are differentiated on the basis of the inequality, subjugation, exploitation, disfranchisement, and discrimination. The weaker sex groups and plurels (usually women) are dominated by the stronger sex groups and plurels (ordinarily men). Whether the differentiation of the sex groups is done along the pattern of equality

or inequality, in both cases the sex groups exist and function as real unities.

When the female sex groups are disfranchised and the male groups are privileged, implicit or explicit antagonism follows. Sometimes it assumes the form of a sharp political struggle by women in suffragist and other movements for their rights, dignity, status, and equality. When sex groups exist on the basis of equality, the antagonism between them may be slight. Nevertheless the functions of sex groups remain tangibly different and they continue to exist as different unities.

Throughout human history we find sex groups differentiated by equality and inequality. Among some 298 preliterate peoples studied by Hobhouse, Wheeler, and Ginsberg, the status of women is good in 10 to 19 per cent of these populations; it is indifferent in 2 to 8 per cent, and bad (subordinated and subjugated) in 73 to 87 per cent of these peoples.[23] According to L. W. Simmons' study of preliterate groups the property rights of

---

[22] See A. Scheinfeld, *Women and Men* (New York, 1944). Some of the differences noted by the author are very questionable.

[23] See L. Hobhouse, G. Wheeler, and M. Ginsberg, *The Material Culture and Social Institutions of the Simpler Peoples* (London, 1915), tables. On the status of women among preliterate populations see R. Briffault, *The Mothers* (New York, 1926-27), 3 Vols.; H. Schurtz, *Alterklassen and Männerbunde* (Berlin, 1902); R. Thurnwald, *Die*

Menschliche Gesellschaft (Berlin, 1932), Vol. II, pp. 29 ff; M. K. Opler, "Woman's Social Status and the Forms of Marriage," *AJS*, Vol. XLIX (1943), pp. 125-146. A one-sided survey of the subjugated position of women is given by Herbert Spencer in his *Principles of Sociology* (London, 1885), Vol. I, pp. 713-732; R. H. Lowie, *Primitive Society* (New York, 1920); W. N. R. Rivers, *Social Organization* (London, 1924).

aged women are much greater among the collectors, hunters, and fishers than among pastoral and agricultural peoples, where the property rights of the aged men are much greater. Likewise the property rights of aged women are better protected in populations with matrilocal residence, matrilineal descent, inheritance, and succession than in populations with the patriarchal type of the family. The same is true of the prestige, political and civil rights, and other privileges.[24]

Likewise among the "historical peoples" both types of differentiation into sex groups and plurels have existed. The early Greek and Roman populations had sex groups and plurels marked by disfranchisements of women and privileges of men. The head of the agnatic family, *paterfamilias*, or husband, had unlimited power and authority (*patria potestas* and *manus mariti*) even to the right of life and death (*jus vitae ac necis*). Women were persons not in their own right but only in the right of the *paterfamilias* or husband (*personae alieni juris*). Their political and most of their civil rights were non-existent, for the women were entirely subordinated to the men. The distinct existence of sex groups in such a population is perfectly clear. Antagonism between them is also present and eventually it becomes explicit, leading to open struggle between the sex groups and plurels which ordinarily results in the emancipation and equalization of women's groups and plurels. So it happened in Greece, Rome, and in many other societies.

Less conspicuous at first glance is the existence and functioning of sex groups in populations where equality is present. None the less it manifests itself in (1) existence of unisexual groups: men's and women's clubs, men's and women's monasteries, schools, clubs, associations or societies, men's and women's journals, magazines, books, and papers. For instance, out of 357 associations in Newburyport (Massachusetts), 143 were male, 110 female,

and 104 mixed membership.[25] Tens of thousands of such unisexual groups exist and function in the United States and in other populations with a rough equality of sexes. (2) It appears in the activities, occupations, and positions inaccessible to the other sex. Even in the most democratic countries such positions as the President of the United States, the Prime Minister, the Commander-in-Chief of the army, the judge of the Supreme Court, the bishop, metropolitan, pope, and so on are closed to women. Many other positions, occupations, and activities are beyond the reach of women. (3) We find it even in the occupations, activities, and positions formally open to both sexes, where distribution of men and women is very different. For instance, in the United States in 1920 in mining occupation there were 99.7 males and only 0.3 females; in manufacturing the percentages were respectively 84.9 and 15.1; in transportation, 93.0 and 7.0; in public service, 97.2 and 2.8; in domestic service, 35.8 and 64.2.[26] The main occupation of adult women has been and still is housewife.[27]

(4) There is hardly any population in which the legal rights and duties of women and men have really been identical or equal. Without exception the political and civil rights of the sexes have always differed in a number of ways. Some of these rights and duties are still reserved only for men or women. In others there is often a great difference in application to the different sexes. For instance, until recently in the French civil code a man was guilty of adultery only if his mistress lived under the same roof with his wife; but a woman was guilty no matter where the adultery was performed. From this standpoint one can find in the totality of the civil, criminal, constitutional, administrative, and commercial laws and mores of democratic populations more than enough differences in the legal and factual status of the sex groups and plurels. (5) The

---

[24] See L. W. Simmons, *The Role of the Aged in Primitive Societies* (New Haven, 1945), pp. 47-50, 79-81, *passim*.

[25] W. L. Warner and P. S. Lunt, *The Social Life of a Modern Community* (New Haven, 1941), p. 122.

[26] *Fourteenth Census*, Vol. XV (1920), *Population, Occupation*, p. 34.

[27] For occupational differences of the sexes throughout history see G. P. Murdock, "Comparative Data on Division of Labor by Sex," *SF* (May 1937); Maroi, "Il lavoro della donna nella sua evoluzione," *Rivista Italiana di Sociologia* (1914), pp. 54-70; Lapie, *La femme dans la famille* (Paris, 1906); Schreiner, *Woman and Labor* (London, 1911).

differentiation manifests itself also in the conduct and activities prescribed for the sexes. In our society this difference comes clearly with the beginning of adolescence. In their dress, recreations, training, manners, responsibilities, even in their associations, boys and girls begin to separate and diverge. The masculine ideal of a manly athlete is not pursued by the girls, just as the pattern of feminine coyness, charm, glamor, and grace is not regarded as becoming to a boy. Drinking, rough fights, sexual indulgences are apportioned to the sexes on a basis of the familiar "double standard." This double standard is applied generally not only in regard to sexual activities but to a large part of the meanings, values, norms, and overt activities of adult men and women. What is becoming to a man is regarded as unbecoming to a woman, and vice versa.

To summarize, there is not the slightest doubt that most democratic populations are separated into many sex groups and plurels with different systems of meanings-values-norms, overt actions, and vehicles, These sex groups in equalitarian societies may live and act without serious conflict; but now and then they do antagonize each other. The ensuing struggle goes on mostly in the form of a decentralized, partisan warfare, without large armies led by general staffs or spectacular battles. It is fought silently in small detachments, daily clashes within the family, school, club, daily newspapers, the occupational union, political party, the courts, and Congress.[28] Once in a while the struggle assumes the character of a broad social movement, like the movement in the last century for women's equality, emancipation, and freedom.

Unorganized at first, it gradually took an organized form, the small women's detachments combining into large armies attacking the citadels of men's privileges all along the front of social life. Parallel with this a change took place also in the technique of the struggle. The age old methods of control of the male by the female—the intricate treatment of the husband by his wife, of a lover by his beloved, of a king by his mistress, or sons by their mothers—are supplemented by more open and effective means: the press and propaganda, boycott and bombs, demonstrations and riots, strikes and organization for the conquest of positions of power. With the growth of woman's organizations, they became more and more influential, leaders of political parties, religious, professional or economic associations vying for their favor. True as the assertion that the history of mankind is a history of class struggle may be, it is no less true that it is a history of the alliance and struggle between sex groups.

The sex co-ordinate is one of the most important to define a person's biosocial profile, mentality, and behavior. Sex is an inherent force working from "the inside," affecting us now unconsciously, now becoming conscious and stimulating an organized pursuit of the values-norms-meanings centered around sex. When men in "silent conspiracy" were introducing and strengthening their privileges throughout the ages, they were following the dictates of their sex, often unconsciously. When the weaker sex struggles to throw off "the tyranny of men" they are again governed by their sex group interests. In short, the conduct of both men and women cannot be well understood without taking into account the influence of their respective sex groups.

The sex collectivity is of the closed type. The passage from one to another is impossible. This explains the stability of the relative proportion of sex-plurels. But this stability does not hinder considerable fluctuations in the size of the organized and the "as if" organized sex groups in different populations at different periods.

---

[28] For instance, at the present moment, in the United States this clash of the sex groups has assumed a sharp form of "the battle for jobs between men and women, of the battle for personal ascendancy of husband or wife, and, perhaps, of the battle for a birth-rate" as, in an exaggerated form, W. Waller puts it. See his "The Coming War on Women" in the Magazine section of the *Boston Herald*, February 18, 1945.

IV. Differentiation into Age Groups and Plurels

Like race and sex, age is also bound up with anatomical, physiological, and behavioral and mental traits which draw persons of similar age together. Each age group has its own interests (meanings, values, norms), partly solidary, partly antagonistic to those of different age groups. Here again the biological differences serve as the fixed bases for sociocultural differences in rights, duties, functions, status, and roles. As a result of these biosocial differentials, real age groups and "as if organized" age collectivities have emerged in practically all populations past and present. The differentiation of the population into real and "as if" age groups is one of the oldest and most universal. It is met in all preliterate societies and it continues to exist in some form in all contemporary societies, as partly legal and partly factual.

In many preliterate and complex societies the division into the age collectivities is legal and real, with a definite set of rights, duties, roles, status, functions attached to each age group, with public and formal rites and ceremonies (*rite de passage*) marking the passage of an individual from one age group to another; with the hierarchy of age groups in their "rank of precedence," prestige, influence, and so on. The number of such age groups is different for different societies, beginning with a few (three or four), and ending with ten and even twenty-three (among the South Andaman Islanders, where some of the age groups are nominal plurels rather than real

groups). The most common division seems to be three or four—the infant, the adolescent, the adult, and the old person.[29] In the most of the contemporary societies there is a legal division into the age of maturity and responsibility (18, 20, 21 years old, depending upon the society and the nature of the rights exercised) and of legal immaturity with full or partial irresponsibility. For instance in the German Civil Code persons up to 7 years old are entirely irresponsible legally, from 7 to 21 they are responsible legally and can transact most affairs, but with the consent of the parents, unless a special act of legal emancipation is performed which makes them legally mature at the age of 18 and over. As a rule legal and social maturity starts in Germany only with the age of 21 and up. Fixed age limits of legal immaturity, or half-maturity and full responsibility are found in all contemporary societies in reference to crimes, exercise of economic and political rights, voting, becoming a congressman or senator, judge or president of the United States, even for college entrance and graduation.[30] This legal division of age groups exists in many forms with painstaking detail.

Among preliterate[31] as well as more advanced populations certain ages enjoy a privileged superiority over the other age groups. In other populations there is a relationship of groups performing different functions and roles, with-

[29] See the details and facts in H. Schurtz, *Alterklassen und Männerbunde*, quoted; the summaries in R. Thurnwald, *Die Menschliche Gesellschaft* (Berlin, 1932), Vol. II, pp. 264 ff; L. W. Simmons, *The Role of the Aged in Primitive Societies* (New Haven, 1945); W. I. Thomas, *Primitive Behavior* (New York, 1937), Chps. 12, 13; G. Landtman, *The Origin of the Inequality of the Social Classes* (Chicago, 1938), Chps. 1, 2. Different divisions among the ancient Greek and Roman thinkers are given in Censorinus, *De die Natali* (Paris, 1843). The problem of age-sex groupings has been studied a great deal and has a considerable literature. It is incorrect, therefore, to state that it "is an almost unexplored field." R. Linton, "Age and Sex Categories," *ASR* (1942), pp. 590-91.

[30] It is incorrect therefore to state that "in our society age grading does not to any great extent, except for the educational system, involve formal age categorization." The author seems to have overlooked a multitude of well fixed and quite formal gradings by age. T. Parsons, "Age and Sex in the Social Structure of the United States," *ASR*, (1942), p. 604.
[31] Among the preliterate populations, according to L. W. Simmons, "in 38 tribes the property rights of the aged men's groups are pronounced, in 8 average, and in 7 slight; for aged women's groups in 7 tribes they are pronounced, in 8 average, and in 13 slight. The prestige of the aged is very widespread, especially among the pastoral and agricultural tribes. So also their political and civil rights and their exercise of leadership in religious, magical, and other activities. See L. W. Simmons, *The Role of the Aged in Primitive Society*, quoted.

out any clear principle of domination or subordination. In the early Roman population young age groups were entirely subordinated to the older groups. The *paterfamilias* had the right of life and death over his children and younger relatives. He could sell them into slavery or do whatever he pleased. The children, as *personae alieni juris*, did not have any civil or political rights; they could not acquire or own any property. At a later stage of Roman history this domination and subordination was replaced, step by step, by greater equality for children and young age groups. They eventually acquired most of their civil and political rights, becoming *personae sui juris*.

In such populations the cleavages between the age groups are deep and clearly discernible; they are definitely fixed by law and by practice. An implicit or explicit antagonism between the most privileged and most disfranchised age groups is a natural result.

In the populations without sharp domination-subordination of age groups, the boundary lines between them are less distinct; nevertheless, the age groups are legally fixed and actually functioning. Their manifestations are (1) fixed, formal, legal divisions of populations into the mature and responsible, the half-mature and responsible, the immature and irresponsible age groups. Every law fixes either implicitly or explicitly the age of the subjects of rights and duties. The concrete age limits fluctuate somewhat, depending upon the nature of the rights and duties. The minimum age for becoming a candidate for the presidency of the United States is different from that for a member of Congress, and both from the voting age or the marriageable age and all from the required age for college entrance. Legal maturity for the majority of civil rights and duties requires the ages of 18, 20, 21 in most contemporary societies. These legal divisions create either real or "as if" age groups.

(2) Many positions, activities and occupations require a certain minimum age and re-

tirement after a certain maximum age, as shown by the changing frequencies of various age groups, (3) in various occupations, positions, and activities. The occupational distribution of age groups in many occupations shows this fact. Persons below fifteen years of age are absent from most of the occupational populations; so also are persons over 60 and 65 years old. Other age groups are distributed differently among different occupations.[32] (4) A different quota of criminality and special types of crimes are furnished by different age groups.[33]

(5) Populations segregate into a multitude of specific age group associations, parties, clubs, societies, organizations, journals, schools, magazines, publications, even movies and shows for young children, youths, and adults. Their variety and number is rather enormous.[34] (6) A different style of training, behaving, and thinking is demanded from contrasting age groups. The style of mentality and conduct appropriate to a young boy or girl is not becoming to persons of the ages above twenty-five, and what is becoming to older persons is not expected from youths.[35] In dress, manners, thinking, behaving, overt activities, affiliations, sympathies, and antipathies these styles are different for different age-groups in practically all populations. (7) Spontaneous "gravitation" of the persons of similar age to one another is evident. Even in daily gatherings of persons, as at a party, there is a spontaneous segregation of persons of similar age (youth with youth, old persons with the old, mature with the mature), unless hindered by some special plan. For a youth to be in company with old men and women is boring. (8) Persons of different ages in the same population react differently to the same phenomena. Other conditions being equal, persons of similar age react more uniformly in their emotions, feelings, approval or disapproval, acceptance and rejection, than persons of widely dissimilar ages. Herein lies one of the sources of the

---

[32] See occupational censuses of the United States Bureau or summaries in such works as G. von Mayr, *Statistik und Gesellschaftslehre* (Tübingen, 1917), parts devoted to occupations.

[33] See the data in any standard text in criminology like E. Sutherland's, J. Gillin's, and others.

[34] In the same Newburyport many associations consisted only of adults, others of sub-adults, others

of the youth. W. L. Warner and P. S. Lunt, *op. cit.*, pp. 122-124.

[35] Cf., on changes in conduct in passage from childhood to adolescence, K. Lewin, "Field Theory," *AJS* (May, 1939), pp. 873 ff.; L. Cole, *Psychology of Adolescence* (New York, 1936); J. E. Anderson (ed.) *The Young Child in the Home* (New York, 1936). See further Ch. 48.

perennial conflict of fathers and sons, the old and the young, the hidden or open antagonism present in all populations between the younger and older generations. Herein lies the source of the "generation-rhythms and periodicities" claimed by many (G. Ferrari, F. Mentré, O. Lorenz, P. Ligeti, K. Joël, and many others).[36]

As with the sex grouping, the struggle is very seldom open, spectacular, and organized. The fight is usually conducted by many small detachments, as a sort of "partisan war." Nevertheless it goes on ceaselessly, without interruption, a continuously flowing river; it constantly undermines and reconstructs the social institutions. When the older age groups establish privileges for themselves at the cost of the younger age groups, as was projected in the Townsend Plan for the old age pensions, this means that the older generation is ascending in power. On the other hand, the growth of rights for childen and young people is a symptom of the growth in strength of the younger generation. In all these changes a struggle for power is evident between the age groups.

As one of the manifestations of conflict of the fathers and the sons we may note a difference in the age of the leaders of radical social movements and revolutions in contrast to the leaders of stable, conservative periods. In a revolutionary era the younger groups predominate and furnish the majority of the leaders as well as the followers of such movements. The fathers and grandfathers, in general, are on the other side of the barricades. During conservative or reactionary epochs the leaders and rulers are usually the older people. A statistical study of various leaders shows the average age of the leaders in ten great reform movements to be lower than that of the leaders in quiet and conservative epochs. The average age of the leaders in the Protestant reformation was 38 years; in the English revolution of 1640 it was 40 years; in the American revolution, 38 years. At the beginning of the French Revolution of 1789 the average age

of eleven persons, who were its leaders, was 34 years. The leaders of the anti-slavery movement in America had an average age of 41 years; the leaders of Japan's Renaissance had an average age of 38 years; of China's awakening, 38 years, etc.[37]

On the whole, then, the leaders and fighters for social innovation are members of younger age groups. So also are the leaders of the unstable, transitory periods, like the recent decades; most of the leaders of the revolutions of this century and the military leaders of World War II have been comparatively younger than those of the stable Victorian period. This shows the indirect role played by age in the large and complicated social processes.

As to the individual man, membership in a definite age group serves as a substantial co-ordinate defining his position and status. Not without reason do identification papers and passports indicate besides one's sex, citizenship, profession, etc., also the age or the year in which one was born. The age, as any other biological factor, influences a person, so to speak, "from the inside." When it is reinforced by social values, meanings, rights, duties, etc., raised upon it, the biological force becomes sociocultural and begins to be controlled by the organized and "as if organized" age-groups.

Since age affects a person's biological, mental, and sociocultural traits, a considerable change in the age-composition of a given population generates many transformations in its organization and sociocultural processes. Through a low birth-rate and low mortality the age-composition of most of the western populations has decreased in the per cent of the young age groups and increased in the per cent of the older age classes. As a result, the whole western population has become somewhat "aged" in comparison with its age-composition in the preceding centuries. Such an "aging" of the western societies is bound to generate many consequences in various fields of its sociocultural and biological life. Beginning with a decrease of the "school

---

[36] This problem is very important in its manifold ramifications. Cf. a survey, analysis, criticism, and the vast literature on the conflict and periodicity of dissimilar age-groups in my *Dynamics*, Vol. IV, pp. 505 ff. The problem has not yet attracted the attention of most American sociologists.

[37] See E. B. Gowin, *Correlation between Reformative Epochs and the Leadership of Young Men* (1909); Also I. Ash, "What Makes a People Lethargic or Energetic," *AJS*, Vol. XIX, p. 374.

population" in our schools and ending with a decreasing population of military age, these consequences are already taking place. If this "aging trend" is not checked, its cultural and social effects are bound to increase. Side by side with some beneficial effects, most of the consequences of "aging" are likely to be grave and disastrous in a long run. "Rejuvenation" of the western population in the form of an increasing birth rate becomes necessary to avoid these dire results. This suggests how in an indirect way the age-composition of a population influences the social structure and sociocultural life of societies.[38]

[38] On the most creative age of scientists and other leaders, see C. W. Adams, "The Age at Which Scientists Do Their Best Work," *Isis* (1946), pp. 166-170; H. C. Lehman, "The Age Factor," *Scientific Monthly* (1945), pp. 127-137; also his "The Age of Eminent Leaders," *A.J.S.* (1947), pp. 342-356.

Chapter 11. Differentiation of Human Population into Sociocultural Groups

I. Differentiation into Kinship Groups

From the biosocial groups we now pass to an examination of the unibonded groups based mainly upon sociocultural characteristics. Among these the kinship groups occupy an important place. *By kinship groups are meant the real groups whose meanings-values-norms, with the respective vehicles, arise from relationships of blood, common ancestry, adoption, totemism, and other equivalents of these ties.* At first glance, the family appears to be the most conspicuous example of the kinship group, and possibly it is the most intensive form. But in several respects the family is more than a mere kinship group. On the other hand, many forms of kinship have quite a remote relationship to the family. As we shall see, the family is not unibonded, but one of the most complex multibonded groups; the tie of kinship is only one of the many bonds uniting the members of a family. For this reason its place is among multibonded rather than unibonded groups. On the other hand, many forms of kinship appeared before the emergence of the family with no relationship to a real marriage, real common ancestry, community of blood, consanguinity, or affinity. For these reasons the kinship tie and the family ties cannot be regarded either as identical or coinciding.

This can be seen from an examination of the nature and variety of kinship forms among the preliterate populations where kinship ties and groups play a very important role. Among such populations the multitude of kinship groups means a differentiation into groups with specified rights and duties, roles and functions of the members and groups toward one another. First of all it is a classificatory device showing each member of a primitive group how to behave with other members. The basis of such inclusion in and exclusion from groups is in no way limited by real consanguinity.

From the point of view of any individual this means that his tribesmen are classified into certain categories, each one of which implies an altogether special set of social rules to be observed by him. He is bound to render services to an individual of one class; with a member of another he may jest and take liberties; with a person of a third category he must have nothing to do except through intermediaries.[1]

The recognition of (kinship) relationship is so extended that everyone with whom an individual comes in contact in the ordinary course of social life is his relative. It is impossible for a man to have any social relations with any one who is not his relative because there is no standard by which two persons in this position can regulate their conduct towards one another.[2]

[1] R. H. Lowie, *Primitive Society* (New York, 1920), p. 80.
[2] A. R. Radcliffe-Brown, "Three Tribes of Western Australia," *Journal of Royal Anthropological Institute*, Vol. XLIII, p. 157. See also G. P. Mur-dock, *Our Primitive Contemporaries* (New York, 1934); A. L. Kroeber, "Classificatory System of Relationship," *Journal of Royal Anthropological Institute*, Vol. XXXIX.

This shows an incomparably wider meaning of the term kinship and of the kinship groups than is implied by the contemporary sense of real consanquinity and affinity. The terms father, mother, brother, sister, uncle, and so on do not mean in such populations what they mean among us, as the terms of the specified members of the family. "Among such preliterary groups if you ask: What is the name of your father? What is the name of your mother? it may be that he will give you successively four or five fathers and as many mothers without including the authors of his being in the numbers . . . If you understand also that every old person is called 'my father' or 'my mother' you will have an idea of the extension of these terms."[3]

From the standpoint of real consanguinity, kinship classes include a very heterogeneous assortment of persons. For instance, among the Haida the term *kwuna* (meaning father-in-law and son-in-law) is applied to a woman's husband's father, her husband's father's own brother, her husband's mother's father, her daughter's husband, her daughter's daughter's husband, and the husband of any clanswoman of the first descending generation.[4] An individual is classified as kin from his father's line of membership, from his mother's line of membership, as a sib, member of a totemic group, age group, blood brotherhood, adopted member, and so on. Consequently a man may be the "grandchild" of a woman and at the same time her "father," or simultaneously be the "son" and the "father" of his father, a woman may be the "daughter" and at the same time "mother" of the same man.[5]

All this is further extended and complicated by many forms of kinship introduced and established by *adoption* and *exchange of children* which makes a "father" of the adopting persons and cancels the fatherhood of the real father; by *blood brotherhood* which makes "brothers" of persons unrelated by blood at all; by *totemic beliefs* and practices with the same spirit, plant, animal, or object as the *common ancestor*; by rules governing *incest* that make kins out of the persons who are not kins by birth and cancelling kinship of persons who are kins by birth. Added to this is the *impossibility of establishing who is the real father and who is a son or daughter of whom* in polyandric, polygynic, and other forms of non-monogamic society; and in many cases of "free" sex-behavior of boys and girls, of those married with the right to use as wives or husbands several "brothers" or "sisters" or all the women and men outside of their incest groups. As a result the consanguineous ties and groups make a small fraction of the much wider and more numerous kinship ties that are based upon other relations.[6]

This explains why kinship and the family ties are very different and cannot be treated as identical as they are commonly treated by textbooks in sociology and the family. As noted above, the kinship groups play a very important role among preliterate populations. There they are possibly the most pervading and powerful groups, when taken in their totality. Even among somewhat more "advanced" populations like the early Egyptians, Babylonians, Greeks, Romans, or the people of Medieval Europe[7] the kinship ties continued

[3] Father Callaud, "A la Côte d'Or," *Les Missions catholiques*, Vol. XXV, p. 284, quoted from W. I. Thomas, *Primitive Behavior* (New York, 1937), p. 100. This work has considerable material on kinship and its equivalents. See Chps. 5-7.

[4] G. P. Murdock, "Kinship and Social Behavior Among the Haida," *American Anthropologist*, New Series, Vol. XXXVI, p. 373.

[5] W. I. Thomas, *op. cit.*, pp. 101-102. See there the material and analyses by R. H. Lowie, R. Kennedy, R. Codrington, J. Roscoe, and others.

[6] See a good digest of the main forms of all these phenomena and a collection of the signficant excerpts from the works of many investigators in W. I. Thomas' *Primitive Behavior*; R. Thurnwald, *Die Menschliche Gesellschaft* (Berlin-Leipzig, 1932), Vol. II, Chps. 7, 8.

[7] Up to the fourteenth century the "kindred" as a broad union of relatives (by blood or other non-biological ties) played a large role in the entire social organization of the rural and partly urban populations. It was the important group that acted on behalf of all kinsmen in civil, criminal, and other matters. The medieval criminal, civil, and constitutional laws were permeated with the principle of kinship We find there the institutions of guardianship by kinsmen, wergilds, blood revenge, maintenance of paupers, and so on. Kinsmen were responsible for the conduct and crime of any kinsman. The kindred also preserved the liberty and rights of its members. For instance, as long as the kindred was strong among the peasants, feudalism and the subjugation of peasants to lords did not thrive. In discouraging the rise of petty chiefs

to play an exceedingly important role in such basic groups as the *gens, gentes, gentiles; phyle and phratry; tribe and clan; estate and caste; and the Gemeinschaft.* We shall see that each of these groups is a multibonded group in which the kinship tie is one of the significant bonds.

Among the more complex industrialized, urbanized, and differentiated populations the role of the kinship tie was progressively diluted. Its power was seized by other groups different from the kinship groups, like the state, territorial, national, and religious groups. On the other hand the *family kinship* became one of the basic ties of this multibonded social group. So long as the family remains a powerful social group (see further Chapter 13), the kinship tie continues to work through the family groups in shaping persons, groups, and the course of sociocultural processes. It continues to work also, though in modified form, through the

state, occupational, territorial, and national groups that have taken something of the kinship bonds into their solidarity and unity. For these reasons the kinship groups, with their respective meanings-values-norms, stand among the important unibonded social groups. They become one of the indispensable co-ordinates determining the individual's position in his sociocultural universe. Most of the kinship groups are neither open nor closed but occupy an intermediary position. The real kinship groups born from the same parents and members of a blood group are nearest to the closed groups. The differentiation along the kinship line does not coincide with any of the previously discussed lines of differentiation into race-age-sex groups nor with any of those which will be discussed further. Each of these unibonded groups is a group *sui generis* and the distinctions into these groups do not coincide with each other.

II. Differentiation into Territorial Neighborhood Groups

A territorial neighborhood is one of the environments from whose influence no one residing in it is entirely free. The fact of living in territorial adjacency with other people (in the same apartment house, village, town, country, city), continually meeting and interacting with territorial neighbors, leads to an exchange and assimilation of many customs and forms of conduct, especially when such a residence is durable or permanent. Likewise territorial proximity imposes upon the neighbors a set of common interests and makes them solidary within the limits of these interests, no matter how different they may be in other respects. Breathing the same air, absorbing the same sociocultural atmosphere, the interacting neighbors cannot fail to develop some similarities and common ways of behavior until eventually they form a group, a local type marked by the "color" of the neighborhood

locality. Such are the regional types of Frenchmen investigated by E. Demolins: the Provençal, Breton, Auvergnat;[8] such are the American local types: the Yankee, Westerner, Kansan, the Ozark Mountaineer, or permanent dwellers of the same slum of a city.

Exposed to the same natural and social environment to which they have to adapt in order to live, individuals develop a community of interests imposed by their territorial adjacency. Harmful cosmic and biological conditions (storms, epidemics, floods, water shortage) usually threaten all within a given locality; unfavorable social conditions (absence of a hospital, school, or church) will also affect the welfare of all residents. Even the most thoroughgoing egoist will not feel safe in a place where an epidemic rages, hunger is rampant, roadways are neglected, hospitals are

---

the kindred tended to keep the status of all freemen equal. See B. S. Phillpotts, *Kindred and Clan in the Middle Ages and After* (Cambridge, 1913), Introduction, Ch. 8 *passim.*

[8] See E. Demolins, *Comment la route crée le type social* (Paris, n.d.) 2 Vols; N. W. Odum and H. E. Moore, American Regionalism (New York, 1938); E. Demolins, *Les français d'aujourd'hui Les types sociaux de midi et de centre* (Paris, 1898).

lacking, where bombs or enemies are menacing. All the inhabitants of the same territorial neighborhood are forced to be similarly interested in good roads, sanitation, and schools, for personal security. To this extent they are compelled to act in harmony, all of which inevitably leads to a kind of local solidarity, local patriotism, a sentiment binding the neighbors into one collective whole. The territory binds them directly in the process of interaction by common interests. It binds them indirectly through a deep attachment to the place where they are born, reared, and acquainted. It becomes a part of their personality, an important part of their values, loved and cherished. "My land," "my home," "my country," "my Fatherland" with all its geographic and social traits becomes the value which one is ready to defend from an enemy, and for which one becomes homesick, if one is absent. Many persons develop a nostalgia or melancholic homesickness when they are far away from home.[9] Our "Carry Me Back to Old Virginny" is an expression of such homesickness. The valiant fight of the soldiers of Russia or of other countries when their "fatherland" is invaded—much more heroic than when they invade other countries—is a manifestation of this deep attachment to one's territorial abode. These facts of homesickness for one's land, home, familiar faces, sights and experiences, as well as the valiant defense of one's abode are especially conspicuous in populations where individuals are born, live, and die in the same territorial neighborhood. Separated from home, members of the Ona tribe feel sad and lonesome; the Maori affectionately call the tribal land "the only surviving parent in the world," "the bed matting of our ancestors"; seized as captives they ask to be permitted to look upon their land or to take a handful of the native earth to weep over. "Every spot of ground is associated with some particular deed connected with their many engagements and triumphs." One is sacred because a man of rank fell there; another because his ancestors are buried there; a third because there he met his wife or sweetheart, or because some other important event of his life occurred there.[10]

The same can be said of all populations that reside where they were born. Even socialists and syndicalists manifest similar attitudes. A. Bebel, one of the leaders of German Socialists, in his speeches at the Reichstag on March 7, 1904 and December 10, 1904, said: "We live and fight to make our Fatherland, our country, ours, even more than yours (of the bourgeoisie), a place to live in for the lowest of us. This is our purpose and we shall with all the means at our disposal fight against any attempt to tear away the smallest parcel of ground from our country. I would gladly take the rifle to fight for the independence of my country."[11]

One of the leaders of the French syndicalists, H. Lagardell, well characterized the importance of the territorial grouping. "Of all the bonds, uniting men, the strongest is the bond of locality, for it creates a community of purposes and interests. Workers of one locality, though belonging to various occupations, have more points of contact among themselves than workers of the same occupation, scattered in various cities. The similarity in the mode of life, family connections, friendships, participation in the same local institutions—sportive, philanthropic, educational—lead to the creation of a living bond."[12]

From the language we speak, on up to our beliefs, tastes, opinions, mores, and manners, everyone who resides in the same locality for a long time is impregnated by its geographic, social, and cultural patterns. An emergence of "the local type of personality," of local patriotism and local culture becomes inevitable in such conditions. *With increasing mobility of the population and with frequent change of*

---

[9] See the facts in R. de la Grasserie: "De la nostalgie et des instincts contraires," *Revue international de sociologie* (1911), pp. 564-610. A good concrete case is well described in G. and N. Papashvily's *Anything Can Happen* (New York, 1940), Chps. 4, 6.

[10] R. Firth, *Primitive Economics of the New Zealand Maori* (New York, 1929), pp. 361 ff. E. Tregear, *The Maori Race* (New York, 1904), pp.

131 ff. W. I. Thomas, *Primitive Behavior*, pp. 32-37.

[11] Bebel in the German Reichstag, March 7 and December 10, 1904.

[12] H. Lagardell, "Revolutionary Syndicalism in France," in *Voprosy Momenta* (Moscow, 1906), pp. 216-217; see also V. Tchernov's *Basic Problems of the Proletarian Movement* (St. Petersburg, 1918); see also A. de Lagardelle, "Le territoire," *Encyclopedie Française*, Vol. X, pp. 10-13.

residence, the importance and effectiveness of a territorial neighborhood progressively declines. That is exactly what has been happening in the mobility of industrial and urbanized people. In such populations the ties of territorial groups have become greatly weakened. In our cities we may live in the same apartment house without even knowing our next door neighbors. In our factories, offices, stores, and other places we may work for a short period shoulder to shoulder without any deep knowledge, attachment, or mutual influence. The psychology of a traveling salesman or of a transient hotel guest develops instead of the psychology of local patriotism. Its place is taken by the attitude *ubi bene ibi patria* ("where is good for me there is my country"), for with increased mobility everyone stays a shorter time in a given locality and is exposed less and less to the influence of his territorial neighbors. Studying the activities that fill every 24 hours of some 100 white collar unemployed persons in Boston, and their interaction with other persons, we find the following indexes of the time-exposure of a person to the influence of the following specified groups: friends, 35.67; family members, 24.09; business associates, 8.85; relatives, 3.15; casual acquaintances, 1.26; neighbors, 0.78; strangers, 0.20.[13]

The figures show that in contemporary urban conditions, for its mobile population, the role of the short-lived and ever-changing territorial neighborhood has greatly declined. It has become in fact one of the least important groups in conditioning human beings. Such a temporary and largely incidental locality group naturally does not provoke local patriotism or attachment and ceases to play the role it formerly had in the immobile, sedentary populations living and dying where they were born.

The decreasing role of the locality group, in the conditions of intense mobility, is due also to the *dissociation of the previously multibonded locality group into a series of unibonded groups.* Among the populations living where they were born, the locality group was in fact a multibonded group in which the

[13] P. A. Sorokin and C. Q. Berger, *Time Budgets of Human Behavior* (Harvard University Press, 1939), p. 153.

locality tie was one of many. Whether in a preliterate tribe or in a Hindu, Chinese, or other village, or in a medieval city with non-migratory and non-mobile population, the locality group was often tied by the bond of kinship, common language, common culture, common religion, common citizenship, even by common occupation and economic interests. Persons who lived all their lives in the same locality composed a multibonded group that molded their personality in all its essential biosocial characteristics. Such a multibonded group, located in a limited area, is what many sociologists still call "community" in contrast to a unibonded association (see above, pp. (117-118).

With the increase of population mobility this multibonded locality group began to dissociate. In the same locality, like a block in a contemporary metropolis, the population is composed increasingly of persons having no kinship whatsoever, belonging to all kinds of racial or nationality groups, members of different religions and occupations, political parties and cultural values, born and reared in different cultural groups. The locality tie has been progressively separated from other bonds and values. The persons settling temporarily within such a locality have been exposed to its influence for a shorter time. This double blow—separation from the other ties and values that previously supported it, and a progressive shortening of exposure—has naturally resulted in its decline. The locality group has progressively become a unibonded territorial group instead of a multibonded group, hence a decline of its importance. Hence also the *notable mistake of many sociologists who continue to treat this unibonded territorial group as an all-important "community" in contrast to unibonded associations.* A purely unibonded locality group has ceased to be a multibonded community and has become one of the insignificant associations as far removed from "community" as any other unibonded group. (See further, Chapter 13.)

However, this does not mean that the locality group as a unibonded group has lost all of its importance. In large areas of population it still remains a variety of the multibonded body. The mobility of the population has not increased to such an extent, even in the urban areas, as to make the residence of its population in the same locality short-lived. Even within a mobile population, where it is transformed into a unibonded group, *it continues to exert a powerful influence in three new ways: (a) as a basis for subdivision of the nonterritorial groups; (b) through extension of the area of one's locality and of the boundary of the local neighborhood group; (c) through emergence of territorially scattered sociocultural institutions similar to one another, therefore acting upon its changing inhabitants in a common way.*

A few comments will explain these new influences of unibonded locality groups. First, even in the most mobile populations of a multibonded locality group, the subdivision of almost all the groups on the basis of locality is still necessary. The nation is divided into territorial states, provinces, counties, townships, electoral and other districts; so also political parties and labor unions are divided into their "locals." Local subdivisions appear in religious groups, especially in large religious bodies like the Roman Catholic or various Protestant churches; and in practically all groups of a considerable size. In this way the locality ties continue to work through practically all of the non-territorial groups.

Second, an immobile population considers "my locality" as just one village, tribe, county, or township; but mobile population extends its boundaries to the larger territory of a whole province or a whole nation. "Fatherland" means, in such a population, the whole of the United States, of England, or of Russia as the entire territory of a population having somewhat similar manners and mores, culture and ways of life. In this greatly extended form the territorial group tends to become again a multibonded group that tends to play an important

role. The patriotism of a vast populated area replaces that of a local parish or village.

Finally, the population of American hotels or cities is very mobile. But if a person spends a few days in New York hotels, then in Chicago and San Francisco hotels, and thus resides most of his life in different hotels, he becomes standardized along the same pattern of "hotel culture." The hotels are scattered widely so far as their location is concerned, but all of them are essentially similar; they all act as one hotel whose population resides for a long time. The same can be said of many cities. American cities are scattered over a vast territory. But as each city is very similar to the others, the persons residing a short time in each city but living long in various standardized cities, with similar hotels, street cars, buildings, newspapers, drug stores, movies, cafeterias, and restaurants—such persons find themselves exposed as though to the same city. As a result they cannot help becoming "cityminded." The multitude of similar cities serve as one city in which individuals live and die. Localities within cities may also have standardized patterns of culture.[14] In this way the territorial group continues to influence individuals, the groups, and the course of human history. It makes an indispensable sociocultural co-ordinate for location of an individual or group in a sociocultural universe. Most of the unibonded local groups are open; one can go and settle wherever he likes, if his financial and other conditions permit. Other groups are semi-open and a few are virtually closed to all who do not have specifications of an exclusive kind (e.g., sacred places, the abodes of kings, presidents, the highly expensive and "select" areas). It is unnecessary to add that the boundaries of various territorial groups follow lines different from those of all other groups.

[14] These localities are represented by the main ecological areas of a city or of any other inhabited place. The areas of a loop, or a transitional area, or residential areas of various cities act in a similar manner upon their changing population. See R. Park and E. Burgess, *The City* (Chicago, 1925); C. R. Shaw, *Delinquency Areas* (Chicago, 1929); M. A. Alihan, *Social Ecology* (New York, 1938); Sorokin, Zimmerman, and Galpin, *Systematic Source Book in Rural Sociology*, Vol. I, Ch. 5.

III. Differentiation into Language, Ethnic, or Nationality Groups

Language is the most important means of communication and meaningful interaction. It is, therefore, the most indispensable condition of the existence of any sociocultural group. As such it becomes one of the most significant values of an individual and one of the strongest bonds of unity or disunity. With no common language people remain largely strangers to one another. They cannot open the world of their meanings-values-norms to others. They remain isolated from one another, no matter how close they may be physically. No common fund of values can be created, and no real sociocultural group can emerge in these conditions.[15]

Furthermore, identity of language means a similarity of many other basic values and norms. E. Durkheim and M. Mauss are not far from the truth when they state that groups having the same language have essentially the same culture, mode of living, manners, mores, beliefs, forms of thinking; in brief, similar mental, moral, and material culture, "All peoples speaking the Indo-European languages have a common fund of ideas and institutions."[16]

In this unreserved form the statement overshoots the mark; but it does correctly show that similarity in language usually means similarity in many basic sociocultural values, meanings, norms, and vehicles. "Members of an ethnic group speak the same language, love a specified land as their own home, obey definite folkways and mores, cherish their own art, venerate a specific past personified in a set of beloved heroes, recognize the offences imposed upon their ancestors by other groups, recognize common symbols such as a script, monuments, places of pilgrimage, and often believe in a common descent."[17] This explains why the persons of the same native language tend to be more solidary with one another than the persons with different languages. Even thoughtful Marxians like K. Kautsky stress that, in spite of the Marxian theory of class differentiation:

Language constitutes the first necessary condition of any joint activity. People who do not understand our language are outside the circle of our associations; we feel more bound socially to those who speak our language, whatever their social position. For a worker in a foreign country the national language difference is often a more powerful factor in life than the sharpest class contrast. A German worker having no knowledge of French, will feel lost and lonely among French workers, in spite of all his enthusiastic talk about international class consciousness. He will greet with great joy the first German he meets, even if the latter were an exploiter, whom he had hated in his own country.[18]

It is no wonder that the language groups emerged a long time ago and from the remote past have played an important role in human history. The most common form of such groups is known as the *ethnic and nationality group*. When we try to analyze so-called nationality groups (in contrast to the nations whose analysis will be given further), we find that the most distinctive trait is language with the many cultural values correlated with it. Individuals speaking the same language and sharing the correlated cultural values compose the nationality or ethnic group. Without a distinct language of its own there will be no nationality. The awakening of nationality often began with the revival of its language and its literature. The struggle for equality of nationalities has usually started with the struggle for equality of their language in the state, court, school, church, etc., for the right to teach it

[15] See A. G. Laguna, *Speech: Its Functions and Development* (New York, 1927); J. Piaget, *The Language and Thought of the Child* (New York, 1926). See other works on language quoted above, in Ch. 3.

[16] E. Durkheim and M. Mauss, "Civilization et types de civilization," *L' Année sociologique*, Vol. XII, p. 47. Cf. I. Vendryes, *Le langage* (Paris,

1921); C. Serrus, *La langue, le sens et la pensée* (Paris, 1941).

[17] N. S. Timasheff, "The Comparative Study of Inter-Ethnic Relations," *American Catholic Sociological Review*, Vol. V (1944), p. 225.

[18] K. Kautsky, *National Problems* (St. Petersburg, 1918), p. 28.

and to use it without discrimination. The total loss of its language by a group means a loss of its individuality and nationality. An expansion of a nationality group is regularly followed by a widening diffusion of its language among other populations; a decline of a nationality group is followed by the restriction of its language. When the power of Arabic nationality grew, the use of the Arabic language spread over wide areas of conquest; it also accompanied the peaceful diffusion of their culture. When Arab nationalism began to decline, the area of the Arabic language declined. So it has been with many other language groups, from the ancient Egyptian, Sumeric, Babylonian, Greek, and Latin, to the widest diffusion of English with the rise in power of the Anglo-Saxon nationalities.[19]

The so-called *nationality movements in history* have been more exactly the *movements of language groups*.[20] Considering that some of the native language groups have had large membership counted by tens of millions, that they have been solidary when fighting against their opponents, that many of them have a rich fund of meanings-values-norms and vehicles at their disposal, we can understand why some of these groups did not hesitate to enter into conflict with powerful states or other groups, and not rarely have come off victorious in the struggle. Concrete examples of this are given by the language group movements in the nineteenth and twentieth century. During this period many a language group like the Greek, the Serbian, the Bulgarian, the Italian, and others absorbed respectively by the Turkish or Austro-Hungarian empires, defeated all efforts to keep them under the conqueror's roof; these language groups finally won independence and created their own states. Likewise the Polish language group, torn between Austria, Germany, and Russia, was able to regain its independence and then to create its own state. The same is true of Czechoslovakia, and for a time at least of Esthonia, Finland, Latvia, Lithuania, and several others. At the present time we witness similar activities of several

language groups to create their own states, a phenomenon which has been occurring throughout history, now with success of the language groups in their struggle with opponents, now with failure, but always with important social consequences. Along the frontiers of history, antagonisms and alliances of language groups have always been significant. The tensions and alliances of the contemporary language groups with one another and with the non-language groups occupy one of the foremost places on the agenda of history.

It must be evident that the differentiation of population into language groups is unique and does not coincide with any other differentiation. That it is different from sex and age groups is obvious. Likewise one racial (zoological) group may be and ordinarily is divided into several different language groups; for instance, the Caucasian race or even its branches like the Nordic or Alpine groups are divided among the English-speaking, Scandinavian, Russian, German-speaking and other language groups. And vice versa: there is hardly any sizable language group which is not made up of several different racial groups, be it Russian, German, English, French, Italian, or any other large language group.

Neither territorial nor kinship nor state groups coincide with language groups. On the same territory of a big city there are found individuals belonging to different language groups. The same language group is ordinarily dispersed over a wide territory, sometimes over entire continents. Members of such language groups as English, German, French, and Russian can be found in the remotest parts of the planet. Kinship groups are incomparably smaller than language groups whose members do not entertain, especially in recent times, an idea of kinship binding them all. Dilution and limitation of the kinship circle in modern times has led, as noted, to replacement of kinship ties with the community of language, or religion, of the state-citizenship, and so on. Such a replacement does not make of them kinship groups. For the same state, like Russia, may consist of several dozens of different language

[19] See the facts in detail in my *Dynamics*, Vol. IV, pp. 217 ff.; A. S. Woolner, *Languages in History and Politics* (Oxford University Press, 1938), *passim*.

[20] H. Kohn, *The Idea of Nationalism* (New York, 1944), though the author does not clearly distin-

guish the language (nationality) groups from the state and the nation. A many volume work on nationality movements was published in Russian, 1910-1915.

groups (Russian, Polish, Bulgarian, Czech, and other Slavic languages, French, German, Latvian—altogether more than one hundred different language groups). And vice versa, members of the same language group belong, as citizens, to different states. The English-speaking groups belong to Great Britain, to the United States of America, to British dominions and in small groups are scattered among the citizens of most of the existing states.

Language makes one of the indispensable co-ordinates defining an individual's or group's position in the sociocultural universe. Language groups, as a rule, are decentralized groups. They are theoretically open groups. Anyone who learns a language and its cultural

values can become a member. Theoretically one can change "language dress"; take off the disliked language and put on one he likes. Actually, the situation is considerably different. To learn perfectly any new language besides one's own is not easy, and for many it is impossible. Still more difficult is it to learn and to make one's own the manner of thinking and the cultural values connected with a new language. For these and similar reasons the language groups are only semi-open. Most of those who can master a new language properly find no legal or biological obstacles. For many others the variety of actual and often legal difficulties make a change of language group quite difficult.

IV. Differentiation into State Groups

The differentiation of human population into state groups like the United States of America, Great Britain, Germany, France, and Russia does not coincide with any that has been or will be studied. As a rule the state group is made up of persons of different race, sex, and age groups, different kinship, territorial and language groups, as well as political, occupational, and religious associations, and conversely, individuals of the same race, sex, language, and other groups are citizens of different states.

It is easy to point out the state groups but it is difficult to define exactly the characteristics that distinguish the state from other groups. The usual definitions of the state found in any text of constitutional law or political science hardly fulfill this task. The state has been defined as an organized people occupying a definite territory and subjected to a sovereign governmental power. In accordance with this definition territory, population, and government have been regarded as the distinguishing marks of the state.[21] The fallacy of this construction can easily be seen. The totality of population, territory, and government is not

characteristic of the state alone. The church, for instance, consists of: (1) the population of the believers; (2) the territory which its buildings, properties, and members occupy; (3) the church government promulgating the sovereign laws by which it regulates the conduct of its members. Likewise the political party, the language, territorial, occupational, and other groups contain these same elements represented by their members, their central committees, and the territories within the boundaries of which their actions take place.

Population is regarded as a distinctive trait of the state because of the false conception that the state exists as one single society. Since, according to this view, all the individuals composing a given society are *ipso-facto* members of the state, the whole population is regarded as an exclusive constituency of the state. We have seen the fallacy of this view. Each individual is a member not only of the state, but also of many other groups, and the population is differentiated not only into state groups but into many others; therefore it cannot be regarded as exclusive property of the state.

The same is true with respect to territory. It

[21] See N. Lasarevsky, *Russian Constitutional Law* (in Russian, St. Petersburg, 1916), pp. 2-10; L. Duguit, *Traité de droit constitutionel* (Paris, 1922), Vol. I, Chps. 1-3; A. Michel, *L'idée de l'état* (Paris, 1902), *Encyclopedie Française*, Vol. X;

L'état Moderne, Studies of L. Febure, Le Fur, Pouget, and others; G. Jellineck, *Das Recht des modernen Staates* (Berlin, 1900); and practically any course in political science and constitutional law.

is usually thought that the state government is the only power in operation within a given territory. But this is a juridical fiction! A simple illustration will show the fallacy of this view. A number of posts located on a piece of ground can be encircled by a number of nets of wires, thus forming several systems of wire netting between the same posts. It would indeed be strange to claim the ground on which the posts are located for one of these systems only; the ground belongs in the same degree to all the netting systems. The relation between the territory and the state is the same as between any system of wire netting and the locality where the posts are placed. To be sure, the state is localized on a definite continuous territory, but the same territory is occupied by the occupational, sex-race-age-language and other systems of interaction.

Even legally the territory is not an exclusive property of the state; it is owned by many other groups and persons. The main difference here is that the state is a group *localized* on a definite, continuous territory (with the exception of its citizens living outside of their state boundary), while many other groups are not so localized. But territorial groups (as a village or city), language, race, and religious groups are also localized within a definite continuous territory. Even in this secondary trait the state is not unique.[22]

Others (anarchists, syndicalists, socialists) find the distinguishing mark of the state in the compulsory character of its government.[23] This view is fallacious. We already know the compulsory relationships are not a monopoly of the state but exist in many other groups, from the family to the labor union, caste and the church

(in some populations). The governments o[f] most organized groups have a degree of compulsory power.[24]

As soon as a group has a governing cente[r] it becomes a power standing above the peopl[e] who are ruled, and employing compulsor[y] measures for the preservation of unity an[d] order. The disciplinary measures which th[e] head of a family takes against disobedien[t] members; the penances, fines, and excommuni cations imposed by church authorities agains[t] wayward members; the reproofs, fines, an[d] exclusion imposed upon unruly party member[s] by the party executive committee are all evi dences of the compulsory character of the gov erning body in many non-state groups.[25] Every where "the rulers" impose their will in variou[s] ways upon the ruled. A group of free peopl[e] achieving its ends without any compulsion i[s] still a rare phenomenon.

Others take as the distinguishing character istic of the state the sovereign character of it[s] power. But this also is far from true. First, no[t] all states enjoy sovereign power. Many state[s] during the Middle Ages, as well as moder[n] states in a federation, like the United States have been without it to quite a degree. Second there are non-state groups which possess bot[h] a sovereign and primary power. The Catholi[c] Church during the Middle Ages never acknowl edged its subordination to the sovereignty o[f] the state; on the contrary, it claimed an[d] actually had supremacy over the secular powe[r] of the state. Neither did the various trade guilds recognize the state sovereignty. Gen erally, the feudal state was a weak group Moreover, even in modern times, when state

[22] On localized and non-localized groups see Lasarevsky's work, quoted, pp. 42-46; R. Maunier, "The Definition of the City," *AJS*, Vol. XV, pp. 536-548; also his *L'origine et la fonction economique des villes* (Paris, 1910); the quoted works of G. Simmel, E. Hugh, W. Firey.

[23] See, for instance, P. Lavrov, *The State Element in the Future Society* (Russian, London, 1876), pp. 12-13; F. Engels, *The Origin of the Family* (Chicago, 1902), and most of the anarchist and syndicalist literature quoted further.

[24] See C. Merriam, *Political Power* (New York, 1934), pp. 20, 48. N. Timasheff views the power of the state in modern times as supreme, but recognizes the compulsory power of other groups. N. S. Timasheff, *An Introduction to the Sociology of*

Law (Harvard University Press, 1939), pp. 161, 218-221, 284-285, *passim*.

[25] P. Lavrov correctly says that "All the political unions organized to fight against state governments were organized upon the compulsory principle often more coercive than the state coercion against which they fought. It permeated practically all the plans of the workers' socialist and communist organizations so far offered"; the plans of K. Marx, F. Engels, F. Lassalle, of the syndicalists, the anarchists, and others. Lavrov, *op. cit.*, pp. 14-15. Lenin's plan of a "destruction of the state" is no exception to this; it consisted in a mere replacement of the state rulers with the ruder coercion exercised by the Communist rulers. See V. Lenin, *The State and the Revolution* (St. Petersburg, 1918), pp. 17-19, 93-94, *passim*.

power increased, there have been numerous collectivities which enjoyed power not only with the consent of the state, but often against its will. Thus the power of the head of the family is derived not from the state, but is a result of independent growth; neither does the priest need the authorization of the state to free a church member from his sins, to impose penance, to excommunicate and to decree various laws regulating the religious life. The heads of the church do not look unto themselves as servants in the employ of the state. Still less does the central committee of an Anarchist, Communist, or Socialist political party or a workers' union owe its existence to the state in capitalist, anti-communistic, or anti-socialist countries. All these organizations emerged, flourished, and sometimes overthrew state governments contrary to the state and its governments in the seventeenth, the eighteenth, nineteenth, and twentieth centuries.[26]

One may say that, though the power of non-state groups is not derived from the state, it does need the latter's recognition and sanction to have any force. But it is easy to see that sanctioning does not transform a primary power into a derivative one; and the fact is that such a sanction does not always take place. The state government hardly ever sanctions the policies of the parties directed against it. Nevertheless, such parties have existed and will continue to exist. The state never gives its sanction to a revolution aimed to overthrow its government; yet such revolutions have occurred and state governments have been overthrown. All this seems to indicate that a number of groups possess primary power not derived from the state, and even independent of state sanction.

To be sure, it may be argued that the state coercively regulating a mass of social relation-

ships and groups "simply does not find it necessary to regulate others in the same way, but reserves for itself the right to do so, when there may be a reason for it. In modern societies any enforcement is possible only if granted by the state laws, every compulsory power is based upon the official state law and is, therefore, derived from the state."[27]

This traditional conception is also a fiction. Were it true that every compulsory power is based upon state laws, the power of a gang of bandits or the power of a party opposed to the state government would also have to be considered as derived from the will of the state, which is absurd. Furthermore, many groups possess power independently and often in spite of the state. But the state, say its proponents, reserves the right to regulate everything. But can it do this? That is the question. Anybody is free, of course, to attribute to himself all sorts of powers, but the essence of the matter is whether one is able to realize them in fact. On paper the state is "sovereign, omnipotent, omnipresent, eternal, and one." These statements, however, are quite fictitious. Were this so, then all parties in opposition, rebels, revolutionaries, and their actions directed against the state government, would have disappeared long ago; for it is inconceivable that a power, capable of doing it, would not desire to uproot all those who seek to destroy it. Yet this has not occurred. No state has ever succeeded in completely suppressing its opponents, for actually it is not omnipotent, and indeed, it may be quite powerless against many non-state movements.

The very fact that most states had to become "constitutional" and limited in arbitrary power by law is convincing evidence; for such limitations of their power have been established not by the free volition of state governments but by the pressure of non-state groups upon the state.[28]

---

[26] See the history of workers' radical movements in N. Kritskaia and N. Lebedev, *The History of the Syndicalist Movement in France* (Moscow, 1908); J. Davis, *Contemporary Social Movements* (New York, 1930); see there literature on the subject.

[27] N. Lasarevsky, *op. cit.*, p. 5; N. S. Timasheff, *op. cit.*, p. 161.

[28] Lasarevsky himself was compelled to recognize this truth. He writes, "The state laws, which are opposed to the prevalent mores and to various groups trying to organize themselves, remain largely a dead letter. . . . To speak of the omnipotency of state laws is incorrect." Lasarevsky,

op. cit., pp. 26-27. These propositions are elaborated in greater detail in the works of the anarchists and syndicalists. See M. Bakunin, *Statehood and Anarchy* (Russian, Moscow, 1919); P. Kropotkin, *Rebels' Speeches* (Russian, London, 1919); Malatesta, *Anarchism*; E. Reclus, *Evolution, Revolution and the Ideal of Anarchism* (Russian tr., Moscow, 1918). See also the works of G. Sorel, Labriola, N. Lagardelle, and other syndicalists, quoted further.

Even in the contemporary totalitarian states with their enormous dictatorial power it turns out to be limited by the other groups: the Communist, the Nazi, the Fascist, and other state powers are compelled, contrary to their will, to change their policies and to limit their arbitrariness under a relentless, anonymous pressure of other groups. The radical reversal of the Communist Government's policies in Russia and the transformation of the Communist Government itself, are especially important from this standpoint.[29] However paradoxical it may sound, one may reasonably assert that the power of many non-state groups is created against the will of the state and in spite of its opposition. Thus sovereignty can not fully serve as the decisive mark distinguishing the state from other collectivities. The traditional definitions of the state are thus inadequate.

What then is the state? In its initial stages it was hardly distinguishable from other groups, as the tribe, clan, gens, horde, and so on. Its power was the power of these groups. Its government was coterminal, often identical, with the government of these groups (whose nature will be discussed in Chapter 12).[30] Only later on is it differentiated from other groups to become a group *sui generis*, with its own organization and government. In its developed form it is a kind of a clearing house, for the interrelations and interpressures of all the groups in a given population over which the state government extends its power. In the second place it has its own set of values-meanings-norms with respective relationships and material vehicles controlled and regulated by the state. The concrete nature of these values and relationships is neither constant nor the same in different states or in the same state at different times. It changes from state to state and from time to time.

The nature of the relationships and values that constitute the state system of interaction is clearly indicated for each state in its official law. The official law codes of France, of Ger-many, or of the United States indicate the relationships (with their components of meanings, vehicles, and human agents) which make up the state system of interaction. In each state a study of its law will show what relationships and values are controlled by the state, and which do not enter its official system of interaction.

Among the changing relationships and values that make a state system of interaction there are some that are comparatively constant and enter into the system of interaction of almost all of the states. They are: (1) *the protection of the independence of the members of the state from outside enemies and maintenance of relationships with other states;* (2) *regulation and control of the monetary system of the population;* (3) *maintenance of some order within the state population regardless of its justice or injustice;* (4) *enactment of the norms of official law for a uniform and obligatory regulation of the main relationships between the individuals and groups within the state population;* (5) *enforcement of this official law; trial and solution of the conflicts between its members so far as they concern the norms of the official state law; apprehension and punishment of the violators of this official law.*

These values and relationships have been the most constant functions of state groups. Other relationships and values so often extolled by idolaters and devotees of the state like protection of freedom, facilitation of sciences and arts, philosophy and religion, promotion of cultural and social progress; facilitation of the mental, moral, and physical well-being of its members have not been so constant in various state systems. Nor when they were included in state systems of interaction were they always managed so as to facilitate, increase, and grant these boons to its members. The objective results of state activity in these fields have even been opposite. Instead of protecting the freedom of its members the state has often suppressed it; instead of liberation of the unfree

---

[29] See my *Russia and the United States* (New York, 1944), Ch. 9; N. S. Timasheff, *The Great Retreat* (New York, 1946).

[30] See W. I. Thomas, *Primitive Behavior*, Ch. 14; R. H. Lowie, *The Origin of the State* (New York, 1927); Herbert Spencer, *The Principles of* *Sociology*, Vol. II, Parts IV and V; M. Kovalevsky, *Sociology* (Russian, St. Petersburg, 1911); L. Hobhouse, G. Wheeler, and M. Ginsberg, *The Material Culture*, quoted; R. Thurnwald, *Die Menschliche Gesellschaft* (Berlin, 1935), Vol. IV, Chps. 4-6; G. Landtman, *The Origin of the Inequality of the Social Classes* (Chicago, 1938), Ch.. 17.

the state often introduced and sanctioned slavery and serfdom; instead of facilitation of science and arts, religion and philosophy, the state often suppressed the cultivation of these values; instead of moralizing its members the state, and especially its government, has sometimes demoralized them; instead of improving health, vitality, and economic well-being the state has frequently ruined them by its incessant wars, its tyrannical laws and agencies, its stupid policies. Such negative results occur not only in the remote past but also in states today. For these reasons many social thinkers from Lao-tzu to anarchists of our day state that "the best state is that wnich governs least"; that "the more restrictions and prohibitions are in the empire, the poorer grow the people. The more weapons the people have, the more troubled is the state. The more mandates and laws are enacted, the more thieves and robbers will there be."[31] Once in a while we have some approach to the government of the people, by the people and for the people, with the state rendering important service in these fields, but such has been the exception rather than the rule.

Generally the relationships and values that make up the state system of interaction fluctuate quantitatively and qualitatively from state to state and from period to period. Quantitatively, in the past as well as in the present there have been "totalitarian" state systems that include in their network an enormous number of relationships and laws controlling almost all the interpersonal and intergroup relationships within the state. In such cases the state is transformed from a unibonded to a multibonded group. The Communist Soviet State of the first period of the Russian revolution especially, the Nazi, the Fascist states, and in a lesser degree other states of the present time are examples of this totalitarian state system controlling and regimenting what to eat, what to wear, where to live, what work to do, what to read, and what opinions to utter. Totalitarian state systems have also been common in the past. The state systems of ancient Egypt, Sparta, and other Greek states; of the

Roman Empire, especially after A.D. 300, the Byzantine Empire, ancient China in some periods of its history, ancient Mexico and Peru; most of the European states of the seventeenth and eighteenth centuries (the period of enlightened despotism and absolutism), are examples of totalitarian state systems.

Side by side with such states there have been the states with very few relationships included in their system of control. Most of the relationships and values in a population with such a "rarefied" network are controlled by the individuals and the non-state groups. The freedom of the population to manage its own affairs, from economic freedom to freedom of religion, press, unions, etc., is much larger under these states. The United States and Great Britain of the nineteenth century are conspicuous examples of such state systems. In the past also there have been states with comparatively few relationships controlled by the state system of interaction. The same state in the course of time may fluctuate between these two types, now becoming more totalitarian, now more *laissez faire, laissez passer*.

The *kind of relationships* of the state system of interaction also fluctuates from state to state, and within the same state from period to period. For instance in early states such relationship as that between the criminal and the victim were not controlled by the state and therefore did not enter its network of relationships but were left to be decided by the parties involved or by non-state groups. Later on this relationship was included in the state network and began to be controlled monopolistically by the state so that all other parties were prohibited from deciding the conflict. Even self-redress of the victim and of his party was forbidden. Most of the economic relationships of production, distribution, and consumption, and most of the relationships between the employer and the employees are not regimented by the "bourgeois" and "capitalist" state. They are outside of its network and are regulated by private persons and non-state groups. In a totalitarian state (Communist, Nazi, Fascist) and to a lesser degree in a "New Deal" state, especially in war time, controls are transferred

[31] Lao-tzu, *Canon of Reason and Virtue*, 9, in W.S.A. Pott, *Chinese Political Philosophy* (New York, 1925), p. 106. For the negative attitude of anarchists see P. Kropotkin, *The Speeches of a* *Rebel* (Russian, Moscow, 1919); M. Bakunin, *The State and Anarchy* (Russian, Moscow, 1919). See also V. Pareto, *Trattato*, quoted, pp. 618-635.

to the state. In many medieval states the religious relationships were included in the state system and prescribed by the state. With the development of freedom in religion such relationships were excluded from the state network and ceased to be controlled by the state. These examples show the fluctuation of the *qualitative kind* of relationships that make up the state system of interaction.

The causes of such a quantitative and qualitative fluctuation of the number and kind of relationships and values that make the state system of interaction will be discussed further (see Chapter 30).[32] For the present the above gives an adequate idea of the variable and relatively constant relationships, values-meanings-norms, with the respective vehicles and members that compose the state group.

It goes without saying that the state group is one of the most powerful groups, especially the state that is a "great power" and whose regimentation has increased to totalitarianism. The "great power" meets all the requirements of political power. (1) The state exerts an enormous influence upon all its members. Since the moment of birth every individual finds himself attached to a state from whose regulations he is unable to free himself. Like an invisible ghost, the state follows the individual everywhere to sanction his birth, regulate his marriage, and note his death. Through its numerous agents it interferes with many of a person's acts, even the most intimate. Its laws and orders determine which norms of behavior are obligatory, permitted, or criminal. The wires extending from the center through all the organs of the state constantly pull the individual in various directions. If he does not show a willingness to follow, he is coerced. Binding the citizens to itself, the state unites them at the same time to one another. During the periods of totalitarian hypertrophy, the state puts its stamp upon all the activities of its members. By a monopoly of the press and all the means of propaganda it molds the citizens in its own image. Constantly watching over them, it compels one and all to obey its ordinances. It removes from life those defying it and elevates to the top of the social ladder those it favors.

(2) The state groups consist usually of large memberships. (3) The state is generally well organized and has at its disposal a large apparatus. A many-storied hierarchy of its agents (officials, the police, the army), where everyone is assigned a definite function, is in its employ. There is a distribution of work between its various organs: legislative, executive, and judiciary. A vast fund of means of influencing human behavior, from persuasion to prison, gallows, firing squad, is at its disposal.

Finally, membership in the same state creates a solidarity among most of its members, except the oppressed part. Whether patriotism is to be regarded as a positive or negative force is a matter of preference, but that it wields power over men is beyond any doubt. A. Herzen was not far from the truth when he declared that "the state fatherland with its zealous patriotism, this cruel virtue, has been responsible for more blood spilling than all the other human vices together."[33] The strength of this sentiment is not denied even by its opponents. The passion with which they fight against it is the best proof of its existence. The sentiment of solidarity created by the state is just as strong now as ever.[34] The "holy union of the classes" proclaimed during the first and second World Wars, the collaboration between various economic and political groups in order to save the state, testifies to the hold of the patriotic sentiment even upon the people opposed to it.

This may explain sufficiently the power of the state over other groups as the family, church, political parties, professional unions, not to speak of smaller organizations. The great power of the state is recognized by most of the historians. Their histories have been largely the histories of the state groups, state governments, state personalities, state wars, state international relationships, and other state

---

[32] See the law of this fluctuation, its causes, the facts, and the literature in my *Dynamics*, Vol. III, Chps. 6, 7. Also my *Man and Society in Calamity* (New York, 1933), Ch. 7.

[33] A. Herzen, *Writings* (Russian), Vol. III, p. 159.

[34] J. Jaurès said correctly, "I never paid any serious attention to the paradox directed against the idea of patriotism. It is not dead; it has only changed." Jaurès, *New Army* (Russian translation, Petrograd, 1919), p. 236. See also his criticism of Marx's proposition that "the proletariat has no fatherland," p. 279.

actions. All other sociocultural groups taken together occupy a very modest place in these histories. Only recently a number of historians began to pay an increasing and long overdue attention to sociocultural history of other than state groups. Yet even now the bulk of histories written are mainly the history of the state Leviathans.

Great as it is, the state power is not as great as we are told by its apologists and enemies. While influenced by the state, the various other organizations influence it in turn. Their interdependence is an obvious fact. History is full of interactions not only among states themselves, but also between states and non-state groups. Their attacks and counter-attacks, alliances and counter-alliances constitute the most important fronts on the battlefield of history. The state decrees, which put into motion multitudes of people and direct them toward some goal, often clash with the orders issued by other groups in their interests. Conflicts result now in the victory of the state, now in that of the opposing non-state groups (religious, occupational, economic, language, and other groups).

We must not overestimate the power of the state and must not describe it in terms which Augustine gave as the properties of God.[35] If these thinkers can be believed the state is omnipotent and there is no power above it; all other powers have their origin in the sovereignty of the state government. It is omnipresent, impenetrable, immortal. It creates law and justice exclusively by its own will, and other groups become negligible units by comparison.

It is hardly necessary to say that all such conceptions are far from the truth. That the state is only one of numerous important groupings follows from the above and subsequent discussion of other important groups. That it is not eternal, the rise and fall of states, and the constant change of state governments, especially conspicuous in our time, shows conclusively. That it shares its power with others is shown by the influence exerted by numerous

organizations existing upon the same territory. That it is not always supreme and omnipotent is shown by its frequent control by other powers (the Catholic Church in the Middle Ages, for instance) and its inability to attain goals it has set for itself without the aid of other groups. State laws which are in open conflict with the interests of non-state groups remain frequently unenforced. *Quid leges sine moribus,* to repeat the pregnant statement of Tacitus. History is crowded with the graves of states destroyed by collision with non-state groups. It was the pressure of language and national groups that destroyed the empire states of the ancient East. During the Middle Ages the superiority of the state did not exist even on paper. During the nineteenth and twentieth centuries states like Turkey and Austria were wrecked by the language or nationality groups that wanted to create their own states (Rumania, Serbia, Bulgaria, Poland, Italy, Czechoslovakia, etc.). The unification of Germany and of Italy, the break-up of the Ottoman and Austrian Empires, the formation of numerous new states after World War I, all testify to the weakness of the state and the strength of the impact of other collectivities upon it. At present the existence of the state is menaced by the nationality, economic, occupational, and class groups.

The statement that "the state is the only creator of law" is as much a jurists' fiction as the statement that the state is an all-powerful organization. The fallacy was shown above, in Chapter 4. L. Petrajitsky convincingly demonstrated its absurdity. The criticism to which J. Cruet has subjected this theory is worthwhile restating here. The idea of the state as the only source of law (says Cruet) is an illusion, for which the dogmatic jurists pay dearly. After attributing to the state an omnipotence and limitless sovereignty, to which the individual is completely subjected, the jurists are forced later to assign to the individual a place independent of the state, small but assured, and must clothe him with "inalienable rights" and "natural rights." Such thinking results in ab-

---

[35] "Quid es ergo, Deus meus? O, Thou supreme, most powerful, most just, most secret, most mighty . . . upholding, filling and protecting, creating, nourishing and perfecting all things." *Confessions,* translated by Sir Tobie Matthew (London, 1923), p. 5. Many descriptions of the state government

differ little from this characterization. Perhaps in Plato's kingdom of ideas such a state and state government may exist; but on earth they have not been known, except as fictitious products of juridical minds.

surdity; the boundless sovereignty of the state appears to be limited in reality by the rights of the individual. *Où est la souveraineté? Il n'y a pas de souveraineté*—ironically concludes Cruet.

He shows further that law is not exclusively established by the state; in actual practice there are numerous norms, created sometimes against the will of the state and often not sanctioned by it. The official law of the state has been largely created not by the state legislative organs, but by the judge, by a scholarly jurist, by the church, or by occupational groups. Such is the praetor's law in Rome, the civil law of the Moslems, the Canon Law of the Middle Ages, the common law of the Anglo-Saxon countries, the occupational guild law of the Middle Ages, and so on. Norms created by the non-state groups often collide with the state law and turn it into a dead letter. The norms created by the non-state group in England made it a constitutional country without a constitution. On the other hand, a number of the state constitutions and laws, promulgated by the state but opposed by non-state groups, have been rendered ineffective, unenforceable, and dead, like three French constitutions of 1790-95, none of which survived; like the charters of 1814 and 1830 in France; or the prohibition law in the United States.[36]

Equally fallacious is the ideology of those who believe that a change in the forms of the political organization of a state (from a monarchy to a republic or to any other form) is sufficient to remove all evils. They forget that the reconstruction of the state organization is the repair of only one of the many systems of interaction of which a population is composed. At best, such reconstruction may produce some changes; at worst, it will remain on paper, powerless to break down the resistance of other collectivities.[37] The same is true of the prevalent belief that an Atlantic Charter or the United Nations Charters, as agreements among the states, are sufficient to insure a lasting peace.

The anti-statists, who see only evil in the state and hope through its destruction to put an end to all inequalities, exploitations, and oppression, are no nearer the truth than the enthusiastic statists. Inequalities and exploitations spring also from other groupings. The oppression of the majority by the minority is not a monopoly of the state, but exists as well in other organized groups. The destruction of the state will not put an end to other forms of evil. The assumption of the functions of the state by the syndicates or churches will only turn them into states replete with the evils which the syndicalists attribute to the state.

Besides the totalitarian and liberal types, there are other differences in state government. They can be classified in a great many ways: autocracies and democracies; monarchies and republics; or (following Plato) on the basis of the dominant passion of the government: (1) aristocracy, or government by wise philosophers seeking for truth and justice; (2) timocracy, or military government motivated by the passion of honor; (3) oligarchy, or government by the rich; (4) democracy, or government by the majority desiring freedom; (5) tyranny, or the government of a despot, cruel, cynical, motivated by lust for power. Also worthy of note is the classification of Aristotle repeated by Polybius, based upon the number of rulers, as states with government by one, monarchy being its good form and tyranny its bad form; of the few, with aristocracy as a good form and oligarchy as a bad form; of the many, democracy and mob rule being respectively its good and bad forms. Other classifications can be found in competent texts and treatises on constitutional law and political science.[38]

The state groups are usually closed groups. The majority of the members of every state are born into it and become members automatically, regardless of their wishes. Likewise, the laws of the majority of the states do not permit change or cessation of membership by the

---

[36] See J. Cruet, *"La vie du droit et L'impuissance des lois* (Paris, 1908) pp. 1-10, 336, *passim*. See also L. Petrajitsky, *The Theory of Law*, quoted. See the treatment of the unofficial forms of law in M. Bourquin, "Les Transformations du concept juridique de l'Etat," *Bulletin de l'Institut de Sociologie de Solvay* (December, 1913).

[37] See V. Pareto, *Trattato*, quoted, Vol. II, p. 597 and ff.

[38] See R. V. Peel and J. S. Roucek (editors), *Introduction to Politics* (New York, 1941), particularly D. Fleming's chapter on "Forms and Types of Government"; V. O. Key, *Politics, Parties and Pressure Groups* (New York, 1942); G. Mosca, *The Ruling Class*, quoted.

choice of a person. A member remains a member regardless of his wishes. Only a few states, like the United States, give a citizen the possibility of renouncing his membership. In most states there are narrow channels of naturalization and denaturalization, but the number of the persons that are naturalized or denaturalized is relatively insignificant. Only in a rapidly growing state needing rapid increase of population like the United States in the preceding centuries, can a large number of immigrants be naturalized. Such states have been few and are rapidly declining in number. Even in the United States, with a reduction of immigration to a mere fraction of what it used to be, the number of the naturalized citizens is bound to decline greatly.

There may be a catastrophic change of citizenship on a mass scale when a whole state or large portion of its population is annexed by a victorious state or is given to another state. Such mass transference of citizenship occurs usually in times of war, or as an aftermath. In most cases it is coercive transfer in which the wishes of the transferred population are neither consulted nor considered. Such transfer does not make the state groups open groups (see further Chapter 23).

V. Differentiation into Occupational Groups

The totality of interacting individuals having the same or similar occupational work comprises the occupational group. Its core is made up of those individuals who stay in their occupation for a considerable length of time and for whom the occupational work furnishes their means of subsistence. In many occupations there are also the individuals that shift from one work to another, staying a short time in each, or those for whom the occupational work is not their chief means of subsistence. Such persons are, so to speak, temporary fellow travelers but not the mainstays of occupational groups.

In a population with several occupations, this occupational differentiation exerts a tremendous influence, first of all in the form of *occupational selection*. Each occupation tends to select as its members only those individuals that can perform it satisfactorily, rejecting those who do not meet its requirements. This is especially true of the qualified occupations. Persons having a poor voice cannot become Metropolitan Opera singers; the weak cannot become heavyweight champions; the stupid do not qualify for the occupations requiring intellectual ability; the careless do not make good accountants or bookkeepers; the inarticulate do not become eminent orators, and so on. Practically all occupations perform, to some extent, this selection.[39] Consequently the members of each occupation have similar traits (partly hereditary, partly acquired), while the members of widely different occupations differ considerably from one another.

A durable occupational work molds the body, mind, and behavior of its members. At the basis of this transforming influence of occupational work lies the principle "function creates organ." An act performed by an organism retroactively changes it. When the same occupational operations are performed from day to day for many years, they effectively modify the mental, moral, social, physiological, and anatomical properties of their members in accordance with the nature and requirements of the occupational work. Each occupation tends thus to remake its members in its own image. And the longer an individual stays in the same occupation the deeper is the transformation.

A long-time professor of physics looks at the world in a way fundamentally different from that of a long-time priest; both view it differently from a long-time factory worker, a druggist, a farmer, a sailor, a banker, a king, a prostitute. From anatomical and hystological differences of the skin of the manual and mental workers, overdevelopment and underdevelopment of muscles, glands, and organs of the body, of the specific occupational diseases, of the rate of suicide, mental disease, and duration of life, to psychological differences in sensation, perception, reproductive

[39] For the details and data see my *Mobility* (New York, 1927), pp. 202 ff.

imagination, attention, feeling, emotionality, will power, and the total mental, moral, and social way of life—in all these respects the members of the same occupation display tangible similarities while the members of different occupations show dissimilarities.[40]

A public prosecutor looks at the world from the standpoint of a code of law, a priest in the perspective of his religion, a pharmacist in the light of his prescriptions, a banker from the viewpoint of money, a farmer from the standpoint of agricultural values. Many ideological differences between the members of different occupations are due to these differences. If priests are predominantly idealistic in their philosophy while the workers in contemporary factories are inclined toward a mechanistic and materialistic outlook, one of the reasons for this difference is the divergent nature of their occupations. If in Germany and in other countries before the World War I the German Social-Democratic Party recruited most of its members from the hereditary or long-time workers in factories,[41] the reason for that is to be found in their occupation. If the mental outlook of a proletarian and of a capitalist has been different in many countries, one of the main reasons has been the dissimilarity of their occupations.

If the same occupation is performed in a family from generation to generation, its selective and retroactive influence becomes so deep

that such persons become distinct "social types," as the "mountaineer" or "hunter of the steppes," often taken as a racial type. E. Demolins has demonstrated this in regard to many "social types" in France and elsewhere.[42] Notable differences of various caste populations where the occupation is hereditary have been due to the hereditary occupation of each caste and not to racial factors, as several scholars have claimed. Likewise many differences between men and women are rooted not in the biological differences between the sexes, but in the different occupations of men and women, which in many populations have been perpetuated from generation to generation. With women taking occupations previously reserved to men and men taking work previously performed only by women, many of these differences tend to weaken and disappear.

This enormous influence of occupation explains why the differentiation into various occupational groups appeared long ago, almost at the dawn of the known human history. It is found among many preliterate populations already organized into guilds; it existed in all the historical societies in ancient Egypt, Babylonia, Persia, India, China, in ancient Greece and Rome, and on through the Middle Ages to the occupational unions of the present time.[43] There are more than 10,000 different

[40] Experimental data are given in my "Influence of Occupation Upon Human Behavior and a Reflexology of Occupational Groups," Journal of Experimental Reflexology, Psychology and Neurology, Vol. II (Russian, St. Petersburg, 1922). See further Langerock, "Professionalism: a Study in Professional Deformation," AJS, Vol. XXI, pp. 30-40; R. F. Hoxie, "Class Conflict in America," AJS, Vol. XIII, pp. 776-81; T. Veblen, The Theory of the Leisure Class (New York, 1912), also his "Industrial and Pecuniary Employments," Publications of American Economic Association (February, 1901); for farmers, peasants, and agriculturists see Sorokin and Zimmerman, Principles of Rural-Urban Sociology, Chps. 3, 12, 14, passim, and Sorokin, Zimmerman, and Galpin, A Systematic Source Book in Rural Sociology, 3 Vols., passim. For many groups see G. Schmoller, Grundriss der Volkswirtschaftslehre (Berlin, 1901), Vol. I, pp. 391-411, Vol. II (1904), pp. 496-557; A. Bauer, Les classes sociales (Paris, 1902), pp. 32 ff; L. Deschesne, La specialization et ses consequences (Paris, 1901); A. Uhl, Arbeitsgliederung und Ar-

beitsvershiebung (Jena, 1924); A. Obrdlik, Povolani (Prague, 1917).
[41] See the data in A. Lurie, The Composition of Proletariat (Sostav Proletariata, Petrograd, 1918).
[42] See his Les français d'aujourd'hui and Comment la route crée le type social, quoted; see also the works of Le Play and of his school, in my Theories, Ch. 3.
[43] See T. Mommsen, De collegiis et sodaliciis Romanorum (Kiel, 1843); E. Ziebarth, Das griechische Vereinswesen (Leipzig, 1896); M. San Nicolo, Aegyptisches Vereinswesen (München, 1913); I. Mendelsohn, "Guilds in Babylonia and Assyria," JAOS (1940); J. P. Waltzing, Etude historique sur les corporations professionneles (Louvain, 1896), 2 Vols; Saint-Leon E. Martin, Histoire des corporations de métier (Paris, 1922); J. M. Lambert, Two Thousand Years of Guild Life (Hull, 1891); K. Bücher, Die Enstehung der Volkswirtschaft (Leipzig, 1921); C. Bouglé "Remarques sur le régime des castes," L'Année sociologique (1900), pp. 28-44; V. Sviatlovsky, Occupational Unions of Labor (Professionalnyie rabotchie soiusy, St. Petersburg, 1908). On the

occupations and each occupation practically is organized into a union. Similar occupations federate and unite into larger unions, and these in turn into the gigantic nation-wide and even international occupational unions of labor, agriculture, management, capitalists, manufacturers, scientists, artists, and other professions.

Occupational federations and unions like the American Federation of Labor and C.I.O., the trade union organization of Great Britain, the General Confederation of Labor in France, or the national and international associations of farmers and peasants, manufacturers and the capitalists have a large membership. They also have important funds of meanings-values-norms at their disposal, a rich assortment of vehicles, including wealth, and other means of influencing human behavior, from strikes to riots and revolutions. They are well organized and solidary within their own groups; consequently they have always exerted a tremendous influence upon their own members, outside individuals, and groups, and on the whole course of sociocultural processes. Not infrequently they have challenged non-occupational groups, including the powerful state groups, and have come off victorious. For these reasons the occupational groups have been among the most powerful groups on the battle front of history.

Their influence at the present time can be observed in many forms. Almost daily we observe how, under the pressure of occupational groups, state governments are forced to comply with the demands of labor, farmer, and capitalist groups. Who can overlook the gigantic national and international conflicts and alliances of larger occupational groups with one another and with the non-occupational collective unities? Reverberations of these activities of occupational groups are felt by almost everyone and their echoes fill the world. Beyond the boundaries of nations we now hear "Proletarians of the World, unite!"; "Manufacturers of all countries, unite!"; or "White Collar Workers, unite!" International occupational solidarity thus becomes an increasing menace to the states.

Finally, the enormous pressure of the occupational groups is manifest in the contemporary social movements of guild socialism, revolutionary syndicalism, and others that aspire after a fundamental reorganization of social life and institutions upon the basis of occupational differentiation. The theorizers of workers' occupational movements, of guild socialism, of labor syndicalism well understand, even overestimate, the enormous role of occupation in determining one's bodily and mental characteristics, interests and behavior, solidarity and ideology. Understanding this they attempt to use it for a reorganization of the social world in conformity with their occupational ideology. They claim that occupational differentiation and grouping is unavoidable, basic, and natural. All other groupings (by states or religion) are neither necessary, natural, nor desirable; they are all to be replaced by occupational federations. These syndicates are to replace states and most of the other social groups and differentiations.

The revolutionary syndicalism brings to life the class struggle in its purest form [says H. Lagardelle, one of the leaders of French syndicalism]. In opposition to the parliamentary state the working class creates bodies, adapted to its struggle as syndicates, and exchanges of labor. The progress of this "State within the State" is marked by the widening of its functions and institutions to the detriment of the functions and institutions of the bourgeois world. The labor organization, taking from the bourgeois state everything which may be of use to it, will continue to grow until it replaces the old state forms. The workers' struggle, as understood by the French syndicalists, must have as its goal the appropriation by the syndicates of all the state functions relating to the labor world.[44]

The occupational organizations are regarded by the syndicalists as the only powerful organs, capable of destroying the present state. . . . Instead of the chaos of anarchism, syndicalism places as the cornerstone of society the power of the occupational organizations.[45]

The state of the future can be nothing else than

occupational unions of the employers and capitalists see A. Kaminka, *Predpinimatelskie soiusy* (St. Petersburg, 1909); A. Goldstein, *Syndicaty i tresty* (Moscow, 1912); A. M. Carr-Saunders and P. A. Wilson, *The Professions* (Oxford, 1933).

[44] H. Lagardelle, "Revolutionary Syndicalism in France" in *Problems of the Day* (Russian, Moscow, 1906); also his "Le fascisme," *Encyclopédie Française*, Vol. X, pp. 84-87.

[45] I. A. Pokrovsky, *The Problems of Civil Law* (Russian, St. Petersburg, 1917), pp. 143-144.

an organization of labor and of toilers. . . . The syndicalist organization is the plan of a new life order. It will concentrate into its hands all the industry together with all other functions of government. The syndicates are the embryo of the future order of things. Only to them belongs the task of organizing production, free from a coercion of government.[46]

The syndicate must become the synthetic organ, embracing the personality of the worker in all its aspects: as a citizen performing political functions, as an economic being earning his daily bread, and as a spiritual individual, says Labriola.[47]

In short, the syndicalist occupational grouping, according to the ideology of the syndicalists, must become the basis of the future society. The other groupings are condemned to death, and syndicalism alone will continue to live, guaranteeing the elimination of exploitation and the realization of the earthly paradise where freedom, peace, and plenty will rule.

Recognizing the importance of the occupational grouping we must, however, point out that the syndicalists overestimate its power and err in assuming that all the other groupings can be replaced by the occupational syndicate. Like many other ideologists of this or that group who do not see the manifold character of social differentiation and the variety of the powerful unibonded and multibonded

groups, they see only the occupational groups, and believe these will supplant all the others in the future society. In this sociological monism they greatly err. Occupational groups and solidarity have not replaced and cannot eliminate the continued existence and solidarity of the racial, sex, age, kinship, territorial, language, the state, religious, family, and other unibonded and multibonded groups. Each of them and all of them are strong enough to defeat the occupational groups in such an effort. The first and then the second World War have shown this. They played an ironical joke on all the syndicalists. The patriotism of the state and of the nation which they declared dead long ago proved to be very much alive; so much so that most of the syndicalists who denounced it before the war, turned themselves into very ardent patriots of their nation. If anything syndicalism itself was defeated and reduced to very modest influence.

Furthermore, their dimly drawn outline of the future occupational or guild or syndicalist society has failed to secure the elimination of exploitation, the establishment of the equality, freedom, abundance, peace, and happiness they expected from it. The complete tutelage of the occupational syndicate over man's whole life would mean nothing but a replacement of the often limited tutelage of the state by that of a new and more monstrous totalitarian Leviathan—the occupational state and government. It would exchange an old, limited,

---

[46] E. Leone, *Syndicalism* (Russian, Moscow, 1909), pp. 38-39.

[47] An excellent collection of the main works of the French syndicalists—G. Sorel, E. Pouget, H. Lagardelle, Leone, Berth, and others—is given in the Russian volumes, *Syndicalism* (St. Petersburg, 1908); a very good history of the French syndicalist movement is given in N. Kritskaia and N. Lebedeff, *History of the Syndicalist Movement in France* (Russian, Moscow, 1908); French works include E. Pouget, *La Confédération Générale du Travail* (Paris, second edition, n. d.); L. Jouhaux, *Le Syndicalisme et la C.G.T.* (Paris, 1920); H. Lagardelle, *Le socialisme ouvrier* (Paris, 1911); Griffuelhes, *L'action syndicaliste* (Paris, 1908); E. Berth, *Les nouveaux aspects du socialism* (Paris, 1908), and his later work in which he renounces some of his previous ideas, *Les Mefaits des intellectuels* (Paris, 1914); G. Sorel, *Reflexions sur la violence*, 3rd ed. (Paris, 1912) and his later work where he also renounces some of his earlier ideas, *Les illusions du progrés* (Paris, 1911); for German-proletarian and capitalist-syndicalism, A.

Thal, "Le syndicalism allemand," in *Grand Revue* (March 10, 1911). For English-American guild socialism and syndicalism see P. F. Brissenden, *The I.W.W.* (New York, 1919); J. G. Brooks, *American Syndicalism and the I.W.W.* (New York, 1913); J. Spargo, *Syndicalism, Industrial Unionism and Socialism* (New York, 1913); M. I. Cole, "Guild Socialist Movement in Great Britain," in American *Labor Year Book*, Vol. III (1919-1920); G. D. H. Cole, *The Next Ten Years in British Social and Economic Policy* (New York, 1929); *Guild Socialism Restated* (London, 1920); N. Carpenter, *Guild Socialism* (New York, 1922). Among the broad and legal theorizers of the state and occupational organizations see L. Duguit, *Law and the Modern State* (New York, 1919); I. Pokrovsky's *Problems of Civil Law*, quoted; P. Proudhon, *Idée générale de la révolution au XIX-e siècle* (Oeuvres complètes, Paris, 1868); G. Taylor, *Guild State, Its Principles and Possibilities* (New York, 1919); H. W. Laidler, *Social-Economic Movements* (New York, 1944).

constitutional state government for a new, un-limited, absolutistic government of occupational groups. This is shown by the experiments of the Communist Government in Russia, of the Corporative Fascist state in Italy and of the corporative government of Nazi Germany. Lenin[48] and leaders of Fascism and partly Nazism wanted also to destroy the non-occupational "bourgeois" state. In creating a "corporative state," based mainly on occupational and labor groups, they realized to a considerable extent the ideals of guild socialism and syndicalism. And yet, instead of all the blessings expected, they created the most monstrous Leviathan, the totalitarian state, that turned the previously free and semi-free proud citizens into mere puppets of the government, autocratically regimented in belief and action, behavior and relationship by the corporative government. No other proof of the illusions of the syndicalists in this field is necessary. These results are comprehensible, when one adequately grasps social differentiation into groups. In such manifold relationships, no single group—be it the state, the occupational, the language, the kinship, or any other group—can take upon itself the task of serving all the needs of human beings without an elimination of their freedom, autonomy, and choice. Such a task would have been possible only if all humans were alike in their tastes, thoughts, beliefs, preferences, inclinations, actions, and so on. In brief they must be similar in all respects. But as a matter of fact they are not. Within the same syndicate some members will be positivists, others mystics, some realists, others futurists, some religious, others atheists, some pacifists, others militarists, some Negroes, others whites, some rich, others poor, some ruling, others ruled, etc. The syndicalist society is not able to satisfy all the different tastes and needs of its mem-bers. Either it will be forced pitilessly to coerce its members to accept its uniform standards, or other organizations will emerge, re-establishing the very inequalities which the syndicalists aimed to destroy. Moreover, as long as the syndicalists admit the necessity of a division into the ruling "initiative minority" and the ruled "passive mass," they introduce inequality between the ruling and ruled with unavoidable consequences of oppression and exploitation of a ruled majority by the active minority with constant struggle between the two. The Communist, Fascist, and Nazi experiments have strikingly corroborated this.

To summarize: The occupational groups are one of the most powerful groups, but their power must not be exaggerated nor their possibilities illusionistically idealized. The occupational group is one of the most indispensable co-ordinates for a definition of the sociocultural position in an individual, a group, or a sociocultural process.

In some populations, like the caste population of India or medieval society, the upper occupational groups are so closed that only a few outsiders can slip into the privileged occupational strata. In other populations like ours occupational groups are theoretically open; but actually the more privileged among these are closed or semi-closed. Formally, there are few religious or legal obstacles to entering any occupation; but actually, due to occupational selection, most of the upper and middle class occupations are inaccessible to an overwhelming majority of the rank and file of the people of lower occupational groups. Theoretically every American boy can become President of the United States; actually, 99.999 per cent of them cannot become even a private secretary to the secretary of the President of the United States.

VI. Differentiation into Economic Interest Groups

Closely related to the occupational group but not identical with it is the differentiation of population into various economic interest

[48] See V. Lenin, *The State and Revolution* (St. Petersburg, 1918).

groups. Among these the most important are groups of the rich and the poor; of the employers-capitalists and the employees-wage earners; of the producers and the consumers; of the sellers and buyers; of the owners and the non-owners: renters and tenants. This differentiation often assumes an aspect of social stratification (see further, Chapter 15), but does not entirely coincide with it. In many populations the groups of buyers and sellers, consumers and producers, owners and renters, employers and employees do not form a hierarchy of superior and inferior, or dominating and subordinated. In such populations they are the groups with different economic interests, but not stratified into a hierarchy of ranks and authorities. Neither do they display a one-sided dependence upon one another. Buyers or consumers depend upon the sellers or producers mutually, as owners and tenants each need the other. Consequently these groups are different from the preceding ones. They are closely related to the occupational division because, as a rule, most of the unskilled occupational groups are poor wage-earners and renters; the semi-skilled are somewhat richer; the skilled still richer; the professional and small business are still higher on the economic ladder, with a larger per cent of employers and owners; while the large land owners, qualified professional, governmental, and big business groups are usually at the top of the scale as capitalists, employers, and owners.

In spite of this tangible correlation with occupational groups, the economic differentiation goes along essentially different trajectories. Among the members of the same occupation there are the poor and the rich doctors, engineers, artists, farmers, scientists, businessmen, workers, literati, clergymen, state officials, and so on. Likewise the groups of producers and consumers, sellers and buyers, owners and tenants are made up of the most different occupations; and vice versa, almost every occupational group is simultaneously selling or buying, producing or consuming, owning or renting.

Economic interests differ more widely from those of race, sex, age, language, religion, and state. The differentiation is in fact *sui generis*. The state of being poor or being rich, being a seller or buyer, producer or consumer, owner or tenant, exerts an enormous influence upon the physical, mental, moral, and other characteristics of a person, upon his values and interests, his behavior and way of living.[49] However different persons may be in other respects, if and when they are equally rich or poor they cannot help becoming similar to one another in a great many respects. Regardless of occupation, the poor in the cities will be found dwelling in the slums of undesirable districts, renting poor rooms, attending poor cafeterias, wearing cheap clothing, having similar diversions and amusements, convictions and beliefs, sympathies and antipathies, forms of activities, and modes of living. A large number of investigations clearly discloses the standardizing effects of poverty upon the personality, behavior, and way of life of people of various creeds, races, nationalities, citizenship, and occupations. Let us consider a few examples.

D. Aeth made an analysis of group differentiation in modern England, from which he drew the conclusion that the standard of life is largely determined by the size of one's income, irrespective of one's occupation or other differences. He recognized seven classes. Those of the first class live in the cellars or filthy rooms in the dirtiest sections of the city; drinking is their pastime; their average income is eighteen shillings per week. Those of the second class live in small apartments and have few changes of clothes; clerks, small employees, and salesmen with an income of twenty-five shillings comprise this class. The third class live in clean five-room apartments, have visiting friends on holidays, are fairly intelligent and give serious attention to work; among these are qualified workers, small office-holders, senior clerks, and some professionals having an income of 45 shillings.

The fourth class have a comfortable apartment, elegant clothes, and a butler. They read magazines, are interested in social life, have been usually graduated from a technical school. These are storekeepers, engineers, commercial agents, teachers, priests, etc. They earn about three pounds a week. The fifth class have a high school education, polished manners, enjoy social visits, late suppers, and cards. They pretend to know much, have a sense of superiority and dignity, and are interested in social, scientific, and cultural affairs. They are composed of small manufacturers, liberal professions, etc. Their average income is

[49] See the facts and the literature in my *Mobility*, Chps. 10-12.

300 pounds a year. The sixth class pay rent from 60 to 80 pounds a year. They are university graduates, their mode of life is fashionable and cultural; they participate in social affairs. They are composed of professionals, high functionaries, big businessmen, etc., with an average income of 600 pounds. The seventh class consists of members who play an influential social role, have a higher education, and an average income of 2000 pounds.[50]

D. Aeth's findings were corroborated later by Descamps' investigation of the same phenomenon. Classifying the social strata a little differently, Descamps outlined in greater detail the similarity of habits, mode of life, and behavior of persons having the same income.[51] Thus persons having a small capital —small bosses, technical employees, teachers, farmers, clerks, bookkeepers, traveling salesmen, priests, etc., persons of various occupations and groups, constituting the so-called "lower middle class"—usually finish a secondary school; their general education continues till they are 14-15 years old, after which they receive a technical education in a technical school. They start to earn a living at the age of 18. In such families servants are employed; they are well educated in special fields; their apartments are decent; they are members of some clubs; they are provided with a pension for old age; and they keep traditions alive.

G. Schmoller came to the conclusion that the size of the income was the basis of class differentiation in German society.[52] A similar richness or poverty makes people solidary with each other and antagonistic toward other groups of different status. This fact has been observed by eminent social thinkers. A state or society divided into rich and poor "is not one but two states [says Plato]; the one of poor, the other of rich men; and they are living on the same spot and always conspiring against one another."[53] With the contrast

of the rich and poor "arises a city, not of freemen, but of masters and slaves, the one despising, the other envying," remarks Aristotle.[54] "Everywhere the poor has an envy and animosity toward the rich. He wants a general revolution; revolt and riots nourish him; he is not apprehensive of any loss because he has nothing to lose," observes Sallustius.[55] Subsequent investigators have uniformly confirmed this spontaneous or organized solidarity of the poor and of the rich and their mutual antagonism. Says Schäffle, "The rich unite by virtue of having common interests, growing out of possession of property. The dispossessed are held together by the struggle for a living wage and by their common hatred of propertied classes."[56]

People similar in other respects, religion, state, profession, etc., but sharply distinct with regard to possession of wealth, have sufficient grounds for mutual conflicts, animosity, envy, exploitation, and struggle.

Wealth to the poor is a striking symptom of the difference in social position between themselves and the rich. A wealthy man "is not one of ours"—such is the logic of the masses. A thoughtful observer could see the striking effects of this logic during the Russian and other revolutions. A decent suit was very often a sufficient cause for placing its owner among the bourgeois and arousing hostile acts on the part of the poor toward him. In order to free themselves of many embarrassments and annoyances, the rich began to dress during the Revolution in the style of the proletariat. In latent form the antagonism between the rich and the poor exists always and manifests itself in hundreds of silent conflicts. In times of social upheavals it explodes strikingly and splits into the inimical armies of the rich and poor members of the same religious, occupational, language, race, sex, age, state, and other groups. In any revolution, whatever the complex alignment of the conflicting groups may be, there is always the "front line" between

---

[50] See D. Aeth, "Present Tendencies of Class Differentiation," *The Sociological Review*, Vol. IV (1910), pp. 267-276.

[51] P. Descamps, *La hierarchie des classes en Angleterre* (Paris, 1914).

[52] G. Schmoller, *Was verstehen Wir unter dem Mittelstande* (Gottingen, 1897). For a vast amount of data and the literature on this question see my *Mobility*, Chps. 3-6.

[53] Plato, *The Republic*, in *The Works of Plato* (New York, The Dial Press, n.d.), p. 317.

[54] Aristotle, *Politics*, Book IV, Ch. 2, § 6-7.

[55] See many similar observations by the Greek and Roman thinkers and description of the conflicts between the rich and the poor in ancient Greece and Rome in R. Pöhlmann's excellent *Geschichte der sozialen Frage und Sozialismus in der antiken Welt* (München, 1912).

[56] A. Schäffle, *Bau und Leben der socialen Körpers* (Tubingen, 1896) Vol. I, p. 93.

the rich and the poor. And the struggle along this front line is one of the basic fronts in every revolution.[57]

In the Russian Revolution of 1917 and subsequent years one of the main conditions determining one's position in the alignment of forces struggling for power, was the possession or lack of property. The poor, consciously or unconsciously, were on the side of the Soviets, the rich in the camp of their enemies. This took place alike in the city and the village in various parts of Russia. The early policies of the Soviet Government were for the sake of the poor. Hence the systematic deepening of the abyss between the rich and the poor, the provocation of the latter to appropriation of the property of the first, the encouragement of the "village poor," "city poor," the constant use of the term "poverty" and its derivatives ("The Village Poor" is the name of a newspaper; sentences like the following "From the time the poorer classes dared to take the power (government) into their own hands"—were common in the Bolshevik literature). The Russian Revolution, like many others, was a spontaneous attempt on the part of the poorer classes to divide and redistribute the wealth, in order to realize a communism of more equal sharing of the goods of life.

The differentiation into the rich and the poor has appeared early in the preliterate populations[58] and has been perennial ever since, varying in degree and contrasts.

The number of the poor is enormous (though as a rule poorly organized); while the number of the rich is smaller but better organized. Each of the contrasting groups is solidary; each has to fight for tangible economic values and "all that money can buy." Each group has a different but potentially vast assortment of means of influencing human conduct. For these reasons this differentiation is one of the most important "fronts" of history. If the poor were organized better the sociocultural role of this grouping would be immeasurably greater than it has actually been. Even so, the differentiation into the poor and the rich is perennial

and significant enough to be included among the most important groupings. In view of the effective influence of poverty and riches upon human life, membership in these groups becomes one of the co-ordinates defining one's position in the sociocultural universe.

The groups of the rich are nearer to closed groups while the groups of the poor are more nearly of an open type. Anyone who so desires can easily become a member of the poor group. Most of those who want to be rich cannot fulfill their wish. In most populations there are no legal prohibitions to becoming rich. But there are hundreds of obstacles for the poor in climbing up the economic ladder, and only a small number of those born poor succeed in becoming rich. In a few rapidly developing countries like the United States this number has been larger; but even there, in the course of time, the opportunities seem to be decreasing. My studies and those of Taussig and Joslyn show that the per cent of the poor-born millionaires and multimillionaires in the present generation has notably declined in comparison with that of the generation around the middle of the nineteenth century.[59] Only in the periods of profound revolutions can a sizable group of the poor become rich. What is said of the poor and the rich can be said of other economic groupings: the buyers and sellers, consumers and producers, employees and employers, and many other varieties of economic interest groups. All consumers as consumers have similar economic interests to buy as good commodities for as reasonable price as possible. This makes them a solidary group, leads to an organization or to conduct as if they were organized into such a group; imposes a series of economic, political, ethical, and other similarities upon their minds and behavior; opposes them often to the groups of the sellers and producers; and in brief, notably conditions their conduct and mentality. In multifarious ways such groups have been among the important groups that have most tangibly influenced the course of sociocultural processes.

---

[57] See the facts in my *Sociology of Revolution* (Philadelphia, 1924).

[58] See besides the quoted works of W. I. Thomas, R. Thurnwald, and others; G. Landtman, *The Origin of the Inequality of the Social Classes* (Chicago, 1938) Ch. 4.

[59] See Sorokin, "American Millionaires and Multimillionaires," *SF*, III (1925), pp. 627-640; F. W. Taussig and C. S. Joslyn, *American Business Leaders* (New York, 1932); S. Riemer, "Soziale Aufstieg und Klassenschiftung," *Archiv für Sozialwissenschaft und Sozialpolitik*, Vol. LXVII (1932), pp. 531-560.

Chapter 12. Differentiation of Human Population into Sociocultural Groups (Continued)

I. Differentiation into Political Parties

By a political party is meant an organized "grouping of individuals for the attainment of a political goal."[1] The concrete nature of this political goal (or set of meanings-values-norms) of the party widely fluctuates, depending upon the conditions in which a given party functions. It is formulated in the platform or the program of the party. Ordinarily it concerns itself with the government of the state, with its personnel, with the political organization of the population, with a set of economic problems urgent in the existing conditions, and with a wide variety of other values mainly but not exclusively of a political and economic nature. Some of the parties have a long series of goal-values in their platforms, while the others, called sometimes a league, association, or union, have only one central goal for realization of which the party is specially organized. The Republican and Democratic, the Communist, Fascist, or Nazi party, the Liberal and Conservative, the Socialist, the Agrarian, the Farmer-Labor, the Centrists, the Christian Democrats, are examples of contemporary parties. Under different names political parties have existed in practically all historical societies and in less crystallized form in many preliterate populations. As soon as two or more organized

factions appear, each endeavors to attain this or that political, economic, or other goal, as a change of the chief, king, or president, of the high administrative personnel, of the political organization, or taxation and distribution of wealth. In regard to many problems there often occurs a difference of opinion among the council of the chiefs or elders, or among the assembly of the grown-up population. The partisans of each opinion group together and try to overcome the opposed group by various means, beginning with argument and ending sometimes with coercion and fighting. All such groups have the basic characteristics of a political party as a temporary league with one central goal and program. As soon as such groups are organized and endeavor to realize their purposes, political parties are established and the population differentiates along party lines.

In clearly developed form they existed in ancient Egypt, for instance the party of the reformer Pharaoh Akhnaton and that of his opponents; in ancient Greece, for instance the party of Pericles and of his opponents; in ancient Rome, for instance the party of Julius Caesar and of his opponents, of Marius, and of Sulla,[2] and in practically all historical socie-

---

[1] M. Ostrogorski, *La démocratie et les parties politiques* (Paris, 1912), p. 642.

[2] On the parties and their struggle in Rome see F. B. Marsh, *A History of the Roman World from*

ties. This means that differentiation along party lines exists not only in recent times or among urbanized and industrialized populations, but is a perennial form of social differentiation.

In some populations like the United States there is a system of mainly two political parties; in others there is a multitude of these, as in most European countries before the war. In a few countries there has been only one legalized, dictatorial party, like the Communist or the Nazi party in Russia and Germany. However, in non-legalized activity there are always parties of the opponents of such a dictatorial party.

The differentiation into political parties is *sui generis*; it does not coincide with any other unibonded grouping. Some may claim that it is identical either with the religious or occupational-economic differentiation. Both identifications are without foundation. Among the members of either the Republican or Democratic party we find persons belonging to different religions, including atheists. And vice versa, the members of the same religion are scattered among different political parties. There is more question about the Communist or Socialist or Nazi parties which are often called Communist or Socialist or the Nazi religions. Though some of the Socialists, Communists, and Nazis may be inimical to established religion, and though some of these may attempt to make out of their party a religion, nevertheless, at no time have these parties coincided with religious groups. Whatever the personal opinions of some socialists, their official programs have always declared that "everyone may believe in anything he likes; as a social-democrat, one may be a Catholic, materialist, or atheist; this has nothing to do with the party. In questions of faith we must maintain absolute neutrality."[3] This platform of the German Social-Democratic

party has been typical for practically all Socialist parties. In spite of the persecution of religions by the Communist Party, the official position of the Communist Party is that "religion is a private affair; the freedom of religion must be guaranteed."[4] At the present time this official program of separation of the party and religion is an accomplished fact. Not only now but even in the earlier period of the Communist revolution, a minority of the members of the party continued clandestinely to belong to the Russian Orthodox or other religious groups. For the atheistic members whose ultimate system of values coincided with those of the Communist party it was then a kind of a multibonded, political-religious group. But this "cumulation" is largely dissociated now, and therefore was a merely temporary phenomenon. Even then such a majority has given not identification of religious and political groups but a temporary cumulation of their bonds. The same can be said of the Nazi party. In addition, as we shall see in the next section, the character of the meanings-values-norms of religion is such that it cannot coincide with those of the political party. An infrequent short-lived cumulation of the two is possible but the groups and lines of differentiation are separate from each other.

Neither can we identify political parties with the occupational groups or with the social classes as some of the Marxians claim. For instance Kautsky says, "The three great parties, liberal, conservative and socialist, correspond to the three great social classes."[5] It is true that in populations with many parties there are some parties, as the labor party and the farmer party, which correspond to occupational groups and social classes. It is true also that there is a tangible correlation between the political parties and occupational-economic groups and social classes.[6]

146 to 30 B.C. (London, 1935); R. Syme, *The Roman Revolution* (Oxford, 1939).

[3] *Protokoll über die Verhandlungen des P.T. der S.D.P.D. abgehalten zu München* (Berlin, 1902), p. 244. Also in *Protokoll uber . . . abgehalten zu Essen a.d. Ruhr* (Berlin, 1907), p. 340.

[4] N. Bukharin, *The Program of the Communists* (Russian, St. Petersburg, 1919), p. 48. *Izvestia*, December 2, 1919. Already in 1918-1919 the Communist party in Russia tried to support some of the liberal factions of the Russian Orthodox religion.

One of the outstanding executioners of the Communist party, Lazis, recommended such a policy explicitly. See Lazis' article in the official *Izvestia*, December 2, 1919.

[5] K. Kautsky, *Today's Problems of International Socialism* (Russian translation, Moscow, 1915), p. 15. For sound critical remarks see A. Bentbley, *The Process of Government* (New York, 1908), p. 421.

[6] For the statistical data and the literature see Sorokin and Zimmerman, *Principles of Rural-Urban*

Nevertheless, the correlation is far from being close or general. In the countries with a two-party system the most different occupational, economic, and social groups make up the membership of each party, and vice versa, the members of the same occupational, economic, and social groups are scattered among both parties. The same is true for the populations with many parties. Even in parties that explicitly claim to be those of a distinct occupational, economic, or social class (as the radical labor party, the farmer-peasant party, the Socialist, Communist, and other parties), their membership has been recruited from a variety of occupational and economic and social groups. Even the leadership of such parties shows the same occupational, economic, and social diversity. For instance, among all the leaders of American Labor listed in the *American Labor Who's Who* for 1925 (whether by the occupation of their fathers or by their own occupations), these leaders in 35.8 per cent belonged to the qualified managerial, professional, and big business occupations; in 30.4 they belonged to the governmental and less qualified managerial, professional, and business occupations; only 0.7 per cent were farmers, and 5.2 and 0.4 per cent were in the semi-skilled and unskilled occupations.[7] Diversity appears in the composition of practically all such parties in Europe and elsewhere. Even the Communist party in Russia is no exception to this rule. It is widely thought to be a party of the factory workers par excellence. But actual factory workers made only 35.7 per cent of its membership in 1926; in 1934 the per cent fell below 9.3. At the present time it is still lower, and the party represents a conglomeration of a managerial bureaucracy engaged in different occupational pursuits.[8]

This applies to all parties. The divergence of party and occupational, economic and social class differentiation is shown also by the violent and short-time fluctuation in the number of votes cast at various elections for this or another party. As we shall see later, the occupational and property status of a population cannot change as quickly as the vote from election to election would indicate. The changes from victory to defeat and from defeat to victory are indicative of a change in the sympathies of the same people. The people who, in one election, cast their votes for one party throw their sympathies to another party at another election.

The German Social Democratic party (before 1914), whose class character has been emphasized by its adherents, is a party of the industrial proletariat exclusively. Yet one-third of the German commercial-industrial proletariat (individuals of identical economic and occupational status) voted for the candidates of the bourgeois parties and not for the Social Democrats. On the other hand, not all Social Democratic voters belonged to the working class; at least half a million of them were drawn from the propertied classes. And the German Social Democratic party has been the most homogeneous of all socialist parties. In other countries such parties have not attained this degree of homogeneity, some of them drawing more votes in localities where the proletariat constituted a very insignificant part of the population.[9]

Blank's findings were also confirmed by other investigators. According to an official investigation conducted by the German statistical bureau the membership of German trade unions in 1913 belonged to various parties; out of 5,391 thousand workmen organized into unions, 2,573 thousand belonged to the Social Democrats; 626 thousand to the Party of the Center; 355 thousand to the Conservative and Non-Liberal; 107 thousand to the Progressive Party; and 7 thousand to the Anarchistic parties. The picture becomes even more striking

---

Sociology, quoted, Ch. 19; Sorokin, Zimmerman, and Galpin, *Source Book,* quoted Vol. II, Ch. 16. Among many works indicated we can note W. Ogburn and D. Peterson, "Political Thought of Social Classes," *Political Science Quarterly,* Vol. XXX (1916), pp. 300 ff; S. Rice, *Farmers and Workers in American Politics* (Columbia University Press, 1924); Sorokin, "Leaders of Labor and Radical Movements," *AJS,* Vol. XXXIII (1927), pp. 382-411.

[7] P. A. Sorokin, "Leaders of Labor and Radical Movements," quoted, p. 399.

[8] For a good summary and analysis on the basis of the official data of the Communist party see B. Moore, Jr., "The Communist Party of the Soviet Union," *ASR,* Vol. IX (1944), pp. 267-278.

[9] See R. Blank, "Die sociale Zusammensetzung der sozial-demokratischen Wählerschaft Deutschlands," *Archiv für Sozialwissenschaft* (1905), heft III.

if we keep in mind that only 27.4% of the German proletariat were in unions and that from the other 72.6%, the greatest part voted for parties other than the socialistic.[10]

R. Michels in his *Les partis politiques* has shown that the membership of the socialist party includes not a few wealthy persons. Beginning with Engels, Lassalle, and Jaurès, many leaders of the socialist parties were men of sufficient means and some quite wealthy.[11] Further, the majority of the leaders were not workers or peasants by profession. Lenin, Trotsky, Kerensky, Chernoff, Plechanoff, Kropotkin, and Bakunin never tended a machine or stood behind a plow.

M. Ostrogorski in his monumental work also points out the heterogeneity of party composition. Members of the conservative, liberal, and labor parties in England are recruited from various occupations, property groups, and legal strata. The only conditions for entrance into the party are a certain age and willingness to pay a membership fee. The party caucuses representing the leading centers of the party are heterogeneous.[12]

Most of the syndicalists emphasize the same fact. "I cannot understand (says Lagardelle) how people with any sense of economic values can identify classes with parties, which are really conglomerations of people drawn from all points of the social horizon and united only by an ideological bond."[13]

That the party and occupational groupings are distinct is shown also by the politically neutral character of the occupational movement. In the United States, England, Germany, and France the occupational unions are organizations independent of the political party; especially explicit is this in France, the first Article of the Statute of the Confederation of Labor stating that "those entering into the Confederation must stay outside of any political school."

It is fairly evident that the party is a grouping *sui generis*, distinct from any other. As such it exerts a notable influence over its members, as well as over other groups and the population in general. All the conditions requisite to a powerful group are present here. First, many parties have a large membership, reaching into the hundreds of thousands and even millions. Second, each party is an organized unity with its own constitution (and fundamental laws, a party program which not only states its attitude on many problems, but also tries to regulate the political behavior of its members. Party laws and dogmas dictate the behavior of the members as imperatively as the state laws. The interests of the party are above those of the individual and unconditional submission to party discipline is its first commandment. The presence of a supreme party government—central committee, leaders, caucus, machine—and of subordinated agencies with their differentiated functions makes the party an organized group par excellence.

Even without such organization the party members usually work in solidarity. Since ordinarily every individual joins a party at his own will and may leave freely, those who remain within its folds must be well satisfied that its aims and principles are completely in accord with their own. Hence a natural harmony obtains between the party members. Loyalty to the party is even more intensified by various artificial means: propaganda, deception, sinecures, and promises of benefits and gains to be derived from unqualified adherence to the party fold. The members are made to think that "the party is above all," "the interests of the party are the supreme law," "the party is infallible"—slogans constantly hammered into the minds of the members. Add to this that big parties have a large fund of means for influencing human conduct.

No wonder, then, that their influence is felt by other groups and the population in general, especially in countries where the party differentiation is sufficiently well established. We shall not go into the trouble of showing in detail the relations between the party and every other group. It would be enough for our purposes to indicate the effects of the party groupings upon the state.

---

[10] See M. Lurie (Larin) *The Composition of the Proletariat* (Russian, St. Petersburg, 1918), p. 10. See there other data.

[11] R. Michels, *Les partis politiques* (Paris, 1911), pp. 186-188.

[12] M. Ostrogorski, *La démocratie et les partics politiques*, quoted, pp. 156 and ff; pp. 164 and ff.

[13] H. Lagardelle, "La Confederation du travail et la partie socialiste," *Mouvement Socialiste*, Nos. 189-190, p. 105.

In the majority of parliamentary states the state governments are under the control of the parties, which create and dispose them at their will; the members of the governments are recruited from the ranks of the victorious party, which has a parliamentary majority or a force of coercion in times of revolution. The essence of parliamentarism is party government. "On ne gouverne qu'avec son parti," said Gambetta; and this is the practice of all parliamentary states. The highly exalted "sovereign state"—the Goliath—is in reality subordinate to a number of small Davids—political parties. Identifying themselves with the state and employing its machinery, the parties become strong enough to exert pressure upon all other collectivities.[14] This is still more true of the one party controlling the state machinery, like the Communist party in Russia, the Nazi party in Germany, the Fascist party in Italy.

Besides, the party acts also directly without the medium of the state. Oral and written agitation—pamphlets and books, lectures and meetings, lies, deception, violence—these are the means and methods which the party uses to promote its interests.

The economic part of the program brings it into contact with the property and occupational groups, the religious with the religious collectivities, the labor and agrarian part with the occupational groupings; by determining the privileges and duties of groups it touches upon the ages, sex, and social groups.

In countries with a developed party life no individual can fully escape its influence. This enormous influence of the parties and their form of organization is regarded by many as the basic source of the defects and faults of modern democracies.[15]

The individual, proclaimed as the supreme value, and independent sovereign of the state, around whom all the relations of public life must revolve, finds himself finally as negligible a unit as before. Modern democracy moves within a tragic circle. The granting of franchise to the masses made imperative the need for organizations for carrying out the election procedure (regulation of votes, recommendation of candidates, promotion of programs). The parties became the mediators between the voters and the state, gradually seizing all the mechanism of elections and deciding their outcome. A group well organized, pretending to work in the name of all the people, became, through a series of various manipulations, the decisive factor in political life, reducing the role and influence of the voter to insignificance. Hence the tragedy of modern political life with its numerous imperfections. Furthermore, the party, through suppressing independent thought and permitting little criticism, turns into a sort of fanatical sect in which dead dogmas replace living creative thought.

The present form of party organization leads also to the selection of mediocrities and hypocrites as its leaders. Independence of thought not being tolerated, individuals with creative minds, courageous and honest with themselves and others, avoid joining the party. If they do enter it, they usually remain an ineffective minority, ruled by second and third rate men whose will stamps itself upon the party as a whole and who speak for the voters. An oligarchy of mediocrities is established. Furthermore, in their endeavor to get as many votes as possible, the parties promise the people "rivers of milk, with ice-cream shores"; the platforms which undertake to satisfy a great variety of interests, often contradictory to each other, remain vague, indefinite, and obscure, and their various points impossible of execution. The real will of the masses, the true public opinion, remains as unknown after the elections as before. Various promises are hardly ever taken seriously by the parties after their candidates have been elected. Hence indifference to matters political, and the decline in the creative spirit of the masses. Party dogmatism and false loyalty are established. The citizens are not aroused by the disorders taking place in public life, for these disorders are sanctioned by the party, and last, but not least, the party, as we have stated, suppresses

---

[14] See details in M. Ostrogorski's *La démocratie et les partis politiques*, quoted. Also J. Bryce, *Modern Democracies* (New York, 1921), 2 Vols.; R. Michels, *Political Parties* (New York, 1915); G. Mosca, *The Ruling Class* (New York, 1939);

W. E. Binkley, *American Political Parties* (New York, 1945).
[15] See the quoted works of Ostrogorski, Bryce, Michels, Mosca, and of the syndicalists and anarchists.

the individuality. Face to face with the party the individual is a negligible quantity, bound hand and foot by it. Any criticism of the party is regarded as a breach of party discipline and is followed by expulsion of critical heretics. Instead of educating the individual to liberty, the party trains men to servility. "Life within the party is a long school of servile obedience. The lessons, the citizen receives here, are lessons in cowardice and cravenness. The better the party is organized, the more demoralized are its members, and the lower the level of social life."[16]

However great is the role of the party, its influence is not to be overestimated, as some are inclined to do. The party is only one of many influential groups, and not of first rate either. In spite of its seemingly extraordinary influence, its potency is limited by the fact that it is as a rule an open grouping. Since ordinarily men are free to join and leave the party at their will, the size of its membership is largely dependent upon the degree with which its policies in general accord with the appetites, desires, aspirations, and value-systems of the masses. As soon as the party begins to pursue policies conflicting with the values and interests of the masses, it loses their support and its membership declines. This is tantamount to a loss of social power; the party either suffers defeat at elections, or, if it continues to rule by violence, is overthrown eventually by an open rebellion against the party despotism, or is slowly "digested" by the population, as the Communist party has been digested and therefore changed by the Russian population. To be sure the party, because of its organization, may be able, by sheer cleverness or through the use of armed forces, to maintain its influence and power for some time, even if its membership is small and its policies are in opposition to the wishes of the masses. This time may be of more or less extensive duration, depending upon a number of conditions, but the result is usually the same; through the ballot or an armed revolt or "digestion" the minority party is eventually reduced to the role of a negligible social force.

Furthermore, the political parties do not comprise all the population of a country; not

all men are politically minded. Thus in England, according to M. Ostrogorski, the proportion of people associated with party organization does not exceed 8 to 10% of the total electorate, the number of those attending the party meetings being even smaller. Not very different is the situation in other countries. The 4,200,000 members of the Russian Communist party constitute an insignificant minority in the population of 190,000,000.

One must not forget also that the active influence of parties begins not with the first moments of the individual's life but usually in later life. The party, in distinction from the state, the family, and other groups, takes no direct part in shaping a man's character; for the individual joins the party when already mature. The party as a rule does not select and prepare the individual, but the latter, fully formed by other groups, selects the party in accordance with his inclinations. The influence of the party is the result of the influences of groups in which man has received his training since the first days of his life. To be sure, from the very moment of joining a party a man is subject to its influences, but the quantity and quality of the latter is usually determined by other groupings. The remedies offered for the amelioration and modification of party life will remain, therefore, ineffective unless the life of the people as a whole changes.[17] Thus the party influence is considerable but far from being as great as many claim. This influence makes the political party one of the co-ordinates, defining man's social position, personality, ideology, and system of values. Even if a person does not belong to any party, such a negative party co-ordinate is important in his sociopolitical relations.

Most of the political parties are open groups, especially for the purposes of voting. Each party welcomes any individual whose main function is to increase the weight of the party and the political power of its leaders and candidates. If the party membership gives a number of privileges and advantages then such a party, for instance the Communist party in Russia or the Nazi party in Germany, is only a

---

[16] M. Ostrogorski, op. cit., p. 642.

[17] The Communist, the Nazi, the Fascist parties tried to "educate" the youth along the party line. However, their efforts have not been very successful.

semi-open group; its gates are open to a limited number of persons and only to the persons that meet the specific requirements of such a party. In such cases the size of the party membership is intentionally limited in order not to make too large a body of the privileged. The Russian Communist party intentionally limited its membership to 4,200,000 members. Even

open parties become fairly closed groups when the distribution of the booty among its members is concerned. The mere voters for the party so "dearly welcomed" as voters have no chance to participate in the distribution of the positions, privileges, sinecures, and spoils of the victorious party after the election or the violent revolution.

II. Differentiation into Religious Groups

Religion is a set of the ultimate values expressed in a credo, objectified by vehicles of a cult and socialized by conduct complying with the religious norms which unite members into one religious group. This definition of religion is clear enough not to confuse it with other systems of meanings and broad enough to embrace the essential character of religion. The ultimate nature of the values is another term for what others call God.[18] It embraces values which are styled "sacred"[19] or "holy" or "*mysterium tremendum et fascinosum!*"[20] It points out the inexhaustible and basic character of the religious values as the matrix from which all other values, including the differentiated categories of the Good, the True, and the Beautiful are derived.[21] Being ultimate the values of religion are not only rational but superrational. J. S. Erigena, Master Eckhart, and the mystics, on one hand, and such sociologists as B. Kidd on the other, state that God is the superlogical *coincidentia oppositorum*, "infinite manifold," "divine nothing."[22] Religion is "a form of belief providing an ultrarational sanction for that large class of conduct in the

individual where his interests and the interests of the social organism are antagonistic, and by which the former are rendered subordinate to the latter."[23] Likewise the definition is free from the defect of making religion something purely subjective and illusory, a "response without a stimulus" as MacMurray aptly calls most of the anthropological and sociological theories of religion.[24] As a system of ultimate meanings religion exists in the form of subjective experience. But as a system of overt actions (cult), ethical conduct, and other vehicles (buildings, religious objects), and as a unified group of believers (church) it exists as an objective sociocultural reality. In fact, as we shall see further (Chapters 40-42), the religious system of values lies at the basis of any integrated culture and clearly determines its essential traits: its science, philosophy, fine arts, law, ethics, politics, and economics. Finally, the ultimate character of its norms goes far beyond any empirical, rational, or logical forms of value. These values and respective experiences become "*the mysterium tremendum et fascinosum.*"[25] If a person does not have any

---

[18] See most of the usual definitions of religion.
[19] For instance E. Durkheim's definition of religion as "a unified system of beliefs and practices relative to sacred things." E. Durkheim, *Elementary Forms of Religious Life* (London, 1915), p. 47.
[20] "Religion is the experience of the Holy." R. Otto, *The Idea of the Holy* (Oxford, 1925); J. Wach, *Sociology of Religion* (Chicago, 1943), pp. 13 ff.
[21] See D. M. Edwards, *Christianity and Philosophy* (Edinburgh, 1932); W. James, *The Varieties of Religious Experience* (New York, 1928).
[22] See a good summary of the mystical experience of God or the ultimate values in E. Underhill, *Mysticism* (London, 1931); Joannis Scoti Erigenae,

De divisione naturae; Migne's *Patrologiae latinae*, Vol. CXXII; Nicolas of Cusa, *The Vision of God* (London, 1928), *De la docte ignorance* (Paris, 1930).
[23] B. Kidd, *Social Evolution* (New York, 1894), pp. 108 ff.
[24] J. MacMurray, *The Structure of Religious Experience* (New Haven, 1936), pp. 4, 23, *passim*.
[25] Besides the quoted works see other definitions and analyses of religion in E. Brightman, *Philosophy of Religion* (New York, 1940); J. M. Moore, *Theories of Religious Experience* (New York, 1938); M. Weber, *Gesammelte Aufsätze zur Religionssoziologie* (Tübingen, 1922-23), 3 Vols. (A part of this work is translated by T. Parsons as *The Protestant Ethic and the Spirit of Capitalism* (Lon-

system of ultimate values and views them all as quite relative, he does not have a religion. If the set of the ultimate values of a person is limited to the purely sensory or empirical world (for instance the set of purely sensory, material, hedonistic, and utilitarian values of a materialist) to the extent that some of these values are regarded by him as ultimate and supreme in contrast to the secondary and relative, such a person and values are religious but in a germinal or limited form. A materialist who ascribes to his matter the properties of an ultimate God (omnipotence, creativity, omnipresence, "emergent evolution"); who regards it as the source, the beginning, and the end of everything; ascribes to it an infinite manifoldedness and supreme value; derives from it the criteria and the norms separating sharply the "holy," "the sacred," from "the unholy" and "profane"; such a materialist is certainly religious. The main difference between him and the true believer in God is partly terminological—he designates by the term "matter" what others call "God" or "ultimate value," or "spirit," or "divine nothing and everything"—and partly the consistency and the degree of refinement of their religion.

The given definition of a religious group (church) is merely an application of our general, three-componential concept of sociocultural phenomena. Like other groups the religious group has (1) the specified component of meanings-norms-values; (2) the components of its interacting members that use, operate, realize, and exchange these meanings; (3) the component of vehicles—the whole set of the ritual of worship and practices, with all the buildings and objects through which the component of meanings is objectified, realized, and socialized. The first component makes the religious *doctrine* or *system of beliefs*; the second, *the members of the church*; the third,

the *religious cult, ritual and conduct*, with all the religious objects.

Each of these components of religion, the doctrine, the cult or worship with all the vehicles involved, leads the believers to communion with the ultimate values or God, and through that directly to their communion with one another. In this way a religion acts as a powerful force uniting into one solidary group of religious fellowship all its believers.[26]

Prayers, rituals, worship, sacrifice, and all the religious vehicles not only objectify and articulate the religious values-meanings-norms but unify and socialize and organize the believers into one fellowship, with all the characteristics of group organization and solidarity. In some of the religions, especially at their initial stages, with great charismatic leaders, this unifying and organizing function of religion appears in the most striking form, unexcelled by any other solidary groupings. Hence the emergence of religions at the earliest period of human history and their existence to the present time.

It goes without saying that the differentiation of human population into religious groups does not coincide exactly with any other. The contemporary religious groups from Confucianism, Taoism, Hinduism, Buddhism, Mohammedanism, Judaism, Jainism, to Christianity and the denominations of each of these religions, do not coincide with race-sex-age groups, or with kinship, territorial, language, occupational, or political party groups. They differ from the state groups and from any unibonded or multibonded group. On the other hand, the members of the same widely diffused religion are found to be scattered among various state, race, territorial, occupational, and other groups. Two exceptions to this rule, however, need to be noted. First, small religious groups have existed as multibonded (cumulative) groups in which the religious tie coin-

don, 1930).) See also C. A. Ellwood, *The Reconstruction of Religion* (New York, 1922); A. A. Bowman, *Studies in the Philosophy of Religion* (London, 1928). See other works in the referred works, especially J. Wach's Moore's, and also my *Theories*, Ch. 12. See also J. M. Yinger, *Religion in the Struggle for Power* (Duke University Press, 1945).

[26] On this unifying role of religion see J. Wach, *Sociology of Religion*, quoted, Ch. 3; J. M. Yinger, *op. cit.*; B. Kidd, *op. cit.*; F. de Coulanges, *The*

Ancient City (Boston, 1900); J. G. Frazer, *Psyche's Task, A Discourse Concerning the Influence of Superstition on the Growth of Institutions* (London, 1913); E. Underhill, *Worship* (New York, 1937); W. E. Hocking, *The Meaning of God in Human Experience* (New Haven, 1912); F. Heiler, *Prayer: A Study in the History and Philosophy of Religion* (Oxford University Press, 1933); A. F. Loisy, *Essai historique sur le sacrifice* (Paris, 1920); P. E. Johnson, *Psychology of Religion* (New York, 1945).

cides with other ties and the religious group has been coterminal with other groups united by other ties. Second, there is a tangible correlation between certain religions and certain social groups.

1. Family Religions

Thus in the history of various populations there have existed the family religions, with each family having its own religion and cult distinct from the others. Such family religions have existed among the Greeks, Romans, Chinese, Hindus, Egyptians, Hebrews, Celts, Japanese, Persians, pre-Columbian Americans, and other populations. The cult of the family ancestors and of the family *lares* and *penates* is an example of such family religions. Here then the family and the religious ties coincide and make a cumulative multibonded group.[27]

2. Kinship Religions and Cults

Certain religions and cults have been coterminous with the kinship groups, each religion being confined within a kinship group. Again such a cumulation of religious and kinship ties has occurred in many populations.[28]

3. Local Religions and Cults

Almost any village and city of ancient Greece and Rome, Egypt and Assyria, Summeria and pre-Columbian America, China, India, and medieval Europe had its own local deities, religion, and cult.[29]

4. Language, National and State Religions and Cults

Certain religions have been diffused mainly within a language group or a state group or a nation (as a multibonded group) especially at the earliest stages of their history. Thus the Greek religion was diffused mainly among the Greeks; Judaism among the Jews; Confucianism or Taoism among the Chinese; the Roman religion among the Romans; the Egyptian religion among the Egyptians, and so on. Many states in the past and recent times have had their own state religion either as the only

religion permitted by the state (*cuius regio eius religio*), and all other religion persecuted, or as a privileged religion officially recognized as the religion of a given state, like the Russian Orthodox religion in pre-revolutionary Russia or the Anglican Church in England. This coalescence of religion with state has been widely spread. Among the preliterate populations and early "historical peoples" such cumulations were common. Even now correlations of a certain religion and certain local, state, language, or kinship groups are quite evident. Judaism is still mainly the religion of the Jews; Confucianism and Taoism are diffused mainly among the Chinese; Shintoism among the Japanese; and Hinduism among the people of India.[30]

5. Cults of Sex and Age Groups

If not the whole of religion then some of its specific cults, rituals, and mysteries have often been confined to certain age and sex groups, especially among the preliterate populations.

6. Cults of Occupational, Economic, Aristocratic, and Underprivileged Groups

Finally, many of the occupational groups have had their own patrons and cults; as the rich and the poor; the privileged and disfranchised; the upper and lower castes, orders and classes. Sometimes the religions of these groups and strata differ greatly; sometimes only in details. Sometimes cultic forms have been reserved only for the upper strata and prohibited to the lower ones; sometimes the difference has been only in secondary traits. Generally, even within the same population adhering to the same religion, there will be found secondary differences in all three components of religion as between the governmental aristocracy, the merchants, the farmers, the military group, the rich, and poor; the clergy and the laity; the old and the young; the men and women; the white and the Negro; the Chinese, Abyssinian, African, and Hindu Christians. In brief, as we shall see further (see Chapters 36, 37) the same religion functions differently among heterogeneous social groups and persons; and the greater their

---

[27] See a good survey of the family cults and respective literature in J. Wach's work, quoted, pp. 58-70; also G. Landtman, *op. cit.*, Ch. 9.

[28] *Ibid.*, pp. 79-88.

[29] See many data, *Ibid.*, pp. 92-97, and Ch. 7.

[30] See Wach, *Ibid*, pp. 97-107; W. J. Cahnman, "Religion and Nationality," *AJS*, Vol. 49 (1944), pp. 524-529.

heterogeneity the greater the difference.[31] Certain forms of religion are congenial to, and diffuse more readily among, some social groups than others. There are also social groups that mingle more easily with certain réligions than with others.

These facts illustrate the two exceptions to the rule that differentiation into religious groups does not coincide with any other grouping. However numerous are these exceptions the rule still remains. The exceptions concern mainly small religious groups. With growth in size any religion tends to dissociate from sex, age, family, kinship, locality, state, language, and occupational groups. Religion transcends these boundaries and diffuses widely among groups of the most different character.

We shall see further that religion creates the solidarity of the co-believers. While it is conditioned by other groups and cultural systems of science, philosophy, fine arts, ethics and politics, economics and law, religion in its turn exerts the most decisive influence upon all groups and systems of culture, from science and the fine arts to politics and economics. Without knowing the religion of a given culture or group—their systems of ultimate values —one cannot understand their basic traits and social movements.

This influence of religion is due to the ultimate character of its meanings-norms-values which affect the mentality and conduct of its members. The influence of the world religion meets all the criteria of the powerful groups discussed above. (1) The membership of the world religions has been enormous. At the beginning of this century the membership of the Christian religion generally amounted to some 500,000,000, of which the Roman Catholics numbered 231 million, the Protestants 143 million, the Eastern Orthodox above 100 million. There were some 256 million Confucianists, 190 million Hindus, 177 million Mohammedans, about 7 million Judaists, and

so on.[32] (2) Religious groups are solidary. (3) They are well organized, with clear-cut constitutions, codes of official and intuitive law, a hierarchy of governmental authorities, a technical division of functions among their government and members, and a rich fund of experience and wisdom accumulated during centuries of their existence. (4) They possess the richest system of ideas-values-norms ultimate in character. (5) They have a vast reservoir of vehicles and means of influencing human conduct: funds, press, schools, pulpits, coercive as well as the most sublime instrumentalities for their purpose.

No wonder that powerful religious groups have constantly modified other groups. Whether among the Christian, Hindu, Mohammedan, or other religious groups, each religion has tangibly influenced the *family*, modifying it in conformity with its pattern. A great change in the late Roman family as well as that of the Teutonic and other barbarian peoples at the beginning of the Middle Ages took place under the pressure of Christianity and in conformity with its norms of the family. The same has occurred with other great religions. Without knowing the norms of sexual life and conduct in this or that religion one cannot understand why the family of a given population has assumed the form of monogamy or polygamy, patrilineal or matrilineal descent; agnatic or cognatic forms.[33]

Likewise religion has tangibly affected *racial and language groups* either in emphasizing the gulf between the "chosen people" and the unbelievers, pagans, gentiles, or "twice born castes" and lower castes; or in filling all such gaps and inequalities by effectively teaching the unity and equality of all races, ethnic, and other groups in Christ or God; and by the actual practice and enforcement of such a unity.

Religion has tangibly influenced all the *kinship groups* by defining consanguinity, affinity, and incest; by establishing a religious form of

[31] Note material and considerations in Wach, Ch. 6.

[32] G. von Mayr, *Statistik und Gesellschaftslehre* (Russian 1907), Vol. II, p. 15. Others, for instance, K. Kautsky, give somewhat different figures: about 600 million Christians, about 250 million Mohammedans, and about 700 million Hindus and Buddhists. K. Kautsky, *National Problems*, Russian translation (St. Petersburg, 1918), p. 37. At the

present time there are about 620,000,000 Christians, 15,000,000 Jews, 250,000,000 Mohammedans, 190,000,000 Buddhists, 280,000,000 Hinduists, 360,000,000 Confucianists and Taoists, 40,000,000 Shintoists.

[33] For the influence of religion upon other groups see Herbert Spencer, *Principles of Sociology*, Vol. III, part VI, "Ecclesiastical Institutions."

kinship through a common totemic ancestor, deity, or other religious kinship. Likewise religion has often tangibly modified the forms of kinship when they contradicted its norms.

Religion has notably influenced the *state groups*. The supremacy of the spiritual power over the secular during the Middle Ages; religious foundation of the caste system in India and the influential role of the priestly Brahmanic caste in the whole history of the states in India, or of the priests in ancient Egypt are enough to indicate such influence. As a matter of fact it has been even wider and more perennial. Many state groups were founded by religious groups and their leaders; and in many states the governmental regime has been theocracy governed by the priesthood of the religion. Many states have been torn apart by the pressure of religious groups; finally, many states have been modified by religion.[34]

Religion has also affected the *occupational groups and political parties*. Hereditary differentiation of occupations among the caste population of India and other countries is inconceivable without the role of religion.[35] Neither can one understand the role of different occupations and their relative social position in Greece and Rome, in Egypt and Medieval Europe, without consideration of the religions of these countries. Directly and indirectly religion continues to affect occupational groups in many ways at the present time. One of these is the existence among the labor groups of denominational trade unions. For example, in Germany of 1913, out of some five millions of organized labor more than one million was organized in religious denominational unions (Protestant and Catholic). The same was true in Belgium and several other countries.[36]

The influence of religion on *political parties* needs no particular discussion. It manifests itself first in the existence of religious denominational parties, like the party of the Center

(Catholic) in Germany, the party of the "Christian Democrats," and the like. Even now such parties are influential in their respective countries. Then, indirectly, the support or rejection of a given party by a large religious body frequently plays the decisive role in the victory or defeat of that party. In the past the political role of religion was still more influential. To sum up, religious groups have been among the perennially powerful agencies that shape the course of history and the destiny of humanity.

Some contend that in the future, religion and religiosity will be replaced by irreligiosity and disappearance of religion.[37] Such contentions are unfounded. While the concrete form of this or that religion may come and go, religion has been the perennial phenomenon of human history and will remain such in the future. As a system of ultimate values-meanings-norms, there is no reason to believe that such systems will disappear, or that mankind will not be able to integrate its ideas, values, and norms to the highest level of ultimate forms, as it has been able to do in the past. Such a theory of a regress is absurd. This or that belief, dogma, ritual, or other concrete form of religion will certainly change as in the past, but religion in new concrete forms will certainly remain.

For these reasons religion is one of the most important co-ordinates of the position of individuals, social groups, and sociocultural phenomena. Some of the religious groups are centralized in their organization and governmental system, for instance the Roman Catholic Church; others, as many of the Evangelical Protestant denominations, are decentralized.

Generally religious groups are nearer to open than to closed groups. Some of these are practically open; any one who desires can become a member or can easily drop his membership. Some religious groups are exclusive, admitting only those who meet their specifications (creed, code of conduct, race, caste), and not admitting any who do not meet these conditions.

[34] Cf. such works as F. de Coulanges, *Ancient City*, quoted; and especially A. Toynbee's theory of the *Universal State* and of the *Universal Church* and their relationship. A. Toynbee, *A Study of History* (Oxford, 1939), 6 Vols.; also J. Wach, *Sociology of Religion*, quoted, Ch. 7; J. M. Yinger's quoted work.

[35] See especially C. Bouglé, *Essais sur le régime des castes* (Paris, 1908), also G. Landtman, *The*

Origin of the Inequality of the Social Classes (Chicago, 1938), Chps. 8-12.

[36] See the figures in M. Lurie, *The Composition of the Proletariat*, quoted.

[37] See for instance J. M. Guyau, *Irreligiosity of the Future* (London, 1897).

III. The Professional and Other Groups

The unibonded groups surveyed above are the most powerful of such groups. Other groups that appear to be important are in fact subgroups within the groups examined.[38] For instance such groups as scientific, artistic, educational, and other professional collectivities are either a variety of occupational-economic groups or religious or state or territorial groups. Some of these professional groups are so important socially and culturally that they deserve to be mentioned specifically.[39] Among these of special significance are scientific, educational, ethical and philosophical, artistic and recreational groups. Except for the educational the membership of these groups is comparatively small; but lack of quantity is compensated by the outstanding quality of the members. Hence the influence of these groups is far greater than their membership would suggest.

1. Scientific Groups

The specific function of such groups is a qualitative enrichment, quantitative increase, and socialization of scientific experience and knowledge. In contradistinction from the ultimate religious values the scientific ideas-norms-values are non-ultimate; they are limited to the cognition of the empirical or phenomenal world and do not deal directly with the transcendental or noumenal world. The totality of persons engaged in this pursuit and united in interacting organized groups constitutes the scientific groups. From the small groups of medicine men, shamans, seers, and inquisitive persons in preliterate populations to the multitude of national and international scientific societies of mathematicians, astronomers, physicists, chemists, engineers, biologists, sociologists, anthropologists, economists, historians, and various academies of science and research institutions, universities and colleges, scientific groups have existed in rudimentary or developed form in practically all populations.[40] Any population in order to live and to survive has to have a minimum of scientific knowledge of its environment. Otherwise, if its members ascribe the properties of cow to a lion and try to milk the lion and kill the cow, or try to eat the uneatables, domesticate the poisonous snakes, and so on, such a population cannot survive. Therefore, a minimum of scientific knowledge has appeared in all populations that have survived.

At the present time there is no need to dwell on the important role of science, of men of science and of scientific groups in human history. It is well known and undisputed. The following computation by N. A. Umov suggests this role. If there were no mathematical, physical, or chemical discoveries or technological inventions made by science for the last two or three centuries the form of motorpower or energy available to man would have been

---

[38] See a survey of a multitude of different groups in A. de LaBorde, De l'esprit d'association dans tous les intérêts de la communauté (Paris, 1821), 2 Vols.

[39] On professional groups generally see A. Bláha, Sociologie inteligence (Prague, 1937); see there the literature. A. M. Carr-Sanders and P. A. Wilson, The Professions (Oxford, 1933); J. Benda, La fin de l'éternel (Paris, 1928) and his La trahison des clercs (Paris, 1927); K. Dunkman, Die Lehre vom Beruf (Berlin, 1922); M. Ullrich, Die psychologische Analyse der höheren Berufe (Leipzig, 1918); M. Feuchtvanger, Die freien Berufe (München, 1922); A. Obrdlik, Povolání, A Verejne Blaho (Prague, 1937); P. de Rousiers, L'élite dans la société moderne (Paris, 1914); H. M. Chatelier, "The Formation of the Elite," Scientific Monthly (September, 1928).

[40] See the varieties and "evolutionary forms" of men of science in Spencer's Principles of Sociology, Vol. III, Part VII, "Professional Institutions," which is still good and is hardly surpassed by recent works. Of these see F. Znaniecki, The Social Role of the Man of Science (New York, 1940); M. Weber, Wissenschaft as Beruf. L. Wilson, The Academic Man (New York, 1942); N. Hirsch, Genius and Creative Intelligence (Cambridge, 1931). Especially important is a general knowledge of the history of science in all its main branches, including that of the humanistic and social sciences. See G. Sarton, Introduction to the History of Science (Baltimore, 1927 and 1931), 2 Vols., also histories of philosophy and respective social and humanistic disciplines. See the curves of the scientific discoveries and technological inventions, together with other relevant data in my Dynamics, Vol. II, Chps. 1, 2, 3, passim.

mainly the physical energy of man himself and of a few domesticated animals. These "motorpowers" were indeed the foundation of the economic life of the societies before the sixteenth and the seventeenth centuries.

How much energy has a man-machine? A free individual working ten hours a day can produce work amounting to 290,000 kilogrammeters, which makes 8 kilogrammeters per second or one tenth horsepower. In these conditions to do the work of a locomotive with 3000 to 4000 horsepower we would need the work of 30,000 human beings moving with the velocity of a fast train. . . . Supposing that the total amount of energy made available through scientific discoveries and inventions of the last two centuries is 20 billion horsepower. A translation of this energy into human machines would require the work of 200 billion human beings ten hours a day. . . . Turning all the human population (about 2 billion) into slave-machines, we could hardly get one hundredth part of the energy granted to us through the discoveries and inventions of the physico-chemical sciences. . . . During millions of years nature brought the human population on this planet to some 2 billion, while the buoyant knowledge of the physico-chemical sciences during two centuries created a hundredfold more units of energy than the number of human servants.[41]

This rough computation speaks for itself.[42] Whether used for constructive or destructive purposes like the atomic bomb, the effectiveness of science has been truly gigantic and rapidly increasing. Its progress is bound to go on in the future. If used for constructive purposes it promises to be an unrivalled benefactor of mankind. If used for destructive purposes, as science has been used in recent times and especially in the first and second World Wars, it may turn into a demonic destroyer of humanity. In either case its effectiveness remains. As the number of persons who have contributed to the development of scientific discoveries and technological inventions has always been small, this smallness is an example of the power of small but highly creative groups.

Scientific groups are, as a rule, decentralized. Centralization would have been detrimental to

their creative activities. No man and no group or government can autocratically prescribe what is true and what is not, nor produce by governmental fiat real scientific discoveries or inventions. Freedom of scientific inquiry is an indispensable condition of its existence and creativeness. Theoretically, scientific groups are open; anyone who is qualified can become a member. Actually only a small fraction of the population possesses such qualifications. Therefore scientific groups in reality are closed to a majority of the population.

2. Educational Groups

A newborn baby is an organism devoid of the meanings-values-norms, the meaningful actions and relationships, and the use of vehicles necessary for living in society. He has to learn all this to become a member of society. Hence in any organized population there are always agencies and groups that perform this educational function of transforming a biological organism into a socialized member. The family, the kinship group, the small groups of a leader and his disciples, the local groups of playmates and friends, the age and sex groups, the school groups, the state, language, religious, political, and occupational groups with all the technical means of communication like newspapers, books, radio, museums, concerts, plays, movies, and so on, are a part of the educational system of a population. Thus the school system in a narrow sense is only a small part of the total educational agencies of any population. The total educational apparatus is rarely united into one real system; it exists as several sets of educational groups and agencies. In this sense it is more or less decentralized, except where in Soviet Russia or Nazi Germany the state government temporarily has tried to control the whole educational process and all of its agencies. Nevertheless, even in such countries the government never fully succeeds in this task, for a large number of educational forces continue to work in different and often in the opposite direction to that dictated by the state government.

Educational groups are largely responsible

[41] N. A. Umov, "Physical Sciences in Servicing Humanity" (Russian) *Priroda* (February, 1913), pp. 149-160.

[42] See other computations in S. H. Slichter, *Modern Economic Society* (New York, 1931), p.

86 on the growth of machine power in the period of 1835 to 1928 (computed in horsepower units). Also R. P. Dutt, *Fascism and Social Revolution* (New York, 1935), p. 25.

for the kind of members a population has: their mentality, sociocultural traits, and conduct; in brief, what kind of sociocultural dress is put on a biological organism.[43] The totality of educational agencies is almost coterminal with all the forces of a given population. Every moment of our living, interacting, and being in a sociocultural world is educational, in a good or bad sense. The influence of the school system in a narrow sense is much more limited than the totality of educational agencies in the above sense. However, it is considerable and exerts a tangible influence upon all the individuals who nowadays pass through elementary, high and vocational schools. Later on we shall discuss the educational processes more fully. For the present we can only mention them and add that the educational status of a person is one of the co-ordinates of his personality and position in the sociocultural universe. Some schools in some populations are open to only a small fraction of their members —the aristocracy, the upper castes or orders, the rich, and the like. Other schools are open for all, even required in many populations of all children of school age.

3. Philosophical, Ethical, Philanthropic, and Similar Groups

Akin to the scientific and educational groups are numerous philosophical societies, ethical and juridical associations, philanthropic leagues, and similar groups. So far as philosophy and ethics were in the past inseparable from science and religion and so far as any science depends upon religion, philosophy and ethics, most of what has been said of science and religion can be said of these groups. The only difference is that the direct influence of philosophical-ethical and philanthropic societies has hardly been as efficient as that of science and religion. Indirectly, however, it has been considerable. First, philosophy and ethics exert a tangible influence upon science itself. Second, they affect also religion and religious groups. Third, we shall see later that it makes

a great deal of difference as to whether a given population has a predominantly mechanistic and materialistic or idealistic philosophy; a universalistic and absolute system of ethics and law or a relativistic, hedonistic, and strictly utilitarian ethics and law; whether in a given society there is a developed altruism and an abundance of mutual help and philanthropic groups, or their scarcity. The mentality, conduct, social relationships, and the whole culture of a given population becomes tangibly different in different philosophical, ethical, and legal atmospheres. Hence the significance of these groups and associations.

4. Artistic and Recreational Groups

The fine arts and recreation in various forms appear in all populations from the most "primitive" to the most modern. Groups engaged in the creation, arrangement, participation, and enjoyment of literature and music, painting and sculpture, architecture and theater, sports, and so on have existed in all populations. So far as fine art or the value of beauty is one of the most important values of any culture; so far as some form of recreation is a physical and mental necessity, these groups have exerted a tangible influence upon their members, upon other groups, and upon the sociocultural life as a whole. If for a moment we imagine that the greatest creations in the fine arts are irretrievably lost, the whole culture of humanity and the richness of every life will be vastly impoverished. We should be robbed of one of the main joys of human life. The same can be said of various recreations and sports. The fine arts and recreations influence every one of us in the more prosaic ways; they are among the most efficient educational agencies that mold our personality; they affect tangibly other groups beginning with the family and touching religious, political, state, occupational, and other groups. Though small (especially the creators of fine art), these groups exert an influence far greater than their size suggests. They have taken a

---

[43] See E. Chalupny, *Sociologie a skoly* (Prague, 1936); F. Roucek (ed.) *Sociological Foundations of Education* (New York, 1944); W. Waller, *Sociology of Teaching* (New York, 1932); J. K. Hart, *A Social Interpretation of Education* (New York, 1931); C. C. Peters, *Foundations of Educational Sociology* (New York, 1930); J. C. Chapman and G. S. Counts, *Principles of Education* (New York, 1929); Sorokin, Zimmerman, and Galpin, *Source Book in Rural Sociology*, Vol. II, Ch. 12; A Todd, *The Primitive Family as an Educational Agency* (New York, 1913); *General Education in Free Society* by the Harvard Committee (Cambridge, 1945).

variety of forms from the schools and academies of the fine arts, to the literary, theatrical, musical, sculpture, and painting associations, societies, museums, theaters, symphony orchestras; football, baseball, and other recreation groups and associations. Some of these groups have been formally closed to the majority of the population; others formally open but actually inaccessible to many who lack the special traits necessary for active participation in them. The products of such groups have been generally open and accessible for most of the people who wanted to enjoy them passively. But even there the financial and similar conditions have often made even the passive enjoyment of a large portion of art creations and recreations inaccessible to many.

5. The Nominal Plurel of the Elite, Great Leaders, and Historical Persons

Finally, we should recognize a nominal group of the elite. Men of genius and of the elite rarely make a real group and appear rather as outstanding individuals whose influence, compared with that of the rank and file of ordinary people, prove to be notably greater. History is not made by heroes, but the influence exerted by various individuals upon the social process is not equally important. The great majority of individuals represent rather insignificant foci of forces with a small circle of influence. They live and die, leaving no memory or historic trace behind them. Others, however, influence the behavior of thousands of men and by actions or words cause extensive changes in social life, leaving their name to posterity for thousands of years to come. As compared with ordinary individuals, if not with groups, the elite represent an enormous historical force.

But what are the "elite"? Who may reasonably be called a great man and why? The usual definitions are highly subjective and therefore scientifically invalid. Thus, a Communist is inclined to regard as great men only Communists; to a monarchist only monarchs are great; a pacifist would protest against the qualifications of Napoleon as a great man; a law-abiding citizen will not include among the great a virtuoso in crimes.

Neither are the attempts at definition made by various scientists free of subjectivity. F. H.

Giddings, for instance, defines the true "elite" as a group of people "who have health and biological vitality, who are most endowed with genius or talent and in whom the social nature is highly developed."[44]

In spite of its attractive and pleasing form, this definition must be rejected, for the simple reason that it does not correspond to reality. One can hardly find great intellectuality, a highly developed moral sense, and abundance of physical vigor in the same man. Many are those who combine a healthy physique with a low intellect and an undeveloped social nature; many intellectual geniuses lack physical vitality and vigor, while not a few of those who possess a highly developed moral sense—ready at all times to sacrifice themselves for others—could hardly be called great intellects. A maximum of good health, outstanding intellect, and high morality in one person is very rare indeed. In accord with Giddings' definition neither Napoleon or St. Francis of Assisi, Bacon or Swift, Byron or Shakespeare, Robespierre or Caesar, could be included among the elite, for none of these men possessed all the characteristics essential to qualify one as a great man. Giddings himself made a serious departure from his own definition by incorporation among the true elite all those who left any trace in history of their deeds.[45] This automatically includes Swift, who betrayed two brides; Herostrates, who is known only as the man who burned a famous temple; Torquemada, the great inquisitor, Napoleon, Lenin, Hitler, and many others whose dubious fame as organizers of mass murder, would hardly satisfy the requirements of his definition. Healthy individuals will agree, but the bodily weak will scoff at the idea that health is an essential prerequisite to greatness. The virtuous will gladly admit that a high sense of morality is a necessary quality of a great man; the selfish, however, will hardly subscribe to that and together with Max Stirner, F. Nietzsche, and other staunch individualists will call such greatness the greatness of a good-natured, sentimental nurse.

Other definitions—such as that given by J. Novikov and those of a majority of American

[44] F. H. Giddings, *The Elements of Sociology* (New York, 1912), pp. 112-118.
[45] Giddings, *Ibid.*, pp. 113-116.

sociologists—suffer from the same fault of subjectivity. Most of them are in the nature of sermons, in which the authors enumerate the virtues they personally approve.[46] Often the elite are said to comprise only the so-called intelligentsia which is characterized as the group whose function is "the creation of new forms and ideals which influence life in the direction of the physical and intellectual liberation of the individual."[47] Subtle, but very vague indeed!

The basic defect of all these definitions is their lack of objectivity. To be scientific a definition must, first of all, be free from too subjective evaluation, praise or condemnation, considerations of good and evil, benefit or harm. In short, it must be based on some objective criterion. Such a criterion, in our opinion, is provided by the *rank one occupies in a given field of human endeavor, estimated irrespectively of whether one's activity is moral or immoral, useful or harmful, beautiful or ugly, just or unjust from the point of view of various people.* In order to clarify this thought we shall make use of an example from Pareto, one of the first sociologists to make an objective study of the elite. In any field of human activity the best specialist, one whose achievements in the estimate of other specialists rank highest, will be designated by 10; others, less successful in their work, will be correspondingly designated as 8, 5, 4, 2, 1 to zero. In the field of making money, for instance, a man making millions will be marked 10, another, earning thousands—6; the one whose income keeps him from starving—1; those who are compelled to beg—0.

"There are people who deify Napoleon, others who hate him as an outstanding rascal. Which of the two opinions is true is not for us to decide. Whether Napoleon was good or bad is not the issue. It is clear that he was an unusual man, very far above other human beings, with exceptional qualities and this is a sufficient reason why we place him among the elite."[48] As a specialist in a definite field, his achievements according to the estimate of other specialists in the same field, far outweigh those of others, and we mark him 10.

It is necessary always, as Pareto remarks, "to take into account the actual, not the potential achievements of a person."[49] All men who excel in some activity and are recognized by specialists in the same field (of different periods, I shall add) as exceptionally able are *potentially* among the elite, irrespective of all ethical and other considerations. Such is the first condition. However, it is not enough. Out of the variegated group of potential leaders a second selection should be made, and again on the basis of an objective criterion. For the objective investigator of social processes such a criterion is *the degree of influence exerted by a given individual upon others and through them upon the social processes as a whole.*

A drunkard or a collector of old heels may be great virtuosos in their special fields, but since their influence is negligible they cannot be included among the elite. On the other hand, a virtuoso in science (Newton, Darwin, Edison), in state administration (Cromwell, Richelieu, Peter the Great, or Lenin), or religious rulers (Gregory VII, Innocent III), exerted a tremendous influence upon other beings and are therefore to be regarded as the true elite. It is debatable whether the roles of Caesar and Marius, Torquemada and Innocent, Robespierre and Lenin, Peter the Great and Napoleon, Mohammed and Bismarck, St. Augustin and Marx, Hitler and Stalin, were of a positive or negative value; but there is no doubt that they were masters of their work and left deep furrows in the field of history. These are truly the elite.[50]

Consequently, those who are the outstanding leaders of influential social groups—the state, church, class, language, and of other groups surveyed, including the professional groups—are the real elite. Occupying outstand-

---

[46] See, for instance, I. Isoulet, *La cité moderne* (Paris, 1901), "The Revolution came in order to replace the false elite by the real one."

[47] Ivanoff-Rasumnik, *The History of Russian Thought* (Russian, St. Petersburg, 1918), pp. 20-27. A more objective study of intelligentsia is given in A. Bláha, *Sociologie inteligence* (Prague, 1937).

[48] V. Pareto, *Trattato*, quoted, Vol. II, pp. 470-471.

[49] *Ibid.*, p. 470.

[50] Compare Furlan, "La circulation des Elites," *Revue international de sociologie* (1911), p. 387; M. Kolabinska, *La circulation des élites en France* (Lausanne, 1912), pp. 5-6; G. Sensini, "Teoria dell 'equilibrio,'" *Rivista Italiana di sociologia* (1913).

ing places in these powerful groups, having at their disposal powerful mechanisms, and having the highest virtuosity in a discharge of their functions, they bring into motion millions of people and press upon the general march of events. That our understanding of the nature of the "Great Man" is correct is shown indirectly by the fact that history records the names not only of the "good" men but also of the "bad," not only of individuals excelling in health, intellect, and sociability, as Giddings thinks, but of all masters in a field affecting the affairs of men.

In Sorokin and Boldyreff's study of *all persons* mentioned in the *Encyclopedia Britannica* from 4000 B.C. up to those born in the period 1800-1849 A.D., the bulk of them fall into the following fields in which they distinguished themselves and became historical: religion, leadership in the state and other important groups, literature, scholarship, science, philosophy, business, music, and other fine arts. Only a very small fraction of the historical persons immortalized themselves in "miscellaneous" fields different from the above nine. Of these nine fields the largest number of the historical persons of all times appeared in the field of leadership in state and other important groups, with a geometric average of 14437; then in literature (10406); then in a decreasing order in religion (9287), humanistic and

social science scholarship (6646), science (5199), fine arts (5423), philosophy (3361), business (1561), music (1077). The total miscellaneous group was slightly larger than music and business (1726).[51]

The number of the elite of first rank is not large. According to Galton[52] there were in 1868 in England 1250 well known men, of whom 520 were eminent. According to Didot's *Nouvelle Biographie General*, only about 100,-000 men left any historical memory out of some 45 billions who have lived on the face of the earth since the days of Pericles to 1850-1870, which means that on the average there was one great man among 450,000 average people.[53] Not very different are the figures obtained by I. V. Boldyreff from his study of all historical persons mentioned in the *Encyclopedia Britannica*.

These are the most important unibonded groups that determine the historical processes, the mentality, conduct, destiny, and social position of individuals. Before drawing a few general conclusions from the above analysis let us pass to a concise analysis and classification of the main multibonded groups.

---

[51] See the detailed figures by fields and periods in my *Dynamics*, Vol. IV, Ch. 7.
[52] F. Galton, *Hereditary Genius* (London, 1892).
[53] See also F. H. Giddings, *The Elements of Sociology*, pp. 115-116.

Chapter 13. Differentiation of Population into Multibonded Groups

I. The Concept of Multibonded Groups

Material bodies such as a table, a stone, a plant, or water are not composed of a single chemical element but of a compound of different elements forming molecules. Similarly, social groups are not composed merely of unibonded groups but often contain multibonded groups made up of two or more unibonded components. For instance the professors and students of Harvard University not only constitute a unibonded group tied together by common membership in Harvard University, but most of them are also linked by a common language (English) and by the tie of a local or territorial group. Part of them, in addition, are related as Roman Catholics or Protestants, Republicans or Democrats, and so on. Almost every population consists of a constellation of diverse multibonded groups. *The totality of interacting persons linked by two or more unibonded ties (values, meanings, or norms) constitutes a multibonded group.*

II. Classification of Multibonded Groups

Since there are many unibonded groups, and since these combine in various ways, any society exhibits an enormous number of diversified multibonded groups. We may classify these groups according to *the number of unibonded ties compounded; the quality of the compounded unibonded ties; the mutual relationship of the compounded ties (antagonism or solidarity, affinity and lack of affinity); the open or closed character of the groups.*

1. According to the Number of Bonds (Meanings, Values, or Norms) Compounded

Just as physicochemical bodies are made up now of two chemical elements, such as H_2O (water), now of three (such as H_2SO_4), now of four (such as $KHSO_4$), and so on, so multibonded groups represent a compounding of two, three, four, or a greater number of unibonded ties. The members of double-bonded groups may be linked together by language plus religion (for example, French Protestants), by occupation plus sex (for example, women factory workers), by race plus locality (for example, Boston Negroes), by kinship plus political affiliations (for example, the Republican faction of the Smith kinship group). The members of triple-bonded groups may be united by such factors as race, occupation, and religion (for example, Protestant Negro porters); sex, age, and locality (for example, a gang of Charles Street boys in their teens); political party, religion, and occupation (for example, Protestant Republican miners), and so on. Quadruple-bonded groups are all illustrated by the following Harvard students who are at once Democrats, Catholics, and Irish or who are French Canadians, members of the same scientific club, and citizens of Quebec. Among Bostonians all persons who are at once electricians, males, Socialists, and Unitarians are examples of a four-bonded group. There are many groups of a still more complex character, whose members are bound together by five, six, or more unibonded ties.

2. According to the Quality of the Ties

Since any unibonded tie may combine with any others, the character of the multibonded group obviously varies according to the character of its components. A double-bonded group may consist of a religious plus a language bond; of a religious plus an occupational bond; of an occupational plus a party bond; of an occupational plus a race, sex, or age bond, and so on. Similarly, a triple-bonded group may be a combination of a territorial with a language and religious tie or of territorial, racial, and sex bonds, and so on. More complex combinations may be represented by N, according to the binomial formula of combinations. The population of modern metropolises, for instance, consists of an enormous number of multibonded groups of diverse composition. It resembles, in a sense, a geological formation composed of multitudes of chemical compounds each of which is formed through the combination of various elements and molecules. The elements are parallel to unibonded social groups; the compounds, to multibonded social groups.

3. According to Mutual Solidarity, Antagonism, or Neutrality of the Compounded Bonds

Like the members of unibonded organized groups, those of multibonded groups may be (a) *antagonistic*, when the compounded bonds repel one another and incite the members to mutually contradictory actions, ideas, and impulses; (b) *solidary*, when the compounded bonds are mutually consistent and induce the same actions, ideas, emotions, and volitions; (c) *intermediary or neutral*. It is usually held that the greater the number of compounded bonds the more solidary the group is. The

actual situation is different. Owing to various factors, sometimes two or more mutually antagonistic bonds are imposed upon a group of individuals; the result is an antagonistic multibonded group. Consider, for instance, the situation of a medieval population who, during the feud between Pope Gregory VII and King Henry IV, were at once Catholics and subjects of King Henry. The religious group headed by Gregory VII issued one set of orders; the state group headed by Henry IV issued a contrary set. As Catholics the population had to follow the injunctions of the church and oppose the king; as the king's subjects they had to obey the orders of the state and denounce the pope. Another example is afforded by the position of "conscientious objectors." Their state citizenship impels them to participate wholeheartedly in war and to defeat the enemy, whereas their pacifist and Christian convictions exhort them to abstain from any active part in warfare.

The solidary multibonded groups are still more numerous and diverse. Americans who at the same time belong to a religious denomination, a trade union, and a political party that urge their members to the maximum war effort constitute a quadruple-bonded group in which all the bonds induce the same action and mentality. Such a group is an inwardly solidary multibonded collectivity.

Finally, if we take the line of conduct recommended by Jesus to Christians who were simultaneously subjects of the Roman Empire: "Render unto Caesar the things which are Caesar's; and unto God the things that are God's" (Matthew xxii, 21), we have (in this matter of paying or not paying state taxes) a neutral double-bonded group, in which the performance of religious duties neither conflicts nor is solidary with that of political duties. (If, however, we consider all the actions prescribed by the Roman Empire and those prescribed by the Christian Church at that period, we find that they conflicted in many ways. Hence the group of Christians who were citizens of the Roman Empire were an inwardly antagonistic body, as evidenced, for instance, by the persecutions of the Christians by the state and the denunciation of the state by the Christians.) A group of Harvard professors who are at the same time Protestants and members of a garden society is a triple-bonded neutral group in which each bond (occupational, religious, and recreational) neither reinforces nor is antagonistic to the others. This inner solidarity, antagonism, or neutrality of a multibonded group notably influences the behavior of its members and the cohesiveness of the group itself.

a. *Effects Upon the Behavior of the Members.* Lucky is the man who is a member of a solidarily compounded group! All the compounded bonds and their groups, with their values and vehicles, impel him to the same kind of actions, thoughts, feelings, emotions, and duties. He is like a ball pushed by several forces in the same direction. He experiences no conflict of duties, no doubts or hesitation. His conscience is clear, and his actions are resolute.

Quite different are the mind and behavior of a member of an inwardly antagonistic multibonded group. The conflicting bonds and values issue, as it were, contradictory orders. Such a person is subjected to forces which tend to push him in opposite directions. Hence he is assailed by conflicting duties, self-contradictions, doubts, and irresoluteness, especially when the compounded bonds are more or less equal in power. Under such conditions there is an incessant struggle in his soul between the conflicting duties, with consequent worry and even remorse. If the conflcting bonds are of an unequal power, his vacillation will eventually result in a voluntary or forced withdrawal from membership in the weaker unibonded subgroup. Such an experience, needless to say, is alike painful and wasteful of one's energy and vitality. Examples of such a situation are afforded by the aforementioned cases of the Catholics who were subjects of King Henry IV, and patriotic citizens who are at the same time Christian pacifists. Hamlet is another example of such a self-contradictory and irresolute type of person placed in this inwardly antagonistic position. Later on we shall discuss this problem more fully (cf. Chapter 19).

b. *Effects on the Cohesiveness and Stability of the Group.* The layman is prone to think that the cohesiveness of a group depends upon the number of ties which bind its members, that the more numerous the ties the more cohesive is the group and the more willingly

will it defend its integrity, unity, and independence. A group whose members are united by numerous ties of common kinship, citizenship, religion, language, and occupation is apparently much firmer than others and cannot be broken up as easily as a group of people united, let us say, only by a common language. This, however, is true only in case the meanings, norms, and values are not mutually antagonistic.

When they are antagonistic, the compounded group will eventually dissolve through inner friction. Those members for whom religious interests are paramount will obey the injunctions of their religion, whereas those who place loyalty to the state above other considerations may refuse to heed them. In this case the group is "a house divided against itself." In its relations with the outside world it will fail to act as a unit. The result will be constant bickering within the group and its eventual dissolution into two or more parts. The fate of the socialist party during the two World Wars is a case in point. In each country the members held a double allegiance: to the party itself and to the state of which they were citizens. This compound was antagonistic in the sense that the state demanded military victory, enforcement of discipline in the army, the mitigation of the class struggle, and reinforcement of class unity, whereas for international socialism the state had value only so far as it promoted the victory of the international proletariat. The latter's interests demanded the sharpening of the class struggle and the end of international war.

This conflict within the socialist organizations resulted, first, in indecisiveness in matters of policy and, secondly, in their gradual dissolution. Three parties finally emerged from the ruins of the socialist party: the left-wing socialists abandoned it in order to devote their energies to the promulgation of straight proletarian internationalism; then the right-wing, or "patriotic" faction, seceded for the sake of a vigorous prosecution of the war; while the middle faction continued to pursue a weak, unstable, self-contradictory policy, vainly striving to reconcile the interests of international socialism with those of the state.

To summarize: The fact that unibonded ties combine to form a single multibonded group does not in itself ensure greater cohesiveness. Everything depends upon the relationship of the compounded bonds. Only a solidary relationship serves to increase the cohesiveness of the group. The greater the solidarity of the unibonded ties and the greater the harmony of their values, the greater the unity of the group. If there is a sufficiently high degree of solidarity, it is not likely to disintegrate. Even if it is temporarily dissolved, its elements inevitably seek to reunite.

The multibonded solidary groups are fortunate in their superior cohesiveness, firmness of policy, and chances for longevity. Groups compounded of mutually antagonistic bonds, on the other hand, vacillating in their policy and torn by internal dissension, eventually disintegrate either through internal friction or through the pressure of some unfavorable external force. Such has been the experience of several contemporary "liberal" and "progressive" groups. The essence of many a revolution, as well as of many orderly processes of social reconstruction, has consisted in the replacement of such groups by solidary social "compounds."

4. According to Their Mutual Affinity or Lack of Affinity

Closely connected with the antagonistic, solidary, and neutral relationships of compounded bonds is their mutual affinity or lack of affinity. Though most antagonistic compounds are unaffined combinations of bonds, whereas most solidary compounds exhibit mutual affinity of the bonds, nevertheless affinity and lack of affinity of bonds are to be distinguished from mutual solidarity and antagonism. The question is this: Which of the bonds most readily enter into a combination with which? Let us concisely outline the problem. In chemistry the term "affinity" means an attraction between certain chemical elements that causes them easily to form compounds. Most chemical elements exhibit an affinity for certain elements and lack it in respect to others. The resulting compounds are met frequently and are relatively stable, whereas those formed by the union of elements lacking such mutual affinity are comparatively rare and are unstable. A similar phenomenon is exhibited by social bonds. A given unibonded

tie A compounds readily with certain other bonds, B or C, producing the multibonded groups AB or AC, whereas it does not easily combine with bonds N, M, or J.

Chemistry has progressed sufficiently to define all the main combinations of elements with other affined elements. Social science and sociology—until recently devoid of even the concepts of unibonded and multibonded groups and of antagonistic and solidary compounded groups—are still unable to determine the precise relationships of affined bonds. It is beyond the scope of this treatise to give a detailed list of all the possible combinations of unibonded ties. The following are a few examples of compounds formed by affined bonds.

A *racial group bond* coalesces fairly frequently (a) with a *kinship* bond, producing a racial-kinship group (R.+K.G.); (b) with a *territorial* bond, creating districts inhabited exclusively or mainly by one racial stock (R.+T.G.); (c) with an *occupational* bond, giving an occupational-racial group (R.+O.G.), with certain occupations monopolized by it and with other occupations prohibited to it; (d) with a *state group bond*, producing a *state* with the overwhelming majority of the citizens belonging to a single racial type, and not admitting to citizenship certain other racial groups (R.+S.G.); (e) with a *language-culture* bond, leading to a racial group speaking the same language or similar languages and having a common fund of certain cultural values (R.+L.G.); (f) with a *political party* bond, exemplified by a political party created by a given racial group or by a political party supported by an overwhelming majority of the members of a given race group (R.+Pp.G.); and (g) with an *economic* group bond, producing either an indigent race group or a rich race group, with different incomes, standards of living, and other economic traits (R.+Er. and R.+Ep.G.). (h) In the past there have been racial religious groups with a religion created by a racial group and almost exclusively confined to it (R.+Rs.G.). At the present time the Hebrews, so far as they still exhibit a fairly distinct racial type, afford an example of such coalescence of racial-religious bonds.

A *kinship group* bond coalesces frequently with (a) *sex or age* bonds, producing special kinship groups restricted to a certain age or sex group (K.+A.G. and K.+S.G.); also with (b) *occupational* (K.+O.G.), (c) *economic* (K.+E.G.), (d) *religious* (K.+Rs.G.), and (e) *political party* bonds (K.+Pp.G.). As a rule, kinsmen belong to the same *state* and the same *language-culture* group (K.+S. L.G.).

The *sex group* bond combines fairly easily with the following bonds: (a) With an *occupational* group bond, giving a double-sex-occupational group (S.+O.G.), with occupations specifically reserved for or predominantly monopolized by either males or females. In some populations the differentiation of occupations along sex lines is sharp and rigid; in others it is less clear-cut. Even in contemporary populations, as we have seen from the foregoing statistical data, there are still important occupations reserved for men, and others monopolized by women. (b) With an *age group bond*, producing double *sex-age* (S.+A.G.) compounded groups of youth, of mature persons, and of old people of each sex. Many associations and organizations, such as the Y.M.C.A., Y.W.C.A., "Spars," "Waves," play groups of children, and the *filii* and *filiae familias* in ancient Rome (formally defined as *personae alieni juris*) are examples of such double componds. (c) With a *political-party bond* (S.+Pp.G.), producing such organizations as the Women's Republican Club, the Suffragist Political Association, the League of Women Voters, and similar political parties reserved for men. (d) With some *Educational* and *professional bonds* (S.+E. and S.+Pr.G.), producing groups such as universities, colleges, and other schools, literary societies, scientific groups, etc. whose membership is confined to either men and boys or women and girls. (e) With an *economic group bond* (S.+E.G.), the women in some populations (as in early Rome), being deprived of all property rights. (f) More rarely with a *religious bond* (S.+Rs.G.), exemplified by monasteries and by male or female religious sects. (g) Very rarely with a *territorial group bond* (S.+T.G.), exemplified by populations with a territorial segregation of the sexes. (h) With a *kinship group bond* (S.+K.G.), yielding double-bonded groups based on matrilineal or patrilineal descent.

The *age group bond* frequently combines with the following bonds: (a) With a *sex group bond* (A.+S.G.). (b) With an *occupational bond* (A.+O.G.), certain occupations being either prohibited to or monopolized by given age groups, as in the case of the prohibition of child labor and of gainful occupations for juveniles, and in that of occupations which either actually or legally (for instance those of the President of the United States and of United States Senators and Congressmen) are reserved for certain age groups. (c) With an *economic bond* (A.+E.G.), the youth being deprived (as in early Rome) of all property rights. Even in contemporary societies the youth up to a certain age are deprived of some economic rights. Moreover, as Bertillon's and other studies show, in France and in certain other countries, the maximum wealth is amassed by persons between the ages of fifty and seventy. "Those who die before the age of twenty-five rarely leave an inheritance. As we pass to higher age groups the proportion of inheritances progressively increases. Between the ages of fifty and seventy about three-fourths of the deceased possess property and leave an inheritance."[1] (d) With a *political party bond* (A.+Pp.G.), giving such double-bonded groups as the Young Republicans and the Communist Youth Organization (Komsomol). (e) With *educational* and *recreational* bonds (A.+E. and A.+Rl.G.), such as those of elementary schools, high schools, and colleges, each of which prescribes maximum and minimum ages for its students. (f) More rarely an age-group bond compounds with *religious, territorial, language, kinship, and racial* bonds (A.+Rs., A.+T., A.+L., A.+K., A.+R.G.).

A *territorial group bond* most frequently forms compounds (a) with a *language group bond* (T.+L.G.); (b) with a *religious bond* (T.+Rs.G.), creating large or small territorial groups with the same religion; (c) with a *political-party bond* (T.+Pp.G.), yielding regional or territorial groups predominantly or monopolistically Republican, Democratic, Communist, etc.; (d) with a *kinship group bond* (T.+K.G.), in the form of a population living in a circumscribed territory, all or most of the

---

[1] J. Bertillon, "Statistique des successions en France et à l'étranger," *Bulletin de l'Institut International Statistique*, Vol. XVIII, Part II, pp. 360-370.

members being blood relatives; (e) with an *economic bond* (T.+E.G.), producing poor and rich urban and rural districts; (f) with a *state bond* (T.+S.), each territory being occupied by citizens of the same state; (g) with an *occupational bond* (T.+O.G.), producing a local population pursuing a single dominant occupation (for example, agriculture or trade); (h) with *educational* and other *professional bonds* (T.+E. and T.+Pl.G.), giving a local population constituting a school center, hospital center, motion-picture and recreational center, and so on; (i) with a *race group bond* (T.+R.G.), establishing racially identical stock inhabiting a certain territory, and racially segregated districts in the cities. It rarely enters into combination with age or sex group bonds.

The *religious group bond* has an affinity for and hence frequently combines with (a) a *language bond*, (b) a *territorial bond*, (c) a *political-party bond*, (d) a *kinship bond* (in early societies), (e) a *state bond*, and (f) a *territorial bond*, leading, for instance, to the predominantly Slavic Eastern-Orthodox double group, the Catholic population of Quebec province, or the "ecological concentration" of a certain religion within a given urban or rural district; (g) an *occupational bond*, examples of which are afforded by the religions of warriors, merchants, peasants, and other occupational groups; (h) a *political-party bond*: the Catholic Centrist Party and the Christian Democrats. Less frequently a religious bond compounds with sex, age, or racial bonds. Finally, especially in the past, the state has prescribed and tolerated only certain religions, thus merging the *state bond* with the religious bond. Even now, despite the general prevalence of religious freedom, there are still exclusively or predominantly Catholic, Protestant, and Mohammedan states.

A *political party bond* easily compounds with *state, language, territorial, occupational* and *religious* bonds, as well as with *sex, age, race,* and *kinship* bonds.

The *state group bond* frequently coalesces with *religious, territorial, language, racial,* and *political-party* bonds.

The *occupational group bond* readily enters into a union with *sex, age, kinship, territorial, political-party,* and *race* bonds. It combines less readily with *religious, state, and language group bonds.*

Such are some of the double "affined" compounds of each of the unibonded ties. The list does not exhaust the double compounds, and it does not include any of the triple and more complex bonded groups. The foregoing discussion furnishes, however, an idea of "sociological chemistry" unknown to contemporary sociology and a chart of what the structural analysis of a group or population really means. The subject opens a practically uncharted field of sociological exploration promising many fruitful results. Some of the most important triple, quadruple, and more complex multibonded groups will be analyzed in this and subsequent chapters.

5. Open, Closed, and Intermediary Multibonded Groups

Like the unibonded groups, the multibonded ones are open, closed, or intermediary from the standpoint of their accessibility to new members and of the ease of withdrawing from membership. The compounded groups made up of closed unibonded subgroups are usually closed; those made up of open or intermediary subgroups are generally open or intermediary, respectively. However, the very fact of compounding may make a compounded group open or closed regardless of the open or closed character of the unibonded ties and subgroups of which it is composed. Groups of Republican Protestants and of Catholic factory workers are examples of double-bonded open groups, since there are no legal or any other formal obstacles to joining or withdrawing from such groups. Such complex multibonded groups as the caste and, in a lesser degree, the medieval estate and groups of slaves or serfs are almost closed groups. Membership in such groups is ordinarily determined by birth and is terminated as a rule only by death. A few other ways exist, such as outcasting, or a change of caste due to some exceptional circumstances; the accident of being taken prisoner in war; the act of voluntarily selling oneself into serfdom or slavery; liberation (*manumissio*) of a serf or slave by his master; and the purchase of freedom from one's master. These methods are, however, comparatively exceptional.

The multibonded groups in which one of the constituent ties is *sex, age, or race* are necessarily closed to all who do not belong to a specified sex, age, or race. Examples are furnished by such groups as Negro Baptists, women journalists, and a society of male septuagenarians.

Multibonded groups such as Democratic university professors, Protestant directors of the United States Steel Corporation, and most of the multibonded groups of more or less privileged character are intermediary between the closed and open multibonded types. Theoretically and legally anyone may become a Democratic university professor, a Protestant director of the United States Steel Corporation or a member of any of the existing social classes. Actually, however, there are hundreds of obstacles which prevent the vast majority of persons from becoming members of the more or less privileged groups. To those who lack the proper qualifications they are closed. In this sense they are intermediary between the closed and the open groups.

6. Multibonded Groups Especially Characteristic of Certain Periods and Populations

Among the various multibonded groups special attention should be given to those which are especially characteristic of the structure of a given population at a certain period. For instance, the specific multibonded group known as the caste is typical of the total structure of the vast population of India, and is absent in almost all other countries. Another powerful multibonded group, known as the social class, is specifically characteristic of the western population of the last few centuries and was nonexistent as an important group in the western population of the Middle Ages. Again, a certain type of family—say, the

patriarchal family—as a multibonded group, is characteristic of certain populations and periods, and is not found as a dominant type in certain other populations and periods.

Such a double-bonded group as socialistic factory workers (a compound of political party and occupation) has been a typical feature of many western countries during the last hundred and seventy-five years, but was virtually nonexistent in western populations before the end of the eighteenth. On the other hand, the double group whose members were citizens of the same state and were obliged to conform to the religion prescribed by the state (*cuius regio, eius religio*) was characteristic of the medieval European population. With the establishment of religious freedom it tended to dissociate and is no longer typical.

7. According to Size, Degree of Centralization, Integration, Organization, Influence

Finally, like the unibonded groups, the multibonded groups may be large or small, centralized or decentralized, possessed of an integrated or unintegrated culture, well organized or poorly organized, and historically influential or the reverse.

For the foregoing reasons, the number and variety of the multibonded groups are enormous. A mere catalogue of all the different forms would fill hundreds of pages. We shall accordingly content ourselves with a survey and analysis of only those multibonded groups that have played an important role in the historical process and that are characteristic of large aggregates of population. These qualifications apply pre-eminently to two series of multibonded groups: (a) *the family, the clan, the tribe, the nation*; (b) *the caste, the estate, the social class*

III. The Immature State of Classification and Definition of Social Groups, Such as the Community, Ethnic Group, and Tribe

Before undertaking a structural analysis of the typical and historically important multibonded groups a few remarks are in order respecting the extremely confused, inconsistent, and immature state of classification and definition of these and other multibonded groups.

It is impossible to define them adequately or properly to analyze their structure on the basis of the current terminology and procedure. For instance, a given term is applied loosely to cover a number of quite different groups; conversely, a given group is designated by a number of different terms. Not infrequently a term lacks any definite meaning. This charge may be substantiated by a cursory analysis of such supposedly well-defined terms as "community," "people," "ethnic group," "gens," "horde," "clan," "tribe," "sib," "society," and "band."

1. The Community

"Community" is one of the basic and most frequently used terms in sociology and social science. Nevertheless, its meaning fluctuates widely, not only from scholar to scholar but from one page to another of the same work of the same scholar.[2] A survey of its meanings reveals that they embrace such diverse conceptions as that of a mere nominal aggregation of individuals, a unibonded territorial group, and any variety of multibonded groups including a territorial bond. What would one say of a chemist who applied the term "water" to cover H_2O, H_2SO_4, and all the other compounds of oxygen, hydrogen, and various other chemical elements? or of a taxonomist who designated a species of plants as "vegetables"? Sociology and the other social sciences are in a precisely analogous situation. They apply the term "community" to the most heterogeneous groups and even to pseudo-groups. If we are to use the term "community," we obviously should apply it to the same kind of group, with the same bonds and other characteristics. If it is used to mean a unibonded territorial or local group in the sense given above, it should not be applied to any other unibonded group nor to multibonded groups, as is regularly done now. If it refers to a multibonded group, with a territorial bond as one of the compounded bonds, the precise kind of multibonded group should be specified, including the number and character of the bonds.

We have seen that there is an enormous number of different multibonded groups. We have seen also that even the multibonded groups with a territorial bond as one of the components yield a great many different double and triple groups, as well as those of a still more complex character. I have pointed out, for instance, that the double groups with the territorial bond as one of the ties include the following types: (a) territorial-religious, (b) territorial-occupational and territorial-economic, (c) territorial-language, (d) territorial-political, (e) territorial-educational, (f) territorial-recreational, (g) territorial-kinship, and (h) territorial-racial. Evidently one should not designate by the same term, "community," without further specification, groups so diverse in their structure and functions. Still greater is the number and variety of the triple groups (territorial plus two other bonds), the quadruple groups, and so on. To cover all these by the same term, without further specification, such as a formula of their composition, is as unscientific as to designate by the term "water" a long series of heterogeneous chemical compounds in which either oxygen or hydrogen is one of the elements, or all substances that are in the fluid form.

The classification and analysis employed in this work serve both to reveal the fundamental defect of the current use of the term and to suggest a radical remedy. This remedy may consist in discarding the term as too vague, or in applying it to all human collectivities in the sense in which "population" is used, or in assigning to it a definite meaning—either that of a unibonded territorial group or that of a specified multibonded group with the territorial bond as one of its components. The terms "unibonded territorial group," "double territorial-language group," "territorial-religious group" (referring, say, to a Baptist parish), and "territorial-occupational group," as well as those referring to other double groups and to more complex groups compounded with a territorial bond, furnish us a much more precise formula of the sociocultural nature of the group than the term "community" employed without any definite specification.

2. The Horde, Clan, Tribe, Gens, People, and Ethnic Group

What has been said of the current use of "community" applies also to that of "horde,"

---

[2] For examples of different meanings of the term, cf. C. Zimmerman, *The Changing Community* (New York, 1938), Chps. 1-4.

"clan," "tribe," "gens," "people," "ethnic groups," "caste," "social class," "estate," and "nation." These terms are used constantly by sociologists, anthropologists, historians, and other scholars. Yet none of them has any definite, uniform meaning in the works of different authors and not infrequently in the works of the same author. Highly pertinent is M. Kovalevsky's observation on the tribe or clan: "Probably I shall surprise many of my readers by the statement that the problem of the origin and initial character of the tribe (or clan) is still an open—that is, an unsolved —problem. 'How!' they may retort: 'is it not established that a tribe (or clan) is an agglomeration of persons stemming from a common ancestor?' Yes, such is the current opinion. It may be found in any text on ethnology or the history of law. Without any further analysis it is repeated in various texts and encyclopedias. And yet, so far, the problem is not solved at all."[3]

The various meanings of "tribe," "clan," and "horde" found in texts of sociology, anthropology, history, and other social and humanistic sciences are suggested by such vague definitions as "By 'tribe' we refer simply to a particular primitive society."[4] Some writers identify a tribe with a kinship group. Again, a tribe, clan, or horde is represented as an indefinite kind of multibonded group. The tribe is depicted also as a variety of state, as a confederation of states, or as a nation. The confusion is further increased by applying "tribe," "clan," and "horde" now to identical groups and now to different groups.

The unbelievable chaos in this field is even greater when one considers the hundreds of tribal groups discussed without any attempt to analyze their real structure. What kind of groups are, for instance, the Dakotas, Iroquois, Crows, Navahos, Sioux, Zuñis, Ashantis, Nandi, Bantus, Zulus, Andamanese, Trobrianders, Mundugmors, etc.? If they are all "tribes," "clans," or "hordes," does this mean that their structure is identical? If so, of what kind is it? If not, why are they all designated by identical terms? Add to these

[3] M. Kovalevsky, *Sociology* (in Russian, St. Petersburg, 1911), Vol. II, p. 91.
[4] K. Young, *Introductory Sociology* (cited), p. 217.

"preliterate" groups the hundreds of "historical" groups referred to by historians as "tribes," "clans," "hordes," or "gens"—the Sarmatians, Huns, Slavs, Scythians, Venetians, Goths, Visigoths, Teutons, Turks, Scots, Mongolians, Manchurians, Koreans, etc. Are these groups meant to be nominal or real groups? If real groups, do they represent merely a language group, a kinship group, a territorial group, or a "camp" (as some anthropologists call a tribe)? Or are they some kind of multibonded group? If so, precisely what kind?

The same objection applies to such terms as "ethnic group," "gens," and "people." We constantly use these terms. Thus we speak of the "American people," "Russian people," "Korean people," "Jewish people," "Tasmanian people," and so on, designating by the same term, "people," quite different groups. The same is true of the terms "ethnic group," "social class," and "nation" and to some extent in the case of "social estate" and "caste."

Such an utterly unscientific procedure cannot be continued if we are to avoid confusion. The best remedy is to substitute a formula for each group, designating its unibonded or multibonded structure, with all the necessary specifications as to its openness or closeness, subgroups and subdivisions, and so on. The terms "tribe," "clan," "gens," "horde," "ethnic group," "people," etc. would then be superfluous, because they would not add anything to the exact formula. If we still wished to retain them, they could be given a definite meaning as designating one of the specified unibonded or multibonded groups.

Precisely this has been the procedure in the few cases where investigators have succeeded in satisfactorily defining the structure of the groups designated by them as "horde" or "clan." For instance, D. F. Thomson defines "clan" (in a patrilineal group) as "a man and all his relatives in the male line: that is, his father, his father's brothers and sisters, his own brothers and sisters, and his sons and daughters, and all the children of the male members of the clan only." "Solidarity within the clan is maintained by the bond furnished by (a) common descent, (b) the possession of common totems, (c) the possession of common territory." Whether we call such a group a "clan" or "abracadabra," its structure is clearly defined. In our generalized terms Thomson's clan is a multibonded group tied together by at least the bonds of *blood kinship* of the specified nature, *common religion* (so far as the totemic tie is a religious tie), *common territory, common language and culture* (unmentioned by him). The essentials of the structure of the group are clear.

No less clearly does he define what he calls "horde" (in contradistinction from, for instance, E. Durkheim's "horde," which is undefined).[5] Thomson indicates that "all these men (of the clan) marry women who are members of other clans, and again their sisters and daughters marry men of other clans, so that the group of people popularly spoken of as a 'camp,' that is found at any time within a clan territory, really consists of members of many clans, and for this group the word 'horde' will be used. Thus a horde consists of all the male members of the clan whose territory it inhabits with their wives, who, though they are members of the horde, are not members of the clan (since entry to a clan is by birth alone), less those women of the clan who have married into other hordes. But while they may change their hordes by marriage, they can never change their clans." None of the bonds uniting the members of the clan unite the members of the horde. "Solidarity of the horde . . . depends solely upon the cohesive force supplied by marriage and the bond set up between a man and a woman (who are members of different clans) by the children and by sharing of normal activities of everyday life, by fighting with other hordes," and by "collective ceremonies of dancing, especially by war, funeral and vengeance dances."[6]

Whether we call such a group by "horde" or "abracadabra," its structure and uniting

bonds are sufficiently clearly defined by the author. In our system of classification his horde is a multibonded group made up of the following compounded bonds: (a) territorial; (b) kinship (through marriage and children); (c) occupational and economic (in the sense of cooperation in securing the means of subsistence); (d) possibly linguistic (though not mentioned by the author); (e) the bond of common experience, common enemies, common recreations, and the semi-religious ritual of the war, vengeance, and funeral cult.

Sufficiently clear are also the meanings of the Iroquois gens, tribe, and confederation in the classical description of L. H. Morgan; for he denotes these in the terms of one of our unibonded or multibonded groups. Thus:

When the Iroquois confederacy was formed, about *A.D.* 1400-1450, the Iroquois were in five independent tribes, occupied territories contiguous to each other, and spoke dialects of the same language which were mutually intelligible. Besides these facts, certain gentes were common in the several tribes . . . The confederacy rested upon the tribes ostensibly, but primarily upon common gentes. All the members of the same gens, whether Mohawks, Oneidas, Onondagas, Cayugas, or Senecas, were brothers and sisters to each other in virtue of their descent from the same common ancestor, and they recognized each other as such with fullest cordiality. . . . Three of the gentes—namely, the Wolf, Bear, and Turtle—were common to the five tribes; these and three others were common to three tribes. . . . Between the separated parts of each gens, although its members spoke different dialects of the same language, there existed a fraternal connection . . . founded upon consanguinity.[7]

Ignoring other details of Morgan's description, we perceive that his tribe is a multibonded territorial, linguistic, and cultural group (with all the common mores, beliefs, and so on

[5] Cf. E. Durkheim, *The Rules of Sociological Method*, pp. 82-83. His statement that it is the "simplest" group, one "which does not include, and has never included, within itself any other elementary aggregate, but is directly composed of individuals," does not serve to define any group. Would the contact of three strangers constitute a horde? or a family which "is directly composed of individuals"? or a small territorial group of primitive collectors of the gifts of nature? What kind of bond unites the members of such a horde is unknown. Its size is also unknown. Is it a uni-

bonded or multibonded group? The same observations apply to Spencer's "simplest" group.

[6] D. F. Thomson, "The Joking Relationship and Organized Obscenity in North Queensland," *AA* (N.S.), Vol. 37, pp. 462-463.

[7] L. H. Morgan, "Houses and House Life of the American Aborigines," *Contributions to North American Ethnology*, Vol. IV, pp. 25-39. For a relatively consistent use of the terms "Horde," "Bande," "Klan," "Sippe," "Stamm," and "Volk," cf. R. Thurnwald, *Die menschliche Gesellschaft*, Vol. IV.

based on these bonds), while his gentes—the Wolf, the Bear, etc.—are multibonded: kinship+dialect of the same language+a somewhat larger territorial group+the common mores, manners, and beliefs based on these bonds. Again, it is unimportant whether we designate these groups as "tribes" or "gentes"; what *is* important is that their bond structure is fairly clearly defined.

We can now turn to a structural analysis of the important multibonded groups. We shall start with the family and its formation.

IV. The Differentiation of Populations into Family Groups and Family Formations

We know that the population of almost any area is differentiated into family units. Contrary to the opinion of many who regard the family as the simplest social unit, it is one of the most complex multibonded groups.[8] Its "sociochemical" formula is as follows: The family in its fully developed form, is (1) highly solidary ("familistic"); (2) highly intensive; (3) highly extensive (coterminous with the total range of important values); (4) semiclosed; (5) a socially sanctioned union of husband(s) and wife (wives), parents and children, and relatives; (6) bound together (ordinarily for life) by an enormous number of bonds (that is, meanings, values, and norms): (a) the satisfaction of the sexual needs of the husband(s) and wife (wives); (b) procreation; (c) procuring for the members the means of subsistence; (d) the socialization and education of especially the younger generation (through linguistic, religious, moral, mental, physical, and occupational training), to fit them for adult life; (e) the protection of the life, integrity, and values of its members from enemies and other dangers; (f) the mitigation of their psychosocial isolation; (g) the promotion of their happiness and development. In other words, it is a multibonded group made up of a unique compounding of heterogeneous and mutually supplementary *sex-group bonds; age and race-group bonds;*

close kinship bonds; territorial bonds (the family dwelling); language and culture bonds (one's native language is ordinarily the language of the family in which one is born); *religious bonds* (the family cult—from 70 to 90 per cent of people share the religion of the family in which they were born); *occupational and economic bonds* (occupational training of the children and transmission of occupation from parents to children,[9] the family acting as a working team in procuring its means of subsistence); and *educational, moral,*[10] and *recreational bonds.* In brief, almost all the important bonds are compounded in the family group. For this reason its solidarity embraces the whole life experience and life values of its members, resulting in the merging of their activities and their individual selves into a single close-knit collectivity. As such it is the only true *Gemeinschaft,* the only all-embracing "community" of bodies and souls, of minds and activities. It is, indeed, as the great Roman lawyer Modestinus defined it, *"consortium omnis vitae, divini et humani juris communicatio."*

This unique structure of the family, and the extremely vital biosocial and cultural functions it performs, explain its extraordinary role in influencing not only its members but also outsiders, as well as sociocultural processes in

[8] Cf. E. Durkheim, "Introduction à la sociologie de la famille," *Annales de la Faculté des Lettres* (Bordeaux, 1888), pp. 257-281.

[9] The children of even the contemporary family follow the occupation of their parents in a higher proportion than any other occupation. Approximately the same ratio applies to their inheritance of the economic and social status of their parents. (For the figures, cf. my *Mobility* (New York, 1926), Chps. 17-18.)

[10] Even the modern family—weakened as it is—still exerts a greater influence upon the children than any other agency. For instance, the coefficient of resemblance between the moral ideas of city children and those of their parents is .545, while the coefficient of resemblance between those of children and their friends is .353, for children and club leaders .137, for children and public-school teachers .028, and for children and Sunday-school teachers, .002. Cf. H. Hartshorne and M. May, "Testing the Knowledge of Right and Wrong," *Religious Education,* Vol. XXI (1926), p. 545.

general. The power of each individual family is, of course, insignificant—its size is too small to be historically and socially effective. However, the *influence of the totality of families of the same type is gigantic, hardly rivaled by that of any other unibonded or multibonded group. The patriarchal, the family-souche,* and *the particularist family formation,*[11] and the monogamic, polygamic, and other types,[12] embrace hundreds of millions of human beings, who enter the family, as the first sociocultural group, immediately after their birth and remain under its monopolistic influence during the formative years of their life, when the organism is plastic and when each influence leaves an indelible impression. Beginning with birth and throughout the first few years of life, the family continuously controls and shapes its members by precept and example, persuasion, and suggestion, constraints and punishment, incessantly inculcating ideas and beliefs, tastes and sympathies, manners and mores. As a result the most essential sociocultural patterning of a newborn human organism is achieved by the family. It is the first and the most efficient sculptor of human material, shaping the physical, behavioral, mental, moral, and sociocultural characteristics of practically every individual. Families of the same type of formation decisively mold millions of human beings who react similarly to an indefinite number of values, who approve or oppose the same phenomena, who strive to achieve similar ends, and who press similarly upon all the other groups.

Moreover, as has been said, the family is the most solidary of social groups. So far as the identical values of all the families of the same formation are concerned, the whole family formation becomes solidary in the defense of these values. Furthermore, directly or indirectly, most of the vehicles and means of influencing human beings are at the disposal of the family, including man power, wealth, and other resources. Thus, from the standpoint of every criterion of power, large family formations have all the characteristics of influential groups: a vast membership; a rich fund of values, meanings, and norms; highly intensive and extensive solidarity; and a huge assortment of vehicles for influencing human conduct. Hence there is much truth in the statement that "what the family is, such will society be."

To be sure, in such a form the statement is one-sided; for if the family tangibly conditions the other groups, these in their turn influence the. family. However, the statement is substantially accurate that the family formation essentially determines all the important groups and institutions of a given population. This fact has been well demonstrated in the past, especially by Confucius, and by F. Le Play and his followers in recent times. They have shown that in a population with a *dominant patriarchal family formation* the other groups and institutions and the entire sociocultural life assume the patriarchal character. Its concomitants comprise the absorption of the individual into the family "we"; the domination of the familistic and paternalistic relationship in the state and other groups; the stability and conservatism of the personality and conduct of the people; the controlling power of tradition in contrast to that of modern fashion; meager scientific and technological inventions; and a slow tempo of sociocultural change. The reason is to be sought in the character of the training which the younger generation receives in the patriarchal family. In populations with a dominant *particularist* type of family formation the institutions and groups, the modes of thinking and acting, are permeated by a spirit of individualism. The prevailing characteristics are the development of self-reliance, initiative, energy, and creativeness; the spirit of innovation versus tradition; a multiplicity of scientific, technological, and other inventions and discoveries; rapid tempo of progress; the control of the state and

[11] For Le Play's types of the family, cf. my *Theories,* Ch. 2, and C. Zimmerman and M. Frampton, *Family and Society* (New York, 1935), pp. 97 ff.

[12] For various types of the family, cf. such works as E. Grosse, *Die Formen der Familie und die Formen der Wirtschaft* (Freiburg, 1896); E. Westermarck, *The History of Human Marriage,* 3 Vols., (New York, 1921); R. Briffault, *The Mothers* (cited); M. Kovalevsky, *Tableau des origines et de l'évolution de la famille et de la propriété* (Stockholm, 1890); and L. Hobhouse, G. Wheeler, and M. Ginsberg, *The Material Culture and Social Institutions of the Simpler Peoples* (cited). Cf. also Sorokin, Zimmerman, and Galpin, *Source Book* (cited), Vol. II, Ch. 10.

the state government by public opinion, and so on. Again, the explanation is that the particularist family molds the younger generations according to this pattern.

(1) The parents of a particularist family do not regard their children as their property but as persons destined presently to be entirely independent of them. They therefore seek to hasten their emancipation.

(2) The children are treated from the very beginning as grown-up persons.

(3) The parents take into consideration not only their own lives but also the future careers of their children.

(4) Great attention is paid to the development of physical strength and to the encouragement of games and sports.

(5) Children are brought early into contact with everyday practical reality.

(6) The boys are taught some manual trade.

(7) The parents and children vie with each other in acquiring the knowledge of new well-verified facts.

(8) There is comparatively little abuse of parental authority.

(9) The children are well aware that parents will not assume the responsibility of establishing them in life.

Finally, populations dominated by an *unstable family formation* neither educate the new generation to have respect for authority nor train them to be independent. Such a type of family develops individuals relying neither upon a stable patriarchal family nor upon themselves, but primarily upon the state. They are trained by the family for bureaucratic positions in the military and civil hierarchy of the state. Hence such societies are marked by a centralized bureaucracy which regulates and controls most of the social relationships, by an underdeveloped public opinion, by the absence of the traditionalism and the rational modernism of the patriarchal and particularist types of society, respectively; and by a general instability signalized by inconsistent and often irrational changes, sometimes of explosive character. The entire family and school education of the young is concentrated on preparation for the official examinations for state positions—not on the training necessary to fit them, as self-reliant

persons, for the free choice of their vocation.[13]

Such are the basic types of the family and the corresponding national types according to Le Play and his school. Apart from the one-sidedness of their thesis, it is approximately valid.

Owing to the complex multibonded character of the family it incessantly interacts with virtually all the other groups. Its interests now coincide, now conflict, with those of certain other groups. When they collide, a struggle of the family formation with the antagonistic group ensues. The struggle is carried on by the family formation with relentless determination, and more often than not results in victory.

This power of the family formation is so great that leaders of conflicting groups have rarely dared to attack it directly. Even major social movements, including revolutions, have seldom ventured to effect a radical change in the family. On the rare occasions that the state and other groups have attempted to destroy or drastically modify the existing family type, they have seldom succeeded; and when they have their success has generally proved short-lived. In its defensive struggle the family formation has sometimes had to yield ground and occasionally has succumbed to the attack; but as a rule it has revived and come back as strong as before. Examples of this successful defensive struggle of the family against the attempts of other groups to make it conform to their own interests are afforded by the various unsuccessful attempts of the state or of religious or other groups to change it. Such were the efforts of the Roman Empire to impose upon the family a universal marriage duty and the duty to have children (*lex Julia et Papia Poppaea*) for all men between the ages of twenty-five and sixty and for all women between the ages of twenty and fifty. Such laws remained largely nugatory. Similar results have attended many analogous laws of states and of religious organizations to increase or decrease the birth rate of the families, to eliminate or liberalize divorces and separations, to prohibit or facilitate extramarital sexual relations, and so on.[14] Only when

---

[13] For the details, cf. my *Theories* and Zimmerman and Frampton, *op. cit.*

[14] For the triumph of the family in its conflicts with the state, cf. J. Cruet, *La Vie du droit et l'impuissance des lois* (Paris, 1908), pp. 125-137.

these measures have been in agreement with the needs of the family itself have they met with any success; otherwise they have proved largely ineffectual.

Striking examples of a seemingly complete collapse of the family under the relentless impact of inimical state or revolutionary groups and of its speedy revival are furnished by the cases where revolutionary movements and their victorious governments have attempted to eliminate the family as a stronghold of capitalism, inequality, or other social evils. In many major social revolutions there have been extreme factions that have demanded such destruction of the family. In most cases they have failed. When, for instance, in the Taborite revolutionary state in Bohemia the family was dissolved and the monogamic form of union was annulled, the family, temporarily crushed, was rehabilitated within a few years. Still more striking was the Soviet experiment. During the first few years of the Communist revolution the government did its best to destroy the family as the cornerstone of private property. A long series of legal and other measures was carried out with a view to undermining monogamic marriage and the family. Divorces and abortions were freely permitted, and even the registration of a marriage was non-obligatory. Legally the difference between socially sanctioned marriage and incidental sex relationships was eliminated by establishing three forms of the contract between the male and female: for an indefinite period, for a definite period, and for a single occasion. The family as a union of parents and children was weakened by inciting the children against their parents; by prohibiting parents from giving religious and other forms of education to their children; by the establishment of state children's homes; and so on. For a few years the family seemed indeed doomed to extinction. Divorces increased at a fantastic rate, as well as desertions and separations; and extramarital sex relations expanded enormously. However, between 1925 and 1930 a reaction to this policy set in and steadily grew. By approximately 1940 the family had

been revived, in many ways even more monogamic and "Victorian" than before the Revolution. The Soviet decree of July 14, 1944, in a sense summed up the process of the revival, making divorce exceedingly difficult —indeed, almost inaccessible to the vast majority of the population, for economic and other reasons. The remarkable feature of this experiment is that the disintegration as well as the reintegration took place under the same government. The family revived contrary to the plans of this government and compelled it to suspend its hostile policy, to legalize the family, and to prohibit the forces undermining its stability, integrity, and solidarity.

These illustrations demonstrate the extraordinary defensive power of the family against attacks. This power is equally in evidence when the family carries on an offensive struggle against other groups. Here also more often than not it has proved victorious. The dissolution of the tribal organization was caused to a large extent by the rising antagonism between its interests and the demands of the family, from which struggle the family emerged firmer and stronger than before. Many small new states have succumbed to the hostile impact of family groups inimical either to the state or to its rulers, or else have been compelled to adapt themselves to the growing demands of the family. This is clearly seen in various official state norms regulating marriage contracts and their dissolution, the rights and duties of the husband and wife, of the parents and children, the family property, the forms of inheritance, etc. A careful study of these norms indicates how they were enacted under the pressure of a family formation upon a state unwilling to enact the measures in question.[15] P. Lavrov sums up the situation thus: "The family submits to the authority of the state only because it considers its . . . interests better safeguarded in a strong political union than outside of it; it causes a commotion within the state as soon as it finds its own interests opposed to those of the state or not sufficiently protected by it."[16] Similarly, the family has

---

[15] Cf. J. Cruet, *op. cit.*, and J. Pokrovsky, *The Basic Problems of Civil Law* (St. Petersburg, 1917). Cf. also the latest civil codes, and the explanatory comments of the latest codifiers.

[16] P. Lavrov, *Works* (in Russian, St. Petersburg, 1918), Vol. V, p. 43. Cf. also N. K. Mikhailovsky, "The Struggle for Individuality," in his *Works* (St. Petersburg, 1904).

exerted pressure, often successfully upon religious, political-party, kinship, language, and other groups, compelling them either to cease their attacks upon the family, or to readjust their policies in the direction demanded by its needs.

On the other hand, the family is constantly subjected to the influence of other groups and is often obliged to adapt itself to their demands. Hence the pressure and readjustment are not one-sided but mutual. The role of the state and the church in modifying the forms of the family, including those of marriage, is fairly obvious. By means of various laws prohibiting marriage without the intervention of the clergy, regulating divorce, and determining the property relations obtaining between the parents and the children, they have effected a considerable transformation of the family in accordance with their own interests. The same generalization applies to the influence exerted by other groups.

As a matter of fact, the entire culture of a given population modified the character of the family, as evidenced by the contemporary crisis of the western family. Owing to the drastic changes in many influential groups and in the total group structure of the western peoples, and to the disintegration of their dominant (sensate) system of culture (cf. Chapters 40-42), the contemporary western family faces a serious crisis involving its structure, functions, and integrity. This crisis is revealed in many different ways. The family as a union of husband and wife is becoming ever weaker and more short-lived, as the steadily rising rate of divorces and separations and of premarital[17] and extramarital sex relations indicates. Similarly, as a union of parents and children it tends to disintegrate, as evidenced by the mounting percentage of childless marriages; the progressively earlier separation of children from their parents; the increasing dispersal of the members of the family; and the marked decline in the monopolistic influence of the family upon the children. Still more striking is its decline as a union of relatives. Its growing structural and functional atrophy is revealed by the dissociation of many of its bonds. The steadily falling birth rate indicates that the family is performing the function of procreation less and less efficiently; its educational and socializing functions are being progressively transferred to the nursery schools, kindergartens, elementary schools, high schools and colleges; and the economic function of furnishing the means of subsistence for its members is being taken over more and more by the state and by occupational and other groups. The same is true of its recreational functions. Finally, it is evident that children are less and less disposed to adopt the occupation, religion, mores, political views, etc. of their parents.[18]

Nevertheless, there is every reason to believe that this crisis, like many others in the past, will eventually lead to a reintegration of the family (in a somewhat modified form in respect to its secondary characteristics). For the family is an indispensable institution and cannot be replaced by any other organized group. The concrete forms of the family and of marriage change, but their essentials are perennial.

The family is in some respects a closed and in others an intermediary group. It is closed in the sense that one is born into a certain family and cannot easily repudiate the relationship, despite the legal possibility of adoption by a different family. It is an intermediary group from the standpoint of the regulations governing marriage, divorce, and adoption, which permit a certain degree of circulation of individuals from family to family. The range of such shifts, for legal and other reasons, is, however, very restricted.

[17] According to Terman, premarital virginity and chastity declined in the United States from 65 to 18 per cent for males born before 1890 and after 1910, and from 85 to 32 per cent for females. Cf. L. M. Terman, *Psychological Factors in Marital Happiness* (New York, 1938).

[18] For the facts and literature, cf. Sorokin, Zimmerman, and Galpin, *Source Book*, Vol. II, Ch. 10. See any of the competent treatises on the family, such as W. Ogburn, "The Family and Its Functions," *Recent Social Trends* (New York, 1933), Ch. 13; E. Mowrer, *Domestic Discord* (Chicago, 1928); and the works of C. Zimmerman, E. Burgess, J. K. Folsom, M. C. Elmer, and others.

V. The Clan, Tribe, and Nation

If we abstract the bonds compounded in the family and add several not present in the family compound, if we reduce the solidarity of the family members, and if we then bring together a sufficiently large number of families, we obtain an aggregation of multibonded groups of a fairly definite composition, three types of which call for special attention—namely, the clan, the tribe, and the nation.

1. The Clan

The clan is a solidary multibonded group consisting of an organized agglomeration of families tied together by the following bonds: (a) mainly blood kinship; (b) territorial proximity; (c) common possession of their territorial abode and of certain cooperative economic enterprises; (d) common race; (e) common language and culture; (f) common religion, especially in the form of a cult of ancestors. It is an almost closed group, with a narrow gateway of marriage adoption, and blood brotherhood, and a few other channels, for an infiltration of outsiders, and with a narrow gateway of marriage, crime, etc. for the voluntary or enforced exodus of members. The solidarity of its members is less extensive and intensive than that of members of the same family. Its authority and government are an enlargement of the family authority, not yet transformed into a full-fledged state government. It is an organized group living and acting as a genuine collective unity. Being an agglomeration of families, a clan is divided into family units, and into combinations of these units as sub-groups within the clan[19] (sibs, sects, and Sippen). In the past especially, before the emergence of larger unibonded and multibonded groups, clans played a very important role. At that period human history was largely the history of the clans and their relationships.

2. The Tribe

The tribe is an organized and solidary agglomeration of two or more clans whose members are united by the following bonds: (a) territorial proximity; (b) frequently the common possession of their territorial abode; (c) common language and culture; (d) common religion; (e) remote, largely "artificial" kinship; (f) a rudimentary state bond, as distinct from "family and kinship" government. Now and then it is racially homogeneous. It represents the multibonded group from which later on, through its dissociation, there developed the multibonded nation and the unibonded state group. It is less closed than the clan, since blood kinship and race play a less important part in it. Through conquest and subjugation, through imperceptible interaction of the neighborhood groups, and through similar channels a number of outsiders may eventually become assimilated by the tribe. Its solidarity is less extensive and intensive than that of the members of the clan. It is subdivided into two or more clans, sibs, and other subgroups. Its stratification is more conspicuous and clearcut and more formalized than in the clan or (especially) the family. Tribal groups have played a very significant role in earlier stages of human history, before the emergence of the state and the nation. The political and social history of that period was largely the history of tribes and their interrelationships. Among preliterate groups, and even among many state-organized populations of the East, such as those of Afghanistan and Abyssinia, tribes or similar groups still continue to play an important role. Many such "states" and "nations" constitute merely loosely knit conglomerations of tribes. In their secondary traits tribes exhibit numerous variations.

3. The Nation

The multitudinous meanings assigned to the terms "nation" and "nationality" reveal once more the crude state of the social science in their group "taxonomy." Precisely what is a nation? Is it the same as a nationality? Webster's dictionary gives the following definitions of these terms: "*Nation*. 1. A people connected by ties of blood generally manifested in community of language, religion, customs,

---

[19] The varieties of such subdivisions of clans are described by anthropologists and ethnological sociologists.

etc. 2. Any aggregation of people having like institutions and customs, and a sense of social homogeneity and mutual interest. 3. The body of inhabitants of a country united under a single government. 4. A multitude; a host." "Nationality. 1. State, quality, or relation of being, or belonging to, a nation. 2. Nationalism. 3. A nation." Thus the term covers at least four groups of basically different composition: a purely nominal aggregation, or "multitude"; a unibonded state group; and two different multibonded groups. K. Kautsky aptly sums up the situation by observing that "a nation (nationality) is like the ancient Proteus, who slips from our fingers every time we try to get hold of him."[20]

The definitions of the term given by various authors[21] range from the downright mystical to the empirically erroneous. The following are the chief types of the conception of nation and nationality. According to L. Frank, "Every national existence is to be thought of as one of the many expressions of the absolute." "A nation is a mystical being, ultrarational and superrational," says Peter Struve. "Nationalism is the active negation of sophia," and sophia is "the world of eternal ideas and primary representations which have been established by God as the foundation of creation," says E. Trubetskoy. In the opinion of I. K. Bluntschli, "The nation is a peculiar material substance which possesses a mystical power to create out of itself a community of national character." "Nationality is rationally undefinable. In this respect the idea of nationality is analogical to the idea of the Church."

Such are the definitions of the term given by N. Berdiaeff. They may be true, but they are unintelligible, at least, devoid of any definite meaning. They do not serve to distinguish the nation from other groups.

Other scholars conceive of the nation (or nationality) not as a metaphysical principle or mystical superrational essence but as a species of social group. Unfortunately they radically disagree as to what kind of group it is. Some, such as A. Gobineau, V. de Lapouge, H. von Treitschke, and the Nazi ideologists, practically identify it with either our unibonded racial group or our double territorial, racial group.[22] By such a pseudo-solution they ignore the problem of finding an important multibonded group distinct from a racial or territorial-racial group, and they contradict their own definition as well as the sociocultural facts. Instead of speaking of Caucasian, Nordic, Mongoloid, or black and white nations or nationalities, as their definition requires, they speak of the French, German, English, and Russian "nations," each of which represents a mixture of several racial types. Such self-contradiction is sufficient evidence of the invalidity of their conception.

Others identify nation with nationality—with our unibonded language group. If we accept this definition, we again ignore the problem of finding an important multibonded group of a specific character. Moreover, if we are to be consistent, we cannot speak of separate British, American, and Irish "nations," as they all use the same language. On the other hand, we cannot properly consider as a single nation the people who employ different languages, like the Walloons and the Flemish in Belgium, or strikingly dissimilar dialects, like the Sicilians and the Milanese in Italy.

For the same reason a nation cannot be identified with a state group. In that case we should again dodge the question of finding an important multibonded group different from the unibonded state group. Likewise, from the standpoint of such a definition we cannot speak of different "nationalities" within the same state or of a given "nationality" scattered among several states. The number and character of the nations must be identical with

---

[20] K. Kautsky, National Problems (Russian translation, Petrograd, 1918), p. 17.

[21] Cf. E. Renan, Qu'est-ce qu'une nation? (Paris, 1882); D. G. Brinton, "The Nation as an Element in Anthropology," Annual Report of the Smithsonian Institution (Washington, D. C.), pp. 589-600; A. van Gennep, Traité comparatif des nationalités (Paris, 1922); J. T. Delos, La Nation, 2 Vols. (Montreal, 1944); O. Jespersen, Mankind, Nation and Individual; Lord Acton, "Nationality," in His-

tory of Freedom and Other Essays (ed. by N. Figgis and R. Laurence; London, 1907); C. A. Macartney, National States and National Minorities (Oxford, 1934); F. J. Brown and J. S. Roucek (ed.), One America: Our Racial and National Minorities (New York, 1944); H. Kohn, The Idea of Nationalism (New York, 1944); and L. Adamic, A Nation of Nations (New York, 1945).

[22] Cf. Hitler's Mein Kampf; W. Darré, La Race, nouvelle noblesse du sang et du sol (Paris, 1939).

those of the states. Similarly, the emergence and disappearance of nations or nationalities must be identical with those of the states. Hence the conquest of the Polish and Czech states by Hitler must have signified the extinction of the respective nations or nationalities.

For similar reasons neither *religion* nor a *community of economic interests* can be regarded as the basic element of the nation. Both conceptions would dodge the problem of discovering a multibonded group playing an important role. The nation and nationality would be identical, respectively, with our unibonded religious and economic groups. Many persons regard themselves as belonging to the same nation in spite of having different religions, and vice versa. Likewise, a worker and a capitalist may both regard themselves as belonging to the same nation in spite of conflicting economic interests. (Workers of different nations, indeed, often have more in common than they have with the capitalists of the same nation.) From this standpoint we should have to speak of Buddhist, Mohammedan, and Baptist "nations" and of rich, moderately well-to-do, and poor "nations."

Nor can the criterion of a nation (or nationality) be the unity of *the royal dynasty* or the community of *mores, institutions, or philosophical outlook*. If Germany or Russia were nations, the replacement of the Hohenzollerns or the Romanoffs by different rulers did not change their nationhood. The mores of a Russian peasant and those of a Russian aristocrat before the Revolution differed much more than those of the Russian and German aristocrats. The same is true of organized or institutionalized forms of behavior. As to philosophical outlook, the views of German, Russian, and American Marxians, Kantians, or Hegelians are very similar, although they regard themselves as belonging to different nations.

Others, like O. Bauer,[23] find the essence of nationhood in the *common culture* of the group. Unless culture is clearly defined, however, such a criterion is too vague to be of any value. In addition, subtract from a culture the factors of language, religion, race, occupations, economics, the state, law, ethics, science, and other values of our unibonded groups, and the result will be a vacuum.

Finally, many regard as the basic element of a nation the *consciousness of belonging to a given nation or nationality or political body*.[24] It is easy to see that the conception is totally ambiguous. Individuals consciously belong to many different groups—state, political party, race, sex, age, language, religious, occupational, and other groups. Which of these groups is the nation? If it is any one of these then the conception has all the shortcomings of the above definitions identifying nation with a race, state, language (nationality), or some other group. If a nation does not coincide with any of the unibonded groups and is some kind of multibonded group, the conception does not indicate its nature at all. The same objections apply to those definitions that make a "collective mind" or "collective soul" the criterion of nationhood.

This survey shows that none of the definitions offered is acceptable; that there is no unanimity in the conception or definition of "nation." Moreover, almost all the conceptions avoid the problem as to whether the nation has been a specific multibonded group that has played an important historic role. Even when some theorists have undertaken to construe "nation" in the sense of a multibonded group,[25] they have actually sought to find a formula that would reconcile all the various meanings assigned to the term by different persons instead of discovering a group of a definite kind marked by the same essential characteristics. The attempt to find such a formula is hopeless and utterly unscientific: it does not seek to separate a class of homogeneous phenomena distinguished by the same traits—a scientific setting of the problem—but attempts instead to perform a mere linguistic feat.

We can now turn to a constructive solution

---

[23] O. Bauer, *National Problems* (in Russian, Petrograd, 1909).

[24] For example, P. Lavrov, *A Treatise on the History of Thought* (cited), p. 620, and M. Laserson, *International Aspects of the Jewish Question* (in Russian, Petrograd, 1917), pp. 12 ff.

[25] For instance, J. T. Delos, in his comparatively thoughtful work. He rightly distinguishes between the nation, the state, and several other groups. Unfortunately, the distinction is not adequately applied.

of the problem—namely, as to whether there has ever been a multibonded group *sui generis*, different from all the other unibonded and multibonded groups, and historically powerful at certain periods and among vast populations. The answer is, Yes. *It is a multibonded, solidary, organized, almost closed group made up of a coalescence of territorial, state, and language bonds.* Whether we designate such a group as a nation or as *X* is of little consequence. What *is* important is that such groups have played a significant role in sociocultural processes. What we call the French nation (in contradistinction to the French state or language group), the British nation, the German nation, the Russian nation, and the American nation are multibonded groups of precisely this composition; for each of them possesses a continuous territory, its own state, and a common language. Even when the language happens to be the same or virtually the same (as in the case of the British and American nations), the other two bonds remain distinctly separate and permit the existence of two different nations.[26] Subtract from any of these nations either its state or its territory or its language, and it could scarcely qualify as such. Subtract two of the bonds and nothing would remain save a unibonded territorial, language, or state group. In addition to these three bonds, some nations have a common religion, are composed primarily of a single racial stock, and so on. These bonds are, however, not common to all nations (in the defined sense) and therefore are not essential characteristics.

We have seen that each of these bonds—the territorial, the state, and the language bond—exerts a tangible influence upon the physical, mental, moral, and behavioral characteristics of the members of the group and upon their organization and culture. When all three are compounded, they exert a still stronger effect. In their totality they produce a "national type." This should not be interpreted, however, as involving the entire personality, all the social institutions, and the whole culture of the nation, which depend on all the important unibonded and multibonded ties. Nevertheless, there is a modicum of truth in

many of the definitions which postulate a common culture, a common body of mores, customs, and institutions, a common psychology, and so forth, in addition to a common state, territory, and language, as the characteristics of a nation. The trouble is that such definitions fail to indicate the exact place which each of these traits occupies in the nation; the specific combination of which they are elements; the precise aspects of psychology, institutions, mores and customs, and culture which are "national"; or the limits of the influence of the national factor upon the personality, social institutions, and culture of the members.

From the formula which I have prescribed it follows that all multibonded groups of different composition should not be designated by the same term. For instance, the multibonded group of the Jews, often spoken of as a nation, is not a nation according to our formula. For some two thousand years the Jews have not possessed a common state, a continuous territory, or even a common language. The majority of them speak the language of the country in which they live. Thus the bonds that constitute the French, the German, the Russian, or the American nation are not strictly applicable to the Jews. Among their essential bonds are rather, those of the Hebrew religion, the Jewish racial type (to a certain extent), and the historical traditions of the Jews.

The dominant role which the three-bonded group in question has played in historical processes has been especially conspicuous during the nineteenth and twentieth centuries—the centuries of national movements and conflicts par excellence.[27]

The nation in the sense of the defined three-bonded group (the term "nationality" should be reserved to designate the unibonded language group), emerged as the successor of the tribe (in the defined sense). When a number of tribes had become merged, the size of the resulting body often greatly increased. At the same time, several of the bonds uniting the tribe—namely, those of a common religion, of a community of ancestors and kinship, and even the tie of common economic interests,

[26] Cf. L. Adamic, *A Nation of Nations* (New York, 1945).

[27] Cf. the works of G. Weill, H. Kohn, J. Delbos, *et al.* (cited).

with the psychological, ideological, and behavioral superstructure built upon these factors —were progressively weakened or eliminated.

Nations are organized groups, since the state component is a well-organized unit. Moreover, nations are relatively closed. As a rule, one must be born within such a group to become a real member. A few channels exist —such as naturalization or the renunciation of state citizenship—for the exchange of members between different nations; but in most countries these channels are very narrow, and permit the infiltration or exodus of relatively small numbers of persons. Even in the United States, where they have been much wider than in most other countries (many of which have granted naturalization to few persons, and some of which have not permitted renunciation of state citizenship on the part of their own citizens), the majority of naturalized immigrants of the first generation have not been appreciably assimilated in respect to language, mental and moral traits, mores and manners, behavior and culture. Not until the second or third generation have they been completely transformed by the "melting pot" into full-fledged members of the American nation.

To summarize: The related multibonded groups of the family, the clan, the tribe, and the nation are among the most important multibonded groups that have influenced the historical destinies of mankind. The transition from family to nation means a progressive loss of many bonds, together with an extension of the size of the group; the family is the most complex in its bonded structure and the smallest in size, whereas the nation is the least complex in bonded structure and the largest in size.

Chapter 14. Differentiation of Population into Multibonded Groups (Continued)

I. What Is a Caste?

In addition to the family, clan, tribe, and nation there are other powerful multibonded groups that have exerted a notable influence upon their members, other groups, and the whole historical process. Of these we shall mention three multibonded groups—the caste, order, and class—that are likewise somewhat related to one another. What is a caste? The term is used in very different senses by different writers. Most of these stress mainly two traits: the closed character of the caste and the hierarchical order (or stratification) of the various castes. For this reason they apply the term even to the position of the Negroes in the United States in their relationship to the white population.[1] If we have in mind the Hindu caste system, such definitions are incomplete. They do not allow for the profound difference between the caste and the estate, and they ignore many essential traits of the caste. When

adequately defined, the Hindu caste is a closed, solidary, organized or quasi-organized multibonded group made up of racial, kinship, occupational, economic, territorial, religious, and language bonds, the state bond playing an insignificant role. These bonds produce fundamental similarities between the members of the same caste in respect to their mentality, culture, conduct, and way of life. Furthermore a given caste forms a definite stratum in the hierarchy of castes ranked by the religious law in the order of their superiority and inferiority. The hierarchy is marked by an almost total lack of vertical mobility.

That the Hindu caste has been (especially at certain periods) one of the most closed of sociocultural groups[2] is unquestionable. With rare exceptions, such as outcasting and a few other channels of intercaste circulation, one enters the caste only through the gateway of birth

---

[1] Cf. for instance, J. Dollard, *Caste and Class in a Southern Town* (New Haven, 1935).

[2] For these and other characteristics, cf. H. H. Risley, *Census of India: 1901*, Vol. I, Part I, pp. 518 ff., and especially his *People of India* (London, 1915); R. V. Russel, *The Tribes and Castes of the Central Provinces of India* (London, n.d.); C. Bouglé, *Essais sur le régime des castes* (Paris, 1908); E. Senart, *Les Castes dans l'Inde* (Paris, 1896); J. Mazzarella, "Le forme di aggregazione sociale nell' India," *Rivista Italiana di sociologia*, 1911; B. K. Sarkar, *The Positive Background of Hindu Sociology* (Allahabad, 1937); A. M. Hocart, *Les castes* (Paris, 1938); A. K. Coomaraswamy,

The Religious Basis of the Forms of Indian Society (New York, 1946)); M. Olcott, "The Caste System of India," *American Sociological Review*, Vol. 9 (1944), pp. 618-665; W. H. Wiser, *The Hindu Jajmani System* (Lucknow, 1936); Ketkar, *The History of Caste in India* (London, 1909); A. K. Mazumdar, *The Hindu History* (Faribadad, 1921); E. J. Rapson (ed.), *The Cambridge History of India* (New York, 1922); S. K. Das, *The Economic History of India* (Howrah, 1925); and the *Laws of Manu, Narada, and Brihaspati*, the *Institutes of Vishnu and Gautama*, and other law books of India, in *The Sacred Books of the East* (ed. by M. Müller), Vol. II (Oxford, 1879), Vol. VII (Oxford, 1880), Vol. XXXIII (Oxford, 1889).

and leaves it only through that of death.[3] In addition, the attachment to the caste in which one is born is obligatory, being sanctioned by the law norms of mores and religion.

That a Hindu caste is a racial group (possessing, however, a considerable mixture of blood acquired during some three thousand years of Hindu caste history) is suggested by the Hindu word for "caste"—namely, *varna*, which means "race" or "color." Even now a darkening of the color as we pass from the highest to the lowest castes is still noticeable. The preservation of racial homogeneity is favored by the fact that one belongs to the caste in which he is born and by the strict endogamic rule of marriage within one's own caste and its subcastes.

That it is a kinship group follows from the fact that members are recruited through births within the caste and from the close in-breeding which prevails.

That it is an occupational group is witnessed by the fact that each caste is assigned its own hereditary occupation. Each individual automatically follows the occupation of his caste as transmitted from generation to generation. "Castes are social aggregates that have the privilege of a hereditary monopoly of their own occupation."[4] Even criminal occupations are the monopoly of special castes. The census of 1901 listed some 4,500,000 persons belonging to such castes. This explains why some of the investigators of the origin of the caste, such as Senart, Niesfield, and Dahlmann, view the castes as a variety of guilds and find in their occupational differentiation the chief source of their origin.

That the caste is an economic group follows from the fact that "each individual has a fixed economic and social status established by his birth in a given caste."[5]

That most of the castes are definite territorial groups is also unquestionable. Even when they move from place to place, they move as a body.

That the caste is a religious group, not only in the sense that the religious values of all the members as such are the same, but especially in the sense that religion profoundly influences the mentality and behavior of its members and is one of the main foundations of the régime itself, is attested by the very name of the system—*varna ashrama aharma* (sacred religious discipline)—and by practically all competent investigators, some of whom (such as C. Bouglé, Hocart, and Coomaraswamy) go so far as to make religion *the* foundation of the system. "One of the principal bonds of the members of a caste is religion, which makes all of them the disciples of the Brahmins," says Ketkar.[6] "Caste is, to a great extent, a product of religion." "Castes are ranked, fixed to their ranks, and kept there mainly through the sentiments of pious respect and of sacred horror. Hindus do not make a distinction between the *jus* (secular law) and *fas* (sacred law)."[7] The prohibition of intercaste marriage, of taking food in the company of members of other castes, of contact and interaction with other castes (which is sometimes regulated up to such details as how near a member of a lower caste may approach a Brahmin or a member of another high caste)—these and many other manifestations of caste differentiation are rooted in religious law norms and not in the secular norms of official state law.

That a caste is a language group, and that its members have in common many cultural values distinct from those of other castes, is also attested by investigators.

That the state, with its official law, has little to do with the caste system is unanimously affirmed by competent observers. Some of these, such as C. Bouglé, go so far as to deny to the state any participation in the origin, maintenance, or functioning of the castes. "All state governments, no matter what, have existed only on the surface of the Hindu world. . . . Because the Hindus live in comparative isolation, confined within their castes, they appear to be created for subjugation by anyone, without, however, assimilating themselves to anyone else and without permitting

[3] For these channels and for horizontal and vertical mobility from caste to caste, cf. B. K. Sarkar, *op. cit.*, pp. 101 ff.; also my *Mobility*, pp. 139-140.

[4] Mazzarella, *op. cit.*, p. 199.

[5] W. H. Wiser, *The Hindu Jajmani System* (cited), pp. 5-6.

[6] Ketkar, *op. cit.*, p. 15.

[7] C. Bouglé, "Note sur le droit et la caste en Inde," *L'Année sociologique*, Vol. X, pp. 148-150; cited works of Hocart and Coomaraswamy.

any outside force to unite them. . . . The *polis*, or political organization, is lacking in India. Instead, a religious tradition dominates it through and through."[8]

The caste is marked, further, by a definite place (legalized through religious law norms) in the entire hierarchy of stratification into superior and inferior castes. In the classical hierarchy of the four main castes established by the ancient law books the order was as follows: Brahmanas, Kshatriyas, Vaisyas, and Sudras. (In addition there were the outcastes.) "Among these each preceding caste is superior by birth to the following one."[9] At the present time there are between 2500 and 3000 different castes. Their ranking is less simple than in the case of the four classical castes; nevertheless it is fairly definite, and is generally reckoned on the basis of the nearness of a given caste to the highest caste—that of the Brahmins.[10]

Finally, a caste is a *solidary and thoroughly organized body*, in which almost all the details of the conduct of its members in relation to one another and to outsiders are regulated by the religious and customary law norms. The caste organization is so detailed and its unity is so close that many investigators compare the group to an organism. "In reality, Brahmanism is nothing less than a body" ("n'est rien moins qu'un corps").[11]

In spite of this closely knit organization of the individual castes, the system as a whole is *decentralized.* Neither the state nor any other central power in India plays an appreciable part in maintaining the caste system. There is no central executive committee of the castes to control intercaste relationships. Moreover,

within a given caste, although there may be a council of elders or a chieftain, their power is limited and in no way comparable to the centralized government of the state. The highest caste—that of the Brahmins—has been rightly called a caste of priests without any church organization, since it has no pope, primate, bishop, central assembly, or any central authority whatsoever. With the exception of the principle of complete prohibition of mixture of blood, it has no credo.

The Hindu caste is one of the most complex of multibonded groups. It differs sharply from the occupational guild (even the type in which the occupation is hereditary). It differs likewise from all the social orders and estates. This type of social group, in fact, seems to have existed on a large scale only in India.[12] Since its emergence in India some three thousand years ago, caste has been the most stable, the most all-pervading, and the most influential social group. States and empires have arisen and passed away; various other associations and groups have appeared and disappeared; but the caste system has persisted. It has, to be sure, known periods of relative weakening and decline, such as the present period, but it is still the basic group in Hindu society, and the most important co-ordinate determining the sociocultural position and character of a person in India. Considering that India embraces about one-fourth of the human race, the important role played by the caste system there has constituted a very significant factor in the entire history of humanity.

---

[8] Bouglé, "Note" (cited), p. 156. The situation is stated more accurately by Mazzarella and others (see Mazzarella, *op. cit.*, pp. 216-219).

[9] Cf. the volumes (cited) of the *Sacred Books of the East: Apastamba, Prashnas,* I; *Patala,* I, *Khanda,* II; *The Laws of Manu,* I, 87-91. For similar statements, cf. *Gautama, Brihaspati, Narâda.*

[10] For the details, cf. the cited works of Risley, Ketkar, Bouglé, Senart, Mazzarella, Hocart.

[11] Bouglé, "Note" (cited), p. 151.

[12] Therefore the various works (such as those of J. Dollard and L. Warner) that apply the term "caste" to the relationship of the Negroes and whites in the United States misuse the term: the Negro-white relationship has a few elements of caste, but is fundamentally different from the real intra- and intercaste relationship. The race and color line, with the respective racial groups, cannot be identified with the castes and their structure and relationships. For a sound criticism of such theories, cf. O. Cox, "Race and Caste; a Distinction," *AJS,* Vol. L (1945), pp. 360-369.

II. The Social Order, or Estate

A loose use of the term "caste" frequently results in its application to the social groups properly known as "orders" and "estates," such as the orders of the noble Spartiates, the free Perioeci, the unfree Helots, and the slaves in Sparta; the noble Eupatridae, the free classes, and the slaves in Athens; the patricians, the plebeians, and the unfree classes in early Rome; the Senatorial and Equestrian orders, the full-fledged citizens, the free but not full-fledged citizens (latini and peregrini), the semifree strata, and the slaves in later Rome;[13] the nobility, the clergy, the bourgeoisie, the free citizens, and the slaves and serfs in medieval Europe; and the somewhat similar stratified orders or estates in many preliterate populations. As such orders are often legally ranked in a definite sequence of superiority and inferiority, and as the respective status passes automatically from the parents to the children, many sociologists have identified the social orders with the caste system. Such an identification is, however, unwarranted, since the structure of the social orders is fundamentally different from that of the castes.

Consider, for instance, the orders of serfs and slaves, on the one hand, and that of the nobles, on the other. In the first place, these orders are not so closed as the castes. One becomes a slave or a serf not only through being born of slave parents, but also through capture as a prisoner of war, through voluntary sale into slavery, through insolvency or crime, through being kidnaped by slave traders (as in the case of free African Negroes), through sale by a free father of his son into slavery, etc. With certain reservations the same may be said of the nobility. One becomes a member of the nobility not only through being born of noble parents, but through the grant of a patent of nobility to a person for his services to the king or other ruler; through the performance of deeds

deemed particularly valuable in a given society (such as certain religious, artistic, political, juridical, economic, scientific, or technical achievements); through the violent overthrow of an existing government, with its nobility, and the establishment of a new order of nobility; through the purchase of a patent of nobility; through military conquest; through intermarriage with the nobility; etc.[14] With the exception of birth, all such methods are ineffective for a change of one's caste position, which, as a rule, is determined only by the caste of one's parents. Herein lies the first fundamental difference between the orders (or estates) and the caste.

The second difference concerns the various ways of terminating the status of slave, serf, or noble. Many a slave or serf is free through the manumissio, or liberation by the master; through a decree of the state or other authorities abolishing slavery or serfdom; through marrying a free person; through the purchase of his freedom; through the performance of certain noteworthy deeds, and so forth. Likewise a noble can lose his status by marrying an unfree person; by adopting a certain occupation or patronage; by selling his patent of nobility; through crime; through the defeat of an army that he has commanded; through a revolution overthrowing the existing order and installing a new order of nobility, and the like. Most of these methods are inapplicable to the position of an individual or a group in the caste system.

Third, some of the legally stratified orders are virtually open groups. Thus the order of clergy of the Christian Church was open to almost all strata, including even the unfree population of the Roman Empire and of medieval Europe. The order of bourgeoisie was likewise open to the free population which

---

[13] For these orders, refer to any competent course in the history of these countries. For Rome see "Cursus Honorum" in Harper's Dictionary of Classical Literature and Antiquities (ed. by H. T. Peck), p. 842.

[14] For the preliterate peoples, cf. G. Landtman, The Origin of the Inequality of the Social Classes (Chicago, 1938), Chps. 13-14; W. I. Thomas, Primitive Behavior, Chps. 13-14. For the historical peoples, cf. the works on the history of their official law and of their differentiation and stratification. Cf. also my Mobility, Chps. 7-9, 13-14.

settled in the cities and succeeded in becoming well-to-do. Such openness does not exist in populations differentiated and stratified into castes.

Fourth, *the orders and estates are much less endogamic and inbred than the castes.* In many cases intermarriage of the nobility with other groups—tribes, states, and so on—is prescribed and endogamic marriage is prohibited. Intermarriage of the nobles with members of the free orders in general is usually not prohibited. Even the marriage of a noble with an unfree person has not been so severely condemned and penalized as that of a Brahmin with a member of one of the lowest castes.

Fifth, as a result practically all the orders have been racially much more heterogeneous and mixed than the castes. Even the royal families of most countries are no exception to this rule. Only in a few societies, as in ancient Egypt (where the Pharoah married his own sister), or where inbreeding has been comparatively strict, do we find a resemblance to the caste system of in-breeding and hence a comparative racial homogeneity in such dynasties. The other orders—the nobility, the middle class, the lower class, and the unfree orders—have been, as a rule, racial mongrels.

Sixth, virtually all the highest orders have been elevated to their rank, at a certain period, from a non-noble or even ignoble stratum. My studies show that the average duration of even most of the royal families rarely exceeds two or three hundred years. A dynasty arises from a non-noble family; reigns for a certain period; then declines and is replaced by a new one, belonging to an entirely different family. The rise and fall of various family, kinship, or racial groups in the case of the nobility contributes markedly to the racial heterogeneity of this order. Still more pronounced is this heterogeneity in the middle and lower orders. This means that, in contradistinction to the castes, which are perpetuated by the same blood, or racial stock, the orders are composed of diverse racial stocks. At the very best, only for a limited period does even the highest order of nobility represent a single, homogeneous stock. The Greek monarchs and nobility of the Hellenistic period had hardly anything in common with the Greek monarchs and nobility of the centuries prior to the fourth B.C. The

Roman Senatorial and Equestrian orders and especially the Roman emperors of the late monarchical period were racial strangers to the Senatorial and Equestrian stocks of the early monarchical and the republican period. As a matter of fact, most of the Roman monarchs and nobles of the late monarchical period were mainly of Oriental origin, hardly related even to the bulk of the Roman population of the earlier periods.

Seventh, the lowest orders, particularly the slaves and serfs, have rarely been organized into genuine groups. They have been at best only quasi-organized groups. As a rule they have been mere social aggregations or collectivities. Most of their members have not even intimately interacted with one another. Only on rare occasions has a given order succeeded in creating an organization (as, for instance, in the case of the slaves' uprising under the leadership of Spartacus). Per contra, a caste is always either a fully organized or quasi-organized group.

Eighth, many of these orders, especially the lower ones (the free class, the serfs, and the slaves), have seldom been confined to any continuous circumscribed territory. Instead, they have been scattered over the whole country. Hence they have not been territorial groups bound by the tie of locality.

Ninth, the lower orders (especially the slaves and serfs, who have often been recruited from war prisoners, kidnaped persons, or persons sold by their masters) have not always belonged to the same language and culture group. Hence not even the language and culture bond has invariably linked them with one another or with the upper orders of the same society.

Tenth, the legal status of each order has rested not so much upon a religious or customary basis (as in the case of the caste system) as upon the official law of the state. The state has played an extremely important role in generating, crystallizing, legalizing, and enforcing the status of the orders, whereas it has exerted little or no influence upon the caste regime in India.

As a result of this analysis we may define *an order or estate as a somewhat organized group so far as the upper orders are concerned,* and largely a quasi-organized or unorganized aggreation or collectivity so far as the lower orders are concerned. It is partly hereditary, but more open than the caste. It is solidary so far as its members are bound together by the ties of similar rights and duties, privileges and disfranchisements (imposed chiefly by the state) and by similar occupational and economic functions (which are less monopolistic than in the caste system). The bond of a common language and race applies to only some of the members; that of kinship, only to an insignificant minority. A given order forms a definite stratum in the hierarchy of orders legally established for the most part by the state.

An order is quantitatively and qualitatively a diluted caste. Several of the ties binding the members of the caste are absent in the order; conversely, the state bond, which is virtually absent in the caste, plays an important role in the order. The closeness of the order is less rigid than that of the caste. In-breeding is also less pronounced. Even the hereditary transmission of status from parents to children is less regular than in the case of the caste.

Orders of various kinds have played an important part in enormous aggregates of state groups and other populations. They have been found in all human populations and have existed for centuries. In such populations the orders have played as important a part as the caste in India and the social class in other populations and periods. In other words, they have been one of the most powerful multibonded groups. Hence the order has represented in such societies one of the most significant co-ordinates of an individual's sociocultural position and characteristics.[15]

In many western societies in particular, the estate regime eventually declined and was replaced by that of the social class, which, in its turn, represents a diluted order stripped of several of its characteristics. Turn now to the analysis of the social class.

III. What Is a Social Class?

Another case showing the prevalent confusion in the definition and classification of social groups is that of the social class. Sociologists and social scientists are vaguely aware that there is some social group that plays an important role especially in modern populations. They try to define it, but as a rule unsuccessfully. In spite of an enormous volume of literature and dozens of definitions of "social class," most of the theories are defective. A large proportion of the theories can be classified in the following categories: (1) Definitions that identify the social class, as a real group, with a mere nominal aggregation; (2) that are exceedingly vague and indefinite; (3) that reduce the social class to a social stratum or rank; (4) that identify it with one of the unibonded groups; (5) which conceive it as a multibonded group, but which are defective in one or more respects.

1. The Social Class as a Nominal Aggregation

Among the classes of contemporary France, L. M. Ferré includes the class "people" (workers, peasants, small proprietors, small and medium merchants, artisans, small industrialists, minor officials, and professionals).[16] The nominalistic character of this congeries of various groups subsumed under the name "people" as a real group is evident. Nominalistic, also is A. Schäffle's conception of class as a mere collectivity of individuals of different degrees of wealth.[17] W. L. Warner and P. S. Lunt divide the population of the "Yankee

---

[15] In the light of the above analysis it is easy to perceive the shortcomings of various definitions of "order" and "estate," such as those of M. Weber, *Wirtschaft und Gesellschaft* (Tübingen, 1922), Vol. I, Ch. 2 and Vol. II, pp. 631-640; W. Sombart, *Der Moderne Kapitalismus* (München, 1922) Vol. II, pp. 1091 ff.; and O. C. Cox "Estates, Social Classes, and Political Classes," *ASR*, Vol. 10, pp. 464-469. All these concepts of the estate are inadequate, either being very vague, like Max Weber's, or ascribing to it properties it does not possess and ignoring those that are essential to it.

[16] L. M. Ferré, *Les Classes sociales dans la France contemporaine* (Paris, 1936), pp. 102, 195-230.

[17] A. Schäffle, *Abriss der Soziologie* (Jena, 1906), pp. 20 ff., 137.

city" into six "classes": "the upper-upper, lower-upper, upper-middle, lower-middle, upper-lower, and lower-lower." When one carefully examines the bases of this division (which, as we shall see, are very vague and virtually unsubstantiated by relevant data), and the connections of each of these "classes" with one another, one perceives at once that the analysis is mainly statistical or nominal, since these six "classes" do not function as tangible units more or less distinct from one another.[18] The "upper-upper" class lives in good and poor residential districts; occupies good and poor houses, and has an unemployed portion. On the other hand, the real estate of such ethnic groups as the Armenians, Jews, Greeks, and Italians, who do not belong to the "upper-upper" or "lower-upper" class, or even form the bulk of the "upper-middle" class, is notably superior to that of the native Yankees who constitute the "upper" and "upper-middle" classes; likewise the occupations of 16.85 per cent of the "upper-upper" are merely clerical, whereas 3.51 per cent of the lower class belong to proprietary and professional groups. The income of the "lower-upper" happens to be higher than that of the "upper-upper," and a portion of the "upper-upper" class has a lower income and a lower level of expenditures than the "middle" class. The "upper-upper" class reads detective and love stories like the "lower-lower" class.[19] If, then, we take the part of the supposed "upper-upper" class that is poorer than the middle class, has poor houses, lives in poor districts, pursues a clerical occupation, associates with all strata, and even intermarries with different classes, the question arises: In what respect is it an "upper-upper" class? According to every characteristic it is evidently not an upper class at all. And if one inquires how the authors obtained their classification into the six classes, the only answer is: "All our informants agreed . . ."[20] On the basis of this alleged agreement the investigators "developed a class hypothesis,"[21] arbitrarily divided the population into six groups, and then presented data that clearly demonstrate the inadequacy of their analysis.

Further examples of nominalistic collectivities treated as social classes are afforded by most of the definitions of the term "middle class." Their authors speak of the "middle class" as a genuine unitary group, whereas they themselves make it abundantly clear that their "middle class" is but a medley of various groups; peasants and farmers, small businessmen, small proprietors, propertyless salaried factory workers, clerks, professionals, minor government officials, etc. Many of the authors ascribe to their "middle class" very different characteristics. The artificiality of the concept is clearly indicated by their own statements: namely, that the "middle class" exhibits "disunity"; that it "is a split personality, tormented by the clash of discordant interests," being "never completely a unity, [but] always of mixed intermediate composition," and so on.[22] If so, then why speak of the middle class as a unit? Why not speak of the middle *classes* and explicitly state that "middle class" is a mere congeries of different groups? The nominalistic character of such definitions is illustrated by the statement that the "middle class" is "the class intermediary between the upper and lower," followed by the acknowledgment that it is a collection of various groups and that the definition is not scientific.[23]

---

[18] W. L. Warner and P. S. Lunt, *The Social Life of a Modern Community* (New Haven, 1941), Ch. 5, *passim*. The artificiality of the division seems to have become clear to the authors, for in their next volume, *The Status System of a Modern Community* (New Haven, 1943), they acknowledge that the members of the same class behave differently and try to remedy the situation by their "positional framework" (of which something will be said further in Chapter 15).

[19] Cf. *The Social Life*, Chps. 9-20.

[20] *Ibid.*, p. 81. This is a very unscientific statement. Quite a number of non-Yankees (all excluded by the authors from the "upper" and virtually from the "upper-middle" class) would disagree with this evaluation. Moreover, such a basis means the assumption of infallible judgment on the part of the informants—rather a strange assumption for a scientific criterion!

[21] *Ibid.*, p. 82.

[22] L. Corey, *The Crisis of the Middle Class* (New York, 1935), p. 151. More accurate is the position of those who recognize that there is no single "middle class," that there are many different groups which can be nominalistically united into the category of the "middle classes." Cf., for instance, J. Lhomme, *Le Problème des classes* (Paris, 1938), pp. 273 ff., and F. C. Palm, *The Middle Classes Then and Now* (New York, 1936), Ch. 1.

[23] For one of the best analyses, cf. E. Mahaim, "Les Classes moyennes," *Revue économique internationale*, November, 1936; also the analyses of

2. Vague Definitions of "Social Class"

"Class is an ensemble of the individuals . . . who are mutually assimilable, eliminating the causes of distinction due to age, sex, or occupation."[24] Evidently one could fit to this definition almost any group, since the members, belonging to the same group, and to this extent solidary, are mutually "assimilable." "A group of people who will . . . and act together when they want approximately the same thing"[25] is another sample of such vague definitions. Any solidary group can fit this definition. More precise, but nevertheless vague, is the following: "A class is really definable only upon the basis of its mores; the code is the class. Terms like 'bourgeoisie' denote a standard of behavior, a set of ideals, in short, a standard of living which is the mores. . . . Classes are formed within a society by interests and modes of life."[26]

So far as the concept of social class is defined in these terms, it cannot fail to be vague. In addition, all social groups can be made to conform to this definition, since the members of any group have similar mores and interests and a similar mode of living. The definition does not indicate precisely how a social class differs from other unibonded or multibonded groups. The vagueness of the definitions of "social class" is typical of social science and sociological literature, especially in America.[27]

3. Definitions That Reduce the Social Class to a Mere Form of Social Stratification with Vertical Mobility

Most of the current definitions of "social class" represent it as a mere stratum in the vertical hierarchy of social stratification, without specifying the characteristics which differentiate it from other forms of social stratification. Such definitions are defective in two ways: first, they do not give the specific characteristics of the social class in contradistinction to those of other stratified groups; second, they assume that all social classes are necessarily stratified, being relatively higher or lower, whereas as a matter of fact they may be on the same level.

Here are typical examples of such definitions. Classes "are more or less homogeneous divisions of the population separated from each other in respect to precedence and privileges."[28] "A social class is any permanent division in society which is differentiated by relatively persistent dissimilarities in rank and separated from other strata by social distance."[29] Of like character are the definitions of M. Ginsberg,[30] W. L. Warner and P. S. Lunt,[31] W. F. Ogburn

---

Oualid, Baudhuin, and Lhomme, *Le Problème des classes* (cited), pp. 273-304.

[24] L. M. Ferré, *op. cit.*, p. 51. Later on the author predicates similarity in the mode of living, which somewhat improves the definition, but this characteristic appears as a *deus ex machina*.

[25] H. Rugg, "The American Mind and the Class Problem," *New Frontiers*, February, 1936. Equally vague are the definitions given in most of the texts in sociology. Cf., for instance, K. Young, *op. cit.*, pp. 477 ff., and Ogburn and Nimkoff, *Sociology* (Cambridge, 1940), pp. 309 ff.

[26] W. G. Sumner and A. Keller, *Science of Society* (New Haven, 1927), Vol. I, pp. 585 ff. Still vaguer is the definition of B. Moore, Jr. He includes in the category of class the caste and practically any group, detecting social classes even in the preliterate populations. For this reason his finding of the class struggle in "stable and unstable societies" is devoid of significance. B. Moore, Jr., "A Comparative Analysis of Class Struggles," *ASR*, Vol. 10 (1945), pp. 31-37.

[27] This is due to the fact that the differentiation of the American population into clear-cut social classes has been less pronounced than in many other countries. C. H. Page, in his monograph *Class and American Sociology* (New York, 1940), observes that American Sociologists of the earlier generation "were imbedded in the soil of the native conditions. . . . They were all impressed by the anticlass elements of American democracy and by the social virtues of that 'classless' segment of society—the middle class." Hence they neglected a scientific treatment of the social class (pp. 250-251). His monograph gives an analysis of the vague, often self-contradictory class conceptions of the eminent American sociologists of the older generation, such as L. Ward, W. G. Sumner, A. Small, F. Giddings, C. H. Cooley, and E. A. Ross. The neglect of the social class as a specific important multibonded group still persists. Even recent monographs, such as J. W. McConnell's *The Evolution of Social Classes* (Washington, 1943), are guilty of similar vagueness of thought. In Europe, where the class distinction has been more pronounced, the problem of the social classes has been studied more attentively.

[28] G. Landtman, *The Origin of the Inequalities of the Social Classes* (Chicago, 1938), p. 36. In addition to the other defects of this type of definition, it treats "social class" as a mere collectivity.

[29] E. T. Hiller, *Principles of Sociology* (New York, 1933), pp. 36-37.

[30] M. Ginsberg, *Sociology* (London, 1934), p. 159.

[31] Warner and Lunt, *Social Life* (cited), p. 82.

and M. F. Nimkoff,[32] and most of the definitions found in introductory texts of sociology.
The basic defect of these definitions is their incompleteness and vagueness. Every organized
group is stratified. In the state groups we find
a long hierarchy of strata, beginning with the
king or the president, passing through the
cabinet members and assistant and associate
secretaries, and ending with the plain citizens.
In the church groups we note a series of ranks
extending from the pope, patriarch, or primate
to ordinary parishioner. A similar hierarchy is
found in business firms and universities. If
stratification—relative superiority and inferiority—is the mark of a social class, then any
organized group is a social class. In that case
we should have to speak of the social classes
of presidents, deans, and full and assistant
professors; of secretaries of state, assistant secretaries, chiefs of divisions, and assistant chiefs
of divisions, and the like. There would be
thousands of social classes, a *reductio ad ab-
surdum*, since we are searching for a powerful
multibonded group. "Social class" would be
identical with the concept of rank, a concept
which does not indicate any characteristic of
a unibonded or multibonded group. Another
error of this species of definition is its assumption that "social class" necessarily presupposes superiority or inferiority of rank.
There are social classes, for instance, the
farmer, peasant, and laboring classes and those
of the large landowners and the big-business-
men, which cannot properly be ranked as relatively superior or inferior. In other words, rank
or hierarchy, though frequently a secondary
characteristic of the comparative position of a
given class, is by no means its essential trait.

[32] Ogburn and Nimkoff, *Sociology* (cited), pp.
309 ff.
[33] For the sake of brevity, instead of giving all
the sources of all the classifications, I refer to the
following monographs, which are about the best in
the field: S. I. Solntzeff, *Social Classes* (in Russian, Tomsk, 1917); J. Lhomme, *Le Problème des
classes* (cited); E. Goblot, *Les Classes de la société*
(Paris, 1899), and his *La Barrière et le niveau*
(Paris, 1930); R. Picard, "La Théorie de la lutte
des classes," *Revue d'économie politique*, 1911; R.
Michels, "Beitrag zur Lehre von der Klassenbil-
dung," *Archiv für Sozialwissenschaft und Sozialpolitik*, Vol. 49, 1922, and his *Nuovi studi sulla
classe politica* (Torino, 1936); L. M. Ferré, *op. cit.*;
A. Bauer, *Les Classes sociales* (Paris, 1902); R.

4. Definitions That Identify the Social Class with One of the Unibonded Groups

This type of definition is suggested by a
mere enumeration of the social classes discussed by various authors. The following list
presents virtually all the principal varieties.[33]

a. *The Poor and Rich Classes.* Our unibonded economic groups of the rich and poor
are recognized in the definitions of Plato,
Menenius Agrippa, Sallust, Enfantin, Con-
sidérant, K. Bücher, Godwin, Mably, L. von
Stein, A. Schäffle, E. Goblot, C. van Overbergh, E. Bernstein, and many others.

b. *Racial Groups as Classes Born to Rule or
to Be Ruled.* Aristotle ("inborn slaves and
inborn rulers"), Caesar, Fénelon, Le Comte de
Boulainvilliers, L. Gumplowicz, A. Gobineau,
G. Ratzenhofer, H. S. Chamberlain, O. Ammon,
V. de Lapouge, and other racialists, and the
protagonists of the theory of the "chosen" race
or people, including the ideologists of the Nazi
"master race." It is easy to see that this conception of the social class represents a distorted
unibonded racial group.

c. *Social Classes as Identical with Occupational Groups.* These definitions exhibit
many varieties according to the classification of
occupational groups, incompletely and incon-
sistently classified. A. Bauer gives the following classification. (1) Ruling classes: legisla-
tors, judges, heads of the state, representatives
of executive power, the army, the clergy, leaders of the intelligentsia; (2) Ruled classes:
peasants, workers, employers, merchants and
bankers, transport workers, paupers, criminals.[34] G. Schmoller, starting with the occupational principle as the foundation of social
classes (though elsewhere he complicates it
with race, education, and wealth), gives the
following classes: (1) big-business men; (2)

Gonnard, "Quelques Considérations sur les classes,"
Revue économique internationale, April 10, 1925;
C. van Overbergh, "Les Classes sociales," *Annales
de la Société belge de sociologie* (Bruxelles, 1905);
P. Mombert, "Zum Wesen der sozialen Klassen,"
Erinnerungsgabe für Max Weber (München,
1923); P. Fahlbeck, *Die Klassen und die Gesellschaft* (Jena, 1922); M. Halbwachs, *La Classe
ouvrière et les niveaux de vie.* (Paris, 1913). Cf.
also the works quoted in this chapter and in the
chapters on social mobility.
[34] A. Bauer, *Les Classes sociales* (cited), pp.
142 ff.

medium employers; (3) small employers; (4) high officials, professionals, and private employees; (5) workers.[35] To this type belongs also Ferré's enumeration of classes in France: remnants of the sacerdotal class; the nobility; the bourgeoisie (businessmen, professional men, officials, judges, and army officers, divided into two subclasses); the popular class, or "people"; criminals and vagabonds, etc.[36]

A variation of this conception of the social class is presented by the physiocrats' classification:[37] (1) the productive (agricultural), (2) the proprietary, and (3) the unproductive classes (industrialists, merchants, and the rest of the population); and by those of L. Duguit, Ch. Gide, and many other sociologists.

d. *Social Class Identified with Rank.* The theories that identify the social class with rank, according to the number of privileges and disfranchisements, rights and duties, or the degree of domination and subordination, are represented by such enumerations as the following: (1) the oppressor and the oppressed, or the ruling and the ruled; (2) the privileged and the disfranchised; (3) the exploiting and the exploited; (4) the conqueror and the conquered; (5) the masters and the slaves (Helvetius, R. Worms, Picard, Saint-Simon, F. Engels,[38] L. Blanc, T. Veblen, J. Blondel, G. Mosca, V. Pareto, and all the others who identify the social class with rank—with relative superiority and inferiority).

All these conceptions of the social class identify it (not always consistently) with one of our unibonded groups: an occupational, an economic, or a race or language group. Their principal shortcomings are as follows. First, none of them furnish an answer to the question: Is there a multibonded group of definite composition that has played a major role among other groups? Designating an important unibonded group is evidently not an answer to the problem.

Second, these theories are inconsistent and even self-contradictory. If, indeed, a social class is merely a racial group, then one should speak of the Nordic, Alpine, Mediterranean, Mongoloid, and other social classes. None of

the racial theories of the social class do that. L. Gumplowicz, for instance, divides the social classes into the nobility, the bourgeoisie, and the peasantry; and G. Ratzenhofer refers to the privileged, the middle, and the disfranchised classes. Again, if the social classes are occupational groups, obviously one should classify them according to occupations. Instead, A. Bauer (who probably offers the most consistent variety of this type of conception of classes) derives, as a sort of *deus ex machina*, the classes of rulers and ruled. Moreover, if the foundation of the social classes is occupational, it is inconsistent to unite into one class, as he does, several different occupations. For instance, in his seventh class, that of the intelligentsia, he groups teachers, historians, journalists, preachers, politicians and state officials, scientists, artists, philosophers, and so on. These groups are united not so much by the identity of their occupation as by the degree of their education. Equally inconsistent are the conceptions identifying the social class with the amount of income or wealth. Some theories of this type, such as K. Bücher's are, in fact, composite, eventually evolving from the social class a multibonded group. Even such relatively sound theories as those of L. von Stein, A. Schäffle, and Overbergh likewise prove inconsistent. Thus L. von Stein, in order to derive his proletarian class, takes into consideration not only its poverty but its lack of education and several other characteristics of a noneconomic nature. Then he is compelled to distinguish between the social and economic classes which do not coincide. In addition to these inconsistencies Overbergh postulates the "middle class," or intelligentsia, which rests not on an economic but on an intellectual basis.

Similar inconsistencies are exhibited by the sociologists who identify the social class with "rank." When they establish the classes aristocracy, bourgeoisie, and proletariat, they are forced to introduce, besides the postulated "rank," the economic criterion of wealth.

The third defect of the theories in question is an over-simplification of the sociocultural facts. Reducing the main line of social dif-

[35] G. Schmoller, *Grundriss der Volkswirtschaftslehre* (Leipzig, 1901), Vol. 1, pp. 392 ff.

[36] L. M. Ferré, *op. cit.*, pp. 102 ff.

[37] Cf. F. Quesnay, *Analise de tableau économique*

(Paris, 1846), Part 1, p. 58, and Turgot, *Réflexions sur la formation et la distribution de richesse. Oeuvres de Turgot* (Paris, 1884), Part I, p. 39.

[38] F. Engels, *Anti-Dühring*, p. 151.

ferentiation to one of the unibonded groups, and contending that this unibonded group is the major group, the social class, they overlook the importance of all other groups, unibonded and multibonded, as well as oversimplify the complexity of social differentiation, postulating a virtually "monistic" unilinear differentiation along the lines of their alleged "social class."

5. Defective Conceptions of the Social Class as a Multibonded Group

The primary defects of the conceptions that represent the social class as a multibonded group are (a) their mutual contradictions and even self-contradictions, (b) their indefiniteness, (c) their predication of the wrong bonds. The first two are exemplified by G. Schmoller. In one place he virtually identifies the social class with a unibonded occupational group; in another, with an aggregation of individuals and families united "not by kinship or neighborhood but by a common occupation, common possessions and education, and not infrequently by similar political rights exercised not for the sake of common economic affairs but for a reinforcement of the consciousness of their unity in the realization of their common interests." Elsewhere he defines class as a resultant of race, occupation, and distribution of wealth.[39] Thus three different formulae of class are offered by the same author. Again, Sumner and Keller declare that classes "are based upon the kin sentiment, upon the results of conquest, upon wealth, trade relations and other distinguishing and unifying factors."[40] From the very enumeration of highly diverse bonds one can easily perceive that their formula can cover any social group (unibonded or multibonded), without specifying any particular group.

Another example of vague, self-contradictory conceptions of "social class" is afforded by T. Veblen in his *Theory of the Leisure Class*. His leisure class is a veritable *coincidentia oppositorum*, a mechanical conglomeration of mutually contradictory characteristics. It is

supposed to be a rich leisure class, excluded from "industrial occupations." Now it assumes the character of the warrior or militant caste, now that of the priestly order, now that of a group of big industrialists and financiers. Now it is parsimonious, now extravagant, with its "conspicuous consumption and ostentation." It is now greedy and predatory, now intent only on achieving honors.[41] I know of no big-business group that is a leisure class. As for rich groups, such groups, as a rule, especially in our society, are not "excluded from industrial occupations"; in the overwhelming majority of cases their members are big industrialists, financiers, or merchants. I can hardly identify the caste of the war lords with the priestly group, or either of them with the rich classes of our time. In brief, Veblen's leisure class can hardly have existed, and certainly does not exist at the present time in any form except perhaps as an insignificant group of the rich who are at the same time parasitic, belligerent (though *rentiers*, as a rule, fear war more than other classes), predatory, ostentatious, and so on. Certainly neither the richest nor the moderately rich groups of modern times correspond to his portrait, nor any upper or middle class of any society at any time. The whole group is a congeries of various bonds assembled in a way that is neither logically nor causally feasible.

The next group of class concepts of this type are the various Marxian doctrines respecting the social class. Most of the Marxians interpret it as a multibonded group. Marx himself did not evolve any definite concept of the social class, in spite of the paramount role played by the class struggle in his theory. In his *Communist Manifesto* he uses the term in the most indefinite way, declaring that "the history of all hitherto existing society is the history of the class struggle. Freeman and slave, patrician and plebeian, lord and serf, guild master and journeyman, oppressor and oppressed, have stood in constant opposition to one another. . . . [in our time] society is splitting up increasingly into two great classes directly opposed to each other: the bourgeoisie and the proletariat."[42] Thus caste, medieval

[39] G. Schmoller, *Grundriss der Volkswirtschaftslehre* (cited), Vol. 1, pp. 392, 395.

[40] Sumner and Keller, *op. cit.*, Vol. I, p. 585. In his "What Social Classes Owe to Each Other" Sumner gives a different, rather Marxian definition of "class."

[41] T. Veblen, *The Theory of the Leisure Class* (New York, 1912), Ch. 1, *passim*.

[42] K. Marx and F. Engels, *Communist Manifesto* (tr. by Kerr; Chicago, 1913).

order, any form of the oppressors and the oppressed, the strata in a guild—all are social classes. In his *Revolution and Konterrevolution in Deutschland*[43] Marx distinguished in Germany prior to 1848 at least eight different classes: feudal nobility, bourgeoisie, petty bourgeoisie, big and medium peasantry, small free peasantry, unfree peasantry, agricultural laborers, and industrial laborers. In another work[44] he defines the peasant class as "millions of families living in *economic* circumstances that distinguish their *mode of life*, their *interests*, and their *culture* from those of other classes and make them more or less hostile to other classes." Here a class is represented as a multibonded group, though very vaguely defined in terms of economic bonds, "mode of life," "interests," and "culture." The precise kind of life, of interests, of culture is not indicated. Marx perceived the nebulous conception of social class characteristic of his earlier works, and in the last volume of *Das Kapital* he undertook to define it more precisely; but unfortunately the volume abruptly ends with the problem merely stated, not developed.

This explains the failure of the Marxians to agree in their interpretation of Marx's class concept. Some, such as K. Kautsky and Overbergh, hold that Marx distinguished three main classes according to the source of their income: the landlords (rent), the bourgeoisie (profit from capital), and the workers (wages), a division that repeats Adam Smith's analysis of classes. Other Marxians, such as Solntzeff and J. Strachey, distinguish only two classes, the bourgeoisie and the proletariat. Still other Marxians, such as E. Bernstein, reject the Marxian classification, replacing it by one based on the amount of wealth. One trait is common to all the really Marxian concepts of the social class, namely, the criterion furnished by the position and role of a group in the *production process*. N. Bukharin's formula is accurate from this standpoint: "A social class is the aggregate of persons playing the same part in production, standing in the same relation toward other persons in the production process." From this basic position it follows, according to Marxism, that the *income, standard of living, mode of life, ideology, culture, psychology,* and *politics,* of the members of the same class will be similar because they are all determined by the position and role of the group in the production process.[45] They derive a concept of the social class as a multibonded group with the bonds of similar income, standard of living, ideology, culture, psychology, and politics, resulting from the similar position of the members of the class in the production process. As we shall see, the definition is more or less valid, apart from the following defects. First, the assumption that all persons occupying a similar position in the production process have a similar income and other common psychosocial and cultural characteristics is not quite accurate. Among the equally rich or poor in our society or any other we find persons and groups occupying very different positions in the production process and pursuing different occupations. Conversely, persons playing the same part in the production process (whether proprietors, highly placed employees, or workers) receive different incomes and are even more divergent psychologically, ideologically, and culturally. The Marxians hence overstress the closeness of the connection between the production factor and other variables. Second, the other bonds which they assign to a social class are not precisely defined. Third, the meaning of the term "position and role in the production process" is too indefinite. The criterion which they emphasize is based on the question whether a person is an owner of the means of production or is merely a wage-earner. If he is an owner, he is a bourgeois; if not, he is a proletarian. This criterion, if consistently applied, leads to absurd conclusions. For instance, a peasant who owns an acre of land must be rated as a bourgeois, whereas an engineer or the president of a large corporation must be regarded as a salaried wage-earner

[43] *Revolution und Konterrevolution in Deutschland* (Leipzig, 1896), pp. 7-11.

[44] K. Marx, *The Eighteenth Brumaire of Louis Bonaparte* (New York, 1926), p. 133.

[45] Cf. N. Bukharin, *Historical Materialism* (New York, 1925), pp. 276 ff.; S. Solnzeff, *op. cit.*, pp. 376 ff.; J. Strachey, *The Theory and Practice of Socialism* (New York, 1936), pp. 96 ff.; and K. Kautsky, *Agrarfrage*, chapter on "Bauer und Proletariat." For a good analysis of the Marxian conception of the social class, cf. J. Delevsky, *Antagonismes sociaux et antagonismes prolétariens* (Paris, 1924).

and hence as a proletarian, even though his income may amount to a million dollars a year. From a behavioral standpoint, from that of the alignment of such groups in politics, from the standpoint of income and mode of living, culture, and ideology, such millionaire "proletarians" have scarcely anything in common with real wage-earners. An independent artisan (owning his means of production), a poor peasant or farmer, and an average factory wage-earner have many more traits in common in all these respects than they share with the rich "proletarians." These and similar difficulties have led many a Marxian to try to modify the essential points of the criterion based on the "production process"; but scarcely any of these attempts have proved successful.[46]

Further examples of the interpretation of "social class" as referring to a multibonded group are afforded by G. Tarde, H. de Man, L. M. Ferré, R. Gonnard, and J. Lhomme, all of whom stress the consciousness of class solidarity on the part of the members of the group, adding to it one or two objective bonds. Thus, for Tarde, persons who intermarry, who eat at the same table without a sense of revulsion, who conform to the same social patterns, and who entertain the same views respecting class distinctions, constitute a socially homogeneous class regardless of their occupational and other differences.[47] This concept is supplemented by another, namely, that in the course of time the technical division of labor and occupations tends to increase, whereas the number of classes tends to decrease. The conception is deficient in that it indicates merely the relative closeness or remoteness of two or more groups without specifying the objective basis of the *jus connubium* and *convivium*, and that it fails to distinguish the social class from other groups, either unibonded or multibonded. In a society with sharp racial differences the members of different races or castes do not regularly intermarry or even eat at the same table. It does not follow that these racial or caste groups are distinct social classes. Conversely, in Russia, Brazil, and several other countries members of different races regularly intermarry. From this it does not follow that the groups into which they are born are not separate classes. The *jus connubium* and the *convivium* may sometimes constitute the *signs* of membership in the same class; but the exogamic and endogamic rules generally follow lines very different from those of the social classes. The prohibition, in western Christian countries, of intermarriage within the limits of close consanguinity and affinity hardly means (as it must according to Tarde's definition) that close relatives necessarily belong to different classes. Conversely, marriages between members of different social groups does not necessarily mean that the classes of the bridegroom and bride are identical.

H. de Man finds the best index of a class "in the common direction of the social will, based on a common mode of evalution of social conditions." This psychological criterion he complicates with the economic conditions that

---

[46] This unclear and inadequate conception, plus the exigencies of pressure politics, led to a peculiar solution of the question as to who is and who is not a proletarian in the practice of the Russian Communist Revolution. Reading the Communist publications for the years 1917-1922, one finds that the Communist government regarded the factory workers generally as proletarians (whose dictatorship it supposedly represented). But when the workers of the Putilovsky, Obukhovsky, and other large factories in Leningrad did not please the government, they were styled "bourgeois," chiselers," "kulaks," "counterrevolutionaries," or "white guards" (in contrast to the Red Army). Peasants were regarded generally as belonging to the petty bourgeoisie, when they pleased the government; in many cases they were styled "honest proletarians." Even the members of the previously rich and aristocratic classes, when they collaborated with the Communist government, were designated as "true proletarians." "The nonparty Red Army soldiers are recruited from the working class and the middle peasant class. They all are honest proletarians, although often devoid of understanding and hence inclined to err" (*Petrograd Pravda*, No. 162, 1919). Since during these years the amount of rations was different for the proletarians and the nonproletarians, the question of who was a proletarian and who was not was of tremendous significance. The problem was, after all, solved by this or that policeman or commissar who, often having no idea of the Marxian conception of social class, had to decide the question in accordance with his likes and dislikes or his intuition, or else on the basis of a prerequisite or even bribery.

[47] Cf. G. Tarde, *Laws of Imitation, passim,* and the discussion in the Paris Sociological Society, *Revue internationale de sociologie,* 1903, pp. 119 ff., 243 ff., 301 ff., 398 ff., 473 ff., 576 ff.

participate in the formation of such a common will.[48] The definition is inadequate. The terms "common will" and "common evaluation" are obscure. The members of a given kinship, religious, political, or any other unibonded group share this common will and mode of evaluation. It does not follow, however, that each of these groups is a social class. Hence the concept does not indicate the *differentia specifica* of either a class or any other organized group.

Similar objections apply to Ferré's definition of "social class" (indicated above). "Mutual assimilability" is applicable to the members of any group. The "mode of life," which the author finally lays down as the fundamental criterion, is an important trait of the social class; but without a further specification it does not delimit the social class. The members of any unibonded group possess a similar mode of life in so far as their membership in the same group is concerned. As already observed, Ferré's concept closely approximates that of an occupational group.

One of the most specific definitions undertaking to combine the psychological criterion with some objective criteria is that given by R. Gonnard. The social class is "a grouping of individuals aware of a certain sort of common life, marked by a certain similarity of needs and aspirations, entertaining similar attitudes toward practical problems as well as ideals, and possessing a comparable degree of general culture, or, at least, of culture oriented in the same direction; who rank similarly the purpose of existence, have similar values, and therefore tend to conform to the same moral pattern and the same social type; who share the same prejudices, the same manners, the same code of honor, and therefore a sense of solidarity binding them together into a single group and linking them with similar extra-national groups."[49]

The definition is all-inclusive; the trouble is that it is too inclusive. The group that it best fits is the family; next, a group of friends or other familistic group. Only within groups of this character can such an all-round similarity be found, embracing virtually the entire range of mentality, interests, manners and mores, conduct, and way of life of the members. Certainly nowhere save in a good family or among friends can such a grouping of individuals be found, especially in a group presumably as vast as a social class.

More adequate is the theory offered by L. M. y Núñez.[50] He rightly construes the social class as a quasi-organized group whose members are united by the similarity of their economic and (especially) cultural bonds. As such they have a similar economic standard of living, similar manners and mores, and a similar mental outlook. In any society there are always three main classes—the upper, the middle, and the lower—together with interclass populations not consolidated into any social class. Following this schema, Núñez describes the characteristics of each of the principal classes. This concept is much more valid than most of the above definitions of "social class." Its shortcomings are: (a) the vagueness of the cultural bonds; (b) neglect of the occupational bond as one of the basic constituent elements of a social class; (c) an undue reduction of all social classes to three strata: higher, middle, and lower. Such a reduction confuses a social class with a social stratum, and also does violence to the actual number of social classes, which varies from population to population, ranging from two to four or more main classes.

Finally should be mentioned the concept of "social class" developed by J. Lhomme in his monograph *Le Problème des classes*. His definition embraces two basic elements: the social function, or mission which the class has to perform in society at large, and the awareness of this function by the members of the class. The social function is something much broader than purely occupational work. In respect to its social function the class exists "for other classes"; in its awareness of this function and of its value the class exists "for itself." Thus a social class is "a human group which, having an important social function to perform, is aware of it and does its best to realize it factually." Only the existence of both these characteristics makes a class a social

---

[48] H. de Man, *Au delà du Marxisme* (Paris, 1929), Ch. 13.

[49] R. Gonnard, "Quelques Considérations sur les classes" (cited).

[50] L. M. y Núñez, "The Social Classes," in *Revista mexicana de sociología*, 1944, 1945.

reality. In the absence of either element the class as such does not exist.[51]

Guided by this conception the author contends that social classes change with a change of the society to which they belong, but that there is no historical trend in the direction of either a steady increase or decrease in the number of classes. In contemporary society there are at least two main classes—the proletariat and the bourgeoisie—together with a conglomeration of intermediate, or "middle," classes. Then he proceeds to analyze the characteristics of each of the principal classes. In his portrait of the proletariat he finds himself in substantial agreement with the analysis given by G. Briefs[52] and others. "A proletarian is a modern salaried person who, in order to live, must constantly renew the offer of his working power and who finds himself involved in a destiny that contains in itself sufficient causes of a perpetual reproduction of the conditions of the salaried worker." The proletarian is not necessarily a manual worker; he may be a mental worker. Moreover, he is not necessarily poor. The important factor is that he must sell his services in order to obtain the means of subsistence, and that such a situation is a permanent necessity for the proletarian class. Such is the objective function of the proletariat. As for its class consciousness, this is characterized (a) by an inferiority complex in the sense of an unduly low social estimate of the value of the labor which the proletarian sells; (b) by the conviction that through his labor he furnishes power to the bourgeoisie and that the entire capitalist and bourgeois civilization is based on his efforts; and (c) by the conviction that the proletariat hence forms a distinct solidary class, with its own interests and values, differing from and opposed to those of other classes. Finally, Lhomme proceeds to analyze the mode of living, the politics, and the values of this class[53] as well as of the bourgeoisie and of the various

intermediate groups which may be spoken of as "middle classes" (not as "the middle class"), though most of them are not classes.

Although Lhomme's position exhibits many strong points, nevertheless it is not entirely satisfactory. First, his conception of the "social function" of the class is somewhat vague. If the social function of the proletariat is the Marxian trait of selling its labor, then all salaried workers, even the president of the United Steel Corporation, must be included in the proletariat. In that case it would consist of groups and persons radically different in their social status, behavior, interests, etc. The greater part of the contemporary bourgeoisie and middle classes would be proletarians, a miscellaneous congeries instead of a homogeneous class. If persons with high salaries are excluded, as the author does exclude them, this means an arbitrary limitation of his own criterion, which is a sign of its inadequacy. Then the proletarian is essentially a poor person, contrary to Lhomme's own position as enunciated elsewhere. Even more pronounced is the vagueness of his "function" as an objective element of a class in the case of the bourgeoisie. The function of this class, "composed of disparate elements," consists in "the assertion of superiority in whatever form: political and economic power, religious influence, moral ascendancy, literary prestige, artistic success, and so on.[54] Such a lust for power and for superiority is present in virtually all unibonded and multibonded groups. Many, like Hobbes, declare it to be a universal human trait. The author himself seems to perceive the inadequacy of his treatment of this function, and therefore, later on, prefers to designate the bourgeoisie in terms of wealth, professional occupations, customs, and education,[55] that is, in terms of a compound of four unibonded ties. This shift of position clearly demonstrates the inadequacy of his notion of the "class function." Still more indefinite is his treatment of class consciousness, the sense of the social mis-

---

[51] J. Lhomme, Le Problème des classes, pp. 78-82. Lhomme somewhat further develops the notion of class given by Plato, that each class has a definite function to perform, and more recently (in various forms) stressed by H. de Man, H. Goblot, W. Sombart, J. Schumpeter and T. Vida. Cf. W. Sombart, Der moderne Kapitalismus (6th ed.), Vol. II, pp. 1091 ff.; J. Schumpeter, "Die sozialen Klassen in ethnisch homogenen Milieu," Archiv für So-

zialwissenschaft, 1927; and T. Vida, Das Problem des Aufstieges (München-Berlin, 1933), Ch. 3.

[52] Cf. G. Briefs, The Proletariat (New York, 1938).

[53] Lhomme, op. cit., pp. 238 ff.

[54] Ibid., p. 264.

[55] Ibid., pp. 268 ff.

sion of the class. Its vagueness is most evident when Lhomme attempts to analyze the specific traits of the bourgeois and the proletarian consciousness and psychology, especially the former.

6. Summary of the Prevalent Conceptions of "Social Class"

The foregoing types of concept of "social class" more or less exhaust the main existing definitions. The primary source of their weakness is the fact that none of the theorizers has evolved a systematic theory of social groups, a consistent and empirically adequate conception of their classification. This basic defect inevitably leads to vague definitions; definitions confusing the social class with nominalistic collectivities; definitions identifying the social class with one of the unibonded groups; faulty definitions of the social class as a multibonded group, and the like. Let us now see how the problem resolves itself from the standpoint of the concept and classification of social groups developed above.

IV. Constructive Analysis of "Social Class"

To reiterate: Our task consists in determining whether there is a specific multibonded group, different from the family, tribe, caste, order, or nation, that in modern times has exerted a powerful influence. We are not seeking for any of the enumerated powerful multibonded groups, which have already been analyzed. Whether we designate the group in question as a social class or by some other term is unimportant. We may call it X, if we prefer.

The answer to the question is in the affirmative. There has been and is such a group. Its formula is as follows: It is (1) legally open, but actually semiclosed; (2) "normal"; (3) solidary; (4) antagonistic to certain other groups (social classes) of the same general nature, X; (5) partly organized but mainly quasi-organized; (6) partly aware of its own unity and existence and partly not; (7) characteristic of the western society of the eighteenth, nineteenth, and twentieth centuries; (8) a multibonded group bound together by two unibonded ties, occupational and economic (both taken in their broad sense), and by one bond of social stratification in the sense of the totality of its essential rights and duties as contrasted with the essentially different rights and duties of other groups (social classes) of the same general nature, X.

Through its legal openness and actual semi-openness the class differs from the closed caste, as well as from the orders or estates whose chronological successor it is. It differs from these also in respect to the number and kind of the compounded bonds, which distinguish it likewise from the family, the tribe, the nation, and any other multibonded group.

By virtue of its occupational, economic, and legal status (values, meanings, and norms) it is broadly solidary (secondary conflicts are present in any class) and now and then antagonistic to certain other social classes.

The coalescence of these bonds in each class is "affined" or "normal": comparative poverty coalesces with manual (unskilled and semiskilled) occupations and with comparative disfranchisement (legal and actual) in respect to rights and privileges; comparative wealth coalesces with creative mental occupations and with privileged status (legal and actual).

If in a given population there exist individuals similar in their occupational, economic, and legal status, but not organized or even quasi-organized, such individuals represent merely a nominal collectivity, not a real social class. To constitute a genuine social class a part of such individuals must be fully organized and another part quasi-organized. When such an organization occurs, a class consciousness arises among the members of the group, as the component of the group meanings, values, and norms, and grows hand in hand with the growth of the class itself. But a mere ideology of the class consciousness, fostered by this or that theorist, does not ensure the objective existence of a class.

This explains why roughly, before the eighteenth century, the social class did not play an important part in western societies. At best it existed only in the form of a few small groups, mostly unorganized and devoid of all but a rudimentary sense of class consciousness. Its place was taken by the social orders or estates—multibonded groups of a different character. The social classes began to emerge in the seventeenth century, and, with the progressive dissociation of the estates, slowly developed, becoming progressively organized or quasi-organized, hand in hand with a parallel development of the ideologies of class consciousness and the class struggle. During the last two centuries the social class has become increasingly powerful, and now constitutes one of the strongest multibonded groups in western societies.

The specific characteristic of the social class is the coalescence of occupational and economic bonds plus the bond of belonging to the same basic stratum, whose properties are defined by the totality of its essential rights and duties, or by its privileges and disfranchisements, as compared with those of other classes. In this sense the social class differs fundamentally from all other groups (multibonded or unibonded).

We have seen that economic and occupational bonds taken separately exert a powerful influence on the body and mind, the behavior and the way of life of an individual. Their combined influence, re-enforced by similarity of status in the stratified pyramid of the population, is still greater. Persons having essentially similar occupations, economic position, and rights and duties cannot fail to become similar in a great many other ways, physical, mental, moral, and behavioral. The similarity of the objective bonds and conditions renders them "mutually assimilable" (Ferré's trait), with a common *lex connubium* and *convivium* (Tarde *et al.*), mutually equal, and possessed of a "consciousness of kind." So far as the theorists of the social class stress the importance of such physical, mental, moral, and behavioral similarities and of similarity in the mode of life, they are right. Their theories are defective in that they do not indicate the objective bases of such similarities, nor their character

and limits. The objective basis of all these similarities is the similar occupational, economic, and legal position of the members. The nature and the limits of these similarities are determined by these bonds: within their orbit the mode of life and other traits of the members of the same class are similar (provided they belong to it for a sufficient length of time); outside of it, in so far as they belong to different state, language, religious, sex, age, or race groups, their psychology, behavior, and mode of life are dissimilar. Although membership in the same class generates many important similarities, these do not cover the whole physical, mental, and behavioral character and the entire mode of life of the members. Through the determination of the kinds of similarities and their limits our definition is free from the vagueness and sweeping overgeneralizations which vitiate other theories.

Additional evidence of the superiority of our definition is furnished by almost all the leading theories of the social class. Although they may seemingly stress one or more other bonds, most of them finally reduce themselves to a compound of occupational and economic bonds plus the bond of stratification. Thus G. Schmoller and others start with occupation as the basis of class, but in the process of analysis are forced to introduce the economic bond and that of sociopolitical stratification. K. Bücher and others start with the economic bond of wealth, but presently inject into their definition the other two bonds. J. Lhomme and others start with the factors of "function" and "class consciousness"; but when they come to analyze definitely the functions and consciousness of the proletariat or bourgeoisie, they are compelled to refer explicitly to occupational, economic, and stratification bonds. The same is true of the Marxian definitions,[56] as well as of many others.

The next question is, What kinds of classes and how many are found within the western population throughout the history of the social class? The answer depends upon how broad or narrow we make the occupational, the economic, and the stratification differences. If we

---

[56] Cf., for instance, K. Kautsky's definition and analysis of the proletariat, bourgeoisie, and peasantry in his *Agrarfrage*. For a good analysis of these classes, cf. V. Tschernov's *Peasant and Worker as*

Economic Categories (in Russian, Petrograd, 1917). The same bonds are given by Max Weber in his very vague definition of the social class. (Cf. his *Wirtschaft und Gesellschaft*, cited.)

make them too narrow—if, say, we take as a separate economic group one with an annual income of a hundred dollars, and as separate occupational groups the carpenters or masons —then, of course, there will be hundreds of different classes. In that case, however, the class is likely to elude our grasp, owing to the excessive minuteness of the economic and occupational gradations. These microscopic gradations are covered by our unibonded groups. In the social class, occupational, economic, and stratification differences operate as broad, fundamental disparities of occupational function and as marked economic contrasts of wealth and comfort—differences which are immediately apparent to even the untrained mind, like the contrast between the occupation of a big-business man and a factory hand, or between the income and luxurious mode of life of a millionaire and the income and standard of living of a poor person. Attention to too detailed differences obscures the similarity of the conditions of the members of the same class and their dissimilarity to those of other classes. Minute differences do not produce either solidarity among the members of the same class or antagonism toward other classes, and hence do not lead to a sense of class consciousness. Even a purely unibonded occupational group not only is organized into small crafts but is affiliated with much larger organizations, such as the American Federation of Labor or the C.I.O., the English labor and trade-union organizations, or the French Confédération du Travail, which embrace hundreds of different occupational groups all belonging to a single broad category, that of labor occupation.

From this macroscopic viewpoint one can easily distinguish the following major classes in the western society of the past two or three centuries: (a) the industrial-labor, or proletarian, class; (b) the peasant-farmer class; (c) the dwindling class of large landowners; (d)

the capitalist class, now being transformed into the managerial class. Each of these powerful classes is divided into several subclasses. In addition, there are a large number of small classes each of which in itself exerts a comparatively slight influence upon sociocultural processes.

What is the laboring, or proletariat, class? First of all it is an *occupational* group. Its bulk is made up of manual workers in factories, mills, mines, and transportation. In addition, it contains groups engaged in mental rather than manual work, the "intellectual proletariat" of clerks and other "white-collar" workers, professional men, and minor government officials, performing predominantly subordinate or semi-routine functions.[57]

In the second place, it is *an economic group* that gets its means of subsistence exclusively or mainly by selling its services in a shifting and insecure market. As G. Briefs rightly points out, this reliance upon the sale of its services is a perennial, not a temporary, phenomenon. Apart from it the bulk of the laboring class has no means of subsistence except perhaps some insignificant subsidiary ones. For the overwhelming majority of the proletariat there is no way of escaping this position by shifting to one of the more privileged classes.[58] Even in populations with a high degree of vertical mobility, as in the United States, only a small fraction of the laboring class is able to accomplish this.[59] Another economic trait of the proletarian class is that it does not own the instruments of production which it uses. A third economic trait is the low scale of its wages and income in comparison with that of other classes, especially of the capitalists or managerial aristocracy or of the large landowners (in the past), and even of many "middle classes." This connection between wage-earning and comparative poverty has long been recognized, as attested by the Roman "*Mercenarii pauperes sunt*"; by Saint Thomas

---

[57] As. P. Fahlbeck, G. Briefs, and others rightly declare, the characteristic of manual work is typical only for the bulk of the laboring class. Another (smaller) part of this class is made up of the "intellectual proletariat or laborers." (Cf. P. Fahlbeck, *Les Classes sociales*, pp. 195 ff.; G. Briefs, *The Proletariat, passim*; and J. Lhomme, *op. cit.*, pp. 239 ff.) The big labor organizations all include many groups.

[58] For an excellent analysis of this point, cf. G. Briefs, *The Proletariat* (New York, 1938), pp. 24 ff.

[59] Cf. in my *Mobility*. For Germany, cf. the summary of the data in S. Riemer, "Socialer Aufstieg und Klassenschichtung," *Archiv für Sozialwissenschaft und Socialpolitik*, Vol. 67 (1932), pp. 531-560.

Aquinas' statement that wage-earners can never accumulate wealth, and that because they are poor they become wage-earners and because they are wage-earners they are poor; and by the reiterated declaration of contemporary investigators "that the poor live by their labor and their labor leaves them poor."[60] Finally, its plane of living is determined by its occupational and economic status.

In the third place, in modern western societies the proletariat and other classes are theoretically equal before the law. Actually, however, and to some extent even legally the totality of their rights and privileges is much more modest than that of other classes. Even legally their civil and political rights have been limited in many countries by requirements of property for the privileges of voting, holding certain offices, and the like.[61] The relative disabilities of the proletarian embrace the following deprivations. The nature of his work is frequently highly monotonous and boring, little calculated to stimulate thought, to say nothing of creativeness. It is often physically disagreeable, being performed under unpleasant and unhygienic conditions. Again, a higher education, desirable positions, and other advantages are ordinarily unavailable. On the other hand, his share of burdensome duties, including subordination to and dependence upon the capitalists, is disproportionately large.

Such are the principal bonds whose coalescence, together with certain additional characteristics (semicloseness, etc.), creates the proletarian class. These objective bonds determine and serve as a foundation for a vast superstructure of important physical and mental traits, interests, beliefs, tastes, aspirations, and ideals, as well as of the mode of living and of various socialistic, communistic, and other movements on the part of the proletariat. In many respects the physical, mental, moral, social, and behavioral character of the laboring class is notably different from that of the other classes.[62]

An analysis of the farmer-peasant class,[63] of the class of capitalists or the managerial aristocracy of corporations, and of the dwindling class of large landowners[64] would demonstrate that each of these classes is likewise made up of a coalescence of the same three primary bonds as the proletariat. Since the present work is not a special treatise on the social classes, the analysis of these classes is omitted.

It is to be noted that of the four big classes the labor and farmer-peasant classes are much more closely related to each other, occupationally, economically, and in respect to their factual and legal rights and duties, than to the other two classes. Hence these classes have exhibited their mutual solidarity more frequently and on more important issues than their affinity to the large landowners and the capitalists. Consequently it is easier to create a farmer-labor party than an alliance between the laboring or farmer class and the capitalistic or large landowning class.

It is to be observed, further, that the sharpness of the class division in a population and the conspicuousness of the class traits in each member depend largely upon the length of time during which the members remain in their class and its unbonded groups. As a rule, other conditions being equal, the longer the period of membership the more class-minded they become. For the same reason, in societies like that of the United States (especially in the past), in which vertical social mobility is strongly developed, the class differentiation is bound to be less clear and effective than in populations with weak vertical mobility. This explains why the proletariat in America has been less clear-cut than in many European countries, and why the social class has played a less conspicuous role in the United States

---

[60] G. Briefs, The Proletariat (New York, 1938), p. 4.

[61] Cf. my Mobility, Chps. 3, 4.

[62] For these traits, cf. the cited works of G. Briefs et al.; the portrayal of the laborer or proletarian, in general literature and the fine arts; statistical surveys (such as that of Booth), and studies of the standards of living such as M. Halbwach's L'Évolution des besoins dans les classes ouvrières (Paris, 1933).

[63] For a definition and analysis of the farmer-peasant class, as well as for the literature of the subject, cf. Sorokin and Zimmerman, Principles of Rural-Urban Sociology; Sorokin, Zimmerman, and Galpin, Source Book in Rural Sociology (cited); L. Smith, The Sociology of Rural Life (New York, 1940); J. T. Sanders and D. Ensminger (eds.), Farmers of the World (New York, 1945); or any other competent works on rural sociology.

[64] The literature dealing with these classes is very copious.

than in Europe. Unfortunately, class differentiation in this country, with the concomitant class consciousness and class struggle, appears to be on the increase.

Finally, it is to be noted that the dominant role played by these four classes in the western world during the last two centuries is well attested by the history of this period. One need not be a Marxian to recognize that this history has been largely the resultant of their mutual alliances and antagonisms, which account for a large proportion of the revolts, revolutions, and social movements of the western nations, as well as for many international wars and alliances. Similarly, a notable percentage of the official laws of these countries have been enacted in response to class pressure. In brief their "operational" effects are undeniable. Therefore no adequate theory of social structure, differentiation, and stratification can afford to neglect this kind of multibonded group. This explains why in this treatise on general sociology the social class is given a comparatively large amount of space.

V. Concluding Remarks

The foregoing analysis of the primary unibonded and multibonded groups gives us the main lines of the social differentiation of humanity into powerful social groups, the structure of the groups themselves, and the principal co-ordinates that determine the position of the groups in the total population, as well as the status and the physical, mental, and behavioral traits of the individual members of these groups. Our next step in this structural analysis will be the study of social stratification.

Chapter 15. Social Stratification

I. The Stratification
of Social Groups

The social structure of the human population does not consist merely in the differentiation of the population into unibonded and multibonded groups. It consists also in the fact of the stratification of organized groups—stratification within any single group and stratification of several groups with respect to one another. Thus to be more or less complete, a knowledge of social structure requires recognition not only of social differentiation but of social stratification as well. The first concerns the division of the population along the vertical lines of the groups; the second refers to the division of the population along the horizontal lines. The real social strata of a group, as well as groups with respect to one another, are ranked as superior and inferior, higher and lower, controlling and controlled, dominating and subordinated, privileged and disfranchised. If the sociocultural world of human groups were only a "one-story structure," the essentials of that structure would be learned through a study of its social differentiation. If it is, as indeed it happens to be, a "many-storied structure," then one must know also its stratificational aspect. This explains why a study of social stratification is now in order.

II. Classification of the Forms
of Stratification or Inequalities

Like social differentiation, social stratification has many forms and can be classified in many different ways. For sociological purposes, the following appear to be the most important: (1) official and unofficial organized real strata, "as if" organized strata, and nominal, statistical pseudo strata (plurels); (2) intragroup and intergroup stratification; (3) unibonded and multibonded stratification. Then each of the unibonded and multibonded strata can be subclassified into open (nonhereditary), closed (hereditary), and intermediary. There are among the intermediary forms those that are *legally sanctioned* by the official law of the state or some other group, and those that are *factual*, that is, without specific legal sanctioning.

The multibonded strata can be classified, according to the number of the stratifying bonds, into double, triple, quadruple, and so on. They can be further classified as a) innerly solidary, or affine; b) antagonistic, or disaffine; and c) neutral. Let us now make an analysis of the nature of each of these forms, one by one, of their combinations, in order to gain a more adequate knowledge of social stratification.

276

1. The Organized Real Strata, the "As If" Organized Strata, and the Nominal, Pseudo Strata

An organized real social stratum of a group, or of a constellation of groups, is composed of the totality of the members interacting with one another and having all the characteristics of a real social group: causal and meaningful unity, reality, individuality, interdependence of its members, government, and so on (see Chapter 8). Whether composed of many or a few or even of one member, the real social stratum lives and functions amidst other strata as a real organized social group with all its essential characteristics (Chapter 4). The real social strata ordinarily are defined legally by the official law of the group, like the ranks of the pope-cardinal-archbishop-bishop hierarchy in the church group, like the full-associate-assistant professor-instructor grading in the university, and so on for other groups. The ranking of the official law may or may not coincide with the ranking of the unofficial convictions of the members of the group. Officially, the rank of the French or the Russian nobility on the eve of the French and Russian Revolutions was the highest among all the estates of the respective countries; but according to the unofficial-law convictions of a considerable part of the French and Russian populations, the "superiority and prestige" of the nobilities was not respected and their official high position was in fact resented and considered unjustified. There are many cases where the rankings of the official and unofficial laws coincide. Now and then the real strata exist factually, that is, without specific legal sanctioning, official or unofficial. Thus in many populations the strata of the rich and of the poor exist as real strata, but they are not defined or sanctioned legally. Whether legally sanctioned or merely existing factually, the real unibonded or multibonded social stratum is always an objectively given real collectivity, easily observable and existing independently of the subjective ranking of observers and investigators.[1]

An "as if" real and organized stratum of a group, or of a constellation of groups, is composed of the totality of the individuals who have the same position—rights, duties, functions, etc.—in the hierarchy of strata, and who therefore think, feel, and act similarly so far as such a similarity is imposed on them by the similarity of their stratum-positions. However, they are not expressly organized into one body, with its own government, regulations, planned and consciously pursued policy, and so on. Many of such members may not even be aware of their co-belonging to the same stratum. The strata of slaves, serfs, and criminals, are examples of such "as if" organized strata. Their social status was precisely defined by law, but did not have any committee, they were often scattered over a wide territory, and they did not react directly with one another. Nevertheless, they acted and felt similarly, like the partisans and guerillas of the same army.

A purely nominal or statistical stratum (a plurel) does not have the essential traits of a real group and does not exist as such in reality. When, for instance, statisticians divide the population into income-groups: below $100, $101 to $150, $151 to $200, $201 to $251, and so on, such economic strata are nominal groups. The persons receiving from all sources an income between $101 and $150 are not necessarily more closely connected with one another than with persons receiving, especially all from the same source, $76 to $100, or $151 to $175. When W. L. Warner and P. S. Lunt divide the population of Yankee City into six strata: upper-upper, lower-upper,

---

[1] For this reason all the studies of social stratification in which the strata are obtained through a ranking of the observers themselves, or through a vague reference to "the status" or "social class" or "prestige" ranked subjectively by one or by a group of evaluators—all these studies actually deal not with the real social strata but with either "as if organized strata" or, in most cases, with purely "nominal plurels" taken incorrectly for a real stratum. Such studies remain largely fruitless. See the examples of such mistakes as well as attempts to avoid them in the works of Warner and Lunt, cited; in W. H. Form, "Status Stratification in a Planned Community," *ASR*, X, pp. 605-13; E. H. Bell, "Social Stratification in a Small Community," *Scientific Monthly*, 1934, pp. 157-164; H. Speier, "Honor and the Social Stratification," *SR*, II, pp. 74-97; M. Smith, "An Empirical Scale of Prestige Status of Occupations," *ASR*, 1943, pp. 185-192; D. Anderson and P. E. Davidson, *Ballots and the American Class Struggle* (Stanford University Press, 1939). See the vast literature on stratification in my *Mobility*.

upper-middle, lower-middle, upper-lower, and lower-lower they are constructing wholly nominal strata. Their own material shows that neither economically, nor by the volume of rights and duties, nor in behavioral, occupational, or any other way, do these strata live and function as real organized or even "as if" organized unities.[2] Still more nominal are most of their 89 stratified positions in Yankee City. These positions are the cuts of a social "mince pie" rather than organs and cells of a living body. Subsequently we shall deal mainly with the organized real and with the "as if" organized strata, paying little attention to the nominal plurels.

2. The Intragroup and Intergroup Strata (Inequality)

We have distinguished further intragroup and intergroup stratification. In our analysis of the organized groups (see Chapter 4), it has been indicated that the distributive and organizational functions of law create a stratification in any organized group. In order to prevent clashes among its members and enforce the official law, any organized group establishes a long or short hierarchy of superior and inferior authorities, and ranks its members into a very definite, clear-cut order in which the decision of each superior authority or stratum is mandatory upon the respective inferior rank or authority. Such an hierarchization of the authority or of the rights and duties leads to a clear-cut stratification of all members of any organized group. This explains why *the organization and stratification are inseparable and why stratification is an inalienable trait of any organized group.* In other words, unequal distribution of rights-duties-roles-functions is an inherent trait of an organization. Whatever organized empirical group we take, from the family, clan, tribe, to age, sex, racial,

language, state, religious, occupational, economic and other groups, they are all stratified into a number of either legal and clearly-cut strata or into a factual and somewhat muddled set of strata, superior and inferior, dominant and subordinate. In both cases these strata exist objectively, making unnecessary the subjective ranking of observers. We shall see this in the next section of this chapter.

Side by side with the intragroup stratification (inequality), there is intergroup stratification, or inequality among groups, whether these groups are of the same or different nature with respect to their unibonded or multibonded characteristics. Different states, different occupational, religious, or other groups, are not situated on the same level, but on different levels so far as their prestige, controlling influence, domination, and other powers are concerned. In other words, groups are stratified one with respect to another. There are big and small state powers; there are the skilled and the unskilled; there are the professional and the big business occupations; there are the monopolistic, privileged religions, and the suppressed, persecuted, and disfranchised ones. These are all examples of such intergroup stratification of groups in the same class. There is also, in somewhat more confused condition, stratification among groups which are of a different nature. There is ranking of the state and religious groups (witness the struggle for supremacy between the state and the church in the Middle Ages); there is ranking of occupational and nationality groups, and so on. In more detailed form, these stratifications will be outlined in the next section. For the present, the above definitions will suffice for the subsequent discussion.

3. Unibonded and Multibonded Stratification

Our concept of unibonded and multibonded groups is also applicable to social strata.

---

[2] See their *The Social Life of a Modern Community and The Status System* (quoted). Somewhat humorous evidence of the nominality of their strata is given in the fact that, having artificially divided the population into these six strata, they subsequently find that members of the same stratum behave differently and that in the associations, cliques, and in many other ways, these strata are intermixed to such an extent that they are forced to make another "discovery," namely, that associations, cliques, occupations, and many other devices

serve as the "integrating links" between the strata, uniting them into one community. The real situation is much simpler. Most of their strata not being real ones, they do not exist. Therefore their members are naturally intermingled. Their second "discovery" cancels their first, and both together show the nominal nature of their six stratified classes. Another conspicuous example of purely nominal plurels substituted for real groups is given in most of the complex and fruitless classifications of S.C. Dodd's *Dimensions of Society* (New York, 1942).

Stratification within any unibonded group is a unibonded stratification; stratification within a multibonded group is a multibonded stratification. It should be remembered that the unibonded groups are those in which the grouping of members is centered around one main class of values-meanings-norms. The multibonded groups are those in which the *raison d'être* of the group is a coalescence of two or a greater number of the sets of the unibonded values-meanings-norms. In accordance with this conception, the stratification in the unibonded groups is based on the same main value on which is based the existence of the group itself. The *raison d'être* of the stratification in such a group is a bigger and better realization of this value: in economic groups of the economic value; in kinship groups, the kinship value; in religious groups, the religious value, and so on. This does not exclude the other values as secondary ones or as a by-product. But, as a rule, an economic group does not exist because of and for the sake of better propagation of religion, nor the religious group for making money. The stratification within an economic or religious group exists for the bigger and better realization of the economic and religious values respectively. For these reasons they are unibonded, the economic with the richer and poorer strata, the religious with the strata of pope, cardinal, bishop, priest, and plain parishioner. Each is based on its own main value, each representing a gradation of this unibonded value in its upper and lower ranks.

Since a multibonded group realizes the main values of two or a greater number of the unibonded groups, its stratification will also be a multibonded stratification whose *raison d'etre* is a realization of these compounded values. Hence the unibonded and multibonded stratification and the strata. A unibonded real or "as if" real stratum is made up of the totality of the members of a unibonded group united into a real stratum by similar rights, duties, and apportionment of the main value of the group, by similar status and role in its realization and enjoyment. The status, role, and apportionment will always tangibly, and sometimes formally, be different from those of the other strata of the same group. A multibonded real stratum in a multibonded group is composed of the totality of the members united into one rank by a similarity of their rights-duties in regard to a similar apportionment, status and role in the realization of the compounded values of the group. This apportionment, role, and status is clearly different from those of other strata in the same group. Hence, *qualitatively there are as many unibonded and multibonded forms of stratification (inequality) as there are unibonded and multibonded groups.* Let us briefly consider these forms of stratification and inequality.[3]

III. Forms of Unibonded Stratification (Inequality)

1. Intra- and Interracial Stratification (Inequality)

If racial groups are organized, we have a racial stratification within each of the racial groups into leaders, influential layers, and plain members. There is also a stratification of the racial groups one with respect to the others, for instance, the white race legally or factually being superior to and dominant over the black race, the ranking involving a series of privileges for the white and disfranchisement for the other race. In some populations and periods, this stratification of different racial groups assumed the sharpest, most rigidly organized legal and factual forms, with the "inferior" race turned into slaves and serfs and with the "superior" race becoming an autocratic master; with the "inferior" race dispossessed of practically all political, civil,

[3] Here I am following the classification of my *Sistema Soziologii* (Petrograd, 1921) Vol. II, pp. 173-178, 249-258. In my monographic *Mobility* I gave a more detailed study of the economic, occupational, and sociopolitical forms of stratification, stressing at the same time that "the concrete forms of stratification are numerous." *Ibid.*, p. 12. The classification of the forms of stratification with the subsequent outline of the main unibonded and multibonded stratifications clarifies, to a considerable degree, the prevalent vagueness of the concept of stratification as well as of its forms.

economic, or other rights, pitilessly exploited by the "superior" racial group, and treated worse than cattle. Human history is full of such racial stratifications. In a population where different racial groups exist side by side, racial inequalities lead often to a clear-cut, legal ranking of different races into several strata from the highest to the lowest, with decreasing privileges and increasing disfranchisement of all kinds as we move from the "superior" to the "inferior" race groups. Thus, even now in the United States, the order of the white, the yellow, and the black "races" is one such form of stratification. Another, and more detailed form, in which the population and lawgivers mix racial and biosocial stocks or nationality groups is illustrated by such stratifications as the Mayflower descendants, the Daughters and Sons of the American Revolution, the native-born Yankees, the Anglo-Saxons, the Dutch-German-Scandinavian-Irish-French, the Italian-Jewish-Russian-Polish-Finnish-Greek-Armenian, the Chinese-Japanese-Oriental, the Negro and other "African" blacks. This order varies, depending upon the state and the stratifiers, but in this or that form it is widely spread, daily used, functions tangibly in hundreds of social relationships, and manifests itself even in legal forms, whether in the size of the quota of immigrants permitted for each "stock," in the total exclusion of Orientals, or in many other forms, not to mention many legal and factual disfranchisements of the Negro and other "Africans."[4]

Regardless of the magnitude of the privileges and disfranchisements of different racial,

or what is thought to be racial, strata, the stratification is unibonded, based upon the assumption of racial heterogeneity, and it is different from all other forms of unibonded and multibonded stratifications. It groups in one stratum, by the bond of racial similarity, and ignores economic, religious, or any nonracial bond. Such interracial stratification is usually followed by the creation of many ideologies[5] rationalizing racial inequality in terms of the notion of a "chosen people," the idea of "blue blood," or some complicated ideology like those theories of A. Gobineau, H. S. Chamberlain, O. Ammon, V. de Lapouge, K. Pearson, and F. Galton, of many eugenists and geneticists, plus the popular beliefs about the inequality of races and the superiority of the ideologists' own race.

2. Intra- and Intersex Stratification (Inequality)

This is another form of unibonded stratification. Biological sex-differences are seized upon for building a superstructure of sociocultural inequalities between male and female groups. It elevates the groups and members of one sex, usually the male, into the superior, privileged, and dominant stratum, and it degrades the other sex group, usually female, to inferior, disfranchised, and subordinate status. In some populations the contrast between the status of men and women is enormous. Women are often deprived of all rights and men, as *paterfamilias*, are given the right of life and death over their women. In other societies the factual and legal difference in the status of the sex groups is not so great. Nevertheless, in whatever form, it exists in practically all

---

[4] The Immigration Acts of 1921, 1924, 1929, and 1934 clearly reflect the United States "official" stratification, ranking, favoring, and discrimination against various European "stocks" and "races." Of the total 100% of immigration, it allotted 55.5% to Great Britain and Ireland, 17.2% to Germany, and only 1.8% to Russia, and from .2% to 4% to all the countries of eastern, southern and central Europe. It excluded entirely the Japanese and most of the other "yellow" races and also the "African" races. It favored decidedly the "races" of northwestern Europe, assigning to them 83% of the total European immigration, instead of the 21% supplied by this area before 1921. It apportioned only 16% of the European total to the eastern, southern and central European groups, instead of the 80% of the total supplied by these areas before the Acts. The

Acts remain the striking evidence of both legal and factual discrimination against and the favoring of specified "racial stocks," and this evidence invalidates all the pious speech-reactions denouncing racial discrimination, all the official and unofficial verbosity that has daily flooded the nation not only during the war, but after it.

[5] See an analysis and criticism of all these theories in my *Theories*, Ch. 5. Characteristic detail: even ranking done by scholars supposedly free from racial prejudice shows its contagious effect. For instance, the ranking of the population of Yankee City by Warner and Lunt is based upon the hidden assumption that the Yankee native population is socially superior and belongs only to the upper-upper and lower-upper. This implicit assumption is the real basis of their stratification into six strata.

populations at all times. Even in the most democratic countries, at the present time, the full factual and legal equality of the sexes has not been attained. The economic, political, and other legal rights of women are still not equal to those of men, in several respects. Factual discrimination against women, beginning with the well-known "double standard of sexual morality" and ending with hundreds of other disfranchisements, still exists. The stratification is unibonded in sexual terms. It is based on the sex-difference and is not reducible to any other basis or form.

There is also intrasex stratification in organized groups of both men and women. Organizations of women are stratified into leaders and led, ruling committee members and ordinary members, influential and less influential. Such layers of "women-aristocrats" and "women-plebs" exist in all local, provincial, state, and national women's organizations. The same is true of all groups of men. In comparison with the intersex stratification, this intrasex hierarchy of men or women assumes other forms of stratification as well, e.g., occupational, political, and so on.

3. Intra- and Interage Group Stratification (Inequality)

All that has been said of sex-stratification is equally applicable to the inequalities of various age-groups. Legally and factually in all societies the age groups have been stratified, with different rights, duties, status, roles, privileges, disfranchisements. In some populations the contrast between age-groups is quite striking, with the younger groups deprived of all rights and subordinated entirely to the older people. In others the differences have been fewer, milder, and more limited. But in none of the populations has there been realized the real legal and factual equality of the status of different age-groups. Even in the most advanced democracies, the younger age-groups are deprived of many rights and privileges —economic, occupational, political, and civic.

There is also an undeveloped stratification within each of the organized age-groups, especially in the disfranchised ones. There are leaders and led, influential and non-influential strata within the same age group. The stratifi-

cation of various "youth organizations" and movements into leaders, committee members, and ordinary members exists in local, state, and national youth groups. Within the organized groups of the same age, say of youth, there are the "youth aristocracy" and the "youth plebs." In such movements and groups as the Townsend movement, an organized elderly age group trying to get privileges at the cost of the younger age groups, there are the national leaders, the state leaders, the county and city leaders of various ranks and degrees of influence, a series of intermediary strata, and finally the ordinary members of the organization—mere voters, payers, and supporters. The concrete forms of the intra-age group stratification or inequality are many. Often they merge with the stratification and inequality in other organized groups.

4. Intra- and Intergroup Kinship Stratification (Inequality)

Each kinship group is stratified into a series of ranks based on blood-kinship, "classificatory" kinship, and artificial-kinship. There are the chiefs of the kins; the high, usually elderly, ranks of the most influential, most honored, most dominating kinship aristocracy; the several intermediary ranks; and the least influential, dominated, and lowest ranks of the kins. The concrete forms of this ranking vary from kinship group to kinship group.[6] Superiority and higher prestige of kinship aristocracy may be due now to age, now wealth, now sacrifice and heroic deeds, now to the number of scalps obtained, now to the endurance of torture, and now to services rendered the group. But, whatever the concrete form, the status of kinsmen in a group is not equal and there is always a clear-cut or somewhat muddled set of ranks of superior and inferior strata.

Interkinship stratification manifests itself in a hierarchy of ranks of different interacting kinship groups. In a conglomerate population consisting of several kinship groups, whether among the preliterate or historical populations, the kindreds, gentes, and families (in which the kinship tie is one of the bonds) have

[6] For examples of concrete forms among preliterate kinship groups, see the cited works of Thomas, Kroeber, Hobhouse, Wheeler, Ginsberg, Lowie, Thurnwald, Radcliffe-Brown, and others.

hardly ever been equal in their status, influence, prestige, honor, and functions. Legally or factually there have always been the leading, the aristocratic, the superior kinship groups, gentes and families and the subordinated, led, uninfluential, and submerged ones. When the kinship tie coalesced with other bonds and there arose multibonded social estates, kinship stratification assumed the legal and clear-cut forms of the hereditary kindreds of the Spartiates and the non-Spartiates and slaves in Sparta; of the Eupatridai, the common Orgeones, and slaves in Athens; the patricians and the plebeians in Rome, with other intermediary and unfree strata; of several orders ranging from nobility to slaves in other populations. Even in contemporary England, the families are still ranked in sixty-five orders of hereditary and non-hereditary dignities— all above the common families. The royal family is at the top, then come the basic ranks of the dukes, marquises, earls, viscounts, barons, knights, baronets, companions, esquires, and gentlemen. In some form, such a ranking of various kindreds and families exists in practically every population. Even in the democratic United States, one can hardly find a village or city, not to mention the nation, in which there is not some stratification of its families into the leading, the higher, the blue blood, the aristocratic, the influential, and into the submerged, the good-for-nothing, with several grades in between. On a nation-wide scale, the kinship groups of the descendants of the Mayflower, of the Daughters and Sons of the American Revolution, of the Sixty Families,[7] to mention but a few, are examples of this kind of stratification. Finally, the role of kinship groups in the appraisal, appointment, and promotion of a person of "good family" in business, the professions, politics, is known to everybody. There is a tendency of kins occupying a high position to open or hidden nepotism. Although denounced incessantly, especially in the so-called equalitarian societies, stratification on the basis of kinship continues to exist everywhere. Its concrete forms change, but its essence remains immortal.

[7] See F. Lundberg, *America's Sixty Families* (New York, 1937).

5. Intra- and Intergroup Locality Stratification (Inequality)

Any territorial group, be it a village, a city, or a precinct, not to mention larger territorial units, has its local aristocracy, its intermediate strata, and its under-dogs. Since any territorial group represents a conglomeration of various unibonded and multibonded groups, the concrete forms of the stratification of local groups are also manifold, overlapping and sometimes "muddled." Nevertheless they all assume a territorially bounded character and manifest themselves in various "locality forms." First, there are the locally elected or appointed authorities in charge of the local needs: economic, sanitary, educational, etc. The local chief, mayor, alderman, selectmen, and so on, make up the upper governing stratum of the population, as a form of local aristocracy. Second, in many cities and even villages the territorial stratification appears in the division of residential areas into exclusive, restricted, plebeian, unrestricted, and slums; into streets and areas occupied by the royal, financial, intellectual, and other aristocracies, as, for example, the Boston Brahmins on Beacon Hill. There are areas for the middle strata and for the lowest, the outcasts and dregs of society. Another form of locality stratification is the division of the local population into "society" and common mortals; into the "exclusive" cliques, the country club sets, and other associations of the upper class; and into the lower plebs not admitted to these aristocratic strata. Even in a village there are several layers of superior and inferior gradations, with the members of the same stratum treating each other as equals and those of different strata discriminating as between superiors and inferiors.[8] Concrete variations on the pattern are numerous, but the general pattern of stratification is essentially constant. The local character is manifest in the fact that most of the "highest local aristocracy" cease to be an aristocracy outside of the limits of the given locality. The "great man" of a given village or precinct turns into an unknown, in-

[8] See concrete examples in Sinclair Lewis's *Cass Timberlane* (New York, 1945). In the city of Grand Republic, Cass Timberlane, Dr. Drover, Bradd Criley, and others are the local aristocracy.

significant common mortal beyond the boundaries of his local group.

Besides the intralocality stratification, there is interlocality stratification. Many national or even international groups like the state, religious groups, occupational unions, political parties, business corporations, are divided into the state, the county, the city, the village, and other local subgroups. In this territorial subdivision of social systems, the leaders or aristocracy of the larger territorial units are factually and often legally superior to those of the smaller territorial units. The president of the state is superior to the governors of the province, and so on. The president of the United States Steel Corporation or of the American Federation of Labor is superior to the presidents or chiefs or managers of smaller territorial units of the Corporation or of the local labor union. As a result, the territorial "aristocracies" of various kinds range into a hierarchy of the superior and inferior strata. There is another variation. In many countries the whole population of a certain territory is deprived of a series of rights and privileges. For instance in pre-revolutionary Russia the population of certain territories did not have the right of self-government (municipal and semstvo) and other privileges. Likewise, in England before the reforms of 1830-1834, the representation in Parliament was grossly favorable to some localities. The variety of interterritorial stratification exists in some form in all countries. In a city not all the "exclusive" areas are equal. At one time the Back Bay in Boston was equal to Beacon Hill, but later it became less aristocratic.[9] There were several "aristocratic" areas of Paris, but not all of these were equal. The same is true of various exclusive localized societies, cliques, Junior Leagues, clubs, and associations. Whatever their concrete and ever-changing patterns, the fact of interlocality group stratification is perennial and general.

6. Intra- and Internationality Stratification (Inequality)

Intranationality stratification exists everywhere. There is the highest stratum, composed of national heroes, of the great political, scientific, artistic, religious, and cultural men and women, who are the pride and glory of the group; then there is the stratum of the members of committees of the various nationality organizations and associations, in the form of the historical aristocracy of a given nationality; there are the middle groups; and lastly, the common people. These strata are relatively clear-cut, especially in the language groups that are suppressed and disfranchised by the state government or other powers. As most of the members of the language groups are hardly organized, their inner stratification is generally somewhat "anarchical," not brought into one clear-cut hierarchy. When a language group creates an almost coterminous state organization, as it often does, purely language group stratification merges with the state hierarchy, assumes its clearness and definiteness, and becomes the same thing as the intrastate stratification.

Internationality stratification is a perennial and practically universal phenomenon. Now and then it assumes clear-cut and objective forms, when certain nationalities are legally ranked in the order of their superiority and inferiority with a respective distribution of privileges and disfranchisements. Thus in ancient Rome the population was stratified into several classes: the full-fledged citizens of Rome, that is, *cives*; the less privileged, like the *latini*; the members of the *civitates cum suffragio* and *sine suffragio*, *civitates foederatae* and *liberae*, subdivided into *aequum* and *iniquum*; the provincial strata of the *peregrini*, *peregrini dediticii*, and so on; each stratum having different status, rights, duties, privileges, and disfranchisements. At the source of many of these divisions lay the fact of conquest, but up to the extension of Roman citizenship upon all the free population except the *peregrini dediticii*, in 212 A.D., the lines of stratification went, to a great extent, along the lines of the nationality or language groups.[10] In Rus-

---

[9] See the facts in an excellent analysis in W. Firey's work, quoted. Also, P. Hatt, "The Relation of Ecological Location to Status Position," *ASR*, 1941, pp. 481-85; also M. A. Gibbard, "The Status Factor in Residential Succession," *AJS*, May, 1941. Cf. C. Shaw and M. McKay, *Juvenile Delinquency and Urban Areas* (Chicago, 1940).

[10] See T. Mommsen, *Abriss des Römische Staatsrecht* (Berlin, 1893); I. Pokrovsky, *Istoria Rimskago Prava* (Petrograd, 1924).

sia before the revolution certain language groups, from the Poles to the many aboriginal groups of Asia, were legally deprived of certain rights and privileges possessed by other language-groups in Russia. Some of the non-Russian groups like the Finns had more political and other rights than the Russian-language groups. In the contemporary French, British, and Dutch empires, not to mention many other states, the subjects in the colonies and possessions, belonging to nationalities different from the French, British, or Dutch, are ranged into several classes according to their comparative disfranchisements. In whatever form, nearly everywhere that state populations are made up of different language groups, there exists either legal or factual form of inter-nationality stratification. Even in the United States there are many forms of it manifest in the ranking of Americans of various nationalities into a series of superiors and inferiors by the native-born of native parents, and by other language groups. The Yankees and Old Americans regard themselves as the highest group.[11] Then come in various orders British-Americans, Scandinavian- or German-Americans, French- or Irish-Americans; all the rest of the other American nationalities are ordinarily ranked below these "aristocratic" groups. The rank order of American nationalities made by the Jewish- or Italian- or Russian-Americans naturally differs in that it puts their own nationality at the top and others in a descending order. But a hierarchical ranking is made by practically all American language groups. It manifests itself in various "exclusive" associations, societies, clubs, resorts, residential districts, and so on, which admit the "superior" nationalities to membership, and exclude the

"inferior" ones. It externalizes itself in other forms of "social distance" which these groups and individuals believe to exist between their rank and that of the other nationalities.[12] It expresses itself in our immigration laws, excluding from immigration and thus from citizenship a large number of racial and language groups of the East, Africa, and other continents.[13] It manifests itself in the terms of *jus connubium* and *jus convivium*, which legally or factually favor or disfavor certain inter-nationality marriages and result in different amounts of intermarriages of different nationalities, even in a democratic country like the United States.[14] To sum up: Intra- and inter-group nationality stratification is almost universal and perennial; its concrete manifestations change, its essence remains.

7. Intra- and Interstate Stratification (Inequality)

The state is the group with possibly the clearest legal and factual stratification. Being a clearing-house for many other groups, its stratification, as we have seen, serves also to express the stratification of other groups. The state constitution and official law give a detailed map of the structure of the hierarchy of its authorities. At the top there is a monarch or president or dictator or Führer. Then comes the cabinet with its secretaries or their equivalent; then undersecretaries, assistant secretaries of various ranks (first, second, etc.); then the chiefs of divisions, assistant chiefs of the divisions, and so on, down to the pettiest official, policeman, and plain citizen. A similarly clear-

---

[11] See Warner and Lunt, *op. cit.* A study shows that sixth grade children found 26 favorable traits in Americans, 6 neutral, and none unfavorable. See R. Zeligs, "Racial Attitudes of Children," *Sociology and Social Research*, XXI (1937), p. 364. See various rankings of nationalities by 1725 adults, 200, and then 12 children, in R. Zeligs, "Tracing Racial Attitudes," *Ibid.*, XXIII (1938), p. 50.

[12] For instance, 269 native American whites, mainly middle class persons, gave the following ranks of social nearness in terms of their neighbor-preferences: Irish, German, Swedish, Jewish, Italian, Armenian, Japanese, Mexican, Filipino, Negro. E. Monjar, "Racial Distance Reactions,"

Sociology and Social Research, XXI (1937), p. 559. In a series of other studies published in this journal, the rank order of language groups varies. On the other hand, the rank of the whites, evaluated by Negroes, is very low. See, for instance, M. C. Hill, "Basic Racial Attitudes towards Whites in an Oklahoma All-Negro Community," *AJS* (1944), pp. 519-523.

[13] See *U.S. Immigration Laws and Rules* (Washington, 1930). E. Bogardus, "From Immigration to Exclusion," *Sociology and Social Research*, XXXIV (1940), pp. 272-278.

[14] See R. Kennedy, "Single or Triple Melting Pot," quoted; J. Drachsler, *Intermarriage in New York City* (New York, 1921); W. Weatherly, "Race and Marriage," *AJS*, XV; A. E. Jenks, "Ethnic Census in Minneapolis," *Ibid.*, XVII; U. Z. Engelman, "Intermarriage Among Jews in Germany," *Sociology and Social Research* (1935), pp. 34-40.

cut hierarchy of ranks may be seen in the judicial order of the state, beginning with the supreme court or judge and ending with the lowest local justices and court agents. There is also a pyramid among the legislative authorities, with the supreme organ at the top—the parliament, congress, the monarch's legislative group; and then a series of subordinated provincial and local legislative organs. The state army and navy have ranks from supreme commander, marshals, down to privates and seamen, with many intervening ranks. Depending on the type of state, these hierarchies vary in their concrete forms, but in all states they are clearly defined and furnish us with a long series of· ranks of authorities.

Interstate stratification is clear in federations and confederations, with the federal authorities being superior to the several state authorities. In some cases there is a legal ranking within these federated states. Less clear-cut, but unquestionable factual stratification exists among the interacting "sovereign" states, where there are "big" and "small" powers. Many interstate relationships are defined by international law. There is an order of precedence of diplomatic representatives of the various states at different seats of government, and there is the comparative prestige and authority of the military, financial, and other agents of a state. The interstate ranking of the "sovereign" states and of their representatives is full of gradations and precedences.

This influential role of the state and its clear-cut stratification explains why an individual's social position is largely determined by his state membership and by the specific stratum in the state hierarchy to which he belongs. Regardless of the individual's positions in other groups, his high state position, e.g., monarch, president, cabinet minister, marshal, or supreme commander, in a powerful state is sufficient to make him a "conspicuous somebody" in the human world and to rank him among "the highest" on earth.[15]

8. Intra- and Interpolitical Party Stratification (Inequality)

Any political party has a long or short hierarchy of its bosses and bossed, ranging

[15] See the details on state stratification in my *Social Mobility*, Chps. II, V.

from the leader, chief, president, to members of the central committee or caucus, to big and small financial supporters, to influential members of the provincial committees, and ending with the precinct leader and plain voting member. Since it is a fighting organization, no political party can be free of such stratification. The Equalitarian, the Socialist, the Communist, the Syndicalist, and the Anarchist (so far as they are organized) parties are not exceptions to this rule. If anything, the rigidity of stratification, the dictatorial autocracy of the higher bosses, is much more severe and autocratic in such parties than in the conservative bourgeois parties. Some of these radical parties, like the Syndicalist, Communist, and the like, explicitly profess the principle of the selected party elite, which is entitled to rule the majority as it pleases, in accordance only with its own decisions. The power of the heads of such Equalitarian, Socialist, Communist, Syndicalist, National Socialist, and Jacobin parties, whether the head be Lenin or Stalin, Robespierre or L. A. Blanqui, Hitler or Mussolini, is autocratic. As to the role of the plain party members in such parties, it is, in the words of a Syndicalist theorizer, E. Fournière, the role of the zeros, whose only function is to increase the weight of the figure on the left, that is, the party leader or boss.[16]

The interparty stratification manifests itself quite clearly in countries with one dictatorial party, as in Cromwellian England, Jacobin France, Communist Russia, Nazi Germany, or Fascist Italy. All other parties are suppressed. The dictatorial party has a monopoly of privileges, and for other parties the concentration camp, confiscation of property, and even execution prevail. In a milder form, this inequality exists also in democratic countries. There is a system of spoils and booty for the victorious party and disfranchisement for the defeated parties. Almost all the coveted state

[16] E. Fournière, *La sociocratie* (Paris, 1910), p. 117. See, on these autocratic, oligarchic features of such parties, V. Pareto, *Systèmes socialistes* (2nd. ed., Paris, 1926); also the quoted works of R. Michels, M. Ostrogorsky, H. Lagardelle, G. Sorel, and others; P. Kropotkin, *The Speeches of a Rebel* (in Russian, Moscow, 1919); M. Bakunin, *The State and Anarchy* (in Russian, Moscow, 1919).

positions, innumerable sinecures, explicit and implicit, direct and indirect economic and other advantages go to the victorious party. There may even be punishing measures against the defeated parties. If the fight for spoils and power flares into civil war between the parties, then their stratification becomes almost limitless; one party tends to exterminate the other with the utmost ferocity.

9. Intra- and Interoccupational Stratification (Inequality)

The members of any given occupation are stratified into many ranks. In the automobile or steel industry we have a long hierarchy beginning with the Henry Fords, the presidents of U.S. Steel and General Motors, and ranging to the lowest unskilled worker and office boy in these occupations, with a large number of intermediary strata. The professions are not excluded from this stratification. In teaching there is a hierarchy topped by the state secretaries of education, presidents of universities and of academies of science and the like, with intermediate strata of university deans, full-, associate- and assistant-professors; then come principals and teachers in high schools; and last there are the elementary school teachers.

The intraoccupational stratification manifests itself in another general form; in almost all occupations there are three main strata. First, the masters or entrepreneurs, those who are their own "bosses" and organize, direct, and control the activities of all the employees; second, the higher employees—directors, managers, high engineers, who, although subordinated to the masters, control and manage those below them; third, the clerical and subordinate employees and wage earners, who do largely routine or manual work, controlled and organized by the higher strata. Each of these basic strata is often stratified within itself.

Under different names these basic intraoccupational strata are found in the past as well as in the present, in private as well as in governmental occupations. In the occupational group of the same caste there is a variation of these divisions. In the Roman or Chinese, medieval or Egyptian guild systems, the ranks of the apprentices, of the ordinary members (*populus, plebs, valets*), and of the *magistri* is an illustration.[17]

The intraoccupational stratification exists in many other forms. The upper strata of an occupational group control the lower ones; they have greater prestige, better economic remuneration, and other advantages. Often the distance between the head of a big occupational enterprise, like Henry Ford, and the lowest wage-earner in the same occupation is as great as between the autocratic monarch of an empire and his humblest subject.

The interoccupational stratification is also a universal and perennial phenomenon. From the standpoint of attractiveness, prestige, remuneration, power, domination and subordination, the unskilled manual occupations have usually occupied the lowest position. Then come the semi-skilled, the skilled; the semi-professional, including the clerical, small business, and petty officials; the highly qualified professionals, including big business and government, being at the top. This basic pyramid of occupations, with minor and temporary variations, is a general uniformity of the interoccupational stratification. The occupations that require a high degree of intelligence, are highly important for the population, and that consist of intellectual creative work of sociocultural organization and control, have regularly been the superior occupations. The occupations consisting of manual, uncreative work, requiring only low intelligence for their performance, have regularly been the most inferior.[18]

---

[17] Cf. Saint Leon, E. Martin, *Histoire de Corporation de Mètiers* (Paris, 1922); J. P. Waltzing, *Étude historique sur les corporations professionelles chez les Romains* (Louvain, 1895), 2 Vols.; J. M. Lambert, *Two Thousand Years of Guild Life* (Hull, 1891); F. Poland, *Geschichte des griechischen Vereinswesen* (Berlin, 1935).

[18] See the facts, details, and literature in my *Mobility*, Ch. 6. The general order of occupations

is similar to F. W. Taussig's, F. E. Barr's, and other generally accepted scales of occupations. As one goes from the top to the bottom occupations, the indices of the required intelligence decrease, economic remuneration decreases; functions of social control and organization (cultural, economic, military, governmental, etc.) decrease; creativeness decreases; subordination increases. The top occupations have always been those of the aristocracy

Within the basic occupational strata there are many subdivisions. These strata have existed partly in an organized, partly in an "as if" organized, and in an unorganized form, from earliest time.

10. Intra- and Intereconomic Group Stratification (Inequality)

All groups, except, perhaps, the familistic family and a small group of the most intimate friends with a real community of economic values, are stratified economically into richer and poorer members. Measured by amount of property, income, economic rights and duties, economic plane of living, or in any other way, the members of the racial-sex-age-kinship-territorial-language-state-occupational-religious or any other group have always been economically unequal. The height and profile of the economic pyramid fluctuate from group to group, period to period, but the stratification remains. Even religious groups with common property, even Communist and Socialist and other groups, could not eliminate the economic inequality, in spite of their intention to do so. Communism in Soviet Russia is typical in this respect. As early as 1918 the Soviet Government had to introduce wage differentials, with a ratio of 175 to 100 as maximum and minumum, and with more than thirty intervening levels. Since then the inequality has kept on growing. In ancient Greece and Rome all the free population was divided formally, e.g., as in the reforms of Solon and Servius Tullius, into several clear-cut economic strata, with respective rights and duties. In other groups the formal stratification may be absent, but the factual stratification stands solid and sometimes strikingly high.

Economic stratification exists not only within a group but also among different groups, either of the same or different natures. Among states, there are the richer and the poorer and less prosperous. This is also true of different religious, political, occupational, and other groups. And it is true in regard to groups of a different nature. Intra- and intergroup equality remains merely an ideal hoped for by many; thus far it has hardly ever been realized in human history. The total social position of every individual depends greatly upon the economic stratum in which he belongs; the rich always occupy a higher position than the poor in the total or integral sociocultural pyramid.

11. Intra- and Interreligious Group Stratification (Inequality)

As soon as a religious group is organized, its stratification emerges. Ordinarily, as in state groups, it is clear-cut. The pope, patriarch, dalai-lama, *pontifex maximus, rex sacrificulus,* the primate, or supreme priest is at the top of the hierarchy; then there is the stratum of cardinals, metropolitans, archbishops, and bishops; then the priests of different ranks and dignities; the various deacons; and finally the plain believers, below whom there may be a stratum of pagans, disbelievers, heretics, and generally the "damned souls." The actual number of the ranks varies in different religions, but in all religions the stratification exists.[19] In almost all religions each superior stratum is believed to be endowed with a greater proportion of divine grace and holiness, has the dominant legal authority, binding the lower ranks, greater prestige, and usually better economic conditions. The contrast between the highest stratum and a disbeliever or heretic is often as great, sometimes greater, than that between an autocratic monarch and a criminal or slave. Many attempts to organize a religious group without stratification have failed as soon as the group reached some modest size. Even such attempts—probably the most earnest—as that of St. Francis of Assisi failed during St. Francis' own lifetime.

---

and upper social strata, while unskilled manual work was the occupation of the strata of slaves and serfs in unfree society and of the least paid, most subordinate unskilled labor in the free societies. See also M. Smith, "Measuring Occupations," *Sociology and Social Research* (1935), pp. 40-50; O. Machotka, "Social Stratification." *Ibid.* (1937), pp. 3-13. Also referred studies of D. Anderson, P. E. Davidson, W. H. Form, H. Speier; A. Obrdlik, *Povolani,* quoted. In this last study the prestige order of various occupations is different, but because they are rated by the members of the respective occupations from the standpoint of social utility. It is to be understood that I state the situation as it has been, regardless of what it ought to be.

[19] See J. Wach, *op. cit.,* Chps. 5, 7, and Appendix, for concrete forms of ranks of the religious hierarchies in various preliterate and historical religions.

There is also interreligious stratification. In populations without religious freedom it manifests itself in the monopolistic position of the obligatory religion and in the suppression of all the other religious groups, including the persecution and disfranchisement of their members. The situation is identical to that in which a monopolistic political party suppresses all other parties. In populations like pre-Revolutionary Russia and in England, the stratification takes a milder form in which one religion is favored as the national religion, the Russian Orthodox and Anglican, for example, with the other religions suffering various degrees of comparative disfranchisement. In many populations there are the religions of the aristocracy, of the middle classes, and of the slaves; religions of different occupations and economic strata; of different kinship groups, and so on.[20]

Subjectively, from the standpoint of a believer, interreligious stratification consists in a belief and in accompanying practices that the believer's religion is the only true one, all the others being untrue, inferior, and "damned." The concrete objective and subjective forms of interreligious stratification are many.

12. Stratification of Other Unibonded Groups

Stratification exists among other unibonded groups. All educational institutions, from elementary school to university, are stratified, each within itself and any one with respect to all the others. The same is true of scientific, philosophical, artistic, philanthropic, and other organized "ideological" groups, e.g., hospitals, symphony orchestras, theaters, the Red Cross, etc. Criminal gangs are stratified into boss, main henchmen, and plain members. The height of the pyramid, the number of ranks, the size of each stratum fluctuate widely from group to group, but intra- and intergroup stratification is present in all of them.

As any stratification means "superiority and inferiority," "domination and subordination," it generates an incessant struggle of the members of the various strata, all seeking to climb up the ladder to a higher place in the hierarchy. There are inflated and deflated ambitions, rivalries, jealousies, envy, hatred, and their consequences: mutual conflict of the members of the different strata for promotion, for differential shares in advantages and disadvantages. The Darwinian struggle for existence is too vague and too general a formula. Intra- and intergroup struggle for higher places in the hierarchy of stratification are more intense forms of the struggle for existence.[21] However, all this will be discussed more fully later.

IV. Multibonded Stratification

1. Double, Triple, and More Complex Strata

Since by definition the multibonded stratification is the multibonded group viewed in its stratified aspect, the multibonded forms of stratification fall in the same classes as those of the multibonded groups. By the number and nature of the unifying bonds we can distinguish the double, the triple, quadruple, and more complex "superior and inferior" strata in the respective double, triple, quadruple multibonded groups. If a person or a set of persons in a given population occupies a high position in both its state and economic stratifications, such a person gives us a double—the state plus economic—aristocracy. If a group occupies a high position in a religious order, say that of bishops, and a high position in a political party and the state as well, such a group gives us a triple upper stratum—the religious, plus political party, plus state. If a set of persons belongs to the chiefs of the noblest kinship groups, are the richest, perform the creative and most aristocratic occupational functions, and at the same time are the highest state officials, such a group gives us a quadruple aristocracy—kinship, economic, occupational, state. On the other hand, a group of persons who are economically poorest, unskilled occupationally, of inferior race, illiterate, belongs to

---

[20] See especially J. Wach, op. cit., Ch. 6.

[21] See N. K. Mikhailovsky, "Struggle for Individuality," in his Works (in Russian).

a quadruple stratum of underdogs, and so on.

Combining the number of the unibonded stratifying ties with their nature we can have as great a number of different multibonded strata in a given population as the binomial formula of Newton defines. Factually, most of such combined strata do exist within any large population.

The stratified system of castes, orders, and classes analyzed in Chapter 14 gives additional concrete examples of multibonded strata. The upper and lower castes are superior or inferior not on a single basis but on a multiple basis. The Brahmins are superior to the Sudras in race, religion, occupation, kinship, language, education, and so on. Likewise, the social estate of the nobles in comparison with that of the free population and slaves is superior not for one reason but for three: occupational, economic, and state. The less strict stratification of social classes is due not to one stratifying factor but at least two factors; the upper classes are richer and discharge higher occupational functions, the state legal stratification playing a much more modest role than in the case of the triple stratum of the social order. In the class population, all citizens are declared to be legally equal in regard to state law.

There are in any population many different double, triple, and quadruple strata. The caste, class, order, family, and tribe, which have been analyzed, with their intra- and interstrata, are only a few, though the most important, of these different multibonded stratified groups.

Here again we see the crude state of the social sciences in respect to their knowledge and classification of the forms of social stratification and of the number and variety of the strata. We have seen that the social sciences do not have any systematic taxonomy of social groups. Now we can note that they do not have any taxonomy of the forms of social stratification and of the social strata. Out of the several dozens, the hundreds even, of various multibonded and unibonded social strata which exist in any large population, especially in urbanized and industrialized aggregations, the current texts in sociology and the social sciences mention only a few, like social class, social order, caste, and even these few are poorly defined in their structural composition.

There is another error: that is the tendency to treat groups and strata nominalistically, to cut them into nice statistical slices of mince pie, to create in this way hundreds of cubes of the social body, and to process them through routine quantitative operations, thus giving "scientific" looking diagrams and formulas and figures which, however, do not give any idea of the real anatomy, cytology, and morphology of the social organism. The works of Warner and Lunt and S. C. Dodd, which have been mentioned, are examples of this error.

The classification of the present work points out a new field of real social taxonomy and stratigraphy in sociology and the social sciences. It enables an investigator to analyze precisely the social differentiation and stratification of any given population into the real and "as if" real groups and strata. As we shall see further, it enables us to define precisely the position of every individual in the complex sociocultural world.

An actual detailed enumeration of all the double, triple, and more complex strata is outside the scope of this work. The definitions being given, any intelligent researcher can apply them to any concrete population under his investigation. Instead of such an actual enumeration, we shall pay attention to other important classes of social strata viewed from additional standpoints.

2. Innerly Antagonistic (Disaffine), Solidary (Affine), and Neutral Multibonded Groups

We must further distinguish the innerly antagonistic or disaffine, the innerly solidary or affine, and the innerly neutral multibonded strata. By the *innerly antagonistic*, and closely connected with it, the *disaffine*, multibonded stratum is meant that made up of the mutually contradictory, uncongenial bonds-values that make the social position of its members innerly contradictory. The members of such an innerly contradictory stratum are urged by the mutually uncongenial or contradictory bonds to the self-contradictory behavior and mentality. Likewise, such a disaffine stratum appears as a self-contradictory stratum to the outsiders who are in contact with it.

The innerly solidary or affine multibonded stratum is that in which the compounded stratifying bonds are mutually congenial, and urge its members to the same behavior and mentality. Finally, the *innerly neutral multi-bonded stratum* is that in which there is no mutual antagonism among the compounded bonds and no mutual solidarity as well. If one imagines a person who is a monarch, a pauper, and a member of a suppressed political party, one has a picture of an innerly antagonistic stratum of the person: highest in his state group, lowest economically, and low in the political party. These three variables are obviously irreconcilable and mutually antagonistic; together they force the person to an impossible and self-contradictory behavior and mentality. As a monarch he has to behave and has to be treated with the dignity, honor, respect, and authority due a monarch. As a pauper he has to behave and be treated as paupers behave and are treated. Two lines of conduct of the person and of the others are obviously irreconcilable, neither objectively nor subjectively possible. "While it is not difficult to preserve one's social prestige by doing nothing, it is difficult to keep it when one possesses nothing," rightly says C. Bouglé.[22] As a result such a coalescence of the stratifying bonds cannot last long and is bound to lead to a decomposition; either the monarch becomes rich and a high member of the dominant party, or he has to cease being a monarch.

There are further examples of anomalous double strata: high occupationally, but low in race and religion; high in nationality or kinship, but low in economic status; rich slaves; poor aristocrats. A member of one of these disaffine strata finds himself "exalted" in one respect and an "underdog" in another. In this way the dilemmas, contradictions, and muddleness of the status of a person appear.[23]

One must not think that such groups are something exotic, infrequent, and without general significance. It is true that the "unnatural" or disaffine strata do not happen as frequently as the "natural" or affine, and when they happen they tend to decompose

rapidly and be replaced by the affine coalescence of the stratifying bonds. Both forms are general forms and have a deep significance for an understanding of many social phenomena and processes. This can be seen from the following typical and factual cases.

The high strata of most of the unbonded groups comparatively easily coalesce together and make an innerly solidary multibonded stratum of the privileged multibonded aristocracy. For instance, the high governmental stratum in the state easily compounds with the rich.[24] These two bonds are mutually affine and solidary; therefore give frequent, durable, and stable coalescence in the form of this double stratum. Once in a while, however, we have in a population two double disaffine groups; one is economically richer but occupies a lower stratum in the state stratification than the other. Such an example is found in the position of the nobility and bourgeoisie on the eve of the French Revolution. The "third estate" was richer, but politically it was, to speak in the terms of its mouthpiece, l'Abbé Sieyès, "nothing" in comparison with the nobility. Two such "unnatural" double strata evidently could not last long; they were bound to decompose and be replaced by two innerly "affine" double strata. Either the rich had to get the high state position or the nobility had to become rich. The French Revolution consisted in the decomposition of these two disaffine strata and in the creation of two new affine strata. The rich third estate "became everything," in the terms of the same Sieyès. The Revolution, in chemical terms, performed a double reaction of transposition of the elements of the two disaffine molecules. Similar was one of the central processes of the Russian Revolution of 1905 and then of the Communist Revolution. At the beginning of the twentieth century, the Russian nobility became impoverished and poorer than the growing industrial, financial, and commercial bourgeoisie, which belonged to a notably lower stratum in the

[22] C. Bouglé, *La démocratie devant la science* (Paris, 1906), p. 92.

[23] See some facts and considerations in E. C. Hughes, "Dilemmas and Contradictions of Status," *AJS* (1945), pp. 353-60.

[24] This is true of the rich and the state ruling class among preliterate as well as historical populations. See facts for the preliterate and historical

populations in W. I. Thomas, *Primitive Behavior* pp. 361-420; G. Landtman, *The Origin*, quoted M. Kovalevsky, *Sociology* (in Russian, St. Petersburg, 1912), Vol. II, pp. 188 ff.; M. Diakonoff *Studies of Social and Political Organization o Russia* (in Russian, St. Petersburg, 1910), pp 82 ff.

state hierarchy. The Revolution of 1905 and subsequent years dissolved both disaffine double groups; the nobility lost its privileges and controlling power in the state while the bourgeoisie elevated itself and became, through the Constitution of 1906, the most important double stratum. In ancient Greece, when the nobles became richer than the king, the monarchy was liquidated and replaced by the aristocracy of the nobility. When the Athenian nobility of the *eupatridae* was economically outstripped by the new rich class, struggle followed and there emerged the Solonian stratification of the free population into four classes on the basis of wealth, the highest with an income of 500 medimni of corn and the lowest with below 200 medimni. At the end of the Republican period in Rome, a new stratum of the Equestrians became richer than the noble Senatorial class. After a series of civil wars and revolutions there was a rearrangement of classes in which wealth and privileged position in the state hierarchy were compounded as stratifying bonds. The same process has gone on for the European nobility and the bourgeoisie since the beginning of the industrial revolution.

In other cases the wealthy may not gain the high state position. The impoverished aristocracy may, by use of force, seize enough wealth to maintain its position. The Spartan aristocracy maintained its position in this way for many decades. Such was also the way of many other aristocracies. Many revolutionary groups obtain wealth after their revolution and thus establish a new "affine" aristocratic stratum. Recent examples are the Nazis and Communists. Poor conquerors who subjugate another country, like William the Conqueror, take for their own group, e.g., the Normans, the riches of the subjugated people, the Anglo-Saxons. The Spanish Conquistadors behaved in the same way and so did practically all the conquerors. These facts—and they occur daily in human history—show that affine and disaffine strata are fairly frequent in populations of all times and all countries. Generally when innerly disaffine strata appear one can expect an orderly or violent liquidation of such strata and the substitution of new affine strata for them. The chemical reaction of transposition is to be expected in such a situation. It may

happen in either of two ways: the rich may get power, or the powerful may seize wealth. Both ways have happened many times in history.

Another general variation of such processes of "transposition" is furnished by the perennial tragi-comedy of history staged by the equalitarian-Communist, Socialist, and Equalitarian-revolutionary groups. The first act of the play consists in the fiery speeches and actions of the equalitarians—mostly poor and disfranchised—who denounce the economic and other inequalities and organize to overthrow the rich strata. The equalitarians make up a triple stratum: economically poor, low position in the state, and members of equalitarian political parties. Its equalitarian, communist, socialist ideology is affine to such a stratum. During the revolution, if the group overthrows the upper economic and state strata and occupies their place, it transforms itself into a conspicuously disaffine stratum: it is in the embarrassing position of finding that its equalitarian ideology does not square with its economic position. Its mottoes—"redistribution of wealth," "expropriation of the exploiters," "take what has been stolen by the rich classes," "down with private property," "down with the government and aristocracy," *"aequatio bonorum," "pecunias a equare,"* and so on—these slogans can now only be directed against the revolutionary aristocracy itself. Evidently such a position is impossible. The new ruling and economic aristocracy must give up its place or the old party standard must be replaced by a new one, fitting to the new position of the party. This second way usually takes place in the form of a gradual transformation of the party's ideology and the party itself from the previous equalitarian, Communist, Socialist, and poor party into a new party rejecting its previous principles and becoming aristocratic. R. Pöhlmann, in his study of Equalitarian, Communist, Socialist, and revolutionary movements of Greece, a study which is still pre-eminent, very well sums up the situation by saying that after an elevation to the top such revolutionary strata "now had every reason to fear the outburst of new revolutions, for in a new revolution with its re-distribution of wealth and privileges they could only lose without any gain; therefore they needed not to go about any more masquerading as proletarian revolutionaries. Usually, in these conditions, they rapidly acquired the most reactionary ideology in economics as well as in politics; they turned into partisans of the *Beati possidentes* (Blessed are those who possess). Now they worried little over the growth of a new inequality. They would not listen to the idea of a new division of property (and of all the other privileges) now that they themselves were the rich and privileged. Consequently their equalitarian-socialist fraternity lasted only till the rich and privileged were conquered and the process of spoliation was accomplished."[25] Such a story has invariably happened with all successful revolutions so far as the economic and social redistribution of wealth is concerned.[26] The latest corroboration of it is given in the facts of the Russian Revolution. Already the ideology, policy, and structure of the Communist Party and the so-called Communist Government are about opposite to what they were before and at the beginning of the Revolution. The party and government are transformed into a new "affine" stratum of triple aristocracy, which has the highest economic, state, and managerial positions. Naturally it has already manufactured a new ideology having little similarity to the previous one.[27]

To give another example, if in the United States the Negro race continues to be considered inferior, and if the Negroes become richer than the whites, two double disaffine strata will be created. Such a situation is bound to provoke, in either way, the "chemical reaction of transposition"; either the whites become richer or the Negroes become an equal race. As a matter of fact, in some of the southern states, where there are prosperous Negroes and "poor whites," such a situation already exists. Now and then it causes one of the reactions of transposition, in the form of lynching and pillaging the Negroes or in the steady elevation of the rank of the Negro group.

Generally the consolidation of the upper

strata of two or a greater number of the unibonded group produces an affine multibonded stratum (*similia similibus curantur*) while a coalescence of the high stratum in one or some of the unibonded groups with the low stratum in others builds an innerly antagonistic, disaffine multibonded stratum, a house divided against itself.

As a rule the multibonded strata of various populations are affine innerly and represent a coalescence of the upper ranks of two or more unibonded groups with one another, and of their lower ranks with the lower ranks of the other. But such an affine coalescence is never perfect. Not one hundred per cent of the upper strata of two or more unibonded groups merge in the multibonded upper stratum, but only a part. The same is true of the lower or middle strata of each of the coalescing unibonded groups. There are always some discrepancies in the secondary rankings and sometimes a sharp disaffinity. Not all the richest persons are highest in the state government, in the religious group, in the blood kinship groups, in the political parties, in the language groups or scientific societies, and so on. Not all the bosses of a political party are the popes or cardinals in the church group, or the presidents or monarchs in the state groups. In short, *the correlation of the affine strata is never perfect.* The stratified pyramids of the unibonded groups never consolidate in such a way that all their strata coincide and create one integral consolidated social pyramid, in which all the tops of the unibonded pyramids make one integral top and all the middle and lowest strata consolidate into one integral middle or lowest stratum. The actual "sky line" of the total stratification rather takes the shape of the skyline of a mountain range with several peaks of different pyramids not entirely merged.

There are several forms of social aristocracy and of social underdogs, not to mention of the middle strata. We have several unibonded aristocratic strata: the aristocracy of the state

---

[25] R. Pöhlmann, *Geschichte der sozialen Frage und der Sozialismus in der antiken Welt* (München, 1912), pp. 469 ff.

[26] See my *Sociology of Revolution, passim*; my *Calamity*, Chps. 8 and 15. See facts and literature in these works.

[27] See my *Russia and the United States* (New York, 1944), Ch. 9; B. Moore, Jr., "The Communist Party of the Soviet Union: 1928-1944," *ASR* (1944), pp. 266-78; N. S. Timasheff, "Vertical Social Mobility in Communist Society," *AJS* (1944), pp. 9-21; N. S. Timasheff, *The Great Retreat* (New York, 1946).

government, of the religious, economic, occupational, racial, language, age, sex, kinship groups; the aristocracy of science, arts, education, and of other unibonded groups. There are several forms of the multibonded aristocracies: upper castes, upper social orders and classes, and many other forms.[28] The same is true of the middle strata and of the lowest ranks in each of the unibonded and multibonded groups. The upper ranks of many unibonded groups in a given population tend to consolidate into several multibonded aristocracies. But the merger is never total and perfect. For instance in the United States, top ranks of the state, of finance, occupational unions, the professions, of the religious groups, of the "blue blood registerites," of the stars of science and the arts, are in fairly close contact with one another. They are interlocked through several groups, institutions, activities, and enterprises. They compose an informal but real multibonded upper stratum that exerts a very strong influence upon the whole course of the sociocultural process. The names of such stars, celebrities, statesmen, captains of finance and industry may be found together in almost every copy of a newspaper. They compose the "cream" of various "Who's Who." They think and act in a fairly concerted way. They make the upper "few hundred families" into an American "consolidated aristocracy."

But since the consolidation is not perfect, another part of the same ranks make up another "consolidated aristocracy," with fairly different policies and activities. Some rich people belong to the Protestant and Catholic and even atheistic religions; some to the Republican, Democratic, and, as a rare exception, even to the Communist Party. Some occupy high governmental positions in Washington, but others are in opposition. Some belong to the "registerites" but others don't. Some prefer Harvard bosses, others Yale or Chicago bosses. Some finance liberal papers, the others conservative ones. On many political and social issues they differ. And so it goes. The same is true of governmental, occupational, scientific,

nationality, and other "aristocracies." The real leaders of even science and religion are often found in different factions and cliques. This is what is meant by saying that the consolidation is not complete or perfect.

The same is still more true of the less organized middle and lower strata in unibonded groups.

Even the highest leaders of some of the unibonded groups find themselves excluded from various consolidated aristocracies. For instance the most prominent leaders of the Negroes are tolerated, but not admitted to the several consolidated aristocracies. Some of these do not admit Jewish or other leaders of the upper ranks. The *nouveaux riches* are often disdained. The leaders of Communist and similar parties cannot become members of the high strata of the Catholic and other religious groups. On the other hand, the Communist leaders or the new millionaires not infrequently scorn the blue blood aristocracy or the upper hierarchy of the Catholic and other churches. The leaders of a given nationality group may humiliate, abuse, and destroy the leaders of another nationality group to which they were inimical. Add to this the incessant change of sociocultural conditions which inexorably leads to the elevation of a new multibonded stratum and undermines the established aristocracy, creating incessantly new innerly disaffine groups.

As a result there are always several discrepancies and contradictions in the consolidation of the multibonded strata, several disaffine strata, small or large, with self-contradictory positions for their members. There are the respective jealousies, disappointments and the ensuing struggle, because in such conditions "those who aim at equality will be ever ready for sedition, if they see those whom they esteem their equals possess more than they do; and those who are not content with equality but aim at superiority, if they think that while they deserve more than they have only are equal with or less than their inferiors."[29]

---

[28] This means that T. H. Marshall's interpretation of my position as denying the existence of social classes is grossly inaccurate. I contend only that social class is one of the multibonded groups and stratifications.

[29] Aristotle, *Politics*, 130-132. In the next chapter it will be shown that there are two different types of the skylines of aristocracies of various populations: one where various peaks are dominated by one tallest peak; another where there is no dominant peak among several tops of various unibonded and multibonded pyramids.

Concrete forms of the innerly disaffine multi-bonded strata have been very diverse in human history. When such strata are small, the decomposition passes without notice. But when they are large, the process of their decomposition and replacement by the new affine multibonded strata becomes quite "noisy" and ordinarily assumes the form of riots, revolts, conquests, revolutions, wars, or radical social reform movements. As a matter of fact there has hardly been any important historical internal revolution or reform which has not been due, to a large extent, to the existence of such "abnormal" strata and has not consisted, to a large extent also, in the "reaction of transposition." Before any revolution or reform in a society there are always some such strata and when the smoke-screen of revolutionary movement has passed, one ordinarily finds new affine strata.

A study of the social processes from this standpoint opens a new and promising field of "sociological chemistry" of social groups, processes, and strata. Herein lies additional evidence of the importance of our classification of groups and strata for scientific purposes.

V. Additional Sub-Forms of the Unibonded and Multibonded Strata

Some of the unibonded and multibonded strata are *legally defined and maintained by the official law of the respective groups.* The legal provisions indicate precisely who can and cannot be their members; what is the position of each rank in the hierarchy of the strata; to what strata it is superior and inferior; what exactly are its rights and duties, its functions and role. Examples of legally defined hierarchies are the official and legal hierarchies of the state, the hierarchy of the church, and the hierarchy of some occupational unions. Among the multibonded strata, the hierarchy of social orders and castes provide an example of the legally defined multibonded pyramid of strata. The official law of the state, together with the official code of the nobility as the upper social order, defines who may become a member, when, and under what conditions, of the nobility, the bourgeoisie, or even of the stratum of the serfs and slaves. The official law of religion plus the official law of the castes themselves determine who may become a member of a caste, when, and under what conditions.

Other unibonded and multibonded strata exist only factually, in the form of less precisely defined layers. There are no legal obstacles, only factual ones, to becoming a member. If one overcomes these, he can enter the stratum. The hierarchy of social classes is an example of a multibonded stratum of the factual character. Also factual in their nature is the intra-group hierarchy of the organized portions of nationality, occupational, and political party groups. So also are some of the "as if" organized strata.

This distinction is important per se, but has a particular significance for the phenomena of vertical mobility which are described further on.

Unibonded and multibonded groups are either legally or factually or in both ways *closed and hereditary* or *open and nonhereditary.* Some are intermediate between these. The caste is a closed and hereditary stratum. The social estate is less closed and less hereditary than a caste, but more so than social class. The upper social classes are more closed than the lower ones. Generally, the upper strata of almost all unibonded and multibonded groups tend to be more closed than the lower strata, so far as an infiltration of outsiders into membership is concerned. Since the upper strata give more privileges and advantages of both economic and non-economic character, the number of vacancies is far fewer than the number of persons who would like to occupy them. Hence the barriers and obstacles of either legal or factual nature. The lower strata have fewer advantages and more burdens; they do not need to bar their gates to newcomers.

Finally, *some of the organized strata are*

"cytological" composition of each of the groups from the standpoint of the nature of its three relationships: familistic, compulsory, and intermediate (contractual); eleventh, the nature of the meanings, values, norms, vehicles, and other componential characteristics of the groups. When this knowledge is supplemented by additional data on the mobility, culture, and other characteristics of the group (discussed further), we have an adequate knowledge of all the important structural traits of the population in question. This analysis gives us a well-rounded and many-sided view of its sociocultural "cytology," anatomy, morphology, and taxonomy, of its "horizontal" and "vertical" aspects; of its real "cells," "organs," and "tissues." This is in contrast to the knowledge of the nominal units of the "social mince-pie" mechanically cut into statistical "cubes" and "slices." Without the outlined analysis, no statistical or other information, no matter how small are the "cubes" of the population treated as a "social mince-pie" and how painstakingly their correlations are computed, can give us even a rough idea of the social structure of the population.

III. The Problem of Classification of the Types of Population Agglomerations ("Societies")

1. Types of Classification

Together with the need for classification of the unibonded and multibonded groups and of their forms of stratification, there arises a need for classification of the population-agglomerations in their main types. The problem has long occupied the minds of sociologists and social scientists. Many attempts to solve it have been made. In Chapter 8 the most important classifications offered have been examined. In spite of their partial value, they were found unsatisfactory. The classifications into "historical and unhistorical"; "Naturvölker and Kulturvölker"; burg, city, metropolis, capital, and center of federation; population-agglomeration with high and low density; "primary and secondary"; evolutionary types based upon psychology or morality: savages of different types, barbarians and civilized, societies of the sub-men, semi-civilized, cultural, and so on; all these classifications have been shown to be inadequate. None of these give an adequate idea of the real structure of types of the agglomerations of populations; nor are most of them in any way "anatomical and morphological" classifications.

2. Spencer-Durkheim Classification

Only Herbert Spencer's and E. Durkheim's classifications try to be "anatomical and morphological." As Durkheim himself explicitly says, "Since the nature of the aggregate depends necessarily on the nature and number of the component elements and their mode of combination, these characteristics are evidently what we take as our basis. . . . Moreover, as they are of the morphological order, one could call the part of sociology which has for its task the constitution and classification of social types, 'social morphology.'"[1] Starting with the concept of the simplest undifferentiated society or horde and then passing to doubly or triply "compounded" or to doubly and triply "polysegmental" societies, Spencer and Durkheim seemingly accomplish the task satisfactorily. However, in Chapter 8 it has been pointed out briefly that both classifications failed to be truly "morphological." The general method they tried to follow was correct, but their concrete results were wrong. They proceed from the simple societies to more and more complex ones, but what is the criterion of simplicity and complexity? Isn't there a hidden defect which will lead to a series of succeeding errors and failures? Yes. First, the concept of simple society is quite indefinite. Spencer himself recognizes that "We cannot say in all cases with precision what constitutes a simple society; for, in common with products of evolution generally, societies present transitional stages

[1] E. Durkheim, *The Rules of Sociological Method*, quoted, pp. 80-81.

which negate sharp divisions. . . ."[2] Spencer, nevertheless, tries to give a characteristic of simplicity and complexity. He regards as simple such a society which forms one acting whole not subject to any other whole, the parts of which cooperate one with the other under the administration of a common, regulating center for the achievement of some general aims. It can be seen that Spencer takes as the characteristic of simplicity or complexity the *political or the state organization* of a group. If one government stands at the head of the group, or there is no government at all, the group is simple; on the other hand, where the heads of the separate simple groups are subjected to some common head, the group is complex. If such groups are in turn subjected to a common government of a higher order, the groups form a doubly-compound society. One more step in the same direction and we receive triply-compound societies, i.e., the great civilized nations.

Spencer's criterion of simplicity is quite insufficient even for defining the complexity of the political organization of the group. According to this criterion a union of states—a confederation or a federal state—is always a more complex and higher society than one unified state. The Confederation of the Iroquois or the Achaean League of Greeks, or the Latin League would have to be regarded, if this were true, as more , complex and therefore more highly developed than England, France, Belgium, and other unified states. Moreover, the more varied the composition of a state is, the higher and more complex it must be. The Empires of Alexander the Great or of Tamerlane, whose power extended over a number of peoples and states, which in their turn were compounded of several groups, should be recognized as triply- and quadruply-compound societies, more complex, for instance, than practically any modern nation. Needless to say, both in the degree of social differentiation and stratification and in the degree of culture, the modern western nations are more complex than the ancient monarchies and eastern despotisms. Furthermore, in order to define the degree of complexity of any group, according to Spencer, one would have to figure

out how many separate groups were merged one with another. This is a problem incapable of solution because of the vagueness of the concept of simple society. If two or more tribes merge into one, the result is a compound society, but the same compound society is obtained also when any two or more separate states of a high degree of social differentiation and stratification join into one state, like the states of the United States. In both cases there are single wholes not subjected to any other wholes. This would mean that the Kabyl tribe, the Iroquois Confederation, the Achaean League, Switzerland, and the United States would have to be regarded as belonging to one morphological type of social group on the same level of sociocultural development. The utter absurdity of such a class is obvious. In short, Spencer's criterion is inadequate even for defining the complexity of the political organization of a group.

This criterion is even more invalid for defining the structure of the whole population (society). Were the population differentiated only into political groups, no other lines of social differentiation being present, the criterion would not have been so bad. Social reality, however, is much different; every population consists, as we have seen, of a number of unibonded and multibonded groups which cannot be reduced to the state-political grouping. Such a classification resembles a taxonomy of plants which would classify all plants only according to the structure of leaves and entirely ignore the other parts. The modern botanists take into consideration all the parts of the plant and the sociologist must proceed in the same way. Two groups may have an identical degree of complexity in the character of organization of the state administrative power, and nevertheless be sharply distinct in all other ways. Both ancient Athens and modern Switzerland are republics, but they are quite distinct in structure and character. Both England and Yugoslavia are parliamentary states but it does not follow that they are identical in all other respects. Federated states are found in the antique world, in the Middle Ages, in modern times, but it would be an absurdity to classify the social structure of their populations into one group and to regard them as similar.

---

[2] Spencer, *Principles of Sociology*, quoted, Vol. I, p. 538.

The objections against Spencer's theory may be applied also, with certain modifications, to Durkheim's. The latter, in distinction from Spencer, seems to offer a clear concept of the simple society. Such is the mono-segmentary group, which consists directly of individuals. Out of this "horde" Durkheim forms his more complex societies by simple addition; two or more joined segments form a simple poly-segmentary society, and so on. This method, however simple, can hardly be applied in reality. First, one can firmly assert that there is no simple society in the sense in which Durkheim uses it; at least, science has not discovered any. The most primitive societies, the totemic groups of the Australians, have some kind of inner differentiation; they consist of sex and age groups, of the governing body, of leaders, of secret societies, and so on. Any organized primitive group is not an undifferentiated mass consisting of individuals directly. The simple society of Durkheim is purely hypothetical, and he himself is compelled to recognize this fact.

Since Durkheim's concept of simple society is devoid of any exactness, his further structure falls down by itself. If the simple society is really poly-segmentary, the distinction between the first and the second disappears. If the concept of the poly-segmentary society is vague, the distinction between simple and complex poly-segmentary societies loses all meaning. It is easy to see that the source of all the errors is again the exclusive dealing with the political state organization without taking into account the other nonpolitical groupings. Durkheim's taxonomy is a purely "artificial" one. Naturally, such a classification does not give us any valid idea of the structure of society and does not classify societies according to their real structures. Had Durkheim attempted to make his propositions more concrete, like Spencer, he would have arrived at the same absurd results. Like Spencer, he would have had to include in one group both ancient Mexico and Assyro-Babylonia, on the one hand, and modern England and France, on the other.

It is obvious from the above why Spencer's and Durkheim's classification should be deemed inadequate. This does not mean, however, that any structural or morphological classification is doomed to failure. The theories of Spencer and Durkheim prove only the failure of their concrete realization of the task, but not the failure of the task itself.

3. A Constructive Classification

That an adequate "morphological" classification of the agglomerations of populations (societies) is possible, is evidenced by our preceding analysis. Such a classification is to be based upon the essential similarities of the agglomerations in regard to all or most of the criteria enumerated above. *All the agglomerations of populations (societies) that consist of not only similar unibonded and multibonded groups but also all the other important characteristics of inner structure and relationships enumerated in our eleven points (see Section II of this chapter) will belong to the same class or type of population agglomerations (societies). The populations that sharply differ in all or most of these points, especially in their important unibonded and multibonded groups and their stratifications, will evidently belong to different types. On this basis one can construct a limited number of main types of populations as agglomerations of stratified groups. If one pays attention to secondary traits of each of the groups into which a population is differentiated and stratified, for instance, to the types of the family, the state, or occupational or economic groups, one can easily establish several subclasses or subtypes within each of the main types.* Such a classification will be adequate, for it will take account of all the main groups and strata, of the lines of differentiation and stratification. Therefore, in contrast to the utterly one-sided and fictitious classifications of Spencer and Durkheim, not to mention the others, it will put into one class the types that are similar and into different classes the agglomerations that are really dissimilar. The classification of the population agglomerates along this line, to be sure, is much more difficult than any existing "simple" classification.

It requires a thorough knowledge of all the main groups into which a given population is differentiated and of all the main strata into which the groups are stratified. Other classifications use not all, but only one main group. The Le Play school takes only the types of *family* (patriarchal, particularist, unstable) and classifies the "societies" on the basis of the prevalent type of the family. The economic evolutionists make the prevalent *occupational and economic group* (the hunters, the pastoral, the agricultural) the foundation of their classifications of populations. Others take either the *state* or the *religious* or the *ideological* (science, philosophy), or other groups and classify the "societies" on this basis. So far as any particular group is concerned, a study of its types and of the distribution of each type (of the family, of the state, of the occupational groups) within various populations is necessary and valuable. Each of these groups, being important, has to be studied and taken into consideration in an adequate classification. The shortcoming of these theories consists in that each of them does not go far enough and does not extend its analysis over the whole constellation of groups and strata of the populations ("societies") studied. Like the Linnaean artificial classification of the plants, they take their pet group and on the basis of its types unhesitatingly classify the populations (societies), irrespective of the extent to which the populations having similar types of family or state or predominant occupation or religion are similar in their other groups and strata. If we could be sure that there is a very close causal correlation between a certain type of family or state or religious group or occupational group, with all the other groups, such a procedure would be adequate and fruitful. If however such a close connection does not exist, if the populations with a similar type of the family, say patriarchal, may have and do have other groups and strata dissimilar from one another, then the inadequacy of such one-sided classifications becomes evident. From the fact that man has a nose and the dog has a nose, it does not follow that man and dog are of the same species. In the light of present-day knowledge, we know that the correlation

between a certain type of one of the groups, say, the unstable family, or the republican state, and the types of the other groups in various populations is sometimes very remote. The populations having the same religion, say, the Roman Catholic, have very different constellations of groups and strata in Catholic Paris, Catholic rural Italy, Catholic Brazil, Catholic Poland, Catholic China, or Catholic America. The predominantly agricultural or pastoral populations have different family, state, religious, artistic, language, and other groups and different forms of stratification. The peoples belonging as citizens even to the same state, for instance, the population of New York and of the Ozark mountains, are as different in their structure of differentiation and stratification as they can be.[3]

These considerations are sufficient to show why the existing classifications are inadequate; why they differ from the only adequate classification, outlined above; and why this last classification does not exist as yet. For its realization an enormous preliminary spade work has to be done. We have to know not only the main types of this or that group (the family, the state, the caste, etc.) and its distribution among the populations of mankind. We have to have such a knowledge in regard to all the main unibonded and multibonded groups and their distribution among the human population. In addition, we have to know all the most frequent combinations of the main types of all the basic groups. Then and only then can we build the classification of the main types of social structure of the populations or "societies."[4] To be sure, many of the best studies done in connection with the one-sided classifications have contributed a great deal toward this goal. In populations with the caste-group we expect to find and do find several groups and forms of stratification different from the populations with the open class

---

[3] Most of the best studies using one-sided classifications themselves disclose the lack of a close causal correlation between the group selected for the basis of the classification of societies and other groups in the populations similar in regard to their selected group. For instance, Hobhouse, Wheeler, and Ginsberg's work has shown that most of the pastoral or agricultural or hunter populations have different types of the family, of government, of

forms of justice, of religion, and so on. Likewise the populations having the same type of the family have different forms of groups and strata. The same has to be said of practically all the classifications based upon only one group, no matter what it is. See the facts of the lack of the close correlation in my *Theories*, especially Chps. 2 and 10.

[4] See several sound considerations along this line in J. Mazzarella, *Les types sociaux et le droit* (Paris, 1908).

system. Likewise in the populations dominated by the patriarchal type of the family, there are groups and stratifications essentially different from those with the unstable family. In the populations with the predominant agricultural occupations, there exist several groupings and strata different from the populations with the dominant industrial and commercial occupational groups. The urban populations have a structure different from that of the rural or pastoral-nomadic populations, and so on. Already there is accumulated so much of the necessary factual material that the first attempts to build an approximation to the adequate classification become almost possible. With a further increase of the factual material, with a clearer, more adequate, and more precise classification of the unibonded and multibonded groups and their stratifications, and with a better realization of the nature of the classification of the populations, such attempts will be more and more frequent and more and more adequate.

It is beyond the tasks of this work actually to give such a complete classification as we did in regard to the unibonded and multibonded groups and their forms of stratification. The outline of its nature suffices for this work. The actual realization of such a classification is a task for special monographic works by a set of future sociologists. For the present we shall denote only several structural formations or types of societies (agglomerations of population) that are important enough and distinct enough to be described specifically. Each of such types or formations is widely used in the historical, sociological, and anthropological disciplines. Some of the formations are specifically studied by special sociologies. In their totality these types are more real, and give a more adequate series of the structural formations than those given by the current, largely artificial, classifications.

IV. Main Types

1. Urban and Rural Agglomerations of Population

On the basis of the number and degree of concentration of a multitude of unibonded and multibonded groups of a certain character within a limited territory, we distinguish, first, the urban and the rural agglomerations of the populations. The profound differences between the urban and the rural agglomerations, with a subdivision of each formation into several subtypes, are so evident and unquestionable that they have led to an emergence of special rural and urban sociologies devoted to a study of each type of agglomeration. The urban agglomeration is characterized by a number of traits. (a) Typologically, as a rule, the total population of the city is bound together only by two main bonds: territorial and state citizenship. In regard to other bonds, it is ordinarily split into different occupational, economic, religious, political, nationality, racial, kinship, and class groups. Exceptions to this rule undoubtedly exist, but they do not invalidate the rule. The rural agglomeration of population is more homogeneous. As a rule it is bound together not only by the territorial and state citizenship bonds, but also by the predominant occupational, economic, language (nationality), kinship, and religious bonds. In all these respects it is more homogeneous than the urban aggregate. Again, exceptions to this rule are given, but they remain exceptions.

(b) The urban aggregate has a much larger multitude of unibonded and multibonded groups concentrated on a limited territory than the rural aggregate of the population; the urban aggregate is therefore notably more differentiated than the rural population.

(c) In the urban population most of the groups are much more stratified than the groups of the rural population. (d) In urban populations the occupational groups engaged in manufacturing, mechanical, commercial, professional, and governmental pursuits predominate, while in the rural populations the agricultural pursuit in its various forms is predominant.

(e) The size of the rural aggregates is notably smaller than that of city populations. (f) The density of the population in the cities is much higher than in rural populations. (g) In the cities a man-made environment predominates, in contrast to the natural environment of the rural populations. (h) The city population has greater vertical and horizontal mobility than the country population.

(i) The urban population is much more heterogeneous racially, ethnically, politically, religiously, morally, aesthetically, ideologically, and so on, than the rural population. (j) The tempo of change is notably faster in the city populations than in the rural ones.

(k) The network of interaction of the city agglomerations is much wider and more complex than that of the country population. In the city there are more numerous contacts per person, wider areas of interaction per man and per agglomeration; predominance of impersonal, casual, short-lived relations over the personal and durable; more complex, manifolded, superficial, and externally standardized relationships than sincere, simple, and deep ones. In the city man interacts as "a number," "address," as an "impersonal" occupational or political or business "agent," whereas in the country man interacts mainly as "an individual human person."

As a result of these differences the whole sociocultural atmosphere, style and pattern of living, psychology and behavior of the city agglomeration is very different from that in the country aggregate. We have, therefore, two basically different sociocultural worlds.[5]

In each country or region, the city appeared later than the villages and hamlets. The last few centuries in the West have been marked by a rapid and steady growth of the cities at the cost of the country agglomerations. The city agglomerations have been playing an increasingly greater and greater role in the molding of human personalities, of social groups, and of culture, and finally, in determining the course of the historical process.

At the present time, in many greatly urbanized and industrialized countries, there seems to have been reached a point of saturation in this trend. Due to the new sources of energy like electricity and radio, railways, automobile, telephone, telegraph, and to many other factors (including the atomic bomb and energy) there has appeared a new trend toward "rurbanization," that would give us a sociocultural world in which the specifically urban and rural traits are merged together, preserving the plusses of both and decreasing the shortcomings of each of these agglomerations. This new trend is emerging in only a few regions and countries, but it is bound to develop more and more, creating thus a new form of sociocultural world.[6]

2. Population Agglomerations With and Without One Dominant Group in Their Total Constellation of Groups

Observing the total constellation of groups into which populations are differentiated and strata into which they are stratified, we can see two different types of social structures. One does not have any single group in the total constellation that unquestionably dominates all or most of the other groups, integrates around itself most of the other groups, determines and dominates the "skyline" of their stratification, and permeates, conditions, and controls the other groups. All or most of the groups of such a population are, so to speak, on equal footing, none of them being dominant. Among the highest strata of all these groups there is no stratum which can be called the highest aristocracy of the aristocracies of the population. If, for instance, we take the population of the United States at the end of the nineteenth century and at beginning of the twentieth, there was no American "aristocracy of the aristocracies" among the highest strata of its unibonded and multibonded groups. Neither the religious, nor occupational, nor state, nor nationality, nor any other of the important unibonded and multibonded groups clearly controlled and dominated all the other

---

[5] A detailed study of the rural and urban agglomerations is the object-matter of the special rural and urban sociologies. Such studies, together with all the important facts and literature, are Sorokin and Zimmerman's *Principles of Rural-Urban Sociology*; Sorokin, Zimmerman, and Galpin, *A Systematic Source Book in Rural Sociology*, 3 Vols.; L.

Smith, *The Sociology of Rural Life*, quoted; N. P. Gist and L. A. Halbert, *Urban Society* (New York, 1933); and many other competent texts in rural and urban sociology.

[6] See on this Sorokin and Zimmerman, *Principles*, quoted, Ch. 27; Sorokin, Zimmerman, and Galpin, *The Source Book*, quoted, Vol. III, Ch. 23.

groups. For some, the highest officials of the U.S.A. were the aristocracy; for others, the multimillionaires; for some the great scientists and artists; for others the great church dignitaries or the "registerites," and so on. The "skyline" of the American population had several high peaks rather than one peak towering over the others. Its aristocracy was a composite, mosaic aristocracy of the upper strata of all the most influential unibonded and multibonded groups.

If we take now the Russian or the German populations of the periods of the Communist Soviet and the Nazi regimes, the unibonded *totalitarian state group* clearly dominated and controlled all the other unibonded and multibonded groups. Likewise the highest stratum of the Soviet and the German state governments was the most powerful "aristocracy of the aristocracies," not by reason of moral or other merits but by virtue of the state control of other aristocracies. Those of the other aristocracies which the Soviet and the Nazi aristocracy disliked were either eliminated, restricted, or demoted. One may like or dislike such a situation, but the dominance of the state group and of its aristocracy in these cases is unquestionable. The "skyline" of the group constellations of these populations was determined by the towering peak of the state group and of its upper stratum.

The difference then between the populations with and without one dominant group in their constellations of groups is clear. These two types differ in their "anatomy and morphology" in a number of important ways. The populations without one dominant group are less centralized, less regimented, each group having more autonomy and its own way of living, functioning and changing, more democratic, more loose in the interconnections of its groups, and less integrated than the populations with one dominant group in its constellation of groups. Furthermore the population without one dominant group does not have one main, central consolidated ladder of stratification, but several ladders of stratification, partly merging in a many-bonded pyramid, but fairly independent from one another. For this reason the picture of the total stratification in such populations is much more muddled, less clear, less definite than in the populations with one

dominant group. Its dominant ladder of stratification gives the "tone" to all other hierarchies of ranks and precedences. Respectively in the former type there are several "equal and different" aristocracies.

Each of these two types has many subtypes. From the standpoint of inner cohesion the population without one dominant group may run from *the free harmonious agglomeration of various groups* up to the *unintegrated, disintegrated, anomic, loose, and anarchic* coexistence of various groups and strata with each group claiming its superiority, each stratum contending for its precedence, making up a somewhat disorderly social aggregate, ever bickering, ever boiling with various pressure groups and antagonisms. Concretely such populations may range from a set of equal families living in the same village up to the big republican and democratic commonwealths.

More numerous and more definite are the subtypes of the population aggregates having one dominant group in its constellation of groups. In accordance with the *kind* of dominant group, one can distinguish the populations in which its total constellation of groups is dominated by such multibonded groups as: *the family, tribe, caste, social order, social class, and nation*; and by such unibonded groups as *religious group* and *state group*. The domination by any of these groups of the total constellation of the groups and their strata in a given population does not necessarily mean that all these other groups are closely connected with the dominating group and would be entirely similar in all populations dominated by the same group, say, by a tribe or by the state. On the other hand, the existing factual material warrants the contention that all the populations dominated by the same kind of a unibonded or multibonded group, say, by the state or by the caste, have several other groups that go with the given dominant group, and thus far their structure will be similar. Being similar to one another, the whole set of such populations will be dissimilar from the set of the populations dominated by a different group, say by a religious group. The dominant group determines not only the skyline and the roof of the social structure of the population but many of the groups or rooms found under such a roof.

a. *The Family-Dominated Agglomerations of Population.* Though the family formations play a very important part in any population (see above, pp. 246ff.) there are some populations, like the Chinese, in which the family plays an exceptionally dominant integrating part. Throughout the long history of China, the structure of its population has been based upon the patriarchal type of family. The state group and government in China has been constructed as a large family group. The religious groups of China, Confucianist and Taoist, have been first of all family groups united by the cult of the family ancestors and by filial piety. The territorial, occupational, and economic groups have also been built around the family and kinship groups. The Confucian-Chinese "five fundamental relationships," integrating the total network of all social (interpersonal and intergroup) relationships, have been taken from the family and extended to all groups and persons: the relationship between a good father and a good son; between elder and younger brother; between husband and wife; between the paternalistic ruler and subject; and between brotherly friends. The ethics and law of such a population is an application of these five relationships. In brief, the family with its filial piety and five relationships is "the root of all virtue, and the stem out of which grows all moral teaching. . . . It commences with the service of parents; it proceeds to the service of the ruler; it is completed by the establishment of character."[7] In and around it the whole structure of the Chinese population is built. Take it out of this total Chinese structure and it crumbles into disintegrated fragments.

Besides the Chinese "ocean of population," there have been smaller populations whose group-strata structure has also been dominated by the family.

b. *Tribal Agglomerations of the Population.* Whatever the secondary differences of all the populations whose dominant group is the tribe (in the defined sense) may be, all such populations are differentiated into tribes, these into two or more clans (in the defined sense), and these in their turn subdivided into several kinship and family groups, each tribe, clan, family being a multibonded group of a definite composition similar in all such populations (see the definitions of the tribe-clan-family). In between the family, clan, and tribe multibonded groups, a rudimentary state group, sex, age, territorial, and a few other unibonded groups, will be given in all populations of the tribal type, but each of such groups plays a relatively modest role in comparison with the three multibonded groups: the family, clan, and tribe. On the basis of the objective similarity of their "anatomy and morphology," the tribal agglomerations of population will have many other social and cultural similarities: religion representing a variety of the cult of ancestors; state (tribal) government closely tied up with the kinship stratification; prevalence of hunting, pastoral, and agricultural occupations as the main ways of getting the means of subsistence, with very little family handicraft and practically no manufacturing industry. Likewise the habitat of the tribal agglomerations will be small hamlets, villages, or dispersed sets of few families in an open country, without a big industrial and commercial city. The mentality of the populations of the tribal type will be marked by a variety of animistic, totemistic, fetishistic psychology and ideology, Materialistic, mechanistic, positivistic mentalities are essentially foreign to it. The main conflicts in such populations are intertribal and not the intercaste or interclass conflicts. In many secondary traits, the separate tribal populations may exhibit variation and dissimilarities; but in their main structural, cultural, behavioral, and mental aspects they display an essential similarity.

c. *Caste Agglomerations of Population.* Some 400 millions of people in India make up thousands of different populations that are dissimilar in many respects. But since the total constellation of the groups of each part of the Indian population is dominated by caste, the social structure, culture, behavior and mentality of these thousand populations exhibit a series of basic similarities typical and unique for the populations of the *caste type*.

The caste principle permeates all other groupings of the India population; it adjusts

---

[7] "The Hsiâo King or Classic of Filial Piety," *The Sacred Books of the East*, Vol. III, pp. 466-467. See all the *Texts of Confucianism, Ibid.*, Vol. III, *passim*; Vol. XXVII, *passim*; *The Texts of Taoism, Ibid.*, Vol. XL, *passim*.

and patterns them along the caste model. The hierarchy of the castes dominates, controls, and unifies all other stratifications. The highest Brahmin caste is the top measure of the ranks of all other castes and groups and persons, and of the outcastes as the lowest stratum, the "untouchables." The caste principle with its rules of strictest endogamy, obligatory inheritance of the total social position of the parents by children, determines the physics and politics, the religion and ethics, the occupation and economic status, in a word, the total social position, mentality, and behavior of practically every member of the population. In accordance with this the main social tensions and conflicts in such formations are the intercaste and religious tensions and conflicts—religious because religion is the basis for caste regime.

d. *The Social Estate Agglomerations of Population.* Both the tribal and the caste types of agglomerations of population differ notably from the agglomerations dominated by the multibonded social estates (see above definition of this social order). The hierarchy of social estates is the controlling group in the constellation of groups and strata of the earlier stages of Greece and Rome, medieval Europe, and of several periods in the history of the populations of China, Egypt, Persia, and other countries. Ranging from the hereditary highest nobility to the order of slaves and serfs, the hierarchy of social orders is the central axis on and around which are built all other groups and hierarchies in such populations. It also determines, though not so rigidly as the caste order, the social position, functions, role, conduct, and mentality of all its members and groups. For this reason, the essential traits of the group and strata structure of such populations must be similar. The same is true of the culture, conduct, and mentality of such populations. In brief, the social estate type of agglomeration of population is a real type widely spread in various periods among various parts of humanity.

e. *The Social Class Agglomeration of Population.* The tribal, caste, and social estate types differ from the populations whose constellation of groups and strata is dominated by *a set of social classes* (see above the definition of social class). In such populations the multibonded groups of tribe-clan-caste-social order

are either lacking or play a very modest role. On the other hand, such groups as occupation, economic, and in part the political, play a decisive role. Likewise, in all populations of this formation, the predominant type of family, of religious, territorial, kinship-age-sex-race-nationality group is the same in many respects, while being dissimilar from those in the tribal-caste-social order formations. Developed commerce, industry, manufacturing, and machinofacturing, numerous urban centers, and so on, are common traits of such class societies. The main tensions and inner wars in such populations assume the form of the interclass struggle for the occupational, economic, and political values. To summarize: the group strata, structure, mentality, conduct, and culture of the populations of the social class formation are similar in many basic respects, no matter in what part of this planet and at what period of human history such type is given. The class-type of society is a real type widely spread in time and in various populations.

f. *The State (or the Nation) Dominated Agglomerations of Population.* In contradistinction to the period of the medieval feudalism when the state group and nation played very modest roles among other groups, we live in a period of the *totalitarian and semi-totalitarian state-Leviathans* decisively dominating practically all the other groups into which the western and in part the eastern populations are differentiated. In the fully totalitarian populations of Communist Russia or Nazi Germany, the state (or the nation) controls all the other groups. Whatever may be secondary and tertiary differences in the groupings and strata of all the populations past and present, whose groupings have been dominated by the state, all such populations exhibit a long series of similarities in their group structure, stratification, culture, behavior, and mentality. The totalitarian Ptolemaic Egypt, Sparta, Lipara, ancient Rome after 300 A.D., Byzantium, China in some periods of her long history, ancient Peru, ancient Mexico, to mention only a few of the totalitarian or the state dominated populations, all illustrate this series of similarities. They are all a variety of the *totalitarian or the state-dominated type of social structure of the population.* In other cases, the place of the state is taken by the nation in the defined sense of this group.

g. *Theocratic Agglomerations of Population.* With the necessary modifications, the same can be said of the populations whose groupings and stratifications are dominated by a *religious group* and its values. The populations of ancient Greece before the fifth century B.C., of ancient Rome before the fourth century B.C., of Tibet, of India, of medieval Europe, are a few examples of such populations dominated by a religious group and its values. However great are their differences, due to the enormous time and space distances and to a lack of contact between them, they have a surprisingly large number of similarities in their social differentiation, stratification, culture, mentality, and behavior. They all give us a *theocratic* type of population-structure, with the spiritual power towering over the secular, or the head of the religious group becoming a secular king; with the stratification headed up by the priest stratum; with predominantly agricultural occupational groups; with the family, marriage, kinship, and sex life regulated by the religious laws; and with the religious values permeating all the others.

Such are the main morphological or structural types of the agglomerations of population differentiated into many groups and stratified into various layers. To recapitulate, we can distinguish:

I. Urban and rural types
II. The types dominated by one group and those without such a domination

Among the populations dominated by one group there are agglomerations dominated by:

    A. The Family,
    B. Tribal,
    C. Caste,
    D. Social Order,
    E. Social Class,

    F. The State- or Nation-dominated, and
    G. The Theocratic Types

These types do not exhaust all the possible types of agglomerations; there are many others, though these are less distinct and less widely spread. A closer study of the problem will undoubtedly supplement and improve this list. However, in comparison with the existing classifications, this series of types or formations seems to be adequate. It is not artificial and one-sided. The populations or societies put into the same class or formation have in fact all-around essential similarity in their group-strata structure, and in the forms of their mentality, conduct, and culture so far as they are connected with the structure (in other parts being different). This similarity goes far beyond the incidental similarity in one or a few insignificant points selected by artificial classifications. Each type is fairly definite and clear and quite tangibly differs from the other types. In the above sketch of each type, no detailed analysis is given. When, however, a microscopical study of all the groups, with their institutions and strata and culture and mentality-behavior has been made, the individuality of each type becomes unquestionable. More than that; a close correlation of the types of family, of government, of religious, judicial, and other institutions, as well as of specific forms of culture, conduct, and mentality with each type, becomes apparent. From this standpoint, each type carefully reflects the main formations actually found in the socio-cultural world. Additional evidence for the reality of the types is that each of them is very widely, though somewhat haphazardly, used by historians, sociologists, anthropologists, and other social scientists. There is no way of avoiding these types. Without reference to them, no adequate history, no anthropology or sociology can be written and articulated.

V. Criticism of the Traditional Theory of Society and Individual

The problem of society and the individual has been one of the most discussed problems in sociology and social sciences. Its traditional setting and assumptions are as follows: (1) On any populated territory, there exists one society consisting of all the persons who inhabit it.

(2) The whole of mankind is divided into a series of such societies, each on its own territory, and no two societies coexist within the same territory. (3) Every individual belongs to one such society only. (4) Sometimes the interests of the individual coincide with those of his society: then we have harmony between the society and the individual; sometimes their interests collide: then we have antagonism. (5) There are no intermediate groups between the society and the individual. The partisans of the individual as well as the partisans of society both are similar in their confrontation of the individual and society. Both assume that the individual faces the society as a whole and that his interests and values are often contradictory to those of the whole society. Respectively, the partisans of the individual and of individualism deplore the trampling of the individual by the society, while the apologists of society denounce the individual for his violation of the values of society. Such are the explicit and implicit assumptions of the traditional but still widely accepted theory of society and the individual.[8]

In the light of the preceding chapters, the utter fallacy of this conception of the relationship between the individual and his one society, with all its assumptions, must be perfectly evident. For example:

(1) If by society is meant just the population of either the whole of mankind or of a certain territory, we know well that such a population is a mere nominal plurel and not an organized system of interaction. However, if it is an agglomeration of several unibonded and multibonded groups, there are several societies, not one "whole" society.

(2) If by society is understood a generic interaction system or group, then, within any populated territory there is not one "whole society" but two or more unibonded and multibonded societies, all of which are real societies. If all these are subtracted there remains no society at all. In both cases, we do not get any one "whole society," but a set of societies, agglomerated, coordinated with, or subordinated to, one another. The belief in the existence of one "whole society" is but a myth. Mythical also are the assumptions that on the same territory or within the same population only one society can exist. We have seen that the same population is differentiated and stratified into several groups and that on the same territory there exist several different groups or societies.

(3) Still more fallacious is the assumption that every individual belongs to one society only. It has been shown that every individual belongs to several unibonded and multibonded groups different from one another: to his or her age, sex, race, language, occupational, economic, religious, state, and other unibonded groups and to several double, triple, and more complex multibonded groups, such as his family, tribe, caste, order, and social class. On the other hand if we subtract all these groups from the social world of an individual, there remains no social group at all and no "society as a whole."

(4) Since every individual belongs to several groups and strata, the traditional confrontation: the individual and society, the individual vs. society, or the individual harmonious with society becomes either meaningless or utterly erroneous.[9] If an individual is opposed to the notion of society as a whole this must mean that he is outside of it and does not interact with its members. If he does not interact with it, he cannot be either antagonistic or solidary with it. In that case no causal-meaningful relationship exists between the individual and the society. If an individual is a member of the society, and interacts with its other members, then we cannot confront him with the society as something "whole" that stands outside and above him. In that case we can confront him only as a member, within this system of interaction, with other members; we can talk of either solidarity or antagonism between our individual and other individuals

---

[8] One of the sharpest settings of the problem of the individual and society in this fashion is found in G. Palante's Les antinomies entre l'individu et la société (Paris, 1913). This conception has largely been constructed under the influence of the state-groups taken for "the society."

[9] See the history of this problem and confrontation in N. Kareeff, Introductory Sociology (Russian, Petrograd, 1917), Ch. 13; H. Michel, L'idée de l'état (Paris, 1898); H. Spencer, The Man Versus State (London, 1896); G. Palante, Les antinomies, quoted; N. Mikhailovsky, What is Progress, The Struggle for Individuality (Russian).

who are members of the same group. More-over, being a member of several other groups, the individual may be and usually is solidary with some of these groups and their members. In fact, it hardly ever occurs that he is either antagonistic or solidary with all the groups and strata he is connected with. Like the early Christians or Communists, he may be antago-nistic with the state government of the Roman Empire or of the "bourgeois state," but he is solidary with his Christian religious group and with his Communist party. Even a criminal-gangster, antagonistic to several groups, is soli-dary with his own gang, often with his family, his friends, and so on. We are told that in the antinomy between the individual and society Socrates was poisoned, Christ was crucified, Danton was guillotined.

When properly analyzed these and all the other cases of the individual *vs.* society appear to be the *conflicts between different groups* or different members of the same group. Socrates, Christ, and Danton were antagonistic to some groups and members and solidary with the

others groups and members. Socrates stood not alone against the alleged one "whole society" but was supported, sympathized with and ap-proved by, his disciples, among whom were such persons as Plato and Xenophon. Christ was perfectly solidary with his disciples and followers and with several other groups of the Jewish, Roman, Gentile population of Jeru-salem. The same is true of Danton.

To summarize: Whatever case of so-called antinomy between the individual and society we take, we find it is not a conflict of the in-dividual and the "whole society" but rather a conflict of individuals with individuals or of a group with a group. Instead of the fictitious unilinear relationship: individual and society, we have a multilinear relationship of in-dividuals to individuals, factions to factions, groups to groups. All the dramatic effusions on the "tyranny of society over the individual" and on the "despotism of the individual over the society" belong to the realm of poetry rather than to social science. The whole prob-lem is a pseudo-problem.

VI. Criticism of the Unilinear Theories of Social Differentiation and Stratification, of Solidarity and Antagonism

Our structural analysis has shown a complex multilinearity of social differentiation and stratification of all mankind as well as of any given population. As a result, at any moment of history we have a complex and ever-chang-ing constellation of solidarities and antagonisms of various social groups and strata. At any his-torical moment we have solidarities and an-tagonisms between various strata of the same group; those between various groups of the same character, for instance, between different states or different occupational groups; finally between different groups: the states and the religious groups, the nationalities and social classes, the race groups and economic groups, and so on. The battlefield of history is the field of many front lines going in different directions, overlapping and criss-crossing one another; with many different armies, each army being solidary with some armies and antag-

onistic to others, with the solidarities and antag-onisms incessantly changing. Now and then among the multitude of front lines and the group-strata armies this or that front be-comes temporarily one of the main fronts in a given population; now alliances and solidari-ties of the states, now of castes, now of reli-gious groups, now of social classes, now of other "dominant groups" (in the above sense of the term). In such populations and periods, most of the other front lines temporarily be-come secondary and tend to align themselves with the main front line and with the main armies of the "dominant groups." But with a passage of time the main front line and the main armies of a given period fade and are replaced by a new front line. *The actual his-torical process is determined at any given moment by the net resultant of all the activities of all the main unibonded and multibonded groups and strata, by all their solidarities and antagonisms, struggles and alliances.* None of our important unibonded and multibonded groups can be excluded from the forces shaping the historical or sociocultural processes, so far as we think of the historical processes within the whole of mankind. Only for some parochial areas and for periods where a given group does not exist or is uninfluential as yet, only for such areas and periods may such groups be excluded from among the shapers of historical processes. From the standpoint of the whole human population, none of our powerful groups can be excluded from the important armies of history that determine its events and course.

In the light of this fact, the fallacy of many unilinear theories of social differentiation and stratification as well as of solidarities and antagonisms and of the groups that determine the course of history, becomes obvious. The theories of A. Gobineau, L. Gumplowicz, and of other "racialists" that stress and see mainly the differentiation and stratification of humanity along the racial lines and that view the historical process mainly as an interracial

struggle are obviously wrong. No less wrong are the theories of Marx and Engels, reducing the multilinear stratification and differentiation to a unilinear main line, and viewing the historical process as a resultant of the class struggle mainly. The same has to be said of *all* the numerous theories that see only one main line of differentiation and stratification, of solidarities and antagonisms, whether among state groups, religious groups, occupational and economic groups, castes, or family formations.

They are all utterly one-sided and inadequate. Their attempts to explain the course of historical or sociocultural processes as a result of the activities of their pet groups only, has always failed and is bound to fail. Their equations that: "X (Historical process) is a function of one variable Y (of their pet group: racial, social class, religious, economic, occupational, caste, the state, the family, or any other group)" is to be replaced by the equation: "X (historical process) is a function of several variables: $A, B, C \ldots N$" (of all the main unibonded and multibonded groups with their unibonded and multibonded strata).

VII. General Conclusion
to the Structural Analysis of Social Phenomena

We have reached the end of our analysis of social phenomena in their structural aspect. We started with the study of the structure of the generic forms of social phenomena, the phenomena of interaction. In this way we obtained our definition of social group. Then we passed to a systematic study of the forms of groups and of their interrelationships. This resulted in the distinction of organized, "as if" organized, and unorganized groups. Having obtained the concept of organized and "as if" organized groups quite logically, we have been brought to the fundamental distinction between the unibonded and multibonded groups. With these conceptions in hand, we proceeded to a systematic "taxonomy" of the most powerful unibonded and multibonded groups, giving as precise a definition of each as it is possible at the present time. Then we passed to a study

of the stratification of the groups and to the classification of the main forms of stratification into unibonded and multibonded types. Starting with the interacting human population at the beginning of our structural analysis, we have now been brought back to it at the end. It appears now as a constellation or agglomeration of various stratified groups. This chapter has given an outline of the main types or formations of population as agglomerations of groups and strata. In this way we have given a "cytological" analysis of the "social cell," the componential structure of the generic social phenomenon of interaction; an "anatomical and morphological" analysis of the social organs and tissues, the unibonded and multibonded groups and stratifications; a "taxonomical" classification of all the main "species" and "sub-species" of groups and stratifications and agglomerations. With this we can end the structural analysis of the *social* universe or of the social aspect of the superorganic world. Now we pass to a concise study of the *cultural* universe or of the cultural aspect of the super-organic cosmos, this being its second aspect. This done, we shall turn to an analysis of the sociocultural structure of personality as the third aspect of the sociocultural manifold.

PART FIVE

Structures of the Cultural and Personality Aspects of the Superorganic Universe

Chapter 17. Structure of the Cultural Universe

I. Ideological, Behavioral, and Material Cultures of Individuals and Groups

So far we have analyzed the structure of the social aspect of the superorganic universe. Now we pass to a study of the structure of its cultural aspect, inseparable from the social but different from it. The social aspect of the superorganic universe is made up of the interacting individuals, of the forms of interaction, of unorganized and organized groups, and of the interindividual and intergroup relationships. The meanings, values, and norms have been studied not for their own sake but merely as the properties of the interacting individuals and as the *raison d'être* of their interaction and of their groups. The cultural aspect of the superorganic universe consists of meanings, values, norms, their interaction and relationships, their integrated and unintegrated groups ("systems" and "congeries") as they are objectified through overt actions and other vehicles in the empirical sociocultural universe. In a study of this aspect, the individuals and groups function not for their own sake but mainly as the agents and instrumentalities of the meanings, values, and norms. Such a shift of the focus of study reveals to us many properties and relationships of the sociocultural universe which pass almost unnoticed in the study of its social aspect. It makes clear also the ontological, logical, and causal relationships between the social and cultural aspects of this universe.

More exactly defined, the cultural aspect of meaningful interaction consists of (1) the totality of meanings, values, and norms possessed by the interacting individual and groups, making up their "ideological" culture; (2) the totality of their meaningful actions-reactions through which the pure meanings, norms, and values are objectified, conveyed, and socialized, making up their behavioral culture; (3) the totality of all the other vehicles, the material, biophysical things and energies through which their ideological culture is manifested, externalized, socialized, and solidified, making up their "material" culture. *Thus the total empirical culture of a person or group is made up of these three levels of culture: ideological, behavioral, and material.*[1]

---

[1] The distinction of ideological, behavioral, and material cultures is logically and factually more adequate than Max Scheler's distinction between "cultural data" and the "real factors" or "cultural and real aspects" of the sociocultural universe. His cultural data are what I call meanings, values, and norms; his "real factors" are sex, hunger, climate, race, and other, mainly physicochemical and biolog- ical phenomena. In Scheler's division the purely biological and physicochemical phenomena are made a variety of sociocultural phenomena, thus making the sociocultural or superorganic phenomena indistinguishable from the inorganic and organic phenomena. On the other hand, it leaves the realm of meanings, values, and norms hanging in a vacuum, separated from their vehicles and

II. Integrated, Unintegrated, and Contradictory Relationships of Cultural Phenomena

Social relationships of individuals and groups are either solidary, antagonistic, or neutral. Similarly, cultural phenomena, in their relationship to one another, also can be either integrated (solidary), unintegrated (neutral), or contradictory (antagonistic). They are *integrated* (solidary) when two or more interacting, that is, causally connected cultural phenomena stand in *a logical or, for art phenomena, aesthetic consistency with one another*. They are *unintegrated* (neutral) *when they are logically or aesthetically unrelated to each other*, being neither consistent nor contradictory. They are *contradictory* (antagonistic) *when they are logically or aesthetically inconsistent and contradictory*. The integration, lack of integration, and contradiction of cultural phenomena concerns

alike all three levels of culture—ideological, behavioral, and material. Not only the meanings, values, and norms can stand to each other in the relationship of logical or aesthetic consistency, unrelatedness, and contradiction, but also the overt actions and the other material vehicles, so far as they articulate and express the respective meanings, values, and norms. The overt actions of an individual or of a group may either practice what their ideological culture preaches, or not practice it at all, or practice something contradictory to it. Similarly, the material vehicles used may either adequately articulate the ideological culture or not express it at all or express meanings, values, and norms contradictory to the professed ones.

III. Integration, Unintegration, and Contradiction of Ideological Culture

1. Of Simple Meanings, Values, and Norms

The relationships of integration, unintegration, and contradiction of meanings, values, and norms pertain first of all to the relationships of single meanings, values, and norms.

Any set of single meanings, values, and norms like a proposition: "A is B," or "Two and two make four," or "All human beings are mortal, Socrates is a human being, Socrates is mortal," in which the subject, predicate, and copula are logically consistent with one another or are so coordinated that they become mutually supplementary, makes any such set a consistent (solidary) system of ideological culture, an integrated unity of meanings,

values, and norms. If a set of aesthetic values and meanings is consistent in its style and content, and makes an aesthetic unity, like the second movement of Beethoven's *Seventh Symphony*, or Homer's *Iliad*, we have an integrated aesthetic culture or fine art.

If a set of single meanings, values, and norms is logically or aesthetically contradictory within itself, we have an innerly antagonistic congeries of meanings, norms, and values or a congeries of ideological culture. Thus the meanings "A is non-A," "Two and two make seven," "All men are mortal, Socrates is man, therefore he is immortal" give us a self-contradictory congeries of meanings; so also the aesthetic values: a part of "Agnus Dei" of the

agents, ungrounded in the empirical sociocultural universe. From this basic error all the subsequent errors of Scheler's *Wissenssoziologie* follows. Similar criticism can be applied to A. Weber's, M. Weber's, and many other theories of the conception of sociocultural phenomena, their divisions, and the divisions of the forms of culture. See Max Scheler, *Die*

Wissenformen und die Gesellschaft (Leipzig, 1926). The mutual relationship of these levels of culture, especially their relationships to the social groups, are exceedingly complex, puzzling, and far from being even remotely cleared by social science and sociology.

Gregorian Chants put together with "No love, no fun, until my baby comes home," and with fragments from the "Star Spangled Banner." In style, in meanings, in norms such a "musical composition" is a self-contradictory congeries. Similar self-contradiction is given by a picture, one part of which is painted in the style of Dürer, another in that of C. Monet, the third in the style of cubism, with parts exhibiting simultaneously saintly asceticism and intense eroticism.

If the single meanings, values, and norms of a given set are logically or aesthetically unrelated to one another, being neither consistent nor contradictory, such a pile gives us an unintegrated conglomeration of meanings, values, and norms. Such a set of meanings is "apple, Hitler, automobile, rain, triangle, fish." Or the set of norms: "water your victory garden," "attend dancing party," "buy a best seller," "pay your bill." Or the set of values: "Iliad, football, Gothic architecture, marriage happiness." They give us an unintegrated dump of ideological cultural values neither consistent nor contradictory from the logical or aesthetic standpoint.

2. Integration of Systems of Meanings, Values, and Norms

If instead of single meanings, values, and norms, we take the integrated systems of meanings, or values, or norms, these systems stand also in the same three relationships with one another: (a) solidary-consistent, in two forms; (b) antagonistic-contradictory; and (c) unintegrated-neutral.

a. *Solidary-Integrated.* These systems of meanings, values, and norms have two forms of mutual relationships, subordination and co-ordination. Two or more integrated systems of meanings stand in the relationship of subordination when one is a part of or a subsystem of the other. The proposition that "the sum of the angles of a triangle is equal to two right angles" is a system, but it is a mere subsystem in the total system of the proposition of geometry. In its turn geometry is a mere subsystem in the still large system of mathematics, and mathematics is a subsystem in a still larger system of science. Even science may be a subsystem in a still larger system of truth when science, philosophy, religion, and the fine arts

all harmoniously work for deeper and more adequate comprehension of a true reality. Thus we have a long series of mutually consistent systems of integrated ideological culture. Similarly, a measure in a musical composition, a "foot" in a verse, is a little ideological system; but both become mere subsystems respectively in a musical period or a couplet; these in their turn are subsystems in still larger musical phrases and strophes or stanzas; these in their turn become subsystems, respectively, in a movement of a symphony or a part of a poem, and the movement is a subsystem in a whole symphony as is a part in a poem. Similarly, long or short series of subordinated sub-sub-sub- . . . systems can be found in science, philosophy, religion, law, ethics, fine arts, political and economic systems of meanings, values, and norms. All the subordinated subsystems of the same integrated system of meanings articulate in various ways and details the same fundamental meanings, values, and norms consistent with one another, with the exception, as we shall see, of some unrelated and contradictory meanings that crop up here and there into any system of meanings, values, and norms.

Two or more integrated systems of meanings, values, and norms are integrated along the line of coordination when neither of these is a subsystem in the other, but both are mutually consistent and supplementary. If we take the systems of meanings, values, and norms that make the science of physics and of chemistry, neither is a subsystem in the other, but both are mutually consistent, supplementary, coordinated systems of physico-chemical science, larger than either physics or chemistry, without any subordination of the one to the other. The same is true of economics and sociology. To take an example of a co-ordination of aesthetic systems. Goethe wrote *Faust.* Gounod created its musical system as an opera. Many an eminent artist has depicted Faust in a series of pictures. Many a theatrical director has staged it as opera. These systems of the literary, musical, pictorial, theatrical Fausts mutually supplement one another and give us an integration of aesthetic systems through co-ordination.

b. *Antagonistic-Contradictory.* When two or more integrated systems of meanings, values, and norms are mutually contradictory, they give us an antagonistic or contradictory congeries of systems of culture. If we take the materialistic and idealistic systems of philosophy, atheistic and Christian systems of beliefs, communistic and capitalistic systems of economy, monarchical and anti-monarchical systems of political ideologies, the ethical systems of hatred and of love, nominalistic and realistic conceptions of reality, these systems (each consistent within itself) give us examples of the antagonistic congeries of sociocultural systems.

c. *Unintegrated-Neutral.* Finally, when two or more integrated systems are neither consistent and supplementary, nor contradictory to one another, we have an unintegrated (neutral) conglomeration of the systems of meanings, values, and norms. A Romantic poem, Republican political ideology, Baptist system of beliefs, Culbertson's bridge playing, give us in their totality an unintegrated conglomeration of unrelated, meaningful systems. Either logically or aesthetically they neither demand one another nor contradict mutually. They are in a neutral relationship. The above makes clear the integrated systems, unintegrated congeries, and contradictory conglomeration of single meanings, values, and norms, as well as of the integrated systems of these in their relationship to one another.

Thus we have a parallelism between the main forms of relationships of human beings and of meanings, values, and norms:

Human Beings
in their relationship with one another give:
1. Isolated human beings
2. Unorganized human groups
3. Organized groups

A) Solidary:
   Subordinated to
   Coordinated with ⎫
B) Antagonistic to   ⎬ one
C) Neutral with   ⎭ another

Meanings, Values, and Norms in their relationships with one another give:
1. Isolated meanings, values, and norms
2. Congeries of meanings, etc.
3. Integrated systems of meanings, etc.

A) Consistent:
   Subordinated to
   Coordinated with ⎫
                    ⎪ one
B) Contradictory to ⎬
C) Unrelated congeries ⎪ another
   neutral to   ⎭

Even more, antagonisms exist not only in the relationship of groups, one to another, but within the groups, in the relationships of their members. Likewise, as we shall see further in this chapter, there are very few, if any, vast systems of meanings, values, and norms which are absolutely free from some inner contradiction or tension and from unrelated congeries in their propositions. Plato's, Kant's, and any other system of philosophy, any of the great religious creeds, any of the sciences, even logics and mathematics, all have some unrelated or contradictory propositions, vitiating the logical consistency of some of their secondary and peripheral propositions. Even the music of Beethoven, Bach, and Mozart have "bridges" that are "neutral" or even contradictory to the main character of their compositions.

From this parallelism it does not follow however, that the total ideological culture of any organized group has only one completely integrated system of meanings, values, and norms, without any congeries, and that any integrated system of meanings is monopolized by one organized group only. We shall see further in this chapter that *such a co-terminality of organized group and of cultural (ideological) system does not exist, and that the relationship between organized group and integrated system of meanings, values, and norms is much more complex.*

Now before going further in the analysis, let us briefly outline the main vast systems of meanings, values, and norms that have been given in the sociocultural universe.

IV. Main Vast Ideological Systems, Combined Systems, and Supersystems

The universe of meanings, values, and norms contains billions of small systems beginning with the simple "A is B," "Thou shalt or shalt not," harmonious musical phrases, simple drawings, short poems, and ending with vast subordinated and coordinated systems made up of many sub-subsystems.

1. Main Ideological Systems

Among the comparatively vastest of these systems are the integrated systems of science, philosophy, religion, ethics, law, the fine arts and the system of oral and written language as the main vehicle for objectification of any system or congeries of meanings.

There is not the slightest doubt that the overwhelming part of each of these universes of meanings, values, and norms is an integrated, logically or aesthetically consistent system. Thus, any *scientific discipline*, beginning with mathematics and logics, passing to physics, chemistry, biology, and ending with economics, sociology, history, and other social and humanistic disciplines is, in the greater part of its propositions an integrated system of meanings, a true ideological system. Almost all its main propositions are mutually consistent and logically interdependent to such an extent that when one of the main propositions in any scientific discipline is changed, many other propositions have to be changed in order to make them mutually consistent. To be sure, each of these disciplines has here and there sets of propositions that are either unrelated to the rest, or once in a while are even contradictory to other propositions. One of the perennial reasons for their presence is the incessant change of any system of meanings. Due to it, at any moment, any system of meanings has survivals from the past, and the newest propositions just discovered, which antiquate and contradict the survivals. Before these are removed and replaced by the new propositions and before the rest of the body of the propositions is logically adjusted to them (which takes time), the whole system contains some mutually contradictory or mixed congeries. But these inconsistent congeries of meanings are an insignificant minority in comparison with the bulk of the propositions of which a given science is made up. And the more the discipline is developed, the more consistent it is, and the fewer are the neutral or contradictory congeries in it. For this reason each science as well as the total body of scientific disciplines makes up an integrated ideological system of science.

The same is true of the great *systems of philosophy* like the philosophy of the Upanishads, of Plato, of Aristotle, of Kant, of St. Thomas Aquinas, of Hegel, and the like. The bulk of propositions of which such a philosophical system is made up is a logically consistent whole, with a few unrelated and contradictory congeries of meanings vitiating it here and there. Likewise all the philosophies of the same kind, for instance, materialistic, make a vast system of materialistic philosophy in which each specific materialist philosophy enters as a subsystem.

Similarly, the main body of dogmas and beliefs, the *Credo* of any of *the great religions*, like the Christian *Credo*, is a logically consistent system of propositions. One cannot change any of the main propositions, for instance, the dogma of the Trinity in the Christian *Credo*, without introducing a contradiction in the rest of the statements of the *Credo*. To be sure, for the general reason of co-existence of the survivals and novelties, some congeries of meanings (unrelated and mutually contradictory) are present in practically all great religious systems, but they are an insignificant minority in the whole system of religious meanings.

Likewise all the *great law-codes or purely ethical codes* from the code of Hammurabi and the Ten Commandments up to the contemporary constitutional, civil, and criminal codes; from the ethical system of Taoism, Brahmanism, Buddhism, Christianity up to ethical systems of Plato and Aristotle, Spinoza and

Kant, Epicurus and John S. Mill—are in their main body of propositions (norms) one consistent whole. Here again one cannot change any of the main norms without making it necessary to modify many other norms in order to avoid their mutual contradiction and unrelatedness. As soon as an important contradiction appears in a law-code, the supreme court or the legislative body have to step in to eliminate it through some modification of the contradictory norms. There is no doubt that any law-code or ethical system contains also unrelated and contradictory congeries but these are again a minority, often latent and invisible.

The same is to be said of the great *art creations* in music and literature, painting and sculpture, drama and architecture; they all give us a marvelous unity of style and content, in their own way sometimes even more consistent than a valid syllogism or mathematical equation. The main creations of Homer, Sophocles, Dante, Shakespeare, Pushkin, Bach, Beethoven, Mozart, Phidias, Praxiteles, Michel Angelo, Rafael, Rembrandt, and the like, are, with the exception of a few "bridges," passages, elements, supreme logico-aesthetic unities.

Finally, any developed *language in its grammar and syntax* is also a logically consistent system of rules or norms vitiated now and then with inconsistent grammatic and syntaxic "exceptions" and "deviations" from the general rules. Like any other integrated system, its grammatic and syntaxic unity is so close that when a new rule enters a given language, many other rules have to be changed in it in order to make it a consistent body. For instance, "if the idea of expressing case by means of a preposition followed by an article comes into language which is already possessed of declensions, either the article and the preposition must eventually eliminate declensions, or the declensions must repel them."[2] In language: "Every element falls into its proper place in accordance with definitely formulable rules." And any infraction of these rules "is resisted as any aesthetic transgression might be resisted— as being somehow incongruous, out of the pic-

ture, or, if one chooses to rationalize the resistance, as inherently illogical."[3]

Since language is a means for expression of any consistent set of ideas or norms, it cannot help being an integrated system in its greater part; otherwise it could not successfully serve consistent sets of ideas, values, and norms.

Thus a truly scientific discipline, great philosophical system, great religion, law and moral codes, great artistic creation, and language are, in their essential body, a vast and complex consistent system of ideological culture.

2. Combined Ideological Systems

Side by side with these vast systems of ideologies, there are *combined ideological systems in which the same or mutually supplementary ideas, values, and norms are articulated by a scientific theory, philosophical system, religious belief, literature or music, painting or architecture, law or ethical norm.*

For example, when a great value like the monogamic family or the capitalist system of economy is claimed by a certain scientific (biological or sociological or economic) theory, by a philosophical system, by a religious dogma; when it is protected by law and ethical norms and glorified by poetry and music, by paintings and plays; then such a co-operation of all these ideological systems, such an articulation of the same basic ideas and values of the family or capitalist economy by these scientific, philosophic, religious, artistic, ethical, and juridical ideologies, makes a combined system of ideology of the family or of capitalism. Another example: In the predominantly Catholic colonial Mexico, its baroque architecture, its hierarchical and monarchical political order, its religion, a great part of its painting and sculpture, its system of education in schools, a considerable part of its musical culture, its law and ethics, manners and mores, scientific and philosophical theories, all articulated the same basic set of ideas, values, and norms, namely, those of medieval Spanish Roman Catholicism. All these ideological systems, belonging to different compartments of culture, joined together into one innerly con-

---

[2] G. Tarde, *The Laws of Imitation* (New York, 1903), p. 175.

[3] E. Sapir, "The Unconscious Patterning of Behavior in Society," *The Unconscious: A Symposium* (New York, 1929), p. 132.

sistent, combined system of ideology articulating in the language of science and philosophy, architecture and literature, politics and economics the same ideas as Spanish Catholicism.[4] These ideas are the presupposition of, and the key to the understanding of why and how colonial Mexico happened to have this kind of architecture, political regime, economic system, religious beliefs, education, and so on. Just so, the system of Marxian ideology is a presupposition and the key to an understanding of thousands of economic, political, scientific, philosophical, artistic, educational, ethical, and juridical ideologies in Soviet Russia. An enormous number of small and vast ideologies in all these fields articulate, in a combined way, the basic ideas, meanings, and norms of Marxianism. In a similar way a large number of scientific, philosophical, religious, artistic, juridical, ethical ideological systems combine in one vast system of American democratic ideology articulated by all these theories, beliefs, artistic creations, and ideologies.

The combined systems of ideologies may be diverse, small and narrow, big and vast. In thousands of forms they are given in the total ideological culture of any population.

3. Various Ideological Supersystems

When in any given universe of ideological systems we find the vastest combined system of ideology, that integrates into one consistent unity most of the essential scientific (including the economic, political, social, and humanistic sciences), philosophical, religious, aesthetic, juridical, ethical, and technological systems; in which all these articulate the same basic meanings, values, and norms, we have the vastest ideological supersystem possible in a given universe of ideological systems. The articulated basic ideas and values make up its major premise.

Concretely, such an ideological supersystem is different in different ideological universes of various populations. The total ideological universe of many preliterate populations is made up of a multitude of little systems and congeries which are little thought through and

are combined, at the best, only into comparatively small "supersystems" of either the totemic beliefs, or cult of ancestors, or cult of the family and tribe or some other relatively narrow principle that unites only a small part of their ideological congeries and systems. A large part of their ideological universe remains eclectic and unintegrated.

In other "historical" cultures and populations the total ideological culture has been integrated into vast supersystems that unite into one consistent whole a greater part of their small and large ideological systems: scientific, religious, artistic, etc. Thus a considerable part of various ideological systems in Soviet Russia is united into the Marxian ideological supersystem. Likewise a considerable part of ideological systems of ancient China has been integrated into the supersystem of the family ideology with the attendant cult of ancestors, filial piety, five fundamental relationships, and other sub-principles of the family ideology. Likewise, a large portion of the ideological systems of ancient Egypt was integrated into the ideological supersystem of the "afterworld." A considerable portion of Egyptian religious beliefs, scientific theories, artistic ideas (pyramids, temples, obelisks), political and ethical ideologies, philosophical, economic, and other ideologies were centered around the central idea of the "netherworld," each articulating it in its own way and language. In several populations the major premise of their cultural supersystem has been "economic prosperity and technological efficiency," and so on.

However, as we shall see further, in *none of the known ideological cultures have the total sum of all its ideological systems and congeries been united into one supersystem. Even the most and best integrated ideological cultures with the vastest possible supersystem have always remained in part eclectic, unintegrated, and, in part, even contradictory.*

4. The Vastest Known Ideological Supersystems

Among the vast ideological supersystems that are known, the vastest supersystem is

[4] See, on this, pointed remarks in F. S. C. Northrop, "Philosophy and World Order," in L. Bryson, L. Finkelstein, R. M. MacIver (ed.), *Approaches to World Peace* (New York, 1944), pp. 642 ff.; Northrop, *The Meeting of East and West* (New York, 1946), ch. 2. See there a similar analysis in regard to the cultures of the United States, Germany, Russia, and other countries.

built on the major premise concerning the ultimate nature of the true reality and value. Is the ultimate true reality and true value sensory, or supersensory, or partly sensory and partly supersensory? By its logical character, the problem of the ultimate nature of true reality and value is the ultimate and most general problem of thought. Being such, it serves as the major premise for building the vastest possible ideological supersystem, integrating into one consistent whole the greater part of the basic principles of science and philosophy, religion and ethics, law and politics, fine arts and economics. The character of an answer to this ultimate problem decisively determines most of the scientific, philosophical, religious, aesthetic, and other ideological systems and congeries. Some ideological cultures answer that the *true reality and true value is sensory*, that beyond the reality and value perceived by our sense organs there is no other reality and no value. Having answered it in this way, such ideological cultures build upon this answer their vastest supersystem in which most of their scientific, philosophical, ethical, and other systems articulate exactly this major premise. Such ideological supersystems can be called *sensate*.

Other highly integrated ideological cultures answer the problem by stating that *the true reality and true value is the supersensory, super-rational God* ("Tao," "World Soul," "Brahman," etc.), *the sensory reality and value being either a mere illusion, or the least important, least real, sometimes even negative, reality and value.* The vastest ideological supersystem built upon this premise can be called *ideational*.

Still other highly integrated cultures assume that the *true reality and value is partly sensory, partly rational, partly supersensory and super-rational infinite manifold.* The ideological supersystem erected upon this major premise can be called *idealistic*.

If we take the total ideological culture—all ideological systems and congeries—of Taoist China, of Greece before the fifth cen-

tury B.C., of Brahmanistic and Buddhistic India, of Christian medieval Europe, of small and large groups of mystics, stoics, and of transcendentally religious populations, of even such preliterate tribes as the Zuni or Hopi Indians, we find that these cultures have had ideational supersystems. In order to understand a greater part of their science, philosophy, religion, fine arts, ethics and law, economics and politics, mores and ways of life, even their behavioral and material culture, one has to be aware of this major premise.

If we take the ideological (and partly behavioral and material) culture of Greece and Rome, after the fourth century B.C. to about the third century A.D.; of the Western World after the fifteenth century A.D.; of "positivistic" and "materialistic" China at some periods of its long history and in some regions; of even some preliterate tribes like the Dobu; of all the positivistic, empiricistic, agnostic, materialistic, utilitarian, strictly "scientific," groups and persons; their culture is found to be integrated into a *sensate* ideological (and partly behavioral and material) supersystem.

Finally, the culture of Confucianist China, of ancient Egypt in some periods and regions, of ancient Greece of the fifth century B.C., of Europe of the thirteenth and fourteenth centuries A.D., and of several other groups and persons, has been integrated by the *idealistic supersystem*. A great deal of the ideologies of these populations have enunciated exactly the idealistic major premise in their science and ethics, law and philosophy, economics and politics, fine arts and other fields of their total culture.[5]

To give a further, slightly more detailed, illustration of ideational and sensate supersystems, let us take the medieval and modern western ideological (and partly behavioral and material) cultures.

If we take the totality of the ideas, norms, values, of the medieval society we find that a greater part (not the whole totality) of the scientific, philosophical, religious, artistic, juridical, ethical, economic, political ideas,

---

[5] See a detailed analysis of all these cultures from this standpoint in my *Dynamics*, Vol. I, pp. 66-101, *passim*, in all four volumes. Cf. further Chps. 40-42. The major premises of Mexican, German, English, Greek, and other cultures, pointed out by H. Danilevsky, O. Spengler, A. J. Toynbee, and F. Northrop, are not the vastest premises, but variations of Sensate, Ideational, and Idealistic premises.

values, and norms were integrated into one vast supersystem that articulated in all these sectors the same basic ideas and values formulated in the Christian *Credo*, with the central idea of *God as the ultimate true reality and the absolute true value*. The ideas of God, of the *Credo*, and of the Bible were explicitly expressed by the medieval Christian religion, by medieval philosophy identified with theology, by medieval science as a hand-maid of religion. Medieval grand literature was religious through and through and spoke of the same *Credo*; grand medieval music was but an articulation of the same *Credo*, being religious music and consisting of a Christian Mass with its Kirie Eleisons, "Agnus Dei," and religious chants; grand medieval architecture of the cathedrals was a veritable Bible in stone; so also was the medieval painting and sculpture, drama and "theater." Likewise, the medieval law and ethics were an expression of the Christian ethics; even medieval economic and political ideas were greatly permeated by the same ideas of Christian religion. So also the manners, mores, and the medieval mentality in general.

If we take the totality of the meanings, values, and norms of the contemporary society, we find in it also, in the vast systems of science, philosophy, religion, the fine arts, law, ethics, and language a still vaster supersystem in which the greater part of these vast systems are united and consistently articulate the central idea that the *true reality and true value is sensory*—the idea opposite to the basic idea of the medieval supersystem. This idea is articulated by the dominant part of science and philosophy, "modern religions," the dominant forms of law and ethics, fine arts, and way of living. In brief, this supersystem integrates into the vastest consistent whole the preeminently larger part of the systems of meanings, values, and norms that are current in our culture. In the later parts of this work we shall study these and other vast systems and supersystems of meanings, values, and norms given in various societies and cultures (see further, Chapters 40-42). For the present the above statements give a preliminary notion of the existence and of the main varieties of the vastest integrated supersystems of meanings, values, and norms.

V. Integration of Ideological, Behavioral, and Material Cultures of an Individual

1. Three Levels of Integration

The above gives us only the ideological integration, unintegration, and contradiction of the meanings, values, and norms of an interacting individual. An individual may have such an ideological integration and yet, in his overt actions, reactions, and vehicles may remain quite inconsistent, not acting at all upon his integrated meanings, values, and norms. For instance, he may have a well-integrated ethical system of norms of the Sermon on the Mount; and yet in his overt actions he may practice the norms of egotism and hatred in regard to his neighbors. He may preach very consistently the system of meanings, values, and norms of sexual chastity and virginity. And yet in his overt actions, reactions, and vehicles he may be a profligate. The historical cases of J. Rousseau, F. Bacon, Voltaire and others give

us instances of such an unintegration or even contradiction of the systems of meanings, values, and norms (ideology) with overt actions and vehicles. Hypocrites who do not practice what they preach supply us with an unlimited number of such discrepancies between the individual's ideological culture and his behavioral and material culture. Hence the full cultural integration of an individual means not only a consistency of his meanings, values, and norms with one another but also that of his ideology with his overt actions, reactions, and vehicles.

We have thus three levels of the integration of the culture and personality of an interacting individual: (a) *Purely meaningful or ideological*, which leaves unintegrated or even contradictory his overt actions, reactions, and the vehicles involved; when he either does not practice what he preaches or practices something opposite to his ideology. (b) *Double, meaningful behavioral-integration*, when he practices most of what he preaches but has some actions and uses some vehicles that either are unrelated to his ideological-behavioral integration, or even contradict it; when he preaches and practices in his overt actions a chastity of monogamic marriage, but at the same time finances "white slavery and houses of prostitution," or when he preaches and practices equality of men and, at the same time, finances slavery ships, as some Boston puritans did in the past. In these cases, the culture and personality of an individual are integrated in their meanings and in the bulk of overt actions but remain unintegrated or even contradictory in another part of his behavior and of vehicles. (c) *Triple, meaningful-behavioral-vehicles integration* of the culture and personality of an individual when his ideological culture is integrated and all his actions, reactions, and the vehicles used consistently articulate and practice his ideology. In this case all three components of sociocultural phenomena are integrated into one consistent unity, and there remains nothing unintegrated or contradictory in the culture and personality of the individual.

2. Purely Meaningful and Meaningful-Causal Integration of Culture of the Individual

These three levels of integration of culture and personality of interacting individuals are very important from another standpoint. (a) *In the case of a purely meaningful-ideological integration there is no causal tie between the component of meaning, values and norms of an individual and other components of his culture, that is, his overt behavior and the vehicles involved.* Meanings function and change without changing respectively the overt actions and vehicles of the interacting person, and vice versa, his behavior and the vehicles used can change without influencing his ideology.[6]

(b) *In the case of the double ideological-behavioral integration of culture and personality the integration becomes not only purely ideological but also causal between the component of meanings, values, and norms and that of the overt behavior of the persons.* The component of ideology is consistently realized and articulated in his overt actions-reactions. A change in the meanings, values, and norms leads to a change in overt actions and reactions and a change in these generates the respective change of ideology.

(c) *In the case of the triple integration, meaningful-behavioral-vehicles, the causal-meaningful ties extend over all three components of culture and personality of the interacting individual.* His culture and personality becomes fully integrated into *one consistent meaningful-causal unity.* His behavioral and material cultures faithfully and consistently articulate his ideological integrated culture.

VI. Integration, Unintegration, and Contradiction of the Culture of a Whole Interaction Group

Up to this point the integration, unintegration, and contradiction of culture has been viewed from the standpoint of an interacting individual. With these categories in hand, we can easily apply them to any group of interacting individuals, to the culture of the interaction systems as such.

1. Ideological Culture

(a) If the set of meanings, values, and norms of each interacting member is integrated and if all the sets of all the members are mutually consistent, the culture of the group is meaningfully or ideologically integrated. (b) If the set of each member is integrated but the sets of different members are mutually contradictory, the culture of the group becomes contradictory on its ideological level.

---

[6] Such a complete rupture of meanings, values, and norms of a person with his actions and vehicles makes him mentally abnormal and leads to his treatment by others as an abnormal person.

(c) When the ideologies of the members are neutral to one another, the culture of the group is unintegrated meaningfully. (d) The ideology of the group becomes also contradictory-unintegrated, if and when the ideologies of each member are self-contradictory or unintegrated. Since the members bring to the group self-contradictory and unintegrated ideologies, the integrated total sum of such ideologies cannot help becoming a hash of unrelated and contradictory meanings, values, and norms.

2. Behavioral and Material Culture

The ideological culture of a group being integrated, it may remain, like the culture of the individual, unintegrated in the components of overt behavior and vehicles of the group. When all members of the group unanimously profess the norm: "love thy neighbour," or "all men are equal," but practice different or opposite norms of selfishness, hatred, indifferentism and discrimination, the integration of the group remains on a purely ideological level, without becoming causal, leaving the culture of the group unintegrated or even contradictory in the relationship between its ideological, behavioral, and material cultures. Hence, the culture of the group may be doubly integrated, becoming meaningful-causal integration, when the integrated ideology of the group is consistently practiced in the overt behavior of its members. The culture of the group becomes triply integrated when the integrated ideology of the group is adequately realized in the behavior and vehicles of the group. In that case the integration of the group's culture becomes complete, meaningful and causal, integrated in its ideological, behavioral, and material culture, with the members solidary in their ideology, behavior, and vehicles.

But shall we regard the culture of a group as completely integrated if all its members profess the norm "hate your neighbor," "hate every member of the interacting group," and each consistently practices it in his actions and the vehicles used? Can we say of such a group that its members are solidary with one another in their ideologies, behavior, and vehicles? The answer is naturally, no. The principle of hatred explicitly and implicitly means a denial of the norms, values, and meanings of the hatred party. Since the group is devoid of even a purely ideological integration of its culture, it naturally remains unintegrated and contradictory in the components of overt behavior and vehicles. Instead of integral solidarity it gives an integral antagonism and unintegration, a Hobbesian conglomeration of individuals in which *homo homini lupus est* and in which *bellum omnium contra omnes* goes on.

VII. Integration, Unintegration, and Contradiction of the Cultures of a Conglomeration of Interacting Groups

The same criteria clearly determine also to what extent is integrated, unintegrated, or contradictory the total, three-levelled, culture of two or of a great number of interacting groups. If the ideological, behavioral, and material culture of each of the interacting groups is entirely integrated and if the total culture of each group is consistent with that of other groups, the total culture of all the interacting groups is integrated into one meaningful-causal unity. If the total culture of each group being integrated contradicts, or is unrelated to that of other groups, their total culture becomes contradictory or unintegrated. If the total culture—ideological, behavioral, and material—of each of the groups is contradictory or unintegrated, the total culture of all the interacting groups becomes also contradictory or unintegrated. If in part the cultures of all interacting groups are consistent, have a common fund of ideological, behavioral, and material culture, while in part their cultures are unrelated or contradictory, the total culture of all such groups becomes partly integrated, partly unintegrated and contradictory.

The preceding analysis describes the essence, forms, and criteria of the integrated, unintegrated, and contradictory culture of an

individual, of a group, and of several interacting groups on all three levels of their ideological, behavioral, and material cultures. Having now these criteria at hand we can ask the
factual questions: To what extent is the ideological culture of an individual, of a group,
and of a conglomeration of interacting groups
integrated? To what extent are their behavioral
and material cultures integrated each within
itself, with each other, and with their ideological culture? We shall begin with the culture of an individual.

Chapter 18. The Actual Structure of the Total Culture of Individuals, Groups, and Areas

I. Extent of Integration of the Total Ideological, Behavioral, and Material Culture of an Individual

1. The Structure of Culture of an Individual

Is the total ideological culture of an individual totally integrated or totally unintegrated or self-contradictory? Is it partly integrated, partly not, and in part contradictory? Does he always practice what his ideological culture preaches? Do the other vehicles he uses always articulate his meanings, values and norms? Is an individual a perfectly rational and consistent creature? Or is he an irrational, self-contradictory creature, or in part rational, in part nonrational, and in part irrational? The theoretical as well as practical importance of these problems is evident. If, indeed, the totality of the ideas, norms, and values (the ideological culture) of an individual were integrated into one consistent whole, an individual would be entirely rational and logical in his total ideology. Then all the laments on illogicality and irrationality of man would be baseless; any reform or change, to be convincing, would need only show its logico-aesthetic consistency and could count for its success upon the fundamental logicality and rationality of individuals. Further, if such a logical mentality of human beings were causally integrated with their overt behavior and vehicles, that merely objectify the logical mentality, then human beings and groups would have been logical, rational or consistent not only in their mentality but also in their overt behavior and in all the vehicles they use.

2. Generalizations

(a) There has hardly ever been any single individual whose total sum of meanings, values, and norms has been either completely integrated or completely contradictory. (b) There has hardly been an individual whose ideological culture has been either fully and closely integrated with his behavioral and material cultures, or entirely unintegrated with these. In other words the causal integration of the meanings, vehicles, and actions of an individual is neither complete nor entirely absent. Therefore the total (ideological and behavioral and material) culture of a person either in each or on all three levels is never completely integrated, nor completely unintegrated and contradictory.

(c) A human being is neither perfectly logical and rational, nor entirely nonlogical, illogical, nonrational and irrational. He is partly both.

(d) The degree and amount of integration of the ideological as well as of all three forms of culture in their meaningful-causal connections fluctuate from person to person, from group to group, from one total culture to another.

Hence all those who claim either a perfect rationality or nonrationality of human beings and groups, perfect integration or a lack of any integration of the total culture of an individual, are flagrantly wrong.

Thus any reasonably good social reform or reformation of a person is neither as easy as the partisans of rationality claim, nor as difficult as the partisans of human foolishness contend. The convincing power of logicality is neither omnipotent and sufficient nor entirely nil. Let us now examine the evidence.

a. *The Structure of Ideological Culture of an Individual.* That the total ideological culture of an individual is in part integrated, and has several consistent systems of meanings, values, and norms follows from the fact that with the exception of complete idiots and "mindless" persons (babies, etc.) all individuals, even most of the mentally abnormal, have in their total sum of meanings, values, and norms at least a few simple consistent systems of these like "two and two make four," "A is A," "this is beautiful," and so on. As a matter of fact even Mortimer Snerd of Mr. Bergen's program has a large number of much vaster consistent systems of meanings, values, and norms.[1] And Mortimer Snerd is probably the stupidest of the stupid persons. It is improbable and impossible that out of many thousands of meanings, values, and norms which an individual has, all the combinations are either contradictory or unrelated; of thousands of contradictions, there will be many contradictions to contradictions which turn into consistent combinations.

Our next evidence is that an individual who does not have any consistent systems in his total ideological culture is an individual absolutely devoid of any sound judgment, of

---

[1] L. Levy-Bruhl's contention that the primitive mentality is alogical, governed not by the laws of logic but the law of participation, is generally considered invalid. If it were even valid, his "loi de participation" has also its own consistency.

any sound knowledge; because any valid scientific proposition means, first of all, a logically consistent system of meanings. Without knowledge, no individual can survive for any length of time. Since even most primitive tribes have existed for many decades and centuries, and if they perished, perished not through their total lack of knowledge, but through disease, enemies, starvation, or other overwhelming calamities, this means that even the most primitive tribes have had a minimum of logic and knowledge necessary for their survival. Any meaningfully interacting individual has and uses his language. Any developed language is an essentially consistent system of meanings. A person who uses a language is constrained by it to be consistent to some degree.

Finally, if we take the total "ideological culture" of any common man we find in it the following picture. Suppose he is a Christian (or Buddhist, Confucianist, or member of any other developed religion). As the bulk of the meanings, values, and norms of Christian and of other developed religions is a consistent system (with some congeries cropping up here and there), his religious ideological culture must be integrated. Suppose he knows mathematics, physics, chemistry, or some other scientific discipline. As the bulk of the meanings, values, and norms of each science is one consistent whole (with congeries here and there), his scientific ideological culture is also consistent in its greater part. Suppose he is an American or French citizen and belongs to the Republican party. So far as the constitution and laws of a nation and the political platform of a party are a logical whole, his political ideological culture is consistent to the same extent. So far as he is a member of a certain occupational or territorial group, of certain associations and societies, clubs and leagues, his respective occupational, neighborhood, aesthetic, etc. ideologies are again somewhat consistent because the official law and constitution of an organized group must and invariably is consistent to a considerable degree.

The totality of the reasons and inductive evidence given show that the total ideological culture of all "mindful" persons is invariably integrated in part and contains a series of small and large logically consistent systems of meanings, values, and norms.[2]

On the other hand, the total ideological culture of a person contains also some unintegrated and contradictory congeries of meanings, values, and norms, first of all, because of the presence of some unrelated congeries and contradictions in practically all vast systems of meanings. Even the most consistent system of mathematics contains some; even the most integrated systems of philosophy and logics have their "antinomies" and unrelated congeries; even the most integrated music of Beethoven, Bach, Mozart, has some "bridges" in it that stand either apart from the consistent parts or sometimes are contradictory to them in style and character. The same is true of practically any other system: law-code, ethical system, social and humanistic disciplines, political ideologies, religious beliefs, language (exceptions to the grammatic and syntaxic rules), fine arts, and so on. Some glaring or obscure congeries and contradictions are present in any system because any concretely given system of meanings, from mathematics up to religious beliefs, is in an incessant process of development or change; some new "discoveries" or "unfoldings of new implications" incessantly go on. These new discoveries are either unrelated or contradictory to the old counterparts in the system. Also, in any vast system there are always some "survivals" that are antiquated and stand either unrelated or contradictory to the rest of the meanings of the system. The perennial presence of "new discoveries" and "survivals" in any vast system are due to the impossibility of continual re-examination and logico-aesthetic "straightening" of the whole system (science,

philosophy, law, etc.). In vast systems it takes time, and sometimes a long time, to understand the unrelatedness or contradiction of a new discovery or implication to the rest of the system, or to grasp the obsolete and contradictory character of the survivals to the other parts and to the new discoveries.[3]

Unintegrated and contradictory parts of the individual's total ideological culture are derived also from the unintegrated and contradictory relationships between the various systems of meanings which he possesses. Thus many subsystems of the Christian ideology of the individual do not deny or affirm, are not logically connected with, many parts of his Republican political ideology. In some other respects, his "political and national ideologies" contradict his Christian ideology. The latter says: "love your neighbor," "love your enemy" while his national and political ideologies say, especially in the time of war, "be patriotic, kill your enemies." Such contradictions between Christian and political ideologies are fairly numerous. Hardly any Christian, whether Republican or Democrat, has ever followed the Christian norm of turning the other cheek. Likewise many of his "occupational" ideologies are partly unrelated and partly contradictory to his religious, ethical, national, and political ideologies. As a Christian on Sundays, in the church, he sincerely professes "love your neighbor." As a businessman in his office, he no less sincerely believes in "business is business," with its cut-throat competition. As a patriotic citizen, especially in the time of war, he sincerely believes in the duty of sacrifice for the country; as a businessman or a workingman he tries earnestly to get all the profit or wages he can, regardless of any duty

---

[2] This consistency is supported also by the experimental studies in psychology that show the tendency of an individual to stick to a standard that he derived himself (autokinetically) in the situation where any other point of reference or standard is absent, and especially in consistency of the standards derived in a group situation. See the experiments and the analysis in M. Sherif, *The Psychology of Social Norms* (New York, 1936), Ch. 6.

[3] The whole dialectic logic of St. Augustine, Erigena, Nicolas of Cusa, Hegel, of most of the Oriental and Occidental mystic thinkers with their claim that every concept contains in itself its own negation, that in its full form any concept is a

coincidentia oppositorum, that there is a dialectical identity of the opposites, that a thesis contains in itself and passes into antithesis and this into a synthesis which as a new thesis contains again its antithesis and passes into it; all this dialectic logic gives systematic evidence of an implicit or explicit presence of inner contradictions and congeries in any concept and in any system of meanings. Karl Marx, Max Scheler, Max Weber, E. Barthel, and others have shown it empirically in the form of an inner tension or split or *Spannung* as an immanent element of practically all problematical meanings. See E. Barthel, *Die Welt als Spannung und Rhythmus* (Leipzig, 1928); the quoted works of Hegel, Marx, Scheler, M. Weber.

of sacrifice. As a Christian and a member of a great democracy he professes equality and brotherhood of all men; as a citizen, businessman, and Southerner he is against complete equality of the Negro and Africans and Orientals. Sometimes he is even anti-Semitic. If, further, we assume that he prefers blondes to brunettes, Gershwin's jazz music to the classical, Scotch to Bourbon or beer; conservative cloth to the loud, these and hundreds of other meanings, values, and norms of our individual are in part unrelated, in part contradictory to his religious, scientific, philosophical, political, national, literary, musical, "feminine," gustatory, occupational, and other meanings, values, and norms.

His ideological culture has also a multitude of unintegrated and contradictory single meanings and "little systems." If he listens to "Information, Please," he picks up a multitude of various unrelated and partly contradictory bits of meanings, values, and norms. He does the same by listening to the radio, reading newspapers and magazines, listening to speeches, sermons, lectures, gossip, talking with others, passing through a vast conglomeration of meanings, values, and norms amidst his family, his kindergarten, his school, his church, his occupational groups, his political and other groups. Throughout his life process he is incessantly exposed to a stream of different, often contradictory and unrelated meanings, values, and norms which he remembers and assimilates, even if he does not want to do so. A short time ago, my radio was on and I heard the advertisement of "Serutan." I did not want to have it in my ideological culture, but, in spite of that, I heard it and assimilated it.

Besides the mentioned "inventions-survivals," the additional reasons for the presence of congeries in the ideological culture of any "mindful" person are three:

(1) Variety, heterogeneity, and partial contradiction of various biological needs of an individual.

(2) Variety and partial contradiction of his sociocultural needs with one another and with biological needs.

(3) Multiple membership in partly contradictory, unibonded, and multibonded groups.

Man's meanings, values, and norms centering around his need of food, various nutritional notions, and food taboos, are very different from his meanings, values, and norms centering around sex. Both are different from those centering around self-protection, shelter, clothing, and other biological needs. The scientific theory of nutrition is very different from the latest architectural theory of building a comfortable house. Both are different from theories of sex physiology or the influence of alcohol upon man's psychology. All these are unrelated to war strategy, and so on. Man has some meanings, values, and norms centered around each and all of these biological needs because he has to satisfy all of these as long as he lives. As a result he possesses many systems and congeries of meanings in each of these fields, and these systems and congeries are only in part consistent with one another; in other parts they are unrelated, now and then contradictory.[4]

Man participates, willingly or unwillingly, in the membership of many groups. Some of these groups are antagonistic to one another and furnish mutually contradictory norms of conduct, values, and meanings to their members. So far as a person belongs to such contradictory groups, he cannot help having "contradictory souls," thus becoming a house divided against itself (see further Chapter 19).

To summarize: We find that our individual has several systems of meanings, values, and norms that within each system are more or less consistent logically or aesthetically. But even within each system, when its meanings and values are analyzed in detail, there will be found some that are either neutral or contradictory congeries. When we analyze the meanings, values, and norms of the different systems he has, we invariably find they are partly consistent, partly indifferent, and now and then quite contradictory. In other words, the totality of the meanings, values, and norms of our individual (his ideological culture) has the following general structure (from the standpoint of their logical and aesthetic consistency).

---

[4] See on this contradiction, Sorokin, *Calamity*, Ch. 3.

Total Ideological Culture of an Individual:

I

Multitude of Ideological Systems
1. Integrated mutually:
   a) subordinated to and
   b) coordinated with one another
2. Unintegrated mutually: logically and aesthetically neutral
3. Contradictory mutually

II

Multitude of Unintegrated and Contradictory Congeries of Single Meanings, Values, and Norms
1. Existing as neutral and contradictory elements within the individual's ideological systems.
2. Existing as unintegrated or contradictory congeries outside his ideological systems.

We can take any individual—past, present or future—and while the concrete forms of his meanings, values, and norms, as systems and as single congeries, may be different from the above, the general structure of his total ideological culture will invariably conform to the above general outline. The only agency that keeps together all this multitude of systems and single congeries is the organism of man (and his superempirical "self," which is not discussed here). But it keeps them together in the same way in which a phonograph plays records as different as is hot jazz from Bach or from Gregorian chants. The tie that binds is not the bond of their mutual logico-aesthetic consistency but the biophysical causal-functional unity of the organism and its nervous system. Man is a veritable *coincidentia oppositorum*. The degree and extent of logico-aesthetic integration of the meanings, values, and norms, of course, fluctuates from person to person.

We arrive at the same conclusions if we consider the problem from the standpoint of varieties of motivations of human actions. If the purposeful motivation is in its essentials a logical motivation, the fundamental motivation of the "because of," the "conditioned," and partly even the normative, have little to do with logical or aesthetic consistency. By their nature, in their meaningful part, they may generate and express very different, mutually neutral, and even contradictory meanings, values, and norms.

b. *The Structure of Behavioral and Material Cultures of Individuals.* We now ask to what extent the overt actions of, and the vehicles used by, an individual correctly and consistently objectify the totality of his meanings, values, and norms? How close is the causal interdependence between these cultures? And finally, to what extent is integrated the total ideological, behavioral, and material culture of an individual in all its three components? The answer to all these questions is as follows.

The "causal" belt uniting the ideological culture of an individual with his over actions and vehicles (his behavioral and material cultures) is imperfect. Therefore not every system or congeries of meanings, values, and norms of an individual is transmitted to, and put into his actions and vehicles. A part of the meanings do not find any expression. Another part of the systems and congeries of meanings, values, and norms finds inadequate articulation and realization in overt behavior and vehicles; these "translate" them defectively and inaccurately. Due to the biological drives, or as we shall see in the next chapter, to the "biological egos" of the individual, his unconscious, subconscious, semi-instinctive, and "conditioned" reflex-actions are, now and then, either contradictory or neutral to the individual's meanings, values, and norms. Likewise some of his actions and vehicles, moved by the motivation of "because of," assume sometimes a form partly neutral and partly contradictory to his ideological meanings, values, and norms.

Consider further that the total ideological culture of a person is only partly integrated and partly not. For all these reasons, *the total overt behavior of a person and the totality of the vehicles used are never completely integrated.* If anything, the behavioral and material cultures of an individual are likely to be integrated less than his ideological culture.

The validity of this generalization is continually corroborated by daily observation and self-observation. All the numerous facts of not practicing what one preaches testify to its validity. We know a multitude of "hypocrites" who practice something partly opposite, partly different, from what they preach. Lying, deceit, insincerity, intentional falsehood, saying what one does not mean, not speaking one's real mind (especially to the bosses), flattery and compliments for the sake of *captatio benevolentiae*, even the bulk of actions of "official" politeness and of "good manners"—all these and many similar actions may be found in the actions of practically every individual. Add to these categories of actions all the numerous actions when, due to biological or other drives, one acts contrary to his meanings, values, and norms. All the honest citizens subscribe to the norms and values of chastity, faithfulness in marriage, a clean sexual life. And yet quite a large portion of these trespass, in their actions, their ideological culture. How many gluttons or alcoholics hold the values and norms of moderation in eating and drinking? How many of them fail to practice it? From time immemorial mankind has extolled the supreme value of peace. In spite of this a just and durable peace is still a mere hope and war is still a stern reality. Almost all of us in our ideological culture are much more generous, altruistic, wise, rational, and noble than in our behavioral and material cultures. Add to these inconsistencies the fact of contradiction between overt actions and real meanings, values, and norms of a person covered up by special "twisting rationalizations," or "derivations," that tend to justify the actions through a special "ideology" contradicting the basic ideology of the person. Their basic norm, "don't kill," "don't lie," or "love your neighbor," is often violated by the actions of killing, mutilating, hurting, ruining, slandering, debasing, and cheating their "neighbors," all in the name of "Humanity," "God," "Proletariat," "Justice," "Progress," "Fatherland."[5]

However, this tells only one side of the true situation. Its other side is that *a part of the ideological culture of an individual invariably finds now adequate, now approximate expression and realization in his actions and vehicles*. In other words, a part of his ideological culture is causally connected with a part of his material and behavioral cultures and in this part all three levels of his culture are consistently and causally integrated. There has hardly ever been an individual who never realized any of his systems and congeries of meanings, values, and norms in any

of his actions and vehicles used. Such an i dividual is a logical, psychological, and soci impossibility. Even an outstanding hypocri and liar is a sincere person in part of h ideology and actions. Even the most errat and inconsistent person expresses adequate some of his ideas and values in his action and material vehicles.

One reason for this is the existence of th purposive motivation in which often, if n always, the actions and vehicles used are pe formed for a realization of the purpose or th value desired. Another reason is the existenc of the normative motivation and the member ship of every individual in an organized grou with its official law. So long as a person is member of an organized group with its code o law, and so long as the normative law convic tions of the person coincide in part with the enforced official law of the group, his action and vehicles express his law convictions values, and norms. Otherwise an organized group becomes impossible; it cannot exist i its members do not practice the meanings, values, and norms for whose realization the group is born and exists. As we shall see further on, when such a minimum of integra tion between the ideological and behavioral cultures fails, the group begins to decline, disorganize, and disintegrate. Almost all aris tocracies entered the phase of a temporary or final decay when their professed noble ideology began to go unpracticed, or practiced in the opposite way, by the actions and material culture of the nobles. So it was with the Eupatridae in Greece, with the patricians in Rome, with the medieval nobility at the end of the Middle Ages, with the aristocracy of the Roman Catholic Church in the period pre ceding the Reformation and then the Counter-Reformation, with the French nobility and Russian nobility before the French and Rus sian Revolutions, and so on.

The facts of coincidence and lack of co incidence are supported also by a systematic analysis of the ideological, behavioral, and material cultures of all the historical persons mentioned in the *Encyclopedia Britannica*, of all the Popes, and of English, Russian, Aus trian, and French monarchs, given in my *Dynamics*.[6] The data of this vast series of

[5] See on this especially V. Pareto's *The Mind and Society*, 4 Vols., *passim*.

[6] See the data and analysis in my *Dynamics*, Vol. III, Ch. 15.

Individual's Total Culture

1. Ideological		Int.			Neutral			C		
2. Behavioral	B	Int.	N	C	Int.	N	C	Int.	N	C	B
3. Material	B	Int.	N	C	Int.	N	C	Int.	N	C	B

Legend:
Int. Integrated, Logically-aesthetically consistent
N Neutral, Unrelated or Unintegrated
C Contradictory

B Purely biological actions and objects used; not followed by mind and consciousness. (Unconscious, subconscious, reflexory, automatic actions and objects used. Not all human actions are conscious and mindful.)

persons show that while in the ideology they differed enormously, some being the adherents of the ideational, others of the idealistic, and others of the sensate ideological cultures, they contrasted much more in these ideologies than in their overt actions and in the vehicles used. Even more, some of the partisans of the ideational ideological culture behaved in a very sensate manner and some of the bearers of sensate ideological culture behaved, to a considerable extent, in an ideational manner. On the other hand, the same data show that, all in all, the partisans of ideational ideology behaved in a more ideational way than the partisans of the sensate ideological culture, and vice versa.

This vast series of data, together with the above reasons, daily observations, and self-observations, confirm the validity of both facts. These facts are essentially similar to the conclusions arrived at in the preceding analysis of the factors of solidarity and antagonism, especially of the factors facilitating and hindering the causal effectiveness of norms and of a realization of these norms in the overt actions and vehicles (see Chapter 6).

These facts mean that practically every individual's total ideological, behavioral, and material culture is partly integrated on all its three levels, partly unintegrated, and partly contradictory. The degree and extent of the in-

tegration naturally fluctuate with different persons and groups. But even the most inconsistent persons have a part of their total culture consistent in all its three components.[7] The whole situation of the meaningful-causal integration, unintegration, and contradiction in the total culture of an individual is depicted by the above scheme.

This diagram shows three levels of the total culture of an individual: meanings, actions, vehicles. We have seen that the totality of the meanings, values, and norms are partly consistent (integrated), partly unintegrated (neutral), partly contradictory. This is shown by the division of this ideological culture into these classes. (The relative length of each class is purely illustrative; it does not pretend to measure the relative amount of the meanings, values, and norms of each class; the amount, as mentioned, fluctuates from person to person.) The second level, the behavioral culture of overt actions, and the third component, the material culture of the vehicles, are shown to be "translating" the integrated, neutral, and contradictory classes of meanings inadequately; only a part of the integrated systems of meanings is adequately "translated" in these components; another part of these integrated meanings is not translated at all (by the neutral actions and vehicles) and the third part of the integrated meanings is "mistranslated" (by

[7] Even most of the patients of mental hospitals. The difference between the mentally normal and abnormal persons is relative, not absolute. All in all the ideological culture of the mentally diseased is less coherent than that of the "normal persons." The same is true of their behavioral culture and of the integration of the ideological with behavioral culture. Finally, the totality of their biological functions and drives gives a less coherent causal

unity than those of the "normal" persons, and these biological drives and functions are less closely related to their ideological, behavioral, and material cultures. Depending on the kind of mental disease, all these "deviations" are quantitatively and qualitatively different with different "mental diseases," but they are all common denominators of the mentally abnormal or normal persons.

the actions and vehicles contradictory to them). The same is true of the unintegrated (neutral) congeries of meanings. In part they are consistently translated into actions and vehicles, find an adequate articulation and realization. Another part of these do not find any manifestation in actions and vehicles. A third part is expressed by actions and vehicles contradictory to these meanings. The same is true of the self-contradictory meanings. A part of these find an expression in actions and

vehicles; another does not find it; the thir part of the self-contradictory meanings i objectified by the actions and vehicles con tradictory to these self-contradictory meanings Finally, the B part of actions and objects mea purely biological actions. As we see the pic ture is complex and far from being as simple as the partisan of man's rationality and of hi nonrationality, of a complete integration o culture and of its complete unintegration, tr to convince us.

II. The Structure of the Total Ideological, Behavioral, and Material Culture of an Organized Group, and of an Area as an Agglomeration of Groups

1. Structure of the Total Culture of an Organized Group

The conclusions reached in regard to the culture of an individual are applicable, with slight variation, to the culture of organized groups. Like the culture of an individual an organized group has its *ideological culture*—the group's official and unofficial Credo, constitution, meanings, values, and norms, ordinarily expressed in its law norms and in its Credo or constitution; its *behavioral culture*—the dutiful and rightful actions of its government and members as these actions are defined in the group's law; and its *material culture*—the totality of the vehicles, including all the property, funds, and means of subsistence of the group. The ideological culture of the Roman Catholic Church is expressed in its Credo, dogmas, canon law, and other meanings, values, and norms of the Church. Its behavioral culture is objectified by all the ritual, actions, and reactions of the members of the Church, beginning with those of the Pope and ending with the actions of a parishioner, the actions and reactions clearly defined by the official and unofficial law of the Church. Its material culture consists of all the funds, property, buildings, objects of religious cult—chalice, cross, and ceremonial vestments. The total culture of the Church consists of all these three cultures. The same can be said of the total culture of any organized group.

If we take the official ideological culture of

a group it always contains, side by side with the integrated part, a small or large part of unintegrated and even contradictory meanings, values, and norms. Among other reasons, a lack of complete integration is due to incessant changes of the group's culture which bring new meanings, values, and norms and make some of the previous values obsolete survivals. The co-existence of the survivals and the new values, given at any moment of the life of the group, makes their partial contradiction and unintegration inevitable, because these factors cannot be at once eliminated. It takes time even for discovery of their contradiction or unrelatedness, and a still longer time to eliminate all the contradictions, hence there is always some contradiction and unintegration in even the ideological culture of a group. Indisputable evidence is that any organized group has in some form a special and perennial organization to decide the incessantly arising contradictions-conflicts in the interpretation of its ideological culture by its various members and outsiders. In Chapter 4 we have seen that some form of judicial authority for a solution of the contradictory ideologies-claims of the members is present in every group. Even more, the judicial authorities are ranked as superior and inferior, with the superior judges deciding the contradictory verdicts of the inferior judges. Not infrequently, even the rulings of the supreme court, when it is made up of several members like the

Supreme Court of the United States, are split by the different interpretations and sometimes contradictory verdicts of its minority and majority judges.

If by the total ideological culture of an organized group we mean the sum-total of all the ideological cultures of all its members, then the ideological culture of the group would contain large amounts of unintegrated and contradictory cultures, side by side with its integrated part. The reason for that is at hand. An individual can have a comparatively consistent system of meanings, say, be a consistent materialist in his philosophy or in his love of gay music. But in the group there may be a member who is a consistent idealist in philosophy and a lover of classical music. The result is that while the philosophical and musical cultures of each member are relatively consistent, the musical and philosophical culture of the group turns out to be unintegrated and contradictory, eclectic and inconsistent, materialist and idealist in philosophy, classical and jazz in music. The same can be said of the total ideological culture of the group.

For similar reasons, the behavioral and material cultures of an organized group are partly integrated with its ideological culture, partly unintegrated, and partly contradictory. In part the group practices what it preaches; in part it does not practice what its ideology professes; in part its practice and material vehicles contradict its ideological culture. One can take any organized group, be it the state, the church, the political party, the occupational union, even the scientific, artistic, educational unibonded and multibonded groups (the family, the caste, the estate, the nation, etc.) and, in the light of the above analysis, one invariably finds in its total culture as well as in each of its levels, integrated, unintegrated, and contradictory parts. There is hardly a single exception to this rule.

2. Structure of the Total Culture of an Area

In the preceding analysis of the social structure of the population of an area we have seen that such a population represents not one society or community but a conglomeration of two or more unibonded and multibonded groups, different from one another, though "located" in the same area. Since the total culture of an individual and of any organized group is partly integrated, partly unintegrated, and partly contradictory, the same picture will inevitably be given by the total ideological and total material cultures, and finally, by the combined total three-leveled culture of the area. The main difference between the total culture of an individual or an organized group, and that of an area, would be that the total culture of an area will contain, as a rule, a still larger proportion of unintegrated and contradictory parts. Since it is made up of the not wholly integrated and different total cultures of two or more groups, it cannot help being less coherent, more eclectic, more of a hodge-podge than even the culture of one organized group. The total culture of even such a small area as that contained in the individual, in a city apartment house, city block, or village, not to mention larger culture areas like the territory of a county, of the whole city, tribe, nation, state, and so on, is always in part a consistent, in part an eclectic, and in part a contradictory mess of various ideologies, actions, and vehicles. This can be seen from a little more detailed analysis of the types of connections between, and of types of unities of, various cultural phenomena found in practically any culture area.

3. Six Forms of Interconnections and Unities of Cultural Phenomena in a Culture Area

In any culture area we find the same six types of connections and unities that were defined in Chapter 7 as the main types of unities generally.

(a) Spatially contiguous and perceptional unities of two or more culture phenomena, united only by their spatial adjacency, for example, *The Saturday Evening Post*, a broken bottle of whisky, and a worn-out shoe lying side by side in a street or on a dump. These phenomena are total logico-aesthetic and causal strangers to each other. In thousands of forms such merely spatially adjacent cultural "bedfellows" are found in practically any culture area, from the smallest to the largest.

(b) Spatially contiguous and mechanically cohesive unities, as a box containing unassembled parts of a radio or automobile, or a scrap book with a page of Plato's *Republic* bound together with a recipe of how to make a mince pie and a picture of a movie star.

(c) Indirect causal-functional objects united by a common external agency: cultural objects gathered together in a study, or cultural objects found on a person—his clothes, hat, letters, money, comb, handkerchief, pencil, cigarettes, and what not in the pockets of his coat. All these cultural objects (with the meanings, values, and norms they objectify) do not have a direct causal-functional interdependence with one another, nor do they logically or aesthetically demand one another; but each of these $A, B, C, D \ldots M$ being causally-meaningfully united with the needs of an individual, the common factor X, are indirectly united with one another not only by the tie of spatial adjacency but also by that of indirect causal-functional relationships.

(d) Direct causal-functional unities, for examples, causal-functional dependence between the social *anomie* and movement of suicide; between depression (in certain conditions) and crimes against property; between war and the change in the rate of divorce or marriage; between a social emergency and growth of the government control and regulation. These unities, again, are given in any culture area in hundreds of different forms.

(e) Pure meaningful, logico-aesthetic unities in the form of small and vast systems of meanings, values, and norms, objectified in the actions and vehicles of the individuals of a given area, are present in any culture area.

(f) Causal-meaningful unities, for examples, an assembled car, meaningfully created, with all parts depending mutually on one another, one part depending upon the whole and the whole depending upon the parts; the cathedral of Chartres; a railroad station with all the rail lines and hundreds of various machines and buildings and warehouses—all causally connected with one another and all created by the purposive activities of the groups; the integrated part of the culture of all the organized groups: church, school, business firm, etc. found in an area.

To illustrate further. If I take such a limited "culture-area" as Harvard Square, its total ideological culture represents a fantastic motley of most different and often contradictory religious ideologies: there are atheists, Catholics, Protestants, Jews, Confucianists, and so on; of political ideologies, because there are Communists, anti-Communists, Republicans and Democrats, Socialists and "Independents," Anarchists and Monarchists. No less heterogeneous are the Square's philosophical, aesthetic, ethical, juridical, economic, scientific, and other ideologies. There are materialists and idealists in philosophy; admirers of Beethoven, Bach, boogie-woogie, and crooning jazz, of Shakespeare, Sophocles, Dante, Gertrude Stein, Steinbeck, and Lillian Smith. A similar eclectic mess is given by other ideologies.

The total behavioral and material cultures of the Square present the most heterogeneous forms of overt actions and reactions, actions and reactions objectifying all the heterogeneous and partly contradictory ideologies described above. The same is true of the material culture of the Square. First we observe the very different buildings of the most widely contrasting architectural styles, from imitative Ionic and Gothic to imitative Renaissance, baroque, Georgian, modern, and Victorian. Second, there are buildings and material objects serving quite different needs, from the subway station, liquor stores, book stores, cafeterias, and garages, to churches, banks, music stores, and so on. On the street one can see lying side by side a broken bottle, a discarded *Boston Globe*, orange peels.

It is obvious that a large part of these heterogeneous and partly contradictory phenomena of ideological, behavioral, and material cultures are united only by their spatial adjacency and by nothing else. A liquor store does not demand as its cause or effect a church or book store or music store or Massachusetts Hall of the University. Only if it were proved that each time when and where a liquor store A is given, the music store B is given; and when the liquor store changes the music store changes, only then their relationship would be causal. Meanwhile we know well that thousands of liquor stores exist without any music store near by; thousands of liquor stores appear, disappear, and change without causing the appearance, disappearance, and change of music stores, and vice versa. This shows that their spatial adjacency at Harvard Square is not causal but purely fortuitous.

Neither are these phenomena united by the

meaningful tie of logical or aesthetic interdependence and consistency. Logically or aesthetically liquor store does not demand music store or church or garage, and vice versa. "Box-type" flat architecture does not demand logically or aesthetically the Gothic or classic or Georgian architecture. If anything, they aesthetically clash with one another. Nor is the *Boston Globe* in a close logical unity with the adjacent orange, bootblack stand, and handkerchief. These and hundreds of other cultural phenomena of the Square are perfect logical and aesthetic strangers to one another, sometimes are even logical and aesthetic enemies. This means that the total culture of Harvard Square contains a large portion of unintegrated and contradictory cultural phenomena devoid of either meaningful or causal ties and bound only by a tie of a perfectly incidental, quite fortuitous spatial adjacency.

Other cultural phenomena of the Square are integrated by causal-meaningful bonds, by causal-meaningful consistency and interdependence. Thus the subway station and many street rails radiating from it, taxicab stands, busses and streetcars, all are parts of one causal-meaningful system of transportation, quite tangibly interdependent upon one another and articulating one set of meanings and values. Likewise the adjacency of University buildings, of book stores, of music stores, of the church buildings, is again causal-meaningful. They are all part and parcel of the complex system of the vehicles of education; all

are the "organs" and instrumentalities of a university education embracing scientific, philosophical, aesthetic, religious and ethical, sport and physical education. As such they are tangibly interdependent and logically and aesthetically consistent.

Finally, if we take such phenomena on the Square, observed during the winter season, as warm overcoats, a party with skis, skis exhibited in some of the stores, trucks unloading coal or heating oil at the houses, street lights burning at much earlier and later hours than in summertime, all these and many other phenomena are united by one factor external to them, by the winter's cold weather and its short daylight.[8]

This short analysis shows that on the very small area of Harvard Square we find indeed all six forms of connections and of "unities" of its cultural phenomena. So far as a mere spatial adjacency and connection through an external factor do not represent either causal or meaningful connection, and so far as the causal-meaningful consistency gives us integrated culture, the total culture of the Square gives us thus portions of contradictory, unintegrated, and integrated cultures.

With some variation the same can be said of the total culture of any area with the possible exception of an area inhabited by two or a very few individuals quite homogeneous with one another. However such culture areas are very few, if indeed there are any at all found in the populated culture areas of this planet.

III. Relationship Between Organized Social Groups and Integrated Cultural Systems

The foregoing analysis shows that an integrated cultural system in each and in all three of its levels, and an organized social group, are not identical unities. *Only in part do they coincide and overlap, namely, insofar as any organized group has a set of meanings, values, and norms as the raison d'être of its existence; and this set must be and usually is integrated in the bulk of its meanings, especially in its law-norms, and in the respective actions and vehicles of the group enforced by it.* Except for this set of meanings, values, and norms,

with their vehicles and obligatory actions and reactions, an organized group and an integrated system of culture (ideological, behavioral, and material) are different unities, having different boundaries, even within the same population. Their difference can be summed up as follows:

Besides its main culture system, the reason

[8] See a more detailed analysis of these four forms of connections between the cultural phenomena of an area in my *Dynamics*, Vol. I, Chps. 1-2; Vol. IV, Ch. 1.

for its existence, each organized group and its members have, as we have seen, not one main ideological, behavioral, material system of culture, but several systems neutral and contradictory to the main system, as well as a multitude of congeries within the systems and outside of them. Some of the multibonded groups, like the family, have a multitude of systems of culture and a veritable encyclopedia of cultural congeries, partly united meaningfully-causally, partly causally, partly through the family needs as their external common agency, partly spatially adjacent. Many systems and congeries have neither direct logico-aesthetic nor direct causal-functional relationship with one another. Unibonded groups like the occupational, religious, scientific, and so on, have a more specific and much less encyclopedic assortment of systems and congeries of meanings, but even these are pluralistic and multitudinous, having several systems and congeries besides their main system.

A given cultural system does not localize and delimit itself within one group, but like an ocean current, washing many shores and islands, spreads over different groups, sometimes an enormous multitude of these. Beginning with the simplest systems of meanings and norms like the table of multiplication, "love your neighbor," the rudiments of science, a belief in God, this or that poetry and fairy tale, this or that language, and ending with many vast cultural systems of science, of idealistic philosophy, of Christianity or Mohammedanism, Beethoven or jazz-crooning, "democratic political system" or "communism, capitalism, fascism," these cultural systems as ideological, behavioral, and material systems of culture spread and root themselves in various occupational, nationality, territorial, economic, political, racial, sex-age groups, in various social orders and classes, the families, tribes, castes, and states. In brief, the same cultural system or congeries of meanings become a part of the total ideological, behavioral, and material culture of very different and extremely numerous groups. The boundaries of diffusion and entrenchment of cultural systems do not coincide with the boundaries of unibonded and multibonded groups. If mapped, they would give very different trajectories. Only the *specific cultural system* that is the reason for

the existence of a given organized group, is somewhat confined within it as an ideological, behavioral, and material cultural system. The cultural system of the Roman Catholic Church is confined within it as an organized social group. The cultural meanings, values, and norms because of and for the sake of which the American Federation of Labor is organized are confined within it. But even this is not quite true and not always true. The ideological system of the Catholic Church is diffused not only among the members of this Church but, as an ideological, cultural system it is known and is present in the minds of many non-Catholics and even of the opponents of the Catholic Church. It is part and parcel of their total ideological culture. The main difference in its existence in the minds of non-Catholics is that they "do not accept it" and especially do not objectify it consistently in their behavioral and material cultures, as the Catholics do. The non-Catholics have and "accept" a different system and now and then objectify this different and sometimes opposite system. *Thus the ideological part of a cultural system specific for a given organized group is not ordinarily confined to it as are the behavioral and material parts of such a system, consistently objectifying the ideological system.*

Furthermore, if two identical or similar cultural systems are invented by different groups independently from one another and these groups are not in interaction, an identical cultural system can generate two organized groups independent from one another. This means that even the coterminality of a given organized group and its specific main cultural system have limitations and exceptions.

The general non-coterminality of organized groups and cultural systems does not exclude some affinity or disaffinity between certain groups and cultural systems. For instance the Communist political and economic system is disaffine to the Association of the Wall Street Bankers. Therefore it diffuses among such a group less successfully than among the poor intellectuals and factory workers. Granting that there are such affinities and disaffinities between certain groups and cultural systems, this fact, plus the confinement of the specific cultural system within the group existing for its realization, do not annul the general rule that organized groups and cultural systems, unorganized groups and cultural congeries are neither identical nor coterminal.

The general reason for the non-coterminality of organized groups and cultural systems is at hand. Any organized group in order to live must have at least a basic elementary scientific system, beginning with the table of multiplication and ending with the A, B, C of physical, chemical, biological, even mental and social knowledge (not necessarily in textbook form) necessary for any group to live, to survive, and to perform its tasks. Likewise any organized group has to have a language which is shared by an enormous number of groups, like the English language. For this reason scientific, language, and other systems are spread, in rudimentary or developed form, among practically all organized groups. In somewhat less degree the same can be said of many other cultural systems.

On the other hand, practically none of the cultural systems, with the exception of the ultimate supersystems taken with all their sub-sub-sub . . . systems, covers the whole realm of inorganic, organic, and superorganic reality and all the needs of the living, thinking, acting individuals and groups. Each of the cultural systems is narrow and specialized and covers only narrow and special needs. Even a scientific system of chemistry or technology, of economics or philosophy, of music or of some applied art, covers only a fraction of the needs of persons and groups.

But in order to live, any individual or member of a group has to deal with many aspects of the reality of the whole manifold universe, has to satisfy not only his religious but also his scientific, aesthetic, ethical, juridical, technical, economic, practical, and bodily needs.

For this simple reason, an individual cannot limit his total ideological or behavioral or material culture to one cultural system. He has to have, in a rude or refined form, most of the main cultural systems: religious and scientific, ethical and juridical, technological and aesthetic, and many practical systems and congeries of how to do this or that, how to satisfy this or that need. Otherwise he will be blind to most of the cosmic, biological, and social universes that surround him, will not know even himself, and cannot satisfy most of his vital needs. Hence the individual's "encyclopedism," the pluralism of his cultural systems and congeries. Hence also the pluralism of the systems and congeries of a social group composed of individuals. In multibonded groups like the family or nation or caste that try to satisfy many needs of their members, it is as inevitable as in an individual. But even in the unibonded groups, side by side with their central culture systems which in groups like the state have to be wide, many-sided and pluralistic also, there always is a need of many accessory neutral and coordinated cultural systems and congeries supplementing the central system.

Neither the state nor occupational group, neither the territorial nor political group can exist and perform their specific functions without language, arithmetic, and the rudiments of other sciences, without any philosophy, ideology, or creed, without any law and ethics, aesthetic and fine arts, and so on. As prerequisites of their specific, main system these systems and congeries must be at the disposal of these groups.

For these reasons, the non-coterminality of the boundaries of the groups and cultural systems is comprehensible.

IV. Critical Remarks on Prevalent Theories of Cultural Integration

In the light of the preceding analysis one can easily see the exceptionally muddled state of the problem of cultural integration in contemporary sociology and social science, and the fallacious character of many prevalent theories.

1. Confused State of Problem of Culture Integration

The terms integration and disintegration of culture are widely used in social science, particularly in sociology and anthropology, but almost always without either any precise meaning or with the wrong meaning. Thus some, like G. Lundberg and N. L. Sims, mix them with the term interaction.[9]

It is evident that such an identification of interaction and integration is erroneous. Interaction may be solidary or antagonistic, organized or unorganized, integrated or unintegrated, on one or all three levels of the culture of the interacting persons, but it is in no way identical to the concepts organized-unorganized, solidary-antagonistic, integrated-unintegrated. One hundred musicians playing each his own music in the small hall certainly interact with one another; but their interaction is neither organized nor integrated, and produces a mere noisy cacophony instead of an integrated system of music. Such authors not only do not define integration satisfactorily, but do not even see the problem or take even the first step in its definition and analysis.

Others use the term "integration" interchangeably with the terms adjustment, adaptation, organization,[10] concentration, coordination, centralization, control, and so on, without clarifying any of these terms.[11] Others mix integration with "solidarity," "approval," "ossifications," and the like,[12] which mixture, especially without a definition of "approval," "ossification," "solidarity," is obviously not permissible. Even when integration is mixed with solidarity as a form of interaction, these two terms and respective phenomena denote two different classes, somewhat related but still neither identical nor coterminal.

Especially surprising is the status of the concept "integration" in so-called "functional anthropology and sociology." For the "functionalists" the integration of culture is the most basic problem and therefore seemingly has to be analyzed and defined in their works. As a matter of fact it is neither analyzed nor defined. One looks in vain for any even remotely clear meaning of "integration of culture" in the works of B. Malinowski and other "functionalists." Malinowski and minor "functionalists" use it incessantly and marvelously succeed in not giving it any definite meaning. Even more, they cover by this term all the six different kinds of unities and connections analyzed above. All these fundamentally different unities they put into one basket of functional-integration. Only through tossing into one hash all these different things is it possible for them to claim that every culture is an integrated unity in which all parts and elements are interdependent and every cultural phenomenon found in the same culture area of either Trobrianders or other primitive groups is integrated with all the other elements. Such a conception of functional "integration" is certainly utterly fallacious in the light of our preceding analysis.[13] B. Malinowski, A. R. Rad-

[9] G. Lundberg, *Foundations of Sociology* (New York, 1939), pp. 290 ff.; N. L. Sims, *The Problem of Social Change* (New York, 1939), pp. 236 ff.

[10] An example of mixing social organization and cultural integration is given by the conception of M. Mead and A. R. Radcliffe-Brown. Even worse, their group organization is mixed with a conglomeration of groups. See M. Mead (ed.) *Cooperation and Competition among Primitive Peoples* (New York, 1937), pp. 467 ff.

[11] Samples of this kind can be found in most of the current textbooks of sociology and in many special monographs and articles. Cf. M. A. Heilperin, "Coördination and Integration in the Realm of Social Sciences"; C. Friedrich, "The Problem of Communication Between Cultures Seen as Integrated Wholes," in *Approaches to National Unity*, ed. by L. Bryson, L. Finkelstein and R. M. MacIver (New York, 1945). The authors cover by the term integration all these and many other meanings, not clarifying any of these terms. Several papers in the same volume suffer from the defect so much that M. Taube is forced to conclude in the process of discussion of these papers: "For some time I

have been interested in the study of what makes any collection of facts an organic unit or intelligible field of study. In all contemporary literature I know of only two discussions which attempt to meet this problem in its most basic forms. These discussions can be found in the works of Sorokin and Toynbee. Both men attempt to define an intelligible field of study, or, if you will, cultural unit." *Ibid.*, p. 705.

[12] See examples in E. Eubank, *The Concepts of Sociology*, pp. 300-301.

[13] This blunder can be found in the works of a large number of functional anthropologists and sociologists. See for instance, B. Malinowski, *A Scientific Theory of Culture, passim*, and pp. 77 ff., 91 ff., 125 ff. His "integration" and "function" now mean a mere spatial adjacency, now "integration" of various cultural phenomena by such external agents as the biological need of reproduction, or of satiation of hunger. This results in the crudest variety of the "instinctivist" interpretation of culture, far clumsier than W. McDougall's instinctivist theory developed in his *Social Psychology*. Now it means a relationship of the means and end, now something near to a causal-func-

cliff-Brown, M. Mead, R. Benedict, partly E. Sapir, R. Dixon, C. Wissler, M. J. Herskovitz[14] and many others are guilty of this fallacy.[15] Their analysis of the concept of integration stops exactly where it has to begin. Slight distinctions which some of them make sometimes, like distinctions between "adhesions," "accidental culture complexes," and "intrinsic associations of cultural phenomena" are mentioned in passing but not developed at all.

Another shortcoming of these theories is a substitution of teleological speculation for causal dependence. Thus, for instance, C. Arensberg and T. Kimball[16] "functionally" explain the relationship between the limited means of subsistence in Ireland and the delayed marriage of the Irish country men. If we accept the tie between the economic and marriage system as causal-functional, then evidently we shall expect that all populations with a scarcity of means of subsistence will show a similar marriage system. Factual data sharply contradict such an expectation. There are hundreds of populations with even greater scarcity of means of subsistence, including land, which have quite different marriage systems. Therefore the relationship of the economic and marriage systems in Ireland cannot be properly styled causal-functional. It is, in fact, mainly the relationship of a unification of economic and marriage systems by a partly common factor external to both; partly the result of many criss-cross efforts of many persons and groups to find a solution; partly, of several possible solutions dictated by the Catholic religion and by many circuitous and incidental factors. In no way is it the relationship of direct causal (functional) dependence. In their valuable monograph Arensberg and

Kimball succumbed in this point to the temptation of finding an easy teleological solution of "means and end" instead of a real causal-functional analysis. They and many other "teleologists" follow the easy solution of the proverbial "birds have wings in order to fly," instead of a scientific solution "birds have wings and therefore they can fly." When we are confronted with the difficult task of analysis of the kind of ties between adjacent cultural phenomena, we are naturally tempted to solve the problem teleologically, inventing some utilitarian explanation of the adjacency according to the schema of means and ends. Almost anything can be easily explained in this way. Even the presence of "vodka," "Volga boat-man," and "samovar" amidst American culture can be easily explained in this way. Many "functional" relationships of the functionalists are in fact nothing but their own teleologically-utilitarian speculations ascribed to the phenomena studied. A scholar should be on guard against this tempting common blunder.

Other scholars seemingly mean by integration something similar to our logico-aesthetic consistency. W. G. Sumner, A. G. Keller, G. P. Murdock, and W. Ogburn say that mores must harmonize with one another because of "a strain toward consistency."[17] Unfortunately they leave the matter at that without any analysis of what kind of consistency? consistency of what with what? what kind of adaptation and of what to what?

To summarize: the prevalent uses of the concept "integration" are indeed highly unsatisfactory. Under the claim of being "scientific," respective "functional" and "integrative" theories represent in fact a hash of the crudest

---

tional unity, and so on. The same mistakes are made by other "functionalists." See W. D. Wallis, Culture and Progress (New York, 1930), pp. 11-12 and Chps. 1, 2; H. Becker, "Culture Case Study," SF XII (1934), p. 32; R. Benedict, Patterns of Culture (Boston, 1934), pp. 46-48; M. Mead, Coming of Age in Samoa (New York, 1928); A. R. Radcliff-Brown, "On the Concept of Functional Social Science," AA, XXXVII (1935), 394-402; M. Mead, Coöperation and Competition, quoted pp. 458 ff.

[14] "No one would deny so obvious a statement that all aspects of a culture are interrelated," M. J. Herskovitz, Acculturation (New York, 1930), p. 21.

[15] Still more recent specimens of this blunder

can be found in several papers published in the volume: R. Linton (ed.), The Science of Man in the World Crisis (New York, 1945).

[16] See C. A. Arensberg and S. T. Kimball, Family and Community in Ireland (Harvard University Press, 1940).

[17] See for instance, A. G. Keller, Societal Evolution (New York, 1931), pp. 246 ff.; G. P. Murdock, "Correlations in . . . Institutions," Studies in the Science of Society, p. 450; W. Ogburn, Social Change (New York, 1921). Much better are the theories of integration of personality and organism in such works as P. Lecky, Self-Consistency (New York, 1945), and K. Goldstein, The Organism (New York, 1939).

metaphysics, mixed with the shreds of biologism, behaviorism, Freudianism, all sprinkled by a poorly understood relationship of means and end, interpreted now as a causal sequence, now as a purposive relationship, now as the relationship of the antecedent and the consequent, now as a mere spatial or time adjacency.

Our concepts of cultural integration, unintegration, and contradiction should not be confused with V. Pareto's "logical" and "non-logical" actions.[18] Pareto's "logical" and "non-logical" actions are very different from my "logical or aesthetically consistent" meanings, actions, and vehicles. In Pareto's use the terms "logical" and "non-logical" are misnomers. The fact of coincidence of the subjective purpose of an action with its objective result (Pareto's "logical action") by itself does not make an act logical or non-logical. The same is true of the discrepancy between the subjective purpose of an action and its objective result (Pareto's "non-logical action"). If I plan to go to New York, and if for a realization of this purpose I choose as a means now the train, now the bus, now an airplane, now a horse and buggy, now a steamer, none of these "means" is either "logical" or "non-logical," logically consistent or inconsistent. Even if I choose such a means-action that would not bring me to New York, such a means-action may be unfit, incapable, ineffective for achieving my purpose, but it is neither "logical" nor "non-logical" because ineffectiveness, unfitness, and incapability are very different notions from those of "logical" and "non-logical," "logically-consistent" and "contradictory," or "neutral." This misuse of the terms "logical" and "non-logical" is the source of many other errors in Pareto's theory.

In contradistinction, the basis of my concepts of integration, unintegration, and con-

tradiction of culture (ideological, behavioral, and material) is logical (or aesthetic, in application to fine arts) consistency or contradiction or unrelatedness of meanings, values, and norms. These criteria can be applied either to propositions or to combinations of meanings (ideological culture). So far as overt actions and vehicles articulate the meanings, they also become either logically consistent, or unrelated, or contradictory. I apply the terms logico-aesthetic consistency, contradiction, and unrelatedness strictly to what they should be applied to: meanings, values, and norms and their articulation in the actions of speech, in other articulating actions and vehicles.[19] I clearly define when, how, and to what extent the pure meaningful integration becomes "causally-functionally" integrated; when and where it is not integrated "causally-functionally"; how much in fact the total ideological and behavioral and material culture of an individual, of a group, of an area is integrated, and what is their general structure from this standpoint.

This analysis of the integration of culture and its criteria seem to be the only possible and valid way. It confirms and somewhat develops further the conclusions reached by other thoughtful investigators of the integration of culture and of cultural unities. H. Danilevsky, O. Spengler, A. Toynbee, A. L. Kroeber and F. S. C. Northrop have taken the criterion of meaningful consistency as the characteristic of a unity or integration of culture. They all find, in terms of A. L. Kroeber, that "all the high-value culture-patterns" are "consistent master patterns" or systems, that when their consistency declines and they become eclectic, they "end in incoherent conflict" and decline as the great achievements of respective persons or groups.[20]

---

[18] See V. Pareto, *Trattato di sociologia generale* (Torino, 1916), Vol. I, pp. 65 ff.; in English translation *The Mind and Society* (New York, 1935), Vol. I, Chps. 1, 2.

[19] For this reason some of my critics, like R. Bierstedt, assert nonsense in contending that logico-aesthetic consistency-contradiction cannot be applied to phenomena of culture. See R. Bierstedt, "The Logico-Meaningful Method of P. A. Sorokin," *ASR*, II (1937), pp. 813-825 and my "Rejoinder," *Ibid.*; see also a toothless criticism by J. H. Randall,

Jr., *Ibid.*, pp. 921-924; also my *Dynamics*, Vol. IV, pp. 12 ff.; 17-32 ff., *passim*.

[20] A. L. Kroeber, *Configurations of Culture Growth* (Berkeley, 1944), pp. 762 ff., *passim*. H. Danilevski, *Rossia i Evropa* (Russia and Europe, *Zaria*, 1869, Nos. 2, 3, pp. 58 ff.) O. Spengler, *The Decline of the West*, Vol. I, Chps. 1-3, *passim*. Unfortunately Danilevski, Spengler, and Toynbee make the mistake of assuming that all the great cultures or civilizations are 100 per cent consistently integrated.

2. Mistaken Theories of Culture Integration of Individual, Group, and Culture Area

The preceding analysis makes invalid several other theories prevalent in the current social science and sociological works. In a brief enumeration, some of these invalid theories are as follows.

(a) All the theories that view man's total ideology either as consistent and rational or wholly inconsistent and non-rational (including irrational) are invalid. Since the most ancient times, passing through the Middle Ages, the Reformation, and the Renaissance up to the present time, such one-sided theories have been widely circulated. Most recently, the theories of Freud and the psychoanalysts, of Pareto, Mannheim, and others, enormously exaggerated the nonrationality, nonlogicality, irrationality and ill-logicality, the nonlogical and nonrational subconscious, unconscious "ideologies," "rationalizations," "derivatives" and "derivations" in the total "ideological culture" of man. On the other hand, the rationalists of all times one-sidedly viewed man's "total ideology" as essentially rational and logical. The truth is in between such extreme views. Man is a creator, bearer and operator of an enormous number of logically and aesthetically consistent systems, even supersystems, and at the same time the creator and agent of many single and intersystem congeries. So also with respect to the total culture of a group of interacting individuals, or of a conglomeration of groups or areas.

(b) Likewise all the theories claiming that man always practices what he preaches, or never practices his ideology, are also one-sided. The causal nexus between man's component of meanings (ideological culture) and those of his overt behavior and vehicles is neither perfect and close nor entirely lacking. In part these cultures are well integrated; in part they remain unintegrated, in part contradictory. As a rule, human beings or a group in part practice what they preach; in part do not practice it; in part man's actions and

vehicles and meanings contradict one another. Here again, man is a *coincidentia oppositorum*.[21]

(c) All the theories of the functional anthropologists and sociologists, historians and philosophers of history—B. Malinowski, Radcliff-Brown, Danilevski, Spengler, Toynbee, and others—that claim a complete logical or causal integration of the total culture of man or of a group are fallacious. There hardly ever has existed a single person or group or area whose total (three-componential) culture has been entirely integrated, either logico-aesthetically, causally, or logico-causally. These theories do not see the unrelated and contradictory congeries.

(d) Likewise all the theories that view the total culture of a person or of a group or of an area as a mere unintegrated congeries, a mere accidental co-existence of single cultural meanings, patterns of behavior and cultural objects, and of their conglomerations and complexes— all such theories are also invalid and one-sided. They are usually preferred by historians, who reduce history to a mere cataloging of contingent, causal, adjacent in time and space, meanings, norms, values, persons, actions, vehicles (material culture), and their combinations and change.[22] Such theories see only congeries and do not see the systems of integrated cultures. The truth lies between these extremes of the "totalitarian integralists or functionalists" and of "the cultural atomists and conglomerationists." We have seen that the total three-componential culture of a person or of a group or of an area have many integrated systems of meanings, actions, and vehicles.

The foregoing analysis and generalized conclusions give a sufficient idea of the integrated, unintegrated, and contradictory cultures of persons and groups, of their main forms and their relationships, and finally, of their difference from the organized-unorganized, the solidary-antagonistic forms and categories. For the present this is sufficient.

---

[21] See on that G. E. Mueller, "What is Man?" *Philosophical Review*, September, 1944, pp. 444-464.

[22] See, for instance, H. Fisher, *History of Europe* (London, 1935), Vol. I, Preface, p. vii. G. von Below, *Soziologie als Lehrfach* (München, 1920);

Sir Charles Oman, *On the Writing of History* (New York, 1939). See a further criticism of the "totalitarian integralists" and of these "cultural accidentalists and atomists" in my *Dynamics*, Vol. IV, pp. 102 ff., 128 ff.

Chapter 19. Sociocultural Structure
of Personality

I. Relationship Between the Social and
Cultural Structures and the Individual's
Self, Mind, and Conduct

After the foregoing analysis of the social and cultural structures of the Superorganic Universe we are prepared to discuss concisely and systematically the relationships of those structures to the individual's mind and conduct.

The first general proposition in this field is as follows: *The social, cultural, and personality structures in a given area of the superorganic universe are three interdependent systems, mutually influencing and reflecting one another.* The social structure of a population is differentiated into groups, some based on one tie and others on many; each group furthermore is subdivided into strata. This total complex is mirrored both in the cultural structure of this population and in the structure of the egos of each member of the group. Likewise, the cultural structure is reflected in the social and personality structures. Finally, the organization of the constellation of egos impresses itself in turn upon the social and cultural structures. All three are interdependent; they are inseparable aspects of the concrete superorganic universe.

The mutual interrelationships of these structures should now be clear. Since individuals are the indispensable components of all social and cultural systems, their personalities (i.e.— the organization of their minds and behavior)

obviously influence the framework of the social and cultural patterns. To this extent Herbert Spencer's thesis, "the character of the aggregate is determined by the character of the units," is correct.[1]

On the other hand, as we have seen, the superorganic aspect of a personality is not determined by or acquired from biological heredity. It is molded by the social and cultural milieu. Man's beliefs, values, and norms, his emotional and volitional expressions and his meaningful actions (but not his purely reflexive and instinctive reactions) are furnished and processed by the social groups with which he interacts. There is no other source for the social and cultural properties of the individual. He has perhaps a margin of selection of these values and meanings, but he can choose and create them only from the material of his social and cultural environment. Even so, the margin of personal creativity is ordinarily fairly narrow, sometimes non-existent. Therefore a *socius*, a person, in contradistinction to a mere biological organism, cannot help becoming a mirror of his sociocultural universe. In this sense the Spencerian thesis must be supplemented by the formula, "The character of the

[1] Spencer, *The Study of Sociology* (London, 1880), p. 48, and Ch. 3, *passim*.

342

individual as a *socius* is determined by the nature of his social and cultural aggregates."

Hence the mutual correspondence of the three aspects of the superorganic: (1) A given individual manifests his social and cultural universe. (2) A culture mirrors its human members and their group organizations. (3) A social structure reflects its component individuals and their cultural patterns. These propositions mean that the quarrel between the partisans of the supremacy of the individual over his society and the champions of the supremacy of society over the individual is meaningless.

The same is true of the parallel controversy between the sociologistic school and the psychological school.[2] Both schools in their extreme forms are one-sided. No sociologistic theory can dispense with the individual because without individuals there can be no group. And no psychological theory can explain the individual if it ignores the fact that social interaction and culture shape the whole personality of the individual. The categories of the *individual*; the *social* and the *cultural* are indeed three inseparable aspects of the same superorganic phenomenon.

This inseparableness is well manifested by (*a*) the concomitant development of the individual mind and the social structure; (*b*) by the close correspondence between the structure of the individual's egos and the structure of the groups to which the individual belongs; (*c*) by the effective determination of the individual's conduct by the groups in which he lives; (*d*) by the general defining of the content of the individual's mind (his scientific, philosophical, religious, ethical, juridical, aesthetic and other values) by the cultural world in which he moves. Let us now briefly substantiate each of these propositions.

II. The Mental Development of an Individual and the Development of Sociocultural Structure

A series of highly important studies of the mental development of the individual have been made by E. De Roberty, E. Durkheim, J. Izoulet, D. Draghicesco, M. Halbwachs, L. Levy-Brühl, F. Paulhan, C. A. Ellwood, C. H. Cooley and others, from the sociological standpoint. The studies of the mental development of the child by W. Preyer, J. M. Baldwin, J. Piaget, G. H. Mead, and others, approach the subject from the psychological standpoint.[3] These works leave no doubt about the close

[2] For a critical discussion of these schools and their representatives, see my *Theories*, Chps. 8-11.

[3] See E. De Roberty, *Sociologie de l'action* (Paris, 1908); E. Durkheim, *The Elementary Forms of Religious Life* (London, 1915); especially D. Draghicesco, *Du rôle de l'individu dans le déterminisme social* (Paris, 1906); J. Izoulet, *La cité moderne* (Paris, 1908); M. Halbwachs, *Les cadres sociaux de la mémoire* (Paris, 1925); L. Levy-Brühl, *Primitive Mentality* (New York, 1923); W. H. R. Rivers, *Psychology and Ethnology* (New York, 1926); P. Radin, *Primitive Man as a Philosopher* (New York, 1936); C. A. Ellwood, *The Psychology of Human Society* (New York, 1925); C. H. Cooley, *Human Nature and Social Order* (New York, 1902); *Social Organization* (New York, 1909); E. Dupreel, *La rapport social* (Paris, 1912); L. Thorndike, *Human Nature and Social Order* (New York, 1940); G. H. Mead, *Mind, Self and Society* (Chicago, 1934); P. Sorokin, *Sociocultural Causality, Space, Time* (Durham,

1943); W. Preyer, *The Development of the Intellect* (New York, 1889); J. M. Baldwin, *Mental Development* (New York, 1895), *The Individual and Society* (New York, 1911), *Social and Ethical Interpretations* (Boston, 1907); J. Piaget, *Moral Judgment of the Child* (London, 1932), *Judgment and Reasoning of the Child* (New York, 1928), *The Child's Conception of the World* (London, 1929); A. Gesell, *Infant and Child in the Culture of Today* (New York, 1938), *How a Baby Grows* (New York, 1945); S. Isaacs, *Intellectual Growth in Young Children* (London, 1930); F. Paulhan, *Les Transformations Sociales des sentiments* (Paris, 1920); K. Levin, *Dynamic Theory of Personality* (New York, 1935); K. Koffka, *The Growth of the Mind* (New York, 1924); E. Westermarck, *The Origin and Development of Moral Ideas* (London, 1906), 2 Vols.; Herbert Spencer, *Principles of Sociology*, 3 Vols. *passim*; L. Hobhouse, *Morals in Evolution* (New York, 1915). A series of detailed experimental studies is listed in my *Theories*, pp. 438 ff.

relationship between individual development and sociocultural organization. They are further reinforced by studies of individuals who have grown up while isolated from human interaction,[4] and by the criminological and psychiatric investigations of mental and moral disorders in their relationship to sociocultural conditions.[5] These studies have demonstrated: (1) Without human interaction the mental development of *homo sapiens* is impossible. (2) Without the interaction of generations of humanity no accumulation of experience or culture can be realized, because thought and cultural values are not biologically transmitted. (3) Without collective experience, no distinction between *true* and *false*, *right* and *wrong*, *normal* and *abnormal* can be made. (4) Without the incessant stimulation of an everchanging sociocultural world, the development of conscious mental life would never have occurred, for man would have sunk into a mental stupor, or, once adjusted to the environment, he would have developed, like other animals, an instinctive mechanism incapable of serious modification. (5) Without a framework of interaction the evolution of such faculties as memory, imagination, analysis, generalization, and synthesis, and the creation of such basic categories as identity, difference, causality, space, time, and number would have been out of the question. Their emergence has occurred only with the development of interaction, of social differentiation, stratification, and integration. More specifically, the appearance of the analytical ability of the human mind is a concomitant of the development of social differentiation. And the growth of the synthesising faculty of man has accompanied the process of integration of social groups and cultural systems. Memory and imagination could occur only within a framework of ceaseless interaction among individuals in differentiated groups.[6] (6) Without interaction, language could not have emerged. Linguistic processes have been closely connected with social change.[7] (7) Finally, without organized and differentiated groups, inventions, the ultimate source of mental and sociocultural evolution, could not occur to any significant extent. Still less could we preserve our inventions. The type of inventions in any given age is determined by the nature of the social structure and the cultural systems.[8]

The investigators of child development have shown that the "ego" of the child, his sensation, perception, memory, language, morality, etc. can grow only in a social milieu. The child's moral and social personality is decisively shaped by this organized, differentiated, and ordered sociocultural universe. If a newly born child is separated from such an environment, and if it survives such a separation, it grows biologically, but it does not grow mentally or morally. As the cases of the "wolf children" show, such "human beings" remain on an animal level of mentality and morality. Even more, when the sociocultural structure and systems of values temporarily become disorganized, as in periods of revolution, wars, and other catastrophes, then the mental and moral life of participants experience disintegration.[9] Crime, mental disorders, and juvenile delinquency invariably flourish in such situations.

---

[4] See the studies of A. Gesell, M. H. Small and others referred to in Chapter 1.

[5] See the literature given in subsequent chapters on revolution and war.

[6] See my *Sociocultural Causality, Space and Time; A Study of Referential Principles of Sociology and Social Science* (Duke University Press, 1943); also C. A. Ellwood, "Culture and Human Society," *SF*, 23 (1944), 6-15; L. Hobhouse, *Mind in Evolution* (London, 1915); *Social Development* (London, 1924); G. Spiller, *The Origin and Nature of Man* (London, 1931).

[7] See A. Pogodin, *Language as a Creation* (Russian, Kharkov, 1913); R. de la Grasserie, *Étude de psychologie et de sociologie linguistique* (Paris, 1909); L. Jordan, "Sprache und Gesellschaft" and K. Vossler, "*Die Grenzen der Sprachsoziologie,*

both in the *Erringerungsgabe Max Weber* (Tübingen, 1921), Vol. I; O. Jespersen, *Language, Its Nature, Development and Origin* (New York, 1925); L. L. Conant, *The Number Concept: Its Origin and Development* (Washington, 1896); E. Sapir, *Language* (New York, 1921); W. I. Thomas, *Primitive Behavior*, Ch. 4; A. S. Woolner, *Languages in History and Politics* (Oxford University Press, 1938); G. C. Schweisinger, *The Social-Ethical Significance of Vocabulary* (New York, 1926).

[8] See my *Dynamics*, Vols. I and II, *passim*; Vol. IV, pp. 234-252; Ch. 7; A. J. Toynbee, *A Study of History* (Oxford Press, 1934-1939), 6 Vols., *passim*. On inventions see also Chapters 35-37.

[9] See my *Calamity* (New York, 1942), *passim.* See in this work Chapters 31-33.

Many studies of the causes of mental disease, especially of various psychoneuroses, have shown that these disorders are due, to a great extent, to sociocultural conditions. In a world where social order and cultural values are unintegrated, psychoneuroses tend to increase with the accompanying disorganization of the personality. This is induced by the complexity and self-contradiction of the respective social and cultural structure, by sudden shocks, by too brusque a passage from one set of social conditions to another.[10]

The evidence given by these studies does not leave any doubt as to the correlation of growth, variation, and decline of social structures and cultural systems on the one hand, and the development and changes of the human personality, on the other hand. They are indeed but two different aspects of sociocultural reality.

III. Pluralism of "Selves" in the Individual as a Reflection of the Pluralism of Groups

1. Biosocial Pluralism of Egos

After these general propositions demonstrating the interdependence of the social, the cultural, and personality, we can now show more precisely the correspondence between the psychological structure of the individual and that of his social milieu. This relationship is so close that the structure of the individual's egos may be considered as a microcosm corresponding to the social macrocosm of the groups to which the individual belongs.

It is commonly believed that the normal individual has a monolithic unity of personality with an indivisible self, one ego. A dualism of different souls in the same individual like that of Dr. Jekyll and Mr. Hyde is admitted, but it is viewed as a purely pathological phenomenon. The belief of some preliterate groups that man has several souls is regarded as a childish superstition. Notwithstanding its popularity, this common opinion appears to me inaccurate and in need of radical revision. Those who hold this view look at the soul of man as the ancient physicists looked at the atom; they view their object as indivisible. In regard to the atom the mistake of the ancients has been corrected; every contemporary physicist knows that atomic unity is a myth, that in fact it is a dynamic constellation of electrons, protons, and neutrons, far from being inseparable and unchangeable. A similar correction is in order with regard to the structure of the empirical ego.

My thesis is that *the individual has not one empirical soul,[11] or self, or ego, but several: first, biological, and second, social egos. The individual has as many different social egos as there are different social groups and strata with which he is connected. These egos are as different from one another as the social groups and strata from which they spring. If some of these groups are antagonistic to each other, then the respective egos that represent these groups in the individual will also be antagonistic.* Such is the first part of my thesis.

Before formulating the second part it is advisable to comment briefly on these proposi-

---

[10] For the influence of war, revolution, famine, pestilence, and other calamities upon man's mental state, see my *Calamity*. In general, see also K. Horney, *The Neurotic Personality of Our Time* (New York, 1937): *Our Inner Conflicts* (New York, 1945); K. Jaspers, *Psychopathologie générale* (Paris, 1928); Sorokin and Zimmerman, *Principles of Rural-Urban Sociology*, Ch. 12; Sorokin, *Mobility*, pp. 515 ff., E. Rüdin, *Über Zusammenhang zwischen Geisteskrankheit und Kultur*, and L. W. Weber, "Läst sich eine Zunähme der Geisteskranken feststellen," both in *Archiv für Rassen- und Gesellschafts Biologie*, 7:704-748. Cf. further Chapter 48 of this work.

[11] Superempirical or transcendental soul is left without discussion: its analysis belongs to religion and metaphysics. See on that self in A. K. Coomaraswamy, "What Is Civilization" in *A Schweitzer's Festschrift* (Cambridge, 1946), pp. 261-274. This superconscious, "egoless soul" is the ultimate agent integrating our biological and conscious egos into unity. It itself is, however, "egoless," being part of the superconscious Godhead. The total structure of personality thus consists of (1) superconscious egoless self, not discussed here; (2) a set of conscious sociocultural egos; (3) a set of conscious biological egos, when a biological drive becomes conscious; (4) a set of unconscious biological drives, reflexes and instincts.

tions. That an individual has a kind of biological ego different from his social egos was known long ago. The ancient views of the conflict between the flesh and the spirit, between carnal temptations and moral duty—the views unanimously held by the great religious and moral leaders—is an explicit recognition of the existence of biological and social selves in a man. In recent decades this dualism of the human being has found an ever-increasing recognition. Freudian psychoanalytic theories, and many other theories as well, hold that there is an unconscious or subconscious ego which is different from, and often hostile to, the conscious and social superego of the individual. However many and great the shortcomings of these theories in other respects, on this basic point they stand on solid ground. One of the best formulations of this dualism of the human soul is that of E. de Roberty[12] and of E. Durkheim. In their works, particularly in Durkheim's study, *Le dualisme de la nature humaine,*[13] it is pointedly stated that "there are two egos in every individual: the biological and social." "Not without reason does man feel himself double: he is dualistic in reality. There really exist two kinds of states of consciousness, antagonistic in their origin, nature, and aims. Some of them express only our biological nature and the objects with which it is immediately tied up. Narrow and strictly individualistic, they bind us to ourselves and we cannot get rid of them, for we cannot free ourselves from our own body. Other states of consciousness, on the other hand, come to us from outside, from society. They are the manifestations of society within the individual and bind us to phenomena beyond the boundaries of our own body. They are impersonal and direct us toward goals common to other people as well as to the self. Only through them is our association with other individuals possible. We are formed of two parts; it is as if we consisted of two beings which, although constantly associated with each other, nevertheless consist of different elements and orient us in opposite directions." The observations and experience of every one

of us repeatedly corroborate this dualism. In the moral sphere it is manifested in the opposition between the egoistic and altruistic wishes and actions; between our carnal and social egos; between the biological temptations and moral and social duty; between the bodily appetites and the social norms inhibiting them: between the flesh and the spirit.

The ascetic who suppresses most of his bodily needs; the soldier who overcomes the biological fear of death and freely sacrifices himself in fulfillment of his duty are examples of persons whose social egos notably triumph over their biological egos. The criminal, the profligate, the glutton, who easily succumb to carnal temptations, are examples of persons with weak social egos easily defeated by their biological selves. In the intellectual sphere the contrast between these egos is equally clear. It manifests itself in the difference between sensations and perceptions which are strictly individualistic and not transferable from one ego to another, and the impersonal and anonymous concepts which are transferable and common to many people, i.e., in the difference between subjective reactions and objective truth, "The old formula *Homo duplex* is thus corroborated by facts." To sum up: the existence in every individual of two different egos—biological and social—is unquestionable.

From this standpoint the theories of De Roberty, Durkheim, and of many others are a step forward from the belief that there is only one indivisible empirical self in every individual. However, they stop short of the goal when they drop the biological ego without further analysis and when they assume that the social ego is one and indivisible. Both conceptions of the biological and the social selves need serious revision. W. James made a further step in his excellent theory of plurality of egos of man: The material me, several social selfs, and spiritual self. The main shortcoming of his sound theory is that he did not closely analyze the relationship between social groups and social "egos."[14] Let us briefly outline the

---

[12] See E. de Roberty, *Sociologie de l'action* (Paris, 1908). This dualism of egos makes the central point of De Roberty's biosocial theory.

[13] *Scientia*, Vol. XV, No. XXXIV, pp. 206-221.

See also Durkheim's *Elementary Forms of Religious Life,* quoted.

[14] W. James, *Principles of Psychology* (New York, 1890), v. I, pp. 294 ff.; *Psychology* (New York, 1892), Ch. 12.

structure of biological and social egos of the person, leaving man's superconscious soul without an analysis.

2. Biological Egos

The prevalent psychoanalytical conceptions of the biological ego are fallacious. Freudian biological "id" as reduced to the libido and instinct of death is phantasmagoric. Better but still incorrect are the conceptions elaborated by C. C. Jung and several other psychoanalysts.[15] The biological ego of an individual is both an unconscious and conscious expression of the biological constitution of the human organism and its physical needs. Latently or consciously it urges us to eat when we are hungry; to do something when we feel physical pain; to satisfy our sex-impulse when it is intensive, and so on. Viewed closely, biological ego is pluralistic in the sense that it consists of several biological needs which now and then are antagonistic to one another. The biological need for food sometimes coincides with the need for preservation of life. But now and then these needs conflict. A soldier prompted by hunger to forage in enemy territory is inhibited by his biological need of life-preservation. The sex-impulse is now solidary with, now antagonistic to, the food need. The same is true of the relationships of all purely biological drives.[16] This means simply that the biological ego is composed of the nutrition-ego, self-protection ego (reflexive running from a dangerous animal, jumping away from a honking car, etc.), sex-ego, and so on. Since these needs now and then clash with each other and give contradictory orders to the organism, they are really separate biological egos, bound together in one organism and constituting in their totality a mosaic-like constellation.

The pluralistic character of the biological ego also appears in the succession of different biological egos in the individual as he progresses from infancy to childhood, then to adolescence, maturity, and old age. Passing from one stage to another, the biological needs of the organism undergo a notable transformation. Some of an infant's bodily needs disappear when he becomes adolescent, and other new ones appear. The biological egos of a child and of a mature organism are essentially different from each other. *This pluralistic and changing character of individual biological egos is generally overlooked by most of the theorizers in the biological field.*

Further, the psychoanalysts ascribe to the biological ego a series of entirely fallacious properties. The Freudian biological id is entirely antisocial; it is depicted as Satan incarnate—cruel, irrational, sexually crazy, destructive. Other psychoanalysts ascribe to it irrationality, aggressiveness, destructiveness, the drive for power, sadism, competitive envy, sexual perversity, hopelessness, Oedipus jealousy and a host of other "regressive" and "recessive" properties.[17] Some, like W. I. Thomas, ascribe to it "four static wishes." Pareto assigns to it six classes of "residues." W. McDougall and others allot diverse sets of instincts to the biological ego.[18]

It is hardly necessary to state that all these bugaboo-paintings of biological ego are mainly degrading fairy tales. As a matter of fact, the biological egos are neither irrational nor rational, neither anti-social nor social. Their relationship to the social egos of a person are much more complex than these theorizers contend. Now and then one or several biological egos may antagonize one or several social egos; sometimes they are mutually solidary. At other times they are neutral to one another. Or a given biological ego may antagonize certain of the social egos, while remaining at the same time quite solidary with other social egos of the same individual. Such is this complex relationship, instead of the utterly one-sided picture suggested by the Freudian "id," almost always antagonistic to conscious ego and social "superego."

---

[15] Cf. S. Freud, *The Ego and the Id* (London, 1927); *Group Psychology and the Analysis of the Ego* (London, 1922); *Civilization and Its Discontent* (London, 1930); C. C. Jung, *Psychological Types* (New York, 1926), and *Psychology of the Unconscious* (New York, 1931); F. Alexander, *Our Age of Unreason* (Philadelphia, 1942); K. Horney, *Our Inner Conflicts* (New York, 1945). See their criticism in I. D. Suttie, *The Origin of Love and Hatred* (London, 1935); Swami Akhilananda, *Hindu Psychology* (New York, 1946), P. Lecky, *op. cit.*

[16] Cf. my *Calamity*, Chps. 3, 5.

[17] Cf. for instance F. Alexander's and Horney's works.

[18] Cf. my criticism of these hypotheses in my *Theories*, Chps. 1, 11.

Occasionally the food or sex ego may urge a hungry person to steal a loaf of bread or to commit the sexual act, thus clashing with the sociocultural egos prohibiting theft and adultery. At other times the biological ego harmonizes with the sociocultural egos of the individual in urging him to eat when he is hungry, to love, kiss, and satisfy his sex appetite, to protect his life when it is in danger. By their nature the biological egos are neither irrational nor rational, neither inherently aggressive nor inherently social. They cannot be said to be intrinsically sadistic or compassionate. All that they tend to do is to satisfy bodily needs. In most cases the social egos sanction and rationally bless such satisfactions of the bodily needs, when they follow socially prescribed means. Only when a biological need urges methods of satisfactions that are tabooed by the social egos does it enter into conflict with them.

To summarize: the biological egos are not a frightful monster, as Freud and other psychoanalysts have depicted. In important ways, they lie at the basis of racial, sex, and age groupings.

3. Social Egos

All individuals, especially those who live in a highly differentiated and stratified society and are members of several social groups, have not one but several social egos, different from, and sometimes contradictory to, one another.

The various egos may appear to be united by means of the integrative functions of the nervous system, by virtue of their incorporation into one body. This superficial semblance of unity is especially impressive when the egos are mutually solidary and harmonious. Nonetheless they remain distinctly different. They may be as different as the music of *Missa Solemnis*, *Old Man River*, *The Blue Danube*, and the *St. Louis Blues*, even though played on the same phonograph—our nervous system and body. The "family self" of an individual contrasts both in mentality and action with his "occupational self"; both these differ from his "religious" and "state-citizenship" selves.

In general, each of us has as many "social egos" as there are social groups to which we belong. Personal experience and daily observation amply corroborate these generalizations.

When we interact with our family we think, feel, and behave like father, mother, sister, brother, son, or daughter. Our ideas, standards, emotions, volitions, as well as our overt actions, are of a certain kind well known to all of us. When we discontinue our interaction with the family, and go to our place of work with our occupational group, our "family ego" disappears and our "occupational self" takes its place. Our conduct is determined by the occupational ego, and there accordingly result the actions of a professor, engineer, doctor, senator, plumber, carpenter, or farmer. The occupational role is quite different from the family role. If one should try to assume his family self in his occupation, he would quickly be fired, to say nothing of being regarded as "queer." When we go to church, the religious self in its psychology and actions is strikingly different from the other selves. The place of "father-mother-brother" or "plumber-professor-doctor" is taken by the self of a Catholic or Protestant or Buddhist. Family or occupational behavior is replaced by kneeling, crossing oneself, praying, singing hymns, and by other religious activities. Similarly, when the religious self is replaced on the "human phonograph" by the state-self, this self appears again quite dissimilar from all the other selves. It pays taxes, sits at trials, obeys government officials, submits itself to penalties, becomes a soldier and unhesitatingly kills the enemies of the state, even though this killing is often strongly disapproved by the religious self of the same individual. As we shall see, such conflicts among the various roles of the individual are fairly common phenomena. Each self is different from all the other selves we have, and this difference comes out in the mentality as well as in the overt actions of the individual. Every individual is like an actor incessantly playing different roles in his life process. The difference between these and those of a theatrical actor lies in the fact that each role of our own self is real, played in life, unlike the make-believe roles of an actor.

Not only are these various selves different, but the stage and co-actors of each self are also dissimilar. Home is the stage of the family self; the office, factory, or laboratory is the stage of the occupational self. The church is the setting of the religious self; Congress, court, jail, battlefield, and governmental bureau, of the state self; stadium, night club, theater, symphony hall, golf links, etc., of the recreational self. Likewise the co-actors of each self are quite heterogeneous. Members of the family are associated with our family role; co-workers, bosses, subordinates, with our occupation role; co-religionists and church officials when the religious self is put into our "phonograph"; and so on. Even the costumes of our various selves are usually different; the family self may show itself in a bathrobe which would be strongly tabooed by our occupational, state, or religious selves, each of which has its own appropriate costume.

Thus *man is indeed a creature of several different empirical roles. Their difference manifests itself introspectively and behavioristically, in man's mentality as well as in his overt actions.* The differences within a single individual may be as great as the dissimilarity between the mythical. "unified" selfs of quite different individual persons.

4. Transformation of Egos

When this is understood it becomes clear that every individual who belongs to different groups daily experiences a series of transformations in his selves. This process consists of a ceaseless replacement of his various selves in his everyday life and activities. The individual indeed resembles a phonograph on which different records are played daily. In the morning when most of us are in the midst of our family, our family self is on the front stage of our personality and we "play the record" of the family self. When we come to our office or place of work the record of the family self is replaced by that of the occupational self. The first role is as different from the second as the record of *Home Sweet Home* is different from that of the *Volga Boatman*. When we are in church on Sundays the record of the religious self replaces all the others, and so on. With each change of the records of various selfs the individual changes in both his internal and external actions. As a result, an objective observer cannot help noticing sharp contrasts in the same individual. Not infrequently they are as great as those between Dr. Jekyll and Mr. Hyde. There is little in common between Robespierre tenderly weeping in his apartment over the sentimental novels of B. de Saint Pierre, and the pitiless, blood-thirsty Robespierre in the Convention, relentlessly demanding the heads of hundreds of persons, even those of his friends. There is little in common between Lenin, overflowing with compassion for a hurt kitten amidst his family and intimate friends, and Lenin as a statesman ordering the extermination of tens of thousands of innocent people. We all know many businessmen, very pious and humanely Christian in church, who are pitiless in their offices, with their cut-throat competition and their stern motto, "business is business." Millions of Christians sincerely profess, "Thou shalt not kill," and "Love thine enemy," when their religious self is in action. Yet the same Christians glorify mass-murder of their enemies and kill them unhesitatingly when they act as the members of their state group. Objectively viewed, these and thousands of other daily transmutations of normal individuals are in fact as great as the transformation of Dr. Jekyll into Mr. Hyde.

5. The Causes of Pluralism

Having established the fact of the plurality of selves in the individual and their incessant change we can ask what is the reason or cause. The answer is at hand. *The diversity of our social roles is due to the fact that we belong to a plurality of organized groups.* Voluntary or involuntary membership in any organized group, whether it is the family, the church, the state, political party, club, or association, quite definitely influences our ideas and beliefs, our values, standards, and emotions, our volitions and overt actions. Each group has its own constitution, its own values, its own norms, with which members must comply. Each of them demands a portion of our time, a portion of our actions, and a portion of our personality. Each imposes upon us certain duties and empowers us sometimes with certain rights. Each has to have its "pound of flesh" from us. Each group puts into us something of itself. One has to have a Catholic ego if he is a member of the Catholic Church. One has to have an occupational self if he is to stay in that occupation. If one does not have the ideas, beliefs, standards, and aspirations required by the group; if he does not discharge the duties imposed by it, or give to it the required portion of his time and energy, then he either terminates his membership or is excluded from the group. In the case of groups wherein one's membership is involuntary, so that exclusion is impossible, the offender is subjected to punishment for violating the constitution of the group. The very structure of the egos of a person, the holy of holies of his personality, is thus a little microcosm that reflects the social macrocosm, the constellation of groups to which he belongs.

These conclusions appear still more significant when we realize that our everyday activities, with the exception of purely physiological activities like sleeping, eating, excreting, and so on, represent nothing but answers to the incessant calls of various groups in which we are embedded. Except for a few physiological actions our whole life is spent in discharge of the duties and functions demanded by groups. Our mornings we spend usually in discharging the activities demanded by our family. Some of us give a few minutes to the duties demanded by our religious group in the form of a prayer or reading the Bible. Then we go to our occupation which takes a lion's portion of our energy and time, several hours each day. During the lunch hour some of us go to a luncheon meeting of our Rotary, scientific, or recreational club. Occupational work ended, we go either to a group of friends, to a political rally, to church, or to some recreational group. In the evening we return to our family and spend within it the rest of the evening and the night. On Sundays we give a part of our time to a religious group. Off and on we perform duties demanded by our state group: pay taxes, function as a member of a jury, go to court and pay the penalty for violating traffic rules. If drafted as a soldier we are obliged to give all our time and energy for several months or years to the state-Leviathan. In this way we spend our day. Of its 24 hours some 14 to 15 hours of our non-sleeping time is spent in answering the calls and pressures of our groups.[19]

And that is not all. Not only is the lion's share of our time and energy spent in responding to the calls of our groups, but each of our responses is definitely patterned by the relevant group. Each group demands from us not just a portion of our time and resources, but it prescribes in detail the qualitative pattern of complying action. One cannot discharge the occupational duties of, say, a professor by behaving like a farmer or a truck driver. If during work hours we are too busy with kneeling and blessing, praying and hymn-singing, we should quickly be fired. If, instead of paying a required tax we were to offer to the state a prayer or a lecture, we would be bound for trouble. Only by paying the tax can we satisfy the state. In this way each group quite definitely molds our behavior, imposes its pattern upon us, and forces us to fulfill it.

Even physiological activities are in fact greatly conditioned by our social groups. Workers on the night shift must work at night instead of sleeping, because such is the demand of their occupational group. Our hours of going to bed and getting up are largely determined by our groups. Sometimes, for instance, on a battlefield, thousands of combatants do not get any sleep at all, or they get only a dismal portion of what is required physiologically. The sort of food we eat, when and how much we eat, again depends upon the totality of our groups, beginning with the O.P.A. Groups may taboo a certain food biologically good for us and prescribe food less nourishing physiologically.[20] In fulfilling the demands of their religious groups, many people fast for days instead of following the physiological demands of our organism. The group constellation through its norms largely determines also the sexual activities of the individual: when, with whom, and under what conditions he may have sexual relationship. Through the totality of controls of the various groups to which the individual belongs, the purely biological spontaneity of such activity

---

[19] See the actual data on how much time and in what kind of activities we spend every 24 hours in P. A. Sorokin and C. Q. Berger, *Time Budgets of Human Behavior* (Harvard University Press, 1939).

[20] See some facts in B. M. Wood, *Foods of the Foreign Born* (Boston, 1922); C. A. Anderson, "Food Rationing and Morale," A.S.R. VIII: 23-33; J. Bennett, H. D. Dickens, "A Study of Food Habits," *Missis. Agr. Exp. Station*, Bull. 245 (1927).

is patterned, greatly limited, sometimes entirely suppressed or perverted.

Not only is behavior of the individual largely determined by his groups, but the content of his mentality is furnished by them also. None of our scientific and religious beliefs, and none of our ethical convictions and artistic tastes is biologically inherited. These are all acquired through and from the groups with which, directly or indirectly, we interact. One's preference for this season's hat or tie, his favorite song or drink, his name, language, convictions, and standards, all these—and these are what constitutes the personality of the individual—are imposed upon him by the groups amidst which he lives. Again, each of these groups has its own soul: a set of ideas, values, norms, and beliefs; and each group tries to inculcate its soul into every member.

These considerations are sufficient to show that we have several different selves, and they indicate the reasons for the pluralism of the empirical egos.

6. Harmonious and Disharmonious Constellations of Egos

From these basic propositions a series of further conclusions follows. First, *if the groups to which a given individual belongs are in a solidary relationship with one another, if they all urge the individual to think, feel, and act in the same way, if they push him toward the same goal and prescribe to him the same duties, then the different egos of the individual which reflect these groups will also be in harmony with one another.* In that case the total ego of the individual will be integrated and unified, free from inner conflict and struggle. The individual will be like a ball pushed by several forces in the same direction—the case of "addition of forces" in mechanics. He will be blessed with peace of mind and by consistency in his conduct. What his rights and duties are, what he shall or shall not do, will be clear to him. No conflict of duties, no inner struggle, no doubt and indecision will worry him. If the family, the state, the church, the occupational group, the political party, and the other groups of the individual issue to him similar commands, for instance, to go and fight the enemy, then all the selves of the person will be unanimously

urging him to do this duty, and he will gladly do it, even sacrificing his life if needed. Happy are the persons who are in this situation. *Only such persons present an integrated and unified personality.* Even though this personality is a mosaic, made up of several component selves, if these components are harmonious with one another, they achieve unity.

If the groups of an individual are in conflict; if they urge him to contradictory actions, duties, thoughts, convictions; if, for instance, the state demands what is disapproved by the church or the family, *then the respective egos will be mutually antagonistic.* The individual will be a house divided against himself, split by the inner conflicts. There will be no peace of mind, no unclouded conscience, no real happiness, no consistency in such an individual. He will be like a ball pushed in opposite directions by several forces—the case of subtraction of forces in mechanics. His conduct will be irresolute and contradictory; so will be his thoughts and utterances. He will be a boat thrown hither and thither by the contrary squalls of antagonistic influences. Like Hamlet he will worry and consume his energy in futile indecision. If the pressure of one group is stronger, then he will follow its orders, but with diminished enthusiasm and power, for the opposition of his other selves will decrease his power of action.

In the past few years the state has demanded from the workers relentless effort in war industries. Their unions now and then have ordered the workers to strike. This objective conflict of the state and the union have generated conflicts within the workers. Their national selves have disapproved what their occupational selves demanded, and vice versa. The result has been hesitant, contradictory conduct. When their national selves prevailed, they did not strike, but were dissatisfied and complained about the state, their employers, factory conditions, and so on. When their occupational selves prevailed, they struck, but without particular enthusiasm or perseverance. Most wartime strikes have quickly ended.

A similar conflict between the national and the religious selves has been generated by the war in thousands of sincere Christians. Jesus' Sermon on the Mount commanded them not to kill but to love their enemies; the belligerent state ordered them to be patriotic and to kill their enemies. In some (for instance, in conscientious objectors), the religious and ethical self prevailed; but their religious enthusiasm has been greatly diminished by the conflict with their patriotic state duty. In others —in the majority of Christians—the national self prevailed, but its impetus has been widely tempered by the doubt and reproach of the religious self, which has led sometimes to unenthusiastic performance of state duties. All sincere Christians who are at the same time good citizens have experienced divided loyalties. Their peace of mind has been profoundly disturbed and their total personality deeply hurt.

We must not think that such split personalities are rare in a population differentiated and stratified into many groups. If not in a sharp, then in a mild form, such inner conflicts are a daily occurrence with most individuals in differentiated societies. In our society there are few individuals who now and then do not undergo a conflict of duties and a clash of loyalties. Sometimes it is only a conflict between two or more meetings of different societies to which we belong; the conflict forces us only to choose which to attend. But there are much more important and painful conflicts between our duties to our family, state, church, occupational group, political party, nationality, friends, and neighbors, which frequently beset us, with all the worries and indecision. When our religious and ethical selves predominate, we are all for the brotherhood and equality of man, and against racial or religious discriminations. But when we are acting as a southern Democrat or as a member of a particular ethnic group, we think, speak and act in the opposite way. Again, acting as a citizen of the nation we profess the duty of universal sacrifice for its well-being; acting as a member of an occupational group we enthusiastically pursue interests contrary to those of the state. We may strike, try to make money at the cost of the state, try to get some special privilege, and so on. Our ethical self proclaims the equal sovereignty of all nations and their right to determine their political regime and policies. But when our national self gets in the saddle, we dictate our commands to weaker nations, interfere in their inner policies, and demand their compliance with our orders on pain of economic, political, or military sanctions. And so this tragic comedy of human inconsistency and self-contradiction goes on. It is not conscious hypocrisy but the unavoidable result of belonging to many different and antagonistic groups. *This explains also why not only the plain citizen but even the most prominent thinkers and leaders display so many contradictions in their speeches, writings, and actions.*[21]

---

[21] V. Pareto demonstrated, in an exaggerated form, the logical inconsistency and self-contradictions of many a prominent thinker: A. Comte and Herbert Spencer, H. Sumner Maine and Hegel, Kant and others (see Pareto's *The Mind and Society*), but he failed to indicate the real cause of such non-logicity. His set of the residues as the source of their non-logicity in no way is the cause of it. Pareto's residues are but a variety of instincts postulated, quite arbitrary, poorly defined, still more poorly classified. They do not explain at all nonlogical actions and speech-reactions. If the residues are constant, as they should be if they are biological residues (sentiments, instincts), then they cannot vary, and therefore cannot explain the changes of human conduct and of human thought. If they are not constant, they are no longer residues. Pareto's operations with the residues are identical with the worst operations of the instinctivists, and amount to a sophisticated kind of animistic procedure. Like primitive animists they first put into man a set of spirits, instincts, residues, four wishes, and so on. Then when they have to account for this or that phenomenon, they pull out a spirit-residue-instinct of war to explain war; of peace, to explain peace; of persistence of aggregates to explain conservatism and stagnation; the residue of combination to explain changes, inventions, machinations; the residue of sex to explain the family and adultery, sexual asceticism and profligacy, polygamy and monogamy, and so on. (See my criticism of such operations in *Theories*, pp. 59-62, 603-617.)

Inadequate also is K. Mannheim's explanation of non-logicity (*Ideology and Utopia*, New York, 1936). He rightly looks for the cause in the group-affiliations of a person; but he does not give any systematic theory of groups or of social mobility. His theory remains vague, and in many respects incorrect.

Meanwhile the real reasons for non-logicity are at hand. They are the nature of one's group affiliations and his cultural affiliations.

When Hegel acts as a member of humanity and a participant in the World Geist, he talks of the world-court as a supreme judge of all states and

7. Some Consequences of Conflicting Groups

In social as well as in individual life, the existence of many conflicting groups generates grave consequences. *It generates an abundance of group egotism, tensions, and clashes, ranging from mild rivalry to riots, revolutions, and wars.* From the end of the Middle Ages to our own time, social differentiation has been increasing, and the common values of different groups, a necessary condition of solidarity, have been shrinking. As a result, competition and conflict between groups, have also been increasing (see further, Chapters 31-33). This is in spite of all the progress in science, education, arts, economic well-being, ethical and religious teachings, etc. In the twentieth century the number of groups, each of which has its own independent system of values, has reached an unprecedented height. Group antagonisms of various kinds have also increased enormously. The international and civil wars of the twentieth century have made it the bloodiest and most turbulent epoch in twenty-five centuries of Graeco-Roman and western history. If not the whole, then at least a considerable part of this increase of group tensions, wars, and revolutions, is due to the factor mentioned. As long as mankind is differentiated into a multitude of various groups whose values are different and not subordinated to a universal set of supreme values, no termination or substantial decrease of wars and revolutions can be expected.

Such a multitude of contradictory values in the individual has many consequences: *it fills him with many inner conflicts and worries; it deprives him of peace of mind, tranquility and happiness; it undermines his mental health and physical vitality; it demoralizes him and may lead him to criminality; it disperses his loyalties and weakens his fulfillment of obligations.* Most psychoneuroses are due not to Freudian fantastic repression of libido or death instinct by the "superego" but to the conflict of various social "egos" with one another and to that of various biological egos with one another, and, finally, to the conflict of some biological with some social egos.

Direct corroboration of this is found in the movement of suicide and mental diseases in western populations during the nineteenth and the twentieth centuries. The growing "parcelizing" of the individual into disharmonious egos is responsible in no small degree for the growth of suicide and mental disease during this period. The improvement of material conditions of the population during this period, the increase of literacy and education, the remarkable progress of medicine and social hygiene, the progress of arts and sciences—all these important factors in human happiness have not been able to restrain the rising level of mental disease and suicide. With minor fluctuations these rates have steadily grown. A happy man does not prefer death to life. If he commits suicide, he is deeply unhappy. If in the west the suicide rate has increased, this means that the proportion of unhappy persons

---

governments. When he speaks as a member of the Prussian State, he makes the Prussian State the supreme and final goal of universal history. When K. Marx speaks in terms of humanity he talks of the movement from unfreedom to freedom, of classless society, and so on. When he functions as a member of the proletarian class, he appears as the ardent ideologist of the dictatorship of the proletariat. When political scientists attribute omnipotency and unlimited sovereignty to the state and then go on to prove "the inalienable rights of man" superior to state sovereignty, they certainly contradict themselves. Their self-contradiction is quite comprehensible: writing about state sovereignty they are the "mouthpieces" of the state group and of their state-self. Insisting on the inalienable rights of the individual, they are the mouthpieces of other selves. Spencer throughout his philosophy contends that societies are organisms and that the higher the biological or social organism, the more integrated it is, and the more "despotic" is the domination of the central nervous system. Such a premise means that the more centralized and despotic the government of society, the higher it is on the ladder of progressive evolution. This conclusion is stated by him, and also by other organicists like P. Lilienfeldt. But the same Spencer in his chapters on militant and industrial types of society, in his *Man Versus the State*, and in the concluding chapters of his *Principles of Sociology*, devoted to socialism and the "coming slavery," sets forth quite opposite claims, i.e., the claims of the individual. There he denounces a centralized regime and pleads for *laissez-faire*. Still more frequently such illogicities occur in the thought and actions of common mortals. Unfortunately how our social affiliations influence our logic and judgments is still but little known. The so-called "sociology of knowledge" has hardly reached a clear formulation of this problem. See R. Merton, "Sociology of Knowledge," in G. Gurvitch, W. E. Moore (ed.) *Twentieth-Century Sociology* (New York, 1945).

has grown. These data directly corroborate our conclusions.

Conflicts of the souls contribute to deterioration of the physical health of the person. They may not affect children and young persons, since their group affiliations are in a fluid state, still limited to the relatively non-conflicting groups—the family, the school, and the neighborhood. Because of their limited group affiliations, they have not yet acquired a number of conflicting egos. Only mature persons experience fully this gnawing process. This explains why the life expectancy of children and younger age groups has increased with the improvement of material conditions, with the progress of medical science and social hygiene, while the life expectancy of the advanced age groups has not shown a corresponding increase. Roughly speaking, the age-specific mortality rates of over 45 are about the same as they were thirty, or forty, or fifty years ago. One of the reasons for this is the prevalence of inner conflicts. These conflicts seemingly annul the beneficial effects of better material conditions, better medical care, and other material factors.

Still more tangible are the demoralizing and criminalizing effects. When a person is placed under a barrage of mutually contradicting norms of conduct; when one group teaches him that property or the marriage vow is sacred while the other group tells him that property is theft and the marriage vow a bourgeois prejudice; then he can scarcely believe that any value is sacred, and any norm unconditionally binding. By such a person all values are apt to be regarded as something relative, as mere conventions that can be broken if the drives of the biological egos so urge. Therefore in such a society an ever-increasing number of persons will violate its ethical and legal standards. Attitudes of extreme ethical relativity, cynicism and amorality, would spread ever more widely under these conditions. The conduct of such a population would be determined increasingly by the biological drives, and by force and fraud.

That is exactly what is happening in western society. In spite of the improvement in material conditions and other moral forces, criminality in western society has not decreased for the last century. If anything, it has tangibly increased. Cynicism too has been spreading. Finally, in this war, all human and divine laws have been violated on a mass scale by all governments. The demoralization has become extreme, and the role of brute force paramount.

In like manner the individual's loyalty to his freely contracted obligations has been shaken. Like an investor who puts his money into too many banks, an individual attached to too many different groups is only slightly loyal to all, and not unconditionally loyal to any. As a result, his sense of loyalty weakens, the boundary line between loyalty and disloyalty tends to vanish, and biological expediency becomes paramount. The rising rate of divorces and desertions proves this in regard to marriage. The wholesale violation of international treaties by practically all governments during the last few decades manifests it on an international scale. Our age may truly be called the age of double-crossing, small and large, individual and collective, national and international.

To summarize: these and many other phenomena we consider undesirable are due, in large measure, to the enormous social differentiation and stratification of human populations into a mass of unintegrated and often conflicting groups, and to the counterpart of this process in the individual, the multitude of different and often mutually antagonistic souls in the individual who belongs to these groups.

As long as such a situation continues, none of these undesirable effects can be abolished. For certain individuals there may be a partial remedy. He can sever his affiliation with all the groups which are contradictory to the groups whose membership he cherishes most. In this way he can extricate himself, to a certain extent, from perpetual antagonism. However, this remedy is limited; an individual cannot terminate his membership in certain groups. In many of them his membership is obligatory and does not depend upon his wishes. For instance, in most states citizenship does not depend upon the individual. This remedy must often fail to solve the problem.

The adequate remedy for the individual as well as for the society consists in *such a rearrangement of the groups that their open antagonism is eliminated*, that they do not press mutually contradictory commands upon the individual, nor force him to conflicting actions. The groups and their orders can be diverse, but as long as their mutual relationship is not antagonistic, the individual can be free from internal conflict and attain unity in diversity.

This perhaps explains why such a rearrangement of social groups is the paramount task of our time. Their values, norms and activities may remain diverse, but they must be freed from mutually antagonistic elements. This can be done only when *all groups subjugate their values to a set of universal norms, or make them concordant.* The essence of these norms for intergroup and interindividual relations has been sublimely formulated in the Sermon on the Mount, and in the Golden Rule. If all groups and their members, no matter how diverse they are, would follow in their ideology and in their activities, these norms, the human world could achieve real unity in diversity, and the individual could integrate his personality. Short of such a reorganization, nothing can help—neither the solemnly contracted Charter of the United Nations, nor increased material prosperity, nor multiplication of schools, nor atomic bombs. Humanity will remain a house divided against itself, suffocating in its intergroup hatred, destroying itself and its culture with the help of its scientific inventions. And the individual will remain an unhappy, tortured, self-contradictory creature, semi-insane and semi-criminal.

IV. The Cultural Content of the Souls of the Individual as a Reflection of the Cultures of His Groups and of Additional Factors

The position of an individual in stratified groups accounts for the complex structure of his egos and for the harmony or disharmony of the component elements of his personality. *The group's ideology, behavioral patterns, and material traits also account for the greater part of the cultural content of the individual mind.* As Charles Blondel rightly says: "The individual does not invent his religion, his morals, his laws, his aesthetics, his language, or the patterns of his everyday behavior with his equals, superiors, and inferiors, his manner of eating, . . . and finally his thought or his conduct. All this he receives ready-made —thanks to education, instruction, and language—from the society of which he is part."[22] For instance, when the religious culture of the group is a set of animistic or totemic beliefs and practices, the individual's religious orientation will also be animistic and totemic. If his religious group is Christian or Buddhist, his religious ego will also be Christian or Buddhist. The same can be said of all the other aspects of the individual personality. The reasons have already been explained. Since the scientific, religious, ethical and other ideas, beliefs, and values are not biologically inherited, the individual acquires these mainly from the groups with which he interacts. Each organized group is organized around a certain set of norms, and each group leaves its impress upon its members. As long as the individual belongs to a group, he must adopt its culture to some extent or his position will become untenable.

Factually, the groups of any society in a particular epoch ordinarily have a common fund of cultural values, such as the elementary practical knowledge necessary for survival, a common language and modes of thought, and an underlying system of culture. Besides this common base, each group has its own specific culture. These cultures are not only diverse, but now and then contradictory. The culture of the individual's economic associations may conflict with the culture of his religious affiliations. The result is that the cultural elements

---

[22] *Journal de psychologie*, 1925, p. 333. Cf. also Charles Blondel, *La conscience morbide* (Paris, 1928) and *Introduction à la psychologie collective* (Paris, 1930).

of an individual are partly consistent, partly antagonistic, and partly indifferent to each other.

In the preceding section I said "the major part" of the individual's culture is determined by the culture of his groups. This means that a lesser portion of the individual's cultural mentality consists of cultural meanings not acquired from organized groups, but from other sources. The latter may include living and dead personalities like Plato or Beethoven, long deceased yet still bearers of great culture. Or they may include cultural elements which the individual contacts as a tourist in a foreign country, or as a visitor at archaeological excavations of ancient civilizations, or as a reader of books. There are hundreds of other ways in which elements of alien cultural systems may enter into our own.

Finally, the individual's culture depends upon *his selectivity and creativity*. No individual can absorb all the cultural elements of his milieu. In one way or another he must select some and reject the rest. This explains why the personalities of members of the same groups are never identical. In secondary points, at least, they differ from one another.

No one is entirely passive. Every person selects, combines, and sometimes even creates,

and he is to that extent an active agent in the social process. True geniuses display great creativity. Out of the existing cultural values they combine something conspicuously different. Most of us display but little genuine creativity, but nonetheless through our selection we function also as active agents. People are not passive *tabulae rasae*, on which society writes its cultural teachings. Whether their selection and creativity depend upon biological constitution or upon something much more subtle and intangible which we can designate as the transcendental soul or as the "creative X" (which hypothesis appears to be reasonable), this problem remains open. What is fairly certain is the importance of the social role of this X-factor.[23]

The factors discussed above adequately account for the essential elements in the personality structure of individuals and for the cultural content of each personality.[24] Only the purely biological properties of the human organism are not accounted for by these factors. But even biological properties are influenced by social factors. Purely biological properties belong to the field of the biological science, and are thus outside of the field of sociology and social science[25] (see further, Chapter 48).

---

[23] It can be called by J. L. Moreno's term, "spontaneity-creativity." See his constructive papers in *Sociometry*, Vols. VII and VIII. Or it may be called "creative intuition," as I and many others have named it. See the bibliography and analysis in my *Dynamics*, Vol. IV, Ch. 16. Plato's "divine madness," *eros*, and "creative mind" are other terms. Cf. A. K. Coomaraswamy's *What Is Civilization*, quoted. Whatever the name, its essence consists in selecting, combining, and creating activity. Its biological counterpart as yet is not found. See further, Chapter 35.

[24] This is more valid and more precise than many other recent formulas of the structure of personality. A pretentious formula is attempted by A. Kardiner and R. Linton. A slight test of the theory shows it is not only not new, but also not clear. It is a vague variation of a very old theme "pilfered" from sociologists (as H. Ozanne rightly remarks). "Structure" and "basic personality" are both undefined. The underlying concepts of institution, group, primary institutions, projective systems all lack clarity, systematic analysis, and elementary corroborating evidence. Other details, like the internal and external ways of resolving tensions, are but a reiteration of my ideational and sensate modes of adjustment. See my *Dynamics*, Vol. I, pp. 66-101, and all four volumes, *passim*.

Cf. A. Kardiner, *The Individual and His Society* (New York, 1939); Kardiner, R. Linton and others, *The Psychological Frontiers of Society* (New York, 1945). See also A. Kardiner's "The Concept of Basic Personality Structure" in R. Linton's (ed.) *The Science of Man in the World Crisis* (New York, 1945). See a good criticism of the theory in H. Ozanne, "Synthesis in Social Science," *Sociometry*, VIII: 208-215, 1945.

[25] We have several classifications of biopsychological types of personality: C. G. Jung's introvert and extrovert; E. Kretschmer's schizothymic and cyclothymic types; L. Klage's "reactability" types; V. Pareto's *rentieri* and *speculatori* types; E. Spranger's theoretical, economic, aesthetic, social, power, and religious ideal types. More complex varieties of personality types are constructed upon the basis of various measurements of biological traits (W. H. Sheldon, E. Hooton), or on the basis of some kind of semi-mechanical tests (H. Rorschach, E. R. Jaensch, G. Ewald, K. Kasper, A. Kronfeld and others). All these types of biopsychological constitutions still remain mainly in the stage of conjectures, and they are far from being proven. Three points are especially questionable in all these typologies. First, to what extent are the differences between the types purely biological? Second, are certain biological traits causally connected with

V. Social and Cultural Position
of an Individual in the Sociocultural World

The very social position of an individual in the sociocultural universe is determined by the totality of the groups and strata to which he belongs. His cultural position is defined by the cultural content of his groups, and by that borrowed from strangers and foreign groups and by the influence of his own selective and creative powers.

In order to precisely determine the *social* position of an individual we must know: (1) the groups of which the individual has been a member; (2) the exact stratum he occupied in each group; (3) the place of each group in the human population. When we know all this, we know all that is essential about the individual as a *socius*. His social position is determined clearly and precisely. For example, Mr. *X* (sex group) comes from the eminent family *X* (family, kinship groups); he is 45 years old (age group), a citizen of the United States (state group), and Secretary of State in the American Cabinet (occupational group and stratum). He is wealthy (economic group), Episcopalian (religious group), Republican (political party), of Dutch stock (ethnic group), married, and has two children (his own family status). He is a trustee of such and such corporations, universities, and museums. He is an honorary member of such and such societies, likes classical music, has certain hobbies (recreational groups). This gives us a fairly definite idea of Mr. *X*'s social position. The complete enumeration of all groups and subgroups to which he belongs will also tell us a great deal about his personal characteristics, his ideas and beliefs, tastes, character, and emotional make-up. There remains little to be known about him as a type of human personality.

This method of fixing the social position of an individual is the only definite one that exists. A mere enumeration of physical or purely psychological characteristics of an individual (his weight, height, emotional traits) does not define his social position at all. Without showing the individual's groups, we cannot determine either his social position or his important personal and behavioral characteristics.[26]

Thus systematically applying the theory of

---

certain psychological and social characteristics of personality? Third, what exactly do various mechanical tests like Rorschach's really measure? One can state with reasonable certainty that some of the purely biological characteristics are really biosocial. Most connections between biological and psychosocial traits of personality are not proven. Finally, the Rorschach and similar tests are now at the stage of the intelligence tests when the latter were first introduced. Enthusiastic partisans of mental tests once firmly believed they were testing native intelligence precisely and accurately. Now this belief has evaporated. Rorschach's test is, if anything, still less reliable. The whole matter is in a state of misty conjecture. Of all these types Jung's "introvert" and "extrovert" types are possibly the most significant. But even these types are far from being purely biological types; they are certainly molded, to a considerable extent, by the sociocultural universe of the individual. When they are reformulated along these lines we arrive at ideational, sensate, and intermediary types of human personality. See my *Dynamics*, Vol. I, Ch. 2, and Vol. III, Ch. 15. Cf. further Chapter 42 in the present work. A good survey of various theories is H. Klüver, "Problem of Types," *Journal of Philosophy*, XXII: 225-234; Klüver, "An Analysis of

Recent Works on the Problem of Psychological Types," *Journal of Nervous and Mental Disease*, LXII: 561-596. C. G. Jung, *Psychological Types* (New York, 1923); L. Klages, *Principien der Caracterologie* (Leipzig, 1920); E. Kretschmer, *Körperbau und Character* (Berlin, 1922); E. Spranger, *Lebensformen* (Halle, 1922); E. Hooton, *The American Criminal* (Cambridge, 1939); *Crime and the Man* (Cambridge, 1939); E. Keiter, *Rasse und Kultur* (Stuttgart, 1938). An uncritical account of the Rorschach test is given in A. I. Hallowell, "The Rorschach Technique in the Study of Personality and Culture," *AA*, Vol. XXXVII, pp. 195-210. Cf. also H. T. Moore, "Innate Factors in Radicalism and Conservatism," *Journal of Abnormal and Social Psychology*, Vol. XX, pp. 234-244; W. H. Sheldon, S. S. Stivens, W. B. Tucker, *The Varieties of Human Physique* (New York, 1940); P. M. Symonds, *Diagnosing Personality and Conduct* (New York, 1931); M. A. Murray, *et al.*, *Explorations in Personality* (Oxford University Press, 1938); G. Allport, *Personality* (New York, 1937).

[26] An additional corroboration of this is the failure of a very complicated technique used by Warner and Lunt. In their first work on Yankee City they artificially ranked the population into six

the structure of the sociocultural aspects of the superorganic, we have been able to lay down a roughly adequate, consistent, and

factually valid theory of personality structure and of personality position in the sociocultural universe.

(nominal) classes. In the process of their study they discovered that "the members of the same class behave differently." (Since the classes are artificial, what else can be expected?) To remedy the situation, they took 357 associations of the city and ranked them in 19 strata. Artificially distributing these 19 strata in the lateral extension of each of the six classes, they obtained 54 still more artificial positions. Not satisfied with these artificial "cubes" sliced out of the social structure of the Yankee City and turned into mince-pie, they divided all the families of the Yankee City into twenty-four classes and then converted them into fifty positions. Next they took all "cliques" of the city and grouped them into thirty-one stratified classes. Mixing the six classes, nineteen associational strata, twenty-four family, and fifty clique strata, they obtained, in a somewhat mysterious way not entirely clear to the reader, 89 positions. Having obtained finally these 89 "cuts" of their "mince-pie" they very laboriously proceeded to describe 89 positions as

behavioral situations. Need one add that none of these positions conveys more meaning than that of a number in the tables? There is no real portrait of any of these behavioral situations. No wonder that the actual results of the study, so far as it deals with the real social structure of Yankee City, are almost nil, in spite of the commendable industry and scientific aspirations of the authors and their field workers.

The method formulated and used in my Russian *Sistema soziologii* (1920) is infinitely less cumbersome and more precise than this complicated mincing of living social structures into artificial statistical pulp, then cutting and slicing the pulp into arbitrary cubes, then laboriously enumerating these cubes, and painfully filling tables with those numbers. I am all for mince-pie on Thanksgiving day, but I am decidedly against it in the study of living organisms and living social structures. See W. L. Warner and P. S. Lunt, *The Status System of a Modern Community*, quoted, Part One, *passim*

Chapter 20. The Structure
of Sociocultural Space[1]

1. Impossibility of Locating Sociocultural Phenomena in Geometric Space

Whatever variety of existing theory about geometric space is taken, be it Euclidean, Lobatchevsky's, Riemann's, Minkovski-Einstein's, or the "n-dimensional" notion of G. Cantor, it cannot be used to locate sociocultural phenomena, nor their spatial relationship to one another. It is enough just to ask: Where is Beethoven's *Missa Solemnis*? a table of multiplication? Shakespeare's *Hamlet*? or the Ten Commandments? to see that they cannot be located in geometric space. They are here and there, everywhere and nowhere in that space. No specification of their latitude, longitude, and altitude can be made or can determine their position in geometric space.

The same is true of the social and cultural *position* of an individual or group; geometric space does not and cannot define it. It is enough to ask: What is my social position? What is the social position of Stalin or Truman? of the Zionist group? or of the Caste of the Brahmins? Where do I stand in regard to slavery or war, to Communism or Buddhism? in order to make this clear. The most meticulous geometric or geographic map cannot answer these questions. These and other sociocultural phenomena simply slip through the meshes of any conception of geometric space.

The identical statements must be made in regard to *social or cultural change, displacement, and change of the position of superorganic objects, persons, and groups in the sociocultural universe*. None of such changes can adequately be defined in terms of the vector-system of geometric space. When President Roosevelt moves in geometric space from Washington to Teheran he does not change his social position, as the President of the United States, at all, and vice versa. Although kings like Louis XVI, Nicholas II, Alfonso of Spain, remained in the same palace, their social position was enormously changed, from all-powerful king to that of a prisoner. The Nazi Swastika remains at the same place in geometric space but its position in the sociocultural universe has changed enormously since the victory of the Allies.

Likewise, when we talk of *social movements, social stagnation, social promotion and demotion, social climbing and sinking, overthrow of a political regime, social rapprochement and social separation, close friendship and social remoteness, social distance*, and so on, we do not mean by these terms something connected with geometric space. The reason is that pure meanings, values, and norms are geometrically spaceless. The category of geometric space is simply inapplicable to them. For the same reason, all objectified socio-

[1] For a systematic analysis of this problem and the literature, see my *Sociocultural Causality, Space, Time* (Duke University Press, 1943), Ch. 3. Also M. Lins, *"La transformación de los valores y objectos en el campo de socialificación de los sistemas sociales,"* and "La tipicidad de las relaciones sociales," *Revista Mexicana de Sociologia,* Vols. V, VI.

cultural phenomena are geometrically space-less, their component of meanings, values, and norms rendering them indefinable and inde-terminate in geometric space. Their material vehicles—this machinery, church building, uni-versity dormitory—are certainly located in geometric space; but by locating these vehicles in geometric space, we do not locate them in the sociocultural universe. The building which houses a church may remain unchanged and in the same geometric place, and yet its position in the superorganic universe shifts enormously when it is transformed into a Communist Club or a warehouse. To sum up: geometric space does not locate sociocultural phenomena or their "spatial relationship," *i.e.*, distance, close-ness, remoteness, and so on.

2. Location of Sociocultural Phenomena in Sociocultural Space

Since a sociocultural phenomenon consists of three components, sociocultural space must be able to locate each of these components as well as that of the total sociocultural phenom-enon in the superorganic universe. The deter-mination of the position and positional rela-tionship must be not merely formal but essential, giving us a knowledge of the nature of the position and of the properties of the relationship. Hence:

(a) The position of a meaning, value, or norm is defined when the place of the given meaning, value, or norm in the universe of meanings, values, and norms is determined.

(b) The place of the vehicle is determined when it is located in the universe of vehicles.

(c) The sociocultural position of a person or of a group is determined when the in-dividual or the group is located in the uni-verse of persons or groups.

(d) When all these components of a given superorganic phenomenon are defined, the total phenomenon's position in the superorganic universe is defined.

Thus the table of multiplication as pure meaning is located in the system of mathe-matics; the Newtonian law of gravitation, in physics; Bach's *Mass in B Minor* in the "field of music"; the Christian *Credo* in that of Chris-tian religion; the *Corpus Juris Civilis* in the field of law, more specifically of the Roman

law, and so on. If we want to specify the posi-tion of any of these meanings still more pre-cisely, we can easily do that through the further specification of exactly the kind of mathematics or physics or music or law or religion to which it belongs. Through deter-mination of the field or system of meanings to which a given meaning belongs and through "location" of this field of meanings in the total universe of meanings, we precisely define the position and positional relationship of any meaning in the universe of meanings.

If we point out the main systems of mean-ings, values, and norms in the universe of meanings and then the main supersystems of these, these main systems and supersystems serve as the chief coordinates or vector system that define the position of meanings in the universe of meanings. *If for instance, we take a manifold of the main systems of meanings such as language, science, philosophy, religion, fine arts, ethics, law, technology, main uni-bonded and multibonded groups, this ten-dimensional manifold permits us, fairly exactly, to locate any meaning, value, or norm in its proper universe.* Dividing each of these ten dimensions into their sub-sub-sub-classes, for instance, science into mathematics, astronomy, physics, chemistry, biology, sociology, psy-chology, and each of these into their sub-classes and concrete derivative scientific dis-ciplines like history, geology, etc., we can define the position of any scientific meaning quite clearly and precisely. The same is true of other dimensions, including the classification of the main unibonded and multibonded groups. If in addition we have a supersystem of meanings of any great heuristic value, like the sensate, idealistic, and ideational super-systems of meanings, these supersystems per-mit a short-cut to the location of any meaning, value, or norm.

In order to define the sociocultural position of an individual or group, we must determine: (a) all the groups, and the exact stratum in each group, to which the person has belonged; (b) the cultural content of "each soul" in the individual, in terms of the ten-dimensional manifold. As we have seen above (Chapter 17), the groups and the strata to which the individual belongs define precisely his social position. The cultural content of the individual: his language, religion, philosophy, science, fine arts, ethics, and law definitely circumscribe his cultural position. *When the position of a person is determined on each of the ten coordinates of our manifold or vector system (with the sub-sub-classes of each coordinate), his or her total position in the sociocultural universe is quite precisely defined.* The same is true of a group.

The same procedure and ten-dimensional system of coordinates determine the position of the vehicles in the superorganic universe. Thus, church building, cross, chalice, statue of St. Mary fall into the field of Christian religion. Court building, jail, volume of criminal law are the vehicles of law. Plow, fertilizer, threshing machine, cow, are the vehicles of the science and technology of agriculture, and so on. The sociocultural position of any vehicle is determined through reference to the system of meanings it objectifies. Finding its place in the system of meanings in the above ten-dimensional vector-system, we find the position of the vehicle in the sociocultural universe.

The physical location of the vehicle in geometric space—*the ecology of vehicles*—can be determined, it is true, through the referential system of geometric space with its latitude, longitude, and altitude or other dimensions. However, such an ecological location of vehicles in geometric space becomes possible only after they are located in the sociocultural universe. Otherwise they remain mere physical or chemical or biological objects whose sociocultural nature and position remain unknown and undetermined.[2]

The above gives an idea of how meanings, vehicles, human agents and any three-componential sociocultural phenomenon is located in sociocultural space, and what such a location means. Instead of the above ten-dimensional vector system another, more detailed or simpler, can be used. The complexity or simplicity depends simply upon the degree of precision with which we want to locate a given sociocultural phenomenon in its position and positional relationship. Whether we use a ten-dimensional or twenty-dimensional vector system, it will have to be similar to the above vector system in that *its dimensions will have to be the main cultural systems and social groups.* There is no other vector system that can catch and locate social and cultural phenomena. The number of the cultural systems

---

[2] Properly understood, sociocultural ecology or geography is nothing but a study of the location, distribution, succession, displacement, and migration of vehicles and human beings as they are reflected on the screen of geometrical space, on the territory of this planet. Such a study is necessary for a full knowledge of the location of the sociocultural phenomena in the sociocultural and geometric space. Studying "crime" or religion or war or a certain art-style, we need to locate not only their members and vehicles in the sociocultural universe but also where, on the territory of our planet, these vehicles and human agents are located, what their frequency is and what their territorial expansion, succession, and migration from place to place are in geometric space. This task can be achieved, however, only if we study the respective vehicles and human members as the components of the respective sociocultural phenomenon and only after having located them in the sociocultural universe. This is necessary for the ecology of any sociocultural phenomenon, be it crime, religion, science, revolution, poverty, genius. The main defect of the existing ecological theories is their vacillating standpoint: They study the ecology of vehicles and human agents partly as sociocultural phenomena and partly as pure physiochemical or biological objects. Such a mixture of ecology of physical phenomena with that of sociocultural phenomena is responsible for many blunders of the existing ecological theories.

Sociocultural ecology gives us some additional knowledge of the phenomenon studied, but this knowledge is limited and of secondary importance. It is limited because the reflection of the position and change of sociocultural phenomena on the screen of geometric space is always imperfect and inadequate. Many changes of the sociocultural position of a given person or phenomenon are not reflected at all on the screen of the geometric space (the territory). On the other hand, the biophysical nature of the vehicle may greatly change without changing its social position. A given building, say Boston Symphony Hall, remains on the same place unaltered, whether it is used now by the Symphony Orchestra, or next day by the Community Church or next day by a political rally. On the other hand, a church building may become old and semiruined physically, still remaining a vehicle of religion.

See a more detailed analysis of this in my *Sociocultural Causality, Space, Time,* pp. 137-139. See there the literature.

and social groups may vary, but the cultural systems and social groups, with their components, are necessary dimensions of the sociocultural vector system.

3. Structure of Sociocultural Space and Distance

The preceding analysis gives us an idea of the nature and structure of sociocultural space. Its characteristics can be tentatively summed up as follows:

(a) Sociocultural space differs fundamentally from any variety of physical or geometric space. It is not as much quantitative, uniform, isotropic space, as qualitative, non-uniform, non-isotropic.

(b) It is a peculiar manifold composed of three main "planes" and of a certain number of "dimensions." It has a plane of meanings, values, and norms; a plane of vehicles; and a plane of human agents. Its dimensions are made up of the main cultural systems and of the main unibonded and multibonded groups, with their subsystems and subgroups. The number of "dimensions" depends upon the degree of precision with which we want to define the social and cultural position of a given sociocultural phenomenon in the superorganic universe.

(c) The location of vehicles and human agents in physical or geometric space, their "ecology," also enters into the total location of the sociocultural phenomenon in the superorganic universe, but it is only one and at that a secondary task in the determination of the positional relationships of the superorganic phenomena.

This conception of sociocultural space contains in itself a definite conception of such derivative notions as "social distance." Sociologically, *two or more sociocultural phenomena are near to one another if they occupy the same or an adjacent position in the vector system of the sociocultural space; and they are distant from one another if their position in the vector system is different.* Two individuals belonging to the same constellation of unibonded and multibonded groups and to the same strata of these groups are very near to one another in the superorganic space; the more different the groups and strata they belong to, the more distant they are to one another. Thus, individuals A and B, who are citizens of the United States, Episcopalians, Republicans, living in the same territorial group, of the same sex and age, equally rich, fond of the same music, literature, drama, and so on, these individuals are very close to one another in the sociocultural universe. Individuals of different race, age, sex, kinship, nationality, citizenship, political and religious affiliation, occupation, economic status, and so on, are very distant from one another. Two Christian denominations, no matter how distant they are in their vehicles and members in physical space, are much nearer to each other in sociocultural space than the Catholic Church and General Motors, or Cubist painting and the science of chemistry. The proposed formula defines clearly the conception of social distance and gives a precise measuring stick for determination of sociocultural distance between various sociocultural phenomena.[3]

4. Concluding Remarks on Structure of Sociocultural Universe

We have come to the end of the structural analysis of the sociocultural universe. Throughout the whole of our exploratory trip between starting and terminal points, we have steadily moved along the same road, guided by the same principles.

---

[3] The proposed conception of sociocultural space and distance is very different from E. Bogardus' conception of social distance. His social distance means the degree of sympathy or antipathy between persons. Such a conception is psychological rather than sociological. If a king and his valet are fond of each other, they are very near to each other according to his conception of social distance. According to the proposed conception of sociocultural distance, they are very far from each other, as far as the position of a monarch differs from that of a valet. Bogardus' conception is valuable for a study of the degree of sympathy or antipathy between persons, but it does not define either sociocultural space or distance; nor is it applicable to the location of sociocultural phenomena in the superorganic universe. It does not answer at all such questions as, where is Beethoven's symphony? how close is it to Bach's music, Steinbeck's novel, United States Steel Corporation, and so on? See, on this and the respective literature, *Sociocultural Causality, Space, Time*, pp. 139 ff. See there also on the *Wissensoziologie of Space Conceptions*, pp. 141-157.

(a) We began our exploration with a microphysical study of the structure of the generic "sociocultural atom"—the inter-individual meaningful interaction. The study yielded the essentials of its complex structure: the three components of meanings, vehicles, and human agents; its three inseparable aspects of the social, the cultural, and the personality of the interacting parties, with all the rich and intricate properties and relationships of each component-aspect to one another.

(b) This knowledge of the generic structure of the "sociocultural atom" as a dynamic constellation of meanings, vehicles, and persons led us to a concise study of its main forms, the types of sociocultural interaction, particularly the antagonistic, neutral, solidary and organized, semiorganized, and unorganized forms of interaction.

(c) The organized interaction "automatically" gave us the concept of an organized group, its unity, and its general properties.

(d) Having the concept of organized group at our disposal, we passed to an analysis of the structure of the social aspect of the superorganic universe. The analysis gave us the classes of unibonded and multibonded groups, powerful and less powerful groups, with their subclasses and subdivisions. Guided by these main forms of social groups, we could easily study the main lines of sociocultural differentiation of a population into the most powerful unibonded and multibonded groups. Their study netted a systematic taxonomy of the unibonded and especially of the little known multibonded groups, with a fairly exact formula of the structure of each of these groups. In this way, we opened up the relatively undeveloped field of the "sociological chemistry" of multibonded social bodies. The total analysis of social differentiation of the whole of mankind as well as of any given population of any area into the powerful unibonded and multibonded groups has supplied us with valid knowledge of the group structure of the social universe.

(e) Then, guided by the same principles, we passed to an analysis of social stratification in all its main forms, and especially of the intragroup and intergroup, the unibonded and multibonded, stratifications. This has given us

an approximate idea of the "vertical aspect" of the many-storied social structures and of human population generally.

(f) An investigation of social differentiation and stratification completed, we have been brought back to the population as a plurel and as an agglomeration of groups and strata. With the knowledge of the main groups and strata, we could easily "dissect" such complex social aggregates into their "organs"—groups and strata—and we have easily singled out the most important structural types of populations as complex social aggregates.

(g) Having finished the analysis of the structure of the social aspect of the superorganic, we passed to that of its cultural aspect. It has given us the classes of the integrated cultural system, and the unintegrated and contradictory cultural congeries, with their relationships of subordination, coordination, coexistence, and contradiction. Likewise it has led us to the distinction of ideological, behavioral, and material cultures. Armed with the concepts of these classes of cultural phenomena, we could easily grasp the structure of the culture of an individual, a group, or a culture area, and could give a fairly exact description of these structures.

(h) Then we passed to an analysis of the structure of personality as the third aspect of the superorganic. We have achieved a definite formula for the structure of the individual's egos, mentality, and overt actions. This formula is likely to be much more adequate and valid than the current Freudian, psychoanalytical, psychiatric, and psychosocial conceptions of the structure of the ego, mentality, and overt activities of an individual. Our formula clearly defines also the exact relationship between the number and content of the different egos in the individual and the social groups and cultural systems in which he is embedded. With the exception of the residual factor, X, the factor of selectivity-creativity, the formula adequately accounts for all the essentials of the structure of the individual egos, their cultural content, and the individual's overt activities. In addition, it defines precisely the individual's position in the superorganic universe.

(i) Finally, the structural analysis of the

social, of the cultural, and of the personality aspects of the superorganic universe has logically led to conceptions of sociocultural space, its vector system, and sociocultural distance. Our conception of sociocultural space and its structure is a mere consequence of the preceding structural analysis of the socio-cultural universe into its three components or aspects.

With this we can terminate the structural analysis of the sociocultural universe and can turn to the study of the main sociocultural processes that recurrently operate in this universe.

PART SIX

Dynamics of the
Recurrent Social Processes

Chapter 21. How Groups Originate and Become Organized

I. The Main Divisions of Dynamic General Sociology

Structural general sociology deals with the structure of the social, cultural, and personality aspects of the superorganic. Parallel with this, dynamic general sociology investigates (1) repeated *social processes* and change, together with the uniformities of the how and why; (2) repeated *cultural* processes and change; (3) the processes and changes of *personality* in its relationships with the social and cultural processes. We begin our analysis with the study of the social processes.

In the study of the social, cultural, and personality processes general sociology maintains its sociological standpoint of a generalizing science. *It does not investigate the specific and unique processes of which the life of a given unique social group is made up, but the processes that are recurrent in the life of any* group, past, present, and future. We are not interested in all the unique features of which the life process of the Roman Empire or Harvard University or the Methodist Church consists. Instead, we are interested in the social processes repeated in the life history of all groups, including the Roman Empire, Harvard University, and the Methodist Church. As in its structural analysis here also sociology represents the algebra and not the arithmetic of the social sciences. Like the physiology of human organisms that studies the basic physiological processes repeated in all human organisms, "social physiology," or dynamics, similarly concentrates its attention on the basic social processes recurrent in the life history of all social groups.

II. The Basic Recurrent Social Processes

The number of concrete forms of the recurrent social processes in the life history of social groups is enormous. Their detailed treatment is the task of special sociologies and of monographic studies. General sociology deals mainly with the limited number of the basic repeated processes. These can be conveniently catalogued in the following classes.

(1) How and why social groups originate; or how and why their members pass from a state of isolation to that of interaction and contact.

(2) How and why they organize, a process which in conformity with the concept of organization, falls into a series of sub-processes: (a) How and why the official law norms emerge in the conduct of their members, and how and why the recommended, required, and prohibited relationships arise. (b) How and why intragroup and intergroup differentiation and

stratification appear, with the government and hierarchy of the respective ranks and authorities.

These complex processes are often spoken of as organization, institutionalization, and adjustment.

(3) How social groups maintain their integrity, the identity and continuity of their existence. This process may be analyzed into its two main ways of maintenance, or the process of the persistence of a group may be resolved, in accordance with their componential structure, into three subprocesses: (a) How the groups maintain the identity and integrity of their component of meanings, values, and norms. (b) How they acquire, exchange, maintain, and lose their vehicles and material means of subsistence. (c) How they maintain their membership: how they recruit, exchange, lose, and distribute their members among their strata (the processes of horizontal and vertical social mobility).

(4) How and why the groups change: (a) in their size; (b) in stratified profile; (c) in the number of the "fibers" in their network of relationships; (d) in the proportion of the contractual, familistic, and compulsory relationships; (e) in association and disassociation of bonds; (f) in the forms of their government and in the amount of governmental regimentation; (g) in the amount and forms of freedom.

(5) How and why groups change now in an orderly and now in a revolutionary manner.

(6) How and why war and peace fluctuate in intergroup relationships.

(7) How and why the groups disintegrate and die (disintegration and dissolution).

(8) How some of the groups revive (regeneration).

Such, in brief, are the basic processes that are repeated, with the exception of (8), in the life history of practically all organized groups that run the complete cycle of their life history. We shall see that each of these processes and subprocesses consists of several sub-subprocesses, to be examined in the chapters that follow. For the present it suffices to say that the totality of these processes embrace almost all the basic *social* processes and all that are usually treated in sociology texts and monographs. *Cultural* processes are not included here; they will be examined in connection with cultural dynamics.[1]

Let us now turn to a concise analysis of these processes.

1. Why and How Social Groups Originate (the Processes of Contact and Interaction)

In a more exact formulation the problem is why and how hitherto isolated human beings interact and thus become a group—a problem

---

[1] Here are a few typical classifications of sociocultural processes by various sociologists.

Invention, imitation, opposition (G. Tarde); organization, disorganization, ascendancy, domination, leadership, formalization, individualization, socialization, conflict, hostility, and suggestion (C. H. Cooley); association, coordination, socialization, adaptation, cooperation, assimilation, organization, continuity, disintegration (C. A. Ellwood); isolation, stimulation, communication, suggestion, imitation, diffusion, discrimination, discussion, accommodation, assimilation, socialization (E. Bogardus); preliminary socialization, genesis of society, association, domination, exploitation, opposition, stimulation, antagonism; competition, conflict, class struggle, war adaptation, cooperation, organization of social effort, will and thought, deterioration, stratification, gradation, segregation, subordination, equalization, selection, socialization, estrangement, social control, individuation, liberation, commercialization, professionalization, institutionalization, expansion, ossification, decadence, transformation, reshaping (E. A. Ross).

L. von Wiese gives a still more detailed classification of social relationships or processes. (Cf.

other samples and references in my *Theories*, pp. 507-513.) Side by side with many merits, these classifications have several shortcomings. (1) They have hardly any definite *fundamentum divisionis*, being frequently casual and haphazard. (2) Many are incomplete, overlooking many a basic process. (3) They repeat the same process under different names. (4) They mix biological, psychological, social, and cultural processes. (5) Detached from their structural or dynamic context, many of these processes are left "hanging in the air," without any specification as to where, when, and in what structures they occur, or how they are related to one another. For these reasons I prefer the outlined method of classification and treatment of the basic processes. As the reader can see, many of these processes have already been treated from the standpoint of structure, but always in connection with either interindividual or intergroup and strata structures. Similarly, in this part all the basic processes are definitely attached to the respective individuals, groups, and strata. Instead of "hanging in the air," all our basic processes, as it were, are "built into" the respective social structures and definitely located in respect to a given group, stratum, or individual.

quite different from that of why and how such a group becomes organized. Two general reasons explain the why, and four types of establishing the contact and interaction, together with the factors involved, explain the how of the problem.

a. *The Why.* Two general and constant reasons why human beings do not remain isolated from one another, why they interact and establish groups amidst which they live and act, are (1) *the lack of sufficiency of the individual;* (2) *the invaluable advantages which the group life offers in comparison with the life in isolation, for the survival of human individuals and of human species, for the development of their creative potentialities, and for the fulfillment of their mission—the realization of the superorganic—on this planet.* Neither biologically nor in any other way is the human individual self-sufficient. Owing to an exceptionally long infancy, all newborn human babies would perish if they were not taken care of by other human beings for a number of years. Without individuals of different sex the procreation of *homo sapiens* would have been impossible. Alone, a human individual, especially in the conditions of a preliterate society, could not protect himself from the attacks of other animals and inimical forces. Alone, he could not learn much, or develop in any significant way his mind and his superorganic potentialities. In a society with a well-developed division of labor the individual alone is as helpless as in a preliterate society. In brief, this extreme lack of self-sufficiency on the part of an individual, the impossibility of his surviving even biologically, is a sufficient reason why he is destined to undergo interactions and to live in the stream of interactions from his birth to his death.

The same is true from the standpoint of the *human species. Homo sapiens* emerged and has been a social animal living in groups be-cause such a life has been much more advantageous for the survival of the whole human species than a life of isolated individuals. The general observation that a social form of life has developed among those species for whose survival it has been advantageous and has not developed among those for whose survival it has been disadvantageous[2] holds also for the species of *homo sapiens.* Still more necessary has been the incessant interaction and group life from the standpoint of the development of the creative potentialities of *homo sapiens* and for his specific mission on this planet: the realization and development of the superorganic mind. In Chapter 1 it has been shown that an individual isolated from the moment of birth from other individuals cannot develop even in a very modest form his creative mental and moral potentialities. This applies to his memory and imagination, to his ideas and beliefs, to his conceptual thought (in science and philosophy, ethics and law), to artistic creation, and to technological invention. Still less possible in isolation is any accumulation and growth of experience and culture.

These two reasons are perfectly sufficient to explain why human beings interact and live in groups.

b. *The How.* We can distinguish four ways in which human beings initiate the interaction process. The interaction may be (1) intentional, or purposeful, sought by all the interacting parties; (2) intentional, sought by some of the parties and opposed or unsought by other parties; (3) intentionally or not, but opposed by all the parties directly concerned; (4) unintentional or fortuitous on the part of all the parties concerned, who interact by reason of various conditions—cosmic, biological, and sociocultural—regardless of their purposes and aims.[3]

(1) The intentional, or purposeful, way is well known to everyone. Millions of human

---

[2] Cf. L. Morgan, *Animal Behavior* (London, 1908), pp. 229 ff.; M. Parmelee, *The Science of Human Behavior* (New York, 1910), pp. 391 ff.; O. Ammon, *Les bases naturelles de l'ordre social* (Paris, 1900), pp. 40 ff. L. Morgan and others rightly indicate that the development of social life among the species is not a criterion of the higher and lower positions of the species on the zoological ladder but is due to its advantages or disadvantages for the survival of the respective species. For

lions or tigers, each of which is capable of protecting itself against its enemies, the developed forms of social life were less necessary than for, say, jackals. Cf. also P. Kropotkin, *Mutual Aid* (London, 1905).

[3] The existence of the fortuitous type, and, in part, of (2) and (3), is evidence of a fallacy of the theories claiming that all interaction processes are initiated purposefully, or according to the schema of means and ends.

beings daily meet one another intentionally and purposefully: for conversation, for business transactions, for political or religious purposes, for scientific or artistic discussions, for a dinner or cocktail party, and so on. Most of the meetings "by agreement," "by appointment," or "by invitation" represent this kind of initiation of interaction. In indirect interactions we intentionally listen to a favorite radio program; read certain newspapers or books; attend a concert, political rally, religious service, club, and the like. The method in question is one of the principal means of initiating interactions.

(2) A gang of criminals trying to escape the group of policemen seeking to arrest them; an army detachment trying to disengage itself and flee from the pursuing enemy; a debtor avoiding his creditor; persons "not at home" to unwelcome visitors; movie or sport stars sought out by admirers to whom they are perfectly indifferent—these furnish examples of the second way of establishing interactions. On a mass scale, examples are offered by conquerors, invaders, and colonizers who, being attracted by wealth or other values, deliberately invade a country, and by the natives who are either opposed to or do not seek interaction with the invaders or colonizers, as in the case of the Spanish *conquistadores* in Mexico and Peru. All the interactions initiated according to the schema "purposefully seeking-avoiding" belong to this type. In various concrete forms this mode has operated in millions of interactions past and present.

(3) Surprisingly for many, a series of interactions may be initiated between parties which are opposed to it. Thus soldiers of two countries unwilling to fight one another may be compelled to meet and to fight as a result of forces outside themselves. The gladiators of the Roman arena were often in the same position. Though this type of initiating an interaction does not operate as widely as the others, nevertheless it exists and operates more frequently than many think.

(4) Finally, we daily because of various conditions enter into many interactions fortuitously, without any purpose, desire, plan, or intention. Absent-mindedly passing the blinking red light in a car without stopping, we suddenly find ourselves interacting with the traffic policeman and then with the traffic court. Riding on a streetcar, we are often addressed by somebody and find ourselves in conversation with a stranger. Resorting to a bomb shelter, not for the sake of interaction but for the sake of safety, thousands of persons initiate contacts with thousands of others. Going to a popular crowded beach for the sake of cooling off, thousands of persons brought together by heat and water undergo interactions. The discovery of gold or other precious metals in this or that part of the world generates a rush of thousands to such places, and then "boom towns," with thousands of interactions of the gold-seekers brought together into spatial proximity. In general, *all the cosmic* factors (light, temperature, water, etc.), as well as *the biological and the sociocultural conditions that bring the individuals together into close spatial proximity, are the factors of the genesis of fortuitous interactions and groups. The same may be said of all the factors facilitating the communication of human beings*. Being placed in physical proximity, the individuals are forced to act and react, mutually or one-sidedly, regardless of any previous purpose or desire on their part. With a few exceptions, under such conditions they just cannot help interacting. Many such interactions are short-lived, while others turn out to be durable, now and then ripening into a close friendship or lasting hatred.

The cosmic, biological, and sociocultural conditions that "bring the individuals together" are numerous and vary for different individuals and groups. But in general, *all the conditions that in some way are advantageous to the given individuals facilitate the interaction processes*; being advantageous, they attract a number of individuals and place them in physical proximity or in contact and thus generate the interaction processes and groups. An oasis in a desert; a fertile valley; a river in a dry country or a beach on a hot day; a comfortable climate; a health resort; iron or oil deposits; a bomb shelter during an air raid; a region safe from an enemy in wartime or rich in food during a period of starvation; a museum; a piece of well-paid work—these and thousands of other cosmic, biological, and sociocultural factors generate or facilitate interaction processes and the birth of groups.

This general rule explains, to a considerable

extent, the past and present density of the population, low in deserts and in frigid and other regions unfavorable for living and high in fertile valleys, in areas with a healthy climate, along the shores of rivers, streams, seas, and oceans, etc.[4]

Still more fortuitous are many indirect and anonymous interactions. An individual living in a city cannot help being influenced by the buildings, subways, streets, voices, noises, and thousands of other "conductors of interaction" and material vehicles created by other human beings and, regardless of the desires of the individual, incessantly affecting his moods, mentality, and actions. In this way we fortuitously interact even with the past generations that built the city, with its buildings and monuments, streets, transportation systems, and material culture in general. We fortuitously interact with the heterogeneous crowd that honks horns, yells and sings, laughs, pushes and pulls us in crowded elevators and subways, exhibiting now animosity or hatred, now love, now joy or sorrow. In the course of a walk or ride from our home to our office we daily experience a series of such fortuitous interactions with the dead and the living, with individuals and anonymous collectivities, interactions that affect us, sometimes deeply and permanently, regardless of any desire or purpose on our part.

If one makes a careful record of all the interactions one undergoes during each twenty-four hours, one will find that every day one experiences many intentional and many fortuitous interactions. When all the miscellaneous interactions are computed, the fortuitous ones will be found to constitute a larger percentage of the whole than the intentional ones. Such are the four principal modes of genesis of the interaction processes and of eventual groups.

2. Why and How Social Groups Become Organized (Processes of Organization, Adaptation, and Accommodation)

Some of the interactions that arise are short-lived, ceasing before reaching the stage of organization. Other interactions continue and eventually become organized.

[4] For a detailed analysis of the various cosmic, biological, and sociocultural factors of fortuitously generated interaction processes cf. my *Sistema Soziologii*, Vol. I, pp. 249-342; also my *Theories*, pp. 106 ff.

a. *The Why*. The general and constant reason why a durable interaction of individuals is bound to pass from an unorganized to an organized form is easily comprehensible. Without a crystallization of the functions and roles, rights and duties, of the interacting individuals, contacts are liable to lead to incessant conflicts. No peace and order, no safety and security, no collective effort and satisfaction of the needs of the members, are possible under conditions of the Hobbesian "war of everyone against everyone." Either such unorganized interactions terminate or else those who experience them harm one another through incessant clashes, thus precluding all the advantages of the group life. Otherwise they must assume the status of organized interactions. Every day thousands of casual reactions occur; other thousands are initiated with the idea of their becoming permanent, but lapse through disagreement and conflict of the parties; finally, other thousands survive through the formation of organized groups. *The organization of a group is the indispensable condition of its survival and durability.* The emerging organization is not necessarily just, fair, or equally beneficial for all its members. It may be, and often is, an organization of powerful conquerors, exploiters, or masters, who vanquish or exploit the other interacting individuals, rendering them subjects, serfs, or slaves. Nevertheless, as has been pointed out in Chapter 4, such a group is an organized group if it possesses a code of law norms, with all the other characteristics of an organized group. Sing-Sing prison represents an organized group, in spite of the animosities between its guards and the prisoners. Generally, what kind of organization emerges from the interaction of the individuals —whether it is familistic or coercive, just or unjust—depends upon the properties of the individuals and the total conditions of the group. It is always the resultant of all the forces of the members and of all the conditions under which they interact.

b. *The How*. As to how a group of interacting individuals assumes the status of an organized group, four principal methods may be enumerated. The organization may be (1) intentional or purposeful on the part of all the interacting individuals; (2) fortuitous or spontaneous, a process of "natural crystallization," of trial and error, on the part of all the parties concerned; (3) intentional on the part of some and fortuitous or even opposed in the case of others; (4) opposed by all the parties concerned.

(1) The first way is quite familiar. Thousands of organized groups—business corporations, and scientific, religious, artistic, political, occupational, familial, and other associations—arise in this way. The interacting individuals with a set of common values purposefully come together and agree to create an organized group for the realization of these common values. They draw up the constitution or the official law of the new group, defining its purpose, its membership, its government, the rights and duties of each member—in brief, all the characteristics of an organized group. The constitution once defined and accepted, on a certain date the group emerges as a full-pledged, organized entity. The whole process of organization requires only a comparatively short time. The official existence of such a group dates from the moment of its formal establishment, or of its incorporation by the state in the case of incorporated groups. Multitudes of familial groups, business firms, and political, occupational, scientific, religious, artistic, philosophical, juridical, ethical, educational and other associations arise in this purposeful "covenantial" and contractual way. Since the known beginnings of history and among the preliterate as well as "historical" populations this mode of emergence of organized groups has been operative.

To this extent the contractual theories of the origin of society or of the state—the theories of Puffendorff and Wolf, of Grotius and Hobbes, of Locke and Rousseau—contain an element of truth. As regards their other claims the contractual theories are, of course, distinctly naïve—for example, in their pictures of the "natural man" and the precontractual "natural society," in their claim that there was a happy anarchic state of unregulated precontractual society or that the contractual way is the only mode of origin of organized groups.

Though *the easiest, quickest, and fairest mode of origin of organized groups, the purposive or contractual way is possible and successful only in groups of individuals whose values, norms, meanings, and respective conduct and ways of living are congenial and similar to a considerable extent, beginning with the common values and meanings they wish to realize through organization, and ending with their belief in the binding and obligatory character of their contract.* In a group of individuals with quite different values and norms, manners and culture, the purposeful way of establishing an organized group either is impossible, is bound to be short-lived, or is liable to miscarry, rendering the organized group a purely coercive pseudo-contractual organization compulsorily or fraudulently imposed by its stronger members upon the weaker ones. In such a case the mutually purposive way becomes, in fact, the third way; purposive on the part of some of the parties and fortuitous or compulsorily imposed in the case of the other parties of the group.

(2) The fortuitous mode of spontaneous ripening of the interaction into an organized form has been operative for a long period of time. For instance, a group of children, unacquainted with one another, meet in a school, new settlement, or neighborhood and begin to interact. In the first stages their interaction is unorganized; the roles, rights and duties of each child remain undefined, their relationships uncrystallized. With the continuation of the interaction, during which many conflicts and clashes occur, step by step the relationships are crystallized: the boss and the bossed, the dominating and the submissive, the leaders and the led, with their specific functions, rights, and duties, progressively emerge. After some time the children assume the status of an organized group. A similar process is observable with grown-up persons.[5]

Many marriage and family groups, as organized entities, also emerge in this way. The ever-repeated story runs something like this. Persons hitherto unknown to each other,

[5] For the concrete facts, for preschool and school children cf. M. Parten, "Leadership among Preschool Children," *Journal of Abnormal and Social Psychology*, 1933, 136-147; Bühler, "Social Behavior of Children," C. Murchison (ed.), *Handbook of Child Psychology* (Clark University Press, 1933); M. L. Page, *The Modification of Ascendant Behavior in Preschool Children* (Ames, 1936); L. Murphy, *Social Behavior and Child Personality* (New York, 1937).

having no idea or intention of falling in love and marrying, meet accidentally at this or that gathering. Sometimes the sequel is a case of "love at first sight"; more frequently it is a gradual crystallization of their feelings, ripening during a series of subsequent interactions. Finally the parties unexpectedly find themselves in love. The question of marriage, however, remains for some time undecided. In many cases the situation does not lead to marriage; in others the intention of marriage arises in one or both parties. Meanwhile, with the relations becoming more and more intimate, crises often occur—misunderstandings, quarrels, temporary separations—until the parties finally marry and establish a family. In some cases the marriage is concluded contrary to the plans of one or both of the parties. The salient points are that the parties do not plan to fall in love, nor do they plan to marry each other until a comparatively late stage in their interactions. Most people marry a certain person not in accordance with any purposeful, rational plan but because of an interaction which spontaneously develops in a way leading to marriage. The purpose to marry emerges relatively late, in most instances as a result merely of the fortuitous mental, emotional, moral, and social situation. Only those marriages in which the parties calculate in advance to marry a certain person for considerations of title, wealth, or similar reasons are the marriages that arise in a purposeful way. Most of the others emerge in the fortuitous way of accidental meeting of the parties and of a spontaneous ripening of their relationships.

In a similar manner many friendship groups are formed, and many a scientific, philanthropic, artistic, debating, political, ethical, or other association or group attains an organized existence. The important point in all such cases is that *the very purpose of creating an organization grows spontaneously, without any*

premeditated plan. In these situations, instead of a preconceived purpose leading to a group organization, an interaction process, spontaneously initiated and spontaneously maturing, eventually engenders the purpose of formalizing and crystallizing an already roughly organized group.

This fortuitous mode of operation was particularly important in the past when mutually unacquainted individuals or groups with different values, norms, and culture happened to come into contact and more or less permanent interaction. A truly purposeful "contractual" organization and unification was impossible in such cases; their values and norms were too heterogeneous to make purposeful cooperation and organization feasible. The contacts and interactions had to continue for a time fortuitously, in hit-and-miss, trial-and-error fashion, with inevitable conflicts and clashes. Many forms of relationship progressively proved unfit and untenable in the given "field of forces" and were eventually eliminated,[6] while others corresponded more closely to the real correlation of the forces. Step by step some persons and groups emerged as leaders or governors, others as the led or the governed. Certain norms of conduct, proving to be the most readily enforceable, were repeated until they eventually became habitual or habitually enforced as the most feasible *modus vivendi*. Reaching this stage of the "folkways," with their further repetition they began to be felt as the "attributive-imperative" rules of conduct, usually dressed up in various religious, ethical, political, and other ideologies. When such rules emerged and covered the basic social relationships, the group finally attained the stage of the organized group, with all the characteristics of organization: official law, the government and the hierarchy of authorities, differentiation and stratification, and so on. In

---

[6] Psychologically the fortuitous emergence of the moral and law norms is essentially similar to the formation of habits out of the random reactions of a person in which the main stimuli are the actions of other parties using all the means of influencing the conduct of the person in question: suggestion, persuasion, rewards and punishments, commands, prestige, authority, and downright coercion. Cf. K. Dunlap, *Habits, Their Making and Unmaking* (New York, 1932); G. Murphy and T. Newcombe, *Experimental Social Psychology* (New York, 1937), Chps. 4-6; R. T. La Piere and P. R. Farnsworth, *Social Psychology* (New York, 1936), Ch. 7; L. L. Bernard, *Introduction to Sociology* (New York, 1942), Chps. 22-25. Cf. also the literature cited in these works. For how these processes proceed among children cf. J. E. Anderson, "The Development of Social Behavior," *AJS*, 1939, pp. 839-957; H. Blumer, *Movies and Conduct* (New York, 1933); quoted works of J. Piaget, M. Parten, C. Buhler.

a stereotyped, generalized way the process may be depicted as a succession of the following phases: (a) spontaneous use of several different and sometimes opposite forms of conduct between the interacting individuals, leading now and then to conflict and clashes; (b) spontaneous process of incessant trial and test of these rules and their incessant selection; (c) progressive decline of the use of the unfit forms and more and more frequent use of the fit forms; (d) progressive elimination of the unfit rule and transformation of the more fit and frequently used forms into the habitual; (e) transformation of habitual rules into customary ones; (f) transformation of the customary rules into the "imperative-attributive" norms (unofficial and then official). With the last phase the organization in the given field of relationship becomes an accomplished fact. When such norms emerge in· all the main fields of social relationships of the interacting members, the group becomes organized completely.[7]

The mode of spontaneous trial and error and of successive selection, with many a conflict and many victims in the interim between the onset of the interaction and its final organization, has been the way of unification and organization of different "families," "hordes," "clans," "territorial groups," "kinship groups," and nationalities, into larger and larger organized groups, up to the emergence of the state organizations.

It continues to play an important role in the process of the international organization of mankind. The need for establishing world peace was felt long ago. For several centuries many plans for its realization have been conceived.[8] However, few have been realized,

and these have proved abortive and short-lived, like the League of Nations. Even when a part of such plans has been carried through, the objective results have invariably been very different from those that were expected.[9] The actual forms of international law, relationships, and organization have by no means conformed to the original plan. A long series of trials and errors, clashes and conflicts, is bound to ensue before a relatively definite and stable international organization emerges, and when established, this organization will be very different from the one intended. Its realization will be due fully as much to the play of fortuitous forces as to purposeful plans and efforts.[10]

From this standpoint the theories respecting the spontaneous growth of religious, customary, tribal, and other law or what is called by many the growth of mores and customs—the theories of Aristotle, Tacitus, Grotius, Hume, A. Ferguson, Adam Smith, Savigny, Puchta, Spencer, W. G. Sumner, M. Kovalevsky, L. Petrajitsky, and others—are undoubtedly valid. Many law-norms have emerged precisely in this fortuitous way, through spontaneous trial and error, the "natural selection" of norms, in the incessant test of the continued process of the interaction of the parties concerned.

In this spontaneous fashion there emerge and develop most of the intuitive or unofficial law-norms. In accordance with the incessant varying conditions of social life our "intuitive" legal convictions undergo constant change (see above, Chapter 4). In this process the factor of spontaneity dominates, instead of the character of the changing norms being determined by the operation of purpose.

As was pointed out in chapter 4, unless law-

---

[7] Compare Waxweiler's scheme: action-repetition-habit-usage or custom-rule-institution (acte-habitude-usage-règle-institution). See E. Waxweiler, Esquisse d'une sociologie (Bruxelles, 1906) and "Avant-Propos" in Bulletin mensuel (Institut Solvay, 1910), No. 1, pp. 1-9.

[8] See S. J. Hemleben, Plans for World Peace through Six Centuries (Chicago, 1943).

[9] The same is true of almost any state constitution and statute: their objective results are invariably different from those expected. The Volstead Act resulted in a bootlegging industry, the gang form of criminality, sordid "speakeasies," and so on, unforeseen by its framers. For a series of striking observations on the discrepancy between the

purposive and fortuitous ways of change of constitutions, cf. J. de Maître's "Considerations sur la France," Oeuvres (Lyon, 1891), Vol. I.

[10] Another formula for a fortuitous origin of law norms within a national or international body is crisis-ordeal-catharsis-charisma-new law. The emergence of the new national and international order in our time follows it closely: the First and the Second World Wars, together with many bloody revolutions, have constituted tragic and instructive crises and ordeals urgently pointing to the necessity of establishing a new order and law. Eventually a new order will be established if meanwhile humanity has not destroyed itself in atomic wars. For this formula cf. my Crisis, pp. 321 ff.

convictions are supported by the members of a group, the official law is doomed to become a dead letter, to be either forcibly nullified or else changed by orderly processes. This means that many purposeful modifications of the official law by legislative bodies, and many purposefully formulated law codes, are governed by the spontaneously evolving and changing intuitive law. Therefore the very purposefulness of such codes is merely rationalization of spontaneous legal convictions. If even the most rational or purposive code runs sharply counter to the spontaneous convictions of the population, it is doomed to be ineffective. The prohibition amendment in the United States is a case in point. Tacitus' *Quid leges sine moribus* sums up well the situation. In other words, under the surface of seemingly purposively enacted official statutes there run the deep currents of the spontaneously evolving and changing law convictions of the population, which eventually manifest themselves in the form of purposive individual or collective legislation. Since a change in the norms of the official law means a change in the organization of the respective group, the fortuitous mode of organization of groups has a much wider and more fundamental application than appears on the surface.[11]

All the theories contending that "not a single institution can appear without the conscious will of man directed toward a definite purpose"[12] are fallacious. Many organized groups and institutions have arisen in a fortuitous way, without such a purpose and volition. Many others, as we shall see, emerged contrary to the will of either all or some of the parties involved. The family consisting of a husband and wife married contrary to their desire and forced to continue to live together irrespective

of the wishes of both offers a cogent refutation of such a claim.

Wrong also are those theories that explain all organized groups as cemented and shaped by conquest and coercion. Some groups are indeed organized in this fashion. But the truly purposive organizations and the bulk of the fortuitously organized groups do not conform to this mode. Its partisans are hence guilty of elevating a particular case into a universal rule.

(3) Many organized groups arise through *the deliberative coercion of parties imposing it upon other parties either antagonistic or indifferent to the organization in question.* When the Spaniards and the English invaded the Western Hemisphere and conquered the native Aztecs, Peruvians, and other Indians, imposing upon them their rules, laws, and organization, the native Americans resisted the invaders; but they were suppressed and compelled to accept the will of their conquerors. The same story applies to almost all invasions and coercive colonizations, such as those of the Aryans in India, the Dorians and other Greeks in Hellas, the Macedonians, the Romans, and the modern Europeans. In other cases the inhabitants of the invaded countries passively submitted to the organization imposed by the colonizers, neither welcoming nor opposing it.

In a different setting the same mode of organization has regularly recurred in various populations when one element, the masters, has imposed its organization upon the hostile or indifferent lower classes, converting these into slaves, serfs, or a submerged and disfranchised stratum. A recent example is afforded by the following case. In 1942 the United States government evacuated from the

---

[11] Cf. M. Kovalevsky, *Modern Custom and Ancient Law* (Russian, Moscow, 1886; French translation, Paris, 1893); E. Westermarck, *The Origin and Development of Moral Ideas* (London, 1906), Vol. I, Chps. 1-13; B. Malinowsky, *Crime and Custom in Savage Society* (London, 1926); W. A. Robson, *Civilization and the Growth of Law* (London, 1935); R. Thurnwald, *Werden, Wandel und Gestaltung des Rechtes* (Berlin-Leipzig, 1934); W. G. Sumner, *Folkways* (Boston, 1906); A. S. Diamond, *Primitive Law* (New York, 1935); J. Cruet, *La vie du droit et l'impuissance de lois* (Paris, 1908); Leo Petrajitzky, works cited above; E. Waxweiler, *Esquisse d'une sociologie* (Bruxelles,

1906); N. Timasheff, *An Introduction to the Sociology of Law* (cited above); P. A Sorokin, *Crime and Punishment, Heroism and Reward* (Russian, St. Petersburg, 1914); W. I. Thomas, *Primitive Behavior* (cited above); P. Kropotkin, *Mutual Aid* (cited above), which gives a series of cases side by side with the purposeful type.
[12] G. Jellinek, *Das Recht des modernen Staates* (Berlin, 1900; Russian translation, p. 30). The similar statement of R. Ihering that "every society emerges purposively, premeditatedly, and consciously," repeated by Makarewicz and others, is likewise fallacious, as are also the recent reiterations of the same idea by the partisans of the "means-end" schema.

Pacific area some 110,000 Japanese to ten "Relocation Centers," where they were subjected to a certain organization which they neither sought nor welcomed.[13]

On a smaller scale this method of organization continues to operate in hundreds of interactions: those of a criminal and of the policemen seeking to arrest him; of the kidnaped and the kidnapers, and so on.

(4) *Finally, there is the type of organization which is opposed by all the parties directly concerned.* A marriage imposed upon both parties by their parents or another group contrary to the inclinations of the parties is a case in point. War prisoners coercively inducted into the German army and forced to fight the army of their own country furnish another illustration. Gangsters confined in a cell and forced to obey the rules of the prison represent a third case.

Such are the four main ways in which an unorganized interaction process is transformed into an organized form and produces an organized group. Negatively, the very existence of these four types testifies to the one-sidedness of the theories whereby each of these methods is represented as the *only* mode of organization of groups. They demonstrate that the purposive, the fortuitous, the purposive-coercive, and the unqualifiedly coercive theories as to the origin of organized groups, while valid in part, are untenable in respect to their claim of exclusiveness and universality.

Invalid in large part is the theory of A. Gobineau that the only basis of social unification is the racial unity of the individuals; for racially homogeneous groups are only one element among many racially heterogeneous groups. Even racially antagonistic persons are often forced to interact and to form an organized group.

One-sided, likewise, are all the theories which, like those of Adam Smith or A. Sutherland, seek the source of society in semi-instinctive sympathy and derive from it all the forms of organized groups. The same is true of the theory of F. Giddings, which finds the roots of social life and of organized groups in "the consciousness of the kind," and that of P. Kropotkin, which stresses the exclusive role

of mutual aid. All such theories elevate a particular case into a universal rule. They ignore the fact that human beings initiate interaction processes and then give them organized form not only in response to such motive forces as sympathy, mutual aid, "consciousness of the kind," "the pleasure of communication" and "enjoyment of interaction," but under the impulse of hatred, the desire to injure, rob, and exploit their fellows.

One-sided, moreover, are the theories that detect the source of organization exclusively in this or that instinct (such as those of W. McDougall, R. Petrucci, and W. Trotter), in imitation (G. Tarde), in mere coercion (L. Gumplowicz, F. Oppenheimer, and others), or in any single factor. The very existence of the familistic, intermediate, and antagonistic forms of interaction and of groups proves that individuals interact willingly and purposefully in the familistic groups, though they cannot do so in the inherently antagonistic groups, nor can they enter purposefully into a group that constitutes for them a prison. The existence of these solidary, intermediate, and antagonistic types of groups presupposes the four different modes of organization in question. Otherwise we are forced to accept the absurd contention that each group is organized willingly and purposefully by all its members—the jail group by its prisoners, the slave-master society by the slaves, the victor-vanquished society by the vanquished. Or, if we accept the claims of the coercion-conquest theory, we must conclude that no groups are organized through free cooperation of all their members for a realization of their common purposes, a conclusion which is emphatically repudiated by the observed facts.

3. Why and How Organized Groups Become Differentiated, Stratified, and Named

The organization of a group means not only the formulation of its official law; the division of actions and reactions into the lawful, recommended, and prohibited classes; and the emergence of government of some sort. It implies also the intragroup differentiation and stratification.

a. *The Why.* Besides the reasons for interaction and organization given above, the additional reasons why organized groups become

[13] For a detailed analysis cf. A. H. Leighton, *The Governing of Men* (Princeton, 1945), Part I.

differentiated and stratified are as follows (1) the biosocial heterogeneity of the individuals; (2) the advantages of social differentiation and stratification; (3) prevention of incessant strife and facilitation of social order and solidarity; (4) incessantly changing sociocultural and partly cosmic and biological conditions.

(1) A child cannot perform various physical and mental functions easily performed by a grown-up person; a man or woman cannot discharge certain functions of the opposite sex; the weak cannot do work requiring considerable physical strength; the stupid are incapable of tasks demanding mental ability; the old and the sick are disqualified for many functions proper to the young and healthy. These purely biological differences of age, sex, health, constitution, and mental ability make the differentiation of roles and functions within a group of interacting individuals unavoidable. If to these biological differences are added those which are acquired, the inevitability of the differentiation becomes still more inescapable. Biologically disparate individuals, even when placed in an identical physical, biological, and sociocultural environment, will not become less disparate; if anything, as a number of experiments show, their innate discrepancies will become more strongly accentuated, because each will react diversely to the environment and because these differences will be intensified in the course of *repetition* of the respective reactions. If, now, the environment —physical, biological, and sociocultural— varies for different individuals (and such is ordinarily the case), many differences will arise in addition to the purely biological ones. As a result of this biosocial heterogeneity of the individuals, social differentiation becomes inescapable for an organized group existing for any length of time. It becomes an inherent trait of any organized group. This explains why there never has been and never will be any organized group without some social differentiation.

For similar reasons the biosocial heterogeneity of the members of the group is a constantly operative cause of the group's stratification. Individuals unequal biosocially cannot be made empirically equal, no matter what devices are employed.[14] The biosocial heterogeneity of the members of the groups does not, of course, determine the concrete forms of differentiation and stratification, but it is a sufficient reason for *some* form of differentiation and stratification.

(2) The second reason for differentiation and stratification is found in the inestimable advantages, economic and otherwise, which they afford the groups and their members. If all the members of a group were to attempt to perform identical functions, without any hierarchy of superior and inferior authorities, the survival of the group would be impossible. Thus if young children were not cared for by older persons, they would die, and with their death the group would eventually disappear. Furthermore, most of the members would perform their functions, particularly those calling for special qualifications, very inadequately. (Nobody, for example, can be an efficient encyclopedist.) The group, as a whole, would hence contravene the fundamental rule that everyone shall discharge those functions for which he possesses special ability. All the economic and other advantages of specialization and of division of labor would be sacrificed. The group in which Beethovens and Mozarts were assigned manual tasks, whereas others, devoid of musical ability were expected to compose music, would not accomplish much in either field. The same applies to practically every other function, such as creative work in the arts and sciences, religion and philosophy, or the management of economic, military, and political affairs.

To summarize: The organized group without any differentiation and stratification is factually impossible; and even if it were pos-

---

[14] Human beings can be made socioculturally equal only if an equal sociocultural status is superimposed upon them; for instance, by virtue of the dogma that all human beings are the children of God, have an equal right to the pursuit of happiness, and so on. This sociocultural equality would, however, be unequal in its concrete manifestations; for some of the children of God become Popes, whereas others remain plain parishioners. For a discussion of how this biosocial heterogeneity of individuals generates social differentiation and stratification among the preliterate groups, cf. G. Landtman, *op. cit.*, Ch. 3, *passim*; W. I. Thomas, *Primitive Behavior*, Ch. 13, *passim*; R. Thurnwald, *Die menschliche Gesellschaft*, Vol. IV, Chps. 4 and 5, *passim*. Cf. also my *Social Mobility*, Chps. 13, 14.

sible, it would be deprived of enormous advantages enjoyed by a differentiated and stratified group. There are, of course, certain limits to the advantages of differentiation and stratification; but within these limits the foregoing propositions are valid.

(3) Furthermore, without a stratified hierarchy of the group's authorities into "superiors" whose lawful orders are obligatory for the "inferior," or subordinate agents, the interacting members would be in a state of incessant conflict, everybody commanding and nobody obeying. With such a *bellum omnium contra omnes* no group could exist for any length of time. Either it would fall apart or it would be in a state of perpetual anarchy. Hence, through the organizational and distributive functions of the law-norms (see Chapter 4), the emergence and crystallization of the official law are inevitably followed by the specified distribution of rights and duties among the members, including the hierarchy of the authorities and the right of the superior authorities to demand the obedience of the inferior authorities and members, and by some form of government to manage the affairs of the group and some form of judicial procedure to decide authoritatively the conflicts between the members. Whether the government is monarchical or republican, that of a chief or a committee, a president-vice-president-treasurer-secretary or just a "boss" and "foreman," some controlling center is indispensable in any organized group, however it may be appointed. Likewise, the hierarchy of agents in a highly developed or a simple form is inevitable. Otherwise group life would be impossible.[15]

(4) Finally, ever-varying sociocultural and, to some extent, physical and biological conditions perpetually create "good and bad luck" for various individuals. Social life is dynamic in its very nature. It constantly changes, and changes more rapidly than the physical and biological conditions. Thus it creates advantageous conditions for the social elevation of

some and for the social demotion of other individuals. The transition of a population from Nazi to Allied domination elevated many an anti-Nazi and demoted many a collaborationist. The last war ruined millions and enriched many thousands. The good luck of a prospector who discovers a vast gold deposit raises him to the upper strata of the economic pyramid. An earthquake ruins many economically and otherwise. Owing to incessant changes of the milieu differently affecting various individuals, they are constantly shifted up or down on the rungs of the ladder of stratification.[16]

These four constant reasons (or causes) are quite sufficient to make it clear why all organized groups are differentiated and stratified. In their totality these reasons mean that the origin and existence of stratification and differentiation are "spontaneous and natural," inherent in the very nature of the organized groups.

b. *Critical Remark.* These four constant reasons for social differentiation and stratification categorically refute all the theories that view social stratification as an incidental trait of organized groups artificially imposed upon them (the theories of L. Ward and others).[17] None of the four reasons is incidental, parochial, or transitory. They are all inherent in the group and are in no way artificial. Artificial are only certain specific exaggerated forms, now and then imposed by a part of the group members upon the others or by one group upon another. In the absence of these artificial forms, all such groups possess some form of differentiation and stratification.

These four fundamental and constant reasons refute also those theories of stratification which explain it almost exclusively through the operation of the war factor, whereby the conquerors make themselves the aristocracy and relegate the vanquished to the lower strata, setting up norms of official law coercively enforced to perpetuate the stratification imposed (the theories of L. Gumplowicz, G. Ratzenhofer, F. Oppenheimer, and others).[18] War has

[15] For a further comment on this point, cf. my *Social Mobility*, Chps. 1, 13, 14, including the literature cited.

[16] Cf. my *Social Mobility*, Ch. 14, including the literature cited.

[17] See L. Ward, "Social Classes in the Light of Modern Social Theory," *AJS*, Vol. XIII, pp. 617-

627; also I. W. Howerth, "Is There a Natural Law of Inequality?" *Scientific Monthly*, Vol. XIX, pp. 502-511.

[18] See F. Oppenheimer, *Der Staat* (Frankfurt am Main, 1908); G. Ratzenhofer, *Wesen und Zweck der Politik* (Leipzig, 1893); L. Gumplowicz, *Der Rassenkampf* (Innsbruck, 1883).

been only one of many concrete ways, not so much of primary origination as of reshuffling and accentuating the forms of differentiation and stratification.[19] In the absence of war, stratification and differentiation would still be found in all organized groups, whether a neighborhood gang of boys, a peaceful group of pioneers, a normal family, a religious group, a cooperative society, or any other organized group. Furthermore, conquerors, such as the Dorians, the Romans, and the Spaniards, did not first introduce stratification into the conquered peoples, but simply replaced a previously existing form of stratification with a different one, with different persons in each stratum. The theories in question furnish simply another illustration of the fallacy of elevating a particular case into an exclusive universal rule.

c. *The How.* All the four ways of initiating interactions and of their organization—intentional and purposive, fortuitous, intentional on the part of some members and opposed or fortuitous on the part of other members, opposed by all the members of the group directly concerned—are the methods of introducing and maintaining social differentiation and stratification within the organized group or in a complex of several groups.

(1) The purposive and voluntary organization of a group includes in its constitution the differentiation of the functions and the stratification of the authorities and ranks of the group.

(2) Fortuitously organized groups emerge with fortuitously developing forms of social differentiation, stratification, and authorities.

(3) In the groups organized coercively, the conquerors, powerful cliques among the members, etc. coercively and purposefully impose their form of stratification upon the unwilling or indifferent parties (the conquered, controlled, or weaker elements).

(4) Finally, there are stratifications and differentiations imposed upon a group contrary to the desires of all its members by an agency external to the group. A state forced by a more powerful state to adopt forms of stratification and differentiation opposed by all its members furnishes an example of such a method of establishing stratification. The reorganization of Japan and Germany by the Allies affords an instance of this type. Intergroup and interindividual relationships present fairly numerous instances. This case may, of course, be reduced to the preceding one, as a special variety.

4. Name and Symbol of the Organized Groups

Practically every organized group has a name, sign, or symbol denoting its individuality. The naming of a group is introduced in one of the same four ways in which the organization of the group is established.[20]

This chapter gives a concise but essentially adequate outline of the why and how of the origin and organization of groups, with their law-norms, their lawful, recommended, and prohibited social relationships, their stratification and differentiation, their government and the organs for the authoritative solution of conflicts. We shall now consider the processes necessary for a continuation of the life of a group.

---

[19] Herbert Spencer has clearly demonstrated this in his theory of the militant and industrial types of society, *Principles of Sociology*, Vol. II, Part V, Chps. 17-18.

[20] The fortuitous mode of designating a group is well illustrated in the case of "Russia," where neither the Russians nor their historians know how the name was given to the group or what it meant. The historians of Russia are still arguing the problem and still entertain divergent hypotheses in the matter. On the other hand, the name "U.S.S.R." is an example of a purposefully adopted name, like those of most business firms and of many other groups.

Chapter 22. How Social Groups
Maintain Their Identity and Continuity

Having once emerged, an organized group has to preserve its unity and identity. This represents an amazingly difficult and complex task. First, the group must retain the identity of its component of meanings, norms, or values; second, it must maintain its set of vehicles; third, its membership; fourth, the meaningful-causal connections between these three components. It must preserve a vital minimum of its organization, solidarity, and cultural integration. The difficulty is enormously increased by the fact that each of the group's components and their causal-meaningful connections incessantly changes. If the group, with all its components and their interconnections, remained static, the task of maintaining its identity, with all that this implies, would be comparatively easy; like a static rock it could exist through inertia until destroyed by some external force. However, the group lives and acts in an incessantly changing environment and itself ceaselessly changes in all its components and in the meaningful-causal ties that unite and bind them together. The United States of America, the Catholic Church, Harvard University, the American Federation of Labor are very different, in all their components and their interconnections, from what they were at the moment of their emergence.

The same may be said of any other organized group. Hence the mystery of the problem: how groups can maintain their identity despite the incessant changes in the groups themselves and in their environment.

Since many groups exist for decades, centuries, or even thousands of years, they evidently solve this problem somehow. The question arises: How do they perform this miracle of preserving their manifold identity despite constant changes in all the components, in the connections of these components, and in the ever changing environment?[1]

1. How Groups Maintain the Identity of Their Component of Meanings, Values, or Norms

a. *The Immanent Dynamism of Meanings.* Practically any idea, meaning, or norm is dynamic in its nature in the sense that when pondered over by human beings it tends to change its characteristics. Meanings, norms, and values contain in themselves many logico-aesthetic implications, variations, developments, and consequences, and sometimes hidden contradictions and tensions, that are not grasped at once, and that become explicit only in the process of unfolding as a result of human contemplation. And the more general the idea,

---

[1] In current literature the problem is often discussed under the name of "social control." However, what is discussed under this name covers only a small part of the problem. From the foregoing it is clear that the problem is much wider and much more complex than a mere question of how and by what means the groups maintain

and at the same time change their sociolegal order, or what is called "social control." See E. A. Ross, *Social Control* (New York, 1901); F. E. Lumley, *Means of Social Control* (New York, 1925); L. L. Bernard, *Social Control* (New York, 1939); and the chapters on social control in all the current texts of sociology.

the richer are its hidden implications. None of the meanings in all the fullness of their implicit content is instantaneously open to those who discover it. But once grasped and thought over, it never rests, and tends to unfold itself more and more in all its implications, consequences, manifoldedness and hidden tensions. And so it moves on and on, ever changing itself, without losing its identity and sameness.[2] Almost the entire history of scientific, philosophical, religious, ethical, and artistic discoveries and creations is but an unfolding of the hidden content of the respective meanings, norms, or values throughout the generations of thinkers and creators. He who for the first time discovered the idea of number and primitive mathematics could hardly have perceived that the concept of number contained such a value as $\sqrt[x]{-1}$, or that his mathematics contained all the formulae of present-day arithmetic, geometry, algebra, and calculus. But once the concept of number had arisen, it tended to unfold its innumerable implications through the thought of the countless mathematicians of subsequent generations.[3] He who first conceived the idea of matter or the atom (for example, Democritus or Parmenides) did not realize the limitless implications subsequently opened up by physicists and chemists. The same is true of the ideas of God, causality, life, goodness, beauty, and practically any meaning, norm, or value. In this sense the component of meanings, values, or norms is dynamic in its very nature.

The immanent dynamism of this component makes the preservation of its identity amidst its own incessant changes and those of the group and its environment especially mysterious.

We know that any group retains its identity and the continuity of its existence as long as its component of meanings, values, or norms remains essentially the same. If the component of meanings of the United States is replaced by that of the Buddhist Church, or that of Harvard University by that of the United Steel Corporation, the United States and Harvard University cease to exist, even if all their vehicles and their personnel remain the same. The component of meanings of these groups at the present time is perceptibly different from what it was originally. Thus the Constitution of the United States possesses many amendments, not to mention the thousands of changes which have occurred in the legislative, executive, and judicial norms since the founding of the Republic. Likewise, the constitution, laws, and by-laws, and the total system of values of Harvard University are very different from those of the original institution. Nevertheless, the contemporary United States and Harvard University are a continuation of their predecessors and not of Russia or Berlin University. Hence the question: What are the necessary conditions for such a preservation of identity amidst incessant change?

b. *Inherent Factors of Continuity of Meanings.* The first condition that makes this possible is *the fairly wide margin of potential variations and unfolded implications which any meaning, value, or norm possesses without sacrificing its identity.* $\sqrt[x]{-1}$ still retains the basic traits of number; matter has preserved its essential, or generic, properties from the time of Democritus down to the present day. However the conception of Christianity may differ among the Aryans and the Nesto-

---

[2] J. S. Erigena, Nicolas of Cusa, and Hegel, in their dialectical method, claimed that any idea contains in itself implicitly its own denial, any thesis its antithesis; therefore no thesis can remain static, but must incessantly change until its implicit contradiction is made explicit. When it reaches this stage the contradiction must be removed through synthesis; the synthesis, in its turn, becomes a thesis again, which must change into its antithesis; and so on. One is not obliged to become a Hegelian in order to perceive the immanent dynamism of ideas, norms, and values. For Hegelian dialectics in their application to social reality, cf. my *Dynamics*, Vol. IV, pp. 630 ff.; Hegel, *Science of Logic* (tr. by W. H. Johnston and L. Struthers, New York, 1929), Vol. I, Book I; H. Marcuse,

Reason and Revolution (Oxford University Press, 1941). In a milder form the Hegelian principle that any idea has in itself its own negation has been reiterated by Max Weber, Max Scheler, and E. Barthel, in the contention that any idea contains in it a tension, or *Spannung*, that leads to its differentiation or variation, cf. E. Barthel, *Die Welt as Spannung und Rhythmus* (Leipzig, 1928). About the inherent dynamism of ideas see E. Meyerson, *Du cheminement de la pensée*, 3 Vols. (Paris, 1931).

[3] See H. Poincaré, *Invention mathématique* (Paris, 1908), and E. Meyerson, *Du cheminement de la pensée* (Paris, 1931), 3 Vols.; Meyerson's work gives rich factual material on how scientific ideas unfold themselves in the process of thought.

rians, the Catholic, Protestant, and Eastern Orthodox denominations; all these still retain the basic traits of Christianity, distinct from those of Buddhism, Hinduism, Judaism, Confucianism, or any other religion. The same is applicable to the meanings, values, or norms that are the *raison d'être* of the existence of any group. Nay, more. The totality of the meanings, norms, or values of virtually any religious, occupational, racial, territorial, political, or any other important group is so broad, complex, and vague ("neutral" or "self-contradictory") that the chief difficulty of an investigator who tries to define them consists precisely in their many-sidedness, complexity, and breadth, which tend to elude exact definition. Such a component is capable of considerable variation without losing its identity.

Another condition that facilitates the preservation of the identity of the component of meanings in the group is *the ingenious device of fundamental constitutions, whereby changes in norms are foreseen and the legitimate methods of change are specified*. Thus, if it were voted, in strict accordance with the rules laid down in the Constitution, that the United States should be an absolute monarchy, and such an amendment were embodied in the Constitution, with a corresponding elimination of all contrary provisions, the identity of the United States, despite the drastic change in its government, would be preserved. The same may be said of practically all groups. Their component of meanings, values, and norms provides this ingenious safety valve permitting a wide margin of change without loss of identity.

For even when such a radical change is effected through revolution, the identity of the system is not necessarily terminated. For instance, notwithstanding the revolutionary change of Russia into the U.S.S.R., the continuity of Russia is not ended by its transformation into the Union of Soviet Socialist Republics so long as the Union considers itself merely an improved version of Russia and retains the historical meanings, values, and norms of pre-Soviet Russia—its vital traditional cultural values and institutions.

The third factor inherent in the component of meanings that favors the preservation of its identity is *its selectivity in adopting certain new elements that do not destroy its identity and in rejecting those elements that are totally uncongenial to it*. In Chapter 8 it was pointed out that each organized group possesses this selectivity. Although the official law-norms of virtually any group contain certain neutral or contradictory elements, the bulk of them constitute a consistent and homogeneous system. If a contradictory norm is adopted, the whole system of law has to be revised, and all the norms that contradict the new one are eliminated. This selectivity of the component of meanings, norms, and values tends to resist the infiltration of contradictory elements, as a rule admitting only those that do not prejudice its identity.

The fourth factor is *the inculcation of the prevalent ideological system into the members of the group, and especially into its ruling stratum, through incessant training, education, enforcement, and similar methods*. We have already seen in Chapter 4 that the norms and meanings of an organized group are regularly inculcated and enforced and that their violators are punished.

The fifth factor is to be found in *the symbols and basic rites* of the group. The component of meanings of each organized group possesses a concrete name, sign or symbol, or rite that serves as a substitute for the rich, complex, and somewhat indefinite ideological system of the group. Not every citizen of the United States apprehends all the meanings, values, and norms which the United States stands for. Hence the various symbolic substitutes: such names as "United States" and "Uncle Sam"; the Stars and Stripes; the national anthem; the oath of allegiance; birth and naturalization certificates; and eminent personalities, such as Washington and Lincoln. Being relatively concrete and simple, and for the most part capable of being apprehended by the senses, they are accessible to all, including children as well as "high brows." They serve to bind together all the members of the United States and to carry on the continuity of the meanings, values, and norms for which they are the substitutes. Especially well do the symbols perform this function when they become a fetish, as they tend to become generally (see Chapter 3). The concrete forms of these symbols are various and numerous. (1) The *name* of the group is one of its most important symbols. Its unifying and perpetuating role is particularly important. "The Roman Catholic Church," "the Communist Party," "Harvard," "Great Britain," "Russia,"—these and multitudes of other names that often remain unchanged in spite of a considerable change in the component of meanings serve to effectively preserve the continuity and identity of the group and of its meanings and values. (2) *Various symbolic signs, gestures,* and the like are another form of symbolic substitutes for the component of meanings. The sign of the cross for the Christian religion; the national flag and anthem for a state; "V" for victory; the elephant and donkey for political parties; coat-of-arms and heraldic devices for families and other groups and what they stand for—these are examples of such symbolic perpetuators of the identity of the group and of the values it embodies. While the values themselves change, the signs, remaining unchanged, maintain the illusion of the identity of the values and meanings in question. (3) *Various basic rites and ceremonies* play a similar role: the rites of naturalization; the rite of baptism; the oath of allegiance; the ceremony of saluting the flag; the legal rites of the transmission of property, of adoption, of marriage, of knighting, of enthronement, of initiation, and the like. (4) *Specific persons*—leaders, heroes, kings, members of the government, the Pope, and so on—often function as symbolic perpetuators of the group and of its values. Not infrequently the constitution of a state, a church, or a political party undergoes a marked change in its meanings and values; but as long as the same *personalized incarnation* of it remains, the values of the group and the group itself appear to be the same as before. The same is true of even the *legitimate successors* of such symbolic persons, such as the heir to a throne, a Pope duly blessed by his predecessor, a revolutionary leader approved by the preceding leader. (5) *Various relics and symbolic objects*—family heirlooms, the relics of a saint, the Holy Grail, the crown of Charlemagne, a will and testament, the Bunker Hill Monument, the Kremlin, etc.—may perform a similar function. (6) Finally may be mentioned *all*

symbolic "*conductors*" discussed above (cf. Chapter 3).[4]

c. *External Factors of the Persistence of Meanings.* Side by side with the immanent factors, the groups contain several components *external to the component of meanings* that facilitate the perpetuation of its identity.

(1) The component of the *vehicles* of the group contributes enormously to the perpetuation in question. Though a notable change in the component of meanings involves some of their vehicles as well, this hardly ever applies to all the vehicles. Any important group objectifies its values and meanings through a host of different vehicles, including its property and material possessions. However great may be the change in its meanings and values, the bulk of its vehicles and possessions remain intact—buildings, instruments and tools, often land, etc. The replacement of the Czarist regime by the Communist regime in Russia modified profoundly its meanings, values, and norms; it altered also many of the vehicles and symbols. But the bulk of the vehicles and possessions of the Russian state remained unchanged: the bulk of its territory; its cities and villages; its museums, churches, schools, factories, and other buildings. The totality of these vehicles objectively, visibly, and tangibly testified to the identity of Soviet Russia with pre-Soviet Russia. They bore witness to the fact that the vague, abstract, complex, and elusive changes in the ideological meanings, values, and norms of the Russian state in no way disrupted the continuity of its existence. Similar observations apply to the bulk of the vehicles of any group. Many of these remain constant in the long process of change of the group and of its values. Their unchanged identity testifies to the identity of the changing component of meanings.

In large groups some of the vehicles play an especially vital role as perpetuators of the identity of the group and its values. For groups that are localized on a certain continuous territory the *territory itself* plays such a role. The territory of a state, of a territorial group, of a

[4] Cf. G. Simmel, "The Persistence of the Social Group," *American Journal of Sociology*, Vol. III, pp. 662-698, 829-836, and Vol. IV, pp. 35-50; also "How Society Is Possible," *Ibid.*, Vol. XVI, pp. 372-391.

nationality or nation, tends to perpetuate their continuity: whatever are the changes in their systems of meanings and values, the territory remains and testifies to the identity of these groups in the process of change. A similar function is performed by a family mansion or homestead for a family; by Beacon Hill or some other exclusive neighborhood for a given "aristocratic" group; and so on. A *certain city, monument* or the like persisting through the centuries plays an analogous role for other groups. London, Westminster Abbey, and the Parliament Building perpetuate the identity and continuity of Great Britain; Mecca does this for the Mohammedans; the Vatican, for the Roman Catholics; Washington, the Federal Capitol, the Liberty Bell, the Bunker Hill Monument, for the United States. Any cathedral, castle, shrine, or other building saturated with the memories of important events in the life history of a given group serves to perpetuate its identity and continuity. A further example is offered by the *funds and property* of a group. A university campus, with its various buildings, together with the funds that remain at the disposal of the university, remains in spite of incessant changes in the administration, professors and students, policies, teaching methods, and laws of the institution. The same is true of business firms, labor unions, scientific and other groups. With a proper modification this observation applies to almost all durable group vehicles. This perpetuating function of the vehicles is especially effective when they become fetishes incarnating the group and its values,[5] so to speak, in their own right (see Chapter 3).

(2) The *component of members of the group* also contributes to the perpetuation of the identity of the group and of its component of meanings amidst incessant change. Every organized group inculcates its values into its members and incessantly enforces its law norms. A solidary group develops in its members a sense of unity, of sympathy and loyalty to the group and to its values. For its responsible leaders it tends to select carefully persons well indoctrinated with its values, meanings, and norms. As a result these values, and

particularly the unity and integrity of the group, become deeply rooted in its members. Though the membership incessantly changes, some members dying or dropping out and new members being born or joining the group, this change goes on in such a way that at any given moment the bulk of the members remain constant. With the exception of periods of catastrophic and spasmodic changes, the incoming and outgoing streams of members flow gradually and imperceptibly. Hence at any given moment of its existence the group and its values are solidly incorporated in the bulk of its membership. Though the meanings may change, the bulk of the members remain, attesting the continued identity of the group and of its component of meanings. Though the Russian revolution profoundly altered the meanings, values, and norms of the Russian state, yet the bulk of its members, the Russian people, persisted, thus perpetuating the continuity of the Russian state in spite of the changes in the component of its meanings and even in its name ("U.S.S.R." instead of "Russia").

The membership component serves to perpetuate the identity of the group and of its values in other, much more positive ways. First, it often perceives the advisability of a modification of its meanings, values, and norms and deliberately effects the modification. Like anyone who, having deliberately changed some of his views, opinions, beliefs, ideas, tastes, and other values, fails to regard such a change as having destroyed his former personality, viewing it merely as its further development, similarly a group may deliberately alter some of its values and meanings without regarding the change as the end of the identity of the group and of its values.

Second, the sense of unity, solidarity, and loyalty to the group developed in the members widens enormously the scope of the changes which the component of meanings may undergo without loss of identity. A person whom we love remains the same beloved person for us despite changes in some of his characteristics—his opinions, beliefs, ideas, tastes, manners, etc. Similarly, the group and its values beloved by the loyal, devoted members remains the same beloved group even if it has altered certain of its characteristics.

[5] For an excellent analysis of this role of *vehicles*, cf. W. I. Firey, *op. cit.*

"My country right or wrong, always my country!" well expresses this idea.

Third, changes in the component of meanings, values, and norms ordinarily proceed gradually. At any given moment they involve only one or a few of the sum total of ideological factors. In addition, at any given moment they usually apply to only a part of the members of the group. Even in an abrupt revolutionary upheaval only a small proportion of the total membership modify their sense of values at any given moment, and only with respect to certain values. Even so drastic a revolution as the Russian revolution altered only an insignificant proportion of the sum total of the meanings, values, and norms of the nation. And this change involved at any given moment only a small fraction of the total population. Some of the values supplanted were eventually revived and reinstated.[6] Such a change, involving at a given moment only a small fraction of the total values of the group and only a fraction of its total membership, and proceeding slowly and gradually, does not disrupt the identity and continuity of the group and of its component of meanings.

(3) Finally, the *identity of the component of meanings and of the group is perpetuated also by other groups with which the given group interacts*. A business firm, a family, a state, or a religious or other organization in contact with other groups enters into many agreements or contracts, with their prescribed rights and duties. As a rule such contracts are not subject by a limiting clause "until some change occurs in the group." A debt contracted by a family, business firm, or the like must be paid even if meanwhile "constitution" and personnel have been modified. An international treaty, signed by the government of a state, remains binding upon the state despite changes in its government and constitution. A married couple, even though they may wish to dissolve the union, are regarded by other groups as duly married, and subjected to the rights and duties inherent in their status, until such time as the union is dissolved through the appropriate legal formalities. In all such cases a given group remains identical for all the other groups, no matter what changes may have occurred within the component of meanings

[6] Cf. my *Russia and the United States*, Ch. 9.

or other components of the group. Its obligations to other groups are enforced by the latter in spite of all changes. Thus the other groups not only facilitate the continuity of the group and of its identity but actually impose this continuity upon it.[7]

The totality of the enumerated immanent and external factors of the identity of the group and of its component of meanings explains the "miracle" of how they remain identical despite incessant change. Later on we shall consider how the component of meanings changes, what quantitative and qualitative processes manifest the transformation, and when the change becomes so great as to destroy the identity of the meanings, values, and norms.

2. What Kind and Amount of Vehicles Facilitate the Maintenance and Continuity of the Groups

(a) Every group must have the vehicles that objectify and manifest its meanings, norms, and values, as well as the members that constitute the group itself. If it loses all its members, it ceases to exist or becomes at best a hollow shell. The excavated civilizations of ancient Egypt, Babylonia, Sumeria, and the Creto-Mycenaean culture afford examples of such dead shells of ancient groups. The excavated cities and buildings represent some of their vehicles and some of the meanings, values, and norms which these vehicles objectified; but in the absence of living members of these groups, they can give us nothing else. Likewise if a group loses all its vehicles, its system of meanings, values, and norms ceases to be articulated; therefore the group as such ceases to live and function. Instead of a group we have in this case only two potential components: the meanings and the human agents, devoid of any empirical collective unity or meaningful-causal connection. In a word, in order to exist, a group must have some vehicles and members, and it must be able to maintain some assortment of these components.

How the groups secure these components will be discussed in subsequent chapters. For

[7] For several sound observations on this point, cf. E. Dupréel, *Le rapport social. Essai sur l'objet et la méthode de la sociologie* (Paris, 1912), pp. 33 ff.

the present it is important to note that merely procuring a certain assortment of the vehicles and members is not enough for the persistence of the group. *Both the vehicles and members must possess certain qualities in order to play this role.*

(b) As to the *vehicles* we know (see Chapter 3) that the connection between the meanings, values, and norms and the vehicles is comparatively loose; the same meaning can be expressed by many different vehicles, and the same biophysical vehicle can objectify a long series of different meanings. Their marriage is, so to speak, polygamous. However, this unspecificity and looseness of their connection is not unlimited. Not all vehicles can equally well objectify the meanings, nor can the meanings indiscriminately select any vehicle for their externalization and socialization or change too rapidly and abruptly. *Language* is a vehicle—the transmitter of ideas. Suppose that a certain nationality group—say, the French—should adopt in swift succession a series of different language vehicles—today English, tomorrow Russian, etc. The result would be the disappearance of the French nationality group in a linguistic sense. Hence the language vehicle, its persistence and preservation, proves to be one of the indispensable prerequisites of the French or other nation.

Territory is one of the material vehicles of the state group. If a state loses its territory, it ceases to exist as such. *The material funds and possessions of the group* constitute another variety of its vehicles. Deprived of the funds used, not for the maintenance of its members, but for the functioning of the group, it would rapidly dissolve, being no longer able to perform its functions. Imagine for a moment that all the books, records, pictures, etc. of a group were destroyed. Such a loss would seriously endanger its continuity; for owing to the limitations of human memory most of its traditions, rules, ideas, beliefs, and values would thereby be sacrificed. If for instance, the scores of all the musical compositions of the great masters were destroyed, most of the musical societies would disintegrate. Nowadays the lack of even such vehicles as radios, telephones and telegraphs, and newspapers would render impossible the functioning of a great many groups.

(c) Moreover, a group cannot afford to change its vehicles, especially the symbolic ones, too rapidly and to use various biophysical objects undiscriminately for its vehicles without endangering its continuity. For example, if the United States should alter its anthem and flag every week, such a rapid change not only would lead to marked confusion but would seriously jeopardize the continuity of the existence of the United States; most of its citizens and the rest of the world would be at a loss to understand precisely what "the United States" stood for. Again, if a church employed as its symbols today a cross, tomorrow a swastika, the next day a crescent, or called itself now "the Christian Church," now "the Woodlawn Church," now "the Mohammedan Church," the result would be hopeless confusion.

In such a rapid change no "marriage" between the meanings and the vehicles could crystallize and become socially apprehensible; no specific vehicle could function as a concrete sign of certain meanings and values; everything would be chaotic and in a state of flux. Under such conditions the vehicles could not serve either as objectifiers of meanings or as perpetuators of the identity of the group and of its component of meanings.

To summarize: *in spite of the looseness of connection between the meanings and vehicles, no group can rapidly change most of its important vehicles, especially the symbolic ones, without endangering the continuity of its existence.* This explains why many religious, political, family, and other groups make their most important symbolic vehicles, such as the name of the group, its flag, its oath of allegiance, its constitution, the symbol of its religion, ikons, important rituals (for instance, religious sacraments), prayers, and so on, hieratic or sacrosanct, not subject to alteration in the slightest detail. The absence of such a provision would lead to incessant fluidity of the vehicles and the loss of their individuality. Of a person whose physical appearance is markedly changed we often say, "That is not the Mr. X we used to know." Still less recognizable is a *group* in such circumstances, since groups are incapable of being sensorily perceived as we perceive a person or a concrete material object.

No group can afford to use indiscriminately any biophysical object or phenomenon as a vehicle for its meanings, values, and norms. Thus, if a group expresses its ideal of sexual chastity through erotic songs, pictures, and books, the vehicles will objectify and induce not chastity but rather sexual licentiousness. If the devotion of a group to its values and heroes is expressed by means of objects and actions ridiculing, "debunking," or debasing these values and heroes, the result will be a degradation of the values and heroes, and thereby of the group itself. If the all-loving God of a religious body is depicted as a monstrous devil, the vehicles in question will not serve their purpose. If a group preaching poverty and self-denial manifests these values through an accumulation of wealth, luxury, and sensuality, its vehicles are of no avail. If a temple presumably devoted to God is turned into a market place of profiteers, the temple as a vehicle will tend merely to undermine the religion. (Jesus had to expel such merchants in order to restore the proper function of the Temple at Jerusalem.) If a state professes the value of enduring peace through ever-increasing armaments and the glorification of war, the cause of peace will scarcely prosper.

(d) Even *quantitatively* there are maximum and minimum limits for vehicles, with an optimum point for the continuity of the group and its system of meanings. The irreducible minimum must obviously preclude the total absence of vehicles, since this would terminate the life of the group as such. If the total mass of vehicles falls below the optimum point (which differs for different groups), it hinders the continuity and the full functioning of the group. Groups with too few material funds, with inadequate means of subsistence for their members,[8] with insufficient advertising facilities and means of communication (radio, telephone, telegraph, press, etc.), with poorly developed linguistic, scientific, and artistic resources, and with too meager symbolic vehicles in all their various forms—such groups are in a less favorable position to assert their individuality, their identity, and the continuity

of their existence than groups possessing more abundant and adequate vehicles.

However, the increase of vehicles beyond the optimum point endangers, rather than promotes, the individuality and continuity of the group, leading to "the curse of bigness," "the disease of quantitative colossalism," and "the intractability of the vehicles," which sap the creative vigor of the group and the integrity and purity of its system of meanings and values.[9] Under such conditions the vehicles as the *means* for objectifying and socializing the meanings, norms, and values tend to become *end* values, and the technique of the vehicles tends to replace the values themselves. Like an organism, the group becomes "obese," and progressively less robust in its creative life. The vehicles become less and less capable of expressing adequately the ideological *raison d'etre* of the group. Less and less energy is left for truly creative activities in developing and enriching the component of meanings, values, and norms. At the same time the group is fatally impelled to accumulate still further vehicles, which it employs for the dissemination of trivial and undigested ideas akin to those of newspaper writers and radio broadcasters whose utterances are distinguished chiefly for their vacuity and vulgarity. The quality of the values is supplanted by the quantity of the vehicles. The result is a situation analogous to the contemporary multiplication of radios devoted to vulgar crooning and similar trash, to the use of churches devoid of the spirit of God, to the functioning of college buildings in the absence of notable teachers and thinkers. (For this type of group see pages 175-177.) When the principal world religions, starting as a rule with a very modest accumulation of vehicles, came to amass wealth, their most vital, creative, and spiritual age was past, giving place to the cult of "bigness," which progressively perverted their system of values and undermined their ethos. Similarly, when a given nation becomes a vast empire, the "curse of bigness" leads to im-

---

[8] The means of subsistence for the members of the groups is not discussed in this work. How groups provide the means of subsistence for their members is properly a question of economics, not of general sociology.

[9] For "the curse of bigness," "the intractability of the vehicles," the role of vehicles as "idols" or

end values, the substitution of technique for creative genius, cf. my *Crisis*, Ch. 7; also A. J. Toynbee, *A Study of History* (Oxford University Press), Vol. IV, pp. 119-585. Toynbee gives a detailed analysis of the "intractability" of institutional vehicles, of the idolization of ephemeral technique, etc.

perialism, to decreasing creativeness, and to
eventual disintegration, as attested by the
experience of Egypt and Babylonia, China and
India, Greece and Rome, and modern empires.
With a proper modification the same may be
said of almost any group. Beyond the optimum
point a further increase of its vehicles disintegrates rather than integrates, hinders rather
than promotes, the individuality of the group
and its creative continuity.[10]

3. The Role of the Members in the Continuity of the Groups

Several conditions in this component promote the perpetuation of the identity and
continuity of the group.

(a) In addition to general biological and
sociocultural properties such as good health,
sound hereditary endowments, and so on,
*an uninterrupted inculcation of meanings,
values, and norms in the members of the group
by every method of indoctrination* is of the
first importance. Especially does this apply
to the leaders and rulers. Only thus can the
group preserve its identity amidst the constant flux of its membership. In earlier sections the point was made that amidst the
changing ideology (meanings, values, norms)
of the group, the vehicles tend to remain
fairly constant, thus creating the illusion of a
relatively static ideology. Also that in normal
times the membership changes very slowly.
Like the vehicles, the membership of any permanent group incessantly changes. Otherwise
every new member would interpret its ideological culture in his own way, the common
denominator of the values would soon disappear, and in a short time the group would
fall apart. This is the reason *why almost every
group possesses devices for an incessant indoctrination of its members*: the ceremonies
of initiation and baptism; rituals and festivi-
ties; indoctrination through the family, through
the school, through the church, through the
press, and through addresses; the commemora-
tion of group heroes; the celebration of im-

portant events (George Washington's birthday, Lincoln's birthday, the Fourth of July,
etc.), and so on. This need explains the various
qualifications which new members must
possess before they are admitted to membership, especially to the responsible positions in
the group. If members of the Roman Catholic
Church are ignorant of its credo and main
values, if citizens of the United States are
unfamiliar with the values the United States
stand for, such a church and state will rapidly
lose their identity in a welter of heterogeneous
values, meanings, and norms.

Indoctrination is especially important *in regard to the law-norms of the group*. In any
long-existing group the law-norms must be
rooted in the law convictions and actions of
its members or at least in the most powerful
elements of the group. As we have seen in
Chapter 4 and shall see in Chapter 33, no lasting order can be maintained through mere
coercion on the part of the bosses. For a short
time the law-norms can be maintained by compulsion. But in the long run the essential prerequisite is efficient indoctrination of the members with the norms in such a way that they
become "second nature." Most of us refrain
from murder, theft, and rape not for fear of
being apprehended and punished but because
the very idea of such actions arouses a sense
of revulsion—because such actions are inhibited by the force of our convictions, backed
by the force of emotion and volition. If all the
members of a group were nihilists and cynics,
or entertained mutually opposed law-convictions and norms, no police or courts could
successfully maintain order for any length of
time; even the authorities themselves would
become unreliable, disorderly, cynical, and
corrupt.[11]

(b) *The development of mutual sympathy,
loyalty, devotion, a sense of oneness, among
the members of the group is a second fundamental factor perpetuating its identity and continuity.* Without such a morale no group can
be permanent. It will lack, as it were, the
cement essential for its unity. Its members not

---

[10] Cf. the excellent analysis in A. Toynbee, *A
Study of History* (Oxford, 1934-1938), Vol. III,
pp. 138 ff., and Vol. IV, pp. 39 ff., *passim*. Cf. all
four volumes of my *Dynamics*, especially Vol. I,
pp. 304 ff., 515 ff., 560 ff:, 666-667, and Vol. IV,
pp. 78 ff., and my *Crisis*, pp. 252 ff. See also Ch.
8 of the present work.

[11] The extreme relativity of the norms and their
contradictory character with different persons and
groups are among the main reasons for the excessive juvenile and other delinquency, lax enforcement of the law, for revolutions, and wars of our
time. Cf. Chapters 33, 42.

only will not strive to preserve it but on the contrary will seek to destroy it. Without this loyalty and devotion of the members to the group and to one another, no genuinely concerted action can be obtained except through coercion. Most of the members will perform their duties and functions in the most inefficient way. As a result the group will exhaust its energies in internal conflicts.

(c) Besides these qualities the *size of the membership of the group* is an important factor in its perpetuation. For its longevity there is an optimum size of its membership, deviation from which in either direction adversely affects its continuity. The adverse effects of too small a membership are well known. All that has been said respecting an excess of vehicles may be said also, with slight changes, about the oversize of the membership. The "curse of bigness" is as applicable here as in the component of vehicles. With an increase of the membership their heterogeneity increases. Thus the indoctrination with the meanings, values, and norms of the group becomes progressively difficult. These come to be articulated less and less effectively until their essence is lost in the variety of the interpretations. The group becomes more and more intractable. When Christianity or Buddhism was disseminated among millions of heterogeneous groups and persons, of varying social status and mentality, the clarity and purity of the religion markedly declined. Frequently only its name and perhaps a few concrete symbols survived as the common denominator. Similarly a political state embracing hundreds of millions of members of the most heterogeneous types, including Fijians and Tasmanians, Hindus and Malayans, up to the British aristocracy, is bound to become for many a mere prison—something negative in value instead of something to be cherished, a unity for which the members are ready to fight and to die. In many cases the only bond is that of coercion. The bigger such an empire becomes, the less united it becomes and the more liable to disintegrate through internal conflicts. This has been the tragedy of virtually all the big empires.[12]

[12] For the facts and a further analysis of this curse of colossalism, cf. the works of Toynbee and mine cited in footnote 10.

With a slight change the same may be said of occupational, political, national, and territorial groups, such as the huge metropolis, the large college, and the big corporation. Having grown beyond the point of their optimum size, they all generate the forces of self-destruction rather than of continuity and self-preservation.

4. The Role of the Causal Bonds Uniting the Group's Components

Finally, the group must have *efficient meaningful-causal bonds to unite all the three components into one structural and dynamic whole.* If there is no meaningful-causal interdependence between the three components, the group does not exist as a real unity. If the connections of the causal-meaningful interdependence are too loose and too weak, the group becomes poorly united, organized, and integrated. In Chapter 17 we have seen that a group is seldom perfectly integrated in all its three components. Only a part of the meanings are consistently and unfailingly objectified in the vehicles and in the actions of the members. Only a portion of the members fully practice, so to speak, what the meanings, values, and norms preach. Between the poles of a perfect meaningful-causal integration of all three components and a total lack of such an integration (which means the nonexistence of the group) there is a wide area of variation in the relative efficiency with which the meaningful-causal bonds unite the three components. Other conditions being equal, *the groups whose three components are united by the meaningful-causal bonds more closely and effectively have a better chance for their continuity than the groups united more loosely.* Laxity of the bonds means that the norms and values are poorly articulated in the vehicles and largely ignored in the actions of the members of the group.

The foregoing analysis shows how groups maintain their identity and continuity and how difficult the task is. No wonder, therefore, that, as we shall see (cf. Chapter 34), many groups are short-lived and that only a few survive for hundreds or thousands of years.

In the following chapters we shall study in greater detail how groups preserve their vehicles and membership, and what processes recur in the maintenance of these components.

Chapter 23. How Groups Acquire, Exchange, Distribute, and Lose Their Vehicles

I. How Groups Acquire Their Vehicles

An organized group must have an assortment of vehicles that objectify, socialize, and solidify its meanings, values, and norms; that allow it to function and to realize its objectives; that make possible the maintenance of the group's members and the performance of their assigned roles and functions. The vehicles embrace (1) the speech and overt actions of the members through which they objectify their rights and duties and articulate the values of the group, and which may be called the *behavioral vehicles, service, or values*;[1] (2) the tools, instruments, equipment, buildings, material possessions, funds, and a multitude of other material or economic objects which articulate the group's objectives and make its functioning possible, and which may be called *material vehicles or values*. In some groups, such as purely religious, philanthropic, or ideological groups, the material vehicles or values do not include the means of subsistence of their members; the group does not take upon itself this task, leaving it to the members to derive them from some other group or source. In other groups the material vehicles or values include also the means of subsistence

of their members. The process of acquiring and maintaining the necessary minimum of the behavioral and material vehicles or values is a universal and perennial process, going on in all groups as long as they exist. Hence the problem: How do groups acquire and maintain their vehicles?[2]

1. Behavioral Vehicles or Values

(a) Almost all organized groups acquire the bulk of the behavioral vehicles *"automatically" through the recruitment and training of their members*. Since actions and reactions are the inalienable property of the members, these supply the group with that kind of services. All that is needed to transform the raw material of their actions and reactions into vehicles is to mold them into the necessary patterns: with respect to how they shall objectify in the assigned language the appropriate meanings, values, and norms; what actions they shall perform or not perform; what kind of ritual to carry on; what functions to discharge; what rights and duties to realize; what manual labor to perform; how to use the instruments, tools, and other material vehicles of the group.

---

[1] Any vehicle objectifying a certain meaning, value, or norm becomes an objectified value itself, in contradistinction to an unobjectified pure meaning, value, or norm.

[2] A part of the material and behavioral vehicles constitute specific economic values which belong properly to economics. Here we are concerned with vehicles or values of a general sociocultural nature.

This kind of vehicle comes to the group automatically through its members. And the more perfectly the behavioral vehicles articulate the ideological culture of the group, the more fully they realize what the group preaches, the better the behavioral vehicles serve the group.

(b) Part of the behavioral vehicles of some groups are not "manufactured," as it were, by the group itself but are obtained from other groups as a *gift, loan, exchange, inheritance, or fraudulent or coercive appropriation*. When a group does not have among its members a person who can perform certain kinds of functions and calls for a doctor, priest, artist, engineer, plumber, or manual laborer from outside the group, the services in question are obtained in one of the enumerated ways. In all such cases the performances of the outsiders are examples of behavioral vehicles acquired from other groups and persons. Through these services the group supplements its own fund of behavioral vehicles.

2. Material Vehicles or Values

These vehicles—funds, possessions, means of subsistence—do not come automatically to the group with its members as their inalienable property. The principal means of acquiring them are as follows: In a really self-sufficient group *the production* by the group of all the vehicles, including the means of subsistence of its members. The clans, the tribes, and sometimes the families of the preliterate populations isolated from the rest of humanity approximate to this extreme type. In the majority of the groups—political, territorial, economic, reli-gious, etc.—the chief ways of acquiring the material vehicles (including or not including the means of subsistence of the members) are as follows: (a) Production of the vehicles by the group plus exchange of its behavioral services and material vehicles for those of other groups. Exchange may be in the form of borrowing, barter, buying, selling, or other forms of trade and commerce. (b) Production by the group plus contribution to it by other groups and persons in the form of a gift, donation, inheritance, or other forms of voluntary contribution free of charge. (c) Production plus coercive or fraudulent appropriation by the group of the services and material vehicles of other groups and persons. (d) A combination of some or all of these ways, sometimes without production by the group in question.

The case of (a) is the prevalent method of securing the material vehicles by most of the groups, including the family and most of the occupational, economic, political, and territorial groups. The case of (b) is prevalent in religious, philanthropic, educational, scientific, artistic, and other predominantly "ideological" groups, often supported by other groups and persons, besides their own members. Cases (c) and (d) are common among states, with their wars and coercive appropriation of the territory, funds, and similar material possessions of other states and groups; also in that of criminal, parasitic, and exploitative groups producing little or nothing and getting their material vehicles, including the means of subsistence of their members, through robbery and plunder, fraud, the coercion and exploitation of other groups and persons.

II. How Groups Distribute Their Vehicles Among Their Members

1. Equal and Unequal Distribution

The official and unofficial law-norms of the groups define the manner of distribution of the behavioral and material vehicles (including the means of subsistence) among their members. The various types of the distribution fluctuate between the poles of *equal and highly unequal distribution*, presenting various gradations of inequality and socioeconomic stratification within the groups. More or less equal distribution occurs very rarely and only within small groups with predominantly familistic relationships, such as the family, the small religious group, and the group of devoted friends. In practically all large groups with predominantly contractual and coercive relationships the distribution of vehicles is invariably unequal. When such groups make an effort radically to equalize the distribution, as many communistic, socialistic, and equalitarian groups have attempted to do (for example, the Communists at the beginning of the Russian Revolution), they generally fail: the strictly equal distribution is usually succeeded by an unequal one. And *the more prosperous the group the less chance is there for a strictly equal distribution. Only in groups with an extreme scarcity of the material vehicles does an equal rationing of the scarce necessities have a chance of success.* Even there several supplementary conditions are necessary, including a considerable development of the familistic or contractual relations. In the needy groups with predominantly coercive and contractual relations the scarcity leads not to equal rationing but to an appropriation of the lion's share by the strong minority, with the majority having little or nothing. In other words, abundance of the vehicles tends to be associated with their unequal distribution, while scarcity leads more often to equal rationing.

The degree of inequality or of socioeconomic stratification fluctuates from group to group, and from period to period in the life history of the same group. As we shall see in Chapters 28 and 30, there is no perennial trend either toward better equality or greater inequality.

2. Private and Group Ownership of the Vehicles

Secondly, some of the groups held the bulk of the behavioral and especially of the material vehicles as the *property or possession of the groups themselves and not of their members.* In such groups the possession, use, management, and disposal of such socialized, nationalized, communized, communal, or cooperative material vehicles are controlled by

the government of the group or by a special body. The group or its government determines what kinds and amounts of vehicles are to be produced or obtained, how they are to be distributed, how and by whom they are to be used or consumed. This system of distribution is ordinarily a "planned" system, with the government doing the planning. In other groups the bulk of the vehicles, including the means of subsistence, constitute the *private property or possession of the members, who enjoy the right of possession, use, management, and disposal of their vehicles.* The distribution of the vehicles in such groups is determined by generosity, private agreements, pressure, and conflicts on the part of the members, through so-called "free market" of exchange (trade and barter), or through coercion and fraud.[3]

Finally, still other groups have an *intermediate system of distribution, partly private and partly public.* The system of American and other corporations in which those who manage—the directors of the General Motors, of the United States Steel Corporation, and so on—do not own even two or three per cent of the property of the corporation, whereas the tens of thousands of owners, the shareholders, do not manage the corporation, affords an example of a combination of the public and private systems of possession and ownership of vehicles.[4]

All these types of distribution of the material and behavioral vehicles have existed in the remote past and in recent centuries, and still exist. Contrary to the common opinion that the system of group property and possession is something new, recently introduced by the Communist and Socialist experiments, such a system was prevalent in many preliterate groups[5] and in many state groups, in ancient

---

[3] One should not confuse equal distribution with the system of group property, and unequal distribution with the system of private property. Almost all the group-property systems in the large state and other groups of the past were very unequal in their distribution, and some of the private-property systems have made for comparatively equal distribution. The widespread opinion that nationalization of the means and instruments of production leads to equality is invalid. The recent Soviet experiment has demonstrated its invalidity as much as all similar experiments in the past. In con-

temporary Soviet Russia there is as little equality in this respect as in almost any "capitalist" country.

[4] Cf. A. A. Berle, Jr. and G. C. Means, *The Modern Corporation* (New York, 1933).

[5] See R. Thurnwaldt, *Economics in Primitive Communities* (Oxford, 1932); M. Herskovits, *The Economic Life of Primitive Peoples* (New York, 1940); L. Hobhouse, G. Wheeler, and M. Ginsberg, *The Material Culture and Social Institutions* (London, 1930); M. Mead, *Competition and Coöperation* (cited above). For the rest of the statements and generalizations of this chapter, cf. my *Dy-*

Egypt, ancient Sparta and Lipara, ancient China (especially at the beginning of our era and again in the eleventh century), ancient Rome after 300 A.D., Byzantium throughout the greater part of its history, and ancient Peru and Mexico. It has been established by many revolutions, such as the Mazdakite revolution in ancient Persia; the oldest known revolution in Egypt (ca. 2500 B.C.), described by Ipuver; several revolutionary movements in Greece and Rome and in the Middle Ages; the Russian Communist Revolution; and the contemporary wave of "nationalizations" of the main material vehicles in England, France, Czechoslovakia, and many other countries of Europe and elsewhere.

Many religious, monastic, family, occupational, and other groups have possessed this type of group or communal property and possession in the distribution of their vehicles, including the means of subsistence.

Similarly, the system of distribution of the type of private property and possession was known to the remotest past and continues to exist in many diverse contemporary groups. The same is true of the third, or mixed type.

As we shall see (Chapter 30), *all these three types fluctuate in the course of time, even in the life history of the same group, presenting no constant historical trend either from communal to private property or from private property to communal, or group, property.* All theories claiming such perennial trends are untenable.

3. The Reasons for Each Type of Distribution

All the perennial factors of stratification enumerated above (see Chapter 21, pages 376 ff), namely, (a) the biological differences of the individuals; (b) the differences in their environment, physical, biological, and sociocultural, especially the ever-changing character of the environment with its "good luck" for some and "bad luck" for others; (c) the advantages of inequality under the given conditions for the survival and well-being of the group or for its most powerful elements; (d)

the potential abundance of the vehicles—all such factors work for an unequal distribution of the vehicles (including the means of subsistence) or for a higher socioeconomic stratification within the group. A decrease of the innate differences of the individuals or of the differences in the total environment of the members, as well as the advantages of a more equal distribution of the material vehicles for the group's survival and well-being (for instance, in those of scarcity of the material vehicles), promotes an equalization of distribution or a reduction of the group's socioeconomic stratification. Ordinarily, excessive inequality of distribution, having passed its optimum point most advantageous to the group, increasingly generates various disadvantages and in this way creates the forces of equalization of distribution. Likewise equalization, having passed its optimum point for a given group, begins to be progressively disastrous and increasingly generates forces that eventually (in an orderly or disorderly fashion) halt further equalization and reverse the trend. Hence there is an incessant struggle of the forces of equalization and stratification within each group, with now one gaining the upper hand, now the other. The result is a constant fluctuation of distribution between the poles of equality and inequality. This mechanism of equilibration is sufficient to explain the fluctuation, as well as the kind of distribution of vehicles within the group (see Chapter 25).[6]

The factors determining the communal or the private-property system of the vehicles are likewise numerous. Of these, four may be mentioned: (a) the nature of the group; (b) the nature of the vehicles; (c) the given constellation of conditions of the group, particularly the presence or absence of emergency; (d) the prevalent type of culture.

a. *The Nature of the Group.* The religious, philanthropic, and similar groups, and the army and navy, by their very nature, are more congenial to the communal system of property than the business groups. As a rule the groups of the first kind have favored the communal type, whereas the groups of the second kind

---

namics, Vol. III, Chps. 7, 8, where the literature is given; also my *Sociology of Revolution* and *Calamity*.

[6] Here, as in many other cases, the groups possess an inherent mechanism for stabilizing their

processes, somewhat analogous to the mechanism of an organism whereby it regulates its temperature and other processes. Cf. W. B. Cannon, *The Wisdom of the Body* (New York, 1933).

have favored the private system of distribution of their material vehicles. *The groups with predominantly familistic relationships are more congenial to the communal system than those with the predominantly contractual type of relationships. The groups with predominantly coercive relationships present both types*: the coercively communal type, imposed by the masters upon the subjugated group (the communal property of prisons, partly of the army, of slaves and serfs, and so on); and the private type, represented by groups of slaves and serfs whose duties to the masters are confined to a certain payment of services, products, or taxes, leaving the rest of the vehicles to their private management.

In a population with both poor and rich groups *the poor groups are more disposed to favor a communal system of distribution than the rich ones*. The history of the diffusion of communistic, socialistic, and similar ideologies, as well as of the predominantly poor groups participating in various equalitarian, communistic, socialistic, and similar movements, illustrates this phenomenon. Such a disposition occurs only in populations composed of both the poor and the rich.[7] In a population devoid of sharply contrasted poverty and wealth it tends to disappear. Finally, *the groups with a dominant ideational or idealistic culture are more conducive to the communal system of possession of vehicles than those with a predominantly sensate culture in its initial virile phase*. In the disintegrating phase of sensate culture there is an overabundance of violent efforts to replace the private system by the communal system; but most of such efforts prove abortive, resulting in a semichaotic redistribution of the nationalized material vehicles.[8]

b. *The Nature of the Vehicles.* Some of the vehicles, by their very nature, are more susceptible to a communal type of distribution than others. To the first group belong the material and behavioral vehicles that are necessary for the welfare of the group but either are unprofitable for private persons and

groups, or exceed the limits of private means for their establishment, operation, and maintenance, or can be created and maintained only through the collective efforts of the group. The buildings, funds, and other instrumentalities of churches and cathedrals; of many public schools, prisons, fortresses, courts, museums, and research institutions; of great ports; of armament factories; frequently of post offices and mail systems; as well as many telegraph and telephone systems, highways and airways, railroads, and other systems of communication and transportation, together with certain lands, forests, lakes, and the like—these and hundreds of other vehicles, especially when their establishment requires an enormous expenditure of capital, material, and labor, and when they cannot be operated profitably by private persons and groups, are possessed, owned, and operated predominantly by the group itself, whether it be the state, a local community, a political party, the army, an occupational group, or a religious or educational organization. Vehicles that can be produced and managed by private persons and are profitable to operate privately have been operated privately. This applies to most commodities produced either by hand or by machine, both producers' goods and consumers' goods. The distinction, however, is only relative, since any kind of vehicle may be owned now in one way and then in another. Nevertheless, it rarely happens that the buildings and other paraphernalia of cathedrals, temples, and other churches or of prisons, fortresses, courts, and the like are owned privately. On the other hand, a large volume of consumers' goods is ordinarily owned privately, even in groups with communal ownership of the means and instruments of large-scale production.[9]

c. *The Given Constellation of Conditions, Particularly the Presence or Absence of Emergency.* In the life history of the same group there is a fluctuation of communal and private distribution of vehicles. Such a fluctuation is due to the changing combination of circumstances of the group, both its internal and external conditions. Precisely what these cir-

---

[7] Cf. my *Calamity*, Chps. 7, 15.

[8] Cf. my *Dynamics*, Vol. III, Chps. 1-8. These cases illustrate the role of the nature of the group as a factor in determining "communal" and "private" systems of vehicles distribution.

[9] These and subsequent factors show the inadequacy of the prevalent opinion that in a capitalist society all kinds of groups are characterized by only private ownership.

cumstances are is still inadequately determined. But one basic condition is fairly well established, namely, the role of acute crises. Whether the emergency is a war or revolution, a famine or grave economic depression, a serious epidemic, a devastating earthquake, drought, or flood, or a notable demoralization of the group, its onset tends to expand and intensify the governmental regimentation of the behavioral and material vehicles of the group. With the expansion of government regimentation the communal distribution of vehicles tends to increase at the cost of private ownership, use, management, and disposal. When the emergency passes, the opposite process ensues. (In Chapter 30 this tendency is discussed more fully.)

d. *The Nature of the Prevalent Culture.* As has been observed, the groups whose dominant culture is ideational are more susceptible to a communal system of distribution of vehicles than the groups possessing a predominantly sensate culture in its initial, virile phase.

4. The Manner of Intragroup Distribution

The ways in which each member of a group or one of its strata obtains a share of the behavioral and material vehicles are essentially the same as the ways in which the group as a whole obtains its vehicles: (a) Through the production of material vehicles and behavioral services. The former may be for one's own use or for exchange with other members of the group or with outsiders. Material vehicles as well as services may be exchanged for the products or services of others or for wages, salaries, fees, rentals, profits, and the like. (b) Through gifts, donations, bequests, and similar contributions, supplemented or not by one's own production and services. (c) Through parasitic, exploitative, coercive, fraudulent, or criminal appropriation of the services and material values of other persons and groups. This type comprises many varieties, including the nominally "legal" appropriation of the vehicles of slaves by masters, those of the colonial peoples by their "civilizers," and of the produce of the lower strata of society by the upper strata; the appropriation of the vehicles of his victim by a criminal, and intricate modes of enrichment of an individual or of a stratum through a combination of some or of all these methods. In the majority of cases of rapid and inordinate enrichment of individuals or strata, their own productions and services, however valuable, are rarely sufficient to account for their acquisitions, which are due to such factors as donations or bequests, the appropriation of the vehicles of other persons or groups, including the Marxian "surplus value"; and sheer "good luck" in discovering an oil field or gold mine or in gambling on the stock market.

III. How and Why Groups Lose Their Vehicles

The continuous process of acquiring behavioral and material vehicles goes hand in hand with the no less continuous process of losing them. In the life history of any group and of any member or stratum within it the production or acquisition of vehicles is paralleled by their depreciation, consumption, or loss; income is offset by expense, renovation by obsolescence, replenishment by depletion. The totality of the vehicles is analogous to a pond fed by an incoming stream and drained by an outgoing stream. *The life processes of the group or of its members are the continuous and necessary cause of the incessant depreciation* or obsolescence, consumption or destruction, and loss of the vehicles. Other factors, internal and external, may play a supplementary role, sometimes a catastrophic one, but they are neither constant nor indispensable elements of the process in question.

The various factors responsible for the loss of group vehicles may be enumerated in detail as follows: (1) The normal depreciation or obsolescence and consumption or destruction inherent in their use. (2) Such intermittent or adventitious physical or biological factors as fires, earthquakes, tornadoes, floods, droughts, crop failures, and epidemics. (3) Excessive donation or gifts to other groups and persons. (4) Various internal or external conditions inhibiting the production of vehicles by the group or by its members or strata, such as religious and ethical precepts condemning riches and glorifying poverty, excessive taxation, and the stifling of incentives for industrious and efficient work and for the application of the inventive and creative genius of the group or of its members. (5) The coercive or fraudulent appropriation of the vehicles of the group or of its members by other groups and members in connection with wars, revolutions, court litigation, the machinations and underhand dealings of competitors, the operations of criminals, etc.

IV. Fluctuation of the Sum Total of Group Vehicles

If the sum total of the "incoming" vehicles is equal to that of the "outgoing" vehicles, the sum total of vehicles remains constant. If the outgoing stream is greater than the incoming stream, the group is impoverished; if the incoming stream is greater than the outgoing, the group is enriched.

Actually it rarely happens that the two streams are equal. If it does occur, it lasts only a short time. During the greater part of the life history of a group the sum total of its vehicles fluctuates. The fluctuation goes on incessantly in all groups even in "normal" times, the given nation, political faction, religious or occupational group, etc. now becoming slightly richer, now slightly poorer. Side by side with these gradual and slight fluctuations there occur sharp and abrupt transitions whereby an impoverished group is suddenly tremendously enriched and a rich group is reduced to the status of paupers. *In periods of war, revolution, and similar catastrophes the fluctuations are more abrupt and violent than in periods of relative order and stability.* For instance, under comparatively normal conditions the material wealth of the American nation increased from $192 per capita in 1890 to $637 in 1919. In Russia, during the seven-year period of war and revolution at the close of the Czarist regime, the per capita wealth decreased from 101.35 rubles (1913) to 38.60 rubles (1921). In America the families of J. D. Rockefeller, Andrew Carnegie, Henry Ford, and others became multimillionaires within the span of a single generation. During the Second World War hundreds of rich families, business and occupational groups, and the like in the occupied countries were utterly impoverished.[10]

As regards their length, the fluctuations range from a comparatively short period (of days, weeks, months, or several years) to one of several decades or even centuries. Business groups fluctuate in their cycles of prosperity and depression in the average periods of three, five, seven, eleven, twenty-five, or more years.[11] Other social groups—the family, religious groups, and all the unibonded and multibonded groups—undergo similar short-time fluctuations in the amount of their vehicles. Many of them lose the bulk of their vehicles and terminate their existence within the brief period of two, five, ten, or more years. For example, the average duration of such small business groups as the grocery, drug, hardware, and shoe stores of Buffalo during the period 1918-1929 was from three to six years. Among large American corporations such as the automobile companies, 64 per cent during the period 1903-1926 survived less than ten years. The median duration of 7338 Swiss joint-stock companies in the period from 1902 to 1920 was only 28.67 years. Similar figures are presented by the Italian and English joint-stock companies.[12] In a subsequent chapter (34) on the duration of social groups it will be shown that many educational, religious, political, and other groups are as short-lived as these business concerns, and that this is due in a large proportion of cases to the loss of

---

[10] Cf. my *Mobility*, Chps. 3 and 18, and my *Calamity*, Ch. 8.

[11] See A. C. Pigou, *Industrial Fluctuations* (London, 1927); W. C. Mitchell, *Business Cycles* (New York, 1930); S. S. Kuznets, *Secular Movements in Production and Prices* (Boston, 1930); J. Schumpeter, *Business Cycles* (New York, 1939); and E. Wageman, *Economic Rhythm* (New York, 1930).

[12] For the sources and other data, cf. my *Dynamics*, Vol. III, pp. 217 ff.

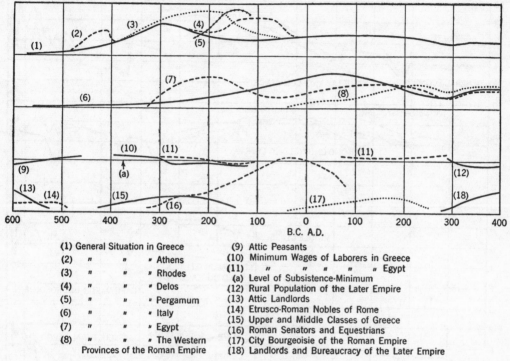

(1) General Situation in Greece

(2) "   "   " Athens

(3) "   "   " Rhodes

(4) "   "   " Delos

(5) "   "   " Pergamum

(6) "   "   " Italy

(7) "   "   " Egypt

(8) "   "   " The Western
        Provinces of the Roman Empire

(9) Attic Peasants

(10) Minimum Wages of Laborers in Greece

(11)   "   "   "   "   " Egypt

(a) Level of Subsistence-Minimum

(12) Rural Population of the Later Empire

(13) Attic Landlords

(14) Etrusco-Roman Nobles of Rome

(15) Upper and Middle Classes of Greece

(16) Roman Senators and Equestrians

(17) City Bourgeoisie of the Roman Empire

(18) Landlords and Bureaucracy of the Later Empire

Figure 1.   Greece-Rome.

most of their material vehicles. Other groups survive longer.

The more permanent groups exhibit, side by side with short-time fluctuations in the sum total of their vehicles, long-time trends with ascending and descending curves representing decades, half-centuries, and even centuries. Figures 1, 2, and 3 show such fluctuations in the material conditions of the Greek, Roman, German, and French populations and of their various groups and classes.[13]

On the basis of these and many other short-time and long-time fluctuations the following tentative generalizations may be formulated.

(1) Most groups existing for a considerable period undergo gradual and abrupt, slight and sharp, short-time and long-time fluctuations in the sum total of their material vehicles and values.

(2) In such groups there is no permanent trend in these fluctuations toward either greater opulence or greater paucity in the sum total of the vehicles.

(3) The fluctuations of various groups of

the same population, such as an agglomeration of unbonded and multibonded groups, do not run parallel: for a given period some of the groups may become poorer, whereas others may grow richer; the "good luck" of one group may prove "bad luck" for another.

(4) However, side by side with such divergent trends in different groups there are periods when the major groups of a given population fluctuate in the same direction, all becoming either poorer or richer.

(5) In periods of serious catastrophe all groups tend to become poorer, with the exception of the small number that profit from the catastrophe.

(6) Under the stress of catastrophe the fluctuations become more abrupt and violent and involve a large number of groups.

(7) The sum total of the material vehicles of the peasant-farmer and laboring classes fluctuates within narrower margins than that of the upper and middle classes.

(8) Groups characterized by a predominantly ideational culture tend to possess fewer material vehicles than those exhibiting a predominantly sensate culture in the phases of

[13] For the details, cf. my *Dynamics*, Vol. III, Ch. 8.

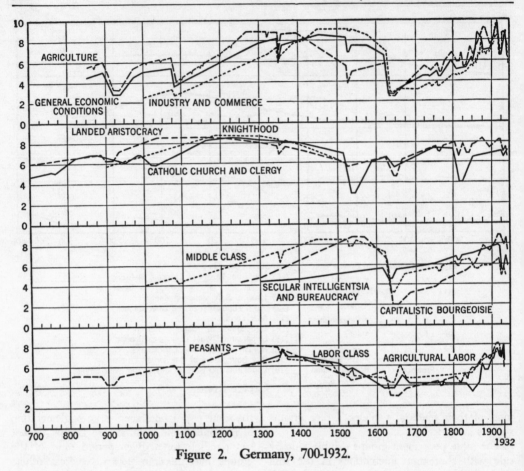

Figure 2. Germany, 700-1932.

the ascendancy and zenith. During the decline of sensate culture its groups tend to become poorer in the sum total of their vehicles, owing to wars, revolutions, anarchy, and other forms of crisis or catastrophe.[14]

(9) In the populations and groups dominated by the ideational and idealistic cultures the material vehicles of the principal religious organizations (associated with cathedrals and other churches, etc.) are much more copious than those of the secular organizations, such as the ruling and the business and professional classes. This is especially true at the zenith and the beginning of the decline of the cultures in question. In populations dominated by the sensate type of culture the converse is true.

V. The Horizontal and Vertical, Intragroup and Intergroup Mobility of Behavioral and Material Vehicles

Since vehicles are acquired and lost through various forms of exchange, gifts and bequests, and compulsory or fraudulent appropriations,

———
[14] Cf. my *Dynamics*, Vol. III, Ch. 8.

they circulate within a group from member to member, stratum to stratum, horizontally and vertically. Likewise they circulate or shift from group to group in both directions. If we desig-

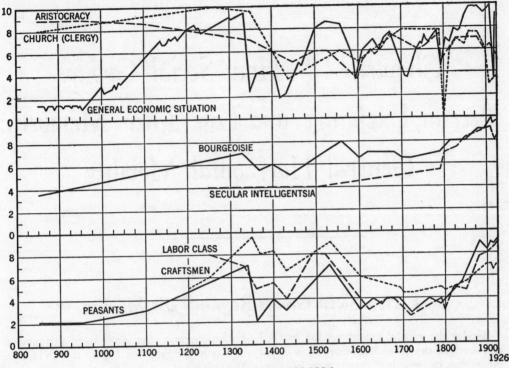

Figure 3. France, 800-1926.

nate a shift of vehicles from one person, stratum, or group to another as *mobility of the vehicles*, we may say that the *mobility of the vehicles is a perennial and universal process in any given constellation of groups*. A shift within a group from member to member, from stratum to stratum, constitutes *intragroup mobility*. A shift from group to group represents *intergroup mobility*. When vehicles move from a lower to a higher member, stratum, or group, we have an *ascending current of vertical mobility*; when they shift in the opposite direction, we have a *descending current of vertical mobility*. The causes and modes, as well as the uniformities, of the mobility of

vehicles will be discussed later (see Chapters 37, 38). The foregoing analysis suffices to show that the process of the mobility of vehicles follows directly from the methods of their acquisition and loss; that it is a perennial and universal process; and that it represents a subclass in a more general process of social and cultural mobility of (1) the members, (2) the meanings, values, and norms, (3) the vehicles. A number of important problems connected with the mobility of vehicles will be treated in the cultural dynamics of this work (Chapters 36 to 38). We shall next turn to a consideration of how groups acquire, exchange, and lose their members.

Chapter 24. How Social Groups Recruit, Exchange, and Lose Their Members: General Horizontal Mobility

I. How Social Groups Recruit Their Members

Besides the general conditions for survival discussed in the preceding chapter, a social group must be capable of maintaining its membership, the component of its human agents. This process falls into two subprocesses: how groups recruit their members and how they exchange them with other groups (social metabolism, or mobility). Let us turn to the process of recruiting the members of the group.

Any organized group existing for any length of time incessantly loses members through their death and in other ways. To maintain its initial size and to grow, a group must continuously recruit new members. Otherwise it will shrink in size and eventually disappear. Hence the problem of the ways of recruiting its members. These may be divided into three main types (each of which presents several subtypes): (1) the automatic, (2) the nonautomatic, (3) the mixed (partly automatic, partly not).

1. The Automatic Way

The automatic method is one of the fundamental means of securing the continuity of a group membership, the component of human agents. The racial and kinship groups (including the family), the state, and (in the past) social orders and castes, religious and occu-

pational groups offer examples of this method. Not only factually but legally the children of the citizens of a state automatically become its citizens, legitimate children automatically become members of a family, and a similar relationship applies to the children of members of a caste or social order, of a race or kinship group. Through this automatic "hereditary" transmission of membership from parents to children these groups obtain an overwhelming majority of their members. Only an insignificant proportion is recruited through such methods as naturalization in the case of states, or of infiltration of outsiders into a caste or social order.

Religious groups and occupational guilds as formerly constituted—that is, as closed groups with a membership legally transmitted from the parents to the children—furnish further examples. Even today, when religious groups are not legally closed, the children of Catholics, Protestants, Jews, and most other religions in from 60 to 90 per cent of cases "inherit" the religion of their parents. Similarly, although the social "inheritance" of the occupation of the father by the children has greatly decreased in western societies in the course of the last century or so, and although the children are now scattered among different occupational groups, nevertheless the occupation of the father is still practiced by a larger percentage of the children than any other occupation.[1] An overwhelming majority of the children of parents of a given nationality automatically become its members. The children of Harvard or Yale alumni favor Harvard or Yale. The children of Republican parents tend to join the Republican party in preference to any other, and so on.

As the easiest and, on the whole, the surest means of maintaining the membership of the group, the automatic method—that of transmission of membership from parents to children—has been widely operative in an enormous number of groups. In many it has been made legally obligatory. All in all, in long-lived groups it has been an indispensable device for maintaining their membership.

2. The Nonautomatic Ways

The main forms of these are (a) voluntary acceptance of membership; (b) appointment; (c) election; (d) employment, or hiring; (e) purchase; (f) and (g) draft and coercion in various forms.

(a) The membership of most scientific, philanthropic, artistic, and other societies, clubs, and associations is recruited through a *voluntary acceptance of membership* by those who are properly qualified and who comply with the conditions of membership (paying fees, and the like). Similarly, the continuity of most families is maintained through voluntary marriage.

(b) In other groups, especially where membership entails certain privileges, *the members are recruited through appointment* by the respective group or by its governing body. Thus professors of many universities are appointed by its governing body. Many officials of the state, the church, and other groups are appointed by their superior authorities: cabinet officers by the president, judges of lower courts by the upper courts, priests by the bishops, elementary schoolteachers by the superintendents, and business employees by their "bosses."

(c) Many groups *elect* their members, especially for their higher strata. In the American federal government this is illustrated by the election of the president, vice-president,

[1] For the data cf. my *Mobility*, Ch. 17.

senators, representatives, and so on. In the Christian Church the positions of Pope or of patriarch are elective, and sometimes those of bishop and priest. Political parties and scientific societies often employ this method.

Election is either by all the members of the group—for instance, by all the citizens of a state who are eligible to vote—or by only a certain stratum (usually the highest stratum), as in the case of the election of the Pope by the cardinals only, of the Emperor of the Holy Roman Empire by its seven electors; of the members of a Masonic Lodge by the upper stratum of the order, of the president of many business corporations by its largest shareholders.

Contrary to the common opinion that the elective method is of recent origin and is necessarily democratic, it is as old as any other mode of recruiting members; and when election is by the highest stratum of the group, for instance, by seven electors among the millions of members of the Holy Roman Empire, or by a few cardinals of the Roman Catholic Church out of a membership of more than a hundred million, it may be as autocratic or oligarchic as any form of *appointment*.

(d) Business firms and other groups obtain their employees by *hiring and by paying the wages agreed upon*. Hiring is a special case of either election or appointment. It is mentioned specifically because of the conspicuous role played by wages in this mode of recruiting membership. They constitute organizations entailing the principal reason why millions of persons agree to become members of such generally monotonous work as that of factories, mills, and offices.

(e) Membership in the upper strata of some groups has often been procured through *purchase* (in an overt or veiled form) by those prepared to pay a high price for the privileges or honors conferred by membership. For example, in certain eighteenth-century monarchies it was possible to purchase a patent of nobility. In a legal or nonlegal, in an open or hidden form, this method of acquiring membership in various groups or strata—ordinarily privileged and especially desirable—has operated on a fairly large scale. Legally or otherwise, this "sale" of membership continues to operate, as in the case of "the Thousand-

Dollar Club" in the election of 1944 and in that of holders of honorary academic degrees, such as those of M.A., LL.D., and Ph.D., liberally granted by our colleges and universities to their benefactors.

(f) The army and navy of most countries recruit their ordinary soldiers and sailors by *drafting* those citizens who have reached a certain age and who meet the necessary conditions. In various forms the draft is used also in other groups where membership entails not so much privileges as burdens.

(g) Finally, *legitimate or illegitimate coercion* supplies members to many desirable or undesirable groups. Through legitimate coercion the membership of prison groups is incessantly recruited by means of arrests and imprisonment of criminals. By coercion hundreds of thousands of persons have their citizenship shifted from one state to another when conquered territories are detached from one state and added to another. By coercion on the part of the state and of the religious authorities, especially in the past, thousands of persons have been inducted into the membership of a given religion. Through overt or veiled coercion hundreds of thousands are forced to vote for a given political party under the threat of the consequences of failure to do so. Similarly, many a marriage undesired by one or both of the parties is concluded under coercion.

3. Some Correlations

Which of the various modes is prevalent in a given group depends upon many conditions. One of these relates to the question whether *membership in a group conveys certain privileges and advantages or imposes certain burdens and sacrifices.*

(a) *Other conditions being equal, groups in which membership entails advantages and privileges—economic, honorary, and otherwise —tend to remain closed to all except the specified limited number of individuals that meet their qualifications.* In these groups the demand for members is smaller than the available supply.

Such groups do not throw their gates wide open for every volunteer who would like to join them. If the ranks of state senators or full professors in the universities, of highly placed executives in business corporations, of exalted dignitaries in religious organizations, and so on were open to all who wished to enter them, there would be millions of senators, Congressmen, professors, Popes, cardinals, bishops, presidents and directors of corporations, and so on. The same may be said of other groups ranging from the Brahmin caste and the nobility to even relatively well-paid occupational groups. Hence all such groups recruit their membership by methods which admit only a limited number of supposedly qualified persons, the automatic way of inheritance of membership by the children of the members, or appointment by the governing body of the group, or election by the upper strata of the members, and so on. Mere willingness to become a member on the part of a volunteer does not suffice.

This explains even such seemingly paradoxical facts as the closed character of the Russian Communist and other revolutionary parties when they assume a governmental dictatorship. After the Communist revolution in Russia the Communist party conveyed a series of important privileges upon its members. If it had been open to all, its ranks would have been flooded by millions of would-be members. No wonder, therefore, that approximately since 1919 and especially since 1922 the party has closed its gates to all except some two or three millions! During subsequent years the maximum size of the membership deliberately controlled by the party fluctuated between 2,600,000 and 4,200,000, hardly ever exceeding the latter figure. Since the Communist party has become a sort of "new nobility" replacing the old Czarist nobility with approximately three million members, such restrictions are quite comprehensible. The same applies to the Nazi party in Germany during the years of its dictatorship.

(b) *The groups in which membership entails mainly burdens and sacrifices rather than privileges and advantages tend to remain open to all who wish to join them.* Everyone is welcome to become a member of the Red Cross, of the Community Chest, of the group of "blood bank" donors; the greater the number of members who are ready to give their monetary contributions, blood, services, time, and energy the better. In such groups the demand for members exceeds the supply. Hence the "open door" policy of recruiting members, reinforced by appeals, such as special publicity campaigns, and sometimes by even prizes and premiums.

(c) Another type of group which welcomes volunteers is represented by *contemporary political parties*, where the rank and file of the members are virtually ciphers, serving the cause of the bosses and of the party candidates. Thus during election campaigns everyone is heartily welcome to join the party and to cast his vote for its candidates. When the campaign is over, the "heartily welcomed dear friends" usually become "forgotten men." Many groups employ a similar procedure.

(d) *Groups in which membership involves notable burdens and sacrifices, disfranchisement, dishonor, or punishment generally employ the compulsory method of recruiting their members.* Even honorable membership in the armed forces in the capacity of a private is sought by far fewer persons than are needed in time of war, hence the draft as a method of recruiting these forces. Few criminals wish to be arrested and imprisoned, hence the resort to compulsion in inducting them into the prison groups. Most citizens of a conquered country are averse to being torn from their allegiance to their state and shifted to another, hence the rude compulsion by which such transfers of citizenship are effected. Again, compulsion has been resorted to by a state or

by the upper castes and strata of a given society with reference to its slaves, serfs, and other submerged castes and strata, who are forced to recruit their members from their children and from a small number of "outcastes."

(e) Finally, *the groups in which membership entails certain advantages and certain disadvantages use several of the foregoing methods.*

4. Critical Remarks

The foregoing ways of recruiting the membership of the groups show the one-sidedness of theories claiming only one of these methods. One-sided is the theory that the membership of all groups is recruited only through a willing, purposive association of individuals. No less one-sided are the theories claiming a coercive method as the only means of recruitment. Like all one-sided theories of the origin and organization of groups, these theories suffer from the "unilateral aberration" of those who perceive only their own "pet way" and are blind to all others. Their authors still view the social processes as an equation in one unknown.

The briefly formulated generalizations concerning the correlation of the type of recruitment with the variables of privileges and burdens suggest that the dominant mode of recruitment of members in this or that group is not something incidental but is deeply rooted in the nature of the group in question.

II. How Social Groups Lose Their Members

Throughout its existence any social group loses its members, either continuously or intermittently. The principal causes may be classified as follows: (1) natural (through death), (2) automatic, (3) nonautomatic, (4) mixed.

1. Natural (Through Death)

The most important and continuous source of loss of members is through their death. In this way every group is incessantly robbed of members, especially those possessing an abnormally large proportion of young children or of old people, the age groups whose mortality rate is particularly high. The periods when the mortality of the members, as a result

of epidemics, war, revolution, etc., is especially high are often critical for small groups or strata that cannot replenish their membership in a short time.

2. Automatic

a. *Expiration of the Term.* In many groups membership, especially in the higher strata, is explicitly limited to a term of one, two, four, or more years. When the term expires, membership automatically ceases. In some groups the tenure may be renewed, in others it can not. Membership in many nonprivileged groups, such as those of hired laborers, servants, and other employees, as well as in more privileged professional groups, is often for a certain term (a week, month, or year, etc.). Another example afforded is by nonre-election or nonreappointment, where elective or appointive membership is for a certain term.

b. *Nonpayment of Dues and Nonfulfill-ment of Duties.* In many groups, particularly in voluntary associations, membership auto-matically terminates with the nonpayment of dues, nonfulfillment of other conditions of membership—for instance, nonattendance at meetings of the group where such attendance is obligatory—also automatically terminates the membership.

c. *Automatic Retirement.* In many groups there is a provision for automatic retirement after a certain age. In many colleges and state groups all members reaching the age of sixty-five or seventy are automatically retired.

3. Nonautomatic

a. *Voluntary Resignation.* In many groups, especially those that are voluntary, members may be lost through their resignation, as in religious, political, occupational, scientific, artistic, and even a few state groups. The method is too well known to call for further comment.

b. *Discharge.* This method, so widely prac-ticed in contemporary relationships between employers and employees, is too familiar to require elaboration.

c. *Expulsion, Ostracism, Excommunication, Banishment, and Imprisonment.* These ways are special forms of discharge. In most cases they are performed by the public authorities of the group, by the group itself, or by its more powerful faction. The reason for such a forcible deprivation of membership is usually some crime or sin, or (in the case of political ex-pulsions) the menace, real or alleged, presented by the victims to the ruling stratum of the group. A Brahmin who commits an unforgiv-able act is expelled from the caste; an officer who compromises the honor of his regiment is discharged; Themistocles and Dante, like thou-sands of other political leaders, were ostracized or banished. A person guilty of heresy is ex-communicated. A criminal punished by the loss of all his political and civil rights ceases to

be a member of the groups to which he has belonged.

d. *Other Compulsory Ways.* A conqueror may deprive thousands of the citizens of a state of their former allegiance and transfer them as citizens to another state. The govern-ment of a state or an autocratic ecclesiastical tribunal (such as that of the Catholic In-quisition), by arresting and imprisoning the members of a prohibited group, may deprive it of many members. By the complete sup-pression of a group or the extermination of its members a government or other power can obviously deprive the group of all its members. The recent Nazi "death factories" in Russia and Poland deliberately used this method for the mass extermination of Russian, Polish, and Jewish groups, and particularly of their leaders.

e. *Correlations.* Like the chief methods of recruitment, the primary causes of the loss of members in this or that group are deeply rooted in the nature of the group itself. The following generalizations can be formulated re-specting the relationships in question.

Automatic ways and voluntary resignation predominate in the groups and strata primarily contractual in character, in contradistinction to the familistic and compulsory types. They pre-dominate in the groups with an elective method of recruiting their members.

Death is the main source of loss of members in the familistic type of group. The very nature of such a group largely precludes both auto-matic factors and the voluntary resignation of the members. The members do not forsake their duties upon the expiration of a certain term; in fact, terms themselves hardly exist in such groups. Likewise, membership is not dependent upon the payment of fees and similar conditions. In exceptional cases other factors may operate, but only in a subsidiary way.

In antagonistic intragroup or intergroup rela-tionships the compulsory methods of discharge, expulsion, excommunication, banishment, ex-termination, and coercive transfer of member-ship from one group to another dominate. The very fact of the exercise of these coercive methods in a group or constellation of groups constitutes substantial evidence of antagonistic relations.

III. How Groups Exchange Their Members

1. Concept and Main Forms of Social and Cultural Mobility

When a group recruits its new members in all the foregoing ways except that of the birth of children among its own members, it acquires them from the members of *other* groups. When it loses members in all the above ways except through death, the loss swells the ranks of other groups. Thus an incessant process of exchange of members occurs. From the standpoint of the individual it represents a process of *intergroup circulation or mobility, of individuals.* Since there are many forms of intergroup and intragroup mobility of individuals, and since these forms represent one of the basic sociocultural processes, it is advisable at this point to define concisely the concept and the main forms of sociocultural mobility.

By *"social mobility" is meant any transition of an individual from one social position to another in a constellation of social groups and strata.* We shall concentrate our attention at this point on the social mobility of individuals, leaving the cultural mobility of the components of meanings and vehicles for subsequent sections of this work. There are two principal types of social and cultural mobility, *horizontal and vertical,* with an intermediary form. By horizontal social mobility is meant the transition of an individual from one social group to another situated on the same level, or stratum. By cultural mobility is meant a similar shift of meanings, norms, values, or vehicles. An individual shifting from a Ford factory to a General Motors factory, at the same salary and doing about the same kind of work, shifts horizontally, without any conspicuous social elevation or demotion. A person who has voted the Democratic ticket and now votes the Republican ticket shifts also horizontally, so long as his position in the two parties remains virtually the same. Cultural horizontal shift is represented by the adoption of telephones, radios, or lipsticks, or the diffusion of the Darwinian theory, communism, and other meanings, values, and norms within a given social stratum, for instance, among farmers of about the same socioeconomic level. In all these cases the shift of individuals or of social values and vehicles takes place without a conspicuous change in the vertical direction, that is, from a lower to a higher stratum or vice versa.

By *vertical social and cultural mobility* is meant the shift of an individual or of a value or vehicle from one social stratum to another—from a lower to a higher rank or vice versa. According to the direction of the transition there are two types of vertical mobility: *ascending and descending: social and cultural promotion, and social or cultural demotion.*

Both horizontal and vertical mobility present *individual and collective forms.* When a factory worker takes the same position in another factory, he shifts individually. When the whole factory shifts to another section of the country, the horizontal mobility assumes a collective form. When an individual rises from the rank of office boy to that of president of a business firm, or from the status of a peasant to the position of a noble at the court of the Habsburgs or Romanoffs, the relative positions of the various social ranks remain unchanged. When a multimillionaire becomes a beggar or a general is demoted to the rank of a captain, he sinks individually. When, however, the entire Romanoff or Hapsburg aristocracy is overthrown by revolutions, its members sink collectively in relation to all the other strata of the Russian or Austrian nation. After the legalization of the Christian Church by Constantine the Great its position underwent a striking upward shift. After the Communist Revolution in Russia the position of the Communist party as a whole was notably elevated among all the other ranks and strata of the Russian population, and with it the social status of its members. When a given system, or congeries, of meanings and values—for instance, the Christian religion or the Communist ideology—was adopted by individuals scattered throughout various countries, the system shifted horizontally in an individual way. When Christianity was imposed upon the entire population of areas of the Roman Empire, or Communism upon the entire population of Russia, the ideology expanded collectively. When a few members of the upper

Social and Cultural Mobility	A. Of Individuals	Horizontal	Intergroup	Similar Dissimilar	General Differential	Individual Collective
			Intragroup			
	B. Of Meanings, values, and norms	Intermediary	Intergroup	Similar Dissimilar	General Differential	Individual Collective
			Intragroup			
			Ascending	Individual Collective		
	C. Of Vehicles	Vertical				
			Descending	Individual Collective		

strata of the Roman Empire embraced Christianity or a few members of the European aristocracy became Communists, the phenomenon represented individual vertical mobility of the ideologies in question. When Christianity became a privileged religion, obligatory for all the upper classes, or Communism was made the official ideology of the ruling class in Russia, these systems of meanings, with their vehicles, climbed the sociocultural ladder in a collective way, the rank of each changing in relation to that of the hitherto privileged and now disenfranchised religions or political credos.

Such are the essential forms of social mobility. The difference between the horizontal and vertical forms is clear, not only theoretically but empirically. There are, however, many shifts and transitions that are somewhat indefinite in character, representing horizontal mobility with a slight admixture of promotion or demotion. These may be regarded as *intermediary, or horizontal-vertical, types.*

The various forms of mobility may be summed up in the scheme shown above. Several of the forms shown there will be subdivided later.

2. Forms of Horizontal Intergroup Mobility[2]

The horizontal mobility of individuals assumes mainly the form of intergroup mobility. Viewed from the standpoint of the groups, it consists in an exchange of their members.

Viewed from the standpoint of the individuals it represents a shift of membership from one group to another. There is, of course, also an intragroup horizontal mobility; but it reduces itself to a mere spatial shift of an individual from one district or community to another, from one factory, office, or house to another.

Intergroup horizontal mobility may be a shift of an individual from one group, such as the Baptist Church, to a *similar* unibonded or multibonded group, such as the Methodist or Catholic Church; from the Republican to the Democratic party; from one occupational group to a similar occupational group. Or it may be a shift of an individual from one group to a *dissimilar* unibonded or multibonded group: from the Methodist Church to the Republican party, from a farmers' occupational group to membership in the National Geographical Society, and so on. In the case of similar horizontal mobility the loss of a member by one group is a gain for another group of the same kind. In dissimilar intergroup mobility the loss by one group is a gain for another of a dissimilar category.

Side by side with the horizontal mobility between *similar and dissimilar* groups we must distinguish *general and differential* horizontal mobility. The general and differential intergroup mobilities are analogous to the general and differential birth or death rate. *General intergroup mobility* means the exchange of the total membership between two or more groups.

---

[2] In these chapters only horizontal and vertical mobility of individuals is treated. The mobility of meanings and vehicles, which enormously increases the total sociocultural mobility within a given population, is treated in the later sections dealing with cultural dynamics.

Its rate is the rate computed for the whole group. *Differential intergroup mobility*, designates the comparative rates of horizontal mobility in the lower and upper strata of the interchanging groups: for instance, the different rates of the recruitment and losses of members among the full, associate, and assistant professors and the instructors of colleges. Do all the strata exhibit the same rate of interchange of their members? Are the rates different for the lower and upper strata? If so, in which are they higher? Are there certain uniformities in the differential rates? Such are the problems of differential horizontal mobility. Having defined the principal forms of mobility of individuals, we shall now turn to a concise consideration of horizontal intergroup mobility.

IV. General Horizontal Intergroup Mobility and Individuals[3]

1. Intergroup Mobility Between Race, Sex, and Age Groups

The purely *biological racial, sex, and age plurels* are not the real social groups; therefore we cannot properly speak of the *mobility of individuals* among interracial, intersex, and interage plurels.[4] Being purely biological, the race, sex, and age characteristics of an individual are congenital and cannot be changed. Such plurels can, through the birth and death rates, change quantitatively, or numerically. But this does not permit a Negro to become a white man, a male to become a female, or an old person to become rejuvenated. In this sense there is no intergroup horizontal mobility of individuals between the bioracial, sex, and age plurels.

There is, however, such a mobility between various racial, sex, and age groups organized as social groups. Among societies for the promotion of the rights of the Negroes there is an exchange of members; indeed white persons now and then become regular or honorary members of such organizations. The same is true of other racial societies. Similarly, women frequently shift their membership from one society of women to another. Not infrequently a person of one sex becomes a member of an organization of the opposite sex. With certain reservations the same generalization is applicable to age groups organized into societies.

2. Mobility of Territorial Groups

An incessant circulation of individuals goes on between one *territorial group* (or "community") and another. In nonindustrialized and nonurbanized populations such *migrations* are comparatively weak; until recently, according to the census of 1901, more than 90 per cent of the population of India died within the territorial group in which they were born. The majority of the remaining 10 per cent were found "only a short distance from their original home and were not emigrants in the ordinary sense of the term." Still more insignificant was the number of persons who went abroad; out of a population of more than three hundred million in 1909 only 11,644 persons emigrated.[5] A similar generalization applies to the population of China and other agricultural countries in normal, peaceful times.

---

[3] In the chapters devoted to the social mobility of individuals I have followed closely, with some variations, the monographic study embraced in my *Mobility* and in the second volume of my *Sistema Soziologii*. The detailed analysis and the conclusions presented by these works are based upon copious facts, statistical data, and other evidences. They supply also an exhaustive bibliography. Few important studies that appeared after the publication of my *Mobility* are referred to in the present work, which confines itself to a concise analysis, a formulation of the uniformities, and a few evidential facts without reproducing the vast body of factual evidence and of literature contained in my *Sistema* and *Mobility*. All the important studies that appeared after the publication of *Mobility* sustain the essential conclusions arrived at in the latter.

[4] The study of an increase or decrease in the population of a given race, sex or age *plurel* is the task of vital statistics. The figures thus obtained have little to do with social mobility.

[5] Cf. my *Mobility*, pp. 382 ff.

Territorial mobility in the industrialized and urbanized countries is incomparably greater and has been increasing, especially in recent decades, since the introduction of railways, steamships, automobiles, and other modern methods of transportation. It has, indeed, become so great that the population of the industrialized western countries in even peaceful times may be regarded as truly nomadic, shifting almost incessantly from locality to locality. Only a small minority in such countries live and die in the territorial group in which they were born. The majority of the population of the big cities was born elsewhere, and a large percentage of those born in a given city no longer live there. In such populations most members change their place of residence (the territorial community) several times throughout their life. Indeed, a substantial percentage change it almost every year, and some are constantly on the move, changing their address almost every week or month. "Trailer homes" are, in a sense, a symbolic manifestation of this increasing territorial nomadism of the industrialized and urbanized countries.[6]

The following generalizations sum up some of the uniformities in the territorial mobility of individuals, or in the exchange of members of the territorial communities.

(a) Weak or strong territorial mobility is characteristic of the population of any locality.

(b) Among the preliterate hunters, collectors of the gifts of nature, and primitive pastoral and agricultural populations it assumes the dominant form of seasonal migrations on the part of groups in their entirety within a certain limited territory. Side by side with this group migration there are occasional individual shifts from group to group.

(c) With an increase of industrialization and urbanization, territorial mobility tends to increase.

(d) Territorial mobility tends to be greater in an urban population than in a rural popula-

tion; in professional, governmental, industrial, and commercial occupations than in agricultural occupations; among men than among women; and among the mature age groups than among the old.

(e) In times of social upheaval and calamity—major reforms, war, revolution, famine, pestilence, floods, drought, earthquakes, and the like—territorial mobility in voluntary and especially in involuntary forms, tends to increase suddenly and sharply in both the individual and the collective forms. These social tornadoes uproot entire communities (thousands and millions of individuals) and often carry them over great distances. The Russian revolution and the Second World War afford concrete examples of this uniformity.[7]

(f) The steadily increasing trend of the territorial mobility of individuals during the last century, strongly re-enforced by the extraordinary upheavals since 1914, renders the population of almost all the territorial communities of the West and partly of the East —village, town, city, metropolitan, and factory settlements—more and more fluid, composed of an ever-increasing proportion of newcomers and strangers, tending to reside in a given territorial group for a shorter and shorter time and bringing with them heterogeneous cultures, mores, and manners. A territorial group thus tends to become a sort of "social hotel" occupied by all kinds of transient guests.

The social and cultural consequences of such increasing fluidity, for the territorial groups as well as for the ever-shifting individuals, are enormous and incalculable. The fluid population regard the territorial community in which they temporarily reside not as a permanent home, as it is viewed by the "sedentary" members who were born there and who spend their entire life there. The fluid population cannot feel any sense of attachment to it such as that entertained by its permanent inhabitants. They are not "impregnated" with the special characteristics of the local culture and mores. On

---

[6] For the figures, cf. my *Mobility*, pp. 382-389.

[7] For the facts, cf. my *Calamity*, Ch. 6, and L. Kawan, *Gli esodi e le carestie in Europa attraverso il tempo* (Roma, 1932). For territorial displacements during the Second World War, see E. M. Kulisher, *The Displacement of Population in Europe* (New York, 1943); also his "Recent Migration in the Soviet Union," *ASR*, Vol. IX (1944),

pp. 223-228. More than eighteen million Americans shifted territorially in connection with war industries in the period from 1940 to 1944. A microscopical picture of this wartime migration from villages to the centers of war industry is given in C. P. Loomis, *Wartime Migration from the Rural Villages of New Mexico*, Mimeographed Bulletin of the United States Department of Agriculture.

the other hand, the incessant influx into a local community of persons from various sections of the world introduces all kinds of cultures, manners, and mores and renders it a "dumping ground" of all sorts of cultural values. This factor increasingly prevents a local community from creating its own individual culture, its own "sociocultural physiognomy," its own sociocultural pattern. The community tends to become more and more standardized and thus experiences a progressive weakening of the attitudes of local patriotism.

Is this trend a permanent one? The probabilities are that it will eventually reach a limit and then will cease and perhaps even reverse itself. For the present and the immediate future, however, it will continue, rendering the population of the local communities still more fluid, with all the positive and negative consequences of such mobility.

3. Interfamily and Interkinship Group Mobility

This mobility is horizontal when marriage, divorce, and adoption does not change appreciably the vertical position of the individuals shifting from family to family. We shall consider here only the horizontal aspect. When a woman marries and comes as a bride into her husband's family (or when, as among certain preliterate peoples, the husband enters the wife's family), the individual shifts from one family or kinship group to another. Through adoption and in similar ways individuals likewise pass from one family to another. Through divorce and subsequent remarriage they again shift from family to family, from one kinship group to another. Considering that among Euro-American populations over eighteen years of age for the males and fifteen years of age for the females only some 20 to 40 per cent remain unmarried, and that among the preliterate and agricultural peoples the percentage is still lower, the interfamily circulation of individuals constitutes a steady and powerful intergroup circulation of individuals. From the standpoint of the family and other kinship groups their "human cells" are in process of constant exchange and renewal. The intensity and other characteristics of the process fluctuate from population to population and from period to period. The following propositions sum up some of the uniformities of this process of interfamily mobility.

(a) In endogamic families the exchange of "cells" takes place between biologically, and often socioculturally, more homogeneous (consanguineous and affined) family and kinship groups than in exogamic marriages. The latter tend to be more efficient mixers of heterogeneous stocks than the former.

(b) In polygamic and polyandric families the interchange of human cells goes on simultaneously among a whole cluster of families and kinship groups, whereas in monogamic families it occurs at any given time, mainly between two of the family or other kinship groups.

(c) The age of marriage tends to be lower and the proportion of the married among the total population tends to be higher among the preliterate, pastoral, and agricultural peoples than among industrialized and highly urbanized populations.

(d) In the western countries the age of marriage in recent times has tended to be lower among agricultural and rural occupations, especially in the case of females, than among most of the industrial, professional, commercial, and other urban occupational groups.

(e) The same is true, in western countries, of the rate of marriage, which tends to be higher (especially in the case of females) in the agricultural and rural occupations than in most of the professional, industrial, commercial, and other urban occupations.

(f) The differences in the rate and age of marriage in western countries are, however, not exceptionally great for different countries, for different occupational groups, and between rural and urban groups.

(g) In time of war the marriage rate sometimes tends suddenly to increase. If the war is prolonged and involves the drafting of most of the marriageable males, the marriage rate goes down until the end of the war. During the first two or three years after the armistice, when many postponed marriages are consummated, the rate rises abnormally and then declines to its prewar level. In some major revolutions and similar calamities it follows this pattern, while in others it does not.

(h) The marriage rate tends to increase in

periods of prosperity and somewhat to decline in periods of depression.

(i) As to divorce and separation, this form of interfamily mobility has been rapidly increasing in most western countries, especially during the past few decades.

(j) This form of interfamily shifting tends to exhibit a higher rate in urban communities than in rural populations; among childless couples than among couples with children; among couples whose members are markedly diverse in respect to race or nationality, religion, cultural values, economic status, age, or health than among couples whose members either are homogeneous or display differences that are mutually supplementary;[8] among atheists than among the devout (unless their religion explicitly approves of divorce or separation); and among liberal Protestants than among Roman or Greek and Eastern-Orthodox Catholics.

(k) In occupational groups the divorce rate tends to be lower among the clergy and the agricultural occupations and higher among actors, showmen, musicians, and the like.

(l) In many countries the divorce rate is higher among the rich than among the poorer classes.

(m) In times of acute social upheaval the rate undergoes a sudden change. With the outbreak of a great war it tends to decline, and continues to decline until the end of the conflict. After the armistice all the accumulated domestic troubles tend to come to a head. This sends the rate of divorce and separation to an abnormally high level during the first two or three years after the armistice. Then the rate returns to its prewar level.

(n) During certain revolutions, famines, pestilences, and similar catastrophes the divorce rate changes in line with the pattern of the catastrophe. In other cases it exhibits a different curve. In revolutions that seek to destroy and then to reconstruct the family, such as the French Revolution and the recent Russian Revolution, the family and the institution of marriage sometimes disintegrate, unlimited freedom of divorce and remarriage is introduced, and monogamy is held in disrepute. As a result the rate of divorce rises to an extraordinary high level, and marriage itself, as a socially sanctioned union, comes to resemble a merely incidental sexual relationship between male and female. Eventually, however, when the destructive phase of the revolution is over, marriage and the family reestablish themselves, and the divorce rate returns to its prerevolutionary level or even falls below it. The Russian Communist Revolution affords a conspicuous example of this pattern. After an almost complete collapse of the family and a fantastically high divorce rate during the first period of the revolution, the family reemerged and became stabilized, and the divorce rate rapidly declined. Especially after the law of July 14, 1944, it became more difficult to obtain a divorce in Soviet Russia than in most of the capitalist countries.

(o) During the first few years after the close of the Second World War we may expect an abnormally high divorce rate. However, there is every reason to assume that, having reached its culminating point, the increase will cease and the trend will even reverse itself, as it did in Russia. So much about this form of horizontal mobility of individuals.[9]

4. Horizontal Interoccupational and Intraoccupational Mobility

When a person shifts from one farm, factory, or office to another of the same kind, without a noticeable change in his vertical occupational position, he shifts horizontally. Interoccupational and intraoccupational horizontal mobility is a universal and perennial process. In some societies, as in that of the Indian caste system, it is very weak. Owing to the

---

[8] Cf. Chapter 7.

[9] For the statistical and other data corroborating these uniformities, cf. my *Mobility*, pp. 397 ff., and *Theories*, pp. 552 ff.; Sorokin and Zimmerman, *Principles of Rural-Urban Sociology*, Ch. 10; E. Groves and W. Ogburn, *American Marriage and Family Relationship* (New York, 1928); W. Thompson, *Population Problems* (New York, 1940); Sorokin, *Calamity*; J. P. Lichtenberger, *Divorce* (New York, 1931); G. von Mayr, *Statistik und Gesellschaftslehre* (Tübingen, 1917), Vol. III; C. Gini, M. Boldrini, G. Zingali, *Demografia* (Torino, 1930); R. Benini, *La demografia Italiana* (Roma, 1911); *Aperçu de la démographie de divers pays du monde* (La Haye, 1929, 1939); A. Bosco, *I divorzi e le separazioni personali dei conjugi* (Roma, 1903); S. A. Stouffer and P. F. Lazarsfeld, *The Family in Depression* (New York, 1937). See also the literature cited in these works.

monopoly of a given occupation by a given caste the members of each occupational group are recruited in India mainly from the children of the parents. On the other hand, among the western peoples of recent times this type of mobility has undergone an enormous development. Various occupational groups exchange their members incessantly and on a very large scale. For instance in the United States in 1917-1918 the labor turnover among industrial workers was such that 2.3 per cent of the employees studied served in a given position for less than one week, 2.5 per cent from one to two weeks, 4.1 per cent from two weeks to one month, 49.5 per cent from one month to one year, and only 27.8 per cent for more than five years. Similar figures are exhibited by the labor turnover in other skilled and semiskilled industrial occupations and to some extent in professional and clerical occupations in this as well as in other western countries.[10] An ever increasing percentage of the gainfully employed remain in a given position for only a short time, tending to shift ever more rapidly to other groups on the same level of occupational stratification. To remain a member of a given occupational group for life becomes an increasingly rare phenomenon.

Among the uniformities observed in this inter- and intraoccupational mobility the following may be noted.

It is lowest in the populations whose social structure is dominated by the caste system. It is low also in populations whose social structure is dominated by the social estate system, with distinct orders of slaves, serfs, free strata, hereditary guilds, and nobility, as in the society of medieval Europe.

It is much higher in populations dominated by the system of social classes. It tends to increase with an increase of industrialization and urbanization. In industrialized and urbanized populations with a system of social classes, horizontal occupational mobility tends to be higher among the unskilled groups than among the semi-skilled, among the semi-skilled than among the skilled and clerical occupations; among unskilled and skilled labor than among the better-qualified and better-paid professional, big business, and highly placed governmental groups. From an economic standpoint it tends to be greater among the poorly paid occupational groups than among the highly paid ones. In periods of prosperity it tends to increase, especially among the laboring classes; in periods of mild depression it tends to decrease.

During wars and other major catastrophes, as well as fundamental technological and industrial revolutions, inter-/and intraoccupational mobility suddenly undergo a marked increase and assume extraordinary forms of individual and especially of collective shifts; the whole occupational structure of the population involved tends to be disorganized from top to bottom.[11]

5. Interstate Horizontal Mobility

Citizenship is rigidly regulated by mandatory provisions in all states. The children of their citizens automatically become citizens. Often all the children born within their jurisdiction to citizens of other states likewise become their citizens. Most states do not allow their nationals freely to choose, change, or renounce their citizenship. Nevertheless, even in normal times there is always a weak or strong current of interstate mobility of individuals. Certain countries like the United States prior to the twentieth century, needing immigrants, liberally granted naturalization, and the immigrants were permitted to renounce their former citizenship. Between 1820 and 1924, 35,974,704 immigrants came to the United States, and most of these became naturalized citizens. Changes of citizenship have always occurred to a certain extent even among the citizens of states more rigorous in their regulation of citizenship than the United States.

This shift of citizenship suddenly assumes enormous proportions, from time to time, in periods of international conflicts or of large-scale revolutions and political and religious movements. An enormous proportion of wars have been followed by peace treaties whereby certain territories have been wrested from the defeated states and annexed to the victorious states. As a result of the transfer of territories

---

[10] For the figures and the literature cited cf. my *Mobility*, pp. 394 ff.

[11] For this particular uniformity cf. my *Calamity*, Chps. 6-8, and *Sociology of Revolution*, Ch. 12; also Kawan, *op. cit., passim.*

from one state to another, thousands and even millions of individuals are suddenly shifted en masse from one citizenship to another. Side by side with such transfers of territory new states may arise during or after such conflicts. Their emergence likewise leads to a mass transfer of citizenship. As a result of the First World War the citizenship of Turkey decreased from 21 million to 13 million; that of Austria from 28 million to 6 million; and that of Hungary from 20 million to 7 million. On the other hand, the citizenship of the British Empire increased from 424 to 449 million; of the French Empire from 81 to 94 million, and so on. Several new states, such as Czechoslovakia, Poland, and Lithuania, were created, their citizens being recruited from those of the defeated states.

Not so extensive perhaps, but also considerable, is the sudden shift of citizenship in times of major revolutions and struggles within a given state involving persecution and oppression of political opponents. Multitudes either are banished or else voluntarily flee to other countries, and many of them become citizens of the state in which they settle. For instance, between 1917 and 1922 more than 1,500,000 citizens of Russia became political émigrés, and most of them eventually became citizens of the states that gave them refuge. After the establishment of the Nazi regime, even before 1939, thousands of Germans and Austrians became refugees and eventually changed their citizenship.

In the various ways enumerated—regular or spasmodic, coercive or voluntary, collective or individual—state groups exchange their members on a fairly large scale. Sometimes a state loses all its members and disappears from the map of bodies politic. A visible manifestation of this process is the fairly frequent and spasmodic alteration of the political maps of states. The alterations are so frequent that beliefs and assurances that a given boundary can be preserved intact in perpetuity are rather naïve. Even more futile are wars undertaken for a modification of state boundaries; for they result at best in a merely ephemeral redistribution of territory, at the cost of perhaps untold thousands of human lives.

Some of these interstate shifts of citizenship constitute merely a horizontal circulation; others are vertical shifts, the status of the shifted population undergoing marked improvement or depression.

Of other uniformities in this type of mobility the following may be mentioned:

Underpopulated states in need of developing their resources tend to welcome the influx of outsiders to a greater extent than overpopulated states.

In the life history of the long-established states there are periods marked by the "open door" policy, and others characterized by the "closed door" policy, when immigration and naturalization are greatly restricted. The latter policy is applied when a state is already densely populated or when it is much more opulent than other states and hence attracts many from the poorer and less well-endowed states. In order to avoid being inundated by immigrants, it is compelled to close its doors to newcomers. Such restrictions tend to be more frequent in the "old age" phase of the life of a state; like a biologically old organism a semi-senile state seems to lose the power to absorb and digest a mass of newcomers.

6. Interreligious Mobility

The interreligious circulation of individuals is somewhat similar to interstate mobility. It goes on in normal times in the form of a moderate but steady stream of persons changing their religious allegiance from one religion to another. Such currents exist even in societies devoid of religious freedom, a few persons transferring their religious allegiance, others abandoning the obligatory orthodox religion to become heretics or schismatics. In countries enjoying religious freedom certain former atheists enter the ranks of one of the religious groups, while some believers sever their connection with any organized religious body. Others pass from one religion or denomination to another. Still others create a new religious sect, and so on. In the United States, during the period from 1926 to 1936, there appeared between 43 and 73 new denominations whose membership was recruited mainly from former members of other denominations, and some ten previously existing denominations disappeared. As regards changes in the size of the membership for the ten years in question, the Methodist Episcopal Church suffered a net loss of 14 per cent; the Methodist Episcopal Church South, 17.1 per cent; the Southern

Baptist Church, 23 per cent, and so on. The total loss in membership for a group of the larger Protestant churches was 8 per cent. At the same time other denominations notably increased their members: the Church of God, by 450.1 per cent; other Pentecostal Assemblies, by 264.7 per cent; the Assemblies of God, by 208.7 per cent; and the Seventh Day Adventists, by 19.4 per cent.[12] For a period of only ten years this gives an extreme example of the "normal" interreligious circulation of individuals. As a result of such shifts some religious denominations rapidly increase in size, while others rapidly decline.[13]

Side by side with this "normal" circulation there occur from time to time "spasmodic" collective shifts from one religion to another, similar to spasmodic interstate shifts. They belong to periods of religious revolution or reformation. Slight changes in the religious attitudes of the population slowly accumulate, finding no outlet in countries devoid of religious freedom. Eventually the accumulations become so great that they split open the existing religious body and lead either to a mass shift to another established religion or to a newly created religion. Examples of such movements are afforded by the rise of Buddhism and Savaism and the reformation of Hinduism between the sixth and fourth centuries B.C. in India; the emergence of Confucianism and Taoism and the rapid spread of Buddhism in China; the origin and growth of Christianity in the Greco-Roman world; the rise and diffusion of Mohammedanism; and the Reformation in Europe.

Sometimes these religious revolutions develop spontaneously. In other cases they are fostered by an application of large-scale coercion. For instance the persecution and suppression of the Russian Orthodox church in Russia by the Communist government from 1917 to about 1928 greatly reduced the membership in that religious organization. When, however, the persecution decreased and finally (in 1942) ceased, membership rapidly increased.

Respecting the uniformities exhibited by the type of mobility under consideration the following tentative generalizations may be made.

(a) In countries enjoying religious freedom interreligious mobility is greater than elsewhere. However, in the totality of interreligious shifts in countries lacking religious freedom the proportion of shifts to no religion (atheism, etc.) is likely to be higher than in those countries which possess religious freedom. In the latter most of the shifts tend to be from one religion to another, not in the direction of atheism or its equivalent.

(b) The rate of "normal" interreligious shifts in the more dogmatic religions tends to be lower than in the less dogmatic faiths, including various semireligious sects.

(c) Interreligious shifts tend to exhibit a lower rate in agricultural and rural populations than in urban and industrial populations, and especially among commercial and professional classes; among women than among men; and among the "low-brow" classes than among the intellectuals.

(d) During wars, revolutions, and other catastrophes interreligious shifts tend suddenly to increase, especially in the form of a marked increase of militant atheists and disbelievers, on the one hand, and of intensely devout believers, on the other.[14] The bulk of the population shifts rapidly from one type of religion to another.

(e) Especially marked is the interreligious shift in connection with the replacement of one dominant type of culture by another dominant type; the sensate by the ideational or idealistic, or vice versa. (Cf. Chapters 40-42.)

7. Interpolitical-Party Mobility

The shifting of individuals from one political party to another exhibits an extremely high degree of dynamism. Political parties resemble hotels, with new guests incessantly entering through one door and others leaving through another door. As a result the victory of a given party is soon followed by its defeat. In the United Kingdom, between 1846 and 1924, there were 27 changes in the cabinet, which meant 27 changes in the party possessing the

[12] See the census *Religious Bodies, 1936* (Washington, 1941); C. S. Braden, "Sectarianism Run Wild," in *Protestantism. A Symposium* (W. K. Anderson, ed., Nashville, 1944), pp. 110-122. For other material cf. my *Mobility*, pp. 402 ff.

[13] For the European countries see *Annuaire international de statistique* for 1916, 1920, 1930.
[14] For this law of polarization cf. my *Calamity*, Chps. 10-12.

majority in Parliament. The average life of a given cabinet was hence only 2.9 years. In France, between 1870 and 1911, the cabinet changed 49 times, giving 9 months as the average duration. In the United States, during the four-year period between successive presidential elections, large-scale shifts of voters from the Republican to the Democratic party or vice versa occur. In 1908 the popular vote for Presidential electors was 7,679,006 for the Republican and 6,409,106 for the Democratic party; in 1912, 3,483,922 and 6,286,214 respectively; in 1916, 8,538,221 and 9,129,606; and in 1924, 15,725,003 and 8,385,586. Millions of voters swing from one party to another during each presidential election. They shift their allegiance in even the shorter period of two years in voting for governors, mayors, and other state or local officials.[15]

In brief, allegiance to political parties is extremely superficial and unstable. In fact, the parties themselves are merely a kind of ephemeral social balloon.

Even in countries with a single dictatorial political party, such as the Fascisti or Nazis, mobility cannot be prevented, in spite of various coercive measures. It manifests itself in the comparatively short life of the dictatorial party; in intraparty splits and factional "purges"; and in the inner transformation of the party itself, which, as in the case of the Communist party in Russia, radically changes its original character within a few years. When these manifestations are properly evaluated the conclusion is inescapable that interpolitical-party shifts proceed in such societies almost as rapidly as in societies possessing several parties freely competing with one another.

8. Internationality Mobility

Much slower and more gradual are the shifts from one language or culture group (nationality) to another. The substitution of one language or culture for another is difficult and takes time. A comparatively small number of people accomplish it successfully within their entire lifetime. Even in such cases the shift must occur at an early age. In an overwhelm-

ing majority of cases a successful shift requires the life span of two generations; only the children of immigrants born within the new language or culture group become thoroughly assimilated to and organically rooted in the new nationality group. Even the second generation retains something of the language and culture of its parents.[16]

In spite of this comparative slowness internationality shifts nevertheless go on incessantly and gradually alter the size and the composition of the nationality groups.

Sometimes they assume a "spasmodic" character, as when a part of a nationality is coercively detached by a more powerful state or other nationality group and an attempt is made to "denationalize" it. Coercive efforts at denationalization, however, meet with much greater difficulties than compulsory changes in mere state citizenship. A state can be more easily destroyed than a nationality. The latter persists much longer and often successfully resists every measure employed to eradicate it.

9. General Conclusion

We thus see that the phenomenon of horizontal mobility is a universal and perennial process. In some groups it proceeds incessantly and on a large scale; in others, more slowly, and sometimes spasmodically.

The western populations of our time exhibit an extraordinarily strong horizontal mobility. Their members are incessantly on the move, shifting from group to group en masse with ever-increasing rapidity. This extraordinary horizontal mobility, together with the pronounced vertical mobility and the mobility of meanings, values, and norms, and of their vehicles, renders the entire western cultural and social structure intensely "fluid" and subjects it to a high degree of disorganization and disintegration. The vast and catastrophic social "squalls" and even "tornadoes" that we witness raging on its surface are unmistakable manifestations of this "fluidity" and "dynamism."

Let us now turn to the question of differential horizontal mobility, a phenomenon which has hitherto received scant attention.

---

[15] For other data, cf. my *Mobility*, pp. 405 ff.
[16] See C. M. Panunzio, *The Soul of the Immigrant* (New York, 1921); F. J. Brown and J. S. Roucek, *Our Racial and National Minorities* (New York, 1937); W. C. Smith, *Americans in the Mak-*

ing (New York, 1939); E. A. Ross, *The Old World in the New* (New York, 1914); and W. I. Thomas and F. Znaniecki, *The Polish Peasant in Europe and America* (New York, 1927).

Chapter 25.[1] The Differential Horizontal Mobility of Individuals

I. Mobility, Assimilation, and Continuity of Social Groups

In Chapter 21 it was shown that to preserve the continuity of its existence an organized group or institution must maintain the identity of its component of meanings, values, and norms, as well as the social relationships regulated by the norms. It was indicated also that for that purpose the general mobility of the members of the group must not be too sudden or too intense. A rapid replacement of nearly all the members of organized groups would lead at once to the disruption of their existence. In order that the set of meanings and values and the network of relationships constituting the "heart, soul, and physiognomy" of a group may be maintained, most of its members must be able to know what they have to do, what their functions, rights, and duties are in regard to one another and toward the outside world. They must not only know what these relations have historically been, but must be able to perform these services in the customary efficient manner. To acquire such proficiency demands some time and practice, particularly with regard to highly skilled functions. Such efficiency and continuity can exist only when the proportion of newcomers at any moment is relatively small, when the old members—the bearers of the individuality of the group—are present in sufficient numbers and can assimilate the newcomers and teach them what they shall do and how they shall do it. In order that this assimilative process shall proceed most smoothly and at the same time not disturb the functioning of the organization, it is essential that the most responsible positions be held by persons previously trained and experienced.

This explains why, as a rule, the general mobility of an organization or institution is gradual even when it is relatively intense, and why, like the metabolism of a biological organism, it ordinarily consists in only a small and partial replacement of the members at a given time. Such gradualness permits an institution or organization to keep its system of values and network of relationships intact or virtually so during a relatively long period in spite of the ever-changing composition of its members. Under such conditions the inevitable changes which do occur in the functions or structure of the organization become almost imperceptible through their gradualness, and in this way the continuity of the existence of the group is not broken.

[1] This chapter is an abridgment of P. A. Sorokin and C. A. Anderson's "Metabolism of Different Strata of Social Institutions and Institutional Continuity," *Comitato italiano per lo studio dei problemi della populazione* (Roma, 1931), reprinted in *Metron*, Vol. X, pp. 319-348, 1932-1933.

II. Differential Mobility of
the Various Strata of a Group

General horizontal mobility does not require that all parts of an organization shall have the same rate or intensity of change in composition. On the contrary, even daily observation shows that the turnover of members of the various departments of an institution is different. For example, as will be shown later in detail, studies of labor turnover in the United States reveal that the semiskilled laborers in industrial organizations have a lower rate of turnover than the unskilled, while the rate for the skilled is the lowest of the three.

While it is true that there are different rates of membership replacement in the several divisions of various organizations, we are mainly concerned in this chapter with the problem of the differences in the intensity and nature of the horizontal mobility of the upper and lower strata of the same group.

The study of differential mobility is particularly important from the standpoint of a proper understanding of the mechanism through which an institution secures the continuity of its existence. In the discussion in the first section of the influence of general mobility upon the continuity of institutions, emphasis was placed upon the dependence upon the degree of mobility. Besides this dependence on the nature and magnitude of the general mobility, an institution depends for its duration and efficiency upon the proper arrangement of the differential mobility of its various ranks of membership. This is especially true of the groups performing delicate, important, and difficult functions. What constitutes the "proper" differential in the rates of the several ranks depends upon the nature of the group.

There are institutions whose "relatively sedentary center of gravity" lies in the lower strata; such, for example, are most of the nations (not their governments) regarded as political bodies. It is evident that no matter how many citizens may emigrate, an enormous proportion of them always remain within the nation and thus automatically secure its membership. This major part is always present,

whatever may be the changes in the government.

Furthermore, there are some organizations whose "centers of gravity," or stable parts, lie in the lower part of the upper stratum or the higher part of the middle stratum. An example of this type is afforded by many contemporary governmental institutions, including the departments and bureaus of administration. In most of the democratic republics the presidents and secretaries follow each other at relatively short and regular intervals as one party replaces another. Yet, except in the cases of serious revolution, the continuity of the government and even its major policies persist. One of the conditions which makes such a continuity possible is the existence of a relatively sedentary stratum in the persons of the many specialists and technical experts in the different bureaus—the civil service, as the British call this group. These persons do not usually occupy the top positions, they are not elected, and they do not change with the fluctuations of parties. These remain, for instance, under Republican, Democratic, Bourgeois or Farmer-Labor governments. The typical term of service of this group exceeds that of the lower grades of employees and also that of the department heads and other honorary functionaires. In these institutions this stratum is the main bearer of the *Gestalt* of the group, and to it is mainly due the continuity of the organization.

Finally, *the greater proportion of existing institutions or organizations have their "center of gravity" at the top of their pyramid.* In such cases the main agents of continuity, or the conservers of *l'ésprit de corps,* the functions, traditions, and network of relationships, are its upper strata. Such upper levels are typically least subject to change in their membership composition. So in this group belong many monarchies; many religious organizations (for example, Roman Catholic, Buddhist, and Mohammedan); some of the highest courts, where the judges hold office for life and may bequeath their position to their children; certain universities and other cultural institutions; and, finally, many economic and industrial institutions, firms, and corporations.

This brief discussion permits an insight into at least the broad outlines of the effect of differential mobility upon the continuity of organizations. When this process of differential mobility contradicts the nature of a given institution, it may seriously endanger the equilibrium and consequently the existence of that group. An improper and excessively strong mobility of one stratum, paralleled by complete stagnation in another stratum, can easily paralyze the institution and thus destroy the structure and functioning of the organization.

After these preliminary remarks and tentative hypotheses we may now turn to an analysis of the results of our factual study of the differential mobility of various strata in a series of institutions which we have investigated. These results throw light upon the details of differential mobility and its mechanism; they reveal also many fluctuations in the intensity of this process under different conditions. When more studies of this type are accumulated, they will permit us to formulate more accurately the uniformities and principal types of differential mobility and to classify human organizations and institutions on this basis.

1. Differential Mobility in College Faculties[2]

This sort of institution has certain advantages of study. The materials are recorded in easily accessible form each year, and the members of most faculties form a closely knit group with clearly distinguished ranks (full, associate, and assistant professors, and instructors) and a systematic policy of promotion and appointment. These ranks are clear-cut, exist as an objective reality, and do not involve individual estimation. We have analyzed the materials for four distinct academic institutions with records extending over some thirty or forty years. These four schools, in the order of discussion, are:

(a) Chicago University, founded about 1890, heavily endowed, and rapidly growing.

(b) Harvard University, second to none of the American universities, marked by a great expansion in size and influence during the last half century.

(c) The University of Minnesota, one of the more important Middle-Western state universities, founded after the middle of the last century but attaining its notable contemporary size and importance within the present century.

(d) Carleton College, an endowed, quasi-denominational college of good caliber, sufficiently scholarly to possess faculty exchange arrangements with the larger universities, and with a fair sprinkling of noted men on its staff.

Comparison of the lists for two successive years permitted an enumeration of the cases in which persons were added to or lost by a given rank, and knowledge of the reason for this change. Additions were considered as due to promotion or to appointment from outside the institution, and losses were attributed to promotion, resignation, or death. The corresponding number of existing staff members could then be counted, and rates of change due to each of these causes separately or in combination easily stated in percentages. The rates for all the years covered were seriated, and a median was taken as a suitable value for the average rate of mobility.

The accompanying tables summarize the rates of differential mobility for the four schools. The median rate was used, as on the whole the most suitable device for comparing the typical mobility of the separate institutions. The median is given for all changes considered together, as well as for the particular causes of change.

The tables given suggest several conclusions. First, *in all of these institutions a differential mobility* of their strata really exists. The rate is different for each of the principal ranks of the faculties.

Second, *the intensity of the mobility increases as we proceed from the highest stratum of the full professors to the lowest rank of instructors*; there is a negative relationship between the frequency of the turnover and

---

[2] Cf. the subsequent studies that largely followed the trend of the study embodied in this chapter: W. A. Lunden, *The Dynamics of Higher Education* (Pittsburgh 1939); E. Y. Hartshorne, "Growth and Metabolism in the Harvard Faculty," *Harvard Educational Review* (1942), Vol. XII, pp. 143-164; and F. Reeves, *The University Faculty* (Chicago, 1933).

University of Chicago (1893-1927)

	Full Professor	Associate Professor	Assistant Professor	Instructors
Total changes	10.2	23.2	28.3	35.2
All additions	7.3	12.1	16.0	18.3
Promotions	4.2	8.6	10.1	11.1
Hirings	1.5	1.5	3.6	6.8
All losses	2.5	7.5	12.4	14.1
Promotions	—	6.0	8.0	8.3
Resignations	1.3	1.5	3.3	8.4
Deaths (few cases)	1.0	—	—	—

Harvard University (1891-1928)

	Full Professor	Associate Professor	Assistant Professor	Instructors
Total changes	9.6	21.1	28.3	62.2
All additions	6.5	16.9	14.8	34.1
Promotions	3.4	11.2	11.3	—
Hirings	2.2	—	3.8	—
All losses	3.0	6.6	11.0	28.0
Promotions	—	—	7.8	3.8
Resignations	2.8	—	3.2	24.7
Deaths	1.7	—	—	—

University of Minnesota (1876-1917)

	Full Professor	Assistant Professor	Instructors
Total changes	11.4	45.7	51.4
All additions	7.4	22.5	32.0
Promotions	3.3	8.0	—
Hirings	2.8	15.7	—
All losses	3.8	23.1	20.0
Promotions	—	7.1	7.6
Resignations	3.2	8.9	8.7
Deaths	2.6	—	—

Carleton College (1895-1927)

	Full Professor	Assistant Professor	Instructors
Total changes	20.0	71.4	61.6
All additions	11.7	33.7	30.8
All losses	7.8	39.2	30.6

the importance of the position on the university faculty. The "sedentary center of gravity," or the main agents of the institutions' continuity, lie thus in the upper parts of these institutions.

Third, *each of the higher strata is recruited more by "inbreeding"—promotion from a lower rank—than from outsiders ("hiring").* This is especially true of the universities of Harvard and Chicago, which are more prominent and more desirable for teachers than the other two. This phenomenon reminds one of the biosocial process of a higher rate of "inbreeding" within the aristocratic than within the lower classes of a population. Such "inbreeding" is one of the chief means of ensuring the continuity of the institution—its functions, network of relationships, and psychosocial *Gestalt*. In addition, when it is considered that the outsiders appointed come from another institution of a similar type and with similar patterns of behavior, functions, and relationships, the appointment of such outsiders means the inclusion of persons with traditions, activities, behavior, and relationships similar to those of the institution's own members who are promoted. In this way the continuity of the institutional work is secured.

Fourth, the figures concerning promotions mean that in all these institutions, besides a mobility in the form of an absorption of the "cells" taken from other social bodies and the loss of their own "cells" to the other institutions, *an exchange between the "cells" of the various social strata of the same institution is taking place.* Each stratum regularly loses a part of its members to the other—usually higher—stratum and absorbs some members from the lower stratum. In these two ways the composition of each stratum is incessantly renewed.

Fifth, *this interstrata mobility within the same institution has an almost entirely one-sided direction, namely, promotion, and almost no downward movement, or demotion.* If one asks how the upper strata avoid the danger of overpopulation, the answer is: partly through death in the higher stratum, but mainly *through retirement, resignation, and rejection* (or involuntary resignation) of the persons ("cells") considered unfit. The social body of the institution ejects such elements and

in this way, plus the other mentioned, avoids the danger in question.

Sixth, when the ratio of the median of "all additions" to that of "all losses" for each of the strata is considered, we see in all three cases a tendency for *the ratio to increase as we pass from the lowest to the highest ranks.* This seems to mean not only that for the period studied the universities have been growing more intensely in their upper stratum and that the healthy growth of a university requires first of all a quantitative and qualitative growth of its full professors, but also that their continuity has been reenforced through the relative strengthening of their upper strata. This shows also that the "profile" of a social institution changes in the course of time.

Seventh,[3] we may next turn to an examination of the *relation between the lapse of time and these various rates;* for it is apparent to even casual inspection that as these institutions have grown in size and importance there have been definite changes in the magnitude and importance of the different forms and sources of mobility. As a rule the total number of changes has tended to increase; the staffs have been becoming more fluid. Among the instructors there has been a marked increase in the total annual rate of mobility; among the assistant professors the rate has also increased, though somewhat less sharply; among the associate professors the increase has been very moderate; while among the full professors there has been a slight downward movement. Thus *we find that in recent years the mobility of membership has become more intense in the lower ranks* and less marked at the higher levels; there has been differential effect of time (or the factors represented by time) upon the rate of total mobility. The same trends may be observed in all losses and gains, but the secular trend is most marked in the case of losses. It is probably true in general that *the mobility of an institution tends to be more intense during the initial stages of rapid growth and to slacken when the institution attains maturity and full growth.*

Eighth, as a special case of secular movement may be mentioned the effect of the First

[3] For the respective data, see the original paper on metabolism from which these conclusions are derived.

POSITION	Period Covered	Number of Men	Mean Service
Secretary	1789-1929	41	36 months
1st Assistant Secretary	1853-1924	36	27 months
2nd Assistant Secretary	1866-1924	2	29 *years*
3rd Assistant Secretary	1875-1924	19	30 months
Chief Clerks	1789-1929	34	50 months

OFFICE	Period	Number of Tenants	Mean Months
Secretary	1789-1877	31	33
Assistant Secretary	1849-1877	16	30
Treasurer	1789-1877	11	95
First Comptroller	1789-1878	15	67
Second Comptroller	1817-1877	10	72
Commissioner of Customs	1849-1874	5	36
First Auditor	1789-1878	9	*118*
Second Auditor	1817-1861	5	*106*
Third Auditor	1817-1879	9	83
Fourth Auditor	1817-1863	9	60
Fifth Auditor	1817-1871	6	32
Sixth Auditor	1836-1875	13	36

World War as an example of a crisis in the life of the larger society of which the universities are a part. So far as our data are relevant the effect was relatively simple. The rate of change of membership increased, and the increase was particularly noticeable among the younger staff members, that is, among the instructors and assistant professors. The change was largely in the form of resignations, and even the highest levels were not immune from this effect. After the war there was a period of unusually rapid change, in many cases marked by extensive additions to staffs.[4]

Turn now to the examination of similar data for other types of groups.

2. Mobility of Higher Federal Officials

In the introductory section of this chapter it was pointed out that many governmental bureaucracies afforded examples of organizations in which the lower part of the upper or the higher part of the middle strata is the least fluid rank. An adequate verification of this conclusion on the basis of the available mate-

rial requires a larger amount of time and effort than it has yet been feasible to expend. We can, however, furnish a few data for the United States which bear upon this point. We have utilized the annual Registers of the Department of State of the Federal Government. In the first of the accompanying tables we present the mean length of service of the men who have held each of the indicated offices.

The positions of the Secretary of State and of one of the assistant secretaries (usually the first) are subject to political tenure and influence and are not technical positions. The latter are usually filled either by specialists or chief clerks. Thus the latter persons actually had, on the average, the longest terms of office. This accords with our hypothesis.[5]

We find a similar picture in the United States Treasury Department.

These data seem to support our hypothesis satisfactorily if we make the reasonable assumption that the clerks and other workers of lower rank have a relatively short tenure.

In the United States Department of Agriculture the mean duration of the tenure of its

---

[4] For a vast body of data, cf. the work by Lunden, cited above.

[5] For more detailed data, see the original paper.

RATIOS OF DESIGNATED CHANGES TO NUMBER OF
PERSONS WITH THE STATED SALARY

| | | Losses | | Gains | | |
| | | | Promo-
tions
& | | Promo-
tions
& | |
Group	Persons	Resigna- tions	Trans- fers	Resigna- tions	Trans- fers	Total Rate
$ 900-1320	2351	11.1	6.7	16.4	4.3	38.5
$1360-2280	3325	7.5	6.5	10.1	8.3	32.4
$2400-7140	1062	6.2	4.1	5.6	8.4	24.3
TOTAL	6738	8.6	6.2	11.6	6.9	33.4

specified ranks during the period 1900-1930 was as follows:

Secretary	about 6 years
First Assistant	about 3 years
Second Assistant	about *14 years*
Third Assistant	about 7 years
Chief Clerks	about 6 years
Bureau Chiefs	about *11 years*
Assistant Chiefs	about 8 years
Chief Clerks	about 6 years

3. Differential Mobility of the Administrative Employees of a State Government

In the preceding section we furnished information concerning the change in membership among those government officials of high status below the cabinet officials. In the present section we turn our attention to a somewhat similar group of state employees in one of the American commonwealths (Massachusetts). Our data refer to the single year 1927-1928 and to the total group of appointive administrative employees of all grades.

By virtue of recent reorganizations the salary schedule of all workers is intended to correspond to the relative skill and importance of the service rendered by each group of persons. Our first analysis, therefore, was designed to divide the salary range into three apparently homogeneous parts.

The categories of resignations and appointments are the most distinct, and here we find the typical pattern of high rank accompanied by low mobility and vice versa. This negative correlation holds also for total rates.

It is possible to break up this total pay roll into smaller, more homogeneous groups. In doing this we encounter small numbers, erratic rates, and data incomplete on many points. Thus a small group of laboratory technicians exhibit the following resignation rates, arranged in order of increasing skill: assistants, 47 per cent; technicians, 40 per cent; junior bacteriologists and chemists, 24 per cent.

A group of engineers (mainly civil engineers) disclose the following resignation rates: junior engineering aids, 15 per cent; senior engineering aids, 7 per cent; junior civil engineers, 6 per cent. For the higher ranks there were no losses during the year in question.

The group of office clerks is much larger, and the data are correspondingly more complete. For resignations we find the following rates: junior clerks, 11.2 per cent; senior clerks, 6.1 per cent; for all higher grades 2.1 per cent. For appointments we find the respective rates to be 17.8 per cent, 4.9 per cent, and 2.1 per cent. There was also a special group of clerks attached to the offices handling finances. Appointments were virtually absent; but the resignation rates were as follows: junior assessing clerks, 18.2 per cent; senior assessing clerks, 7.7 per cent; deputy assessors, 4.4 per cent.

We may also compute the rates for total changes in these two categories of clerks as listed above. The respective rates by ranks are as follows: lowest rank, 39.2 and 31.8 per cent; middle rank, 25.6 per cent; highest rank, 14.4 and 15.2 per cent. There is excellent agreement in the rates for the two groups.

It would be possible to give additional figures for other small groups; but there is no point in doing so. In this particular group of civil servants in administrative and clerical positions—a stratum within the larger pyramid of state officials—there is the typical inverse relationship between high rank and low turnover.

4. Differential Mobility in Industrial and Occupational Groups

Numerous studies of the turnover of various strata in industrial and occupational groups exhibit, with a few exceptions, the same rule, namely, that *differential mobility increases as we go from the upper strata to the lower*. The following is a typical example: In a certain industrial organization the rate of turnover in 1916-19 for the skilled workers was 22.6; for the semiskilled, 65.6; for the unskilled, 250.5. S. H. Slichter summarizes the situation for America as follows: "In general there is an inverse relationship between the degree of skill and the rate of turnover. The higher the degree of skill the lower is likely to be the turnover rate. There are exceptions to this rule, but in most plants it holds true."

On the basis of a vast body of data similar conclusions were reached in my *Social Mobility*[6] for a variety of occupational groups and their strata in a number of different countries. Here are some of the most salient uniformities discovered.

(a) *Hereditary transmission of occupational status from father to son in intergenerational mobility tends to be higher and differential occupational mobility lower in the occupational groups and strata which demand greater technical experience or larger financial resources or which entail more privileges and honors than other groups and strata*. In contemporary western societies the hereditary transmission of occupation from father to children fluctuates between 3 and 70 per cent. It is high in the skilled, well-paid, and privileged occupational groups and comparatively low in the relatively unskilled, poorly paid, and unprivileged occupations.

(b) *"Within the same occupation, in the life-time of one generation, the more qualified and better-paid strata shift less intensively than the less qualified and more poorly paid groups."*

(c) *"Members of occupations which disappear or decrease (like agricultural occupations in the United States) shift more*

[6] For the data, see Chapter 17, *passim*.

intensively than members of occupations which develop and prosper."

(d) *"Unskilled labor is more mobile than skilled labor; business and professional groups (their higher strata) are likely to be still more stable even than the group of skilled labor."*

(e) *"In a country where agriculture does not rapidly disappear, the occupational mobility of the agricultural group is likely to be low; in a country where agriculture dies out, the shifting of agriculturists to other occupations is likely to be high."*

(f) Finally, *"occupational mobility of the young people who have recently entered an occupation and are in the process of finding a suitable occupation tends to be greater than that of persons at the age of forty and over."*[7]

Such are some of the salient approximate uniformities directly and indirectly related to the differential mobility of groups and strata.

5. General Conclusion

The foregoing analysis shows that differential mobility occurs in all kinds of social groups. The discussion elucidates also its significance for the continuity of organized groups. The data indicate that the dominant method of securing this continuity is a gradual absorption of new personnel into the institution and their gradual promotion to the higher and more responsible positions. As a rule, the upper stratum of the institution is the most important agent of its continuity; therefore it is the least exchangeable and the most deeply "inbred." There are, however, deviations from the prevailing rule in certain institutions, of which an example was afforded by the federal government of the United States. In such institutions the sedentary center lies in the lower part of the upper class or in the upper part of the middle class, mainly according to the type, structure, and social functions in question.

Finally, *in periods of severe upheaval, such as war or revolution, the dominant pattern of differential mobility is disrupted and the trend is partly reversed. The upper strata tend to be overthrown and replaced in their entirety by newcomers either from outside or from the lower strata.*[8]

[7] *Mobility*, pp. 426-427. See also the factual evidence.

[8] Cf. my *Calamity*, Chps. 6, 7; *Sociology of Revolution*, Part III; and *Mobility*, Chps. 17-19.

Chapter 26. How Groups Exchange, Test, Select, and Distribute Their Members (Vertical Mobility)

I. Uniformities in Vertical Mobility

Every organized group exhibits not only horizontal, general and differential mobility, but also vertical mobility. This consists in the individual and collective shift of members of the group from stratum to stratum, either upward (social climbing) or downward (social demotion).[1] In other words, the various strata of a given group incessantly exchange their members through promotion and demotion. Besides intragroup vertical mobility there is also intergroup vertical mobility, individuals passing vertically from one group to another, for instance, from a lower caste to higher or vice versa.

Like horizontal mobility, vertical mobility proceeds unceasingly in "normal," gradual forms and occasionally in "spasmodic" forms. Normal mobility usually assumes the form of individual shifts, whereas the "spasmodic" type ordinarily consists in collective vertical shifts.

Let us first set down a few general propositions before undertaking an analysis of the more specific aspects of vertical mobility.

(1) *Any organized group, being stratified, has a strong or weak current of vertical mobil-*

ity. The membership of each stratum of a group is recruited in various ways, including the birth of new members. A group can recruit the membership of all its strata exclusively by the latter method only under three exceptional conditions: (a) a perfect correspondence between the births and deaths of its members in the sense that there is neither a surplus nor deficit of births relative to deaths; (b) the ability to fill in this way any sudden need for a rapid enlargement or reduction of the size of a given stratum; (c) the ability of the children of the members of each stratum to perform successfully the functions of the stratum. As we shall see, none of these ideal conditions can be realized by any group. Births and deaths, as a rule, do not balance one another over a long period; they are not so elastic and controllable as to enable each stratum of the group instantaneously to adjust them to the incessantly changing needs for expansion and reduction; and the children of capable parents frequently do not possess the abilities of their parents or else possess abilities quite different from those necessary for the satisfactory performance of the functions in question.

Hence none of the strata of any organized group have ever been completely closed to persons born outside the stratum (see Chapter 21). The most nearly closed strata are

---

[1] The total vertical mobility in a given population is made up of the mobility of individuals and groups plus that of meanings, or cultural values, and vehicles.

probably castes; as a rule the members of each of the stratified castes are recruited from the children of the members. Yet even in the periods of greatest rigidity of the caste system at least a weak stream of vertical mobility has always flowed from caste to caste. Even the relative hierarchical position of castes in a system embracing some 2500 to 3000 different castes has been subject to change.[2]

The foregoing proposition applies with even greater force to the social orders, ranging from slaves and serfs to the highest nobility; their members have been recruited not only from their children but from outsiders. Similarly, hereditary royal families are not closed groups, but are replenished from the outside through intermarriage. Most of them rarely lasted longer than 250 to 300 years. New dynasties now and then were started by the "upstarts."

Only the racial, sex, and age plurels as purely biological entities cannot be penetrated by persons of a different race, sex, or age. Such plurels, as a rule, are not stratified and organized social groups. When they do exist as organized social groups, membership is ordinarily open to sponsors, leaders, honorary members, sympathizers, and supporters of a different race, sex, or age.

(2) *No organized group has ever existed in which the vertical social mobility has been absolutely unrestricted and the transition from one stratum to another has encountered no obstacles.* Apart from periods of acute disorganization and of disintegration, the vertical mobility has always been controlled by mechanisms for the testing, selection, distribution, promotion, and demotion of its members. Absolutely free vertical mobility would presuppose a group in which every member could occupy any stratum or position which he wished to occupy. In such circumstances, in an army there would be chiefly generals and hardly any privates; in a state, largely monarchs and high-ranking officials and few subjects; in a business corporation, principally presidents, directors, and managers and scarcely any wage workers; in a university, chiefly full professors and relatively few in-

structors and students. Such a group obviously could not function. Hence in any organized group there is always a complex device that sifts its members, assigning some to the upper positions and relegating others to the lower ranks. The familiar "equality of opportunity" in democracies is no exception to this rule. The theoretical possibility for every boy to become President of the United States or president of the United States Steel Corporation does not translate this possibility into fact. We shall consider the obstacles to a perfectly free vertical mobility at greater length later on.

(3) *The rate of vertical mobility varies in different groups, as well as in groups of the same unibonded or multibonded type.*

(a) Vertical mobility in a caste is lower than in a system of social orders, and in both it is lower than in a system of social classes. The proportion of people that inherit their status is higher in a caste than in a system of social orders, and in both it is higher than in a class society. Similarly, the proportion of newcomers is lower in the case of a caste than in that of a social estate and especially a social class. More specifically, the hereditary transmission of occupational, or economic, status from father to son in castes is not very far from 100 per cent; in social orders it is somewhat lower; and in social classes it is still lower, fluctuating between 3 and 70 per cent, with an average index of transmission ranging from 20 to 60 per cent.

(b) It tends to be lower in the predominantly agricultural and pastoral populations (where these occupations do not tend to decrease) than among the highly commercialized, industrialized, and urbanized peoples.

(c) As a rule, among groups of the same kind, vertical mobility tends to be lower in those characterized by the hereditary status of their members (recruited mainly through birth) than in those whose members are recruited through election by the rank and file of the members (in contrast to oligarchic election by the top ranks), through voluntary influx, through personal achievement, etc. Likewise, vertical mobility tends to be higher in groups with "automatic" loss of membership in the upper strata than in those with life membership in the upper strata.

---

[2] For the facts and the sources, cf. my *Mobility*, pp. 139 ff.; also B. K. Sarkar, *The Positive Background of Hindu Sociology* (Allahabad, 1937), Ch. 3, *passim*.

In other words, vertical mobility *tends to be higher in groups enjoying a real equality of opportunity, and in open groups than in closed ones. Vertical mobility in the ranks of state strata, from the plain citizen up to the head of the state, tends to be higher in the states with a democratic elective system than in those with the hereditary status of ranks and social positions, and in the former it is higher for limited terms of office than for a life tenure.* The turnover among the members of hereditary dynasties is much slower than that among elected presidents or monarchs; and the proportion of persons attaining the position of monarch among the lower strata in the monarchical countries tends to be lower than that of the elected presidents of states with non-hereditary rulers. The dynasties of ancient Egypt (with the exception of a few short-lived upstarts), beginning with the third and ending with the twenty-sixth, reigned, respectively, 80, 150, 125, 150, 30 (the seventh and the eighth are ranked together), 285 (the ninth and tenth), 160, 213, 208 (the thirteenth to the seventeenth), 230, 145, 5, 110, 145, 200, 27, 6, 50, and 138 years. In China its various dynasties, beginning with the Yao and ending with the Tsing dynasty lasted, respectively, 96, 50, 439, 644, 862, 44, 422, 154, 28, 287, 57 (five dynasties of the period of anarchy), 316, 149, 90, 275, and 267 years. In Rome and Byzantium hardly any dynasty reigned longer than 100 years; most dynasties reigning during periods of upheaval lasted only a few years, a few months, or even a few days. The Merovingians reigned about 269 years; the Carolingians, about 235; the Capets, 341; the Valois, 261; the Bourbons, 204, and so on. Except for self-appointed monarchs during periods of war, revolution, or anarchy—which are always marked by an enormous collective vertical mobility—royal dynasties retain their position much longer than presidents of a given family or kinship group. In France after 1870 practically all the presidents came from different families. In the United States, though the Adamses and the Roosevelts furnished two Presidents each, all the other incumbents of the White House belonged to different families. Within a comparatively short period there were 32 Presidents belonging to different families. In normal times, free from notable anarchy

or other catastrophes, a larger proportion of persons from the lower and middle strata are able to attain the position of head of the state in countries with the elective system than in hereditary monarchies. Among the presidents of France and Germany the percentage of such persons was 23.1, and among the Presidents of the United States, 48.3; whereas among the monarchs of Russia it was only 5.5, among the kings of England, 5.0, and among the kings of France, 3.9. Only among the emperors of the Western Roman Empire (owing to the fact that the period after the second century A.D. was largely unstable) the percentage of upstarts was 45.6, and among the emperors of the Eastern Roman Empire it was 27.7.[3] What has been said of monarchs and elective presidents is even more true respecting the upper ranks of the state authorities in general; in states with the elective system the turnover of the upper strata in the official hierarchy tends to be greater than in states with the hereditary system. Above (pp. 417 ff.) some figures were given for the average tenure of British and French cabinets and for that of the officials in the higher ranks of the federal government of the United States. They revealed an average tenure of very short duration. In the monarchical states, on the other hand, the tenure of the upper ranks of officialdom is notably longer and replacements are made from the upper strata of the state aristocracy in a much greater proportion than in the democratically elective state systems. The vertical currents in the monarchical states or those with oligarchical or aristocratic elective systems circulate only within the upper strata, whereas in the democratically elective state systems they circulate from the bottom to the top of the state pyramid.

(d) As has already been observed, in occupational and economic groups and strata vertical mobility tends to be lower in those that occupy the apex of the pyramids than in the lower groups and strata. The upper groups and strata tend to be more closed than the middle and lower ones. In the occupational groups we have seen that the groups and strata with a notably high hereditary transmission of occupational status from the father

---

[3] Cf. my "Monarchs and Rulers," *SF*, May and September, 1925.

to the sons tend to possess a lower mobility than those with a lower hereditary transmission of occupational status. The occupations demanding considerable technical training or capital or entailing special privileges belong to the former category. In Taussig-Joslyn's study the percentage of occupational transmission from father to sons is as follows: unskilled and skilled laborers, 33.3; skilled laborers, 37.3; farmers, 29.1 (decreasing group); clerical and small business, 49.9; professional and big business, 75.5.[4] Similarly, among the *economic strata* the upper ranks of the millionaires exhibit the highest rate of hereditary transmission of occupational status and a very high rate of transmission of economic status. In my study of the American multimillionaires of two generations (deceased and living) 49 and 72 per cent, respectively, pursued the same occupation as their fathers, or a similar occupation; and only 38 per cent of the deceased and 19 per cent of the living generation started their life poor. More than 52 per cent of the living multimillionaires inherited their wealth from their parents.[5] Likewise, 70.9 per cent of Germany heavy industrialists, 67.2 per cent of the large merchants, and 85.2 per cent of the large estate-owners came from the highest economic stratum; only 15 per cent of the wealthiest originated in the middle and lower class.[6] Again, among the German upper intellectual ranks studied, 56.1 per cent of the males and 69.7 per cent of the females came from the upper intellectual ranks; 22.7 per cent and 20.8 per cent, respectively, from the upper economic class; and only 21.2 per cent and 9.5 per cent, respectively, from the middle and lower professional and economic classes.[7]

With an appropriate modification this proposition may be applied to many other groups, including the army and navy, universities and colleges, and business corporations.

(e) Among similar unibonded or multibonded groups vertical mobility tends to be higher in those which promote or demote their members on the basis of personal achievement rather than on the basis of the prestige and social standing of the family, of kinship, of caste or social order, of creed, of political party, of race, sex, or age, of seniority, or of wealth or other criteria distinct from personal achievement. In groups distributing their members on the basis of personal achievement the circulating currents pick up for promotion more persons from the lower strata and for demotion more persons from the upper strata than in groups possessing other criteria of promotion and demotion. An army with a personal achievement basis promotes more privates to the rank of general and demotes more generals than an army promoting only the members of aristocratic families or the rich or basing promotions on seniority. A similar observation applies to religious organizations, political parties, and other groups.

(f) Among similar groups vertical mobility tends to be higher in those in which the abilities of the members of the upper strata are subjected to crucial tests vitally important for the existence and welfare of the group. In time of war, army and political leaders are subjected to such tests. The battlefield quickly demonstrates which generals and commanding officers are capable and which are not. Under such conditions the promotion of the capable

---

[4] F. W. Taussig and C. S. Joslyn, *American Business Leaders* (New York, 1932), p. 142.

[5] Cf. my "American Millionaires and Multi-Millionaires," *SF*, Vol. III (1925), pp. 635 ff.; F. W. Taussig and C. S. Joslyn, *American Business Leaders* (New York, 1932), Part III; *Mobility*, Chps. 17-19; S. Riemer, "Upward Mobility and Social Stratification" (translation of his article "Sozialer Aufstieg und Klassenschichtung", *Archiv für Sozialwissenschaft und Sozialpolitik*, Vol. 67 (1932), pp. 507-560; P. E. Davidson and H. D. Anderson, *Occupational Mobility in American Community* (Stanford University Press, 1937).

[6] *Sozialer Auf und Abstieg im Deutschen Volk, No. 117 der Beiträge zur Statistik Bayerns* (München, 1930), p. 61.

[7] *Ibid.*, p. 56. In this study, as in several others, the higher artistic, sport, political, and religious (Catholic) strata are recruited in a larger proportion from the middle and lower economic and intellectual ranks: 71.1 per cent of the male and 53.4 per cent of the female upper political, sport, and welfare ranks, and 31.2 per cent of the males and 12.3 per cent of the females in the upper artistic professions. However, it is to be kept in mind that the Germany of 1920-1930 was in a state of political upheaval. Therefore lower-class labor and political leaders could easily climb the social ladder. In the Germany with a system of social orders, and even in that of the Hohenzollerns, such a large proportion of social climbers would have been impossible.

leaders and the demotion of the inefficient assume much greater proportions than in time of peace, when many pseudo-abilities pass for real abilities, and many real abilities are overlooked.

With a proper modification the same may be said of virtually any group which periodically confronts a crucial test. A business firm faced by an economic depression; a religious organization or political party subjected to persecution; a university which is suffering from very unfavorable financial circumstances or whose teachers are undergoing persecution—these and other groups under similar conditions tend to reshuffle their members more intensely than under conditions of comparative well-being, prosperity, and complacency. Under the latter circumstances the "brass hats" and mediocrities may for a long time occupy high positions and parade as capable leaders without fear of being disturbed.

(4) *Varying from group to group at one and the same time, the rate of vertical mobility also fluctuates in the life history of the same group from period to period.*[8] This general proposition can be broken down into a few more specific uniformities.

(a) In the life history of any organized group the vertical mobility tends notably to increase, becoming often collective and catastrophic, in periods of crisis and calamity, such as those marked by major wars, revolutions, famines, pestilences, or economic depressions. Each of such crises serves as a crucial test for especially the upper strata of the group. Hence it eliminates the failures and promotes the persons and groups that show the necessary ability. Some of such crises, for instance, pestilence and war, lead to a higher mortality rate within the group and often to a particularly high rate of mortality in the upper strata, rapidly creating vacancies which can be filled only through the promotion of suitable persons from the lower strata. Some crises, such as revolutions, represent the culmination of long-accumulated maladjustments and injustices, for example, an accumulation of incapable "aristocracy" in the upper strata and of capable potential rulers in the lower strata. Owing to these and similar circumstances the vertical

mobility becomes much greater than in normal times and often assumes a mass character, pulling down the entire upper strata and pushing up large groups from the lower layers.

In major political revolutions a part or even the whole of the previous ruling class is overthrown and is replaced by groups and individuals from the lower strata. If a revolution is not only political but also social and economic, the rich and well-to-do classes are impoverished through "communization," nationalization, or confiscation of their property and many formerly impoverished groups and individuals become comparatively rich and well-to-do. In such "total" revolutions as the Russian Communist revolution, and to some extent in the French revolution of 1789, Bohemian revolution of the fifteenth century and the oldest recorded revolution in ancient Egypt (ca. 2500 B.C.) similar convulsions occurred within the religious, occupational, political, kinship, nationality, race, sex, and age groups, and among most of the scientific, philosophical, artistic, and other groups. Their upper strata are partly or wholly supplanted, and new persons and groups are promoted to take their place. In the "total" revolutions there is hardly any important social group that does not experience a similar disruption, especially during the first phase of the revolution. (For a further discussion of revolutions, cf. Chapter 31.)

Wars, even if not followed by a revolution, likewise greatly accelerate vertical mobility in the various governmental, occupational, and other groups of the belligerent countries. The rate of promotions and demotions in the armed forces notably increases. So also does the rate of vertical circulation within the governmental strata; within the hierarchy of the occupational groups and within the strata of each of these; and within the economic pyramid, impoverishing many well-to-do and enriching many poor persons and groups. A much larger number of those previously poor become millionaires, and many more millionaires are impoverished. Some formerly well-paid groups are now poorly paid.[9] In brief, war is also a great re-

[8] For a long series of relevant facts, cf. my *Mobility*, pp. 142 ff. 414-490.

[9] For statistical data of some of the European and other wars and for the United States during the First World War, cf. my *Mobility*, Ch. 18; also my *Calamity*, Chps. 7 and 8.

shuffler of the social stratification of all the important groups.

A similar, though perhaps less marked, increase and acceleration of vertical mobility regularly occurs during disastrous famines, epidemics and pestilences, earthquakes, floods, fires, and the like.

(b) In all large and important multibonded and unibonded groups, but especially in the occupational, economic, and political groups, vertical mobility increases in periods of far-reaching scientific discoveries and of the widespread application of new technological inventions. Such discoveries and inventions create new sources of wealth, sometimes undermining the former sources, and call into existence new occupational groups, undermining the functional basis of some of the former occupational groups. They elevate, economically or occupationally, certain groups and demote certain others. Less directly they affect also the distribution of political power. Through these and similar channels they notably reinforce the individual and collective vertical circulation within stratified economic, occupational, and political bodies. Such discoveries and inventions lead to what is commonly called "the industrial revolution," a revolution embracing economic, occupational, and eventually political changes in these groups and especially in their stratification and vertical mobility. Whether it be the discovery of a new land, or the invention of the steam engine, telegraph, telephone, automobile, airplane, radio, or atomic bomb, every such discovery and invention has led to the appearance of new industries, new occupational groups, new groups of wealthy persons, new political forces, and, as a result, has notably increased the vertical mobility of especially the occupational, economic, and political groups.

(c) Other conditions being equal, economic and occupational vertical mobility within the upper strata tends to be higher in the populations with vast unexploited natural resources than in the populations without such unexploited resources. The United States of the frontier days and of the present day affords an example of the two cases. According to this proposition, we should expect that before the end of the nineteenth century there must have been a higher rate of economic and occupational mobility within the upper ranks of the millionaires and occupational groups than at the present time (although, as we shall see, the vertical occupational and economic mobility has tended to increase in the last few decades within the whole population when all the economic and occupational strata are considered). This expectation seems to be corroborated by the relevant facts so far as they have been studied. For instance, among the deceased generation of American multimillionaires active around the middle of the nineteenth century the percentage of those who started their career poor was 38.8, and the percentage of those neither poor nor rich was 31.5; whereas among the living generation of multimillionaires these percentages were only 19.6 and 27.7 respectively. In the deceased generation in question only 29.7 per cent started their career rich, while in the living generation this percentage was 52.7. This means that in the past there was a larger opportunity for a poor man to become very rich than at the present.[10] Similarly, in the deceased generation only 49 per cent pursued an occupation similar to that of their fathers, whereas in the living generation the percentage is 72.[11]

(d) In most ideological groups, such as religious, scientific, and philosophical bodies, political parties, and artistic associations, and to some extent in sex, age, nationality, and racial groups, vertical mobility tends to increase in periods marked by the discovery and diffusion of new and important scientific theories, religious beliefs, philosophical systems, social and humanistic theories, artistic styles, and ethical and juridical norms. Such discoveries and such diffusion lead to religious reformations and revolutions, to the reorganiza-

---

[10] P. A. Sorokin, "American Millionaires" (cited), pp. 635-537. See also F. W. Taussig and C. S. Joslyn, *American Business Leaders* (cited), Chps. 12-14; S. Riemer, "Upward Mobility" (cited), pp. 10 ff. For other data, cf. my *Mobility*, Chps. 17-19.

[11] See my *Mobility*, pp. 142 ff. This slackening trend of vertical circulation within the upper occupational and economic strata in countries without vast areas and natural resources to be exploited has occurred many times in the past, in the history of several societies. Under such conditions the upper classes tend to become more closed to outsiders.

tion of political and other groups, and to revolutions in science and philosophy, ethics, the fine arts, and eventually in the system of values of the respective populations. Hence a process of intense vertical mobility occurs in these groups. Certain of the previous groups disintegrate; certain new ones arise, grow in prestige, and attain a high social position. In all groups many of the upper strata and individuals are demoted, and new groups and persons rise to take their places. Occasionally such discoveries and diffusions become most important factors of political, economic, and social revolutions. The rise and diffusion of Buddhism, Christianity, Mohammedanism, and the European Renaissance and Reformation furnish examples of such factors and of the attendant enormous reinforcement of vertical mobility, whether in India, in the Graeco-Roman or Arabic world, in central and western Europe, or in other countries. The collective and individual vertical mobility during the decades and centuries of their initial diffusion was truly revolutionary. Vast groups among the older religious, philosophical, and ethical systems swiftly declined, and new religious groups rapidly appeared and mounted the ladder of the total social stratification. All the other groups, including the governmental hierarchy and political parties and the racial, ethnic, kinship, and caste groups, experienced a notable dislocation and vertical displacement in their intergroup position and their intragroup stratification.

In a lesser degree the same is true of the new scientific, political, social, philosophical, artistic, and other ideologies. Such ideologies as the Copernican cosmology, the Darwinian theory of evolution, the philosophies of Plato, Aristotle, and Saint Augustine, the utilitarian system of ethics, Marxian economics and sociology, Comptian positivism, and the foremost theories of equality and democracy are among the principal factors accelerating vertical mobility in many groups.

(e) As we shall see later, vertical mobility tends to be higher in populations and groups with a predominantly sensate culture than in those with a predominantly ideational culture, reaching its peak during periods of transition from the sensate to the ideational types; or vice versa. This proposition embraces, in im-

plicit form, virtually all the preceding propositions respecting the fluctuation of vertical mobility in a framework of time. We shall see that the ideational type of culture, being essentially static, and the sensate type of culture, being essentially dynamic, respectively slacken and accelerate the tempo of sociocultural change, including the tempo of vertical mobility. Periods of transition from one such dominant cultural form to another are characterized by acute political and social revolutions, civil and international wars, and other factors of mobility. As such they exhibit a fundamental restratification of all the main social groups and a wholesale reshuffling of most of the strata of the groups involved.[12]

(f) Because the western populations are in a stage of transition from the previously dominant sensate culture to an idealistic or ideational form of culture (cf. Chapters 40-42), the normal and orderly as well as the spasmodic and revolutionary vertical mobility in practically all their important groups have been rapidly increasing during the last few decades. The spasmodic and revolutionary mobility of the twentieth century has reached an extraordinarily high degree of intensity. In subsequent chapters we shall see that the twentieth century in the West has been the most revolutionary and most belligerent century among some thirty centuries studied. Each revolution and war, as has been pointed out, means a sudden and widespread dislocation that displaces most of the existing strata. Several times within the twentieth century such violent disturbances have made havoc of political, economic, occupational, and many other stratifications. Politically almost all the monarchies and their aristocracies have been overthrown; likewise the successors of the monarchical ruling classes, and the ruling classes in many republics and dictatorships. In Russia the monarchical regime was entirely liquidated, being replaced by the liberal-democratic group of Kerensky's regime; this was supplanted by the Communist ruling class of the Lenin - Trotsky - Kamenev - Zinoviev - Rykoff period; this, in turn, was liquidated by the Stalin group; and now the original composition

[12] Cf. my *Dynamics*, Vol. IV, Ch. 11, and all four volumes, *passim*; also *The Crisis of Our Age*, *passim*.

of Stalin's ruling class is being replaced by Stalin's "nationalist bureaucracy."

In Germany the Hohenzollern regime was succeeded by the Weimar Republic; this gave place to the short-lived Hindenburg regime; this, in turn, succumbed to the Nazi ruling class; and finally, this class was displaced by the military government of the Allies, with a new ruling stratum.

A parallel experience is that of Austria, where the Hapsburg ruling aristocracy and its successors gave way to the Nazis, and they in turn to the post-Nazi ruling groups.

As violent and abrupt changes have happened in Italy and Greece, Hungary, Rumania, Bulgaria, and Yugoslavia, Turkey and Persia, and many other formerly monarchical countries. The new republics, such as Czechoslovakia, Finland, Poland, Lithuania, Latvia, and Estonia, have undergone a series of similar convulsions, some of them temporarily disappearing as sovereign states. In other countries, like France, Great Britain, and the United States, where there has been no open revolution, profound changes have occurred also. The contemporary ruling class in these countries is very different from the one in power before the First World War. In Britain and America the old ruling class has been replaced in large part by the "new-dealers" and "new new-dealers," new labor groups, new industrialists, new wealthy groups, and new professional groups—elements that played a very insignificant role in the nineteenth century and before the First World War. The total effects of such "landslides" have become so great that today's ruling class bears only a remote relationship to that of the beginning of this century.

Similar dislocations have occurred in the *economic pyramids* of the western populations. In most of the western countries the wealthy stratum consists today mainly of newcomers (*nouveaux riches*), the greater part of the wealthy class of the beginning of the century now being impoverished. During the last thirty years several "landslides" on a large scale have happened in this stratification in practically all the western countries, and landslides continue to occur daily in various forms.

Enormous and striking changes have taken place also in the occupational composition of the populations of nearly all the western countries. Even in nonrevolutionary countries, such as the United States, these occupational changes have been profound. Per million of the occupational population of the United States, the number of farmers decreased from 103,097 in 1850 to less than 40,000 in 1940 and that of the wheelwrights from 1323 to some 30; that of the clerical employees increased from 4369 to more than 43,000, and so on. Such changes mean not only horizontal but also vertical alterations of the occupational structure of the population. An enormous horizontal and vertical occupational mobility was introduced by the Second World War. More than 10,000,000 were taken into the armed forces; and more than 20,000,000 civilians shifted to wartime industries from occupations considerably different from their pre-wartime occupations. The subsequent reconversion gives a new reshift.

In countries that have experienced revolutions as well as wars during the twentieth century the occupational horizontal and vertical mobility has been still greater than in the United States.

Owing to the revolutions and wars of this century the collective and spasmodic vertical circulation in other groups, such as political parties, religious organizations, nationality groups, and family and kinship groups, has been exceptionally great. Hardly any important unibonded or multibonded group has escaped "landslides" in its stratification. As a matter of fact, within a few years of the Second World War enormous "landslides" occurred in almost all unibonded and multibonded groups, in the form not only of vertical mobility but of a rearrangement of the relative positions of the strata themselves. In a concise way the phenomenon may be summed up as follows.[13]

In intersex stratification the position of women relative to that of men rose, and the gap of the sex inequalities considerably narrowed.

In interage stratification the younger groups especially between the ages of eighteen and twenty-one, rose in their comparative status.

In interrace stratification the status of the

---

[13] For the details, cf. my "War and Post-War Changes in Social Stratifications of the Euro-American Population," *ASR*, Vol. X (1945), pp. 294-303.

"inferior" races—black, yellow, and others, subordinated race groups—was elevated, while that of the "master race" (or white Euro-American race) declined, the gap of the race inequalities becoming narrower and less pronounced than before the war.

In interstate and international stratification several great powers, such as Germany and Japan, declined to the point where they actually disappeared as sovereign states, whereas other powers, such as the United States, Russia, and China, conspicuously mounted the ladder of interstate stratification.

In interfamily and kinship stratification many aristocratic, patrician, blue-blood families and kinship groups gave place to plebeian upstart families and kinship groups.

In economic stratification the pyramid was greatly flattened in most of the European countries (cf. the next chapter). The composition of the upper and lower strata is now considerably different from that of prewar days; and the value of wealth as the basis for prestige and high social position has notably declined in the total system of values.

Similar rearrangements of the relative positions occurred in the *occupational* groups. The position of many unskilled and semiskilled occupations classified as "essential" to the war effort rose, while that of many clerical, small business, and professional occupations regarded as "non-essential" deteriorated.

A comparable transformation occurred in the relative positions of many *religious groups and political parties*. Some of these, such as the Russian Orthodox Church and the "suppressed" or "underground" political parties, rose to a position of dominance, while many others declined.

In the stratified structure of *social classes* the class of large landowners almost disappeared. The status of the capitalist class conspicuously sank, and that of the laboring class sharply rose. In addition, a new class of managerial bureaucracy emerged and rapidly grew.

Finally, among all the multitudinous groups and their aristocracies the relative position of *the state hierarchy*—especially of the upper strata—and that of the *highest ranks in technology and the physical sciences sharply rose*.

To summarize: there is no doubt as to the extraordinary increase of the collective and spasmodic vertical mobility in the western populations of the twentieth century.

Besides this spasmodic and mass-scale increase, vertical mobility has been increasing in extent and intensity in its "normal" form in many groups among the western populations. In *occupational* groups, with the exception of the highest strata (spasmodically changed by war or revolution), the increase has manifested itself, first, *in a systematic decrease in the inheritance of the occupational position of the parents*. For instance, in the sample of United States populations studied by myself the percentage of transmission of occupation from the great-grandfathers to their sons was 72; from the grandfathers to their sons, 38.9; and from the fathers to their sons only 10.6. A similar decrease was revealed by several other studies.[14] Second, the totality of available data shows that, all in all, the vertical occupational mobility within the lifetime of one generation has tended also to increase in most of the occupational groups studied.[15] Nowadays people tend to change their occupation, either in an upward or in a downward direction, more frequently than one or more generations ago. There is an unquestionable increase of not only horizontal but also vertical interoccupational and intraoccupational mobility.

As to "normal" economic vertical mobility, it has hardly increased within the upper economic stratum during the last few decades. In the American multimillionaire group and several other groups studied by the author the transmission of economic status from parents to children has not decreased from generation to generation. Similar results have been obtained in several German studies.[16] In the middle and lower economic strata an intense vertical "normal" mobility has been observable. However, in view of the enormous increase of spasmodic vertical economic mobility due to the wars, revolutions, and other crises of this century, a huge net increase in vertical mobility would have been virtually inevitable, even in the absence of a "normal" increase.

It goes without saying that the twentieth century has witnessed a notable increase, both spasmodic and "normal," in the vertical circula-

---

[14] Cf. my *Mobility*, Ch. 17; also Taussig and Joslyn, *op. cit.*, Ch. 13.

[15] *Ibid.*, pp. 42 ff.

[16] See, for instance, *Die wirtschaftliche und soziale Lage der Angestellten* (Berlin, 1931).

tion of individuals and groups within *the political parties*, which have been incessantly appearing and disappearing, rising and declining. Today a given party is dominant; tomorrow it is declared illegal, its leaders being imprisoned or executed, or at least dragged down from their elevated positions. In any case the personnel of the upper strata undergoes a rapid change, today's leaders being replaced by new persons tomorrow.

The same may be said of many *religious groups*. The relative positions of various denominations in the constellation of stratified denominations have been changing rapidly in various countries. Certain denominations have been increasingly splitting into two or more sects, each split representing a mass promotion and demotion of the hierarchy. Within otherwise stable denominations the vertical shift of the members, especially of the higher ranks of the hierarchy, has been accelerating and involving larger numbers of persons.

In a word, vertical mobility—individual and collective, normal and especially "spasmodic" —has been steadily increasing in most of the important groups of the western populations until it has produced a state of feverish disorder akin to that of a disturbed anthill!

(5) From this temporary trend it would be fallacious to conclude that such an acceleration of vertical mobility is going to continue indefinitely, or that such a trend has been perennial throughout the whole of human history. *According to all the available data, there seems to be no definite perpetual trend toward either an increase or a decrease in the intensity and volume of vertical mobility. Instead we note simply a fluctuation of its increase and decrease in the course of the life history of practically all long-lived social groups.* Hence the recent upward trend of vertical mobility in the West is likely sooner or later to slow down and even reverse itself.

The reasons for such a fluctuation are not far to seek. So far as violent, "spasmodic," and collective shifts are concerned, they must fluctuate because the magnitude and frequency of wars, revolutions, and other calamities fluctuate in the course of time (cf. Chapters 31 and 32).[17] Since most of the spasmodic and mass mobilities are due to these factors, their fluctuation determines that of the spasmodic and mass mobility.

As to "normal" vertical mobility, it also is limited in its increase or decrease. For a satisfactory performance of the functions of especially the upper strata special talent is often necessary. Such talent is possessed by only a limited number of persons; not everyone can become a Beethoven or Newton, a Saint Paul or Napoleon, a great ruler or a great organizer of business. Hence only the limited number of potentially capable persons can climb to the top strata. Even these persons need a long preliminary training in order to discharge their functions successfully. This introduces a time limitation of vertical mobility, reinforced by several other conditions inherent in the mechanism of testing, selecting, and promoting or demoting the individuals concerned. Moreover, as we have seen, unlimited vertical mobility is detrimental to the continuity of social groups. It encounters a series of brakes and obstacles in all "normal" groups. Then there is often a lack of vacancies within the upper strata. For all these reasons normal vertical mobility cannot increase indefinitely. Having reached its optimum point (different for different groups), it is bound to slow down and frequently to reverse itself.

These general considerations are supported by the actual facts so far as they have been studied. A more or less systematic study of vertical mobility in the state hierarchies, occupational and economic groups, religious organizations, and political parties, and even in the emergence, growth, fluctuation, and decline of castes and social orders, demonstrates that vertical mobility in all these groups has fluctuated, now increasing and now decreasing, instead of perpetually growing or declining.[18]

---

[17] For the wars and revolutions of the last twenty-five centuries, cf. my *Dynamics*, Vol. III, Parts II and III. My pioneer study of these movements, adversely criticized by several "experts" (who actually were incompetent pseudo-scholars), has since been confirmed in all its essentials by a sub-sequent study of the problem by Q. Wright in his *A Study of War* (2 Vols., Chicago, 1942). So far only these two works present a systematic study of the trends of war during a period of some twenty-five centuries.

[18] For other considerations, cf. my *Mobility*, pp. 142-160, *passim*.

Even in the most recent period we have noticed that within the upper occupational and economic strata normal mobility has tended to decrease rather than to increase.

When the contemporary "fluidity" ceases; when the currents of anarchy, revolutions, and wars are over; and especially when the transition from the present declining sensate culture to a different type of culture is accomplished, there is every reason to expect a decrease of "spasmodic" and even of "normal" vertical mobility. In any case, the evidence in favor of a fluctuation hypothesis is much more substantial than that in favor of a perpetual trend of either increasing or decreasing vertical mobility.

(6) Among other approximate uniformities in the field of "normal" vertical mobility the following may be mentioned.[19] *"Normal" vertical mobility takes place in all groups gradually, from one stratum to the next, proceeding in orderly fashion and being controlled to a considerable extent by the mechanisms of social testing, selection, and distribution of individuals.* Whether in the occupational, economic, political, or other pyramids, the majority of individuals move up or down gradually, step by step, without skipping the intermediate ranks. From an unskilled occupation they climb to a semiskilled occupation, then to a skilled or clerical position, then to a less highly qualified profession, or small business, or modest governmental position. From a condition of poverty they climb gradually through the various economic strata. Similar gradualness is exhibited by the downward movement. The same may be said of promotion and demotion in the army and navy, in religious groups, in state officialdom, and in scientific, artistic, and other groups and organizations, whether the shift is accomplished in several generations or in only one generation. With reference to occupations the proposition may be formulated as follows: *The closer the affinity between occupations, the more intense is the mutual inter-*change *of their members; conversely, the greater the difference between occupations the smaller is the number of individuals who shift from one group to another.* This proposition does not mean that all the shifts occur gradually, from one step to the next, without skips. There are always certain individuals who move faster and who occasionally skip some of the intermediate stages. Hence the following propositions:[20]

(a) Different individuals move in the vertical direction at different velocities.

(b) The greater the number of political, occupational, economic, or other social strata to be crossed, the smaller is the number of those who make such shifts. A slave may rise to the position of a king, or a king sink to the status of a slave; a poor man now and then becomes a millionaire, and vice versa; and an unskilled person occasionally rises to the apex of an occupational pyramid. But the number of such "jumpers" has always been small.

(c) In many stratified groups the tendency is for the members of the upper strata to sink and for those of the lower strata to rise.

(d) The middle strata seem to be more stable than those at the two extremes; though some of their members shift upward and others downward, the proportion of those who remain within the same stratum appears to be greater than the proportion remaining in the upper and the lower strata.

(e) Since "normal" climbing is gradual and takes time, the average age of the active new members of the upper strata in the same group (not the age of their children who do not actively discharge the respective functions) tends to be higher than the average age of the active members of the lower strata.[21]

(7) *As a consequence of these features of vertical mobility, particularly in western populations, the following propositions ensue:*

(a) Children of different fathers belonging to a given stratum of economic, occupational, religious, political, state, and other groups, and

---

[19] Formulated in my *Mobility* on the basis of considerable factual evidence, these generalizations have since been confirmed by a number of studies. See especially Taussig and Joslyn's study (cited); S. Riemer's summary of the German studies (cited); and several of the German studies, especially *Sozialer Auf und Abstieg* (cited), *Die*

wirtschaftliche und soziale Lage der Angestellten (cited), and others mentioned in Riemer's paper.
[20] For the actual evidence cf. my *Mobility* and other works cited in the preceding footnote.
[21] For the facts, cf. my *Mobility*, pp. 453 ff., and *Die wirtschaftliche und soziale Lage der Angestellten* (cited), p. 36.

now and then even the children of the same family, are dispersed among various strata in these groups.

(b) The membership of practically all the strata in almost all the groups of the western populations is recruited from the offspring of highly dissimilar strata.

(c) Among the upper strata are found to some extent the children of the parents belonging to the lower strata, and vice versa.

(d) This means that different groups and strata of the western populations are considerably interwoven and linked together through this interchange—horizontal and vertical—of the members and their offspring.

(e) As a result the cleavages between various strata and groups are not clear-cut. When one son becomes a laborer, another a physician, and a third a businessman, it is difficult to decide to what group and stratum, occupational and economic, such a family belongs. Since members of the same family enter different strata and groups, these strata and groups are more or less interlinked, ceasing to be as remote from one another as they would be if their members were recruited from only those who were born in the groups or strata in question. Hence the blurred character of the stratification and the class struggles among societies made up of classes which incessantly interchange their members.

(f) This vertical and, to some extent, horizontal mobility reveals the one-sidedness of extreme theories of the class struggle, as well as the fallacy of many eugenic theories. Extreme proponents of the class struggle depict the social classes as though they were closed

castes, without a perennial interchange of their members and without connections with other classes, groups, and strata through a dispersion of members of a given family, stratum, or group throughout different classes, strata, and groups. "Marxian social theory in neglecting vertical mobility does so at the expense of depth of insight into the stratification of modern society."[22] When the innumerable interconnections and incessant vertical shifts of the population of each social class are considered, class differentiation and the class struggle are seen to be merely relative phenomena. The rapidly shifting element of each social class is, at best, only a temporary and highly diluted agency of the class struggle, class psychology, and class interests. As such it is a fluctuating factor that links different classes together, cushioning their clashes and conflicts and blurring the class differentiation and stratification. It explains why, in reality, the alleged class conflicts and class differences are neither so sharp and clear-cut nor so "absolute" as Marxians and others depict them.[23]

Since the upper classes in the contemporary western populations represent a *mixtum compositum* recruited from all strata, it is fallacious to depict them as the biological offspring of long-existing aristocratic families separated for generations from the common stocks and peoples, as some eugenists and radical theorists do. The contemporary upper classes are, biologically and socially, "mongrels" or "hybrids" and in no way represent either biological or social castes. As such they deserve neither the eulogy of the eugenists nor the condemnation of the "anticaste radicals."

---

[22] S. Riemer, *op. cit.*, p. 6.

[23] The phenomena of mobility, interchange, and interconnections of the groups and strata render superfluous any "cliques" and "associations," created *ad hoc*, that allegedly link the otherwise unconnected social classes of a "community" and integrate the various groups and strata into a single system. They allegedly play a role similar to that of boards nailed across several otherwise unconnected logs. Such is the theory offered by W. L. Warner and P. S. Lunt in their *Social Life of a Modern Community*, pp. 110 ff. It is unnecessary to point out that this conception of interconnections through the "planks" of associations and cliques is untenable. We have seen that through horizontal

and vertical mobility all strata and groups are interconnected and integrated. This role is played by any family, group, or stratum of a mobile population. The "cliques" and "associations" do not occupy in this respect an exclusive position as "integrators." Being comparatively unimportant and superficial factors, they possess much less interconnecting efficiency than the main groups and their strata. Any individual, as a member of several different groups, serves to connect them. Through the mobility of the individuals the groups are linked by hundreds of ties. The Warner-Lunt theory is based on the false assumption of a unitary society (see above, pp. 306-307, and 357).

II. General Causes of Vertical Mobility

Since vertical mobility is an inherent and perennial trait of all organized and stratified groups, its causes are also inherent and perennial though somewhat different for different groups. Among these may be mentioned the following.

(1) In groups electing or appointing the members of their upper strata for *a definite term, this feature of their organization is the basic cause of their horizontal and vertical mobility.* On the expiration of the term, the previous incumbents must be replaced. Hence the inevitability of new persons being elevated to high positions. If the candidates are recruited from all the strata of the group, the vertical current circulates from the bottom to the top of the pyramid and now and then elevates to the upper positions members of the lower strata. If the candidates are limited to the middle and upper strata, the current catches up only the members within these strata.

(2) A similar cause operates in the Roman Catholic Church, whose high dignitaries are *elected or appointed for life* but, being celibate, do not transmit their position to their issue. After the death of a Pope, bishop, or cardinal their positions must be filled by persons recruited from the lower strata of the Church. Here again *the cause of vertical mobility is inherent in the very organization of the group.*

(3) In many groups vertical mobility is caused by *an insufficient self-perpetuation of the upper strata.* Through a low birth rate or through high mortality a number of vacancies are created within the upper layers which can be filled only by persons recruited from the lower layers. In such groups the insufficient self-perpetuation of the upper classes creates an "upward draft" that picks up and promotes persons from the lower classes. For instance, in Sparta the number of Spartiates (the upper social order) before the Persian Wars was 8000. Through high mortality and possibly a low birth rate it had decreased by *ca.* 420 B.C., to 6000; by *ca.* 371 B.C. to 1500; and by 244

B.C. to 700, of which only 100 were full-fledged Homoioi. Among the Roman patricians (the upper social order) only about 15 families survived to the time of Caesar. Even among the equestrian and noble families that arose during the age of Augustus most were extinct by the time of Claudius. The number of full-fledged citizens of Athens decreased from 16,000 at the beginning of the Peloponnesian Wars to some 2500 by the time of Sulla.[24] In all such cases the vacancies had to be filled by persons from the lower strata.

Similarly, in medieval and modern Europe most of the aristocratic families became extinct within 300 years. Of 500 English aristocratic families of the fifteenth century hardly any exist at the present time.[25] In specific aristocracies such as military castes and royal dynasties, extinction has often been due to a notable degree, to the dangerous character of their position and hence to an unusually high proportion of deaths through violence. While for the entire population of the United States suicide and other forms of violence constituted only 7.2 per cent of the total causes of death, for the monarchs of Rome, Byzantium, Turkey, England, Austria, Prussia, Russia, and Germany they fluctuated between 20 and 66.3 per cent. For the presidents of Bolivia they represented 40 per cent; for presidents of the United States and France, 12.1 per cent; for prominent military men of various countries, 20 per cent; for statesmen, 10 per cent, and for Roman Catholic Popes, 9 per cent.[26]

In recent decades the upper classes of the West have also possessed a birth rate often insufficient to fill the vacancies created by death.[27]

The foregoing observations demonstrate that a "social vacuum" is incessantly created through the inability of the upper strata to perpetuate themselves sufficiently to fill the vacancies and that these must be filled through promotions from the lower strata. This factor does not operate in all social groups, because in some the upper strata (for instance, the

[24] Cf. my *Mobility*, pp. 357 ff., for an exhaustive series of facts of this kind.
[25] *Ibid.*, pp. 347-360.

[26] Cf. my *Mobility*, p. 356.
[27] *Ibid.*, pp. 347-356.

Brahmin caste of India) reproduce themselves sufficiently to fill the vacancies.

(4) *The next general cause is the unfitness of many individuals to perform the proper functions of their social stratum, arising from the dissimilarity of parents and children, and from the profound change which many persons undergo in the course of their life.* If the members of a group, especially those of the upper strata, regularly fail to discharge satisfactorily their duties and functions, the group will progressively suffer and eventually disintegrate. If the government of a state shows increasing incapacity; if the commanders of an army display a lack of organizational, strategic, and other military ability; if the leaders of a religious organization exhibit greed, sensuality, and ignorance, the state, the army, and the church are bound to suffer. If, on the other hand, their lower strata contain "born rulers," "born military geniuses," or genuine spiritual leaders, such persons are likewise unsuited to their lower positions. Directly or indirectly they will undermine the group from below. In other words, *a fairly high degree of correspondence between the social positions of the members and their ability to perform the proper functions of their strata is a prerequisite for the continued existence of the group. When the discrepancy becomes too great, the group must either correct it by reallocating its members according to their ability or else to suffer, even perish.* Hence the unavoidableness of vertical mobility under the circumstances in question.[28]

Several forces generate such discrepancies in the life process of every group. One such force is the *dissimilarity between the parents and children in regard to the specific ability necessary for the successful discharge of the functions of their stratum.* A portion—perhaps the lesser portion—of the children are born with qualities dissimilar from those of their paren For example, the children of Hippocra Socrates, Aristotle, and many other emin thinkers lacked the genius of their parents; children of many capable rulers, such as Pe the Great, Charles V, and Napoleon, failed display any of the ability possessed by th parents; and the children of builders of bu ness empires not infrequently are wastrels Conversely, the children of slaves may be bo rulers.

To prevent an unduly large accumulation unfit persons, the group is forced continuous to shift a part of its members to the stra corresponding to their abilities, to demote t incapable children of capable parents and promote the capable children of incapab parents. The concrete methods of promotic and demotion are of various sorts: on the o hand, impoverishment, outcasting, dethron ment, discharge, revolutionary overthro failure to reelect, etc.; on the other, norm promotion, elevation through revolutions palace coups, election, etc.

Owing to physical or mental sickness, acc dents, excess, and other causes, *persons some times undergo a profound change in the cours of their lifetime* whereby they lose their abilit properly to perform their functions. Henc the need of replacing such persons with differ ent ones. In this way again a steady stream o vertical mobility is generated: sick monarch and other rulers are eliminated; the rich be come poor; religious and ethical leaders los their prestige, and so on.

(5) *Another cause of vertical mobility is a incessant change in the environment—espe cially in the sociocultural environment—o groups and their individual members.* Change in the sociocultural environment ceaselessly create favorable conditions for some members and unfavorable conditions for others, leading

---

[28] A. Toynbee (cf. his *Study of History*, Vol. III, *passim*) has demonstrated that in all civilizations during the period of their growth their "creative minority" adequately meets challenges to the group's existence and growth, but that in periods of decline this creative minority is replaced by an uncreative "dominant minority" that fails to meet the challenges successfully.

[29] Ibn Khaldun made the generalization, on the basis of his observations of the life cycle of prominent Arabian families, that the son of the founder of a great family is often a mere continuator of his father's work, and that the grandsons and great-grandsons are regularly wastrels. See Ibn Khaldun, *Prolégomènes historiques, Notices et Extraits des manuscrits de la Bibliothèque Imperial* (Paris, 1862), Vol. XIX, p. 287. Pareto's cycle of the *speculatori* and *rentieri* is merely a special case of the general rule of the dissimilarity between parents and children. For the facts and the literature, cf. my *Mobility*, pp. 360 ff., and *Dynamics*, Vol. IV, pp. 505 ff.

respectively to their promotion and demotion. Rich deposits of oil or manganese among a population that is aware of their industrial and economic uses serve to enrich the owners of such land. The invention of the automobile has enriched many of its manufacturers and impoverished many manufacturers of horse-drawn vehicles. A whimsical change in public taste makes millionaires out of Sinatras and beggars out of many "old-fashioned" singers. The replacement of a monarchy by a republic elevates a host of adherents of the republic and drags down many a monarchical aristocracy. A declaration of war automatically demotes many a pacifist and elevates to the rank of hero many a belligerent. Victory or defeat in war is followed by a mass displacement of groups and their members. The vicissitudes of the stock market enrich many a gambler and ruin many an unlucky investor. In general, any change in the economic, political, scientific, technical, ethical, religious, judical, aesthetic, philosophical, and other sociocultural conditions of a group, as well as any profound change in its physical and biological condition (such as epidemics, floods, droughts, and earthquakes), cause a horizontal and vertical displacement of its members.

This dynamism of sociocultural life alone is sufficient to produce an incessant stream of vertical mobility within any group or constellation of groups. Considering that other factors of mobility—such as election or appointment for a limited term, the dissimilarity of parents and children, and the profound changes experienced by persons in the course of their lifetime—are also more or less inherent in the component of members of the groups, *the main cause of vertical mobility is seen to be immanent, or inherent, in the sociocultural groups themselves.* Even in a constant natural milieu, with an adequate self-perpetuation of the upper strata, vertical mobility would inevitably occur in all organized groups. *Factors external to the group may reinforce or hinder it, but they are merely secondary.*

III. The Mechanisms of a Group for the Testing, Selection, and Distribution of Its Members

The preceding analysis suggests that the distribution of the group's members among its various strata is not a matter of mere chance. It is not simply by good or bad luck that some of the members of a state become its king or president while others remain plain citizens or are electrocuted as criminals, or that some become Popes or bishops of an ecclesiastical organization whereas others are plain parishioners or heretics. Nor is the distribution due principally to the personal virtues or vices of the members. *The first determining factor is the group organization itself, which defines who shall occupy each of its strata and positions and under what circumstances. The second factor is the presence or absence of certain specific qualities in the respective individuals, as tested by the group's devices.* These two factors determine largely the position, promotion, and demotion of the members.

(1) The official law of a group defines the status open to its members and prescribes the conditions. The constitution of a hereditary monarchy excludes as possible candidates for the position of monarch all citizens except the children of the monarch, and prescribes in great detail which of these may become his successor and in what order. Thus virtually all citizens are excluded as possible candidates for a throne, regardless of their personal qualities. In the elective republics likewise the constitution of the state determines which of its citizens may become president, and the provisions are as rigorous as the law of succession in the monarchies.

The constitution of a caste or social order determines that only the children of Brahmins or of the nobility, respectively, may, as a rule, become Brahmins or nobles; that the children of the lowest caste or of slaves may automatically become members of the lowest caste or of the stratum of slaves, respectively. The constitution of the family determines under what conditions a person may become a husband or *pater familias*, a wife, a son-in-law, etc., with the respective rights and duties of each position. The constitution of a privately owned business firm defines clearly who may become its head or president, its higher or lower employees, with the respective functions of each position. According to the constitution of the Roman Catholic Church, only celibates may become its priests or higher dignitaries. Only possessors of the Ph.D. degree may become professors in many colleges, and so on.

These examples clarify the meaning of the statement that the first and probably the most important factor which determines the position of each member of a group is the group organization itself. Regardless of the personal abilities of the members, the organization of a monarchical state or of a caste, as has been said, is such that it excludes from the throne or from membership in the caste all who are not born, respectively, within the royal dynasty or the caste.

In other groups the provisions are different, but similar provisions are a part of the organization of every group and constitute a substantial portion of its "constitutional law." They not only determine what positions each member is obliged or entitled to occupy or prohibited from occupying but also contain the rules governing the promotion and demotion of the members, as well as the rules for ascertaining their qualifications. Whether the members of the group are promoted on the basis of seniority, of wealth, of political affiliations, of race or creed, of their belonging to a patrician family, or of personal achievement of this or that kind—all this is determined by the constitution of the group. As a result, in two similar groups, for instance, in two armies or college faculties or business firms, persons are promoted and demoted on different bases.

The constitution of the group determines by what kind of test and by whom the qualifications of its members are ascertained. In caste populations and those with social orders, parentage is accepted as the supreme criterion of the position of individuals. In populations with open social classes such a test is not regarded as of paramount importance. Instead, wealth is frequently accepted as the principal evidence of fitness of a person for membership in the upper social strata. In other groups, side by side with wealth other criteria are accepted, such as race, nationality, age, sex, political party, religion, education, ideology, I.Q., manners and mores. In monarchical states republican sympathies militate against membership in the state hierarchy; in a Republican regime in the United States, affiliation with the Democratic party becomes an obstacle to promotion and a reason for the dismissal of many a government official, and vice versa. In Communist Russia or Nazi Germany a lack of sympathy with the Communist or the Nazi credo could be sufficient cause for execution or imprisonment, or at least for demotion to the lowest social position. A non-Catholic cannot become a dignitary of the Catholic Church. In several "democracies" a Negro is ineligible for admission to any high social or governmental position. The same applies to many races and nationalities. Without a Ph.D. degree few persons can obtain a professorial position in colleges and universities.

Having been accepted by a group, any kind of "evidence of fitness"—no matter how childish it may appear to this or that person— serves to determine the social position, the promotion and demotion, of its members. Even where, according to contemporary notions, the criteria appear to be reasonable and "scientific," we find a wide variety of applications of such evidence and correspondingly a notable difference in the occupants of the upper and lower strata. In universities the instructors and professors are supposedly selected and promoted on the basis of their scientific qualifications and achievements. But when such a rule is examined in its actual operation, it is found that some colleges emphasize research; others, teaching ability; still others, efficiency in obtaining considerable funds for the college; some others, "yes, men" of the administration. By "research" is meant in some colleges a painful elaboration of the obvious; in others, a monographic interpretation of this or that passage of some classic author; in still others, something susceptible of "practical application." In monarchical China the highest ranks of the statesmen were recruited from students who exhibited superior knowledge of the Chinese classics and possessed a graceful style.

The above shows how decisive a role is played by the organization of the group in the selection, placement, promotion, and demotion of its members within its stratified pyramid. Such is the first factor determining the social position of an individual.

(2) Its second factor is the totality of characteristics, relevant to the group's criteria of fitness, possessed by each member. Individuals differ widely in their characteristics, both positive and negative. *In each group the members that possess the traits required by the group for a certain stratum have a much better chance of being placed in that stratum than those who lack such traits.* In groups attaching paramount importance to parentage only the children of the monarch can become monarchs, regardless of their other qualities; only the children of Brahmins or nobles can become Brahmins or nobles, respectively; to all others, no matter how capable they may be and no matter how dull the royal-born, the Brahmins, or the nobles may be, the upper positions, as a rule, are closed. In the groups where wealth plays the dominant role, it is chiefly the rich who climb to the top positions. In the Nazi "Aryan" state the "non-Aryans" have no chance to occupy the top political or social positions. A scholar like G. Vico, whose theories radically deviate from the prevalent theories governing university administration and faculties, has little chance for academic promotion, or even for a university appointment, no matter how epoch-making his theory may be. The same is true of other eminent scholars who entertain unorthodox views. A person who is perfectly frank and sincere can seldom become a high-ranking diplomat; one of the prerequisites of such a position has traditionally been a marked ability to use words in such a way as to mask one's real intentions. Again, in many political campaigns, candidates with too high ideals—those who scorn demagogy, flattery, and hypocrisy, and are unwilling to hold out the prospect of unattainable goals—have little chance of being elected. (Indeed, most idealistic persons do not even offer themselves as candidates in such cases.) If a university diploma is made the prerequisite for becoming a doctor, a lawyer, or an engineer, all persons lacking such a diploma are automatically excluded from such positions. Persons who do not pass the civil-service examination in the state requiring it for official positions are similarly debarred.

Such is the second factor determining the social position of a member in the group. Thus *the nature of the testing mechanisms of the group, and the presence or absence in a member of the requisite characteristics for the upper strata in particular, essentially determine the social position, promotion and demotion, and "success" and "failure" of each member of the group.* The incessant operation of these two factors makes comprehensible the statement that the social position of individuals is not a matter of mere chance, of good or bad luck, but is definitely determined by the organization of the group—by its mechanisms for testing and selecting its members—and by the respective qualities of the individuals.

This raises the question: To what extent does the position of individuals within the strata of the group correspond to the principle *"To everyone according to his ability"?* The wide variety of criteria of fitness used by different groups give the impression that the selection and distribution of members bear scant relationship to their real abilities. The answer to this problem is approximately as follows: *There has scarcely ever existed a social group whose members were distributed according to their real ability.* Among the upper strata there have always been members whose place, according to their ability, should have been in the lower strata, and vice versa. On the other hand, *in every long-existing group the distribution of the members within the strata cannot completely ignore the principle "To everyone according to his ability."* If its born rulers and leaders were all placed within the lower strata and its upper strata were filled completely with stupid persons or slave types, such a group could not exist for any length of time; either it would rapidly disintegrate or a revolution would occur, overthrowing the stupid and incapable aristocracy and replacing it with capable leaders from the lower classes. *This means that in a long-existing group with criteria of fitness that appear strange to us the criteria must possess a cer-*

tain element of validity and rationality, must test and select the members of its various strata to some extent according to their ability.

For example, the automatic assignment of children to the social stratum of their parents in castes, social orders, and royal dynasties appears to us one of the least adequate criteria of vertical distribution of individuals according to their ability. However, when the conditions of the castes, social orders, the royal dynasties are thoughtfully studied, such a mechanism of testing and distribution of their members appears to be not entirely invalid. First, it has behind it the principle of heredity that capable parents produce a larger proportion of capable children than incapable parents. Though the biological inheritance of the mental qualities of the parents by their children is never perfect, it is more than a chance expectation. Secondly, when the castes, social orders, and so on arose, there were no tests for determining the mental, moral, and social aptitudes of individuals. School education was either entirely lacking or else limited to the family circle. In such circumstances the children of capable parents were better-educated and better-trained than the children of the lower strata, who had no schooling or training at all. Biologically as well as educationally the children of the higher castes or orders were better equipped as rulers and leaders than those of the lower strata. Hence the status of the family as a criterion of the ability of the children was far from being entirely unreasonable; in the circumstances such a criterion was certainly one of the best available. Thirdly, in hereditary royal dynasties additional considerations played an important part, especially the necessity of eliminating any struggle for the position of monarch on the part of ambitious pretenders; the position having been made hereditary within the royal family and the order of succession to the throne having been clearly defined, the danger of civil war and similar disturbances was greatly reduced.

The validity of these considerations is well supported by the relevant facts. First, take the extraordinarily long existence of the Brahmin aristocracy in the caste population. Its unquestionable superiority has lasted possibly longer than that of any other aristocracy

known; for more than two thousand years it has maintained its social supremacy among all the other castes. This is the more significant in that the Brahmins are neither the wealthy nor the military caste, nor even an organized group like the Roman Catholic Church. They have maintained their superiority without wealth or military power or the power of organized machinery, the usual means for the maintenance of most other aristocracies. Such an exceptionally long superiority could not be maintained by a caste recruited from persons devoid of ability. Moreover, during this long period of Brahmin domination India has known several periods of notable cultural and social distinction. Likewise, we cannot brand as stupid most of the Egyptian royal dynasties, despite the fact that they were strictly inbred groups. The extraordinarily long duration of Ancient Egypt, with its series of social, cultural, and political renaissances unexcelled for these centuries by any other people, clearly proves that Egypt's royal dynasties and its aristocracy were not composed of stupid or mediocre persons exceeded in ability by the lower classes. Finally, a study of the mental and moral caliber of the European royal families shows that they have contributed as many persons of genius as any other stock in human history.[30]

Though family status still plays a certain role in the vertical distribution of individuals in the contemporary West, its role, and the inheritance of social position, are much less conspicuous than in the caste and social orders. The reasons are fairly obvious. Under contemporary conditions such criteria, as exclusive factors, would be out of place, and, if applied, would tend to miscarry. The various strata of the western peoples are not inbred groups but a mixture of various stocks of different groups and strata. The family is unstable. Education is supplied by a variety of schools, and is thus no longer restricted to the facilities offered by the family. We have at our disposal several supposedly scientific tests of the aptitudes of individuals, including

---

[30] Cf. F. A. Woods, *Mental and Moral Heredity in Royalty* (New York, 1906), and *The Influence of Monarchs* (New York, 1913). Somewhat more conservative is my study "Monarchs and Rulers," *SF*, 1925-1926.

the so-called "intelligence tests." In other words, neither biologically nor educationally may the children of the upper strata be assumed in general to be greatly superior to those of the middle and lower strata and as such automatically entitled to inherit the social positions of their parents.

Let us next turn our attention to the *religious groups*. In many "ideational" populations, such as those of India and medieval Europe, the Church played an exceptionally important role in testing and selecting the individuals and distributing them among the various strata. When the Church branded certain individuals or groups as pagans, heretics, or schismatics, or as sinful or immoral, these persons and groups were debarred from high positions and often demoted to the lowest social ranks. On the other hand, by approving the others as pious or virtuous, the Church elevated them and sanctioned their high positions. Constituting, as it did, the main agency of intellectual, moral, religious, and social education, the Church played a decisive role as the testing, selecting, and distributing agent in such societies.

In the contemporary West the Church still plays an important role in this respect, but much less conspicuously than formerly. The reason is that the principal educational and selective functions have passed from the Church to secular agencies. Moreover, the general influence of religious groups has notably declined. Under these altered circumstances the decrease of the role of the Church as a testing, selecting, and distributing agency, with its own criteria of ability and fitness, is easily comprehensible.

These examples illustrate the point that most of the criteria and agencies employed by various groups in the vertical distribution of their members are more or less sensible, serving to some extent to allocate their members according to their ability.

When social conditions undergo a radical change, the mechanisms for the testing, selection, and distribution of individuals change also. Hence in the contemporary western populations the tests, techniques, and agencies are distinctly different from those employed in many other populations with a different culture and social structure. Though the old criteria of ability and of the vertical distribution of individuals, such as family status, religious position, wealth, race, political party, nationality, age, and sex, continue to play an important role as criteria of the individual's fitness for the upper or lower strata, two agencies—*schools and the occupational group*—now play an extraordinary role in the western populations. Not only do they test, select, and distribute the individuals within the school or the occupational group, but they perform these functions for all the other groups. Their "certificates" of ability or inability are "honored" by practically all the other groups. Of these two testing, selecting, and distributing agencies the school tests, selects, and distributes individuals according to their general intelligence and fitness, whereas the occupational groups test, select, and distribute them according to their specific occupational aptitudes.

Many do not realize that our schools are not only training and educational agencies but also —and perhaps even to a greater extent—testing, selecting, and distributing agencies for all the other contemporary groups. Beginning with the kindergarten and elementary schools and ending with the university, they are the selective agencies that determine to a great extent the future social position of their pupils. How inexorably they perform these functions is evident from the fact that in the nineteen twenties in the United States out of every 1000 pupils entering the first grade only 263 reached the eighth grade and only 56 the fourth grade of the high school. Making the necessary allowance for the death of pupils between the first grade and the eighth grade, in the eighth grade there should have been 871, whereas actually there were only 263. This means that more than 600 out of 1000 could not reach the eighth grade; the school had eliminated them as socially incapable. This selection continues even more rigorously in the high school and in college. Only an insignificant percentage of the children entering the elementary school become college graduates.[31] The overwhelming majority of those who fail to do so are automatically excluded from the professional and high-ranking governmental

---

[31] For the data, cf. my *Mobility*, pp. 187-193.

and business positions because in our society a college diploma or its equivalent is the prerequisite for becoming a doctor, teacher, lawyer, engineer, or civil servant, or for occupying a comparatively advanced position in business or obtaining a commission in the army or navy. Only a few individuals succeed now to enter and to climb these ladders without being graduated from a college or an equivalent technical and military school. The vast majority of those who are dropped by the schools before graduation are doomed to remain in the lower social strata. The schools, then, are the institutions that test and select the possible candidates for all the social strata. Their marks and grades are not only indices of how well the students have digested their textbooks and the lectures of their teachers, but also certificates of the abilities and aptitudes of the students for positions in the various strata.

So far as the upper strata of our societies are thus sifted and largely determined by the schools, the characteristics of our aristocracies depend essentially upon the nature of the school tests and selections. If these are inadequate, the upper strata will be defective. In passing, it may be noted that the contemporary school tests are inadequate in several respects. First, they test mainly the purely intellectual capacity of the pupils, relatively ignoring their social, moral, and personality traits. An intellectually superior student may graduate with honors though morally—in his character, personality and conduct—he may be thoroughly mediocre. This explains why our upper classes—economic, political, professional, religious, and social—have exhibited so little moral heroism, altruism, or even honesty and integrity. If anything, they have been below the average level of the middle and lower classes in this respect. Large sections of the upper strata have proved to be rapacious, egoistic, sensual, or corrupt.[32] In brief, since the school system is one of the most important testing and selecting agencies, the successful pupils who climb to the upper strata naturally reflect the strong and weak points in the testing and selecting system of the schools.[33]

Secondly, our schools are concerned primarily with cramming information into the minds of the students, instead of teaching them to think seriously. The dominant method of teaching is semimechanical, addressed not so much to the mind of the students as to their memory and "conditioned" reflexes. The result is an abundance of "well-informed" persons who are poor thinkers; mechanical experts who, as a rule, perceive and precisely measure only the details, overlooking the basic factors of the complex problems they are confronted with.

Side by side with the schools the occupational groups of our society reexamine the tests and selections made by the schools and render the final verdict. Like the schools they perform these functions not only for themselves but for all the other groups. They do this in three forms: (a) prevention; (b) promotion and demotion; (c) shifting to a different type of occupation. The preventive testing and selection of individuals by the occupational groups consists in nonadmission of unsuitable individuals to certain occupational groups. Millions of persons having poor voices cannot become professional singers; millions of persons lacking a Ph.D. or a college diploma cannot enter most of the professional occupations. Millions of would-be presidents, governors, mayors, and other high governmental officials, as well as of big-business leaders, are similarly debarred. The very fact of the existence of such qualifications for membership prevents millions of persons from entering the corresponding groups. In this way occupational groups exert an enormous and decisive influence upon the vertical distribution of individuals.

The promotional-demotional selection by occupational groups manifests itself in promotion of capable members and in demotion or discharge of incapable members. From the very first, every member of an occupation is constantly tested by his group respecting the fitness with which he discharges his functions. In this incessant trial some show themselves to

---

[32] Some of these, such as some of the heiresses of large fortunes, or as the Hollywood movie, the stage, and the radio "aristocracy," have given rise to more scandals and exhibited more libertinism in

a period of only several decades than the old royal and aristocratic families during several hundred years of their existence.

[33] Cf. my *Mobility*, pp. 187-193.

be competent in their work and are therefore slowly or rapidly promoted; others fail, and are demoted or discharged or else voluntarily give up their position. Hence the occupational groups determine not only the social position of each member within the occupational group itself, but, to a considerable extent, his general social position. Persons who rise in a governmental group from the position of clerk to that of a member of the cabinet of the United States government elevate themselves not only in the governmental group but on the economic ladder, on the political ladder, and on the social ladder in general. The same is true of persons who, from the position of an unskilled laborer, climb to that of the president of a railroad, bank, or a business corporation; of persons who become eminent authorities in the arts or sciences, high dignitaries of important religious groups, or bosses of powerful political parties.

Finally, through the nonadmission of unqualified persons and through the discharge of failures, occupational groups force them to shift from occupation to occupation until they find the occupation best suited to their abilities. Through these processes the occupational groups again decisively determine the social position of individuals.

In all three forms of test and selection occupational groups give finality to the results of the testing and selection carried on by the schools. In some cases they fundamentally alter the verdicts of the schools. A number of school "failures" prove highly successful in a given occupational activity. For instance, in terms of

scholastic rating and academic diplomas, Hegel was deficient in philosophy; the greatest poet of Russia, Pushkin, and one of its greatest prose writers, Leo Tolstoi, received poor grades in the Russian language at the university. Their occupational group reexamined this scholastic verdict and found it fallacious; Hegel proved to be one of the foremost philosophers, and Pushkin and Tolstoi stand in the front rank of poets and writers. Conversely, in the occupational retesting many scholars graduated "Summa cum laude" turn out to be failures. In still other cases the occupational retest merely confirms the verdict of the school test and selection.

Let us consider a few concrete cases. A Chicago firm advertised a number of vacancies to be filled. It received 11,988 applications. Of these, 54 per cent were rejected at once. Of the remaining 46 per cent only 33 per cent were interviewed. Only 4.4 per cent of the total number of applicants were hired. Thus 95.6 per cent of the applicants were eliminated before they even entered the firm. In more highly skilled occupational groups the preliminary elimination is still more rigorous.

The demotional selection made by occupational groups is illustrated by the discharge of some 30.7 per cent of the employees of a leading metal corporation in 1915; of 40 per cent in the printing industry; and of 46.4 per cent in stores. In the highly skilled occupations this form of selection is still more drastic.[34]

IV. Bodily, Vital, and Mental Differences in the Members of the Various Strata

Since the second factor in the vertical distribution of individuals consists in the specific differences in their family status, their wealth, their race or nationality, their sex or age, and their various aptitudes for passing successfully the tests of the schools and of the occupational groups, we may ask; Do the members of the upper and lower strata differ from one another also in their general physical, vital, and mental characteristics?

[34] For other details, cf. my *Mobility*, pp. 202-206.

A careful study of this problem leads to the following conclusions.[35] Regardless of whether the differences are inherited or acquired, or both:

(1) The upper classes tend to be taller and heavier, to possess greater cranial capacity, to be better-looking, and to exhibit less serious and less numerous anomalies and defects than

[35] For statistical data and literature, cf. my *Mobility*, Chps. 10-12. Here I merely sum up the conclusions reached in these chapters.

the lower classes. The difference between the two in respect to these traits is, however, small, and overlapping; a part of the upper classes is less tall and heavy than a part of the lower classes.

(2) The claim, frequently advanced, that the upper classes are more dolichocephalic and blond than the lower classes, which are supposed to be more brachycephalic and darker—that is, the claim of the superiority of the "Nordic" racial type—is essentially without foundation. The existing factual evidence does not support such a theory. In other words, there is no constant or significant correlation between social status and the physical characteristics in question.

(3) Side by side with the more or less constant or general differences in stature, weight, physiognomy, etc. there are others which are temporary and local, changing from time to time and from group to group.

(4) The upper social classes are stronger physically and have greater vitality than the lower strata. Their life span is longer, their mortality lower, and their health better than those of the lower classes.

Like the differences in stature and weight, these vital differences are probably due, in part at least, to better environment. Again, these differences are by no means uniform; for instance, a part of the upper classes exhibits a vitality only equal to or actually inferior to that of the lower classes.

(5) In the preliterate groups and in the less civilized populations the physical differences between the upper and lower classes have possibly been more pronounced than in modern society, where physical strength and prowess do not play such an important part as formerly.

(6) The upper strata display higher intelligence than the lower strata. Social stratification and distribution of intelligence are positively correlated. However, this difference is due not merely to different hereditary endowment but also to different environment, training, and education.

(7) The correlation between intelligence and social stratification is subject to many exceptions, showing a great deal of overlapping and fluctuating from group to group and from time to time.

(8) During the decline of a given aristocracy the above differences, physical and mental, tend to decrease and even to disappear.

(9) Save during periods of decline the upper classes tend to possess a larger proportion of ambitious, bold, and adventurous characters; of hard, unsentimental, uncompassionate, egoistic, and even cruel persons; of cynical hypocrites and liars; and of bold sensualists. In periods of decay these differences tend to disappear. Aristocracy becomes sentimental, soft, timid, nonadventurous and secretly sensual. Such an aristocracy, as a rule, is then superseded by newcomers from the middle and lower strata. All the foregoing differences are due in part to heredity and in part to the environment and mode of living of the upper and lower strata.[36] A mere enumeration of these differences shows that they are more numerous than those indicated by Pareto and others, and that Pareto's are open to question.

[36] For the facts and evidence, cf. my *Mobility*, Chps. 10-13.

Chapter 27. Two Modes of the Maintenance of Groups

I. Modes of Self-Adjustment and of Adjustment of the Environment

1. A Twofold Task

As long as a group exists, it must maintain its unity and a certain degree of adjustment to its environment. Ceaselessly changing itself in an incessantly changing environment, it must preserve its internal equilibria. The groups solve this twofold problem through constant adjustment to their environment and through the adjustment of their environment to themselves. To some extent all groups use both modes of adaptation. However, some groups follow mainly the way of inner transformation, without a notable change of their biophysical or social environment; while other groups solve the problem predominantly through a modification of their physical, biological, and sociocultural environment, to suit it to their needs. Even the same group at different periods uses now the one, now the other, of these methods. Like the two different forms of freedom (Chapter 30), there are thus two different ways in which a group adjusts its relations to its environment. One is the path of inner modification of the group: (a) voluntary and (b) imposed; the other is the path of transformation of the external, mainly biophysical, environment.

2. Two Forms of Self-Adjustment

The way of self-adjustment is prevalent in groups (a) that are relatively indifferent to the external environment and hence not very eager to change it; (b) that attach importance to it but are unable appreciably to modify it.

(a) The groups possessing a *predominantly ideational culture*—the ascetics, the stoics, the mystics, and others that neither take seriously nor value highly the sensate, material environment, that regard contemplation as the supreme value, that are absorbed in "the inner immaterial values" of their soul, of the transcendental kingdom of God—such groups follow mainly the way of *inner, spiritual self-adjustment*. Being little interested in the physical, chemical, and biological properties and relationships of their environment, they do not study it from these scientific standpoints; therefore do not go in for technological inventions and do not possess efficient means for —in fact, are not interested in—the transformation of the material environment to fit it to their needs. They agree with the Taoist dictum that "doing nothing is better than to be *busy* doing nothing." They reduce their physical needs to the barest minimum; concentrate upon self-control, self-discipline, and self-sufficiency; and try to detach themselves as far as possible from their external milieu.[1] In this

---

[1] For a series of formulas respecting the relative value of contemplation, action, and social utility offered by Hindu, Buddhist, Chinese, and Christian thinkers, cf. A. Huxley, *The Perennial Philosophy*

way such groups sometimes achieve a degree of self-adjustment that permits them to exist without a serious modification of their milieu for a long time. The populations of the countries and periods characterized by the ideational type of culture, such as a considerable part of the populations of India, China, and medieval Europe, depended for centuries principally upon this mode of maintaining their internal and external equilibria, transforming their material environment only slightly and existing predominantly (though not exclusively) through self-adjustment.

(b) Another form of the group adaptation through imposed self-adjustment occurs ordinarily in groups *dominated by sensate culture,* which in spite of their desire to change their environment, are frustrated by the overwhelmingly adverse forces of the environment. In conditions of calamity—famine, plague, depression, war, defeat by victorious rivals, persecution, etc.—such groups are forced to maintain their existence through an involuntary rearrangement of the structure and functions of the group. Many families, business firms, state hierarchies or political parties, occupational groups, and similar associations are subjected to conditions in which the adverse forces of their environment are overwhelming, when all efforts to change it fail. Under such circumstances many groups disintegrate. Those that survive do so mainly through a drastic self-transformation of various kinds: through a change of their constitution, through shifts in the personnel of their government, through curtailment of their expenses, through the sacrifice of a part of their material vehicles and wealth; through the increased industry, labor, and self-discipline of their members; through patient endurance of various hardships; through compliance with the orders of other groups; through revaluation of their values, that is, through a mental, moral, and social renaissance, and so on. The imposed self-transformation of Japan, Germany, or other states under the pressure of their conquerors; the self-adjustment of many business concerns during periods of acute depression; the

self-modification of a defeated and persecuted political party; the inner revolution of a family in periods of distress and misfortune; the self-reconstruction of an occupational union under conditions of adversity—these are concrete examples of such a survival through imposed self-adjustment.

3. Transformation of the Biophysical and Material Sociocultural Environment

This method ordinarily prevails in groups marked by the sensate type of culture in its virile phase. Such groups do not seek primarily to change themselves but, rather, to change their milieu. Being reluctant to reduce their desires and appetites, especially the sensate ones, they try to develop and inflate them. Believing mainly in sensory realities and values, they do not seek any "supersensory" or transcendental value. Their energies are directed principally toward a study of the physical, chemical, and biological properties of sensory reality; in the course of such a study they make many a scientific discovery and achieve many a technological invention. Thus they acquire the efficient means for the transformation of the empirical milieu in the desired direction. Applying scientific knowledge, employing technological devices, and exploiting all the powers they possess, such groups transform the physical, chemical, and biological environment; overcome, through force or fraud, the resistance of other groups; expand at their cost; if need be, defeat and conquer them in cut-throat competition, in skillful political machinations, or even in war. In these and similar ways they create powerful ruling families, colossal business empires, mighty states and kingdoms, dominant political parties, great imperialistic "religions," and various other influential associations, employing science and technology for the control and transformation of the environment. In such groups action, not contemplation, is the guiding motto and ethos.

Many a group employs both of the foregoing methods of maintaining their equilibrium.

(New York, 1945), Ch. 27, *passim.* Huxley contrasts the groups that regard a society as good only so far as it renders contemplation possible for its members with the groups that envisage the objec-

tive of human life in action, in the progress of technology, and in the transformation of their milieu (*Ibid.,* pp. 294 ff.).

4. Fluctuation of the Two Methods in the Life of a Group

Finally, as has been said, these two main ways of adaptation fluctuate in their domination in the life history of many long-existing groups. In varying degrees almost any family, business firm, and religious or political group, and even the state, at one period successfully adjusts its environment to itself, expands its needs and expenses, increases in size and influence, and subjugates its adversaries. Then it enters the "phase of adversity," when it must curtail its desires and expenses; retreat from previous positions; reinforce its self-discipline and self-control; and subsist with fewer means, vehicles, and members. Thus the Christian Church survived during the first centuries of its existence mainly through ideational self-adjustment to the inimical external world. Then, after its legalization, it entered upon the phase of expansion and of transformation of the external sociocultural world according to its aspirations. In this phase it acquired enormous power and wealth, a colossal mass of vehicles, and a huge membership. In this process of modification of its environment it inevitably suffered a loss of self-control and inner unity, with ever-increasing schisms and dissensions, culminating in the disintegration of the Church. Being in danger of utter demoralization, the Church undertook, beginning with the twelfth century, a series of self-adjustments and self-reformations which continued up to the Counterreformation, effected chiefly by the Council of Trent. Since that time, in a less acute form, the Catholic Church has undergone several "swings" from one way of adjustment to the other. The Russian Orthodox Church likewise underwent a drastic self-adjustment during the first period of the Communist Revolution, when it was subjected to persecution and suffered acute adversity. The German Empire, especially after 1871, adjusted itself mainly through an efficient modification of its environment which reached its culminating point in 1914. After the defeat of 1918 it temporarily entered the phase of self-adjustment; but soon, particularly after the accession of Hitler's regime, it feverishly reentered the phase of violent transformation of its environment which, after years of unparalleled success, brought it to utter defeat and to the phase of rigorous imposed self-adjustment.

Similar fluctuations occur in the life history of almost every organized group.

II. Reasons for Fluctuations Between Self-Adjustment and Modification of the Environment

The reasons for such a rhythm of the modes of adaptation are partly external, and are largely immanent in the group in the sense that the fluctuations would occur even if the external milieu were constant. When a group undergoes increasingly drastic self-adjustment, it generates forces that impel it toward the transformation of its environment, and vice versa. With an increasing transformation of the environment there emerge in the group forces that tend to reverse the trend and that lead to self-adjustment. For example, the saintliness and self-discipline of many small ascetic and monastic groups increasingly attract followers and believers, as well as donations and contributions. As a result the group grows, its possessions increase, and it ultimately develops or acquires rich and powerful abbeys, monasteries, and religious, political, and business centers with an effective power for transformation of their environment. Such was the cycle passed through by thousands of Christian, Buddhist, Hindu, and other monastic and ascetic groups. Such also was the cycle traversed by the Christian Church, which was transformed from a small, poor, and otherworldly group into the most powerful, influential, and wealthy organization of the Middle Ages.

Sensate groups subjected through adversity to the phase of self-adjustment never accept it voluntarily, always seeking to overcome it and to pass to the phase of expansion and transformation of their environment. Every state or business firm tends to expand, to become powerful and prosperous, and to transform its environment. Hence the internal forces of such groups incessantly operate in favor of transition from the state of self-adjustment to that of modification of their environment.

On the other hand, when a group enters the phase of a modification of its environment, it tends progressively to neglect its self-control and the maintenance of its inner order; the more energy it expends in expansion, the less energy is left for keeping its house in order. The more it overcomes external obstacles, the more obstacles it has to cope with: with the extension of the circle of its transformed environment, the adverse forces grow in proportion to the increase of the radius of the circle. The more it expands beyond the optimum point of its meanings, vehicles, and members, the more difficult becomes its successful and creative functioning. Sooner or later the group experiences a decline in its transforming power and extension and has to undertake a retreat and to pass into the phase of self-adjustment. The history of families, of business firms, of states, of religious and political groups, of occupational and other associations, presents innumerable cases of such a shift from one phase to the other. The history of individuals, on the one hand, and of vast civilizations, on the other, demonstrates this process. In regard to major civilizations, A. Toynbee's rhythms of "withdrawal and return," of "rout and rally," of "schism and palingenesis," serve to corroborate the fluctuations in question. Toynbee gives a copious series of such facts in his work.[2]

Such are the immanent forces that render the fluctuation process unavoidable. These immanent forces alone are sufficient to explain the phenomenon. When innumerable external forces are added to them, the rhythm of self-adjustment and adjustment of the environment becomes thoroughly comprehensible.

III. Mechanism of Groups for Self-Regulation in the Maintenance of Their Life and Individuality

The foregoing illustrations of how the immanent forces of groups generate the rhythm in question are not something exceptional but are characteristic of organized groups. When a certain process goes too far and threatens the existence of the group, the group itself generates forces that serve to inhibit the process and to reverse it. We have met this immanent self-regulation of processes many times before and will continue to encounter it in the fluctuation of the basic forms of social relationships, of the forms of government, of the type and amount of freedom, of evolutionary and revolutionary changes, and so on. Hence a few generalizations respecting its "mechanism" are advisable at this point.

This property was noted long ago. Beginning with the most ancient theories respecting the immanent self-control of groups and their life processes and ending with the most recent theories of the economic, political, social, and other equilibria of groups, all such theories point to this property. When they state that any group attempts to maintain its equilibrium in the sense that, on being disturbed, it tends to return to its previous status, or that it possesses organs or mechanisms of limitation or inhibition, a system of checks and balances, they refer to precisely this general property of immanent self-regulation of groups.[3]

The existence of this property means that groups have a certain mechanism that controls such self-regulation. This mechanism is analogous to the complex mechanism of a biological organism that regulates its temperature and many of its vital processes.[4] In a more precise sense the social mechanism of self-regu-

---

[2] Cf. A. Toynbee, *Study of History*, quoted (all 6 volumes).

[3] For a detailed history of the theories of self-regulation of group processes and the theories of

group equilibrium, cf. my *Dynamics*, Vol. IV, Chps. 13, 14.

[4] For this mechanism, cf. W. B. Cannon, *The Wisdom of the Body* (New York, 1933); K. Goldstein, *The Organism*.

lation of group processes does not inhere in a specific part of the group but is diffused throughout the whole group, though it is somewhat more intensely concentrated in the governmental hierarchy and in the intellectual, ethical, artistic, and practical elite. Now and then there are special devices in the group organization that perform the function in question.

Like the nervous system in a biological organism, the mechanism is diffused throughout the whole group; for when a certain process goes too far and begins to generate a series of painful, disintegrating consequences, these negative effects are felt by most of the members of the group. All such members constitute a "general sensorium" that registers these negative results and that tends to resist them, to eliminate them, and to replace them with processes that promise an alleviation of the disastrous effects.

The mechanism is more highly concentrated in the elite and the governmental strata because, as a rule, these elements of the group detect the negative effects earlier and locate their source more accurately than the rank and file of the members. Not infrequently these group organs make such observations one of their special functions, in the form, for instance, of systematic registration of births and deaths, marriages and divorces, sickness, crimes, employment and unemployment, prices and wages, business indices, international relations, etc. Hence they are more sensitive organs of the group than the rank and file of its members. They are charged with the task of coping with changes more immediately and directly, in their executive capacity, than the ordinary members.

Finally, groups possess special devices for the detection and control of their processes, especially for the inhibition and reversal of processes that go too far in a certain direction and become dangerous for the well-being of the group. These devices are both numerous and diverse. All the devices for observing and registering the effects of important processes; all the scientific agencies of investigation and research; all the instrumentalities dealing with the invention and application of remedies for alleviating or eliminating dangerous processes, including legislative, judicial, and executive organs; all the devices designed to prevent one-sided development of certain processes, such as "the division of powers," the system of checks and balances, the referendum, the veto, the clothing of the government with dictatorial powers in cases of emergency—all such devices, agencies, and organs are part and parcel of the social mechanism for the self-regulation of groups. Since the sensitive "receptors," "conductors," and "effectors" of such a mechanism (to use Sherrington's terms for the nervous system of a body[5]) are spread throughout the whole group, the mechanism is an inherent part of it. The process of self-regulation of the group is thus not something metaphysical, artificially imposed upon the group,[6] but one of the essential and basic processes and properties of groups in general.

[5] Cf. Sherrington, *The Integrative Functions of the Nervous System* (London, 1906).

[6] As some of the pseudo-empiricists claimed in their adverse criticism of the theory of immanent self-regulation of group processes set forth in my *Dynamics* (Vol. IV).

Chapter 28. Fluctuation of the Size and Stratified Profile of the Groups

I. Fluctuation of the Size of the Groups

Since the influx of new members and the exodus or loss of old members of a group are rarely equal, the size of the group's membership does not remain constant and almost incessantly fluctuates, with the exception of the groups whose membership is intentionally fixed at a certain number.

For the same reason the size of the membership of each stratum of the group undergoes fluctuation, resulting in a comparative expansion or shrinking of the size of this or that stratum, which, in its turn, leads to a modification of the stratified profile of the group. Hence *the fluctuation of the size of the group and of the profile of its stratification as a universal, ever-repeated process.*

When the total influx of new members is greater than the total exodus or loss of old members, the size of the group or stratum grows. When the total influx is less than the total loss, the size of the group or stratum decreases. When the total exodus and loss are equal, the size remains constant.

Almost any group existing for an appreciable length of time fluctuates in the size of its membership, now growing, now declining, now remaining stationary. The extreme minimum of this fluctuation is the loss of all its members, which means the extinction of the group; the extreme upper limit is different for different groups and exhibits a wide margin of expansion.

The patterns and curves of the fluctuation vary in many respects. (1) *The succession of phases—increase, decrease, and stationary phase—does not exhibit any uniform order of sequence for all groups.* In some groups, after their emergence, we observe a decrease in their members, followed by either increase or a stationary phase; in others the succession follows the order increase, stationary phase, decrease; in still others the order is stationary phase, decrease, increase or stationary phase, increase, decrease. The order of succession of these phases may vary even in the life history of the same group in the process of several increases, decreases, and stationary phases repeated throughout its existence. In brief, there is no uniformity in the succession of the phases and no uniform curve of either growth or decline of the size of the group.[1]

---

[1] This means that the theories of V. Pareto, C. Guignebert, K. Leontieff, O. Spengler, O. Ammon, and many others who claim that social institutions or organized groups uniformly show the sequence increase, plateau, and decline unduly elevate a partial pattern to a universal rule.

The same is true of all theories asserting the existence of "a normal curve of growth of social groups" or of a diffusion of cultural values (recently reiterated by H. E. Pemberton, R. Pearl, and others). They also elevate a partial pattern to a universal rule. As a matter of fact, in the fluctuation of the size of groups and strata, as well as in practically every other field of sociocultural processes, there hardly exists any "normal curve." Cf.

(2) *The curves of the fluctuation vary also in symmetry and asymmetry, in the skewness of their general pattern.* In some groups they rise slowly and decline abruptly or remain for some time stationary; in others they rise rapidly and decline gradually; in still others the rise and decline are more or less symmetrical, and so on. *No normal or uniform curve of fluctuation of the size of different groups, or of the same group in its repeated fluctuations, is detectable.*

(3) *The fluctuations vary also in their gradualness and abruptness.* In normal periods the fluctuation of the size of the family, the church, the state, and occupational and other groups is gradual and is limited by a comparatively narrow margin; in periods of "spasmodic" mobility—under conditions of war, revolution, and other calamities—it becomes sudden and abrupt. Entire families are wiped out; others increase in their membership. Kingdoms, political parties, religious organizations, and many other groups are suddenly obliterated or greatly reduced in their membership, while other are abruptly increased in their membership through the annexation of new populations, the mass conversion of new followers, and similar acquisitions, either voluntary or coercive.

(4) *The sizes of groups fluctuate widely, also, in the number of members gained or lost and in the minima and maxima of their membership.* Some groups, like the family and kinship groups, by their very nature are limited in the size of their membership; for families it fluctuates between zero and a few dozen members; in monogamic families the margin is still more limited, rarely exceeding ten to fifteen members. In other groups, such as political parties, religious organizations, the state, and occupational groups, the upper limit of membership exceeds several hundreds of millions. Theoretically it appears to be unbounded. Even in groups of the same kind the size fluctuates widely. As has already been mentioned, groups in which membership conveys certain distinct privileges tend to limit their maximum size more drastically than groups in which membership does not convey any special advantages.

(5) Is it probable that among the *groups of the same kind* the size of one of these groups can grow indefinitely until mankind is united into *one* group only—into one state, one race, one religion, one political party, one occupation? In respect to practically all unibonded and multibonded groups the answer is in the negative.[2] *Such a growth of a single group would mean the disappearance of social differentiation.* A return to such an undifferentiated status is highly improbable. One can hardly imagine all families and kinship groups being absorbed by a single family or kinship group. If such a situation were to arise, it would mean not an increase in the size of one family until it embraced all humanity, but simply the disappearance of the family and kinship groups. Their forms may change, but their complete disappearance is impossible.

The same is true of the sex and age groups. They are here to stay. No more probable is the disappearance of either racial or ethnic differentiations. Certain racial or ethnic groups may disappear; others may decrease or increase in size; new racial or ethnic types may emerge; new hybrids may come into existence. But it is quite improbable that at any future time all human beings will be racially or ethnically homogeneous.[3]

Various language groups may eventually produce a world language used by all humanity; such a world esperanto would not, however, erase a multitude of various languages, with their respective cultures, used by various ethnic groups for intragroup communication.

The same may be said of religious, political, occupational, and state groups. Obviously, all occupations can not be reduced to a single occupation. Nor is it probable that all mankind would have the same religion, the same political party, or even the same state. As in the case of ethnic groups, it is conceivable that all the states might be united into one super-

---

my *Dynamics*, Vol. IV, pp. 279 ff. See also A. L. Kroeber, *Configurations of Culture Growth* (University of California Press, 1944), Chps. 10-11, *passim*.

[2] For a detailed discussion of this problem, cf. my *Sistema Soziologii*, Vol. II, pp. 347-442, and G. de Greef, *La Structure générale des sociétés*

(Bruxelles-Paris, 1908), Vols. II, III, *passim*, and Vol. III, Ch. 21.

[3] The theory of L. Winiarsky and A. de Gobineau that eventually all men will be racially similar to one another is ill-founded. Cf. A. de Gobineau, *Essai sur l'inégalité des races humaines* (Paris, 1855), Vol. IV, pp. 318 ff.

state; but such a superstate would not be an expansion of the membership of one state through the absorption of all the others, but a federation of several states into one superstate organization. Its emergence and development would not lead to the disappearance of a multitude of different states. Like intragroup languages existing side by side with a world esperanto, different states would continue to exist, with a limited number of their functions transferred to the world superstate; for mankind is too vast a body for all its political affairs to be successfully managed by the government of a world federation. If the creation of the federal government of the United States did

not eliminate the existence and functioning of separate states of the union, it is still less probable that the emergence of a world federation would lead to the extinction of all the states on this planet.[4]

To summarize: however elastic may be the maximum limit of the size for all groups, such a limit, varying for different groups, seems to exist. *It is improbable that any of the groups could grow to such proportions as to swallow up all the groups of the same kind*, the more so since virtually all social groups have a limited life span. Having reached their maximum possible size, sooner or later they decline in size, disintegrate, and eventually disappear.

II. Fluctuation of the Stratified Profile of the Groups

What has been said of the size of the group may be said of the relative and absolute size of each of its strata. As a rule *the size of each stratum fluctuates also*. Thus in the universities

the size of the strata of deans, of full professors, of associate and assistant professors, of instructors of various ranks, and even of the graduate students and seniors, juniors, soph-

---

[4] Before the eighteenth century, and even in the eighteenth and nineteenth centuries, most thinkers firmly believed that there was a basic historical law of a steady expansion of the area of pacific relations, with a progressive decrease of war, ignorance, injustice, and so on, and with a prospective unification of mankind into a single federated society. J. G. Herder, J. Fichte, I. Kant, F. Hegel, A. Comte, and many others have formulated such a historical law. See J. G. Herder, *Outlines of a Philosophy of the History of Man* (tr. by T. Churchill; London, 1803); I. Kant, *The Idea of Universal History on a Cosmo-political Plan* (tr. by T. DeQuincey; Hanover, 1927); J. Fichte, *Characteristics of the Present Age* (1804); and Hegel, *Philosophy of History* (tr. by J. Sibree; New York-London, 1900). In the second half of the nineteenth century a host of philosophers, sociologists, political economists, and political scientists repeated such a contention. Among the many recent reiterations of the theory, H. Hart's is probably the most mature. With a wealth of statistical and historical material he tries to demonstrate that in the course of time there has been an accelerating trend from smaller to larger political units or states—a trend which will result around 1950 in a single world government. His theory is based upon the assumption of a close relationship between technological and political development and upon accelerating trends in both variables. His demonstration consists in a series of data that show an ever-enlarging size of the territory controlled by governments, beginning with the earliest Mousterian groups and ending with the great empires of the present time. Cf. H. Hart and D. L. Taylor, "Was There a Prehistoric

Trend from Smaller to Larger Political Units?" *AJS*, Vol. XLIX (1944), pp. 289-301, and H. Hart, *Can World Government Be Predicted by Mathematics?* (Durham, 1943). In spite of his ingenious and painstaking study, the conclusions of H. Hart are questionable. First, most of his data, expecially those on the prehistoric political units, are of a highly conjectural character. Second, the large territories of some of the contemporary empires, such as the British Empire, are obtained through an inclusion of the territories of all their colonies and dominions past and present. The separation of such colonies and dominions from the empires (British, French, Spanish, and others) reduces their territorial size to a comparatively modest area, no greater than that of several old empires such as those of Genghis Khan and Tamerlane. Third, if the territories of all the past empires were taken, with all their dependencies, their sizes would be seen to compete with those of most of the biggest empires of the present time. Moreover, the size of the territory is not an adequate measure of the existence or nonexistence of a trend toward bigger and less numerous states. The number of states existing on this planet at different periods is a much more accurate index of the reality of such a trend. Disregarding the prehistoric age and even ancient times, and taking simply the last few centuries—especially the last two, during which, according to Hart, his trend has been especially accelerated—we can hardly detect any certain trend toward a decrease in the number of states on this planet. Of some seventy-six independent states which, according to Hart, existed in 1939 (H. Hart, *Can World Government Be Predicted by Mathematics?* p. 2),

omores, and freshmen fluctuates from year to year, from season to season.[5] The same is true of the marshals, the five-star generals, and all the other ranks in the army or navy. Nor does the number, absolute or relative, of state officials remain constant. Even in normal times it fluctuates within narrow margins. In abnormal periods these margins expand considerably. A similar fluctuation we find in the strata of religious bodies, economic or occupational bodies, and even in those of the family and other kinship groups. Their pyramids exhibit a comparative increase of the size now of the upper strata, now of the middle strata, now of the lower layers. *The profile of the stratified pyramids is not constant but changes in the course of time.*

This means that theories such as Pareto's claim that the profile of the economic pyramid is constant are not corroborated by the relevant empirical facts. Pareto asserted that the profile of economic stratification or the frequency distribution of income in any society (earlier contention) or, at least, in many societies (later contention) represents something constant, like crystals of the same form, and can be expressed by a definite mathematical formula. His contention is not supported by the facts; they show that the frequency distribution of income in various groups, and in the same group at different periods, varies sharply. Therefore the profile

of the economic stratification varies also from group to group, from period to period.[6]

Nor may we contend that in these fluctuations of the profile as well as of the height of the stratified pyramid of social groups there is any perpetual trend either toward a certain kind of profile or toward an increase or decrease of the height. In the middle of the nineteenth century Karl Marx contended that in the economic pyramid of European countries the middle economic strata tended to become more and more narrow; the economic strata of labor larger and larger and poorer and poorer; while at the top of the pyramid wealth tended to be concentrated in fewer and fewer hands. During the ninety-odd years that have elapsed since the publication of this theory, the economic facts have not supported it; the poor have not become poorer; the middle economic strata have not decreased; nor has wealth been concentrated in fewer and fewer hands.[7] Equally untenable are the opposite theories which claim a steady historical trend toward greater economic equality; at the present time the economic contrasts between the rich and the poor are as great as ever. No eternal historical trend toward economic equality can be discovered. Instead, we note in the life history of a given population certain periods when economic inequality and the height of the economic pyramid grow, and other periods when they decrease. At one period the forces of inequality gain the upper hand; at another, the forces of equalization. This applies to the

---

thirty-six emerged as sovereign states during mainly the eighteenth, the nineteenth, and twentieth centuries: Albania (1912), Greece (1830), Bulgaria (1878), Belgium, Rumania, Luxemburg, Germany, Poland, Czechoslovakia, Hungary, Norway, Finland, Lithuania, Estonia, Latvia, Italy, Yugoslavia, almost all the Latin-American states, the United States, Persia (1730), Afghanistan (1750), Siam (1782). (See Sorokin, "Life-span, Age-Composition, and Mortality of Social Organizations," *Mensch en Maatschappij*, Vol. IX, p. 79.) Such a situation does not point to any accelerating trend, during these centuries, toward a decrease in the number of states.

What is going to be the situation in the future nobody can definitely predict. It is not even certain that any enduring superstate will emerge. Even if it should, this would not mean the disappearance of national states and of state differentiation.

[5] Cf. the figures for several universities in Sorokin and Anderson's "Differential Metabolism" (cited), and the works of W. A. Lunden, E. Y. Hartshorne, and F. Reeves (cited).

[6] For the statistical data and literature, cf. my *Mobility*, pp. 36 ff.

[7] For the statistical data, cf. my *Mobility*, pp. 38 ff. According to L. Corey's study of the United States from 1870 to 1940, among the strata of gainfully employed in all occupations the main gainers were the middle strata (small-business, professional, technical-managerial, and other salaried employees). Thus in the period 1910 to 1940 the total working class increased from 19,730,000 to 29,518,000, while the total middle-strata groups increased from 8,870,000 to 16,633,000—an increase much greater than that of the laboring class. For the detailed figures, cf. W. Lessner, "United States Middle Class on the Increase," *New York Times*, May 27, 1945; A. M. Edwards, *Comparative Occupation Statistics* (Washington, 1943); T. Sogge, "Industrial Classes in the U. S.," *J. Am Statist. Assn.*, 1944; Anderson and Davidson *Recent Occupational Trends* (Stanford U. Press, 1946); L. Corey, "The Middle Class," *Antioch Review*, 1945.

history of virtually all large countries and their populations.[8]

Such is the situation in the field of economic stratification. A similar situation obtains in the field of other stratifications. Many believe that in the field of political stratification there is a trend toward greater equality, or a flattening of the pyramid. When the belief is seriously tested, it is found wanting, so far as a perennial trend is concerned, operating throughout the whole history of mankind. If anything, the political stratification among the preliterate and prehistoric peoples is less conspicuous than among the more "advanced" historical peoples. When we examine the political stratification in Egypt and Babylonia, Greece and Rome, India and China, medieval and modern Europe, and other countries, we do not find that in the later stages of their history these states were less stratified than during the initial stages. Indeed, the later stages reveal a higher and steeper political pyramid. When we come to our own times, we find that the state pyramids are as highly stratified as ever, with political inequality as great as before. In totalitarian states of all kinds the political inequality between the dictators and their henchmen, on the one hand, and the masses, on the other, is as sharp as that to be found in the history of any state. The same is true of the inequality between the full-fledged citizens of European countries and the downtrodden, unprivileged populations of their colonies. Neither is there any perennial trend from the government of minorities to that of majorities, from monarchies to republics, from autocracies to democracies, from appointive to elective offices.[9] Here, as in the field of economic stratification, we can detect merely temporary trends: now toward political equal-

ity and a flattening of the political pyramid, now in the direction of political inequality and intensification of the political stratification.

The same may be said of the profile and height of occupational and other stratified pyramids.[10] However measured, their height and profile display only temporary trends, now toward greater occupational democracy and equality, now in the opposite direction. Beliefs in the existence of a permanent trend in either direction are, for the most part, merely the result of wishful thinking.

The fluctuation of the height of the stratification has occurred in both orderly and gradual fashion and abrupt and spasmodic manner in the life history of practically every organized group. Most of the time it proceeds in an orderly, gradual, almost imperceptible way. From time to time this mode is replaced by spasmodic, abrupt, violent, and disorderly changes. In major revolutions the pyramid is temporarily flattened—economically, politically, and otherwise—to the shape of a trapezium, with its upper strata cut off, their members demoted or overthrown, and some of the members of the lower strata placed on the top of the trapezium. This was what happened, for instance, to the economic, political, occupational, and other stratifications during the first phase of the French, the Bohemian (15th century), the Russian, and many other fundamental revolutions. However, when the destructive phase is over and the reconstructive phase is entered, the flattened pyramid tends to be quickly rebuilt, increasing in height and, after a few years or decades, reappearing in a new form, being about as high and steep as it was before the revolution. Such is the eternal cycle, or rhythm, of social processes in this field.

III. Immanent and External Factors of the Fluctuations

The factors responsible for the fluctuation of the height and the profile of the stratifications fall into two classes: immanent and external. We have seen (in Chapter 4) that the very nature of an organized group demands stratification and that the stratification hence cannot

be flattened beyond a certain limit. Stratification and organization of a group are inseparable. This means that the antistratification or equalizing forces cannot eliminate it as long as the group remains organized. Thus every

---

[8] For the facts of the history of the preliterate peoples, ancient Rome, Greece, China, Egypt, the Roman Catholic Church, and the modern European

and American populations, cf. my *Mobility*, pp. 46 ff.

[9] For the facts, cf. my *Mobility*, Ch. 5.

[10] *Ibid.*, Ch. 6.

organized group contains within itself forces opposed to a complete equalization of the members. When the equalizing forces begin to press too far in the direction of flattening the stratification, the organizational forces increase their counterpressure. Either they check any further flattening of the pyramid or else if they are unsuccessful, the group becomes disorganized, without any hierarchical distribution of its ranks and members.

On the other hand, when the stratification becomes excessive, entailing enormous privileges for the upper strata and the disfranchisement of the lower strata, it begins to menace the existence of the group. Dissensions and antagonisms among its members increase; the coercive official law of the group loses its authority; the functions of the group begin to be performed less and less adequately by the upper and lower strata; its energy begins to be increasingly wasted in internal friction. With an increase of these maladjustments the forces of equalization increase their pressure and, unless the group goes to pieces, eventually check a further increase of the height of the stratification and, in an orderly way or by means of revolution, decrease it. At the same time, we have no reason to assume that the stratifying and equalizing forces are always equal and always perfectly balance each other.

The work of these two forces is complicated by a multitude of forces external to a given group that incessantly press upon it. Some of these external factors facilitate an increase, others a decrease, of stratification. So far we know very little as to which of the external agents work in favor of equalization and which favor inequality, or as to the conditions under which they operate. Many theories seek to explain an increase of equality through various demographic conditions, claiming that with an increase of the size of the group, of the density, heterogeneity, and mobility of its population, equality within the group tends to increase.

Unfortunately, when tested, these theories prove to be invalid in their essential claims.[11] Other theories stress the social division of labor and social differentiation as a factor of equality.[12] Contrary to such claims, the development of division of labor has not been followed by a decrease of either economic, occupational, or political stratification; certain forms of the social division of labor have led to caste, semicaste, and social-order regimes instead of leading to equality. For these and many other reasons such theories are untenable. Equally untenable are those theories that ascribe, without serious qualification, an equalitarian role to religion or to science, technology, and economic factors. Certain religions, like Hinduism, have been one of the main factors of caste inequality. Even Christianity, with its basic principle that all men are children of God, created in God's image, did not prevent the rise of the feudal social orders or the inequalities of the post-medieval period. The capitalist economy, whose protagonists stress its equalitarian role, has not reduced either economic, political, or occupational inequality. Under the capitalist system, assisted by modern science and technology, the so-called backward peoples, including almost all the eastern populations, have become victims of economically and technologically progressive white "civilized" peoples who have brought to them exploitation, serfdom, slavery, and even extermination. Viewed realistically, most of the contemporary democracies, such as Great Britain, France, the Netherlands, and Belgium, are, indeed, highly stratified oligarchies, exhibiting enormous political, economic, and social inequality between their upper strata and the lowest strata of their colonial populations. These democracies are superimposed upon the vast strata of their unprivileged, exploited, politically and otherwise disfranchised colonial populations. They do not differ markedly from the Athenian "democracy," in which some twenty thousand citizens dominated much

[11] For instance, C. Bouglé, Les Idées égalitaires (Paris 1908); also his La Democratie devant la science (Paris, 1923) and the theories of M. Kovalevsky, F. Carli, A. Coste, E. Durkheim, and others. For a detailed characterization and criticism of these theories, cf. my Theories, pp. 417 ff. and Ch. 7, passim.

[12] E. Durkheim's De la division de travail social is a good example of such theories. However, in his later works Durkheim himself acknowledged the one-sidedness of his theory that an increase of social differentiation and of division of labor leads necessarily to equality. For a criticism of his theory on this point, cf. C. Bouglé, "Revue générale des théories récentes sur la division du travail," L'Année sociologique, Vol. IV; L. Deschesne, La Spécialisation et ses conséquences (Paris, 1901); and N. Mikhailovsky, The Struggle for Individuality (Russian).

vaster strata of slaves, semislaves, and disfranchised "barbarians." Even among the
"civilized" peoples themselves, as has been
said, capitalism, science, and technology have
not established an equalitarian millennium, and
since 1914 have led to political tyranny, dictatorships, and autocracies.

Among many possible generalizations in this
field, the following may be mentioned as the
most plausible.

*All the main factors of stratification indi-
cated in Chapter 20 operate in favor of its
intensification.* Reducing this proposition to
more specific formulae and supplementing it
with other approximate uniformities, we arrive
at the following tentative generalizations.

(1) Other conditions being equal, *when the
size of the body politic abruptly increases, the
political stratification tends to increase,* and
vice versa.

(2) When the biosocial and cultural *heterogeneity* of its members increases, especially
their ethical and law convictions, the stratification tends to increase, and vice versa.

(3) When a given group *is subjected to
war, revolution, famine, or other serious emergencies,* the political stratification increases in
the special form of an enormous autocratiza-
tion of the government and of expansion of its
functions of regimentation and control (cf.
Chapter 30). A sudden enlargement of the
body politic requires an expansion of the
political machinery. This expansion entails an
increase of various superior and inferior ranks
which heightens the stratified political pyramid. Its heightening means an increase of
political inequality. A "town-hall" democracy
is possible only in small communities. Direct
democracy is feasible only in small political
groups, religious sects, and so on. A large
group eliminates it in favor of representative
democracy or autocracy, with a hierarchy of
officials and ranks.

The more heterogeneous a population is in
its hereditary make-up, in its social and cultural characteristics, especially in its ethical
and juridical convictions, the more difficult it
is to make the members equal and to control
them as equals. In a group consisting of
geniuses and idiots, babies and grown-ups,
"savages," paupers and millionaires, conquerors and victims, Hindu outcastes and English peers, criminals and saints, one may preach

equality, but in vain. And the greater the
heterogeneity, the more rigid and more autocratic the political regime has to be to keep
such a group in order. When such a completely
heterogeneous body as India is incorporated in
the British Empire, or Indonesia in the Dutch
Empire, though the British and Dutch may be
the most sincere "levelers," they cannot establish genuine political equality. When a "civilized" nation annexes a subjugated preliterate
population, no equality can be expected in the
resulting society. When the law-convictions of
the citizens divide them sharply into revolutionaries and counterrevolutionaries, inequality
is bound to increase.[18]

(4) More generally, *a group with predominantly familistic relationships tends to be
less rigidly and highly stratified than a group
with predominantly contractual relationships;
and a contractual group is less disposed to an
increase of inequality than a group with predominantly compulsory relationships.* An increase of compulsion and antagonism engenders greater inequality and stratification;
an increase of a truly familistic relationship
promotes an increase of real (in contradistinction to formal) equality. This proposition applies not only to political but to all other
stratifications and inequalities. In a group
whose members are united by mutual love,
inequality becomes superfluous and tends to
be nonexistent, in spite of the separate functions of the mother, father, grown-up brothers
or sisters, and so forth.

In a contractual group, stratification of the
bargaining partners is inevitable, but it is
moderated by the interests of the freely contracting parties.

A compulsory group represents the quint-
essence of inequality and stratification of the
coercing, more powerful, party and the coerced
victim, unmitigated by love, sympathy, or compassion, the respective parties hating and
despising one another.

(5) Finally, under ever-changing environmental conditions *all the factors that give
special advantages to some of the members or
groups and place other members and groups
at a disadvantage operate in favor of increasing stratification and inequality.*

[18] For a more substantial corroboration of these
propositions cf. my *Mobility,* pp. 85 ff; also *Dynamics,* Vol. III, pp. 595 ff.

Chapter 29. Changes in
Social Relationships

I. Fluctuation of Familistic, Contractual, and Compulsory Relationships

1. Europe and America

From the fluctuation of the size and the vertical profile of the groups we can now turn to a study of the repeated changes that occur in the inner structure of the groups, in the "fibers" of which their network of relationships (or meaningful forms of interaction) is made up, in the functions of their government, and in the freedom of their members.

We have seen that the total network of social relationships of a group is made up, in various proportions, of three kinds of relationships: familistic, contractual, and compulsory (see Chapter 5). *In the life history of an organized group the relative proportions of these relationships do not remain constant but fluctuate in the form of an increase of one or two of these relationships at the expense of the remainder. Even in the total constellation of the main unibonded and multibonded groups of a given population, the proportions change, making most of the groups now predominantly familistic, now mainly contractual, now conspicuously compulsory.* In a family initiated through a compulsory marriage the parties married against their will may in the course of time become deeply attached and devoted to each other. The compulsory union thus turns into a familistic one. Or those freely and contractually entering the marriage union may subsequently discover their mutual incompatibility. If, in spite of their desire to terminate their marriage, they are unable to do so, the contractual relationship becomes a compulsory one. Sometimes we observe the degeneration of one-sided and weak familistic relationship into the contractual or compulsory type in the relationships of friends, members of the family, and other groups. Similar transformations of the "fibers" of the network of social relationships take place in practically all groups: in the state, in political parties, in territorial groups, in occupational groups and business firms, in religious organizations, etc.

Let us consider the European states. The early Carolingian state in its relationship between the monarch and the free classes was predominantly familistic, with the paternalistic monarch as a *pater familias*, the subjects, the *fideles*, being regarded as the children of a big family, with the relationship of *fidelitas*. In the relationship of the state with the unfree classes it was mainly a compulsory system. When, from the Carolingian state, we pass to the feudal state of the twelfth or thirteenth to the sixteenth century, we observe a decrease in the network of relationships of the familistic type and an increase of contractual and, to some extent, of compulsory relationships: the monarchy becomes largely elective; the relationship between the monarchs and the other free strata becomes contractual, with a stipulation of the rights and duties of each party, and so on. Turning to the European state of the sixteenth to the eighteenth century inclusive, we notice a further decrease of the familistic and a great increase of the compulsory relationships in the absolutistic monarchies of that period. With the end of the eighteenth and throughout the nineteenth and the prewar twentieth century we observe that the state system of relationships becomes mainly contractual, with a notable decrease of compulsory relationships among its members and strata; it is the liberal, constitutional state typical of this period. Finally, after the First World War the state again greatly changed through an enormous decrease of the contractual fibers in its network and a great increase of compulsory relationships, with a considerable augmentation of the familistic ones in the whole state system. The Communist, Nazi, and other totalitarian states afford examples of the state system made up chiefly of compulsory and partly of familistic-paternalistic "fibers," with a small proportion of contractual "threads" in their network.[1]

A careful analysis of the fluctuations that have occurred in the family and other kinship groups, religious organizations, occupational groups, territorial communities, and social orders and classes in the European population from the early medieval centuries up to the present time suggests the following generalizations. In all the principal unibonded and multibonded groups:

(a) The social texture of relationships from the eighth to the twelfth century appears to have consisted primarily of familistic and in lesser degree of compulsory fibers, the contractual relationships (in spite of the fact that many familistic and compulsory relationships originated contractually) playing a relatively minor role.

(b) Toward the thirteenth century the familistic forms begin to decline in most of the unibonded and multibonded groups, while the contractual and compulsory relationships begin to multiply.

(c) The period from the sixteenth to the middle of the eighteenth century is marked by a notable growth, in most of the unibonded and multibonded groups, of the compulsory relationships at the expense of the familistic and, to some extent, of the contractual relationships.

(d) Beginning with the end of the eighteenth century, the compulsory relationships rapidly decrease and the contractual ones strikingly increase, making the nineteenth century the golden age of contractualism.

(e) The period from 1914 up to the present time is marked, in most of the unibonded and multibonded groups and especially in the state groups, by a rapid decline of the contractual relationships in favor chiefly of the compulsory and in lesser degree of the familistic relationships.[2]

This gives a fair idea of the fluctuation in the proportions of these relationships in the constellation of the main unibonded and multibonded groups. In various forms such fluctuations occur in all populations.[3]

2. Contemporary Decline of Contractualism and Growth of Compulsory Relationships

The enormous importance of the changes in the proportions of these "fibers" in the total texture of group relationships must be clear to every thoughtful person. Such changes are fundamental and underlie most of the impressive changes on the surface of the group organization, such as the shift from capitalism to communism, or from monarchical to republican government. Let us accordingly, make a brief analysis of the Euro-American social groups of the nineteenth and twentieth centuries.

As has been said, the nineteenth century was the golden age of contractualism in the Euro-American populations. Its dominant economic system, called capitalism, with all its merits and defects, was, strictly speaking, merely a contractual system. In contradistinction to the compulsory economic system of

---

[1] For a detailed corroboration of these changes, cf. my *Dynamics*, Vol. III, Chps. 2-4.

[2] For a detailed corroboration of these conclusions, cf. my *Dynamics*, Vol. III, Chps. 2, 3, 4.

[3] A recent concrete example of such fluctuations within the Japanese Relocation Camp in Poston is given in A. H. Leighton's *The Governing of Men* (Princeton, 1945), Part I. In this group, within a short space of time, the mixed social relationships between the Japanese and the administration became sharply compulsory (the prestrike and strike period). After the end of the strike contractual relationships increased ("self-management").

slavery and serfdom or the familistic system of economic relationships, the capitalist economic system rests upon a free contract between the employer and the employee; the employer agrees to pay certain wages, the employee, to render certain labor or services. The parties are not bound by ties of affection, as are the members of the familistic group, nor does one party coerce the other, as in a compulsory system.

In the political field the contractual relationship resulted, during the nineteenth century, in the elimination of autocratic, coercive governments and in their replacement by democratic political regimes, with the government contractually elected, contractually limited in its power, contractually bound to respect the inalienable rights of the citizen—his liberty, equality, and individualism. The elective principle became the chief method of recruiting public officials in the state, in the municipalities, and in most of the other governmental groups. Government of the people, by the people, and for the people is contractual government *par excellence*.

Religious groups were also organized on a contractual basis. In many countries even the army and navy become voluntarily contractual. The same was true of the family, with marriage declared to be a purely civil contract, freely entered into and often terminated at the will of the parties. In brief, the contractual relationship became the principal fiber in the texture of virtually all unibonded and multibonded groups of the nineteenth century.

In the twentieth century, especially after 1914, this contractual system began rapidly to crumble, being replaced by chaos or compulsory and, in a lesser degree, familistic relationships in most of the unibonded and multibonded groups of the western populations. The capitalist economy has been progressively superseded by the compulsory "planned" economy of communism, Nazism, state socialism, or state capitalism, the government prescribing what is to be produced and how it is to be distributed and consumed, with an obligatory assignment of economic functions, and with an obligatory regulation of wages, prices, dwellings, and the like. Of "free enterprise" and free contractual relations between employer and employees little remains.

In the political field most of the nineteenth century democracies have given place to various dictatorial, autocratic regimes. In practically all Euro-American states, especially in time of war, the inalienable liberties and rights of the citizens, including their contractual rights, have been either entirely abolished, as in Communist Russia, Nazi Germany, and Fascist Italy, or else greatly curtailed. Government regimentation and regulation has invaded all the fields of social relationships and all the unibonded and multibonded groups. In the nineteenth century citizens and private organizations could do many things without asking the permission of the government; at the present time we can do hardly anything without such permission.

The decline of contractual relationships in the family has assumed a different form, that of the disintegration of the contractual family. As a union of husband and wife it has become less and less stable; an increasing number of marriages end in divorce or separation. As a union of parents and children it has likewise been disintegrating; the number of childless marriages has been rapidly increasing; the ties uniting parents and children are weaker and less binding than before and are broken earlier. In Soviet Russia the free contractual family, having reached the maximum of disintegration in the years 1918-1925, eventually began to revive; but the revival was followed by a progressive increase of governmental regimentation of it, with prohibition of abortions and illicit sexual relationships, and with a drastic limitation of divorces which, after the law of July 14, 1944, became practically unavailable for the overwhelming majority of the Russian population. In brief, many contractual fibers in the fabric of the family were replaced by coercive and familistic fibers.

A similar decline of contractual relationships has occurred in many other groups. Free contractual labor unions have been progressively replaced by compulsory government unions or by political machines and labor gangs manipulated by politicians and racketeers and coercively imposed upon a vast proportion of laborers. In the totalitarian and semitotalitarian countries all other associations—even scientific and aesthetic associations—have been increasingly regimented and controlled by the government.

Finally, contractualism has failed notoriously in the field of international relationships. In many countries international treaties have been violated and the solemn contractual obligations of the government thus repudiated. The League of Nations has ceased to exist. Coercion and brute force have been unleashed in the form of vast world wars and many lesser wars, as well as a host of bloody revolutions. The twentieth century, indeed, has been the bloodiest and most turbulent in the entire course of the twenty-five centuries of western history.

In a word, within a few decades the texture of the social groups of the West has drastically changed through a replacement of most of its contractual fibers by compulsory and familistic ones.[4]

3. Reasons for Fluctuation

The factors responsible for the fluctuation of group relationships are immanent and external. The immanent factors are inherent in the group and in the nature of its relationships. The compulsory and contractual relationships bear in themselves the seeds of their own decline, which inevitably ensues when these relationships attain their extreme form and fully unfold their immanent potentialities. The coercive relationship, when it becomes excessive, leads to disorganization. The coerced party may die out, or at least exhibit increasing inability to serve its masters. Or the exploited party may revolt against its masters, with disruption of the group and consequent separation of the coerced party. The only alternative to the disintegration of the group is a mitigation of coercion, its orderly or revolutionary limitation and transformation into either contractual or semifamilistic relationships between the two parties.

To repeat: Any coercion, when fully developed, generates forces leading to its inhibition, either through the disruption of the group or through the substitution of contractual or familistic relationships for the compulsory ones.

Similarly, under certain conditions the contractual relationships generate forces that tend to undermine them. Any genuine contractual relationship requires: (a) equal freedom of

the parties to make or not to make the contract; (b) the fulfillment of the contractual obligations by each party; (c) avoidance of misuse of the contract; (d) harmlessness of the contractual actions of the parties to other members and other groups. Otherwise the contractual relationships easily degenerate into pseudo-contractual or compulsory ones—into a contract made under duress, or occasionally into semifamilistic relations. The equal freedom of the parties enjoyed at the time the contract is formed often disappears later. For instance, in the capitalist contractual economy, with its inevitable phase of depression and mass unemployment, the workers, being unemployed, and confronted with the starvation of their families, frequently have to accept employment under conditions which they would not accept if they actually enjoyed the same degree of freedom as their employers. Often, in spite of the alleged "equality of contractual opportunity," they cannot find any employment. In such circumstances the contractual relationship loses its benefits and appeal for these workers. As such it ceases to command their devotion and allegiance and is easily replaced by either compulsory forms such as the state W.P.A., state obligatory employment on public works, etc., or familistic ones.

Likewise, a genuine contract, beneficial to all the contracting parties, requires that the parties should be fair, honest, devoid of a disposition to misuse the contract, and willing to fulfill their obligations. Frequently, especially in a society possessing an ethically nihilistic, relativistic, and highly egoistic sensate culture (cf. Chapters 40 to 42), a party is disposed to use a contract to the detriment of the other party and not to perform unpleasant duties. In recent business and political relationships such misuse of contracts and nonfulfillment of duties have become quite frequent on the part of employers as well as employees and trade unions, and of governmental regimes as well as the opposition. Under such conditions contractual relationships become harmful for the weaker party, being transformed into either compulsory or, more rarely, familistic relationships. They lose their utility, prestige, and the allegiance of the masses, and thus their very raison d'être.

When a group of gansters make a contract

---

[4] For the details, cf. my *Dynamics*, Vol. III, Chps. 3, 4, and *Crisis*, Ch. 5.

to murder or rob, in organized fashion, the rest of the population, or a group of selfish businessmen agree to exploit the public, they become a menace to the security, property, and other values of the rest of the population and, as such, arouse its opposition. At the same time they tend to discredit the value of contractual relationships and to alienate many from their allegiance to contractual relationships.

In these various forms contractual relationships, which flourish usually in societies characterized by the relativistic, materialistic, hedonistic, sensate type of culture, generate forces leading to their decline and to their replacement by either compulsory or familistic relationships.[5]

Somewhat different is the situation with familistic relationships. By their very nature they seem to be free from the generation of the forces leading to their undermining; loving and devoted friends or family members are not inherently bound to become either egoistic contractualists or bitter enemies. The reasons for the decline of familistic relationships lie elsewhere. By their nature the familistic relationships are the finest flower of human relationships. But they can thrive only if they are carefully and incessantly cultivated. Without an incessant effort they cannot grow. This is why such relationships, in their sublimer forms, have been comparatively rare phenomena. Having arisen among a few friends or family members or persons overflowing with love for all, including their enemies, persons like Buddha and Saint Francis of Assisi, these relationships do not continue automatically among the children of the friends or parents or new members of the familistic (religious, social,

or ethical) group. Owing to incessant changes in the membership of the groups, in their qualities and conditions, the familistic relationships tend to disappear with the death of the original members if they are not cultivated by the new members. When a wise, just, and compassionate ruler of a group or head of a business firm or leader of a given village is replaced by a successor devoid of wisdom, justice, and love, the familistic relationship obtaining between the former leader and his followers inevitably disappears, being replaced by either a contractual or a compulsory relationship. For these and similar reasons, inherent in the life of the group, even the familistic relationships cannot endure forever. They also are destined to emerge and disappear, to grow and to decline.[6]

Thus the immanent factors of fluctuation are sufficient to explain why the proportions of contractual, compulsory, and familistic relationships in a group are not constant, and fail to exhibit any permanent trend, but endlessly fluctuate.[7]

The external factors of fluctuation are numerous and diverse. Their primary role consists in reinforcing or weakening, in accelerating or retarding, the rise and decline of each of the three forms of relationships in question. In each case of fluctuation the external forces contributing to it must be carefully considered; otherwise many specific traits of a given fluctuation cannot be accounted for. Even if the general character of the fluctuation is satisfactorily accounted for by the immanent causes, the specific traits of a given shift, occurring in a certain constellation of conditions, can be explained only in terms of the specific external factors operating in a given case.

---

[5] None of these immanent causes of the decline of contractual (and capitalist) relationships is correctly assessed by such works as F. A. Hayek's *The Road to Serfdom* (Chicago, 1944). This and similar works merely idealize the contractual economy and politics and "debunk" the coercive and familistic systems, without any proper analysis of the real causes of their rise and decline.

[6] Plato expressed this in his statement that even his ideal republic was not eternal and, like all empirical phenomena, would eventually degenerate and disappear. A. Toynbee presents a series of facts respecting the transformation of the "creative minority" (familistic leaders) into the "dominant minority" (coercive and contractual) in some

twenty civilizations. His otherwise excellent analysis has this defect: he claims that in the life history of each civilization such a transformation occurs only once, namely, when the civilization passes from the phase of growth into that of breakdown and disintegration. In the life history of all organized unbonded and multibonded groups, including Toynbee's "civilization," it actually occurs several times, sometimes within the short period of a few years or even months. (A. Toynbee, *op. cit.*, Vol. III, *passim.*)

[7] For a more comprehensive analysis of the problem, cf. my *Dynamics*, Vol. III, pp. 124 ff. For the decline of the contemporary contractual relations, cf. my *Crisis*, Ch. 5.

II. Fluctuation of the Number of Classes of Relationship in the Group Network

Not only do the proportions of familistic, contractual, and compulsory relationships fluctuate in the fabric of the groups, but the total number of the classes of relationships that make it up likewise fluctuates. At one period it increases through the inclusion, in the fabric, of one or more classes of relationships that hitherto were not among its fibers. At another period the number decreases through the exclusion of one or more kinds of relationships that hitherto were a part of the system. Thus most of the economic relationships of production, distribution, and consumption were originally not a part of the texture of the capitalist state and were accordingly not controlled and regimented by their governments. They constituted fibers of the fabric of private business groups and were hence controlled by business-labor groups. After the Russian Revolution almost all economic relationships were embraced in the fabric of the Communist state. Upon the entry of the United States and other countries into the First World War many economic relationships were similarly included in the texture of these states and, as such, came to be controlled by their governments. In Russia virtually no relationships remained in the network of the private business groups, and consequently these groups almost entirely disappeared. In the Middle Ages religious relationships were controlled by the states, which prescribed the obligatory religion (*Cuius regio, ejus religio*). Upon the promulgation of religious freedom they were excluded from the state network and thus ceased to be regimented by the respective governments.

Similar reduction and multiplication of relationships occur in virtually all groups. The Christian Church in the Middle Ages included many social, educational, cultural, registrational, political, and other functions which in modern times were transferred to other groups, particularly to the states. Conversely, at the beginning of the Middle Ages many social relationships hitherto not embraced in the religious system came to be controlled by the Church.

A century ago the family network of relationships comprised among its fibers most of the educational, religious, recreational, occupational, and economic relationships of its members. During the last few decades many of these relationships have been transferred to other groups: the educational relationships, to the school systems; the religious, to the Sunday School and the Church; many economic relationships (insurance, social security, etc.), to the state or to insurance companies; occupational relationships, including vocational training, to vocational schools, occupational groups, and so on. As a result the family now controls a much smaller number of social relationships than formerly. Conversely, at the beginning of the Middle Ages, the family underwent the process of multiplication of the number of relationships comprised in its system.

The opposite pole to the situation we have been considering is the theoretical case where *all* the relationships of the members of a given population are embraced in and controlled by a single group. Such a body—whether the state, the Church, or what not—would be an extremely multibonded and self-sufficient body comprising the relationships, functions, and controls of the state, of territorial communities, of political parties, of the Church, of occupational groups, of the family, and of all the other unibonded and multibonded groups. It would represent the maximum possible multiplication of social relationships within a single group.

The actual fluctuation of the number of social relationships making up the network of social groups rarely presents such extreme cases of either diminution or multiplication. The number of relationships fluctuates within a much narrower margin, now decreasing, now increasing, but rarely, in the basic groups, falling to zero or rising to the point where one group becomes absolutely self-sufficient and includes in its network all the relationships of all the members of a given population. Such a situation would mean the elimination of the social differentiation of the population, a case virtually unknown in any society.

III. Transfer and Migration of Social Relationships from Group to Group

The reduction of the number of relationships in the network of this or that group does not mean that they cease to exist but, rather, that they are transferred to some other group, which thereupon assumes their control. Similarly, when the number of relationships in the network of a given group increases, the multiplication is achieved not through the creation of new relationships but through a reduction in the texture of some other group or groups. Reduction as well as multiplication of relationships is the result of transfer and migration of these relationships from the network of one group to that of another.

The transfer of social relationships from group to group means also the transfer of the control of these relationships from one group to another. When the registration and certification of marriages, births, and deaths was taken from the hands of the Church and transferred to the state, the control of this function likewise passed from the Church to the state. When occupational training was taken from the hands of the family and shifted to the medieval guilds, the control of this function was assumed by the guilds. Again, when economic relationships were shifted from private business groups, representing "free enterprise," to the state, the state governments assumed the control of production, distribution, consumption, prices, wages, and similar economic processes.

When the production, distribution, and consumption of alcoholic beverages in the United States were included in the governmental network through the prohibition amendments, the state assumed the control of functions which had hitherto belonged to other groups. When occupational unions embrace in their network the political relationships of their members, they assume the control of these relationships.

The transfer and migration of social relationships from group to group ordinarily proceeds slowly and gradually. Consequently the network of the respective groups now becomes denser and now thinner. Occasionally the transfer and migration of relationships assume an abrupt and spasmodic form in which a large number of relationships pass from one group to another. This occurs primarily in revolutionary periods. During the French revolution and the recent Russian revolution most of the relationships hitherto controlled by the Church were abruptly shifted to the control of the revolutionary state. During the Russian revolution virtually all economic relationships were suddenly transferred from private business groups to the government, with the result that most of the business organizations, disappeared.

The transfer and migration of social relationships is not a mere academic phenomenon but one of the highest practical importance. When economic relationships are shifted from private business-labor groups to the state, the economic regime is changed from one of capitalism to one of state socialism or communism. When educational relationships migrate from the network of a religious group to that of the public schools, religious education is replaced by secular education. If the state group includes in its network all the main educational, economic, occupational, political, religious, and other relationships, it becomes totalitarian, fundamentally different from the liberal state, with a limited number of relationships in its network and under its control.

Viewed in this light most of the conflicts between capitalism and communism or state socialism, between syndicalism and free labor and capital, between religious and secular education and culture, between totalitarian and democratic states, between "free religion" and "imposed religion," are essentially conflicts between different viewpoints as to whether certain relationships should belong to this or to that social group; to the private business groups or to the state; to the religious groups or to the secular public schools; to the occupational unions or to political or other groups. To sum up: Any transfer of a major social relationship from one group to another is a social process of notable practical importance for the groups involved as well as for the total population concerned.

If a totalitarian state appropriates most of the relationships, there remain few to be regulated by the other groups. Many of these will lose all their functions and disappear. In such conditions all save the dominant group will be weak and comparatively unimportant in their functions and controls.

Thus it is seen that in any population with a multitude of groups there is *an eternal intergroup struggle for the appropriation of social relationships*. In this struggle the family or a religious group may seize most of the relationships; in many cases the state succeeds in monopolizing the relationships and their control; now and then a caste, a social order, or

an occupational guild accomplishes this. Eac of such groups becomes one of the dominan groups of the population (cf. Chapter 16). W live in a period when the state has arrogate to itself an enormous number of social rel. tionships. Hence it has become "totalitarian in many countries, with a corresponding redu tion in the number of social functions con trolled by most of the nonstate groups, th religious, economic, occupational, territoria kinship, and family groups. The momentou consequences of such a concentration of rel. tionships in the state network are obvious.[8]

IV. Accumulation of Unibonded Ties and Dissociation of a Multibonded Complex

If several relationships (ties) migrate and accumulate within the network of a given unibonded group, such a group becomes a multibonded group, and vice versa. If, *per contra*, a given multibonded group loses all its relationships (bonds) except one, through their migration to the networks of other groups, the multibonded group is transformed into a unibonded one. If the family loses most of its former relationships and functions and becomes merely a sexual union of male and female, the family as a multibonded group disappears, giving place to a unibonded group of male and female bound together by the satisfaction of their sexual urge, and vice versa. If, as has happened in the past, several ties or relationships shift from a tribe or clan to the unibonded union of male and female, and such a group embraces the procreational, kinship, educational, economic, and other functions of a full-fledged family, the unibonded group is transformed into a multibonded group, the fully developed family as it was analyzed above.

The dissociation of multibonded groups into less complex multibonded groups or into unibonded groups, as well as the emergence of multibonded groups through the association and accumulation of two or more unibonded

ties, is explained by the migration of soci relationships from group to group. The group which acquire two or more relationships be come multibonded groups of varying degree of complexity. *Per contra*, those that underg the progressive loss of relationships are ult mately transformed into unibonded groups an may cease to exist altogether.

This process of association and dissociatio occurs in various forms incessantly. In the pas at some periods of Hindu history, the mult bonded caste tended also to dissociate int several groups of a lesser complexity than th caste; at other periods, the opposite process association of several unibonded ties into multibonded caste group occurred. With proper change the same can be stated of th social estates or nations or social classes, in th above sense of these terms.

In the early Vedic period India did not hav castes. Eventually the religious, occupationa racial, territorial, and family, kinship, an language ties coalesced to form the mult bonded caste. Later several of the multibonde castes tended to dissociate into groups of le complexity. Many a population in the pa has lacked a territorial + state + languag group called a nation. In the course of tim through the association of the correspondin ties within vast groups, nations have arisen Some of these, such as ancient Egypt, ancie Greece, and ancient Rome, eventually dissoc ated into several unibonded groups which

---

[8] Cf. W. Firey, "The Responsiveness of Interaction Patterns to Emergency," *SF*, October, 1942, in which the above and subsequent generalizations are tested experimentally.

in their turn, became extinct through the loss of either members, vehicles, or relationships. Some of the smaller nations of recent times have likewise tended to dissociate and disappear.

With appropriate modifications the same may be said of the social estates or social classes (in the foregoing sense of the terms). The social estates eventually disappeared in many countries through the dissociation of their bonds, being superseded by the social classes. In some countries, such as the United States, the latter are still in the process of growth and qualitative differentiation.

In hundreds of less spectacular forms and on a smaller scale the dissociation of groups into unibonded ones, as well as the association of unibonded groups in multibonded bodies, incessantly occurs in every differentiated and stratified population. For instance, a group of Italian or Irish Catholics settle in the same area of Boston, and all the members engage in the same occupational pursuit, a quadruple multibonded group (national, religious, territorial, and occupational) is formed. When in the course of time some of its members change their occupation, and shift their residence to a suburban town, the group undergoes the process of dissociation into simpler groups. If some members of the second generation substitute English for Italian and adopt other religions, the former quadruple multibonded group tends to disappear through dissociation into unibonded and double or triple multibonded groups.

These processes of association and dissociation, as we have seen, are closely connected with the process of migration and transfer of social relationships, ties, or functions from group to group. Although they are hardly even mentioned in most of the texts of sociology and social science, they are important processes, generating significant sociocultural effects, and as such need to be seriously investigated.

In the light of the existing knowledge of these processes the following tentative generalizations may be formulated.

(1) The intensity and magnitude of the processes of association and dissociation are not constant in different populations or in the same population during different periods.

(2) They are more marked in populations exhibiting notable horizontal and vertical mobility than in less mobile populations.

(3) They are more intense in urban and industrialized populations than in preliterate, pastoral, and agricultural populations.

(4) They increase enormously during periods of war, revolution, and other catastrophes.

(5) They increase sharply in periods characterized by a fundamental transformation of the basic cultural systems of a given population—in periods signalized by great scientific discoveries and technological inventions and a drastic transformation of religious, ethical, philosophical, artistic, juridical, economic, and political ideology.

(6) They are more typical of populations dominated by the sensate type of culture than of those dominated by the ideational type.

(7) There is virtually no perpetual historical trend in the direction of either increase or decrease of these processes.

Chapter 30. Fluctuation of Government Regimentation, Forms of Government, and Freedom

I. Basic Law of Fluctuation of Governmental Control

Tangibly related to the preceding fluctuations of the quality and quantity of social relationships, of their transfer and migration, of their association and dissociation, is another universal and ever-repeated process—that of the expansion and contraction, the hardening and softening, of governmental control over the groups. This fluctuation is so well known that we can formulate the basic law governing it. The uniformity runs as follows. *When a given organized group faces a grave emergency menacing its existence or its basic values, the governmental control over it tends to become more rigid and severe and tends to expand to embrace many social relationships of its members hitherto free from such control. As the emergency passes and conditions become more nearly normal, the governmental controls tend to relax.* Great emergencies comprise wars, revolutions, and other severe internal disturbances, famines and grave economic depressions, plagues and other epidemics, earthquakes, volcanic eruptions, floods, droughts, and so on—in general, all the conditions that menace the existence and the basic values of the groups. Therefore, when a given group passes from a state of peace to that of war; from prosperity to im-

poverishment (with unemployment and othe "satellites" of economic depression); when tends to be disrupted by revolution, riots, dis sensions, and anarchy; when earthquake floods, droughts, epidemics, or similar calam ties assail it; or when it is menaced by othe groups—in all such cases the governmenta control over the group tends to increase in it extent and severity, and vice versa.

This uniformity is well corroborated, firs of all, by the fluctuation of governmenta control in the state groups. Under condition of grave emergency, from ancient times u to the present, governmental control in a state groups has invariably expanded, some times resulting in communistic, absolutist, o other varieties of the totalitarian state. Th greater the emergency, the greater has bee the increase of governmental control, and vic versa. Conspicuous examples of the operatio of this rule have been afforded in the twentiet century by the First and the Second Worl War and by the depression of 1929 and th subsequent years. In all western countries, in cluding the United States and other democra tic countries, governmental control and regi mentation markedly expanded and becam more exacting and severe during the tw

World Wars and the great depression. In Russia, where the war factor was reinforced by revolution, famine, epidemics, and other calamities, governmental control began rapidly to expand during the First World War under the Czarist regime, continued to increase under the Kerensky regime, and reached its maximum possible limit under the Communist regime. The Communist regime itself, during the first years of its existence, with its unlimited regimentation, was essentially but a manifestation of the tendency toward unlimited governmental regimentation elicited by a multitude of grave emergencies, such as war, revolution, famine, and epidemics. When, after the First World War and the termination, in 1921, of the civil war, conditions began to improve, the control exercised by the Communist government began to relax, especially during the years between 1932 and 1939, prior to the outbreak of the Second World War.

Owing to the First World War and its "satellites," in almost all western countries there was a sharp increase of governmental regimentation after 1914. In many western countries it manifested itself in a replacement of the liberal, democratic state, with its limited governmental control, by various totalitarian regimes and dictatorships; in others, by a marked increase of governmental regimentation, carried on under the name of the "New Deal" in the United States and under different names in other countries. During the Second World War the increase became especially rapid and spectacular. What has been said of war applies equally to emergencies.[1]

When this uniformity is understood, most of the changes of the political and socioeconomic regimes in the same state and most of the differences between the political and economic regimes of different states become readily comprehensible. If, for instance, the United States, prior to the present war, had a political regime with a very modest governmental control of the life and relationships of its citizens, and with a minimum of autocracy and militarism, the main reason was

that, being protected by two oceans, the country was relatively free from the danger of wars and invasions; that it was very rich in resources and very prosperous; and that it had suffered few major calamities. As a result it was democratic, liberal, and nontotalitarian in its political and socioeconomic networks. With an increase of danger due the less highly protective role of the oceans and to other conditions, the governmental regimentation and autocracy began to increase.

On the other hand, Russia, occupying an open Euro-Asiatic plain incessantly invaded by Europeans as well as Asiatics throughout its whole history, had been exposed to the constant threat of war, had had to wage many wars, and hence could not fail to develop an autocratic and quasi-totalitarian government, with much more rigid controls than those exercised by the United States. Russia could survive only by becoming more centralized, and governmentally more autocratic than the United States.

When other emergencies, such as the famines, epidemics, and internal dissensions that have frequently befallen Russia, were added to the constant threat of reality of war, the relatively autocratic political regime, beginning with the Tartar invasions of the thirteenth century and extending up to the present time, is easily comprehensible.

When applied to the economic regime, the law under discussion explains why certain countries have had a state-socialist or communistic regime largely managed and controlled by the government, with a meager development of "free enterprise," whereas other countries have possessed capitalistic and "free enterprise" economic systems directed mainly by private individuals and organizations.

The law explains also why the economic regime of the same country fluctuates between the pole of free enterprise, with its *laissez faire, laissez passer,* and that of an economy managed and controlled principally by the government.[2] Even the most capitalistic country, with virtually no governmental domina-

---

[1] For a factual corroboration of this law in the history of Egypt, Babylonia, Persia, Greece, the Hellenistic states, Rome, Byzantium, medieval and modern European states, ancient Peru and Mexico, etc., cf. my *Dynamics*, Vol. III, pp. 192 ff., and *Calamity*, Ch. 7. These works contain also copious bibliographical citations.

[2] Contrary to widespread opinion, the economic systems managed by the government—the totalitarian, communistic, state-socialist, and similar economies—have been as common in the past as the economic regimes of "free enterprise," managed by private persons and groups. For the facts, cf. my *Dynamics* and *Calamity.*

tion of economic relationships, tends to develop a communistic, state-socialist, or totalitarian system, if for a decade or so it is subjected to such calamities as wars and famines. Conversely, the most communistic or totalitarian nation, with an economy entirely managed by the government, becomes progressively "capitalistic," with decreasing governmental control of economic relationships, when it enjoys for a few decades internal and international peace, prosperity, and freedom from grave calamities. Such fluctuations depend little upon the actions of this or that individual, be he a king, dictator, or president. Only the *details* of these sociocultural processes are determined by the wisdom, ability, and experience of the rulers.[3]

What has been said of the fluctuation of governmental control in the state groups may be said, with an appropriate modification, of the expansion and contraction, the hardening and softening, of governmental control in other organized groups. When a given local community is visited by a devastating flood, fire, calamitous earthquake, or the like, the normal laws are replaced by martial law or a state

of siege, with a sudden corresponding increase in the severity of the laws and their enforcement and with an expansion of governmental control of the community.

When a religious organization is menaced by heresies, dissensions, and internal conflicts, as in the case of the Christian Church in the thirteenth century and the period of the Reformation, the control exercised by the Church government tends to expand and to become much more rigid. The phenomenon is illustrated in the case of the Catholic Church by such measures as the Inquisition; the founding of the Society of Jesus; and the Counter-reformation, with its various reforms aimed at the cleansing of the Church and the centralizing of its control over the entire Catholic world.

Again, when a family or a business firm enters a period of adversity, it must tighten its controls or else disintegrate.

To summarize: The fluctuations under discussion are ever-repeated and universal processes. In large and well-organized groups like the state they manifest themselves unequivocally; in smaller groups, in a less definite form.

II. Fluctuation of the Forms of Government

We may classify the forms of the state and of group government into theocratic and secular; into republics and monarchies; into autocracies and democracies; into aristocracy, timocracy, oligarchy, democracy, and tyranny (as Plato did). Or we may adopt Aristotle's classification: (1) the government of one, with monarchy as its good form and tyranny as its bad form; (2) the government of the few, with aristocracy as its good form and oligarchy as its bad form; (3) the government of the many, with democracy and mob rule, respectively, as its good and bad forms. In the life history of long-existing groups these forms fluctuate from group to group, and from period to period in the existence of the same group. The prevalent popular opinion that in the

course of history there has been a steady trend from unlimited and bad autocracy to greater and better democracy, from monarchism to republicanism, from tyranny to government consecrated to social service, is not corroborated by the facts. Republican forms of government, as well as government of the people, by the people, and for the people, in the pattern of direct democracy, have existed and still exist among a number of preliterate groups; and in the early stages of some historical peoples. Similarly, monarchical, tyrannical, autocratic, aristocratic, and oligarchic forms of government existed in the remote past and still exist. If we examine the history of the Greeks and the Romans, we find that the state started as a monarchy; then became in turn an aristocracy, an oligarchy, and a demo-

---

[3] This law of fluctuation of governmental control is evidently unknown to such scholars as F. A. Hayek (*The Road to Serfdom*, cited above), and to most Chambers of Commerce, Senators, and other public officials, who preach the virtues of capitalism and the vice of regimentation. No wonder they cannot forecast the increase or decrease of regimentation and are impotent to change its course in the time of emergency.

cratic republic (for the full-fledged citizens); and in the Hellenistic and later Roman times degenerated partly into tyranny, and again became an autocratic monarchy. In the history of other states the sequence of forms has been different, fluctuating without any universal uniformity. In this respect Aristotle's statement that there is no uniform sequence in the succession of these forms remains valid.[4] No perennial historical trend and no ever-repeated cycle of the forms of government can be detected in the fluctuation of the forms of government in the state or Church, in political parties or occupational unions, or in the family or most other organized groups. The factors that determine this or that form of government in a group are numerous, embracing the nature of the group itself, as well as a host of internal and external conditions. For instance, in groups that are predominantly executive, centralization and autocracy tend to be greater than in deliberative groups. The army and the executive branch of the government are uniformly more autocratic, centralized, and regimented than a deliberative academy of science or legislature. It would be a misfortune if academies of science or universities were to be as autocratic and centralized in their government as the army. On the other hand, the army would be a highly inefficient organization if it possessed as "liberal" a government as universities or academies. One of the factors determining the form of government is the factor of emergency; it tends both to expand governmental control and to make it autocratic. Another factor is the dominant type of culture; in an ideational culture, theocracy tends to prevail, while in a sensate culture a secular type of government prevails. (Cf. Chapters 40 to 42.) The detailed discussion of these factors, however, lies outside the scope of this work.

III. Fluctuation of Freedom of the Groups and Their Members

1. Formula of Freedom

An individual is free when he can satisfy all his desires by the means he has at his disposal. If the sum total of his desires exceeds the sum total of the means for their satisfaction, he is unfree. Hence the following general formula of freedom:

$$\frac{\text{Sum total of means } (S.M.)}{\text{Sum total of desires } (S.D.)}$$

When the numerator exceeds or is equal to the denominator, one is free; otherwise one is unfree.

2. Two Forms of Freedom

The formula suggests two different ways to become free. One is to decrease one's desires so as to make their sum total either equal to or smaller than the sum total of the available means for their satisfaction. The other is to expand the means of their satisfaction to equal or exceed one's expanding desires. The first

[4] Cf. Aristotle, *Politics*, 1316, a, b, in Everyman's Library edition.

gives us the ascetic, stoic, or ideational type of freedom; the second, the sensate, hedonistic, or utilitarian type. The first form of freedom is essentially inner; the second, mainly external. The first is achieved through the inner control and transformation of one's ego; the second, through a transformation of the external milieu of the individual. Job's "The Lord gave, and the Lord hath taken away; blessed be the name of the Lord" is the supreme expression of ascetic-ideational freedom. "The more I have the more I want" is a concise formulation of sensate freedom.

In our sensate culture the ascetic-ideational freedom is almost entirely overlooked; indeed, it is interpreted as a lack of freedom. Nevertheless, it has been and is as real as the sensate freedom. By many persons and groups it has been regarded, and sought for, as the only real form of freedom. Ascetics and stoics of all countries and times—the genuine Hindus, Buddhists, Taoists, Stoics, mystics, early Christians, and many other groups—consciously strove for precisely this form of freedom. From their standpoint, sensate freedom is nothing but foolish licentiousness and the subjection of man to the tyranny of incidental environmental forces. From the standpoint of an objective observer, both forms are real; both are warranted by, and follow from, the above formula of freedom.

3. Distribution and Fluctuation of Ideational and Sensate Freedoms

Ideational freedom is dominant in populations controlled by the ideational form of culture; sensate freedom, in societies in which the sensate form is prevalent.

When a given culture passes from the ideational to the sensate form, ideational freedom passes into the sensate form, and vice versa.[5] Thus, for instance, among the Hindus whose Hindu and Buddhist cultures have been predominantly ideational, the prevalent form of freedom has likewise been the inner, ascetic, ideational freedom achieved through the suppression and control of the desires and lusts. The same may be said of the true Taoist culture of China; of the culture of the Graeco-Roman Stoics, Cynics, mystics, ascetics; of the ancient and medieval culture of the Christians, and the like. Even the preliterate groups, such as the Zuñis, or the Hopi Indians whose culture was mainly of a primitive ideational or idealistic character, possessed a primitive ideational or idealistic form of freedom. Among populations characterized by the sensate type of culture—as, for instance, among the western populations since the thirteenth century—the predominant type of freedom has been sensate. In brief, there is a close causal connection between the dominant types of culture and freedom. This causal connection explains the distribution of the three principal forms of freedom.

When, as we shall see later (cf. Chapters 40 to 42), the culture *of a given population shifts from the dominant ideational form to the idealistic or sensate form, or vice versa, a corresponding fluctuation takes place in the forms of freedom. In other words, the causal connection between the dominant forms of culture and liberty applies also to their time sequence.* Thus when, in India, at the height of the Gupta and Maurya empires, Hindu culture became more sensate, the form of liberty also became sensate. When the sensate culture of the Graeco-Romans between the fourth century B.C. and the third century A.D. began to be replaced by the rising ideational culture of Christianity, the sensate liberty of the previous period was superseded by the ideational liberty of Christianity. The ideational type of culture and liberty dominated Europe up to the end of the twelfth century. When, after the thirteenth century, the sensate form of culture came to dominate the West, the sensate type of liberty similarly began to gain the upper hand. First the upper class sought to secure it for themselves through such measures of Magna Charta, limiting the arbitrariness of the kings; then, commencing with the thirteenth century, the middle classes endeavored to obtain it through the revolutions of the urban communes; still later, especially after the revolutions of 1688 and 1789, the lower classes engaged in the struggle on their own behalf. The guiding motto of all such struggles has been "Give me (sensate) liberty or give me death!" Hence the preoccupation of these centuries with the inalienable rights of man; with constitutional guarantees of freedom of speech, religion, the press, and so on. At the present time, when the dominant sensate culture of the West is disintegrating, sensate freedom is beginning to disintegrate also. Its formulae are increasingly used for a hypocritical justification of the tyranny of one group over the others: the conquerors over the vanquished, the colonial masters over the colonial serfs, and so on. It steadily degenerates into the rule of brute force, assisted by fraud, and leads to a succession of conflicts of nation with nation, class with class, pressure group with pressure group. In these and many other ways, in this *bellum omnium contra omnes*, an increasing number of groups and persons progressively lose their sensate freedom, safety, and security. They sacrifice these also through a disproportionate expansion of their sensate desires relatively to the available means of their satisfaction.

---

[5] For a definition and analysis of the ideational and sensate forms of culture, and for their distribution and fluctuation in the life history of the Graeco-Roman, western, and other cultures, cf. my *Dynamics* (4 Vols., New York, 1937-1941). See further Chapters 40-43.

4. Uniformities in the Fluctuation of Sensate Liberty

Turning from the fluctuations of the basic forms of liberty to the quantitative fluctuations of sensate liberty, the following generalizations may be formulated.

(a) *The amount of sensate liberty is not constant but fluctuates from group to group, and from period to period in the same group.* The proposition is fairly self-evident, whether we take the groups of the same kind or of different kinds. The amount of liberty of speech, of religion, of the press, of assembly, of autonomous management of one's economic affairs, of choice of occupation, of marriage and divorce, and the like fluctuates from state to state, from religious group to religious group, from occupational to occupational group, from family to family, and so on. In states with slavery or serfdom it is much more limited for the lower classes than in states without slaves or serfs. "The four freedoms" have hardly existed in certain state groups, whereas in others they have been realized to some extent. In the army and the navy, in monastic orders, and in prison groups which drastically regiment the conduct and relationships of their members, it is much more limited than in various free associations—scientific, artistic, etc. In castes it is much more limited than in social classes.

(b) *If we assume the total sum of the sensate desires of the upper and lower strata to be equal, then at any given moment the amount of sensate liberty tends to be greater in the upper strata than in the lower strata.* The proposition is again almost self-evident. Masters are more free from the sensate standpoint than slaves and serfs; the dominant strata than the subordinate strata; the rich than the poor; the privileged than the disfranchised; the superior authorities than the inferior ones, and so on. The upper strata have larger means at their disposal for the satisfaction of their sensate desires than the lower strata of the same group; therefore, by definition, they are more free than the lower strata.

(c) *If, however, we assume that the sum total of the sensate desires of the upper strata is larger than that of the lower classes, the upper classes may not be freer than the lower classes; they may be even less free.* Sensate desires, by their very nature, tend to increase indefinitely. The more sensate values one possesses, the more one desires, especially in regard to such values as wealth, luxuries, physical comforts, power, popularity, and fame. The sum total of the sensate desires of the upper classes is, as a rule, much greater than that of the lower strata. Though the upper strata have a greater amount of means for the satisfaction of their desires than the lower classes, these means may fall short of the enormously expanded sensate desires of the upper classes; hence the latter are frequently less free than the lower strata.

(d) *The contrast in the amount of sensate liberty of the upper and lower strata, measured by the amount of their means of satisfying their sensate desires, is not constant but fluctuates from group to group, and from period to period in the same group.* In groups with slavery or serfdom the contrast in sensate liberty is much greater than in groups without slaves or serfs. In castes and social orders it is greater than among social classes. In autocratic monarchical states it is more conspicuous than in constitutional and democratic states, with various freedoms guaranteed for all members and with the government limited in its rights and privileges. In economic groups exhibiting marked economic inequality of the poorer and richer strata it is greater than in a more equalitarian economic society. In populations in which the women and the lower age groups are entirely subordinated to the men and the higher age groups, respectively, it is greater than in populations with a more nearly equal status for men and women and for the different age groups.

In Greece and Rome, and, indeed, in almost all countries, with the abolition of slavery and serfdom in the later stages of their history, and with the elimination of the autocratic power exercised by the men over the women, and by the higher age groups over lower ones, the contrasts along these lines sharply decreased. On the other hand, when a given society introduces slavery or serfdom, when the status of slaves and serfs becomes worse instead of better, and equality of the sexes or age groups is replaced by their inequality, such changes involve an increase of the contrasts in the respective liberties of the masters and slaves, the men and women, and the upper and lower age groups. We have seen also that the severity and scope of governmental control fluctuate. Most cases of increase of governmental regimentation mean an increase of the contrast between the freedom of the rulers and that of their subjects, and vice versa.

When India developed the caste system, the contrast between the upper and lower classes in respect to sensate liberty increased; so also upon the rise of social orders. When the opposite process occurred—the replacement of the castes or social orders by social classes—the contrasts of freedom decreased.

When the free Roman population passed from the republican to that of unlimited monarchy, the contrast between the upper and lower social strata of the Roman state in respect to political liberty increased, and vice versa.

In a less spectacular form the inequality in the liberty of the upper and lower strata fluctuates in practically all organized groups. In the family there are periods of its increase, when the head of the family becomes more absolute and autocratic, and periods of its decrease, when its head ceases to be an autocrat and suffers a limitation of his power and authority. In political parties and occupational unions there are periods of genuine autocracy on the part of their bosses, and of drastic subordination of the rank and file of the members to the boss and his henchmen; and there are other periods marked by greater relative equality of their upper ranks and the ordinary members. Similar fluctuations occur in religious, territorial, kinship, racial, and other organized groups.[6]

(e) *The amount of sensate liberty fluctuates in the life history of the same group from period to period.* When a given population is conquered by another, its liberty is sharply curtailed; conversely, when it is victorious over another group, its liberty increases. We have observed that the relative proportions of the familistic, contractual, and compulsory relationships in the network of a group fluctuate. When the proportion of familistic or of truly contractual relationships increases, the freedom of the group likewise increases. When the pro-

portion of coercive relationships increases, its liberty correspondingly diminishes. So far as freedom from adverse natural forces is concerned, most long-existing groups experience now and then some calamity such as a drought, flood, earthquake, or epidemic. Under such circumstances the liberty of the group temporarily declines, since many of its desires cannot be satisfied as under normal conditions. Again, in periods of impoverishment and depression the economic liberty of the group obviously decreases; for it can no longer satisfy certain needs as during periods of prosperity.

If we turn to a systematic study of the various liberties of a group—political, economic, occupational, and religious, freedom from want and adverse natural forces, freedom from fear, and so on—we can readily perceive how these liberties fluctuate in the course of time. Political and civil liberties and equality of opportunity at some periods of a nation's history do not exist or are very meager; at other periods they are relatively abundant. Similar fluctuations occur in the economic liberties of a group. These increase with an increase of its prosperity and decrease with its impoverishment. The same is true of the freedom from fear. Wars, revolutions, and similar calamities breed fear. Since, in any long-existing group, periods of peace and war, of well-being and calamity, incessantly alternate (cf. Chapters 31 and 32), freedom from fear now increases, now decreases.

(f) *Different groups, as well as the same group at different periods, differ widely in the kind of liberties they permit or prohibit. Side by side with the quantitative fluctuation of liberty from group to group, and from period to period in the same group, we observe a qualitative fluctuation.* Thus Mohammedans allow polygamy, but prohibit the use of alcohol and pork, while Christians permit the consumption of alcohol and pork but prohibit polygamy. Many groups allow polyandry or fairly promiscuous sexual life while prohibiting any deviation from the established religion. Other groups prohibit polyandry and promiscuous sexual life while allowing complete religious freedom. Caste and, to some extent, guild societies deny freedom of choice of occupation but grant considerable latitude in the matter of religious beliefs and political affili-

[6] For the details, cf. my *Dynamics*, Vol. III, Ch. 6.

ations. In other groups there is freedom of occupational choice but a minimum of political and religious liberty.

If we consider specific liberties, similar differences are observable. As regards *freedom of speech and thought*, certain groups allow unrestrained criticism of God and religious beliefs while prohibiting and punishing any criticism of monarchs, dictators, the wealthy, and the powerful. In other groups a criticism of God or religious dogma is strictly forbidden, whereas that of monarchs and the rich and mighty is tolerated. Some groups ban the criticism of monarchs and the hereditary aristocracy, but not that of the rich, of labor leaders, of socialists, communists, and anarchists, and so on. In other groups a denunciation of monarchs, princes, Popes, and aristocrats is fostered, whereas criticism of the rich, of labor leaders, of communists and socialists, or of Nazis is made a *crimen laesae majestatis*. In certain groups criticism of foreigners or Jews is suppressed; in others, welcomed. Liberty of speech, thought, or the press, in fact, is not something definite and uniform but represents the widest diversity of "freedoms," some of which are actually opposed to one another.

A similar situation obtains respecting *religious freedom*. Few societies have ever accorded complete liberty to all religions. In the United States the Mormons, so far as they advocated polygamy, and several quasi-religious anarchistic and pacifistic organizations have been directly or indirectly suppressed and even punished. In Communist and Nazi states all religions incompatible, respectively, with the dogmas of Communism and Nazism are severely persecuted. In caste societies all religions advocating intercaste marriage are likewise prohibited. In the Christian populations of the Middle Ages all non-Christian religions were persecuted, suppressed, or inhibited. In Catholic countries non-Catholic Christian denominations have been persecuted; in Protestant countries Catholics have been disfranchised, and so on.

The same is true of *economic freedom*. As regards unlimited competition or *laissez faire*, monopolies and cartels, the choice of occupations, child labor, the employment of women, the distribution of incomes, taxes, imports and exports, and dozens of other economic factors, there has been the widest variety of liberties and prohibitions in various groups, and in the same group at different periods.

Still more true is this of *freedom from want and freedom from fear*. In certain societies, for instance, in medieval Europe, want and poverty tended to be commended and wealth and prosperity denounced, in accordance with the Gospel dictum that it is easier for a camel to pass through the eye of a needle than for a rich man to enter the Kingdom of Heaven. The divine Lady Poverty, asceticism, the suppression of all carnal desires, and so on have been strongly urged in such societies. In others, such as the contemporary ones, poverty and want have been condemned, and prosperity, physical comfort, and the satisfaction of bodily desires have been extolled. Even within such societies, however, not all forms of freedom from want are equally encouraged. In some groups the use of alcoholic beverages is prohibited; in others it is allowed, whereas the use of tobacco and of certain foods and beverages is taboo.

Likewise not all types of *freedom from fear* are equally tolerated in different societies. In time of war, persons who exhibit fear of the enemy are branded as deserters, cowards, pacifists, or even traitors. In religious societies the fear of God is one of the basic injunctions; in non-religious societies it is discouraged, whereas fear of kings, dictators, presidents, bosses, or foremen is strongly encouraged.

(g) *Seldom, if ever, has there been a group in which complete freedom has been realized. Per contra, there has existed scarcely any group totally devoid of freedom.* The first kind, that of absolute anarchists, could exist only among 100 per cent socialized persons or else angels; among ordinary human beings it has never been realized. It would presuppose an organized group without obligatory law-norms and governed exclusively by one-sided imperative moral norms absolutely identical and equally strong among all the members. On the other hand, a group utterly destitute of freedom is likewise a logical and factual impossibility. Factually, it simply could not survive. Logically, it would mean a group whose members deliberately deprived themselves of all freedom and established law-norms contradictory to all their convictions and interests.

(h) *In general, freedom tends to decrease with the transition from familistic to contractual and compulsory forms of social organization.* In a familistic society all members are free; in contractual groups, a part of the members; and in compulsory groups, only a small minority. In familistic groups only a few of the relationships of the members are subject to coercion, and the means of restraint (the penalties for violations) are very mild; whereas in compulsory groups a much larger area of conduct is coercively controlled, and the methods of control (the penalties for violations) are extremely severe. The contractual type of society occupies an intermediary position. Since the familistic society is essentially harmonious and is permeated by mutual love and devotion, it does not require much coercive restraint. Its members are naturally and spontaneously social in their actions and relationships. Since, per contra, a compulsory group is cemented into oneness mainly through coercion of the majority by the more powerful minority, the latter has to restrain most of the actions of the majority, must deprive it of most of its freedom, and must enforce its control by drastic punishments and repressions.[7]

5. Mistaken Theories of Trends Toward Freedom

When the whole range of the fluctuation of liberty is considered in its sensate, idealistic, and ideational aspects, *the widely accepted opinion that the main historical trend consists in ever-increasing freedom is rather questionable.*[8] The proponents of this theory concentrate exclusively on certain forms of political freedom, overlooking all the others. Even in the field of political freedom they admit only those facts which support their thesis, ignoring the rest. They make arbitrary assumptions as

to what prohibitions and punishments constitute violations of freedom and what do not. In a concise criticism of the theory the following weaknesses may be mentioned.

(a) The theory assumes that there is a definite trend from autocratic monarchies to democratic republics. The assumption is, however, not borne out by the facts. There is no such trend, and, in addition, many republics are more autocratic than many limited monarchies.

(b) Mere wishful thinking is also the assumption that autocratic governments tend to disappear in the course of time. Even in the state groups contemporary dictatorships are as autocratic as any autocracy in the past. The fluctuation of governmental control and of the coercive, familistic, and contractual relationships testifies definitely against such an assumption.

(c) The theory likewise takes for granted that slavery and serfdom have disappeared. This assumption also is questionable. Slavery and serfdom in their worst form appeared not at the dawn of human history, not even at the earliest stages of the history of different nations, but at their later stages. In our day more than twelve million foreign workers were enslaved in Germany, and in the occupied countries even greater numbers were treated worse than slaves. In our day the bulk of the labor in the totalitarian countries—Communist and Fascist—attached to the factories or collective farms (*ad glaebae adscripti*) are as little able to move about freely and to choose their occupations, to oppose their Communist or Fascist bosses, as the serfs and slaves of the past. During the Second World War similar trends appeared in most countries. Not infrequently the subordination of employees to their capitalist or Communist bosses is not essentially different in degree from that of serfs and slaves to considerate masters. Add to this the millions of natives in the colonies of Euro-

---

[7] For a corroboration of this proposition, cf. my *Dynamics*, Vol. II, Chps. 13-15.

[8] An overwhelming majority of the thinkers, philosophers, and scholars of the nineteenth and the twentieth centuries believed in such a law. At the dawn of human history, they held, there was no freedom. According to Hegel, there then appeared, in the Oriental monarchies, liberty for one; at the next stage, in the Graeco-Roman and medieval worlds, there emerged freedom for the few; and

finally, at the time of Hegel, freedom began to be realized for all. The main trend of history thus consists in the realization of ever-increasing liberty. (Cf. Hegel's *Philosophy of History*.) This idea has been reiterated by Kant, Herder, Fichte, Condorcet, and Comte, and is being reiterated by a host of scholars, scientists, statesmen and politicians, journalists, and plain people. The "four freedoms" of our time are among its many variations.

American countries, whose treatment by the "civilized" nations has been hardly better than that of slaves. The elimination of slavery on paper has not eliminated it in reality. There is no convincing evidence that such domination and mistreatment of groups by other groups have been on the wane.

(d) The same may be said of the alleged trend toward the equality of men and women, of the upper and lower age groups, of races and ethnic groups. In many of the early and preliterate societies there was as great an equality of these groups as in contemporary peoples, and certainly greater than in many recent societies. One does not find any steady historical trend toward such equality; instead one notes merely local and temporal fluctuations.[9]

(e) Equally unwarranted is the claim that elective government tends progressively to supplant the self-appointed type. Elective government was known to many preliterate and early historical tribes, and it has functioned throughout the course of history among various groups and populations. On the other hand, the governments of many contemporary groups are self-appointed or pseudo-elective. Again, instead of a linear trend we find merely temporary fluctuations.

(f) Highly dubious is also the claim that freedom of thought, speech, the press, religion, and association has emerged only in modern times. As a matter of fact, religious freedom existed in many preliterate groups, in ancient Egypt, China, and India, and in certain periods of Greek and Roman history. On the other hand, acute religious intolerance swept over the western countries during the centuries of the Reformation and the religious wars. Even in the nineteenth century, in many democratic populations, there was a great deal of intolerance. There is no linear trend from an absolute lack of religious freedom to the complete religious liberty.

Freedom of association, including the formation of secret societies, guilds, and similar organizations, has always existed. Its limitation appeared at a comparatively late stage of human history, amidst complex civilizations.

The same is true of freedom of speech and

[9] On this point cf. B. Malinowski, *Freedom and Civilization* (New York, 1944).

political thought, which existed in many past societies and cultures and even in preliterate groups. Such restrictions as were imposed were no greater than in the "freest" societies of our time. Moreover, freedom of speech may be permitted in one society in regard to certain matters but prohibited in respect to others, whereas in another society the situation may be exactly the reverse. In certain societies obscene speech is prohibited, but political speechmaking is allowed; in others the converse is true.

(g) Since there is no certain trend toward a decrease of compulsory relationships, and no similar trend toward a decrease of governmental control and regimentation, we have no solid basis for claiming a linear trend toward greater liberty.

(h) If there is no trend toward a decrease of social stratification, there is again no valid ground for the claim in question.

(i) When we consider other spheres of social life, we have still less reason to assume a trend toward greater liberty. It is not evident in sex relationships. The same applies to food and drink; the prohibition of certain foods and of alcohol and other beverages is a contemporary reality. Freedom from intense, monotonous, and sometimes harmful work likewise does not exhibit such a tendency. Many primitive pastoral and agricultural peoples have been much freer in this respect than the laboring groups and other occupational populations of the modern industrial countries. Freedom from want has likewise not been growing steadily throughout the course of history. At the present time hundreds of millions lack the minimum amount of bread and other necessities. Similarly freedom from fear fails to exhibit any such trend; for the principal factors which elicit it—calamities (such as wars and revolutions) and insecurity (such as that introduced by the invention of the atomic bomb)—show no signs of abating. To conclude: *When carefully tested, the law of progressive increase of freedom is found to be little more than wishful thinking.* Instead of such a linear trend, we can detect only quantitative and qualitative fluctuations of freedom from group to group, from period to period.

The sensate freedom of an individual is the sum total of freedoms he enjoys in all the groups and strata of which he is a member. It must not be judged or appraised by the freedom he possesses in *only one* of the groups he is affiliated with. This is the mistake ordinarily made by most theorizers on freedom and its growth. Considering the state only, and in the state only certain political rights, they often overstress the freedom of the individual in modern times. In the discussion of the transfer and migration of social relationships it was pointed out that social relationships, when no longer controlled by a given group, usually pass into the control of some other group. For instance, in India the state has played a comparatively minor role in many periods and has controlled a comparatively insignificant portion of an individual's conduct and relationships. A similar situation obtained in medieval Europe; the feudal state was weak and controlled relatively few relationships. To conclude from this that the individual enjoyed a high degree of freedom in the caste or feudal society would, however, be quite unwarranted. The caste, the family, the local community, and other nonstate groups meticulously controlled most of the relationships and conduct of the individual in India; the Church, the local community, the social order, the guilds, and the family likewise rigidly controlled most of the relationships and behavior of the individual in the Middle Ages. The liberal state of the nineteenth century dominated a limited section of an individual's relationships and conduct; but his family, his local community, his social stratum, and his occupational and economic groups regulated his conduct and relationships in the most meticulous fashion, including even his clothes and manners. The contemporary, especially the totalitarian, state controls a very large part of the individual's relationships and conduct; the rest is controlled by other groups of which he is a member, especially by occupational groups and unions, economic organizations and bosses, political parties, the schools, and his family and neighbors. His total freedom is about as limited and his cherished desires as much thwarted as ever before. When he violates the norms of his groups, he is penalized about as severely as in the past.

We have scarcely any solid basis of claiming that the total freedom of the contemporary individual is substantially larger than that of an individual of earlier generations. In some respects the preliterate individual may have enjoyed a wider range of freedom than contemporary laborers and business executives, professional men and even rulers. Even dictators are not free: virtually all their activities are inexorably prescribed and regimented by the forces inherent in the various groups of which they are the avowed bosses.

6. Factors in the Fluctuation of Liberty

The reasons for the fluctuation of liberty between the minima and maxima are fairly comprehensible. Any long-existing group must have *some* freedom; otherwise it cannot function and survive. I. P. Pavlov has shown that it is a biological necessity for the survival of an organism.

"The freedom reflex is one of the most important reflexes, or, if we use a more general term, reactions, of living beings. If the animal were not provided with the reflex of protest against boundaries set to its freedom, the smallest obstacle in its path would interfere with the proper fulfillment of its natural functions. Some animals, as we all know, have their freedom reflex to such a degree that when placed in captivity they refuse all food, sicken and die."[10]

When totally deprived of freedom, animal organisms sooner or later die. The same is true of human beings. Confinement in prison cells, especially solitary confinement, even when all other conditions such as food and air are satisfactory, proves detrimental to their health, though the confinement may leave them a considerable margin of freedom. When bound and thus deprived of freedom of motion, they deteriorate still more rapidly, both physically and mentally. When preliterate natives have been conquered by the "civilized" nations and drastically limited in their freedom through the prohibition of their mores and way of life, a high death rate has generally resulted. Under such conditions the Melanesians, Tasmanians,

---

[10] I. P. Pavlov, *Conditioned Reflexes* (tr. by G. Anrep, Oxford, 1927), pp. 12 ff. This gives an account of his experiments with dogs, some of which had a comparatively weak reflex of freedom, whereas others had a very strong one, refusing food when their freedom of motion was limited.

Fijians, Aztecs, and hundreds of other peoples have lost the will to live and have eventually died out.[11]

A certain minimum of freedom to follow one's inclinations, regardless of their wisdom or folly, proves to be a necessary condition for health, happiness, and survival. When deprived of this minimum one inevitably suffers physically, mentally, and morally. Under these circumstances one resists such suppression; but if one is unsuccessful, one eventually succumbs. It follows that the surviving preliterate, and even paleolithic and neolithic, groups must have possessed a certain minimum of liberty and can by no means be considered as entirely unfree, as the theory of the progressive historic growth of liberty assumes.

When the amount and the kinds of liberty in any group notably decrease, the group generates an increasing resistance against such a trend, and either succeeds in stopping or even reversing the trend or else soon perishes. Those groups that have survived have been able to preserve the necessary minimum of freedom. In other words, in the surviving groups there is a limit below which their freedom does not and cannot fall; for when it begins to decrease, the group generates the forces of expansion of its liberty or else perishes.

Side by side with this minimum there is also a maximum limit of freedom beyond which it cannot go without causing the disorganization of the group. If every member were perfectly free to satisfy all his desires, the result would be an incessant *bellum omnium contra omnes*, perpetual conflicts and anarchy, owing to the selfishness, greed, and passions inseparable from ordinary human nature.

When a group develops its freedom to a level approaching the extreme maximum, it is faced with the choice of either developing it still further and eventually perishing, or of checking the trend and reversing it. Many groups have proved unable to halt the trend and have perished in the flames of riots, revolts, anarchy, and civil wars. Those that survived generated increasing opposition to the degeneration of liberty into license and often reversed the trend.[12]

Thus freedom has maximum and minimum limits, different for different groups, which a group cannot exceed without endangering its existence. When liberty falls close to the minimum level, the group tends to generate counteraction and reverse the trend. When it approaches the maximum level, the group likewise tends to develop a counteraction and to reverse the trend. Those groups that cannot accomplish this task perish. Hence the fluctuation of freedom and the improbability of an eternal trend toward more unrestricted freedom. External factors now reinforce, now weaken, the immanent forces of "equilibration" of freedom, but the inherent forces of the group are sufficient in themselves to account for the fluctuation.

As to why different groups have various kinds of freedom and restraint, the main reason is the sociocultural difference of the groups themselves. In the first place, a series of actions and relationships detrimental to the survival or welfare of the group are almost universally prohibited—the murder of a member of the group, treason, rape and illicit sexual relationships, and similar acts.[13] Secondly, the differences in the kind of free and prohibited relationships appear in the fields where the groups differ from one another partly in their biological nature but mainly in their sociocultural system. *With substantial exceptions, each group tends to permit those actions which are harmless or beneficial to the group or its*

---

[11] Cf. Louis Le Fevre, *Liberty and Restraint* (New York, 1931); W. H. R. Rivers, "The Psychological Factor," in *Essays on the Depopulation of Melanesia* (Cambridge University Press, 1922); and A. H. Engelgardt, *Progress as the Evolution of Cruelty* (Russian).

[12] Plato admirably describes this process. "An excess of liberty, whether in states or individuals, seems only to pass into an excess of slavery. . . . And so tyranny naturally arises out of democracy, and the most aggravated form of tyranny and slavery out of the most extreme form of liberty."

Cf. *The Republic*; in *The Works of Plato* (the Dial Press, New York, n.d.), Vol. II, p. 336. Pages 323 ff. of the latter work describe in detail the process of degeneration of unlimited liberty into anarchy and then into slavery and tyranny.

[13] For a detailed study of crimes and punishments in various societies, cf. my *Dynamics*, Vol. II, Chps. 13-15. The prevalent opinion respecting the relativity of the prohibited acts is fallacious. Such acts as murder, perpetrated against other members of the group, are prohibited in practically all groups.

dominant faction, and tends to prohibit those which are actually or potentially dangerous to the welfare and unity of the group or its dominant element.

Furthermore, when a group or subgroup begins to suffer increasingly from the lack of a certain kind of liberty (such as freedom of speech, of religion, of sexual life, of divorce, or of competition), it becomes vociferous in its demands for the establishment of such a liberty. Conversely, when a group or a subgroup suffers increasingly from the overexpansion of a certain type of freedom—unrestrained freedom of speech or the press, or an excess of divorces and sexual licentiousness, competition, cartels and monopolies, drug addiction and drunkenness, insubordination of inferiors to their superiors, atheism and cynicism, or demoralizing philosophies, novels, pictures, plays, and so on—it generally makes a strenuous effort to curb the excess in question. The reaction may be caused by an inordinate decrease or increase of liberty, the desires of the group or of its most powerful element remaining constant; by a change in the level of the desires of the group or its leaders, the amount of liberty remaining constant; or by a change in both factors.

These approximate rules explain an enormous number of concrete cases of demands for certain forms of liberty and of demands for curbing their excesses. When recently the American movies became saturated with crime and sensuality, there arose a demand for their restraint. When America began to suffer from the unrestrained liberty of the speculative stock market, there developed an effort to curb it. The same applies to the unlimited freedom of monopolies, corporations, and cartels, and to that of the press, literature, and indoctrination. When the United States needed a full development of its natural resources, and hence free business enterprise and competition, a strenuous agitation for such freedom arose. When, in the early history of Massachusetts, the control of religious and ethical relations became too rigid and inquisitorial, insistence on religious and ethical freedom finally curbed the intolerance of the ruling group in the commonwealth; the hanging of "witches" and heretics was checked, and a reasonable minimum of religious and ethical freedom was secured.

Chapter 31. Fluctuation of Orderly and Disorderly Change of Groups

I. Prevalence of Orderly Change

1. Lawful, Orderly Change

Tension and relaxation, sickness and health, crisis and repose, incessantly alternate in the life process of an individual. They usually coexist; but now one alternative, now the other, becomes dominant. Similarly, in the life process of an incessantly changing group; periods of orderly, lawful change are followed now and then by periods of disorderly, revolutionary upheaval. Both forms coexist to some extent; even in orderly change there is always an element of disorder, and vice versa. However, the element of disorder in an orderly period and that of order in a disorderly phase constitute only minor factors.

The periods of orderly change are marked by the fact that the change proceeds according to the official law of the group. As mentioned before, explicitly or implicitly the official law of the group provides in advance for its change and often prescribes detailed rules as to how such a transformation is to be effected. The constitutions of the state, of the church, of business firms, of trade unions, of political parties, of the family, and so on, contain precise provisions defining the ways of abrogating obsolete norms, of enacting new laws, and even of amending the constitution itself. Many of these groups have specific law makers and law interpreters—legislatures, judicial committees, courts and judges, jurisconsults, monarchs, the *pater familias*, Popes, councils of elders, and so on—that either function perennially or are created *ad hoc*. In other groups, such as castes and sex, age, race, and nationality groups (so far as they are organized) either the organized parts perform this function or it is performed through the resolutions of congresses of the group leaders or through the laws of the state, the church, or some other well-organized group that regulates their relationships.

As long as the change proceeds according to the official law of the group, it is a legal and orderly change, no matter how radical it may be, how fast its tempo, or how drastically it transforms the rights, duties, functions, and relationships of the members, the hierarchy of ranks, or the forms of government of the group. For instance, the thoroughgoing reforms carried out by Peter the Great and Alexander II in Russia, or by the Japanese government in the second part of the nineteenth century, were very radical changes, accomplished in a relatively short period. Nevertheless, they were orderly, lawful transformations effected in accordance with the provisions of the official law of Russia or Japan.

Such orderly changes are possible only under the following conditions. First, the legal norms of the group must be incessantly impressed upon the minds of the members and incorporated in their behavior through all the available means of impregnation and inculcation: suggestion and example; precepts; indefatigable enforcement, reinforced by demotion or punishment of offenders and promotion and other rewards in the case of law-abiding members; and various ingenious devices that serve to impress the norms indelibly upon the intellectual, emotional, affective, and volitional nature of the members, such as the cult of heroes, religious and ethical rites, legal rituals, ceremonial festivals, parades and exhibitions, and stimuli appealing to all the sensory perceptions of the masses. Through praise, flattery, and persuasion; advertising, slogans, and propaganda; satire and ridicule, commands, threats, and punishments, plus the pressure of other groups, the group incessantly strives to pattern the mind and shape the conduct of its members in accordance with its law-norms, developing a deep sense of group loyalty, devotion, pride, patriotism, and solidarity.[1] The second condition is that (a) for the bulk of the members the norms shall become their "second nature," controlling their mentality and conduct; (b) that the unofficial law-convictions of the members shall not sharply deviate from or contradict the norms of the official law; (c) that the proportion of the members unimpregnated by the norms and uncontrolled by them shall not be too great; (d) that the dominant element of the group shall succeed in enforcing the official law, in spite of dissenters and would-be violators.

2. Criminals and Dissenters as Disorderly Elements in Orderly Group Change

This second condition is seldom fully achieved. Only in small groups permeated with a sense of familistic solidarity, where the official law coincides with the unofficial legal convictions of all the members, is it fully achieved. In an overwhelming majority of groups and in almost all the larger groups the official law is violated (a) by members who easily succumb to temptation (ordinary criminals); (b) by members who do not fully practice what their norms preach (ordinary violators); (c) by members whose unofficial law-convictions sharply deviate from or even contradict the official law of the group (religious,

ethical, and political dissenters and protestants, or "ideological" violators).

In any extensive group there are always some members insufficiently indoctrinated with the norms of the group or any other norms. This is sometimes due to mental or physical deficiency; more often, to inefficient and even contradictory socialization, to the failure to impress them with the norms and to insist upon their application. Their personality remains unintegrated, with poorly developed and perhaps mutually contradictory "sociocultural egos" and with a comparatively strong biological egos, likewise unorganized and disharmonious (cf. Chapter 19). Such persons are "rudderless boats," thrown hither and thither by the currents of their biological drives. This type of persons makes up the bulk of the ordinary criminals and violators of group law.

In the chapters on the structure of culture and personality we have seen that there are few, if any, persons who practice one hundred per cent what they preach. This applies also to the law-norms. Even among "law-abiding" citizens there is always a tendency to avoid the performance of burdensome duties, to circumvent the unpleasant provisions of the law through secret violations, through sham observances, through bribery, or through resort to clever lawyers and court machinery.

Unofficial law-convictions change almost incessantly, hand in hand with any fundamental change in the composition of the group or in its environment. But the official law cannot incessantly change; for the enactment of basic statutes requires putting into motion the huge, complex, and expensive legislative machinery of the group. Hence its official law almost always lags behind the unofficial law-convictions of certain members (cf. Chapter 4). Such "ideological" dissenters and protestants violate the norms of the official law not because they are victims of their biological impulses but because they follow the imperatives of their unofficial norms, which they regard as more just than those of the "obsolete and unjust" official law.

---

[1] For the detailed means of so-called "social control," cf. F. E. Lumley, *Means of Social Control* (New York, 1925); E. A. Ross, *Social Control* (New York, 1902); A. D. Weeks, *The Control of Social Mind* (New York, 1923); L. L. Bernard, *Social Control* (New York, 1939); L. A. Boettiger, *Fundamentals of Sociology* (New York, 1932), Chps. 10-12, 32; P. A. Sorokin, *Crime and Punishment, Heroism and Reward* (Russian, St. Petersburg, 1914).

Another reason for the continuous generation of ideological violators is the multigroup membership of individuals (cf. Chapter 19). We have seen that the law-norms of the groups to which an individual belongs are often mutually contradictory. Obeying the norms of his religious group, he may violate certain norms of the state; following the norms of his family, he may violate the rules of his political party, and so on. Such situations arise in practically all differentiated and stratified populations.[2]

To summarize: *In virtually all extensive populations there is a certain amount of maladjustment in the form of discrepancy between the official law and the unofficial law-convictions of a part of the members, between the official laws of different groups, and between the official law and its inculcation in another part of the members. This maladjustment calls forth the phenomenon of crime or violation of the official law by ideological and ordinary criminals or offenders. Criminality generates sanctions and punishments. In this sense, crime and punishment are immanent consequences of the existence of organized groups, with their official law and its enforcement.* They constitute the normal disorderly element in an otherwise orderly change of the groups. The less the official law is supported by the members of the group, and the greater the number of its ordinary and ideological violators, the more abundant and severe tend to be the penal sanctions invoked (in groups of the same kind). In a group whose official law is imposed by an insignificant minority, where it contradicts the unofficial law-convictions of the majority, where it is weakly rooted in the mind and behavior of its members, its enforcement is possible only through the most severe punishments. This explains the severity of the punishments imposed by a conqueror upon the conquered; by a dictatorial minority upon the coerced majority; by the masters upon slaves and serfs; by colonial "civilizers" upon the colonial natives, and so on.[3] Ordinarily, however, the element of disorder involves too small a fraction of the members and too few legal relationships seriously to menace the orderly functioning of the group.

II. Revolutionary Change

1. Widening Discrepancy Between Official and Unofficial Law

The widening discrepancy between the official law of the group and the unofficial law-convictions of some of its members now and then assumes extraordinary proportions in the absence of any adequate modification of the official law to bring it into harmony with the unofficial law-convictions of an ever-increasing number of members. Thus an irreconcilable antagonism respecting the main values of the group emerges. The official law finally begins to contravene the law-convictions either of an enormous majority of the group or of a sufficiently powerful element of the membership. In this way an unbridgeable chasm appears between the system of values of the partisans of the official law and that of its opponents. If under these conditions the official law is not changed peacefully, its opponents strive to overthrow it, and the system of values defended by it, by violent, unlawful, revolutionary methods. Their efforts are usually reenforced by the violations of ordinary criminals. When the contradiction between the value systems of the defenders and opponents of the existing law increases, the proportion of the "unimpregnated violators" increases also.

2. Definition of Revolutionary Change

A comparatively sudden, rapid, and violent change of the obsolete official law of the group, or of the institutions and system of values which it represents, may be called a revolutionary change. (a) In contrast to orderly change, a revolutionary change is carried on contrary to the rules of the official law. (b) Slowly gathering momentum, a revolutionary change suddenly "explodes," as it were, proceeding at a much more rapid tempo than ordinary change. (c) A revolutionary change

---

[2] The immanent generation of ideological criminals is largely overlooked by criminologists; likewise the inherent causes of criminality itself.

[3] For a detailed factual corroboration of this proposition, cf. my *Dynamics*, Vol. II, pp. 523-627.

attacks not just one or a few norms of the official law, a few details of this or that governmental institution, or a few minor values, but the entire body of the official law or a substantial part of it, and either all social institutions (including the existing government) and the whole system of values protected by the official law, or at least several fundamental institutions and values. (d) Revolutionary change involves the direct or indirect participation of a considerable part of the membership of the group. Through (c) and (d) it differs (quantitatively and qualitatively) from the violation of certain norms of the group by its ordinary and ideological offenders, who usually attack only a few of the legal norms and constitute a comparatively small group. (e) Finally, a revolutionary change always results in the use of force and violence, either on a moderate scale or in the form of civil war entailing considerable bloodshed and destruction.

3. Varieties of Revolutionary Change

If a revolutionary change is directed exclusively against the political regime of the group, it is a *political revolution*, ranging from a comparatively limited "palace revolution" to a drastic transformation of the ruling class and the government. If a revolutionary movement attempts a violent change in the economic system of the group—its forms of property and possession, of production, distribution, and consumption—it may be called an *economic revolution*. If revolutionary movement aims primarily at a change in the religious values of the group, it may be designated as a *religious revolution*. This type is exemplified by the violent struggles of the Reformation and Counterreformation. If a revolution is directed against the existing family and marriage system, it may be correspondingly labeled. This type is illustrated by the plebeians' struggle for the *jus connubii* in Rome, by the Mazdakite and Taborite revolutions, and by such minor revolutions as those of the Mormons and other groups who have attempted to substitute polygamy for monogamy, or vice versa.

If the institutions, relationships, and values attacked are *racial* or *national* the revolutions are respectively *racial* or *nationalistic*. Finally, if a revolutionary change attempts to transform the entire body of official law and all the important institutions and values of the group —political and economic, religious and ethical, legal, and domestic—it is a *total revolution*. The Communist revolution in Russia, the Taborite revolution in Bohemia, and the oldest known revolution in ancient Egypt (*ca.* 2500 B.C., well described by its contemporary Ipuver) furnish examples of total revolutions.[4]

4. The Frequency and Movement of Revolutions

There is hardly any long-existing group which does not experience from time to time a major or minor revolutionary change. The family, caste, or social order, occupational or economic organizations, religious bodies, political parties, the state or nation, and other unibonded or multibonded groups all pass from time to time through periods of tension and violent crisis, sometimes disintegrating as a result of the strain. Though no systematic

---

[4] For a substantiation of the above and an analysis and factual corroboration of the subsequent propositions, cf. my *Sociology of Revolution* (Philadelphia-New York, 1925); my *Dynamics*, Vol. III, Chps. 12-14; and my *Calamity*, *passim*. See also Plato, *The Republic*, Bk. VIII; Aristotle, *Politics*, Bk. V; Thucydides, *History of the Peloponnesian War*, Bk. III; R. Pöhlmann, *Geschichte der sozialen Frage und des Sozialismus in der antiken Welt* (München, 1912); A. H. Gardiner, *The Admonitions of an Egyptian Sage* (Leipzig, 1909); H. Taine, *The Origins of Contemporary France* (6 Vols., New York, 1876-1894); J. de Maistre, "Considerations sur la France," *L'Oeuvres* (Lyon, 1891), Vol. I; E. Burke, *Reflections on the Revolution in France*; A. Bauer, *Essay sur les revolutions* (Paris, 1908); G. Lebon, *The Psychology of Revo-lution* (New York, 1913); T. Geiger, *Die Masse und ihre Aktion* (Stuttgart, 1926); A. J. Toynbee, *A Study of History*, Vols. IV-VI; W. H. Chamberlin, *The Russian Revolution* (New York, 1935); L. Trotsky, *The History of the Russian Revolution* (3 Vols., New York, 1936); C. Cossio, *El concepto puro de revolución* (Barcelona, 1936); A. Povina, *Sociología de la revolución* (Cordova, 1933); N. S. Timasheff, *The Great Retreat* (New York, 1945); G. S. Pettee, *The Process of Revolution* (New York, 1938); C. Brinton, *The Anatomy of Revolution* (New York, 1938); K. Kautsky, *The Social Revolution* (Chicago, 1912); M. A. Elliott and F. E. Merrill, *Social Disorganization* (New York, 1932), chapter on revolution; R. A. Orgaz, *Ensayo sobre las revoluciones* (Cordova, 1945). Cf. also the literature cited in these works.

study has been made of the frequency of these crises in different groups, it may be tentatively stated that there is no periodicity in such revolutionary upheavals, their frequency fluctuating widely not only among different groups but even among groups of the same kind. There is no perpetual trend toward either increasing or decreasing frequency of revolutions.

Such is the situation with respect to the important internal disturbances in the history of states, nations, and other major groups. The author made a study of all the important internal disturbances (revolutions, riots, revolts, and civil strife) recorded in the history of ancient Greece and Rome, Byzantium, Italy, Spain, France, Germany, Austria, England, the Netherlands, Russia, Poland, Lithuania, etc., a period extending from the sixth century B.C. to 1925 A.D. and comprising some 1622 major internal disturbances. On the basis of this systematic (and so far unique) study of revolutions, plus the study of internecine wars in China, the following conclusions were reached as to their frequency, distribution, and trends.[5]

(a) On an average one important internal disturbance occurred in most of these countries in every five to seven years, in the Netherlands once in twelve years, and in Byzantium once in seventeen years. The longest peaceful periods ranged from sixty to some ninety years, but such periods were few.

(b) There is no strict periodicity in the occurrence of revolutions.

(c) There are no particularly "orderly" and particularly "disorderly" nations, the only difference being that a nation peaceful at one period becomes disorderly at another.

(d) There is no tangible difference between various countries in respect to the violence, bloodshed, cruelty, and destructiveness of their revolutions.

(e) The duration of major disturbances fluctuates widely, ranging from a few days to several decades. The predominant duration is several weeks.

(f) The curve of the disturbances of various countries throughout their history differs widely: there is no uniform pattern of these curves for the countries studied. Nor is there any uniform pattern in the movement of these curves in the history of the same country.

(g) Neither in the history of individual countries nor in that of Europe as a whole is there any permanent trend toward more frequent and more violent revolutions or toward their disappearance. The notion of the progressive replacement of violent change by orderly evolution in the course of time is not supported by the facts.

The foregoing propositions, as well as subsequent ones, are demonstrated by the curves and indices of movement of the revolutions in the history of ancient Greece and Rome and in that of the other European countries mentioned. Here are the comparative indices of the magnitude of revolutions in these countries by centuries.[6] The indices of the total magnitude of revolutions in Greece are as follows: for the sixth century B.C., 149; for the fifth, 468; for the fourth, 320; for the third, 259; for the second (first three quarters), 36. The figures for Rome are as follows: For the fifth century B.C., 130; for the fourth, 291; for the third, 18; for the second, 158; for the first, 556. For the first century A.D., 342; for the second, 267; for the third, 475; for the fourth, 368; for the fifth (first three quarters), 142. For subsequent centuries in the rest of Europe the figures are as follows:

Century	Index of Magnitude of Disturbances
VI (three quarters)	446
VII	458
VIII	733
IX	589
X	537
XI	693
XII	763
XIII	882
XIV	827
XV	748
XVI	509
XVII	605
XVIII	415
XIX	766
XX (1901-1925)	295

[5] For the details, cf. my *Dynamics*, Vol. III, Chps. 12-14; cf. also I. S. Lee, "The Periodic Recurrence of Internecine Wars in China," *China Journal*, March-April, 1931.

[6] For the method by which the indices are derived, cf. my *Dynamics*, Vol. III, Chps. 12-14. Detailed data for each of the European countries are also given.

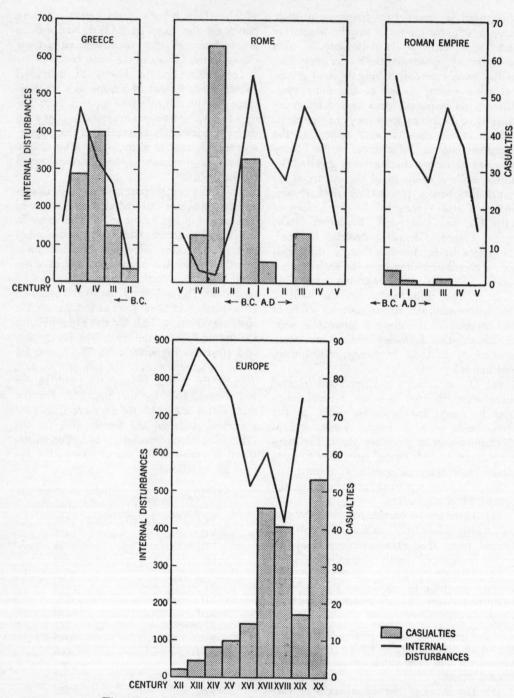

Figure 4. Movement of War and Internal Disturbances
in Greece, Rome, and Europe

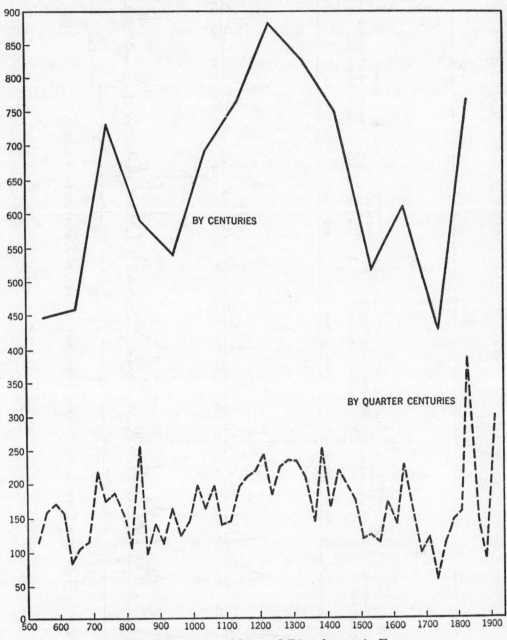

Figure 5.   Movement of Internal Disturbances in Europe.

Figures 4 and 5 show this movement of internal disturbances pictorially. Figures 6 shows the movement of civil wars in China.

(h) There is a slight tendency for internal disturbances to occur more frequently during and immediately after wars, especially in the defeated countries; but it is neither pronounced nor uniform.

(i) There is a tendency for domestic disturbances to multiply during the periods of particularly rapid development of a given civilization and during the periods of marked

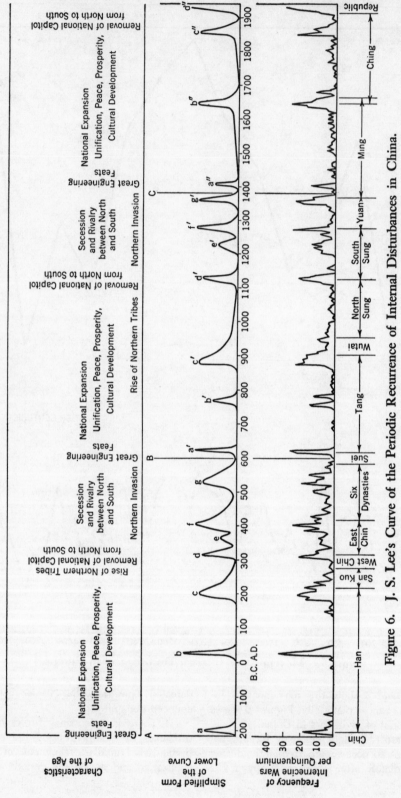

Figure 6. J. S. Lee's Curve of the Periodic Recurrence of Internal Disturbances in China.

decline and disintegration.[7] The revolutions of the first kind may be compared, according to Karl Marx, to the birth throes of a new creative order, whereas those of the second type may be likened to the agonies of dissolution.

(j) Propositions (h) and (i) may be subsumed under the proposition that, quantitatively and qualitatively, the curve of revolutions reaches its maximum in periods of transition and unsettlement of social institutions, cultural values, and norms of conduct and falls to its minimum in periods of stable and well-crystallized social institutions, cultural values, and norms of conduct.

III. Uniformities in Revolutionary Change

A fully developed major revolution entails manifold changes in various life processes of the group involved: in its vital processes; in the psychology and behavior of its population; in its social institutions and government; in its cultural values. Let us briefly sum up the uniformities in the modification of these processes in revolutionary upheavals.

1. The Cycle of Revolution

The first uniformity in revolutionary change consists in the often repeated cycle of revolution. Almost every revolution consists of two phases. The first is *the destructive phase*, in which the revolution destroys not only institutions and values that are moribund and that would perish anyway, but also institutions and cultural values that are vital, creative, and growing; these are temporarily disrupted and checked in their developments. The second is *the declining phase* of the revolution, in which the vital institutions and values re-emerge, resume their growth and induce the destructive forces of the revolution to recede. In this second phase the revolution destroys much of what it sought to accomplish in the first period, and rebuilds much of what it destroyed in its first phase. Generally only the moribund institutions, values, and trends eliminated in the first phase fail to re-establish themselves. In other words, a revolution in its second phase makes a volte-face and continues the vital processes of the prerevolutionary period, regardless of who is in the saddle, revolutionaries or counterrevolutionaries. Such is the essence of this ever-repeated cycle of revolutions, pointed out by many eminent investigators. Only the groups that perish in the first phase fail to experience it. This cycle is the key to an understanding of the bulk of the complex and numerous changes effected by revolutions.

2. The Law of Polarization

Another general uniformity in revolutionary change is the law of polarization. It relates to the opposite effects of revolution upon different elements of the population and upon their activities. The overwhelming majority of the population in normal times is neither distinctly bad nor conspicuously virtuous, neither very socially-minded nor extremely antisocial, neither markedly religious nor highly irreligious. In times of revolution this indifferent majority tends to split, the segments shifting to opposite poles and yielding a greater number of sinners and saints, social altruists and antisocial egoists, devout religious believers and militant atheists. The "balanced majority" tends to decrease in favor of extreme polar factions in the ethical, religious, intellectual, and other fields. This polarization is generated by revolutions in all fields of social and cultural life. Negative polarization usually prevails in the first, or destructive, period, whereas in the second phase the positive polarization increases and the negative declines.[8]

In the interest of economy, in subsequent formulas of changes in the first period of revolutions only the dominant negative polar-

[7] The same may be said of much milder forms of social disturbance, such as industrial strikes. They also tend to multiply in periods of prosperity and in lesser degree in periods of acute depression. Cf. A. Hansen, "Cycles of Strikes," *American Economic Review*, 1921, pp. 616-621, and J. V. Spielmans, "Strike Profiles," *Journal of Political Economy*, 1944, pp. 319-339. Spielman's study shows more precisely the relationship between the duration and number of strikes and the number of wage-earners involved.

[8] For the law of polarization and its inductive corroboration, cf. my *Calamity*, pp. 79 ff., 158 ff., Chps. 10-12, *passim*.

ization is mentioned; in the second phase only the dominant positive polarization.

3. Changes in Vital Processes

In fully developed major revolutions resulting in civil wars the *birth rate* of the population usually begins to decline nine months after the beginning of the civil war; after the end of the destructive phase it rises and during the next two or three years remains above the prerevolutionary level; then it resumes its prerevolutionary trend. The *death rate* of even the civilian population tends to increase with the outbreak of civil war. After the end of the destructive phase it drops, sometimes to a point even below the prerevolutionary level; then it resumes its prerevolutionary trend. If the revolution does not attack the family and marriage, the *marriage rate* begins to decline with the advent of the violent phase of the revolution. When the destructive phase terminates, it rises above the prerevolutionary level during the first two or three years and then returns to its prerevolutionary trend. Under these conditions the rate of *divorces or separations* tends to decline during the first phase, thereafter rising and then returning to its prerevolutionary trend. If the revolution seriously undermines the family and marriage, marriages as well as divorces greatly increase, as a rule, during the initial stage, sometimes—as in the Russian revolution—reaching a unique height amounting to an utter disorganization of the family and marriage. In the second phase both rates rapidly drop, returning eventually to their prerevolutionary levels.

Owing to destruction, the lack of vital necessities, epidemics, and terrorism, the death rate rapidly mounts, sometimes attaining an extraordinary height. For instance, during the first five years of the Russian revolution at least thirteen to fifteen million persons perished. *Suicide*, for the reasons indicated in Chapter 3, tends to decline during the first phase of a revolution, rising during the second phase, and then returning to its prerevolutionary level. *Morbidity* sharply increases. Various plagues and epidemics are typical of especially the first phase of a revolution.

Finally, the kind of *net selection* effected by revolutions is approximately *neutral* in most of them; if during the phase of terror and civil war the leaders and those mentally and otherwise more fit succumb on both sides to a greater extent than the average mediocrity, through starvation, epidemics, and other factors the weaker elements are probably decimated at a higher rate than the stronger and more fit. The Russian revolution exterminated in its civil war about two million persons. It eliminated through starvation, epidemics, etc. from eleven to thirteen millions. If the victims of the civil war were more "fit," those who perished from other causes were weaker than those who survived. The net result is approximately neutral.

The reasons for these phenomena are apparent. The increase of the mortality rate is due to the increase of hardships, the lack of necessities, famines, epidemics, and the anxiety and fear characteristic of the first phase of a revolution. With the improvement of conditions in the second phase and with the elimination of a large proportion of the weaklings during the first period, mortality declines in the second phase. Owing to the famine, hardships, and anxiety, conception and the growth of the foetus become more difficult. The percentage of amenorrhea and of venereal disease, rendering conception impossible, increases. Moreover, many prospective bridegrooms are inducted into the armies of the civil war. All this leads to a decrease of the birth rate during the first phase. In the second phase, with an improvement of conditions, with soldiers returning home, many postponed marriages are realized, which nine months later leads to an abnormally high birth rate. If the revolution attempts to destroy the family and marriage, the extraordinarily large number of sex unions concluded during the first phase of the revolution rarely produce a proportional increase in the birth rate, owing to the prevalence of contraception, abortion, venereal disease, and amenorrhea associated with such incidental sexual relations. Later on, during the second period of the revolution, with the revival of the family and of real marriage, the birth rate goes up.

With the drafting of husbands, divorce decreases in the first period when the revolution does not destroy the family and marriage. When the husbands return from the civil war in the second period, accumulated disloyalties and other causes of discord lead to an increase of divorce. If the revolution destroys the family and marriage, divorces soar during its first phase to an unprecedented level. Marriage and divorce become little more than a change of sex partners in incidental liaisons. With the revival of the family and of the sanctity of marriage during the second phase, when legal and other obstacles to divorce sharply increase, the number of divorces markedly decreases.

The decrease of suicide during the first stage of a revolution is due to a decrease in the psychosocial isolation of the individuals; with the outbreak of revolution the collective élan breaks the hard shell of the individual, as it were, and merges him with the "common soul," so to speak. With the advent of the second period the psychosocial isolation of many individuals detached from the circle of their intimate friends and placed among strangers increases; the collective élan and intoxication of the common cause decline; and disillusionment respecting the anticipated miracles of the revolution sets in. Hence the tendency to suicide increases.

Finally, starvation and other hardships, epidemics, and anxiety produce an increase of sickness and morbidity.

4. Changes in Psychology and Behavior

A considerable proportion of the population undergo notable changes in their psychology and overt behavior. In their concrete forms these are very numerous and diverse, and as such cannot be described in this work. In a generalized form they may be summed up as follows.

a. *Breakdown of Personality Structure.* Since the first period of revolutions manifests itself in a sudden collapse of social and cultural institutions and values, and since personality structure is inseparably connected with social and cultural structures, the collapse of the latter is paralleled by a corresponding breakdown of the personality structure of a considerable portion of the population. Other elements of the population, less exposed to the revolution, may not experience such a breakdown; in fact, the personality of a minority, freed from antagonistic group membership and membership in antagonistic cultural systems,

may be more strongly integrated than before (positive polarization). However, the portion that undergoes a breakdown of its personality structure is far larger than the positively polarized element. The most notable trait of this phase consists therefore in the fact that the mental apparatus of a considerable percentage of the population tends to be disorganized, becoming "recessive" (to use the terminology of psychoanalysis). This manifests itself in (1) an increase of mental disease in the form of various psychoneuroses, especially the anixety and fear complex, paranoia, schizophrenia, maniacal depression, delusions of grandeur, and *idées fixes*; (2) in an increase of mob psychology at the expense of the normal psychology of the individual; (3) in an upsurge of sadistic and similar tendencies; (4) in an enormous outburst of emotionalism and passion little controlled by reason or intellect; (5) in a replacement of the logic of common sense by that of the *loi de participation*, ascribed by Levy-Brühl to primitive man; (6) in a somewhat abnormal modification of the processes of sensation, perception, association, and reproductive imagination, these processes undergoing a "recessive" twist; (7) in a disintegration of the prerevolutionary composite social egos, and a corresponding strengthening of the biological egos, as a result of the displacement or annihilation of various groups and strata represented by the social egos of the individual. Certain new social egos are injected into individuals as a result of their affiliations with new groups and strata. Some egos are re-enforced with the growth in power of the corresponding groups and strata; others are weakened as a consequence of the weakening of the corresponding groups and strata. The net results of these processes are that the total composite personality becomes highly confused and amorphous, losing its unity, integrity, and harmony; individuals are far less controlled by their social egos and much more by their biological egos, now largely freed from the control of the social egos. (8) Revolution and everything connected with it occupy the central place in the popular mind and drive out of the field of consciousness everything not connected with the revolution. People begin to sense, think of, and evaluate everything *sub specie revolutionis*.

In the second period of the revolution the opposite process occurs: that of the reintegration, resocialization, and consolidation of psychical processes and the structure of the egos. With the improvement of material and other conditions and the elimination or mental rehabilitation of the fanatical and unbalanced elements, the balanced and especially the highly integrated and positively polarized elements finally succeed in restoring the normal mentality of virtually the entire population.

b. *Effect on Overt Behavior.* In the field of overt behavior a similar negative polarization dominates the first phase of revolution, reflecting the typical collapse of social and cultural structures. It may be styled the process of desocializing, "deculturizing," and "biologizing" the conduct of the population particularly exposed to the revolutionary impact. Since conduct is largely a response to stimuli exerted by the groups and strata to which one belongs, when these groups and strata collapse their members tend to be deprived of their corresponding social egos. Their biological egos are thus liberated from the control of the social norms and become the decisive factor in the determination of social conduct. However, owing to the fact that the human biological egos, in contradistinction to the excellent reflex and instinctive apparatus of animals, are poorly integrated and function inefficiently, the human beings controlled by such a biological mechanism easily become "the worst of beasts," as Aristotle and Plato observed. They are driven hither and thither in response to the whim of diverse and often contradictory urges only slightly controlled either by the mechanism of reflexes and instincts or by sociocultural forces. This explains the violent, cruel, destructive, and frequently unstable and contradictory behavior of mobs in the first phase of revolution. (The opposite, or positive, polarization also occur, but on a much smaller scale.)

In the second phase of revolutions the opposite processes assert themselves. Positive polarization prevails over negative polarization in this phase. It is initiated by the catastrophic consequences of the first phase, whereby the population is faced with the alternatives of either perishing or restoring a modicum of solidarity and cultural order. Through the efforts of the positively polarized minority and the stern decrees and penalties of the government, the process of rehabilitation proceeds until the necessary level of sociality is attained. The groups that fail in this effort usually cease to exist as social and cultural individualities.

The desocialization, or "biologization," characteristic of the first phase of revolutions manifests itself in many forms, including civil war between the members of the same group, with its unspeakable bloodshed and cruelty, and a tremendous increase of antisocial acts in the relationships of the population in general. For instance, whereas the average annual number of executions in Russia in the orderly period of 1881-1905 fluctuated between 9.6 and 18.6, in the revolutionary years 1905-1908 it rose to 547 in 1906, 1139 in 1907, and 1340 in 1908; then it subsided, falling to 73 in 1911. During the revolution of 1917 and the subsequent years it reached the fantastic level of some 150,000 annual executions in the years 1918-1922. With the passing of the destructive phase it began slowly to decline. A similar phenomenon is exhibited by all revolutions,[9] from the Egyptian revolution of *ca.* 2500 B.C. to the present day. Says Ipuver, a contemporary of the Egyptian revolution: "A man smites his brother of the same mother. . . . Behold a man is slain by the side of his brother. . . . A man regards his son as his enemy. What men do is iniquity." Declares Thucydides, a witness of the Corcyrean revolution of 427 B.C.: "Death thus raged in every shape; and there was no length to which violence did not go; sons were killed by their fathers. . . . Some were slain for private hatred; others, by their debtors."[10]

The infliction of bodily and mental torture, rape, deprivation of freedom, theft, banishment and ostracism, and the like are typical of the relationships of members of a revolutionary society during the phase in question. To be sure, the positive polarization of conduct in the form of altruism and self-sacrifice is not lacking; but it is much weaker and involves a much smaller proportion of the population than the negative polarization.

[9] For the data, cf. my *Dynamics*, Vol. II, pp. 600 ff., and *Calamity*, pp. 184 ff.

[10] For similar testimony, cf. my *Calamity*, pp. 184 ff., and *Sociology of Revolution*, Chps. 4-10.

c. *Speech Reactions and Corresponding Ideologies.* In the field of oral and written speech reactions and the corresponding ideologies the change, observable even before the revolution and during its first phase, consists in loosening the tongue from all restraints and inhibitions. Wholesale condemnation and vilification of the old regime or of the opposite faction—its personnel, institutions, values, and actions—floods the country, as well as unqualified justification and glorification, in simple and complex ideological forms, of everything pertaining to one's own faction, however horrible it may be. "Down with . . . !" "Long live . . ." become the guiding mottoes. Unlimited freedom of speech is demanded for one's faction, and freedom of speech is entirely denied to one's opponents. The ethos of the flood of speech reactions is mainly hatred, enmity, and animosity directed against one's opponents, and passionate enthusiasm for one's own faction, only to a slight extent love, altruism, or sociality. Speeches, articles, pamphlets, treatises, sermons, songs, plays, etc. are all marked by these traits, and their total volume enormously increases.

In the second phase of revolutions the opposite process begins to assert itself. Various inhibitions and limitations of freedom of speech and the press are introduced and enforced by the dominant power. Although the latter still reserves complete freedom of speech for its own faction and denies it to its opponents, increasing moderation gradually appears. Censorship is established; silence is imposed upon the conquered factions side by side with progressively increasing restrictions upon the freedom of speech enjoyed by the dominant faction itself. Presently a modicum of freedom of speech is achieved even by the vanquished parties. "Down with . . . !" is progressively replaced by the slogan "Restrain!" and liberating ideologies by restraining ideologies. The favorite mottoes of the first phase give place to opposite mottoes in the second. Eventually the population enters its normal post-revolutionary phase.[11]

d. *Property Relationships.* In the field of property relationships the first period is marked, among the revolutionaries and the poorer classes, by weakening or collapse of most of the norms prohibiting the violation of the property rights of others, especially of the well-to-do and the counterrevolutionary groups. Within the latter groups it is marked by a decline in the measures for the protection of their property against such violations. As a result, economic revolutions lead to wholesale confiscation, nationalization, communization, and equalization of the possessions of the upper, well-to-do classes and often of the middle classes. To a lesser extent this process occurs even in political and other types of revolution. An increase of crimes against property is a regular consequence of the change of behavior in this field. An upsurge of greed and cupidity is another regular satellite of the change in question.

In the second phase of revolutions the converse process asserts itself, that of re-establishing the inhibitions against the violation of the property rights of the new well-to-do and governing groups; re-enforcement of protective actions within such classes; suppression of crimes against property; limitation of unbridled greed; and often the "denationalization" and "decommunization" of property. This is achieved through drastic punishment of would-be violators by the governing class. Even communist and socialist revolutions are no exception to the foregoing rule. Ordinarily the communists and socialists who in the first phase have clamored most loudly for the nationalization and equalization of property, in the second phase, when they are in the saddle, change their attitude, re-establishing economic inequality, vigorously protecting their own possessions, and ruthlessly suppressing crimes against property. In brief, in a somewhat modified form they restore the sacredness of property rights and become fervent partisans of the *beati possidentes.* Even in the Communist revolution in Russia, where the land and the large-scale factories remained nationalized, a new form of economic inequality appeared, with a new rich governmental managerial bureaucracy, with vigorous suppression of crimes against property, and with unqualified glorification of the regime of economic inequality. This tragi-comedy has repeated itself many times in the various economic, com-

---

[11] For the detailed facts of the transformation of speech reactions and ideologies, cf. my *Sociology of Revolution*, Ch. 4.

munistic, socialistic, and equalitarian revolutions.[12]

e. *Sex Behavior and Relationships.* A somewhat similar relaxation and collapse of inhibitions takes place in the sphere of sex behavior and relationships in the first phase of revolutions. In those that undermine the family and marriage, the collapse is most thoroughgoing, resulting in a riotous freedom of sex activities. In the Soviet revolution in Russia, the Taborite revolution in Bohemia, and the Mazdakite revolution in ancient Persia sexual license manifested itself also legally, in the form of laws dissolving the family and marriage and sanctioning free sex liaisons. In revolutions not directly involving the family and marriage a perceptible breakdown of sex inhibitions and an upsurge of sexual license also regularly occurs, though to a lesser degree than in the revolutions of the foregoing type. In addition to illicit sex relations among the young, marital infidelity, and an increase of divorces and separations, the first phase is marked by such sex crimes as seduction, rape, and various forms of perversion.

In a much smaller section of the population the opposite polarization takes place, in the form of a purification of sexual life—of marital fidelity, chastity, and even asceticism.

In the second phase the opposite trend sets in. It is initiated by recognition of the disastrous results of the sexual license of the first phase, by purposeful activity on the part of the positively polarized elements, and by the laws and punitive measures of the government. These measures now curb sex freedom; exalt the sacredness of marriage and the family; glorify marital fidelity and chastity; and penalize fornication, adultery, seduction, and the like. The Communist revolution in Russia affords a conspicuous example of this transformation of sex behavior during the first and second periods. Other revolutions likewise conform to the "two-phase law" under discussion.[13]

f. *Labor Activities and Behavior.* A similar cycle is typical of labor activities and behavior.

In the first phase of revolutions productivity and efficiency decline among large sections of the industrial and clerical workers and even among managerial and professional groups. Strikes, reduction of working hours, and even total abstinence from labor increase apace.

In the second period the process reverses itself. Necessity dictates the motto "He who does not work shall not eat." Under the pressure of starvation, re-enforced by stern measures on the part of the new government, strenuous discipline is imposed upon the workers, not infrequently exceeding in its rigor that prevailing before the revolution. This is especially true of communist and other totalitarian revolutions, which nationalize labor and subject it to the management of the government bureaucracy.[14]

g. *Ethical and Religious Conduct.* An analogous transformation takes place in ethical and religious conduct. A sharp polarization into "sinners" and "saints," into militant atheists and devout believers appears, but the negative polarization into sinners and atheists is much more pronounced in the first period of revolutions than the positive polarization into saints and fervent believers. Hence an increase of crimes, immorality, and antisocial conduct and a decline of religious sentiment and fervor regularly occur in that phase in practically all major revolutions. In the second phase the opposite trend sets in, leading, in various forms, to a revival of religious sentiment and the emergence of more highly ethical and less antisocial conduct in the revolutionary society.[15]

With a corresponding variation the same may be said of other spheres of human behavior and relationship. The law of polarization and the two-phase cycle of overt behavior are outlined above very schematically; in reality, these uniformities manifest themselves in much more diverse and complex forms than those indicated.

5. Changes in Social Structures

a. *In Intergroup Social Differentiation.* Owing to a sudden and large-scale transfer

---

[12] For the concrete facts, cf. my *Sociology of Revolution*, Ch. 5, and *Calamity*, Ch. 15.

[13] For the details, cf. my *Sociology of Revolution*, Ch. 6. For the Russian revolution, cf. my *Russia and the United States*, pp. 182-184; N. S. Timasheff, *The Great Retreat*, Ch. 13.

[14] For the details, cf. my *Sociology of Revolution*, Ch. 7.

[15] For the details, cf. my *Calamity*, Chps. 10-12, and *Sociology of Revolution*, Chps. 7-9.

of social relationships from group to group, many groups within the revolutionary population disappear and new groups appear; many groups suddenly decline in their membership and other groups increase in size. As a result, intergroup differentiation undergoes an extraordinary change. In the first phase of revolutions, when the prerevolutionary lines of intergroup differentiation are effaced, the entire intergroup structure of the population becomes blurred and gravely impaired. In the second phase a new system of intergroup differentiation emerges.

b. *In Intergroup Stratification.* A similar dislocation occurs in the relative position of various groups. The previously dominant religious or political party or social estate sinks to a lower level, whereas the formerly disfranchised sect, faction, or party is elevated to a dominant position. In the first phase the intergroup stratification becomes confused and chaotic; in the second it grows in definiteness and clarity.[16]

c. *In Intragroup Differentiation.* Intragroup differentiation undergoes a like transformation. Owing to the collapse of the official law and of the intragroup relationships of the members, their rights and duties, functions and roles become unsettled and confused. An upstart now seeks to perform the functions of a monarch, and a monarch is compelled to discharge those of a prisoner; a private plays the role of a general, and a general the role of a gardener, and so on. In the second phase the internal structure of the group is rebuilt in a new form, crystallized, and solidified. A new official law emerges, with a corresponding distribution of rights and duties, functions and roles, among the members.

d. *In Intragroup Stratification.* In the first phase the intragroup stratification also crumbles. Its upper strata are cut off, and the whole pyramid flattens into a kind of trapezium. Several of the previous lower strata are elevated, either in their entirety or in part. The group as a whole suggests a territory shaken by an earthquake, with the upper, middle, and lower strata moving upward or downward, some tilted at a crazy angle, others shattered and dispersed here and there.

In the second phase a new stratification be-

16 For the details, cf. my *Calamity*, Chps. 6-7.

gins to crystallize. The height of the stratification increases, and the trapezium is reconverted into a social pyramid, of a somewhat different height and profile than before, with a mixture of old and new elements in each stratum. The hierarchy of ranks, of superior and inferior authorities, reappears and becomes stabilized.

6. Changes in the Mechanism of Social Testing, Selection, and Distribution of Individuals

In the first phase the previous mechanism is disrupted and ceases to function efficiently. The principle "to everyone according to his ability" is disregarded much more than in normal times. Its place is now taken by a different principle: "According to devotion and faithfulness to the dominant political party." Ability, talent, and training count for little. If persons with such qualifications are opposed to the dominant party, they are demoted, persecuted, or executed. If they are neutral, they are not promoted and may even be demoted. "Revolution does not need scientists"; therefore the French Revolution executes Lavoisier and appoints ignorant or mediocre chemists. The Russian revolution dismisses the rector of the University of St. Petersburg, the eminent biologist Shimkevitch, and appoints a mere freshman, Zweiback. It dismisses the dean of the same university, replacing him with Mr. Serebriakov, a semiliterate sailor from the Baltic fleet. Similar appointments, promotions, and demotions are made on a mass scale. As a result the bulk of the persons distributed among the various strata, ranks, and positions during the first phase have little aptitude for their functions. Consequently the social life of the population begins increasingly to suffer. Neither economic, political, scientific, technical, cultural, nor military functions are performed satisfactorily. Alarming maladjustments and suffering, which threaten to undermine the power of the dominant party, finally force the government and the population to restore, at least in part, the mechanisms for the testing, selection, and distribution of members.

This process sets in toward the end of the first phase and continues in the second. A remote approximation to the principle "To everyone according to his ability" reappears, begin-

ning with military and economic positions and
ending with cultural and professional posts.
Faithfulness to the ruling faction becomes a
less important criterion for appointment to responsible positions, giving place to talent and
competence. Hence many incapable upstarts
that gained a foothold in the upper strata in
the first phase are supplanted, and many capable persons are elevated. By the end of the
second period the occupants of various strata
constitute a mixture of the old and the new
elements, prerevolutionary aristocracy intermingled with the new aristocracy in the upper
layers, and old and new "under dogs" in the
lower layers.[17]

7. Changes in Social and Cultural Processes

*Voluntary and especially involuntary migra-
tion, general and differential horizontal mobility, and vertical mobility increase on a vast
scale.* In the first phase, owing to the weakening of the mechanism of testing and selection,
they are indiscriminate and chaotic. Social
life suggests a gigantic waterfall uprooting a
mass of individuals and tossing them hither
and thither, with little chance to occupy a
given position for any length of time. Individuals change their economic, occupational, political, territorial, family, religious, and other
affiliations much more rapidly than in normal
times, and the changes are far more striking.
Today's multimillionaire is tomorrow's pauper;
yesterday's slave is today's dictator; within a
short period an army private becomes a general, and a general becomes a prisoner. "Indeed, the land [that is, the order of things]
turns as does a potter's wheel. He who was a
robber is now lord of wealth; the rich man is
plundered." Thus Ipuver, a contemporary of
the Egyptian revolution of about 2500 B.C.,
sums up the situation.[18]

Economic life becomes disorganized during
the first phase. Economic inequality decreases
through equalization, confiscation, and the nationalization of wealth. The standard of living
declines, sometimes catastrophically. Poverty,
misery, and mass famine often ensue. In the
second phase the process of equalization and
confiscation declines, economic inequality
grows, and the standard of living rises.

Political life becomes unsettled in the first
phase of a revolution. With the former government overthrown and a new one not firmly
established, political confusion and anarchy
reign. One regime rapidly succeeds another.
Eventually a dominant faction emerges. For
the maintenance of its power it has to resort
to dictatorial, autocratic, and tyrannical
methods, supplemented by certain constructive
reforms. Regimentation, coercion, and terrorism characterize the latter part of the first
phase, as well as the second phase. The government exterminates thousands, hundreds of
thousands, or even millions of its opponents;
millions are imprisoned, confined in concentration camps, or banished. Eventually coercion and terrorism gradually subside, and a
new period of order and normality is ushered
in, marked by the restoration of civil and
political liberty. All compartments of culture—
science and philosophy, religion and ethics,
literature and the fine arts, politics and jurisprudence, etc.—are indelibly stamped with
the imprint of the revolution, which becomes
the central object of attention.[19]

Cultural life likewise undergoes many diverse transformations. In the first phase most
or a considerable part of the cultural values
of the old regime are denounced and vilified
by the revolution and its partisans. In total
revolutions such as the Russian Communist
revolution, almost all social institutions and
cultural values—science and philosophy, religion and the fine arts, ethics, mores, law, politics, economics, etc.—are branded as "bourgeois," "capitalist," or "degenerate," and an
attempt is made to replace them with revolutionary institutions and values. Likewise the
creators of these values, eminent statesmen,
poets and writers, composers, scientists and
philosophers, religious and moral leaders, are
denounced as "mouthpieces of the degenerate
aristocracy or bourgeoisie."

In the second period the opposite process
sets in, that of reinstating and exalting most
of these values and their creators. Conversely,
the revolutionary pseudo-values substituted for
the eternal values in the first phase are now
usually repudiated and fall into oblivion. Here

---

[17] For the details, cf. my *Sociology of Revolution*,
Ch. 12.

[18] For the details, cf. my *Sociology of Revolution*,
Ch. 12, and *Calamity*, Ch. 6.

[19] Cf. my *Calamity*, Ch. 9.

are a few typical illustrations. In the first phase the Russian revolution denounced "bourgeois science" and tried to create a system of revolutionary, proletarian mathematics, physics, chemistry, and biology, and social and humanitarian sciences. By the end of the nineteen-twenties it had to abandon this fatuous attempt and reinstate the traditional exact sciences, as well as, later on, most of the humanistic and social sciences. In the first period the revolution imprisoned, banished, or executed a host of genuine scientists and scholars and disparaged many of the eminent scientists and scholars of the past. In the second phase it began to praise and cherish them and to exalt the most illustrious of them.

In the first phase the revolution persecuted religion as "the opiate of the people's mind," exterminated thousands of religious leaders, closed many churches, dissolved religious organizations, and slandered foremost religious leaders of Russia and other countries. In the second phase, at the beginning of the nineteen-thirties, it mitigated and then abandoned the persecution of religion, legalized religious organizations, extolled notable religious leaders, and reversed its position in general.

In the first phase it denounced all idealistic philosophies and philosophers and discredited such Russian poets and writers as Pushkin, Tolstoi, and Dostoevski, composers and musicians like Chaikovski and Rimski-Korsakoff, and the czars, statesmen, and military leaders. In the second phase it reversed its position in this respect.

In the first phase the revolution endeavored to destroy the monogamic family and marriage, the prerevolutionary system of education, manners and mores, sports and recreation. It

banned even such details as the uniforms worn by students and the titles and shoulder epaulettes of military officers. The second phase ushered in the usual reaction.

Only moribund cultural values are permanently extinguished in the first phase of a revolution. Practically all the vital values finally reassert themselves. Just as a revolutionary group comes into power on the crest of the wave ushering in the first phase of a revolution, so it can survive in the second phase only through riding the reverse wave—through a volte-face and drastic readjustment.[20]

Such are the basic uniformities in the manifold changes inaugurated by revolutions. They mean much more than a superficial change of government or of the personnel of the various strata. Some societies cannot survive the havoc wrought during the first phase and perish as social groups. Others withstand the ordeal.

In any case, the cost in human life, suffering, and cultural values is so great that it is evident that orderly, evolutionary processes of change are distinctly preferable from every standpoint. If Russia had been spared the Communistic revolution, it would have achieved greater progress politically, economically, intellectually, morally, aesthetically, and otherwise, as indicated by the rapid tempo of its advance in all these fields from the middle of the nineteenth century up to 1914.

Incidentally, it may be pointed out that the latter phenomenon disproves the common assumption that revolutions of the Russian type occur only, or principally, in stagnant societies. On the contrary, they generally occur in societies characterized by a particularly rapid development.[21]

---

[20] Cf. my *Sociology of Revolution*, Chps. 13-16, and my *Russia and the United States*, Ch. 9.

[21] Cf. my *Russia and the United States*, Ch. 7, and N. S. Timasheff, "On the Russian Revolution," *Review of Politics*, July, 1942.

Chapter 32. Fluctuation of Peace and War in Intergroup Relationships

I. Orderly and Disorderly Change of Constellation of Groups

1. Recurrence of War in Changing Intergroup Relationships

Like the intragroup changes, the intergroup relationships in a given constellation of interacting groups also incessantly change. This change proceeds for the most part in an orderly and peaceful manner, but now and then it assumes a disorderly and violent character, often resulting in bloody internecine struggles. Such violent interludes occur in the history of almost all long-existing groups: nationalities and states, territorial communities, political parties, religious organizations, occupational groups, castes, social estates and classes, tribes, clans, families, and other unibonded and multibonded groups.

2. Varieties of Wars

In accordance with the character of the warring groups there are internationality and interstate wars, inter-political-party wars, interreligious-group wars, interoccupational wars, intercaste wars, inter-social-class or inter-social-estate wars, intertribal and interclan wars, interfamily feuds, and so on.

Side by side with such wars there are also the wars between different kinds of groups: the state and the church, occupational groups and the nationality, the nation and economic groups, social classes and the state, and so on.

Though, as we shall see in the next chapter, most wars are fought for the sake of several values, nevertheless in many cases a single basic value becomes the paramount cause. Wars are fought primarily for economic values, for political values, for nationalistic values, for religious values, for ethical and juridical values, for the values of freedom or domination, and even for scientific, philosophical, and aesthetic values.

3. Frequency, Duration, Cycles, Trends, and Movement of Wars

Though lesser wars between various social groups, with the exception of states, have been inadequately studied, it may be tentatively stated (a) that the frequency of wars in the shifting interrelationships of various groups fluctuates strongly from one constellation of groups to another and from one period to another; (b) that even in the interrelationships of groups of the same kind the frequency fluctuates from period to period; (c) that there is in general no strict periodicity in the alternation of warlike and peaceful periods; (d) that there is scarcely any perceptible historical trend toward the abolition of war.

Such are the conclusions derived from a systematic study of all the recorded major interstate wars (some 967 in number) in the history of Greece, Rome, Austria, Germany, Eng-

496

land, France, the Netherlands, Spain, Italy, Russia, Poland, and Lithuania from 500 B.C. to 1925, A.D.[1] Taking as a measure of magnitude the size of the casualty lists per million of the respective populations, the figures are as follows for each specified century.

For Greece the index of magnitude for the fifth century B.C. is 29; for the fourth, 36-48; for the third, 18-33; for the second, 3-3.6. For Rome the index for the fourth century B.C. is 12; for the third, 63; for the first, 33; for the first century A.D., 5; for the third, 13. If we take the entire Roman Empire, the indices are 3 for the first century B.C.; 0.7 for the first century A.D.; and 1.3 for the third century A.D.

For Europe as a whole the indices are as follows:

Century	Index of Magnitude of War
XII	2-2.9
XIII	3-5
XIV	6-9
XV	8-11
XVI	14-16
XVII	45
XVIII	40
XIX	17
XX (1901-1925)	52

Figure 4 shows the trends pictorially.

With the growth of population the casualties naturally increased sharply, whereas the total casualties of the wars from the twelfth to the nineteenth century inclusive amounted to some fourteen millions, those of the First World War reached some twenty millions, while those of the Second World War exceeded fifty millions. During the last three centuries, not only has the size of the armies notably increased but also the number of casualties in proportion to the strength of these armies, as indicated by the following figures.

Century	Casualties in Terms of Percentages of Army Enrollment
XII	2.5
XIII	2.9
XIV	4.6
XV	5.7
XVI	5.9
XVII	15.7
XVIII	14.6
XIX	16.3
XX	38.9[2]

The invention of gunpowder and similar devices for the more effective elimination of the enemy is one of the principal reasons for the increasingly destructive character of warfare in the course of these centuries. Another important reason for this characteristic is the increasing continuity of actual fighting during the wars of the present century in contradistinction to those of the past—notably the Hundred Years' War and Thirty Years' War—in which battles were often separated by long intervals of relative inactivity amounting to an armed truce.

On the basis of my studies, and those of Q. Wright and J. S. Lee (cited) the following conclusions may be drawn respecting the frequency, movement, and trends of wars between large and powerful groups.

(a) In the history of states and nations a war occurs on an average in every two or three years. In every hundred years of the history of the following nations or states the percentage of years marked by war was 57 for ancient Greece, 41 for ancient Rome, 40 for Austria, 28 for Germany, 44 for Holland, 67 for Spain, 36 for Italy, 50 for France, 56 for England, 46 for Russia, 58 for Poland and Lithuania, and 39 for the United States (exclusive of wars with the Indians). If the Indian wars are included, the figures for the United States exceed 60 per cent.

These figures, of course, do not mean that the nations in question actually devoted as many years to warfare as the data suggest; for many wars lasted less than a full year. Never-

---

[1] For the detailed figures and other relevant data, cf. my *Dynamics*, Vol. III, Chps. 9-11. My pioneer study has since been repeated along somewhat similar lines in the substantial work of Q. Wright, *A Study of War* (2 Vols.) (Chicago, 1942), which covers several other aspects of war phenomena. Wright's curves of the movement of wars agree essentially with my curves. An extensive bibliography is given in these works. For further literature, cf. my *Theories*, Ch. 6.

---

[2] In the First World War. In the Second World War the percentage was probably much higher for Russia, Germany, and other leading belligerents. For the sources of these and other figures, cf. my *Dynamics*, Vol. III.

theless, the figures show that the frequency of war is considerably higher than most of us usually think.

Moreover, the average of one war every two years does not mean that wars are distributed evenly. There are certain periods when warfare goes on uninterruptedly for a number of years, even for decades; and there are other periods marked for a number of years, even for one or two decades, by peaceful conditions. However, periods of peace as long as a quarter of a century have been exceedingly rare in the history of these countries, and such a phenomenon as an entire century of peace (in the case of Holland) is almost unique.

(b) The data indicate, further, that there are no marked differences between nations in respect to their peacefulness or belligerency. If Germany has exhibited a lower frequency than other nations, this is because its wars were much more substantial in their magnitude than those of other nations. The principal difference is merely that a certain nation is peaceful at a given period and militant at another, whereas in another nation the converse is true.

(c) The data show also that democracies and republics are not more peaceful than autocracies and monarchies, that with an increase of literacy, educational institutions, scientific discoveries, and technological inventions war has not tended to decrease. The medieval centuries were predominantly monarchical and autocratic, illiterate, and possessed of very few scientific discoveries and technological inventions; yet the level of war was low. In the subsequent centuries, beginning with the thirteenth, discoveries and inventions, literacy and education grew steadily, especially in the nineteenth and twentieth centuries (cf. Chapter 41); yet wars constantly increased from the twelfth to the eighteenth century, and in the twentieth reached a magnitude probably unequaled in the entire history of the human race.[3] After the thirteenth century, monarchies came to be more and more limited, and beginning with the end of the eighteenth century they tended to disappear in favor of republics and democracies. After the First World War they almost entirely disappeared. Nevertheless, wars grew in number from the thirteenth to the seventeenth century, increased enormously at the end of the eighteenth and the beginning of the nineteenth century, and reached their maximum in the present century.[4]

Applying the same method of concomitant variation to the curve of the movement of war and its magnitude in different countries, one is forced to reject as invalid the theory that prosperous societies are less belligerent than poor societies; that in periods of prosperity war tends to decrease while in times of depression it tends to increase; that a decline of religious sentiment operates in favor of peace; that relativity of values, utilitarian ethics, utilitarian rationality, empiricism, positivism, pragmatism, skepticism, and so on, tend to inhibit warlike tendencies. Most of these and similar forms of "patented insurance" against war, so widely accepted by statesmen, scholars,[5] journalists, and the common people, either are negative in the effects or actually operate in favor of war.

(d) There is no strict periodicity in the occurrence, frequency, and fluctuations of war magnitude.[6]

(e) The duration of wars fluctuates widely. But most of the major wars exhibit a modal duration of from 2.5 to 4.5 years.

(f) In the history of a nation wars tend to multiply during the periods of political, social, economic, and cultural growth and expansion, as well as during those of its decline and decay.[7]

---

[3] Experimental studies of solidarity show also that there is no close connection between intellectual alertness and high morality and altruism. (See above, Chapter 6.)

[4] For the increase of wars with the growth of democracy, cf. A. Toynbee, op. cit., Vol. IV, pp. 143 ff.; also Q. Wright, op. cit., Ch. 22.

[5] These theories as sponsored by Q. Wright in his Study of War (Chps. 8, 14, 19, 37, passim) are not borne out by even his own data. Thus, his own evidence shows that the most primitive peoples— that is, the least literate—are the most peaceful;

that with an increase of "liberalism," "humanism," "modernism," and "relativism" wars have not decreased, and so on.

[6] Q. Wright's claim of a periodicity of fifty years in the increase and decrease of war remains unproved. He himself claims it for only the last three centuries; but even for these centuries it is very doubtful. (Cf. Wright, op. cit., pp. 227 ff.; also my Dynamics, Vol. III, pp. 352-360.)

[7] Cf. my Dynamics, Vol. III, pp. 363-370. A. Toynbee's contention that wars occur chiefly in connection with the dissolution of civilizations is

(g) In the history of a given constellation of interacting nations or groups wars tend to increase during periods of acute transition and change occurring nonsynchronously in the nations or groups involved. The periods of transition from one fundamental type of culture to another—for instance, from the sensate to the ideational or idealistic type, or vice versa—are those in which wars attain their maximum height. With the crystallization of any of these types of culture the curve tends to decline.

(h) One of the long-time cycles in the history of war is represented by the transition from *total* war during the early stages of human history and in that of many preliterate groups, where the entire population is involved, to *the wars waged by professional soldiers* or by a relatively small part of the nation, and finally to the intensely totalitarian type of wars characteristic of our own time.

The initial thesis gives place to antithesis and finally to synthesis.[8]

(i) The evolution of war magnitude in the history of nations does not reveal any uniform curve of fluctuation. Instead we observe sharply different curves for different nations.[9]

(j) There is no perpetual historical trend toward either a decrease or an increase of war. The process fluctuates, exhibiting short-time trends of either kind and then a reversal or other change. The theories claiming a progressive pacification of the race constitute merely wishful thinking.[10] The unprecedented outburst of wars in the twentieth century, the bloodiest and most turbulent century in human history, is sufficient in itself to refute such utopian theories, to say nothing of the trend of war during the preceding centuries. The only groups which have enjoyed freedom from war have been a few primitive preliterate clans and tribes!

II. The Social and Cultural Effects of War upon the Belligerent Nations and Other Groups

Like the process of revolution, the war process is woven of many strands in the constellation of the warring groups. In essence most of them are similar to those of revolutions. As in revolutionary changes, there is also the phase of "conversion," on the outbreak of war, and that of "reconversion" when peace returns. The processes of the reconversion period are in part the reverse of those of the conversion period. Here is a list of the most important uniform changes characteristic of periods of war.

1. Change in Vital Processes During War

The change in vital processes is similar to that effected by revolutions, with the exception that the marriage rate in strenuous wars entailing the drafting of a considerable percentage of the youth of marriageable age declines, as a rule, with the outbreak of war and continues to do so until the end of hostilities. During the first two or three years after the

armistice it rises above the prewar level, owing to the realization of many postponed marriages, and then resumes the prewar trend. In some cases, when a society does not immediately throw itself wholeheartedly into the struggle, there is a temporary rise in the marriage rate at the beginning of war.

The divorce rate tends to drop with the outbreak of war; but upon its conclusion, when long-accumulated maladjustments come to a head, the divorce rate ordinarily soars during the first two or three years and then returns to its prewar level. With some variations, selectivity and morbidity (including suicide) follow the pattern typical of periods of revolution.[11]

2. Changes in Mental Life

In mental life war, like revolution, operates along the line of the law of polarization. (a) In combatants exposed to the dangers and privations of battle it *accentuates mental disorders and functional neuroses*; the same is

---

highly doubtful. Cf. A. Toynbee, *op. cit.*, Vols. III-V, *passim*.

[8] Cf. my *Dynamics*, Vol. III, pp. 360 ff.

[9] For the curves for various nations, cf. *Ibid.*, Chps. 9-11.

[10] For a survey of such claims, cf. my *Theories*, Ch. 4.

[11] For the data and literature, cf. my *Theories*, pp. 329-338.

true of the civilian population exposed to the dangers and hardships of war. A smaller proportion of the combatants and civilians are affected positively; their mental life becomes more strongly integrated than in peacetime. (b) *The field of consciousness of the combatants as well as the civilians tends to be dominated by ideas, images, associations, and judgments directly or indirectly related to war.* (c) As in revolutions, there is an outburst of emotionalism, passion, and hysteria, which usually exhibit the opposite extremes: *fear and courage, hatred* of the enemy and of those who hinder the war effort, and *ardent affection* for one's country and for those who undergo danger, suffering, and hardship on its behalf. The sense of patriotism is generally intensified except in unpopular wars. (d) *The disintegration of the constellation of individual egos also occurs in wartime, but far less markedly than in revolutions.* The constellation of social groups and strata in the belligerent population partially changes, but does not ordinarily collapse, as in revolutions. The nation goes to war preserving virtually intact its structure of groups and strata. The individual continues to be embedded in most of his groups as before the war. Hence the structure of his egos is altered far less than in revolutions. Some of his affiliations are severed, and certain new ones are established, but on a much smaller scale than in revolutions. Only in wars that lead to the virtual collapse of the group structure of the nation does the disintegration of the individual's egos and of the integrity of his personality, become as marked as in revolutions. The principal psychological change consists in the cleavage of one's personality into two opposing selves, the one animated by hatred for the enemy and the lust to kill and destroy, the other by a sense of love, self-sacrifice, and patriotic devotion vis-à-vis one's country and its loyal citizens. (e) *Many opinions, evaluations, attitudes, and ideologies undergo an acute change, both in the armed forces and in the civilian population, with the outbreak of war, and change again, sometimes in the opposite direction, soon after the armistice.*[12] Many a prewar

pacifist becomes militant upon the declaration of hostilities, and many a militarist turns pacifist after the war. Many a fervent peacetime protagonist of freedom clamors in time of war for its drastic limitation and for the imposition of ironclad discipline. The military profession, often disparaged in peaceful times, tends to be exalted in time of war, and frequently loses its glamor after the armistice. Many ideologies popular in peacetime are branded as "treason" or "fifth-column propaganda" in time of war, and so on.

3. Changes in Overt Behavior

In the field of overt behavior the main transmutations among the combatants are as follows. (a) Activities directly or indirectly unrelated to the war effort tend to disappear, or are weakened or driven into the background, whereas the activities connected with war tend to increase. Combatants are frequently compelled to refrain from eating, sleeping, bathing and many other activities invariably performed in normal times. On the other hand, they often have to march for hours, undergo extreme hardships, and expose themselves to grave danger. Luxuries and even ordinary comforts have to be dispensed with. War tends to transform the human organism into a mere mechanism. In a lesser degree much the same is true of the civilian population. War eliminates hundreds of public and private activities that fail to promote or actually hinder the war effort, and introduces and reinforces hundreds of other activities that make for victory. The profoundness of these changes is suggested by the terms "war mobilization," "war conversion," and "postwar reconversion." (b) Among the combatants engaged in battle the activities motivated by fear and directed to liberation from it enormously increase, to say nothing of various purely physiological processes induced by fear, such as urination and hysterics. Under conditions of total war these changes occur also among the civilian population. With the return to normal conditions these changes tend to disappear, but their consequences survive for some time in the form of functional nervous disorders, psychoneuroses, and the like. (c) Since war is dual in its psychosocial nature—at once highly antisocial and highly altruistic—it "polarizes" human be-

[12] Cf. my *Calamity*, pp. 40 ff., 275 ff.; also A. L. Lowell, *Public Opinion in War and Peace* (Cambridge, 1916), Ch. 5, *passim*.

havior, markedly accentuating selfish and anti-social actions, such as profiteering and crime, as well as acts of altruism, self-sacrifice, and heroism, at the expense of the relatively neutral actions that constitute so large a part of one's normal conduct. The Nazis exhibited this polarization especially clearly. On the one hand, they performed the most bestial actions in relation to millions of their victims; on the other, they unflinchingly sacrificed their lives for the Führer and the Third Reich.

4. Changes in Differentiation—Stratification and Mechanism for Testing, Selecting, and Distributing Individuals

The changes effected by war in the field of social differentiation and stratification, and in the mechanism for the testing, selection, and distribution of individuals, are chiefly as follows. (a) Groups and strata that hinder or fail to promote victory tend to be demoted or penalized, to decline in numbers, or even to disappear; whereas those that assist the war effort tend to expand and to be promoted or rewarded. Typical examples are furnished by the increase of the armed forces, their prestige, and their remuneration, on the one hand, and by the prohibition and penalization of various pacifistic, unpatriotic, or treasonable groups and strata, on the other. (b) The social position of the defeated nation as a whole declines and that of the victorious nation rises in relation to other nations. The decline and rise in question mean a corresponding demotion and promotion, respectively, for most of the members of the two nations. (For an outline of the essential changes in stratification during the Second World War, cf. Chapter 26.) (c) In the victorious nation the strata and groups that served as leaders during the war are elevated, whereas in the defeated country such groups and strata sink and are sometimes overthrown. (d) The mechanism for the testing and selection of individuals undergoes a change in that it gives much greater weight to military qualities than in peacetime, specific tests being devised to determine these qualities. Persons and groups that display notable military ability are promoted much more rapidly than in normal times, whereas those that are devoid of such ability are often demoted, even though in peacetime they may

have risen rapidly in the social scale. After the armistice the mechanism for the testing and selection of individuals tends to resume its normal character.

5. Changes in Social and Cultural Processes

(a) Voluntary and especially involuntary migration, general and differential horizontal mobility, and the vertical circulation of individuals and groups sharply increase. Qualitatively these processes differ from those typical of revolutions.[13]

(b) In the economic field, war leads to waste of wealth and a lowered standard of living (especially in the defeated nation); to a considerable redistribution of wealth; to centralization and regimentation of economic processes by the government; sometimes to inventions and to rationalization of the processes of production and distribution of the necessities of life.

(c) In the political field the principal changes are as follows: (1) an increase of governmental centralization, control, and regimentation at the expense of freedom and autonomy on the part of private groups and persons; (2) in the defeated countries, occasional revolution and anarchy, leading to the imposition of control by the victorious nation over the vanquished; (3) compulsory changes in the territories of the states or groups involved; (4) loss of the sovereignty and independence of the defeated groups, and the acquisition of sovereignty by the victorious groups; (5) sudden changes in the relative strength and position of various political parties, social estates and classes, etc.; (6) the appearance, especially in the vanquished country, of strongly developed reform and revolutionary movements.

(d) In ethical and religious processes the basic transformation consists in the polarization of the population into sinners and saints and into extremely religious and irreligious factions. Whether the positive or the negative polarization is the stronger depends upon various conditions. This explains why criminality increases in some wars and decreases in others. Positive polarization has often resulted in an expansion of the area of peace and solidarity. Positive polarization explains also why

[13] Cf. my *Calamity*, Chps. 6-7, and *Mobility*, Chps. 18-19.

virtually all notable progress in ethical codes and religious beliefs has occurred either during or immediately after major wars, revolutions, and other calamities, rarely in periods of prolonged prosperity and physical well-being. On the other hand, the same periods have been marked by an upsurge of criminality, depravity, cynicism, atheism, and so on.[14]

(e) In the field of science, technology, philosophy, and the fine arts the effects of war, like those of revolution and other calamities, are also polarized. On the one hand, war, revolution, and other tragedies greatly stimulate the creative and inventive faculties, resulting in many important scientific and technological inventions, and the creation of notable religious,

philosophical, literary, and artistic values. On the other hand, by their very nature, war and revolution are destructive forces and destroy directly or indirectly many values, creative powers, and scientific, artistic, and other institutions. The net result in this respect is mostly negative, but in a minority of cases the positive results are very considerable.[15]

(f) In all fields of cultural life, war stamps with its own image the arts and sciences, philosophy and law, religion and ethics, economics and politics, in the sense that they all become concentrated upon war and the phenomena connected with it. Upon the cessation of hostilities this preoccupation with war tends to decline and disappear.

[14] For the facts and the literature, cf. my *Calamity*, Chps. 7-12, and *Theories*, pp. 337 ff.

[15] Cf. my *Calamity*, Chps. 13-15, and *Theories*, pp. 349 ff.

Chapter 33. The Cause and Factors
of War and Revolution

I. Criticism of the Theories of Causation
of War and Revolution

The existing literature on causation of war and revolution reveals the almost hopelessly muddled condition of our knowledge in this field, and in that of causality generally.[1] We find in this literature, first, an almost unbelievable diversity of causes set forth by different, and sometimes even by the same, investigators. The causal factors evoked include: sunspots, climate, conjunctions of planets, and other cosmic factors; instincts of pugnacity, of war, of fighting, of herd, and of aggressiveness; overpopulation, underpopulation, high and low birth and mortality rates; universal law of struggle for existence, and other biological factors; fear, fight for freedom, relaxation from inhibitions imposed by civilization, sadism, lust for power, ostentation, vanity, and dozens of other psychological forces; a long list of economic, political, dynastic, religious, aesthetic, educational, and other social factors; diverse cultural conditions like "the true and false culture," *mores*, and the like; philosophical abstractions like destiny, providence, and so on; and finally, various "wicked," great- and small-men and groups. This enormous diversity of the causes is sufficient evidence of a lack of a real knowledge of the problem. What would we say if such an agglomeration of diverse causes were listed, let us say, for diphtheria, or for the birth of a child?[2]

---

[1] As a sample of the enormous amount of literature and theories in the field, the two following symposia may serve: H. J. Stenning (editor), *The Causes of War* (London, 1935). This includes articles by Dean W. R. Inge, Lord Beaverbrook, G. D. H. Cole, Sir Josiah Stamp, Sir Norman Angell, Aldous Huxley, Major Douglas, Sir Austin Chamberlain; Arthur Porritt (editor), *The Causes of War* (New York, 1932) includes articles by Sir Arthur Salter, Sir Arthur Thompson, G. A. Johnston, A. Zimmern, C. F. Andrews, F. J. Libby, H. Atkinson, W. Steed, and others. See also H. Fielding Hall, *The Nature of War and Its Causes* (London, 1917); R. Hubert, *Les interprétations de la guerre* (Paris, 1919); G. L. Dickinson, *War: Its Nature, Cause and Cure* (New York, 1923); T. Veblen, *An Inquiry into the Nature of Peace* (New York, 1917); Paul Lacombe, *La guerre et l'homme* (Paris, 1903); Tell A. Turner, *Causes of War and the New Revolution* (Boston, 1927); A. C. Pigou, *The Political Economy of War* (London, 1921); John Bakeless, *The Economic Causes of Modern War* (New York, 1921); Q. Wright, *The Causes of War and the Conditions of Peace* (London, 1935); *A Study of War* (quoted), S. R. Steinmetz, *Soziologie des Krieges* (Leipzig, 1929); Jules Sageret, *Philosophie de la guerre et de la paix* (Paris, 1919); L. L. Bernard, *The Causes of War* (New York, 1944); cf. other literature cited in P. Sorokin, *Theories*, Ch. 6; *Dynamics*, Vol. 3, Chps. 9, 10, 11, and pp. 543-577; *Sociocultural Causality, Space, Time*. On Theories of causation of revolution see the literature on revolution given in the Chapter 31.

[2] Cf. H. J. Stenning, *op. cit.*, 96.

1. Inconsistency of Proffered Theories

This depressing situation is aggravated by many additional sins. One of these is the internal inconsistency of many of the theories offered. For instance, many of these claim that the main cause of war is economic: "to keep what we have got and to take more,"[3] or "the Imperialist rivalries stirred by our present economic system,"[4] and the like. And then the same authors assure us that "war does not pay," that the conquerors and the conquered alike usually lose economically. Unless we assume an absolute stupidity and unteachability of all the peoples, these two statements, that the cause of war is economic, and that war does not pay, are hard to reconcile. The assumption of absolute stupidity is hardly sound. Therefore, either the cause is indicated incorrectly, or it is false that war never pays.

Still more clearly does such a self-contradiction stand out when we confront the causal diagnosis and the cures of war offered by the same author. For instance, Aldous Huxley regards as the causes: geography, climate, racial and economic factors, boredom, passions, nationalism, fear, and wicked men; in brief, a number of deep forces, some of which do not depend upon human control. In spite of this, he does not hesitate to offer as the cure for war such measures as: "psychoanalysing our politicians and newspaper proprietors," "abolition of boredom," and, of course, united propaganda against war.[5] If his causes of war are real, then evidently the means suggested to prevent or abolish it do not touch most of these causes, and therefore have to be impotent; if they are effective, then evidently the causal diagnosis is wrong. Similarly, G. D. H. Cole regards economic imperialism and rivalry in its deepest sense as the main cause of war. Yet, as the patented cure for war he suggests socialism, without explaining how it can abolish the economic rivalries, and especially, "nationalisation of the manufacture of armaments and the complete stopping of the international trade in arms" which "would decrease the amount of military preparation in the world and make war less likely."[6] Lack of correspondence between the column of the causes and that of the cures of war is again striking. When one considers a series of magical effects ascribed to nationalization of armaments and stopping the international trade in arms, it becomes still clearer. For instance, nationalization of manufacturing of armaments in all probability would cause, not an abolition of war or its decrease, but a particularly strong development of manufacturing of armaments by the governments of all countries; stopping of international trade in arms (like some neutrality pacts) would stimulate the strong nations to become more aggressive, and would make the nations with little development of the arms industry the prey of the strong nations. In brief, instead of "making war less likely" such measures may increase the explosions, or, at any rate, can hardly decrease them. Again, if the causes are indicated adequately, then the cures cannot be effective; if the cures are valid, then the causes are fallacious. One could continue *ad libitum*.

2. Weakness of Theory of Multiple Causation

Still another defect that aggravates the above sins is a most pitiable application to the study of war of the principle of so-called multiple causation. After stressing this or that particular causal factor of war, most of the authors finally rely upon some variety of multiple causation. A typical example is Dean Inge's enumeration of the factors of war: pugnacity, plus artificial stimulation, plus pressure of the population, plus machinations of the government to distract the attention from internal affairs and to stop a revolution at home, plus aggressive imperialism, plus fear, plus drive for unification, plus something else.[7] Aldous Huxley's multiple causation is as follows: geographic and climatic conditions; racial factors; economic factors; passions; wicked great men, plus a series of psychoanalytical factors which he stresses as the most important.[8] Sir Josiah Stamp agrees that wars are caused by a "collection of conditions," among which he particularly mentions: economic penetration, economic inequality, differentiated population,

---

[3] G. L. Dickinson, *op. cit.*, 50.

[4] G. D. H. Cole, in H. J. Stenning, *op. cit.*, 59; Sir Josiah Stamp, *op. cit.*, 83-85.

[5] In Stenning's *The Causes of War*, pp. 47-58.

[6] *Ibid.*, pp. 59-62, 71.

[7] Dean Inge in Stenning, *op. cit.*, pp. 15-19.

[8] *Ibid.*, pp. 47-58.

and some others.[9] Professor James Ford enumerates the following elements of the multiple
causation of war: economic factors, private
manufacturing of armaments, dictatorships,
totalitarian regimes, misguided education, mob
psychology, emotionalism, wrong attitudes, ambitions, anger, avariciousness, and so on.[10] Sir
Arthur Salter enumerates religious, dynastic,
political, and economic causes, each consisting
of several subclasses.[11] G. A. Johnston mentions
specifically among many causes: social injustice, monotony of industrial life, the artificial
stimulation of consumption, unemployment,
etc.[12]

The slogan of multiple causation is very
popular nowadays. We use it all the time as
something quite definite, sound, and unquestionable. As a matter of fact, the problem of
multiple causation is neither clear, nor unquestionable, nor free from serious logical
difficulties. It may be valid and meaningful
when all the variables belong to a commensurable, homogeneous class, but it is meaningless
when the factors are quite incommensurable
and belong to profoundly different planes of
phenomena. Suppose we take as the formula
of multiple causation the following one: universal law of struggle for existence, instinct of
pugnacity and herd, fear and lust for power,
existence of wicked rulers, division of mankind
into different nations, the sunspots, and some
religious and economic factors. One can see
that these factors belong to fundamentally
different planes of reality, and as such are
neither commensurable, nor comparable, nor
generally capable of being united into any
real unity. How is it possible to compare and
co-measure the role of the sunspots and that
of fear or lust; the weight of fear and that of
the universal law of struggle for existence;
the weight of these and of the division of
mankind into nations, or of the religious factor? It is evident that they cannot be measured,
or even roughly appraised in any comparative
way; there is no measuring stick applicable
to all of these. In brief, such a use of multiple

causation is logically unpermissible.[13] For this
reason only, this kind of formulae of the
multiple causes are worthless.

Furthermore, even when they are free from
this error, the formulae of multiple causation
do not give *per se* any criterion for choice of
the real causes out of millions of circumstances
under which a war or revolution breaks out.
Suppose we take the First World War as an
illustration. Here are a few out of millions of
attendant circumstances: shot at Sarajevo; Vis-
count Gray's psychology; bad influence of
Rasputin upon the Czarina; economic imperialism of Germany; vast territory of Russia; low
birth rate in France; Hegel's and Nietzsche's
philosophy; private manufacturing of armaments in England; German "fear" of the Russian rearmament; great popular reception of
President Poincaré in Russia in the summer of
1914; Polish aspirations for independence; desire of the military class for elevation of its
prestige; departure of Emperor Wilhelm II
for a sea trip a few days before the opening
of the war; supposed backward culture of Russia and her slavophil policy; heavy rain in
parts of Austria in the summer of 1914. . . .

All of these conditions indeed were present
immediately before and at the beginning of the
war, but shall we take them all as causes, just
because they were existing before and at the
beginning of the war? If so, we must then consider millions of other conditions existing then
as part of our multiple causation. Evidently
such a catalogue is neither a causal formula,
nor has any cognitive value; there is no end
to the enumeration of the infinite number of
the items and conditions present before and at
the opening of war or revolution, and if there
were, such a list could not be remembered.
If we exclude all these millions of conditions,
then what reasons can we give for their exclusion, leaving only those enumerated above?
We do not have any criterion for judging that
the enumerated conditions are more important
than those not enumerated. Even if we pass by
this difficulty, the above conglomeration of the
factors of our "multiple causation" is still

---

[9] *Ibid.*, pp. 83-95.
[10] James Ford and K. M. Ford, *The Abolition of
Poverty* (New York, 1937), p. 259.
[11] Cf. Porritt, *The Causes of War*, pp. 1-25.
[12] *Ibid.*, 26-62. See there many other forms of
multiple causation.

[13] "Fear does not 'combine' with a gun to explain
a case of manslaughter as wind combines with
water to produce a storm at sea," R. M. MacIver
indicates rightly. See his *Society, a Textbook of
Sociology* (New York, 1937), pp. 476 ff.

nothing but enumeration of a few incidental conditions, chosen haphazardly or arbitrarily, mistaken for the causes. Even so, the number of the factors in the enumeration is too large and their nature is too incommensurable to be of any value as a causal formula.

These remarks show why the causal formulae surveyed are logically unpermissible, factually fruitless, or, at best, represent a mere haphazard description of some of the circumstances present in one or a few wars—which description in no way is causal analysis and has practically nothing to do with it. This conclusion is reinforced still more by the fact that *few, if any, of the above theories concerning the causes either of war or revolution take into consideration the relevant factual material concerning war and revolution* as a check on the validity of the theories. It is almost unbelievable how almost all the theories on the causes of war and revolution are completely free from any factual material concerning war and revolution and their movements. In a very few of the studies some material can be found; all the rest of the theories are practically devoid of any factual, and especially, of relevant factual, corroboration. From this standpoint, they represent a pure and unadulterated speculation at its worst, logically incoherent, factually unchecked, lacking any inductive confirmation.

If such a study of the relevant facts of war were made by the authors, most of the theories would never have appeared, or would be removed to a morgue at once. Why? Because they either do not solve the problem of the causes of war as an empirical phenomenon, or they are contradicted by the relevant facts. Let us take a few examples. In order that a theory of the sunspots or climatic or other astrophysical causes of war or revolution be entitled to any consideration, it must at least show that fluctuation in the sunspots or the conjunction of the planets goes on in a tangible association (positive or negative) with the fluctuation of the war-peace, revolution-order periods in a given country or several countries, and with the increase and decrease of the magnitude or frequency of war phenomena. For this purpose, all such theories need a sufficient series

of facts, giving the periods of peace and war, of revolution and order and the data of their increase and decrease. With the exception of half-fantastic theories in this field like that of K. Mewes,[14] almost all the theories do not even try to give any series of data, or even *any* data, about the war-peace, revolution-order, movement. Therefore, they remain mere conjectures hanging in the air, unrelated to the facts, without any attempt at inductive testing. More than that, when they are tested, as I tried to do, no tangible association is discovered between the movement of either the sunspots or climatic or astrophysical factors and the movement of war and peace, revolution and order.[15] The same goes for all the theories of various instincts, prepotent reflexes, drives, residues, fear, lust for power, aggressiveness, and other instinctive or psychological forces as the causes of war and revolution. Likewise, such causes as "the universal law of the struggle for existence" fall into the same objectionable category in accounting for the presence or absence, or the magnitude of war and revolution. If any of these "factors" is assumed to be constant, then it flatly fails to explain why a given country or a universe of several countries now has peace and now has war, now revolution and now order, why war or revolution is now increasing, now declining. The alleged cause being constant, while its effect varies, the alleged cause cannot be the real cause. If any of these forces is assumed not to be constant, then the theories must explain why the force fluctuates, and that its fluctuation is tangibly parallel to the fluctuation of war-peace phenomena. Such a test has scarcely been attempted by any theories of this sort. They have hardly, if ever, gone beyond a purely dogmatic assertion, and rarely have tried to secure a minimum of the relevant facts about the movement of war and peace. Therefore, they also remain void.

With slight variations these considerations bear upon most of the other theories of the causes of war and revolution. Until they all attempt to secure a modicum of the relevant facts concerning the movements of war and revolution and their increase and decrease and until they account satisfactorily through their

---

[14] K. Mewes, *Krieges und Geistesperioden im Völkerleben* (Leipzig, 1922). See my criticism of it in *Dynamics*, Vol. III, pp. 352 ff.

[15] See P. Sorokin, *Dynamics*, Vol. III, pp. 352 ff.; *Theories*, Chps. 3 and 6.

"causes" for the real movement of war and revolution, they are all void and worthless. Thus, when the above fallacies of the existing theories of war causation are considered, the net result is that either we do not know anything real about the causes of war and revolution or if we do know something, the theories, remaining pure conjecture, do not show it.

II. Main Cause and Supplementary (Positive and Negative) Factors

Since in view of multiplicity and incommensurability of various conditions in which war and revolution explode the formula of multiple causation: War=f(A,B,C . . . N); Revolution=f(B,D,E . . . X) is inapplicable,[16] more fruitful seems to be the way of discovery of *the main, the necessary cause of these phenomena with an indication of the supplementary factors that facilitate and inhibit the effects of the main cause.* By the main or necessary condition is meant the factor without which war or revolution cannot occur. By the supplementary factors are meant the numerous and diverse conditions that either facilitate the realization of the effects of the necessary cause or neutralize them. Thus, in diphtheria the necessary cause is infection. Positive supplementary factors are those conditions favoring the spread of germs and decreasing the immunity of the human organism to infection; negative supplementary factors are inoculation and similar influences that neutralize or inhibit the effects of infection, thereby turning the necessary cause into an *insufficient* cause. The necessary cause of birth is conception. The positive supplementary factors are all the conditions that favor the growth of the fetus into a child. Negative supplementary conditions are those which, like abortion and disease, inhibit this development of the fetus. The main cause of a given phenomenon is always the same, but the supplementary factors are diverse, variable, and shifting in their nature as well as in their combinations.

I am perfectly aware of the many objections against distinguishing between the necessary cause and the supplementary factors. These objections can be found in almost all the serious treatises on inductive logic, such as those by J. S. Mill, A. A. Tshuproff, J. Venn, C. Sigwart, and others, as well as in a number of special monographs on causality. However, the logical and investigational advantages of such a distinction are so great, and its disadvantages so comparatively small, that the objections can be disregarded. They are really far from decisive. The principle of the main cause and supplementary factors is generally used in causal analysis throughout the natural sciences. Their experience confirms its validity and fruitfulness. Nearly all the advances in the natural sciences have involved the discovery of the main or necessary cause of a given phenomenon and some of its supplementary factors.

1. Main Cause of Internal and International Peace and War

(a) *The main cause of internal social peace is the presence in the given society of a well-integrated system of basic values, with their corresponding norms practiced in overt conduct.[17] The fundamental values of the various factions and members of the society must be essentially in harmony with this system and with one another. The values must be based on the principle of the Golden Rule and not on that of hatred.*

(b) *The main cause of international peace is the presence in each of the interacting societies of a well-integrated system of basic values and their norms, all of which are compatible with one another, practiced by the societies involved, and based on the Golden Rule.*

(c) *In a given universe of societies or within a particular society the probability of*

---

[16] Where the variables A, B, C . . . N are homogeneous and commensurable the formula of multiple causation should be applied.

[17] Every basic value has its set norms of conduct, with their "thou shalt" and "thou shalt not." Religious, ethico-juridical, scientific, economic, political, aesthetic values—each has its code conduct.

peace varies directly with the integration of the systems of the basic values and their mutual compatibility. When their integration and harmoniousness decline, especially suddenly and sharply, the chances for international or civil war increase.

Before elaborating these propositions, a few clarifying comments are in order.

Our attention is focused on the main values and not on the minor values of the given societies. What exactly are the major values of any society must be found by factual investigation. In general they are composed of the basic ethico-juridical, religious, scientific, economic, political, and aesthetic values and those of self-respect and independence. This does not prevent different societies from stressing now religious, now economic, now political values as *primus inter pares*. In spite of such concrete differences from society to society and from period to period, these values are generally fundamental ones.[18]

We are concerned with the compatibility of the systems of values but not with their similarity, homogeneity, or identity. The point is that two systems of values may be heterogeneous and yet not incompatible with one another. In a society like ours, the citizens have different religions, aesthetic tastes, and political ideas. Yet they are compatible with one another, and their heterogeneity does not lead to civil war.

The positive supplementary factors of war and revolution are all forces that generate and facilitate the conflict of the main values of a given society or of a universe of interacting societies. They are numerous and changeable. Extreme poverty of one part and richness of another part of society or societies; impossibility of satisfaction of the basic biological needs in food, shelter, sex, safety; technological inventions that lead to a cleavage of the values of the societies involved and give advantages to one part and disadvantages to the other; ideologies and beliefs that spread the gospel of superiority-inferiority, hatred, domination, national-class-group struggle; extreme relativization of values leading to *anomie*; accelerated tempo of disharmonious change in different parts of the society(ies); paramount impor-

tance given to certain scarce material values whose scarcity and high estimation generate intense competition and struggle for these; the gospel of unlimited rivalry and competition; the extremely egotistic and individualistic system of education; disintegrated state of the family, the neighborhood; the state; sensualistic and hedonistic character of literature, theater, fine arts, science and philosophy; moral cynicism and nihilism; up to "dynastic" or trade-union rivalries; these and many other conditions have played, under certain circumstances, the role of the facilitating factors of war and revolution.

Similarly *the negative supplementary factors* of war and revolution have been diverse and numerous. The efficient and fair legislative apparatus promptly removing the discrepancy between the old official law and the new unofficial law convictions of the population; ideologies and practices of love, solidarity, common interests; universally binding system of values and norms; educational system cultivating solidarity and sacredness of main values; technological inventions weakening the lag of the values of one part from those of the others; decrease of excessive economic and political inequalities; creative and unselfish leadership of the ruling groups; alleviation of misery and poverty; idealistic arts, sciences, philosophy and religion; common great danger for all the societies involved; distribution of individuals according to their ability; the family, the school, the state and other groups, well integrated and mutually cooperating; favorable geographic and biological conditions (sound heredity and the selection of the fit)—these and hundreds of other conditions have played the role of inhibitors of war and revolution.

Having clarified these propositions, we may ask what are the evidences of their validity.

2. Evidence of the Validity of the Propositions

Each of the subsequent sets of evidence sums up a regularly repeated uniformity, and therefore is a more adequate proof than a mere collection of singularistic facts.[19] All these uniformities show either an *explosion or increase of war and revolution whenever the inte-*

---

[18] See on this my *Dynamics*, IV, Chps. 1, 2, 3.; above Chapter 17.

[19] Factual data for corroboration can be found in my *Dynamics*, III, Chps. 9-14; and in Quincy Wright, *A Study of War*, 2 Vols.

gration of the main values or their compatibility decreases. If this decrease occurs among the factions and members of a given society, the result is civil war (revolution) or severe and bloody punishment. If the decrease of integration and harmony occurs among the value-systems of different societies, the result is international war.

(a) The first set of corroborations consists of the countless outbreaks of war when two hitherto isolated societies, with different and contradictory systems of values, come for the first time into direct and durable contact. The contact makes real the potential irreconcilability of their contrasting main values. According to the proposition, such a situation must lead to war, and it has done so fairly uniformly, in ancient as well as in more recent times. Quincy Wright's study shows that the warfare of comparatively isolated peoples has the lowest mean index (2.03); next come peoples with moderate intercultural contacts (index 2.59); finally the peoples with wide and close cultural contacts (index 2.91).[20] Early history and anthropology give us hundreds of cases of wars occasioned by the meeting of two formerly isolated tribes. If their basic values were different such a contact has almost invariably been followed by warfare. The same is true of historical societies. A notable portion of the wars of these societies occurred precisely when, in the process of migration or expansion or colonization, one society met another for the first time. The contact was almost invariably followed by wars, whether of defense, offense, misunderstanding, subjugation, or colonization, even when the societies had no conscious military objectives. So it was in the history of Egypt, Babylonia, China and Persia, Greece and Rome, Europe and the Americas. When Egyptians met Nubians or Palestinians or Hyksos or any other group with different values, war followed. When in the process of peaceful colonization the Greeks met other peoples and societies, war took place. The same is true of the Macedonians and the Romans throughout their history. The expansion of these empires meant contact with other societies having different systems of

[20] Q. Wright, *Ibid.*, p. 559. See also Table 12, p. 557.

values. The resultant wars lasted until one part was destroyed or subjugated, or their values became compatible. The same is true when West met East; when the Spaniards or Pilgrims met the aboriginal Americans, and so on through the chronic colonial wars that have been going on continually.

(b) This partly explains why the *rapid expansion of contact and communication after the thirteenth century has been followed by an increase of war on this planet.* New technical means of communication and transportation have brought face to face an ever increasing number of tribes, societies, nations, and empires. The irreconcilability of their value-systems was thus systematically intensified. Consequently wars, especially colonial conflicts, increased until, in the nineteenth century, the truly isolated groups had almost disappeared. They were all subjugated by force and then divided between the great powers.

In all these wars the real cause is not the fact of contact and expansion of intersocietal interaction. By themselves contact and interaction are neither war-making nor peace-making factors. Contact and interaction as such are not the cause of diphtheria; a person can have thousands of contacts with other persons and still be free from diphtheria. He may be in touch with a sick person and yet remain healthy as long as he does not get the infection. The cause is infection by the germs; contact is a facilitating circumstance. Similarly, intersocietal contact and interaction do not lead to war, if the value-systems of the respective societies are not incompatible. The cause is the incompatibility. Social contact and interaction are facilitating factors.

(c) *The third set of corroborations is given by civil wars (revolutions) arising from a rapid and fundamental change in the basic values of one part of a given society while the other part either does not undergo it or moves in the opposite direction.* This means a rapid increase in the incompatibility of the main values of the two parts of the society. According to the present thesis, some sort of civil strife should follow such a transformation. And this has uniformly been the case. Practically all the civil wars (revolutions) of the past have emerged from a sudden increase of the contrast in the major values of revolutionaries and counter-revolutionaries. From the civil wars of Egypt and Persia to the recent upheavals of Russia and Spain, history consistently offers evidence of the validity of our proposition.

(d) *The fourth set of proofs consists of the cases where in the universe of interacting societies a profound transformation of the value-systems occurs only in one or a few without occurring simultaneously in the other interacting societies.* Such a situation means again a greater incompatibility of the values of these societies. The result of such an increase has uniformly been an outbreak of war between the societies involved. Take, for instance, the historical cases of profound religious transformation. When Achenaton's religious revolution occurred in ancient Egypt, the result was civil and then international war. When the Buddhist religious transformation occurred in India, a similar series of conflicts followed. The emergence of Christianity, the Byzantian iconoclastic reformation, and the Protestant Reformation each resulted in a long series of wars. The same is true of such religious variations of Christianity as the Hussite movement and the Albigensian "heresy." The story has been repeated many times in human history with monotonous uniformity.

If the transformation occurs in the realm of *political* or *politico-economic* values, it assumes the form of a political or politico-economic revolution. If the changes in one society are sufficiently radical, they are generally followed by a series of "revolutionary wars" with the unrevolutionized neighbors. The wars of the Cromwellian, French, Russian and Nazi revolutions are typical illustrations of the uniformity. There are few profound political or economic-political revolutions in history without their aftermaths of war.

(e) A fifth group of proofs is epitomized by the *fact of the increase of war and civil war attendant upon an acceleration of sociocultural change in a given universe of interacting societies or of a given society. This is especially true in the West and throughout the world during the last five centuries.* The real cause of an increase of war in such periods is not acceleration. If it proceeds at an orderly and uniform pace in all societies, or among all parts of a society, no intensified irreconcilability of the value systems occurs, and therefore no

internal or external war follows. This is witnessed, for instance, by the rapid rate of change in Europe and America during the second part of the nineteenth century. Variation in the tempo of change *per se* is neither a war-making nor a peace-making factor. It is neutral. If it has made for war in certain cases, the reason is that not all the societies or not all the parts of a given society changed at the same rate. This made for greater incompatibility in their value-systems; hence the increase of bloody conflicts. During rapid change the main values are in a state of flux and do not have time to "settle" and become universal; they become somewhat disintegrated, thereby further facilitating war.

(f) The sixth category of evidence includes the following facts. Empires composed of *highly heterogeneous and conflicting populations and cultures* often initiate wars in order to prevent a development of internal movements threatening their unity. In cases of this kind the incompatibility first manifests itself internally, in the form of struggle and civil war. This eventually provokes international war.

(g) We next consider the opposite instance, where the nation is perfectly integrated internally, in other words, *highly nationalistic.* But being thus unified, it differs fundamentally from other societies with respect to its system of values. Its norms are incompatible with theirs. An ultra-nationalistic state does not respect or tolerate its neighbors' ways. The uniform result of such arrogance and intolerance has been war.

In both of these cases the cause of the wars is not heterogeneity or homogeneity per se. In different situations they could lead to other results. In the situations described they lead to war because they produce a clash of the values of the given societies.

(h) The next corroboration is given by the noted fact that *revolutions and wars crowd particularly into the periods of blossoming and decline of a given nation.* Such periods are the times of a rapid and disharmonious transformation of the values of the nation, which sharpens conflicting values among the different parts of the nation. A widening discrepancy between the official law supported by the old regime and the unofficial law-convictions of the "radical" part of a given society, an invariable condition of revolution, points at the same fact, an increase of incompatibility between the main values of different parts of a given society.

(i) The next series of corroborations involves *the major movements in the magnitude of war and revolution in the history of Greece, Rome, and European countries* from the sixth century B.C. to the present time (see the figures above).[21] The major fluctuations of these curves cannot be accounted for by any hypothesis except the one proposed herein. *According to our hypothesis we should expect the greatest magnitude of war and revolution, in the periods of radical transformation of the societies* (war) *or of a given society* (revolution). That is exactly what these curves show.

In Greece the most belligerent centuries are the fourth and fifth B.C. We know (see further Chapters 40 to 42) that these centuries saw a most profound and rapid transformation of the value-system of Greek society. The old religious or ideational system was crumbling, the new sensate system was not yet built. All Greece was in a state of immense flux. No value or norm remained universally binding for all states, groups, or individuals. Sociocultural *anomie* became supreme. In these conditions the incompatibility of the common values enormously increased.

When values cease to be universally binding, their controlling power evaporates. Human beings and groups become dominated mainly by blind, egotistic, biological impulses. Brute force supplemented by fraud becomes supreme. It would be a miracle if under these circumstances wars and civil strife did not enormously increase. Indeed, war reached its highest level in Greek history during these centuries.

For the same reason the maximum of revolution was reached in Greece in the fifth and then fourth centuries B.C. Comparing the curves of revolution and of war in Greece, Rome, and European countries one sees that in some periods their main ups and downs go on parallel; in other periods the war curve lags by decades, sometimes even by a century or so, the curve of revolution. In a comparatively small universe of states like the Greek states or Italy (Rome), the lag of war curve from that

[21] For detailed data see *Dynamics*, Vol. III.

of revolution is the lag of a few decades. In a vaster universe of states embracing Europe and a part of other continents there is sometimes a lag, as for instance in the centuries from the fourteenth and fifteenth to the seventeenth, of two and a half centuries. To summarize, in most of the main ups and downs, the curves of war and revolution go on parallel, sometimes synchronously, more often with a lag of war curve from that of revolution.

The reason for such a lag of war curve and for the lag-period now being short, now long, is comprehensible. Revolution is a business of one society; as soon as an incompatibility of its values ripens, revolution explodes. War is a business of two or more societies. For its explosion a longer time is necessary than for explosion of revolution; not only a new system of values in one of the interacting societies must mature, but a new system of values in such a society must consolidate, become explicitly incompatible with the old system of values in other societies, and actually spread and involve these other societies. For all this an additional time is needed, and the vaster the universe of several states involved, the greater the number of such vast states and the poorer the means of contact, communication, and interaction among them, the longer the time required. These reasons explain why the curve of war tends to lag behind that of revolution and why in a vast universe of states with poor means of communication a much longer time is needed to generate their conflict, to make the incompatibility of values explicit, than in a small universe like Greece or Italy (Rome). Add to this the necessity for a state to have a strong inner order in time of strenuous war that leads often (as in Rome of the third century B.C. or in the European states at several periods) to a decrease of revolution in the times of strenuous wars.

These considerations, then, explain the lag of war curve from that of revolution, the length of the lag, and some other deviations of these curves from one another. Due to a complex play of a multitude of positive and negative supplementary factors there must be several other deviations of these curves. However, in most of their main movements they go on parallel, with a lagging war curve.

The most belligerent centuries in the history

of Rome were the third and first B.C. and the third A.D. Why? The third century witnessed the long and bloody conflict between irreconcilable value-systems of Rome and Carthage. The first century B.C. saw the great transmutation of the formerly semi-ideational values of Rome to an overripe sensate form. The transformation was enormously accelerated by the impact of the sensate Hellenic culture upon the Roman society. At the end of the second and during the first century B.C., as in Greece, it led to *anomie*. In this situation, as we would expect, an increase of civil and international wars occurred. Finally, a rise of the "curve" in the third century A.D. is again quite comprehensible. In the third century A.D. Christianity, with its ideational system of values sharply opposed to the dominant sensate system, came to the surface as a tangible power. The struggle between the pagan (sensate) and Christian (ideational) systems assumed public form. Hence, according to the proposition, war had to increase. (For the next few centuries no reliable data are available.)

The first important upswing of revolution in Rome was in the fifth and fourth centuries B.C. when the incompatibility of the value-systems of the patricians and plebeians, not to mention of the monarchy and aristocracy, became irreconcilable. With an achievement of the last demand of the plebeians, the *jus connubii*, a new order of values was set forth. For this reason, and because of the most strenuous Punic wars, the revolutions greatly decreased in the third century B.C. Then with the gigantic change in the values from the semi-ideational to sensate in the second and first centuries B.C. (the change greatly stimulated by the impact of the sensate Hellenistic culture), the Roman society became sharply split into irreconcilable factions. Hence a conflagration of revolutions in the first century B.C. In the first and second centuries A.D. a new sensate system of values becomes dominant and settled. The irreconcilability decreases. Hence a decline of the revolutions in these centuries. In the third century A.D. Christianity with its ideational system of values became already an important power and entered an open struggle with hitherto prevalent sensate culture. Hence a new flare-up of revolutions in Italian Rome. In the fourth century A.D. Christianity was legalized, became the dominant religion and system of values, and subsequently established a new ideational system of culture and society. Parallel with this the curve of revolutions tended to decrease in the fourth and especially in the fifth century A.D.

If we take eight main European countries and study the most belligerent periods of their history, the results are similar. Their war-maxima fall in the periods of increasing incompatibility and disintegration of the value-systems.[22] Without going into details for each country, we can summarize the movement of war in Europe as a whole, from the twelfth century to the present time.

From its initial low point the curve begins to rise very slowly in the thirteenth and fourteenth centuries, then faster during the fifteenth and sixteenth centuries, until it reaches its first peak in the seventeenth. Then it declines slightly in the eighteenth, and much more in the nineteenth century, although there is a minor rise at the close of the eighteenth and at the beginning of the nineteenth. In the twentieth century it soars to a point unprecedented in all the twenty-five hundred years of western society.

Our hypothesis well accounts for these three maxima of war. The period from the end of the twelfth to the seventeenth century saw the profound transformation of the European system of values from the medieval ideational to the modern sensate. The ideational values were disintegrating and the modern sensate system was not matured. The atomization and relativization of values resulted in the collapse of their stabilizing power. Their incompatibility—interindividual, intergroup, and interstate—became much greater than before. Hence an increase of international as well as civil wars throughout Europe. But by the seventeenth century Europe had attained a new integrated system of ultimate values (sensate). Disintegration gave way to integration. Consequently there occurred the decline of the curve of war-magnitude during the eighteenth and the nineteenth centuries.

Its temporary rise at the end of the eighteenth and at the beginning of the nineteenth centuries is easily explained. It was due to the

---

[22] See *Dynamics*, Vol. III.

clash between those who wanted to liquidate the last remnants of the feudal order and of the ideational culture and those who wanted to preserve them. After this short-lived clash, the curve of war markedly declined throughout the nineteenth century. These decades were the zenith of a well-integrated sensate culture and social order. The clash of values within the European universe was at its minimum. Hence the peaceful character of these decades.

With the beginning of the twentieth century we witness a rapid disintegration of sensate culture.[23] All its values were relativised and atomized to such an extent that none of them remained universally valid. Marriage, private property, God—all these values were undermined, criticized, and ground to dust. Social anarchy became supreme. No single value was recognized as binding equally the Hitlerites and anti-Hitlerites, communists and capitalists, rich and poor, religious believers and atheists. As a result, the values lost a great deal of their restraining power. An ever-increasing part of the population was guided by sensual, egotistic, and biological impulses. Force and fraud became again the chief norms of conduct. This incompatibility of values, together with a tremendous growth of interindividual, intergroup, and intersocietal relationships, made inevitable an unprecedented explosion of civil and international wars. Thus we find ourselves in the bloodiest century of the last twenty-five hundred years of human history.

Of three main peaks in the movement of revolution, the peak of the eighth century occurs in the time of Carolingian Renaissance —when in many populations of Europe a split in values widened and grew. The second, much higher peak occurs in the centuries thirteenth to fifteenth. Exactly these centuries were the most transitional in the passage from the declining ideational supersystem of values to the rising sensate, the period of the greatest transmutation of main values with the respective split of the population into the irreconcilable parties. The temporary peak of the end of the eighteenth century was again produced by the increase of conflict in values of the

defenders of the old regime and of the partisans of the new political and economic systems. Finally, the unprecedented explosion of revolutions in the twentieth century has been and will be due to the great transition from the decaying sensate culture to the new-idealistic or ideational-order of tomorrow. The irreconcilability of values of different factions reached its zenith. As a consequence the curve of revolutions has gone also up into the stratosphere.

In this manner the actual maxima of war and revolution-magnitudes in the history of at least ten countries (Greece, Rome, and eight European countries) unequivocally support our hypothesis.

(j) *Murder is individual war.* What is the cause of murder, and how does it increase and decrease in the course of time? We know that murders are committed for many different reasons. In spite of this variety all murders have one and the same cause, although their supplementary factors vary. The cause is the same as that of war. This is true of murders committed for material advantage, murders by fanaticists, murders of revenge, feud, passion, or insanity, and of murders for self-preservation. In all these cases, the cause is either the irreconcilable nature of the parties' basic values (murders of fanaticism, altruism, revenge, feud, passion), or an extreme atomization thereof (killings committed for material gain, self-preservation, or insanity). In the latter instance, these murderers are governed primarily by blind and disorganizing biological impulses. Both types reproduce in miniature the aforementioned condition of social *anomie*.

This theory of murder-causation is supported by the fact that persons with strongly integrated values do not commit murders of the second type, no matter how dire the emergency or how tempting the profit. My study shows that the per cent of persons taking the lives of their fellows during famine or other great emergencies is no more than one per cent. The rest may perish, but they will not slay.[24] Similarly, murders of the first type (feud, revenge, passion, fanaticism) are committed only by persons whose norms are diametrically and uncompromisingly opposed to those of their victims.

---

[23] See the evidences in my *Dynamics*, all volumes, and in my *Crisis of Our Age*; cf. further Chapters 40 to 42 in the present work.

[24] See my *Calamity*, pp. 81-82; *passim*.

(k) Further evidence is offered *by changes in the severity and extensity of punishment for crimes, especially capital punishment.* Severe punishment is an index of irreconcilable conflict between those who punish and those who are punished. In this sense it is also a form of interindividual and group war. We know that the severity of punishment for crimes is not constant but fluctuates, in penal codes as well as in concrete practice, from period to period and from society to society. Elsewhere[25] the criminal codes of Greece, Rome, and of the main European countries have been studied in considerable detail. Changes in the severity of punishment both in the penal codes and in actual practice in these countries were systematically investigated. When the periods of increase and decrease of the severity of punishment were defined, the problem of the cause of these fluctuations was studied. The solution was as follows: *"Each time, when in a given group, the ethico-juridical heterogeneity and antagonism of its members increase, the amount as well as the severity of punishment imposed by one part of the society upon the other tends to increase; and, other conditions being equal, the greater the incompatibility, the greater is the increase."*[26] A sufficient body of evidence was given in *Dynamics* to demonstrate the validity of the proposition.

(l) Finally, our proposition is supported by the inadequacy of all the other theories of the causes of war and revolution. These take the form of either a theory of multiple causation or of some exclusive specific-factor hypothesis. The latter emphasizes some particular variable such as economic or political elements, sunspots, density and size of population, climate, etc. None of these, however, can stand even an elementary test. One can take either mine or Professor Wright's war curves and try to explain their "ups and downs" in terms of any of these theories. The result is failure. These theories simply do not fit the data, and the data do not fit the theories.

The inadequacy of the multiple-causation type of theory has been set forth above. We may add one more point to that discussion. When multiple causation assumes the form of some kind of equilibrium theory, stating that a change of any variable of the equilibrium system is one of the causes of war or peace, it does not get us anywhere. Since the variables are numerous, they are arbitrarily chosen from the countless antecedent conditions amidst which war or peace occur. They remain incommensurable and incessantly varying in each case. The concept of equilibrium is inapplicable to social systems. This conclusion is reinforced strongly by Wright's attempt to use such a theory of multiple causation. In spite of the enormous material collected, and the many valuable contributions made, his attempt is unsuccessful. He leaves unsolved the problem of the causation of war and peace.[27]

III. The Conditions of Lasting Internal and International Peace

1. No Lasting Peace Within Decaying Sensate Culture, Society, and Man

Within the framework of the contemporary (sensate) culture, society, and man, no elimination, even no substantial weakening of national and international group tensions—economic, racial, ethnic, occupational and others —is possible, because this framework is shot through by a multitude of irreconcilable clashes of values. Neither most intensive sensate propaganda nor sensate education, nor political and economic measures, so far as they remain within the framework of sensate society and culture, can perform this task. At the best, they may shift the center and *loci* of the tensions, may change their color and concrete forms, but that is all they can do. Taken as a

---

[25] See my *Dynamics*, II, pp. 515-627.
[26] *Ibid.*, p. 595. See there the factual corroboration. This law of fluctuation of the severity and magnitude of punishment is more accurate than "two laws of evolution of punishment" formulated by Durkheim. See my criticism of his "laws" *Ibid.*, II, pp. 515 ff.
[27] Cf. Wright, *op. cit.*, Vol. II; my criticism in *Ethics*, April, 1942, pp. 202-207.

whole they are utterly inadequate to achieve the purpose, because they neither touch nor eradicate the deep cause of the intergroup tensions and conflicts.

The first reason for this somewhat pessimistic statement is the predominant nature of the contemporary culture and society and, as their resultant, of contemporary man. Their sociocultural nature incessantly generates a multitude of tensions and conflicts and cannot help doing that.

(a) They all are permeated by the spirit, ethos, and pathos of rivalry, competition, and desire of victory over the rivals and others in all fields of sociocultural activity, from science, football, fine arts, and business up to the "imperialistic superiority" of religions and their Gods and followers. This spirit ceaselessly generates a striving for superiority, power, and prestige of the competitors over their rivals, and a deep desire for their defeat and "lower place" in the universe. This passion leads to a cultivation of the "fighting spirit" and an indefatigable and never ceasing fight with the rivals. An unavoidable result of such a situation is a multitude of intergroup antagonisms and clashes between the rivals, the victors, and the vanquished, "the superior and the inferior" (in politics, business, science, arts, religion, etc.), "the parties of success and of failure." *In other words, interindividual and intergroup conflicts are an inseparable, immanent, or inherent trait of the contemporary culture, society, and man.* These are inherently belligerent in their sociocultural nature.

(b) To the same result these lead through their assigning paramount importance to the sensory, material, hedonistically-utilitarian values in their total scale of values. Notwithstanding the hypocritical, half-mechanical preaching of the values of "the Kingdom of God," the contemporary culture, society, and man, in their actual functions, make the sensory, material, hedonistic values paramount —the supreme goal of human aspirations, ambitions, and desires. These values range from money, wealth, material comfort, material security, and conspicuous consumption up to the kisses, copulation, popularity, fame, power, and prestige. As these values are scarce and limited in their quantity and cannot be spread in unlimited abundance among all in-

dividuals and groups, the paramount value given to them by our culture and society produces ceaselessly a never ending, intense, often bloody and antisocial struggle of every group with every other competing group for as large a share of these values as can be obtained at the cost of others. This results again in tensions and conflicts.

(c) The same result is generated by the contemporary culture, society, and man through their dominant hedonistic and egocentrically utilitarian ethics, law, and mores, and especially through the excessive relativization of all norms and values devoid of any universal binding. This atomization leads to moral, mental, and social anarchy and to cynicism in which each rival group regards itself as the supreme arbiter entitled to use any means for its victory. As a consequence, the emergence of rude force masked by fraud and other more subtle screens becomes inevitable. Force becomes the supreme judge. "The weapon of criticism turns into the criticism by the weapon of force." Tensions and clashes follow.

(d) Incessant clashes are also generated by the dominant—sensate—man of our time. He is, first of all and most of all, a fighter, intoxicated by lust for victory, power, influence, fame, pleasure, and sensate happiness. "To suppose that men who are filled individually with every manner of restlessness, maddened by lust of power and speed, votaries of the god Whirl, will live at peace whether with themselves or others, is the vainest chimera," rightly remarks one of the eminent American humanists.[28]

(e) This conflagration of war and violence is hastened along by the general degradation of man's value by sensate culture. Quite consistently with its major premise, that true reality and value are sensory, it views man as a mere empirical "electron-proton complex," a "reflex mechanism," a mere "animal organism," a "psychoanalytical bag filled with libido," devoid of anything supersensory, sacred, or divine. No wonder that in such a culture man is treated in the same manner as we treat all the other sensory "complexes," "mechanisms,"

---

[28] Irving Babbitt, *The Breakdown of Internationalism* (a reprint from the *Nation*, June, 1915), p. 25.

and "animals"; any individual or group that hinders the realization of one's wishes is eliminated in the same way in which we liquidate a mosquito or a snake or "neutralize" any organic or inorganic object that impedes the fulfillment of our desires. This explains why, in spite of all the vociferous claims by our culture as to its humanistic, humane, and humanitarian mission, it is, objectively, in its decadent phase, one of the most inhuman of all cultures, killing, mutilating, and degrading human beings by the tens of millions.

(f) Similarly, the basic institutions of contemporary society are permeated by the same militarism and are incessantly generating interindividual, civil, and international conflicts. *Private property*, with its inevitable differentiation into the excessively rich and the utterly miserable, generates persistent criminality, class antagonism, and class war. The *state* with its naked power policy of the Machiavellian *raison d'état* is an openly militaristic institution unrestrained by any of the ethical norms that are obligatory for private conduct. The same is true of our *political parties*: first and foremost they are fighting machines, using the spoils system, bribery, vituperation, murder, and civil war as instruments in their struggle for spoils and power. Our *occupational unions*, beginning with labor unions and ending with capitalists' associations, are organized primarily for militant purposes, namely, the successful defeat of antagonistic organizations by whatever means may be necessary, whether there be strikes and lockouts or revolution and civil war. Even the *family*, so far as it imbues the children with the cult of family egotism, power, and "success," is shot through with the same militaristic spirit. Finally *almost all our institutions* glorify sensate *power and success* as the highest virtues. They methodically inculcate a "fighting spirit" into everyone from the day of his birth to the day of his death. Our heroes are invariably fighting persons who successfully crush their rivals, whether on the football field, in cut-throat business rivalry, on a battlefield, in political machinations, or in class war; and they are typified by our "world champions" in tennis, swimming, coffee-drinking, pole-sitting, and jitter-bugging. Even our "Superman" is the superman only because he "is faster than a bullet, more powerful than a

locomotive," and more militant than Mars; he is forever in a fighting mess.

Thus, whether we study the objective movement of war and revolution that has grown with the emergence and growth of modern culture or whether we study the essential characteristics exhibited by it and the society and man expressing it, we cannot fail to see their preeminently militant sociocultural nature, especially in its decaying phase. War in its various forms, and especially the war for sensory values, is their ethos, soul, and heart. Within the framework of sensate culture, society, and man, no lasting national or international peace has ever been or ever will be possible.

This means also that most of the contemporary plans for a lasting peace are doomed to failure so far as they hope to achieve it within this framework by a mere job of repatching. Elementary inductive considerations will show this unequivocally. As patented panaceas against war, these plans offer an enlightened self-interest; a specious "utilitarian rationality"; emancipation from religion and absolutistic ethics; a greater and more extreme relativism of all values; a still greater dose of positivism, empiricism, materialism, utilitarianism, and mechanisticism in all their varieties; a further expansion of literacy, schools, universities, newspapers, magazines, movies, the radio, and other "educational" instrumentalities; a still more rapid increase in scientific discoveries and technological devices; a replacement of all monarchies by republics, of all autocracies by democracies, of capitalism by communism, socialism, and other sensate "isms"; dismemberment and disarmament of the vanquished; a bigger and better "balance of powers" and various "Unions Now" in the form of diverse double, triple, and quadruple alliances, on up to the United Nations, armed with a crushing military and police force; a higher economic plane of living, at least for the victorious nations; a more just distribution of natural resources, and so on and so forth. The hopelessness of all these hopes is unquestionably shown by "an ugly fact," that with the emergence and growth of our modern culture and society from the thirteenth on to the twentieth century all these panaceas have been growing also; and yet their growth has been paralleled during these centuries by an increase of war and revolution rather than by the decrease for which the plans contend. From such a "concomitant variation" only an idiot can conclude that these panaceas are suffocating war and that, when applied in a still greater dose, they could kill it forever. The only sound conclusion is that either the panaceas are perfectly impotent in the eradication of war and revolution or that, within the framework of this modern culture, society, and man, they work in favor of war and revolution, rather than against it. For this reason these plans, especially those that call themselves "practical," "realistic," and "scientific," are nothing but an illusion and self-delusion. Within a different framework, as we shall see, some of these measures can be helpful; within the contemporary one, they cannot and will not build a temple of enduring peace.

2. The Culture and Society Necessary for an Enduring Peace and Order

These gloomy conclusions do not mean that an enduring peace is generally impossible. They signify only that for its realization a new culture, with an appropriate kind of society and man, different from the contemporary one, is in order. The essential characteristics of these can be briefly summed up.[29]

(a) The new culture must put less emphasis upon purely sensory reality-value and more upon the truly rational and upon the supersensory-metarational reality-value, viewing the true reality-value as an infinite manifold with three main aspects: sensory, rational, and supersensory-metarational, each within its sphere being a true reality and a true value. This conception of the true reality-value, sponsored by Plato and Aristotle, Erigena, Thomas Aquinas, and Nicholas of Cusa, to mention but a few names, must replace the major premise of our sensate culture. Accordingly, the new culture must be an articulation of this new major premise in all its main compartments: in its science, philosophy, religion, fine arts, ethics, law, and forms of social organization on up to the manners, mores, and ways of living of its individual and group members.

(b) Its science must study, through sensory observation, the empirical aspects of the in-

finite manifold; its philosophy must investigate through mathematical and syllogistic logic the rational and logical aspects of the true reality-value; its intuitive wisdom must give us the notion of the supersensory-metalogistic aspects of it through the intuition of great religious and ethical seers, great scientists like Sir Isaac Newton, great philosophers like Plato, great artists like Beethoven and Shakespeare, and great technological inventors inspired to their achievements by intuition.[30] The history of human knowledge is a cemetery filled with wrong empirical observations, false logical reasonings, and misleading intuitions. This means that, taken separately, each of these ways of cognition is fallible and that if it is to achieve validity it must have the cooperation and mutual verification of the other two ways of cognition. The outlined integralist system of truth gives us precisely this organic integration, cooperation and mutual verification of all three ways of cognition. As such, it promises to give a more valid, richer, and better-tested truth than that which the dominant, one-sided sensory cognition can give. It eliminates also the contemporary antagonism between, and mutual undermining of, science, philosophy, and religion.

(c) Instead of the excessively relativized and atomized utilitarian and hedonistic pseudo-norms of our culture—devoid of their universal binding-power, transgressed at every suitable occasion, and degraded to the level of mere Paretian "derivations," Freudian "rationalizations," Marxian "ideological beautifications" of the economic, sexual, and other sensate "residues," "complexes," "drives," and "interests"—the ethics and law of the new culture in accordance with its major premise must be embodied in a set of universal norms binding and effectively controlling the behavior of all, unquestioned and undisputed in their ethical prestige by any other conflicting norms. In their content these universal norms must be a variation of the main ethical norms of practically all great religions and moral codes, from the elementary Golden Rule and Ten Commandments on up to the norms of the Sermon on the Mount as their sublimest ex-

---

[29] See a more detailed analysis of this new culture, society, and man in my paper, "The Task of

Cultural Rebuilding," F. E. Johnson (ed.), *World Order* (New York, 1945).

[30] Cf. on rule of intuition further, Chapter 35.

pression. Such an ethics and law will stop the atomization of moral values, eliminate ethical and legal cynicism, and abolish the dictatorship of rude force and fraud as the supreme arbiters of human conduct.

(d) Instead of the spirit of rivalry and cult of success over the others, human relations must be permeated by the spirit of "oneness," of all groups and persons, by the psychology of the free and real "we," extended over humanity. Instead of incessant stimulation of "fighting spirit" to overcome the rivals, they must be filled with the pathos of mutual service, by profound ethics of humility and sacrifice, by love at its noblest and best. Instead of glorification of "success" and the successful champions they must inculcate a sincere, wholehearted teamwork without the superiors and inferiors, the heroes, and the failures. The spirit of a good family in which every member is honestly doing his work, according to his ability, and where nobody thinks of a superiority and inferiority, is a rough approximation to this spirit of the culture and society necessary for the elimination of tensions, revolutions, and wars.

(e) Again in accordance with its major premise, the painting and sculpture, literature and music, drama and architecture, of the new culture must be quite different from contemporary fine arts. Integralist beauty must be reunited with truth and goodness, so that the new fine arts will become a value-laden art instead of being an empty art for art's sake. Instead of debunking the immortals, the new art must immortalize the mortals, ennoble the ignoble, and beautify the ugly. Instead of being negativistic, centered around the police morgue, criminal's hideouts, insane asylums, and sex organs, it would reflect mainly the eternal values, positive ideals, heroic events, and great tragedies and dramas. Like the comparable art of Greece in the fifth century B.C. and of Europe in the thirteenth century A.D., it must be an inspiring, ennobling, educating, and truly beautifying art instead of a degrading, demoralizing, and enervating cult of social pathology, as contemporary art largely is.

(f) In such a culture man will again be regarded as an end-value, as an incarnation of the divine manifold rather than as a mere biological organism, reflex-mechanism, or psychoanalytical libido, as he is usually regarded now. The value of man must again be lifted far above the utter degradation into which he is now thrown. Accordingly, the practices, institutions, and relationships that turn man into a mere means for predominantly sensate ends will largely disappear.

(g) Most of the social institutions that contradict the total character of this new culture must be eliminated. The dominant form of social relationships in such a society must be neither contractual nor compulsory, but familistic. The economic and political regimes of such a society must be neither capitalistic, communistic, nor socialistic, but familistic. The enormous contrast between multimillionaires and paupers, the rulers and the ruled, must disappear. Private property shall be limited and turned into a kind of public trusteeship. A decent minimum of the necessities shall be secured for all. The main motives for a socially useful economic and political life should be neither profit nor power but the motive of creative service to the society, similar to the motivation of great artists, religious leaders, scientists, and true philanthropists. Social institutions that contradict these purposes shall largely disappear, those that serve them will be established and reinforced.

The practical consequences of the establishment of such a culture and society will be immense, especially in the field of human mentality, conduct, and interrelationships. The new system of values and truth will abolish the contemporary antagonism between science, philosophy, and religion; they will all be inseparable organs of a unified system of truth, all pointing toward the same verities, validities, and values. The contemporary atomization and relativization of truth, goodness, and beauty will have been terminated. With this there will be an end to the contemporary mental, moral, and social anarchy. An age of certitude will replace our present age of uncertainty. Liberated from the gnawing tortures of uncertainty, the sapping poison of contradictions, and the weariness of confusion, the human mind will once more regain an inner harmony, peace, and happiness. With these qualities its creative vigor, self-confidence, and self-control will be restored. In such conditions most of the contemporary psychoneuroses will evaporate. Universalized truth will unite into one mind all of mankind.

The general devaluation of that which is purely sensate will greatly weaken the contemporary struggle for existence and for material values and will reinforce the quest for the rational and metarational values. As a result interindividual and intergroup antagonisms will greatly decrease, their brutal forms will wither, and man's conduct will be ennobled and made truly social. The same result will follow from the universalized ethical norms rooted into the heart and soul of men. Not so much by external sanctions as by inner power they will inhibit most of the antisocial actions and relationships, particularly the bloody mistreatment of man by man, of group by group. The most brutal forms of crime, civil strife, and international warfare cannot thrive in such a cultural climate and will greatly decrease. The same is true of brute force and fraud as the arbiters of human conduct.

The new fine arts will contribute their share to the same effect. By virtue of their positive beauty they will educate, inspire, instruct, fascinate, and control human beings fully as much as the new science and religion, philosophy and ethics. Primarily devoted to eternal beauty, the fine arts will serve also, as a by-product, the task of true socialization of *homo sapiens*. In this way they will contribute generously to an elimination of antisocial activities, relationships, and institutions in the human universe.

Finally, through its regained harmony, peace, and happiness of mind the new culture will make human beings less egoistic, irritable, quarrelsome, violent, and antisocial. Through a release of new creative forces in all fields of sociocultural activity it will make everyone a partner and participant in the most sublime form of happiness, the happiness of a creative genius.

In these and thousands of other ways the new culture will develop a new man, happy, generous, kind, and just to himself and to all his fellowmen. Within the framework of such a culture, society, and man neither interindividual war (crime), nor civil war, nor international war can flourish. If they do not disappear entirely, they will certainly decrease to the lowest minimum known in human history.

Such are the essential traits of the culture, society, and man necessary for an enduring peace in interindividual, intergroup, and international relationships. Without this framework as the main condition of peace, all the other panaceas against war and revolution are futile. With it, many of these will facilitate its realization. For instance, with this sociocultural foundation the United Nations and other forms of superstate government will faithfully and fruitfully serve the cause of peace. Without it, such a superstate government will be either as impotent as the defunct League of Nations or, what is still worse, may turn into a world tyranny as cruel as some of the "world empires" of the past or will lead to an increase of civil wars.[31] Without it the military and police forces of such a world government will certainly be misused and will eventually serve the cause of war instead of the cause of peace. With it, all the state and superstate governments, no matter what may be their technical forms, will be true familistic democracies. As such they will actively facilitate the maintenance of peace. Without it, no formal republican or democratic regime, even if universally diffused, can ever help—no more so than in the past, when the democratic and republican countries were at least as belligerent as the monarchical and autocratic nations and when the growth of republican and democratic regimes for the last few centuries has been followed by an increase, rather than by a decrease, of war. Without this framework the further increase of scientific discoveries and technological inventions will be of just as little avail as in the past, during which, beginning with the thirteenth century, they have steadily and rapidly increased up to the present

---

[31] From 500 B.C. up to 1925 A.D. there were in the history of the Greco-Roman and western societies some 967 international and 1623 civil wars. Great civil wars were as bloody and destructive as big international wars. A mere replacement of international wars by civil wars does not give any decrease of war and increase of peace. Hence —the futility of a mere establishment of the world government, without the other conditions necessary for a real peace. Cf. on number of wars and revolutions *Dynamics*, Vol. III.

time and have been followed by an almost parallel increase of war and revolution. The same is true of the development of schools, universities, books, magazines, papers, movies, radio, theaters, and all the other means of contemporary education. Beginning with the thirteenth century, they have been steadily increasing without any resulting decrease of war, revolutions, or crime. This is still more true in regard to such panaceas as a more equitable distribution of the natural resources or a higher material standard of living or a more enlightened self-interest and utilitarian "rationality." Without the foregoing framework any truly equitable distribution of the natural resources throughout all mankind is impossible, just as it has been impossible in the past. The states and nations will remain as egotistic and rapacious as they have hitherto been. Those who believe that a diffusion of democratic forms of government would change this forget that the so-called democracies of the past and the present have been fully as imperialistic as the autocracies. They forget also the unpleasant but unquestionable fact that almost all such democracies, beginning with the Athenian and ending with the contemporary ones, have been based upon the severest exploitation of colonies and "spheres of influence" or have consisted of a vast layer of semifree and unfree population many times larger than the full-fledged citizenship of such democracies.

Likewise an "enlightened self-interest" and utilitarian "rationality" have been growing ever since the thirteenth century, without being accompanied by any decrease of war. One of the reasons for this is the fact that from a deeper standpoint this self-interest turns out to be a blind egotism, and utilitarian "rationality" a most irrational illusion. Utilitarian rationality is defined as the use of the most efficient means for the realization of an end desired. Typically, it has in view only the rationality of the means, and it neglects the rationality of the ends. The present war, which uses the most efficient and scientific means available for the defeat of the enemy, is perfectly rational from this standpoint; so also is the activity of a gang of efficient murderers, armed with the best techniques of murder, which is never caught or punished. These considerations show clearly that the

truly rational action is that in which the ends as well as the means are rational. An action that uses rational means to irrational ends is particularly irrational. For this reason the utilitarian rationality of our society cannot regard war or revolution as irrational, and still less is it able to achieve the abolition of both.

Likewise, without this framework, the panaceas suggested for the eradication of crime, rioting, revolution, and civil war cannot be effective. These irrational phenomena will remain and may even grow in spite of the panaceas, just as they have remained and grown during the centuries of the domination of modern culture. Notwithstanding the fact that these panaceas have been applied with especial liberality in the twentieth century, the glaring fact remains that neither crime, rioting, nor revolution has decreased; nor has the family become any better integrated; nor have suicide and mental disease declined; nor has the intensity of the interindividual and intergroup struggle for existence diminished; nor, if we can measure happiness by the movement of suicide, has man become any more happy. If anything, the objective results have been exactly opposite to what might be expected from the application of the panaceas.

The net result of the preceding analysis is that the suggested framework of the new culture, society, and man is not the manifestation of a preacher's complex, nor is it the "impractical" indulgence of an armchair philosopher in his pet preoccupation, but rather is it a most practical, scientific, and matter-of-fact indication of the *necessary conditions* for a realization of the objective—a lasting peace. Without it, all the other means to building a temple of lasting peace and order are bound to be impotent or will only produce even bigger and more terrible wars and revolutions.

3. Prospects

To this conclusion may be raised the objection that the new sociocultural framework is itself unrealizable and utopian. If such an objection were valid, it would only mean that an enduring peace is impossible. In that case all rational persons should stop fooling themselves and others with the utopia of a mankind without war, bloody revolution, and crime and should resignedly accept them as inevitable in the same manner in which we accept death. However, after a careful scrutiny, the objection turns out to be far less axiomatic and unquestionable than it appears at first glance. In other words, the chances for a realization of the new framework, with the enduring peace that it implies, are not at all nil.

First, if mankind is going to live a creative life and is not going to sink either into the somnolence of "a benumbed and ruminating human herd" or into the tortuous agony of decay, the new framework is the only way that is left. The existing framework is so rotten and is progressively becoming so destructive and painful that mankind cannot creatively and contentedly live within it for any length of time. If it cannot be replaced by the new framework, then the end of mankind's creative history, in one of the two ways just indicated, is inescapable, and science, having invented its atomic bomb, will hasten it. But such a conclusion is not inevitable; in spite of the gravity of many of the great crises that have beset mankind throughout history, human beings have always been able somehow to create new forms of culture and society that have eventually terminated the crisis. For the present there is no unquestionable evidence that a new sociocultural renaissance is impossible.

Second, the shift from a withered sensate culture to a form of culture somewhat akin to that just outlined has happened several times in the history of Greco-Roman, western, and certain other great cultures. If it has been possible of occurrence in the past, there is every reason to suppose that it can recur in the future.

Third, if the birth of the new culture were dependent entirely upon contemporary "utilitarian rationality," its emergence and growth would be uncertain indeed. But fortunately such is not the manner in which one form of culture is ordinarily replaced by another. The replacement is usually a result of the historical process itself, of gigantic, impersonal, spontaneous forces immanent in a given sociocultural framework; and only at a later stage does it become facilitated by truly rational forces that plan and endeavor to build the new culture with all available scientific means. The spontaneous forces immanent in our modern culture have already brought about its phase of decline and crisis; they have already undermined its prestige and fascination to a considerable degree; they have already alienated from it a considerable portion of the population; they have robbed it of most of its charms —its security, its safety, its prosperity, its material comfort, its happiness, its sensate freedom, and all of its main values. Not in the classroom but in the hard school of life millions of people are being incessantly taught by these forces an unforgettable and indelible lesson, comprehensible to the plainest human being, that the existing framework is going to give them "stones" and bullets instead of bread; gigantic destruction in place of creative construction; misery instead of prosperity; regimentation in lieu of freedom; death, mutilation, and suffering instead of security of life, integrity of body, or bigger and better pleasure. With these charms progressively evaporating, this modern culture of ours has no other great values by which to hold the allegiance of humanity. Like a pretty woman whose bodily charms have gone, it is destined to lose more and more the adherence of humanity until it has been entirely forsaken and dethroned from its dominant position in favor of a different sociocultural framework. This point has about been reached by our culture. Its magnificent creativeness, its prestige, and its charms are about over.

Parallel with this defection of humanity from contemporary culture, the same spontaneous forces are generating and increasing the quest for a different sociocultural framework, one which is more creative and adequate and less destructive and painful. This quest is at the present moment the main item in the order of the day; almost everyone is busy with the problems of the future society and culture. Only a few, who nothing forget and nothing learn, still cherish ideas of a restoration of the past and a revitalization of a withered framework. The overwhelming majority understand —if not by calculation and logical analysis, then by plain horse sense—that that is impossible. They recognize the necessity of some framework different from that which we have now.

At this stage the truly rational forces enter the play and take a guiding hand in it. With all the available wisdom and knowledge and with a sense of supreme duty they endeavor to create various systematic blueprints of the new sociocultural framework, to test and improve them, rejecting the less adequate ones and perfecting the better ones. New plans with their philosophies, ideologies, and ways and means of realization, multiply, become more and more coordinated, more and more diffused, continually accumulate a momentum and an ever increasing legion of adherents, until they become a tangible social force. This force grows and in thousands of ways begins significantly to influence human mentality and conduct, science and religion, philosophy and ethics, fine arts and social institutions. The process is slow, develops erratically from day to day, and has many deviations, mistakes, and

miscarriages of its own. Altogether, it takes several decades, even a few centuries, for its full realization. Sooner or later, however, it terminates in a dethronement of the sociocultural framework that was previously dominant, and in a rise to ascendancy of the new framework.

In the case of our contemporary culture we have reached the point at which the rational forces are about ready to enter the play. Together with the spontaneous forces of the historical process itself, they may be able to create a new sociocultural framework that will be a rough approximation to the one outlined above. When this objective has been reached, the utopia of a lasting peace and order will become a reality. If this is not achieved, apocalyptic catastrophe is ahead.

Chapter 34. Life-Span, Mortality, and Resurrection of Groups

I. Life-Span and Mortality of Organized Groups

1. Groups Are Mortal

A further, ever repeated process in the life-history of groups is their dissolution. Already Plato has rightly remarked in connection with his ideal republic: "Seeing that everything which has a beginning has also an end, even this perfect constitution will in time perish and come to dissolution."[1] The end of a social group comes when one or all of its components are lost or the meaningful causal belt, uniting them, disappears.[2]

At one time-moment an organization emerges as a separate and recognizable collective unity and begins to function as an individuality among thousands of other organizations and institutions. This functioning may be shorter or longer. Sometimes it is so short that the organization dies at its "pre-natal stage" before it emerges. Sometimes the organization lives for a certain length of time, and then, either suddenly or gradually losing its essential traits, it begins to disintegrate and becomes more and more unidentifiable, until finally, like a wave which exists for some time and then disappears in the midst of other waves, it dissolves in the ocean of other organizations and institutions.

The beginning and the end of some organizations and institutions is clearly marked and can be established definitely in terms of a year, a month, sometimes even a day or an hour. Such are, for instance, most of the organizations whose beginning and end are determined by juridical incorporation and dissolution. Other organizations and institutions, like many states, religious organizations, educational institutions, sometimes the family, and so on, often do not have such definite marks of their emergence and end, either because they are not recorded and are lost in the gray past, or because they have grown and dissolved, gradually and imperceptibly. In such organizations the life-span either cannot be established at all or can be determined only very approximately, liable to a considerable error.

2. Economic Organizations

It is comprehensible that in our "economically-minded society" the fullest data are collected in regard to various business organizations. The first impression which these data convey is that an enormous majority of business organizations in contemporary society have a life-span much shorter than is usually thought. Here are some typical data.

If we take retail trade business enterprises, as they are represented by grocery, drug, shoe, and hardware stores, their median longevity in Buffalo, in the period of 1918-1928, was about

---

[1] Plato, *The Republic*, Chapter 8, p. 257, in Everyman's Library edition.

[2] See a more detailed analysis of a dissolution and disintegration of social and cultural systems in my *Dynamics*, Vol. IV, pp. 85 ff. Cf. further Chapter 47.

three years for the grocery stores, and about six years for the drug, shoe, and hardware stores. From 17 to 60 per cent of them died out (withdrew from business) during the first year of their existence, and only 5 per cent of the grocery stores, 28 per cent of the drug stores, 13 and 21 per cent of the hardware and shoe stores, respectively, survived ten years.[3] R. S. Vaile's study of grocery stores in Duluth, Minnesota, showed that only 28.6 per cent of the independent grocery stores and 77.8 per cent of voluntary chain stores survived to four years.[4] E. Heilman's study of 16,089 business firms in Minnesota[5] gave 6.6 years as the average length of these firms, with 5.2 years for the firms with capital below $2000, and 33.2 years with the capital of $500,000 and over.

Similar results are given in the less extensive studies of Kolb and Wileden, J. W. Barger, and P. H. Nystrom.[6] It goes without saying that the longevity of these institutions fluctuates considerably in different localities and countries; but, when a sufficiently large sample is taken, in most of the contemporary urbanized and industrialized societies (with their intensive mobility), it is hardly probable that the results would be radically different from the above. Even if their longevity would be two or three times longer or shorter than in the mentioned studies, it still would be relatively short; at any rate, much shorter than the average life-expectation for man.

R. C. Epstein's study shows that in the period from 1903 to 1926 in the United States, 181 automobile concerns were engaged in the manufacture of passenger automobiles on a commercial scale. Of these only 66 remained in business for ten years or longer. This means that about 64 per cent of these—relatively big industrial organizations—had a duration of less than ten years. And this is an expanding industry in the period of its boom![7]

That this short life-span of the contemporary economic organizations is not exceptional but typical is evidenced further by a series of studies of large samples of the joint-stock companies and economic limited companies in various countries. From the nature of such economic organizations it follows that they represent a rather typical cross-section of all the business organizations—all the important industries, trades, etc.—of the contemporary economic world. At the present time we have the data for Switzerland, Italy, and Great Britain.

A study of the age-composition and duration of life of 7,337 Swiss joint-stock companies for the period 1902-1920 shows that the median life-expectation at the moment of the founding for all the companies is about 28.67 years. Of all the companies existing in any of the years from 1902 to 1920, from 42 to 45 per cent (according to the year) had a life-span below seven years; from 18 to 31 per cent between seven and fourteen years; from 11 to 13 per cent between fourteen and twenty-one years. Thus more than 75 per cent of all the companies had an age under twenty-one years. Only from 13 to 25 per cent of them existed over twenty-one years.

If we take the companies which were dissolved their average life-span was 10.06 years; the median, about five years. Only 1.3 per cent of them existed over fifty years. The third year of the existence of the companies was

[3] See E. D. McGarry, *Mortality in Retail Trade* (Buffalo, 1930), pp. 52, 57-61; 6,268 stores were investigated. Many interesting and important details are given in this study.

[4] R. S. Vaile, *Studies in Economics* (Minneapolis, 1932).

[5] E. A. Heilman, *Mortality of Business Firms in Minneapolis, St. Paul and Duluth, 1926-1930* (Minneapolis, 1932). See also R. A. Stevenson (ed.), *A Type Study of American Banking* (Minneapolis, 1934); F. S. Chapin, *Contemporary American Institutions* (New York, 1935), Chapter 5.

[6] See P. H. Nystrom, *Economics of Retailing*. See J. H. Kolb and A. F. Wileden, *Special Interest Groups in Rural Society* (Wisconsin, 1927). Kolb and Wileden studied the longevity of various organizations among the rural population of Wisconsin; the organizations for "better business" had a mean duration of 12.1 years, for "better farming" 7.2 years. See also J. W. Barger, *The Rural Community Clubs in Montana* (University of Montana, 1930); Barger's study of rural organizations in Montana, where the organizations of economic nature were also included, gives 6.8 years as the average duration of the existing organizations.

[7] R. C. Epstein, "Producers' Growth Curves in an Expanding Industry," *Harvard Business Review*, Vol. VI, pp. 270-277, 1927-1928; see also Epstein's, *The Automobile Industry: Its Economic and Commercial Development*, 1928.

the most critical and gave the highest rate of dissolutions.[8]

Similar results are obtained by G. Lasorsa for the Italian joint-stock companies for the period of 1902-1922. The Italian companies had a still shorter duration of life than the Swiss. The expectation of life at the moment of founding is here 24 years 10 months instead of 28.67 years for the Swiss. The average duration of the dissolved companies is here 6 years 9 months instead of 10.06 years. While 86.49 per cent of the Swiss companies reach the duration of five years, here the percentage is only about 72.24; about 74.22 per cent of the Swiss companies reach the age of ten years; here only 61.67 per cent. Except these differences in detail the essential results are similar. Here also the first three years of existence of the companies were the most critical and gave the highest rate of dissolutions.[9]

The picture given by about 5000 English limited companies founded in the period from 1856 to 1865 and whose life-career is studied up to 1928 is not materially different:

The facts of duration show that almost 36 per cent of the ordinary companies formed in the decade (in 1856 to 1865) ceased to exist in any form within five years promotion, with an additional 4.5 per cent having to be sold or reconstructed. Some 54 per cent had ceased to exist within ten years, with an additional 7 per cent having to be sold or reconstructed. Eight per cent exist today in original form. . . . Expressed in quartiles and medians, the facts of duration for companies, entirely ceasing to exist in different industries show that only two groups have lower quartiles of over five years, that only two have medians over ten years, and that only four have upper quartiles of over twenty years. No important industry (except cotton) shows companies of great longevity, and none shows a really high survival rate.[10]

This means that the gross duration of the English limited companies has been somewhat shorter than even that of the Italian. The large samples of the last three studies,

their substantiality and the remarkable similarity of the results, in spite of the fact that they concern three different countries, this, together with the other data given, strongly warrants the conclusion that the results are typical for the economic organizations and institutions of all the modern capitalistic industrial societies. There may be some variation in either direction—to greater or lesser longevity—but that would hardly change the general picture of a relatively short life-span of the modern economic organizations. This does not preclude, of course, a possibility of much longer duration for a few economic institutions. But they cannot change the general picture and a short existence of the majority of the modern economic organizations.

3. Various Private and Local Cultural Associations

The data relating to this class of social organizations are unfortunately much more scarce than those for the economic institutions. Nevertheless, so far as private and local cultural organizations are concerned (clubs, literary, musical, oratorical, and other local associations) the existing data are, at least, significant for a large portion of such associations in the modern urbanized and industrialized societies. These data, like the preceding, again disclose a life-span of such organizations much shorter than it is usually thought. Here are some examples.

In the quoted study of Kolb and Wileden 351 rural organizations were studied in a county in Wisconsin (organizations for "better business," "health and social welfare," "young people's cultural organizations," "parent-teacher associations," "better farming," "home improvement," recreational clubs and groups, etc.). Their modal length of life was only about two years. Of 351 organizations only three (or less than 1 per cent) have existed over 50 years; 87 dead organizations had four years for the mean length of life; for the

---

[8] See "Bestand der Schweizerischen Aktiengesellschaften nach ihrem Alter," *Schweizerische Statistische Mitteilungen,* IV (Jahrgang, 1922), 4 Vols.; also for 1920, 4 Vols. See also H. Gaedicke, "Altersaufbau, Abgangsordnung und Lebensdauer von Aktiengesellschaften." *Allgemeines Statistisches Archiv,* Vol. 19, pp. 513-529, 1929.

[9] See Giovanni Lasorsa, "Indagini sulla mortalita delle societa italiane per azioni." *Giornale degli economisi e rivista di statistica,* 1928, pp. 838-858.

[10] H. A. Shannon, "The First Five Thousand Limited Companies and Their Duration," *Economic History,* A Supplement of the Economic Journal, January, 1932, pp. 396-419, 418-419.

264 existing organizations the mean is 7.4 years.[11]

Barger's study of 50 rural organizations in Montana has shown that their age ranges from one to eighteen years, giving an average of 6.8 for all the existing ones.[12]

F. S. Chapin studied 533 student organizations at the University of Minnesota since 1887. The organizations consisted of musical, literary, debating and oratorical societies, athletic and military associations, sororities, fraternities, honor, religious, and political groups. Between 1887 and 1924, 43.7 per cent of all these societies died and only 56.3 per cent were in existence at the moment of investigation.[13]

Not very different are the results of L. A. T. Haak's study of similar organizations at Harvard University, for the period of 1875-1925, made in my seminar. Of 464 organizations studied, 27.6 per cent had a duration of less than three years; 20.7 per cent from three to five years; 18.1 per cent from five to ten years; 22.8 per cent from ten to twenty-five years; and 10.8 per cent existed for more than twenty-five years. Thus about one-half of these organizations did not exceed a life-span of five years.[14]

4. The Family

We must distinguish between the life-span of the family as a union of husband and wife, and that of parents and children. As a union of husband and wife it ends with the death of one or of both, or with a divorce or desertion. In this sense the duration of a given family is limited to the period from a few days to that of some seventy or eighty years. Through divorce this span is cut still shorter in its maximum. Of some 2651 marriages in Wisconsin (1929) that ended in divorce, 13.9 per cent lasted less than one year; 8.9 per cent less than two years; 7.7 per cent less than 6.6 years. All in all 87.9 per cent lasted less than 20 years.[15] Generally in the populations with a

high divorce rate the span of life of husband-wife union is much shorter than in the populations with a low divorce rate.

When we take the family as a union of parents and children, we must distinguish between its social and biological longevity. The social life-span of the family, like other social organizations, does not necessarily coincide with its biological duration. As a social unity, a given family may exist socially, through adoption and similar means, after it ceases to exist biologically through the death of all its biological offspring. And vice versa, socially it may disappear though its biological posterity, in the form of illegitimate children, and the offspring whose connection with a given family become intangible, may continue to exist. In our study we have in view not the biological but the social continuity of the family. The life-span of the family as a union of parents and children again fluctuates from a short duration, limited in the childless families with the duration of life of the married, up to much longer periods of continuity of the family in several generations. Obviously in the populations with a high and increasing per cent of childless families the duration of the family longevity is lower than in the populations with a low per cent of childless marriages. As to the longest span-life of the family in this field the existing material is scarce and relates mainly to aristocratic and privileged families which, for various reasons, have been more interested in the continuation of their history and existence than most of the families of the lower classes whose history usually is not known beyond three or four generations. It is reasonable to assume, therefore, that the social existence of the families of the lower classes is rather of a shorter duration than that of the families of the upper classes, whatever may be their biological durations. As to the social longevity of the upper class families, the following data are representative.

According to the well-known Fahlbeck study of the Swedish nobility, of 1219 families about

---

[11] See Kolb and Wileden, *op. cit.*, pp. 47 ff.

[12] See Barger's work, quoted.

[13] F. S. Chapin, *Extra-Curricular Activities at the University of Minnesota*. (University of Minnesota Press, 1929), p. 11 and *passim*.

[14] L. A. T. Haak, *Student Organizations at Harvard*, 1875-1925. Unpublished study, presented as

a term-paper in Sorokin's course: "Social Dynamics," p. 13 (Harvard, 1932).

[15] K. Young and C. L. Dedrick, "Variation in the Duration of Marriages," *Journal of American Statistical Association*, Vol. XXVII, June, 1932. F. S. Chapin, *op. cit.*, p. 72.

77.6 per cent existed less than 100 years; about 20 per cent from 100 to 200 years; and about 3 per cent from 200 to 300 years. Only one family out of 1,547 families lived over 300 years. In other words, about 84 per cent of the families ceased to exist socially in the third generation, only two families reached the ninth generation, and none lived longer.[16]

The existing data relating to royal families of various countries and periods, Greek and Roman upper classes, medieval nobility, and so on, are not essentially different. For instance, most of the ancient Egyptian dynasties existed about 150 years; the Chinese dynasties about 300 years; the Merovingians, 269; the Carlovingians, 235; the Capets, 341; the Valois, 261; the German dynasties, about 120 years, and so on. Longevity of the majority of the aristocratic families in medieval Europe was definitely under 200 years; a few families exceeded this duration, but most of them existed socially not much longer than 100 years.[17]

If the duration of life of a family with children does not go usually beyond two or three hundred years, it also does not go under the span of two or three generations in the upper as well as the lower classes. This means that though the family is a small group so far as its membership is concerned, nevertheless, all in all its duration has been conspicuously above that of most of the economic and private cultural organizations.[18] It lives socially (and also biologically) several times longer than most of the business and cultural unities, though these latter have often much larger membership and much larger economic means. The explanation of this fact lies evidently in the nature of economic and cultural organizations which bind their members together only by special economic and special cultural ties, while the family binds its members by almost all the important social ties and interests. It is a *"consortium omnis vitae, divini et humani juris communicatio,"* as the *Corpus Juris Civilis* of Justinian puts it. Its members are bound together for life and death; their interests are

similar in many vital points; they are bound by ties of kinship, friendship, by community of life-experience, by similarity of mores, language, and so on; therefore, the family persists where other organizations disintegrate. Such seems to be the secret of this relatively longer duration of the family with children as a social organization.

5. Universities and Colleges

If we turn to larger social organizations like the universities, the cities, and finally to states and religious organizations, the problem of their duration often cannot be determined definitely. Nevertheless, something can be said which would convey at least an approximate idea of their life-span. In regard to such social institutions as universities and colleges the data are more satisfactory than for the others, and probably do not deviate much from the reality.

In cooperation with Dr. Walter Lunden, we made a study of the age-compositions of all universities, colleges, and other institutions of higher learning existing in 1930 and enumerated in the well-known "Minerva."[19] Of 779 institutions listed, for which the data of their foundation are given, 602 or 77 per cent had been founded since 1800, 48 or about 6 per cent were founded in the eighteenth, 31 or about 4 per cent in the seventeenth, 41, 27, 12, 13, and 5 respectively in the sixteenth, fifteenth, fourteenth, thirteenth, and twelfth centuries. Few, if any, go beyond the twelfth century. This shows that almost 80 per cent of them have an age not exceeding one hundred years; and quite an insignificant percentage are of an age extending over several centuries. There is no doubt that many institutions of higher learning have been founded and have died since the twelfth century, but the data of their duration are lacking. Likewise, in the past in China, India, Ceylon, Babylonia, Greece, and Rome, the universities and the centers of higher learning existed, but unfortunately reliable data of their life-span are lacking. The

---

[16] P. E. Fahlbeck, *"La noblèsse de Suède,"* *Bulletin de l' Institut International de Statistique*, Vol. XV, pp. 173 ff.

[17] See the detailed data in Sorokin, *Mobility*, pp 156-157; 357 ff.

[18] See on this correct remarks of F. S. Chapin, *op. cit.*, pp. 72 ff.

[19] *Minerva*, 1930. *Jahrbuch der gelehrten Welt* (Berlin, 1930). See many details in W. A. Lunden, *The Dynamics of Higher Education* (Pittsburgh, 1939), pp. 93 ff.

data show that even such institutions rarely gave a duration extending beyond one or a few hundred years. On the other hand, they seem to exist for a longer time than most of the economic institutions and organizations.

6. Cities as Territorial Groups

Although the cities represent not any one social unity but a conglomeration of many social organizations, nevertheless, as a territorial abode for many social organizations which have occupied it, the city can be taken as a pseudo-unit for our investigation.

Adolphe Quételet, in one of his essays on the duration of nations, governments, and cities, thought that the average duration of big cities was about 627 years. This figure he obtained from computing the average of the durations of three cities, Tyre (680 years), Carthage (701 years), and Syracuse (501 years).[20] At the present moment we can hardly accept such a method or such an average. In our mobile age, in the regions of the "boom-cities," we have cities which appear and disappear within a few years. For instance, Dr. N. L. Whetten in his doctor's thesis has shown the following picture of appearance and disappearance of the cities of over 5,000 population in the Canadian Prairie provinces. The number of such cities was eight in 1910, ten in 1915, twelve in 1920, eleven in 1925, and eleven in 1930.[21]

The figures show that within the period of five years two new cities of over 5,000 population sprang up, and within the same period one of them disappeared. His data show also that in regard to smaller cities such appearance and disappearance has been still more sudden and violent. Similar was the situation in the "boom-areas" of the United States. This means that in such areas in our modern age a sudden appearance or disappearance of a city and its longevity amounting only to a few years is a real phenomenon.[22]

If we turn to cities which are not "boom-cities" their duration is difficult to compute on account of a lack of accurate data and sufficiently large samples. But it is possible to measure the age-composition of the existing cities. In a way it gives an idea about the longevity of at least the existing cities. With Dr. C. A. Anderson we made such a study of the age-composition of the largest cities of the world (over 100,000 population) as well as smaller cities. The samples were not only representative, but in regard to the largest cities, all such cities about which the data of their appearance exist, were included. Smaller cities were also represented by a very large sample selected at random. The cities about which no data could be secured were excluded. In regard to other cities it was possible to secure in many cases the year or the decade of its foundation, in other cases at least the century when it emerged as a notable social center. Main results show the following picture:

The Great World Cities
(100,000 population and over in 1920)

Period of Emergence	Number	Per cent
B.C. to 5th century A.D.	67	18.8
6th to 10th century	69	19.4
11th to 15 century	75	21.2
16 to 20th century	144	40.5
Total	355	99.9

If we take the great cities which were founded in the sixth century A.D. and later (288 cities), 16.3 per cent of them were founded in the nineteenth century, 13.9 in the eighteenth, 9.0 in the seventeenth, 10.7 in the sixteenth, 3.1 in the fifteenth, 3.1 in the fourteenth, 4.5 in the thirteenth, 7.6 in the twelfth, 7.6 in the eleventh, 11.1 in the tenth, 4.9 in the ninth, 3.5 in the eighth, 2.1 in the seventh, and 2.4 in the sixth century. All in all, about 50 per cent of the great cities of the world

---

[20] A. Quètelet, *Du système social et les lois qui le régissent*, p. 163-164 (Paris, 1848).

[21] N. L. Whetten, *The Social and Economic Structure of the Trade Centers in the Canadian Provinces with Special Reference to Its Changes*, 1910-1930. Unpublished Doctor's thesis, submitted to the Division of Sociology (Harvard University, June, 1932).

[22] Passing by it is proper to notice that in the past, in such countries as Egypt, Assyro-Babylonia,

and other Oriental countries, the cities were also erected and abandoned suddenly, according to the whim of the Pharaoh or ruler. Almost every Pharaoh used to build his own city, and after his death it was usually abandoned or greatly diminished. See data in P. A. Sorokin, C. Zimmerman, G. J. Galpin, *A Systematic Source Book in Rural Sociology*, Vol. I, Chapters 3, 4 (Minneapolis, 1931). Thus the "boom-cities," though of a different form, were not unknown to the past also.

have existed, so far, less than about 450 years; and about 30 per cent less than about 230 years.[23]

If we take the cities in a relatively new country like the United States of America, they are naturally much younger. Of 66 American cities with the population of 100,000 and more in 1920, 24.3 were founded in the seventeenth century; 31.8 per cent in the eighteenth; and 43.9 in the nineteenth century. If we take a representative sample of the smaller cities, for instance up to 5,000 population, then 15.8 per cent of them were founded in the seventeenth century, 24.1 in the eighteenth, and 60.1 per cent in the nineteenth century.[24] Thus about one half of the American cities are only centenarians or still younger.

If we take the cities of an older European country, for instance France, then the picture looks as follows. (Our sample includes 234 cities taken from the French Census of 1926, for which the data of their foundation could be found.) Of the 234 cities, 155 are from 10,000 to 25,000 population, 64 from 25,000 to 100,000 and 15 are over 100,000 population. Of these cities about 40.1 per cent were founded before the fourth century of our era and were Roman cities. But as the continuity between these ancient and the new cities founded on the same place was broken, it would be more appropriate to take only those cities which were founded in the sixth century A.D. and later (128 cities). Of these 8.6 per cent were founded in the sixth century, 15.6 in the seventh, 12.5 in the eighth, 13.3 in the ninth, 16.4 in the tenth, 11.7 in the eleventh, 7.8 in the twelfth, 6.2 in the thirteenth, about I per cent in the fourteenth and fifteenth, 1.6 in the sixteenth, 4.7 in the seventeenth, and about 1 per cent in the eighteenth and nineteenth.

This shows that the French cities are much older than the American ones; and that most of them approach one thousand years in age.

However, as was mentioned, the city as it is taken here is not a social organization, but rather a territorial abode of numerous social organizations. Therefore the above ages of the cities are not the durations of social organizations proper, but durations of the locus which has been, interruptedly or not, occupied as their stage by many and quite different social organizations.

7. The States

A. Quételet contended that the average duration of the state is 1,461 years, the average obtained by him on the basis of the rightly or wrongly computed durations of Assyria, Egypt, the Jewish State, Greece, and Rome.[25]

We can scarcely agree with this conclusion, because even the slightest attempt to compute the durations of a number of the states shows at once an evident arbitrariness of the above figure. As a matter of fact such an attempt shows a great variation in the states' duration. Some, like China, are still in existence after four thousand years. Others, like most of the South American states or the newly created states after the World War, like Esthonia, Latvia, etc. have existed only a few years, or a few decades.

Generally, on account of the vagueness of the concept of the state, the phenomena of discontinuity and revival in the States' existence, absorption of one state by another and their parcellation into several states, unification of the independent states, and often a mixture of the state with the nation and nationality; because of these and similar circumstances, it is exceedingly difficult, almost impossible, to compute the states' duration without a somewhat arbitrary standardization of what is to be regarded as the beginning and the end of the state. If we agree to regard as the state's beginning any latest period before which the population of a certain territory was not a sovereign body and after which it became such, or out of several states was made one united state which did not exist before, then the majority of existing states are rela-

---

[23] The list of the cities was taken from the *Aperçue de la démographie des divers pays du monde, 1925.* The data of the foundation of the cities were secured from various encyclopedias and historical works.

[24] There is a slight correlation between the age of the cities and their present size; but it is slight and inconsistent for various countries. Many of the old cities are small at the present moment. A popular opinion that the older the city the larger it tends to be is thus not quite accurate.

[25] A. Quételet, *Du système social,* quoted pp. 158-161 (Paris, 1848).

tively young. Such are Albania (independent since 1912); Greece (since 1830); Bulgaria (since 1878, and completely independent since 1909); Rumania (since 1878); Belgium (since 1831); Luxemburg (since 1867); Germany (since 1871); Poland (1920); Czechoslovakia (1918); Hungary (1920); Norway (1905); Finland (1917); Esthonia (1920); Latvia (1918); Lithuania (1920) (these three have already lost their independence); Italy (1870); Jugoslavia (1920; before Servia, 1880). Add to this Chile, Bolivia, Peru, Ecuador, Colombia, Venezuela, Brazil, Paraguay, Uruguay, Argentina, Mexico, Guatemala, Salvador, Honduras, Nicaragua, Panama, Costa Rica—all made independent in the nineteenth century. In addition the United States of America, Persia (since 1730), Afghanistan (1750), Siam (1782) became independent in the eighteenth century. Under our agreement at least 36 states have an age either about or much below one hundred years; and a few others between one and two hundred years.

If we agree to regard as the beginning of a given state its first emergence on the political scene as an independent political union, and pay no attention to the subsequent loss of sovereignty and its absorption by another state, provided that state at the present time (like Poland, Czechoslovakia, and many others) is a sovereign body, then the duration of most of the above states, as well as those which have existed for centuries without loss of their sovereignty (like France, Russia, England, etc.), is much greater and approaches one thousand years, some longer, like China, and some shorter, like the United States, Turkey, Hungary, and some others. None of the states of Europe and western civilization exceed much the duration of fifteen centuries. Only a few Oriental states can boast an age considerably longer than fifteen centuries, and even these states have not an uninterrupted existence for such a period; they have been conquered several times, and several times have lost their sovereignty and ceased to exist as independent states.[26]

All in all, the duration of the states, regardless of the criteria of the beginning and the end accepted, shows an enormous variety, from the short-lived states whose duration sometimes does not go beyond a few decades or even a few years, to the states with uninterrupted sovereignty of several centuries, and with interrupted existence for more than two thousand years.

8. Religion and Denominational Religious Groups

If we take the great world religions as social organizations they have a duration longer than any of the social organizations examined, and possibly longer than most or all social organizations of any kind. Indeed, Hinduism and Judaism are already more than 3,500 years old; Buddhism, about 2,500; Confucianism and Taoism, also about 2,500; Christianity, about 1,900; Mohammedanism, about 1,300; and this is also true of some other, though not so diffused, religions and their organizations.

If we take, however, various denominations of one of these great religions, for instance, various Christian denominations, their age is, of course, much younger, and their duration generally much shorter. Protestantism as a whole is about 500 years old. The separation of the eastern Christianity from the western Christianity and a formal existence of each of the main separated branches of Christianity is also less than 1,000 years old.

If we turn to the still smaller denominational organizations, their age and duration is again much lower than those of the main branches of Christianity. To avoid bias in selection I undertook to give the real picture of the whole situation of "age-composition," and with the help of Dr. C. A. Anderson I made a study of the existing religious denominations in the United States, as they are represented in the U. S. Census of Religious Bodies for the periods of 1890, 1906, 1916, 1926 and 1936.[27] Part of the religious denominations of the United States were "imported," that is were started elsewhere; the other part is

---

[26] The few cases like Egypt, Persia, and Greece are hardly an exception to this rule, because the connection between the ancient and contemporary Egypt, Persia, and Greece hardly goes beyond the mere name.

[27] See the volumes of the *U. S. Bureau of the Census of the Religious Bodies* for 1890-1906, 1906-1916, for 1916-1926, 1926-1936.

"native," that is, originated in the United States. All in all, in 1926, there were 196 various religious denominations (excluding those which had only a few followers). Of these, 46 were "imported," 150 were "native." If we take the "native" denominations (mostly Christian) only 16.4 per cent of all such were founded before the nineteenth century (in the seventeenth and eighteenth centuries); the remaining 83.6 per cent were started in the nineteenth and twentieth centuries. This shows that the majority of the denominations in the United States are relatively young. In other countries where traditionalism is stronger and complete freedom of religion is lacking, the picture will probably be different, and most of the denominations older. Nevertheless, it is probable that even in such countries there will be a number of open or secret denominations and sects of a relatively recent foundation.

As to the data of the importation of the "non-native" denominations and their foundation in the United States, 67.4 per cent of all those imported denominations were imported (started their religious organization in the United States) in the nineteenth century. The remaining 32.6 per cent were imported in the seventeenth and eighteenth centuries. These data show that the denominational organizations in the United States are all relatively young.

In order to have a clearer idea of the longevity of the denominations and their organizations we studied the intensity of changes in the denominations as they were reflected in the Census data for the periods 1890-1906, 1906-1916, 1916-1926, and 1926-1936. The essentials of this study can be summed up in the following figures: in the period between 1890 and 1906, 68 new denominations or 46.9 per cent of the existing ones were added and 20 denominations or 13.8 per cent of the existing denominations ceased to exist. This gives the total change

(new additions plus dissolutions) of 60.7 per cent of the existing denominations; corresponding figures for the period 1906-1916 are 21.2 per cent of additions, 8.8 per cent of dissolutions, total 30.0 per cent of the existing denominations; for the period 1916-1926 the corresponding figures are 6.9, 8.4, and 15.3 per cent; for 1926-1936, 12.1, 4, 16.1 per cent.

These data show that in the United States during a short period of ten to sixteen years, a considerable number of the denominations appear and cease to exist, having thus a very short duration of life. In other countries the picture may be different; but it is probable that when all the open and secret sects and "religious groups" of a personal nature, often not registered in the official statistics, are taken, they would show something similar to the above picture of a relatively rapid appearance and disappearance of religious organizations. This suggests that only the broad rivers of the great religions flow for a long time; the small rivulets of various denominational organizations and sects flow for a short time and then dry out.

If instead of the denominational organizations one would take still smaller religious organizations of a given church, of parish, they seem to appear and disappear still more quickly than the denominational organizations.

9. Multibonded Groups

We have seen the duration of the family. The duration of some multibonded groups like castes in India is one of the longest; they have existed there for more than 2000 years. Much shorter is the duration of *social estates*; on the average these ranged between one and five centuries. The life-span of tribes and clans cannot be computed on account of lack of data. Some of these in the past seemingly existed for the fairly long period of one or more centuries; others were short-lived.

II. Factors of Longevity

In the above a large amount of the data about the life-span of various types of social organizations have been given. They show that the whole ocean of social life is in an in-

cessant motion and consists of an enormous number of various social organizations in an incessant process of appearing and disappearing. Each social group is like a wave which comes and goes, to be replaced by new waves. All in all, the duration of these "social waves" is rather short for the smaller social organizations. Only the big social organizations like world religions, empires, and castes persist for a relatively long time. But even they can hardly be regarded as having unlimited life-span, or lasting as long as the human social life itself.

Now the question arises: What are the factors which are responsible for the death of social organizations, and which factors facilitate and which hinder the longevity of social groups?

These problems are too complex and too difficult to be discussed here at any great length. All that I can do in this chapter is merely to put down dogmatically some tentative conclusions reached in the process of the study of these problems. I have some evidences supporting these hypotheses but on account of the lack of space, I have to omit them.

As to the problem of why social organizations do not last forever and sooner or later cease to exist, the answer is almost the same as that for the question: why biological organisms die. Style the cause as "destiny," as "immanent," as "law of life and death," or as something else, the names do not matter. What matters is that the duration of social organizations seems to be finite: "what has a beginning in this empirical world has an end." "That is that," and all the numerous words can hardly add much to this.

The next question is: Why do some of the social organizations have relatively longer, some others shorter durations? The answer is very unsatisfactory and yet seems to be the only possible one, namely: it depends mainly upon the nature of social organizations (besides environmental conditions). Just as various biological species have different durations of their life, some very short and others like the elephants long, similarly various "species" of social organizations, for instance, a great religious organization and a great industrial corporation, have different length of life. The main difference from the biological species is that the variability of durations of social organizations even of the same type (as well as of different types) seems to be much greater and less definite in their uniformity. We have seen that there are states and religious and

other organizations of an exceedingly short duration (a few days, months, years), and that there are states, religious and other organizations of a duration computed by hundreds and thousands of years. In biology such a contrast in the duration of the organisms of the same species hardly ever exists. Social institutions are then incomparably more variable in this respect than the biological organisms. Among different kinds of social groups, the *groups bound together by several important values harmoniously combined with one another tend to live longer than the groups united only by one narrow and comparatively unimportant value-meaning.* The family, the caste, the tribe or clan, the state and religious organizations— as the groups with several important value-meanings—tend to live longer than an enormous number of "associations" whose members are united only by one narrow and comparatively unimportant value. This proposition explains also a comparatively short duration of economic groups. Contrary to the opinion that the business and economic organizations tend to be particularly long-lived because they have a better economic foundation for the satisfaction of their needs, without which satisfaction no organization can exist, we have seen that the non-economic organizations like the religious, the political, and even the family, live longer than the purely economic organizations, which are possibly of the shortest duration of any other type of social groups. The most uncertain way to insure one's immortality is an investment of one's total energy into the economic organizations.

More answerable is the problem concerning some of the factors of longevity of the organizations of the *same type or class.* There is a tangible correlation of the longevity of the organizations of the same type with several "variables."

(1) The longevity seems to be *negatively correlated with the rapidity of the creation of the organization.* Hastily concluded marriages, hastily built empires (the empires of Genghis-Khan, Tamerlane, Alexander the Great, Napoleon, Hitler, etc.); rapidly created religious organizations; political parties; industrial and economic enterprises; and generally most of the artificially and hastily built organizations, tend to be of a shorter duration than

those which have grown spontaneously, and ripened more slowly and "naturally" without artificial "pull."

(2) There seems to be *an optimum size of an organization* of a given type in given circumstances. A great deviation from such an optimum size either in the direction of overgrowth or undergrowth, seems to be negatively correlated with the longevity of the institutions of the same kind. Too small and too great empires, corporations, political organizations, cultural associations, denominations, and some other organizations, especially when they have been built quickly, tend to disintegrate, to split into parts and factions, or to be wiped out by the "competitors" more easily than the "optimum size" organizations of the same kind.

(3) *Within an optimum point, the larger the group the longer its life-span.* Small groups tend to live a shorter life than larger groups.

(4) A similar "optimum point" seems to exist in regard to the *homogeneity and heterogeneity of the members of the organizations of the same kind.* Too much heterogeneity as well as too much homogeneity tends to shorten the duration of the organization. The predominant opinion is that homogeneity favors, heterogeneity disfavors the life of the organization. Such an opinion is hardly supported by the facts. Too great heterogeneity leads to conflicts, inner struggle, factions, and similar "diseases" inside of the organization. Too much homogeneity renders it rigid, inelastic, stagnant, and incapable of adapting itself to the ever-changing environmental conditions. Such an organization cannot use profitably the pluses of the division of labor, cannot have at its disposal a variety of functions which any long-lived organization has to perform in an ever-changing social world. These are some of the reasons for my statement and accumulated data seem to confirm it.

(5) Again, there seems to exist an optimum point in *the rigidity and elasticity of the constitution of the organization of the same type.* The organizations whose members have too little freedom while the governments have too great a right of interference and control in the management and regulation of the affairs of the organization and the relationships of its members; and the organizations which give an enormous freedom to their members and impose little, if any, obligatory rules upon them, are likely to be more short-lived than those which hold "the optimum point policy" in these respects. The same is to be said for too great and too small changeability of the constitutions of the organizations. Contrary to the popular opinion that the more liberty is given to the members and the "more progressive," "changeable," and mobile is the organization the more vital and long-living it tends to be, the facts do not warrant at all this "liberal illusion" of the nineteenth century. As Aristotle and Plato have noted, too much "progressiveness" and "freedom" lead to anarchy, do not permit the organization to be crystallized and integrated well; make it, in the process of incessant "progressive" change, skeletonless, unstable, inefficient, and "protoplasmic," and thus endanger its longevity. The more rigid Roman Catholic organization has existed longer than many a "liberal" and "free-thinking" religious sect. More rigid political bodies have existed also longer than the majority of similar bodies but "too liberal," "too progressive," and "too free."

On the other hand, too much governmental control, too much compulsion, too much rigidity and ossification in the constitution and functions of the organization lead to similar results. Here as well as in many other respects, the happy optimum point seems to be the best condition for the longevity of the institutions of the same kind.[28]

(6) Similar *"optimum points" seem to exist in regard to the "openness and closeness"* of the doors of the organization for the newcomers; to *the equality and inequality* of the members (contrary to the popular opinion, too much of the arithmetical equality is as harmful as too much inequality); to the rapidity with which the composition of the membership changes (too much "hereditarism" in the positions of the members and their posterity is as bad as too rapid and incessant change of the members and rapid shifting of the positions from member to member); too much "hereditarism" leads to senility; too much of "the new blood" when it is not carefully selected and not properly trained disrupts the organization and does not permit its strong integration and crystalliza-

[28] P. A. Sorokin, *Mobility*, pp. 533 ff.

tion, shatters all the time its network of values and of social relationships and makes it exceedingly fragile.

(7) Other conditions being equal, the organization (of the same type) which succeeds in such a distribution of its members among the group's positions which is nearest to the principle "*to everybody according to his talent,*" such an organization has greater chances to survive than the organizations which greatly deviate from that rule.

(8) Further on, *the more creative minds has the group, the richer and better integrated is its system of meanings, values, norms, the more solidary are its members, the nearer— qualitatively and quantitatively—is the total sum of its vehicles to their optimum point, the greater is the longevity of a group among the groups of the same kind.*

(9) In such groups as the family, caste, social estate, nation, nationality, or racial group, the longevity is decisively determined, among other factors, by their birth and mortality rates, or by the net increase of such groups. When the net difference between death and birth rate is either zero or negative, such groups begin to die out and have a longevity shorter than the groups with a high rate of natural increase.

(10) Without going into other important conditions within the organizations themselves, it is proper to mention further that the longevity of the organizations depends not only on their inner conditions but *also on their environment.* The environment may be favorable or unfavorable. It happens sometimes that even the inwardly best organizations die quickly in an exceedingly unfavorable milieu; and vice versa, the exceedingly poor organizations sometimes live a relatively long life in the favorable constellation of the environmental circumstances.

III. Resurrection of Social Groups

Most of the groups die and fall into oblivion forever, but some groups die and then revive in a somewhat modified form. The process of group resurrection is thus a repeated or recurring process, though it is not universal in the sense of occurring in the life-history of all organized groups. A number of states like Poland, Bohemia, or ancient Egypt; or several states conquered and dissolved by Hitler temporarily die, and lose their sovereignty sometimes for a period of several decades or centuries, and then revive and regain their sovereignty and identity with their previous social "self." The same is true of several nationalities and nations; suppressed and dissolved and then revived political parties, religious sects and denominations, scientific, educational, artistic, philosophical, occupational, and other groups. Even a defunct family through adoption or through transfer of its name, fortune, status, and title to another family is regularly resurrected, for instance, in England, where the name-title-status of the defunct aristocratic families are annually transferred and granted by the crown to some distinguished persons.

In these and similar ways the process of resurrection of social groups indeed occurs and is ever repeated. As such it has to be mentioned among the important repeated social processes.

IV. General Conclusion to This Part

The preceding processes, ever repeated in the life-history of social groups, give us most of the important social processes. In their totality they furnish us with the approximate knowledge of the essentials of "physiology of social groups." Now we can turn to the study of the repeated cultural processes with their approximate uniformities and then to the investigation of the dynamics of personality. The repeated processes and uniformities in the life-process of social systems, of cultural systems and of personality, are mutually supplementary to each other and in their totality they give us some comprehension of the dynamics of the sociocultural universe in its three aspects.

PART SEVEN

The Dynamics of Cultural Processes

Chapter 35. The Conception of Cultural Systems

I. The Law of Three Phases in the Genesis of Cultural Systems

The first basic, ever-repeated, and universal process in the field of cultural dynamics is that of the birth of cultural systems and congeries. It corresponds to the birth of organized and unorganized social groups, though it does not coincide with this entirely—social groups and cultural systems and congeries are not co-terminous. A study of it introduces us to the microdynamics of the conception of systems and congeries of meanings, values, and norms, which was taken for granted in the study of the birth of social groups. There we noted how and why human beings interact and become organized around the central meanings, norms, and values of the group as the *raison d'être* of its existence. Here we have to inquire how and why these meanings, norms, and values coalesce into systems and congeries and become the component of meanings, values, and norms around which individuals interact and are organized into groups.

The basic uniformity in the genesis and emergence of cultural systems or congeries is as follows: *Any empirical cultural systems or congeries passes through three fundamental phases: (1) the conception (invention, creation, and unification) of two or more meanings, values, and norms to form a consistent system or congeries; (2) the objectification of the ideological system or congeries in the vehicles; (3) its socialization among human beings in* either an ideological form only or behavioral and material forms.

Now and then these three phases may be telescoped in their time sequence, the onset of each phase being almost simultaneous with that of the others. As a rule, however, the conception phase is the first, the objectification phase the second, and socialization the last phase in the time sequence. Sometimes these phases are separated from one another by considerable periods of time.

We know that systems of meanings, norms, and values represent logically or aesthetically consistent combinations ranging from the simple proposition "A is B or A is non-B" to vast scientific, philosophical, religious, ethical, and other systems and supersystems. Before any system or even congeries of meanings, norms, and values is born, it has to be conceived by the human mind in the form of a lucky or unlucky marriage of two or more ideas, patterns, or values. Before the Newtonian system of physics and the Darwinian theory of biological evolution could be objectified in an address or published in the form of a book, they had to be conceived in the minds of Newton and Darwin, respectively. (Even inconsistent and haphazard ideas, norms, and patterns must be imagined and thought out before they can be objectified. The phase of objectification thus always follows that of conception.) Finally there came the phase of socialization of these systems. Through their lectures and addresses (sound conductors) and books and articles (color and light conductors) the systems became accessible to other persons and began to be diffused or to socialize themselves among other human beings. Before Beethoven's symphonies were composed or Raphael's pictures were painted, they had had to be conceived by their creators; having been conceived, they were then written or painted (objectification); finally they became socialized through the performance of Beethoven's music or the exhibition of Raphael's pictures to the public. Three similar phases occur in the birth of cultural congeries.

Sometimes these phases follow one another rapidly. Again, there may be a long and painful period of conception, lasting for years, before a scientific, philosophical, religious, legal, or artistic system is even roughly formulated. Even then a long period may elapse before it is fixed in a final form, and a still longer period before it finds an audience or publisher. Finally, a long interval may pass before the objectified system is socialized among a considerable number of persons. Thus G. Vico's theory

of social dynamics had to wait some 120 years after its publication before it attained real recognition. Similar examples of belated recognition are found in all fields of creative genius. After the general formulation of this law we must turn now to a detailed study of the hows and whys of each of these phases. First, how and why are ideological systems or congeries conceived? What are the factors and conditions that favor the conception of major creative systems? Second, how and why are systems and congeries of meanings objectified in vehicles, and why is a given system or congeries of meanings "materialized" in a particular kind of vehicles? Third, how and why are the objectified systems and congeries socialized in one or the other of two fundamental forms of socialization, purely ideological when the systems and congeries become known to a number of persons but do not tangibly influence their behavior, and behavioral socialization when they effectively influence not only the mentality but also the actions of the persons to whom they become known? What factors facilitate, and what factors retard or diminish, the diffusion and effectiveness of the objectified systems and congeries?

II. The Conception (Invention and Creation) of Ideological Systems and Congeries

1. The Conception of Simple Systems and Congeries

With the exception of babies, persons isolated since birth, and idiots, every human being has an assortment of single meanings, congeries of meanings, and even a few simple ideological systems in the form of "Snow is cold," "This tree is green," "We went to the lake," "Do this," "Don't do that," "This is tasty," "One and one make two," and so on. Single images, patterns, notions, and meanings incessantly throng the human mind, appearing and disappearing, coalescing with or becoming dissociated from one another, following in this or that sequence, now agreeing, now disagreeing; finally they combine with one another in various congeries and systems, now quite spontaneously, now following the path

of association of images, now that of Pavlov's conditioned reflexes, now that of Levi-Brühl's "law of participation," now that of more complex patterns of combination, and occasionally that of the laws of logic and of aesthetic consistency. The tendency toward a combination of images, patterns, and ideas is one of the primary propensities of the human mind, as primary as the reflex of cognition or curiosity, which, according to I. P. Pavlov, is one of the fundamental reflexes of animal organisms.

If an individual were entirely isolated from others and could not profit by their experience, his fund of images, patterns, and ideas would be very meager, probably incoherent and chaotic, constituting mainly a congeries and rarely a system (cf. Chapter 1). Born, reared, and educated among other persons, being incessantly stimulated and taught by interaction processes, the overwhelming majority of people, after their infancy, can and do combine single meanings not only into congeries but also into at least simple systems. With the help of others, every person discovers, conceives, invents, or creates for himself a multitude of various systems of meanings, norms, and values. We do not know any primitive group which does not have some simple magical, religious, aesthetic, or scientific system of meanings, norms, and values. Not all the combinations of ideas, patterns, and norms of the preliterate peoples are mere congeries, devoid of any logical or aesthetic consistency. Many of these are real systems.[1] In other words, the generation of simple cultural congeries and systems is coextensive with the sociocultural life of mankind as an inseparable concomitant.

2. The Conception of Great Ideological Systems and Supersystems

Very different is the situation in regard to the conception of vast new ideological systems. *Only a small number of individuals, in only a small number of groups, are capable of conceiving such systems.* Out of several billions of human beings who have lived on this planet only some 150,000 to 200,000 names are preserved in the annals of history, and not even all of these represent inventors, discoverers, and creators of great new ideological systems. Part of them were destroyers, murderers, monstrosities, freaks, and other rarities. Even assuming that the names of many great creators and inventors of the remote past remain unknown —such as the anonymous discoverers or inventors of fire, the wheel, and the lever, the domesticators of animals and plants, the discoverers of the rudiments of agriculture, arithmetic, the fine arts, religion, law, and ethics, and so forth—the fact remains that the total number of creative minds constitutes an insignificant minority among the human beings who have lived on this planet. Even in contemporary societies, only an insignificant fraction become discoverers, inventors, and creators of important new systems of meanings, values, and norms.[2] Approximately one creative genius occurs for every four to five hundred thousand uncreative persons.

Similarly, among the many thousands of nationalities, tribes, clans, and other racial and ethnic groups that have existed on this planet, only a very few, hardly more than fifty, have originated notable cultural systems. A somewhat larger number of such groups have created a language system. The vast majority of tribes and peoples have not displayed any substantial creativeness in other fields of culture, and hence have remained at the level of so-called nonhistorical, or preliterate, groups. According to A. Toynbee,[3] only twenty-one historical groups have evolved sociocultural systems or civilizations of the first rank: the western, two Orthodox Christian (in Russia and the Near East), the Minoan, the Hellenic, the Hittite, the Syriac, the Sumeric, the Babylonic, the Arabic, the Iranic, the Egyptian, the Hindu, the Indic, the Sinic, two Far Eastern, the Andean, the Mexican, the Yucatec, and the Mayan. To these are added five "arrested civilizations" that did not evolve the higher types of civilization: Polynesian, Eskimo, Nomadic, Ottoman, and Spartan; and three "abortive" civilizations: Old Irish, Viking (Scandinavian), and Far Eastern.

The number and classification of the great historical creative groups may be somewhat different. H. Danilevsky[4] finds only ten great cultural, or historical, types: Egyptian, Chinese, Assyro-Babylonian (Ancient Semitic), Hindu, Iranian, Jewish, Greek, Roman, New Semitic (Arabian), and European. Almost

---

[1] Even Levi-Brühl's alleged "law of participation," supposedly governing the combination of notions, meanings, and patterns of the primitive peoples, produces not only congeries but systems in our sense, such as "This is not that," "This fish is edible," "This snake is poisonous," "This man is an uncle," "This is taboo," "This is enjoyable," and even much more complex systems. Levi-Brühl's theory is essentially invalid. (L. Levi-Brühl, *Les Fonctions méntales dans les sociétés inférieures*

[Paris, 1910]; also his *L'Expérience mystique et les symboles chez les primitifs* [Paris, 1938]).

[2] The experimental study of the "creative spontaneity" of various persons initiated by J. L. Moreno confirms the wide discrepancy between individuals in this respect. (Cf. J. L. and F. Moreno, "Spontaneity Theory," *Sociometry*, 1944, pp. 339-356.)

[3] A. Toynbee, *A Study of History*, Vol. I, pp. 132 ff., and Vol. IV, pp. 1 ff.

[4] H. Danilevsky, "Russia and Europe," in *Zaria*, 1869, Nos. 1-10, No. 2, p. 87.

identical is the number of civilizations of the first rank given by O. Spengler, whose theory in many essential points repeats that of H. Danilevsky.[5] From ten to twenty-five, varying according to the field of culture, is the number of great cultures treated by A. Kroeber.[6] Nevertheless, the fact remains that only a limited number of ethnic groups or nations have created great new cultural systems, scientific, technological, philosophical, artistic, religious, ethico-juridical, political, economic, and the like. Even within such groups, only the small "creative minority," to use Toynbee's term, has been instrumental in creating such systems.

On the other hand, various congeries and simple systems, as has been said, are incessantly conceived by virtually everyone. Even a four-year-old baby or an inmate of an insane asylum is able to conceive nonlogical, illogical, or inconsistent combinations of images, patterns, ideas, or meanings. They are produced still more prolifically by mature and normal persons. Hence congeries of meanings, values, and norms abound in the total culture of any people, at any period.

In contradistinction to ideological systems, especially to the major systems, nonlogical, illogical, and inconsistent congeries are comparatively unstable and short-lived. They come and go, easily combining and as easily dissociating. Possessing no inner connections—logical or aesthetic—and representing a mere promiscuous agglomeration of meanings, norms, and values, congeries disintegrate under the impact of the slightest adverse influence. They fail to afford a basis for the individuality, persistence, and growth of any culture, to say nothing of a great culture. No group can long survive if it has at its disposal only a fund of illogical, inconsistent, or fallacious congeries. If, for instance, such a group ascribes the properties of a cow to a lion and tries to milk the lion and to kill the cow, if it tries to eat what is uneatable, if it has no adequate idea of the measurement of space and time, if its norms of conduct are mutually contradictory, if its magical and religious beliefs are false and self-contradictory, such a group cannot long survive. Still less is it capable of evolving a great culture. The cultures devoid of systems and supersystems that integrate a large part of their cultural elements "play the role of mere ethnographic material, similar to the inorganic material entering into the historical organisms, that is, the cultures possessing highly integrated systems. They enrich the variety and wealth of the historical cultures, but they do not attain the level of historical individuality." "Sometimes moribund and disintegrating great cultures sink to the level of mere ethnographic material until a new formative principle reintegrates their elements, mixed with new elements, into a new great culture."[7]

For these reasons we shall pay less attention to congeries than to systems of meanings, norms and values. The integrated major systems are the backbone of persisting cultures and surviving groups. Only those cultures that create notable ideological systems attain first rank, and only here can one expect to find the uniformities and regularities in which sociology is primarily interested. Congeries, being incidental combinations, lack inward logic and therefore uniformities. The logic of their appearance and disappearance, modification and transformation, association and dissociation, is the logic of accidental, fortuitous forces quite distinct from that of cultural systems.

III. The Chief Facilitating Factors of the Discovery, Creation, and Invention of the New Major Ideological Systems

1. Five Basic Factors

Why among a multitude of groups only a few conceive new major cultural systems, and why among millions of individuals in a given population only very few become the originators of such systems in science and technology,

---

[5] Cf. O. Spengler, *The Decline of the West* (New York, 1929).

[6] A. Kroeber, *Configurations of Culture Growth* (Berkeley, 1944).

[7] H. Danilevsky, "Russia and Europe" (in Russian), *Zaria*, 1869, No. 1, p. 90. Danilevsky, whose theory in many respects was repeated by O. Spengler fifty years later, divides all nationalities

philosophy, ethics, religion, the fine arts, law, politics, economics, and the like, remains a mystery. This mystery, however, may be somewhat elucidated by the following fundamental conditions: (a) a favorable biological heredity; (b) an urgent sense of need for a new system; (c) the cross-fertilization of two or more different systems which are in direct contact with one another; (d) good luck; (e) cultural freedom.

a. *Favorable Heredity.* The necessity of these factors for the creation of basic ideological systems is rather obvious. One is not obliged to subscribe to the claims of extreme hereditarians and racialists to perceive that a fortunate heredity is a prerequisite condition. Otherwise no amount of training can make one a Mozart or Beethoven in music, a Homer, Dante, or Shakespeare in literature, an Isaac Newton or Galileo in science, a Plato or Kant in philosophy, a Buddha or Saint Paul in religion, an Edison or Bell in technology, a Carnegie or Ford in economic organization. The precocity of certain eminent composers, such as Mozart, the unfavorable conditions which many creative personalities have had to overcome, including the lack of adequate technical training—these and a host of other evidences all point in the same direction. The fact that few tribes and other social groups have been creative suggests the same conclusion, especially when it can be shown that the environmental opportunities of many uncreative groups have been better than or as good as those of the few creative groups.[8] Even the conception of comparatively simple systems requires a normal hereditary endowment. Precisely what this "fortunate heredity" is we do not know; but, whatever it is, it is an indispensable factor.

b. *The Social Need for a New System.* Favorable heredity is, however, not sufficient in itself. If persons or groups feel no urgent

need for a new system—if their lives are well balanced and their needs are tolerably well satisfied—a hereditary advantage may remain latent or may be wasted in the invention of petty combinations and systems. For instance, groups of persons living in a mountainous region do not require safe and convenient means of maritime transportation and hence have no incentive to invent them, in contrast, for example, to the Eskimos and Polynesians. Groups that are not menaced by enemies, and are hence free from invasion and conquest, do not invent systems of military art, with their organization of fighting forces, weapons, strategy, and leadership. Conversely, groups subject to the perennial threat of war, invasion, and conquest, are in urgent need of just such a system and accordingly devote themselves to its invention and perfection. Recently we have seen many nations, like the United States, slacken their inventiveness in the military field in time of peace and suddenly expand it on an enormous scale in the face of a threat of war. During the Second World War more manpower, brain power, and material resources were probably spent in the United States in the conception and creation of new weapons, ships, airplanes, and other implements of warfare than during all the peaceful periods of the last two centuries combined. Similarly, groups not suffering from internal anarchy and disorder rarely devote much effort to the conception and creation of ethical, legal, and political systems that make for internal stability. Until the need for a stable international system became an urgent necessity, only a few isolated efforts were made in this direction. Now that a lasting peace has become a matter of life and death for the whole of humanity, efforts to evolve such a system have enormously multiplied.

To repeat, an urgent sense of need stimu-

---

or nations into three main classes according to their historico-cultural roles (*ibid.*, pp. 88 ff.); (a) ten great cultures or civilizations integrated into one consistent whole; (b) temporary nationalities or nations, such as Huns, Mongols, and Turks, whose principal historical role is the destruction of decadent great cultures, and which suddenly emerge as military-political bodies and rapidly sink back into oblivion, becoming mere ethnographic material; (c) the eclectic, unintegrated cultural groups destined to serve as mere cultural material for the great cultures. This statement of

Danilevsky's is reiterated, with some variations, by O. Spengler, A. Toynbee and A. Kroeber. I find it fairly valid.

[8] A. Toynbee's theory of a not too unfavorable and not too favorable environment as the main factor in the emergence and growth of major civilizations is quite inadequate, for millions of individuals and the majority of populations and groups live in such an environment without becoming creators of notable cultural systems. Cf. Toynbee, *op. cit.*, Vol. I, pp. 271 ff.; also my *Theories*, pp. 137 ff.

lates efforts to create the needed system.[9] In creative individuals this need, stimulated by a social demand, is often experienced, so to speak, inwardly. They experience an urgent impulse, frequently manifest in their early life, to write, to compose music, to paint, to preach, to teach, to experiment with tools and mechanisms, or the like. This inner stimulus is the mainspring of their creative activity, monetary and other considerations often constituting purely subsidiary factors.

c. *Cross-Fertilization.* The third fundamental condition is the situation of a group or person at the point of intersection of crosscurrents of various appropriate or relevant systems of meanings and values. Since any new system of meanings is a blend of two or more existing systems, such a union occurs more naturally amidst several crosscurrents of different ideas, beliefs, and patterns. Such a milieu contains richer material for a new synthesis or creative combination than a cultural milieu of monotonous stereotypes.

The point of junction of various cultural streams supplies a larger number of the elements necessary for a new creation. No great invention, discovery, or creation has been conceived in a fully developed form by one person. All of them are based upon the achievements of predecessors and contemporaries, each of whom has contributed to the building of the system. For example, no system of railroad transportation could have been invented without the prior invention of the steam engine. Without the internal-combustion engine the airplane could not have been invented. The incandescent electric light required some twenty-three inventions prior to the work of Edison and Jablochkoff, and some twenty-four subsequent inventions were needed to improve Edison's and Jablochkoff's invention. A similarly long list may be cited for such as the wheel, the lever, the plow, and the steamship, as well as the telephone, the telegraph, the airplane, radio, the jet-propelled plane, the atomic bomb, etc.[10]

The same may be said of scientific, philosophical, religious, ethical, artistic, economic, and political systems. All the major scientific discoveries have been the collective achievement of many generations of creative minds.

Without the scientists of the Graeco-Roman world and of later European civilizations (including Copernicus, Galileo, and Kepler) who developed mathematics, mechanics, and physics, Sir Isaac Newton's work would have been impossible. Buddhism was an outgrowth of the Hindu Vedic religion. Without Judaism, Mithraism, Neo-Platonism, and Neo-Pythagoreanism, Christianity could not have arisen. Without Socrates and the pre-Socratic philosophers, Plato's and Aristotle's philosophy would never have evolved. Without Turgot, Condorcet, Saint-Simon, etc. Comte's system of positivist philosophy and sociology could not have been formulated. To multiply instances, Karl Marx's dialectical materialism presupposed the work of Hegel and materialistic philosophers, and Hume and Descartes were indispensable forerunners of Kant. In the absence of the pioneer work of Bach, Handel, Haydn, and Mozart, Beethoven's music could not have been composed. Without the artists of the fourteenth and fifteenth centuries the paintings of Raphael, Leonardo da Vinci, Michelangelo, and Titian could not have been achieved.

Scarcely any notable system has been originated by a single isolated genius alone. Such seemingly isolated creative geniuses as Erigena in philosophy, Diophantus in mathematics, and Villon and Chaucer in literature represented a "minority stream" among their contemporaries, instead of belonging to the "majority stream." Thus Plato, Gregory of Nyssa, Pseudo-Dionysius, and Saint Augustine were the forerunnners of Erigena; a similar observation applies to the others, all of whom were influenced by earlier systems which they utilized for the purposes of a new synthesis. In short, every notable system is a stream fed by currents derived from many known and unknown sources.

On the other hand, when there is an urgent need for the creation of a new system, when all the necessary elements for its invention are at hand, the discovery is frequently made simultaneously by two or more persons working independently of one another. The invention of calculus by Newton and Leibnits and that of the electric lamp by a Russian, Jablochkoff, and by Thomas Edison are examples of

---

[9] Toynbee's "challenge [my urgent need] and response" is valid. (*Op. cit.*, Vol. I, pp. 249 ff.)

[10] Cf. S. C. Gilfillan, *The Sociology of Invention* (Chicago, 1935), and *Inventing the Ship* (Chicago, 1935); G. Bouthoul, *L'invention* (Paris, 1930).

the numerous scientific and technological inventions and discoveries made simultaneously by two or more creative thinkers.[11] The same applies to the creation of cultures by groups. Being exposed to the fertilizing crosscurrents of various cultural systems and congeries, such groups have at their disposal far richer and more stimulating material for a new synthesis than groups isolated from other cultural systems and congeries; for the latter cannot profit by the different patterns created by other groups, lack the elements essential for a new synthesis, and are restricted to the same systems and congeries, varying them at best only in certain details.[12]

On the other hand, this factor alone is insufficient to explain the process. Persons and groups devoid of a fortunate heredity and possessing no need for a new creation will not conceive new major systems.[13] Moreover, too great a variety and richness of foreign cultural elements often leads to "mental indigestion," resulting in an incoherent agglomeration of cultural congeries instead of a system, as in the case of the Hellenistic and the contemporary eclectic western culture.[14]

d. *Good Luck.* To these three factors should be added the residual factor of good luck. By this is meant a specific, incidentally favorable event, situation, or constellation of circumstances that attracts the attention of or suggests the idea to, the potential conceivers. Many creations, inventions, and discoveries have been accidental in this sense. The swaying lamp noted by Galileo in the cathedral at Pisa or the apple falling with a thud in the garden of Newton served as the impetus that led to their discoveries. In a number of cases the acci-

dental setting of conditions has been such that all that was needed was to observe the conditions and to draw the conclusions suggested by them. Persons and groups endowed with a fortunate heredity, experiencing an urgent sense of need, placed amidst crosscurrents of cultural streams, and concentrating upon a problem, notice such lucky accidents and profit by them. Others pass them by without grasping their import.

e. *Cultural Freedom.* H. Danilevsky regards political independence as a necessary condition for a group to become creative. "In order for the civilization of a potentially creative group to be conceived and developed, the group and its subgroups must be politically independent"[15] (his second law of the dynamics of great cultures). A. Kroeber declares: "It is certainly true that high achievements by suppressed nationalities are rather rare. If such a nationality contributes, it is usually through the medium of the culture of the ruling people," like the Irish through English literature. However, he indicates several exceptions to this rule, such as pre-Islamic poetry in Arabia and Polish literature of the early nineteenth century.[16]

On the other hand, A. Coste claims that political independence is not indispensable for creativity in the fields of religion, ethics, philosophy, and the fine arts. The religious systems of Buddhism, Judaism, Christianity, and Mohammedanism were conceived and emerged in either subjugated or politically insignificant groups. Ionia and other Greek states were more creative in the spheres of the fine arts, philosophy, and ideology than the powerful Roman Empire. From the fourteenth to the sixteenth

---

[11] For a list of 148 such independent inventions, cf. W. Ogburn, *Social Change*, pp. 90-102.

[12] This proposition is unanimously accepted by virtually all serious investigators of the dynamics of leading cultures. H. Danilevsky's "fourth law" states that any major civilization attains its fullest development and its climax when its ethnographic elements are diversified. He declares, furthermore, that the subsequent "related cultures" profit substantially by the creative achievement of preceding and contemporary cultures. The fact is stated in virtually the same terms by O. Spengler and A. Toynbee. Toynbee acknowledges that contact with the elements of other cultures "may provide a stimulus to creation" (*op. cit.*, Vol. I, p. 440, and Vol. V, pp. 338 ff.); that "the related civilizations," through the "internal proletariat," pass their herit-

age on to the subsequent civilization; that other groups, with their civilizations, may play the role of the challenging force, and even be imitated, to some extent, in the fundamental processes of "challenge and response" and mimesis. A. Kroeber (*op. cit.*, pp. 795 ff.) likewise states that other cultures may supply the material and may render the "content" of a culture richer, thus facilitating the creation of new "patterns" (or systems).

[13] H. Danilevsky, *op. cit.*, Chps. 1-3.

[14] Cf. my *Crisis*, Ch. 7; Toynbee, *op. cit.*, Vol. V, pp. 432 ff., *passim*; and Kroeber, *op. cit.*, pp. 795 ff. These authors declare that creation is the task of the group itself. Mere imitation of various patterns does not make a group or person creative.

[15] Danilevsky, *op. cit.*, Ch. 5.

[16] Kroeber, *op. cit.*, p. 794.

century Italy was weak and divided politically, and yet it was more creative in the fields of the fine arts and ideology than strong and united countries such as France, England, and the Netherlands. In several nations the most brilliant ideological achievements often occurred when they were politically decadent and in a state of disorganization.[17] For instance, the blossoming of poetry, painting, philosophy, and science in Persia occurred when it had been subjugated by the Arabs, not when it was a powerful empire. Likewise, the most notable development of religion and ethics among the Jews took place after they had lost their political independence. The upsurge of cultural activity among the Germans around 1200, in the sixteenth century, and between 1750 and 1850 occurred in periods of political disorganization. A. Toynbee goes so far as to claim a negative relationship between the expansion of a given group into a "universal state" and its creativeness. In his twenty or so civilizations the most creative period is found to occur when the respective group is comparatively small, before its geographical expansion and transformation into a universal state. The "creative minority," freely imitated by the rest of the group, of the first phase, is replaced in the second phase by the "dominant uncreative minority," not freely followed by the rest of the state.[18]

The truth seems to lie somewhere between these opposite theories. In a large number of cases Danilevsky's "law" is confirmed by the following facts. (1) There are not many creative groups politically dependent and suppressed. (2) In many nations the climax of their creativeness in various fields was attained at the climax of their political power or after their liberation from foreign domination: the period of Sargon I in Akkad; of Hammurabi in Babylon; of the fourth, fifth, and sixth dynasties in the Old Kingdom of Egypt, of the twelfth dynasty in the Middle Kingdom, and of the eighteenth and the nineteenth dynasties in the New Empire of Egypt; during the reign of Solomon among the Hebrews; in the fifth century B.C. in Athens and in certain other Greek states; in the time of Caesar and Augustus in Rome; at the climax of the Maurya and Gupta empires in India and the T'ang dynasty in China; in the time of Charlemagne in the Frankish kingdom; between 800 and 1050 in Arabia; during the reign of Charles the Fifth in Spain, of Elizabeth and Queen Anne in England, of Peter the Great and Catherine the Great in Russia, and of Louis the Fourteenth in France. (3) During periods of subjugation several nations and groups experienced a decline of creative activity.

On the other hand, Coste and Toynbee (to some extent) are also right in the sense that creativeness in several fields of culture, particularly in those of religion, ethics, philosophy, the humanities, and the fine arts has frequently occurred either in periods of political decline, disorganization, and even subjugation in small nations, sometimes not independent politically but possessed of the necessary cultural freedom. *Such cultural freedom is to be regarded as the necessary minimum without which it is difficult for a group to become creative.* Any additional freedom, including political sovereignty and independence, may facilitate creativeness up to a certain point, but is neither a necessary nor a sufficient condition for originating great systems, particularly in the fields of religion, ethics, philosophy, the humanities, and the fine arts. According to the law of polarization, creativity, especially in the religious and ethical fields, increases mainly in periods of catastrophe (or immediately thereafter), including the loss of political independence. On the other hand, several powerful empires, such as those of the Huns, the Mongols, and Turks, were fairly sterile in respect to great scientific, philosophical, humanistic and religious systems.

What has been said of political empires applies also to economic empires. Economic prosperity and power are, up to a certain point, favorable conditions for creativity; but above minimum satisfaction of basic needs they are neither necessary, nor sufficient, nor even favorable conditions. Many a group, having become economically affluent, proves less and less creative, even in the economic and technological fields. This applies still more to individual creators, many of whom have been poor, limited in their sensate liberty, like Epic-

---

[17] A. Coste, *Les Principes d'une sociologie objective* (Paris, 1899), Chps. 2, 22, and *L'Experience des peuples* (Paris, 1900), Chps. 1, 2.

[18] Toynbee, *op. cit.,* Vol. IV, pp. 2 ff., and Vol. I pp. 52 ff., *passim.*

tetus, actual slaves.[19] To be more precise, economic well-being may promote creativeness in science, technology, and sensate art, but tends to hinder it in religion, ethics, and possibly nonsensate philosophy and law.

Taken alone, each of the five factors is insufficient to explain the mystery of the origin of major cultural systems. Taken together they account for the greater part of this mystery. Toynbee's twenty-one civilizations were evolved during periods when the respective groups possessed all five favorable factors. An overwhelming majority of individual creators whose career is known to us have likewise enjoyed these five variables.

2. Independent Inventions, Rediscoveries, and Diffusion

Are ideological systems conceived only once, by a single person or group, eventually spreading to other groups, or are they now and then conceived independently by different persons and groups? The ascertained facts respecting hundreds of inventions and discoveries made independently by several different individuals and peoples testify against the theories of G. E. Smith, W. J. Perry, and others who claim that most important inventions were made only once, having originated in Egypt and thence having spread to other regions.[20] Cultural systems, once invented, do tend to diffuse and do often spread far beyond the area and groups in which they were conceived. This, however, does not refute the fact of independent discoveries, inventions, and creations. Practically all great cultures, while borrowing and adapting elements of other cultures, have invented certain important systems themselves, sometimes even rediscovering independently those of other persons and groups. It is doubtful whether any first-rate culture could have evolved through mere borrowing and imitation. We have recently observed several independent inventions in the fields of atomic energy, rocket guns and planes, etc. in various countries. Even though their basic principles were a common possession of such countries, the essential modifications of their applications to different types of instruments of war have proceeded independently.

IV. The Role of Intuition, Reason, and Sensory Experience in the Creation, Invention, and Discovery of Major Systems

1. Necessity for All Three Forms of Cognition

If by intuition (or inspiration) we mean a sudden, direct, and valid initial conception of a new system occurring spontaneously in the mind of the conceiver;[21] by reason a consistent, logical (mathematical, syllogistic, or dialectic)

---

[19] Several anthropologists and sociologists set forth many other conditions necessary, in their opinion, for a group to become great. For instance, J. Lippert contends that "no race or group has ever risen to a high level of culture without the milk of domestic animals." He seems to be unaware of the fact that the Chinese and Hindus abhor milk, just as the Mohammedans abhor pork. Yet they have created noteworthy cultures. Most of these theories are either clearly fallacious or else elevate a mere predisposing condition to the rank of an essential factor. Cf. J. Lippert, *The Evolution of Culture* (New York, 1940).

[20] Cf. G. Elliott Smith, *The Migration of Early Culture* (Manchester, 1929), and W. J. Perry, *The Children of the Sun* (London, 1927). In a much milder and modified form, not denying even reinvention and rediscovery, but underestimating the role of independent invention and overestimating the role of diffusion, the theory is set forth by F. Graebner, W. Schmidt, W. H. R. Rivers, and others. See F. Graebner, *Methode der Ethnologie* (Heidelberg, 1911); W. Schmidt and W. Koppers, *Völker und Kulturen* (Leipzig, 1924); W. Schmidt, *The Culture Historical Method of Ethnology* (New York, 1939); W. H. R. Rivers, *History and Ethnology* (London 19—). For a criticism, see R. B. Dixon, *The Building of Culture* (New York, 1928), pp. 212 ff.; A. L. Kroeber and C. Holt, "Masks and Moieties as Culture Complex," *Journal of the Anthropological Institute*, Vol. L, pp. 452-460; G. E. Smith, B. Malinowski, H. J. Spinden, and A. Goldenweiser, *Culture: the Diffusion Controversy* (New York, 1927); *Independence, Convergence and Borrowing* (Harvard University Press, 1937); W. I. Thomas, *Primitive Behavior*, Ch. 16; P. Honigsheim, "The Problem of Diffusion," *Michigan Academie of Science*, Vol. XXVII, pp. 515-524.

[21] After a survey of the meanings of intuition by various philosophers and scientists K. W. Wild finds the following common element in their definitions

process of thinking the idea through in its inductive, deductive, analytical, and synthetic aspects; by sensory experience a perception of the sensory phenomena related to the idea and a sensory verification of it through empirical evidence (experimental, observational, statistical, and practical), then all three types of mental activity are necessary for the discovery, creation, or invention of a significant cultural system. Neither intuition, nor reason, nor empirical experience alone is sufficient. Innumerable scientists have spent their lives in an empirical (sensory) study of phenomena without achieving any notable discovery. Multitudes of teachers of philosophy, logic, and mathematics have failed to conceive any new philosophical, logical, mathematical, or other system. There have been millions of intuitional day-dreamers who, having stumbled upon an idea, have failed to clarify, develop, verify, and apply it in constructing an original system. Truly creative thinkers have been fortunate in possessing and exercising all three types of mental ability.

2. Role of Intuition in Initiating Discovery, Invention, and Creation

There is hardly any doubt that the conception of most great systems has been initiated by intuition. A study of how the minds of inventors work shows this in the field of technological inventions. They themselves almost unanimously point to intuition as the initial impulse and the most important factor in their inventions. "In my own experience many decisions were made on the basis of intuition," testifies I. I. Sikorsky, inventor of clippers, helicopters, and so on.[22] "Ideas come when I least

expect them, often when I am half asleep, or day-dreaming," state American inventors.[23] The same principle applies to scientific discoveries. In mathematics, according to the testimony furnished by such eminent mathematicians as H. Poincaré and G. Birkhoff, a great many discoveries have been made through intuition. Poincaré's own experience is typical. "For fifteen days I tried to demonstrate that no function analogous to what later on I called les fonctions fuchsiennes could exist. During all these days . . . I attempted a great number of combinations, but arrived at no result. One evening . . . I could not get to sleep; ideas appeared in throngs . . . until two of them hooked together, so to speak, and made a stable combination. In the morning I established the existence of the class of fonctions fuchsiennes. All that I had to do was to repeat the results, which took me only a few hours."[24] An apple falls with a thud, and Newton suddenly gets the idea of the law of gravitation; a lamp is observed to sway in the cathedral at Pisa, and Galileo conceives, as by a short circuit, the law of oscillation of the pendulum. A similar experience has occurred repeatedly in connection with most scientific discoveries.[25]

Still more striking is this role of intuition in the conception of philosophical, religious, ethical, juridical, artistic, social, and political systems.[26] Mozart's testimony is typical. Answering the question as to how he creates his musical compositions, he answers: "What, you ask, is my method of writing and elaborating my large and lumbering things? I can, in fact, say nothing more about it than this: I do not know myself and can never find out. When I am in particularly good condition, perhaps riding in a carriage, or on a walk, or during a

---

of intuition: "An intuition is an immediate awareness by a subject of some particular entity, without such aid from the senses or from reason as would account for that awareness. . . . It gives us insight into reality as opposed to or supplementing appearance." (K. W. Wild, Intuition [Cambridge University Press, 1938], pp. 226 ff.) For other literature, cf. my Dynamics, Vol. IV, pp. 746 ff.

[22] I. I. Sikorsky, The Story of the Winged-S (New York, 1942), p. 227. Cf. the whole of Chapter 22.

[23] Cf. J. Rossman, The Psychology of the Inventor (Washington, 1931), pp. 101-116.

[24] H. Poincaré, Science et méthode (Paris, 1908), pp. 52-55. Cf. also his Inventions mathématiques (Paris, 1908), and G. Birkhoff, "Intuition, Reason

and Faith in Science," Science, December 30 1938.

[25] Cf. E. Meyerson, Du cheminement de l pensée (Paris, 1931), Vol. I, pp. 23 ff., Vol. III pp. 719 ff.; T. Langmuire, "Science, Common Sense and Decency," New York Times, December 27, 1942; N. Lossky, Sensory, Intellectual and Mystical Intuition (Paris, 1938); F. Kretschmer The Psychology of Men of Genius (London, 1931) pp. 141 ff.; and J. Venn, The Principles of Empirical or Inductive Logic (London, 1907) pp. 352 ff. Cf. also my Dynamics, Vol. IV, pp 746 ff.

[26] Cf. I. Lapshin, Philosophy of Invention and Invention in Philosophy (in Russian, Prague, 1924)

sleepless night, then thoughts come to me in a rush . . . Whence and how—that I do not know. Those which please me I retain in my head and hum perhaps to myself. . . . (Everything) goes on in me as in a very vivid dream. All that remains is to put them on paper."[27]

Practically all the major religious, ethical, aesthetic, and philosophical systems, and many other such systems, were conceived through intuition.[28] "Genius" is another term for it. Without such genius even the application of all of F. Bacon's "logistic rules" would fail to produce creative results. "Superconscious" is a still different name for it. All the consciously rational knowledge of the rules of musical composition or of English language does not make professors of music or of English Beethovens and Shakespeares, respectively.

This does not mean, of course, that intuition alone is sufficient. First of all, it must be sound; second, the initial enlightenment it supplies must be checked, tested, and developed by logic, or reason, and by empirical sensory observation.

3. Intuition as the Ultimate Foundation of Science, Philosophy, Ethics, and the Fine Arts

Besides being the initiator of original conceptions, intuition serves as the foundation of the validity of the basic propositions not only of religion, ethics, philosophy, and aesthetics but also of mathematico-logical and scientific thought.[29]

To summarize: The cooperation of the senses, of reason, and of intuition is indispensable for the conception of original systems in all fields of culture. As Edison put it, the inspiration of intuition must be supplemented, developed, and tested by "perspiration," by a vast amount of empirical observation and logical or mathematical reasoning.

V. Why Different Groups Create Major Systems in Different Fields of Culture; Why a Given Group Shifts Its Creativeness to Other Fields

1. No Encyclopedically Creative Genius or Group

None of the individual originators of major systems creates these in all cultural fields. The overwhelming majority of men of genius evolve an important system in only one field—on rare occasions, in two.[30] Homer and Plato, Phidias and Beethoven, Shakespeare and Michelangelo, Galileo and Newton, Edison and Madame Curie were all creators in only one field. There has hardly ever been a truly encyclopedic creator. The same is true of creative groups. None of these has been creative in all fields of culture at the same period of its existence or even throughout its entire history. Apart from language, the greatest achievements of a given nation or group have usually been confined to one or a few fields. Thus the Macedonians, Huns, Mongols, and Turks construc-

ted great political empires, and Carthage built a vast economic empire; but none of them evolved great systems in other fields of culture. Arabic culture achieved little in the drama, sculpture, or painting; Russia and England failed to develop any noteworthy sculpture. Egypt did not distinguish itself in philosophy or the drama; Greece, through the creation of a great religion or political or economic empire; Rome, in philosophy or science. Japan has not excelled in architecture, religion, philosophy, or science (except mathematics), or modern western culture in religion or ethics. The principal achievement of Greece was limited to the fine arts and philosophy; that of Rome, to the creation of a great political empire, military system, and system of law; that of the Hebrews, to religion, ethics, and literature; that of medieval Europe, to the organization and development of Christianity,

---

[27] O. Jahn, *W. A. Mozart* (Leipzig, 1856-1859), Vol. III, pp. 423-425.

[28] For the data and literature, cf. my *Dynamics*, Vol. IV, Ch. 16.

[29] Cf. my *Dynamics*, Vol. IV, Ch. 16.

[30] Cf. A. Kroeber, *Configurations of Culture Growth*, pp. 377 ff., *passim*.

theology, and philosophy; that of the modern western world, to science, technology, philosophy, and the fine arts.

2. Fallacy of Invariable Specificity of Cultural Creativeness

On the other hand, we must avoid the mistake of H. Danilevsky, O. Spengler, A. Toynbee, and F. S. Northrop who claim that each great culture, throughout its entire history, has been creative in only one field: the Hellenic culture, in the aesthetic field; the Hindu culture, in the religious field; western culture, in that of science and technology, and so on.[31]

Such theories are sharply contradicted by the general facts and by the specific fact of shifts of the field of cultural creativeness in the course of the existence of a group. Western culture was highly creative in the field of religion and theological philosophy and deficient in science and technology through the medieval period, but uniquely creative in science and technology and relatively backward in religion and theological philosophy throughout the modern period. Likewise Greek culture from the ninth to the sixth century B.C. exhibits scarcely any aesthetic originality in painting, architecture, or sculpture, but evolved epoch-making systems in these fields from the end of the sixth to the third century B.C. Such shifts have occurred repeatedly in virtually all cultures of the first rank.

3. Shifts of the Fields of Cultural Creativeness

As to the shifts of the field of creativeness of major cultures in different periods of their existence, the following historical data sum up roughly the fluctuations in the specified fields. They are approximate, and they reflect predominantly the sensate standpoint. Nevertheless, viewed from a given standpoint, whether it be sensate or ideational, the stream of creativity does not appear to be either constant or limited to one field. Furthermore, the data supply the factual basis for several other conclusions of a fairly general character.

THE SEQUENCE OF CLIMACTIC PERIODS IN THE
DEVELOPMENT OF THE LEADING CULTURAL SYSTEMS[32]

EGYPT

Religion	c. 3500-3000 B.C., c. 2500-2300 B.C., c. 1580-1490 B.C., c. 1370-1352 B.C.[33]
The State and (to some extent) Economics	2895-2540 B.C., 2000-1785 B.C., 1580-1200 B.C., 663-525 B.C.
Science	c. 4241 B.C., 1900-1500 B.C.
Literature	2000-1225 B.C., 1300-900 B.C.
Sculpture	2840-2575 B.C., 1580-1350 B.C.
Architecture	1580-1250 B.C.
Music	1411-1284 B.C.
Painting	1580-1250 B.C., 750-525 B.C.

INDIA

Religion	c. 1000 B.C., c. 600-400 B.C., c. 272-232 B.C. c. 1-100 A.D., c. 788-860
The State (native, not foreign) and (to some extent) Economics	c. 321-186 B.C., 78-96 A.D., 320-500, c. 606-647, 1350-1600
Philosophy	600-400 B.C., 100-500, 600-1000
Science	700-500 B.C., 400-1150 (Climax c. 500-625)
Literature	400 B.C., -100 A.D., 350-750

---

[31] A. Toynbee, op. cit., Vol. III, pp. 128 ff. In a somewhat different form the same theory of the specificity of the creative potentiality of leading cultures is one of the main principles of Danilevsky's, Spengler's, and Northrop's theories.

[32] Cf. my Dynamics (all four volumes; more specifically, Vol. I, pp. 209 ff., passim; Vol. II passim; Vol. III, Ch. 8; and Vol. IV, Ch. 7); my Calamity, Ch. 12; Kroeber, op. cit., passim.

[33] Periods of creative innovation and ennoblement of religious systems.

INDIA (*Cont.*)

Sculpture	*c.* 150 B.C., 400-725 A.D.
Architecture	1489-1706
Music	1600-1771
Painting	450-750, 1615-1800

CHINA

Religion[34]	550-400 B.C., 350-230 B.C., 140-110 B.C., 9-23 A.D., 184-280, 317-650, *c.* 841-953, *c.* 1100-1400, 1600-1650
The State and (to some extent) Economics	*c.* 950-770 B.C., 230-210 B.C., 196 B.C.-0, 43-184 A.D., 618-738, 1020-1100, 1368-1620, 1662-1795
Philosophy	550-400 B.C., 350-230 B.C., 100-650 A.D. (eruditional and organizational, less creative), 1050-1200
Science	200 B.C.-265 A.D., 420-740, 1240-1320, 1720-1880
in Medicine	500-150 B.C., 175-325 A.D., 960-1280
Literature:	
Poetry	*c.* 650 B.C., 300-100 B.C., 200-900 A.D. (peaks *c.* 400 and 750), 1000-1100, 1700-1800
Drama	1200-1450
Novel	1250-1700
History	*c.* 650 B.C., 145 B.C.-50 A.D., 1050-1200
Sculpture	618-960 A.D. (peak *c.* 700-750)
Painting	*c.* 750 A.D., 960-1200, 1450-1500
Architecture	1400-1500
Music	*c.* 1400-1500

JAPAN

Religion	*c.* 550-650, *c.* 1720-1800
The State and Economics	*c.* 700-900, 1200-1300, 1400-1490, 1650-1800, 1920-1940
Philosophy	Very little developed
Science	1600-1800 (mathematics)
Literature	700-1200, *c.* 1400, 1700-1800
Music	806-1146
Sculpture	700-750, 1000-1150, 1200-1250
Painting	1350-1650
Architecture	1350-1600

GREECE

Religion	850-500 B.C., 350-300 B.C.
The State and Economics	750-430 B.C., 500-300
Philosophy	585-270 B.C.
Science	585 B.C.-100 A.D.
Music	750-600 B.C., 450-350 B.C.
Literature	800-700 B.C., 550-350 B.C.
Architecture	550-430 B.C.
Sculpture	559-350 B.C.
Painting	450-300 B.C.

ROME[35]

Religion	50-450 A.D.
The State	500 B.C.-200 A.D., 284-337, 379-395
Economics	200 B.C.-100 A.D.
Philosophy[36]	100 B.C.-450 A.D.
Science	100 B.C.-300 A.D.

[34] Emergence, revival, and diffusion of Confucianism, Taoism, and Buddhism, together with ethical reforms.

[35] Includes all creative minds in the Roman Empire, regardless of their nationality.

[36] Including the Neo-Platonists and Church Fathers.

Rome (*Cont.*)

Literature	80 B.C.-0, 50-120 A.D.
Sculpture	30 B.C.-100 A.D.
Painting	50-110 A.D.
Architecture	20-140 A.D.
Music	0-50 A.D., 460-495 A.D.

Arabic—Islamic World[37]

Religion	622-1258
The State	632-833
Philosophy	800-1200
Science	750-1250
Literature	530-1200

France[38]

Religion	Decline after the thirteenth century
The State	1050-1325, 1600-1715, 1800-1815, 1850-1870, 1890-1940
Economics	1100-1325, 1475-1560, 1840-1914
Philosophy	1075-1160, 1300-1350, 1600-1700, 1750-1850
Science	1580-1660, 1750-1870
Architecture	1050-1350
Sculpture	1140-1325, 1450-1550, 1850-1910
Music	1100-1350, 1650-1750, 1850-1910
Painting	1620-1670, 1760-1880
Literature	1070-1300, 1520-1580, 1630-1700, 1780-1900

Germany

Religion	Decline after the thirteenth century. The Reformation: 1517-1555
The State	919-1000, 1024-1056, 1190-1197, 1493-1556, 1713-1786, 1870-1940
Economics	1150-1400, 1800-1914
Philosophy	1220-1300, 1700-1890 (culmination 1780-1850)
Science	1450-1550, 1600-1716, 1800-1940
Architecture	1120-1260
Sculpture	1120-1260, 1400-1550
Painting	1450-1560, 1800-1900 (slight wave)
Music	1720-1890
Literature	1190-1225, 1750-1880

Great Britain

Religion	Decline after the thirteenth century
The State	1272-1307, 1509-1547, 1558-1603, 1689-1940
Philosophy	1200-1320, 1640-1730, 1740-1795, 1820-1880
Science	1600-1710, 1750-1880
Architecture	1189-1377
Painting	1715-1850
Sculpture	1220-1250, 1758-1787
Literature	*c.* 1400, 1525-1700, 1760-1875
Music	1520-1710

[37] Sculpture, painting, and, for the most part, drama are poorly developed.

[38] For the European countries religion is omitted, because formally they are all Christian. The most vigorous phase of Christianity in all countries occurred during the medieval centuries—roughly, prior to the fifteenth. Christianity had split into the eastern and western branches in the eleventh century. After the fifteenth it split into various sects, and then into the Protestant and Catholic branches, the former subsequently breaking up into a progressively increasing number of sects. The Renaissance brought an intensification of secularism, and thereafter the entire body of European culture tended to become more and more secularized or sensate and less and less religious and Christian. (Cf. Chapters 40-43 and especially my *Dynamics* (all four volumes) and *Crisis.*)

ITALY

Religion	Decline after the thirteenth century
The State	(Practically absent in its history)
Philosophy	1240-1300, 1500-1600, c. 1700
Science	1520-1670, 1770-1810
Architecture	1440-1600
Sculpture	1420-1800 (climax 1420-1600)
Painting	1420-1600
Music	1530-1650, 1680-1800

RUSSIA

Religion	Decline after 1700
The State	1000-1200, 1480-1600, 1700-1914, 1940—
Philosophy	1850-1917
Science	1860-1947
Architecture	1100-1400
Music	1820-1947
Literature	c. 1200, 1800-1917
Painting	1400-1500, 1860-1917
Sculpture	(Little developed)

However approximate may be the periods of comparative creativeness in the history of the specified countries,[39] the data nevertheless show that the creativeness in various fields is intermittent, is largely nonsimultaneous, and rarely occurs in all fields of culture at the same time. They demonstrate also the fallacy of Spengler's, Toynbee's, and Danilevsky's theories that a given civilization exhibits only one creative period in this or that cultural field. Moreover, they refute the claims for a uniform time sequence in the *Blütezeit* of various fields of culture.

4. Causes of the Shifts

The shifts observed raise the question as to why some groups are creative in certain fields and uncreative in others, and why the same population exhibits creativeness in different fields of culture at different periods. The answer is to be found *in the five factors of creativeness, plus the meaningful-causal rela-*

tionships that exist between various cultural systems and supersystems.

If a given group possesses the right hereditary endowment, at the intersection of cultural streams, and enjoys good luck, *it tends to evolve great systems in those fields of culture in which it urgently needs them for its unity and for the continuity of its existence.* Groups living on islands, such as the Polynesians, or on the seashore, such as the Eskimos, devise ingenious methods of maritime transportation; pastoral and agricultural peoples invent systems of pastoral and agricultural technology and science; industrial and manufacturing groups originate corresponding mechanical systems. Peoples like the Hindus, incessantly subject to invasion and subjugation by various foreign conquerors, or the Hebrews, who, very early in their history had to wander in the desert (after their exodus from Egypt), were attacked by other peoples, and, after their subjugation, were scattered over the earth— such groups can preserve their unity and con-

---

[39] The creative and uncreative periods are noted by historians without regard to the content and character of architecture, sculpture, literature, music, philosophy, religion, etc., the creative and uncreative periods being selected arbitrarily, principally on the basis of what I call sensate criteria of greatness, criteria which are the opposite of those of ideational and idealistic greatness. If the latter are applied, the creative and uncreative periods in these various fields prove to be very different from those given above. From this standpoint the philosophy of many of the Church Fathers

may be possessed as an achievement of the first rank; so also medieval music, sculpture, painting, and so on. At a later stage I shall list the periods of the rise and decline of systems in these fields of culture by their content or character, instead of arbitrarily determining what is of major importance and what is of only subordinate importance. For the present the foregoing discussion may suffice to demonstrate the intermittent character of creativeness (of essentially the sensate type) in the various fields of culture.

tinuity only through close religious and moral unity, since political unity and a strong governmental organization are denied them. Hence they evolve great religious and ethico-juridical systems that help to maintain their identity and solidarity. Without the Vedic and Hindu religion and the subsequent caste regime; without the Hebrew religion and Ten Commandments, the continuity and sociocultural survival of these groups would hardly have been possible. For the same reason many nations and peoples experience notable religious creativeness in periods of anarchy and peril.

Other groups, permanently menaced by invasion and extermination and forced by their conditions to adopt a program of expansion, colonization, and conquest, meet the need by the creation of powerful state and military systems.

So far as major systems of the fine arts are concerned, the fine arts serve different needs and therefore assume different characters according to circumstances. As we shall see, among the peoples dominated by ideational cultures the fine arts are the servants of religion and ethics, and as such are fundamentally religious and ethical. They function hand in hand with religion and ethics, constituting one of the most effective techniques for that purpose. This explains, for instance, the predominant religious forms of the fine arts in India, among the ancient Egyptians and Jews, among the early Greeks and Romans, and in medieval Europe.

In groups and cultures possessing a predominantly sensate character the social function of the fine arts is an increase of sensate pleasure and diversity of life. Hence they assume a secular character—that of art for art's sake—quite different from that of the religious or ideational fine arts.

A change in the nature of the urgent needs experienced in the life history of a given group explains in large measure the shift of creativeness from one field of culture to another. In a long-existing group its urgent needs do not remain the same throughout its entire history but change with the incessantly changing internal and external conditions of the group. Now the most urgent need may be the protection of its independence or the maintenance of internal order and discipline, met

by the creation either of a powerful political and military system or, if this is unavailable, of a great religious, philosophical, and ethico-juridical system. Now the paramount need may consist in securing the means of subsistence, met by devising scientific, technological, and economic systems ensuring the necessary minimum of economic well-being. Now the paramount need may be a multiplication of the group through a rising birth-rate and a declining mortality rate. Various of the fine arts serve these and other purposes either as ennobling, moralizing, unifying agencies (religious, ethical, patriotic, and the like) or as instruments of *joi de vivre*, of refined pleasure, of love or eroticism, of diversity and richness of sensate life. The groups in question will, accordingly, seek to create notable systems of ideational, idealistic, or sensate fine arts in one or several fields.

A systematic study of the periods of creation or ennoblement of major religious and ethical systems in the history of various nations and groups yields the following fairly general uniformity. *In the history of many creative groups the leading religious and ethical systems have ordinarily originated or been notably ennobled and perfected during periods of internal anarchy, tragic and devastating wars, grave pestilences or famines, or similar major calamities and crises, or else immediately after such calamities.*[40] This is especially true of groups that have been unable to cope with the emergency, for instance, through the creation of a powerful state or a prosperous economy. Periods of marked prosperity and sensate well-being have rarely, if ever, witnessed the rise or perfection of any first-rank religious or ethical system. As was explained above, under conditions of catastrophe religious and ethico-juridical systems are the most indispensable, most effective, and most accessible means for maintaining the unity of the group, for terminating internal anarchy, for reviving internal order and discipline, and for lifting its members to higher levels of social responsibility. Under the stress of such catastrophes as major wars and revolutions, famines and pestilences,

---

[40] These periods are also marked by the opposite "polarization" of irreligiousness and demoralization, according to the law of polarization formulated in my *Calamity*.

floods and droughts, earthquakes and conflagrations, a portion of the population exhibits a marked intensification of religious sentiment and moral heroism, while another portion becomes more irreligious and demoralized.[41]

In ancient Egypt the first important religious and ethical systems emerged or were markedly perfected in periods of severe calamity, such as those of around 3500-3300 B.C. and at the end of the Old Empire, the Middle Kingdom, and the New Empire.

In China the ethico-religious systems of Confucianism and Taoism emerged in the sixth century B.C., a period of grave internal anarchy and other calamities. A further ennoblement of Confucianism by Mencius and of Taoism by Chuang-tsze, and the creation of a moral philosophy of universal love by Mohtih, occurred in the fourth century B.C.—another century of major crises and calamities. The subsequent spread of Buddhism, of Neo-Confucianism, and other important religious movements occurred likewise in periods of disaster.

In India the religion and morality of the *Rig Veda* emerged about 1000 B.C. during a protracted crisis. The greatest ennoblement of the Vedic system of religion and morality, and the rise of Buddhism, of Jainism, of the philosophy of the *Upanishads*, and of the ethical systems of the *Bhagavatas* and *Saivas*, took place between the sixth and fourth centuries B.C., during another disastrous epoch. On the other hand, the periods of comparative prosperity and of powerful empires (such as those of the Guptas and Mauryas) in India, as well as similar epochs in the history of China, were marked by a comparative decline in religious sentiment, morality, and heroism, to say nothing of their failure to evolve any noteworthy religious or ethical systems.

The first substantial ennoblement of the Jewish religion and ethics—the work of Moses —occured under the catastrophic conditions of the exodus. The second notable step, marked by the charismatic leaders (*c.* 1020-960 B.C.)—the Judges, Samuel, Saul, and David—likewise

took place in very critical times for the Jews. The prosperous reign of Solomon, on the other hand, was marked by a decline of religious and moral sentiment. Possibly the climax of the Jewish religious and moral development — the rise of the great prophets and prophetic movements—was attained under the stress of the heaviest calamities that had befallen the Jews from 925 to the fourth century B.C.: the complete loss of their independence, the destruction of Jerusalem, and the Babylonian and other captivities.

In Greece and the Graeco-Roman world Stoicism, Neo-Platonism, and Neo-Pythagoreanism emerged and developed in a period of decline and calamity. The emergence of many religious and ethical sects (eventually absorbed by Christianity) and the rise and growth of Christianity and its sublime ethical system occurred also during periods of grave and protracted disaster.

Similarly, every disastrous period in the history of the western countries has been marked by an intensification of religious sentiment and morality and by the appearance of new sects and ethical currents,[42] side by side with negative polarization.[43]

In other groups, war, revolution, famine, etc. have led to the creation of a strong state, with a powerful governmental and military machine capable of establishing and maintaining internal order, waging defensive or offensive warfare, or coping with famine. Sometimes the establishment of such a state system occurs side by side with that of religious and ethical systems; more frequently, however, it is an alternative method. Periods of grave crisis are regularly marked by the expansion of governmental centralization, regimentation and control, by an accentuation of the role of the state and its political, administrative, and military forces. From the remotest past up to the latest World War, in which the United States was transformed from a nation with comparatively insignificant military forces and limited governmental control into a nation with

---

[41] For this and for subsequent uniformities, cf. my *Calamity*, Chps. 9-12.

[42] Cf. my *Calamity*, Chps. 9-12.

[43] For instance, the sudden emergence of Messianic movements among the American Indians

(the ghost dance, the prophet dance, and the Smohalla and Peyote cults) after 1870 occurred during a highly calamitous period for the Indian tribes in question. (For an outline of the movement and the relevant literature, cf. W. I. Thomas, *op. cit.*, pp. 680 ff.)

a gigantic military machine and enormously expanded federal and state governmental regimentation, the creation and growth of great political (or economic) systems in periods of grave crisis have repeatedly occurred.

The factor of the existence and transformation of urgent social needs fails, however, to account for all differences in creativeness, or for all shifts of creativeness from one field to another in the history of a given group. For such an explanation one has to take into consideration not only the periods of blossoming and decline of each system of cultural phenomena but the *character, content, and social functions* of each system. The organization and government of a state may be now religious and theocratic, now purely secular. Philosophy may be idealistic or materialistic, empirical or rational, agnostic or mystic. The fine arts may be now religious and ethical and now secular and hedonistic, if not actually sensual. Science may now be a handmaid of religion and now independent. Again, religion may be subservient to science. It is obvious that opposing philosophies—say, materialistic and idealistic philosophies—or religious and secular music, painting, sculpture, architecture, and literature, cannot be expected to develop and decline in parallel fashion. A materialistic philosophy may arise when an idealistic philosophy wanes; religious architecture may flourish when secular architecture deteriorates; theocratic government may emerge when secular government declines. The wholehearted devotion of a society to a religion that frowns upon material wealth and economic well-being is obviously not calculated to promote economic development.

---

[44] This is the reason why works such as that of A. Kroeber (cited), which attempt to analyze these phenomena regardless of the character and content of philosophy, the fine arts, etc., have arrived at very meager conclusions, why the *Blütezeit* in certain fields is arbitrarily determined, and why some of the deductions are highly questionable. One

For this almost axiomatic reason, merely noting the periods of an assumed blossoming of philosophy or science, the fine arts or religion, without an analysis of their content and character, can afford no valid conclusion as to why each field of culture blossoms or remains undeveloped, or as to how their movements are interconnected (if they are connected at all). Indeed, without such a preliminary analysis of the content and character of the systems in all fields of culture we can hardly even determine in which periods they flourished and in which they remained static.[44] The periods enumerated in the foregoing table, according to the judgment of the leading historians, are rather arbitrary, as most historians are definitely biased in favor of the sensate forms of philosophy, scholarship, the fine arts, statesmanship, etc. In their opinion the Church Fathers were poor philosophers, whereas Locke, Rousseau, and Voltaire were eminent philosophers; religious literature is not literature at all, only secular literature being worthy of the name, and so on.

Later on (see Chapters 40-42) we shall discuss this matter with due consideration for the character and content of all the cultural systems. Even assuming that the data given in the foregoing table are heavily weighted on the sensate side, they nevertheless show that even the predominantly sensate forms of various systems of culture fail to rise and decline simultaneously or to develop continuously, that groups are not equally creative in all fields, and that a given group does not evolve the same systems at different periods of its life history. They demonstrate also the role of the five factors of creativeness, especially that of an urgent sense of need.

---

cannot, indeed, expect to find religious and idealistic types of philosophy and the fine arts blossoming side by side with atheistic, mechanistic, and materialistic philosophy and sensuous fine arts. The same may be said of most historical and sociological works subject to the same shortcoming.

Chapter 36. How Ideological Systems Are Objectified

I. Unborn and Stillborn Systems

As long as a system of meanings remains at the stage of a mere mental conception, it does not constitute a part of empirical sociocultural reality. It must first somehow be objectified through vehicles and then socialized through becoming known to other human beings. If the conception of an ideological system may be compared to the conception of an organism, its objectification may be likened to the birth of an organism.

Like the process of birth the objectification process is difficult and precarious. Many ideological systems die at this stage. The conception of a beautiful poem frequently miscarries when an attempt is made to translate it into words. The same often occurs with a musical composition. A painting or sculpture objectifying a concept may prove to be crude and immature. The model of an invention may prove to be unworkable. A scientific, philosophical, or religious idea, when an effort is made to formulate it, may be found to be self-contradictory or fallacious, unverifiable, platitudinous, unutterable, or the like. Hence there are many more conceivers of poems, symphonies, pictures, philosophical and religious systems, technological and scientific theories, ethical and legal codes, than there are capable objectifiers of such systems. At the stage of conception there are multitudes of great poets, philosophers, scientists, lawgivers, etc. At the stage of objectification the overwhelming majority fail and are eliminated; they either do not attempt to give birth to their concep-

tions or else give birth to a stillborn child.

Such failure is due, first of all, to the immaturity of the concept itself. It is due, secondly, to the lack of sufficient technical skill for an adequate objectification of the conception. It is not enough to have the mind of a great writer or composer, painter, scientist, or philosopher: one must possess the skill to put a poetic concept into effective words, to translate a musical inspiration into an adequate score, to shape a scientific idea into a competent, logically developed, and well-tested theory. This is even more true of a technological invention: the idea of a flying machine occurred to Leonardo da Vinci and to certain other persons in the fifteenth and sixteenth centuries, but only during the twentieth century did airplanes become a reality. A primitive steam engine was conceived in the third century B.C. in China, but not until the nineteenth century was it actually objectified.

Thirdly, the objectification of the conception of a new system requires the prior existence of all its components, in the absence of which it cannot be realized. Without the invention of polyphony, the fugue, counterpoint, harmony, and so on, Beethoven's musical conceptions could not have been objectified. Without a system of musical notation and scoring, great compositions could not be written. Without the invention of paper (c. 105 A.D. in China) the art of printing would have been impossible.

Fourthly, in addition to these obstacles,

there are various other impediments, partly economic and partly social, to the successful objectification of a conception. A highly religious society, for instance, may persecute a materialistic philosopher or an atheistic poet; a caste or aristocratic society may suppress an equalitarian political thinker; a communistic society may frown upon an anticommunist ideologist. Under such circumstances many a conceiver of such systems abstains from their objectification. The hostility of a given culture to a certain system may hinder its objectification in many other ways. Instead of being subjected to outright persecution, a creative personality may be deprived of the means of subsistence, or at least denied sympathy and encouragement. The full objectification and propagation of religion and theology, with the concomitants of temples and cathedrals, an ecclesiastical hierarchy, rituals and ceremonies, and objects of veneration, is possible only in a highly religious society; the sucessful objectifi-

cation and development of a science demands a sensate culture, and so on. Even when a culture is not inimical to a given conception, its objectification may require larger funds than are available. Sometimes vested economic and other interests endeavor to suppress a new system at its conceptual stage because it is inimical to these interests. Thus many industrial concerns shelve inventions that would render obsolete the products manufactured by these concerns. Dominant scientific, philosophical, religious, ethical, political, and economic systems are prone to prevent the objectification and particularly the socialization of competing systems by such means as denunciation or hostile criticism, discrimination against their originators in the matter of appointments or promotion, and even more drastic and ruthless measures. This explains why objectified systems of meanings are less numerous than those which are conceived, why a vast proportion of the latter are either never born or else stillborn.

II. Relationship Between Nature of Meanings and That of Vehicles

Why is a given meaning objectified by a given kind of vehicle? Why is the same meaning objectified by different sounds (words) in different languages, for instance, "sun" in English, "soleil" in French, and "solntze" in Russian? Why in the same language is each meaning expressed by a given word? Likewise, why is a given meaning objectified by different written characters in different languages— Egyptian, Chinese, Sanskrit, Greek, Arabic, or English? Why, for instance, is the meaning of "two" objectified by the figure 2 in one case and by II in another case? How did it happen that in one language the written figures are of one kind and in another language of a different kind? Why is one of the vehicles of Christianity a cross; of Mohammedanism, a crescent; of the United States, stars and stripes; of the Third Reich, a swastika? Why did the system of Greek religion and civic virtue find its expression in the form of Doric, Ionic, or Corinthian temples; that of the Christian religion in the form of Romanesque or Gothic cathedrals; that of the Chinese in the form

of a pagoda; that of the Mohammedan in the form of a mosque? Why are governmental or military ranks symbolized by different types of uniforms and insignia in different countries? Why are religious services and rituals of one kind in one religion and of a different kind in another?

The problem is a very complex one and in large part still remains a mystery. A few reasons, however, can be indicated that elucidate a part of the problem. These factors may be summed up as follows.

An overwhelming proportion of the vehicles used by individuals and groups for the objectification of their ideological systems and congeries are inculcated by the *socio-cultural milieu* in which the individuals and groups are born and reared and in which they interact. These vehicles include languages and music, or sound conductors; letters, signs, and pictures, or color and light conductors; gestures, actions, ceremonies, and rituals, or pantomimic conductors; objects, and other conductors.

This proposition, however, is not concerned with the *original* "marriage" between the meanings and the vehicles but takes for granted the prior existence of a vast number of such "marriages." The difficulty lies not in the acquisition of the vehicles but in the original establishment of a connection between the given meaning and the given vehicle, as in the case of the idea "sun" and the spoken and written symbols in which it is objectified in various languages.

By way of approach to this central problem the following propositions may be laid down.

1. Influence of Existing Vehicles on Creation of New Ones

In already objectified systems and supersystems the nature of the existing body of vehicles decisively determines the character of the new vehicles or of the modification of the old vehicles in the sense of patterning the new vehicles after the relevant existing vehicles as a variation and of avoiding extraneous vehicles. Every system is selective, and as such admits for the most part only new elements that are congenial to it. This proposition follows as a corollary of the essential nature of meaningful-causal systems, in contradistinction to ideological congeries. Any vehicle—whether language or music, a certain style of painting or architecture, or what not—changes in the course of time. But such changes are limited by the nature of the sum total of existing patterns. The following are typical examples.

a. *Changes in Oral Language Vehicles.* Spencer reports that English greengrocers in his time abbreviated "artichokes" to "chokes" and changed "asparagus" to "asparagrass," "sparrowgrass," and finally "grass."[1] Such changes of English sound conductors accord, however, with the general character of the language. Similar phonetic changes occur incessantly in virtually any language. Not only do words change, but now and then certain grammatical and syntactical rules undergo modification. These modifications, however, take place within the framework of the general grammatical and syntactical idiom of the tongue, in distinction from that of an alien tongue. There is a large number of very different language structures, ranging from the extremely analytic type, such as the Chinese, where a word expresses nothing but the notion of an object, quality, activity or relation, to such types as the Yana Indian language, where one word expresses the idea "Shall I have the people move across the river to the east?" Nevertheless, in each case the existing structure of the language patterns the new words or structural changes after its own peculiar character.[2]

b. *Changes in Writing.* What is said of oral language applies also to the signs that constitute its written form. The existing body of written signs determines the character of the new signs introduced into a given written language. Thus, the orthography of many English words has changed within the last few centuries, but the characters have remained English (or Roman). The infiltration of foreign or extraneous characters has been a very rare phenomenon.[3] After the invention of an alphabetic system of writing, in the process of its diffusion it was modified by each principal language in accordance with its existing body of phonetic properties and written characters yielding the Greek, the Ogam, the quadratic Hebrew, the cursive Syriac, the highly cursive Arabic, and the still more divergent Brahmi, Sanskrit, Korean, and Manchu scripts.[4]

c. *Variations in Other Vehicles.* A similar generalization applies to other vehicles of any system (not congeries). Thus, the patterns of the Christian cross varied in size, material, shape, and the number of points, but all the variations retained the basic pattern of the

---

[1] Herbert Spencer, *Principles of Sociology* (London, 1885), Vol. I, p. 831.

[2] For the details of the described manner of linguistic change, cf. E. Sapir, "The Unconscious Patterning of Behavior in Society," in *The Unconscious: A Symposium* (New York, 1925); *Language: An Introduction to the Study of Speech* (New York, 1921); O. Jespersen, *Language, Its Nature, Development and Origin* (London, 1924); H. Delacroix, *Le Langage et la pensée* (Paris, 1930); H. Delacroix, E. Cassirer, L. Jordan, A. Meillet, et al., *Psychologie de langage* (Paris, 1933); and A. S. Woolner, *Languages in History and Politics* (Oxford University Press, 1938).

[3] For the modification of the ancient Egyptian writing, cf. A. H. Gardiner, "The Nature and Development of the Egyptian Hieroglyphic Writing," *Journal of Egyptian Archeology*, Vol. II, pp. 63-68.

[4] Cf. R. B. Dixon, *The Building of Culture*, pp. 136 ff.

cross in all Christian denominations, in contra-distinction, for instance, to the Mohammedan crescent or the Hebrew star of David. The flag of the United States has also varied from time to time, but all the changes have kept the basic pattern of the stars and stripes. The written constitution of the United States has likewise been modified, but its amendments have not deviated from the fundamental principles of the instrument. The patterns of Gothic, Romanesque and baroque architecture vary, similarly, in different Gothic, Romanesque, and baroque buildings; but all the variations preserve the essential features of each style. To repeat, the initially established character of the vehicles of a given ideological system exerts a very decisive influence upon the new vehicles and upon the modifications of the old. To use W. I. Thomas' expression, this existing body of vehicles "defines the situation" and serves as a selecting and patterning agency.

Only when the meaning of an ideological system radically changes is there a corresponding revolution in the vehicles. Such a change means, however, the disruption of the old system and its replacement by a new one.

2. Manner of Selection of Vehicles

Returning now to a consideration of the first, original expression of a given meaning through a given vehicle, (a) a part of such marriages between the meanings and vehicles is due to the instinctive, reflexological properties of the human nervous system, and to the human vocal apparatus; (b) a large proportion is determined by the combining function of the human mind, especially in the form of associations of phenomena on the basis of similarity, of spatial and temporal contiguity in perception, of contrast, etc.;[5] (c) a substantial percentage of the vehicles is determined by the abstracting activity of the human mind; (d)

perfect objectifications of great ideological systems are due to the creativeness of developed minds, including the purposeful creation of the vehicles. A few comments on each of these factors are in order.

a. *Instinctive, Reflexological, and Unconscious Emergence of Vehicles.* An animal or human organism, when it experiences intense excitement of either a painful or a pleasurable character, emits many different sounds and produces a variety of facial expressions, gestures, and expressive movements. It snarls, growls, roars, laughs or cries, moans, groans, or sighs; it shows its teeth or glares with its eyes; it shivers or trembles; it caresses, fondles, licks; it slaps with its paws, bites, or pecks; it attacks or runs away, and so forth. These and many other expressions of emotion occur reflexologically, without any purpose, premeditation, definite awareness, or fixed habit pattern.[6] This reflex expression of emotion (or Pareto's residue of the manifestation of sentiments through external acts)[7] led, through repetition, to the use of sounds, gestures, and motions as the vehicles for an objectification of many emotional and other states of mind, congeries, and systems. Eventually these conductors began to be utilized intentionally and resulted in vocal, pictorial, gestural, and other rudimentary language. When we are cheerful, we laugh; when we are sad, we cry or sigh; when we suffer pain, we groan or moan; when we are angry, we shake our fists; when we love, we embrace, caress, or kiss; when we are afraid, we turn pale, tremble, or run, and so on. Eventually, as Spencer and others have shown, these reactions led to the appearance of ceremonies and rituals, manners and mores, badges and other object vehicles, etc., expressing a multitude of meanings, values, and norms.[8] Among preliterate groups the language of "manual concepts," of gestures and signs, is enormously developed. Among civi-

---

[5] This combining function of the human mind is somewhat similar to what V. Pareto calls the residue of combination. (Cf. his *Mind and Society*, §§. 889-1396, 1687-2059.) Its simplest forms are based on the mechanism of conditioned reflexes. (Cf. J. P. Pavlov, *The Conditioned Reflexes*, cited.)

[6] Cf. C. Darwin, *The Expression of the Emotions in Man and Animals* (New York, 1873); Spencer, *The Principles of Sociology* (London, 1885), Vol. II, Part IV (Ceremonial Institutions), Ch. 1, *passim*; V. Bekhtereff, "Mimika i eie biologitches-

koie znachenie," *Vestnik Znania*, 1910, and *General Foundations of Reflexology, in Russian* (Leningrad, 1921).

[7] Cf. Pareto, *Trattato* (cited), sects. 889-1396, 1687-2059.

[8] Cf. Spencer, *Principles of Sociology* (cited). The part "Ceremonial Institutions" still contains many valid generalizations. Cf. also the cited works of Jespersen, Sapir, and Delacroix—Meillet on the origin of language.

lized peoples the language of deaf mutes and the oral, expressional, and histrionic language of actors on the stage are derived to a considerable extent from this reflex expression of emotion in terms of sounds, gestures, and actions.

b. *Emergence of Vehicles Through the Combining Power of the Human Mind.* The well-nigh incessant combination of ideas, patterns, and images of objects, phenomena, events, and qualities perceived is the most general and fundamental function of the human mind. Such a process takes place even in our dreams. The combinations are extremely heterogeneous, ranging from logical ones to the fantastic and bizzare combinations characteristic of dream states. Most typical are the associations of phenomena on the basis of similarity, contiguity, and dissimilarity, or contrast.[9]

Many meanings, values, and norms are objectified through a given set of vehicles because these vehicles are associated in our perceptions with the respective phenomena on the basis of some *similarity*. Many words in various languages are imitations of the sounds produced by animals, inanimate objects, and phenomena, for example, "cuckoo," "bang," and "pop." In the language of children and of several preliterate groups such imitative, or onomatopoetic, words occupy a considerable place.[10] Musical compositions in the minor key—for instance funeral marches and such movements as the last section of Tchaikovsky's *Pathétique* symphony—frequently suggest lamentation, moaning, crying, or sighing; while many compositions in the major key are imitatives in melody, tempo, and rhythm, of the sounds associated with cheerful moods. Much "program music" suggests the songs of birds (for example, Beethoven's *Pastoral Symphony*, Wagner's *Tristan's Journey*, and Liszt's *Préludes*), thunder, storms, the winter wind (as in several compositions of Sibelius), the noises of factories, war, falling bombs, and explosions (for example, Prokoffiev's and Shostakovitch's compositions), and the like.

Association by similarity plays an important role also in poetry, metaphors, etc. (Cf. Gogol's "The river glistened like glass, like a Damascus blade.")

Likewise many color and light conductors are based upon this principle. Pictorial signs of the triangle, square, and so on are reproductions of the respective geometric figures. Hieroglyphic writing (in Egypt and elsewhere) is a pictographic reproduction of various objects, phenomena, and processes.[11] An enormous proportion of painting, sculpture, and architecture reproduces, sometimes illusionistically, persons, animals, landscapes, objects, and so on.

Similarly, many expressive gestures, ceremonies and rituals (religious, juridical, military, and political), and objects are vehicles based upon the same principle of association through similarity.[12] Phallic cults and ceremonies imitate sex organs and functions. War dances, with their objects, imitate the actions and objects of war. Red wine functions in religious and other ceremonies as a substitute for blood; a red flag has often objectified bloody revolution; an engagement or wedding ring "binds" the parties, and so on. The same principle underlies the construction of cathedrals, with quintuple cupolas symbolizing Christ and the four Evangelists, and the ground plan simulating the Cross.[13]

What has been said of the principle of association through similarity applies also to that of *association through spatial and temporal contiguity*. A complex idea of a phenomenon is objectified through a simpler vehicle associated spatially or temporally with the phenomenon. The Cross thus became a symbol of

---

[9] Cf. especially L. Lévy-Brühl, *Les Fonctions mentales* (Paris, 1912), pp. 149 ff., 175 ff., summing up the observations of many ethnologists and anthropologists.

[10] Cf. Lévy-Brühl, *op. cit.*, pp. 192 ff.

[11] Cf. A. H. Gardiner, *op. cit.*; M. Verworn, *Die Anfänge der Kunst* (Siena, 1909); J. W. Danzel, *Die Anfänge der Schriften* (Leipzig, 1912); also the quoted works of F. Boas and H. Read on the primitive arts.

[12] For such vehicles in the field of law, cf.

Chassan, *Essai sur la symbolique du droit* (Paris, 1847), and Leo Petrajitzky, *Theory of Law*, Vol. I, pp. 51-57: For military ceremonies, uniforms, actions, and gestures, cf. Lieutenant Jaray, *Du formalisme au "Débrouillez-vous!"* (Paris, 1912). Cf. also the "Ceremonial Institutions" of Spencer (cited).

[13] Cf. especially Schlesinger, *Geschichte des Symbols* (Jena, 1912), chapter on "Symbolik in der Baukunst," and F. R. Webber, *Church Symbolism* (Cleveland, 1927).

Christianity partly through its connection with the crucified Christ; "Washington" often typifies the federal government of the United States, and so on. The objectification of the meaning of a certain object, phenomenon, event, or value—especially when these are complex—by a vehicle that is adjacent, simpler, and more concrete is a fairly typical process.[14]

"White" often calls forth in our mind "black"; "saintly," "sinful"; "big," "small"; "beautiful," "ugly"; "God," "devil"; "communism," "capitalism," and so on. Some of the vehicles seemingly emerged through this process of *combination by contrast*. It is observable in pictures of gods and devils, saints and sinners; in various vehicles expressing the distinctions between superiors and inferiors; masters and slaves, conquerors and the vanquished, aristocracy and plebs; and so on.[15] As has been observed, dreams and daydreams evoke the most incongruous combinations of images, ideas, patterns, and forms. Some of these are retained, often being manifested in a use of the corresponding vehicles determined by the combinations.

(c) *Emergence of Vehicles Through the Abstracting Function of the Mind.* One of the highest forms of combining activity of the mind is its abstracting function. It consists in an ability to observe and abstract similarity, uniformity, and connection among the apparent disparities and perceptual dissimilarities of the phenomena. This mode of combination is not confined to perceptual similarity, contiguity, or contrast. It goes beyond such combinations and gives us, in its mature form, the *causal* connections of the phenomena,[16] *causal uniformity, and the typical in the arts and sciences*: the aesthetic type and the scientific "ideal type," or adequate definition (for example, the definition of the triangle, square,

or circle in geometry, and any adequate definition in science, philosophy, religion, or law).[17]

In its immature form the abstracting function produces all kinds of noncausal, nonlogical, atypical combinations, and pseudo concepts, types, patterns, and forms.

W. I. Thomas rightly remarks that anthropologists and social scientists have largely neglected this abstracting property of mind "in their attempts to explain origins, particularly the origins of savage inventions." Their "explanations" rarely go beyond the mere reflex, instinctive, and associational factors.[18]

A systematic study of the development of language and numeral systems in the case of Helen Keller, Laura Bridgman, and Marie Heurtin, who either were born deaf mutes or became deaf mutes soon after birth, shows clearly the role of this power of abstraction; without it they could not have developed their intelligence and their language and other vehicles to the same extent as they actually did.[19]

To this abstracting ability is due also the extension of meanings and their vehicles and their transfer to other fields and vehicles, for instance the extension of the meanings and sound vehicle "firelight" or "sunlight" to "light," "enlightenment," "the light of truth," "Lead, kindly light," "heavenly light," etc. in oral and written speech and in various pictorial and sculptured symbols of light. A similar extension and transfer through the abstracting function of the mind occurs in all fields of ideological systems and congeries. Similarly, the idea of "balance" has been extended and then objectified in various vehicles in the sense of weighing machine, mental equipoise, harmony between parts, adjustment of an account, amount on hand, remainder, equilibrium in physics and science, justice

---

[14] For the details, cf. my *Sistema soziologii*, Vol. I, pp. 153-176, and W. I. Thomas, *Primitive Behavior*, Chps. 4, 18.

[15] For examples of this combination by contrast and difference, cf. Pareto, *op. cit.*

[16] The essence of causal relationship is the existence of identity among perceptionally different phenomena and of difference among phenomena that appear to be similar. (Cf. my *Sociocultural Causality, Space, and Time*, Ch. 2.)

[17] The geometrical definition of a triangle represents its "ideal type" in the strictest sense of the term. So also does an adequate definition of any

class phenomenon. From this standpoint Max Weber's conception of the "ideal type," so far as he distinguishes it from such adequate definitions, is faulty. Even more mistaken are many commentators upon Weber's "ideal type," who fail to realize the identity of the "ideal type" of the triangle and its adequate definition.

[18] W. I. Thomas, *Primitive Behavior*, pp. 774 ff. Cf. the analysis of the role of abstraction in the development of language and of other vehicles among preliterate and advanced groups.

[19] For a detailed analysis, cf. W. I. Thomas, *ibid.*, pp. 776 ff.

(represented by a goddess with scales in her hand), the Apocalyptical "weighed in the balance and found wanting," and so on.[20] The vocal, written, musical, pictorial, sculptural, architectural, and other objectifications of these meanings of balance are extremely varied, and in all of them the abstracting ability plays a decisive role.

When a writer, painter, sculptor, or composer creates a Don Quixote, Hamlet, Babbitt, or other type, they abstract certain traits from a multitude of concrete persons, combine them into a typical unity, and give us not only the ideological type but also its objectified portrait in written, painted, sculptural, auditory, or other forms. (Cf. Beethoven's *Coriolanus*, Gounod's *Faust*, Richard Strauss's *Till Eulenspiegel*, Wagner's *Lohengrin*, etc.)

When scientists or scholars formulate the definition of a triangle, a chemical element, a physical force or mass, a biological cell, or of feudalism, urban versus rural habitats, capital and labor, and so on, they abstract the generic properties from a great number of concrete triangles, chemical bodies, cells, cities, etc. and give us a concept, or "ideal type." These generalized conceptual types find their objectification in oral, written, pictorial, and other vehicles—formulas, definitions, symbols, etc.

Through the abstracting property of mind many inventions have been conceived and objectified, ranging from primitive boats or arrows to the most complex modern inventions.

As this abstracting ability is almost unlimited in respect to the traits and phenomena from which it abstracts and which it generalizes and combines, it is evident that the relationship between meanings and vehicles is often loose and "polygamic" (cf. Chapter 3). Through this abstraction the same meaning may objectify itself in very different vehicles, and the same vehicle (for instance, money) may objectify very different meanings. The idea of a lethal projectile has objectified itself in a stone and in stone-projecting machinery, in bows and arrows (of poisonous and non-poisonous varieties), in guns, in rocket projectiles, in atomic bombs, and the like.

(d) *Invention of Vehicles Through the Intuitional, Logical, and Sensory Creativity of the Mind.* An enormous number of vehicles

has been invented through the creative power of the developed mind, especially those of the dominant ideological systems. Contrary to the behaviorists, reflexologists, and other partisans of distorted mechanistic interpretation of the human mind as something little different from an inorganic mechanism or biological reflex, the creative function of the developed mind is fully as well established as the various problematical subconscious and unconscious instincts, reflexes, complexes, "residues," and mechanisms which they postulate. The creativeness of a Plato, a Beethoven, Phidias, or Shakespeare, or of a Newton or Euclid is undeniable.

Creativeness[21] is marked by the following characteristics: the conception of an original system, the development of a logically or aesthetically consistent system, and an adequate objectification of the system in its vehicles. Originality requires the ability to combine the elements of the system and its vehicles in a way inaccessible to uncreative or less creative minds, transcending combinations based merely on similarity, contiguity, or contrast, and even those derived from a low-grade power of abstraction. An eminent scientist, for instance, discovers laws (such as that of gravitation) beyond the grasp of less creative minds. The same applies to the achievements of original poets and other writers, composers (like Bach, Beethoven, Wagner, and Chaikovsky), painters, sculptors, and architects.

In this sense the margin of freedom of truly creative combinations of either ideological systems or their vehicles is incomparably greater than that of less creative combinations based on instincts, associations, and low-grade abstraction. Truly creative combinations are largely unforeseen and unpredictable. Not infrequently even the creators themselves are not aware in advance just how they will develop their initial ideas, as is evident from the numerous preliminary sketches, outlines, drafts, models, and patterns of the final creative product of many poets, artists, composers, scientists, lawgivers, and ethical and religious leaders.

Since truly creative work is essentially unpredictable and enjoys a wide margin of free-

---

[20] *Ibid.*, p. 779.

[21] Cf. J. Moreno's paper (cited on *Creativity-Spontaneity.*

dom in its combinations of ideas and values, of vehicles and "materializations," the connections between original ideological systems and their vehicles are naturally loose, in the sense that creative minds may choose the most diverse combinations of sounds, colors, lines, patterns, and materials for the objectification of their systems. No rigid or narrow determinism between a system of meanings and its vehicles can be established in advance.

This does not mean, however, that a creator is absolutely independent of the language or idiom of his milieu and epoch. He can articulate his system only in the language—oral, literary, musical, artistic, religious, philosophical, technological, or scientific—of his culture and groups. But within these limits he is free to make any combination of elements. Now and then he even transcends these limits and introduces certain new elements not present in his social and cultural milieu. The wide margin of freedom possessed by the creative function of the mind explains why the objectification of a given ideological system in a given set of vehicles still remains to a considerable extent a mystery. The explanation of the mystery must be sought in the very nature of the creative process itself. When the nature of creativeness is understood, the complexity and many-sidedness, the apparent indeterminateness and unpredictability, of the connections between the ideological system and its vehicles will be understood. The abstracting and creative functions of the developed mind (under the favorable conditions of the five basic factors indicated in the preceding chapter) explain why the great ideological systems in all fields of culture have manifested themselves in a given set of vehicles.

One of the partial forms of the abstracting and creative mode of objectification of ideological systems is the *purposeful invention or selection of the vehicles*. Many scientists and scholars invent or select a new term, sign, or symbol for the objectification of their system of meanings, values, and norms. Thus, many mathematical symbols, such as the triangle, the square, the integral and differential in calculus, were purposefully created for an adequate expression of the respective meanings. The Latin nomenclature of taxonomy, many terms in the biological and social sciences, and most of the physical and chemical terms and formulas have been created in this purposive way, as well as the choice of such vehicles as the Nazi swastika, Soviet Russia's sickle and hammer, and the flags of various states. Other illustrations are afforded by technological inventions, painting and sculpture, architectural works, the objectification of law-norms and ethical principles, political reforms, and economic measures.

The purposeful origin of vehicles is only one of the modes of creative origination of vehicles. As we have seen, many systems and sets of vehicles are produced intuitively, without a pre-existing purpose or plan. They arise spontaneously, requiring only to be verified, elaborated, and embodied in various material forms.

(e) *The Cooperation of Several Methods.* Finally, many vehicles emerge through the cooperation of various methods. The totality of the foregoing factors—instinctive, reflex, associational, abstractive, and creative—explain to a considerable extent how and why given ideological systems and congeries are objectified through given vehicles. Guided by these principles in each specific case of a meaning and its vehicle, one can largely decipher how and why this particular "marriage" has occurred.

Chapter 37. Socialization of Objectified Systems and Congeries: Mobility of Cultural Phenomena

I. Forms of Socialization of Cultural Phenomena

If an objectified system or congeries is not to be confined to its creator, it has to become known to other persons, it has to acquire, that is, other human agents; in brief, it has to be socialized among individuals and groups. Thus the process of socialization becomes a universal and ever-repeated phase of the grounding of any living system or congeries in sociocultural reality. The systems and congeries that do not succeed in becoming socialized at some time after their birth, die with the death of their creators: they do not become a tangible part of the given empirical culture. Some objectified systems and congeries become socialized very soon after their objectification; others have to wait years and even decades before they become widely known to many persons and groups.

Socialization of a cultural phenomenon may be ideological, in the sense that the system or congeries becomes known to others only ideologically, without tangibly affecting their behavioral and material culture. But it may also be ideological, behavioral, and material, changing the ideology, behavior, and material culture of the persons and groups that receive it. The purely ideological as well as the behavioral and material socialization may be positive when the persons accept the cultural phenomenon and practice it, negative when they reject it, neutral when they are indifferent to it. Thus, if a Communist theory becomes known to a person intellectually and does not affect his behavioral and material culture, that person's "infection" with Communism remains mainly ideological (positive or negative). If the theory visibly changes the person's behavior and material culture, Communism has become socialized in the person ideologically, behaviorally, and materially (in a positive way when the person supports it, spreads it, contributes his money, time, energy; in a negative way, when he criticizes it and fights it).

Socialization of a given cultural phenomenon increases when it "infects" an ever-growing number of persons, groups, and strata; in that case the phenomenon spreads, multiplies, expands. When the number of previously infected persons, groups, and strata decreases, its socialization declines or contracts. An increase of socialization of a cultural phenomenon may be either mainly ideological or it may also be behavioral and material, when the ideology begins to be practiced and used in the material culture of an increasing number of persons, groups, strata. Similarly, the decrease of socialization of a given cultural phenomenon may be either mainly ideological or ideological-

563

behavioral-material. This distinction is important because, as we shall see, the magnitudes of the ideological, and the behavioral and material socializations of the same cultural phenomenon are rarely identical. More, now and then the socialization of a given cultural system, for instance, of Christianity, may be growing ideologically, but at the same time its behavioral and material socialization may be decreasing.

Ideological or behavioral and material increase of socialization of a given phenomenon may mean also: (1) an increasing number of persons and groups coming into contact with and learning about a unique cultural phenomenon, for instance, visiting a museum to see a picture of Raphael or some other master; (2) increasing multiplication of the copies of a given cultural phenomenon, e.g., a best-seller, a car, a cathedral, a picture, a symphony, or a play; (3) both types of increase. The same is true of a decrease of socialization of a given cultural phenomenon. The following scheme sums up these forms of socialization.

| Socialization of objectified cultural systems and congeries | Mainly Ideological | positive negative neutral | Increasing in the forms of: 1, 2, 3, and others: diffusion, multiplication, expansion decreasing in the forms of: 1, 2, 3, and others: contraction, rarefication, disappearance |
| | Ideological-Behavioral-Material | positive negative neutral | increasing in the forms of: 1, 2, 3, and others: diffusion, etc. decreasing in the forms of: 1, 2, 3, and others: contraction, etc. |

II. Mobility of Cultural Phenomena: Its Forms, Routes, Directions, and Kinds

1. Horizontal and Vertical Mobility of Cultural Phenomena

For a given objectified cultural phenomenon to be socialized, it must pass or be transmitted from person to person, from group to group, stratum to stratum. Any such passage or transmission of a cultural value gives a process of mobility (migration, circulation) of cultural phenomena, the counterpart of the mobility of individuals and groups already studied. In this sense the processes of socialization and mobility of cultural processes are inseparable from each other.

Like the mobility of individuals, the mobility of cultural phenomena may be *horizontal*, when the phenomenon passes from person to person, group to group, of the same or similar social stratum and position; *vertical*, when it passes from upper to lower and from lower to upper strata; *intermediary*, when the ranks and strata of the persons and groups remain undetermined or blurred. Mobility may be *intentionally selective and controlled*, when a cultural phenomenon is desired to be known and socialized only within definite persons and groups; *spontaneous and unselective*, when nobody tries to select the recipients of a cultural value or, on the contrary, some persons or groups desire it to be known to all or to as many persons and groups as possible. The selective mobility is directed only toward the select areas, persons, groups. The spontaneous may be not directed at all or, as in advertizing, directed to all.

2. Channels, Routes, and Directions of Mobility of Cultural Phenomena

Cultural phenomena tend to move from the center of their objectified emergence (inventors, creators) or from their given place (persons and groups that have them) along all the channels of communication and interaction that exist between their given place, and human agents (inventors, possessors) and other areas, persons, and groups. The more developed is the total system of communication between these points the more easily they move; the directions of their mobility are determined by the directions of the routes of communication. They move especially easily and rapidly within the network of the communication to points, persons, and groups to whom they are addressed by either the inventors and creators, or human agents, of a given cultural phenomenon or to those who seek for the given cultural phenomenon selectively directed mobility, and vice versa. They either do not pass at all or move with difficulty to areas, persons, and groups having no lines or poor lines of communication with the place, persons and groups that have a given cultural phenomenon. The proposition is practically self-evident. It explains why a newly invented fashion in dress moves quickly and easily from New York to Chicago or Los Angeles and passes slowly and with difficulty from New York to a much nearer Adirondack or Ozark mountain village; why a foreign or a new cultural phenomenon penetrates first to the urban centers and often leaves much nearer rural areas and populations untouched. Since the total network of communication of big cities is incomparably more developed, and since they have more contacts with foreign cultures, persons, and groups than the rural areas, the foreign cultural phenomena flow into the culture of the cities faster, in fuller and more numerous streams than into the rural areas. In the past, for instance in the Graeco-Roman world, the foreign cults of Mitra, Cybele, Great Mother, Isis, Osiris, and others reached and penetrated the cities, seashore ports, along the maritime routes, among the merchants, legionnaires, officials. They penetrated very little and only much later to the rural areas and populations. In mountainous, steppe, or desert regions in the past, lacking means of communication, cultural phenomena travelled along the mountainous paths and caravan routes and reached the border regions and border populations first, although these places and peoples were often very distant from the place of departure of a given cultural phenomenon. Our proposition explains the map of the spread of various other cultural phenomena, for example, the Greek or Latin, Arabic or English languages. The Greek, the Malayan, the Polynesian navigators carried their respective languages along the shore of the Mediterranean or among the islands of the Malayan and Polynesian archipelagoes. The Berbers, Arabs, and Turks disseminated their languages and other culture traits in and along the borders of the steppes and deserts which they travelled. The English, with Britannia ruling the waves, carried their language and culture traits to the areas and peoples of their empire.

The proposition also shows why in the past, and partly at the present, epidemics move along the highways, waterways, and railways connecting the place of their emergence with other places. The same is true of most other cultural phenomena, whether tobacco, certain writing and script, architectural style, fashions, or music. It explains also the extraordinarily fast and many-directional mobility of cultural values disseminated by telegraph, telephone, and radio, by airplanes and rocket planes, by newspapers and television. Through these means of communication a cultural phenomenon almost instantaneously reaches millions of listeners, readers, places, and groups in all parts of the world.

In regard to the vertical mobility of cultural phenomena the proposition is equally valid. In the past many cultural traits of the masters and serfs passed vertically through the valets and servants of the lord, who interacted with both strata. Other traits passed between these social orders because both strata were exposed to the same cultural influences: the church, the religious service, a song, a landscape, and so on. So far as various strata nowadays listen to the same radio program, attend the same church service, read the same paper or book, are exposed to the same objectified cultural objects, mix in school and at political rallies, in short, generally share many channels of communication, the upper and lower classes transmit traits from one to another incessantly.

The proposition specifies farther why the invention of the atomic bomb, with its "know how," is known only to a limited number of persons in the United States, Canada, and England, and remains unknown (at this moment of writing) to millions of persons who live right in the places where it was invented and is manufactured (a typical case of directed and controlled mobility of many inventions, of "secret societies," etc.). It explains also why the spies and their governments, the persons who are anxious to know the secret inventions of other countries, now and then succeed, with the rest of the populations remaining ignorant of the invention, why often an inventor, scientist, scholar, poet, reformer, or religious apostle communicates his invention, theory, poem, plan of reform or religion to a few scientists, inventors, scholars, poets, or religious disciples living far from him, without broadcasting the system to millions that live right next to him.

On the other hand, the proposition makes obvious the fallacy of many theories of migration, diffusion, and shift of cultural phenomena, such as the theory of a concentric spread, of the northward, the eastward, the coldward, the westward mobility of cultural systems. As the total network of conductors connecting a given cultural phenomenon with other persons and groups is rarely, if ever, evenly spread by concentric circles, C. Wissler's "law of concentric diffusion of culture," according to which a cultural phenomenon spreads from the center of its origin concentrically, is no law at all. At best it is a partial case.[1] As the existing network of conductors from a given cultural phenomenon does not always spread to the north or to the east or the west, as a rule it is diffused in several directions, all the theories claiming either a northward or coldward, westward, or eastward course of cultural streams with the passage of time—the theories of S. Gilfillan, V. Stefansson, P. Mougeolle, R. Mewes, E. Sasse, E. Smith, S. Reinach, etc.—are fallacious; they unduly generalize a partial case into universal uniformity.[2]

3. Two-Sided Cultural Mobility

The direction of any current of cultural phenomena moving from one locus or person to another point or person is rarely one-way. It is usually a two-way current: from A to B and from B to A; from the city to the country, and vice versa; from civilized groups to the preliterate ones, and vice versa; from aristocracy to the lower classes, and vice versa. Only the current that flows from the dead to the living, from Plato or Beethoven to us, is a one-way current. The city and the industrial country send their industrial products to the rural areas and to preliterate populations. From these they receive raw materials, agricultural produce, and so on. If a missionary, a rich man, a lord, an educated person passes some of his cultural properties to a pagan, a poor man, a slave, an illiterate, in their turn the former are affected by some of the cultural traits of the latter. All commerce and trade consists of giving something and getting something. There are a few exceptions to this rule of cultural current and countercurrent, but they do not annul the dominant uniformity.[3]

[1] Cf. Kroeber, op. cit., pp. 813 ff.

[2] See on routes of mobility the data and literature in Dynamics, Vol. IV, pp. 202-206. For the routes of travel and spread of epidemics see J. Brownlee and M. Greenwood, "Epidemic" and "Plague" in Encyclopedia Britannica, Vols. VIII and XVII; C. Creighton, A History of Epidemics in Britain, 2 Vols. (Cambridge, 1891-1893).

For mobility and spread of tobacco, R. U. Sayce, Primitive Arts and Crafts (London, 1933), Chps. 6, 7; for those of script, writing, and other cultural phenomena, W. I. Thomas, op. cit., Ch. 16; for foreign religions, J. F. Toutain, Les cultes paiens dans l'empire romain, 3 Vols. (Paris, 1907-1920); for mobility and spread of Christianity, K. S. Latourette, A History of the Expansion of Christianity, 3 Vols. (New York, 1939); for rural-urban differences in the infiltration of foreign cultural phenomena, Sorokin and Zimmerman, Principles of Rural-Urban Sociology (New York, 1929); for

languages and other cultural phenomena, A. J. Woolner, op. cit.; A. Toynbee, op. cit., Vol. III, pp. 391 ff. For C. Wissler's theory, see his The Relation of Nature to Man (New York, 1926); criticism in R. Dixon, The Building of Culture, pp. 69 ff. For criticism of the westward, the northward, the eastward, and other theories of migration of culture see my Theories, pp. 106 ff.; A. Deonna, L'archeologie (Paris, 1912), Vol. II, pp. 193 ff.

[3] See G. Tarde, The Laws of Imitation (New York, 1903), pp. 215 ff., 371 ff. Tarde's work still remains an unexcelled treatise on mobility of cultural phenomena, in spite of its somewhat unfortunate title and terminology. Concrete cases may be found in Sorokin, Zimmerman, and Galpin, Source Book, quoted, Vol. III. G. H. Danton, The Culture-Contact of the United States and China (New York, 1931); W. M. Webb, The Heritage of Dress (London, 1907), pp. 223 ff.; my Dynamics, Vol. IV, pp. 207 ff.

4. Streams of "Finished" Cultural Systems and of Congeries of "Raw" Material

This two-sidedness of cultural diffusion does not mean that both streams are equally strong, nor that they are made of the same kind of cultural phenomena. A teacher passes to his pupils mainly "finished" cultural systems (in arithmetic, science, language, history, etc.), while he gets from the pupils mainly congeries of questions and remarks. The situation is similar in many other cultural streams and counterstreams. If we take the cultural stream from the city to rural areas, from a "civilized" country to an "uncivilized," from the upper to the lower strata, its main difference from the counterstream consists exactly in that it carries mainly finished and polished systems and sometimes congeries: industrial products, aesthetic, religious, political, scientific, and other systems. However, the counterstream brings to the city, the civilized country, and the upper classes, cultural phenomena that enter these centers as raw material, to be modified and transformed into finished products, even if this material functioned in rural-un-civilized-lower strata centers as finished systems. Nails, lipsticks, cars, radios, machinery of all kinds, candy, canned food, papers, books, religious creeds, political ideologies, scientific theories, hospitals, baseball, bridge, crossword puzzles, songs, fads, and fashions, and thousands of other cultural phenomena flowing from the urban-civilized-upper centers enter and function with some modifications in the rural-uncivilized-lower centers as finished products. Furs, ivory, ore, agricultural and pastoral products, folklore, folk tunes, customs, patterns, and beliefs make up the counterstream and enter the urban-civilized-upper centers as raw material to be processed, manufactured, and modified into the finished products.

This uniformity has several important exceptions. (a) In periods of the decline of urban centers, of a civilized culture, and of upper classes, the contents of the streams tend to reverse themselves. Then the urban-civilized-upper class products tend to become raw decadent materials entering the culture of the rural-uncivilized-lower classes, while the products of the counterstream tend to enter and function in the culture of the urban-civilized-upper centers as virile finished products. In Tarde's terms, in this situation, the imitation reverses itself. The upper classes begin to imitate the lower; the civilized, the uncivilized; and the urbanites, the rustics. That was what happened in the period of decline of Rome during the centuries after the third A.D.; what happened to the decadent French and Russian aristocracies on the eve of the French and Russian revolutions. The culture of the sugar-coated *paysans* and shepherds, romantic savages and exotic primitives, of Rasputins and the "common people," became the dominant fashion within the culture of these aristocracies and their urban centers. "Primitivism" and "archaism" invade, in these conditions, the arts and fashions, manners and mores, costumes, ethics, and philosophy of the civilized-urban-upper centers.[4]

(b) When a "barbarian" conquers a "civilized nation," or the lower and rural classes overthrow the upper and urban groups, they impose their own culture and treat the culture of the vanquished as decadent raw material. Imposed by coercion, the culture of the barbaric-lower-rural groups becomes, at least temporarily, the finished culture.[5] When they conquered "civilized populations," the Mongols, the Dorians in Greece, the Arabs, the Sumerians, the Assyrians, the Scythians in India, the Normans in England, all imposed their own language, their own religion, many of their manners and mores upon the conquered population as the "finished" and aristocratic culture.[6]

---

[4] See the facts and the literature in *Dynamics*, Vol. IV, pp. 210 ff. Toynbee, *op. cit.*, Vol. IV, pp. 131 ff.; Vol. V, pp. 20 ff., 430 ff., 441 ff.; Vol. VI, pp. 86 ff.; A. Challamel, *History of Fashion in France* (London, 1882), pp. 208 ff., 216 ff.; S. Dill, *Roman Society from Nero to Marcus Aurelius* (London, 1905), pp. 73 ff.; H. Taine, *The Origins of Contemporary France* (New York, 1876), Vol. I. Contemporary fashions of jazz and boogie-woogie, of primitivistic and archaistic patterns imitated in all fields of our culture, the cult of the "common man" are further illustrations of the exception discussed.

[5] "Temporarily" because many conquerors of that kind succumb eventually to the charms of the culture of the vanquished and absorb it in considerable degree. Previous proletarians, becoming rulers, begin to imitate the culture of the old aristocracy. The Communist ruling class of Russia, *Anno Domini* 1946, is already imitating an enormous part of the culture of the Czarist ruling class.

[6] See the facts and literature in *Dynamics*, Vol.

(c) If the cultures exchanging their products are not clearly different, e.g., civilized and uncivilized, urban and rural, upper and lower, then the streams of exchange do not exhibit the uniformity of the "finished" and "raw" products. Rather, their exchange of cultural phenomena is determined by many different conditions, to be discussed further. The equally, or even more civilized conqueror may borrow the cultural values of the vanquished, as Europeans borrowed tobacco-smoking from the Indians, coffee and tea-drinking, polo-playing, pajama-wearing, and hot-bath taking from the Turks; as the conquering Romans adopted the Greek equipment of the cavalry man, and the Greek gods with latinized names; as the Turks borrowed firearms; and as Peter the Great borrowed military techniques from the conquered Swedes.

III. Leadership of Upper-Urban-Civilized-Male Groups in Creation and Importation of Foreign Cultural Values

1. Importers and Earliest Recipients of Foreign Culture

The preceding general rule about the streams of finished and unfinished cultural phenomena is connected with another uniformity in cultural mobility. Assuming that various groups of a given population are equally congenial or indifferent to a foreign cultural value, then the traveling merchants, officials, army men, missionaries, scholars, scientists, intelligentsia, journalists, the upper strata, the professionals, and the urban upper and middle classes are the earliest importers and recipients of foreign cultural phenomena. The lower classes and the rural population ordinarily lag in the importation and adoption of foreign cultural values. The reason for this uniformity is clear. The upper-middle-urban groups have a more developed network of communication, reaching more numerous and remote foreign cultures than do the lower-rural groups. As a result they are "infected" with, import, and adopt the elements of foreign culture, both systems and congeries, earlier than the rustics and unskilled, semi-skilled and even skilled labor.

For the same reason, especially in the past, when they were more secluded than men, women and children of the same groups and strata lagged in the importation and adoption of foreign cultural elements.

This general rule has some exceptions. (a) If there is a large immigration of foreign population into a given country, the immigrants bring with them their foreign culture. This may diffuse first within the lower strata of the receiving population. Such was the case with the United States in the period of enormous immigration from Europe, Africa, and Asia; with Rome around the beginning of our era, when large masses of Orientals, barbarians, and Greeks migrated into Italy and settled there. However, even in these conditions, the rural population of such countries lagged in adoption of the respective foreign cultures, compared with the urban. The Roman *pagani*, agricultural population, lagged by some 400 years in the adoption of Christianity, as compared with the urban population. In the United States even now, "foreign" religions and other foreign cultural values are more widespread in the cities. The percentage of Protestants (the native religion for the United States) is still notably higher in the rural areas and the percentage of Jews, Catholics, Greek and Russian Orthodox, Buddhists, Confucianists, and so on, is lower than among the urban populations.

(b) In periods of the decline of upper classes, or of disurbanization, the disorganized and decaying upper and urban classes cease to be the earliest importers and recipients of foreign culture. (c) Where the network of communications of the urban-rural, upper-lower classes is equally developed, the lead and lag discussed does not exist.

With these few exceptions, the above uniformity is well corroborated by the relevant facts of history. It is not the low-brows who are

IV, pp. 217 ff. A. S. Woolner, *Languages in History and Politics*, pp. 12 ff. Toynbee, *op. cit.*, Vol. I, pp. 116 ff., Vol. V, pp. 527 ff. G. Tarde, *op. cit.*, pp. 169-170, 368 ff.

seen first wearing the latest model from Paris, or a Chinese dress, or adopting a foreign religious, political, or other creed, exhibiting a foreign art-object, showing foreign manners and tastes. It is the highbrows, the rich, the aristocratic strata, the travellers, missionaries, the government officials, journalists, the cruising army and navy men, the globe-trotters, who regularly show such "infection." The upper-professional-urban groups were the early importers of Buddhism into China; Oriental cults into the Graeco-Roman Mediterranean region; of Christianity into western countries; of Protestantism into the previously Catholic populations; of Oriental cultural systems and congeries into the western world; of Fascism and Communism into the non-Fascist and Communist countries. The same groups first import and adopt the latest technological inventions and gadgets from foreign countries.[7]

2. Prevalent Downward Current of Newly Created Values from Upper to Lower, Urban to Rural, Civilized to Uncivilized Populations

Being situated at the cross-currents of various cultural streams, having a more developed system of communication, better training, and, possibly, a better hereditary fund (with the exception of periods of decay), the upper and middle strata are more creative culturally than the lower strata, and the bulk of the urban and civilized populations creates more cultural systems and congeries than the bulk of the rural and uncivilized population. Therefore, as a rule, new cultural values appear first within the upper-professional-urban-civilized populations and then, with a lag, they flow downward to the lower-rural-uncivilized populations. The main exception is that in the periods of decline, the creative activity of the upper-urban-civilized groups slackens and the downward stream dries up.

Again, the relevant facts of the present as well as of the past corroborate the proposition.

In our time almost any technological invention, new fashion of dress, new dance, song, or music, new social, economic, political, religious, scientific, or philosophical system, new law and ethical norm, new literary, architectural, or sculptural creation, emerges in and is adopted by, first, the upper, middle, professional, urban, civilized populations; then with some lag it descends into the lower-rural-uncivilized populations. This lag in the past was sometimes of several decades, even centuries. At present it is shortened, but still exists, especially in the field of complex scientific, philosophical, artistic, political, and economic systems. Sometimes what is already outmoded in the first groups of the population enters the culture of the second groups, so great is the lag.

This lag and downward current of the new cultural creations was manifest even more clearly in the past. The fashions of dress of the upper and lower classes show this systematically. So also do folk-songs and folk-tales. Most folk-songs are only belated modifications of the songs of the upper, middle and urban groups, but long ago forgotten within these circles. The same is true of language, scientific and philosophic theories, religions, and vices. In recent times, with a lag of several decades, such systems as Darwinian evolution, Marxian ideology, socialism and communism, began to reach the lower, rural, and uncivilized populations. We must not forget, in regard to such ideologies as revolution, socialism, and communism, that their creators and earliest exponents—Saint-Simon and Mabley, Morelli and Cabet, Fourier, Marx, F. Engels, F. Lassalle, J. Jaurès, Bakunin, Kropotkin, Trotsky, Lenin, and Stalin—all came out of the upper, middle and professional populations.

In other words the upper, middle, professional, urban, and civilized populations are the innovators,[8] and the lower, rural, uncivilized groups are the followers. The new finished products and systems go mainly downward, while the raw material for manufacturing the

---

[7] See the corroborations and literature in *Dynamics*, Vol. IV, pp. 227 ff.; J. F. Toutain, *op. cit.*, Vol. I, Ch. 1; Vol. II, pp. 24-30, 58, 65; Vol. III, pp. 102-109; *passim*; Sorokin, Zimmerman, and Galpin, *op. cit.*, Vol. II, pp. 373 ff.; F. V. Cumont, *Oriental Religions in Roman Paganism* (Chicago, 1911), pp. 53, 56, 83; *passim*.

[8] Cf. Tarde, *op. cit.*, pp. 221 ff. "The principal role of a nobility is its initiative, if not its inventive character. Invention can start from the lower ranks but its extension depends upon the existence of some lofty social elevation, social water-tower, whence a waterfall of imitation descends. As long as its vitality endures, a nobility performs this function."

systems and finished products flows upward. Only in the period of disurbanization and decline of the upper, middle, and professional classes may the roles be reversed.[9]

The propositions on five factors of creativity, on the streams of finished and raw cultural

products, on early importers and adopters of foreign culture, and on the innovating role of the upper, middle, professional, urban groups all are mutually connected, each supports the others, and all together reinforce their mutual validity.

IV. Mobility of Congeries, Systems, Supersystems, Total Cultures, and of Great Creative Centers of History

1. Forms in Which Cultural Phenomena Travel

Along the lines of interaction and communication, the cultural phenomena move from area to area, person to person, group to group, stratum to stratum in the forms of single cultural congeries, a cluster of congeries, simple systems, vast systems, supersystems, and total cultures of given populations.

In the present American culture we find Russian *vodka*, *samovar*, songs like "Black Eyes," and "Volga Boatman," words like "soviet" and "ikon," a Chinese dress or dish, a Gothic building on a university campus, and many similar congeries. All were torn from their Russian or Chinese or medieval culture systems and drifted into this country as single congeries. Since prehistoric times, a similar mobility of cultural congeries has been incessantly going on in thousands of concrete forms. Frequently such congeries or their clusters have crossed enormous distances.

Cultural phenomena move also in the form of small and vast systems. A language, a religion, a scientific theory, telegraph and telephone systems, Communist ideology, Parliamentarism, planned economy, Plato's philosophy, Bach's music, the Bible, Shakespeare's tragedies, Buddhism, Roman law, classic or

Gothic architectures, and thousands of other cultural systems have been ceaselessly moving from area to area, person to person, horizontally and vertically.

The same is true of supersystems. Originating within a small group of early Christians, Stoics, neo-Platonists, neo-Pythagoreans, the ideational supersystem of culture moved from Palestine in several directions, further and further, until it spread over all parts of the globe and became, as we shall see, the dominant system in medieval Europe. The same is true of the western sensate supersystem. Emerging at the end of the twelfth century within a small and dispersed group, it moved and spread among an ever-increasing number of persons, groups, and areas throughout the whole world; since the sixteenth century it has been the dominant supersystem of the whole western world and in many areas and groups on other continents. Similarly, in the past, the Buddhist and the Mohammedan supersystems of culture (not religions only) moved from India or Arabia to many other parts of the world.

Each time a group of migrants moved from one place to another, they carried with them their total culture with all its congeries and systems, and planted it at the place of their settling.[10]

---

[9] See the data and literature in *Dynamics*, Vol. IV, pp. 221 ff.; G. Tarde, *op. cit.*, Ch. 6, pp. 223 ff. Tarde especially well demonstrated this downward current of the new cultural values. In his terminology the lower strata imitate the upper strata, with some lag. Even a passage of the political regime from aristocracy to democracy is, in Tarde's interpretation, nothing but a belated imitation of the political activities of the great lords and ladies after they ceased to be interested. On popular art as a belated reiteration of previous aristocratic art, see C. Lalo, *L'art et la vie sociale* (Paris, 1921),

pp. 142 ff.; about lag on language and dress see A. Challamel, *History of Fashion in France*, pp. 36 ff.; R. Maunier, "Invention and Diffusion," *Melanges D. Gusti* (Bucharest, 1936), pp. 6 ff.; in religion, C. Guignebert, *Christianity, Past and Present* (New York, 1927), pp. 175 ff.; in technological, economic fashions of the recent time, P. H. Nystrom, *Economics of Fashions* (New York, 1928), pp. 36 ff.

[10] See the facts and literature in *Dynamics*, Vol. IV, pp. 230 ff. *Independence, Convergence, and*

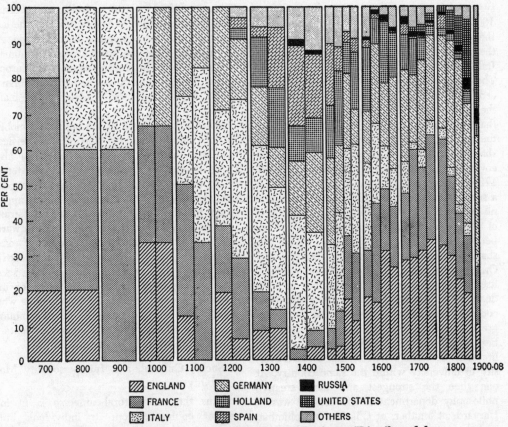

ENGLAND
FRANCE
ITALY
GERMANY
HOLLAND
SPAIN
RUSSIA
UNITED STATES
OTHERS

Figure 7.   Important Discoveries and Inventions. (Distributed by
country of origin.)

2. Shift of Creative Centers of Culture

As the five factors of creativity (fortunate hereditary fund, being at a cross-current of diverse cultural streams, the nature of the urgent needs, "good luck," and cultural freedom) incessantly change in the course of time for the same group, now being favorable, now unfavorable, and change among different groups, in the course of time the change leads to a shift of cultural creativity from area to area, population to population. For some time its centers are in groups A and B; then they move to groups C and D and M, and from these to others, sometimes even returning to one of the previous centers. At one time the

creative centers of a great political system are in Egypt and Babylonia; at another they shift to Persia, Macedonia, and Rome, to India and China, then to Arabia and Europe, with now Spain, now Austria, now France or the Netherlands, England, Germany, or Russia playing the roles of great powers. At the present time the United States has become such a center. Likewise the great centers of musical creativity in Europe were at one period in Sparta and Syria; then in Rome and Milan; then, after the medieval period, in France and Italy, the Netherlands and England, Austria and Germany, and finally in Russia, Norway, and Finland. For the last ten centuries the creative centers of economic empires were in Spain, Portugal, and Italy, then in the Netherlands, France, England, Austria, Germany; now the center has shifted to the United States. The same is true of scientific and technological

Borrowing, quoted; the quoted works of Dixon, W. I. Thomas, Sayce, Toynbee, Latourette. J. Jensen, *Geschichte der Schrift* (Hanover, 1925); T. F. Carter, *The Invention of Printing in China and Its Spread* (New York, 1931).

systems. While in the period from 800 to 1600 Italy made some 25 to 41 per cent of all the discoveries and inventions in Europe, in the period from 1726 to the present time the Italian share dwindled to from 2 to 4 per cent. The United States contributed only 1.1 per cent of the total discoveries and inventions in the period 1726-1750, and nothing before that; this share increased to 25.3 per cent for the periods of 1900-1908. The Netherlands' share was from 10 to 21 per cent of all the discoveries and inventions in the period of 1300-1725; it decreased to some 2 to 3 per cent in a subsequent period. Russia's share was almost nil before 1600; it increased to 3.7 per cent of all the discoveries and inventions for the period 1900-1908.[11] (Figure 7 shows the share of the main countries from 700 to 1908.) On a smaller scale, this kind of shift manifests itself in the rise and decline of the main industrial and financial cities within the same country. There is also the rise and decline of great universities; within the universities the best departments, of philosophy or science, literature or social sciences, shift from university to university within the same country. At one time the strongest and most creative philosophy department in the country was at Harvard; at another, at Chicago or Columbia, and then at some other university. The same can be said of the shift of all creative centers from country to country, even from continent to continent, on a large scale; and from city to city, university to university, church to church, studio to studio, on a smaller scale.

3. Shift of Centers of Human History

The vastest form of the shift of the creative centers of culture is that of the centers of human history. The earliest "historical" stage was centered in the East, in Mesopotamia, Egypt, and Central Asia with the Sumerians, Egyptians, and Babylonians as the main actors.

Then it shifted to China, India, and Persi; then to Greece, Rome, Arabia; and for the la four centuries its center has been Europe. A the present time the main center of huma history seems to be shifting again from Europ to the Pacific, with the United States, Russi; China, India, and Latin America as its mai; players.[12]

What has been said of the horizontal mobil ity of culture can be said of its vertica mobility. Vertically, cultural phenomena als; move in congeries, systems, and supersystems As to the vertical shifts of the creative cen ters, these tend to remain mainly in the uppe; strata, but the human personnel of these strata is incessantly changing through the downward mobility of the uncreative aristocracy and through an upward elevation of the creative members of the lower strata. As we have seen in our analysis of the social mobility of individuals and groups, the Mohammedans who inhabit the creative peaks of the mountains incessantly change but the creative centers remain at the tops of the mountains.

4. Social, Cultural, and Intrapersonality Mobility

Thus the sociocultural universe is in incessant double motion; its individuals and groups move horizontally and vertically, and its cultural congeries, systems, supersystems, and whole continents of culture move to and fro, up and down. The total dynamism of the sociocultural world is therefore much greater than may be suggested by either a mere social or mere cultural mobility. This dynamism may even be said to be triple; besides the social and the cultural there is the intrapersonal dynamism, to be studied further. As a result of this triple dynamism, the sociocultural ocean is never static; it ever changes and ever creates in all its aspects—social, cultural, and personal.

---

[11] See the detailed figures by countries and by periods in *Dynamics*, Vol. II, pp. 150 ff.

[12] See E. Fischer, *Passing of the European Age* (Harvard University Press, 1942), *Dynamics*, Vol. IV, pp. 234 ff.

Chapter 38. Socialization of
Objectified Systems
and Congeries (Continued)

I. Transformation of Cultural Phenomena
in the Process of Mobility

1. The Laws of Transformation

When a cultural phenomenon, whether a simple congeries or a complex system, passes from person to person, from group to group, or from one stratum to another, it remains essentially unchanged if the culture of departure is identical with the culture of infiltration, and if the mechanical means of standardization are present. If the two cultures differ, the migrating cultural phenomenon changes, and the greater the difference, the more it changes. If the two cultures diverge fundamentally, their components can hardly be interchanged and socialized, least of all the behavioral and material components.

When the difference between the culture of departure and that of infiltration remains constant, the extent of the transformation of the migrating phenomenon depends upon its own nature. The more complex, refined, and intricate the phenomenon, and the greater the training required for its use, the more profoundly it changes in the culture of infiltration. This explains why some phenomena can migrate without change, while others cannot, and it also indicates the extent and causes of the transformation of the latter variety.

2. Comments

Two specialists in the same science can adequately understand and transmit to one another their respective scientific theories. English-speaking persons can pass to each other, either orally or in written form, an enormous mass of values and norms. If the conductors of interaction are mechanically standardized, like the printing press, thousands of cultural meanings can be conveyed clearly to all who know and read the language. The existence of such mechanically standardized vehicles greatly facilitates the passage of cultural phenomena with minimum change. Persons and groups having similar cultures can thus exchange great numbers of cultural elements without seriously distorting them.

However, since there are scarcely any individuals or groups with identical cultures, an overwhelming majority of migrating cultural phenomena undergo a transformation. Pupils learning English from the same teacher read and write, each in his own individual way.[1] The same is true of other social activity. Although

[1] See G. W. Allport and P. E. Vernon, *Studies in Expressive Movement* (New York, 1933), and the literature there cited.

we are born and brought up in the same general cultural universe, we have our individual peculiarities in shaking hands, wearing our clothes, dancing, eating, and so on. Therefore the more notable the biocultural contrast between persons, the greater the transformation in the cultural phenomena circulating among them. Plato's teachings can pass from one professor of philosophy to another with ease, but hardly to a preliterate person. The effects of Bach's music upon a professional musician and upon a Trobriander differ enormously. Between the Christianity of the theologians and that of the newest preliterate converts is a deep chasm, bridged only by a very few concrete symbols.

When the cultures of two persons or groups are thoroughly dissimilar, most cultural phenomena cannot pass from one to the other. Once my three-year-old son asked me "Who brings the moon?" In spite of my strenuous efforts to explain to him the revolution of the moon around the earth, I dismally failed, until I had an inspiration. "Santa Claus!" Santa Claus passed as a substitute for the theory of celestial mechanics. Similarly, calculus cannot be taught to persons ignorant of arithmetic.

When the complex philosophical systems are transmitted to the masses, they have to be popularized and simplified, often to the point of complete distortion. Even so they cannot be grasped by children, preliterates, or mentally defective people. Intricate machines cannot be used properly without the requisite training. Still less can they be repaired and maintained. It is a daily experience of professional teachers of sociology that advanced scientific ideas cannot be completely comprehended by many students.

If the difference in the cultures of the interacting groups is constant, then the degree of change in the migrating trait depends upon its relative complexity. Elementary mathematics can migrate more easily than calculus or the theory of relativity. A spade is more quickly accepted and mastered than is an elaborate steam shovel. The more complicated the system, and the more training required for its use, the smaller is the area of its potential diffusion.

Such are the main uniformities in the transmission of cultural phenomena from person to person, group to group, and from one culture to another.[2]

II. Successful and Unsuccessful Cultural "Best-Sellers"

Observation shows that some new books, songs, plays, creeds, theories, and other cultural congeries and systems become "best-sellers," rapidly spreading among thousands of persons and groups. Yet other new cultural values find only a few "customers" and are "poor sellers." Why this difference? What are the factors in successful and unsuccessful socialization (diffusion) of cultural phenomena?

The general answer seems to point to a law of demand and supply. Those cultural phenomena for which there is intense demand become best sellers; those for which the demand is negligible are poor sellers. Unfortunately, this answer is tautological. It does not tell us why the demand for women's veils is great in the Mohammedan population but small among Christian groups. Why does the demand for certain styles of clothes vary from season to season? Or why is isolationism popular at one time, but not at another? What explains the changes in the public's taste for books?[3] The law of demand and supply does not answer these questions at all. Although the problems involved are not fully understood, a few instrumental factors can be indicated.

[2] Further material and literature will be found in *Dynamics*, Vol. IV, pp. 252 ff. For an example of changes in Christianity in various preliterate groups, see E. C. Parsons, *Mitla* (Chicago, 1936), pp. 204 ff.; L. Spier, "The Prophet Dance," *General Series in Anthropology*, No. 1 (1935). On Buddhism in China see Hu Shih, "The Indianization of China"; on Roman Law in medieval Europe, see L. Wenger, "Ancient Legal History," both articles in *Inde-*

pendence, Convergence, and Borrowing. Cf. also H. Jensen, *Geschichte der Schrift*; T. F. Carter, *The Invention of Printing in China*; W. I. Barnet, "Culture Processes" and "Invention and Cultural Change," *AA*, Vol. XLII, pp. 21-48; Vol. XLIV, pp. 14-30.
[3] A. P. Hackett, *Fifty Years of Best-Sellers: 1895-1945* (New York, 1945), p. 3.

1. Urgent and Universal Needs

The cultural values that satisfy the most urgent and universal needs of many human beings are the most easily spread and socialized; the values that satisfy the secondary needs of a few individuals are less widely socialized. The less urgent the needs and the smaller the universe of human beings with such needs, the more limited the diffusion of the corresponding values. The biosocial needs of food, drink, clothing, shelter, and sex are, in their generic form, the most urgent and universal for all human beings. Therefore the cultural values of food, drink, clothing, love, marriage, and sex relations, as necessary for the very maintenance of life, are universally socialized in their generic form. (Specific patterns of food, clothing, etc. cannot be defined as generic.)

Also universal in their generic form are such cultural values as language, script, rudimentary arithmetic, practical lore, ethico-legal norms, and elements of the fine arts. Each of these generic classes of cultural phenomena is an indispensable condition of life in groups, and therefore is found everywhere in the human universe. But if we take particular varieties of these cultural categories (golf club, Homer, Shakespeare, radio, corn flakes, bicycle, whiskey), such phenomena are much less widely socialized than their generic archetypes. The reason is that they meet the less urgent needs of smaller circles of human beings than do the general values of food, language, script, etc.

This proposition must be qualified. The two variables, urgency of need and its universality, do not always go hand in hand. Some needs may be extremely urgent for a small number of individuals, and other needs may be universal but not urgent.[4] Therefore we may say (a) of the cultural values that satisfy equally urgent needs, the values satisfying the more numerous needs will be made widely socialized. If in a given human universe the need X is felt by ten times as many persons as are subject to need Y, then the value satisfying X would tend to be more widely socialized than the value

satisfying Y. (b) Of the cultural values that satisfy equally frequent needs, those values satisfying the more urgent needs will tend to be more widespread than those satisfying less urgent needs.

This proposition gives an orientation to the problem. To be more concrete it would require factual studies of the comparative urgency and frequency of the needs of various individuals and groups.

2. Complexity, or Refinement of Values of the Same Kind, Price, and Culture

A more precise and concrete formula can be given if we assume that cultural values are of the same kind and price, and are circulating in the same cultural population. Our observation shows clearly that such values (for instance, three-dollar novels in the United States) do not socialize equally. Some become best-sellers and are sold by the thousands; of others, only a few dozen are sold. Some new songs become "hits," others die almost immediately.

Among the cultural values of the same kind, price, and cultural milieu, the more refined and complex the value, and the more special training is required for its use, the less widely it spreads, in comparison with less complex values.

Most values of a given class are not equally simple. They can be arranged in a pyramid of increasing complexity. Thus in mathematics we proceed from arithmetic to algebra, then to trigonometry and calculus. Each preceding branch is prerequisite to the next. Therefore arithmetic is more widely socialized than algebra; geometry and trigonometry are more generally diffused than calculus. The most complex problems of mathematics can be understood by only the few greatest mathematicians.

The number of pupils enrolled in the elementary courses in any field of study is far greater than the number enrolled in graduate courses. Likewise the output of elementary texts far surpasses that of advanced monographs. Will Durant's *Story of Philosophy* and H. G. Wells' *Outline of History* have sold more than one million copies. Yet none of the works

---

[4] Similar indeterminacy is found in the famous formula of Jeremy Bentham: "greatest happiness of the greatest number of human beings." What gives happiness to the greatest number of human beings does not necessarily bring the maximum of happiness for some individuals; and what gives the most happiness to some persons does not necessarily give the maximum happiness to all.

of the great philosophers or historians has ever (within a correspondingly limited time) been a best-seller.[5] Despite the efforts to popularize art, the number of performances of the greatest musical compositions cannot match that of popular jazz. The radio time given to the broadcasting of classical music is only a fraction of that assigned to popular music. In this country there are only about ten great orchestras, each playing intermittently. Their concert halls are not always filled. Meanwhile there are thousands of dance bands whose performances are eagerly sought by millions. To bring a classical composition to the masses it must first be jazzed up. Only thus did Tchaikovsky's Concerto gain its great popularity.

It is the same story with literature and drama, painting and sculpture. Tens of thousands fill the movie theatres daily, while the few great plays are staged infrequently, and draw but small audiences. Oscar Wilde said correctly that the classics (in literature) are those whom everybody praises but nobody reads. If in the long run the classics in all fields of culture are the best sellers, in a short period of time they are very rarely such. In the United States from 1880 to 1945 there have been some 180 novels selling 500,000 copies or more. On this list are only two books by Mark Twain, one by Jack London, one by Pearl Buck, one by Booth Tarkington, one by Ernest Hemingway, and two by Sinclair Lewis, and these are at the bottom of the list. More than 95 per cent of the best-sellers consists of books that are sold feverishly, and are soon gone with the wind into oblivion.[6]

During the period studied, other best-sellers were cook-books, dictionaries, primers of various kinds, comics, juveniles, some 120,000,000 to 250,000,000 copies of Horatio Alger's works, cross-word puzzle books, religious hymnals, and the like. With the exception of the Bible and Shakespeare, there are no advanced works in any field among them.[7]

Some qualifications and exceptions should be noted. The first relates to the *span of time*. The less complex and less refined values are best-sellers only for short periods of time. In the long run of time it is the truly great and refined values that last. The works of Plato, Aristotle, Kant; of Homer, Shakespeare, and Dante are re-issued and re-translated for centuries. Among the short-time, best-seller novels in the United States C. M. Sheldon's *In His Steps* seems to top the list, with 8,000,000 copies sold since 1897. Simultaneously some 33,259,919 Bibles and several million copies of Shakespeare were sold. If we estimate all the copies of these two works that have circulated in all languages from the moment of their appearance, and if we include second-hand sales, the number would run into billions.

Even American classics in the long run are fairly good best sellers. The total sales of the works of Jack London, H. W. Longfellow, R. W. Emerson, Mark Twain, J. F. Cooper, Walt Whitman, H. Melville, F. Parkman, N. Hawthorne, W. Irving, H. B. Stowe, and H. D. Thoreau reach a mark of over a million.[8] Including second-hand sales, their circulations would amount to tens and hundreds of millions. The life-curve of the short-time best-sellers soars and immediately falls. The life-curve of the great works rises moderately, sometimes with minor fluctuations, to a fairly high level, where it remains for an indefinite period.

The second qualification is that sometimes, especially in fine arts, ethics, and religion, there appear creations combining *sublimity with simplicity*. The Bible, the Mahabharata, the Iliad, and the Sermon on the Mount are examples of such creations. Accordingly they appeal to both intelligentsia and to the masses. However, exceptions of this kind are relatively rare.

3. Adequacy and Economy in the Satisfaction of a Given Need

Given the same economic cost and culture, among values satisfying the same need, those that satisfy it more efficiently and adequately tend to be socialized more successfully. The less adequate values are relegated eventually to a secondary status, and they are used only as substitutes for the more efficient ones, or as ornamental values in sports, plays, rituals, and the like. The need for artificial light is better satisfied by kerosene lamps than by wooden

---

[5] A. P. Hackett, *op. cit.*, pp. 95 ff.
[6] Hackett, *op. cit.*, pp. 95-134.

[7] *Ibid.*, pp. 95 ff.
[8] *Ibid.*, pp. 116 ff.

splinters, and still better by electricity. For this reason electricity has relegated the cruder means of artificial lighting to an unimportant and ornamental position in civilized populations. This has happened also to the bow and arrow and the flintlock musket. Similar examples can be indicated in all areas of social activity. If there are two different but equally efficient values available for the satisfaction of the same need, both will be equally diffused, given the same conditions.

Rum, gin, whiskey, and wine exist side by side in the same population, because each meets the need for intoxication. Other examples are different types of literature, automobiles, etc.

4. Congeniality of the Receiving Culture

Other conditions being equal, the more congenial the migrating trait is to the receiving culture, the greater are its chances of wide socialization. The more antagonistic it is the less are its chances of successful diffusion. Neutral values occupy an intermediate position between these two extremes.

Revolutionary Communism does not spread successfully among the capitalistic captains of industry, nor does capitalism win adherents among revolutionary Communists. The belief in the immaculate conception of Christ does not diffuse among atheists nor a philosophy of mechanistic materialism among ardent Catholics. Pro-Nazi propaganda had as little success among the Allies during the late war as pro-American propaganda among the Germans. An ideology of equality cannot survive in a strong caste society. The Divine Comedy of Dante would not win any literary prizes if it were first published in a sensate culture. The erotic plays and novels of our time would find no great audiences in medieval culture.

On the other hand, in a vodka-drinking population, new brands of vodka would spread more easily than whiskey. Propaganda for contraception would gain a more favorable response from populations whose religious and ethical values do not forbid birth control. Congenial values are welcomed; uncongenial

ones are resisted. Adam Ferguson correctly said that "they borrow often that which they are disposed to invent." G. Tarde and a legion of sociologists and anthropologists have shown the validity of this proposition.[9]

5. The Elements of Force and Coercion

Cultural values have often been imposed by pressure, ranging from mild persuasion through economic and political reprisals to the rudest forms of torture and death. If the coercion is maintained relentlessly and systematically for a sufficient length of time, the coercively imposed cultural values are often injected into the subjugated culture, and they thus become socialized. Nearly every extended domination of one culture by another has resulted in the transfer of many cultural phenomena from the dominant group to the subordinate group. Examples may be drawn from the history of the Sumerians, Egyptians, and Babylonians. The Dorians imposed their culture upon the conquered population of southern Greece; the Romans left their mark upon their Mediterranean empire, as did the Tartars upon Russian culture. Today we see the imposition of "democratic" and "soviet" cultural features upon Japan, Germany, and other defeated (or liberated) countries. Civil wars invariably reveal the same process.

In a milder tradition, dominating minorities have imposed many cultural phenomena upon the lower strata, quite aside from cases of voluntary imitation of the upper classes by the lower ones. Public administrations, labor unions, religious groups, universities, and business firms transmit daily, through various modes of pressure, a legion of cultural values upon their members.

Although not all the imposed cultural values become deeply rooted, since coercion often provokes a negative reaction, nonetheless many cultural phenomena in the long run are acculturated in the subordinate society. Preliterate groups and practically all historical societies contain clearly discernible cultural elements taken over from former conquerors. The role

---

[9] See the facts and literature on uniformities of socialization in *Dynamics*, Vol. IV, pp. 268 ff. Also G. Tarde, *Laws of Imitation*, quoted; *La logique sociale* (Paris, 1895); *L'opposition universelle* (Paris, 1897); M. J. Herskovits, *Acculturation*, quoted; H. C. Peterson, *Propaganda for War*

(New York, 1919); H. D. Lasswell, *Propaganda Technique in the World War* (New York, 1927); J. H. Mueller and Kate Hevner, *Trends in Musical Taste* (Bloomington, n.d.). For the anthropological literature, see W. I. Thomas, *op. cit.*, Ch. 16.

of force and coercion in various forms has always been a considerable one in socialization.[10]

6. Influence of Lines of Communication and Interaction

Finally, other conditions being equal, a cultural value with access to a more developed system of communication and interaction will reach a greater number of persons and groups. In the terminology of our time, the more advertised goods attract a greater number of customers. Often, indeed, inferior goods, if well advertised, have better markets than superior but poorly advertised goods. Advertising is not omnipotent, despite enthusiastic beliefs to the contrary, but it is one of the important elements in the diffusion and socialization of cultural values.

Advertising, however, is only one form of contact between the value and its potential customers. When all forms of contact are considered, the spread of the value is often observed to be proceeding hand in hand with the growth of the total network of interaction. Thus, for instance, ownership of radios in the United States is relatively greater in metropolitan areas than elsewhere, "because the residents of each unit of a region of metropolitan influence have culture contacts with the urban center of diffusion in inverse ratio to the time-and-convenience distance from the city," or in inverse ratio to the communication and interaction lines.[11]

Such are some of the more important factors explaining why some cultural values become "best-sellers" while others do not. Any one of these factors by itself cannot account for this phenomenon, but together they present an adequate understanding of this problem.

III. What Happens When Two Different Cultures Meet

1. General Uniformities

Certain general uniformities explain what happens when two entire cultures come in contact with each other.

(a) Their most congenial systems and congeries tend to pass most easily from one culture to the other. The less congenial they are, the more transformed they become in the process of diffusion.

(b) The simplest, most urgent, most efficient, and most accessible tend to pass the most rapidly.

(c) If one of these cultures is "superior" to the other, then the downward stream from the superior to the inferior culture will be stronger than the upward stream, and the products of the superior culture will enter the inferior as finished products.

(d) The most uncongenial elements of the two cultures have little chance to intermix, unless pressure in various forms is applied.

(e) The most contradictory values of the two cultures will clash with one another. For some time they can co-exist as congeries, but eventually they are bound to conflict. If they are of equal strength, they will weaken one another, so that a basic transformation becomes prerequisite to reconciliation. But if one of them is more efficient and more adequate than the other, this one will drive out or subordinate the weaker. However, the victorious value will probably also undergo some modification.

(f) If the values are neutral, they will intermingle to some extent, though not so easily as will the congenial values.

(g) Under favorable conditions, from this clash of contradictory values and intermixing of neutral and congenial ones there may arise a new invention or new creation, resolving the conflict by establishing a new system.

In the meeting of two entire cultures, all these mutations except the last one occur regularly. Each may predominate at different times. The mutation (g) happens only in creative

---

[10] See G. Sorel, *Reflection on Violence* (New York. 1912); F. Oppenheimer, *Der Staat* (Berlin, 1908); M. Vaccaro, *Les bases sociologiques du droit et de l'Etat* (Paris, 1898); or any substantial social history of any nation.

[11] H. E. Pemberton, "Culture-Diffusion Gradients," *ASR*, September, 1936, p. 221. See also R. W. Bowers, "The Direction of Intra-Societal Diffusion," *ASR* (December, 1937), pp. 826-836, though his census data hardly permit an accurate analysis.

groups. These propositions are algebraic formulae summarizing an enormous number of concrete cases described by anthropologists, historians, sociologists, economists, and other scientists.

2. Values That First Penetrate the Other Culture

The foregoing propositions suggest the answer to the question: What kind of values first penetrate the other culture? They also indicate the one-sidedness of several current theories in this field. It is widely believed that when two diverse cultures meet, the material or economic and technological values penetrate first, then the political, and finally the nonmaterial or ideological. This school includes K. Marx, A. Coste, L. Weber, A. Weber, W. Ogburn, R. M. MacIver, A. Toynbee, W. G. Sumner, A. G. Keller, J. G. Leyburn, R. Linton, and others.[12]

This theory logically presupposes that the material, economic, and technological values of two cultures are always the most congenial, while the religious, artistic, ethical, and other nonmaterial values are always the most antagonistic. Such a presupposition is evidently fallacious, for there is no logical reason for *a priori* congeniality between the economic or technological values of two cultures, or for disharmony between their nonmaterial values. The theory is also contradicted by the facts. In some cases the economic values diffuse first; in others, the technological; in still others, the religious and ethical. Usually several different categories of values socialize simultaneously. The daily meeting of two individuals does not cause one to borrow from the other his economic traits, and then his political opinions, and lastly his ideological culture. If we meet a priest, we notice first of all his priestly traits. In the case of a scientist, we are interested primarily in his scientific theories. Which of the various aspects of a personality we finally absorb depends upon the configuration of our respective interests.

The same is true when group cultures as a whole come into contact. When European immigrants landed in America, they absorbed simultaneously from American culture some elements of the English language, manners and mores, political and legal values, as well as the purely economic or technological values.[13] Likewise the Zapotecans took from the Spanish culture not only tiled roofs, but wedding rites, elements of Catholicism, and patterns of social organization. The Mexicans of Tepoztlan borrowed chiefly the elements of the nonmaterial culture of the Spanish. A South African tribe, Kxatla, likewise took from western culture first Christianity, then elements of law, and finally economic elements.[14] Among the first values taken from Byzantium by the Russians were religion, architectural styles, the Greek language, etc. When Chinese culture came into contact with the West, "the sequence of social change in China does not appear to be from material technique to social ideologies. . . . The elements borrowed from Western culture have been (first) in the realm of social ideologies rather than of material technique."[15]

---

[12] See A. Coste's quoted works; A. Toynbee, *op. cit.*, Vol. IV, p. 57; A. G. Keller, *Societal Evolution* (New York, 1931), pp. 208 ff.; J. G. Leyburn, *Frontier Folkways* (Yale University Press, 1935), pp. 229 ff.; C. Wissler, "Aboriginal Maize Culture," *AJS*, March, 1916, p. 661; R. Linton (ed.) *Acculturation in Seven American Indian Tribes* (New York, 1940), pp. 485 ff.; W. Ogburn, *Social Change, passim*. The works of L. and A. Weber, MacIver, and others are quoted further, in this and the next chapters.

[13] See E. A. Ross, *The Old World in the New* (New York, 1914); W. I. Thomas and F. Znaniecki, *The Polish Peasant* (New York, 1927), Vol. II, pp. 1646 ff.; C. M. Panunzio, *The Soul of an Immigrant* (New York, 1921); R. Park, and E. Burgess, *Introduction to the Science of Sociology*, pp. 769 ff.; F. J. Brown and J. S. Roucek (ed.), *One America* (New York, 1945); G. Tarde, *The Laws of Imitation*, pp. 199 ff.

[14] E. C. Parsons, *Mitla*, quoted, p. 536; *passim*; R. Redfield, *Tepoztlan* (Chicago, 1930), p. 31; I. Schapera, "Contributions of Western Civilization to Modern Kxatla Culture," *Transactions of the R. So. of Africa*, Vol. XXIV, pp. 221-252; A. I. Hallowell, "Recent Changes," etc., *Atti de XXII Congr. Intern. degli Americanisti* (Rome, 1928), pp. 97-145; T. Lynn Smith and V. J. Parenton, "Acculturation among the Louisiana French," *AJS*, November, 1938. All other literature in *Dynamics*, Vol. IV, pp. 282 ff.

[15] R. T. LaPiere and Cheng Wang, "The Incidence and Sequence of Social Change," *AJS*, November, 1931, p. 401; Ching-Yueh Yen, "Crime in Relation to Social Change in China," *ibid.*, November, 1934. Often "fables precede commodities in the intercourse of peoples," states Masaharu Anesaki, on the meeting of Japanese and western cultures; cf. his "East and **West**," in

Unless coercion enters, the only general uniformity is that the most congenial elements tend to penetrate first, the contradictory ones last.

If the first human agents that come into contact with a given culture are missionaries, then religious values enter the other culture first, provided that the religions of both cultures are in some degree congenial. If the first human agents are traders, then economic values are the first infiltrators.

Other values of secondary importance may be associated with the main diffusing elements. Besides language and religion, missionaries often bring medicine, knives, calico, and other gifts. The traders leave not only their merchandise but something of their beliefs, ideas, and mores. Conquerors often plant their whole culture upon the conquered. Such are the main uniformities in the intermingling elements of two cultures.

IV. Comparative Socialization of Ideological, Behavioral, and Material Cultures

1. Greater Swiftness in Spread of Ideological Culture

Ideological culture moves faster and more easily than behavioral and material cultures of the same system or congeries. Is a cultural phenomenon socialized simultaneously in its ideological, behavioral, and material aspects, or is there a lag in the diffusion of some of these elements? The ideological element tends to diffuse first, and more rapidly than behavioral and material aspects. Whether the cultural phenomenon is religious, scientific, artistic, or economic, its idea or meaning first has to be communicated to others. Then it begins to influence behavior and material culture. Sometimes there is considerable lag between the indoctrination of a meaning and its realization in behavior and material vehicles. In many cases the behavioral realization of the ideological element is meager and inadequate, and occasionally only the ideological form moves without a corresponding behavioral manifestation. The myriad cases where persons and groups do not practice what they preach prove this. The ideology of the Golden Rule is more widespread than its practice. Millions of Christians know the Sermon on the Mount; only a fraction adheres to it in everyday life. G. Tarde correctly stated that "imitation . . . proceeds from the inner to the outer man. . . ." In the seventeenth century French fashions began to diffuse throughout Europe because French literature had preceded them. "The desire to imitate a certain value must precede and usually does precede the overt diffusion of it." The diffusion of religious dogmas pre-

cedes that of rituals, the diffusion of scientific or philosophical ideas anticipates their overt realization in material institutions.[16]

To summarize: The ideological elements of cultural phenomena move earlier, farther, and faster than their behavioral and material forms. For this reason *the ideological culture of persons and groups is richer than their total behavioral and material cultures.* For example, my ideological culture includes a knowledge of Confucianism, Buddhism, Hinduism, Taoism, Jainism, Shintoism, Mohammedanism, and Judaism. In my behavioral culture I do not practice these religions, and in my material culture I have scarcely any of their vehicles. Similarly, my ideological culture contains a fair knowledge of the various kinds of gardens, past and present. But the garden I cultivate is of but one type.

The rule has, however, a few exceptions. One case is that of material traits whose meaning has been lost. Thus archaeologists sometimes excavate an object whose meaning is unknown. Preliterate tribes may acquire an item whose ideological nature is a mystery.

2. Criticism of the Dichotomic Theories of Diffusion

In the light of the preceding propositions it is easy to see the error in the prevalent dichotomic theories of diffusion. Their authors are F.

Independence, Convergence, and Borrowing, pp. 249 ff. See also G. H. Danton, *The Cultural Contacts of the United States and China* (New York, 1931).

[16] G. Tarde, *The Laws of Imitation*, pp. 199 ff.

Bacon, Campanella, Leonardo da Vinci, John Locke, Saint-Simon, many Marxians, many economists like M. Tugan-Baranovsky, many sociologists like A. Coste, L. Weber, A. Weber, T. Veblen, W. G. Sumner, A. Keller, W. Ogburn, R. M. MacIver, and others.[17] They divide all cultural phenomena into two classes, *material and nonmaterial, civilization and culture, social and ideological, economic and noneconomic.* What exactly is meant by each of two classes is not easy to define; the concepts are very vague. A general description, in my own words, runs as follows. By *material, civilizational, and economic* are indicated the material components of scientific, technological, and economic phenomena, minus their ideological aspects. Pure scientific theory is, according to their somewhat contradictory statements, a part of the nonmaterial or ideological culture. An automobile, airplane, or atomic bomb is a material trait, but the theoretical physics or chemistry that invented these devices is not. By nonmaterial culture is denoted the ideological components of religious, philosophic, ethico-juridical, literary, musical, and other phenomena. That seems to be a fair description of what the dichotomic categories of cultural phenomena signify.

The dichotomic theories next contend that material-civilizational-economic culture spreads earlier and faster, and diffuses more widely than the nonmaterial, noneconomic or ideological culture. These theories are defective logically as well as factually. First, each of these classes is a strange concoction of phenomena. Material vehicles of science or technology are separated from their component of meanings—respective scientific, technological, or economic theory; and this theory (scientific, technological, economic "ideology") is united with the "ideology" of religion, fine arts, law, ethics etc., separated again from the behavioral and material components of religious, artistic, ethical phenomena. Both classes obtained are thus the worst kind of congeries,

devoid of any unity. The whole operation is akin to that of a biologist who would classify all the phenomena of life into the class of "material life" made up of horses' body, birds' wings and bees' honey; and into the class of "nonmaterial life" composed of horses' breathing, birds' flying, and bees' buzzing, with horses' tail thrown in. Biologists do not make such monstrous classifications. Social scientists seemingly do that. Such classes evidently cannot serve as real classes for any scientific purpose.

On the factual side, no technological device is more widely spread than the idea of it. In other words, the ideological aspects of scientific, technological, or religious phenomena are no less widely diffused than their behavioral and material elements. As a matter of fact, as I suggested above, ideological elements are more widely diffused than material elements. The same is true of any other cultural phenomenon.

Factually, pure science in the form of a table of multiplication or elementary biological knowledge is diffused among a much larger number of persons than all the recent material gadgets invented by the scientists.

If the dichotomic theorists mean that scientific, technological, and economic phenomena (and not simply their material vehicles) diffuse faster and more universally than the religious, ethical, artistic, legal, philosophical, and linguistic phenomena, then their statement is also questionable, even in this more logical formulation. To clarify the proposition, we must distinguish between the generic and particular types of cultural phenomena of the same class. Generically, some devices are diffused everywhere in the human universe. But so also are language, scientific and religious ideas, legal norms, and social organization. Likewise the elements of the latter class are far more widely diffused than the elements of the former. The table of multiplication is certainly much more widespread than any particular technological device.

---

[17] See Bacon, "De dignitate et augmentis scientiarum," *The Works of Francis Bacon* (London, 1803), Vol. VII, p. 24; M. Marx, *Contribution to the Critique of Political Economy* (New York, 1904), pp. 11-13; M. Tugan-Baranovsky, *Osnovy politicheskoi economii* (Riga, 1924), Ch. 1; A. Coste, quoted works; L. Weber, *Le rythme du progrès* (Paris, 1913); A. Weber, *Ideen zur Staats- und Kultursoziologie* (Karlsruhe, 1927); A. Keller, *Societal Evolution* (New York, 1931); W. Ogburn, *Social Change* (New York, 1922), pp. 195 ff., *Recent Social Trends* (ed., New York, 1933), pp. xiii ff.; T. Veblen, *The Place of Science in Modern Civilization* (New York, 1919); R. M. MacIver, *Society*, quoted. See also *Dynamics*, Vol. IV, Chps. 4, 6, 7. Most of the introductory textbooks of sociology put forward the dichotomic theory in some version or other.

If we take a particular form of either gadgets or religion, both particular forms are diffused only within certain groups and the particular technological culture, say, Chevrolet or Philco radio, are diffused in a less number of copies than, say, the Bible or Shakespeare. English language ("nonmaterial, particular culture") is diffused among a much larger number of persons and groups than all the automobiles taken together. The same is true of such particular ideological cultural phenomena as the idea of Golden Rule, a belief in some kind of god, the visual or symbolic painting, singing and dancing, festivals and ceremonies, crime and punishment, some kind of alphabet and writing, and a host of other nonmaterial traits. In their generic form they are as universal as scientific, technological, and economic phenomena. In their particular forms they are diffused as much as any particular form of science, technology or economics.

Even in recent years the ideologies of Communism, Fascism, jazz, and lipsticks infected a greater number of persons and groups than radio or telephone, airplane or television.

On the other hand, among the material and nonmaterial cultures there are purely local phenomena that do not migrate. The techniques of navigation do not spread among populations living far from rivers, lakes, oceans. Irrigation does not diffuse among peoples who do not need it. Hence in both interpretations the dichotomic theories of diffusion are invalid, logically as well as factually.[18]

V. Diversity of the Curves of Socialization of Cultural Phenomena

With commendable zest for preciseness, several sociologists have claimed the existence of a uniform curve of diffusion of cultural phenomena. Thus F. S. Chapin suggests that cultural growth involving diffusion tends to follow an S curve.[19] H. E. Pemberton contends that "within any given area the diffusion of a culture trait tends to occur at a rate which may be described by the cumulative curve of normal distribution.[20] H. Hart[21] marshals a mass of data on growth of subhuman and human populations, cities, of the number of governmental functions, growth of production, inventions, state laws, and so on, to show that their growth and diffusion follows the logistic curve. A Davis[22] suggests the Gompertz curve.

There is no doubt that any of these curves can be fitted to the data of growth and diffusion in many of these cases. However, there is but slight logical or factual basis to argue for the existence of any one type of growth curve. For such a curve to exist in the field of cultural diffusion, the factors influencing the diffusion would have to be uniform in time and space. The urgency of the value-need, the frequency of its distribution among human beings, its simplicity or complexity, the nature of the culture of the diffusion, the amount of coercion, the lines of communication, etc. would all have to be consistently the same. Such an identity does not exist. Consequently there are no logical or mathematical grounds for a general diffusion formula.

Indeed, the contrasting formulae offered for such a curve are factual evidence that there are different rates of diffusion for different cases. Further, each of these fitted curves covers but an infinitesimal fraction of the phenomena of growth. The series studied are specifically selected as suitable for mathematical treatment, while unsuitable cases are excluded, such as all the cultural phenomena that do not diffuse at all and die at the moment of their emergence; all the cultural phenomena, like some best sellers, that diffuse

---

[18] See a more developed criticism of these theories in Dynamics, Vol. IV, Chps. 4, 6, 7.

[19] F. S. Chapin, Culture Change (New York, 1928).

[20] H. E. Pemberton, "The Curve of Culture Diffusion Rate," ASR, August, 1936.

[21] H. Hart, "Logistic Social Trends," AJS, March, 1945, pp. 337-352; see there the literature.

[22] A. Davis, "Technicways in American Civilization," SF, March, 1940. An eminent mathematician rightly said: "One can manage to obtain a variational principle appropriate to almost any physical or mathematical theory." G. D. Birkhoff, Scientific Monthly, 1944, p. 54. See also A. Lotka, "The Law of Evolution," Human Biology, 1945, pp. 17 ff.

at once and then suddenly stop and decline; all the phenomena that have several waves in their socialization, with several ups and downs; the phenomena that diffuse very slowly and for an indefinitely long time, sometimes with an increasing trend or plateau; sometimes with several plateaus and ups and

downs, each of somewhat different patterns, and so on. Whatever examples of diffusion we select for study, they reveal a variety of rates and types, with no tendency toward uniformity.[23]

In brief, several formulae can be fitted to a limited series of diffusion, but there is no single curve that fits all cases of diffusion.

---

[23] For epidemics see C. Creighton, *A History of Epidemics in Britain*, 2 Vols. (London, 1891-1894); compare for instance the curves of deaths from plagues in 1563, 1636, 1625; from smallpox epidemics in the sixteenth, seventeenth, and eighteenth centuries. See also W. H. Davis, "The Influenza Epidemics," *American Journal of Public Health*, No. 9 (1919); M. Greenwood, "Factors that Determine the Rise, Spread, and Degree of Severity of Epidemic Diseases," XVIIth *International Congress of Medicine* (1913), Sec. 18, pp. 49-80.

On the diffusion of musical compositions as measured by the frequency of their performance by leading orchestras in the United States, see J. Mueller and K. Hevner, *Trends in Musical Taste,* quoted. On hybrid seed corn diffusion, see B. Ryan and N. C. Gross, "The Diffusion of Hybrid Seed Corn," *Rural Sociology*, March, 1943, pp. 15-24. See also my *Dynamics*, Vol. IV, pp. 279 ff.; and A. Kroeber, *Configurations*, quoted, pp. 773-776.

Chapter 39. How Cultural Systems and Supersystems Grow and Decline

I. Infant Mortality of Systems

Having been objectified and socialized, a cultural system emerges as a concrete individuality. At the moment of its birth any cultural system is infantile, so to speak, in all its components. Its meanings are as yet comparatively simple and undeveloped; its vehicles are meager and imperfect; its human agents are few in number. Plunged into a world of many systems and congeries, it begins its struggle for survival and growth. It must be able not only to preserve its own ideological identity, its vehicles and agents, but to withstand successfully the attacks of inimical systems and congeries. Any new "A is B" or "A is not B" finds among other systems not only its

allies but also its adversaries. Amidst a multitude of cultural systems and congeries a relentless struggle goes on for existence and individuality, each system trying to survive and to expand at the expense of others.[1] *An enormous percentage of cultural "infants" cannot endure this struggle and soon perish.* Since man is a thinking and talking creature millions of little systems in the form of "A is B," or the like, relating to scientific, practical, religious, and other subjects are incessantly born in the conversations of millions of human beings. They live for a moment, die, and are speedily forgotten.

II. Little Systems That Grow Into Great Systems

Since a large proportion of cultural "infants" die prematurely, only a small percentage growing into big systems, the question arises: What kinds develop and by what methods? We must bear in mind that main systems are not born, like Athena from the head of Zeus, in a fully developed form. Many preparatory efforts and considerable time are required for the ideological integration of minor systems

into a vast ideological system, and for the development of all three of its components. Hundreds of years ago there were no systems of chemistry, physics, biology, or technology as we know them today. Instead there were merely separate chemical, physical, biological, or technological ideas and practices, often unconnected with each other, supported by a meager number of corresponding vehicles and agents. Likewise, none of the major religious systems were born in a fully developed form; many decades and even centuries of germination, differentiation, combination, and general-

[1] For an excellent study of the struggle for individuality vs. the struggle for existence, cf. N. K. Mikhailovsky, *Struggle for Individuality* (in Russian, St. Petersburg, 1904).

584

ization of various disparate religious ideas and practices preceded the birth and the ideological, behavioral, and material growth of these systems to their full stature. The same observation applies to any mature, aesthetic, ethical, juridical, or political system.

A petty system must possess three characteristics in order to evolve into a great system. (1) Like the seed of a giant tree, it must contain the potentialities of unfolding into a vast system, meaningfully and practically important. Like the seed of a tiny plant, explicitly and implicitly trivial ideas, values, and norms cannot grow into vast systems; at best they can form merely a detail of such cultural giants. Such ideas as "a pink tie," "a stone," or "Put on your left shoe first" can never lead to significant systems. But such concepts as "atom," "wheel," "fire," "lever," "line," "number," "soul," "god," "relationship," "love," "justice," "beauty," and "cause and effect" contain the potentialities of vast ideological and cultural systems. (2) A minor ideological system must correspond to some genuine *need on the part of a given population*.[2] Ideological systems that are of no service, that do not bear any vital relationship to existing realities and values, may enjoy a momentary success, but cannot develop into major systems and cannot survive amidst the intense struggle for existence of a multitude of systems. (3) Finally, to be durable, a minor system must be related to some *perennial reality and value*.

1. Factors of Growth

The means of attaining this growth are neither easy nor simple. The chief factors in the development of potentially creative minor systems are as follows:

(a) The "self-unfolding" of ideas when they are thought over and exchanged in meaningful interaction. On pages 380 ff., 538 ff., it was pointed out that meanings are highly dynamic

forms of reality. They are, so to speak, always on the move, unfolding themselves, eliminating their hidden tensions and contradictions, the phase of thesis passing (in Hegelian terms) into antithesis and then into synthesis. Without premeditation, in the process of meaningful interaction this or that potential meaning, hitherto hidden, frequently comes out, as it were, into the open, is objectified in this or that vehicle, enters into the behavioral and material culture of the group, and undergoes further development.

(b) Quantitative and qualitative accumulation of the unfolded meanings, vehicles, and agents in the process of individual and group interaction and of articulation of the system.

(c) Attacks by inimical systems and congeries in the incessant struggle for survival and growth in the total constellation of congeries and systems. Inherently inferior and meaningfully weak systems succumb to such attacks, either perishing or being relegated to the position of a mere detail in a virile system. Strong and creatively pregnant minor systems often profit by such attacks, which stimulate the unfolding of their potentialities, bring into the open what was before hidden, and contribute to their development and growth. Under extremely unfavorable conditions, of course, even certain of these systems may succumb to such attacks.

(d) The cross-fertilization and the merging of two or more congenial minor systems in a single vast subordinated or coordinated system. Two or more hitherto independent simple ideological systems—for instance two arithmetical processes, or ideas of supernatural agents, or several notes or tunes, or simple stories, or two cases of using a stick as a lever—may sooner or later become linked in some one's mind (often spontaneously) and lead to a more generalized, but still very rudimentary, mathematical, magical or religious, musical, poetic, or technological system. Eventually two or

---

[2] Even mythologies, magical beliefs, and other systems of fantastic ideas of preliterate peoples have reflected in a bizarre way some aspects of reality and have served many a vital need of such peoples. Cf. J. G. Frazer, *Psyche's Task* (London, 1913); G. Sorel, *Reflections on Violence* (New York, 1912), pp. 133 ff., dealing with the usefulness of myths; and Pareto, *The Mind and Society, passim*, on the usefulness of many "derivations" and nonlogical ideologies. For the services rendered by religious beliefs, cf. Durkheim, *Elementary Forms of Religious Life*; J. Wachs, *Sociology of Religion*; M. Weber, *Religionssoziologie*, F. de Coulanges, *The Ancient City* (Boston, 1900); B. Kidd, *Social Evolution* (New York, 1894); C. Bouglé, *Essais sur le régime des castes* (Paris, 1908); and B. Malinowski, *Myths in Primitive Psychology* (New York, 1926). For other literature on this topic, cf. my *Theories*, Ch. 12.

more of these systems repeat the same process and produce a still more generalized system, and so on.

(e) Unfolding immanently under the attacks of hostile systems, becoming more and more generalized through spontaneous inter-linking, potentially great systems are even more stimulated in their growth by the factors of good luck and incidental genius (cf. Chapter 35). An exceptionally favorable constellation of circumstances and the occurrence of a creative genius enormously promote the unfolding of the system in one or all of its components. Hitherto isolated, several systems of addition, substraction, division, and multiplication are finally generalized into a more comprehensive system of arithmetic. Numbers and their relationships become detached from concrete objects (such as hands, fish, and apples) and carry on an independent issue as an abstract system, applicable to anything possessing a quantitative aspect. Eventually there emerges a full-fledged, closely integrated mathematical system as a scientific ideology, a cultural system objectified in billions of vehicles, realized in billions of overt actions, and socialized in millions of human beings. A similar generalization applies to the unfolding and development of minor religious, philosophical, artistic, legal, political, and technological systems.

2. Various Forms in the Growth of Systems

Minor systems grow quantitatively and qualitatively, in part or all of their components.

a. *Quantitative Growth.* In the *ideology* of a system, growth consists in an increase of various meanings, values, and norms without an essential change of its framework. An increase in the number of words in a language without a notable change in its grammar and syntax, of prayers, myths, and legends in religion, of single norms in a law code, of specific facts in a science, of lines in a poem, or of bars in a musical composition is an example of the quantitative growth of the component of meanings. Quantitative growth of the vehicles means an increase of the sum total of behavioral and material vehicles without a marked improvement in their quality—a multiplication of wealth, property, tools, means of communication, and rituals, ceremonies, and other actions that objectify the ideology of the systems. The quantitative growth of the third component is represented by an increase in the number of persons, or *human agents*, among whom the system is socialized.

ˈb. *Qualitative Growth.* This signifies the qualitative improvement of a system in part or all of its components. The growth of its *ideology* consists (1) in a better logical or aesthetic *integration* of its meanings, values, and norms; (2) the *generalization of its basic principle*, one set of such principles or one principle, value, or norm replacing a multitude of separate partial principles; (3) in the *extension of the principle* to all logically or aesthetically subordinated and coordinated meanings, subsystems, and systems, in the sense that the principles become their major premise; (4) in *ever-greater development, differentiation, and diversification of* the specific forms or articulation of the basic principles.

The qualitative growth of mathematics and the natural sciences has consisted in the evolution of poorly integrated, specific mathematical ideas into better integrated, generalized, extended, and diversified systems, and in the replacement of a multitude of specific scientific rules, facts, and ideas by more and more precisely formulated and more highly generalized laws or basic principles. A similar observation applies to religious, philosophical, and other systems. The definitive formulation of the Christian Credo was derived from many separate religious, philosophical, and ethical concepts, including those of Judaism, Mithraism, Platonism, Pythagoreanism, Manicheism, and so on. In a long process both antedating and following the teachings of Jesus these separate ideas and systems were pondered and discussed, tested, sorted, and combined and recombined by many thinkers, including the Church Fathers, until they culminated in the formulation of the Nicean *Credo*, with a multitude of subordinate ideas, subsystems, and systems. The principles of the *Credo* were extended, moreover, to the fields of medieval theology and philosophy, science, literature and drama, the fine arts, ethics and law, politics, and economics, becoming their major premise. Much the same may be said of the qualitative growth of ideological systems in any field of culture. Plato's and Kan't philosophical systems integrated, generalized, extended, and differentiated many of the narrower, less consistent, less generalized, and less differentiated philosophical ideas and systems of their predecessors. Bach, Mozart, and Beethoven performed the same service in relation to the music of their predecessors. The *Corpus Juris Civilis* summed up, integrated, and generalized a host of earlier law-norms of the Graeco-Roman civilization. The growth of the technological systems of the wheel consisted in the integration, generalization, and extension of the principle with reference to transportation, the generation and transmission of power, and the like, with ever-increasing diversity of mechanisms applying this principle.

The qualitative growth of the *behavioral and material vehicles* of a system consists in their increasing capacity to embody and objectify adequately its ideology. The progressive integration and coordinated diversification of the vehicles renders them capable of articulating a system of meanings, values, and norms more and more fully and efficiently through a multiplication of bio-physical instruments. Thus the replacement of picture writing by the rebus and by alphabetic writing permitted a better expression of meanings and ideologies. The replacement of vague written symbols and terms by more precise symbols and terms, and that of rudimentary instruments and techniques by more precise instruments and techniques, marked the development of scientific vehicles. The invention and improvement of a system of musical notation, as well as the introduction of new musical instruments ranging from a primitive drum or harp to the elaborate equipment of a contemporary symphony orchestra, typified the growth of musical vehicles. The perfection of religious rituals and ceremonies, ikons and other symbols, songs, temples, etc., and the substitution of the locomotive, steamship, automobile, and airplane for more primitive modes of transportation, afford further examples of the qualitative growth of vehicles.

The qualitative growth of *human agents of the system* means an improvement of their qualities as active operators, manipulators, and propagators of its ideology. The replacement of unskilled musicians in an orchestra by virtuosi, of incompetent preachers or professors by competent and inspiring ones, of the mediocre among political leaders by real statesmen, illustrates the factor in question.

3. Uniformities in Relationships of Quantitative and Qualitative Growth of Systems

There is a closer connection and greater parallelism between the quantitative growth of the vehicles of a system and that of its members than there is between the growth of these two components and that of its ideology. When a given system, whether that of early Christianity, of the Russian Communist party, of a state in its initial phase, or of a given cultural fad or fashion, grows in respect to its membership, it ordinarily expands also in the sum total of its behavioral and material vehicles: funds, property, tools and instruments, territory, activities, etc. And vice versa: an increase in the sum total of its vehicles is usually accompanied by that of its human agents. Sometimes the growth of members leads in the quantitative increase, sometimes that of the vehicles. The growth of these components is not always followed by a corresponding growth of its ideology in the sense of an increase of its meanings, values and norms. The ideology often remains essentially the same from the quantitative viewpoint. In spite of the enormous momentary spread of this or that fad or fashion, "best seller," radio broadcast, or language, their basic ideologies may remain virtually unchanged. Now and then all three components develop *pari passu;* but as a rule there is a lag between the quantitative growth of the ideology of the system and that of its vehicles and agents. In other words, the quantitative growth in the objectification and socialization of a system may take place without a respective quantitative increase of its ideology.

The relation between the quantitative and the qualitative growth of systems exhibits several different types: (a) systems may develop quantitatively, without a corresponding qualitative growth; (b) in certain systems the quantitative growth lags considerably behind the qualitative growth; (c) in other systems the two may proceed more or less *pari passu;* (d) still others may grow qualitatively, without a corresponding quantitative growth.

a. *Quantitative, Without Corresponding Qualitative Growth.* The aforesaid fads and fashions, short-lived cultural best sellers, and evanescent radio talks, crooning, and jazz, broadcast to millions of listeners, afford petty examples of ideological systems that expand rapidly in respect to their vehicles and human agents, without any perceptible growth in their ideologies. They are born, multiply quantitatively, produce an "epidemic" of objectification and socialization, and swiftly pass into oblivion. In a somewhat more lasting form many political empires have expanded through conquest, like those of Genghis Khan, Tamerlane, Napoleon, and Hitler, with a rapid increase in population, territory, and other vehicles, without any essential growth of their ideological system. Many financial and business concerns likewise expand principally in the number of their patrons and vehicles, without a marked qualitative growth in their ideology, vehicles, or human agents.

Essentially quantitative growth is typical also of the "post-creative" or decadent period of systems which have exhausted their creative potentialities. Many of them, not being able to grow qualitatively, increase for the most part quantitatively, especialy in respect to the components of vehicles and agents. Hence the "disease of colossalism," or the "cult of bigness," which frequently characterizes such systems in their post-creative phase.[3] For instance, the creative possibilities of the Gothic style of architecture were essentially exhausted by the thirteenth century. After that it grew mainly quantitatively. The truly creative phase of almost all great religions falls within the initial period of their existence, when their systems grow ideologically, as well as in respect to their vehicles and adherents. Subsequently they expand chiefly in the number of their vehicles and members, without a corresponding improvement of their quality. Much the same may be said of philosophical, artistic, ethical, legal, and other systems whose creative potentialities are limited and cannot grow indefinitely. At this stage a system tends to deteriorate qualitatively, to become distorted, vulgarized, and more primitive in the

process of further socialization among huge masses of adherents.

b. *Qualitative, With Quantitative Lag.* Many cultural systems first grow qualitatively, especially in their ideological component, with a pronounced quantitative lag. Thus the cosmogonic system of Aristarchus of Samos had to wait some nineteen hundred years before it became widely objectified and socialized through a perfected form of the Copernican system. The steam engine, invented in a rudimentary form in China in the third century B.C., had to wait until almost the nineteenth century to become objectified and socialized on a large scale for purposes of transportation and manufacturing. G. Vico's philosophy of history and J. S. Bach's system of music became widely objectified and socialized only about a century after their creation. It required from one to five centuries for Christianity to expand quantitatively to the position of the dominant religion of the Graeco-Roman world.

c. *Pari Passu.* Many systems tend to grow quantitatively and qualitatively *pari passu.*

d. *Qualitative, Without Corresponding Quantitative Growth.* Finally, there are perennial minor groups in all fields of culture whose members constantly perfect their system without any appreciable increase in the number of its vehicles and human agents. Esoteric and secret societies, exclusive cliques and oversophisticated factions, as well as groups of mathematicians, biologists, historians, philosophers, artists, and lawgivers dealing with the most complex problems of their systems, furnish examples of this type of growth. The profoundest mathematical, philosophical, artistic, and ethical problems are always confined to a handful of the most eminent mathematicians, philosophers, artists, and ethical ideologists, respectively. They cannot be widely objectified and socialized because they are inaccessible to the masses. Although such systems may be constantly perfected in their ideology, they rarely, if ever, expand in respect to their vehicles or their membership.

Potentially great cultural systems, as a rule, represent in their growth principally types b and c and to some extent type d. Systems devoid of creative pregnancy but meeting a

---

[3] For this disease of colossalism, cf. my *Dynamics, passim,* and Toynbee's work, *passim.*

widely felt temporary need belong chiefly to type a. *This type of growth is followed also by systems whose creative period is over and which have entered the decadent phase of their life career.* Finally, *the highly esoteric systems and the most complex and creative of the upper range of subsystems of various cultural systems represent type* d.

A purely qualitative growth of systems takes place ordinarily in all components of the system, but not necessarily to the same degree. Some systems develop uniformly in their ideology, vehicles, and human agents. Others improve for a given period mainly in either their ideology, their vehicles, or their membership. In religious, scientific, and educational systems there are periods marked by a galaxy of eminent religious leaders, scientists, and educators, respectively, without a corresponding improvement in the material vehicles. Again, there are periods characterized by the construction of elaborate cathedrals, research laboratories, and educational institutions, but by a mediocre body of clergy, research workers, and teachers. Finally, in the development of science, philosophy, the fine arts, religion, politics, and economics there are periods when a notable improvement of the ideological systems is effected without any conspicuous improvement of the vehicles or human agents. As already observed, considerable time elapses, as a rule, before an enriched, integrated, and generalized ideology finds its adequate objectification and socialization in improvement of vehicles and human agents.

III. The Growth of Supersystems

1. The Gradation of Supersystems

Through the operation of the same factors, and qualitatively and quantitatively in line with types *b* and *c* and to some extent with type *d*, various cultural supersystems arise. Step by step the basic principles of a supersystem are integrated, logically or aesthetically; then generalized and extended to several major systems in a given total culture; and finally embraced by most of the larger systems until the supersystem has integrated the greater part of these major systems into one consistent whole. Parallel with this ideological growth it develops, qualitatively and quantitatively, in respect to its vehicles and agents until it becomes the most inclusive and important element of a given total culture, endowing it with both individuality and a high degree of integration.

As was pointed out in Chapters 17 and 18, not all total cultures attain the level of integration into a single vast supersystem; many remain eclectic, integrated into several major systems of science, art, religion, philosophy, economics, politics, technology, and law, each of which remains more or less unrelated to the others. Only truly great cultures achieve the degree of integration requisite for a fully developed supersystem.

Other cultures create some kind of supersystem uniting important segments of their major systems. These supersystems differ in size and comprehensiveness, some being less generalized and integrating a smaller percentage of the major systems of a given total culture and a smaller portion of each of the integrated systems than the others. Among other things, the vastness of supersystems depends upon the degree of generalization of their major premises. And these premises, as we shall see, are different in different supersystems.

It should be reiterated that even the vastest supersystems known—the ideational, sensate, and idealistic—do not integrate 100 per cent of all the systems, congeries, the phenomena of a given total culture, but only the major portion of its major systems. Less comprehensive supersystems integrate a still smaller percentage of the cultural phenomena. For instance, the mutually integrated and generalized principles of filial piety and of the five fundamental social relationships of Confucianism created a cultural supersystem that was articulated by the majority of the Chinese family and kinship systems; by a part of the political and economic systems; by Confucian religion, philosophy, ethics, and law; by some of the fine arts; and by a portion of the Chinese mode of living. This supersystem and its major premises permeated, integrated, and animated a very substantial section of the major and minor systems and congeries of the total Chinese culture; they have endowed it with its dominant individuality. When one knows its basic principles, one has the key to an understanding of an enormous percentage of cultural phenomena during the periods of dominance of this supersystem in the history of China.

It would be a mistake to conclude, however, that this supersystem integrated Chinese culture 100 per cent. Besides thousands of minor systems and congeries which remained outside the Confucian supersystem, occupying a position of relative neutrality or even antagonism, Chinese culture possessed another supersystem, based upon different premises from those of Confucianism, namely, Taoism. This Taoist supersystem existed side by side with Confucianism throughout virtually the entire history of Chinese culture, and at some periods achieved a position of dominance. Finally, there were several much smaller supersystems, of a sensate type, that coexisted with the two major supersystems.

Turning to western civilization, we note that the economic system of capitalism grew during the nineteenth century into a supersystem far transcending the limits of a purely economic system; a portion of our civil and criminal law, of our ethics, of our literature and architecture, of our political and philosophical systems, of our science and way of life, has been clearly stamped with the basic principles of capitalism. Marxianism has been right in stressing the capitalistic character of many of our noneconomic cultural systems and congeries. Its error consists in an undue generalization of this supersystem; not all phenomena of western culture have embodied the principles of capitalism, and not even the greater portion of the majority of the systems and congeries of this culture. The assertion that the basic principles of capitalism have completely

permeated the Catholic or Protestant religion or western science, philosophy, law, ethics, and fine arts is thoroughly fallacious. Capitalism itself is merely one of the systems comprised in a vaster sensate supersystem that has dominated western culture for the last few centuries. Like sensate science, philosophy, fine arts, law, and ethics, the fundamental principles of capitalism are but an application of the major principle of the sensate supersystem, namely, that the true reality and value are sensory. Hence the similarity of the essential principles of capitalism and of those of many other cultural systems of the West is due not to the extension of capitalist principles to these other systems, but to the fact that they are all the offspring of the same parent—the sensate supersystem.[4]

2. The Ideational, Idealistic, and Sensate Supersystems

The vastest known supersystems that have actually been embodied in various cultures are the sensate, idealistic, and ideational supersystems (outlined above in Chapter 17). They are based upon the most comprehensive and general of all the ontological principles, namely, *the one defining the ultimate nature of reality and value.* Ontologically there are no more all-embracing concepts than the three following definitions of the ultimate nature of reality and value: (a) True reality and true value are sensory—the major premise of the sensate supersystems. (b) True reality and value consist in a supersensory, superrational God, Brahman, Atman, Tao, or its equivalent—the major premise of the ideational supersystem. (c) True reality and value are an infinite manifold, partly supersensory and superrational, partly rational, and partly sensory—the premise of the idealistic supersystem. Implicit within each of these major premises is the definition of the kind of science, philosophy, fine arts, ethics, politics, economics, mentality, and way of life that must be created to make them consistent with itself and with one an-

---

[4] The same mistake, in reverse, is represented by such theories as that of Max Weber, who contends that the capitalist system has been a function rather than the cause of the Protestant religion. According to Marx's equation, religion and other ideological systems are functions of the capitalist system of economy. According to Weber, capitalism is a function of Protestantism and its *Wirtschaftsethik.*

The real relationship is that capitalism, Protestantism (in part), individualism, political democracy, contractual relations, utilitarianism in ethics and law, and sensate art, science, and philosophy are all functions of the sensate supersystem that dominated western culture after the sixteenth century. (cf. Chapter 43).

other. If a given total culture succeeds in creating one of these supersystems with an adequate qualitative and quantitative development, such a culture accordingly attains the highest degree of integration possible for human beings with limited logical and rational endowments.[5]

A detailed study of the nature and dynamics of each of these supersystems and of the modes of their growth, changes, and decline is indispensable for a proper understanding of the nature, structure, and changes of the highly integrated cultures, of the supersystems themselves, and of virtually all cultural phenomena

in general. Such a study represents an integration, generalization, and extension of a multitude of valid theories of cultural change in the form of a single consistent theory of cultural dynamics. The subsequent chapters devoted to these three supersystems and their dynamics in the history of the Graeco-Roman and western cultures present a crucial "clinical" case.

Since in this study we are concerned not only with the growth of these supersystems but with their decline, it is advisable at this point to outline the relationships between the decline of a system or supersystem and its growth.

IV. The Decline of Systems and Supersystems

In their total life history cultural systems and supersystems exhibit periods of growth and periods of decline. Contrary to Spengler and other theorists, many systems and supersystems experience several periods of growth and of decline. The decline of systems and supersystems is characterized by the same forms and relationships as their growth.

1. Quantitative Decline

Quantitative decline may concern the ideological component of a system, consisting in a decrease of its elements, or it may mean a decrease of the vehicles and human agents. We are well aware, for instance, that the funds and material possessions or the members of a religion, university, scientific system, or political party now and then decline.

The quantitative decline of the members and of the vehicles of a system ordinarily go hand in hand, just as they do in connection with its growth.

2. Qualitative Decline

Qualitative decline may consist in the deterioration and logico-aesthetic disintegration of the ideology of a system, or it may consist in the deterioration of its vehicles or human agents when these come to embody the system of meanings and values less and less adequately. It occurs also when the meaningful-causal connection between the ideology and the vehicles and human agents becomes looser.

3. Connection Between Quantitative and Qualitative Decline

As in the process of growth, the connection between quantitative decline and qualitative decline presents the following four types: (a) a system declines chiefly quantitatively, without a serious qualitative deterioration; (b) it declines principally qualitatively, the quantitative decline showing a time lag; (c) it declines quantitatively and qualitatively approximately *pari passu*; (d) it becomes "petrified,"

---

[5] The main differences between these supersystems and the major systems of each of ten cultures of Danilevsky-Spengler, each of twenty cultures of Toynbee, and specific cultures of Northrop are as follows: (1) they assume that the total culture of each of their cultures is integrated into its major system; I claim that only the major part of each of these cultures is integrated into one system or supersystem; (2) the major premises of their systems of each culture are outlined very vaguely, often left without any definition; (3) they tried to discover the specific major system of each

of their cultures, Mexican, or American, Chinese or Hindu, and so on. My supersystems are the most general types of supersystems given in various cultures, of which their major systems are but species. Even Northrop's "aesthetic and theoretic components" are a mere species of my sensate, ideational, and idealistic supersystems, torn from these organic unities and somewhat artificially combined. Cf. the quoted works of Danilevsky, Spengler, Toynbee, and Northrop. See further on this, Chapter 43.

mechanically continuing its existence with its creative forces exhausted, but outwardly stationary in respect to the quality and quantity of its components.

(a) Owing to persecution and other factors, between 1918 and 1932 the Russian Orthodox religion suffered a marked decrease in its membership and vehicles (all its funds and property being confiscated by the Soviet government), but without any qualitative deterioration of its remaining ideological component; if anything, it showed an improvement during this period of quantitative decline. Many cultural systems of various kinds have experienced a similar decline.

(b) A qualitative deterioration of the Russian Orthodox Church in respect to its ideology and agents set in at the beginning of the nineteenth century. Thereafter, for several decades, it exhibited a quantitative growth of its vehicles and agents. A similar retrogression has occurred in the Catholic, Protestant, Buddhist, Hindu, Taoist, and Mohammedan religions, as well as in various systems of politics and economics, philosophy and law, and even science and the fine arts. At the present time we observe a marked qualitative deterioration in most of these fields, sometimes accompanied by a continued quantitative growth.

(c) The parallel qualitative and quantitative decline of systems is an ever-present phenomenon, requiring no illustration.

(d) The fourth type is represented by various systems whose creative period is over, but which continue to function through sheer inertia, without any visible sign of their quantitative or qualitative decline. Such a stationary existence is in reality a slow decline, for in the cultural world those persons and systems that have ceased to be creative inevitably retrogress. Systems of this type are characterized chiefly by well-organized machinery, rigidly established rituals, and entrenched dogmas, formulae, and rules.

The decline of a system does not necessarily entail its dissolution or extinction, for it frequently recovers its vitality in one or more respects. Only when its ideology disintegrates to such an extent that it loses its identity or when it loses all its vehicles or members does it actually become extinct. Moreover, the decline and even the death of a cultural system do not mean the death of its members or the destruction of its vehicles. As a rule these are simply transferred to other systems.

We shall now undertake a more detailed study of the growth and decline of supersystems.

Chapter 40. Growth, Fluctuation, and Decline of Main Forms of Fine Arts

Each of the major premises of these supersystems defines clearly what kind of the fine arts, of science, philosophy and religion, law and ethics, economics and political systems are contained in, and consistent with it. As the major premises are profoundly different from one another, different also from one another must be the ideational, idealistic, and sensate fine arts, science and philosophy, law and ethics, or other cultural systems, as the subsystems in these supersystems. In other words, logically and factually there must be three different forms of each of these systems. Let us outline these forms in each of the main compartments of culture, and see whether these forms have really been given in empirical cultures and if so, where and when.

I. Ideational, Idealistic, and Sensate Fine Arts Defined

1. Ideational Art

Ideational, idealistic, and sensate arts profoundly differ from one another in their external. style as well as internal content. In accordance with the major premise ideational art articulates exactly the premise that the true reality-value is God. Therefore internally *the topic of ideational art is the supersensory kingdom of God or its terminological equivalent.* Its "heroes" are God and other deities, angels, saints and sinners, and the soul, as well as the mysteries of creation, incarnation, redemption, crucifixion, salvation, and other transcendental events. It is religious through and through. It pays little attention to the persons, objects, and events of the sensory empirical world. Its objective is not to amuse, entertain, or give pleasure, but to bring the believer into a closer union with God. It is a part of religion, and functions as religious service. It is a communion of the human soul with itself and with God. As such it is sacred in its content and form. As such it does not admit any sensualism, eroticism, satire, comedy, caricature, farce, or anything extraneous to its nature. Its emotional tone is pious, ethereal, and ascetic.

Its style is and must be symbolic. It is a mere visible or sensory sign of the invisible or supersensory world of values. Since God and supersensory phenomena do not have any material forms, they cannot be perceived and depicted naturalistically, as they appear to our senses. They can only be denoted symbolically. Hence the transcendental symbolism of ideational art. The signs of the dove, anchor, and olive branch in the early Christian catacombs were mere visible symbols of the values of the invisible kingdom of God, as distinct from the empirical dove or olive branch. Such an art is wholly internal and therefore looks externally simple, archaic, devoid of sensory trimmings, pomp, and ostentation. It suggests a marvelous soul dressed in shabby clothes. Its significance is not in its external appearance but in the inner values it symbolizes. It is not an art of the professional individual artist but the creation of the anonymous collectivity of believers conversing with God and with their own soul. Such a communication does not need any professional mediators or any beautifying externalities.

2. Sensate Art

Sensate art lives and moves entirely in the empirical world of the senses. Farmers, workers, housewives, girls, stenographers, teachers, and other human beings are its personages. At its overripe stage, prostitutes, criminals, street urchins, the insane, hypocrites, rogues, and other subsocial type are its favorite "heroes." Its aim is to afford a refined sensual enjoyment: relaxation, excitation of tired nerves, amusement, pleasure, entertainment. For this reason it must be sensational, passionate, pathetic, sensual, and incessantly new. It is marked by voluptuous nudity and concupiscence. It is divorced from religion, morals, and other values, and styles itself "art for art's sake." Since it must amuse and entertain, it makes wide use of caricature, satire, comedy, farce, debunking, ridiculing, and similar means.

Its style is naturalistic, visual, even illusionistic, free from any supersensory symbolism. It reproduces empirical phenomena as they look, sound, smell, or otherwise appear to our sense organs. It is dynamic in its very nature: in its emotionality, in the violence of the passions and actions which it portrays, and in its incessant modernity and change. It has to be externally changing, presenting a constant succession of fads and fashions, because otherwise it will be boring, uninteresting, unenjoyable. For the same reason it is the art of external show, dressed up for an exhibition. Since it does not symbolize any supersensory value, it stands and falls by its external appearance. Like a pretty but stupid glamour girl, it succeeds only as long as it is tricked out and

retains its superficial beauty. To retain its charm, it has to make lavish use of pomp and circumstance, colossality, stunning technique, and other means of external adornment. Furthermore, it is an art of professional artists catering to a passive public. The more it develops, the more pronounced become these characteristics.

3. Idealistic Art

Idealistic art is an intermediary between the ideational and sensate forms of art. Its world is partly supersensory and partly sensory, but only in the sublimest and noblest aspects of sensory reality. Its heroes are partly gods and other transcendental creatures; partly the empirical man, but in his noblest aspects only. It is an art intentionally blind to everything debasing, vulgar, ugly, and negative in the empirical world of the senses. Its style is partly symbolic and allegoric, partly realistic and naturalistic. In a word, it represents a marvelous synthesis of the ideational and the noblest forms of sensate art.

4. Eclectic Art

Finally there is a low-grade of an unintegrated or little integrated art, representing a mechanical mixture of anything and everything. It has no internal unity or consistency of style. It is the art of a bazaar, a congeries of different topics and diverse styles.

5. Historical Examples

Ideational, idealistic, and sensate supersystems are perennial, given in a rudimentary or full-grown form in many cultures of the past and of the present, among the preliterate as well as historical cultures. Ideational fine arts in an impure and rudimentary form occur among many primitive peoples such as the Hopi[1] and Zuni Indians, the Negro tribes of Africa, and certain Australian tribes. Likewise the geometric art of Neolithic man, when it was symbolic, was typically ideational. In the so-called historical cultures, ideational art dominated at certain periods the art of Taoist China, Tibet, and Brahmanic India, Buddhist culture, and ancient Egypt; that of Greece

---

[1] Cf. L. Thompson, "Logico-Aesthetic Integration in Hopi Culture," *AA*, 1945, pp. 540-553; on primitive art see W. Deonna, *L'archeologie*, 3 Vols. (Paris, 1912); F. Boas, *Primitive Art* (Oslo, 1927); H. Read, *Art and Society* (New York, 1937). Cf. other literature in *Dynamics*, Vol. I, *passim*.

from the ninth to the end of the sixth century B.C.; that of the early and medieval Christian West, and so on. The sensate form of the fine arts, in turn, has been scattered everywhere and at all times. It is the prevailing form of the art of early Paleolithic man, of many a primitive tribe, such as the Bushmen of Africa, of many an Indian and Scythian tribe, and the like. It pervaded the fine arts of Assyria, at least during some periods of its history, and those of ancient Egypt in the later stages of the Old Kingdom, Middle Kingdom, and New Empire, and especially during its latest periods—the Saite, Ptolemaic, and Roman epochs. It definitely characterized the later known era of the Creto-Mycenaean culture and the Graeco-Roman culture from the third century B.C. to the fourth century A.D. Finally, it has been dominant in western culture during the last five centuries. The idealistic form of art has not been so widespread as the other two, but has occurred many times. Its best examples are furnished by the Greek fine arts of the fifth century B.C. and by the western art of the thirteenth century.

However different in many respects are the fine arts, for instance of primitive and civilized peoples, they all exhibit a series of similar internal and external characteristics when they belong to the same type. Among other things, these facts mean that the domination of this or that form in the fine arts is not a matter of the presence or absence of artistic skill, but is the result, rather, of the ideational, sensate, idealistic, or mixed mentality of the respective peoples and cultures. Living in a sensate age, we are prone to interpret ideational art as more primitive than the sensate, and the ideational artist as less skilful and masterly than the sensate artist. Such an interpretation is, however, without foundation. Paleolithic man or the man of the early Stone Age was a sensate artist, highly skilful in the visual reproduction of the empirical objects he was interested in, such as animals, hunting scenes, and the like. Neolithic man or the man of the more highly developed culture of the late Stone Age was essentially an ideational artist, and his work revealed little traces of sensate art. Thus the later and more developed stage of culture produced ideational art, rather than the sensate art which had preceded it. Likewise, the perfect sensate art of the Creto-Mycenaean Age was replaced after the ninth century B.C. by the ideational art of early Greece. Similar shifts from one form of art to another we observe in the fine arts of ancient Egypt, China, and several other countries. Finally, the perfect sensate art of Graeco-Roman culture from the third century B.C. to the fourth century A.D. was replaced by the ideational art of the medieval Christian West.

All this means, as we have seen, that the preeminence of each form of the fine arts is not a question of the presence or absence of artistic skill but of the nature of the dominant supersystem of culture. In a culture marked by the ideational supersystem, its fine arts will be prevailingly ideational; and a similar generalization holds true for the cultures dominated, respectively, by the sensate, idealistic, or mixed supersystem.[2]

II. Notable Shifts in the Forms of the Fine Arts

When in a given total culture the dominant supersystem changes, the dominant form of the fine arts changes in the same direction. If the sensate supersystem is superseded by the ideational, sensate art gives way to ideational art, and vice versa. An example of this phenomenon is furnished by the shifts of the Graeco-Roman and the western fine arts from one dominant form to another. Let us glance at these shifts, not only for their own sake but also for an understanding of the nature of the contemporary crisis in the western fine arts.

The story begins with the Creto-Mycenaean art, which, exemplified by the famous Vaphio cup, is a perfect visual art, showing an unexcelled sensate mastery on the part of the artists. It gives us a superlative impressionistic rendition of the taming of a bull. We know also that the late period of the Creto-Mycenaean culture was decadently sensate.

When we come to the Greek art of the eighth century to the end of the sixth century

[2] For the facts, details and statistics, cf. my *Dynamics*, Vol. I, Chps. 5-7.

B.C., we encounter the realm of so-called archaic or, more exactly, ideational art, with all the characteristics proper to such an art. It is symbolic, religious, and other-worldly. It does not depict things as they appear to the eye; instead, it employs geometric and other visible symbols of the invisible world of pre-dominantly religious values.

Beginning with the end of the sixth century B.C., we note a decline of ideational art in all its aspects and the emergence of an idealistic art which reaches its climax in the fifth century B.C. with Phidias, Aeschylus, Sophocles, and Pindar. It is probably the example *par excellence* of idealistic art. Exemplified by the Parthenon, it is half religious and half empirical. From the sensory world it derives only its noble types and positive values. It is an idealizing, typological art. Its portraits are beautiful types, not realistic representations of a given individual. It is marred by nothing low, vulgar, or debasing. It is serene, calm, and sublime. Its idealism manifests itself in the artist's excellent knowledge of human anatomy and of the means of rendering it in an ideal or perfect form, in the type of persons represented, in their postures, in the abstract treatment of the human type. There are no concrete portraits, no ugliness, no defective traits. We are introduced to immortals or idealized mortals; the aged are rejuvenated; infants are depicted as grown up; the women reveal few traits that are specifically womanish, and appear in the guise of athletes. There is no concrete landscape. The postures and expressions are free from anything violent, from excessive emotion and distorting passion. They are calm and imperturbable, like the gods. Even the dead reflect the same serene beauty. These characteristics are the result not of technical limitations but, rather, of the artist's desire to avoid anything that might disturb the harmony or ideal order of the idealistic scheme of life. Finally, this art was deeply religious, moralizing, instructive, ennobling, and patriotic. It was not just art for art's sake, but an art indissolubly connected with other values, religious, moral, and civic. The artist was self-effacing and merged his identity in that of the community: Phidias, Polycletus, Polygnotus, Sophocles, and other masters were just *primi inter pares* in a collective religious or patriotic

enterprise embracing the whole community. They had not yet turned, like the sensate artists, into professionals wholly absorbed in art for art's sake and therefore liberated from civic, moral, religious, and other duties. In brief, it was an art perfectly blending heavenly perfection with the noblest earthly beauty, interfusing religious and other values with those of sublime sensory forms. It may be designated as a "value-laden" art, in contradistinction to the "value-empty" art of the pure aesthetician.

After the fifth century B.C. the sensate wave began to rise, and the ideational wave to decline. As a result the idealistic synthesis was shattered, and sensate art came to dominate the field from approximately the third century B.C. up to, roughly, the fourth century A.D. During the first centuries of our era it entered its over-ripe phase, marked by realism and by an ever-accelerating tempo of imitation of the archaic, classic, and other styles. This same period witnessed the emergence of Christian ideational art, which kept pace with the growth of Christianity, becoming in the sixth century A.D. the dominant form.

With the advent of the fourth century A.D., the sensate Graeco-Roman art underwent a significant change. Though many an historian characterizes this mutation as the decay of classic art, it may be more accurately interpreted as the decay of the sensate form and its eventual replacement by a new dominant form, namely, by the Christian ideational art, which held sway from the sixth century to the end of the twelfth century.

The supreme examples of medieval architecture are the great cathedrals and temples, buildings devoted to God. Their external forms —the cruciform foundation, the dome or spire, and almost every architectural and sculptural detail—are symbolic. They are truly the Bible in stone. Medieval sculpture, in turn, is religious through and through. It is once again the Old and the New Testament "frozen" in stone, clay, or marble. Medieval painting is likewise overwhelmingly religious, a pictorial representation of the Old and New Testaments, almost entirely symbolic and other-worldly. There is no attempt to reproduce in two-dimensional terms the illusion of three-dimensional reality. There is little nudity, and what little there is is ascetic. There is *no paysage, no genre, no realistic portraiture, no satire, caricature, or comedy.*

Medieval literature is derived mainly from the Bible, certain comments on it, prayers, the lives of the saints, and other religious literature. Literature of a purely secular character occupies scarcely any place in it. If some secular Graeco-Roman literature is used, it is so fundamentally transformed and so symbolically interpreted that Homer, Ovid, Virgil, and Horace constitute a mere simulacrum. We have to wait until almost the twelfth century for a genuine secular literature. The entire empirical world is ignored. The medieval drama and theatre consists of the church service, religious processions, and mystery plays. Medieval music is represented by the Ambrosian, Gregorian, and other plain chants, with their *Kyrie eleison, Alleluia, Agnus Dei, Gloria, Requiem,* and similar purely religious songs.

All this is externally simple and austere, archaic and traditional, and hieratic. Externally, for a sensate person accustomed to the luxurious trimmings of sensate art, it may appear very bleak and unattractive, devoid of technical mastery, of entertainment, of beauty. Nevertheless, when it is understood that ideational art is subjective, immersed in the supersensory world, it is seen to be as impressive in its own way as any known sensate art. The ideational art of these centuries is ethereal, admirably expressive of its supersensory orientation, and eminently consistent. It is the art of the human soul conversing with its God. As such it was not designed for the market, for purposes of profit, for fame, popularity, or other sensate values, or for sensual enjoyment. It was created, as Theophilus has observed, *nec humane laudis amore, nec temporalis premii cupiditate . . . sed in augmentum honoris et gloriae nominis Dei.* Hence its anonymity. The artists were collective; the whole community built a cathedral or church. Individual leaders did not care to affix their names to their creation. With very insignificant exceptions, we do not know even the identity of the creators of the foremost cathedrals, sculptures, or other masterpieces of medieval art. Such were the pre-eminent characteristics of medieval art from the sixth to the end of the twelfth century.

These traits are not derived from superficial impressions, but from a systematic quantitative and qualitative analysis of more than one hundred thousand medieval and modern pictures and sculptures, of most of the medieval literature extant, of the greater part of the surviving medieval music, of the bulk of medieval architecture and drama. Later on, the principal data of this statistical study will be given. They will show clearly the ideational character of the dominant medieval art. For the present, let us continue our brief characterization of the main swings throughout the later centuries.

At the end of the twelfth century we witness the first signs of the decline of the ideational fine arts in most fields except that of music, where the decline appears somewhat later. The fine arts pass from the ideational form to the idealistic form of the thirteenth century and of part of the fourteenth century. This is similar in certain respects to the Greek idealistic art of the fifth century B.C. In both cases it is moored to the supersensory world; but in either case it begins to reflect more and more the noblest and most sublime positive values of the empirical world, whether they relate to man and civic institutions or to idealized beauty. In its style it unites the ripest technical mastery of the sensate artist with a pure, noble, and idealistic *Weltanschauung.* It is a highly selective art, so far as the sensory world is concerned, chosing only the positive values, types, and events and ignoring the pathological and negative phenomena. It embellishes even the positive empirical values, never depicting them as they actually look, sound, or otherwise appear to the senses. It is an art of idealized types, and rarely of sharply individualized persons or events. As in the Greek art of the fifth century, its portraiture is not a bald reproduction of the traits of a given person, but an abstract and noble type having remote, if any, resemblance to the real traits. Its *genre* reflects only the noble events. Its heroes are the immortals and semidivine beings—heroic figures, whether in their achievements or in their tragedy. It immortalizes the mortals. Even when it depicts the dead, it often represents them with open eyes, as if they beheld the light inaccessible to us, and free from any symptom of decomposition and death. It is serene, calm, free from any frivolity, comedy, or satire, violent passions or emotions, anything debasing, *pathétique*, or macabre. It is the art of a pure nun who for the first time notes the beauty of the empirical world—the spring morning, the flowers and trees, the dew, the sunshine, the caressing wind and blue sky. These traits are conspicuous in all the fine arts of these centuries, though in music they are markedly weaker. Music still remains mainly ideational; only about a century later does it come to assume the noble forms of the beauty of idealistic music.

The idealistic period ends with the close of the fifteenth century. The continued decline of the ideational form and the progressive rise of the sensate form result in the dominance of the sensate form in most of the fine arts. This domination increases, with slight fluctuations, throughout the subsequent centuries, reaching its climax and possible limit in the nineteenth century.

We already know the characteristics of this sumptuous sensate art. It has been overwhelmingly *secular*, aiming to reflect sensory beauty and to provide sensory pleasure and entertainment. As such, it has been an art for art's sake, divorced from religious, moral, and civic values. Its heroes and personages have been common mortals and, in its later stage, preeminently the subsocial and pathological types. Its emotional tone has been passionate, *pathétique*, sensational. It has been marked by voluptuous and sensual nudity. It has been an art of *paysage* and *genre*, of portraiture, of caricature, satire, and comedy, of vaudeville and operetta; an art of show, decked out "a la Hollywood"; an art of individualistic, professional artists catering to a passive public. As such it has been devised for a market, as a commodity to be bought and sold like any other commodity, depending for success on competition with other commodities.

In its external style it has been *realistic, naturalistic, or visual*. It has depicted empirical reality as it appears to our senses. In music it has presented a combination of sounds that please or displease, as such, through their sheer physical qualities, without any symbolism or transcendental meanings behind them. In this sense it has reflected merely the *surface of empirical phenomena*—their superficial forms,

appearances and sounds—instead of penetrating the three-dimensional depth of the object in painting, and the essence of the reality that lies beneath the surface; hence its *illusionistic* character. A sensate picture, with its foreshortening and perspective, aims to give an illusion of three-dimensional reality through a two-dimensional medium. Similar illusionistic devices have been abundant in sculpture and even in architecture. They tend to produce a show, reflecting surface appearances rather than the substance itself. In brief, we find all the characteristics of a full-fledged sensate art as indicated above.

In order to perceive the essential differences between this sensate art and the medieval ideational and idealistic art, to obtain a clearer conception of the major shifts of the western fine arts, and to procure the necessary evidence for the correctness of the foregoing outline, let us glance at some summary statistics taken from my *Dynamics*.[3] The figures are based on a study of more than one hundred thousand pictures and sculptures of the eight principal European countries from the beginning of the Middle Ages up to 1930. This cross section, embracing as it does the overwhelmingly greater part of the pictures and sculptures of these countries known to the art historian, is thus the most representative ever given. While the details may exhibit certain inaccuracies, the essentials are certainly reliable. Likewise the conclusions concerning music, literature, drama, and architecture are based on similarly representative samples of the foremost known musical, literary, dramatic, and architectural creations of the eight countries.

One of the most important characteristics of ideational, idealistic, and sensate art is the nature of their topics, whether in the field of the supersensory-religious or in that of the sensory-empirical. From this standpoint the history of European art is well depicted by the figures on page 599.

Among all the pictures and sculpture studied, the percentages of religious and secular works are as follows for the specified centuries.

The figures show that medieval painting and sculpture were overwhelmingly religious. This

[3] See for enormous factual material and detailed statistics *Dynamics*, Vol. I, *passim*.

	Before the 10th	10th-11th	12th-13th	14th-15th
Religious	81.9	94.7	97.0	85.0
Secular	18.1	5.3	3.0	15.0
Total	100.0	100.0	100.0	100.0

	16th	17th	18th	19th	20th
Religious	64.7	50.2	24.1	10.0	3.9
Secular	35.3	49.8	75.9	90.0	96.1
Total	100.0	100.0	100.0	100.0	100.0

religious factor began to decline after the thirteenth century, becoming quite insignificant in the nineteenth and twentieth centuries, whereas the percentage of secular pictures and sculptures, virtually absent in the Middle Ages, has risen since the thirteenth century to approximately 90 to 96 per cent of all the known pictures and sculptures of the countries in question.

It is to be added that the growth and decline of each form *has not been a unilinear trend but a steady trend with minor fluctuations. If instead of the century figures shorter periods were taken they would show more numerous ups and downs or minor growths and declines of each form.*

Sensate art in Europe first emerged in Italy and France, then within a few decades spread over most of the European countries, the trend reaching Russia with a lag of about 100-125 years. However, from the end of the eighteenth century the trend grew in Russia very rapidly, putting her at the end of the nineteenth century in the same position as the other countries.[4]

A similar situation has prevailed in music, literature, and architecture.

Medieval music is represented par excellence by the Ambrosian, Gregorian, and other plain chants of a religious character. As such, it is almost 100 per cent religious. Between 1090 and 1290 there appears for the first time a secular music, that of the troubadours, trouvères, and minnesingers. Thereafter secular music becomes more and more dominant. Among the leading musical compositions the percentage of religious compositions falls to 42 per cent in the seventeenth and eighteenth centuries, 21 in the nineteenth, and 5 in the

[4] Cf. the figures and diagrams in *Dynamics*, Vol. I, Chps. 10-13; *passim*.

twentieth. The percentages of secular compositions rise, respectively, to 58, 58, 79, and 95 per cent.

In literature likewise, for the period from the fifth to the tenth century, there is almost no secular masterpiece. The works of the Graeco-Roman poets and other writers used are so drastically remodelled and subjected to such rigorous symbolic interpretation that they have little in common with their originals and serve as a mere adjunct of religious literature. In the ninth, tenth, and eleventh centuries and at the beginning of the twelfth there appear a few semisecular or semireligious works, such as the *Heliand*, the *Hildebrandslied*, *La Chanson de Roland*, and *Le Pèlerinage de Charlemagne*; but we must await the second half of the twelfth century for the emergence of genuinely secular literature. On the other hand, in the literature of the eighteenth to the twentieth century the percentage of secular works rises to 80-90 per cent, according to the country.

In architecture virtually almost all the foremost creations of the Middle Ages were cathedrals, churches, monasteries, and abbeys. They dominated the skyline of the cities and villages, embodying the creative genius of medieval architecture. During the last few centuries, on the other hand, the overwhelming majority of architectural creations have been secular in character—the palaces of the secular rulers, the mansions of the rich and powerful, town halls, business buildings, railroad stations, museums, concert halls, theatres, opera houses, and the like. Amid such structures as the Empire State and Chrysler Buildings, Radio City, and the towers of the great metropolitan dailies, even the vast cathedrals of our cities are lost.

These unquestionable facts leave no doubt

Style	Before the 10th	10th-11th	12th-13th	14th-15th
Visual (sensate)	13.4	2.3	6.0	53.6
Ideational (formal, symbolic)	77.0	92.2	51.1	29.2
Expressionistic	....	....	....	....
Mixed	9.6	5.5	42.9	17.2

Style	16th	17th	18th	19th	20th
Visual (sensate)	72.0	90.6	96.4	95.5	61.5
Ideational (formal, symbolic)	20.3	5.9	2.5	0.3	0.7
Expressionistic	....	....	....	2.8	35.5
Mixed	7.7	3.5	1.1	1.4	2.3

as to the ideational character of the medieval fine arts and the secular nature of those of the last four centuries, especially from the eighteenth to the twentieth. They show how exactly this change proceeded, from century to century. Among other things, they indicate that in the topics treated the art of the thirteenth century was still overwhelmingly religious.

Another important aspect of ideational-idealistic and sensate art is its external style, whether it be formal and symbolic or visually and audibly sensate. The change in this respect is outlined by the above summary data concerning the percentage of each specified style of European pictures and sculpture for the centuries in question.

(Figure 8 sums up pictorially the preceding figures, showing the rise of the sensate wave from 1200 to 1930. It shows also the movement of other additional characteristics.)

The overwhelmingly ideational (symbolic, hieratic, formal) style of the medieval centuries and the pre-eminently visual, or sensate, style of the last five centuries are now sufficiently clear. The thirteenth and fourteenth centuries mark the first sharp decline in the domination of the ideational style in favor of first the idealistic and then the sensate form. The twentieth century is characterized by a sharp decline in the visual-sensate style and a marked increase in the expressionistic manner, thus breaking the trend that prevailed from the thirteenth to the nineteenth centuries, inclusive. In a modified form similar great shifts have occurred in other fine arts.

In literature we witness a decrease, after the twelfth century, in purely religious—and thus symbolic—literature in favor of the essentially allegorical literature of the thirteenth to the fifteenth century and of the realistic, naturalistic manner of the last four centuries.

In music we observe a decrease in the simple, ethereal music of the chants and an increase in music ever richer in its sensory embellishment and trimmings. This manifested itself in a replacement of the unadorned unisonous music of the chants by polyphony, counterpoint, and fugue; by harmony, or monophony; by complicated rhythms and dynamic contrasts; by an increasing number and diversity of instruments; and by all the other elaborate technical means characteristic of the music of the seventeenth to the twentieth century. Finally, the present century introduced such innovations as the wholenote scale, atonality, and cacophony. We must not forget that the famous Roman *Schola* in the time of Saint Gregory had only seven singers. Even much later, despite the luxury of the papal Sistine Chapel, there were hardly more than thirty-seven singers, and these were reduced in the time of Palestrina (*c.* 1565) to twenty-four. There was no orchestra and no instrumental accompaniment. Then, step by step, the choruses and instrumental means progressed both in quantity and in quality. Monteverde's *Orpheus* (1607) was scored for about thirty instruments; the orchestras of Bach, Lulli, and Stamitz were of the same size. Most of the notable symphonies of the eighteenth century (from Mozart to Beethoven) were scored for a still larger number of instruments, about sixty. Those of the nineteenth and twentieth centuries (from Berlioz and Wagner to Mahler, Richard Strauss, and Stravinsky) are scored for a hundred or more

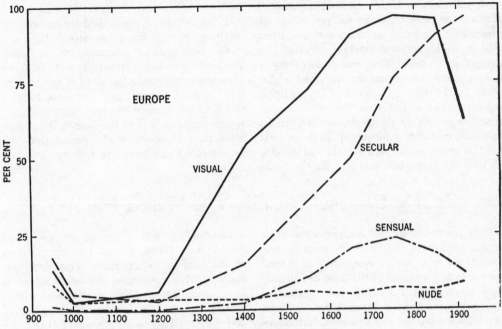

Figure 8. Rise of the Sensate Wave.

instruments. Such has been the course of the qualitative and quantitative evolution of music during the sensate centuries.

In architecture the trend, up to the recent years of the twentieth century, was in the same direction, that of sensateness—from the Romanesque and Gothic to the over-ornate flamboyant Gothic, the imitative styles of the Renaissance, the showy baroque, the still more puerile rococo, and finally, in the nineteenth century, the over-decorative, incoherent Victorian manner and successive waves of imitation of the Gothic, Romanesque, Moorish, and so on. These styles are marked by display and ornamentation, utility, and eclecticism. The twentieth century gives, as we shall see, the

first signs of hope, that of a new integration.

Other relevant characteristics demonstrate the same shifts of the western fine arts as are indicated by the transformation of their topics and style. Take, for instance, the *other-worldly-ascetic* and the *sensual atmosphere* of pictures and sculptures. In those of the medieval period from the sixth to the fourteenth century the percentage of sensual works fluctuates between zero and 0.8 per cent. In recent centuries it rises to 20.2 for the seventeenth, 23.6 for the eighteenth, and 18.4 for the nineteenth; and then recedes to 11.9 for the twentieth, as the crisis century. The Middle Ages disclose no picture or sculpture of extremely sensuous or sexual character, and a notable proportion of

Centuries	Paysage	Portrait	Genre	Love Scenes
Before the 10th	0	1.4	5.4	0
10 to 11th	0	0.4	1.6	0
12th to 13th	0	0.9	0.5	0
14th to 15th	0.1	6.6	4.1	0
16th	1.6	11.5	5.3	(From 3 to 47
17th	2.9	17.8	14.9	per cent, de-
18th	6.6	21.8	25.3	pending upon
19th	15.4	18.9	35.9	the country)
20th	21.6	18.0	37.4[5]	

[5] Those who desire more detailed figures as to these and several additional traits can find them in my *Dynamics*, Vol. I, Chps. 5-13.

medieval works are highly spiritual and ascetic. For the last three centuries the percentage of preeminently spiritual paintings and sculptures falls to an insignificant fraction, whereas the percentage of strongly sensual pictures shows a sharp upswing, especially from the eighteenth to the twentieth century. In medieval representations of the nude the percentage of eroticism is zero up to the thirteenth century; in recent centuries it mounts to 21.3 per cent for the seventeenth, 36.4 for the eighteenth, 25.1 for the nineteenth, and 38.1 for the twen-

tieth. Other symptomatic characteristics for the pictures and sculptures studied are represented by the percentage figures on page 601.

For our present purposes the foregoing statistics are sufficient to corroborate the above statements concerning the trend of the western fine arts from the medieval ideational form to the idealistic form of the thirteenth and fourteenth centuries and to the sensate form characteristic particularly of the period from the seventeenth to the twentieth century.

III. The Contemporary Crisis in the Western Fine Arts

This brings us to the contemporary crisis in the fine arts of the West. Wherein does it consist and what are its symptoms? A general answer as to the nature of the crisis has already been given; it consists in the disintegration of the sensate form of the fine arts that has been dominant for the last five centuries. In the second part of the nineteenth and in the twentieth century it reached its over-ripe stage, and it has subsequently tended to become progressively more hollow and self-contradictory. This increasing vacuity makes it more and more sterile and should enlist increasing revolt. Its mounting self-contradictions widen enormously its inner dualism and progressively destroy its unity, indeed, its very nature.

1. The Achievements of Our Sensate Art

The achievements of sensate western art are both prolific and illustrious. In its technical aspects it is possibly more masterly than the sensate art of any other age or culture. Our art masters are unequalled in their command of technical resources. They can imitate primitive art, the art of Phidias or Polygnotus, that of the Gothic cathedrals or Egyptian temples, of Raphael or Michelangelo, of Homer or Dante, of Palestrina or Bach, of the Greek or medieval theater. In addition, the fine arts of modern western culture have achieved chefs-d'oeuvre unknown to previous periods.

Quantitatively, our culture has produced art creations unexampled either in volume or in size. Our buildings dwarf the hugest structures of the past, our orchestras and choruses make those of the past seem actually Lilli-

putian, and the same is true of our novels and poems. As a result, our art touches the lives of the masses to an extent heretofore unknown. It has penetrated the whole of social life and all the products of civilization, from prosaic tools and instruments (such as knives and forks, tables, and automobiles) to the appointments of the home, dress, and what not. Whereas music, pictures and sculpture, poems and drama, were formerly accessible only to the select few who were fortunate enough to be in a room where the music was played, the picture or sculpture was exhibited, the poem was read, or the drama was performed, at the present time almost anyone can enjoy symphonies played by the best orchestras, dramas performed by the best actors, literary masterpieces published in thousands, sold for a price available to millions, and accessible in multitudes of public libraries; sculpture and pictures in the original, exhibited in public museums and reproduced in millions of excellent copies, and so on. With the expenditure of the slightest amount of energy almost anyone can be in touch nowadays with almost any object of art.

Another significant merit of our art is its infinite diversity and variety, a typical characteristic of any sensate art. It is not restricted to any one style or any one field, as was the art of many past epochs. It is so rich in its variety that almost anyone possessed of any degree of taste can find in it something that meets his approval. Primitive, archaic, Egyptian, Oriental, Greek, Roman, medieval, classic and romantic, expressionistic and impressionistic, realistic and idealistic, Renaissance, baroque, rococo, visual and tactile, ideational and sensate, cubistic, futuristic, and old-fashioned, religious and secular, conservative and revolutionary, saintly and erotic—all these styles and patterns, and hosts of others, are present in our art. It is like an encyclopedia or gigantic department store where one can find anything he is looking for. Such diversity, on so vast a scale, has never before been exhibited by any sensate art. It is a unique phenomenon, one meritorious rather than blameworthy.

Finally, respecting the inner value of its foremost creations, western sensate art requires no apologia. Bach, Mozart, and Beethoven; Wagner, Brahms, and Tschaikowsky, need not apologize to any composer of any previous period. A similar generalization holds good for Shakespeare, Goethe, and Schiller; Chateaubriand, Hugo, and Balzac; Dickens, Tolstoi, and Dostoevski; for the builders of the mightiest skyscrapers; for the most eminent actors; or for the most distinguished painters and sculptors from the Renaissance to the present time. Any master of our sensate art is as competent in his own field as almost any master of earlier periods and cultures.

In all these respects contemporary art has enormously enriched man's culture and immensely ennobled man himself.

2. Maladies of Our Sensate Art

But side by side with these superlative achievements, our sensate art contains the inherent disease germs of its own decay and degeneration. So long as it is still growing and maturing, they are not virulent. But when it has finally exhausted most of its truly creative forces, they become active and turn many a virtue of sensate art into a vice. The process usually leads to the growing aridity and sterility of its decadent stage, and then to its disintegration.

More precisely, first, *the function of giving enjoyment and pleasure leads any sensate art at its decadent stage to degrade its own values to a mere means of sensual enjoyment.* As a mere means of amusement, contemporary art naturally degrades itself to this level. From the realm of the absolute it sinks to the level of commodity values. No wonder that it even-

tually comes to be so regarded both by the public and by the artists themselves! It becomes a mere adjunct of advertisements of coffee, drugs, gasoline, chewing gum, and the like. This is clearly brought out by radio, newspaper, poster, and movie art. Not only the dubious art values of the moment but even the greatest art values of the masters are nowadays degraded to the level of such an adjunct. Any day one may hear a selection from Beethoven or Bach as an appendage to the eloquent advertising of such commodities as oil, banking facilities, automobiles, cereals, and laxatives. Rembrandt's or Praxiteles' creations are used as labels for soap, beer, razor blades, or silk stockings. They become mere "satellites" of the more "solid" enjoyments, such as a bag of popcorn, a glass of beer, a highball, or a pork chop consumed at popular concerts or art exhibitions.

The second malady of sensate art is its *tendency to become more and more superficial in its reflection and recreation of the sensory world itself.* As we have seen, it strives to reproduce the world as this appears to our sense organs. It does not posit any supersensory value behind the sensory forms. It stands or falls according to its ability to reflect and reproduce this sensory world as faithfully as possible. Such a function necessarily restricts it chiefly to mere surface phenomena. Sensate music stands or falls in accordance with its surface values, as a combination of sounds. Behind and beyond the sounds there is no supersensory value to refer to. Sensate literature, again, is simply the "behavioristic reflection" of surface psychology, surface events, surface personages. Every one of the sensate arts, even at its climax, is thus doomed to portray merely the superficial appearance of the phenomena depicted. In this respect it is a twin sister of snapshot photography. It was no accident that the latter art was invented exactly at the moment when the sensate art of the West had become decadent and impressionistic. Like photography, sensate art can "shoot" any object or phenomenon of the sensory world in its surface aspects. No wonder that photography, being simpler, more mechanical, and cheaper, has successfully driven many a form of sensate art from the market.

The foregoing malady leads, in turn, to a

third: *the morbid concentration of sensate art on pathological types of persons and events.* Both Greek art (before the third century B.C.) and that of the Middle Ages immortalized the mortals, shunned the prosaic and mediocre, as well as the vulgar and the negative and pathological.

As we pass from the Middle Ages to more recent centuries the scene changes. These ennobling and idealizing tendencies tend to disappear, their place being taken increasingly by their opposites. When we come to the art of the present day, the contrast, as has already been observed, is well-nigh shocking. Contemporary art mortalizes the immortals, stripping them of everything divine and noble. Likewise, it ignores almost all that is divine and noble in man, in his social life and his culture, sadistically concentrating on the mediocre, and especially on the negative, the pathological, the subsocial and subhuman. In music and literature, painting and sculpture, the theater and drama, it chooses as its "heroes" either the ordinary, prosaic types of human beings or the negative and pathological. The same is true also of the events with which it deals. Housewives, farmers and laborers, businessmen and salesmen, stenographers, politicians, doctors, lawyers, and ministers, and especially detectives, criminals, gangsters, and "double-crossers," the cruel, the disloyal, hypocrites, prostitutes and mistresses, the sexually abnormal, the insane, clowns, street urchins, or adventurers—such are the "heroes" of contemporary art in all its principal fields. God, saints, and real heroes are, as a rule, conspicuous by their absence. Even when—as an exception—a contemporary novel, biography, or historical work chooses a noble or heroic theme (such as George Washington, Byron, or some saint), it proceeds, in accordance with the prevailing psychoanalytical method, thoroughly to "debunk" its hero.

Contemporary art is primarily a museum of social and cultural pathology. It centers in the police morgue, the criminal's hide-out, and the sex organs, operating mainly on the level of social sewers.

Fourth, *the diversity of sensate art results eventually in a growing incoherence and disintegration.* What a medley of heterogeneous styles, patterns, and forms it displays, from the imitative archaic, primitive, classic, and romantic styles to the most bizarre modern forms! Taken as a whole, it is an inchoate complex, devoid of unity or harmony. Inasmuch as any art worthy of the name must be integrated, this unintegrated agglomeration is inevitably incoherent.

This incoherence is still further accentuated by the waves of imitation which have uniformly emerged during the later stages of sensate art. The more decadent it becomes, the more imitative it grows and the swifter becomes the tempo of the successive phases of the process. Its creative potentialities being exhausted, sensate art relies increasingly upon a sophisticated imitation of earlier styles and patterns, beginning with primitive and archaic art and ending with the classical, ideational, idealistic, romantic, neo-classic, or neo-romantic style, according to the preference of the artist and the demands of the market.

Finally, the disintegration manifests itself *in increasing subordination of quality to quantity, of inner content and genius to means and techniques.* Sensate art has to be sensational, so it achieves its effects by quantitative appeal. Hence the disease of colossality, typical of the decadent sensate phase of Graeco-Roman and present-day art. A confusion of greatness calls the biggest the best. This leads inevitably to qualitative deterioration; hence the inner emptiness of our biggest creations. Decadent periods are marked by the substitution of means for ends, of technical skills for genuine creativeness. The greater the attention to technique, the greater the neglect of the central, inner end-values. We seem to forget that, after all, technique is a mere means, not the end of creative work. Concentration upon technique, instead of upon the creative end-values, is a sign of the bankruptcy of genius.

3. The Revolt Against Sensate Art

All these consequences are spontaneously generated by sensate art in the process of its development. They are definite symptoms of its growing disintegration, which became so unequivocal that the revolt against sensate art had already broken out at the close of the nineteenth century, after the decline of the impressionistic school in painting and sculpture and in other fields of the fine arts. Impressionism represented the farthest limit of sensate art. Its motto was to reflect the surface of sensory reality as it appears to our eyes or other senses at a given moment. *What* to render was wholly unimportant. The important thing was to produce an illusion of the appearance of the person, landscape, or thing represented. Hence a given landscape, since it looks different at different times, might become the subject of a series of different paintings. In all these respects the impressionistic school constituted the uttermost limit of a sensate art based on momentary glimpses of mere surface phenomena. No further development in this direction was possible.

After its brief heyday, impressionism declined under the assaults of hostile criticism. Its place was taken by cubists, surrealists, futurists, pointillists, expressionists, Dadaists, constructivists, and other "ists," not only in painting and sculpture but also in other fields of the fine arts. Whether in painting and sculpture, in architecture, in music, in literature, or in the drama, these modernists openly revolted against the decadent sensate art. They refused to reproduce the mere visual surface of phenomena, as does sensate art. What they strove to present is substantiality, the three-dimensional materiality, beneath the visual surface. Hence their cubist planes and similar technical devices, so strange to a sensate person. Again, they rebelled against an art debased to a mere instrument of pleasure and entertainment. Hence their music, so discordant to the habitual sensate ear; hence their literature, which appears so unpleasant and indigestible to the habitual readers of sensate fiction; hence their eccentric and incomprehensible sculpture. In a word, the modernists take issue with almost all the basic characteristics of declining sensate art. The revolt is both fundamental and relatively successful. Modernism is destined to enjoy a fairly long lease of life. It may be seen at any museum or it may be heard at almost any concert; it is solidly entrenched in the field of architecture; it has invaded both literature and the drama.

Most of the leading composers—for example, Stravinsky, Prokofieff, Hindemith, Honegger, Schönberg, Berg, and Shostakovitch —are modernists. In painting and sculpture the proportion of modernist works rose from zero in the eighteenth century to 2.8 per cent in the nineteenth and 35.5 per cent in the period from 1900 to 1920. A similar situation prevails in the other fine arts. Such a successful revolution is in itself sufficient evidence of the disintegration of our sensate art. Together with other symptoms, it establishes beyond any doubt the profound gravity of the crisis.

Does this mean that modernism is a new organic form of western art destined to dominate the succeeding decades or centuries? Such a diagnosis is hardly sound. More accurate is the conclusion that modern art is one transition from a disintegrating sensate to an ideational or idealistic form. As such, it is revolutionary vis-à-vis the dominant sensate form. But it has not yet arrived at any definite goal. Whereas its negative program is as clear as any merely negative program of revolution can be, its positive program has not yet emerged. If the style of modernist art is definitely divorced from that of sensate art, its content still remains thoroughly sensate. It does not attempt to depict anything supersensory.

The communists and fascists in politics are the analogues of the modernists in the fine arts. Both groups are in rebellion against the dominant sensate politico-economic and art systems; but both are essentially sensate. Accordingly, neither group can constitute the politico-economic or art system of the future. They are mainly destroyers and rebels, not constructive builders. They flourish only under the conditions peculiar to a period of transition. Whether we like it or not, sensate art seems to have performed its mission. After the decline of the ideational culture of the Middle Ages, it infused new vitality into the art of the West; produced for four centuries notable values and evolved unique standards; and finally exhausted its creative forces and, together with the whole system of sensate culture, began to show increasing signs of fatigue, sterility, perversion, and decadence. This decadence is now in full swing. After the travail and chaos of the transition period, a new art, ideational or idealistic, will perpetuate in a new guise the perennial creative élan of human culture.[6]

---

[6] See the details in *Dynamics*, Vol. I, Chps. 8-13.

IV. Conclusion

We have demonstrated above that there are indeed ideational, idealistic, and sensate fine arts, and that these forms have been given in many cultures of the past and of the present, as dominant forms (never embracing 100 per cent of all fine art phenomena of a given culture). In their life history these forms fluctuate in their growth and decline, now one, now another form becoming dominant; in the history of the Creto-Mycaenean, Graeco-Roman and the western cultures we marked the centuries of emergence, growth, and decline of each form of art. We have diagnosed the process of disintegration of sensate art of our times, and we can now see and test whether the fluctuation of domination and decline of these forms of the fine arts have been going on hand in hand with the fluctuation of domination and decline of ideational, sensate, idealistic systems of truth (science, philosophy, religion), law and ethics, economics and politics. Let us glance at these fluctuations.

Chapter 41. Growth, Fluctuation, and Decline of Main Systems of Truth, Cognition, and Knowledge

I. Three Systems of Truth

1. The Problems

Testing our hypothesis respecting the existence and dynamics of three supersystems, let us now see whether there are actually three different systems of truth, congnition, and knowledge, each corresponding to the three major premises of the supersystems; whether such systems have been embodied in empirical cultures; whether they have fluctuated in their domination; and, finally, whether the main fluctuations of each system in the history of the Graeco-Roman and western cultures went hand in hand, in the major movements, with the fluctuations of the corresponding form of the fine arts. If the answers to all these questions are in the affirmative, this will prove that there have indeed existed sensate, idealistic, and ideational supersystems consisting, at least, of integrated systems of the fine arts and of systems of truth (namely, science, philosophy, and religion).

The answers are indeed in the affirmative. There have been three major systems of truth, cognition, or knowledge each corresponding to the meaningful nature of each of the major premises.

2. The Ideational System (or Ideational Religion, Science, Philosophy)

Ideational truth is indeed the truth revealed by the grace of God through his mouthpieces (the prophets, mystics, oracles, and founders of religion), disclosed in a supersensory way through mystic experience, direct revelation, divine intuition, and inspiration. *It is the truth of faith.* Since the true reality or value is a supersensory God, it cannot be adequately apprehended through sensory experience or logical reasoning. Ideational science, philosophy, and religion are concerned primarily with supersensory reality and values. The basic truth of the ideational system is that of its religion, next to its theology, and then of its philosophy and science as handmaids of religion and theology. The revealed truth appears to its followers as absolutely valid and infallible, free from any relativity and doubt. Since, according to the major premise, sensory reality and values are not the true reality and values, the ideational system of truth is little interested in the study of the physical, chemical, and biological properties of the empirical world. Hence it makes few, if any, discoveries in the field of empirical science, and few technological inventions calculated to increase material comfort and raise material standards. It is engrossed in the supersensory world, dedicated to the eternal verities, in contradistinction to the temporal truth of the senses. It is absolutistic, nonutilitarian, and nonpragmatic.

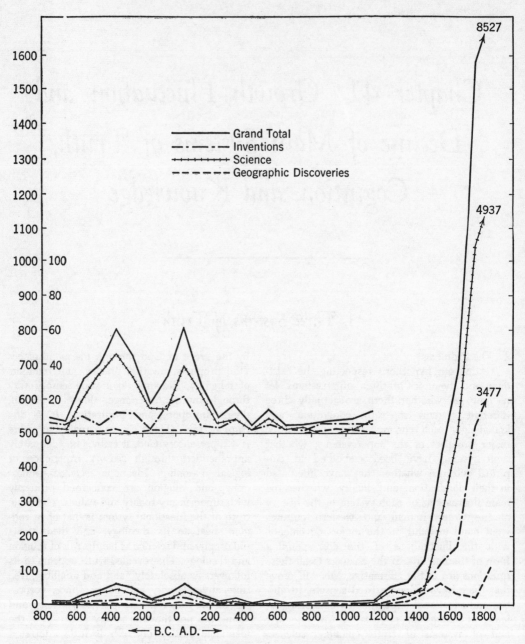

Figure 9. Number of Scientific Discoveries and Inventions,
800 B.C. to 1900 A.D., by Centuries.

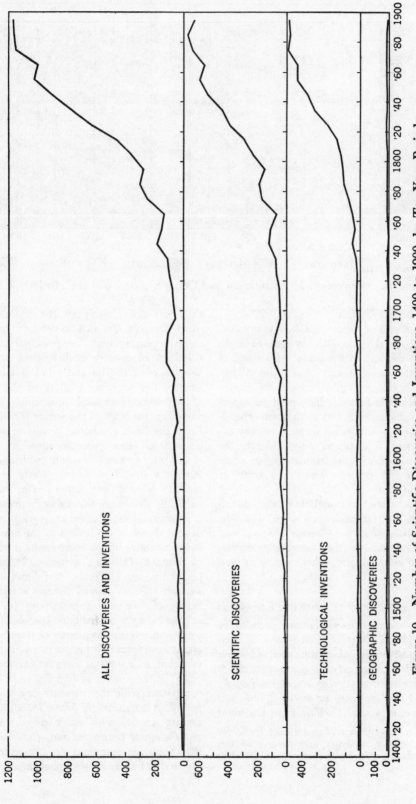

Figure 10. Number of Scientific Discoveries and Inventions, 1400 to 1900, by Ten-Year Periods.

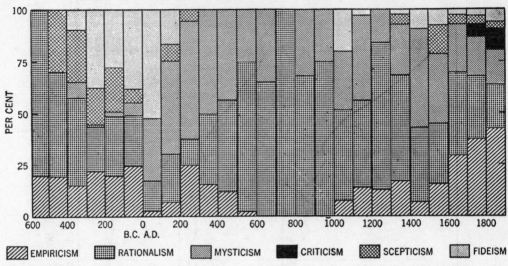

Figure 11. Movement of Empiricism and Other Systems, 600 B.C. to 1900 A.D.

3. The Idealistic System

As a synthesis of sensory, rational, and supersensory truth the idealistic system of truth recognizes the role of the sense organs and of reason as the source and criterion of the validity or invalidity of a proposition concerning sensory and rational phenomena. In regard to supersensory phenomena it claims that any knowledge of these is impossible through sensory experience and is obtained only through the direct revelation of God. Human reason combines into one organic whole the truth of senses, the truth of faith, and the truth of reason. These are the essentials of the idealistic system of truth and knowledge. The systems of Plato, Aristotle, Albertus Magnus, and Thomas Aquinas are the supreme examples, embracing in one organic whole, divine as well as sensory and dialectic truth.[1]

4. The Sensate System of Truth and Knowledge

Since, according to the major premise of sensate culture, the true-reality value is sensory, cognition is obviously derived only through the sense organs. Sensate truth is mainly the truth of the senses. John Locke's dictum, *Nihil esse in intellectu quod non fuerit prius in sensu* (Nothing is in the mind

[1] For the development of systems of truth, for detailed statistics, analyses, and sources of this chapter, cf. my *Dynamics*, Vol. II, Chps. 1-3; *passim.*

that was not already in the sense), is its exact formula. In this system of truth the sense organs become the principal source of cognition of sensory reality; their testimony decides what is true and what is false; they become the supreme arbiters of the validity of any experience and proposition. Another name for this truth of the senses is empiricism. From the basic character of sensory truth are derived its other characteristics.

(a) Any system of sensate truth and reality implies a *denial of, or an utterly indifferent attitude toward, any supersensory reality or value.* By definition, supersensory reality either is nonexistent or, if it exists, is unknowable to us and therefore equivalent to the nonexistent. Being unknowable, it is irrelevant and devoid of interest (Kantian criticism, agnosticism, positivism, etc.). Hence it follows that the sensory cultures regard investigations of the nature of God and supersensory phenomena as superstitious or fruitless speculation. Theology and religion, as a body of revealed truth, are at best tolerated, just as many hobbies are tolerated, or are given mere lip service.

(b) If the sensate system disfavors any preoccupation with the supersensory aspects of reality, *it most strongly favors the study of the sensory world, with its physical, chemical, and biological properties and relationships.* All the cognitive aspirations are concentrated on the study of these sensory phenomena, in their materiality and observable relationships, and on the technological inventions that aim to serve our sensory needs. Knowledge becomes equivalent to the empirical knowledge represented by the natural sciences. Hence in a sensate system of truth natural science replaces religion, theology, and even speculative philosophy; scientific discoveries and inventions tend to flourish. This generalization is well supported by the data of scientific discoveries and technological inventions. The figures on pages 608 ff. summarize this movement during the centuries studied.

During the ideational centuries of Graeco-Roman fine arts (from the eighth to the sixth centuries B.C.) the number of discoveries and inventions is low. With the second half of the sixth century B.C. the number greatly increases, remaining on a high level up to the fourth century A.D., a period dominated (as we have seen) by a sensate art and (as we

Number of Scientific Discoveries
and Technological Inventions

Centuries	Greece and Rome
8 B.C.	6
7	5
6	31
5	40
4	57
3	45
2	17
1	32
1 A.D.	60
2	18
3	6
4	16
5	4
6	4

	Western Christian Europe
7	4
8	4
9	6
10	7
11	8
12	12
13	53
14	65
15	127
16	429
17	691
18	1574
19	8527
20 (1901-1908)	862

shall see) by the truth of the senses. Beginning with the fifth century A.D., it sharply declines, remaining very low until the thirteenth century, a period dominated by an ideational art and (as we shall see) by ideational truth. Starting with the thirteenth century, it begins to rise more and more rapidly, until in the eighteenth and nineteenth centuries it reaches an unprecedentedly high level, the nineteenth century alone yielding more discoveries and inventions than all the preceding centuries together. Figures 9, 10, and 11 give a pictorial summary of these and subsequent facts.

(c) Sensate truth, or empiricism, as we have seen, rejects any revealed supersensory truth. It discredits also, to a certain extent, reason and logic as the sources of truth until their deductions are corroborated by the testimony of the sense organs. If deductive logic contradicts the testimony of the senses, its deductions are ruled out as false. Therefore in sensate cultures and societies *the empirical systems of philosophy gain in strength, while the systems of philosophy based upon ideational or idealistic truths decline.* This is well attested by the relevant historical facts. For instance, the relative percentages of empiricism among all the other philosophical systems of truth have been as follows in the specified centuries: zero per cent from 600 to 1000 A.D.; 7.7 in the eleventh century; 14.3 in the twelfth; 12.8 in the thirteenth; 7.2 in the fifteenth; 15.8 in the sixteenth; 29.6 in the seventeenth; 37.5 in the eighteenth; 42.6 in the nineteenth; and 53 in 1900-1920. If we add to empiricism the other related systems, such as criticism and scepticism, the empirical system reaches a total of 47.5 per cent in the eighteenth century, 55.7 in the nineteenth, and 72 in 1900-1920. Thus throughout the greater part of the Middle Ages, empiricism remains close to the zero line (Figure 11 gives a pictorial reproduction of the movement of empiricism from 600 B.C. to 1900). We have seen that these centuries were the Blütezeit of the ideational fine arts; they represented likewise *the nadir of scientific discoveries and inventions.* As we pass to the centuries marked by the re-emergence of sensate art and culture we observe that, with minor fluctuations, empiricism, as the truth of the senses, begins to parallel the rising tide of scientific discoveries and inven-

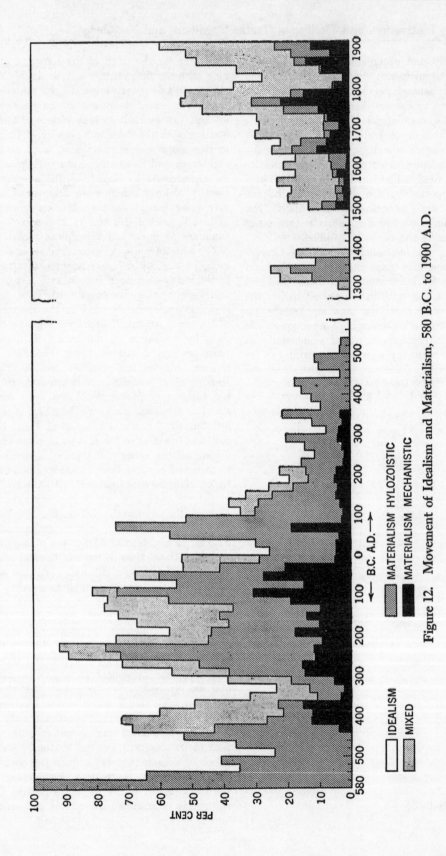

Figure 12. Movement of Idealism and Materialism, 580 B.C. to 1900 A.D.

IDEALISM

MIXED

MATERIALISM HYLOZOISTIC

MATERIALISM MECHANISTIC

B.C. A.D.

tions. In the last two centuries both reached an unprecedentedly high level. On the other hand, the systems of philosophy based upon ideational and idealistic truths move in the opposite direction, constituting from 80 to 100 per cent of all the systems of truth in the period from 600 to 1000 A.D., declining thereafter, with minor fluctuations, to approximately 30 and 12 per cent, respectively, in the nineteenth and twentieth centuries.

In a word, the sensate form of art, the empirical systems of philosophy, sensory truth, scientific discoveries, and technological inventions move in conjunction, rising or declining with the rise or decline of the sensate supersystem of culture. Similarly, ideational and idealistic art, and nonempirical philosophies based upon ideational and idealistic truths, likewise move together. Their movement is essentially opposite to that of sensate art, science, technology, and empirical philosophy.

(d) A fully developed sensate system of truth and cognition is inevitably *materialistic*, viewing everything, openly or covertly, in its materialistic aspects. Whereas the mentality committed to the truth of faith spiritualizes everything, regarding even matter as a mere appearance of supersensory reality, the mentality dominated by the truth of the senses materializes everything even spiritual phenomena themselves, viewing the latter as a mere appearance or as a by-product of material phenomena. Hence the general tendency of the sensate mentality to regard the world—even man, his culture, and consciousness itself—materialistically, mechanistically, behavioristically. Man becomes, in sensate scientific definitions, a "complex of electrons and protons," an animal organism, a reflex mechanism, a variety of stimulus-response relationships, or a psychoanalytical "bag" filled with physiological libido. "Consciousness" is declared to be an inaccurate and subjective term for physiological reflexes and overt actions of a certain kind. All the conceptions and theories predicated upon a spiritual, supersensory, immaterial reality are dismissed as a sort of superstition or ignorance or as a result of the tyranny of misused words. Such a trend manifests itself in hundreds of ways. Our statistical studies show that the periods marked by the growing domination of sensory truth have always been parallel by an intensification of the materialistic mentality and by a corresponding decline of idealistic and ideational philosophy. Thus during the medieval centuries the percentage of the materialistic philosophy among all the other philosophies from 500 to 1300 was zero, and that of the idealistic philosophy and *Weltanschauung*, 100. In the nineteenth and twentieth centuries materialism increased, respectively, to 12.7 and 23.3 per cent; whereas idealism decreased, respectively, to 55.9 and 40.3 per cent, the remainder being represented by composite philosophies blending materialism and idealism. Figure 12 shows this movement pictorially. Scientific theories based upon the truth of the senses tend, as we have seen, to become progressively materialistic, mechanistic, and quantitative, even in their interpretation of man, culture, and mental phenomena. The social and psychological sciences begin to imitate the natural sciences, attempting to treat man in the same way as physics and chemistry treat inorganic phenomena. In the field of the social sciences all mental and cultural phenomena come to be treated behavioristically, physiologically, "reflexologically," "endocrinologically," and psychoanalytically. Society becomes economically minded, and the "economic interpretation of history" begins to hold undisputed sway. A quasi-pornographic conception of human culture acquires a wide vogue in biographies, history, anthropology, sociology, and psychology. Anything spiritual, supersensory, or idealistic is ridiculed, being replaced by the most degrading and debasing interpretations. All this is closely analogous to the negative, warped, subsocial, and psychopathic propensities exhibited by the fine arts during the decadent phase of sensate culture.

In such a culture, material values naturally become paramount, beginning with omnipotent wealth and ending with all the values that satisfy man's physiological needs and material comfort. Sensory utility and pleasure, as we shall see, become the sole criteria of what is good and bad.

(e) A further consequence of such a system of truth is the development of a *temporalistic, relativistic, and nihilistic mentality*. The sensory world is in a state of incessant flux and becoming. There is nothing unchangeable in it, not even an eternal Supreme Being. Mind dominated by the truth of the senses simply cannot perceive any permanency, but apprehends all values in terms of shift and transformation. Sensate mentality views everything from the standpoint of evolution and progress. This leads to an increasing neglect of the eternal values, which come to be replaced by temporary, or short-time considerations. Sensate society lives in, and mainly appreciates the present. Since the past is irretrievable and no longer exists, while the future is not yet here and is uncertain, only the present moment is real and desirable.

Hence the sensate *Carpe diem,* as tomorrow is uncertain; snatch the present kiss; get rich quick; seize the power, popularity, fame, and opportunity of the moment, because only present values can be grasped. As the tempo of change accelerates, this "present" grows ever shorter and more transitory. To the same source is attributable the stupendous role of time in the life and activities of such a society. *Tempus fugit, tempora mutantur et nos mutamur in illis,* and *tempus edax rerum* become the mottoes of the sensate mentality.

(f) From the same system of truth and values follows the doctrine of *relativism.* Since everything is temporal and subject to incessant change, and since sensory perception differs in the case of different organisms, individuals, and groups, nothing absolute exists. Everything becomes relative—truth and error, moral and aesthetic considerations, and what not. A thing may be good today and bad tomorrow; in a given set of conditions a proposition may appear to be true, and under other conditions false. Sensory observation shows that scientific, philosophical, religious, moral, aesthetic, and other values, norms, and beliefs vary according to the individual, the group, and the period. Hence the dictum, "Everything is relative in this world," as the motto of sensate truth; hence its negative attitude toward any absolute whatsoever. But relativism, once accepted, inevitably becomes more and more uncompromising, until finally all relative truths and values are completely "relativized" and reduced, so to speak, to atoms. Sooner or later, relativism thus gives place to scepticism, cynicism, and nihilism. The very boundary line between the true and the false, between right

and wrong, disappears, and society finds itself in a state of veritable mental, moral, and cultural anarchy. No society can long exist under these conditions. Either it perishes or it substitutes another system of truth, one sounder and more adequate to its needs. (See the figures and the diagrams on movement of relativism in Chapter 42.)

(g) All this means that sensory truth, when made exclusive, inevitably develops into a kind of *illusionism,* a replica of impressionistic painting, in which it undermines itself. Instead of valid cognition of the true reality and values, it increasingly gives us relative and conditional hints respecting the ever-fleeting shadows of ever-changing sensory impressions, which differ with different individuals, groups, and conditions. Instead of revealing truth as the *adaequatio intellectus et rei,* it yields mere impressions and artificial constructions relating to something essentially unknowable. Decadent sensory science even declares that it is not concerned with any true reality. In this way sensory truth eventually digs its own grave.

(h) The same system of truth gives rise to the *nominalistic and singularistic mentalities* characteristic of sensate society. Sensory impressions are always singularistic. For example, we cannot perceive the *genus* horse or the *genus* homo, that is, essences, categories, and universals. We perceive only an individual horse or other object, in its sensory appearance. Hence the vogue of nominalism, with its axiom *Universalia sunt nomina;* all universals, categories, concepts, and essences are but mere words, unscientifically used, and corresponding to no objective reality. They are merely the result of the tyranny of words over unscientific minds. Hence the reluctance to recognize the reality of universals and essences. Men prefer, and delight to deal with, concrete phenomena. Such a mentality regards society as simply a sum of interacting individuals. It cannot see the forest for the trees.

(i) Finally, sensate science, philosophy, pseudo-religion and ethics are *utilitarian, hedonistic, pragmatic, operational, and instrumental.* Science and philosophy, as we have seen, come to be imbued with utilitarian aims. Only those disciplines which, like physics and chemistry, biology and medicine, geology and geography, technology, politics and economics, are eminently practical and serviceable are intensively cultivated. Hence the aforesaid progress of the natural and technological sciences. Other disciplines, either metaphysics and "nonpragmatic" philosophy, or transcendental religion and absolute ethics, are relatively ignored. So far as they are cherished, they assume the same utilitarian, sensory, and pragmatic, or instrumental, character. Psychology, as a science of the human soul, turns out to be a physiology of the nervous system and its reflexes. Religion, as a revelation of God, degenerates into a second-hand "social gospel," a sort of political creed. Philosophy turns out to be a second-class sensory utilitarian science composed of empiricism, positivism, neopositivism, pragmatism, criticism, agnosticism, scepticism, instrumentalism, and operationalism—all marked by the same utilitarian and economical traits.

And so with other disciplines. *Savoir pour pouvoir* becomes one of the supreme criteria. Anything that does not permit a utilitarian control tends to be neglected; anything that does is elevated to the dignity of a scientific or valid proposition.

Of like character is the educational system, which is first and foremost a training school devoted to "useful knowledge" and the crafts. Its chief business is to prepare successful businessmen, craftsmen, engineers and technicians, politicians, lawyers, doctors, teachers, preachers, and so on. Mastery is sought in such arts as amassing a fortune, farming, home cooking, barbering, the invention of machines, research work, teaching, and preaching. Elementary, high-school, and college education, all are oriented principally in the same direction, paying scant attention, if any, to the forgotten purpose of real knowledge and wisdom: the nature of true reality and true values. Since this is deemed devoid of any immediate, short-time sensory utility, it is given merely lip service, playing little part in the actual curriculum of the schools of sensate society.

Such, in brief, are some of the characteristics of the system of sensory truth.

5. Contrast Between Ideational and Sensate Truths

The foregoing discussion of the three systems of truth has shown that each is derived from the major premise of one of our three supersystems of culture. It is necessary to realize clearly the profound difference, in particular, between the ideational truth of faith and the sensate truth of the senses. *If either is regarded as "the truth, the whole truth, and nothing but the truth," the two become mutually irreconcilable.* What appears true from the standpoint of ideational truth is ignorance and superstition from the standpoint of sensate truth, and vice versa. Many a revealed truth of religion is utterly false from the point of view of an exclusive truth of the senses, and vice versa. This explains the sharp clash of these systems of truth that marks especially the periods of decline of the one and the rise of the other. The shifts from one system to the other give us the greatest mental revolutions. An excellent example is furnished by the clash between the emerging revealed truth of Christianity and the sensory truth dominant in the Graeco-Roman society of the first centuries of our era. To the Pagan Graeco-Roman thinkers, swayed by the truth of the senses, Christian revealed truth appeared but mere superstition and ignorance. The foremost intellectuals of the time, like Tacitus, called it "dangerous superstition," "infamous and abominable." Pliny characterized it as "nothing but a debased superstition carried to an extreme." To Marcus Aurelius it was only an unreasoned and intemperate spirit of opposition; to Suetonius it was "a novel and maleficent superstition." Celsus regarded the Christians as "illogical folk. . . . They will not reason or listen to reason about their faith, but stick to their 'Ask no question but believe,' or 'Thy faith shall save thee,' or 'The wisdom of the world is a bad thing and the foolishness a good.'" To Celsus, as to other partisans of sensory truth, the Christians, with their truth of faith, were mere charlatans, ignoramuses, prestidigitators, and the like. Even Christ and the Apostles were ignorant and "notorious vagabonds"; the Virgin Mary, a girl with an illegitimate child, and so on. From the point of view of sensory truth, the Christian truth of faith, revelation, and God—indeed the whole Christian religion and movement—could not appear other than an absurdity and superstition.

On the other hand, from the standpoint of

the revealed truth of Christianity, the truth of the senses and the sensory knowledge derived from it could not appear anything but foolishness. As Saint Paul formulates the principle, "The wisdom of this world is foolishness with God." Other early Christians and all the Church Fathers designate sensory knowledge as "doubtful, uncertain, and probable rather than true" (Minucius Felix); as a mere "vanity" (Basil the Great); as "deceit and tricks," "babbling," "lies," "errors," and the like (Saint Augustine); as something that is misleading; and, finally, as something opposed to the truth (Tertullian, Origen, *et alii*). Tertullian's famous statement sums this up very cogently: "*Cruxifixus est Dei Filius; non pudet, quia pudendum est. Et Mortuus est Dei Filius; prorsus credibile est, quia ineptum est. Et sepultus resurrexit; certum est, quia impossibile est.*" [The son of God is crucified; that is not shameful because it is shameful (that is, from the sensate standpoint). And the Son of God died; that is credible because it is absurd. And He rose from the dead; that is quite certain because it is impossible.]

In this statement the clash is formulated in the most masterly manner. What is impossible or untrue from the sensate standpoint may be possible and quite true from the standpoint of the Christian truth of faith, and vice versa.

The clash of these two systems was as sharp as possible and lasted for centuries, until Christian faith emerged victorious around the sixth century. This system was not much concerned with empirical knowledge, which was deemed a second-hand truth, being admitted as a "handmaid" so far as it did not contradict the supersensory, superlogical, and superrational revealed truth of Christianity. Its simple objective was excellently formulated by Saint Augustine. It reduced itself exclusively to the knowledge of God and of the soul. *Deum et animam scire cupio. Nihilne plus? Nihil omnino*—such is the categoric formula of this system of thought.

If we now turn to the Renaissance, when the submerged truth of the senses re-emerged and began rapidly to drive out the revealed truth of Christianity, we note that the clash was as sharp then as it was at the period of the rise of Christian truth, with revealed truth now on the defensive and sensory truth taking the offensive.

It must be clear that the whole mentality of human society—what is regarded as true or false, knowledge or ignorance, the nature of education and the curricula of the schools—all this differs according to the dominant system of truth accepted by a given culture and society.

II. Fluctuation of the Growth and Decline of the Three Systems of Truth

1. Parallel Fluctuations in Systems of Truth and Those of the Fine Arts

When the totality of the relevant evidence is considered, it demonstrates clearly that in the history of the Creto-Mycenaean, Graeco-Roman, and Western cultures the three systems of truth fluctuated in their rise and decline and that the principal fluctuations of each system of truth were tangibly parallel to those of the corresponding systems of the fine arts.[2]

The latest stage of the Creto-Mycenaean culture was characterized by the dominance

of the sensate fine arts as well as the sensate system of truth.

From the eighth to the sixth century B.C., Greek culture was essentially ideational both in its system of art and in that of truth. Homer's, Hesiod's, and the Orphic and Pythagorean worlds are those of gods. The ideational mentality was even more strongly developed among the less sophisticated masses. Hence there were few scientific discoveries and inventions. Empiricism and mechanistic materialism, as philosophies, were either nonexistent or played a minor role.

From the second part of the sixth century B.C., when sensate truth began to re-emerge and ideational truth began to decline (parallel

---

[2] The tables and diagrams given above show the fluctuations outlined in this summary. They are taken from my *Dynamics*, Vol. II.

with a similar change in the fine arts), to the end of the fourth century B.C., the idealistic system of art and truth prevailed, as a synthesis of the sensate and ideational systems. It exhibited a notable increase of scientific discoveries and inventions.

With considerable fluctuations, due to the merging of Hellenistic, Roman, and Oriental cultures, the period from the end of the fourth century B.C. to approximately the close of the fourth century A.D. presents a mixed picture, with the sensate system of art and truth dominant over its opponents. It is marked by a decline of the traditional Graeco-Roman religion; by a fairly large number of scientific discoveries and inventions, and other sensate traits.

The fourth century witnessed the legalization and socialization of the ideational system of Christianity, which emerged at the beginning of our era and slowly developed during the first centuries of its existence. Now it became the dominant religion and system of truth, and with its further growth it ushered in the Christian medieval culture, with its ideational fine arts and its system of truth, ethics, law, and so on. The period from the fifth century to the end of the twelfth century was characterized by an exceptionally strong development of ideational art and truth, not to mention other fields of medieval culture. This is witnessed by a marked decline of empirical and materialistic philosophy, relativism, utilitarianism, temporalism, and other traits of the sensate mentality, as well as of scientific discoveries and inventions.

Between the end of the twelfth and that of the fourteenth century idealistic systems of art and truth prevailed. Empiricism and a mild form of semimaterialistic monism, utilitarianism, and scientific discoveries and inventions re-emerged. The ideational systems began to decline, the sensate to rise, both currents meeting and producing a synthesis of idealistic forms of art, science, philosophy, and religion.

After the fourteenth century sensate systems of truth and of the fine arts reasserted themselves and have dominated up to the present time. This is revealed by the growth of sensate philosophy (empiricism, materialism, skepticism, and agnosticism); the rapid multiplication of scientific discoveries and inventions;

the pagan spirit of the Italian Renaissance; and the split of Christianity and its ideational culture into the western and eastern branches and later into Catholicism and Protestantism, each of which exhibited a further cleavage into various sects, heresies, and schisms. All branches of Christianity henceforth showed decreasing creativity, some becoming mainly ritualistic and dogmatic institutions, while others represented a sort of second-hand social gospel.

Finally, the present time witnesses the disintegration of sensate art, as well as of the sensate system of truth.

Thus both "variables"—the systems of art and of truth—have proceeded in their major movements in the same direction, tangibly parallel, each, however, exhibiting its own peculiar minor deviations and fluctuations. When the movements of each system of truth and of its subsidiaries are studied in detail, the curves prove more complex than they are outlined here. Each variable shows many secondary ups and downs, and the periods of rise and decline are less sharply defined and change less abruptly than the outline suggests.

Once again the re-emergence of sensate truth occurred in Italy and France, then spread to other countries, reaching Russia after a lag of from one hundred to one hundred and fifty years. During the nineteenth and twentieth centuries Russia finally attained a position roughly analogous to that of other countries.[3]

2. Crisis of Contemporary Sensate System of Truth

The crisis of the contemporary sensate system of truth is parallel with the crisis of contemporary sensate art, and is at once theoretical and practical. Both aspects manifest themselves in many ways.

(a) The theoretical phase is revealed first, in *a progressive obliteration of the boundary line between sensory truth and falsehood,* reality and fiction, validity and utilitarian convention. Its temporalistic, relativistic, nominalistic, materialistic, and other traits lead to an increasing relativization of sensory truth until

---

[3] For a vast amount of statistical and other evidence, as well as a development of these statements, cf. my *Dynamics*, Vol. II, Chps. 1-4; *passim.*

it becomes indistinguishable from error. The same result is produced by its utilitarian and pragmatic properties. And this is exactly what is happening before our very eyes. The western truth of the senses faces the tragic denouement of its own dethronement. When it is declared that scientific propositions are mere "conventions," and that, of several different conventions, the one which under the circumstances is most convenient, "economical," expedient, useful, or "operational" for a given individual is most true (cf. Henri Poincaré, Karl Pearson, Ernst Mach, William James, *et alii*), the whole fabric of truth and knowledge itself is threatened with collapse. According to this criterion, the dogmas of Stalin or Churchill or Hitler are true because they are most convenient to them. Truth reduced to a norm of mere convenience, or to a mere ideology or "derivation" that glorifies and rationalizes economic and other interests neutralizes itself; for everyone is equally entitled to claim that any ideology is true for the simple reason that it is useful to him. Thus, in this maze of conveniences, conventions, and utilities, thousands of contradictory truths appear, each claiming to be as valid as the others: the truth of capitalists and proletarians, of communists and fascists, of liberals and conservatives, of believers and atheists, of scientists and Christians Scientists, of the privileged and the underdogs.

All this facilitates an explosive upsurge of man's elemental forces and leads men to treat their fellows, individually or in groups, as mere material atoms, electron-proton combinations, or biological organisms. If man is only an atom or electron or organism, why stand on ceremony in dealing with him? (We do not hesitate to scotch a snake or crush an atom!) The halo of sanctity having been stripped from man and his values, human relationships and sociocultural life degenerate into a savage struggle (witness the endless succession of contemporary wars and revolutions!) whose issue is decided by sheer physical force. In this struggle many values are destroyed, among them those of sensory science, or materialistic truth itself.

(b) Sensory science has still further undermined its own values through a progressively increasing relativism and *thin and narrow empiricism divorced from other social values— religion, goodness, beauty and the like.* The divorce of the empirical aspect of reality from its other aspects has tragically narrowed the world of meanings and values and enormously impoverished the infinite richness and creativeness of sociocultural life and cosmic reality, including even sensate happiness itself.

This indifference of empirical science to goodness and beauty has rendered it amoral, even cynical. It has thus become an instrumentality ready to serve any master, whether God or Mammon, and any purpose, whether socially beneficial or disastrous, constructive or destructive. On the one hand, it has created a world replete with beneficial gifts; on the other hand, it has created the most devilish means for the destruction of human life and culture. Poisonous gas, bombs and other explosives, are just as truly the children of empirical science as are refrigerators, medicine, tractors, or similar inventions.

Throughout one half of this planet, freedom of thought and research during at least a decade preceding the Second World War were muzzled by those who specialized in the control of precisely the destructive forces unleashed by empirical science. Science was degraded to the role of a mere handmaid of contemporary "barbarians" who learned well the motto of empiricism: Truth is what is convenient and useful; of several possible conventions, that which is most convenient for me is most true. Hence empirical science, carried to its logical conclusion, once again paved the way for its ultimate downfall and became the greatest danger to humanity.

(c) Finally, because of its enormous and complicated assortment of facts—poorly integrated, often irrelevant, and, despite their alleged precision, frequently contradictory— *empirical science has distinctly impaired our understanding of reality.* The bewilderment engendered by its complexity is heightened by a feeling of uncertainty. Indeed, sensory truth may be said to have ushered in the Age of Incertitude. Its theories are at best hypotheses, marked by contradictions and by incessant change. The world proves increasingly a shadowy jungle, at once unknown and incomprehensible. Such incertitude cannot be tolerated indefinitely. It is inimical to man's happiness, his creativeness, even his survival. In the absence of adequate certainty, he seeks an artificial substitute, even though it be but an illusion. So he did during the decline of the Graeco-Roman sensate culture, in favor of the absolute verities of Christianity; and so he is already doing at the present.

In the face of this difficulty we elaborate endless mechanical indices and bibliographies, digests and abstracts, indices of indices, bibliographies of bibliographies, digests of digests, and abstracts of abstracts. Human life is too short to master such an overwhelming and indiscriminate agglomeration of facts. In our frantic eagerness to know "more and more about less and less" we miss the really essential things. So empirical science eventually begins to obey the law of diminishing returns. It fails increasingly to satisfy man's need for proper orientation in the universe and for an adequate understanding of this universe. Hence the increasing sterility of sensory social and related sciences. Notwithstanding their imposing array of historical, statistical, pseudo-experimental, clinical, and observational data, during the last three decades they have not produced a single new valid generalized theory. At the best they have only reinstated, in a vulgarized and more primitive form, the generalization of the preceding centuries.

The practical failure of the decadent empiricism of contemporary culture is demonstrated by our increasing inability to predict or control the course of the sociocultural processes. On the eve of the war and of enormous economic misery most of the empirical scientists were predicting bigger and better prosperity and lasting peace. As to control, the more economists have tampered with economic conditions, the worse they have become; the more political scientists have reformed governments, the more are governments in need of reform; the more sociologists, psychologists, anthropologists, and lawyers have tampered with the family, the more the family has disintegrated; the more "scientific" solutions are offered for

crime, the more numerous become the crimes, and so on. Despite all the natural and social sciences at our disposal, we are unable either to control the sociocultural processes or to avoid the historical catastrophes. Like a log on the brink of Niagara Falls, we are impelled by unforeseen and irresistible sociocultural currents, helplessly drifting from one crisis and catastrophe to another. Neither happiness, nor safety and security, nor even material comfort has been realized. In few periods of human history have so many millions of persons been so unhappy, so insecure, so hungry and destitute, as at the present time, all the way from China to western Europe. Wars and revolutions, crime, suicide, mental disease, and other evidences of deep-seated social maladies flourish apace, some of them on a scale hitherto unknown. We are witnessing a veritable "blackout" of human culture. Atomic bombs, cosmic-ray bombs, bacteriological means of warfare are hanging over humanity, ready to end its history.

Such are the how and the why of the contemporary crisis of sensory truth, and such are its symptoms. As in the case of other one-sided systems of truth, the immanent forces of sensate truth have eventually wrought its own decline. Whether we want it or not we are in a transitional stage from the declining sensate truth to another more adequate system of truth.

3. Conclusion

The above has shown the fluctuation in togetherness of the fine arts and of systems of truth. Let us now inquire as to whether the supersystems have been embracing also the ethical and law systems and whether art, science, philosophy, religion, of each of the three types have been changing hand in hand with fluctuation of ideational, sensate, and idealistic forms of law and ethics.[4]

[4] See the data, literature and more detailed analysis in *Dynamics*, Vol. II, *passim*.

Chapter 42. Growth, Fluctuation, and Decline of Main Systems of Law, Ethics, and Types of Personality

I. Three Systems of Ethics

Logical deduction from the major premises of each supersystem defines the nature of the ideational, idealistic, and sensate systems of ethics and law. Observation shows not only the empirical existence of such systems in various cultures but also their growth, fluctuation, and decline in parallel to those of the corresponding systems of art and truth in the Graeco-Roman and western cultures. The following are examples of each type of ethical norms and ideals.

1. Ideational Ethical Norms

Lay not up for yourselves treasures upon earth, where moth and rust doth corrupt. But lay up for yourselves treasures in heaven, where neither moth nor rust doth corrupt.

No man can serve two masters: for either he will hate the one, and love the other; or else he will hold to the one, and despise the other. Ye cannot serve God and Mammon. Therefore I say unto you, Take no thought for your life, what ye shall eat, or what ye shall drink; nor yet for your body, what ye shall put on. But seek ye first the kingdom of God, and his righteousness; and all these things shall be added unto you. . . . Love your enemies, bless them that curse you, do good to them that hate you, and pray for them which despitefully use you, and persecute you. Be you therefore perfect, even as your Father which is in heaven is perfect. . . . Our Father which art in heaven.

. . . Thy kingdom come. Thy will be done in earth, as it is in heaven. (*Matthew*, vi: 24, 25, 33, 9, 10; v: 44, 19, 20)

Different in form but similar in content are the ethical systems of Hinduism, Buddhism, Taoism, Zoroastrianism, Judaism, and any other ideational mentality. They all see the supreme ethical value not in this sensory world but in the supersensory world of God or the Absolute; all regard the empirical world of the senses with all its values as a pseudo-value or, at best, as an unimportant and subordinate value.

The good is one thing, the pleasant another; these two, having different objects, chain a man. It is well with him who clings to the good; he who chooses the pleasant misses his end.

Look on this world as you would at a bubble (or mirage). . . . The foolish are immersed in it, but the wise do not touch it.

Wise men . . . care for nothing in this world.

There is no satisfying lusts, even by a shower of gold pieces; he who knows that lusts have a short taste and cause pain, he is wise. He delights only in destruction of all desires.

A man who is free from desires . . . sees the majesty of the nonempirical Self, by the Grace of the Creator. . . . He is the greatest of all men.

The mind approaching the Eternal has attained to the extinction of all desires.

Such are Hinduist and Buddhist expressions of the negative attitude toward all the sensory values—riches, gold, pleasure, and power.

Ideational ethics aims not at an increase of the sensory happiness and pleasures of this world but at the union with the Absolute, which is supersensory. The norms of such ethics are regarded as revealed by, or emanating from, the Absolute; therefore as absolute, unconditional, unchangeable, and eternal. They cannot be disregarded under any conditions or for any other value. If the fulfilment of such norms gives as a by-product some happiness and joy, these remain mere by-products, not the objective of such ethics. If the moral commandments lead to sensory pain and grief, that does not matter either. Sensory happiness or unhappiness, pleasure or pain, are utterly irrelevant for such an ethical ideal.

2. Sensate Ethical Norms

Any ethical system that regards sensory happiness, pleasure, utility, and comfort, in their refined or unrefined form, as the supreme value, is a sensate system of ethics. All purely utilitarian, all hedonistic, even many eudemonistic systems of ethics are varieties of this kind of ethical ideals. Its formulae are well known to us:

The maximum happiness for the maximum number of human beings.

The supreme end is pleasure.

Let us eat, drink, and be merry, for tomorrow we die.

Wine, women, and song.

Follow thy desire, so long as thou livest. . . . Do what thou wishest on earth, and vex not thy heart.

Time is short; let us enjoy it.

There is no heaven, no final liberation, nor any soul in another world. . . . While life remains, let man live happily, let him feed on glee, even though he runs in debt. When once the body becomes ashes, how can it ever return again?

Carpe diem.

Buy a car and be happy.

Such are the eternal Chinese and Hindu, Greek and Roman, Italian and French, English and American, past and present formulae of the more rude and more refined sensate systems of ethics. Their supreme aim is to increase the sum of sensate happiness, pleasure, utility, and comfort, because they do not believe in any supersensory value. Their rules are therefore not absolute but relative, expedient, and changeable, according to the persons, groups, and situations involved. They are regarded as man-made rules. If they serve the purpose of happiness, they are acceptable; if they do not, they may be discarded.

3. Idealistic Ethical Norms

Idealistic ethical norms are an intermediary synthesis of ideational and sensate values. Like ideational ethics, idealist ethics perceives the highest value in God or the supersensory Absolute; but, in contradistinction to ideationalism, it views positively those sensory values that are the noblest and that do not militate against the Absolute. Its formulae likewise have been many.

The perfect happiness of man cannot be other than the vision of the Divine essence. (Saint Thomas Aquinas)

The soul being immortal and able to bear all evil and all good, we shall always hold to the road which leads above. And justice with prudence we shall by all means pursue in order that we may be friends both to ourselves and to the gods, . . . and we shall both here and in that thousand years' journey . . . enjoy a happy life. (Plato-Socrates)

[The *summum bonum,* or perfectly happy life] will be higher than mere human nature, because a man will live thus, not in so far as he is a man, but in so far as there is in him a divine principle. . . . We must . . . make ourselves like immortals and do all with a view to living in accordance with the highest principle in us. (Aristotle)

Be mindful of death. . . . Possessions do not make for happiness. Wealth is unstable. Eat no bread, if another is suffering want, and thou dost not stretch out the hand to him with bread. . . . Be pious, diligent. Be not a drunkard. Lead an honest life. Be respectful. Learn: knowledge is useful. . . . Be careful of women. (Egyptian moral norms)

These formulae range from the highest ideational-idealistic plane almost to the utilitarian-sensate level, as in the Egyptian moral maxims. But the first three formulae are a variety of idealistic ethics. They virtually merge with eudemonistic ethics.

FLUCTUATION OF GROWTH AND DECLINE OF THREE SYSTEMS OF ETHICS

These three systems of ethics have fluctuated in their domination throughout the history of Graeco-Roman and western cultures. Each of them has prevailed in about the same periods during which the ideational, idealistic, and sensate systems of art and truth have been in the ascendancy. The dominant Greek ethics from the eighth to the fifth century B.C. was mainly ideational—that of Greek religion, of Hesiod, Aeschylus, Sophocles, Herodotus, Pindar, and others. They all considered that "human happines does not stay long," is far from being the main value; all regarded the ethical norms as absolute.

This system of ethics began to decline in the fifth century B.C. and was replaced by the idealistic ethics of Socrates, Plato, and Aristotle, with the norms quoted previously. The period from the third century B.C. to about the fourth century A.D. was marked by sensate ethics in its nobler Stoic and Epicurean forms, as well as in the crude forms of naked hedonism and of the code of *Carpe diem*. Even on many a tombstone were inscribed such vulgar sensate maxims as *Es, bibe, lude, veni* (Eat, drink, play, come hither); and "Let us eat, drink and be merry, for tomorrow we die."

After the fourth century A.D. the ideational ethics of Christianity achieved supremacy, remaining unchallenged to the thirteenth century. We know well its maxims. In their sublimest form they are summed up in the Sermon on the Mount. Being derived from God, the moral values of Christian ethics are absolute. Their cardinal principle is the all-embracing, all-bestowing, and all-forgiving love of God for man, of man for God, and of man for man. Their pathos and ethos are derived from this boundless love, and from the charismatic grace, duty, and sacrifice implied in it.

From this attribute of Christian ethics followed the medieval—either negative or indifferent—estimation of all the values of the sensory world as such, from wealth, pleasure, and utility to sensory happiness, when divorced from the supersensory value. This attitude is stressed by medieval monasticism and asceticism and by the medieval outlook on this life as a mere painful preparation for the transition from the sinful City of Man to the eternal City of God.

The uncompromisingly ideational system of ethics then began to give way to the less rigorous idealistic ethics of the thirteenth to the fifteenth century. In the fourteenth and fifteenth centuries sensate ethics re-emerges, flourishing apace during the next century, that of the Renaissance and the Reformation. The hedonism, sensuality, and paganism of the ethics of the Renaissance are well known. Less sensual, but nevertheless sensate and utilitarian, was the ethics of most of the sects of the Reformation, with perhaps an exception in ascetic Protestantism (Calvinism, Pietism, and Methodism). Though masked by its ideational phraseology, the real character of the ethics of Protestantism was largely utilitarian and sensate. Money-making was declared the sign of God's grace; it was elevated to the rank of a primary duty. Says Benjamin Franklin: "Honesty is useful because it assures credit: so are punctuality, industry, frugality, and *that is the reason they are virtues. . . .*" A similar gospel was preached by representatives of other Protestant currents. Early and medieval Christianity had denounced wealth as the source of perdition; money-making, as *summae periculosae*; profit, as a *turpe lucrum*; money-lending, as a grave crime; the rich man as a first candidate for perdition, for whom it was more difficult to enter the kingdom of God than for a camel to go through the eye of a needle. Now the Reformation and the Renaissance made an about-face. "On Sundays he [the Puritan] believes in God and Eternity; on week days, in the stock exchange. On Sundays the Bible is his ledger, and on week days the ledger is his Bible." Hence the parallel growth of Protestantism, paganism, capitalism, utilitarianism, and sensate ethics during the subsequent centuries. The last four centuries have witnessed the supremacy of sensate ethics in western society.

The following tabulation, presenting the per centages of the partisans of the Absolute (ideational and partly idealistic ethics) and of the relative sensate ethics of happiness (hedonism utilitarianism, and eudemonism) among all the eminent ethical thinkers in each specified century, gives a fairly definite idea of the shift outlined.

Period	Sensate Ethics of Happiness (Percentage)	Absolute Ideational Ethics (Percentage)
A.D. 400- 500	0	100
500- 600	0	100
600- 700	0	100
700- 800	0	100
800- 900	0	100
900-1000	0	100
1000-1100	0	100
1100-1200	0	100
1200-1300	0	100
1300-1400	0	100
1400-1500	8.7	91.3
1500-1600	43.5	56.5
1600-1700	38.4	61.6
1700-1800	36.3	63.7
1800-1900	38.0	63.0
1900-1920	43.0	57.0

We have seen that throughout the Middle Ages sensate ethics was practically absent, appearing in a clear-cut form only in the fifteenth century, attaining a rapid growth in the sixteenth century, and maintaining thereafter a high level, with minor fluctuations reaching their maxima in the period of the Renaissance and the Reformation and in the present century. Figure 13 shows these shifts pictorially. Looking at the movement of the sensate ethics of happines we see clearly the periods of its rise and decline from 500 B.C. to 1920 A.D.

A similar picture is presented by the following figures, which indicate the percentages of the partisans and the absolute and the relative—ethical, intellectual, and aesthetic—values among all the eminent thinkers of these problems in each specified period.

The table indicates how the relativism of all the supreme values, from the ethical *summum bonum* to truth and beauty, absent in the medieval period, re-emerged in the fourteenth century and, with some minor fluctuations, grew during the subsequent centuries, reaching its maximum in the present century. These figures and Figure 14 show also the progressive relativization of all the values mentioned in the preceding and subsequent chapters, a relativization that tends to rob them of their very identity, so that they cease to be norms and values. Here, as in several other tables, the

Period	Relativism (Percentage)	Absolutism (Percentage)
A.D. 400- 500	0	100
500- 600	0	100
600- 700	0	100
700- 800	0	100
800- 900	0	100
900-1000	0	100
1000-1100	0	100
1100-1200	0	100
1200-1300	0	100
1300-1400	20.8	79.2
1400-1500	23.1	76.2
1500-1600	40.4	59.6
1600-1700	38.0	62.0
1700-1800	36.8	63.2
1800-1900	37.9	62.1
1900-1920	48.6	51.4

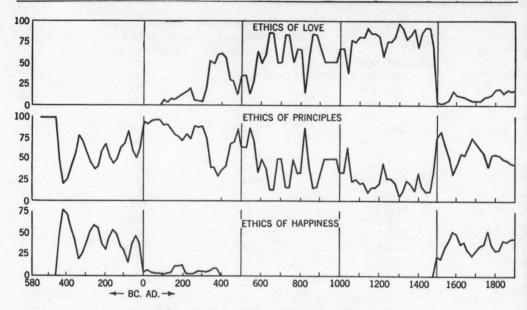

Figure 13.   Ethics of Love, Principles, Happiness.

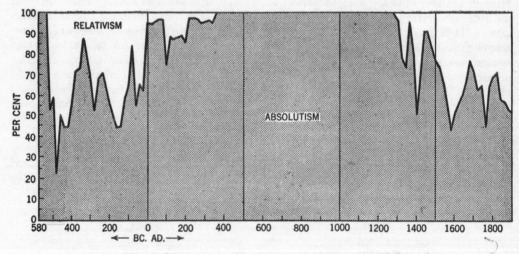

Figure 14.   Relativism vs. Absolutism in Ethics and Philosophy.

fact that absolutism is numerically still slightly greater (51.4 per cent) than relativism (48.6 per cent) must not mislead us. A small portion of whiskey or a few drops of poison are sufficient to make the water intoxicating or poisonous. The same principle should be applied to relativism and several other items discussed. The crux of the matter is the relative increase or decrease of each of the currents studied. A jump of relativism from zero to 40 or 48 per

cent is sufficient to weaken, atomize, and disintegrate ethical or any other values. In regard to all these values, we live in an age of extraordinary relativization and atomization. They in their turn, are the signs of mental and moral anarchy; for a value that is no longer universal becomes a pseudo-value, a plaything of individual fancy and wishes.[1]

———

[1] Cf.*Dynamics*, Vol. II, Chps. 13-15.

IDEATIONAL, IDEALISTIC, AND SENSATE SYSTEMS OF LAW

1. Ideational Law

Like ethical systems, the integrated systems of law are also ideational or idealistic or sensate. The ideational code of law is viewed as given by God or the Absolute. It is always largely *jus divinum* or *sacrum*. Its norms are regarded as the commandments of God. As such they become absolute, not to be set aside for any utilitarian or other considerations. Often nothing is allowed to be changed in these rules. Here are typical examples of such a law code.

Now therefore hearken, O Israel, unto the statutes and unto the judgments, which I teach you. . . . Ye shall not add unto the word which I command, neither shall you diminish aught from it, that ye may keep the commandments of the Lord your God which I command you. (Deuteronomy iv: 1 and 2)

And for another example:

Now for the sake of preserving all this creation, the most Glorious [Lord] ordained separate duties for those who sprang from His mouth, arms, thighs, and feet. . . . The Lord created . . . punishment, the protector of all creatures, an incarnation of the law, framed of Brahman glory. (*The Laws of Manu*, I, 31; VIII, 14)

For verily I say unto you, Till heaven and earth pass, one jot or one tittle shall in no wise pass from the law, till all be fulfilled. (Matthew v: 18, 19)

The norms of ideational law are not aimed at an increase of sensory happiness or pleasure or utility. They are to be obeyed unquestionably as the commandments of the omniscient and ever-just Absolute. Being such, the ideational codes of law protect many a value that seemingly has no sensory utility or pleasure. On the other hand, they probibit many a pleasure and utility as sinful.

In such codes crime and sin are synonymous, just as obedience to the law is synonymous with obedience to God and salvation. Therefore in *its criminal part the ideational code of law always has among its prohibited and punished actions many an action that violates the prescribed rules in man's relationship toward God and supersensory values.*

Prescriptions directed against heresy, apostasy, sacrilege, blasphemy; violation of the Sabbath, or holy day; violation of the prescribed sacred rituals; non-fulfilment of the sacred ceremonies of baptism, marriage, and funeral; infraction of the sacred rules respecting either intermarriage or contact with gentiles and disbelievers and so on—these laws comprise a large part of the punishable actions of such criminal codes. *Their system of punishment is likewise made up not of sensory punishments only but of supersensory penalties as well.* Punishment ranges from the eternal damnation of the sinful, and often of his progeny, in some inferno, or purgatory, to excommunication from the society of believers, to deprivation of the sacraments and of the blessings of the religious rituals in burial and other events. The objective of the punishment is not so much prevention of crime, or education of the sinner-criminal, or protection of the utilitarian interests of the society, as an *expiation* of the sin committed against God; any violation of the absolute norm requires the vindication of the norm and cannot pass without expiation for the sin performed. A criminal is always *sacer esto*; therefore he must be punished, no matter whether, from a sensory standpoint, such a punishment is useful for the culprit or society, or not. The system of the *judicial evidence of such a law contains, moreover, an assortment of supersensory evidence in the form of the ordeals,* "*the judgment of God,*" the dicta of oracles, prophets, and pythias, and other "supernatural techniques" for finding out whether or not the accused party is guilty. This system of judicial evidence is based upon the assumption of the interference of the Absolute in judicial affairs. *Almost every law action,* be it the exchange or purchase of property, or conclusion of a contract, or payment of a debt, *is prescribed to the last detail through the pronouncement of certain sacred formulae, through definite sacred actions, without the possibility of changing anything, even a single letter or detail, in this sacramental procedure.* Just as no change in an important religious ritual is permitted, so no change is permitted in any judicial procedure, in the interest of the parties involved, or any one else. Finally, *the judges in such a system of law are always—directly or indirectly—priests, pontiffs, and other members of the sacerdotal order, assisted by oracles, prophets, seers, saints, and the like.* In brief, the norms of the law are absolute and rigid; the forms of its enforcement and application are also absolute and formal. No vagueness, uncertainty, relativity, ambiguity, or expediency is admitted. The legal conscience of ideational society is clear-cut, free from any doubt, and not open to any questioning or criticism. It embodies in detail the major premise of the ideational mentality.

Accordingly, ideational law is not controlled entirely by considerations of utility, profit, expediency, and sensory well-being, even in such utilitarian matters as production, exchange, and consumption of economic values: trade and commerce, money and banking, profit and interest, property and possession, rent, the relationship between the employer and employees, and other property and economic relationships. On the contrary, these are all subordinated to the ideational norms of the law, and are admitted only so far as they do not contradict ideational values. If they do contradict these norms and values, they are rejected, prohibited, or punished, no matter how useful they may be for the society or the parties involved. This fact explains the expulsion of the merchants from the temple at Jerusalem by Jesus, with his rebuke, "My house shall be called the house of prayer; but ye have made it a den of thieves"; Christ's dictum, "Verily I say unto you, that a rich man shall hardly enter into the kingdom of God"; and the prohibition by the canon law and Christian morals upon money-lending, profit, devotion to money-making, and other economic—and profitable and useful—activities. All these activities are restricted by, and subordinated to, ideational values. This applies also to the personal relationships of marriage and the family. The considerations of happiness in marriage receive little attention. Because marriage is a recognized sacred bond, no divorce was possible under medieval Christian law, whether the parties were happy or unhappy. In brief, ideational values transcend all other values in such a code of law.

The same is true of any other association, contract, and social relationship envisaged by ideational law. The twofold, divinely authoritarian regulation of social relationships, (a) through a negative limitation of contracts and compulsions contradictory to the absolute norms of God, and (b) through the positive stimulation of duty, sacrifice, love, altruism, and good will, regardless of any considerations of profit, utility, pleasure, and happiness, is the specific characteristic of ideational law.

Finally, *such a code regards the legitimate authority of government as derived ultimately from the Absolute, or God,* not from physical force, wealth, or popular mandate. A government with authority not based on the sanction of the Absolute, and not obedient to its commands, is invalid for such a system of law and such a society. Hence in all societies ruled by ideational law the regime is always either explicitly or implicitly a *theocracy.*

Such, in brief, are the typical traits of ideational law. These traits one finds in the secular and canon law of medieval ideational Europe, of Brahmanic or Hinduistic India, or of Tibet; in the law of early ideational Rome and Greece; in that of the Incas; and in any other ideational culture.

2. Sensate Law

The characteristics of sensate law present a very different picture. It is viewed by a sensate society as man-made, frequently, indeed, as a mere instrument for the subjugation and exploitation of one group by another. Its aim is exclusively utilitarian: the safety of human life, security of property and possession, peace and order, the happiness and well-being of either society at large or of the dominating faction which enacts and enforces sensate law. Its norms are relative, changeable, and conditional. Nothing eternal or sacred is implied in such a system of law. It does not attempt to regulate supersensory values or man's relationships toward them. It contains few, if any, provisions respecting man's relationship to God, the salvation of the soul, or other transcendental phenomena. Its criminal code virtually ignores the ideational crimes of heresy, apostasy, sacrilege, and the like. Its punishments are wholly sensory, devoid of supersensory sanctions. Their purpose is not expiation but revenge, the re-education of the culprit, the security of society, or similar utilitarian objectives. Its judicial evidence is invariably sensory; no "judgment of God" or ordeals are admitted. Its judges, again, are secular. Its rules and procedures are elastic, variable, free from the rigid formality of ideational law.

The social relationships regulated by sensate law are subject to the same sensory, utilitarian considerations. In this regulation the law does not invoke any divinely authoritarian sanction. All the relationships are either contractual (left to the agreement of the parties) or compulsory (imposed by the stronger party upon the weaker); and all are sanctioned by law. No nonutilitarian or antiutilitarian limitations are imposed on property relationships, personal relationships, or any other relationships so far as they are not required in the interest of other groups.

Finally, *the government that enacts and enforces such a code is a secular—not a theocratic—government*, based either upon military and physical power, upon riches and abilities, or upon the mandate of the electorate. Since no divine, supersensory sanction is demanded for the legality and authority of the law, there is no opportunity for the rise of an influential theocracy.

Such are the essential characteristics of sensate law, whether it be the western law of the last few centuries, the law of the sensate period of Greece and Rome, or that of other sensate societies.

3. Idealistic Law

Idealistic law, in turn, occupies an intermediate position between ideational and sensate law.

4. Shifts in the Domination of Ideational, Idealistic, and Sensate Law

As in the field of ethical ideals, the fine arts, and the systems of truth, each of the main forms of law, in the history of the Graeco-Roman and western cultures, rose to a position of dominance and then declined in favor of one of the other forms of law. The early Greek and Roman law before the fifth century B.C. was mainly ideational. It was largely the *jus divinum or sacrum*, with the priesthood as the ruler, law-giver, and judge, and with the legal norms prescribed by the gods. It was therefore sacred and inviolable. The transgressor became the *sacer esto*. The objective of punishment was expiation. In the words of a certain

historian, "religion in early Greece was an absolute master; the state was a religious community, the king a pontiff, the magistrate a priest, and the law a sacred formula; patriotism was piety; and exile, excommunication." According to another historian, in ancient Rome (before 510 B.C.) the king was the supreme priest (*pontifex maximus, rex sacrificulus*). "He held intercourse with the gods of the community, whom he consulted and appeased (*auspicia publica*), and he nominated all the priests and the priestesses." The criminal law was sacral; many of the most flagrant crimes were of religious character. In a word, the situation exhibited all the characteristics of ideational law. Toward the end of the sixth century B.C. there appeared symptoms of its decline, and in the fifth century B.C. sensate law re-emerged. Between the third century B.C. and the fifth A.D. it grew to a position of dominance, revealing all the usual characteristics. The rise of Christianity brought with it the rise of ideational law, which after the fifth century became dominant and remained so until about the end of the twelfth century. During this period the Christian law of medieval Europe—both secular and canon law—assumed all the typical traits of ideational law. Medieval criminal law, for instance, as compared with the law of the pagan barbaric tribes or of late Roman law, introduced many new, severely punishable crimes of a purely religious character, such as blasphemy, apostasy, heresy, schism, sorcery, hindering religious services, nonfulfilment of religious rites, nonobservance of Sunday, violation of "God's peace," abuse of corpses, suicide, usury, contact with Jews, abduction, adultery, panderage, incest, fornication, and abortion. Most of these new crimes are, from the purely utilitarian and hedonistic standpoint, not necessarily harmful or painful to the parties involved. From the ideational Christian standpoint they were transgressions against the commandments of God, a violation of ideational values; therefore they were treated as criminal and severely punishable.

As we move from the codes of medieval law to those of the seventeenth and more recent centuries, most of these offences cease to be crimes and are excluded from the list of criminal and punishable offences. The few that remained criminal changed their nature and were punishable for purely utilitarian reasons. The terminal point in this trend toward increasingly sensate criminal law was reached in the Soviet criminal laws of 1926 and 1930, where all religious crimes were entirely abolished and, with their elimination, many a crime connected with ideational values, such as seduction, adultery, polygamy, polyandry, incest, sodomy, homosexuality, fornication, and public indecency, ceased to be regarded as crime. All such actions have become noncriminal. A similar transformation occurred in the field of constitutional and civil laws. In practically all western countries they became almost purely sensate, and they remain predominantly sensate at the present time.

We come now to the present crisis in ethical ideals and in law. Since their dominant forms in western countries are sensate, the crisis evidently consists in the disintegration of the sensate ethics and law of the western countries.[2]

5. The Disintegration of Sensate Ethics and Law

The essence of the crisis consists in a progressive devaluation of our ethics and of the norms of our law. This devaluation has already gone so far that, strange as it may seem, they have lost a great deal of their prestige as ethical and juridical values. They have little, if any, of the sanctity with which such values and norms were formerly invested. More and more present-day ethical values are looked upon as mere "rationalizations," "derivations," or "beautiful speech reactions" veiling the egotistic interests, pecuniary motives, and acquisitive propensities of individuals and groups. Legal norms, likewise, are increasingly considered as a device of the group in power for exploiting other, less powerful, groups, a form of trickery employed by the dominant class for the subjugation and control of the subordinate classes. Ethical and juridical norms have both become mere rouge and powder to deck out a fairly unattractive body of Marxian economic interests, Paretian "residues," Freudian "libido," Ratzenhoger "interests," the psychologists' and sociologists' "complexes," "drives," and "prepotent reflexes."

[2] Cf. *Dynamics*, Vol. II, Ch. 15; Vol. III, Ch. 5.

They have turned into mere appendages of policemen, prisons, the electric chair, "pressures," and other forms of physical force. They have lost their moral prestige and have been degraded and demoted to the status of a device used by clever hypocrites to fool the exploited simpletons. With the loss of moral prestige, they have progressively forfeited their controlling and binding power as effective factors of human conduct. Their "Thou shalt not" and "Thou shalt" have more and more ceased to affect human conduct as moral commandments or to guide it according to these commandments, and have grown progressively null and void.

Having lost their "savor" and efficacy, they opened the way for rude force as the only controlling power in human relationships. If neither religious nor ethical nor juridical values control our conduct, what then remains? Nothing but naked force and fraud. Hence the contemporary "Might is right." This is the central feature of the crisis in our ethics and law.

The crisis did not originate either suddenly or recently. It is not due to some unforeseen factor external to sensate ethics and law. On the contrary, it has been generated slowly by the sensate system itself, in the course of its development, from the pathogenic germs implicit in the system.

These poisonous germs of sensate ethics and law were inherent in the utilitarian and hedonistic—that is, relativistic and conditional —nature of the ethical and legal values of the system. Any sensory value, as soon as it is put on a plane of relativistic and utilitarian convention, is bound to retrogress, becoming more and more relative, more and more conventional, until it reaches a stage of "atomization" in its relativism and of utter arbitrariness in its ever thinner and less universal conventionality. The final stage is bankruptcy. This is a brief summary of how and why the salt of sensate ethico-juridical values came to lose its savor. If the essence of moral and juridical values is utility and sensory happiness, then everyone has the right to pursue these values *ad libitum*. As pleasure, utility, and sensory happiness differ with different persons and groups, one is entitled to pursue them in the way one pleases and by any means one has at his disposal. As there is no limit to the expansion of sensory desires for sensory values, the available amount of these sensory values finally becomes insufficient to satisfy the desires and appetites of all the individuals and groups. The dearth of these values in turn leads to a clash of individuals and groups. Under such circumstances the struggle is bound to become ever sharper, more intensive, and more diversified in its means and forms. The ultimate result is the emergence of rude force assisted by fraud as the supreme and sole arbiter of the conflicts. Under such conditions no logic, no philosophy, and no science can invoke any transcendental value to mitigate the struggle and to distinguish the right moral relativism from the wrong, the right means for the pursuit of happiness from the wrong, or to distinguish moral obligation from selfish arbitrariness, and right from might. The simple reason is the nonexistence of any transcendental value or norm in sensate ethics or law. Aside from subjective utility and happiness, relativism and convention, sensate ethics and law have no absolute judge, no objective and universal criterion to decide the issue. Hence we can deduce the inevitable "atomization" and self-annihilation of the sensate system of values from the very process of its development.

Coming on the historical scene as a successor to, and as a substitute for, Christian ethics and law, the modern system of sensate ethics and law in its immanent development sowed the seeds of the degradation of man, as well as of the moral values themselves. Declaring the moral values to be mere conventions, it dragged them down to the level of utilitarian and hedonistic calculations, completely relative in time and space. If they were expedient for a given man and group, they could be accepted; if they were a hindrance, they could be rejected. In this way a limitless relativism was introduced into the world of moral values, whose arbitrariness engendered conflict and struggle. This, in turn, produced hatred; and hatred led to rude force and bloodshed. In the chaos of conflicting norms moral values have been more and more ground to dust; they have progressively lost their binding power and given way to rude arbitrary coercion. The pathos of binding Christian love has tended to be supplanted by hatred—the

hatred of man for man, of class for class, of nation for nation, of state for state, of race for race. As a result, might has become right. *Bellum omnium contra omnes* has raised its ugly head. These are exactly the conditions we face.

At the present time there is hardly any ethical value common to and equally binding upon communists and capitalists; Hitlerites and Jews; Italians and Ethiopians; the British alliance and the German alliance; Catholics and atheists; multimillionaires and the underdogs; employers and the employed; oppressors and the oppressed, and so on. Their ethical and juridical values are quite contradictory and irreconcilable. What one faction declares good, another brands as bad. And the tragedy of it is that there is no sensate arbiter, acceptable to all these factions, whose decision is equally authoritative for all. If any mediator attempts such arbitration, he becomes, in turn, only an additional faction denounced by the others. We are thus a society of endless contesting parties without a moral judge to decide the contests. The result is moral chaos and anarchy. Every one becomes his own law-giver and judge, deeming his own standard just as good as anybody else's. Inertia still causes appeals to "public opinion" or to "the world's conscience," but they are either voices crying in the wilderness or else smoke screens masking the egotistic aspirations of this or that "pressure group." Instead of one genuine public opinion, we have thousands of pseudo-public opinions of factions, sects, and individuals. Instead of a "world conscience," we have millions of contradictory "rationalizations" and "derivations." The whole body of ethics accordingly becomes a plaything of unscrupulous "pressure groups," each of which tries to snatch as big a share of sensate values as possible at the cost of other groups. Under these circumstances the motivating, binding, and controlling power of ethical ideals tends to vanish. Since there is no uniform moral code, there is no united pressure of homogeneous public opinion to mould one's sentiments and convictions during his early formative years. Hence there is no uniform moral conscience to wield an effective motivating power in human behavior. Is it any wonder that crimes, wars, revolutions, have increasingly afflicted western society? "Everything is

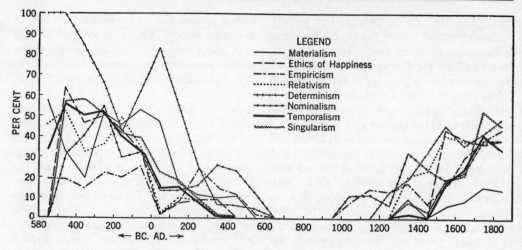

Figure 15.   Subsystems of Sensate System of Truth.

permitted, if you can get away with it" is the main moral maxim of our time.

Thus sensate society, with its sensate ethics, has prepared its own surrender to the rudest coercion. "Liberating" itself from God, from all absolutes and categoric moral imperatives, it has become the victim of undisguised physical coercion and fraud. Society has reached the nadir of moral degradation and is now paying the tragic price of its own folly. Its vaunted utilitarianism, practicality, and realistic expediency have turned into the most impractical and unrealistic disutilitarian catastrophe. Nemesis has at last overtaken it.

Hence the contemporary tragedy of sensate man himself. Stripping man of his divine charisma and grace, sensate mentality, ethics, and law have reduced him to a mere electron-proton complex or reflex mechanism devoid of any sanctity or end-value. "Liberating" him from the "superstitions" of the categorical imperatives, they have taken from him an invisible armor that unconditionally protected him, his dignity, his sanctity, and his inviolability. Divested of this armor, he finds himself but a plaything in the hands of the most fortuitous forces. If he is useful for this or that, he may be treated decently and cared for as we care for a useful animal. If he is harmful, he can be "liquidated," as we exterminate harmful snakes. No guilt, no crime, no valid reason, is needed for such a liquidation. Without any compunction, remorse, regret, or compassion, millions of guiltless people are uprooted, deprived of all possessions, of all rights, of all values, subjected to all kinds of privations, banished, or killed by bombs and bullets, simply because their mere existence is an unintentional obstacle to the realization of a lust for power, for wealth, for comfort, for some sensate value. Rarely, if ever, have even cattle been treated with such cynicism! Released from all the inhibitions of supersensory values, sensate man suicidally murders sensate man—his pride and self-confidence, his values and possessions, his comfort, pleasures, and happiness. In this tornado of unleashed sensate passions, the whole of sensate culture is being blown to pieces and swept away.

As has happened several times before, in the insanity of a decadent mentality, sensate man again today is destroying the sensate house he has so proudly been building for the past five centuries. Sensate ethics and law have once again entered a blind alley. This alley marks their *finis* for the present epoch. Without a shift toward ideational or idealistic ethics and law, without a new universalization of the values, they cannot escape from this blind alley. Such is the verdict of history in regard to the past crises of sensate ethics and law, and such must be its verdict regarding the present crisis.[3]

6. Conclusion

The foregoing shows that there have indeed been ideational, idealistic, and sensate systems of ethics and law; that in the Graeco-Roman and

[3] For further evidence, cf. my *Dynamics*, Vols. II and III *passim*.

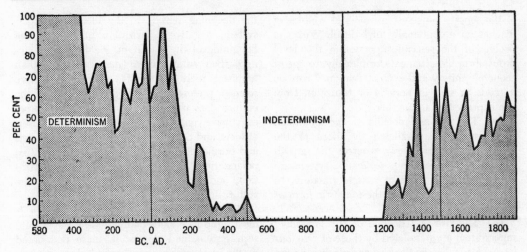

Figure 16. Movement of Deterministic and Indeterministic
Philosophies, 580 B.C. to 1900 A.D.

western cultures they fluctuated hand in hand with the respective systems of fine arts and truth; and that there have existed three supersystems, each consisting of systems of the fine arts, of truth (science, philosophy, and religion), and of ethics and law, with a multitude of subsystems.

Figure 15 gives an idea of the parallel fluctuations of eight subsystems of the sensate system of truth from the sixth century B.C. up to the present time. Though the fluctuations of these eight sensate "variables" were not strictly parallel so far as minor fluctuations are concerned, nevertheless in their major movements

they oscillated together, exhibiting a high level of sensate culture between the fifth century B.C. and the third century A.D.; an enormous decline between the fourth century A.D. and the latter part of the Middle Ages; and an upsurge which set in during the twelfth century and which has continued up to the present time.[4]

In the next sections it will be demonstrated that our supersystems have been still vaster, embracing several other systems and being connected with various other processes and their fluctuations. Let us briefly enumerate some of these.

II. Other Developments from the Three Supersystems

(1) The rise and decline of the *ideational* supersystem are tangibly connected with those of the *familistic and partly compulsory* relationships in all social groups, whereas the rise and decline of the *sensate* supersystem is tangibly connected with those of the *contractual* relationships,[5] exhibiting a notable increase of compulsory relationships in its declining phase.

(2) The rise and decline of the *ideational*

supersystem is meaningfully and causally connected with those of *theocratic* government, while the fluctuations of the *sensate* wave are accompanied by parallel fluctuations of *secular* government,[6] democratic at its zenith and totalitarian in its declining stage.

(3) The rise and decline of the *ideational* supersystem are marked by *a stationary level of economic well-being* or by its *moderate decline*. The rise of the *idealistic* supersystem is characterized by a *notable improvement* in the *material standard of living*. At the zenith

---

[4] For the actual figures, cf. my *Dynamics*, Vol. III.

[5] See above, Chapter 5. For further evidence, cf. my *Dynamics*, Vol. III, Chps. 1-4.

[6] For the evidence, cf. my *Dynamics*, Vol. III, Ch. 5.

of the sensate supersystem material well-being reaches an exceptionally high level. With the decline of the sensate supersystem this level drops abruptly, often catastrophically, to one of economic misery and even starvation. Likewise it tends to sink in periods of transition from one supersystem to another.[7]

(4) The rise and decline of the *ideational* supersystem are paralleled by those of the ideational form of *liberty*, whereas the growth and fluctuations of the *sensate* supersystem are accompanied by those of *sensate freedom*. In the *idealistic* supersystem the *idealistic form of liberty prevails*.[8]

(5) The rise and decline of the *ideational* supersystem are paralleled by those of *religious leadership*, whereas the rise and decline of the *sensate* supersystem go hand in hand with those of financial and business leadership, economic organization, and sensate politics, technology, science, and arts. Leadership during the dominant period of the *idealistic* supersystem is partly religious and partly sensate.[9]

(6) Wars, revolutions, and social movements tend to assume a *religious* character in populations dominated by the *ideational* supersystem; a *secular* character (especially in the interest of economic and material power) in *sensate* populations; and *a mixed* character, partly religious and partly sensate, in *idealistic* cultures.

(7) Wars, revolutions, crime, and mental disease tend to increase sharply in periods of transition from one supersystem to another, increasing particularly in connection with shifts from the declining sensate supersystem to the ideational or idealistic supersystem.[10]

(8) Positive and negative polarization (ethical, religious, scientific, philosophical, artistic, etc.) becomes particularly conspicuous during periods of transition. If the transition is from the declining ideational supersystem through the idealistic to the sensate supersystem, at the beginning of the transition period the positive polarization still prevails, producing at the end of the period a balanced idealistic-sensate type. If the transition is from

the declining sensate to the ideational supersystem, negative polarization prevails at the beginning of the transition, yielding more sinners than saints; more demoralization than heroism; more destructive than constructive science, philosophy, ideologies, and art. If the culture does not perish in the transition process, then eventually, through a series of crises, ordeals, and catastrophes, a process of catharsis and purification leads to a decrease of negative polarization, an increase of positive polarization, and a revival and reintegration of the culture in question.[11]

(9) *The tempo of sociocultural change* is most rapid in periods dominated by the sensate supersystem, and slowest in those dominated by the ideational supersystem, idealistic periods occupying an intermediary position. Sociocultural change is rapid and disorderly in transition periods.[12]

(10) Horizontal mobility and especially vertical mobility tend to be most marked and most chaotic in transition periods, less so in sensate periods, and least of all in ideational periods (after a consolidation of the ideational supersystem).[13]

(11) Periods dominated by the ideational supersystem tend to create somewhat closed multibonded groups, such as *castes and social estates*, whereas those dominated by the sensate supersystem favor the emergence of *more open social classes*. In periods of transition most of the lines of social differentiation and stratification, together with the mechanism for testing and distributing individuals, as well as the character of the main unibonded and multibonded groups, become disorganized and confused.

1. Extension of the Supersystems Over the Greater Part of the Total Culture

The above eleven processes, meaningfully and causally connected with the supersystems of art, truth, ethics, and law, extend the supersystem over the major part of the economic, political, and leadership systems; the domain of the basic social relationships and groups;

---

[7] Cf. my *Dynamics*, Vol. III, Ch. 8.

[8] *Ibid.*, Vol. III, Ch. 6. See also above Chapter 30.

[9] Cf. my *Dynamics*, Vol. IV, Ch. 7, and Vol. II, Ch. 5.

[10] *Ibid.*, Vol. III, Chps. 9-14.

[11] For the evidence, cf. my *Calamity*, Chps. 4-15, and *Crisis*, Ch. 9.

[12] Cf. my *Dynamics*, Vol. IV, Ch. 11.

[13] *Ibid.*, Ch. 11. Cf. also my *Mobility*, passim.

and such fundamental processes, factors, and phenomena as war, revolution, crime, mobility, tempo of change, polarization, and differentiation and stratification—in a word, over the greater part of all the major systems and processes of the Graeco-Roman and western cultures. Taken together with the systems of the fine arts, of truth and knowledge, of ethics and law, these additional systems and processes make each of the three supersystems a vast sociocultural "organism" that integrates most of the leading social and cultural systems and processes into a single unit. Sensate literature, painting, drama, music, sculpture, and architecture; sensate science and technology; sensate philosophy and ideologies (materialism, empiricism, temporalism, relativism, singularism, nominalism, and individualism, with skepticism and nihilism in the declining phase); sensate ethics and law; predominantly contractual relationships (with compulsory relationships at the stage of decline); some kind of secular regime in the state and other groups; a high level of material well-being (except during the phase of decline); the sensate form of liberty and leadership; sensate wars, revolutions, and crimes; a swift tempo of social and cultural change; intense mobility; and predominantly open social classes—all these and some other systems and processes are "organs" of the sensate supersystem. Like those of biological organism, they all are connected with one another and with the entire supersystem by meaningful and causal ties. This double bond makes them interdependent in their static and dynamic aspect. When one of the systems is present (as a part of such a supersystem), the other systems and processes are ordinarily also present; when one of the systems or the supersystem as a whole changes, the rest of the systems change also.

The same generalization applies to the idealistic and ideational supersystems. Each of these is a vast "organism" made up of idealistic or ideational systems and processes in all the enumerated fields of culture and social groupings. Just as the static (anatomical) interrelationships and dynamic (physiological) functions of organs can be adequately studied only as actual parts of an organism, so also the static and dynamic causal and meaningful interrelationships of the systems and subsystems of a supersystem can be adequately understood only when they are studied as parts of the whole. Sensate fine arts and philosophy cannot be detached from their supersystem and studied as "independent variables," existing by themselves and changing independently of the rest of the organism.

III. Four Types of Personality

The ideational, sensate, idealistic, and eclectic cultures are characterized, respectively, by ideational, sensate, idealistic, and eclectic types of personality. In a rudimentary or developed form these are perennial and basic types.

1. The Ideational Type

The ideational type, in its active and passive forms, is characterized by the following traits. Such a person conceives the true reality and value essentially as a supersensory and superrational God or its equivalent. Sensory reality is regarded either as an illusion or as a low-grade or negative pseudo reality. He overstresses spiritual needs and values and underestimates sensory needs and values. Sometimes, as an ascetic, he reduces the latter to an almost unbelievable minimum. He tries to adjust himself to sensory reality principally through self-modification. He is preoccupied primarily with the inner, mystical, supersensory, and superrational world. He contemplates the eternal, unchangeable Being as the true reality or value, change and becoming being considered as either unreal or unimportant. His activities are mainly those of the "introvert." For him truth is absolute, revealed through the grace of God—through mystic experience or divine intuition—and not through sensory perception. His moral system is absolutistic. His art is purely ideational. He either remains aloof from empirical reality as an ascetic or tries to reconstruct it in accordance with his system of ideational values. He is, however, little interested in purely external reconstruction of empirical sociocultural reality. He does not believe in purely externalistic reforms. His motto is, "Seek ye first the kingdom of God and his righteousness; and all [sensory] things shall be added unto you." In the passive, or ascetic, type the overt behavior of the ideationalist adequately articulates his ideological culture. In the active type the behavioral and material culture less adequately expresses the ideationalist's ideological culture.

2. The Sensate Type

The sensate type of personality, in its active and passive forms, is the opposite of the ideational type. A sensate person is a noisy, active extrovert. For him reality and values are sensory and largely material; the transcendental he does not recognize. He expands his sensory needs as much as possible and does not strive to develop spiritual needs. He seeks to satisfy his sensory needs through an energetic modification of his empirical environment; if he is of the passive type, he spends his life in snatching the maximum of sensory pleasure according to the "Wine, women, and song" formula. The active sensate person is a fighter against nature, against human beings, against anything or anybody that hinders the satisfaction of his sensory needs. He is not given to self-analysis or introversion. He views everything dynamically, as an incessant becoming. Hence he is a firm believer in change, evolution, progress. His norms of truth and beauty and his ethical norms are all relative and changeable. He regards them as mere human conventions. He is an empiricist and relativist in his science and philosophy; a hedonist in his fine arts; a utilitarianist and hedonist in his ethics and law. He does not believe in any "kingdom of God," as something apart from or above sensory reality. His freedom is purely sensate. His prescription for any social evil is a reconstruction of external empirical reality.

3. The Idealistic Type

This type is intermediary between the ideational and sensate type. An idealistic personality tries (with considerable success) to unite into one balanced whole the noblest traits of the sensate personality and the less extreme characteristics of the ideational type.

4. The Eclectic Type

This type (found in all cultures, at all times) is unintegrated and inconsistent, whether in its rudimentary, low-brow form or in its high-brow and sophisticated form. The ideological culture of the eclectic is a mixture of various systems and congeries; his behavioral and material culture is a medley of disconnected incidental, inconsistent patterns of conduct and material vehicles. In the case of the rich and sophisticated the stock is ample, sometimes containing many masterpieces of artists and thinkers, and various luxurious and costly articles. In the case of poor, low-brow eclectic slaves and serfs, unskilled laborers and paupers, the stock of material culture is pitifully meager and primitive. In both cases, however, the total culture of the eclectic is heterogeneous in character. Since his ideological and behavioral cultures are unintegrated, his total behavior is largely incidental, determined chiefly by fortuitous external factors. When these are painful or extremely unfavorable, the eclectic type of person tends to disintegrate or to experience a recession to nihilism, skepticism, cynicism, or even animalism.[14]

The last three chapters have demonstrated the existence of three vast supersystems of culture, their empirical fluctuations in the course of time, and certain details of the manner of these fluctuations. We can now pass to a systematic analysis of the principal causes and modes of cultural change in general and of its uniformities in particular.

[14] For the details of these types, cf. my *Dynamics*, Vol. I, Ch. 2, and Vol. III, Ch. 15.

Chapter 43. Modes of Change of Systems, "Civilizations," and Congeries

I. Basic Differences in Change of Meaningful-Causal Systems and Causal Unities and Congeries

1. Change in Meaningful-Causal Togetherness in Culture Systems

After examination of the how and why of conception, objectification, socialization, mobility, growth and decline of cultural systems and supersystems, we can study more closely and analytically the modes of change of cultural systems and congeries, the relationship of various systems to one another in this change, and the modes of change of whole "civilizations."

Since by definition and by fact a cultural system is a unity whose parts are bound together by a meaningful-causal tie, it cannot help changing as a whole, in togetherness. The tighter the general and differential integration of its parts the more conspicuous is its change in togetherness.[1] An important change in one important part demands a corresponding meaningful-causal change in other parts and in the whole system; similarly the change of the whole system effects a corresponding change of its parts.

Such interdependence or togetherness of change within the system is a function only of the inherent relationships between its parts. Whether the changes occur simultaneously or not is in large part irrelevant to their togetherness. For one thing, the criterion of simultaneity is relative and may mean at the same instant of time or within the same span of five hundred years, depending on an arbitrary standard selected by the investigator. Furthermore simultaneity is not per se proof of causality. Two phenomena, such as the birth of a child in an African jungle and the meeting of the Rotary Club in Boston, may occur in the same hour and yet be entirely unconnected with each other causally or otherwise.

In considering the relation between causal connection and time, two basic facts should be kept in mind: different or identical causes operating under different circumstances require differing amounts of time to produce their effects; the effects of an important change in a part of a system may reach some parts quickly but others only after a considerable time lag. Water which boils over a gas fire in

[1] See the analysis of general and differential conductivity in Chapter 8. This principle is similar to the holistic-biological interpretation of the organism. Cf. K. Goldstein, *op. cit.*

a few minutes might require half an hour to boil over a wood fire. The cause, heat, in each case is the same, but the disparity in the intensity of the cause is reflected in a disparity of the time required for its characteristic effect on water. Tubercular infection or cancer of one part of an organism does not spread instantaneously over the whole; a considerable span of time is necessary before the disease affects all organs and the organism as a whole. Furthermore the condition of the organism may hasten or retard the development of the disease so that the time required for the cause, tuberculosis or cancer, to produce the ultimate effect, death, is likely to differ widely as between different organisms. Finally within any given organism different parts may manifest different degrees of resistance or susceptibility to a cause. Thus in an aging body not all parts grow equally old at the same time. In all these phenomena the causal connections are clear and continuously operative, but the time spans, the "synchronicities or non-synchronicities" are different.

The same is true of the sociocultural systems in their change. Depending upon the vastness of the system or supersystem, the degree of its meaningful-causal integration, general and differential conductivity between its parts, a change in one part of the system may and does reach the other parts not at the same but at different moments of time. The same is true when the system as a whole undergoes its immanent change, inherent in its nature. Like an aging organism, a sociocultural system immanently changing as a whole, say from the sensate to the ideational type, does not necessarily change simultaneously in all its parts; some parts may show the characteristics of the change earlier than the others. A narrow synchronicity of change is therefore not a necessary characteristic of a change in togetherness nor does a lack of such synchronicity argue against the existence of causal-meaningful ties between the parts of a system.

More symptomatic of a change in togetherness is the meaningful character and direction of the change of the parts of the system. If various sociocultural phenomena believed to be parts of the same causal-meaningful system change in the same direction (that is, for example, if literature and painting, music and

sculpture, science and philosophy, ethics and law, economics and politics in a given population all show an increase of materialism, irreligiosity, sensualism, and nihilism), such a meaningful identity of change in all these phenomena is a significant symptom of their causal-meaningful relation as parts of one causal-meaningful system or supersystem. If a further study discloses that through human agents and the vehicles or conductors of interaction these cultural phenomena are indeed connected with each other, such a causal connection reinforces the hypothesis of these phenomena being parts of one causal-meaningful system or supersystem, and of their changing in meaningful-causal togetherness. In that case it is nonessential whether the change is manifested simultaneously throughout the system or not. For instance, in the transformation of the largest supersystems from sensate into idealistic or ideational and vice versa, a time-span of one or two centuries was required to perform the change and in this transformation of the whole supersystem some of its subsystems, for instance music, lagged behind the other fine arts by about one century and a half at the end of the Middle Ages. On the other hand, in its change from sensate to ideational form at the beginning of the Middle Ages, music preceded the change of the other fine arts by about a century. Due to the vastness of the supersystem, to its complex and discreet character, to poor communication and conductivity in the past, such non-synchronicities in change of subsystem or system in a supersystem are as natural as the non-synchronicities in the analogies of the changes wrought by tuberculosis, cancer, or aging in an organism. The meaningful connection of the change, identical direction of it (say, from sensate to ideational), the ascertained interaction and communication between the changing systems are fairly sufficient evidence that these systems are parts of the same supersystem, that they have a meaningful-causal connection, and experience a change in togetherness.[2]

[2] On the other hand, A. Toynbee goes too far in that direction, stating that in most of his civilizations a span of some 500 to 2000 years was necessary before the consequences of "the breakdown of civilization" were manifested in their disintegration. Such periods are too long for one to believe in

When on the other hand, the problem is to determine whether a given set of cultural phenomena are parts of a single system or merely coexisting congeries, the question of synchronous occurrence of change may be significant. If change is found to be more or less regularly synchronous (that is, occurring within a few months, years, or decades of each other depending upon the vastness of the set and other conditions), this may be a symptom of some causal or meaningful connection. This is the reason for our especially statistical observation and time-series analyses along the lines of correlation and contingency techniques. A high coefficient of correlation in the fluctuation of two or more variables is a symptom of a possible causal relationship between the variables studied and this causal relation may be the reason for their concomitant variation. However, it is not sufficient evidence; many high correlations may be spurious and many others inconclusive. On the other hand, a closer experimental, inductive, or meaningful-causal study can disclose the existence of causal ties between phenomena of which the statistical examination yields only an insignificant correlation.

One cannot therefore rely on the mere synchronous change of the phenomena; their connections must be tested further by experimentation, observation, clinical analysis, and so on. If such tests cannot be made, one good "clue" is the criterion of meaningful relation. If the phenomena examined are meaningfully related, the synchronicity of the change acquires a strong support as evidence of the phenomena being parts of a system. If no meaningful relationship between the phenomena can be discovered, even a high coefficient of correlation in their variation becomes insufficient evidence for their causal relationship. Thus if a high coefficient of correlation is found between the variation of the

birth rate of an African tribe and the number of courses given by a professor of entomology in a college unconnected with the tribe, the coefficient is likely to be spurious; no meaningful relationship can be found between two variables. On the other hand, when we know what a war between the United States and Japan means, and when we observe a sudden increase of American warships sunk, sudden expansion of the American army, scarcity of meat and butter available to the civilian population, an increasing number of war books becoming best sellers, a sudden decrease of regular students in the colleges, we have no hesitation in claiming the existence of meaningful-causal ties between these and hundreds of other phenomena, in spite of their difference from one another, and in spite of their nonsynchronous occurrence; they all are meaningful-causal manifestations of the war between the United States and Japan. As a matter of fact, in an enormous number of cases, this meaningful clue, plus the factual interaction alone, is sufficient to give us a firm ground for conclusion that the phenomena $A, B, C, \ldots X$ are parts of one causal-meaningful system, no matter how different they are in outward appearance. Missionary activity of a Catholic priest in China, demonstrations by Catholics in Mexico, Vatican protest against secularization of churches, elevation of a bishop to the cardinalate, opening of a new Catholic school, resumption of diplomatic relations between a given state and the Vatican, campaign against demoralizing movies—all these different phenomena, happening at different times, leave no doubt in us that they are all manifestations of a many-sided change of the same meaningful-causal system, the Catholic Church, in its various parts.

In other, less obvious cases where the meaningful relationship between the set of phenomena is comprehensible but we are not sure

---

the existence of a meaningful-causal relationship between the breakdown as a cause and disintegration as effect. See Toynbee, *op. cit.*, Vols. III, IV, V, VI, *passim.* See my criticism in "A. J. Toynbee's Philosophy of History," *Journal of Modern History*, Vol. XII, pp. 374-387.

It is to be noted further that the discussed change in meaningful-causal togetherness has nothing to do with A. Kroeber's problem: do various systems blossom together and simultaneously? The

criteria of blossoming are arbitrary; therefore the fact of synchronous or nonsynchronous blossoming of, say, painting and philosophy does not say anything of their meaningful-causal connection. Without a consideration of the *content* of the systems we cannot say anything of their relationship. When the content is considered, for instance, religion and materialistic philosophy, we cannot expect their simultaneous blossoming; they are incompatible. Cf. Kroeber, *op. cit.*, pp. 773 ff.

whether the connection is causal (for instance roughly concomitant explosions of unrest among American soldiers in Germany, Japan, and China; or an emergence of a similar ideology, similar materialistic or pragmatic philosophy in America, China, and Russia; or the development of a religious trend in best-selling novels, in the latest paintings and sculpture, in radio talks of news commentators, in philosophical and scientific works, in the school curricula, etc.), we must find out whether there is a factual contact and inter-action between these phenomena through their human agents, or vehicles of interaction and communication. If such connection is found, the meaningfully related phenomena can be considered, with reasonable certainty, to be connected also causally; therefore making one meaningful-causal system, changing therefore in togetherness.

Thus in the determination of whether any set of cultural phenomena constitutes a mean-ingful-causal system or a group of congeries, synchronicity plays some part, but it is never decisive or conclusive. The meaningful relation and factual contact between the phenomena in the set remain the most important criteria.[3]

2. Incidental, Disconnected Change of Cultural Congeries

By definition and fact the cultural congeries do not change in causal-meaningful together-ness. Since there are no meaningful-causal rela-tionships between congeries $A, B, C, \ldots X$, the change of A in a cultural dump does not lead

[3] See a development of this in my *Dynamics*, Vol. IV, Chps. 4, 6, 7; my *Sociocultural Causality, Space, Time*, Chps. 2 and 4. This shows that J. S. Mill's inductive rules have to be modified con-siderably in their application to the study of the causal relationships between sociocultural phe-nomena. The meaningful character of these often permits one to establish with reasonable certainty the existence of causal relationship by a "short-cut" method of ascertaining meaningful relatedness between two or more phenomena, and then of a factual contact between them. On the other hand, a strict application of either method of identity or difference or of concomitant variation is rarely possible in sociocultural phenomena because in their appearance they are radically different and rarely give the necessary number of identical repetitions of the same variables. If we had not known what the Catholic Church was meaning-fully, we should never have been able to connect

to the change of $B, C, \ldots X$; since congeries are not a meaningful-causal unity, they do not have any "whole" and "parts." Not being a unity, they do not have an immanent course of change in the sense of unfolding their inherent potentialities, as the system has. Therefore, the change of congeries depends mainly upon the forces external to them (besides purely physico-chemical and biological changes in their material vehicles). The change is acci-dental, unforeseen, and largely unpredictable. In a study of the change of cultural congeries we cannot rely on the meaningful "clue" but have to proceed by the empirical methods of the natural sciences. The cardinal difficulty is that sociocultural congeries manifest much fewer identical repetitions than physical or chemical phenomena and thus provide fewer opportunities for the discovery of uniformities. Their study is thus largely unrewarding for a generalizing, nomographic science like sociol-ogy. For this reason our attention will continue to be given mainly to the investigation of the change in time of sociocultural systems and supersystems. A descriptive narrative of a change of congeries we leave to the historians and to other individualizing sciences.

3. How "Civilizations" Change

A profound difference in the manner of change of systems and supersystems, on the one hand, and of congeries, on the other, raises the question: in which way do the Danilevsky, Spengler, and Toynbee "civilizations" change? Do they change as systems in meaningful-

causally all the above manifestations of the Catholic sociocultural system: from the phenom-enon of a missionary activity in China to the support of the Polish London government and creation of five new American cardinals. Without the meaningful clue we should never have been able even to guess the existence of a causal-mean-ingful relationship between this motley of externally different things and events. No Mill's method of identity, difference, or concomitant variation would be able to disclose to us this relationship. Many of the social scientists seem to be still unaware of this and of other differences in the discovery and establishment of causal relationships between the purely biophysical phenomena, devoid of com-ponents of meaning and of meaningful "clues," and sociocultural phenomena. It is high time these elementary but basically important things were understood. Such an understanding would save a useless waste of research energy mechanically

causal togetherness, or do they follow the way of congeries, changing disjointedly, accidentally? The answer evidently depends upon their nature. If each of these "civilizations" is a unified meaningful-causal system, it will change in togetherness. If it is a congeries it will change in the pattern of congeries. Danilevsky, Spengler, and Toynbee regard each of their ten or nine (Danilevsky, Spengler) or twenty-one "civilizations" (Toynbee) as a unified organism, born, growing, declining, and dying as a unity. They do not distinguish between the meaningful, meaningful-causal, causal, and purely spatial unifications of cultural phenomena, but they leave no doubt that the *total sum of cultural phenomena* of either Greek or Chinese, of Arabic or Hindu, of the Western or Eastern Christian "civilization" makes one unified whole living and changing in togetherness, and as a unity passing through the states of spring, summer, fall, and winter (Spengler), or childhood, youth, maturity, old age, and death. Each civilization, having lived its cycle, dies. According to all of them at the present time most of their "civilizations" are already dead; for Toynbee, of his 21 civilizations only the Western still lives and that is in a half-dead agony.

Can we accept such a theory with its basic principle that each civilization is a unified whole? On the basis of the analysis of the structure of the total culture of an individual, group, and of an area (see Chapters 17 and 18) the theory is obviously untenable. Not only must it be denied that the total culture of such enormous areas as the western world or Greece, Rome, or India makes one logically or aesthetically consistent system, but it is not even true that the total culture of the smallest component areas constitute such a system. From the standpoint of their logical or meaningful consistency they represent rather a conglomeration of a multitude of systems and congeries partly consistent, partly neutral, partly contradictory to one another. There is not the slightest evidence of a meaningful consistency in such total cultures or civiliza-

tions. The claim to such consistency was largely due to the vagueness of criteria of unity; the criterion of logico-aesthetic consistency is entirely lacking in the Danilevsky, Spengler, and Toynbee conceptions. Even the criterion of causal interdependence is unclear: Instead of showing such interdependence they assume it by the use of analogical terms like "organism," "species," which attach to the cultural phenomena an unwarranted concept of biological unity.

If their "civilizations" are not meaningful systems, what are they? Why and how have these thinkers arrived at the conclusion that they are unities? The answer to the second question is that *they confused two different things: an organized or "as if organized" group and a cultural system.* Their very classification of the "civilization"—be it Egyptian or Sumeric, Greek or Roman, Arabic or Iranic, Chinese or Hindu—is really a classification of *social groups* and not of systems of culture. Even as a classification of social groups it is not quite consistent.

Most of their "civilizations" are really the language groups as a unibonded group in our sense; others are either the unibonded *state groups* or *nations* as a three-bonded group united by the ties of common language, state, and territory; still others are partially *territorial*, partly *religious* groups. Such "civilizations" as Greek are first of all the Greek language group, because Greece hardly ever was united into one nation or state. Such "civilizations" as Roman or Spartan or Ottoman are mainly the *state* groups, because Sparta differed from other Greek states not by language but by being an independent state. The same is true of the Ottoman empire, a multitude of subjugated language groups with different religions and mores, never amalgamated into a single nation. "Civilizations" such as the Russian, Chinese, or Iranian denote essentially nations. "Civilizations" like Toynbee's Buddhistic Chinese, or Islamic or Hindu or Near East Christian are mainly *religious* or *territorial* groups. Finally such "civilizations" as the Hellenic did not represent even any organized group; during the short-lived unification by conquest, under Alexander the Great, the Hellenic world was a conglomeration of groups, united neither by state, language, religion,

---

aping the inductive methods as they are and have to be applied in the natural sciences and would lead to a discovery and establishment of causal-meaningful relationships among many phenomena in a simpler and more valid way.

territory, or any other bond. Still less did it represent any even remotely unified culture. Except for the scattering of Greek exploiting settlers and Hellenized barbarians, and the superficial diffusion of various odds and ends of Greek or Roman culture, there was no social or cultural unity. In a word, the Hellenic world was just a vast "dump" of most heterogeneous social groups and cultural systems and congeries.[4]

This point reached, several conclusions follow as to what represents the *total culture of each of these social groups.* (a) So far as some of these groups are real organized groups—as the state group or as religious groups or as nations—they have a set of meanings, values, and norms that make one meaningfully consistent whole, the set because of which and for the sake of which the respective social groups were organized and functioned.

Outside of this set of meanings, values, and norms, the *total culture* of the members of each of these groups was a conglomeration of different, partly consistent, partly neutral, partly contradictory, systems and congeries. From the fact that a set of individuals have the same language and belong to the same language group, say Greek or Chinese, it does not follow that all these members have the same religion, philosophy, aesthetic tastes, ethical and juridical norms, manners and mores. We know that among the Greeks there were believers and atheists, ethical absolutists and nihilists, materialists and idealists in philosophy, and so on. The same is true of any other language group. From the fact that some 400 millions of Europeans, Hindus, Malayans, Canadians, and Fijians belong to the same state system, the British Empire, it does not follow that their total culture is identical or that even the total culture of each component is consistent. The same observation can be made of the total culture of the members of any state. Similarly it cannot be inferred from the diffusion of the Islamic or Christian religion over various areas of the world that the total culture of all Mohammedans or of all Christians is consistent. Precisely the same objection applies to any territorial group or nation. In the total culture of each of these groups there is a small portion

that is meaningfully integrated, the systems around which and for the sake of which the group was organized and functioned. Outside of this portion, the rest of its total culture is in no way a consistent whole. In no way, therefore, can it be regarded as one meaningful system or supersystem. None of the "civilizations" of Danilevsky, Spengler, or Toynbee is such a meaningful unity. All of them are a vast and complex conglomeration of a multitude of systems and congeries. This conclusion is still less questionable in regard to such "cultural and social dumps" as the "Hellenic civilization." *For this reason none of these "civilizations" can change as a real system in meaningful-causal togetherness.* Only in that portion of their total culture that is the *raison d'être* of the group can it change in the togetherness of a real meaningful-causal system.

(b) *This premise does not exclude, however, the existence of a vaster portion of the total culture of these "civilizations" that is bound together by a sort of causal interdependence, mainly by an indirect causal relationship through a common agent to all of them.* We have seen (Chapters 17 and 18) that an individual or group has many cultural systems and congeries that are partly neutral, partly consistent, partly contradictory to one another. So far, however, as all these systems and congeries are united in the same person or group, being directly connected with the same bearer or agent, they happen to be indirectly connected with one another in their causal interdependence. Systems A, B, C . . ., meaningfully and causally unrelated to one another, each being connected with the same person or group X, find themselves in indirect causal connections with one another. A serious change in one of these systems therefore may, and often does, causally influence some of the other systems of the same person or group. For example, if the religion or economic system or language or any other important system in the total "civilization" notably changes, its change may cause a change of some other systems and congeries in the total given "civilization."

Nevertheless, in a change brought about through indirect causal relationships, no meaningful consistency is to be expected. The

---

[4] Cf. its characterization in M. I. Rostovtzeff, *A History of the Ancient World,* 2nd ed. (Oxford University Press), Vol. I, Chps. 25-26; also his

The Social and Economic History of the Hellenistic World (Oxford University Press, 1942), Vol. I, Ch. 1.

change is caused by indirect causal dependence which, as such, is neither logico-aesthetically consistent nor inconsistent. "Meaningful induction" cannot foresee or predict its direction or character. In addition, the direct and indirect causal interdependence in such meaningfully unrelated phenomena may and often does exist not only within the parts of a given "civilization" but quite as much between its parts and the parts of some other total "civilization." Causally, the Crusades of the Christian group depended for their success and failure as much upon the Christian world as upon the non-Christian Mohammedan world; the resistance of the Mohammedan and non-Christian world determined their failure as much as the insufficiency of the efforts of the Christian groups. In other words, the causal interdependence does not cut out the criticized total "civilizations" into a closed causal system; it often extends beyond such "civilizations" and happens to be as intense, even closer, between some parts of a given "civilization" and some "total cultures or civilizations" outside of it. The destiny of Chinese total "civilization" in this war was more intensely determined by the "civilizations" of other Allies, than by the feud between the "Nationalist" and "Communist" parts of the supposed Chinese total "civilization."

(c) The conclusions following from the preceding analysis are as follows: Each of the supposed "civilizations" under examination when taken in its totality is neither meaningful, nor meaningful-causal, nor even a causal unity. In the small part—within the system which is the *raison d'être* of the respective group—there is meaningful and meaningful-causal unity. If there is some sort of vaster system or supersystem, then within the limits of these can be found a vaster meaningful-causal system or supersystem. Side by side with this in a vast part they are mainly indirect causal unities. None of these meaningful, meaningful-causal, and indirect causal unities cover the total "civilization."

In a large part the "civilizations" remain conglomerations of neutral and contradictory meaningful systems and congeries and of non-causal spatially adjacent congeries. From a purely causal standpoint, some parts of the total "civilization" are in as close causal interdependence with the sociocultural phenomena outside of the given "civilization" as with those inside. None of the civilizations in its totality can be regarded, therefore, as a closed causal system.[5]

If the above conclusions are correct, others follow as to the nature of the change of such "civilizations." Contrary to the claims of Danilevsky, Spengler, and Toynbee none of the "civilizations" taken as a whole can change in meaningful-causal togetherness as the real systems and supersystems change. None of the "civilizations" can change as a unified causal system. Not being a meaningful-causal or causal unity none of the "civilizations" can be born as a unified system; they cannot grow, cannot pass the stages of childhood and maturity, then die, because social and cultural dumps cannot be born, organically grow, and then die. What has not been a unity cannot grow as a unity and cannot be disintegrated, since it never was integrated. All the sweeping conclusions made by their authors from the false premise of the unity of such "civilizations" are untenable. To illustrate this let us take "the death of civilizations" so categorically stated by the partisans of the criticized theory. First, hardly any of their civilizations have ever died *in toto*, as a unified organism. As a matter of fact, a large part of their total culture, many systems and subsystems, have passed into other cultures and are still alive even in the contemporary western culture. Take, for instance, the oldest "civilization," the Egyptian. Many Egyptian religious and ethical systems and subsystems have passed into the cultures of other groups, particularly into the Jewish culture; through the Bible and through the early cults of Isis and Osiris they came into Christianity; they are living now through the Christian religion as well as through others closer to the Egyptian at the present time.[6] Similarly the Egyptian political system and their law-norms have passed into the cultures

---

[5] In a milder and more indefinite form A. Kroeber also rejects the rigid unity of the total civilizations, though his concept of the unity— "the key pattern"—remains somewhat vague. Cf. *op. cit.*, pp. 826 ff.; *et passim*. With a modification the above criticism applies also to the East and West of Northrop.

[6] Cf. J. Breasted, *Dawn of Conscience* (New York, 1933); F. Cumont, *Les religions orientales dans le paganisme romain* (1920).

of the Hellenistic world, thence to the Roman empire and to most of the European states.[7] The same is true of Egyptian art; even the contemporary art of the West still shows traces of Egyptian influence, in pattern, style, and even content.[8] Many other systems, subsystems and congeries of the total Egyptian culture are still alive. One is not obliged to subscribe to the extreme theories of G. E. Smith and W. J. Perry in order to see that a considerable part of the old Egyptian civilization has never died at all but still forms an element of other cultural systems as a distinct Egyptian system or subsystem.

What really died out of the total Egyptian civilization was *language, the independent Egyptian state*, and some other systems and congeries. As the Egyptian "civilization" in the theories of Danilevsky, Spengler, and Toynbee is the total culture of the Egyptian language, territorial, and state group (Egyptian nation), the disappearance of the Egyptian language and state led these authors to the conclusion that the total Egyptian culture and civilization had died. Baselessly making the total Egyptian culture one system, they no less baselessly concluded that with the death of some of many systems and congeries of this civilization, the total Egyptian civilization died. Still clearer is the situation with the newer Graeco-Roman civilization, which is also much nearer to our own. An enormous part of this "civilization" has never died and is still very much alive. Greek and Latin language systems; Greek and Roman art as a living art imitated by and influencing the contemporary architecture and sculpture, painting, and drama; and Roman and Greek philosophical and ethical systems; Roman law, especially the *Corpus Juris Civilis*; Greek and Roman political and military organization, and many other vast cultural systems and subsystems are living and functioning, both in their Greek and Roman forms and as the formative elements of many western culture systems. The creations of Phidias and Praxiteles, Homer, Sophocles, Aristophanes, Thucydides, Herodotus, Socrates, Plato, Aristotle; of Cicero, Horace, Virgil, Lucretius, their creations and hundreds of other Graeco-Roman

cultural systems are carrying on a very vigorous life. The notion of the death of the total Graeco-Roman "civilization" is derived mainly from the disappearance of the Greek and Roman state systems as living realities and from the relegation of Latin to the Christian clergy, scholars, and classically educated groups.

But the death of these groups does not mean the death of a civilization. On the contrary, almost all of the great Graeco-Roman cultural systems are very vigorously alive. They make up a very large part of the western "civilization."

With a slight modification the same can be said of practically all other "civilizations." The Chinese, Russian, Islamic, Arabic, Hindu, and Jewish civilizations continue to exist even as language, state, territorial groups, not to mention their continuance as sociocultural realities. The languages and state systems of some have disappeared, but the bulk of their religious, philosophical, ethical, legal, aesthetic, and other systems and congeries continue to function with all three components of human members, meanings, values, and norms, and a vast assortment of vehicles. Moreover some, like the Hindu, the Chinese, the Arabic are even showing clear signs of a political renaissance. Only perhaps a few either small or very old "civilizations" like the Hittite, the Sumerian, the Mayan, have in large part died, but even these have survived in at least a few systems and congeries.

To summarize: there is a little ground for contending that all or any of the truly great "civilizations" died *in toto*. Not being unities but a conglomeration of many systems and congeries, these civilizations have lost some of their systems and congeries (mainly their language and independent state system); other systems and congeries of the conglomeration of each "civilization" have survived and still live and function either as systems in the contemporary "civilizations" or as three-componential realities. This conclusion means that in its systems or supersystems each of these "civilizations" changes as systems change, in

---

[7] Cf. on that M. I. Rostovtzeff, *A History of the Ancient World* (Oxford University Press, 1926), Vol. II, pp. 325 ff.

[8] Cf. the evidence in H. Schäfer, "Ägyptische und heutige Kunst," *Die Antike*, Vol. III (1927), pp. 195 ff. J. Capart, *Lectures on Egyptian Art* (Chapel Hill, 1928).

meaningful-causal togetherness. To this part of the "civilizations" many of the conclusions of Danilevsky, Spengler, and Toynbee are applicable; as a matter of fact many of these conclusions display a remarkable keenness of observation and insight, and a deep understanding of the complex processes of cultural change. That part of the "civilizations" which is united only by direct or indirect causal but not by meaningful ties, such a part does not follow the same course of change as the meaningful-causal unities. It is free from the pressure of logico-aesthetic consistency, and moves and changes along patterns "neutral" to such consistency. Finally, the part of the "civilizations" which is unintegrated meaningfully and not interdependent causally, changes as congeries, disjointedly, accidentally, mainly through the fortuitous pressure of external factors.

Despite the basic misconceptions of the structure and movement of the civilizations which Toynbee, Spengler, and Danilevsky premise for their thinking, certain of their conclusions are nevertheless valid if divorced from their false frame of reference. Reinterpreted and placed within the scheme of sensate, idealistic, and ideational supersystems and less integrated eclectic cultures, they agree essentially with the conclusions of my analysis of these systems and greatly reinforce them. For instance, what Danilevsky, Spengler, and Toynbee regard as the phase of growth in their "civilization" corresponds essentially with what I have called the ideational phase of the great cultures. My characterization of the ideational supersystem and their concept of the phase of growth, especially Toynbee's description of this phase and partly of "petrifaction," are essentially similar. What they call the youth-maturity phase or the period of the "breakdown of civilization" (which in Toynbee's scheme has a specific meaning) coincides again in many points with my idealistic supersystem, occurring as a passage between declining ideational and rising sensate supersystems. What they style as the decline and then disintegration phase (Toynbee's phase of "the Universal State and Universal Church") coincides again in many essential traits with my sensate supersystem, especially at its overripe stage. This concurrence of conclusions reached by different authors working independently of one another and approaching the problem from quite different viewpoints deserves to be noted; it is cumulative evidence that in these points the conclusions are likely to be valid.

The basic difference between these theories and my own begins with the fundamental premise. They regard their "civilization" as a real unity; I regard it as a conglomeration of various systems and congeries, only in small part integrated meaningfully-causally, in larger part unified through indirect causal bond, but in still greater part an unintegrated conglomeration of systems and congeries. They view each civilization as an organism or "species" that follows the biological life-cycle of growth, youth, maturity, old age and death. For me such a life-cycle is neither logically nor factually tenable. Unintegrated cultures cannot grow, age, or decline; they need not have identical life-cycles, occurring only once and ending always with death. They cannot have a uniform life career. From their false premises many other fallacious conclusions are drawn by Danilevsky, Spengler, and Toynbee.[9]

In my works, instead of these false premises, a more valid and precise distinction between the cultural systems and supersystems and cultural congeries and conglomeration of congeries is carried through, with the necessary distinction between the meaningful unities, meaningful-causal, direct and indirect causal unities and, finally, spatially adjacent congeries. Meaningful-causal systems and supersystems change in togetherness, congeries not in togetherness; purely causal unities change in togetherness, if they are close unities, but this togetherness is purely causal, very different from the meaningful-causal togetherness. The total cultures that are little integrated change mainly in the way of congeries. Total cultures that are highly integrated up to the vastest possible sensate, idealistic, and ideational supersystems, change in these supersystems as meaningful-causal unities. Changing in this way, such total cultures shift from one supersystem to another, and having run their cycle repeat it, without dying or being "petrified" for a thousand or more years. In the rest of such total cultures, some of their minor supersystems and systems

[9] Cf. my "A. J. Toynbee's Philosophy of History," *Journal of Modern History*, 1940, pp. 374-387.

may change in causal dependence on the changing of the dominant supersystem, but this causal dependence does not make them a meaningful part of the dominant supersystem. Finally, a part of the total culture that is a real congeries to the dominant supersystem changes as congeries do.

The real picture of the change of so-called total cultures or civilizations is thus much more complex than the partisans of their alleged unity claim. And there is hardly any doubt that the proposed conceptual framework is more valid than the too simple theories of the unity of civilizations.

II. Inadequacy of the Prevalent Factorial Analyses in Application to Cultural Systems

The basic difference between the meaningful-causal cultural system, the purely causal interdependent systems, and congeries, and the deep dissimilarity of the why and how of their change dictate two fundamentally different approaches to the study of their static and dynamic relationships.[10] In application to congeries and partly purely causal systems the prevalent way of factorial or causal analysis of taking any cultural phenomenon as an independent variable and studying its relationship to another phenomenon as a variable, through observational, statistical, experimental, and other procedures is legitimate. Each variable can be taken *per se*, in isolation from other variables.

In application to meaningful-causal subsystems, systems, and supersystems, this procedure is entirely inadequate and can lead only to a series of blunders. A biologist cannot study the relationship between, say, the heart and digestive system of an organism, each organ being cut out of the organism, and treated as an independent variable. He would find he had only a dead heart and dead digestive organs, whose real relationship and function in the system of the whole organism would remain unknown to him. Still more distorted and blundering will be the results if a biologist, having no idea of the organism, should take half a heart and three-quarters of a stomach as two independent variables and try to study their causal and functional relationships. Fortunately such biologists hardly exist nowadays. But unfortunately in the social

sciences similar procedures are still prevalent. Without realizing at all the fundamental difference between a cultural system and congeries, the rank and file of the factorial analysts unhesitatingly take any social or cultural phenomena, treat them all simply as "variables" regardless of whether they may be a part or subsystems in a system. They handle all cultural phenomena as a congeries, as variables. Worse still, as we saw and shall see in the case of the dichotomic theories (see Chapter 44) their proponents take for one of their variables ("material culture"), only the component of material vehicles (gadgets, instruments of production) of several systems cut off from their ideological component. For their other variable they take the ideological component of some other systems, cut off from their material vehicles. They then confront these two variables and deduce pseudo-uniformities of a "nonmaterial culture" lagging behind the "material one."

The whole procedure is as sound as that of a biologist who takes for one of his variables the "material tail of a horse" and for the other variable the "nonmaterial breathing" of a bird and tries to find which of the two variables leads and which lags in a change. Without a preliminary investigation as to whether a given cultural phenomenon is a part of a system or independent congeries most "factorial analysts" take any cultural phenomenon as just a variable and try to discover statistically its relationship to another variable. In this way they often pick up a variable

---

[10] Even in physical and biological disciplines a sharp distinction is made between their systems and congeries. See A. J. Lotka, "Evolution and Thermodynamics," *Science and Society*, 1944, pp.

161 ff. "The Law of Evolution," *Human Biology*, 1945, 168-194. In psychology K. Lewin and others begin to carry it through. Cf. K. Lewin, "Field Theory in Social Psychology," *AJS*, 1939, pp. 884 ff.

that, like the horse's tail or bird's breathing, is a part of a system and study it as an independently existing variable. They butcher a living unity into mechanical cuts; unite several cut in a dead unity; chop several living systems into cubes; and then laboriously study the coefficient of the correlation between these cubes. The insanity of such handling of systems must be glaring. And yet it is still prevalent in the factorial analyses of social scientists. As mentioned in our study, we shall try to avoid it and treat the causal-meaningful relationships in systems and between the systems along fundamentally different lines than the relationships between independent congeries.[11]

III. Under What Conditions Systems Grow and Blossom Together

This question can be answered now, after the preceding analysis of sensate, ideational, and idealistic supersystems, more adequately than it was answered before, in Chapter 35.

1. If the Culture Has a Supersystem

If a given culture is integrated into one of three supersystems, then the following systems will grow and blossom in togetherness.

(a) When the *ideational* supersystem is rising we can expect: a creative blossoming of religion and theology; of idealistic and mystical philosophy, with its ontological idealism, eternalism, mysticism, religious or transcendental rationalism; ideational fine arts in all main fields; deep and real psychology of human mind and soul; ideational-absolutistic ethics and sacred law; theocratic, political, and social organization; developed familistic social groups; and other systems and subsystems of the ideational character, mentioned above. All these systems will be growing and blossoming together, though not all necessarily will be equally great creative systems. Likewise they will be growing together even if all systems remain only rudimentary. The dominant rudimentary ideational supersystem of such cultures as that of Tibet, or of the Zuni and Hopi Indians are examples.[12] On the other hand, science, natural science, technology, and economic empires; materialistic and empiricist philosophy, relativism, singularism, nominalism; sensate fine arts, sensate-relativistic, utilitarian, hedonistic, and sceptical ethics and law; these and all other sensate systems and sub-

systems will develop little in such a culture and at such periods. They will show little creativeness and little growth.

(b) When the *sensate* supersystem is rising, all sensate systems will be growing together, though not necessarily with equal creative splendor and magnificence. When the sensate supersystem begins to decline, all its systems and subsystems begin to decline also.

(c) When the *idealistic* supersystem emerges —usually as a passage between the declining ideational and emerging sensate systems— idealistic systems of religion and philosophy, science and arts, ethics and law, politics and economics emerge and grow. When the idealistic supersystem declines, all its systems and subsystems decline also.

Such is the change when a given culture is integrated into one of the supersystems. This answer takes into consideration the content and character of each of the systems. It is more precise than the answer given in Chapter 35 when the content and nature of each system was not considered and when the criteria of growth and blossoming were rather arbitrary, based upon the mainly sensate estimates of historians. For them there was no great medieval literature or music, no great medieval sculpture or philosophy, no development of psychology or social science. Consciously or unconsciously imbued with sensate standards they do not see any greatness in ideational

---

[11] See a development of this criticism in my *Sociocultural Causality, Space, Time,* Ch. 2, *et passim.*

[12] See a good analysis of Hopi culture from this standpoint in L. Thompson's "Logico-Aesthetic Integration in Hopi Culture," *AA* 1945, pp. 540-553. Especially good is the analysis of Hopi arts from this standpoint.

Table 1. World. Geometric Averages

Period	I	II	III	IV	V	VI	VII	VIII	IX	X	Arithmetic Average
B.C. 4000–3951	—	8.4	—	—	—	—	—	—	—	—	0.8
3000–2951	—	6.4	—	—	—	—	—	—	—	—	0.6
1500–1451	39.0	—	—	—	—	10.0	—	—	—	—	1.0
1050–1001	17.9	48.3	—	—	—	—	—	—	—	—	8.7
950–901	13.7	—	44.6	—	—	—	—	—	—	—	1.8
900–851	—	21.8	—	—	—	—	—	—	—	—	7.9
850–801	10.6	18.0	10.9	—	—	—	—	—	—	—	1.8
800–751	53.4	19.2	—	—	—	—	—	—	—	—	4.1
750–701	9.8	18.2	—	—	—	—	—	—	—	—	7.2
700–651	—	—	19.3	—	—	—	—	—	—	—	2.9
650–601	36.2	21.7	34.8	—	—	—	—	—	—	—	9.3
600–551	69.5	39.2	25.7	—	—	41.0	—	—	6.6	—	18.2
550–501	42.3	104.4	12.8	—	—	122.7	—	—	7.6	—	29.9
500–451	30.8	96.7	105.8	5.9	3.8	64.8	—	8.7	26.9	—	33.3
450–401	3.6	168.0	144.4	80.3	14.1	110.4	—	2.8	48.4	—	58.3
400–351	2.8	175.0	26.3	57.4	10.3	214.3	—	9.3	27.1	3.1	52.2
350–301	—	281.7	32.1	31.2	4.4	145.3	5.5	5.2	50.6	—	54.4
300–251	—	70.4	51.7	1.7	30.9	91.6	14.3	—	—	—	26.0
250–201	—	155.0	42.7	5.8	33.6	8.5	—	—	—	—	24.6
200–151	—	111.7	81.0	38.6	—	13.0	—	4.6	—	—	24.9
150–101	6.7	37.5	12.3	5.4	12.9	11.4	2.2	—	—	—	8.6
100–51	5.6	265.9	95.2	23.2	7.5	14.8	—	—	—	—	43.8
B.C. 50–1	13.1	216.0	219.5	128.1	23.2	4.0	—	26.0	15.3	—	61.9
A.D. 0–49	253.4	125.6	41.3	41.1	8.4	55.3	—	18.5	2.8	2.2	54.9
50–99	36.4	170.7	159.8	55.1	14.1	46.8	—	3.7	—	—	48.7
100–149	132.3	37.3	54.1	71.7	38.7	2.2	—	11.2	—	—	34.7
150–199	97.3	70.4	68.3	34.4	10.3	38.6	—	—	2.6	—	32.2
200–249	155.2	77.3	16.7	15.2	—	19.6	—	—	—	—	28.4
250–299	135.6	36.6	3.8	1.7	4.3	—	—	—	—	—	18.2
300–349	200.0	75.8	—	29.5	9.4	22.9	—	5.7	—	—	34.3

Period	I	II	III	IV	V	VI	VII	VIII	IX	X	
350- 399	307.9	78.7	41.9	34.7	15.0	18.0	—	—	3.3	—	50.0
400- 449	197.3	83.7	33.8	50.6	—	—	—	—	—	—	36.5
450- 499	35.5	86.8	—	53.1	4.7	20.1	—	—	—	—	19.6
500- 549	56.4	119.3	11.9	58.8	7.4	28.6	—	—	—	—	28.0
550- 599	80.3	40.6	22.4	15.2	4.1	—	—	—	—	—	16.6
600- 649	199.4	52.4	44.2	7.2	—	—	—	—	—	—	30.7
650- 699	78.5	1.7	14.6	—	12.0	—	—	—	—	—	9.5
700- 749	54.0	34.1	—	12.2	—	—	—	—	—	—	11.2
750- 799	34.4	55.2	—	8.1	—	—	—	—	—	—	9.8
800- 849	76.3	60.8	4.6	24.1	—	—	—	—	—	—	16.6
850- 899	129.8	80.4	—	45.0	8.9	—	—	—	—	3.1	28.4
900- 949	80.2	54.0	7.8	15.5	3.3	16.6	—	2.4	—	8.0	18.1
950- 999	59.1	93.1	48.0	19.7	—	9.7	—	—	—	—	22.6
1000-1049	94.6	129.3	14.3	8.8	29.2	5.8	—	—	—	10.5	28.7
1050-1099	195.1	211.6	23.1	25.5	6.3	—	—	—	—	—	49.0
1100-1149	152.6	132.7	20.0	110.0	—	28.3	3.0	—	—	—	44.8
1150-1199	222.4	182.0	63.9	54.4	—	29.7	—	—	—	—	58.4
1200-1249	136.9	195.1	41.4	62.6	18.9	56.3	—	4.5	4.7	—	47.7
1250-1299	156.3	185.0	47.2	64.4	13.2	8.8	16.9	8.6	35.8	—	54.0
1300-1349	108.7	180.8	108.2	53.1	8.8	21.4	15.0	—	78.1	—	58.7
1350-1399	195.8	193.8	142.5	32.5	14.8	34.3	29.5	5.0	36.6	—	65.1
1400-1449	161.4	222.0	56.0	90.8	4.6	33.2	40.1	14.3	157.7	—	78.0
1450-1499	231.9	393.4	120.2	213.5	12.1	8.9	100.7	29.0	442.1	12.1	156.4
1500-1549	805.8	504.4	409.2	220.3	96.3	65.3	82.3	116.6	790.4	10.8	310.1
1550-1599	626.6	782.3	782.1	363.9	187.0	49.1	70.0	149.2	262.3	75.9	334.8
1600-1649	512.6	927.0	828.9	441.7	295.0	328.5	71.7	138.2	686.0	38.4	426.8
1650-1699	901.1	1063.1	942.8	389.3	420.7	303.2	67.1	57.7	560.1	78.1	478.4
1700-1749	634.2	786.4	842.6	527.7	451.0	318.8	77.9	181.2	249.0	149.1	421.8
1750-1799	452.4	2329.9	1666.5	995.2	1318.0	404.5	271.3	397.3	597.9	295.8	872.9
1800-1849	944.6	3201.0	2765.0	2022.2	2042.2	535.3	692.7	530.2	1327.7	390.4	1445.1
Totals	9287.3	14937.4	10406.2	6646.4	5199.4	3361.6	1561.2	1726.3	5423.3	1077.5	5962.9

I, Religion; II, State; III, Literature; IV, Scholarship; V, Science; VI, Philosophy; VII, Business; VIII, Miscellaneous; IX, Fine Arts; X, Music.

TABLE 2. WORLD. GEOMETRIC AVERAGES, PERCENTAGES

Period	I	II	III	IV	V	VI	VII	VIII	IX	X	Total Percentage
B.C. 4000–3951	—	100.0	—	—	—	—	—	—	—	—	100
3000–2951	—	100.0	—	—	—	—	—	—	—	—	100
1500–1451	—	—	—	—	—	100.0	—	—	—	—	100
1050–1001	44.7	55.3	—	—	—	—	—	—	—	—	100
950– 901	17.1	27.2	55.7	—	—	—	—	—	—	—	100
900– 851	—	100.0	—	—	—	—	—	—	—	—	100
850– 801	26.0	47.2	26.8	—	—	—	—	—	—	—	100
800– 751	74.6	25.4	—	—	—	—	—	—	—	—	100
750– 701	33.7	—	66.3	—	—	—	—	—	—	—	100
700– 651	39.1	23.4	37.5	—	—	—	—	—	—	—	100
650– 601	38.3	21.5	14.1	—	—	22.5	—	—	3.6	—	100
600– 551	14.2	34.9	4.3	—	—	41.1	—	2.9	2.6	—	100
550– 501	9.2	28.7	31.4	1.7	1.1	19.2	—	0.8	7.9	—	100
500– 451	0.6	29.2	25.0	13.8	2.4	19.1	—	1.6	8.3	—	100
450– 401	0.5	33.6	5.1	11.0	1.9	41.1	—	1.0	5.2	0.6	100
400– 351	—	51.2	5.8	5.6	0.8	26.4	1.0	—	9.2	—	100
350– 301	—	27.0	19.8	0.7	11.9	35.1	5.5	—	—	—	100
300– 251	—	63.1	17.7	2.3	13.4	3.5	—	—	—	—	100
250– 201	—	44.9	32.5	15.5	—	5.2	—	1.9	—	—	100
200– 151	7.6	42.4	14.0	6.1	14.6	12.8	2.5	—	—	—	100
150– 101	1.2	60.7	21.7	5.3	1.7	3.4	—	6.0	—	—	100
100– 51	2.1	34.9	35.4	20.7	3.8	0.6	—	—	2.5	—	100
B.C. 50– 1	46.2	22.9	7.5	7.4	1.5	10.1	—	3.5	0.5	0.4	100
A.D. 0– 49	7.5	35.1	32.8	11.3	2.9	9.6	—	—	0.8	—	100
50– 99	38.1	10.8	15.8	20.5	11.1	0.5	—	3.2	—	—	100
100– 149	30.2	21.9	21.2	10.7	3.2	12.0	—	0.8	—	—	100
150– 199	54.7	27.2	5.9	5.3	—	6.9	—	—	—	—	100
200– 249	74.5	20.1	2.1	0.9	2.4	—	—	—	—	—	100
250– 299	—	—	—	—	—	—	—	—	—	—	100

Period	I	II	III	IV	V	VI	VII	VIII	IX	X	
300– 349	58.2	22.1	—	8.6	2.7	6.7	—	1.7	—	—	100
350– 399	61.8	15.7	8.4	6.9	3.0	3.6	—	—	0.6	—	100
400– 449	54.0	22.9	9.2	13.9	—	—	—	—	—	—	100
450– 499	18.1	44.4	—	27.2	—	10.3	—	—	—	—	100
500– 549	20.2	42.7	4.2	21.0	1.7	10.2	—	—	—	—	100
550– 599	48.4	24.5	13.5	9.1	4.5	—	—	—	—	—	100
600– 649	65.0	16.9	14.5	2.3	1.3	—	—	—	—	—	100
650– 699	82.8	1.7	15.4	—	—	—	—	—	—	—	100
700– 749	48.1	30.3	—	10.9	10.7	—	—	—	—	—	100
750– 799	35.2	56.5	—	8.3	—	—	—	—	—	—	100
800– 849	46.0	36.7	2.8	14.5	—	—	—	—	—	—	100
850– 899	45.7	28.3	—	15.9	3.1	5.9	—	—	—	1.1	100
900– 949	44.3	29.8	4.3	8.6	1.8	5.4	—	1.4	—	4.4	100
950– 999	26.2	41.2	21.3	8.7	—	2.6	—	—	—	—	100
1000–1049	33.0	45.1	4.7	3.1	10.3	—	—	—	—	3.8	100
1050–1099	39.8	43.2	4.7	5.2	1.3	5.8	—	—	—	—	100
1100–1149	34.1	29.6	4.5	24.5	—	6.6	0.7	—	—	—	100
1150–1199	38.1	31.1	11.0	9.3	—	9.7	—	—	1.0	—	100
1200–1249	28.7	40.9	8.7	13.1	3.9	1.9	—	1.8	6.6	—	100
1250–1299	28.9	34.3	8.8	11.9	2.4	4.0	3.1	2.5	13.3	—	100
1300–1349	18.5	31.0	18.4	9.0	2.3	5.8	4.5	—	5.6	—	100
1350–1399	30.1	29.8	21.9	5.0	0.6	—	5.1	4.3	20.2	0.8	100
1400–1449	20.7	28.5	7.2	11.6	0.8	4.3	6.4	5.1	28.3	0.3	100
1450–1499	14.8	25.2	7.7	13.6	3.1	0.5	2.6	6.4	25.6	2.3	100
1500–1549	26.0	16.3	13.2	7.1	5.6	2.1	2.1	2.6	7.8	0.8	100
1550–1599	18.7	23.4	23.4	10.7	6.9	1.5	1.7	2.1	16.1	0.9	100
1600–1649	12.0	21.8	19.4	10.3	8.9	7.6	1.4	1.7	11.7	1.6	100
1650–1699	18.8	22.2	19.7	8.1	10.7	6.4	1.8	1.4	5.9	3.5	100
1700–1749	15.0	18.6	20.0	12.4	15.1	7.6	3.1	1.8	6.8	3.4	100
1750–1799	5.2	26.8	19.1	11.4	14.1	4.6	4.8	4.5	9.2	2.8	100
1800–1849	6.5	22.2	19.1	14.0	14.1	3.7	4.8	3.6	9.2	2.8	100

I, Religion; II, State; III, Literature; IV, Scholarship; V, Science; VI, Philosophy; VII, Business; VIII, Miscellaneous; IX, Fine Arts; X, Music.

forms of religion, philosophy, fine arts, law or ethics, politics or economics.[13]

When we divest ourselves of these perfectly subjective and arbitrary standards, we clearly see that ideational systems in their super-systems are great in their own way, and are very consistently integrated with their major premises and with one another. As such they are great creations, emerging, growing, and declining in togetherness.

2. If the Culture Does Not Have a Super-system

If a given culture is not notably integrated into one of our supersystems, then growth and blossoming of its various systems is likely to be somewhat incidental, devoid of the above togetherness. In such a culture, depending on the urgent nature of its needs and their shift, now science may blossom either alone or side by side with some sort of philosophy or one of the fine arts; now creativeness may develop in politics or economics with some sort of legal system; now architecture or music may produce great systems, perhaps sensate, perhaps idealistic or ideational. Under such conditions we should expect what A. Kroeber actually found: in two out of thirteen cultures sculpture and painting developed and blossomed simultaneously; sculpture blossomed earlier than painting five times; later than painting twice; and four times blossoming of one of the other of these arts was lacking entirely.[14] Study of the interrelationship of growth of other cultural systems would yield similar results. Not united by logico-aesthetic ties and at best only causally interdependent, various cultural systems grow and decline in these conditions at random.

3. Additional Evidence

Besides the data given in the chapters on fluctuation of supersystems, additional solid evidence for the validity of these propositions is supplied by the preceding summary table compiled by John V. Boldyreff for my *Dynamics*. All historical persons mentioned in all volumes of the *Encyclopedia Britannica* were classified according to the periods and the fields of activities through which they became noted. After that the geometric average of the number of persons and lines devoted to them was computed for all the persons in a specified activity for a given half century. Table 1 gives the geometric averages, Table 2 the percentages of these averages for each ten fields for each period, all ten fields making 100 per cent.[15]

The absolute or percentage figures for each specified field for each period may serve as a rough measure of the comparative creativity in each field in the same period. Increase and decrease of these percentages of geometric averages from period to period serves as a rough indicator of increase and decrease of creativity in these fields. If not all historical persons have been strictly creative in a constructive sense of the term, the bulk of these were, and the rest "immortalized" themselves by some actions and deeds—destructive or constructive—far beyond the deeds of the non-historical bulk of human beings. For all these reasons the table gives us, as far as it goes, a systematic and solid index of the field: periods in which a creativity or "blossoming" was strong or weak; how the creativity changed from period to period; where it exploded synchronously; where it appeared earlier and where later; and finally, how it proceeded continuously or intermittently, in a cumulative or noncumulative way. The tables give summarized data for all cultures thrown together, and in this sense do not deal strictly with one culture. However, due to an enormous neglect of all the cultures except the Graeco-Roman

---

[13] The same mistake lies at the very foundation of A. Kroeber's work, which tries to find out how, when, and whether in togetherness or not, great "growths" of nations, religions, science, philosophy, fine arts occur. Entirely ignoring the content and nature of each system, relying entirely on estimation of a limited number of historians with their sensate standards of "growth and blossoming," the work gives somewhat incidental, mainly sensate periods of blossoming. As a result, the subsequent

analysis could not yield and did not yield many significant uniformities and conclusions. A few conclusions reached are typical mainly for cultures which were not integrated into the vastest supersystems, the case examined in section 2, that immediately follows.

[14] Kroeber, *op. cit.*, pp. 779 ff.

[15] Cf. the details of the computation and other technical procedures used in *Dynamics*, Vol. IV, Ch. 7. See there also several tables for separate countries.

and the western in our history and the encyclopedias, even "The World" tables are made up mainly of historical persons of the Graeco-Roman and western cultures. When similar tables computed separately for Egypt, Persia, India, China, Greece, Rome (Italy), France, England, Germany, Austria, Central Europe, Russia and Poland, and the United States are examined, they all agree with the main movements of the tables for the whole world. For the sake of economy these tables for separate countries are not reproduced here.[16]

Creativity in Religion and Business. After these remarks let us turn to the examination of the tables for the whole world. First, let us glance at the figures concerning religion and business (columns I and VII). We already know that in predominantly ideational periods religion becomes the main field of creative activity, while economics and business are neither cultivated, nor attract many creative minds. In the sensate period, on the contrary, religious creativity is largely neglected, while business activity is much more cultivated. From the preceding chapters on the rise and decline of ideational, idealistic, and sensate super-systems in the Graeco-Roman and the western world we know at what centuries each of these supersystems was dominant and at what periods it was in decline. The table confirms indeed that the periods of a great creativity in religion, like the periods from 1050 to 501 B.C. and especially from 750 to 501,[17] and then from 200 A.D. to about 1300 A.D. (ideational periods) are marked by an almost entire lack of creativity in business; throughout these periods there is almost a complete lack of persons who became historical through busi-ness creativity, and vice versa. The periods when the business field gives historical per-sons, like the periods of 350-100 B.C. and then 1250 to 1849 A.D., are marked by a notable decrease of creative historical persons in the field of religion. We know already that these periods in Greece and the western world were marked by the rise and domination of the

sensate supersystem. While in ideational periods from 30 to 100 per cent of all the historical persons became historical through religious activity, in the sensate period the percentages of such persons fell down to either zero (350-151 B.C.) or to a mere 5 to 6 per cent (1750-1849). Thus *the creativity in partic-ularly ideational systems of religion and in particularly sensate systems of business are mutually exclusive.* Indeed "no man can serve two masters . . . Ye cannot serve God and Mammon." This mutual exclusiveness of creativity in these ideational and sensate sys-tems par excellence is shown by the data of all separate countries studied (given in *Dynam-ics*).

This is the direct corroboration of the above propositions.

Movement of Creativeness in Religion and Statesmanship. At first glance the move-ments in these fields appear to be erratic, the reason being that our tables do not separate theocratic or ideational statesmanship from secular or sensate. When such a separation is made, the relationship of the creativity in these systems becomes comprehensible in a greater portion of the respective columns. First, we see that their movements are *mutually exclusive in several periods.* The periods 400 to 1 B.C. and 1750-1849 are marked by almost complete disappearance of creativity in religion and an enormous increase in political activities. On the other hand, a period like 100 to 1200 A.D. is marked by a comparative increase in creativity in religion and a decrease of creativ-ity in statesmanship. In the data for separate countries this exclusiveness is shown in a very clear-cut way.[18] In other portions of the two columns *the movement of creativity in both fields grows and declines in togetherness. In still others they vary without apparent relation to each other.*

This seemingly erratic relationship is not erratic at all, when the theocratic and secular forms of statesmanship are distinguished. In the periods of domination of sensate super-systems its statesmanship and political leader-

---

[16] Cf. the tables for most of these countries in *Dynamics*, Vol. IV, Ch. 7.

[17] The period of emergence and growth of Taoism, Confucianism, Hinduism of the Upani-shads, Savaism, Buddhism, Jainism, Zoroastrian-

ism, the Orphic-Pythagorean movement, and of the great Jewish prophets, and so on. See G. F. Moore, *History of Religion* (New York, 1913), Vol. I.

[18] See the data in *Dynamics*, Vol. IV, Ch. 7.

ship become secular or sensate; as such it rises while in such periods religious creativity and leadership decline. Hence their mutually opposite movements in the periods of 400 to 1 B.C. or 1750 to 1849. In the ideational periods the government becomes either explicitly or implicitly theocratic. It is carried on either by the explicitly religious leaders, making separate secular government unnecessary, or by political leaders in appearance different from the spiritual powers but in fact working hand in hand with them, controlled by them and representing disguised theocratic statesmanship. When religion and statesmanship work hand in hand, the indicators of their creativity parallel each other, rising and declining together. This is clearly shown in many of the ideational periods in our tables.

Finally, religious and political systems may now and then be little integrated with one another, neither working hand in hand nor in opposite ways to each other. In such cases their mutual movement is to be erratic and unrelated, as is shown by several periods in our tables.

Movement of Creativity in the Fine Arts. Since in the tables the ideational, idealistic, sensate forms of the fine arts are not distinguished; since art creators in ideational periods remain mainly anonymous and therefore do not enter individually the annals of history, and since, as mentioned, the encyclopedias compiled by sensate scholars are blind to ideational forms of the fine arts, it is apparent that our list is made up mainly of sensate and partly idealistic literati, painters, sculptors, architects, musicians, and playwrights. For these reasons it is comprehensible that the indicators of creativity in the fine arts *move in the opposite way from those in religion, tend to decline in dominantly ideational periods, and to rise in dominantly sensate periods.* With the exception of early leaders in the field of the fine arts who, like Homer or Hesiod, must be classed among religious leaders as much as among the fine arts creators, the indicators of creativity in the fine arts tend to rise with the idealistic period and then to grow in the vigorous stages of sensate periods. Only when the fine arts and religions are unintegrated do they move independently.

Movement of Philosophical, Scholastic, and Religious Creativity. The above considerations are quite applicable to the relationship between the movement of creativity in religion and in philosophy and scholarship. Since our data here do not distinguish the sensate, idealistic, and ideational forms of philosophy and scholarship, the first impression is that they move independently of each other. A *slightly greater concentration of philosophers and scholars in idealistic and sensate periods* marked by low creativity in religion is partly explainable by the prevalent anonymity of philosophical and scholastic creators in ideational periods, partly by merging philosophy and scholarship with religion in such periods, and partly by greater conformity of philosophical thought in ideational periods. For these reasons such periods dominated by religious creativity do not yield as many individual thinkers in these fields as idealistic and sensate periods.

When, however, a clear distinction between ideational, idealistic, and sensate forms of philosophy and scholarship is made, as we did in the preceding chapters, *then ideational forms of philosophy and scholarship* (*idealism, transcendental rationalism, mysticism, fideism, ontological realism, eternalism, etc.*) *grow with religious creativity in ideational periods;* similarly *sensate forms of philosophy-scholarship* (*materialism, mechanisticism, scepticism, nominalism, empiricism, singularism, temporalism, relativism, utilitarianism, etc.*) *grow with the sensate supersystem and in the periods of decline of religious creativity.* The same is true of idealistic philosophy and scholarship.

Finally some systems of philosophy and scholarship may not be integrated with either ideational religion or sensate supersystems, and therefore may grow independently of other sensate or ideational systems.

Movement of Science-Creativity. Science embodies mainly the truth of the senses assisted by that of reason. As such it is predominantly a *sensate system.* It can hardly flourish in ideational cultures but begins to rise in idealistic supersystems and to flourish in sensate ones. *Its creativity thus tends to grow when religious creativity declines, and vice versa.* That is exactly what our data show, partly for the world as a whole, despite masking of part of the data by Arabia and some other countries. In ideational periods of Greece, later of Rome, and then throughout the western medieval periods there were very few, sometimes no scientific discoveries and technological inventions; in idealistic periods they began to grow and the growth assumed enormous proportions in sensate periods. In the western sensate period especially, after the sixteenth century, the development proceeded so rapidly that the nineteenth and twentieth centuries produced a greater number of discoveries and inventions than almost all the preceding centuries together.

Now and then some scientific systems embody not only the truth of the senses and of reason but also of faith. Creation of such rare scientific systems may parallel religious creativity. However, such a situation occurs mainly in idealistic periods and is an exception to the rule.

Thus, on the basis of these data which sum up an enormous number of facts, the propositions formulated at the beginning of this section of the chapter are well corroborated. Together with the evidence cited in our study of the supersystems they form solid grounds for maintaining the validity of the propositions.

IV. Additional Propositions

Tables 1 and 2 and the data given in Chapter 35 suggest additional conclusions important per se as well as for a criticism of several theories of the temporal order of sociocultural change examined in the next chapters.

(1) *Creativity in the fields of religion and statesmanship, measured by the time of emergence of historical persons, appeared earlier than in any other field of culture. Next comes the field of literature, and at about the same time creative historical persons emerge in the fields of philosophy, fine arts, science, and scholarship; creativity in the field of business comes last in the course of time.* This proposition repudiates the theories that economic and technological change regularly lead all the others, especially the creative "ideological" changes.

Considering that at the dawn of history religion embraced the elements of science, scholarship, and philosophy, and that religious, moral, social and political organization is the paramount requisite for the existence and survival of any group, the early emergence of religious creativity is not surprising. L. Petrajitzky, R. Stammler, J. G. Frazer, F. de Coulanges, C. A. Ellwood, and several other scholars have indeed shown that such an organization is the necessary condition of not only organized economic and technological activity

but even of the very existence of any group, especially at the dawn of history.[19]

(2) *This conclusion is corroborated further by the fact that not only does creativity emerge earliest in the field of religion and statesmanship but it is the most continuous and engages the largest number of historical persons in comparison with all other fields. On the other hand, creativity in business is the most intermittent and engages the fewest historical persons of all fields of culture.* This conclusion sharply contradicts the theories claiming a perennial leadership of economic changes as the starting point for all other sociocultural changes. It contradicts also the theories claiming technological creativity as the perennial leader of all other changes. From the table, especially the tables for separate countries[20] and the data of Chapter 35, we clearly see many periods devoid of any historical person creative in the field of science and technology; and yet during such periods creative changes, particularly in the fields of religion, statesmanship, and literature continued to take place.

(3) *In the table covering the whole world and especially in the tables for separate countries, the creativity in all specified ten fields of culture is intermittent and nonlinear.* The same is shown by the summary data given in Chapter 35 and by other tables furnished later. In each field creativeness flowers suddenly,

---

[19] Cf. R. Stammler, *Wirtschaft und Recht* (Leipzig, 1896); L. Petrajitzky, *Die Lehre vom Einkommen* (Leipzig, 1893); F. de Coulanges,

The Ancient City (Boston, 1900); J. G. Frazer, *Psyche's Task* (London, 1913).

[20] Cf. these tables in *Dynamics*, Vol. IV, Ch. 7.

then declines, sometimes to the vanishing point, then rises again. There is no field and no country in which such ups and downs have not occurred. This supports the statements in Chapters 35 and 37 and in chapters on the supersystems, on shift and fluctuation of creativity from period to period and from country to country. No single country, even the world, can expect creativity in a given field of culture to increase continuously. On the contrary, any creative culture should expect in each field an alternation of the bursts and lulls of creativity. Now a galaxy of creators suddenly or gradually appears; now it decreases and vanishes. Even the unusually long rise of scientific and technological creativity in western culture from the thirteenth century on is likely to be slowed down and decline in the future, through a decline of interest in its promotion, or through the destructive forces released through science and technology by sensate man at the overripe stage of the sensate era. It has happened many times in the past, particularly at the end of the Graeco-Roman sensate period and during the rise of the ideational phase (see the figures on scientific discoveries and inventions in the next chapters). For separate countries such a decline of scientific and technological creativity has happened several times.

(4) *The same data show, however, that even in the culture of separate countries the blossoming periods in each or in most of the fields of culture happen not once, as Danilevsky, Spengler, and Toynbee contend, but several times.* In any of twelve cultures given in Chapter 35, as well as in the tables on historical persons (in *Dynamics*, Vol. IV), we observe several ups and downs of creativity in practically all fields of culture. There is no objective possibility of claiming that one of these peaks is the greatest while the others are just little "introductory" or "post-creative" ripples. Still less is it possible to claim that each great culture blossoms in all its compartments only once, or passes through the stages of childhood, maturity, old age, and

then death. As it was partly indicated before, there is no real ground for such contentions. The forms of systems and supersystems change in their domination, creativity fluctuates up and down in each field, but neither the change of supersystems nor creativity happens only once in the life history of a great total culture. They have happened several times and, if humanity is not destroyed, will happen again and again.

(5) *When in each field of culture the indices of historical persons are added from each preceding to each subsequent period, from the earliest to the latest, all series become naturally cumulative. And the accumulation of the indices in the fields of religion, statesmanship, and literature is rather faster and greater than in the field of science and technology, and especially of business.* Such a cumulative index rates religion at 9287.2, statesmanship at 14937.4, literature at 10406.2, while for business it is only 1561.2; for science 5199.4. Such a result evidently contradicts the contentions that only science, technology, and economic discoveries and inventions are cumulative.

(6) Finally, the data answer the question of what fields attract the best creative minds and brains. Contrary to the prevalent opinion that they always go into science, technology, and business and that only poorer brains go into religion, philosophy, the social and humanistic sciences, and the fine arts, all the preceding data show that *in highly integrated cultures, the best creative minds in ideational periods go into the fields of religion, ideational statesmanship, and ideational fine arts and humanities, while in sensate periods they enter mainly the fields of science, technology, business, and sensate forms of statesmanship, fine arts, and humanities.* There are only the slightest grounds for claiming that they always go into the same fields. Our contemporary obsession that the best brains invariably enter business, science, or technology is but the pleasant delusion of our business, science, and technology representatives.

V. Change of Systems by Variation and Substitution

In considering a change of a total culture or "civilization" one should distinguish two different kinds of change of its systems and supersystems. One is a change of the same system by variation; the other is a much deeper change by substitution of a new system for the old one. A cultural system in any field of culture, science or philosophy, fine arts or religion, law or ethics, politics or economics, hardly ever appears immediately in a fully developed form. It emerges ordinarily in a somewhat rudimentary form as a mere germ of the system rather than its full realization. Then if it is destined to grow qualitatively, it begins to unfold itself more and more fully, shedding some heterogeneous traits and adding or developing characteristics that are typical of it. In this growth it incessantly varies. Often several generations are required for it to grow to its full stature. It varies also in passing from one group to another, acquiring local variations in its process of socialization. In due course of time it eventually unfolds all its potential variations of growth because no concrete system (as we shall see in Chapter 46) is an inexhaustible omnivariant God but a finite system with a limited number of possible variations. Continuing its existence it does not stop its variations, but beyond the point of its full realization, these variations begin to add the characteristics that are foreign to it, that disfigure its real physiognomy, that overload it with an ever-increasing number of traits distorting its real nature, functions, and value. In this process of the qualitative decline of the system comes a moment when the system breaks down. Then it may become a fundamentally different system or a pile of congeries or be replaced by a new system which serves the old functions. In that case we have not a change of the same system by variation but a change by substitution of a new system for the old one. Sometimes the old system, having reached a clear-cut crystallization, tends to become static, hieratic, and repeated endlessly in its hieratic form. Such hieratic petrifaction of the system means a complete cessation of its creative growth. Becoming petrified, it ceases to be the center of creative forces, less and less successfully performs its sociocultural functions, and sooner or later is replaced by a new, more creative system that takes over its functions and relegates the petrified system to the position of a museum-piece.

The new system, replacing the outworn one, emerges sometimes through a gradual transformation of the old system; by shedding an increasing number of its real traits and adding new ones, it becomes at a certain point so basically changed that further transformation means the end of its existence and the beginning of a new system. Using Toynbee's expressions, such old and new systems may be said to be related to each other as "*apparented and affiliated*" systems.

In other cases the new system does not emerge through the transformation of the old system but through its radical replacement by a system growing from quite different sources, representing a basically different type. In that case the relationship of the old and the new system is the relationship of strangers devoid of any apparentation and affiliation. Thus the relationship of the present romance languages to Latin is that of "apparented and affiliated" language systems. But when Latin was replaced by, say, Chinese or Russian, the relationship is not one of apparentation or affiliation. Similarly early Christianity was replaced sometimes by such affiliated systems as Eastern Orthodox, Catholic, or Protestant denominations; elsewhere it gave way to an unrelated, stranger system, like atheism, Buddhism, or Confucianism.

It goes without saying that the change by variation of the same system is less radical than the change by substitution; the change of an apparented system by a new affiliated system is less basic than the replacement of the old by a new unrelated stranger. All these forms of change of systems occur in practically all total cultures or civilizations. Change by variation proceeds incessantly, but substitution occurs infrequently, separated by comparatively long intervals of time.

To illustrate: After its invention the horse-system of transportation passed through a large number of variations—horse-back riding, horse and buggy, horse and carriage, and so on. In the course of time all the main variations were exhausted; therefore they began to be repeated at various periods and in various cultures without producing any new types of this system. Then steam, electricity, and gasoline systems of transportation were invented. The new systems were not mere variations of the old one but radically new, scarcely affiliated with the old system. The new systems represented a much deeper revolution of the transportation system than all the previous variations of horse transport.

Similar kinds of change can easily be observed in practically all technological systems. An enormous number of variations of the bow and arrow systems eventually gave way to the gunpowder system, unrelated to it, and this system in turn is now being supplanted by the atomic power system.

In the field of writing there were many variations of picture writing; when, in many cultures, it was replaced by rebus writing, this last system was new but somewhat affiliated with the picture writing; when both were replaced by alphabet writing the new system was an unaffiliated one.

In philosophy there has been an endless variation of either idealistic or materialistic philosophical systems. When, however, a given idealistic system of philosophy is replaced by a materialistic one, or vice versa, we have again a radical change by replacement.

In science all basic theories in mathematics, astronomy, physics and chemistry, biology and social sciences have undergone countless variations. When, however, the geocentric system of cosmogony was replaced by the Copernican system, when the theory of separate creation was replaced by the doctrine of evolution, when vitalism in biology gave way to mechanism or vice versa, the atomistic theory to the nonatomistic or vice versa; when the emanation theory of light was replaced by the wave theory, Euclidean geometry by Lobachevskian or Riemanian—all such changes were the changes by substitution of a new system for an old one. In all fields of science changes by variations go on incessantly, but from time to time these are interrupted by the replacement of a basic scientific theory.

A similar pattern of change can be observed in the fine arts. In Greek architecture variations of the Doric order eventually gave way to the Ionic and the Corinthian, different though affiliated systems. The emergence in Europe later of the Gothic architecture was a radical departure from all the Greek orders. Gothic began in a rudimentary form in northern France, then developing and spreading through local variations it reached its fullest expression in the thirteenth century. As variations continued it departed from its essential style and became more and more ornate, flamboyant, rococo, more and more distorted. Thus eventually it exhausted all its main possibilities and succumbed under the weight of its atypical variations. It was then replaced either by the imitative Renaissance or by the baroque architecture, each basically different from the Gothic. Still more striking is the change in the fine arts when its ideational variations are replaced by sensate or vice versa.

In politics there are many variations of either monarchical or republican regimes; now and then it happens that a republican regime is replaced by a monarchical one, or vice versa.

In economics the capitalist regime has had many variations at different periods and in different populations; when the Communist system of economy replaced the Russian capitalist system, a basically different system of economy was established instead of the old one, and so on in all fields of culture.

As we shall see in Chapter 46, practically all concrete cultural systems are finite and limited in the basic types of their variations. When they complete the possible variations, the creative possibilities are exhausted. If they continue to exist, they begin to repeat the basic types. Thus if there were no new systems to replace the old ones, the history of culture would be a cycle of narrow repetitions. Its creative drive would have become progressively weaker.

If this has not happened it is thanks to constant creation of new systems to take the place of the old ones. Through changes by substitution, cultural life renews its parts and its creativeness. Viewed from this standpoint, the replacement of one supersystem by another represents the deepest cultural upheaval which renovates all parts of the system, producing a new creative flare-up by unfolding new horizons and new values. There is little ground to regret such profound revolutions. No matter how magnificent a particular supersystem may be, it eventually becomes exhausted of its creative genius. One can and should have all the reverence and gratitude for the dying creator who achieved all he could, but this reverence and appreciation should not prevent the welcoming of new creators to replace the dying one and to continue in their own way the creative life of human culture and of man himself. Change by substitution of a new creative system or supersystem is absolutely necessary for the maintenance of the creative continuity of human sociocultural history.

VI. Critical Remarks

In this and preceding chapters the untenability of several current theories of sociocultural change, particularly those of Marx and Max Weber, becomes rather evident. Marxianism contends that economic and technological changes (as "means and instruments of production") determine the changes in religion and other "ideological" systems of law, ethics, fine arts, and humanities. Max Weber, on the other hand, though equally stressing the interdependence of all the systems, gives causal precedence to religion and its resultant *Wirtschaftsethik* as the preponderant factor in the change of the economic system. According to Marx, the emergence of the capitalist system of economy and technology led to the emergence of Protestantism and subsequent changes in the ideological systems of the West. For Max Weber, on the contrary, the emergence of Protestantism with its *Wirtschaftsethik* was the preponderant factor of the emergence of the capitalist system of economy and its characteristic technology, of rationalism, of utilitarian ethics, and even of the development of science in western Europe.[21] In a somewhat simplified form Marxianism supposes the equation: Protestantism is the function of capitalism: $P=f(C)$. Max Weber turns it around making capitalism the function of Protestantism and its *Wirtschaftsethik*: $C=f(PW)$. As a matter of fact both equations and related theories are fallacious. The adequate formula is: capitalism, Protestantism, utilitarian ethics and law, science and technology, rationalism, individualism, contractual relations, visual-sensate art, materialistic philosophy, empiricism, temporalism, singularism, nominalism, and relativism —all are the manifestations of the decline of the ideational and rise of the sensate supersystems. As parts of one supersystem they are all dependent upon one another and upon the whole. Protestantism was not the cause of capitalism, nor was capitalism the cause of Protestantism; both were interdependently changing in togetherness with the supersystem as a whole. We have seen this in the chapters devoted to the rise and decline of sensate, ideational, and idealistic supersystems.

The situation is analogous to a large number of anatomical, physiological, psychological, and sociocultural changes experienced by an organism when it passes from childhood to youth and maturity: weight and stature increases; muscles, glands, and organs undergo important changes. All these changes proceed interdependently, in togetherness, as manifestations of the basic change of the whole organism. It is ridiculous to separate out of these multiple interdependent changes one system like the increase in stature or the appearance of a mustache as the cause of all the other changes. In biology the absurdity of the procedure is evident. Unfortunately it seems not so evident

[21] Cf. for a somewhat diluted Marxian interpretation H. M. Robertson, *Aspects of the Rise of Economic Individualism* (Cambridge University Press, 1933); M. Weber, *The Protestant Ethic and the Spirit of Capitalism* (New York, 1930); R. H. Tawney, *Religion and the Rise of Capitalism* (New York, 1926); R. K. Merton, *Science, Technology and Society in Seventeenth Century England, Osiris*, Vol. IV (Bruges, 1937). Contains a good bibliography, important material, but unfortunately the author succumbed to M. Weber's theory, overlooking its weak points. A. Fanfani, *Catholicism, Protestantism and Capitalism* (New York, 1935) gives a substantial criticism of the one-sidedness of Marxian as well as Weberian theories. For general criticism of Marxian and Weberian theories see my *Theories*, Ch. 10, and pp. 673 ff.

in the similar change of the supersystem when it passes from one of its basic forms into another. The Marxians persist in regarding the economic mustache as the cause of all the other changes while the Weberians find it in the religious stature.

Actually, the fallacy of both theories is clearly demonstrable by the facts. Practically all the changes which Weber ascribes primarily to Protestantism and its *Wirtschaftsethik* appeared from one to three centuries before the emergence of Protestantism. We have seen that the ideational supersystem had already begun to decline in most of its parts by the end of the twelfth century, passing into the idealistic one in the thirteenth and fourteenth centuries with an ever-increasing number of characteristics of the sensate supersystem. Scientific discoveries and technological inventions began notably to grow after the end of the twelfth century and originated in Catholic countries; utilitarian ethics and Weberian rationalism likewise began to emerge at about the same time or some one hundred and fifty years before the Reformation; visual and sensate fine arts, empiricism, materialism, hedonism, individualism, nominalism, and singularism all appeared one to two hundred years before Protestantism. Business leaders reappear on the historical scene in 1100-1149. The capitalist system of economy even in the Weberian sense emerged and began to develop in Italy, Spain, and Portugal some two hundred years before Luther published his theses. In short, most of the phenomena that Weber regards as consequences of Protestantism were already well along in their development long before the advent of the Reformation.

Even after its emergence all the sensate systems continue to grow in the Catholic as well as in the Protestant countries, and some of these sensate systems (individualism, secular rationalism, science and technology, hedonistic and utilitarian *Wirtschaftsethik*, the contrac-

tual system of political and economic regimes, materialism, sensualism, sensate fine arts, and so on) grew first in Catholic Italy as products of the Renaissance rather than in Protestant Germany, England, or the Netherlands.[22]

The Marxian theory is no less untenable. First of all, no radical economic or technological changes took place in Europe before 1300. Among the historical persons, business leaders emerge in Italy only after 1350, in France, for a short period in 1100-1149, then in 1250-1299, but only after 1500 do their series become continuous; in England they emerged only after 1350; in Germany after 1600, in Russia and Austria still later, in the United States after 1650.[23] They then postdate by hundreds of years the decline of the ideational supersystem at the end of the twelfth century. Furthermore, notable development of the truly capitalistic system did not take place until the seventeenth century, when the sensate supersystem was already dominant in practically all other compartments of the western culture. Without any other evidence this would be sufficient to vitiate the Marxian theory.

As mentioned before, the basic fallacy of both theories is that they do not distinguish between the change in meaningful-causal togetherness of systems and supersystems and that of the congeries. Both theories treat their "economic" and "religious" factors atomistically, as congeries in regard to each other and to all the other systems of the supersystem. They naturally, therefore, arrive at the "mustache" theory of causes. It is about time to abandon such childish statements of the problem. Both these theories and any other theory which neglects the difference between change in systems and in congeries cannot help arriving at logically and factually wrong conclusions.[24] A great deal more will be said of these fallacies in subsequent chapters in the criticism of various theories of the lead and lag in change of various classes of cultural phenomena.

---

[22] Cf. the detailed data on growth of all these sensate systems in *Dynamics*, all volumes. There the data are given also by separate countries, Catholic as well as Protestant.

[23] Cf. *Dynamics*, Vol. IV. pp. 333 ff.
[24] For a more detailed criticism of other points of these theories cf. my *Theories*, Chps. 10 and 12. Cf. also Fanfani's referred work.

Chapter 44. Time-Sequence Uniformities in the Change of Systems

1. Tentative and Pseudo-Uniformities of Cultural Lead and Lag

From a study of the essential modes of change of systems and supersystems we can now turn to a more systematic investigation of what kind of time-sequence uniformities, if any, are found in their change. Do some cultural systems always lead in change and others always lag? This chapter attempts to answer this old problem, on the one hand, in a constructive way by formulating some tentatively valid uniformities, and on the other, in a critical way by exposing the fallaciousness of several pseudo-uniformities claimed by many current theories. Besides the discussed uniformity of changing in togetherness of systems and supersystems, the following uniformities of the temporal order of change can be stated.

(a) *In a qualitative change of a system its component of meanings, values, and norms—its ideology—tends to change first while its component of behavioral and material vehicles, including technique, tends to lag in the change.* (In a purely quantitative change of the system the order of the change of the components may be different.) The behavioral and material cultures of a system contain also the technique of the objectification of the system's meanings or ideology: the religious system has a technique of praying, conducting religious services, of using and making religious objects, etc.; the scientific system has its technique of research; the law-system, its technique of crime-detection, court-procedure, evidence, and punishment; economic systems contain the techniques of business management, production, advertising, or salesmanship; the medical system, the techniques of medical diagnosis, treatment and cure; the literary system, the techniques of writing; the system of music or painting, the techniques, respectively, of composing, singing, or playing a musical instrument, and of painting or staging a play; the educational system has its techniques of teaching and training. In brief, each system has in its behavioral and material cultures the techniques for the realization of the system's ideology. *So far as the technique is a part of the component of the vehicles, it also lags in comparison with the component of the meanings (ideology) of the system in the qualitative change.*

A few exceptions to this uniformity exist, mainly in the form of the retroactive influence of the behavioral and material vehicles, including the technique upon the ideology, but they do not invalidate the rule.

We have seen that in an emergence of any system the phase of the conception of its ideology precedes the phase of its objectification in overt actions and material vehicles. It is the conceived ideology that chooses its vehicles and not the vehicles that determine the ideology. This lead of ideology continues in the change of the system, after its emergence. Before the conception of Christianity there could be no Christian religious behavior or ritual, no Christian cathedrals, frescoes, ikons, statues, ceremonial vestments, and so on; before the conception of a scientific or artistic or ethical ideology there can be no objectification in overt actions and material vehicles. Similarly, before a change in a given ideology there is rarely a change in its behavioral and material manifestations. Before a different airplane or gun or spade or any variation of a particular gadget is built, there is a prior variation of the controlling ideas. Change in a scientific theory precedes its objectification in a lecture, in manuscript, on the pages of the textbooks, in overt actions of the scientists, and in other material vehicles of science, including appropriate techniques, instruments, laboratory equipment, research institutions, and so on. Only after an Arian or Monophysitic modification of Christian ideology, did the new idea manifest itself in a legion of behavioral and material forms; just as after an ideological split between the partisans and opponents of the *filioque* or the Protestant variation of Christian ideology came the behavioral and material split of Christian system into the Western and Eastern, into the Catholic and Protestant Christianity. Before the law-norms are changed on the statute books, and in application within the material culture, they first had to be changed in the minds of the lawmakers and in the ideological convictions of the populations. We have seen that the unofficial law-convictions change incessantly whereas institutionalized law, with its cumbersome behavioral and material machinery, tends regularly to lag behind these preliminary ideological changes.

Sometimes a considerable time elapses before a changed ideology, for instance, a new scientific theory, a new philosophy, or political, economic, and sociological system, a new invention, a new style of music or literature, succeeds in changing the existing behavioral and material forms of the prevalent old ideology. The inertia of the old behavioral and material forms, together with the vested interests involved, resist their change sometimes for decades or longer. Sometimes contradiction between the changed ideology and the antiquated behavioral and material forms accumulates and, if not removed in time, explodes in revolutions. All this means that thought is the most dynamic form of reality, and certainly more dynamic than its materializations. As we have seen, it is never static and always contains in itself tensions that, demanding resolu-

tion, produce continual change and new creation.

A few seeming exceptions to this generalization exist, but even these exceptions are more apparent than real. They mainly take the form of the already examined retroactive influence of the behavioral and material cultures upon the ideological.[1] The existing behavioral and material cultures certainly condition our ideologies; their "lucky combination" suggests sometimes a new idea (as we have seen), or a new technique helps new discoveries, but conditioning, suggestion, and help do not mean that the behavioral and material vehicles change into a new system before the respective ideologies are changed. The existing scientific and technological cultures two decades ago did not permit the invention of radar or the atomic bomb. However, within these decades radio research and the development of sub-atomic physics, chemistry, and mathematics changed so notably that the practical realization of the respective mathematical, physical and chemical theories in the form of radar, rocket plane and guns, and of the atomic bomb became possible. Before these material and behavioral culture systems appeared their blueprints were drawn up, and before these blueprints could be made a long and complex change of the theories involved was required.

(b) *In a supersystem or a vast system consisting of several subordinated and co-ordinated subsystems, a tangible change first appears in one of the small subsystems, then in larger systems, then in vast systems, and finally in the supersystem as a whole. Some of the superficial changes in the smaller systems do not diffuse over their larger systems (as ripplings on the ocean surface do not disturb the deep currents); the tempo of the change in the smaller systems tends to be faster than in the larger systems and supersystems.*

Though any mechanical, biological, and sociocultural system incessantly changes as a whole in the process of its living and acting, a tangible change does not take place instantaneously in the whole system. It enters first some of its smallest subsystems and, if it is a serious change, it spreads over one or several subsystems which are causally and meaning-

[1] See Chapter 3.

fully closest to the one changed; only later does it affect the entire system and become noticeable in it as a whole. In a similar way it spreads only gradually over the vaster systems, until it makes itself felt in the whole super-system.

In an automobile some changes in one or a few of its subsystems take place annually in every new model. A serious change in the whole character of an automobile, leading to its radical transformation, occurs only after many years of accumulation of the changes in its important and unimportant parts. A revolutionary change-over to a basically new system of transportation, as from horse and buggy to automobile or to airplane; from rowboat or sailboat to steamship, takes still longer. The vaster the given technological system the slower the tempo of its tangible transformation in comparison with that of its subsystems.

The changes in this or that narrow theory of physics or chemistry, biology or social science are almost weekly phenomena; here and there something is changed in almost any new edition of standard texts. Changes in more basic theories of any science, involving several of their divisions, are more rare. The revolutionary reconstruction of the whole system of physics or chemistry, economics or sociology is still rarer. A revolutionary change of all the sciences, physiochemical, mathematical, biological, social, and humanistic in their basic system of truth and general principles are, as we have seen, still less frequent.

A change in this or that prayer, ritual, or material vehicle of a religion is more frequent than changes in basic Credos and dogmas. Small Christian denominations change, appear, and disappear within every year or decade.[2] The large religious systems like the Catholic, the Protestant, the Eastern Christianity, Hinduism, Buddhism, Confucianism, Taoism, endure for centuries changing basically as a whole only rarely, once in a century or in several centuries.

While changes in the small subsidiary political systems—in local government, or in sections of civil, criminal, municipal, and administrative law go on almost incessantly, replacing one statute with another, one norm with a different one, the basic change of the whole corpus of criminal or civil law happens more rarely; and the change of the whole fundamental law of a given state, including the change of its constitution, occurs still more rarely.

The same is true of economic systems and subsystems. While the changes in the organization of small business firms are almost continuous and, as we have seen, the firms themselves emerge and disappear within a few years, both the changes and the life span of larger industrial corporations take a longer period; finally, the change of the whole economic system, say, from capitalist to communist economy, occurs still more rarely.

Changes in little subsystems of music or painting, sculpture or architecture are again quite frequent; changes in the whole character of music or architecture, literature or painting are less frequent; changes in the whole character of all the main fine arts are still more rare. Shifts from ideational to idealistic or sensate fine arts have occurred in the past only at intervals of a few centuries. Despite a few exceptions, this rule holds generally true of almost all cultural systems.[3]

(c) *Within a cultural system or super-system, basic principles and their vehicles tend to change less, and change more slowly than the peripheral, secondary meanings and their vehicles. So far as the subsystems incorporate these peripheral and secondary values, while the system or supersystem is based upon and articulates the basic principles of the whole system, this proposition is connected with the preceding generalization and each supports the other.*

In any science, its basic principles and methods change less, and more slowly than its peripheral theories and propositions. The central credo and principal dogmas of a religion change much more slowly than its various prayers, myths, legends, secondary rituals, objects of veneration, and so on. In a language system grammar and syntax undergo much less change than words, intonation, and pronunciation. In the totality of the law-norms of the state or any organized group, the basic constitution with its norms changes less and

[2] See the data on such denominations and their span of life, above, in Chapter 34.

[3] Cf. A. Kroeber, *op. cit.*, pp. 304 ff. In a different way he arrives at similar conclusions.

more slowly than the norms dealing with various peripheral relationships, rights, and duties. In an economic system principles like that of private ownership or communal or state ownership change little, while its peripheral details of renting, buying, selling, distributing, advertising, promotion, and demotion of the employees, and so on, change much more easily and quickly. The same can be said of any social system. In a system of music or painting, literature or architecture, sculpture or drama the secondary details vary from artist to artist, often even from one creation to another of the same artist. Basic styles, like the naturalistic or symbolic, visual or ideational, romantic or classic, impressionistic or expressionistic, linear or *malerisch*, fluctuate much more slowly, as we have seen. The same is true of the principal subject matter of the fine arts: A shift, for instance, from religious (ideational) subjects to the secular (sensate) ones is slower in the total system of painting, sculpture, music, architecture, and literature in a given culture than variations of religious topics in ideational art, or secular topics within sensate art. Such variations occur in the paintings, literary works, musical compositions, or sculptures of the same creator while shift from the dominant ideational to the prevalent sensate subjects, or vice versa, have taken usually a period of one or more centuries.

In technological systems of transportation or communication, of warfare or machinofacturing, changes in the peripheral gadgets go on much more easily and quickly than those in the basic principles of the respective technologies. Peripheral variations in prevalent methods of cattle breeding or crop cultivation occur from breeder to breeder, farmer to farmer, gardener to gardener. Changes in the basic methods of cattle breeding, agriculture, or horticulture happen much more rarely and have taken centuries to come to pass.[4] From a different standpoint A. Kroeber arrives at similar conclusions: whole cultures change more slowly than their parts; great qualitative growths of cultural systems take a longer time than the growth and decline of some parts of the systems.[5] This principle has important bearing on a number of problems of cultural change to be discussed further.

(d) *No generalization can be made as to the order of change among subsystems. It is unlikely that any subsystem uniformly leads or lags.* In a complex system set in a dynamic environment, there seems to be no obvious or logical reason why change should always affect one subsystem first or another last. Such uniformity could only be looked for if the system contained some inherently and specially sensitive or insensitive systems and if the stimulus of the environment was always directed at the most sensitive and withheld from the least sensitive. Since such constancy is scarcely to be expected either of the nature of cultural systems or of the environment, no theoretical priority of change among subsystems can be established.

This logical consideration is supported by observations of comparatively simple and spatially compact mechanical and organic systems. A "pathological" change in a car or airplane does not always begin with the same part, say, the battery or spark plugs. Some varieties of azaleas respond to the spring by opening their flowers first and then their leaves; in other varieties the order is reversed. Some human babies begin to walk before they can talk; others learn first to talk, and then to walk. Disease strikes some human organism first in the lungs, to spread later (if not checked) to other organs; in others a disease begins first in the digestive system, or attacks the nervous system, the bones, or other organs.

Such a lack of uniformity in relatively simple organisms must be expected still more in cultural systems which are more complex, more disparate, more discrete, more dynamic and more continually subjected to changing conditions of the physical, biological, and especially sociocultural milieu. This expectation is corroborated, first, by the patent inadequacy of many theories that attempt to prove the existence of such uniformity and second, by the facts as observed in phenomena of sociocultural change.

2. Criticism of Current Theories

Several theorists have thought to find a uniform order of change among cultural subsystems. Sir Flinders Petri and O. C. S. Crawford claim that cultural changes generally affect

---

[4] Cf. G. Tarde, *The Laws of Imitation*, pp. 174 ff.
[5] Cf. A. Kroeber, *op. cit.*, pp. 804 ff.

first architecture, then sculpture, then painting, then music, mechanics, theoretical science, and lastly wealth.[6] P. Ligeti also found that in the system of the fine arts architecture always leads, followed by sculpture and painting.[7] Hegel and V. de Laprade are in agreement with this dogma.[8] There are also several other variants of the order of change in the whole system of the fine arts.[9] The theories are certainly interesting; some, like Ligeti's, are elaborately developed and apparently well corroborated. Unfortunately none of these beautiful theories can meet the test of "the ugly facts." Tables in Chapter 35 summarizing the data on the blossoming of the various fine arts as well as the other systems in the culture of some twelve countries, are sufficient in themselves to refute the theories. As the data of Chapter 35 are more systematic, continuous, and complete, their testimony must overrule the rather haphazard selections of evidence presented by the theorists. In addition there are other facts which contradict the theories discussed.[10]

In the system of science A. Comte's theory can serve as one of the best theories of a constant predictable time sequence in the change of the basic scientific disciplines from the theological to the positive stage. His sequence is mathematics, astronomy, physics, chemistry, biology, and sociology.[11] As a classification of basic sciences according to their increasing complexity and decreasing generality, it is excellent. As dogma on the time-order in which the disciplines become "positive" it is quite unsatisfactory: First, Comte's fundamental assumption that mankind and its whole culture pass in the course of time uniformly through three stages, from theological through metaphysical to positive stage, is unwarranted and contradicted by both facts and logic. Second, even if these disciplines were moving to positivism in the above time-order this would not mean that in all other respects they were changing in the same order. In the tens of thousands of years between the beginning of human history and the point at which culture arrived at Comte's "positivistic" stage the cultural subsystems have undergone hundreds of changes. Because they may have reached the "positivistic finish" in the order in which Comte assigns them it does not follow that they have undergone all their other numerous changes in the same order. Furthermore it is folly to talk as though a uniform change through Comte's three main stages took place in all the scientific subsystems. Mathematics as mathematics has always been positivistic; two and two must universally and eternally make four wherever and whenever elementary mathematics exists. One cannot therefore talk of the passage of mathematics from the theological to the metaphysical to the positivistic stage. It is equally clear that though the other branches of science might be considered to pass through such stages, they could not have done so in strict chronological order. To assume that up to the fourteenth century A.D. all human culture, including the sciences, remained largely in the theological stage and that no "positive" knowledge of physics, chemistry, biology, or sociology existed, is fantastic. Had that been true mankind could not have survived. A minimal real knowledge of physical, biological, and social phenomena is a condition of survival for a man or a group even for a period of a few weeks. Persons or groups who confused the physical properties of a banana and a stone and who therefore tried to eat stones and make slingshots out of bananas, such persons and groups would in their theological ignorance soon perish from the earth. This is the logical refutation.

The fact is that a large number of the most revolutionary scientific discoveries and inventions were made in the immemorial past:

[6] W. F. Petri, *The Revolutions of Civilizations* (London, 1912), p. 97; "History in Art," *Antiquity*, September, 1931; O. G. S. Crawford, "Historical Cycles," *Antiquity*, September, 1931.

[7] P. Ligeti, *Der Weg aus dem Chaos* (München, 1931), pp. 34; *passim*.

[8] G. W. F. Hegel, *The Philosophy of Fine Arts*, 4 Vols. (London, 1920), Vol. I, pp. 110-147; Vol. III, pp. 18 ff.; V. de Laprade, *Le Sentiment de la nature avant le Christianisme* (Paris, 1866), preface and *passim; Le sentiment de la nature chez les modernes* (Paris, 1866).

[9] See discussion of these in *Dynamics*, Vol. I, pp. 198 ff.; Chps. 5 and 6; *passim*.

[10] Cf. also A. Kroeber, *Configurations*, quoted, pp. 779 ff.

[11] See A. Comte, *Positive Philosophy*, tr. by Martineau (New York, 1855), Vol. I, pp. 1-33, *passim; System of Positive Polity* (London, 1875), Vol. I, pp. 27 ff.; *passim*.

Table 3. Western World Output of Natural Science, Technological, and Geographical Discoveries and Inventions By 100-, 50-, and 25-Year Periods

Period	Mathematics	Astronomy	Biology	Medical Science	Chemistry	Physics	Geology	Total (Science)	Technology	Geographical Discoveries	Grand Total	Boldyreff's Geometric Averages
3500- 801 B.C.	1	2	—	—	2	—	—	5	17	—	22	—
800- 701	—	3	—	—	—	—	—	3	6	—	9	—
700- 601	—	—	—	—	—	1	—	2	5	—	7	—
600- 501	2	7	2	3	3	2	1	20	10	1	31	17.9
500- 401	3	8	2	8	4	8	1	34	5	1	40	14.7
400- 301	8	5	14	8	5	6	—	46	12	2	60	64.5
300- 201	7	9	7	4	—	11	—	33	12	1	45	12.9
200- 101	2	5	4	2	—	—	—	14	2	1	17	30.7
100- 0	—	2	—	6	1	4	—	14	17	—	32	22.5
1- 100 A.D.	1	2	1	15	5	10	—	39	21	1	61	49.0
101- 200	2	7	6	9	—	2	—	23	4	—	27	4.3
201- 300	2	—	3	2	—	1	—	5	3	—	8	24.4
301- 400	—	—	—	4	1	3	—	8	8	—	16	0.0
401- 500	—	—	1	1	—	—	—	2	2	—	4	12.1
501- 600	—	2	—	4	1	1	—	8	5	1	13	4.1
601- 700	2	—	1	2	—	—	1	2	2	—	4	0.0[2]
701- 800	—	2	—	—	—	—	—	3	1	—	4	0.0[2]
801- 900	—	—	1	—	—	—	—	—	5	1	6	0.0[2]
901-1000	—	—	—	—	—	—	—	—	5	2	7	0.0[2]
1001-1050	—	—	—	—	—	—	—	1	3	1	5	0.0[2]
1051-1100	1	—	—	2	1	1	—	1	5	—	3	0.0[2]
1101-1150	—	—	1	3	—	1	1	3	3	—	8	0.0[2]
1151-1200	1	—	—	4	—	6	1	4	—	—	4	0.0[2]
1201-1250	2	—	5	3	3	—	—	15	3	2	20	12.2[2]
1251-1300	1	—	2	5	12	6	—	24	6	3	33	13.2[2]
1301-1350	3	7	3	5	1	1	1	20	12	4	36	8.8[2]
1351-1400	—	1	3	—	2	3	2	11	13	5	29	5.8[2]
1401-1450	1	2	3	1 (2)[1]	3	1	1	12	17	10	39	0.0[2]
1451-1500	10	4	2	5 (29)[1]	4	7	7	33	32	23	88	12.1
1501-1525	3	3	1	7	3	4	—	24	27	26	77	96.3
1526-1550	7	5	4	40 48[1]	10	2	6	76	28	17	121	
1551-1575	3	13	10	25	4	9	6	60	28	6	94	187.0
1576-1600	14	24	13	17 68[1]	8	6	3	85	38	14	137	
1601-1625	14	31	3	13	19	16	—	86	31	12	129	295.0
1626-1650	28	13	3	10 66[1]	24	14	3	97	32	5	134	
1651-1675	23	24	16	56	34	14	3	170	53	6	229	420.7
1676-1700	61	24	20	112[1]	33	18	1					

Period					Medicine[1]						Total	
1701-1725	12	15	10		107[1]	6		111		1	340	} 451.0
1726-1750	46	25	30	73		40	6	249	90	1	383	} 1818.0
1751-1775	21	20	32	58	165[1]	83	5	258	121	4	691	
1776-1800	24	26	37	64		191	7	416	261	14		} 2042.2
1801-1825	19	34	113	82	269[1]	307	21	686	378	26	1090	
1826-1850	22	42	231	137		478	39	1191	803	27	2021	
1851-1875	19	37	382	178	455[1]	489	27	1443	1073	39	2555	
1876-1900	7	55	371	263		459	32	1617	1223	21	2861	
1901-1908	—	15	77	114		216	7	552	309	1	862	
Total	329	478	1415	1268		2469	175	7645	4830	286	12,761	

[1] Figures taken from F. H. Garrison, An Introduction to the History of Medicine (1929).
[2] Without Arabia and Persia.

TABLE 4. CURVE OF SCIENTIFIC DEVELOPMENT FROM 800 B.C. TO 700 A.D. BY CENTURIES

PERIOD	GREECE[1]	ROME[1]	GREECE AND ROME (total)	ARABIA[2]								
				Period	Mathematics	Physics	Chemistry	Natural History	Medicine	Geography	Humanistics	Total
800-701 B.C.	6	—	6	700- 750	—	—	—	1	4	—	6	6
700-601	3	2	5	750- 800	18	—	7	1	16	—	15	45
600-501	26	5	31	800- 850	61	7	1	4	25	6	47	142
500-401	39	1	40	850- 900	72	7	6	6	11	3	28	147
400-301	52	5	57	900- 950	33	6	1	2	29	35	35	123
300-201	42	3	45	950-1000	52	—	9	8	43	9	49	156
200-101	14	3	17	1000-1050	48	21	5	5	7	18	56	196
100- 0	12	20	32	1050-1100	27	2	—	3		6	37	82
1-100 A.D.	25	35	60	1100-1150	25	14	1	5	23	11	40	119
101-200	5	13	18	1150-1200	23	2	1	18	26	22	67	159
201-300	—	6	6	1200-1250	18	4	3	12	17	20	64	138
301-400	1	15	16	1250-1300	25	14	5	10	19	26	58	157
401-500	4	—	4									
501-600	3	1	4									
601-700	4	—	4									

[1] Computed from Darmstaedter's work.
[2] Derived from the previously cited paper by P. A. Sorokin and R. K. Merton, in which the sources and procedure of deriving these figures are fully described. It should be noted that, whereas the figures for Greece and Rome refer to the number of discoveries (listed by Darmstaedter), those for Arabia refer to the number of scientists of sufficient importance to be discussed by G. Sarton, in his Introduction to the History of Science, 2 Vols. (Baltimore, 1927-1931).

domestication of fire, of animals, discovery of the edible and inedible plants and animals (some 90 per cent of these discoveries were made in the remotest past); the principle of the lever and the wheel; the pastoral and agricultural arts, and so on. As shown by the data in Chapter 35 as well as in this and the following chapters, a notable development of science in the Egyptian and other old cultures took place one to four thousand years before our era. The same data show that creation of great systems in the mathematical, natural, humanistic, social, and biological disciplines proceeded, with some fluctuations and deviations, in Greek, Roman, Arabian, and western cultures.[12] Neither logic nor facts therefore can support Comte's sequence of the sciences through his three stages.

Besides the summary data given in Chapter 35, above are a few tables of the movement of discoveries and inventions in various sciences for the whole world, and separately for Arabia.[13] An important discovery or invention —and historical records note only those that are important—is one of the most vital changes in any system; therefore the movement of these is an incomparably better measure of a change than a semi-mythical assumption of when a science reaches a stage of positivism.

The data on discoveries in various scientific disciplines in Arabia does not show that discoveries began first in mathematics, then passed to physics, chemistry, biology, and the social and humanistic disciplines. On the contrary discoveries and creations in humanistics appear before those in mathematics. Secondly, discoveries in mathematical, chemical, and biological disciplines emerge in the same century. Thirdly, their course in time is marked by indefinite fluctuations in all disciplines. One period witnesses a blossoming particularly in mathematics or humanistics, another sees other disciplines flourish and nowhere is there any perceptible regular relation in time between the rise of one and the rise of another.

The fluctuation of the discoveries and inventions in various mathematical, physical, biological, and technological sciences in the Graeco-Roman and western world points a sim-

ilar moral. In addition these tables show that there are centuries when discoveries and inventions blossom in all sciences (sensate periods); and there are the periods, like that from 300 A.D. to about 1250 A.D., when they become scarce in all sciences (ideational period). This is to be expected in view of the hypothesis already developed of the change in togetherness of all the scientific subsystems in the total system of science and technology. The evidence of several other tables to be given later on will all testify to the same conclusions. For the present, these considerations and data are sufficient to refute Comte's doctrine of temporal sequence in the change of the various sciences.

Other theories of a uniform time-sequence in the change of subsystems in a cultural system will stand the test of fact and logic no better, and we may dismiss the notion that any such uniformity exists.

The foregoing conclusions about subsystems apply equally to systems. There is no system which within a supersystem tends consistently to lead or to lag in a cultural change.

As we have seen, all systems within the same supersystem change in togetherness but at different times different systems may experience the change first. When, for instance, the order of change of various fine arts from the sensate to the ideational form or vice versa is examined closely, we see that now music leads the change (in Greece of the eighth to the fifth century B.C. and in the fourth to the sixth century A.D.), now it lags behind the other fine arts (in the centuries from the sixteenth to the nineteenth). Sometimes philosophy leads religious change (in Greece from the seventh to the fourth century B.C.), sometimes religious change leads the change in philosophy and science (as during the first centuries of our era in the Graeco-Roman world or again in the first half of the European medieval period). Change in law sometimes precedes religious change, sometimes follows it. However, all these leads and lags are secondary, within the understandable span of nonsynchronicitiy, and in no way nullify the change in togetherness

[12] Cf. A. Kroeber, *op. cit.,* pp. 782-791.

[13] These tables will be used also for the demonstration of several other propositions in later chapters. They are taken from my *Dynamics,* Vol. II, pp. 134-139. See there the detailed data, the sources, and the methods of compiling these tables.

of all these systems of the same supersystem.[14]

The positive reasons for a lack of such a uniformity are those already given for subsystems. Facts corroborate the conclusion. Nevertheless theories asserting this uniformity have been developed.

3. E. de Roberty's Sequence

One of the most logical theories is that of E. de Roberty. According to it any culture is composed of four main forms of collective thought or systems: analytical thought or science; synthesizing thought or philosophy and religion;[15] symbolic, concrete thought or the fine arts; applied thought or technologies of all kinds, representing a practical application of the other three kinds of thought to a practical need, from the physico-chemical technology of industry and the biological technology of medicine and agriculture to all kinds of practical ethics, law, and social engineering.

In a cultural change these four systems change in the time-order of science, then philosophy or religion, then fine arts, and finally, applied technological disciplines. Synthesizing philosophy or religion depends upon analytical thought or science and therefore changes later than science; the fine arts depend upon the scientific and philosophical or religious thought and therefore lag behind science and philosophy and religion; similarly applied or technological thought lags behind all the other three. Without a development of physicochemical sciences there can be no developed physicochemical technology; without biological sciences, no advanced and scientific medicine or cattle breeding or agriculture; without social sciences, no scientific social engineering.

When science radically changes in its principles and propositions, religion and philosophy have to change also. Without knowing Egyptian religion and philosophy, Egyptian fine arts, beginning with the pyramids and obelisks and ending with their sculpture, is incomprehensible. Without knowing Greek religion and philosophy, Greek art, beginning with statues of Zeus, Athena, Venus, and Apollo and ending with the Parthenon, temples, and Greek tragedies, is also incomprehensible.

Such in brief is this highly logical theory of time-sequence in the change of the great systems in the total culture.[16] Now and then such a sequence does in fact occur. But it is not at all a universal rule, for it posits the complete rationality of man and complete integration of all his systems and congeries into one supersystem, as well as either a constant or a uniform "dynamic equilibrium" of all the forces of his environment. We know already that none of these conditions are actually realized. Man is only partially rational; only a part of his total culture is integrated into one supersystem; his milieu is incessantly changing and changing in varying ways.

For these reasons man often changes his scientific ideas without changing his religious or aesthetic or practical thought and actions. Man often changes his philosophy or aesthetic tastes without changing his scientific ideas. Finally, as we have seen, he changes many of his scientific, religious, philosophical and aesthetic ideologies without a corresponding change of his "applied thought and behavior." Furthermore, his behavior and material culture frequently condition his ideologies in the form of Pareto's "derivations," the psychoanalysts' "rationalizations," or Marxian "ideologies." If apologists of the "subconscious," and of biological drives enormously exaggerate this "nonrationality" of man, they nevertheless are right in claiming its existence. In analyzing the structure of personality we have seen them too, and the reasons for their existence and their inevitability. It turns out thus that the uniform sequence of de Roberty is not uniform at all.

This conclusion is corroborated by a series of facts. First, the data on the "blossoming periods" in the main fields of various cultures given in Chapter 35 show that the blossoming in science was not the earliest in time, but was preceded by religion in most of the cultures. Second, and more to the point, the data on the movement of the scientific discoveries and

---

[14] See the facts in *Dynamics*, all volumes.

[15] He regards philosophical and religious thought as identical, both being synthesizing kinds of thought on the ultimate reality, values, and problems.

[16] See E. de Roberty, *Nouveau programme de sociologie* (Paris, 1904); *Sociologie de l'action* (Paris, 1908).

technological (applied) inventions show that
the applied inventions, instead of notably
lagging behind scientific discoveries, in accordance with de Roberty's theory, have actually
proceeded hand in hand with them (with
certain minor deviations), in the physicochemical as well as biological and other theoretical
and applied disciplines. The above Tables 1-4
and Figure 10 show that technological inventions move parallel with the discoveries
of analytical science; and that the inventions in
medicine (applied biology) again move hand
in hand with the discoveries of theoretical
biology. One may at times move faster than the
other but by and large their movement is
concurrent.

This is still more clearly corroborated by
other, more detailed data and tables when we
take shorter periods of 10 years.[17] A series of
other statistical and historical data cited in
Chapter 43 supplies additional corroboration.

If in the history of any total culture we ask
in which field the earliest "blossoming" occurred, the answer will not be science but
usually religion and political organization.[18]
This is shown in the data on blossoming given
in Chapters 35 and 43.

In the world as a whole as well as in the
main European and American countries the
persons that became historical through their
creativeness in the fields of religion and statesmanship emerged invariably several centuries
before the persons that became historical
through their scientific discoveries and technological inventions.[19]

The foregoing considerations and facts are
sufficient to refute de Roberty's theory so far
as it claims a universal uniformity in time
sequence of four forms of thought.[20]

---

[17] See the more detailed tables on the movement
of scientific discoveries and technological inventions by 10-year periods, in *Dynamics*, Vol. II, p.
136; Vol. IV, pp. 328-353.

[18] See also A. Kroeber, *op. cit.*, pp. 782 ff.

[19] See *Dynamics*, Vol. IV, Ch. 7. See there also
material on the sources and methods of computation.

[20] To the credit of de Roberty it should be noted
that he himself admits many exceptions to his rule,
due to the interference of physical and biological
forces in the pure sociocultural process. See a more
detailed criticism of de Roberty's theory in *Dynamics*, Vol. IV, pp. 292-302.

4. Dichotomic Theories of Uniform Lead and Lag

Almost directly opposed to de Roberty's
theory are the Dichotomic theories of Karl
Marx, T. Veblen, L. Weber, A. Weber, R. M.
MacIver, W. Ogburn, and others.[21]

According to these theories the "material,"
"technological," "economic," and "civilizational" culture leads in change while the "nonmaterial," "ideological," and "clutural" culture
lags. The reasons are that the inventions in
material culture are more numerous and frequent than those in nonmaterial culture; that
there are more obstacles to the change in
nonmaterial culture than in the material; that
vested interests in the given society are more
opposed to the changes in nonmaterial than in
material culture; that material culture is cumulative while the nonmaterial is not; that material culture diffuses universally, the nonmaterial only locally. For instance, according to
this theory the material culture of the West
changed enormously during the last few
decades while our family, our political and
other nonmaterial institutions and culture remained in the form adapted to the material
culture of the preceding centuries.

Such is the essence of this old theory, not
invented but repeated with some variations by
the scholars mentioned above and by many
others. Its basic, crucial weakness has already
been indicated in the preceding chapter.

(a) Unaware of the distinction between a
cultural system and congeries the authors do
not indicate whether *each of two classes* of
material and nonmaterial culture is a system or
congeries; (b) they do not define, with even
a minimum of clarity, what exactly they mean
by each class; therefore each class remains

---

[21] See their quoted works. In a more careful and
much better form essentially deviating from one-
sidedness of other theories it is restated by F. S.
Chapin in his *Cultural Change* (New York, 1928),
Ch. 7. In an uncritical form it is repeated as valid
in most of the introductory texts on sociology. For
its criticism see my *Dynamics*, Vol. IV, pp. 302
ff. R. Merton, "Civilization and Culture," *Sociology
and Social Research*, Vols. XXI, 1936; the papers
of M. Choukas, W. Wallis, H. J. Mueller, J. W.
Woodward and others referred to in *Dynamics*,
Vol. IV, pp. 311 ff.

vague and ambiguous.[22] The same phenomenon by the same author now is put in the first, now in the second class. (c) Having no theory of the componential structure of cultural phenomena they tear out of different systems their behavioral and material vehicles and unite these vehicles into one congeries or class of "material culture," (its alias) which is further congerialized by inclusion of some of the components of meanings ("inventions," "ideological values as means,") of some systems. Similarly they cut out the ideological components of many different systems and unite them into the class of the "nonmaterial" (and equivalent) culture, increasing the confusion of this "cultural dump" still more by relegating to it some of the behavioral and material vehicles of religious or artistic or ethical systems. It is scarcely necessary to comment on the utterly concoctive character of these congeries and classes. One can confront a system to system, say, economic to religious system, and may try to find their relationship and their lead and lag; but one cannot confront and look for a uniformity of lead and lag between two artificial congeries brewed illogically out of different components of different systems. In this form the theory is obviously untenable and does not need any criticism. It deserves it, however, in some of its more logical modifications. (d) If the theory means that in emergence or change of any given cultural system the material and behavioral vehicles emerge and change first, then the theory can at least be tested, but the test shows it fallacious. As we have seen, ideas, concepts within a system, including technological invention, precede their material objectification and socialization. Similarly a change in the system's component of meanings precedes as a rule a qualitative change in its other components.

(e) If the theory means that practical technological invention precedes in time theoretical discoveries in the corresponding "pure science," as, for instance, that "physicochemical technology" precedes the development of mathematics, physics and chemistry, or that medicine and agronomy precede the discoveries and

development of theoretical biology, then the theory is equally untenable. If de Roberty's opposing claim is not valid, still less valid is this thesis of the dichotomic theorists. Sometimes the technological inventor in the process of his work discovers an essential theoretical principle, but even then, it can only be one of the many theoretical discoveries which must have been known before his invention was possible. The tables given in this and earlier chapters show clearly that discoveries and inventions go hand in hand in their major movements although in minor fluctuations now one and now the other may seem leading.

(f) If the theory means that in the life history of a given total culture the scientific and technological and economic discoveries emerge, blossom, and change first, while religious, artistic, sociopolitical, philosophical and "ideological" discoveries and creations, emerge, blossom, and change later; the theory is again untenable both logically and factually. Again the data referred to, especially Tables 1-4 explicitly contradict such a generalization.

Historical persons who created important religious and political systems emerged several centuries before the scientific, technological, and economic discoverers, creators, and inventors. This is true of all the separate countries studied.[23]

(g) If the theory means that the natural science disciplines and technologies emerge, develop, and change earlier than the social, humanistic, religious, artistic, philosophical and ethical ones, in the sequence: mathematics and mathematical technology, astronomy, physics, chemistry and their technologies, biology and its technologies; then the theory becomes essentially similar to A. Comte's theory and, like it, is untenable for the reasons given above.

The figures on discoveries in science and humanities in Arabia, as well as in various natural sciences throughout the world, given in Table 1 and further Table 2 on historical persons creative in specified fields, all these, together with several others given in *Dynamics*, in no way corroborate such a claim. They

[22] This ambiguity permits some of its partisans to shift their ground indefinitely when one of their interpretations is successfully attacked. An example of such shifts is supplied by R. M. MacIver in his

"repudiation" of my criticism of his variant of the theory. See the specific criticism of MacIver's variant in *Dynamics*, Vol. IV, pp. 166 ff.; 305 ff.
[23] See the tables in *Dynamics*, Vol. IV, pp. 330 ff.

show rather that invention or creation of a new system in religion or politics, social science or the humanistic disciplines, philosophy or the fine arts, occurred either before or at the same time as discoveries in the mathematico-physico-chemical and technological fields.[24]

This is corroborated by the data on the paleolithic and neolithic cultures. In all primitive tribes we meet not only the rudiments of physicochemical sciences and their technologies but often much better developed systems of religion and magic and the fine arts,[25] and well integrated family and political organizations, laws and mores.

Furthermore, up to comparatively recent times, no sharp divisions existed between science, philosophy, religion, and technology. Almost all of the eminent thinkers of Greece and Rome and medieval Europe were at once scientists, philosophers, moralists, and political and social ideologists; many were also technological inventors like Thales of Milet, Pythagoras, Anchitas, Anaximander, Archimedes, Democritus.[26] The host of others like Hesiod, Homer, Pythagoras, Philolaus, Thales, Heraclitus, Empedocles, Zeno, Anaxagoras, Leukippos, Socrates, Protagoras, Georgias, Plato, Aristotle, in Greece; J. S. Erigena, St. Thomas Aquinas, Albertus Magnus, Duns Scotus, Nicolaus Cusanus, Roger Bacon, and others were simultaneously "philosophers," theologians, scientists, social, political, juridical, ethical thinkers and artists. One could not expect that the scientist in these men would change earlier and faster than the philosopher, the theologian, the lawgiver, or the political thinker. If each of these individual thinkers is assumed to be logical, his total ideology must have changed more or less consistently, in togetherness. On the other hand, if each is assumed to be illogical, the very fact of illogicality precludes the possibility of any uniform change which would give consistent precedence to the change of his scientific and technological ideologies.

(h) As to the seemingly convincing argument that the rate of change in material culture is faster than in nonmaterial, the argument breaks down on their failure to adduce any unit of velocity of change. Without such a unit, comparison of the amount or rate of change as between material and nonmaterial phenomena becomes impossible. Which change is larger or faster: from Paganism and Judaism to Christianity, or from horseless transportation to horse transportation? From polygamy to monogamy or from pastoral economy to agricultural? From Classic architecture to Gothic, or from "natural" economy to money economy? From capitalism to communism or from steam to electricity? From gunpowder to atomic fission or from national sovereign states to a world-state? Which of these changes covers the greatest sociocultural distance in the smallest periods of time? Without yardsticks to measure by the question is unanswerable.[27] The argument of the dichotomists becomes entirely void.

(i) No less void is their argument that, while the material culture of the last few decades has changed enormously, the nonmaterial culture lagged and is now hopelessly obsolete. The argument is purely subjective and arbitrary in the choice of criteria. The sublimest norms of ethical conduct, the Golden rule, the ethical systems of practically all the great religions, and especially the norms of the Sermon on the Mount were discovered and formulated in the ethical or nonmaterial culture of thousands of years ago. Behavioral and material cultures have lagged hopelessly behind these norms up to the present time. Science and technology, triumphing with the atomic bomb, have not yet objectified in their own or in the total material culture these nonmaterial discoveries. Similarly, the just

---

[24] Cf. A. Kroeber, op. cit., pp. 779 ff. He does not find any single people in whose culture science emerges first followed by religion. The rule is that religion reaches first a high degree of integration and then science, arts, etc.

[25] See especially F. Boas, Primitive Art (Oslo, 1927); H. Read, Art and Society (New York, 1937); R. H. Lowie, Primitive Religion (New York, 1925); see other references in Dynamics, passim.

[26] See P. M. Schuhl, Machinisme et philosophie (Paris, 1908), Ch. 1; H. Diels, Antike Technik (Leipzig-Berlin, 1924), pp. 98 ff.; L. Robin, Platon (Paris, 1935); F. M. Feldhaus, Die Technik der Antike und des Mittel-alters (Potsdam, 1931); A. Rey, La science dans l'antiquité, 2 Vols. (Paris, 1930-1933).

[27] See a development of this in my "Recent Social Trends," Journal of Political Economy, April, 1933.

"familistic" economic and political systems were formulated by religious, ethical, political and social thinkers long ago, thinkers like Ipuver, Moses, Confucius, Lao-Tze, Hesiod, Plato, to mention only a few. And yet the respective "material and technological" economies and political regimes have been unable up to the present to realize these ideological systems. Some of the greatest aesthetic values in literature and painting, sculpture and architecture, music and drama again were developed long ago in ancient Egypt and China, India and Greece, Rome, Persia, and other countries. The material, technological, and economic culture contemporary with these creations was, by comparison, infinitely more primitive, imperfect, inefficient; even today's material culture cannot boast any comparable perfection in its own field. These nonmaterial creations have already waited a few thousands of years for corresponding achievement in the material culture and they are still waiting. The nonmaterial "utopias" of beautiful garden cities; of flying carpets and machines, even of intra-atomic fission, dissolution, recreation emerged several thousands of years ago; and still many of these utopias are not realized at all.

Actually the argument on either side is equally fallacious since it makes the two basically false assumptions discussed above: first, that the ideologies and material vehicles of cultural systems may be separated and, second, that all material components and all nonmaterial components may be combined in two pseudo-supersystems and meaningful assertions then made about their character and movement. We have already seen that such a procedure ignores the true togetherness of cultural systems and assumes, on the other hand, a wholly spurious togetherness of the artificial "material" and "nonmaterial" cultural dumps.

(j) Meaningless also are the statements of the kind that while the material culture of the last century has enormously changed, our family, political, artistic, ethical, and religious cultures remain unchanged and obsolete. First, it is untrue to say that for the last century or few decades or even years our nonmaterial culture has not changed; it has enormously changed in all its compartments. Second, even if they had not changed, what grounds would

there be for calling them obsolete or antiquated? Suppose the family has remained strong, truly familistic, with few divorces, a high birth rate, with generally sound and healthy domestic conditions and relationships insuring good education for the children and minimizing juvenile delinquency, would such an institution need to change to avoid obsolescence? If it did and the change took the form of an enormous increase of divorces, separations, sex scandals, childless marriages, juvenile delinquency, could it then be said to be keeping up with material changes and becoming only modern? Is the music of Bach, Mozart, and Beethoven obsolete? Do swing, blues, and boogie-woogie represent progress in music which corresponds to the change in material culture? Is Shakespeare obsolete and only the latest best-seller the representative of modern literature?

It is meaningless to talk about the enormous change of the material culture and obsolescence of the "lagging" nonmaterial culture. The fact that the Beethovens and Shakespeares emerged several centuries back evidences the leading role of the nonmaterial fine arts rather than their lag in comparison with the material culture.

In all their deploring of the supposed lag of nonmaterial culture, the dichotomic theorists never pause to reflect exactly what kind of nonmaterial culture would correspond with each stage of material development. What sort of family institution, or music, philosophy, law, painting, sociology would be appropriate to "atomic material culture?" Is "obsolescence" of the family in such a culture to be avoided by a change to the polygamic, monogamic, promiscuous, patriarchal, or matriarchal form? Should the birth rate be higher, the divorce rate lower, or vice versa? What kind of music should accompany atomic fission? What religion, if any? What ethics?

These questions have never been answered because technology itself could never supply criteria for judging the level of nonmaterial culture. Criteria of obsolescence in music, religion, family, law, philosophy must be drawn respectively from music, religion, family, law, and philosophy. No other judgments can have any meaning because, lacking any appropriate standard, they must break down in vague generalizations.

(k) If the theories claim that technology changing itself always forces a change in nonmaterial culture, the statement is again largely fallacious. We know a large number of cases when an existing technology decayed not through technology but through the impact of nonmaterial culture. A. Toynbee cites a long series of facts on how the splendid Roman roads, magnificent irrigation systems of the Tigris and Euphrates, Ceylon, the Pontine marshes, the irrigation canals in China went to pieces not because of a decay in technical skill but because of the incidence of social, political, and moral anarchy among the respective peoples. We have witnessed gigantic destruction of technological culture on the surface of this planet in the wars and revolutions of this century.[28] Contemporary historians have found that the economic and technological decline of the Graeco-Roman world was "not the cause, but one of the aspects of the more general phenomenon of social disorganization."[29] On the other hand, as we have seen, the development of modern technology, modern capitalism, and modern material culture came not before but partly later than, partly simultaneously with the development of sensate fine arts, and of materialistic and utilitarian philosophy, utilitarian and hedonistic ethics, secular law, new forms of political and social thought, individualism, singularism, nominalism, the Renaissance, the Reformation, and a host of other nonmaterial cultural systems.[30]

Fallaciousness of the theory of the unilateral effectiveness of material culture may also be demonstrated by examination of primitive peoples where different forms of nonmaterial culture are found to exist among peoples with similar technological and material cultures. On the other hand, similar religion, fine arts, literature, marriage and the family, political and judicial institutions are found among the populations with dissimilar technological and material cultures.[31]

(l) We have already seen in the preceding chapter the invalidity of the claim that material culture diffuses universally, the nonmaterial only locally.

(m) Finally, it is also false to contend that material culture is cumulative while the nonmaterial is not. This statement is again so ambiguous and vague that several possible meanings of it must be considered. If it means literally what it says, then it is obviously wrong; as time goes on nonmaterial culture accumulates in all its forms. At the present time we have much greater mass and diversity of musical compositions, literary works, sculpture, pictures, buildings, philosophies, religions, ethical systems, law codes, social and political theories than we had one hundred, five hundred, or five thousand years ago. Tables 1 and 2 show that religious and political series of historical persons are the longest, the most continuous and accumulate fastest, and that the business series of historical persons is the shortest, the most discontinuous, and the least accumulative.

If the statement means that only in science and technology do new discoveries or inventions actually produce new things, it is also wrong. Important religious, aesthetic, or philosophical innovations are no less new. Confucianism, Taoism, Judaism, Christianity, Mohammedanism are each as novel as any new gadget in comparison with its predecessors. The same is true of important philosophical, literary, architectural, musical or legal creations. Actually the novelty is not absolute in either nonmaterial or material fields. The "new" technological invention or scientific discovery is generally a combination of old elements or a variation of an old principle. The basic principles even of atomic structure, fission, and destruction are very old, dating back to Democritus and Leukippos and still older thinkers of ancient India. Principles of atomic structure, fission, and destruction are fairly accurately formulated in several old Hindu sources which suppose a cycle of "elemental dissolution" of all material elements: space, smell, color, form, flavor, sound, ether, and

---

[28] See Toynbee, op. cit., Vol. IV, pp. 40 ff.

[29] M. I. Rostovtzeff, The Social and Economic History of the Roman Empire (Oxford University Press, 1926), pp. 302 ff., 432 ff.

[30] See M. Weber, Gesammelte Aufsätze zur Religionssoziologie, 3 Vols. (Tübingen, 1922-

1923), though he enormously exaggerates the role of Protestantism; A. Fanfani, Catholicism, Protestantism and Capitalism (New York, 1936).

[31] See Hobhouse, Wheeler, and Ginsberg's work, quoted. See other relevant facts in my Theories, Ch. 10.

matter with all their properties to occur periodically every 311,040,000,000,000 mortal years.[32]

Creation in nonmaterial cultures similarly involves the combination and variation of older systems. Bach's music in comparison with its predecessors is as new as a locomotive in comparison with a horse and wagon; but both Bach's music and the locomotive represented "a lucky marriage of two or more ideas" existing before. Both combined in a new way old existing elements. There is no basis for claiming a distinction between the material and non-material cultural systems in respect to the novelty of their creations. In both cases accumulation means replacement of the old with the new which is itself compounded of the old.

If, finally, this thesis means that only in material culture is there a progression of change toward perfection, the proposition is again very questionable. Are English whisky or German beer more perfect samples of material culture than Graeco-Roman wine? The answer is purely a matter of personal taste, which cannot be decided objectively and scientifically. The same must be said of the latest fashion in dress, food, even fuel (oil or coal vs. wood) in comparison with the old. If we had the courage of our convictions, many of us would prefer old-fashioned dress, food, and even wood-fire (as we do in our summer homes), to many modern forms of these material cultures.

This is true even of more complex gadgets. Many of our contemporaries, including a number of scientists, wish that the atomic bomb had never been invented; like General Arnold, our Air Corps chief, many of us would prefer to dispense with the disturbing, threatening mass of noise-making planes, rocket bombs, and similar gadgets, if we could. Because in an increasingly complex life they became all but inevitable it does not follow that we must make a virtue out of the necessity. Still a large number of city dwellers see no virtue in the necessity of living in crowded tenement parts in big cities with all their bustle and hustle, dirt and glitter, excitement and killing monotony. Similarly a host of people do not

feel they are better off in the deadly monotonous life of a modern factory than their grandfathers were on the farm.

All this means that as soon as the principle of "more perfect" and "better" is introduced, an investigator abandons the ground of scientific objectivity and begins to evaluate his personal preferences.

From the standpoint of a killer and perhaps of an inventor the atomic bomb is a better instrument of destruction than its predecessors; from the standpoint of humanity, and especially the victims, it is a hellish invention. The position of the "objectors" is at least as defensible as that of its proponents. The same can be said of other gadgets. Judging by the rapidly increasing suicide rate, it would seem that the last century of great technological progress has not made humanity happier or better satisfied with life.

On the other hand, on the ground of this subjective preference a better case for "progress" could be made out for advances of nonmaterial culture. There are few people who desire to reject the Copernican, Newtonian, and latest astrophysical cosmologies and return to the Ptolemaic system. After the emergence of the great religions and ethical systems few wished to return to religious primitive animism, fetishism, totemism. After the great philosophical systems we do not aspire to return to primitive philosophies. After Bach, Mozart, and Beethoven we can hardly go back to the mere plain chant. After great historical works we can no longer accept the primitive fantastic histories.

If such reversions to the more primitive occur, they happen in both material and non-material cultures. War destroyed Europe, Asia, and part of Africa and has returned them to a material culture even worse than that of many primitive tribes. Somewhat similar relapses in nonmaterial culture now and then also occur.

5. Tarde's Proposition; Conclusion

The totality of these considerations and evidence shows the untenability of the dichotomic lead and lag theories. At best they fall into the familiar error of elevation of a partial fact into

[32] See among many Hindu sources *The Vishnu Puráná*, tr. by H. H. Wilson, 5 Vols. (London, 1864-1877), Vol. V, pp. 55, 162, 195 ff.; Vol. I, pp. 114 ff. See other sources and quotations in my *Dynamics*, Vol. II, pp. 353 ff.; Vol. IV, pp. 442 ff.; on variations of atomic theories see *Ibid.*, Vol. II, pp. 439-446.

a universal rule.[33] There is, however, one roughly valid generalization related to this whole problem. It is the proposition formulated by Tarde on the accumulative and non-accumulative parts of the same system. It may be restated as follows: *In any cultural system the central core of its basic and integrated principles, values, and norms is only moderately accumulative while its peripheral meanings and parts are much more accumulative and often admit almost an unlimited accumulation.*[34] Words in a system of language can accumulate almost without any limits; the grammar and syntax cannot. If these fundamentally change, such a change means the replacement of this language by a new one. In religions, myths and legends, stories of the saints and of the sinners, various prayers and even rites can accumulate widely; the main dogmas can do so only within very narrow limits. If and when a given religion admits all kinds of dogmas it loses its individuality and ceases to be an integrated system. In science, including sociology, concrete facts and data can accumulate without limits; basic principles admit only a narrow accumulation within limits of its integrated referential framework. If the basic principles of a scientific discipline are fundamentally transformed through an accumulation such a change means again a replacement of the old discipline by a new one. The

basic principles of a technological system, be it the principle of wheel, of steam, electricity, gas, or atomic energy, admit very limited accumulation, for the wheel or steam engine still remain wheel, or steam engine in spite of infinitely great variation of these. When the basic principles of a given technological system are radically modified through an accumulation, such a change means again a replacement of the old by a new technological system. Detailed laws and bylaws of the state (or of any other group) admit endless accumulation; its constitutional principles admit only a limited number of amendments. The same can be said of practically any system. This proposition is most closely connected with, and restates the above propositions (b) and (c) and the proposition that there is no system which within a supersystem tends consistently to lead or to lag in a cultural change. Thus these propositions plus Tarde's, plus proposition about change by variation and substitution, mutually support each other. In this formulation the proposition is equally valid for material and nonmaterial cultural systems.

For the present the above propositions on the valid and invalid uniformities sum up the existing knowledge in the field. They usher us into a study of other sets of temporal uniformities in the change of cultural systems and supersystems.

---

[33] See a further criticism and the literature in *Dynamics*, Vol. IV, Chps. 4, 6, and 7.

[34] Tarde's proposition is that there are two distinct kinds of discoveries or inventions: "those that are capable of indefinite accumulation and

those that, after a certain degree of accumulation has been reached, must, if progress is to continue, be replaced" by quite a different system, with different principles, patterns, values, and styles. *The Laws of Imitation*, pp. 174 ff.

Chapter 45. Direction, Rhythm, Periodicity, and Tempo in Sociocultural Change

I. Direction in Sociocultural Change

1. Three Patterns of Direction

Any cultural phenomenon changes from something to something. This *"from-to,"* from a state A to a state B, is the direction of the change. As in a vector system a given direction may have two senses, from A to B or from B to A. There are three main patterns of direction: linear, cyclical, and variably recurrent.

a. *Linear Direction.* If both the sense of a given direction from A to B and the direction itself remain the same throughout the process of change, its pattern is linear. It may be *spatially* linear, as when a given cultural system moves steadily in space from one place to another, from the north to the south, from the east to the west, or from mountains to plains. It may be *quantitatively* linear, when the change involves either a quantitative increase, decrease, or constancy throughout its existence. It may also be *qualitatively* linear in the sense of a *uniform order of sequence* of qualitative states A, B, C, . . . N leading from the state A, through the intermediary stages B, C, . . . to the final state N; as, for instance, from the "theological" through the "metaphysical" to the "positive" stage according to A. Comte. Though the intermediary states appear to be different from one another, nevertheless each subsequent state manifests a

greater congeniality and nearer approach to the final state. The metaphysical state of Comte is more congenial and is qualitatively nearer to positive state than is the theological. In other words, the qualitative linearity consists in a more adequate potential realization of the final stage in each subsequent state of the uniform sequence of states from A to N. In its patterns linear direction may be *unilinear*, along a straight line leading from A to B without any deviation from it for any moment; *oscillating*, admitting minor deviations from the straight line, nevertheless with oscillations leading steadily from A to B; *spiral* where minor deviations consist in spirals but, like a spiral spring, these spirals lead also steadily from A to B; *branching*, as in an upward growing tree, although the branches grow in various directions, the main direction remains, nevertheless, linear, from A to B.

b. *Cyclical Direction.* This means either an absolute or relative recurrence of a given state or states; the cultural phenomenon having completed one spatial, quantitative, or qualitative cycle of change, the process is repeated again and again, moving spatially in a variety of circles, quantitatively passing through the same phases of increase-decrease, increase-decrease, qualitatively passing through the same stages of *ABC, ABC,* and so on. When all the repeated cycles are identical, we have absolutely cyclical direction; when they are not quite identical, we have relatively cyclical direction. In all these varieties cyclical direction differs from oscillating, spiral, or branching linear direction in that it does not have any linear trend from A to B extended without limit in time.

c. *Variably or Creatively Recurrent Direction.* This pattern comprises in itself a combination of linear and relatively cyclical directions. In a part it may have a linear link, but its direction is changed in the next link; it contains in itself a rhythmic repetition of some relative cycles, but these cycles are never identical, nor do they return back to their previous position; each cycle is an ever-new variation of the preceding cycle, or more exactly, rhythm or oscillation.[1]

2. Fashionable Patterns of Direction in Various Cultures

(a) *In dominantly ideational periods of culture in ancient Babylon, India, China, Greece, Rome, Persia, and medieval Europe the cyclical direction was thought to be the master-pattern of change and was applied to the whole world as well as to sociological processes.* The whole history of the world as well as of mankind and its sociocultural life was thought of as an infinite recurrence of either identical or essentially similar cycles. The life of the universe consists, first, of an endless series of cycles of the Great Year (varyingly estimated from 311,040,000,000,000 years to the most popular 432,000 years duration). Each Great Year cycle is supposed to be an exact reproduction of the preceding ones, with all the phenomena contained in it. Within this great cycle there is a multitude of smaller cycles which also repeat themselves either identically or approximately. Any change in direction has been repeated an infinite number of times in the past and will recur an infinite number of times in the future. The Babylonian, Hindu, and Persian cyclical conceptions, the Chinese eternal rhythm of the Yin and the Yang, the prevalent cyclical conceptions of the over-whelming majority of Greek, Roman, and medieval thinkers, the idea which appears in Ecclesiastes: "The thing that hath been, it is that which shall be; and that which is done is that which shall be done; and there is no new thing under the sun," are examples of such conceptions.[2]

(b) *In predominantly sensate cultures the linear conception in one or all its varieties is most fashionable and under the name of evolution and progress is thought to be the master pattern direction in physicochemical, biological, and sociocultural change.* The last four centuries of our predominantly sensate culture give an example of this. Beginning with the sixteenth century and on up to the twentieth, linear conceptions progressively grew and became dominant in the scientific, philosophical, social and humanistic thought of the West. The central content of the historical process of mankind was conceived as an unfolding and ever fuller realization of this "trend of progress and evolution," of steady "historical tendencies" and of "the law of sociocultural development." Some delineated these trends as unilinear, others as "spiral," still others as "oscillating and branching," with minor deviations and temporary regressions; nevertheless in all these varieties the conception of a linear direction of the central sociocultural process remained intact. Consequently the main ambition and central preoccupation of scientific, philosophical, social and humanistic thinkers in these centuries consisted in the discovery and formulation of these "eternal laws of progress and evolution," and in an elaboration of the main stages or phases through which the trend passes as it comes to fuller realization in the course of time. Discovery, formulation, and corroboration of the existence of such trends and their stages was the focal point of biology and sociology, of philosophy of history and social philosophy, and of the other social and humanistic sciences of the nineteenth century. If in some disciplines like history they did not occupy a very large space in the actual narration of historical events, they served as the guiding stars and referential principles for ordering and interpreting the concrete factual

---

[1] For details and developments, cf. *Dynamics,* Vol. I, Chps. 4, 5; Vol. II, Chps. 4, 5, 10; Chps. 8-10.

[2] For a detailed survey of such conceptions and their connection with ideational culture, cf. *Dynamics,* Vol. II, Ch. 10.

material. In this sense, the social thought of especially the eighteenth and nineteenth centuries was indeed stamped by a faith in linear laws of evolution and progress.

In the *physicochemical sciences* this faith expressed itself in an emergence and rapid acceptance of the principle of entropy of Carnot-Clausius as a perpetual and irreversible direction of change in any thermodynamic system[3] as well as in the whole universe.

In *biology* the belief discussed expressed itself in an emergence and general acceptance of the "law of evolution," almost unanimously interpreted in the sense of a linear trend (in its unilinear, spiral, branching, oscillating variations) of a progressively growing differentiation and integration; of a passage from the simple to the complex; from "the lower to the higher"; from "the less perfect to the more perfect," "from amoeba to man," from reflexes and instincts to intelligence and reason; from the solitary individual to the family, the tribe, and the modern state, on up to a "Federation of the World." "Throughout the course of evolution there has been a continual elimination of the least fit and a survival of the fit . . . the elimination of the antisocial and the increase of specialization and cooperation."[4] The linear interpretation of biological (and social) evolution was and still is (though less pronounced now) the main dogma of biology.

The same is true of the dominant conception of sociocultural change in the *philosophy, social philosophy, and philosophy of history* of the eighteenth and nineteenth centuries. The conceptions of Herder, Fichte, Kant, and Hegel are typical in this respect. Herder and Kant both saw the central trend of historical processes as a progressive decrease of violence and war, as a steady increase of peace area, and as a growth of justice, reason, and morality in the course of time.[5]

For Fichte the whole of human history is a sequence of five stages, an ever fuller realization of freedom, truth, justice, and beauty. For Hegel the central trend of the historical process consists in a progressive growth of freedom, beginning with freedom for none at the dawn of human history, passing through the stages of freedom for one, then freedom for some, and ending with the stage of freedom for all.[6]

In the *sociology and social philosophy* of the nineteenth century the general conceptions of social dynamics held by Turgot, Condorcet, Burdin, Saint Simon, and Comte, and of evolution by Herbert Spencer, are fully representative. For Comte the whole process of history is but a steady passage from the theological, through the metaphysical, to the positive stage of human mentality, culture, and society. Consequently, Comte's "social dynamics" hardly deals at all with repeated sociocultural processes; it is devoted almost entirely to a formulation and corroboration of his "law of the three stages." Spencer's "social dynamics" is simply an application of his formula of evolution-progress, according to which the whole sociocultural universe passes in the course of time from an indefinite, incoherent homogeneity to a definite, coherent heterogeneity, with a progressively growing dif-

[3] On the entropy, cf. R. Clausius, "Le second principe fondamental de la théorie mécanique de chaleur," *Revue des cours scientifique*, 1868, p. 158; P. Duhem, *L'évolution de la mécanique* (Paris, 1902); H. Poincaré, *Thermodynamique* (Paris, 1892).

[4] E. G. Conklin, *The Direction of Human Evolution* (New York, 1925), pp. 15, 17, 75, 78. Conklin's conception of biosocial evolution is quite typical of the prevalent conception of biological evolution in the nineteenth and partly in the twentieth century. In a similar linear manner though not so anthropomorphically biological evolution was interpreted by the rank and file of biologists of the nineteenth century. The formulae of evolution of Milne-Edwards, K. von Baer, Herbert Spencer, and E. Haeckel run along the same lines. The concepts of biological evolution of

J. Arthur Thompson, J. S. Huxley, C. L. Morgan, Sir Arthur Smith Woodward, and many biologists of even the twentieth century are also similar. They are all not only linear but identify evolution with progress. Cf. E. Haeckel, *Prinzipen der generellen Morphologie* (Tuebingen, 1906); J. C. Smuts, *Holism and Evolution* (New York, 1925); and two symposia on evolution: *Creation by Evolution* (New York, 1928), and *Evolution in the Light of Modern Knowledge* (New York, 1925).

[5] Cf. Herder's *Outlines of a Philosophy of the History of Man*, tr. by T. Churchill (London, 1803); Kant's *The Idea of a Universal History on a Cosmo-Political Plan*, tr. by T. DeQuincey (Hanover, Sociological Press, 1927).

[6] Cf. Fichte's *Characteristics of the Present Age* (1804) and Hegel's *Philosophy of History*, tr. by J. Sibree (New York and London, 1900).

ferentiation and integration of human personality, culture, and society.[7]

Dominated by this linear conception of sociocultural change, most sociologists and social scientists of the nineteenth century reduced their study of a dynamics of sociocultural phenomena, even in purely factual investigations, mainly to a discovery and formulation of various linear trends, successive stages of development, historical tendencies, and laws of evolution of the phenomena investigated. As a result most of the "uniformities of change" they discovered assumed a linear character. Here are a few examples out of many.[8] Ferdinand Toennies' theory of the passage of human society in the course of time from the *Gemeinschaft* to the *Gesellschaft* type is a linear theory. Emile Durkheim's theory of a gradual change from a state of society based upon the "mechanical" solidarity to one based upon "organic" solidarity, with a subsidiary trend of replacement of "repressive" by "restitutive" law, is also a linear theory. Similar in its linearity is the social dynamics of Lester F. Ward, which posits a progressively increasing teleological, circuitous, artificial, self-directed, and self-controlled character of human adaptation in the course of time; or H. T. Buckle's dynamics of a "diminishing influence of physical laws and of an increasing influence of mental laws" as time passes by; or Herbert Spencer's and Durkheim's laws of the passage of societies from the "simple" to the "compound" ("doubly compound," "triply compound," and so on), in the course of their history. No less linear is J. Novicov's law of the evolution of the struggle for existence from the earliest form of a bloody "physiological extermination," through a less bloody "economic," then "political" struggle, to a final bloodless form of purely "intellectual" competition; or the alleged historical trend of a progressive widening of the area of peace and of shrinking of the area of war in the course of history, claimed by dozens of social scien-

tists; or Novicov's, William F. Ogburn's, and Hornell Hart's law of acceleration of the tempo of change; or A. Coste's law of the five stages of evolution of social structures from the "burg" to the "city," "metropolis," "capitol," and finally to a "world center of federation"; or P. Mougeolle's "law of altitude," according to which the most densely inhabited areas and the cities descend, in the course of time, from the zones of high altitudes to those of low altitudes; or similar historical trends of the westward, eastward, or northward movement of civilization with the passage of time (according to different authors); or A. Gobineau's historical trend from the pure and unequal races to the progressively blended and equal ones with the degenerated "human herds, benumbed in their nullity," and the end of human civilization as a terminal point of the trend; or L. Winiarsky's law of social entropy leading progressively to greater sociocultural equalization of castes, orders, classes, races, and individuals, with the final state of a dead sociocultural equilibrium and the end of mankind's history; or the perennial trend toward a bigger and better equalitarianism interpreted as the positive trend of history (in contradistinction to its interpretation as a death of society and culture) by a crowd of sociologists, anthropologists, political scientists, ethicists, philosophers, and historians. Even such social dynamics as those of E. de Roberty and of Karl Marx were not quite free from this linear "obsession" of the nineteenth century. If Marx himself did not give a clear-cut theory of successive stages of social evolution, he nevertheless postulated one eschatological linear trend of history, the trend toward socialism as the final stage of social development of humanity. His followers, from Engels, Bebel, and Kautsky to H. Cunow and a legion of lesser Marxists, manufactured a series of historical laws in the evolution of economic, political, mental, religious, familial, and other sociocultural phe-

[7] Cf. Auguste Comte, *Cours de philosophie positive* (Paris, 1877), Vol. I, pp. 8 ff. and through all volumes. About the theories of his predecessors, cf. R. Mathis, *La loi des trois états* (Nancy, 1924). See also Herbert Spencer, *First Principles* (London, 1870), Ch. 22; *passim; Principles of Sociology* (London, 1885), 3 Vols. Though the Spencerian formula of evolution and progress includes the

opposite process of dissolution, Spencer fails to deal with the dissolution aspect in his study of sociocultural evolution and progress. Such a neglect of this opposite process is also symptomatic of the preoccupation we have noted.

[8] Cf. the bibliography and details in my *Contemporary Sociological Theories* (New York, 1928) and *Dynamics*, Vol. II, Ch. 10 and *passim*.

nomena, with appropriate stages of development.

Like Marx, E. de Roberty and certain others were little concerned with the manufacturing of various eternal trends and stages of development, but even they assumed the growth of conceptual thought in one or more of the four forms as formulated by de Roberty (scientific, philosophical or religious, aesthetic and rationally applied thought) as a central tendency of the historical process. G. de Greef, together with many political scientists, posited a trend of political evolution from the earliest regimes based upon force to social organization based on free contractual relationships. G. Ratzenhofer's and Albion Small's trend from the "conquest state" to the "culture state," or the somewhat opposite trend, claimed by P. Lilienfeld, from the earliest type of decentralized and unregimented political groups to regimes of centralized, autocratic, and regimented political control; or L. T. Hobhouse's trend of social development from a stage of society based upon kinship, through one based on authority, toward a final stage built upon citizenship; or F. H. Giddings' "zoogenic, anthropogenic, ethnogenic, and demogenic" stages of sociocultural development (the latter stage divided into linear substages: military-religious, liberal-legal, and economic-ethical); all of these are further varieties of the linear type of trends so extensively manufactured by social scientists of the nineteenth and beginning of the twentieth centuries. To these may be added the dozens of historical trends manufactured by sociology and anthropology, law and history, concerning the evolution of the family, marriage, and kinship, all of them with uniform stages of development, from promiscuous "primitive" sex relationships to the monogamic family (passing through three or four or five stages, according to the fancies of the authors like J. Bachofen, J. F. McLennan, Sir John Lubbock, F. Engels, A. Bebel, L. H. Morgan, and many others); from the patriarchal to the cognatic family based upon equality of the sexes; from the patrilineal to the matrilineal system of descent and kinship, or vice versa; from equality to inequality of the sexes, or vice versa; all sorts of trends were claimed. These and all the other social and humanistic sciences vociferously "discov-ered" a host of eternal historical trends with their stages of development: from fetishism or totemism to monotheism and irreligiosity; from religious and magical superstitions to a rational scientific mentality; from ethical savagery to the rational ethical man; from primitive ugliness to a bigger and better beauty, and so on.

Writers in *political science* unhesitatingly formulated a series of various "laws of political progress-evolution" from "autocratic monarchy to democratic republic" or vice versa (depending upon the political sympathies of the scholar); from "direct democracy to representative democracy" or vice versa; from primeval anarchy to centralized government or vice versa; from "government of force" to that of "social service"; all with various intermediary stages definitely following one another in a more or less uniform sequence. In *economics* likewise a large number of eminent thinkers were busy with economic trends and stages of development through which all peoples were supposed to be passing. F. List's five stages of economic development: barbarian, pastoral, agricultural, agricultural-manufacturing-commercial; B. Hildebrand's theory of the three stages: *Naturalwirtschaft, Geldwirtschaft,* and *Creditwirtschaft;* Karl Buecher's law of the three stages: closed self-sufficing, city, and national economy; and Gustav Schmoller's theory of five stages may serve as typical examples of this linear "economic dynamics." The economics of the last century treated in the same linear fashion economic evolution from collective to individual agriculture or vice versa; from primitive collectivism to capitalist individualism, or vice versa; and so on, up to the still narrower trends allegedly given in the process of economic change.

Archeology and history likewise were dominated by the same linear conceptions of historical change. If in the actual narrative of historical events a discussion of such trends, tendencies, and laws of evolution-progress did not occupy a very large space in factual historical works, such trends and laws (assumed by the archeologists and historians) served as the guiding stars and referential principles for the ordering of chaotic historical material and especially for interpreting it. The archeological and historical "law of technological evolution" with its standardized stages: paleolithic, neo-lithic, copper, bronze, iron, and machine age is one of their linear laws serving as a funda-mental referential and ordering principle. The idea of progress itself, interpreted linearly, is actually another such principle—an idea which served as the veritable foundation for the bulk of historical works in the nineteenth century. Even the explicitly factual histories openly inimical to any "philosophizing" in history did not escape it. The *Modern Cambridge History* provides a typical example of this; in spite of the aversion of its editors and authors to any philosophy of history we read in its opening pages: "We wish to dis-cover the tendencies which are permanent. . . . We are bound to assume as a scientific hy-pothesis on which history is to be written, a progress in human affairs. This progress must inevitably be towards some end."[9] It is hardly necessary to add that in other supposedly purely factual narratives, the historians of the nineteenth century, from Mommsen, L. von Ranke, Fustel de Coulanges, and F. Guizot up to the authors of *Cambridge Modern History* actually formulated a large number of linear laws of evolution, in all fields of social and cultural life.[10]

To summarize: sociology, the other social, philosophical, and even natural sciences of the nineteenth century viewed the central problem of physical, biological, and sociocultural dynamics in a fairly simple way; the problem was one of discovering and formulating the linear trends believed to be unfolding in the course of time. In the field of sociocultural change the task assumed an almost unbeliev-ably easy character; it simply amounted to drawing a unilinear or oscillating or branch-ing or spiral main line from the "primitive" man, society or culture to the present time.

The whole historical process was thought of as a kind of well-ordered college curriculum, with primitive man or society as a freshman, subsequently passing through the stage of sophomore, junior, senior (or others when the classification contained more than four stages), and then graduating either in the class of "positivism" or "freedom for all" or any other final stage suggested by the fancy and taste of the scholar.[11]

In a less pronounced form a similar rise of linear conceptions occurred in the dominantly sensate periods of past cultures.

3. Faults in Conceptions of Eternally Linear and Cyclical Directions of Change

In application to the direction of sociocul-tural processes, and to that of biological proc-esses also, the conceptions of identically cycli-cal and limitlessly linear change can hardly be accepted as valid. For a limited span of time these processes may be linear; in the form of nonidentical rhythms or oscillations (see next sections) they may contain recurrent "cycles," but an overwhelming majority of these proc-esses are neither limitlessly linear nor eternally cyclical. Each process when taken in all its characteristics constantly involves new ele-ments and at the same time represents an ever new variation of old themes, recurrent rhythms and "cycles." All in all the variably recurrent pattern seems to be the only ade-quate master-pattern of the direction of an overwhelming majority of sociocultural proc-esses. The reasons for such a conclusion will be given in the next chapter. For the pres-ent we shall pass to an analysis of sociocultural rhythms, periodicities, and tempo closely related to the direction of these processes. After this analysis the reasons will be given in the next chapters.

---

[9] The *Cambridge Modern History* (Pop. ed., New York, 1934), Vol. I, p. 4. Note that the work was executed in the nineteenth century. A con-temporary example is that of H. Fischer's *History of Europe* (London, 1905), where an aversion to historical generalizations is contradicted with "the fact of progress is written plain and large in the pages of history." Vol. I, p. vii.

[10] Cf. *Dynamics*, Vol. II, Ch. 10.

[11] Thus in the quoted *Cambridge Modern History* we read: "The practical applications of scientific knowledge will go on extending and . . . future ages will see no limit to the growth of man's power over the resources of nature, and of his intelligent use of them for the welfare of his race." Vol. XII, p. 791.

II. Uniformities of Rhythm, and Periodicity

1. The Concept of Rhythm and Its Forms

In music rhythm is the repetition of units consisting of an accented note a accompanied by one or more unaccented notes, $b . . c . . d$ which together with caesuras, the masculine and feminine harmonic closes, combine to make up the larger units of the whole composition. Two or more rhythms make a period as two verses in poetry make a couplet; two or more periods make a musical phrase as two or more couplets make a poetical strophe or stanza; several phrases make a movement in music and several movements make a symphony or given musical composition.

Repetitions similar to musical or poetical rhythms occur in social and cultural phenomena. A *sociocultural rhythm* is a recurrent unit of process consisting of two or more different phases such as: AB-AB-AB or ABC-ABC-ABC, or some more complex series of phases.

(a) Sociocultural rhythms may recur *in time*. A given series of phases may be repeated many times in the life-process of the same system or organized group. They may recur *in space*. The given series of phases may be found only once in the life history of each system or group, but the same order of phases will be found to be repeated in the life process of other similar systems and groups. Finally, rhythms may be recurrent *in time as well as in space*; the series of phases is repeated many times in the life history of each system and of all similar systems.

(b) Sociocultural rhythms may be *quantitative*, that is, the phases may consist of an increase and decrease of some sociocultural phenomenon, or the pattern may be one of increase-plateau-decrease, or may have some still more complex quantitative form; they may be *qualitative* when the phases A and B, or A, B, and C differ from one another qualitatively; or they may be *qualitative-quantitative*.

(c) There may be rhythms consisting of two phases: AB, AB . . . ; of three phases: ABC, ABC . . . ; of four, or a greater number of phases.

(d) Rhythms may be *embraced as subrhythms in a larger rhythm*, this larger rhythm being in its turn a subrhythm in a still larger embracing superrhythm. Thus the daily rhythm of day and night is a subrhythm in a weekly rhythm, the weeks form a subrhythm in a seasonal rhythm, and the seasons form a subrhythm in the annual rhythm.

(e) Rhythms may be *periodic or nonperiodic*. They are periodic when each complete rhythm ABC is of the same duration as measured by astronomical or watch time, say, one week; they are nonperiodic when the chronological duration of each complete rhythm is different, as when ABC is completed in one hour on one appearance, and takes a week for completion on another appearance. Nonperiodic rhythm is still real rhythm; there is a repetition of the same succession of phases ABC, though each phase or the whole rhythm varies in time duration.

(f) Rhythms may be of *short or long-time durations*; ordinarily the embraced rhythms are of a shorter duration than their embracing rhythm.

(g) Finally, it is to be noted that *two or more different rhythms may exist simultaneously in the same embracing system*. For example, heart-beating, breathing, peristaltic motions, and other rhythms exist simultaneously in the human organism, each as a part of its life process. Likewise, within every twenty-four hours of our existence the rhythms of sleeping-walking, hunger-satiation, tiring-resting, feeling cheerful-feeling depressed, and many other phase-like processes go on simultaneously, each constituting a rhythm different from the others.

With the general forms of rhythm defined we can now turn to an inquiry as to whether rhythms appear in sociocultural processes and if so, what kinds, how they are related to each other, and what temporal uniformities are observed in the rhythmical change of systems and supersystems.

2. Kinds of Rhythms Appearing in Sociocultural Processes

An enormous number of claims as to the most diverse sorts of sociocultural rhythms repeated in time and space have been advanced by writers in the various social and humanistic disciplines. A mere survey of all such theories would require a substantial volume.[12] Here we can touch the problem only very briefly. There is no doubt that in the embracing life process of individuals, organized groups, and cultural systems, there are many rhythmic processes. However, the following reservations must be made: (a) not all sociocultural processes are necessarily rhythmic; and (b) the majority of rhythms recurrent in time or in space are neither universal, that is, given in the activities of *all* persons, groups, and systems, nor do they eternally repeat themselves. Most similar rhythms are confined to persons, groups, and cultural systems of the *same type*. In persons, groups, and systems of different types the rhythms are different. Each such rhythmic process continues only so long as the given type of person, group, or system continues; if the given type undergoes either a dissolution or a basic change the rhythm changes also. (c) Finally, a given rhythm *ABC* does not repeat itself identically in all its traits but always with some variation of its secondary traits. With these reservations we can glance briefly at the kinds of sociocultural rhythms punctuating sociocultural processes.

a. *Quantitative Rhythms.* Most sociocultural processes have some kind of quantitative rhythm such as increase-decrease, increase-decrease; or increase-plateau-decrease, increase-plateau-decrease. We find quantitative rhythms repeated in the diffusion of cultural traits; the growth or decline of many sociocultural systems and groups is expressed by a logistic curve with the formula $Y_c = K_1 + \dfrac{K_2}{1 + 10^{g\,(d_a - d_i)}}$, an S curve and formula of a less refined kind, a Gompertz curve, an Orthogonal Polynomial curve, normal frequency ogives, or some others. So long as the same logistic pattern of quantitative growth or diffusion is repeated in subaspects of a given system, such as in the growth of its cities, its crop or cement production, its inventions, its railroad mileage, or the like, it is possible to speak of quantitative

logistic rhythms.[13] Other social phenomena seem to follow a rhythm of increase and decrease, such as that given in the movement of crime, suicide, many diseases, the quantitative increase and decrease in the influence of many ideologies, groups, and cultural systems up to business fluctuations, rhythms, and cycles. Caution should be exercised not to universalize any particular quantitative rhythm, for instance, the logistic one, as characteristic of all phenomena, groups, and systems. It was pointed out in Chapter 38 that each of these curves is limited to certain kinds of groups or systems or congeries and is in no way universal for all groups, systems, and congeries.

In spite of considerable work in this field it is still largely unexplored; actually only a few quantitative rhythms within a negligible fraction of sociocultural processes have been explored. It remains for the future to construct a systematic theory of the forms of quantitative rhythms and of the processes in which they are found.

b. *Periodic Rhythms.* Past and present thinkers have advanced an enormous number of theories concerning all sorts of periodic rhythms in various sociocultural processes. Many of them have been based on mere statistical averages of duration which in no way constitute real sociocultural periodicities. The length of periods range from 311,040,000,000,000 mortal years in Hindu theories up to periods of a few years in business fluctuations, of a few weeks, days, hours, or minutes[14] in various processes. The most popular periodicities have been those of 4,320,000 years, 720,000 years, 432,000 years, and 2484 years for the *annus magnus*, or the Great Year during which the world, including the sociocultural world, was supposed to repeat itself in elemental dissolution and regeneration. Shorter periods of 1,000, 600, 300, 100, 60, 50, 49, 30, 33, 25, 12, 11, 9, 7, 5, and 3 years have been often claimed in various sociocultural processes: wars, revolutions, political, religious, economic, and other processes. Of these shorter periodicities the "generation-

---

[12] Such a survey is given in *Dynamics*, Vol. IV, pp. 388-583. To date this is by far the most complete survey of the problem of rhythms and the relevant literature.

[13] For an analysis of the logistic curve and an enumeration of the phenomena to which it applies,

cf. H. Hart's *Logistic Social Trends*, quoted. The literature is cited there also.

[14] For a critical survey of these theories, cf. *Dynamics*, Vol. IV, Chps. 9-11; Vol. II, pp. 353 ff.; *Theories*, pp. 730 ff. The literature is cited there.

periodicity" of some 25 to 30 years has also been popular. All in all, nearly every number of years or days has been claimed by somebody.

The existence of such periodic rhythms has been explained by some on metaphysical grounds, by others on the grounds of physical, geographical, or cosmic factors; by others on the grounds of biological factors (especially the generation-periodicity); by still others on the basis of economic or sociocultural factors.[15] Most of the fantastically long periodicities can be dismissed as unprovable and irrelevant in regard to sociocultural processes whose total known duration is hardly beyond several thousands of years.

Likewise, most of the pseudo-periodicities that are based on mere statistical averages of duration (like "business cycles" of 3 or 7 or 11 or 25 years) can be dismissed; a statistical average of duration is not a real period but just the result of the addition and division of several figures; as such it has little to do with the real duration of periods in a real periodic rhythm.

Furthermore, almost all periodicities claimed on the ground of geographic, cosmic, metaphysical, or biological factors can be dismissed; they are not far from the multitude of "astrological" periodicities claimed by all kinds of charlatans and in most cases not even corroborated by a minimum of necessary evidence. Another part of these periodicities are based on mere statistical averages.

The proponents of these theories have been looking for the explanation of sociocultural periodicities in the wrong fields. *Real sociocultural periodicities in the main are not due to cosmic-geographic or biological factors but are of sociocultural origin. In each society the real periodicities reflect the socially established punctuations in its sociocultural processes as measured by the system of social time and its units established by the given group or culture.* So far as social time with its units of minutes, hours, weeks, or months is a consciously or unconsciously established social convention, different in different societies and cultures and little related to cosmic or biological processes, the sociocultural periodicities in a given society or culture are reflections of social convention and are of sociocultural origin.

One has to keep in mind that the systems of time reckoning and time-units are different in different societies. Most of these units, like the minute or the hour, the week or month are "clock" time artificially established in social life. In the endless uniform flow of astronomical time there are neither seconds, minutes, hours, weeks, nor the equally arbitrary time-units of other groups and cultures. These units are different in different societies, for instance, there are "weeks" of five, six, seven, nine, fourteen, and twenty-six days' duration in various societies.

Therefore whether a given time-duration is equal to, shorter, or longer than another is determined by the socially established time unit that measures the duration. Durations that in astronomical time are unequal (for instance, from Christmas to Christmas, from lunch to lunch) are made equal, and chronologically equal durations are made unequal. Whether two time-durations are equal and thus whether the associated rhythm is periodic is determined by the time-system of a given society. For this reason all sociocultural periodic rhythms are sociocultural conventions, determined by the time system of the given culture or group.[16]

So understood, there certainly are many periodic rhythms in the sociocultural processes of groups and cultural systems, though most sociocultural rhythms are nonperiodic. The durations of periodic rhythms in each society and culture correspond to its time-reckoning system and its units, or to the calendar of the group. If the time-systems and their units are different in different groups and cultures, the duration of periodic rhythms in its sociocultural processes will also be different.

In conformity with the time-system and time units of western populations and culture there are in several countries periodic rhythms of a certain *number of minutes or hours*' duration; our buses and trains, elevateds and planes repeat the same trip within the same number of

---

[15] A critical survey and analysis of such theories is given in *Dynamics*, Vol. IV, Chps. 9, 10.

[16] This complex question is discussed at length in my *Sociocultural Causality, Space, Time,* Ch. 4.

For different systems of time-reckoning in various groups see M. P. Nilsson, *Primitive Time Reckoning* (Lund, 1920) and F. H. Colson, *The Week* (Cambridge, 1926).

minutes or hours scheduled; work periods in office or factory, lectures, radio programs, and plays are repeated from day to day, sometimes with an overtime payment if the work lasts a few minutes beyond its strictly determined length. Generally with the complication of sociocultural life the tyranny of time grows; we begin more and more to live by watch-time which determines to the minute many of our repeated hourly and daily activities and sociocultural processes.

There are many *daily periodic rhythms*. An enormous number of social processes go on within certain hours of daytime and cease for certain hours during the night. Industrial, commercial, educational, religious, and many other types of organizations experience this daily rhythm in their life-process. The rhythm of breakfast-lunch-dinner; of sleeping and waking, the twenty-four hour rhythm of suicide and death with their maxima about 6-7 A.M. and 7-10 P.M. and minima about 12-2 P.M. (in several populations), and many others go on from day to day.

There are *weekly periodic rhythms* measured by the seven-day week of our time system. On Monday or Thursday many of our activities are repeated from week to week on the same day, with Sunday having its own pattern of activities repeated from Sunday to Sunday; rooms and services are hired by week; certain events and processes repeatedly happen once in a week.

There are several *monthly* and *seasonal* periodical rhythms such as the seasonal curves of births, with maxima from January to April, minima in November, December (June to August in European countries); of death with maxima in January to April; of suicide, with maxima in May to July (for European countries); of many diseases (especially pulmonary); of crimes; of economic activities; of recreation and many other phenomena.

There are many *annually rhythmic processes and events* such as Christmas, New Year's Day, the Fourth of July, Washington's Birthday, Memorial Day, and Thanksgiving Day; the annual celebration of birthday, wedding day, and certain other annual dates; work and salaries are computed often on an annual basis; stocktaking or housecleaning processes likewise repeat themselves from year to year,

now and then on the same day of the year. Certain religious ceremonies or political elections are repeated on the same days from year to year, and so on.

There are further *biennial rhythms* and rhythms of three, four, five, ten, fifteen, twenty-five years or longer in political processes (elections in every two or four years), religious, educational, economic, and other processes, which repeat themselves periodically within each of such periods. The business cycles of three, four, seven, eight, and eleven years are mainly statistical averages, however, and not real periodic cycles.

Generally, organized groups and cultural systems have a calendar of activities and periodic events. This calendar may or may not be written, but it exists factually in each organized group or system as a blueprint of the coordinated activities of its members. A University calendar determines in detail which courses are repeated on which week days at which hours; on what day weekly or bi-weekly there are the meetings of various committees and associations, religious services or concerts. Most of these events repeat themselves periodically from hour to hour, from day to day, week to week, semester to semester, even from year to year. In this way the bulk of the activities of each professor, student, and administrator in the University are defined, coordinated, and made periodic. The same can be said of a business firm, a religious group, a government, or practically any sort of association. The very organization of a group or the integration of a cultural system implies the existence of this largely periodic coordination of activities and processes. This understood, the existence of various periodic rhythms, sometimes several rhythms running simultaneously in various processes of the group or system, becomes certain, and they appear to be more numerous than is usually thought.

These considerations also indicate that the periodicities in the total life-process of various groups and systems are bound to be diverse and will fail to coincide with each other. To repeat: a legion of investigators have been looking in the wrong places for the explanation of periodicities. They have been looking for the causes in cosmic and biological factors instead of in the calendar of groups and systems. For this reason the real periodic rhythms have been little studied. It is about time to begin their investigation more earnestly and along sounder lines than has hitherto been done.

As to longer periodic rhythms of 100, 300, 500, 600, 1200 years claimed to mark either extraordinary increase or decrease of wars, revolutions, radical changes in religion, political regimes, etc., most such rhythms still remain insufficiently proven and uncertain. There are certain periods of extraordinary upheavals, revolutions, wars, and innovations succeeded by the periods of comparative order, peace, and stagnation, but such rhythms are nonperiodic—the periods have varying time-durations.

c. *Nonperiodic Rhythms.* The majority of sociocultural rhythms are nonperiodic: war and peace, order and disorder, prosperity and depression, organization and disorganization; these and many other qualitative rhythms repeat themselves but not at a periodic interval. Similarly, long time increase and decrease of birth, death, marriage, divorce, suicide, and crime rates are also mainly nonperiodic. The periods of 5, 7, 11, 16, 30-33, 48-60, and 100 years claimed by some for such long-time fluctuations are mainly statistical averages and not real periodicities. The number and diversity of nonperiodic rhythms is enormous. Here are a few examples of double, triple, quadruple, and more complex rhythms consisting respectively of two, three, four, or a greater number of phases.[17]

(1) Repeated in the life process of the same organized group or cultural system, nonperiodic recurrent *two-phase rhythms* of war-peace, order-disorder, prosperity-depression, increase-decrease of crime, stratification, differentiation, convention-revolt, tradition-fashion, expansion-contraction of governmental regimentation, polarization-equilibration, integration-disintegration, challenge-response, withdrawal-return, are recurrent in many organized groups and cultural systems.

Many investigators of the fine arts have claimed the existence of a recurrent alternation of the following styles in the same or in different systems of fine arts: mechanical-organic, gothic-Greek, classic-romantic, static-dynamic, idealistic-naturalistic, and others. In some art systems such alternation has occurred, but none of these rhythms can be claimed to be universal, valid for all art systems.[18]

In scientific and philosophical systems, according to several investigators, there is a double rhythm of fact-finding and synthesis; these phases and the rhythm have been found in the life-process of physics and chemistry, biology and sociology, giving periods mainly devoted to the collection of facts and periods devoted mainly to synthesis and generalization. It seems reasonably certain that such rhythms occur in several scientific disciplines, at least in some periods of their existence and development.

Others have claimed the existence of a rhythm consisting of a phase of intuitive creativity supplanted by a phase of scholarly elaboration in the development of philosophy, fine arts, religion, and science. It is true that in some systems of art, science, philosophy, religion, ethics, and law such a rhythm has indeed existed. Athens from the sixth to the fourth century intuitively created great systems of art and philosophy; the Alexandrian Hellenic world elaborated in an erudite and scholarly way, but showed little real creativity. However, this rhythm can hardly be extended over all arts, sciences, and cultural systems of all periods and times. It is rather a limited rhythm applicable only to some systems at some periods of their existence.

The same can be said of a still larger double rhythm posited by St. Simon, consisting of the alternation of critical and organic periods in the life history of social and cultural systems. According to St. Simon there is an organic phase in which science, philosophy, religion, arts, law, and ethics all work harmoniously with one another to give the society a period of peace, order, and well-being. This organic phase is followed by a critical phase in which these systems conflict with one another and lead to social antagonisms, revolution, disorder,

---

[17] All metaphysical and cosmic double, triple, and other rhythms like the Chinese Yin-Yang, the Persian Ahura Mazda-Angra Mainyu, Empedocles' rhythm of Strife-Love, and so on are omitted.

[18] For a developed analysis of these and all subsequent rhythms, cf. *Dynamics*, Vol. IV, pp. 388 ff.

and anarchy. This phase is again succeeded by a new organic phase, and so the rhythm goes on. In application to the Graeco-Roman and western cultures as well as for some periods of the great Oriental cultures the rhythm has been roughly valid. But it cannot claim to be universal nor given at all times.

The situation is similar with regard to L. Weber's theory, according to which there is in the history of "civilization" a two-phase rhythm of domination of technical and material values and of domination of religious, spiritual, and ethical values. St. Simon's and Weber's rhythms denote less accurately the superrhythm of domination of sensate and ideational supersystems.

(2) The Hegelian dialectic triad of thesis-antithesis-synthesis is a general formulation of a *three-phase rhythm*. There is hardly any doubt that several sociocultural processes show a three-phase rhythm. Quantitatively, all processes that follow the formulae of increase-plateau-decrease, or increase-decrease-plateau exhibit this kind of rhythm. There are several processes which fluctuate according to this type of rhythm, at least for some periods of their existence. Qualitatively, the ever-repeated rhythm (once in the life of each cultural system, but recurrent in the life of all fully grown systems), the conception-objectification-socialization of cultural systems developed previously, is an example of a qualitative three-phase rhythm. Tarde's rhythm: invention-imitation (diffusion)-opposition is another. Rhythms of three meals per day, of three movement concertos, of three-day weeks or holidays among some populations, of three generations from shirt-sleeves to shirt sleeves (given in a limited number of systems), are prosaic varieties of such rhythms.

Among the less prosaic and more embracing three-phase rhythms is that of V. Hugo and E. Bovet, who claim that the literature of all peoples in its whole life history passes through the stages lyric, epic, and dramatic. According to them this three-phase rhythm is found in the life history of all literatures and is even repeated in the life history of the same literature. According to W. Deonna and others, the sculpture and painting of the paleolithic, neolithic, Graeco-Roman, and Christian (western) cultures have uniformly passed through the phases

archaic-classical-decadent. In each of these cultures sculpture and painting passed through this three-phase rhythm only once but the rhythm is found in the life history of all four cultures. C. Lalo and others have tried to show that the music of each culture passes through three phases: preclassical, classical, and postclassical, the rhythm repeating itself even in the life history of music of the same culture. Greek music, the music of Christian melody, the poliphony of the Middle Ages, and modern harmony are all supposed to have passed through these phases.[19] My own theory of the recurrence of a three-phase rhythm of ideational, idealistic, and sensate forms of art in the Graeco-Roman, western, and some other cultures is an example of a three-phase rhythm.

In regard to all these theories, some of which like Deonna's and Lalo's were developed in detail with a vast body of corroborative factual evidence, it can be stated that in the painting, sculpture, music, architecture, literature, and drama of some cultures such rhythms have indeed appeared. However, this is true only for those cultures in which art has been sufficiently integrated. Just as the series of ideational, idealistic, and sensate phase occurs only in highly integrated art cultures, so Lalo's and Deonna's rhythms, congenial to and embraced by my rhythm, occur only in some highly integrated art cultures, and not in all. With this limitation and reservation, their theories are roughly valid. Hugo's and Bovet's rhythm is at best applicable only to exceptionally few literatures and even in these cases is very doubtful.

There are theories of vaster three-phase rhythms such as the emergence, growth, and decline of civilizations, types of philosophy, of fine arts, etc.; most such theories are vague and untenable. Still more embracing three-phase rhythms repeated in the history of different cultures are exemplified by G. Vico's and my own theories. According to Vico the culture of great nations passes through a great rhythm consisting of three phases: the phase of gods, of heroes, and of men. In the phase of gods the religion, art, philosophy, law, political and social organization are permeated by

[19] For a detailed characterization of these theories, criticism and literature, cf. *Dynamics*, Vol. I, chps. 5 and 6.

religious principles; in the phase of heroes by heroic principles; in the phase of men by the characteristics of common men. The rhythm may also be repeated in the life history of the same culture.

Stated in a more precise and accurate form, with much greater reservation, my theory of fluctuation of the domination of sensate, ideational, and idealistic supersystems in some highly integrated cultures is an example of a great three-phase superrhythm congenial to Vico's theory.

Turgo, Condorcet, and Comte's "law of three stages," if it is applied to different cultures, furnishes a further example of a great three-phase rhythm. However, its linear character and the other invalidities discussed above make this law very questionable. The theories just discussed give an idea of the enormous variety of three-phase nonperiodic rhythms in sociocultural processes.

(3) There are many small and vast *four-phase rhythms* in sociocultural processes. The four-day week in some populations, the cycle of morning-afternoon-evening-night, the four-season rhythm of social life in many countries repeated from year to year; the four-year curricula of schools and colleges, four-movement symphonies and four-act plays, the biosocial rhythm of childhood-adolescence-maturity-old age passed through by a full human life, are all examples of small quadruple rhythms repeated in time and space.

The four-phase rhythm of childhood, youth, maturity, old age through which nations, societies, cultures, fine arts, and other cultural systems are supposed to pass has been defended by many thinkers, past and present, from the Roman historian Florus up to O. Spengler and A. Toynbee. Unfortunately, in this analogical formulation the theory remains vague and very doubtful, even in application to the few cultures with which these writers have dealt.

The rhythm of four generations from the ascendance to the decay of certain aristocratic and royal families, observed by Ibn Khaldun and others, and the rhythm of four generations of "predecessors, revolutionaries, reactionaries, and successful accomplishers" observed by J. Ferrari, are again examples of rhythms found only in certain cultures and periods and are in no way universal (contrary to the claim of Ferrari).

(4) Plato's famous theory of the regular succession of five forms of government: aristocracy, timocracy, oligarchy, democracy, and tyranny (supposedly repeated in several cultures); and Polybius' no less famous rhythm of monarchy, tyranny, aristocracy, oligarchy, democracy, and mob rule, are examples of *five- and six-phase rhythms*. Aristotle has shown that they can in no way be regarded as universal or even more or less general. At best they occur only in a few cultures and groups. Our seven-day week is an example of a seven-phase rhythm. There are other still more complex rhythms, punctuating sociocultural processes.

These examples give an idea of the variety of real sociocultural rhythms pulsating in sociocultural life, in the life history of persons, organized groups, and cultural systems.

3. Rhythmic Time-Sequence Uniformities

On the basis of the foregoing analysis of rhythms the following formulae on time-sequence uniformities can be added to those of the preceding chapter:

(a) If and when it is ascertained that certain processes of a given social group or cultural system are rhythmic, and when the phase-structure of the respective rhythms is known, it can be expected that the phases of the rhythms and the rhythms themselves will continue to occur in their ascertained order, so long as the groups and systems retain their essential character. If the ascertained rhythm is a two-phase rhythm AB, then the phases AB, AB, . . . will continue to repeat themselves in that order. If the ascertained rhythm consists of three-phases: ABC, ABC, . . then after A we can expect B, then C, and after C again A, and so on, as long as the group or system retains its essential identity.

(b) However, the probability of such an expected temporal sequence of the phases is naturally not the same in all rhythmic processes. In some it is high, in others, low. The greater the number of observed repetitions of a given sequence of phases, and the lesser the known number of the exceptions to the sequence, the greater is the probability of the expected sequence of phases.[20] The number of day and night sequences observed is enormous, and the number of exceptions to this alternation is nil; therefore with the highest probability (a coefficient of 1) we expect that after this night a day will come and after the day a night again will follow. In the sociocultural rhythms observed there are few, if any, that can have this high probability. Some simple rhythms such as the alternation of public activity by day and of its cessation at night have repeated themselves many, many times, and therefore have a comparatively high probability of recurrence, but not so high as the cosmic alternation of day and night because there have been several known exceptions when public activities did not stop in the night time, when offices, factories, stores, churches, etc. remained open and filled with activities.

Vaster rhythms and superrhythms like the succession of sensate, idealistic, and ideational supersystems have been observed only a few times; on the other hand, this sequence has been either blurred or absent in several total cultures. For this reason the probability of the repetition of this sequence is comparatively low. In the cultures where such supersystems are given it is not certain that after a sensate supersystem there must necessarily come the domination of an ideational, rather than an idealistic supersystem, or even a period of eclectic disintegration. In some thirty centuries, from the late Creto-Mycenaean culture up to the present time, this sequence has been repeated two and a half times. On this and also on some logical grounds it is probable that after the decline of the present sensate supersystem a new ideational supersystem will rise to domination. But this probability is low; therefore we cannot be certain that after the decline of the present sensate supersystem an idealistic or eclectic phase will not come, nor even that the whole of western culture may be destroyed.[21]

With proper modification these considerations can be applied to all other ascertained sociocultural rhythms, especially to vast rhythms. Thus G. Vico's claim of an invariable sequence in his ages of gods, heroes, and men in unduly universalized and rigid. There is still less foundation for a universalization of the Spenglerian and Toynbian rhythms of childhood, youth, maturity, and senility of societies and civilizations, or of the other vast rhythms mentioned.

In spite of all these reservations, the observed recurrence of rhythms with their phases provides a more solid basis for prediction within certain degrees of probability of the sort of changes to be expected in given groups or systems than most of the dichotomous theories of "lead and lag" criticized above. With further study of sociocultural rhythms we can improve their "predictive" value a great deal.

4. Value of Rhythms and Superrhythms in Analysis of Causal-Meaningful Relationships

Besides their superior "predictive" value over dichotomous theories a knowledge of rhythms, and especially of the superrhythms, has a much greater significance for the unraveling of relationships between the multitude of subsystems of a given culture and for an understanding of the direction of their concerted change. It gives us a key to a whole network of multilinear, causal-meaningful relationships, static and dynamic, between a multitude of systems or "variables" in a given culture. This network of relationships is so complicated that it can hardly be grasped by any other means.

a. *Multilinear Static Causal-Meaningful Relationships.* Suppose some investigator states that a given total culture is dominated by an ideational supersystem. This general statement, if valid, is sufficient for us to make a number of deductions concerning the general character of many systems and subsystems of such a

---

[20] This is a somewhat simplified version of the more general formula of probability $\frac{m}{n}$ in stochastic relationships. On this cf. A. A. Tschuprow, *Grundbegriffe und Grundprobleme der Korrelationstheorie* (Leipzig, 1925); also his *Studies in Statistical Theory* (Russian, Moscow, 1909), Ch. 3.

[21] Several critics have wrongly ascribed to me the contention that there is an invariable and certain character to the succession of sensate, ideational, and idealistic phases. Throughout all volumes of *Dynamics* and explicitly in the fourth volume (pp. 770-773) I stressed again and again that the order is neither invariable nor certain; here I only reiterate these statements.

culture and of their mutual relationships. Thus we can deduce with reasonable degree of certainty: (1) that the dominant topic of all its fine arts will be religious and transcendental; (2) that the dominant style of the art will be symbolic; (3) that religion will dominate its philosophy and science; (4) that purely empirical science and technological inventions will be little cultivated; (5) that in the total scale of values in such a culture economic and material values will occupy a comparatively low place; (6) that its ethics and law will be sacred, absolutistic, and universalistic; (7) that the economic plane of living will be modest; (8) that familistic and coercive relationships will be developed more than contractual relationships; (9) that the governments of the groups of such a culture will be explicitly or implicitly theocratic, and so on. We grasp at once a whole "bundle" of causal-meaningful ties between all these phenomena as causally coexisting with one another, according to the multilinear causal formula: "if A (an ideational supersystem) is given, $B,C,D, \ldots N$ (the above characteristics of all the systems and subsystems) are given." Such a formula gives us at once, so to speak, a comprehension of the bulk of the static causal relationships of coexistence of many of the systems (variables) in such a total culture.

b. *Multilinear Dynamic Causal-Meaningful Relationships.* Similarly, the knowledge of supersystems and of their superrhythms gives us a comprehension of the direction of the change of all the systems and subsystems of such a supersystem, and of their interrelationships in the change. When in the seventeenth century Vico stated that European culture was passing from the phase of heroes to that of men, he correctly diagnosed the direction in which religion and ethics, political and economic institutions, science and arts, language and mores were changing, the forms toward which they were moving, which traits they were losing and acquiring. Unappreciated during his lifetime, the predictions of Vico have subsequently proven to be valid in major essentials. His predictions constitute one of the best examples of a roughly accurate diagnosis of the direction of the change of most of the systems and subsystems of European culture, much more valid than many narrower and more precise appearing predictions of specialists in economics and politics, in prices and wages.

Similarly in the nineteen twenties the author of this work was already predicting, contrary to the prevalent predictions of economists and political scientists, statesmen and scholars, press and public, that instead of a generally expected peace the western world was moving to bigger and more terrible wars; that instead of order and streamlined progress we were moving toward revolutions and disorders; instead of prosperity to misery; instead of democracy to dictatorships; instead of higher morality toward demoralization; instead of constructive application, toward increasingly destructive application of science and technology; instead of overpopulation to depopulation; instead of a stronger and better family to its disorganization, with a subsequent increase of divorces, desertions, juvenile delinquency, etc.; that further on there would be a replacement of emphasis on quality by an emphasis on quantity, and a replacement of creativity by technique. These and many other still more specific predictions as to what changes we should expect in various fields of the fine arts, ethics, law, philosophy, religion, and so on; all these predictions, which so far have proven valid, were based exactly upon a roughly correct grasp of the decline of the modern sensate supersystem and of the superrhythm of the supersystems in the history of the Graeco-Roman and western cultures. The nature of the sensate supersystem correctly understood, the general direction of its decline rightly diagnosed, these premises gave a firm foundation for predicting the direction in which all its systems and subsystems would develop; which traits they would gradually lose; which traits they would acquire, and other subsidiary consequences which would be forthcoming. So far the events predicted have come to pass and the predictions have turned out to be incomparably more accurate than the host of predictions by narrow specialists in economics and sociology, politics and business, by statesmen, educators, and the public. Most of their predictions, based upon purely mechanical manipulations of special and narrow variables torn from the organic context of the real systems and their supersystem, have turned out to be entirely wrong; others essentially incorrect. The reason for their failure was exactly that they did not have any idea of systems and supersystems; of the fact that systems and supersystems change in togetherness; that they are subject to rhythms and superrhythms. Cutting their variables (whether prices and wages, business indices and bank failures, a half dozen international treaties and internal statutes, the latest results of a Gallup poll of public opinion, or some other variable) from the living unity of the systems of which they are only tiny sub-sub-subsystems, they were like a fantastic physician diagnosing the course of development of an organism on the basis of two hairs, a few nails, and a few drops of blood taken from the organism and studied as independent variables, without any consideration of the organism as a whole.

This unsound procedure is still being continued. Dozens of precise looking "scientific" predictions are manufactured every day which prove themselves wrong, and will continue to prove wrong until this mechanical procedure is abandoned.

The general formula for grasping the multi-linear dynamic change of a multitude of systems and subsystems in their rhythms and superrhythms is this: If A (a given supersystem or vast system) is changing in a given direction, the $B,C,D,E, \ldots N$ (all its systems and subsystems) vary in the same direction together. "If A passes into X (if a sensate supersystem passes into an idealistic or ideational supersystem), then all its systems and subsystems are bound to pass also into X."

Such a grasp of a whole network of the causal-meaningful relationships between a host of variables (systems and subsystems) cannot be obtained at all without an understanding of systems, supersystems, their rhythms and superrhythms. Any mechanical manipulation of the variables cut out mechanically cannot yield a grasp in any way comparable. Herein lies the enormous cognitive, practical, and predictive value of the method of systems and supersystems, and of their rhythms and superrhythms.[22] This means that the prevailing methods of studying the causal-functional relationships between sociocultural phenomena are in need of a drastic revision and modification.

III. Tempo Uniformities in Change of Cultural Systems

1. Tempo and Rhythm

Tempo should not be confused with rhythm. The same phonograph record with the same rhythms can be played at 78 revolutions per minute or at 156 revolutions per minute. The rhythm of the music remains unchanged; the tempo is twice as fast in the second case as in the first.

The tempi of qualitative changes of qualitatively different sociocultural systems are incommensurable, not comparable; therefore no meaningful statement can be made about comparatively faster or slower tempi of such processes; if a statement is made, it becomes meaningless and empty. We do not have any unit of velocity of change applicable to such qualitatively noncomparable processes. There is no sense in saying that a change from the Gothic to the baroque style was slower or faster than the change from the horse and buggy to a

system of transportation by automobile, or from monarchy to republic. We do not know whether the "distance" from the Gothic to baroque is greater or smaller than that from horse and buggy to automobile. We do not have any unit of velocity to measure these "distances," therefore we cannot say anything as to which of these changes has the faster tempo. The various statements, still often made, about either "accelerated" or "slowed" tempi of such noncomparable changes are thus completely meaningless.

If tempo or velocity is defined as $V-T = \dfrac{M \text{ (Magnitude of change)}}{T \text{ (time)}}$ the notion of tempo-velocity is applicable and can be measured or compared only in purely quantitative changes and in a very approximate manner in the qualitative changes of the same kind or within the same system.

Quantitative changes with the same unit of change can be compared, measured, and de-

[22] For a development of this, cf. *Dynamics*, Vol. IV, pp. 423 ff.; *Causality*, Ch. 2.

scribed as faster or slower, accelerated or retarded in a large number of sociocultural processes: in production of automobiles or radios, in faster or slower growth of the population, in hundreds of quantitative increases and decreases. Statistics of population, of production, of trade and consumption, of movement of disease, of diffusion of certain values, and so on, give hundreds of examples of the legitimate application of the measurement of tempo or velocity of quantitative change. If 1,000 automobiles are produced in one month, while in another 10,000 are produced by the same firm with the same capital and labor, the tempo of the production in the second month is ten times as fast as in the first. Similarly we can compare and measure the tempi in various quantitative processes.

Much more roughly the idea of tempo can be applied to two or more *qualitative* changes of the same kind in the same or different systems. Thus the idealistic period in the sculpture, literature, and architecture of Greece of the fourth and fifth centuries B.C. lasted about one hundred and fifty years; an imitative wave of idealistic art in Rome in the time of Augustus lasted only about seventy years. On this basis we can say that the tempo of change of the imitative idealistic wave in its emergence, growth, and decline was about twice as fast as that in the original idealistic wave in Greece.

2. Tempo-Uniformities in Sociocultural Processes

a. *Law of Acceleration.* The most popular theory in this field is that of a progressive acceleration of tempo of change in all sociocultural processes in the course of time. The alleged "law of acceleration" is taken for granted and stated as a kind of axiom by a legion of sociologists, social thinkers,[23] and the public. We are told that "the tempo of

social life has speeded up," "the tempo of change is always more rapid," and so on.

For a corroboration of the law its proponents inform us that in biology "the most ancient species underwent the slowest evolution," that the duration of the Stone Age was 228,000 years while that of the Metal Age was only 18,000 years; that Egyptian art hardly changed during 3,000 years while Greek art ran its course in 700 years and Italian art in only 400 years. "Progress is but an acceleration of adaptation."[24] H. Hart furnishes a large series of facts along similar lines, beginning with the accelerating tempo of increase of brain power from Propliopithecus, through Pithecanthropus up to modern man, and ending with an ever-increasing velocity of locomotion, and the unification of humanity into larger and larger states up to the world state.[25] G. Tarde contended that in the course of time wars were of shorter and shorter durations and peace periods longer and longer.[26] C. Lalo claims that the Greek musical system changed slowly and lasted 1,200 years; Gregorian music lasted only 600 years; modern harmonic music only 300 years.[27] Similarly A. Niceforo, H. Adams, F. Tönnies, W. Willcox, and almost all authors of texts in sociology repeat the law of acceleration of tempo of change in the course of time.

b. *Critical Remarks.* The law of acceleration in its all-sweeping, unlimited formulation by Novicov and partly by Hart, which holds that everything in the course of time changes faster and faster, is obviously untenable. If valid it would mean that as we refer back into the past we would find the whole universe and all its processes changing more and more slowly until at the "beginning of time" the whole universe would be found to be static and unchangeable. Neither the beginning of time, nor the static state of the universe, nor the emergence of change from what was un-

[23] Possibly the most systematic formulation of the law of acceleration as a universal law valid in inorganic, organic, and superorganic processes is given by J. Novicov, *Les luttes entre sociétés humaines* (Paris, 1896), pp. 187-196 and *passim.* In American literature H. Hart, W. Ogburn, N. L. Sims, H. Adams, and almost all authors of texts in sociology repeat it as an unquestionable verity. See especially H. Hart, *The Technique of Social*

Progress (New York, 1931) and also his quoted works. Also H. Adams, *The Degradation of the Democratic Dogma* (New York, 1919), pp. 302-311.

[24] J. Novicov, *op. cit.*, pp. 48 ff., 187 ff.

[25] H. Hart, *op. cit.*, pp. 27 ff.; *passim.*

[26] G. Tarde, *Social Laws* (New York, 1899), pp. 109 ff., 132 ff.

[27] C. Lalo, *L'Esquisse*, quoted, p. 320.

changeable; nor any reason why a mere flow of time from the past to the present must lead to a progressive acceleration of change, have any tangible meaning nor can any of these hypotheses be demonstrated either logically or empirically. The whole conception is super-metaphysical in a bad sense of the term. Empirically, there is no ground to assume there was any "beginning of time," nor that the physical or chemical processes going on in nature at the present time require a mere fraction of the time which they required, say, a million of years ago, nor that instead of nine months required now from the conception to the birth of a human being, nine hundred and ninety-nine months were necessary several thousands of years ago, nor that the average duration of life of man or any other organism was a hundred or a thousand times longer in the past. We can assume with a reasonable degree of certainty that about the same nine months were necessary from the conception to the birth of a human being in the past as at the present. Similarly, it is very unlikely that the life duration of *homo sapiens* or any other species has changed radically in the course of tens of thousands of years of human or animal history. If it has changed slightly for human beings it has increased rather than decreased. Finally, there is no reason to assume that a given chemical or physical reaction in the same conditions requires less time now than in the past. All this means that there are a multitude of inorganic, organic, and, as we shall see, superorganic processes with *constant tempo*. For these reasons the law of acceleration of everything in the course of time as we move from the past to the present can be dismissed.

The law is untenable also in its somewhat more limited sense as applied to either sociocultural or biological processes. At the beginning of this section it was pointed out that the notion of tempo or velocity is inapplicable to qualitatively different sociocultural processes. Most of the concrete cases given by the proponents of the law as a demonstration of its validity compare the velocity of change of qualitatively different, and therefore non-comparable, processes; from the fact that elephants or alligators live longer than butterflies it does not follow that alligators change more

slowly than butterflies. The fact is simply that the duration of life of these species is different. Differences in the duration of life of different species tell us nothing about the tempo of change of these species.

On purely empirical grounds most of the sociocultural evidence given by the proponents of the law is false. It is not true that as time goes on the duration of wars becomes shorter and shorter; the actual facts of war disprove such a contention. It is not true that Egyptian art did not change at all during 3,000 years, and that Greek art existed only 700 and Italian art only 400 years. Egyptian art underwent many changes; Greek art continues to exist up to the present time; Italian art existed before Cimabue and continues to exist up to this day. The metal age likewise is very much alive and does not show any sign of disappearance. The Greek musical system did not remain unchanged during 1,200 years but underwent a series of the most radical changes from sensate to ideational and idealistic and then again to sensate, not to mention a great many changes of a less radical character. Gregorian music was only a new ideational phase of Greek music complicated by Oriental music, and in this phase lasted longer than the idealistic or sensate phase of Greek music; plain chant music lasted from the Ambrosian chants of the fourth century to the thirteenth century at least, while the Graeco-Roman sensate music lasted at best from the third century B.C. to the fourth century A.D. Gregorian music continues to exist up to this moment; it is sung daily in church services, played on records, and performed elsewhere.

Even the valid factual evidence given by the proponents of the law demonstrates not a law of acceleration but an earlier or later emergence of the respective phenomena in time. Since the stone age emerged earlier than the metal age, the stone age has existed for a longer time than the metal age; but such a longer existence does not at all mean a progressive acceleration of change within the stone or the metal age. Both ages continue to coexist side by side without any sign of disappearing; stone is still used for hundreds of purposes, and metals do not show any sign of falling into disuse. From the fact that in a family one child was born earlier than another it does not follow that the tempo of change of the later born child is faster than that of the first child.

When the evidence of the partisans of the law is tested along these lines not much is left, either of the evidence or of the law. What is left, as we shall see later, is the fact that in a given sociocultural process, or in several sociocultural processes which are qualitatively comparable, the tempi of change are not always constant. In some processes or periods the tempi are faster than in others; the tempo of a given process sometimes is accelerated, sometimes constant, sometimes slowed down. All this, however, is something very different from the law of acceleration of anything and everything in the course of time, from the past to the future. Such a law does not exist, nor has it any meaning; there is no comprehensible reason why everything should change faster and faster in the flow of time.[28]

c. *More Valid Tempo Uniformities.* (1) There are biosocial and sociocultural processes with constant and variable tempi of change. Biosocial processes such as the change of the foetus from its conception to birth, the passage from childhood to puberty, from puberty to maturity and then to old age, and many others are roughly constant in the course of time. Disregarding individual variations these changes require at the present time about the same amount of time as they did in the past. They do not show any accelerating or retarding trend in their tempi in the course of time. Likewise the strictly periodic sociocultural rhythms examined in the preceding sections remain also roughly constant as long as the system does not change in other major essentials. The daily rhythms of sleeping-waking, of social activity in day time and of its cessation at night time; weekly rhythms, monthly rhythms, seasonal rhythms, annual rhythms, biennial rhythms, and so on remain constant; each rhythm with each of its phases repeats itself within the same unit of time, as long as it exists. As the number and variety of such periodic rhythmic processes is considerable, this means that in sociocultural life there are processes with constant tempi of change. Throughout their existence the tempi show little variation in the course of time. Even the tempo and duration of the

growth and blossoming of a number of great cultural systems in the past and at the present remain, according to A. Kroeber, essentially unchanged. "They seem to take about as long now as they did one or two thousand years ago."[29] The periods of blossoming of Chinese, Greek, Arabic, medieval and modern philosophy are of some three to four centuries duration; Greek, Latin, Japanese, Chinese, French, Spanish, and English drama grew and blossomed within periods of some one or two centuries. In other words, in this process of growth and flowering of great systems there is hardly any evidence of an acceleration of tempo.[30]

Having shown the existence of processes with constant tempi let us pass now to those with varying tempi—those which show acceleration and slowing down. The most significant uniformities here can be put as follows.

(2) When a given cultural system or supersystem passes from an ideational to an idealistic and then to a sensate phase, the tempo of change tends to accelerate and become faster. When it passes from a sensate to an ideational phase, the tempo of change tends to slow down.

(3) Within the sensate phase the tempo of change in the system or supersystem tends to become particularly fast in the later, superripe stage of that phase.

(4) The tempi of change in a system or supersystem during the transitional period of its passage from a sensate to an ideational phase or vice versa tend to become chaotic or similar to a chaotic noise in which it is difficult to discern clearly any more or less regular tempo.

(5) When a system or supersystem passes several times through the sensate, ideational, idealistic phases, the second or third sensate (or ideational or idealistic) phase tends to have tempo of change faster and endures a shorter time than the preceding sensate phase. The same is true of the second and third recurrence of an ideational or idealistic phase in comparison with its former appearance.

(6) These propositions are valid only for sensate, idealistic, and ideational systems and supersystems, they are inapplicable to other

28 Cf. further *Dynamics*, Vol. IV, Ch. 11.

29 A. Kroeber, *op. cit.*, p. 808.
30 *Ibid.*, pp. 809 ff.

systems and especially to congeries of cultural phenomena.

(7) In regard to congeries hardly any tempo uniformity can be formulated or discovered.[31]

The logical reason for these uniformities lies in the nature of the values characteristic of each type of system. An ideational culture by its very nature tends to be a static culture, immersed in the eternal, everlasting, unchangeable true reality-value. It is a culture of Being par excellence. A sensate culture on the contrary is a culture which places a high value on empirical Becoming, ever changing and never static. Idealistic cultures occupy an intermediary position.

The empirical evidence amply corroborates this logical expectation. The Graeco-Roman and western supersystems in their ideational phases changed so comparatively slowly that historians often depict these phases as quite static, unchangeable, "archaic." One can take the tables and diagrams given in the preceding chapters for these cultures and can easily see, for example, that the number of scientific discoveries, the number of technological inventions, the content and styles of the fine arts, the content of philosophical and ethical systems, etc., all change little in the ideational phase and much more in the sensate phase. A culture in the ideational phase, having discovered its eternal verities, stays satisfied with them, and does not seek to replace them by ever new and different values. It is hieratic, traditionalistic, and in this sense changes little and slowly. A culture in the sensate phase, on the contrary, unceasingly tries to be "progressive, dynamic," seeking forever new empirical values, looking not to the eternal values discovered in the past but to the newer and better, most modern values. It values the latest fashion instead of the old-time consecrated tradition. It tears down the building just erected to replace it by a new one. It puts a premium upon anything swift, fast, dynamic, modern, "up to the last minute" and even beyond it. Hence its feverish tempi of change, its insatiable lust for change, its never-resting Becoming.

In the light of these considerations and em-

pirical evidence it is comprehensible also why the tempo of change of a supersystem slows down when it passes from a sensate to an ideational phase. The tempo of change of medieval culture from the sixth century up to the thirteenth was much slower than that of the preceding Graeco-Roman sensate phase from the third century B.C. to the fourth A.D. Such a slowing down of tempo must be expected each time a given system passes from a sensate to an ideational phase. For the same logical and especially empirical reasons it is comprehensible that the sensate phase changes faster and faster as it approaches its last stage, its superripe period. The feverish tempo at that stage of sensate supersystem is caused by its disintegration.

The processes of change in a system or supersystem during the most critical transitional period from one basic form to another become so chaotic that one cannot clearly discern any regular tempo, just as in a cacophony of diverse deadening noises one cannot discern any clear tempo. Possibly each of the processes in that great transition has its regular tempo; possibly these tempi are even very fast; but since we can hardly isolate each process in the general noise, the term chaotic seems to be most accurate for the description of such tempi.

Finally, since the second or third recurrence of any of the three phases in the same system takes place in the matrix of a total culture already greatly enriched by the preceding phases, especially with regard to empirical aspects beginning with science and ending with technology, it is quite comprehensible that the tempo of each second or third or fourth repetition of the same phase should be faster than at its preceding recurrence. The modern sensate phase of western culture emerged amidst the culture of the thirteenth century, which was empirically much richer in science and technology than the emerging sensate culture in Greece of the third century B.C. For this reason, and especially during the nineteenth and twentieth centuries, the modern phase of sensate culture has been changing at a tempo notably faster than that of the Graeco-Roman sensate phase. A glance at the movement of discoveries and inventions in particular, shows that during the last hundred years there have been more discoveries and

---

[31] For an elaboration and substantiation, as well as qualification of these propositions, cf. *Dynamics*, Vol. IV, Ch. 11.

inventions than during almost all the preceding centuries.

Similar considerations are applicable to the second, third, and each additional recurrence of ideational or idealistic phases. If, for instance, a new ideational phase comes after the decline of the present sensate phase, this ideational phase will start in a milieu consisting of the contemporary scientific and technological knowledge—amidst radio, airplanes, cars, atomic machines, and so on—which will make the tempo of its change much faster than that of the medieval ideational phase. We can be certain that a new ideational phase will not abolish most such knowledge and technology but will divert their functions from destructive to constructive purposes. Airplanes can be used for bombing or for missions of mercy. Atomic energy can be used for the destruction of millions of lives or for service to God and man. As a result of its emergence in such a milieu the new ideational phase is bound to show faster tempi of change in the field of empirical realities than its predecessor.

However, this acceleration of tempi with each subsequent recurrence of a given phase must not be regarded as unlimited, and as applicable to all systems and supersystems, existing independently from one another. In all probability there are limits to such an acceleration. Beyond a certain point it may not go and in catastrophic or other conditions it may even be reversed. If for instance, there should be a third atomic world war, the destruction might be so catastrophic that most of the accumulated culture on this planet would be destroyed. The surviving fraction of humanity would find itself amidst a litter of pitiable cultural debris, with most of its scientific knowledge and technology lost. Starting in such conditions a new ideational culture might turn out to be even more static than its medieval predecessor.

Such are some of the comparatively valid generalizations in the field of tempo-uniformities in sociocultural change.

Chapter 46. Reasons for Sociocultural Change and Variably Recurrent Processes

I. Principle of the Immanent Change of Systems and Supersystems

Having analyzed sociocultural changes— their forms, directions, and rhythms—we must now inquire into their causes. Why are socio-cultural phenomena not static? Why do not sociocultural changes pursue a uniform linear or cyclical course instead of exhibiting varying rhythms and tempos? As Aristotle rightly ob-served, "We cannot feel that we understand a thing until we can give an account of its causes and its *modus operandi*."[1]

Most of these questions are satisfactorily explained by two general principles or uni-formities: by the principle of immanent change of sociocultural systems, assisted by the prin-ciple of facilitating external factors, and by the principle of limit in its three fundamental forms.

(1) Any system, especially a sociocultural system, being a "going concern," incessantly functioning, inevitably changes as long as it continues to exist and function, even if it is placed in a wholly static environment.[2]

Change is an inherent property of all function-ing systems. The most efficient automobile engine is bound to change if it is left running, even under the best conditions. Likewise any biological organism or system inevitably changes as long as it lives, even if the external conditions are static. As the experiments of S. Metalnikov and others show, the simplest organisms, such as the amoeba or paramecium caudalum, having reacted to a given stimulus A, react to the same stimulus a second time in a different way, although the stimulus and the other conditions of the environment may remain unchanged; their third reaction is dif-ferent from the second, and so on.[3]

To reiterate, the cause of the changes in a social system is inherent in the system itself. Whether the system is scientific or religious, aesthetic or philosophical, whether it is rep-resented by a family, a business firm, an occu-pational union, or a state, it bears within itself the seeds of incessant change, which mark

---

[1] Aristotle, *The Physics*, 194 b.
[2] For a development of this and subsequent statements cf. my *Dynamics*, Vol. IV, Chps. 12, 13; also for a history of theories of immanent change and examples of contemporary explanations of busi-

ness fluctuations and political and other trans-formations.
[3] Cf. S. Metalnikov, *La Lutte contre la mort* (Paris, 1937), p. 74 and Chps. 1-7; also K. Gold-stein, *op. cit., passim.*

every action and reaction even in a fixed environment.

(2) An additional reason for the change of a sociocultural system is its milieu, which is made up mainly of a multitude of other changing systems and forces. The total constellation of interacting systems necessarily intensifies the process of change inherent within each member system. Thus the change implicit in a family or a scientific or philosophical system is stimulated through the interaction with other families or the state and with other scientific or philosophical systems.

(3) The immanent change of a sociocultural system or supersystem means, furthermore, the generation of a series of consequences affecting and largely determining its subsequent career. The effects of a given change are not evanescent. In most cases they are lasting and engender a cumulative series of consequences, even if the environment remains static. Thus the marriage of a member of a family or the division of the family property produces a train of consequences that induce further changes in the family. The consequences of a war do not cease with the armistice and peace, but usually continue to operate long after the end of the war.

(4) Hence, changing immanently and generating a cumulative series of consequences of each change, a system incessantly transforms both itself and its milieu.

(5) Through this incessant generation of consequences attending each of its changes a system perceptibly determines the character and course of its own future career. The whole series of changes it undergoes throughout its existence is to a large extent *an unfolding of its inherent potentialities*. From an acorn can spring only an oak. From the seed of any organism can emerge only the respective organism. In spite of the vicissitudes of their subsequent life history, the main line of the changes which such organisms undergo is merely the result of the inherent properties of the seed. The same is true of sociocultural systems. For instance, implicit in the family system are the main lines of its subsequent development; the course of the change of a family is different from that of a political party or state, regardless of its environment. Likewise the course of the changes experienced by

a musical system is different from that of a scientific or ethical system. As we shall see, the forms of change of "univariant" sociocultural systems are different from those of "bivariant" or "multivariant" systems; the forms, rhythms, periodicities, and directions of their quantitative and qualitative changes differ in each system according to its nature. In this sense any sociocultural system largely molds its own destiny.

(6) This fundamental characteristic of systems or supersystems does not preclude the influence of external—geographic, biological, and sociocultural—factors. However, their role consists largely (a) in the acceleration or retardation of the immanent change of a system; (b) in facilitating or hindering the realization of its potentialities; (c) in the suppression, distortion, or overdevelopment of some of its characteristics; (d) in a modification of its secondary traits, or in its mutilation or destruction. External factors cannot transform a given system into something fundamentally different from its essential nature, cannot make it unfold properties which it does not possess, cannot radically alter its immanent course. They can crush the system, or they can use its components—its members and some of its vehicles and meanings—for the creation of another system. This means, however, not the radical transformation of a given system into another quite different one, but rather the substitution of another in its place. No external conditions can force a corn seed to grow into a rose bush, or transform a scientific system into a symphony or a work of sculpture, a novel into a law code, or a family into a political party or a state. External factors can promote or hinder the full development of an oak or a scientific theory; they can accelerate or retard their growth; they can merge the family with a political party, thus making a multibonded group out of two unibonded groups, or they can crush systems and groups. That is all.

The outlined functions of external factors concern equally the geographic, the biological, and even the sociocultural factors external to a given system. Geographic factors exert a perceptible influence upon the distribution of population; upon the character of dwellings, roads, means of transportation, clothing, and food and drink. But they do not rigorously determine the forms of population groups, the essential architectural forms of buildings, or the essentials of food and drink and modes of transportation. They influence to some extent wealth, the distribution of industry, and the seasonal fluctuation of business; possibly (though more questionably) vital processes— energy, efficiency and mental creativity, forms of disease, and the like. This influence is neither decisive nor rigorous. Changing socio-cultural conditions convert into wealth materials which under other circumstances are not regarded as potential wealth. Mental creativity, health, and sickness depend still less upon geographic conditions. As for religion, science, philosophy, the fine arts, law and ethics, language, politics, and economics, probably only certain subsidiary traits are determined by geographic factors. The essential nature of these systems and their changes depend little upon geographic factors.[4] The various effects of geographic conditions do not exceed the formulated functions of external factors so far as sociocultural systems are concerned. In regard to cultural congeries their effects may be somewhat more decisive.

What has been said of geographic factors applies to biological forces external to a system. The biological factor of heredity is an internal factor of a sociocultural system because human beings, with their hereditary properties, are components of sociocultural systems. The effects of other biological factors, such as density of population, natural selection, and the so-called "struggle for existence," are confined to the outlined effects of external factors.[5]

More decisive is the influence of sociocultural factors external to a given system or supersystem. But even this is confined to the enumerated functions of external forces. Only when a given system actually becomes a part of a larger system or of a supersystem does it begin to change in close accord with all the parts of the larger system or the supersystem.

(7) This means that any system (or subsystem or supersystem) possesses a certain measure of self-determination and a certain margin of autonomy from the operation of external forces in its functioning and changes. The degree of self-determination and the margin of autonomy differ for different systems, depending upon their nature, their milieu, and other conditions.

(a) Other conditions being equal, the lowest degree of self-determination and the narrowest margin of autonomy are found among unorganized groups and cultural congeries; they are the prey of external forces.

(b) In systems of the same kind the degree of self-determination and the margin of autonomy tend to increase with a better organization of the groups and with a closer integration of the cultural systems.

(c) In subsystems and systems that are a part of a larger system or a supersystem, the self-determination and the margin of autonomy of each are limited not only by external forces but also by the other subsystems and systems of the more inclusive system. Each part retains a certain degree of autonomy, but this is restricted by the close meaningful and causal interdependence of the parts upon one another and upon the system as a whole. Hence the component parts tend to change in togetherness often synchronously, though at somewhat different rates.

(8) So far as the self-determination of any system is equivalent to its freedom, it is free, within the margin of its autonomy, from the deterministic influence of external forces. The systems are somewhat indeterminate also in the

---

[4] For a detailed study of the relationship between various geographic factors and diverse sociocultural phenomena, cf. my *Theories*, Chps. 2, 3. Since these chapters give a survey, analysis, and criticism of these relationships and the respective literature about as complete as in any earlier work, and since the conclusions given are still as valid as at the time of its publication, the present study does not devote special chapters to the role of external factors. Among the works published recently G. Dykmans' *Introduction critique à la science economique* (2 Vols. Bruxelles, 1945) gives the most complete survey, criticism, and bibliography dealing with the role of geographic factors; Dykmans' conclusions agree in all essential respects with those arrived at in my *Theories*. L. Deschesne's *La Localization des diverses productions* (Bruxelles, 1945) furnishes a very detailed study of the effects of geographic conditions upon the localization of industry, together with the most highly generalized rational principles of such localization and of sociocultural ecology.

[5] For a detailed analysis and criticism of the role of biological factors, together with the relevant literature, cf. my *Theories*, Chps. 4-7.

sense that the very notion of the potentialities of a system necessarily contains a marginal element of indeterminacy. A potentiality A with traits $a, b, c, d, \ldots n$ implies the possibility of a realization of traits a and c in one case; of $a, d,$ and n in another; of $b, c,$ and d in a third, etc. Thus the potentialities of the system permit a measure of choice in the realization of its secondary traits.

(9) Beyond the limits of self-determination and the margin of autonomy the life course of systems is determined by external factors and by other systems with which they are united into a more comprehensive system. Principles (8) and (9) thus afford a definite answer to the question: Are social and cultural systems deterministic or indeterministic? Each system is in part self-deterministic, or free, and in part deterministic, unfree.

This conclusion appears to be much sounder than many others, for instance, those that claim the complete determinism of sociocultural sys-

tems or their complete indeterminism and freedom of will; or such theories as that of A. Eddington, who postulates chance or indeterminacy for inorganic phenomena and an "objective law of direction" for organic and superorganic phenomena,[6] or that of Max Planck and others, who proclaim the rule of "statistical and dynamic determinism" in the inorganic world, with regions of "ego" and "free will" exempt from such determinism.[7] All such theories are both one-sided and in certain respects inconsistent.[8]

(10) Since every system changes immanently and since it changes also under the influence of changing external factors and of changes in the supersystem to which it belongs, it can never return to its original state, can never reproduce itself in absolutely identical fashion. *Hence the strictly cyclical conception of the change of systems is untenable. The principle of immanent change emphatically contradicts it.*

II. The Principle of Limits

The principle of limits is the second general principle or law that accounts for an enormous number of characteristics of sociological change, particularly of rhythms and of variations in recurrent trends, and for the improbability of any permanent linear course of change in sociological systems. The principle of limits exhibits the following three main forms.

1. Limits in Causal-Functional Relationship of Interdependent Variables

According to the first form of the principle of limits the causal-functional relationship between two or more variables A and B has certain definite limits; beyond a given value of A and B it ceases to exist or undergoes a radical change. Within certain limits the more firmly we strike a piano key, the louder the resulting sound. Beyond this point the result will be

not a louder sound but merely a broken keyboard.

The physicochemical and biological sciences are well aware of the principle of limits in the causal-functional relationships of their variables. They have formulated a number of general principles relative to the "stability limit" (Knorr and others), "critical temperature," "critical pressure," "critical concentration," and the like, representing points beyond which the causal-functional relationship between the given variables either undergoes a radical change or ceases to exist. For example, "Chemical reactions do not take place completely in one direction, but proceed only to a certain point and there make a halt." Thus the upper limit in the vaporization of water or the equilibrium between liquid and vapor is reached at the critical temperature of 364.3 degrees and the critical pressure of 194.6 at-

[6] Cf. A. Eddington, *The Philosophy of Physical Science* (New York, 1939), pp. 61, 89-90; *passim.*

[7] M. Planck, *Where Science Is Going* (New York, 1932), pp. 145-169, and A. Lotka, "Evolution and Thermodynamics," *Science and Society,* 1944, pp.

169 ff.; J. Frank, *Fate and Freedom* (New York, 1945).

[8] For the fluctuation of deterministic and indeterministic conceptions in their application to the ideational and sensate supersystems, cf. my *Dynamics,* Vol. II, Ch. 9.

mospheres. At higher temperatures no pressure, however great, can induce the liquid phase. Such limits are typical of a vast number of causal-functional relationships between physicochemical variables.[9]

Sociologists and social scientists are imperfectly aware of this principle. When they formulate valid or invalid causal relationships between business depression and criminality, prosperity and the birth rate, poverty and the mortality rate, education and criminality, economic conditions and the forms of the arts, farm income and illiteracy, and so on, they rarely mention any limits within which the causal relationship between their variables holds. They seemingly assume that it has no limits no matter what values we assign to the variables.

On the basis of both logic and observed facts it is reasonably certain that in practically all causally connected sociocultural variables there are limits beyond which the causal-functional relationship ceases or else assumes another character. Poverty below the level of physiological necessity depresses the birth rate and increases the mortality rate; an improvement in material well-being up to and above the level of physiological necessity causes an increase in the birth rate and a decrease in the mortality rate. However, there are limits beyond which a further improvement of material conditions does not lead to a further rise of the birth rate or decline of the mortality rate; it may even produce the opposite results. The same is true of practically all causal relationships between sociocultural variables; they apparently all have their limits. A precise causal formula demands, therefore, the specification of the limits within which it is valid and beyond which it becomes invalid. This principle of limits in causal-functional relationships is one of the reasons why most sociocultural processes have their "optimum" points and fluctuate without any definite trend between certain limits in their direction and course.

2. Limits in Linear Direction of Sociocultural Change

Contrary to the claims of a host of biological and social "linearists," the theory of a permanent linear trend of biological evolution or sociocultural progress is hardly tenable on either logical or empirical grounds. In virtually every sociocultural process there are limits for a linear trend. Within a limited time and a limited segment of the process some linear trend is possible, but it is scarcely possible for an unlimited period or for the entire process.

A linear sociocultural change is a complicated variety of the uniform rectilinear motion observed in mechanics. Newton's law declares that such motion is possible only when there is no interference from external forces, or when the moving body is completely isolated from all environmental factors, or when all the external forces at any moment mutually cancel one another and permit the body to move according to the law of inertia, uniformly and rectilinearly. The motion of material bodies, including the heavenly bodies, is, however, not subject to these conditions. Gravitational forces, for instance, interfere with it and divert it into a circular or elliptical orbit.

Still less do these conditions apply to sociocultural phenomena. They are subject to the constant operation of physical, biological, and sociocultural factors. No systems or congeries exist in a vacuum, isolated from the forces of the environment. Nor do the innumerable forces external to a changing sociocultural phenomenon perpetually annul one another. Moreover, even if this were true, the principle of immanent change would preclude the possibility of limitless linear trends in the change of sociocultural systems and congeries.[10]

These logical reasons are well corroborated by factual evidence. Practically all the permanent linear trends postulated by biological and social scientists have proved spurious when subjected to the acid test of empirical observation.

[9] A. Findlay, *The Phase Rule and Its Applications* (London, 1904), pp. 96, 200, 234; *passim.* W. Gibbs's phase rule and the theorems of van't Hoff, Le Chatelier, and others present the general principles of such limits.

[10] There are many other reasons for this conclusion. For a more precise elaboration of this and subsequent statements, cf. my *Dynamics*, Vol. IV, Ch. 14.

3. Limited Possibilities of Basic Variations of Systems

Since every empirical sociocultural system is finite, and since there are limits beyond which any further change renders it unrecognizable and unidentifiable, therefore it is capable of only a limited number of basic variations or types of change. Having exhausted these types, the system either disintegrates or repeats these types in a new setting, with different secondary characteristics. Hence on the one hand the recurrence, or rhythm, of sociocultural processes, and on the other, the variations in their course.

Natural scientists are thoroughly familiar with the principle in question, and, in contrast to social scientists, they incessantly apply it. Every physicist knows that water has only three basic types, or phases of variation—vapor, liquid, and solid—which are repeated endlessly. Chemical systems with more than one component exhibit a greater number of phases and greater degrees of "freedom" in their changes; but, according to W. Gibbs's formula: $P+F=C+2$, or $F=C+2-P$ (where P denotes the number of phases, F the degree of freedom, and C the number of components of the system); virtually all chemical systems are limited in their transformations and therefore repeat their phases in time and space.[11]

Similarly, the number of basic physical forms of energy, such as heat, sound, electricity, and magnetism, is strictly limited; therefore they endlessly recur in the physical world. The same is true of biological systems; whether it is the number of species, or the number of dominant characteristics or variations of a given species, or the number of fundamental biological processes (adaptation, natural selection, the struggle for existence, reproduction,

and so on), they are all limited in their fundamental types, and therefore recur in time and space.

No less true is this of sociocultural systems. Whatever classification of the basic types of *economic organization* is adopted, these rarely exceed six or eight in number, as in the classification given by K. Bücher, G. Schmoller, E. Meyer, and W. Sombart, who list hunting, the collecting of natural products, pastoral life, agriculture, and industry. If a given economic system runs through all these types and continues to exist, it must necessarily repeat them, with variations. Similarly, the cardinal types of the *family* and *marriage* do not exceed ten in number. The same is true of the chief types of *political regimes* and the *forms of government*; the five forms given by Plato and the six of Aristotle and Polybius embrace all the principal variations. No different is the situation with respect to the basic forms of *religion, language and writing, ethics and law, philosophy,* or the *fine arts*. The same is true of *technological systems* (as illustrated by the paleolithic, the neolithic, the copper, the bronze, the iron, and the machine age), and of systems of mechanical energy.

Even if we take *the main patterns of minor social and cultural* phenomena, such as styles of dress and coiffure,[12] of arrow points, of sword handles, and of drums, or systems of matrilineal and patrilineal descent and forms of kinship, we find that they too are limited and therefore repeat themselves in secondary variations at various periods in various societies.

Summarizing, the basic forms of almost all sociocultural phenomena are limited in their number; hence they inevitably recur in time, in rhythmic fashion, and in the course of their changes do not follow a strictly linear trend.[13]

[11] Cf. A. Findlay, *The Phase Rule*, pp. 16 ff. H. Poincaré rightly stresses the importance of the limited number of chemical elements, whose recurrence makes possible the science of chemistry. If, instead of 92 chemical elements, there were 92 billions, "each time we picked up a new pebble, there would be a strong probability of its being composed of an unknown substance. In such a world there would be no science." Even life itself would hardly be possible under such conditions. For a further comment on this statement, cf. P. L. du Nouy, *Biological Time* (London, 1936), p. 34.

[12] G. Glotz remarks that the modern Parisian coiffure and dress are strikingly similar to those

of the Minoan culture. (*La Civilization Egéenne* (Paris, 1923), pp. 88 ff.) W. Deonna gives a large number of such recurrences in dress, coiffure, manners, etc. (*L'Archéologie*, 3 Vols., *passim*.)

[13] For a development of this proposition, cf. my *Dynamics*, Vol. IV, pp. 701 ff.; A. Goldelweiser, "The Principle of Limited Possibilities," *Journal of American Folklore*, 1913, pp. 259-290; R. Thurnwald, "The Spell of Limited Possibilities," *ASR*, 1937, pp. 195-203; and R. Lowie, "On the Principle of Convergence in Ethnology," *Journal of American Folklore*, 1912, pp. 37 ff. For other literature, cf. my *Dynamics*, Vol. IV, pp. 704 ff.

III. Immanent Change and Limits and Rhythms of Sociocultural Processes

From the principle of the immanent change of systems, re-enforced by the ever-changing consellation of external factors, there follows the impossibility of an absolutely cyclical direction of change.

The principle of immanent change, re-enforced by that of limits (in its three forms), precludes a limitless linear direction of change in sociocultural systems. Theoretically such a limitless trend is possible in the case of an "invariant" social system, that is, one which possesses only a single basic type, variant, or phase, which cannot change into any other form, variant, or phase.[14] Even an "invariant" sociocultural system can pursue a linear trend only in a vacuum or in a milieu where all the external forces cancel one another out. Such a theoretical case is hardly ever realized in the sociocultural universe. First, we are not sure that there are any invariant sociocultural systems; second, the necessary milieu, with a mutual annulment of all the external forces for an indefinite period, does not exist; third, it is certain that no sociocultural system operates in a vacuum, completely isolated from all external forces. Hence such unlimited linear directions are hardly possible in the actual change of a sociocultural system. What may resemble a limitless linear trend is likely to be merely a limited trend of considerable du-

ration exhibiting many deviations from strict linearity even within this segment, and becoming explicitly nonlinear when a longer period is considered. Even such possibly linear processes as the increase of the population of the earth, the multiplication of inventions and discoveries, and the intensification of social differentiation and division of labor are, in fact, linear in only a limited sense; viewed even in their known span of existence, they reveal many deviations from linearity, and if considered from the standpoint of their entire life history, they would probably be found to pursue a parabolic course or to fluctuate without any definite trend.[15] Ninety-nine per cent of all other linear "laws of evolution and progress" are definitely untenable, figments of the imagination of theorists rather than accurate formulae of the actual direction of sociocultural processes.

This generalization applies also to the laws of the "universal stages" through which mankind as a whole or a given society or cultural system is supposed to pass. Apart from the sequence of phases of repeated rhythms, no such law of stages has been established. When empirically tested, most of such laws, including Comte's law of three stages, Spencer's law of evolution, and hundreds of similar laws of historical development, prove untenable.[16]

---

[14] The term "invariant" is borrowed from Gibbs's phase rule. It designates chemical systems that do not possess any degree of freedom, whereas chemical systems that possess two or more degrees of freedom are designated, respectively, as "univariant," "bivariant," and "multivariant." (Cf. A. Findlay, *op. cit.*, pp. 17 ff.)

[15] Cf. my *Dynamics*, Vol. IV, pp. 715-726.

[16] Recently L. A. White attempted to defend such linear laws of evolution and of the universal linear sequence of its stages. He is right so far as he asserts that many evolutionists do not claim that every culture or society passes through these stages in their universal sequence. He fails, however, to demonstrate what exactly are these evolutionary stages and who and what passes through them, and where. "The evolutionists described the development of writing as follows: first there was picture writing; out of it grew a form of rebus writing; and out of this emerged the alphabet.

What they have done is to describe a cultural process; they have said that these stages follow one another in this order. They have said nothing about any tribe or nation, or about the order in which it might acquire one or another of these forms of writing." (L. White, "Diffusion vs. Evolution," *AA*, 1945, pp. 343 ff. Cf. also his "History, Evolutionism and Functionalism," *Southwestern Journal of Anthropology*, 1945, pp. 221-246.) This order of emergence of the forms of writing is the best case cited by White in support of his claim. Taking his statement at its face value, we are entitled to conclude that even this sequence of the forms of writing is not a universal law of evolution; for many tribes and nations have not passed through this sequence. Those which have done so represent neither mankind as a whole nor even the majority of social groups. Therefore they give only a partial, limited sequence of no more general significance than the following sequences:

The *number of phases* in the rhythm of a given sociocultural process roughly corresponds to the number of basic types or variations of a given system. If the system is "univariant" and has two basic types, then its rhythm will exhibit two phases, such as the sequences increase and decrease, materialism and idealism, peace and war, depression and prosperity, or the diurnal-nocturnal rhythm of activity and rest. If the system is multivariant and has, say, six main types or variants, such as the Aristotelian forms of government (monarchy, tyranny, aristocracy, oligarchy, democracy, mob rule), then its changes will present a six-phase rhythm, and so on. If one knows how many fundamental variants a given system possesses, one can predict what kind of rhythm, with how many phases, it will display in the course of its existence. This statement must, however, be accepted with certain reservations. Sociocultural systems are much less rigid than chemical systems, and the sequence of their phases is more variable. For instance, between clear-cut phases of economic prosperity and depression there may be intermediate "bridges" that cannot be properly designated as either definite prosperity or definite impoverishment. In bivariant system with three basic variants, these are repeated again and again, but not necessarily in the same order; between these phases there may be subsidiary phases.

The *less numerous the principal variants* of a given sociocultural system, the *simpler, more pronounced, and more readily observable are its rhythms*. If it has only two main variants and consequently a two-phase rhythm, this rhythm repeats itself more frequently and is hence more easily observed and apprehended than one with 500 phases in a system with 500 basic variants.

In systems with a *large number of main variants the rhythm is so complex, consisting of so many phases, that we can hardly grasp its nature or observe its recurrence*. The change of such systems, even if they have a fairly definite rhythm, appears nonrhythmical and nonrecurrent. It suggests an ever-new process, without any repetitions or recurrences, incessantly varying and unpredictable.

The two preceding propositions explain why many sociocultural processes appear unique at any moment of their existence. They account also for the actual novelty of most sociocultural processes considered not only in their main aspects, but in all their secondary and detailed characteristics. Since the number and variety of these secondary characteristics are enormous, and since the conditions of the milieu are also highly varied, the number of combinations of these secondary traits and of the milieu is practically unlimited. In respect to the secondary traits of a system and of its milieu we cannot expect any repeated uniformity, any recurrent rhythms. It is only in its main types or variants that the history of a system repeats itself in the form of recurrent rhythms, and even these can be properly apprehended only if the basic variants and the phases of the rhythm are not too numerous. Thus the total change of most systems reconciles the two extremes; it is in part a repetition of the old, and in part ever new. The new factors preclude a recurrence of identical cycles.

Understood in the above sense, the dominant form of the direction of sociocultural processes is neither permanently cyclical nor permanently linear, but varyingly recurrent, with incessant modifications of the old themes.

The task of the historical, ideographic, or individualizing sciences consists in the descrip-

---

picture writing, alphabetic form, rebus writing, alphabetic form; alphabetic form only; picture writing only; rebus writing only. We have no reason to elevate one of the sequences—say, picture, rebus, and alphabetic writing—into a universal law of evolution, leaving the other sequences in the inferior position of a mere deviation from the alleged universal law. Furthermore, even the allegation that there first appeared picture writing, then rebus writing, and finally alphabetic writing is a mere guess. Third, even if they did emerge in that order, such an emergence, happening only once in the course of history, in no way establishes a law of evolution. Again, the fact that the classical

Greek style of architecture was followed in turn by the Romanesque, Gothic, baroque, rococo, and other styles does not establish a law of architectural evolution. To elevate such a local, particularized sequence into a law of evolution of architecture means to deprive the term "law of evolution" of its central meaning. The overwhelming majority of social and cultural forms exhibit no universal stages of evolution. White is correct in distinguishing repeated sociocultural processes from unique historical events and from nonrhythmic, ever varying processes; but his valiant effort to champion the linear laws of evolution, with their universal stages, is futile.

tion of the new, unique features of a given system, whereas the task of sociology and of the nomographic, or generalizing, sciences consists in the observation and abstraction of re- peated uniformities in the process of change, of established rhythms, however approximate and subject to variation these uniformities may be.

IV. Backward Glance, in Light of Immanent Change and Limits

These principles sum up what we have met in the study of the fluctuations of virtually all the preceding social, cultural, and personal processes. We have observed that social organization, differentiation, and stratification grow immanently until they reach their optimum point in a given group; when the optimum point is exceeded, groups generate forces that inhibit further differentiation and stratification. On the other hand, when immobility persists too long, social systems generate forces working for differentiation. If systems do not succeed in regaining their optimum equilibrium, they tend to disintegrate. The same immanent reaction of systems and the same fluctuation between the optimum limits have been observed in the alternations of freedom and restraint, of expansion and contraction of governmental regimentation, of increase and decrease of mobility, etc. Too much sensate freedom, laissez faire, or mobility generates forces within a system that tend to limit these factors and to reverse the trend. Conversely, too much restraint, governmental regimentation, or immobility elicits the opposite reaction in favor of more freedom, less governmental control, and greater mobility.

We have seen also how and why compulsory or even contractual relationships contain within themselves the seeds of their own destruction and of their transformation into a different kind of social relationships. The same has been demonstrated with respect to the leading cultural systems and supersystems. Each of the principal supersystems possesses the germs of its own decline. With the development, and especially the overdevelopment, of a sensate, ideational, or even idealistic supersystem these germs develop, become more virulent, and eventually undermine the supersystem and pave the way for the emer-

gence and growth of a different system. Even if the external milieu were completely static, each supersystem would immanently follow this course, just as a human organism inevitably pursues its predetermined course from childhood to old age.

The principles of *immanent causes* and of *limits* must be and are applied to explanation of all such sociological phenomena as changes of political or economic systems, business cycles, changes in styles of art or in patterns of cultural growth in various preliterate groups, the rise and decline of historic civilizations, or the maintenance of social equilibrium. Thus the overwhelming majority of theories of the business cycle find its cause in the immanent forces of the capitalist system of economy that inherently generates waves of prosperity and depression (the theories of M. Tugan-Baranovsky, A. Spiethoff, G. H. Hill, J. Schumpeter, M. Bouniatian, A. Aftalion, A. H. Hansen, E. Wagemann, and others).[17]

Geographic, biological, and other forces external to an economic system play merely the role of accelerating (facilitating) or retarding (hindering) factors, or, in extreme cases, that of catastrophic agents. Even in a static milieu, fluctuations of the capitalistic economic system would inevitably occur. Regardless of the milieu, the capitalist system bears within itself the seeds of its own destruction. Hegel and Marx are correct in predicting its immanent, or "dialectical," self-destruction.

Similarly, any political regime, religious creed, or style of art is immanently bound to change and eventually to bring about its own decline. Plato and Aristotle demonstrated this principle in their analysis of how and why each political regime—whether it be an aristocracy or timocracy, oligarchy or monarchy,

---

[17] Cf. my *Dynamics*, Vol. IV, pp. 660 ff., and *Theories*, pp. 120 ff.

democracy or tyranny—generates the forces of its own destruction.[18] When anthropologists declare that the nature of the initial culture of a given preliterate group "defines the situation" and becomes the decisive determining factor in the subsequent development of such a culture, they are merely enunciating the principle of immanent self-determination and development of cultures.[19]

When Toynbee, Spengler, Danilevsky, et al. seek to explain why civilizations decline and disintegrate, they unanimously affirm that they perish "not through murder but through suicide" immanently generated by each civilization in the process of its growth. When social scientists speak of social, economic, or political "equilibria," they all apply the principle of immanent self-adjustment of social, economic, or political systems. The very statement that any social system, when disturbed, tends to reestablish its initial position, or to restore its equilibrium, is a clearcut formulation of the principle of immanent change and self-adjustment.[20]

V. Decline of Systems and Exhaustion of Their Creative Forces

Viewed ontologically, the decline of most cultural systems and supersystems is due largely to the growing inadequacy of their intrinsic values—their deviation from genuine reality—or to the exhaustion of their creative functions. Millions of uncreative systems arise, flourish for a time, and quickly disappear. The longevity of most cultural systems and supersystems is due to the fact that they embody genuine reality and values; in other words, that they are creative.

Being, however finite, limited in the quantity and quality of the true reality-value which they embody, they unfold in the course of their existence merely the potentialities of their finite system of values. Having fulfilled this mission, they eventually become devitalized, a liability rather than an asset. When they have reached this point, their decline is inevitable. Through sheer inertia they may perpetuate their existence for a brief period, an existence (to use Toynbee's phrase) which is rather "death in life" than actual life. Ultimately they are banished from the stage of history and relegated to a "museum" status.

A pertinent illustration of this generalization is afforded by our supersystems. In spite of the richness of their values, even they are finite, each incorporating only one aspect of ultimate truth, reality, or value. The ideational supersystem unfolds the supersensory and superlogical aspect of the infinite manifold; the sensate supersystem, its sensate aspect; the idealistic supersystem, its rudimentary idealistic aspect. Having fulfilled its mission, each supersystem becomes increasingly sterile and progressively hinders the emergence of a new and vital supersystem representing an aspect of reality largely neglected during the domination of its predecessor. Such a situation presents, as it were, an ultimatum to the society and culture in question; they are forced either to replace the exhausted supersystem with a creative one or else to become stagnant and fossilized. Some cultures succeed in making the necessary substitution and survive. Others perish or else become fossilized, being converted into mere raw material, so to speak, for more creative cultures.

When the sensate supersystem of the Creto-Mycenaean culture was exhausted, it was replaced by the creative ideational supersystem of the Greeks. When this declined, it was superseded by the idealistic supersystem of the fifth century B.C. Being highly unstable

---

[18] Cf. Plato, *The Republic*, Books VII and VIII; also Aristotle, *Politics*, Book V; *passim*.

[19] Cf. W. I. Thomas, *Primitive Behavior*, Ch. 2; R. Lowie, "Some Problems in Ethnology," *AA*, Vol. XIV (1912), pp. 68-71; C. Wissler, "Ceremonial Bundles of the Blackfoot Indians," *Anthropological Papers of the American Museum of*

Natural History, Vol. VII, Part 2 (1912), pp. 100-106; and F. Znaniecki's "closed system" in *The Method of Sociology* (New York, 1934), pp. 11 ff.

[20] For an analysis of equilibrium theories, cf. my *Dynamics*, Vol. IV, pp. 677-693.

and fragile, this, in turn, gave way to the sensate supersystem of the period from the third century B.C. to the fourth A.D. By the fourth century A.D. this supersystem had become depleted, and it was replaced by the ideational Christian supersystem of the Middle Ages. By the thirteenth century the latter had fulfilled its mission and was succeeded by the idealistic and then by the sensate supersystem of the last five centuries. Each supersystem, during its ascendance and at its climax, has been marked by creative genius. Each has contributed immeasurably to humanity's store of truth, beauty, and goodness.

The rhythmic succession of the supersystems is hence not a monotonous cyclical recurrence, but an ever-creative process constituting a progressive realization of the infinite manifold in the empirical world of humanity.

The contemporary sensate system, in its virile stages, contributed markedly to the values of science and technology, the fine arts, and, in lesser degree, philosophy and ethics. But it is clearly approaching the end of its career, indeed, it is rapidly crumbling under our very eyes. In its present decadence phase, characterized by increasing wars and revolutions, by the perversion of science in the interest of ever more lethal weapons of destruction, by progressive sensualism and the like, it has begun to menace the further existence of humanity. If civilization is not to perish, our moribund sensate supersystem must be replaced by a new ideational or idealistic supersystem. Sooner or later such a supersystem will emerge, destined to continue the creative role of the superorganic on this planet.

Chapter 47. The Life Span, Death, and Resurrection of Cultural Systems

I. The Life Span of Cultural Systems

In Chapter 34 typical life spans of various organized groups were given. The data exhibit a very wide range. The range of spans of empirical cultural systems seems to be even wider than that of social groups, fluctuating from the near-zero point to several thousands of years. In several cases their life span is almost coextensive with that of human history.

Any system of meanings as pure meanings is timeless. Such a proposition as "Two and two is four" is permanently valid. When the question of the duration of cultural systems is raised, it applies not to systems of pure meanings but to empirical three-componental systems, objectified in material vehicles and socialized among human beings.[1]

The death of such a system means either the complete loss of its vehicles or agents or the logico-aesthetic disintegration of its system of meanings, or a combination of the two.

1. Relative Longevity of Systems

There is a multitude of petty systems that are either never objectified and socialized or

else only for a moment. Millions of propositions of the type "A is B," uttered in our daily conversation, are forgotten almost as soon as they are enunciated.

Then there are thousands of minor systems that endure for only a few weeks, months, or years, comprising books in various fields of culture, drawings, paintings, works of sculpture, buildings, and the like. To the same category belong sundry economic, political, educational, religious, and other minor systems evolved by various groups as the *raison d'être* of their existence. Such groups exist on an average for only a few years, and with their disappearance the respective cultural systems become extinct.

When we turn to such systems as *a given language, a major religion, notable philosophical, ethical, juridical, aesthetic, scientific, technological, economic, and political systems, we find that most of them endure for decades*

---

[1] The question can hardly be raised respecting the life span either of congeries or of the conglomeration of systems and congeries called "civilization." The notions of life and death are applicable only to living and functioning unities, either biological or sociocultural. They become meaning-

less in regard to unintegrated and undifferentiated organic matter or cultural congeries. This is the reason (as we have seen in Chapter 43) why the statements of Danilevsky, Spengler, and Toynbee on the death of "civilizations" are rather meaningless, and why even Kroeber's position is likewise vague, since he fails to differentiate clearly between systems and congeries. (Cf. A. Kroeber, *op. cit.*, pp. 818 ff.)

or centuries and that the greatest of them function for a thousand or more years, fluctuating qualitatively and quantitatively, but maintaining an uninterrupted existence. Chinese, Greek, Latin, and several other languages have persisted for more than two thousand years, and such tongues as Russian, German, French, English for almost as long a period.

Such *religious systems* as Confucianism, Taoism, Hinduism, Buddhism, Judaism, Jainism, and Christianity have existed about two thousand years, or over.

Among *philosophical systems*, the Vedanta and the Upanishad philosophy and those of Plato and Aristotle, Democritus and Plotinus, have endured for two or more millenniums. Those of Saint Augustine and Erigena, Albertus Magnus and Saint Thomas Aquinas, Descartes, Hume, and Kant continue to retain their vitality.

Such *scientific systems* as the basic elements of arithmetic and geometry date back to an early period of human culture. The same is true of the rudiments of astronomy, physics, chemistry, and biology. Without a practical knowledge of the basic elements of physics, chemistry, and biology not even a primitive society could have long survived. In the course of time these have been supplemented by the discovery of various uniformities and general laws and principles, leading to more comprehensive and more consistent scientific systems.

A similar observation applies to the major and minor systems in the field of *the social and humanistic disciplines*. The histories of Herodotus and Thucydides are still vital. The same is true—at least, within the limited circle of specialists and scholars—of the sociological, political, and economic generalizations of Confucius and Mencius, anonymous ancient Hindu and other thinkers; Plato, Xenophon, Aristotle, Ibn Khaldun, and later social thinkers.

The basic *ethical and juridical* principles, such as the Golden Rule, the Ten Commandments, and their equivalents, and the developed ethical systems, such as those of love, utilitarianism, hedonism, eudemonism, skepticism, and cynicism, formulated centuries and even thousands of years before our era, continue to live and function.

Both major and minor juridical systems, such as the *Corpus Juris Civilis*, the *Laws of Manu, Brihaspati*, and *Narada*, and the *law of the first books of the Bible*, survive not only in books and in the studies of scholars but also in social life, as vital norms practiced and enforced.

A similar situation obtains in the case of great *aesthetic systems*. The Mahabharata and Ramayana and the works of Homer, Sophocles, Aristophanes, Dante, and Shakespeare—these and many other literary creations persist as empirical cultural systems. So also the major architectural systems, embracing the Egyptian pyramids and temples, notable Greek and Roman buildings, Hindu temples, the medieval Christian cathedrals, and the like.

The same is true of great works of sculpture and paintings. Again, many folk songs and religious and magical incantations which originated in the remote past continue to be sung. Since the invention of musical notation, such musical systems as the Gregorian chants of the Middle Ages, various motets, and much more elaborate musical creations have been bequeathed to posterity in written form and still pulsate in the contemporary musical world.

Finally, such ancient *technological* systems as the use of fire, the lever, the wheel, and several pastoral and agricultural techniques survive in even the most advanced technological countries. Likewise, many notable technological systems subsequently evolved in various fields of technology have continued to function up to the present time. Even technological systems later supplanted by more perfect ones have not entirely disappeared; as secondary, or auxiliary, systems they are practiced side by side with their successors. In spite of the locomotive, steamship, automobile, and airplane, such ancient means of transportation as walking, horseback riding, sailing, and rowing are still used. Notwithstanding gas and electricity, wood and coal continue to be widely used for heating purposes. Indeed, many technological systems originating in the stone, copper, bronze, and iron ages survive as supplementary systems in our technological machine age.

Notable cultural systems seem to last somewhat longer than major organized groups. These now and then disintegrate and cease to exist, whereas the great cultural systems evolved by them often find new human agents to perpetuate their existence.

Finally, if we take not a given concrete cultural system or supersystem but its *generic and typical form*—not a given great religion but the main types of religion, such as theism, deism, or pantheism; not a given scientific or philosophical theory but a system of mathematics or physics, or a materialistic, idealistic, empirical, rationalistic, mystical, or skeptical system of philosophy—we find that in *these generic and typical forms the great systems in all the principal fields of culture are virtually "immortal."* This or that particular language may disappear, but language in general, and even its main types, is perennial. This or that specific religion may become extinct; but religion per se never dies. Its main types (monotheism, polytheism, theism, pantheism, etc.), however classified, have perpetuated themselves, with various modifications so far as their secondary characteristics are concerned, throughout the entire history of human culture. Certain major philosophical systems of the past have disappeared, and some of the contemporary ones are also likely to disappear. But philosophy itself and its primary types (materialism, idealism, rationalism, empiricism, mysticism, skepticism, and so forth) are perennial.

The same is even more true of science—of the basic scientific disciplines and principles. This or that scientific theory may decline and be forgotten; but science per se, and even the essential scientific disciplines and principles (such as atomism and vitalism), are "immortal"; in one form or another they will continue to exist in spite of the growth or decline of a given type in a given period or culture.

A similar continuity is characteristic of the fine arts in general and their main types— ideational, idealistic, sensate, eclectic, symbolic, naturalistic, classic, and romantic. They have existed since the remote past and will exist, in one form or another, in the future.

The same observation applies to ethical, juridical, and technological systems and their basic types, and even to political and economic systems. A given monarchy or republic may be ephemeral; but monarchical, autocratic, aristocratic, oligarchic, republican, and democratic forms of government are perennial. So also are privately managed and governmentally managed economic systems, "free enterprise," and communist enterprise.

Finally, the same is true of ideational, idealistic, and sensate supersystems, not to mention eclectic total cultures. In a rudimentary or developed form all these supersystems have existed since the remote past, since the paleolithic and neolithic eras. They have developed and declined (but never entirely disappeared) many times in the cultural history of the Orient and the Occident, and in a modified form they will continue to exist.

2. Factors in the Life Span of Systems

The factors determining the duration of cultural systems are very numerous, embracing all the geographic, biological, or sociocultural conditions that facilitate the preservation of the human agents of the system, its vehicles, and its logico-aesthetic unity. Their mere enumeration would require many pages. However, most such factors are secondary and supplementary.

The decisive factor is the greatness of the system itself. The more universal, the more essential to the survival and creativeness of humanity, the meanings, values, and norms of the system are, the longer its span of life is likely to be. Conversely, petty systems, whose value is purely temporary, limited to their creator or to a small group, and representing something unnecessary for either biological survival or a full mental, moral, and sociocultural development—such systems are very short-lived.

However subjective and arbitrary the division of cultural systems into "great" and "small" in the above sense may appear to be, nevertheless such a division has objective existence. The sociocultural process itself effects this objective division; it inexorably sifts the cultural grain from the cultural chaff, quickly disposing of the chaff and preserving the most valuable grain, its main types, and especially its generic seeds. In this rigorous selection some grain may be destroyed and some chaff retained. Occasionally, cultural chaff enjoys temporarily a sensational vogue that promises immortality; conversely, many a truly great system fails to attain recognition and large-scale objectification and socialization until long after it has emerged. But all in all, in spite of these defects of threshing, winnowing, and sifting, only the great systems in the above sense are permitted to live for long periods of time.[2]

II. The Death of Cultural Systems

As we have seen, myriads of petty systems expire daily, such as radio programs and innumerable newspaper and magazine articles, pictures, and cartoons. Many language systems pass away, except perhaps as "museum pieces." Minor religious systems are likewise evanescent. (In the United States several denominations become obsolete every decade.) Even larger religious systems may be denied immortality. The Babylonian and Sumerian, Egyptian, Hittite, Greek, and Roman religious systems no longer exist as living religious systems in their total character. Their elements have entered into other (later) religions as building material, so to speak. Similarly, a whole series of philosophical systems, in their total character, have become defunct, at best continuing to exist merely as component elements of greater philosophical systems subsequently evolved. Even scholars and specialists know only fragments of several ancient Chinese, Hindu, Egyptian, and Persian philosophical systems. Even those of Pythagoras, Heraclitus, and Empedocles are known only in fragmentary form and only to a limited circle of scholars.

Sundry scientific discoveries and systems of the remote past, likewise perished, to be rediscovered later, in other cultures and populations. As certain papyri and other documents, unearthed during the last century, attest, several astronomical, mathematical, biological, medical, and physical systems, discovered in the early stages of Egyptian or Babylonean history, eventually became extinct and had to be rediscovered.

The same is true of technological systems, with all the practical knowledge involved. The art of regulating the level of the Nile, which flourished during the prosperous periods of Egyptian history, later declined; the excellent irrigation systems practiced in central Asia and elsewhere before our era and during its first centuries eventually decayed; the Roman art of roadbuilding similarly lapsed, and was forgotten during the medieval centuries; even such technological systems as those of gunpowder, the steam engine, and printing, discovered in China before the Christian Era, ultimately declined and had to be rediscovered.

Aesthetic systems also perish, especially great architectural, sculptural, and pictorial creations that are unique. Their material incarnations, subjected to the vicissitudes of physical, biological, and sociocultural forces, are often destroyed or irretrievably decay through neglect. A large percentage of the aesthetic creations of ancient cultures have perished completely; others, like the Parthenon and a few Egyptian temples, survive only in fragments. The Second World War destroyed a large number of even comparatively recent aesthetic systems. Many major musical systems, created before the discovery of musical notation, have likewise perished. In a lesser degree the same is true of great literary systems.

Do cultural systems die a "natural death," or perish only through the influence of inimical external forces? Are they mortal in the same sense in which every human organism is mortal, or are they potentially immortal in the absence of a hostile external force? The answer is that they die by both methods.

(1) *An overwhelming majority of petty systems die a natural death.* In radio talks,

---

[2] This sifting and survival of the major cultural systems are possibly more real than the natural selection and survival of biological organisms in the struggle for existence. Fitness in the biological sense does not always mean greater perfection; not infrequently, retrogressive organisms survive, whereas higher types perish. In the competition of cultural systems the proportion of pseudo-systems that survive is possibly less than that of "fit" but inferior biological organisms. Cultural selection apparently makes fewer mistakes than biological selection.

newspaper and magazine columns, public addresses, and so on, millions of petty systems expire daily without the intervention of inimical forces. They are forgotten as soon as they are objectified and socialized. The same is true of many drawings and petty technical pictures, songs and tunes, sculpture, and the like. They perish because they lack the stuff of true greatness and real value. They are mere cultural "chaff," not worth preserving.

Even larger cultural systems die naturally, either because they have exhausted their real value or are incapable of competing with systems of greater merit. Almost all the extinct major systems enumerated in earlier paragraphs died a natural death for one or the other of these two reasons. The Egyptian, Greek, and Roman religions were not victims of persecution. They gradually deteriorated, giving place to more vital religions, such as Christianity. No one exterminated the hieroglyphic or the cuneiform script; they died out because they were unable to compete with alphabet writing. Similarly, no one prohibited or destroyed the classical type of Greek and Roman architecture; it simply became obsolescent after the fourth century A.D. A. Toynbee gives a long and impressive series of such instances, embracing many major systems. During the vigorous, creative phase of a given cultural system neither adverse physical, biological, nor sociocultural forces suffice, as a rule, to destroy it. On the contrary, such adverse forces tend to invigorate and reenforce the system.[3]

Although there are exceptions to this rule, it is valid in application to the majority of cultural systems and supersystems. Both their extinction and their temporary decline have been due primarily to the deterioration caused by the exhaustion of their creative forces. Having run the gamut of its variations, having delivered, so to speak, all its real values, a given system necessarily ceases to be creative. Hence it becomes a liability rather than an asset, and is eventually eliminated. It may be quickly supplanted by a new, more creative system, or it may linger for a while in a "petrified state," to the detriment of the society and the total culture to which it belongs. The immanent deterioration and natural death of

outworn systems are exemplified especially clearly in the case of "petrified" systems. Many of them exist in this uncreative "petrified" state for centuries, without the intervention of any hostile external force intent on their destruction.

This inherent deterioration explains the extinction of most of the defunct systems and of most cases of the temporary decline of various systems and supersystems, including notable religious and artistic creations, philosophies and scientific theories, law codes, and political and economic systems. Each of them contains the seeds of its own degeneration. When their creative potentialities are exhausted, religions enter the phase of "petrified" rituals, mechanically repeated dogmas, highly organized administrative machinery, and material opulence. An originally creative style of art comes to be imitated and reimitated, with increasingly finical and puerile variations, until it degenerates into an empty, meaningless triviality. The same sort of thing happens in the case of a philosophical system: its incessant repetitions render it progressively more insignificant, vacuous, and barrenly "scholastic" until it becomes a mere uncreative "incantation."

Similarly, the decay of the capitalistic economic system is due not to its enemies but to the inherent deterioration of the system itself. In the absence of further creative potentialities, it engenders increasing social difficulties, ranging from business depressions and unemployment to national and international strife. As such it has become a public liability rather than an asset. No wonder that it is declining and that its grave-diggers are multiplying!

(2) *Other cultural systems expire through violence—through the operation of inimical external forces.* These forces either exterminate the human agents of the system or deprive it of its vehicles; sometimes they do both. As a rule, they compel its adherents to abandon it, imposing upon them a different religious, juridical, political, economic, philosophical, or aesthetic system. Applying coercion in all its forms, both crude and refined, with a view to prohibiting the objectification and socialization of the suppressed system (including inculcation by the family, as well as by school

[3] A. Toynbee, *op. cit.*, Vol. IV, pp. 40 ff.

and religious groups), and disseminating the new system by every means of propaganda. Through these and similar measures they often succeed in undermining or eradicating a system and in replacing it with a different one.

In this way many a language system has been destroyed by a conqueror. Many a religion has similarly been suppressed. Many a scientific, artistic, ethical, juridical, political, and economic system has been extinguished by conquerors, by victorious revolutionaries or counterrevolutionaries, by autocratic governments, or by western missionaries, merchants, and "civilizers" in the so-called "backward" regions of the world.

Nazi Germany followed this practice in unrestrained fashion in regard to the cultural systems of all the conquered countries, systematically exterminating the population of especially Poland, Russia, Yugoslavia, and Greece, employing all sorts of torture and punishment, robbing the conquered countries and their cultural systems of most of their vehicles, and so forth. The Nazis thus obliterated thousands of cultural systems. If they had been victorious, there is not the slightest doubt that they would have continued this practice on a still larger scale until the "new order" was universally established.

In a less brutal form the same extinction of cultural systems is being perpetrated by the Allies in the case of the Fascist powers. Giving it the highfalutin name of "democratic reeducation," the Allies are seeking to eradicate most of the cultural systems of Germany, Japan, Italy, and Austria—in particular, the economic, political, philosophical, and (in the case of Japan) religious systems.

III. The Resurrection of Cultural Systems

The cultural systems whose creative potentialities were not exhausted before their extinction, or which acquire such potentialities in a new setting, occasionally revive. This resurrection sometimes applies to only a single system; sometimes a whole group of formerly connected systems revive together. The resurrection of cultural systems is a counterpart of the restoration of organized groups.

The movements frequently designated by the term "renaissance" afford pertinent examples of the phenomenon in question. The renaissance of *language systems* is illustrated by revivals of the Czech, Bulgarian, and Serbian tongues and literatures in the nineteenth century, and by contemporary revivals of the Estonian, Latvian, Lithuanian, and other languages and literatures. Such languages, while not entirely extinct, had been relegated to the status of inferior, nonliterary idioms. The revival of Greek and Latin during the Renaissance is another case in point. Although they were not dead languages, they had been limited to a narrow circle of ecclesiasts or had become "inferior" tongues confined to the illiterate masses. The rehabilitation systems often coincides with or precedes the restoration of a given nationality culture, resulting now and then in the creation or resurrection of a state coterminous with the corresponding linguistic group.

A typical instance of the resurrection of a *major system* of law is furnished by the revival of the Roman system of law. After having remained dormant for about six centuries, it was resuscitated by the University of Bologna in the twelfth and subsequent centuries, in southern France during the thirteenth century, and finally in Germany and other European countries in the course of the fifteenth and following centuries.

The rebirth of *artistic systems* is exemplified by several imitative revivals of earlier styles in Egypt; by the adoption, on the part of the Romans, of Greek archaic, classical, and Hellenistic art; by the striking revival of Greek and Hellenistic art during the Italian Renaissance; by the Gothic revivals in nineteenth-century Europe and America, and so on. Revivals of *religious systems* occurred several times in ancient Egypt, especially under the later dynasties, when earlier religious cults were reinstated. Julian the Apostate attempted to restore Roman paganism. The resuscitation of the national religions of various peoples after their suppression by a foreign conqueror is a typical phenomenon. The rebirth of Platonism and Aristotelianism in Europe after the twelfth century, and the contemporary revival of Thomism and Augustianism, serve as examples of the renaissance of *philosophical systems*.

The rehabilitation of monarchical and republican regimes in various countries is thoroughly familiar to all political scientists. The overthrow and subsequent restoration of slavery and of systems of free labor, of capitalism and state socialism, represent a frequently repeated sociocultural rhythm in the field of *economics*. The vicissitudes of *manners and mores* are illustrated by the decline and revival of forms of the family, occupational unions, and the like, and even of fashions of dress.

The Italian Renaissance furnishes an instance of the simultaneous revival of a whole group of cultural systems. Not only the Graeco-Roman languages, but the classical systems of literature, painting, sculpture, architecture, philosophy, ethics, law, and politics were suddenly "unearthed" and vitalized.

Finally, the rise and decline of the *sensate, idealistic, and ideational supersystems* serve as an example of the decay and revival of vast cultural supersystems. After several centuries of virtually latent existence each of these supersystems has reemerged and, in a modified form, has achieved the position of a dominant supersystem. In a sense, all the fluctuations of materialism and idealism, determinism and indeterminism, realistic and symbolic painting, and ideational, idealistic, and sensate music, indeed, all the sociocultural rhythms, are merely manifestations of relative decline and revival, and so on.

The revival of the major portion of a given total culture is especially accentuated when it is connected with that of a nationality, nation, or state. The nation or other group, during the initial period of its restored independence and freedom, tends to reinstate everything that it regards as belonging to its historical culture. Even trivial values are sometimes reestablished in place of the hated culture of the oppressor. The operation of these processes may be clearly seen today. Just as everything German was repudiated by the peoples liberated from the Nazi yoke, so, upon the termination of the Allied occupation of Germany and Japan, a violent reaction against the culture of the Allied "oppressors" may be expected in these countries. Only petty and relatively valueless cultural systems and congeries fail to revive (and there are exceptions even to this rule). Truly great cultural systems and supersystems are virtually indestructible. They may be enfeebled, suppressed, or temporarily extinguished; but ultimately most of them reassert themselves and renew their development until they have achieved their creative mission.

Chapter 48. Dynamics of Personality

I. Parallelism of Social, Cultural, and Personality Processes

Personality is a microcosm reflecting the sociocultural macrocosm wherein the individual is born and lives (see Chapter 19). The life of an individual is a great drama determined first by his social universe and then by the biological properties of his organism. Even before the organism is born, the sociocultural universe begins to influence and to determine the properties of the organism, and it relentlessly maintains this molding process till the individual's death and beyond.

(1) *Sociocultural conditions determine first whether or not a given organism shall be born.* If current norms prescribe the wide use of contraception, abortion, and other means of birth control, the number of potential births is greatly reduced. If such measures are prohibited, millions of often unwanted organisms are born into this world.

(2) *Sociocultural forces tangibly determine even the biological properties of the organism.* They do this by prohibiting sexual intercourse and marriage between the members of certain age groups, races, castes, social estates, families, religions, occupations, and the members of ethnic groups; by prescribing monogamous or polygamous marriages, or exogamic and endogamic restrictions. Cultural norms may taboo sex relations between individuals with certain diseases or other characteristics. They regulate extramarital sex relations, marriage and divorce, and such customs as infanticide. By such means the sociocultural "boss" becomes the most important agency of biological selection affecting

the destiny and the properties of an organism. Furthermore, it tangibly affects the foetus in its prenatal stage, now mutilating and harming it, now favoring its healthy growth.

(3) *The sociocultural universe determines the environment and the first role of the newly born organism.* Whether born in a king's palace or a slave's hut; whether heir to a throne or to slavery; whether illegitimate or legitimate; endowed with a silver spoon or burdened with poverty and the sins of his forefathers—these questions of environment and first roles are almost entirely determined by the sociocultural milieu.

(4) *All subsequent multifarious roles to be played by the newly born organism are determined by the sociocultural universe.* This is true even of the individual's posthumous fate. Shall he disappear into oblivion or become an historical figure of heroic or criminal character? Such questions can be answered only by the sociocultural environment.

(5) *The biological organism of the individual determines further the irreversible cycle of childhood, adolescence, maturity, and old age; the discharging of physiological needs such as eating; the quality of performance of sociocultural roles.* However the concrete forms of these biological functions (how, when, where, with whom, etc.) are determined again by the sociocultural "boss." Social conditions choose which of thousands of different child or youth roles he will play—child-prince, street urchin, or juvenile delinquent. What kind of

food, how much, how often, and in what ways he will eat or fast; when, where, with whom, and how often he will satisfy his sex-needs; what kind of shelter and dress he will have or lack—all these biological forms are defined by the sociocultural milieu. Health and even longevity depend upon sociocultural conditions as much as, and often more than, upon biological constitution. Some fifty millions of young healthy lives were terminated or mutilated by the Second World War, lives which otherwise would have lasted much longer, had they depended solely upon biological conditions.

(6) *The kind of personality, mentality, and behavior which will be grafted upon the somewhat indefinite biological framework depends almost entirely upon the individual's sociocultural environment.* If living in an ideational culture, he will be notably ideational; in sensate culture, sensate. What roles he is destined to play throughout his life depend again upon the "sociocultural playwright," who writes the plays and assigns the roles. The biological constitution limits the freedom of the sociocultural playwright in the following ways: (a) heredity determines how well the individual plays his assigned roles; (b) the playwright cannot assign a baby's roles to an old man, or male roles to a female; (c) the biological constitution now and then forces the playwright to reassign the roles and to change "the stars" in the play, transferring, for instance, the role of a ruler to a person previously a slave. With these limitations, the freedom of the playwright in patterning the personality of each individual, in assigning his roles, in deciding the character of the play, its acts, scenery, makeup, and costumes, is practically unlimited. The whole life-drama of each person is thus shaped and directed by the sociocultural macrocosm in which he is born and lives.

(7) *Since the playwright constructs the sociocultural personality, it patterns also in its own image the dynamic processes of human life.* These inevitably mirror the corresponding processes of social groups and cultural systems. (a) Like the dynamics of social groups, the dynamics of personality is made up of repeated and unique processes. Taken in all its detailed characteristics, any human life is unique. But considered in terms of its basic processes, it is woven out of elements recurring in the individual's life and in the lives of other persons. (b) Like the social and cultural systems, an individual passes through three stages: he is conceived, born (objectified), and eventually socialized or organized. (c) Individuals, like groups, die prematurely or survive to an advanced age. (d) Some individuals remain poorly organized and badly integrated; others become highly organized and well integrated. (e) The growth of the individual's personality consists in the unfolding of his potentialities in a given setting, in the increasing differentiation of his abilities and functions, in the structure and integration of his egos, and in the qualitiative and quantitative enrichment of his world of meanings, actions, and vehicles. (f) Like any social system, an individual eventually begins to decline and to deteriorate. (g) And like all sociocultural processes, the life processes of the individual have their states of development, their directions, their rhythms and periodicities.

Let us now discuss further some of these recurrent processes.

II. Repeated Processes and Rhythms in the Life-Process of the Individual

1. The Great Cycle of Human Life

The most embracing cycle in every full human life is the passage from the roles of infancy to those of old age. The irreversible direction of the drama is determined by the biological organism, but the number of the acts—the age stages—into which the whole passage is divided, the roles which an individual has to play in each age grade, and the total meaning of each stage are determined by the individual's sociocultural universe. They have but a remote relation to the biological changes in his organism.

Whether the whole drama is divided into

our four phases of infancy, adolescence, maturity, and old age, or into a larger number of grades as among certain other populations, the important point is that *the passage of an individual from one age-division to another denotes not so much the physical changes in his organism as the changes in his personality and his sociocultural roles.* Before the individual is born, the script, the stage, and the role he has to play at each age-division are already prepared for him in great detail by the sociocultural milieu. The culture sets the pattern for each age-act, and it expects from the individual a lusty performance of his assigned roles. It attempts roughly to time with the biological changes in his organism his transfer into the next age-act, but this timing is never accurate. When the socially determined occasion arrives, the individual is passed into the next age group, whether or not his biological organism is ready to perform the new roles. If he performs these successfully, well and good; if he fails, then other and less pleasant roles are assigned to him: the roles of a defective delinquent, truant, rebel, and the like.

The drama opens with the act of *childhood or infancy.* If the newly born infant happens to be in the exclusive control of one group (say, the family), there is but one script prescribing his role in detail. If he happens to be under the control of several groups (his family, his playmates, the nursery school, the state), then there are several scripts. These may prescribe the same role to the infant, or they may set forth different roles, sometimes contradictory with one another. They define in detail how the child is to be treated and how he must play his role, and they meticulously differentiate the roles of the infant-prince and infant-peasant, infant boy and infant girl, legitimate infant and illegitimate, first-born and second-born, and so on.

Each group tries to "socialize" the infant by inculcating a "self" or "soul" patterned in the group's own image, the self and personality of the prince-infant or slave-infant, the Brahmin-infant or Sudra-infant. *If one group monopolizes the child, and if its own "soul" is integrated, then the child receives one integrated "self" from this group. If several mutually contradictory groups are in control, then the infant receives correspondingly discordant*

"selfs." Hence at the very start he tends to become a split personality, with conflicting roles molded by very different cultural patterns. In such situations the infant naturally fails to play well some or all of the contradictory roles. In the first case he becomes a "complete failure," antagonizing all the groups. In the second, he becomes a "good child" in the opinion of the groups whose roles he plays well, and "an unruly child," in need of "real discipline" in the opinion of the groups whose roles he fails to play. In both situations, however, he becomes a split personality. This initial "split personality" is a tragic burden; it weighs heavily upon his subsequent development, and often prevents the ultimate integration of his character. *The mutually contradictory "scripts" of the infant's roles prescribed by mutually antagonistic groups are the real culprits responsible for the greater part of social delinquency.*

The socially determined time assigned for childhood being over, the individual is relentlessly moved into the next act of his life; in our society this is the phase of elementary school. In many contemporary societies, when a child reaches the chronological age of eight years, he has to enter elementary school. In other societies the chronological age may be different, but the passage itself nonetheless takes place as relentlessly and abruptly as in our society. The child is suddenly placed on a new stage, with different roles to play, and with different co-actors. He must drop a large number of the habits, acts, and saying of his infant role, and he must quickly acquire a set of entirely new habits. Ready or not, he must play his new roles, and these roles are again prescribed in detail by the school and by all the other groups in direct or indirect control of the "first grader." From A to Z the roles and the ideological, behavioral and material cultures are prescribed by the controlling groups.

Again, if the groups are concordant, they build an harmonious self in the boys and girls of this age. If the roles prescribed by each group are discordant, they plant several discordant selfs and mutually contradictory cultural systems and congeries in the young actors.

Between birth and the early teens each child experiences so many different conditions and roles, that all talk about equality of opportunity is pious nonsense. There never has been any equality of opportunity between foetuses with good and bad heredity; between prince-infant and slave-infant, rich infant and poor infant; between infants surrounded by harmonious groups and those reared among discordant groups. From the very moment of conception, the destinies of these individuals are anything but equal.

Boys and girls pass next into the phase of *adolescence*. This period is again determined not so much by the biological conditions of their organisms as their sociocultural universe. Biologically some of them reach the stage of puberty before the sociocultural phase of adolescence, and some attain it afterward. Again there is an abrupt transference from the preceding scenery, roles, and co-actors to a conspicuously different pattern. The adolescents must suddenly drop a large part of their former ideological, behavioral, and material culture; they must forget their pre-adolescent roles. Their rights and duties, liberties and taboos are now quite different from those of childhood. And here again the adolescent's roles are prescribed in detail by the groups about him, with all their differentiations and complexities.

Then comes the stage of *maturity*, followed by *post-maturity* and *old age*. The individual passing from one of these roles to another must be as versatile as the best dramatic actor playing in turn the roles of Tom Sawyer, of Father in *Life with Father*, and of King Lear.

To summarize: this great cycle of human life, with all its sudden transitions and modifications of the personality, is experienced by every individual who lives out his term. In the course of this Odyssey the dynamics of personality has an irreversible direction from infancy to old age. However different are the details of the journey for each individual, his self, his conduct, and his total culture are fashioned and determined at each state by the sociocultural milieu. The social environment determines whether an individual can change the role of a poor child for that of a rich one; the role of a slave for that of a freeman; the role of a Chinese coolie for that of Russian factory hand. It decides whether he will acquire an integrated or an unintegrated personality, and whether he will be a hero or a criminal. It decrees whether he will be forgotten after his death or will live in the memory of posterity. All in all, the dynamics of personality is essentially determined by the sociocultural universe of the organism.

The only liberty left to the individual is the margin of selection and creativity mentioned in Chapter 19.

2. Other Cycles and Rhythms in the Dynamics of Personality

Each act of the great cycle of human life—infancy, adolescence, maturity and old age—has a duration of several years. The activities that fill every twenty-four hours of this duration change incessantly, but this change is but variation on familiar themes. In other words, the bulk of the activities with which the individual fills his time is made up of repeated processes, punctuated by a variety of double, triple, quadruple, periodical, and nonperiodical rhythms. These rhythmical processes and periodicities are a counterpart of corresponding social and cultural processes. The life-processes of the individual are largely constructed in their image. This structuralization means that, in an orderly social universe, all individual activities are "budgeted" into daily, weekly, seasonal, and annual "blocks."

Every day the individual gets up at about the same time, and goes through the routine of his morning toilet, breakfast, proceeding to school or his place of work, undertaking there the same educational or occupational work. Then comes lunch and supper, reading the paper, listening to a favorite radio program, and finally, going to bed. This *daily cycle* of repeated activities fills the greater part of every twenty-four hours and occupies approximately the same part of each day. Details vary with each individual, but the basic routines are similar for many people. And each routine is strictly determined by the totality of the groups to which the individual belongs. Even more, these groups make *most of these daily routine activities periodical*. The individual spends about the same time for each of his routine activities; he begins and ends each at about the same hour; he meets in each activity about the same persons; he performs each activity in about the same place. Thus a group of white-collar employees in Boston spends on the average from weekday to weekday every twenty-four hours in the following fashion: 11 hours in satisfaction of various physiological activities; about 8 hours in their occupational work; 1 hour and 20 minutes in various societal activities; 8 minutes in religious activities; 1 hour and 24 minues in intellectual pursuits; 24 minutes in artistic activities; 8 minutes in courting and love; 1 hour and 30 minutes in various recreational activities.[1] Detailed "time-structure" of daily activities of various individuals is diverse, but some common or similar "time-structure" is found in the daily activities of most people.

Besides the daily rhythms, the individual's activities involve *weekly rhythms*: the seven-day week in western society, and the five, eight, nine, or sixteen-day week in other populations. The time-structure of activities of every Monday or Sunday repeats itself again and again in the activities of the individual. Similarly there are *monthly, seasonal, and annual rhythms*. Birthdays, Christmas, Thanksgiving Day, Fourth of July, and so on, are marked by similar activities of the individual from year to year—the same routine on Christmas, the same turkey dinner on Thanksgiving. There are also biennial, five- ten-, and twenty-five year rhythms.

All these rhythmical activities cover most of the movements of the individual. All such repeated activities are determined by the corresponding rhythms in the sociocultural processes of the groups amidst which the individual lives. Groups constitute the sociocultural "grooves" defining the trajectory of the "individual needle" in its life-processes. They give an orderly structure to the personality, guiding its incessant changes into fixed channels. In this manner they make the changes in personality gradual and imperceptible within each main act of the great life-cycle. Only when the person has to pass from one age-phase to another does the change become somewhat abrupt and difficult. But as soon as the individual overcomes the first difficulties of the new role, his activities again assume a specific structure, and the routine of rhythmical activities becomes habitual. These socially imposed repetitions help the individual "needle" to move along the socially established "grooves" of his life-symphony.

III. Transformations of the Individual's Egos and Culture

1. Formation and Transformation of the Egos

We already know that the self of the individual is mosaic and pluralistic; that each individual has, besides his biological components, as many selfs as there are social groups in which he participates; and that these sociocultural egos are as different from one another as are his groups (see Chapter 19). We know also that the cultural content of each self consists mainly of elements from his groups, and that each self is conditioned by the selective and creative functions of the individual.

The first rudimentary constellation of selfs is patterned in the individual during childhood. It is not unchangeable, but nevertheless in many ways it is decisive. It defines, to a con-

[1] P. A. Sorokin and C. Q. Berger, *Time-Budgets of Human Behavior* (Harvard University Press, 1939), p. 76.

siderable extent, the subsequent structure of the egos, for it is the foundation upon which subsequent selfs are built. Reconstructing the early constellation is always an exceedingly difficult task. *The initial constellation of the child's selfs consists of his biological selfs surrounded by his sociocultural selfs.*

The same is to be said of the child's culture. His ideological culture-language, ideas, beliefs, tastes, ethical convictions, and so on, are defined by the ideological culture of his groups. Similarly with his material and behavioral culture. A child born among Chinese-speaking groups, with Confucian religion, with the Chinese aesthetic tastes, ethical norms, manners and mores, would absorb these Chinese cultural elements. In a culture dominated by an ideational supersystem, the child's total culture will be ideational. Because of the heterogeneity of hereditary biological organisms and the X-factor of selectivity and creativity, children will make somewhat different selections from their cultural milieux. But whatever selections they make will all be variations of existing cultural values.

Subsequent transformations of the child's egos are determined by the immanent and irreversible changes in his biological selfs and by changes in his position in social groups. These are the two variables that account for most of the transformations in the individual's selfs. The passage of the organism from childhood to adolescence involves numerous anatomical and physiological changes, which modify substantially the biological needs of the organism. Sex impulses hitherto dormant become real. Physical helplessness is replaced by strength. New activities emerge, and childish pastimes vanish. The new biological egos tangibly affect the individual's sociocultural egos.

A similar transformation of the biological egos occurs when the individual passes from adolescence to biological maturity, and thence to an old age. *This immanent and irreversible evolution of the organism and of its egos makes inevitable the transformation of all the selfs of the individual.* It is one of the "river beds" determining the course of change in the individual throughout his life.

However, biological growth is only one side of individual evolution. If it stood alone, changes in the complex personality structure of human beings would be very few and simple. They would be reduced to the four main biological phases of childhood, adolescence, maturity, and old age. Actually, the number of transformations in the structure of the individual's egos are incomparably greater, infinitely more complex, and bewilderingly diverse. Their general formula is as follows:

Whenever the social position of the individual changes, the constellation of his sociocultural selfs undergoes a corresponding transformation. This formula means that the structure of the sociocultural selfs of the individual changes (a) when his group membership changes; (b) when his strata membership changes; (c) when his direct and indirect cultural affiliations change; (d) when the groups, strata, and cultural systems with which he is affiliated change. A few comments on this precise formula are in order.

If a communist becomes a Catholic, he cannot help changing his previous communist ego for a Catholic ego. If a poor, unskilled, disfranchised worker in the automobile industry becomes the rich and powerful head of a vast automobile concern, he cannot avoid the transformation of his former proletarian ego into that of a captain of industry. Otherwise he could not remain in his new position; he would lose it, be ousted or go bankrupt. If an emperor were overthrown and imprisoned permanently, he would relinquish his imperial self and acquire the ego of a prisoner. "Once a grand duke" ceases to be a grand duke in these conditions.

In brief, any shift by the individual from one group or stratum to another is followed by a corresponding transformation in his egos; and the more contrasting are the groups and strata to which he moves, the more contrasting are the egos lost and the egos acquired. Though unnoticed, such replacement of the individual's egos are daily occurrences. In societies with intense horizontal and vertical mobility, these transformations of the egos proceed incessantly on a large scale. This explains the surprising changes in poor workers, who only yesterday hated and denounced the rich "robbers"; becoming rich, they soon begin to defend the sacredness of property, to denounce strikes and the "impudent demands" of workers. In a word, their "souls" have changed, and not infrequently such self-made millionaires turn into the worst slave-drivers.

The transformation of souls explains why every ruler, even one of proletarian origin, inevitably exhibits interests, psychology, and conduct quite different from those of the ruled; why every worker performing the functions of a delegate and representative for a long time is inevitably transformed into an oligarch and bureaucrat; why extreme radicals elevated into the ranks of the rulers become traitors to the proletarian cause. This is why the communist proletarians of Russia, having become dictatorial rulers, have radically changed their egos, their values, ideology, and conduct; why practically all the "socialist" and "labor" leaders lose their previous egos, once come to power, and acquire new ones. They change their ideology, behavioral, and material cultures and often become the sternest and most autocratic oppressors of the peasant and labor classes. Herein lies the "secret" of the eternally tragical comedy of "mutation" of the Oliver Cromwells, Robespierres, Lenins, Stalins, and of the lesser changes in the Noskes, Vivianis, Mac-Donalds, Clemenceaus, Bevins, and so on. From immemorial times such mutations in the souls of slaves become kings and in kings become slaves have occurred again and again.[2]

These mutations do not necessarily indicate the "rascality" or the "nobility" of man; they are merely the inevitable result of changes in the individual's social position. Very often these readjustments are accompanied by the acquisition of a narrow group spirit, by an intolerance toward one's former group. The main antidote for such narrow-mindedness is more frequent change in the individual's status, for this will lead to a decrease in mutual intolerance and will do away with the necessity and habit of identifying man by one label or another (proletarian, monarchist, atheist, Russian, German, etc.), a habit which often prevents us from seeing the man behind the label. Unfortunately, the increase of such transfers from one social group to another meets today with many difficulties and cannot therefore be easily accomplished.

This explains also the inevitability of the mass "deformation" of the souls and behavior of men during revolutions. As we have seen (in Chapter 31), in each revolution a very intensive shift of social positions by multitudes of individuals takes place. Such a change must inevitably bring about a mass transformation of the minds and behavior of all displaced and dislocated men. At the beginning of the revolution, when the old system of groups and strata breaks down and new organized constellations are not crystallized as yet, the whole social structure is in a fluid state. The old faiths, convictions, and norms of behavior disappear, and the displaced individuals, having lost their previous "souls," resemble individuals in a trance. They are like a frail canoe carried away by a storm. They fail to recognize their responsibilities and duties. Like somnambulists, individuals with confused and muddled egos perform acts which they would have regarded as obnoxious before the revolution.

But the first period of the revolution ends,

[2] Cf. V. Pareto, *Trattato*, quoted, v. II, p. 541.

the agitated social sea calms down, a new system of social differentiation and stratification crystallizes, and a new social structure finally emerges from the ruins of the old. This process is concomitant with the crystallization of new "souls" in individuals. Men gradually become adjusted to their new occupations, they master their new roles, and each acquires the "souls" suitable to his new social position. If the new position differs radically from the old, the individual's mentality and behavior will be different also. There is nothing strange then, if a former monarchist assumes the role of a fanatical communist, or a former capitalist the role of a proletarian. For all this is inevitable, because the change in the individual's position induces a change in his soul.

Individuals changing their cultural affiliations change their egos also. Having come in contact with a new political or philosophical or religious cultural system, individuals may exchange their old ideologies for a new one, often without notably changing their group memberships. A professor or public official can change his cultural affiliations considerably without being obliged to change his social position. Such a shift in cultural affiliations also changes somewhat the individual's souls. Instead of a subscriber to Plato's philosophy, he may become a materialistic philosopher. An admirer of jazz may become a devotee of classical music; a Catholic may become a Christian Scientist. All such changes are followed by notable modifications in one's souls and actions. Of course, when the shift in cultural affiliation is great, it is regularly followed by a change in the social position of the person.

Finally, *individuals experience a mutation of their souls when the situation of their groups and cultural systems notably changes.* In such cases the mutation is due not to a shift in their group and cultural affiliations, for they remain the same, but it is due rather to the change in the state of their groups and cultural systems. For instance, when a rich group becomes poor, or a persecuted group becomes privileged, the members of the group undergo similar changes. When the Russian communists climbed from a persecuted status to a privileged one, their souls changed from persecuted and disfranchised "souls" into the proud and authoritarian souls of the elite. When the Russian or the Nazi aristocracy was overthrown, the souls of all the members of these former aristocrats became transformed into the souls of underdogs.

In times of revolutions, wars, and other catastrophies such sharp changes in the status of many groups occur on a large scale, and likewise occur also the mass-mutations in the souls of the members of all promoted and demoted groups.

2. Mutation of Selfs and of the Culture of the Individual

Mutation of the individual's souls means transformation of his ideological, behavioral, or total culture. Cultural transformation is the other side of the mutation of egos. As such, it is due to the same biological transformation of the organism resulting from changes of the biological egos and from changes of the group and cultural affiliations of the individual.

If the change in the selfs of the individual is slight and somewhat superficial, it results mainly in changes of his *ideological culture*, without a serious mutation of his behavioral and material cultures. The individual simply reshuffles some of his ideas and beliefs, tastes and convictions; he replaces, say, his "new deal" ideology with "an old deal ideology," his preference for Plato with that of Aristotle, and so on. The reshuffling involves some modifications of the affective, emotional, and volitional states of his personality, but neither too deeply nor too seriously. Ideological mutation proceeds without a serious disturbance of one's behavioral and material culture.

This explains the already noted fact (see Chapters 17 and 18) that *the ideological culture of the individual can change without a proportional change in his behavioral and material cultures*. Somewhat different ideas, beliefs, tastes, and norms come into the field of consciousness of the individual; they expel some of his old ideas and beliefs, without directly affecting his overt actions and material culture. Observation and self-observation show that such a current of changing meanings, values, and norms almost incessantly flows through a person's ideological culture. The results of practically all public opinion polls show that the opinion of the same persons on the same problem changes from poll to poll.[3]

"Changing one's mind" is in no way limited to women, as the proverb has it. It is a universal phenomenon. Every individual changes his mind or some elements of his ideological culture without correspondingly changing his overt actions and his material culture. Any new movie he sees; any book, paper, or magazine he reads; a lecture or sermon he listens to; an event he observes, all bring new elements into his ideological culture and obliterate some old elements. Who does not know thousands of "ideological conversions" to fascism, democracy or communism without any tangible change in the behavior and material culture of the respective "converts." They change their ideologies about as easily as their seasonal clothing.

This means that the *dynamics of the ideological culture of the individuals is more mobile and changeable, has a faster tempo of modification than the dynamics of behavioral and material cultures*. Change in public opinions about various matters is more frequent and contrasting than changes in respective public actions. We daily change something in our ideological culture without disturbing at all the routine of our daily activities. The immanent stirring of our ideas, beliefs, and convictions; the urges of our biological egos; all the external cosmic and sociocultural forces incessantly influence some part of our ideologies. When we are hungry, a stale piece of bread is "delicious." When we are satiated, a good meal is styled "tasteless." Having listened to an eloquent sermon, we decide to change our defective conduct, but the next moment we forget the decision and continue in our old ways. Studying carefully great world religions or great ethical treatises, we make the respective ideologies of Buddhism or Taoism part and parcel of our own ideology. These ideological systems become intellectually interiorized and our total ideology correspondingly enriched. Such a notable change of our ideology does not, however, disturb our religious and ethical practices. They remain often unchanged.

When our biological organism changes profoundly, when our group and cultural affiliations undergo serious modification, when the

---

[3] Cf. for instance, J. S. Bruner, *Mandate From the People* (New York, 1944).

status of our groups basically changes, the ensuing radical change of our biological and sociocultural egos causes a tangible mutation of our ideological, behavioral, and material cultures. In that case the change is not limited to mere ripplings on the ideological surface, but it goes deep into the layers of our behavioral and material cultures and transforms them according to its nature. When a mature organism becomes senile; or when a healthy organism becomes seriously ill; when a king becomes an imprisoned criminal; or a dictator becomes a "war-criminal"—all such changes are invariably followed by a corresponding change of the ideological, behavioral, and material cultures. *In part this mutation of our behavior and of our material culture is coercively imposed; in part it comes by itself, spontaneously.* An old or sick man cannot behave physically like a young or healthy person. An imprisoned king cannot behave physically like a free autocrat; the material culture of his resplendent palace is replaced by that of a prison. Spontaneously, the feelings, emotions, ideas, and actions of an old man differ from those of a young person. Imperceptibly, similar change occurs in persons transposed to different sociocultural positions. Otherwise, without proper readjustment of their ideologies, actions, and material culture they cannot stay in their new position. They either leave or are expelled from it. Even a minor custom like wearing evening dress has to be observed by a former laborer elevated to cabinet minister when such dress is prescribed. Otherwise he finds himself in an embarrassing situation, and he will embarrass others to the point of provoking protests, indignation, and outright pressure to comply with the dignity of his new office.

When, finally, the status of the individual's groups is sharply changed by demotion or elevation, enrichment or impoverishment, improvement or aggravation, war or peace, the total culture of the individual's personality undergoes a notable change.

Any of the changes of the individual's selfs and total culture means serious emotional, affective, and volitional shocks, stresses, strains, and excitations. Whether an intense elation by promotion or mental depression from demotion, any transposition of the individual

profoundly disturbs his affective-emotional life. Any replacement of the old selfs by the new ones is a painful experience where the joy of acquiring a new ego is always mixed with the sorrow of losing the old one. Any new shift requires from him a strenuous effort to adjust himself to his new position. He must rearrange his ideas, values, and norms, his overt actions and manners and his material vehicles. Any transposition severs some of his previous social ties and for some time leaves him suspended in a "social vacuum," because new intimate ties cannot be established in a short time. Temporarily at least a change in social status disorganizes and disintegrates one's personality by breaking his old ego-constellation. If such shifts are sharp and frequent, the individual is subjected to perennial affective and emotional tensions and to chronic disorganization of his selfs and culture. Before he can crystallize and integrate his new egos and culture, he is again shifted to a new position, and he has to begin once more to build up another personality structure.

Shall we wonder that under these conditions a series of psychological consequences occur in these personalities.[4] (a) Some individuals save themselves by becoming "plastic and fluid" in their personalities, not taking seriously any value or loyalty, to expel or receive any soul and culture at a moment's notice. Such plasticity and cynicism is the only way many retain their sanity. (b) Other individuals incapable of becoming sufficiently "fluid" tend to become neurotic, melancholic, paranoic, and to suffer from various other psychoneuroses. In such conditions some of them commit suicide. (c) Some individuals polarize "negatively" by turning into cynical sensualists and devotees of *"Carpe diem."* Others polarize positively by becoming religious, saintly, ascetic, and stoic. (d) Some individuals expand their mental and cultural vistas, enrich their ideological, behavioral, and material culture, and even create a new system from the diverse elements they absorb. Others, on the contrary, suffer from inability to digest, interiorize, and integrate their incessantly changing egos and culture. They become eclectic, superficial, characterless individuals.

[4] See the facts and details in my *Mobility*, Chps. 21-22 and *Calamity*, Chps. 4, 10, 11, 12.

Like rudderless boats they are the playthings of external sociocultural waves and currents, incessantly thrown hither and thither by the latest fashion, event, or leader. (e) When the individual is transposed upward to better material and sociocultural conditions, the neurosis and melancholy, the disintegration of his personality, and the negative polarization are somewhat mitigated by his elation at his suc-cess in sociocultural climbing. When he shifts downward, these psychological afflictions are aggravated by the deterioration of his material conditions, and by his sense of "failure" and social sinking. However, in both cases, the transposition produces emotional and affective shocks and stresses; in both cases it tends to disorganize the individual.

IV. Conclusion

Such in brief is the drama of human life, with its tragic and comical roles, its joys and sorrows, its integrity and disintegration. The life-drama of each individual is indeed a microcosm reflecting the gigantic sociocultural processes in which he is embedded. Whatever the individual's specific biological constitution, his group affiliations, his culture, such will be the structure of his personality and the dynamics of his life.

With this we can close our analysis of the structures and dynamics of the social, cultural, and personality aspects of the superorganic world. We see that they are indeed inseparable and indivisible. We have obtained some under-standing of these structures and dynamics, of their interrelationships and uniformities. However, this understanding is neither complete nor adequate. It is only a first step in the unravelling of this most mysterious universe wherein we live. Playing the double role of observers and actors, future generations will continue to enlarge and to deepen the understanding of the universe and of themselves.

At the present moment this universe is in the midst of a vast transformation. So also are the souls and actions of its human members. Let us hope that the great passage to a new and integrated society will be made without additional tragedy or apocalyptic catastrophe.

Index of Subjects

Ability, and social position, 436-439, 444; and social stratification, 377; social test of, 438-441
Absolute ethics, 620-623
Absolute law, 624
Absolute reality, 607
Absolute truth, 607
Absolute value, 623
Abstract generalizing science, 16
Abstracting activity of mind, 560-561
Acceleration, law of, 691-695
Accident in discoveries and inventions, 543
Accidental change of congeries, 638
Acculturation, 578-581
Accumulation, in material and non-material culture, 672-673; of basic and peripheral values, 674; of social bonds, 464-465
Acquisition of group vehicles, modes of, 390-391
Action-reaction, immanent, 447-449, 455, 460-461, 477-478
Actions, forms of, 43-46
Actuality and potentiality in growth of systems, 697-698
Adaptation, and integration, 338-340; and organization, 371-372; group, two forms of, 445
Adequacy, in classification of groups, 159-160; of satisfaction of need, 576-577
Adjacency, spatial, and causal unity, 145-146, 333-334; temporal, and causal relationship, 635-638
Adjustment, see Adaptation
Adolescence as age-group, 191-194
Aesthetic consistency, 314-315
Aesthetic systems, duration of, 708

Affinity and disaffinity of groups, social bonds, and strata, 239-240, 289-293
Age, as a basis of differentiation, 191; of leaders, 193
Age groups and plurels, 191-192, 281
Agents, human beings as culture, 313, 342-343
Agglomeration of groups, population as, 296; rural-urban, 301; society as, 297; types of, 302-307
Aggression, see Crime; Revolution; War
Agnosticism, 610, 617
Agricultural classes, 273; economic position in Greece, Rome, France, Germany, 397-399
Alternation, see Fluctuation; Rhythm
Anarchy, and freedom, 477; and law, 77; and stratification, 378
See also Revolution
Ancestors, 676
Animistic theories of instincts, 352
Annual rhythms, 684
Annus magnus, 676, 682
Anomie, 334, 513
Antagonism, social, and coercion, 94-95, 106-109; classification of, 95-99, 110-116; factors of, 119-124, 127, 507-508, 514-515; role of similarity and dissimilarity in, 133, 141-143; uniformities in, 128
Antagonistic interaction, 70, 93-94; forms of, 95-99
Antagonistic relationship, between egos, 347, 351-352, 718-722; between meanings, norms, values, 314-

316, 323; between social bonds, 239-240, 289-293
Antagonistic trend, contemporary, 130-131
See also Revolution; War
Anthropological branch of sociology, 23
Architecture, idealistic, ideational, sensate, 596-599
Area, structure of culture in, 333-335
Aristocracy, as elite, 233-235, 646-648; as form of government, 174, 176, 468; characteristics of, 443-444; decadent, 176, 289-293, 439-440, 493-494, 567-568, 588
Army, wartime casualties in, 497
Aquatio bonorum, 291
Art, as a cultural system, 318; contemporary, crisis of, 602-604; eclectic, 599; fine, blossoming and creativity in, 548-551, 646-649, 652; forms of, 593-601; idealistic, 594; ideational, 593; sensate, 594; naturalistic, 594; personages in, 604; religious, 593, 597-599; secular, 594, 598-599; symbolic, 593
Artist, anonymous, 596-597; individualistic, 604-605
"As if organized" group, 182, 277
Ascetic adaptation, 445
Ascetic freedom, 469
Aspects, of infinite manifold, 321-322; of sociocultural phenomena, 63-64
Assimilation, 415
Association, and community, 116-117, 243; of ideas, 538, 559-560; of social bonds, 464-465

Index of Names

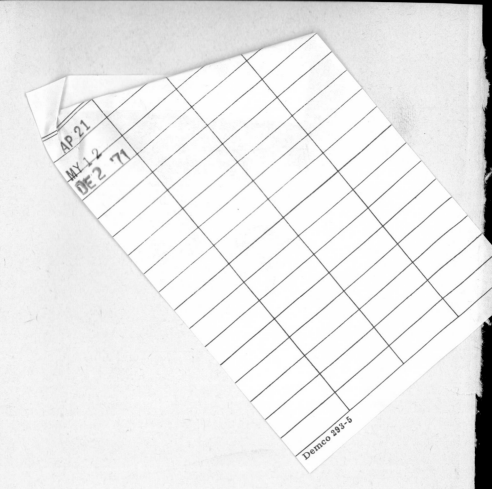